IS IT RELEVANT TO YOU AND THIS COURSE?

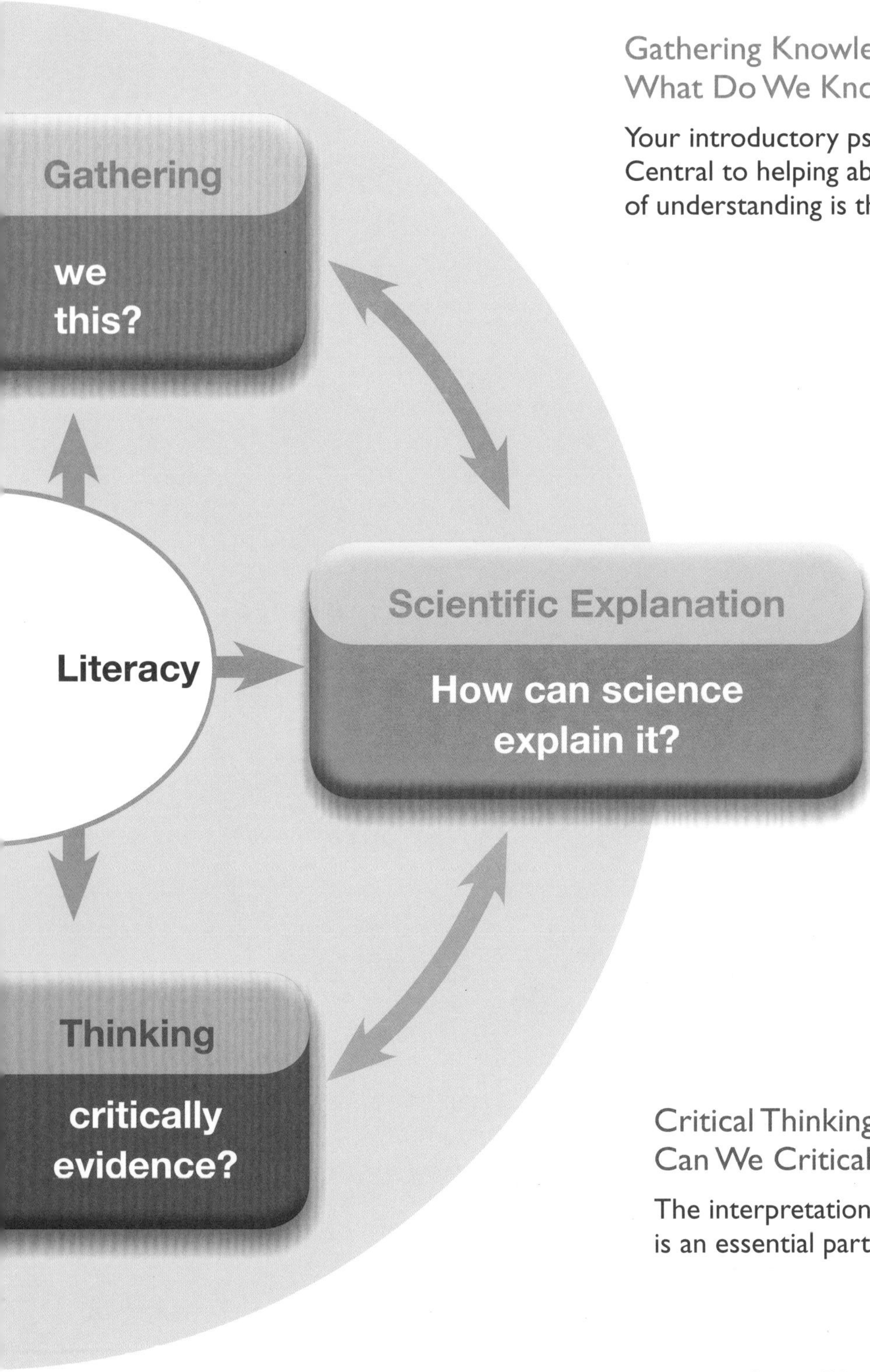

Gathering Knowledge and Learning Concepts: What Do We Know about This?

Your introductory psychology course covers many content areas. Central to helping absorb this content and getting a strong base of understanding is the way the material is organized.

Scientific Explanation: How Can Science Explain It?

This element of scientific literacy encompasses a basic understanding of research methodology and thinking about problems within a scientific framework.

Critical Thinking: Can We Critically Evaluate the Evidence?

The interpretation of information and observations is an essential part of scientific literacy.

AN INTRODUCTION TO PSYCHOLOGICAL SCIENCE

AN INTRODUCTION TO PSYCHOLOGICAL SCIENCE

CANADIAN EDITION

Mark Krause
Southern Oregon University

Daniel Corts
Augustana College

Stephen Smith
University of Winnipeg

Dan Dolderman
University of Toronto

Toronto

Editor-in-Chief: Michelle Sartor
Acquisitions Editor: Matthew Christian
Senior Marketing Manager: Lisa Gillis
Program Manager: Söğüt Y. Güleç
Project Manager: Marissa Lok
Developmental Editor: Johanna Schlaepfer
Media Content Editor: Sonia Tan
Media Producer: Tiffany Palmer
Production Services: Tania Andrabi, Cenveo® Publisher Services
Permissions Project Manager: Daniela Celebre-Glass
Photo Permissions Research: Carly Bergey, PreMediaGlobal
Text Permissions Research: Jill Dougan, EPS
Art Director: Zena Denchik
Cover Designer: Miguel Acevedo
Cover Image: Sarjeant/Getty

Credits and acknowledgments for material borrowed from other sources and reproduced, with permission, in this textbook appear on the appropriate page within the text or on page C-1.

10 9 8 7 6 5 4 3 2 1 [CKV]

Library and Archives Canada Cataloguing in Publication

Krause, Mark A. (Mark Andrew), 1971–, author
An introduction to psychological science : modeling scientific literacy/ Mark Krause, Southern Oregon University, Daniel Corts, Augustana College, Stephen Smith, University of Winnipeg, Dan Dolderman, University of Toronto.—Canadian edition.

Includes bibliographical references and index.
ISBN 978-0-13-292450-4 (bound)

1. Psychology—Textbooks. I. Corts, Daniel Paul, 1970–, author II. Smith, Stephen D. (Stephen Douglas), 1974–, author III. Dolderman, Dan, 1972–, author IV. Title.

BF121.K73 2014 150 C2013-907851-7

ISBN 978-0-13-292450-4

To my partner in life, Andrea Krause.
And many thanks to Gordon Burghardt and
Michael Domjan for instilling in me a
passion for science and discovery.

Mark Krause

To Kim, Sophie, and
Jonah . . . for everything.

Dan Corts

To my wonderful wife, Jenn, and
our amazing children, Oliver
and Clara. Thank you for
putting up with me.

Stephen Smith

To my partner, Safa Ali, who is my unfailing
support and inspiration toward wisdom. To
my children, Alexandra, Kate, and Geoff,
who love this world so deeply. And
of course, to Steve, without whom
this textbook would never
have gotten finished!

Dan Dolderman

Brief Contents

Contents

6 LEARNING 225

7 MEMORY 269

10

LIFESPAN DEVELOPMENT 391

14 HEALTH, STRESS, AND COPING 585

15 PSYCHOLOGICAL DISORDERS 623

From the Authors

A well-rounded university education requires a healthy dose of science. This means not just a memorized list of scientific terms and famous names, but rather the abilities and disposition that allow students to encounter, understand, and evaluate scientific as well as nonscientific claims. This is true regardless of an individual's personal and career goals. As this text and MyPsychLab program emphasize, the science of psychology reaches across disciplinary boundaries and addresses numerous complex issues affecting individuals and society. To effectively use what they learn about psychology, students need to carry with them a scientific perspective. *An Introduction to Psychological Science* is written from the perspective of scientific literacy—the ability not only to define scientific terminology, but also to understand how it functions, to critically evaluate it, and to apply it to personal and societal matters.

Psychological science is in a privileged position to help students hone their scientific literacy. It is both a rigorous scientific discipline and a field that studies the most complex of all phenomena: the behavioural, cognitive, and biological basis of behaviour. With this focus on behaviour, one can rightly argue that psychology resides at the hub or core of numerous other scientific disciplines; it also shares connections with neuroscience, education, and public health, to name a few linkages. From this perspective, the knowledge acquired by studying psychological science should transfer and apply to many other fields. This is great news when you consider that psychology is one of few science courses that many undergraduates will ever take.

To make scientific literacy the core of our text and MyPsychLab, we developed content and features with the model shown in the graphic as a guide. The competencies that surround the scientific literacy core represent different knowledge or skill sets we want to work toward during the course. The multidirectional nature of the arrows connecting the four supporting themes for scientific literacy demonstrates the interrelatedness of the competencies, which span both core-level skills, such as knowing general information (e.g., terms, concepts), and more advanced skills, such as knowing how to explain phenomena from a scientific perspective, critical thinking, and application of material.

We used this model in developing all aspects of this program, the topics included in the book, the execution of the writing, the learning objectives we established, the quizzes, and other features. We believe a scientific literacy perspective and model will prove useful in addressing two course needs we often hear from instructors—to provide students with a systematic way to categorize the overwhelming amount of information they are confronted with, and to cultivate their curiosity and help them understand the relevance, practicality, and immense appeal of psychological science.

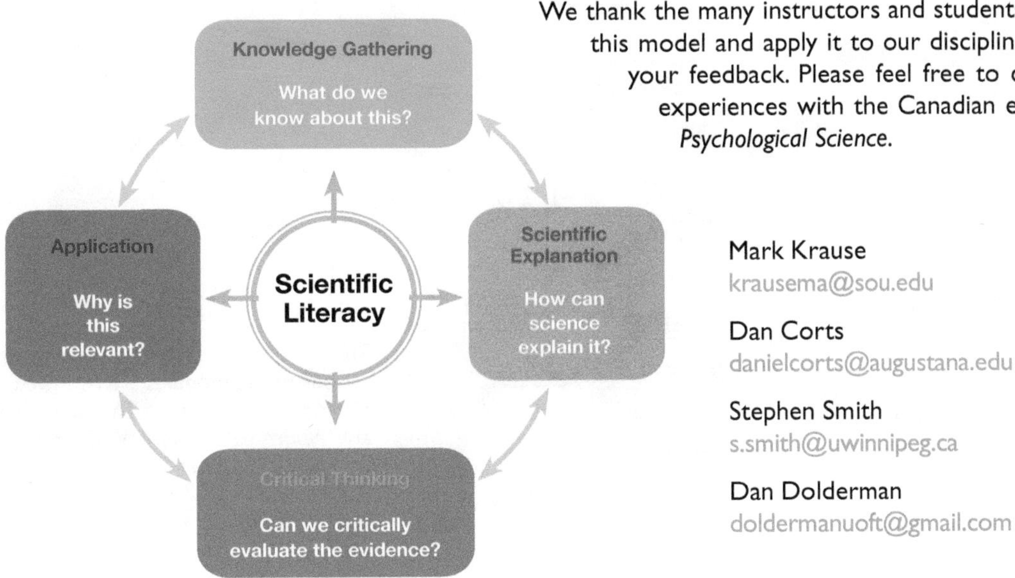

We thank the many instructors and students who have helped us craft this model and apply it to our discipline, and we look forward to your feedback. Please feel free to contact us and share your experiences with the Canadian edition of *An Introduction to Psychological Science*.

Mark Krause
krausema@sou.edu

Dan Corts
danielcorts@augustana.edu

Stephen Smith
s.smith@uwinnipeg.ca

Dan Dolderman
doldermanuoft@gmail.com

Content and Features

Students in the general psychology course are inundated with many disparate pieces of information at a time when they are still developing the skills and strategies for organizing and making sense of that information. How do the scientific literacy model and supporting features in *An Introduction to Psychological Science* address this issue?

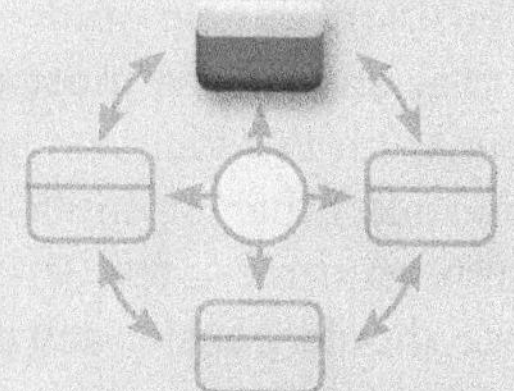

Knowledge Gathering

What do we know about this?

Introductory psychology courses cover a vast amount of content drawn from diverse specialty areas. The organization of the material is central to helping students absorb this content.

Modules

Chapters are divided into modules to make it easier for students to organize content as well as to self-test and review their learning at regular intervals. It also transforms lengthy chapters into nice "bite-sized" chunks of information that students can read in a single sitting (e.g., between classes). For instructors, the modular content makes it easy to customize delivery based on their preferred syllabus.

Learning Objectives

Learning Objectives organized around an updated Bloom's taxonomy aim to guide students to higher-level understanding. Summaries of the key points related to these objectives are provided at the end of each module. Objectives are listed at four levels of increasing complexity: know, understand, apply, and analyze.

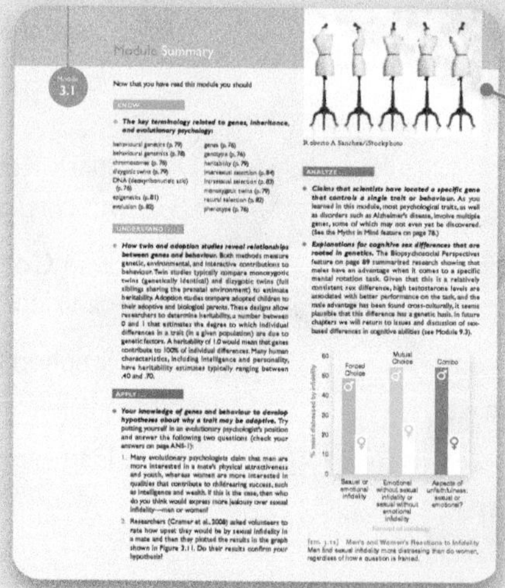

Module Summaries

The major terms, concepts, and applications of the modules are reviewed in the Module Summaries. The summaries also return to and address the original Learning Objectives from the beginning of the module and include application questions (with answers in the back of the book).

Another major set of forebrain structures comprises the **limbic system**, *an integrated network involved in emotion and memory* (Maclean, 1952; see Figure 3.25). One key structure in the limbic system is the **amygdala**, *which facilitates memory formation for emotional events, mediates fear responses, and appears to play a role in recognizing and interpreting emotional stimuli, including facial expressions.* In addition, the amygdala connects with structures in the nervous system that are

Key Terms

Key Terms are defined within the narrative, helping students place them in context, and are then listed again within the Module Summaries. A complete glossary is also included at the end of the text.

Quick Quizzes

Quizzes appear at the conclusion of major sections of the module (typically two to four quizzes per module). These quizzes contain multiple-choice questions that enable students to assess their comprehension and better prepare for exams. Like the Learning Objectives, the Quick Quizzes assess understanding at the four levels of Bloom's taxonomy and are marked accordingly.

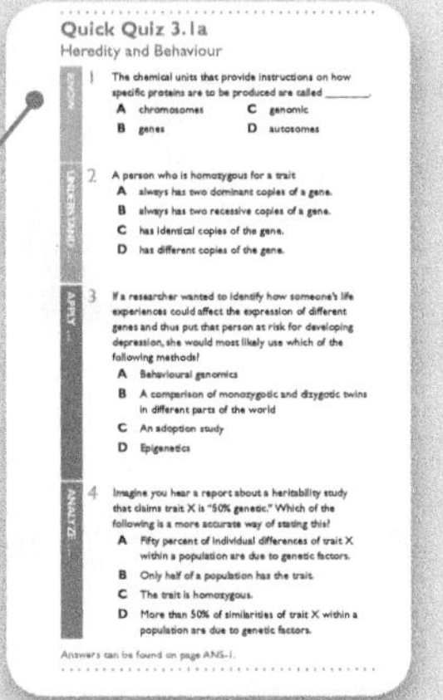

Quick Quiz 3.1a
Heredity and Behaviour

KNOW ...
1 The chemical units that provide instructions on how specific proteins are to be produced are called ________.
A chromosomes
B genes
C genomic
D autosomes

UNDERSTAND ...
2 A person who is homozygous for a trait
A always has two dominant copies of a gene.
B always has two recessive copies of a gene.
C has identical copies of the gene.
D has different copies of the gene.

APPLY ...
3 If a researcher wanted to identify how someone's life experiences could affect the expression of different genes and thus put that person at risk for developing depression, she would most likely use which of the following methods?
A Behavioural genomics
B A comparison of monozygotic and dizygotic twins in different parts of the world
C An adoption study
D Epigenetics

ANALYZE ...
4 Imagine you hear a report about a heritability study that claims trait X is "50% genetic." Which of the following is a more accurate way of stating this?
A Fifty percent of individual differences of trait X within a population are due to genetic factors.
B Only half of a population has the trait.
C The trait is homozygous.
D More than 50% of similarities of trait X within a population are due to genetic factors.

Answers can be found on page ANS-1.

Active Illustration

For key figures and illustrations, animations are provided within the eText to deliver greater clarity and understanding. For example, readers are much more apt to understand the structures of the brain when they can click on a diagram of it and see a fully rotating illustration. The Pearson eText for the Canadian edition of *An Introduction to Psychological Science* is designed with alternative delivery models in mind. Highly visual, clearly laid out, and with integrated video and media, it is optimal for online reading and interaction. Students can access their textbook anytime, anywhere, and any way they want, including listening online or downloading it to their iPads.

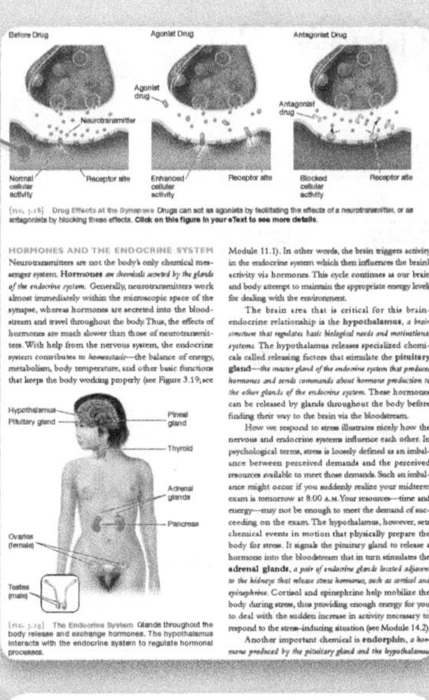

[FIG. 3.18] Drug Effects at the Synapses Drugs can act as agonists by facilitating the effects of a neurotransmitter, or as antagonists by blocking these effects. **Click on this figure in your eText to see more details.**

HORMONES AND THE ENDOCRINE SYSTEM
Neurotransmitters are not the body's only chemical messenger system. **Hormones** *are chemicals secreted by the glands of the endocrine system.* Generally, neurotransmitters work almost immediately within the microscopic space of the synapse, whereas hormones are secreted into the bloodstream and travel throughout the body. Thus, the effects of hormones are much slower than those of neurotransmitters. With help from the nervous system, the endocrine system contributes to *homeostasis*—the balance of energy, metabolism, body temperature, and other basic functions that keeps the body working properly (see Figure 3.19; see Module 11.1). In other words, the brain triggers activity in the endocrine system which then influences the brain's activity via hormones. This cycle continues as our brain and body attempt to maintain the appropriate energy levels for dealing with the environment.

[FIG. 3.19] The Endocrine System Glands throughout the body release and exchange hormones. The hypothalamus interacts with the endocrine system to regulate hormonal processes.

The brain area that is critical for this brain-endocrine relationship is the **hypothalamus**, *a brain structure that regulates basic biological needs and motivational systems.* The hypothalamus releases specialized chemicals called releasing factors that stimulate the **pituitary gland**—*the master gland of the endocrine system that produces hormones and sends commands about hormone production to the other glands of the endocrine system.* These hormones can be released by glands throughout the body before finding their way to the brain via the bloodstream.

How we respond to stress illustrates nicely how the nervous and endocrine systems influence each other. In psychological terms, stress is loosely defined as an imbalance between perceived demands and the perceived resources available to meet those demands. Such an imbalance might occur if you suddenly realize your midterm exam is tomorrow at 8:00 A.M. Your resources—time and energy—may not be enough to meet the demand of succeeding on the exam. The hypothalamus, however, sets chemical events in motion that physically prepare the body for stress. It signals the pituitary gland to release a hormone into the bloodstream that in turn stimulates the **adrenal glands**, *a pair of endocrine glands located adjacent to the kidneys that release stress hormones, such as cortisol and epinephrine.* Cortisol and epinephrine help mobilize the body during stress, thus providing enough energy for you to deal with the sudden increase in activity necessary to respond to the stress-inducing situation (see Module 14.2).

Another important chemical is **endorphin**, *a hormone produced by the pituitary gland and the hypothalamus*

MyPsychLab

MyPsychLab icons in the margin call out important information students can access online—for example, videos, simulations, and hands-on experiments.

Watch the Video
Listen to the Chapter Audio
Explore the Concept
Simulate the Experiment
Study and Review

Scientific Explanation

How can science explain it?

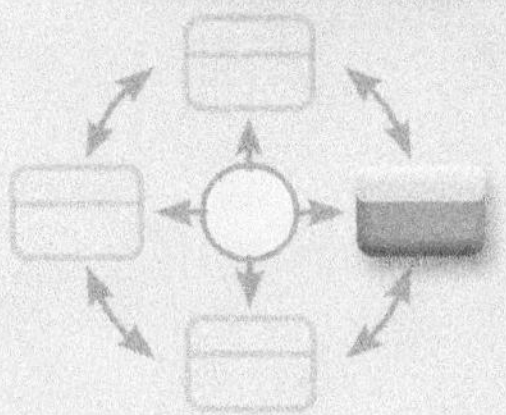

This element of scientific literacy encompasses a basic understanding of research methodology and thinking about problems within a scientific framework. *An Introduction to Psychological Science* integrates and reinforces key research methodology concepts throughout the book. This interweaving of methodology encourages students to continue practising their scientific thinking skills. Learning science is more than accumulating facts; students learn to ask questions, construct explanations, test those explanations, and communicate their ideas to others.

Module Opening Vignettes

Each module opens with a short vignette emphasizing the personal and societal relevance of certain topics to be covered. The vignette concludes with Focus Questions preparing the reader to think about the content found within the module.

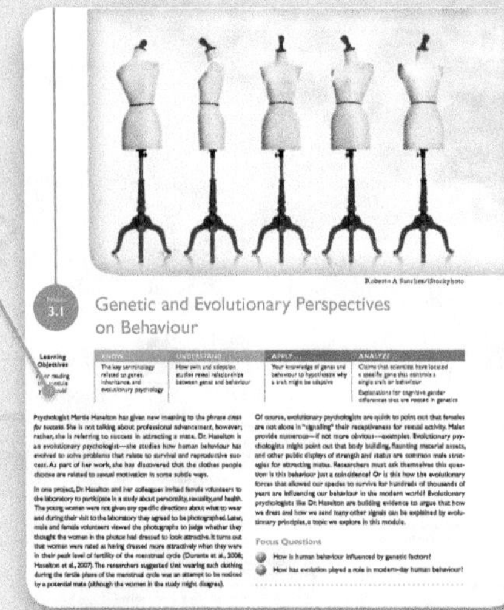

Module 3.1

Genetic and Evolutionary Perspectives on Behaviour

Biopsychosocial Perspectives

To emphasize the complexity of scientific explanations, students are reminded throughout each chapter that behaviour includes biology, individual thoughts and experiences, and the influence of social and cultural factors.

BIOPSYCHOSOCIAL PERSPECTIVES

Hunters and Gatherers: Men, Women, and Spatial Memory

Evolutionary psychologists claim that the brain consists of a set of cognitive adaptations for solving problems related to survival and reproductive fitness. They also hypothesize that male and female brains will differ in some ways because males and females have had to solve a different set of problems in order to survive and reproduce. Specifically, due to their size and strength, males were traditionally responsible for tracking and killing animals. These responsibilities would require males to travel over long distances without becoming lost. Females, due to the fact that they cared for children, remained closer to home and instead spent time foraging for berries and edible plants. Males' responsibilities would favour individuals with good spatial skills; females' responsibilities would favour memory for the location of objects (e.g., plants). The question, then, is whether the abilities that were adaptive for males and females over the course of our species' evolution are still present today. Put another way, will modern males and females show performance differences on different tests of spatial abilities that are consistent with their historic roles as hunter (males) and gatherer (females)?

One sex difference that has been reported involves solving the mental rotation task seen in Figure 3.9.

Instructions

1. Take a close look at standard object #1 in Figure 3.9. One of the three objects to the right of it is the same. Which one matches the standard? Repeat this with standard object #2 and the three comparison shapes to the right of it.
2. Many researchers find that, on average, males and females differ in their ability to perform this task. Do you think that

Myths in Mind

Many commonly held beliefs people have about behaviour before taking a psychology course are half-truths or outright falsehoods. This feature sets the record straight in a concise and informative way. The selected examples are likely to have personal relevance to many readers and deal with important scientific issues.

MYTHS IN MIND

We Are Born with All the Brain Cells We Will Ever Have

For decades, neuroscience taught us that nerves do not regenerate; in other words, scientists believed that we are born with all of the brain cells we will ever have. This conclusion made perfect sense because no one had ever seen new neurons form in adults, and severe neurological damage is often permanent.

MyPsychLab Simulations

MyPsychLab Simulations allow students to participate in experiments online to reinforce what they are learning in class and in their book. More than 50 experiments, surveys, and inventories are available through this online tool (available at MyPsychLab).

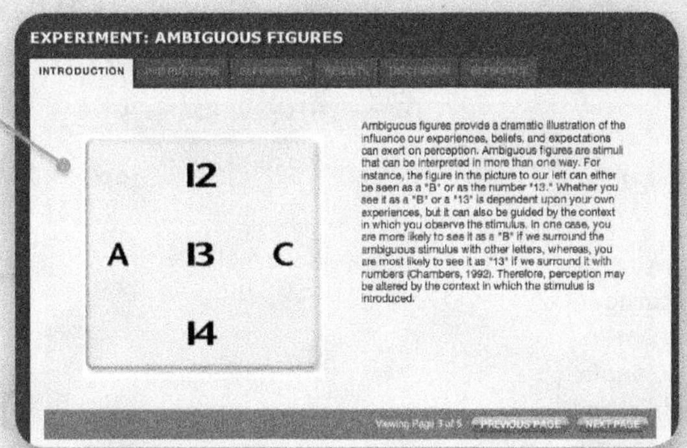

In recent years, an increasing number of instructors have begun to focus on telling students how psychological science fits within the scientific community. Psychology serves, in essence, as a hub science. Through this emphasis on scientific literacy in psychology, students begin to see the practicality and relevance of psychology and become more literate in the fields that our hub science supports.

Critical Thinking

Can we critically evaluate the evidence?

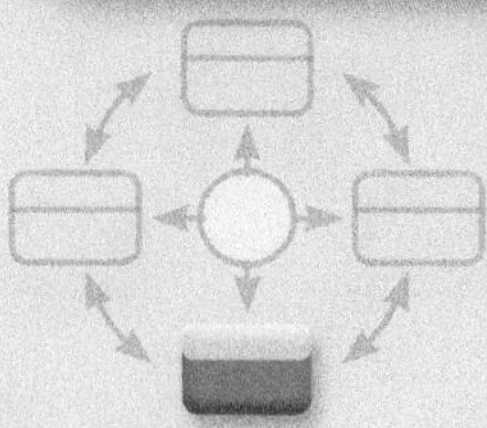

Many departments are focusing to an increasing extent on the development of critical thinking, as these skills are highly sought after in society and the workforce. Critical thinking is generally defined as the ability to apply knowledge, use information in new ways, analyze situations and concepts, and evaluate decisions. To develop critical thinking, the module objectives and quizzes are built around an updated Bloom's taxonomy. Objectives are listed at four levels of increasing complexity: know, understand, apply, and **analyze**. The following features also help students organize, analyze, and synthesize information. Collectively, these features encourage students to connect different levels of understanding with specific objectives and quiz questions.

Working the Scientific Literacy Model

Working the Scientific Literacy Model, introduced in Chapter 1, and then featured in each module in the remaining chapters, fully integrates the model of scientific literacy. Core concepts are highlighted and students are walked through the steps of knowledge gathering, approaching the problem from a scientific standpoint, using critical thinking, and revealing applications.

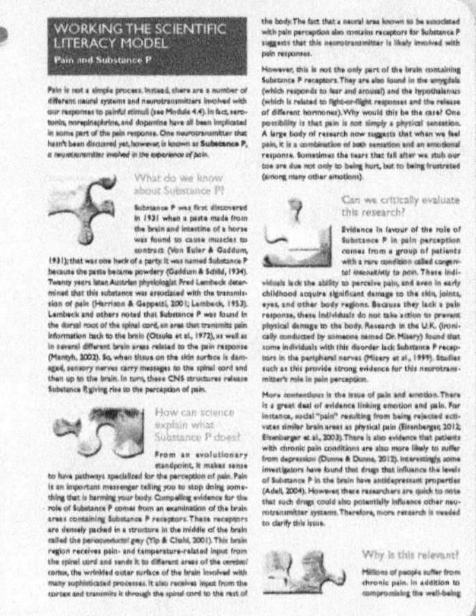

WORKING THE SCIENTIFIC LITERACY MODEL

Pain and Substance P

What do we know about Substance P?

How can science explain what Substance P does?

Can we critically evaluate this research?

Why is this relevant?

Work the Scientific Literacy Model

At the end of every chapter, students have an opportunity to "Work the Scientific Literacy Model" themselves. The Work the Model feature walks students through content from the chapter, providing study tips and reminders for key content areas. Students are asked to critically evaluate what they have learned by accessing a video clip, either through MyPsychLab, the Layar app, the QR code on the page, or YouTube. They are then provided with a question prompting them to apply relevant content to the scenario depicted in the video. These questions can be assigned as either a classroom discussion or a writing assignment.

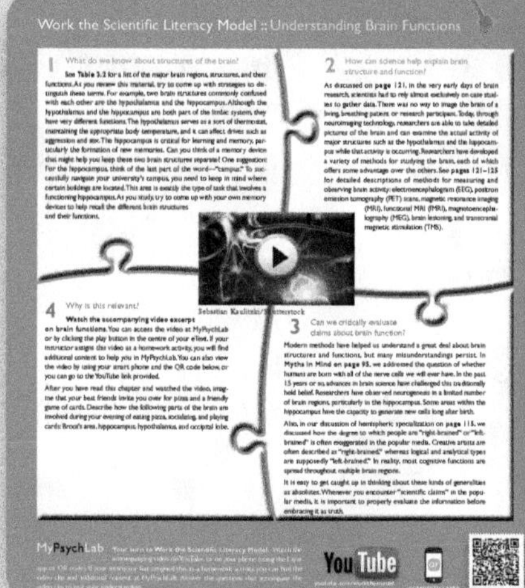

Work the Scientific Literacy Model :: Understanding Brain Functions

1 What do we know about structures of the brain?

2 How can science help explain brain structure and function?

3 Can we critically evaluate claims about brain function?

4 Why is this relevant?

INTERACTIVE PRINT

Download the free Layar App

Scan pages featuring the Layar logo

Discover interactive content

Study Plan

Through MyPsychLab (www.pearsonmylabmastering.com), students have access to a *personalized study plan*, based on Bloom's taxonomy, that arranges content from basic level thinking (such as remembering and understanding) to more complex critical thinking (such as applying and analyzing). This layered approach sharpens critical thinking skills, and helps students succeed in the course and beyond.

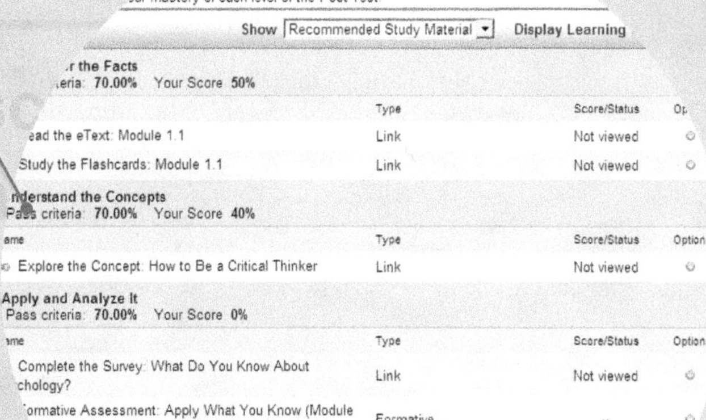

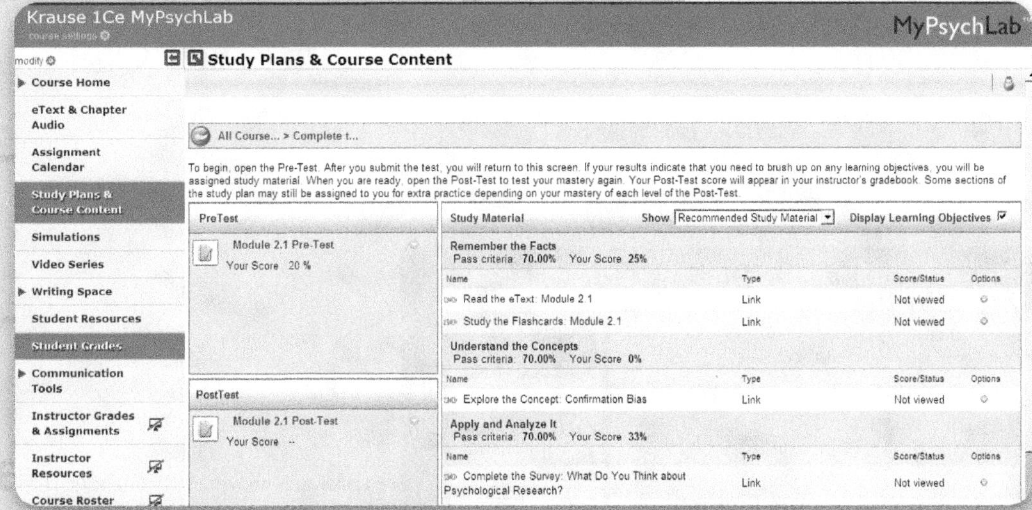

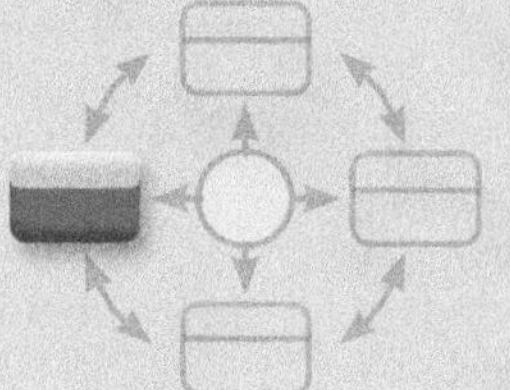

Application

Why is this relevant?

Psychology is a highly relevant, modern science. To be scientifically literate, students should relate psychological concepts to their own lives, making decisions based on knowledge, sound methodology, and skilled interpretation of information.

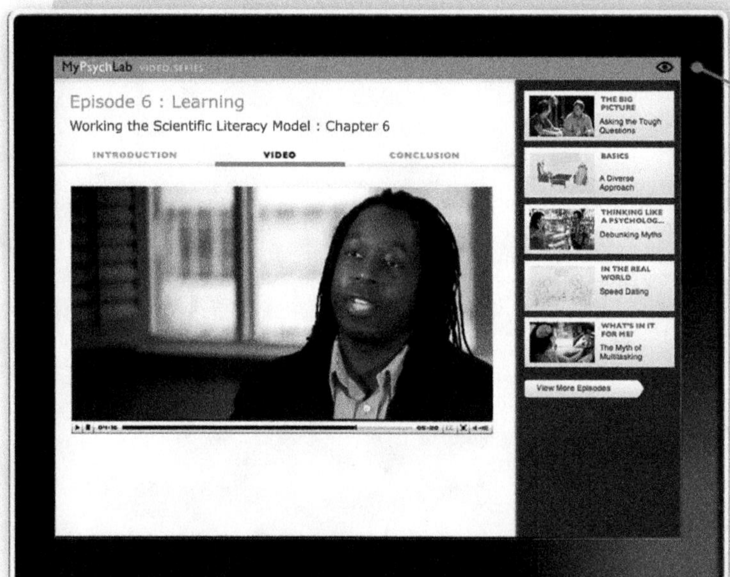

MyPsychLab Video Series

Links are provided throughout the eText to relevant episodes of the MyPsychLab Video series—a comprehensive, current, and cutting-edge series featuring 17 original 30-minute videos covering the most recent research, science, and applications and utilizing the most up-to-date film and animation technology.

Why is this relevant?

PSYCH @

The Artist's Studio

Although we often think of painters as being eccentric people prone to cutting off their ears, they are actually very clever amateur vision scientists. Rembrandt (1606–1669) varied the texture and colour details of different parts of portraits in order to guide the viewer's gaze toward the clearest object. The result is that more detailed regions of a painting attract attention and receive more eye fixations than less detailed regions (DiPaoloa, Riebe, & Enns, 2011).

In addition to manipulating a viewer's eye movements, painters also use a variety of depth cues to transform their two-dimensional painting into a three-dimensional perception. This use of *pictorial depth cues* is quite challenging, which is why some paintings seem vibrant and multilayered (like nature) while others seem flat and artificial. So what are some strategies that artists use to influence our visual perception?

To understand how artists work, view the painting by Gustave Caillebottein shown in Figure 4.26. In this painting, you will notice that the artist used numerous cues to depict depth:

Psych @

The "Psych @" feature reveals an everyday, personally relevant application of psychological science. The content of these features is geared toward issues and concerns that many university students care about.

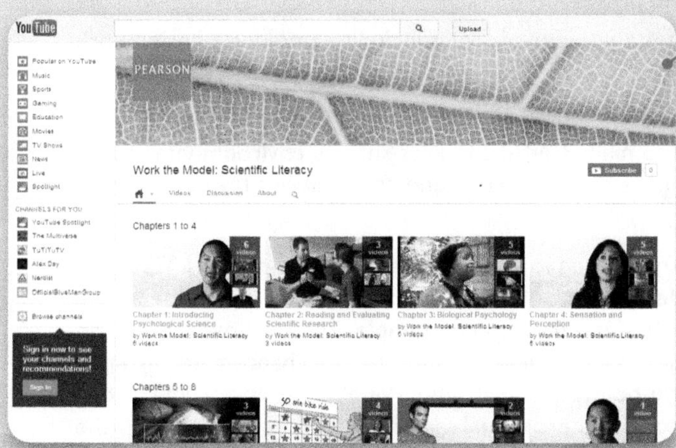

YouTube Scientific Literacy Site

YouTube has become one of the most popular social media resources for both instructors and students. The challenge, of course, is to find clips that are relevant to key content areas. To help instructors access valuable open-source content and further bring to light the relevance of the discipline of psychology, a YouTube channel, found at

www.youtube.com/workthemodel

has been developed to accompany *An Introduction to Psychological Science*. The book provides relevant video links for instructor and student access, in addition to the videos that frame the end-of-chapter "Work the Scientific Literacy Model" activity.

What's New in the Canadian Edition?

When we started writing the Canadian edition of this textbook, we assumed we'd just add the letter "u" a few hundred times and insert some pictures of Sidney Crosby. We did add several thousand u's and one photo of Crosby—but, as we began to write the different chapters, we became amazed at how important Canadian researchers have been to the study of psychological science. In boxing, there is the phrase "punching above your weight." It is used when a smaller fighter's punches feel like they are coming from a larger, stronger fighter. Canadian psychology is like that. Despite the fact that we are a relatively small country (in terms of population and the number of research institutions), we have made incredibly important contributions to a number of areas of psychology. The work of Canadian researchers served as the foundation for many areas of neuroscience, perception, memory, social, and health research. So, although we rewrote large chunks of the book, the Canadian content isn't just added as a bonus. The Canadian content is actually an essential part of psychological science *in general.* As a result, we ended up adding over 1400 *new* references to the U.S. edition of this book. These include the following additions:

- highlighting the importance that Canadian research has had on the development of modern psychology;
- adding research conducted by Canadian researchers from all 10 provinces;
- incorporating research related to cultural psychology and the experiences of first- and second-generation immigrants to Canada;
- discussing bilingualism and its effects on culture, cognition, and the brain;
- providing a thorough discussion of Canadian legal decisions (including references to specific Supreme Court rulings) related to issues such as sexting, hypnosis, and recovered memories;
- discussing Canadian statistics and laws related to drug use and possession;
- providing Statistics Canada and Health Canada materials for a number of topics including smoking, obesity, work stress, gambling, and clinical conditions;
- clarifying the ethical requirements for conducting research at Canadian universities and hospitals;
- incorporating discussions of social issues that are central to many Canadians' lives such as environmental issues, the increased role of technology in our lives, and the influence that marketers and corporations try to have over us all.

We have also made an effort to make psychology less "abstract" than it is often portrayed in textbooks. Throughout this book, we use examples from the real world in order to demonstrate that the concepts the students are learning about affect *their own* behaviour. Although we include some traditional examples such as how to improve study habits, we go beyond that. For example, we use the concepts learned in different chapters to highlight tricks used by advertisers (including those used in negative political advertising). We also point out interesting things to look for in social interactions, such as the tendency of heterosexual males to stand up straighter in the presence of women in order to appear more powerful (discussed in Evolutionary Insights into Human Behaviour in Module 3.1). Our hope is that these engaging examples will allow the students to see the world in a slightly different way.

In addition to these examples, *we also try to show the students how they can use psychology to change the world that they live in.* An example found in many chapters is that of changing people's environmental behaviours and their attitudes toward issues such as climate change. Our hope is that by seeing how psychological science can be used to change behaviours for the better, students will be motivated to take the information from this book outside of the classroom to create the types of changes that our world desperately needs.

When you begin any course, it is like starting a journey. We hope you enjoy your journey through the Canadian edition of *An Introduction to Psychological Science* as much as we enjoyed writing it.

For Instructors

SCIENTIFIC LITERACY is a key course goal for many introductory psychology instructors.

Learning science is an active process. How do we help instructors model scientific literacy in the classroom and online in a way that meets the needs of today's students?

ORGANIZATION

Instructors consistently tell us one of the main challenges they face when teaching the introductory psychology course is organizing engaging, current, and relevant materials to span the breadth of content covered. How do we help organize and access valuable course materials?

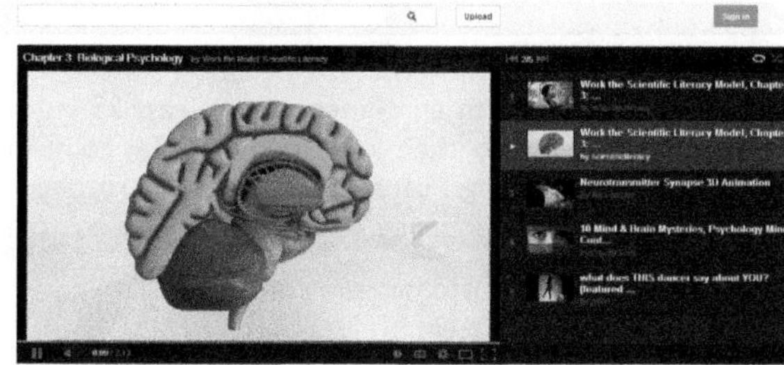

YouTube Scientific Literacy Site

As mentioned earlier, a YouTube channel, found at www.youtube.com/workthemodel, provides a wealth of videos to help engage students and enhance their learning. The ready access provided to these videos, with content spanning the breadth of psychological science, means that instructors no longer have to search for just the right video links to material that meshes with the text's content.

LECTURE GUIDE

I. MODULE 1.1: THE SCIENCE OF PSYCHOLOGY (Text p. 2)
▲ Return to Table of Contents

Learning Objectives

- ✓ **Know** the key terminology of this module.
  - See bold, italicized terms below.
- ✓ **Understand** the steps of the scientific method.
  - The basic model is in figure 1.1. Basically, scientific theories generate hypotheses. If a hypothesis is confirmed, new hypotheses may stem from in, and the original theory receives added support. If a hypothesis is rejected, the original hypothesis may be modified and retested, or the original theory may be modified or rejected.
- ✓ **Understand** the concept of scientific literacy.
  - Scientific literacy refers to the process of how we thinking about and understand scientific information (figure 1.3). Working the model involves answering a set of questions:
    - What do we know about the phenomenon?
    - How can science explain it?
    - Can we critically evaluate the evidence?
    - Why is this relevant?
- ✓ **Apply** the biopsychosocial model to behavior.
  - Psychologists examine behavior through three main perspectives: biological (e.g., brain and genetics), psychological (e.g., thinking, learning, and emotion), and sociocultural (e.g., family, gender, and social context).
- ✓ **Apply** the steps in critical thinking.
  - It is important learn how to use and apply these steps, versus just memorizing them. Remember, critical thinking involves (1) being curious, (2) examining evidence, (3) examining assumptions and biases, (4) avoiding emotional thinking, (5) tolerating ambiguity, and (6) considering alternative viewpoints.
- ✓ **Analyze** the use of the term scientific theory.
  - The term theory is often used interchangeably with opinion in casual talk, but not in science. A scientific theory is an explanation for a broad range of observations, integrating numerous findings into a coherent whole.

Instructor's Resource Manual

The Instructor's Resource Manual includes suggestions for preparing for the course, sample syllabi, and current trends and strategies for successful teaching. Each chapter offers integrated teaching outlines, lists the key terms for each chapter for quick reference, and provides an extensive bank of lecture launchers, handouts, and activities, as well as suggestions for integrating third-party videos and web resources. This resource saves prep work and helps professors use their classroom time more efficiently.

ORGANIZATION

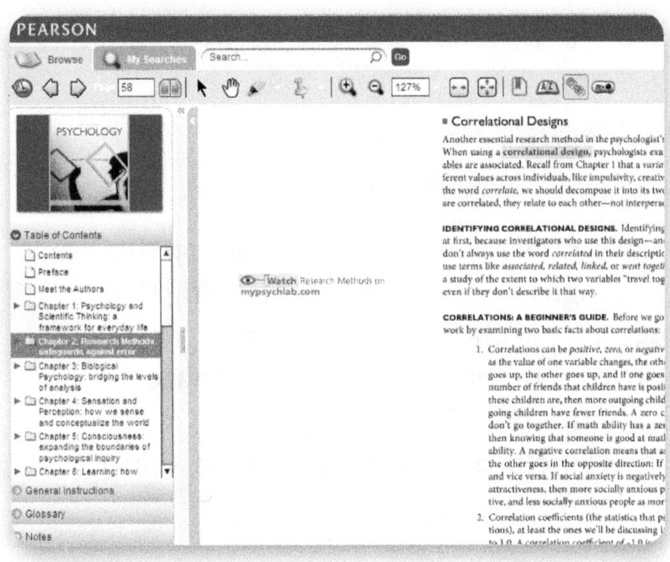

Pearson eText

The Canadian edition of *An Introduction to Psychological Science* is designed with alternative delivery models in mind. Highly visual, clearly laid out, and with integrated video and media, it is optimal for online reading and interaction. Instructors and students can access their textbook anytime, anywhere, and any way they want, including listening online or downloading it to an iPad.

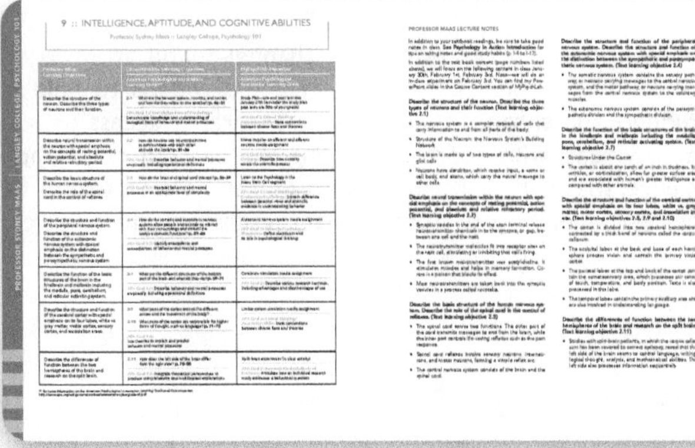

Create a Custom Text

For courses with enrollments of at least 25 students, instructors can create their own textbook by combining chapters from best-selling Pearson textbooks or reading selections in a customized sequence. To begin building a custom text, visit

www.pearsoncustomlibrary.com

Instructors can also work with a dedicated Pearson Custom editor to create the ideal text—publishing original content or mixing and matching Pearson content. Contact a Pearson publisher's representative to get started.

PRESENTATION

Instructors consistently tell us making their classroom lectures and online instruction exciting and dynamic is a top priority so they can engage students and bring psychology to life. We have been listening and have responded by creating state-of-the-art presentation resources, putting the most powerful presentation resources at your fingertips.

ClassPrep

Finding, sorting, organizing, and presenting instructor resources is faster and easier than ever before with ClassPrep, which is available in MyPsychLab. This fully searchable database contains hundreds of our best teacher resources, such as lecture launchers and discussion topics, in-class and out-of-class activities and assignments, handouts, and video clips, photos, illustrations, charts, graphs, and animations. Instructors can search or browse by topic, and readily sort their results by type, such as photo, document, or animation. Instructors can create personalized folders to organize and store the content that they like, or can download resources if they prefer. In addition, instructors can upload their own content and present directly from ClassPrep, or make it available online directly to their students. Also available—a ClassPrep app that allows access to all favourite resources via any mobile device.

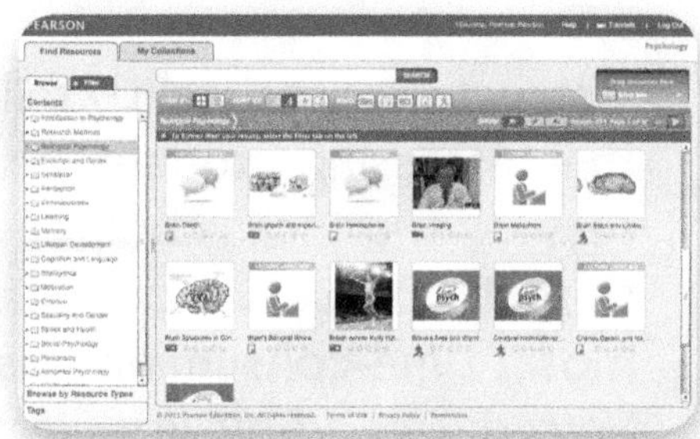

PowerPoint Presentations

Engaging PowerPoint slides bring the powerful Krause/Corts/Smith/Dolderman design right into the classroom, drawing students into the lecture with interesting information and rich visuals. The slides are built around the learning objectives in each module and offer key material that is provided in the text. In addition, interactive presentations with "clicker" questions are provided for instructors using classroom response systems.

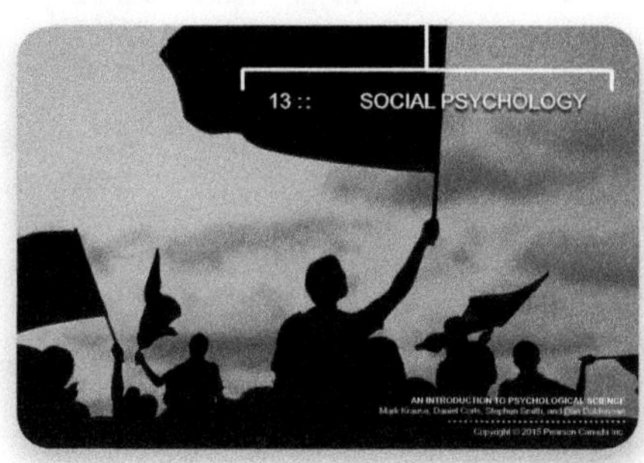

MyPsychLab Video Series

The MyPsychLab Video series is a comprehensive, current, and cutting-edge series featuring 17 original 30-minute videos covering the most recent research, science, and applications and utilizing the most up-to-date film and animation technology. Questions are provided within MyPsychLab so that instructors can assign relevant clips from the series as homework; they may also use the series in the classroom to illustrate the many fascinating topics in the field of psychology as part of their lectures. Guided by the Design, Development, and Review team—a diverse group of introductory psychology instructors—each episode is organized around the major topics covered in the introductory psychology course syllabus. Find out more about the MyPsychLab Video Series: www.pearsonhighered.com/showcase/mypsychlab_videos/

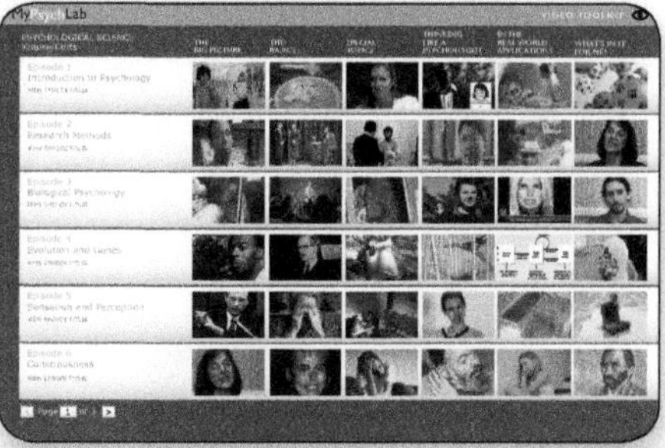

For maximum flexibility, each half-hour episode features several brief clips that bring psychology to life:

- The Big Picture introduces the topic of the episode and provides the hook to draw students fully into the topic.
- The Basics uses the power of video to present foundational topics, especially those that students find difficult to understand.
- Special Topics dives deeper into high-interest and cutting-edge topics, showing research in action.
- In the Real World focuses on applications of psychological research.
- What's in It for Me? clips show students the relevance of psychological research to their own lives.

ASSESSMENT

Instructors consistently tell us that assessing student progress is a critical component to their course and one of the most time-consuming tasks. Vetted, good-quality, easy-to-use assessment tools are essential. We have been listening and we have responded by creating the absolutely best assessment content available on the market today.

Test Bank

The Test Bank (Test Item File) contains more than 3000 questions, many of which were class-tested in multiple classes at both 2-year and 4-year institutions prior to publication. All questions have been thoroughly reviewed and analyzed line by line by a developmental editor and a copy editor to ensure clarity, accuracy, and delivery of the highest-quality assessment tool. All conceptual and applied multiple-choice questions include rationales for each correct answer and the key distracter, which serve both as an added guarantee of quality and as a time-saver when students challenge the keyed answer for a specific item.

In addition to this high-quality Test Bank, a second bank containing more than 2000 questions is available for instructors looking for more variation.

The Test Bank also comes with Pearson MyTest, a powerful assessment generation program that helps instructors easily create and print quizzes and exams. Questions and tests can be authored online, providing instructors with the ultimate in flexibility and the ability to efficiently manage assessments wherever and whenever they want. Instructors can easily access existing questions and then edit, create, and store them using simple drag-and-drop and Word-like controls. The data for each question identifies its difficulty level and the text page number where the relevant content appears. In addition, each question maps to the text's major section and learning objective. For more information, go to www.PearsonMyTest.com.

1) In order to be scientific, it must be possible to test a hypotheses.

Correct: *A testable hypothesis is one that can be confirmed or rejected (you do not prove a hypothesis), and a scientific hypothesis must be testable.*

Diff: 1
Type: FIB
Page Reference: 3
Skill: Conceptual
Objective: Understand the steps of the scientific method.

2) For psychologists, critical thinking means that we apply scientific methods carefully, examine our assumptions and biases, and tolerate ambiguity when the evidence is inconclusive.

Correct: *Critical thinking involves exercising curiosity and skepticism when evaluating the claims of others, and with our own assumptions and beliefs.*

Diff: 2
Type: FIB
Page Reference: 9
Skill: Conceptual
Objective: Apply the steps in critical thinking

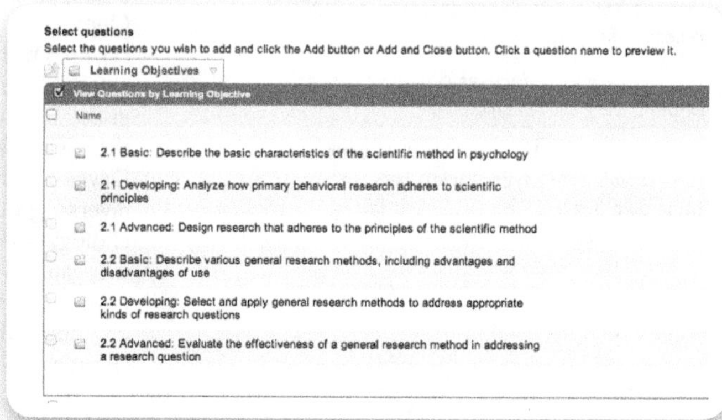

MyPsychLab

Educators know it. Students know it. It's that inspired moment when something that was difficult to understand suddenly makes perfect sense. MyPsychLab was designed and refined with a single purpose in mind—to help educators create that moment of understanding with their students.

MyPsychLab offers students useful and engaging self-assessment tools, and it provides instructors with flexibility in assessing and tracking student progress. For instructors, MyPsychLab is a powerful tool for assessing student performance and adapting course content to students' changing needs, without requiring instructors to invest additional time or resources to do so.

Instructors and students have been using MyPsychLab for more than 10 years. To date, more than 600 000 students have used MyPsychLab. During that time, three white papers on the efficacy of MyPsychLab have been published. Both the white papers and user feedback show compelling results: MyPsychLab helps students succeed and improve their test scores. One of the key ways MyPsychLab improves student outcomes is by providing continuous assessment as part of the learning process. Over the years, both instructor and student feedback have guided numerous improvements to this system, making MyPsychLab even more flexible and effective.

Pearson is committed to helping instructors and students succeed with MyPsychLab. To that end, we offer a Psychology Faculty Advisor Program designed to provide peer-to-peer support for new users of MyPsychLab. Experienced Faculty Advisors help instructors understand how MyPsychLab can improve student performance. To learn more about the Faculty Advisor Program, please contact your local Pearson representative.

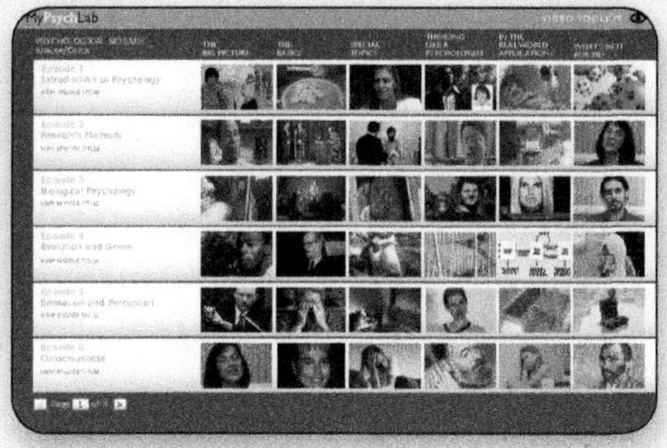

MyPsychLab includes the following features:

MyPsychLab Video Series

The MyPsychLab Video Series is a comprehensive and cutting-edge series featuring 17 original 30-minute videos covering the most recent research and utilizing the most up-to-date film and animation technology. Multiple choice and short answer essay questions are provided within MyPsychLab so episodes can be assigned as homework.

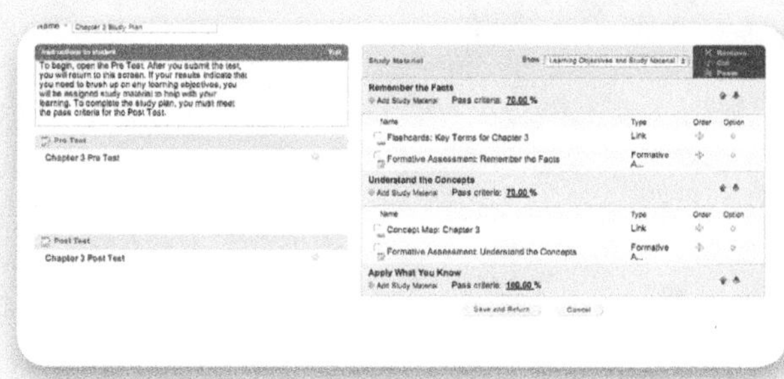

MyPsychLab Study Plan

Students have access to a personalized study plan, based on Bloom's taxonomy, that arranges content from less complex thinking (such as remembering and understanding) to more complex critical thinking (such as applying and analyzing). This layered approach promotes better critical thinking skills and helps students succeed in the course and beyond.

ASSESSMENT

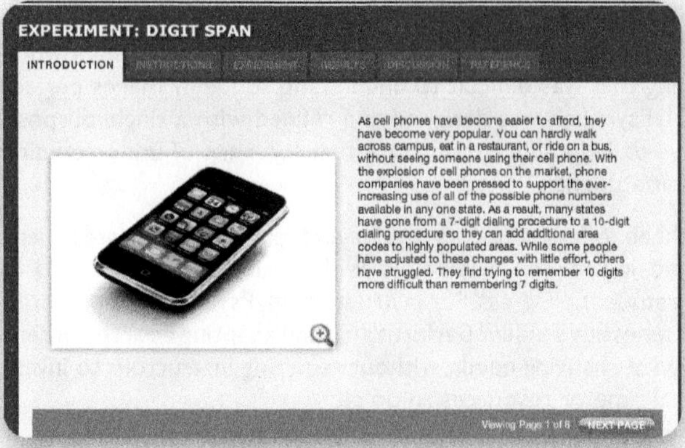

MyPsychLab Simulations

Online simulations help students understand scientific principles and practise through active learning. Over thirty experiments, inventories, and surveys are available through MyPsychLab.

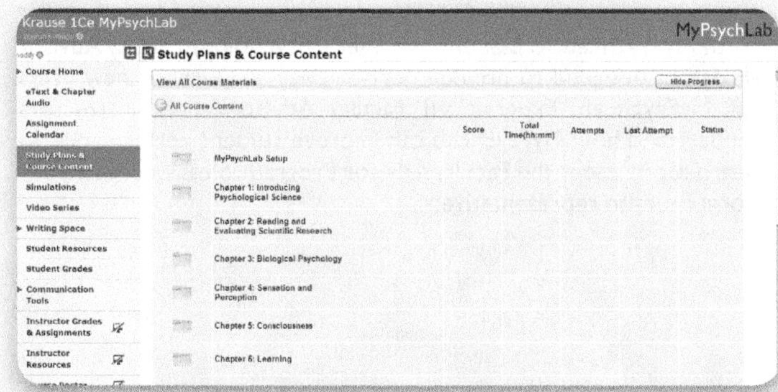

For access to all instructor supplements for *An Introduction to Psychological Science*, go to vig.pearsoned.ca and follow the directions to register (or log in if you already have a Pearson user name and password). Once you have registered and your status as an instructor is verified, you will be emailed a log-in name and password. Use your log-in name and password to access the catalogue. Click on the "Browse by Discipline" link, click on "psychology" and then "introductory psychology," and finally select the Krause/Corts/Smith/Dolderman, *An Introduction to Psychological Science*, text. Under the description of each supplement is a link that allows you to download and save the supplement to your desktop.

For technical support for any of your Pearson products, you and your students can contact http://247.pearsoned.com.

Acknowledgments

We cannot fathom completing a project like this without the help and support of many individuals. Through every bit of this process have been our families and we thank you for your love, patience, and support. Although our children will be disappointed that this book is not about princesses, Spiderman, or sea creatures, we hope that they'll read and enjoy this book one day. Our extended families, particularly Peggy Salter, also provided immense support and helped our children feel loved even when we had to work late to finish this book. In addition, our departments have been wonderfully understanding and helpful, offering advice with their various specializations, providing examples and tips, reviewing drafts, and tolerating our occasional absences.

The Canadian edition of this textbook involved a small army of helpful people. Our Developmental Editor, Johanna Schlaepfer, was incredibly supportive and patient throughout this entire process. We cannot thank her enough. We are also indebted to Matthew Christian, the Acquisitions Editor, who got this project started and helped motivate and organize us throughout the writing of this textbook. Duncan Mackinnon, the Pearson Sales Representative for Manitoba and Saskatchewan, also helped with the initial stages of this book and provided useful information about the level of writing and analysis that were missing from the Canadian introductory psychology textbook market. Marissa Lok, Nidhi Chopra, and their production teams worked tirelessly in order to turn our Word, Excel, and PowerPoint files into a beautiful textbook. Susan Bindernagel's copyediting and encouragement were also much appreciated. We would also like to thank the entire Pearson sales team for promoting this book as well as the supplements team for editing the MyPsychLab and other online materials.

The Canadian edition of this book benefitted from conversations with a number of colleagues. Amy Desroches was immensely helpful in making suggestions for Canadian content for the language module (Module 8.3). Beverley Fehr provided useful articles and suggestions for the new section on love (Module 11.3). Doug Williams provided us with a number of helpful ideas that ended up influencing parts of Chapters 6 (Learning) and 14 (Health, Stress, and Coping); he gets bonus points for doing this while at a Winnipeg Jets game (Washington won . . . stupid Ovechkin). Lars Gustav Fjordlund provided insights that helped us add new content to the module on drugs (Module 5.3). Danielle Gaucher made a number of useful content and editorial suggestions throughout the writing of this book. Michelle Di Nella, Steve's research assistant/teaching assistant/lab coordinator/former graduate student/friend, typed up and organized over 1300 references. We cannot thank her enough for her patience and work ethic. We also thank Jen Kornelsen, Steve's research collaborator and friend, who provided a tremendous amount of support throughout this project and who was always willing to listen to different ideas (and jokes) that we had for this book. Finally, we extend a heartfelt thanks to Safa Ali, for her tireless support, and tremendous amount of research and editing work, particularly for Chapters 10 (Lifespan Development), 15 (Psychological Disorders), and 16 (Therapies), for which her wisdom and insight were invaluable.

Finally, the many reviewers and students who carefully read over earlier versions of each chapter have been immensely helpful. We are very grateful that you shared your expertise in the field of psychology, and in teaching, to help bring this book to life.

List of Reviewers

Jeffrey Adams, Trent University

George Alder, Simon Fraser University

Stephanie Denison, University of Waterloo

Stephane Gaskin, Concordia University and Dawson College

Peter Graf, University of British Columbia

Rick Healey, Memorial University of Newfoundland

Denise M. Iacobucci, Camosun College

Alison Luby, University of Toronto

Laura MacKay, Capilano University

Stacey L. MacKinnon, University of Prince Edward Island

Jamal K. Mansour, Simon Fraser University

Geoffrey S. Navara, Trent University

Wayne Podrouzek, University of the Fraser Valley

David Reagan, Camosun College

Biljana Stevanovski, University of New Brunswick

Cheryl Techentin, Mount Royal University

Jennifer Tomaszczyk, University of Waterloo

Randal Tonks, Camosun College

Ashley Waggoner Denton, University of Toronto

Susan G. Walling, Memorial University of Newfoundland

Stacey Wareham-Fowler, Memorial University of Newfoundland

Ross Woolley, Langara College

We value feedback from both instructors and students, and we are sure that we will need it for our second Canadian edition. Please do not hesitate to offer suggestions or comments by writing to Steve Smith (s.smith@uwinnipeg.ca) or Dan Dolderman (doldermanuoft@gmail.com).

1

Introducing Psychological Science

Sarah2/Shutterstock

FotosearchRF/Glow Images

Module 1.1

The Science of Psychology

Learning Objectives

After reading this module you should

KNOW ...	UNDERSTAND ...	APPLY ...	ANALYZE ...
The key terminology of the scientific method	The steps of the scientific method The concept of scientific literacy	The biopsychosocial model to behaviour The steps in critical thinking	The use of the term *scientific theory*

Almost everyone has misinterpreted someone else's meaning in a conversation. You could misinterpret someone leaning closer to you as flirting when really you were just talking too softly. You could mistake someone's tone of voice as being annoyed when that person was actually talking loudly to be heard over other people in the room. We also frequently misjudge other people's attitudes and personalities. The unfriendly and arrogant person at work might actually turn out to be a shy person who dislikes crowded social events. In all of these situations, we make inferences about another person based on the different cues they provide us. But how do we decide which cues are important? Are they really the right cues to be using when we want to explain other people's behaviour?

The situation is even more complicated in the wired world of the 21st century, with everyone plugged in to email, online gaming, and social networking sites like Facebook. But these new ways of interacting with people from around the world also come with their own set of challenges. How do you interpret someone's behaviour or intentions when all you have to go by is words on a screen and cartoon-like happy faces? How much information do you need to (safely) disclose in order for other people to understand you? These puzzles have led researchers to develop a new line of research, *cyber emotional intelligence,* that examines the assumptions that we make about people based on their online personalities (Ben Youssef & Ben Youssef, 2011).

The purpose of this opening section isn't to depress you; instead, it is to show how complex human behaviour is and how challenging it can be to try to understand it. In this textbook, we will examine many different aspects of behaviour—from basic brain and perception functions to memory to social behaviours. But all of these chapters have the same central theme: the quest to understand *why* and *how* we behave the way we do.

Focus Questions

 How can the human mind, with its quirks and imperfections, conduct studies on itself?

 How can scientific and critical thinking steer us toward a clearer understanding of human behaviour and experience?

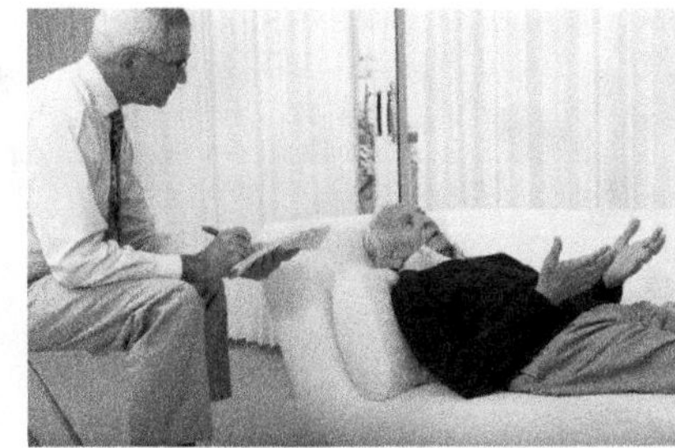

Left: AF archive/Alamy; centre: sextoacto/Shutterstock.com; right: Flirt/SuperStock

Television personalities such as Phil McGraw, experiments involving animals running mazes, and sessions between a therapist and client are common notions about the work of psychologists. But how well do they represent the field?

Which words and images come to mind when you hear that someone is a psychologist? Many of us think of professionals conducting therapy or people in white lab coats watching rats run through mazes. The field of psychology is also viewed through the lens of "pop" psychology—the scores of self-help gurus on TV, on the radio, and in the books lining bookstore shelves. Although these images are not necessarily false, they don't fully capture the scope of the field of psychology. One goal of this book is to challenge your expectations about psychology and to show you that psychology—and psychological research—affect almost every aspect of your life.

To begin, we should acknowledge that psychology is a vast discipline; in fact, we might do better to consider it to be a collection of disciplines composed of many overlapping fields of study. Two unifying qualities allow us to group all these fields into the category of psychological science. First, psychology involves the study of behaviour that, broadly defined, can include perceptions, thoughts, and emotions. Second, psychologists employ the *scientific method* in their work. On these grounds, we can define **psychology** *as the scientific study of behaviour, thought, and experience, and how they can be affected by physical, mental, social, and environmental factors.* In the following sections, we will discuss some basic principles of science. As you will see, psychologists share with other sciences a common set of methods and perspectives for understanding the world.

The Scientific Method

What exactly does it mean to be a scientist? A person who haphazardly combines chemicals in test tubes may look like a chemist, but he is not conducting science; a person who dissects a specimen just to see how it looks may appear to be a biologist, but this is not science either. In contrast, a person who carefully follows a system of observing, predicting, and testing *is* conducting science, whether the subject matter is chemicals, physiology, human memory, or social interactions. In other words, whether a field of study is a science, or a specific type of research is *scientific*, is based not on the subject but on the use of the scientific method. The **scientific method** *is a way of learning about the world through collecting observations, developing theories to explain them, and using the theories to make predictions.* It involves a dynamic interaction between hypothesis testing and the construction of theories, outlined in Figure 1.1.

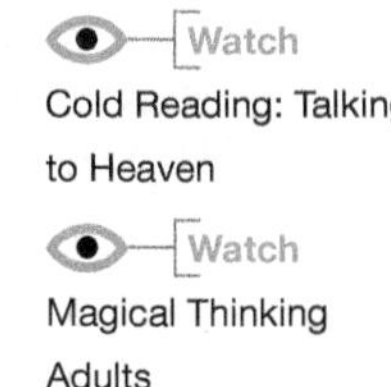

HYPOTHESES: MAKING PREDICTIONS Scientific thinking and procedures revolve around the concepts of a hypothesis and a theory. Both guide the process and progress of the sciences; however, it is important to differentiate between these terms. A **hypothesis** (plural: hypotheses) *is a testable prediction about processes that can be observed and measured.* A hypothesis can be supported or rejected (you do not *prove* a hypothesis), and a scientific hypothesis *must* be testable. These rules are regularly broken by people claiming to be scientific. For example, astrologers and psychics are in the business of making predictions. An astrologer might tell you, "It's a good time for you to keep quiet or defer important calls or emails." This sounds like a request to not even bother

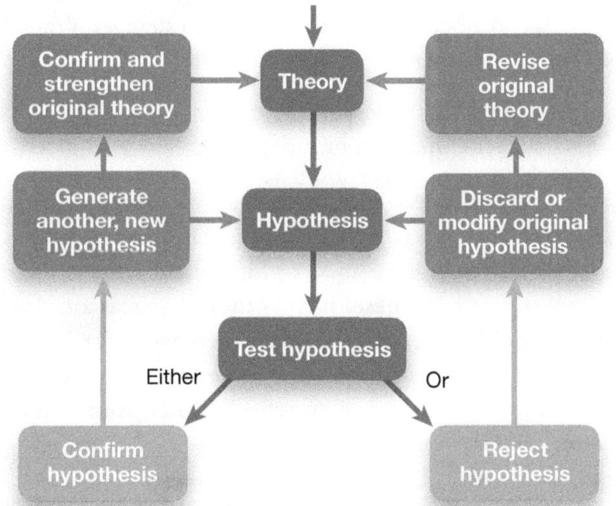

{FIG. 1.1} **The Scientific Method** Scientists use theories to generate hypotheses. Once tested, hypotheses are either confirmed or rejected. Confirmed hypotheses lead to new ones and strengthen theories. Rejected hypotheses are revised and tested again, and can potentially alter an existing theory.

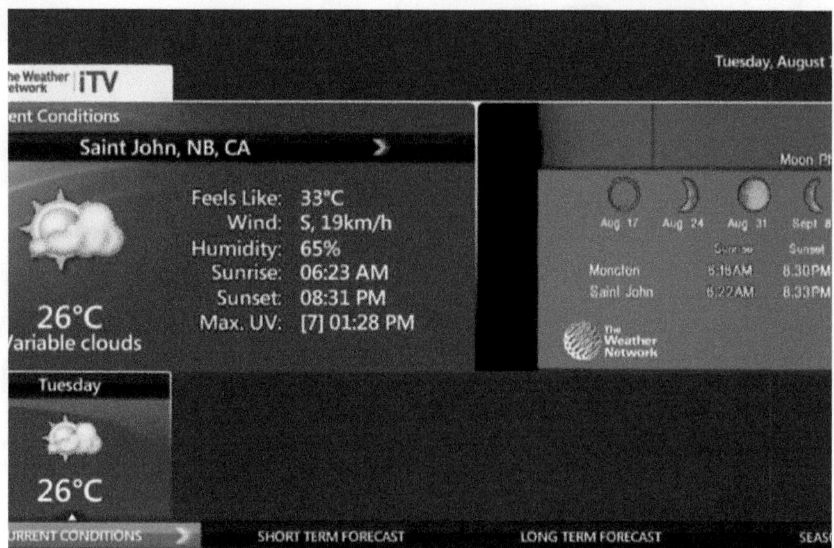

Hand-out/BELL ALIANT INC./Newscom

Supporters of psychics and astrologers often point out that scientific fields (such as meteorology) do not always make correct predictions. A key difference between science and pseudoscience is that in science an incorrect hypothesis is rejected and an alternative can be stated and tested.

testing the prediction, because it might come true. The horoscope leaves two courses of action: (1) cave in, fully accept the prediction, and heed the advice or (2) take your chances. If you take your chances, it is very likely that by the end of the day you can find at least a grain of truth in the prediction. Horoscopes make *very* general predictions—typically so much so that you could easily find evidence for them if you looked hard enough, and perhaps stretched an interpretation of events a bit. In contrast, a good scientific hypothesis is stated in more precise terms, such as the following:

> "People become less likely to help a stranger if there are others around."
>
> "Cigarette smoking causes cancer."
>
> "Exercise improves memory ability."

Each of these hypotheses can be confirmed or rejected through scientific testing. An obvious difference between science and astrology is that scientists are eager to test hypotheses such as these, whereas astrologists would rather you just take their word for it. We do acknowledge that astrology is a very easy target for criticism. In fact, it is often referred to as **pseudoscience**, *an idea that is presented as science but does not actually utilize basic principles of scientific thinking or procedure.* Incidentally, a 2005 Gallup poll found that 25% of Canadians (17% of males and 33% of females) believe that the position of the stars in the sky can affect a person's behaviour.

THEORIES: EXPLAINING PHENOMENA In contrast to hypotheses, a **theory** *is an explanation for a broad range of observations that also generates new hypotheses and integrates numerous findings into a coherent whole.* In other words, theories are general principles or explanations of some aspect of the world (including human behaviours), whereas hypotheses are specific predictions that can test the theory or, more realistically, specific parts of that theory. Theories are built from hypotheses that are repeatedly tested and confirmed. If a hypothesis is supported, it provides more support for the theory. In turn, good theories eventually become accepted explanations of behaviour or other phenomena. However, if the hypothesis is not supported by the results of a well-designed experiment, then researchers may have to rethink elements of the theory. Figure 1.1 shows how hypothesis testing eventually leads back to the theory from which it was based.

Similar to hypotheses, an essential quality of scientific theories is that they can be proved false with new evidence. In fact, any scientific theory must be *falsifiable*: Just as researchers can discover strong evidence in support of a theory, they can also discover evidence that challenges a theory. As Figure 1.1 shows, theories can be updated with new evidence. The process helps to ensure that science is *self-correcting*—bad ideas typically do not last long in the sciences.

The term *theory* is often used very casually, which has led to some persistent and erroneous beliefs that many people have about scientific theories. So to clarify a few common issues:

- **Theories are not the same thing as opinions or beliefs.** Yes, it is certainly true that everyone is entitled to their own beliefs. But the phrase "That's just *your* theory" is neither the correct use of the term "theory," nor an argument that a scientist would make.
- **All theories are *not* equally plausible.** Groups of scientists might adopt different theories for explaining the same phenomenon. For example, several theories have been proposed to explain why people become depressed. This does not mean that anyone can throw their hat into the ring and claim equal status for his or her theory (or belief). There are good theories, and there are not-so-good theories.
- **A measure of a good theory is not the number of people who believe it to be true.** According to a 2009 Gallup poll, only 61% of Canadians (and only 39% of Americans) believe in the theory of evolution by natural selection (Angus Reid Opinion, 2012), despite the fact that it is the most plausible, rigorously tested theory of biological change and diversity.

Testing hypotheses and constructing theories are both part of all sciences. In addition, each science, including psychology, has its own unique way of approaching its complex subject matter as well as its own unique set of challenges. In the case of psychology, we must remember that behaviour can occur on a number of different levels including the activity of cells in different parts of the brain, thought processes such as language and memory, and sociocultural processes that shape daily life for millions of people. Therefore, psychology examines the individual as a product of multiple influences, including biological, psychological, and social factors.

THE BIOPSYCHOSOCIAL MODEL Because our thoughts and behaviours have multiple influences, psychologists adopt multiple perspectives to understand them. The **biopsychosocial model** *is a means of explaining behaviour as a product of biological, psychological, and sociocultural factors* (Figure 1.2 on p. 6). Biological influences on our behaviour involve brain structures and chemicals, hormones, and external substances such as drugs. Psychological influences involve our memories, emotions, and personalities, and how these factors shape the way we think about and respond to different people and situations. Finally, social factors such as our family, peers, ethnicity, and culture can have a huge effect on our behaviour. Importantly, none of these levels of analysis exists on its own. In fact, these levels influence each other! The firing of brain cells can influence how we think and remember information; this, in turn, can affect how we interact with family members or how we respond to social situations like a concert. But, these influences can occur in the other direction as well. Social situations can affect how we think (e.g., getting annoyed at the crowded hallway at your university), which, in turn, can trigger the release of chemicals and hormones in your brain.

Ellie Rothnie/Alamy

"All swans are white" is a falsifiable statement. A swan that is not coloured white will falsify it. Falsification is a critical component of scientific hypotheses and theories.

The take-home message of this section is that almost every moment of your life is occurring at all three levels; psychologists have taken up the exciting challenge of trying to understand them. Indeed, behaviour can be fully explained only if multiple perspectives—and their interactions—are investigated. This "systems perspective" will become particularly apparent as you read about psychological research that tackles complex topics.

Throughout this text, we will apply the biopsychosocial model to many of the topics we will cover. An icon, like the one in the margin, will appear in these sections, prompting you to apply the biopsychosocial model to a specific problem or question about multiple influences on thinking and behaviour. Our hope is that by the end of this textbook, you will use a similar strategy when examining the events of your own life.

Quick Quiz 1.1a
The Scientific Method

KNOW ...

1 A testable prediction about processes that can be observed and measured is referred to as a(n)______.

- **A** theory
- **B** hypothesis
- **C** opinion
- **D** hunch

2 A theory or prediction is falsifiable if

- **A** it has been proven false.
- **B** it is impossible to test.
- **C** there can be evidence for it or against it.
- **D** if and only if it comes from pseudoscience.

APPLY ...

3 How would you apply the biopsychosocial model to a news report claiming that anxiety is caused by being around other people who are anxious?

- **A** Recognize that the news report considers all portions of the biopsychosocial model
- **B** Recognize that psychologists do not regard biological factors when it comes to anxiety
- **C** Recognize that the only effective treatment of anxiety must be drug based
- **D** Recognize that the news report only considers one portion of the biopsychosocial model

ANALYZE ...

4 The hypothesis that "exercise improves memory ability" is a scientific one because

- **A** it cannot be confirmed.
- **B** it cannot be rejected.
- **C** it makes a specific, testable prediction.
- **D** it can be proven.

Answers can be found on page ANS-1.

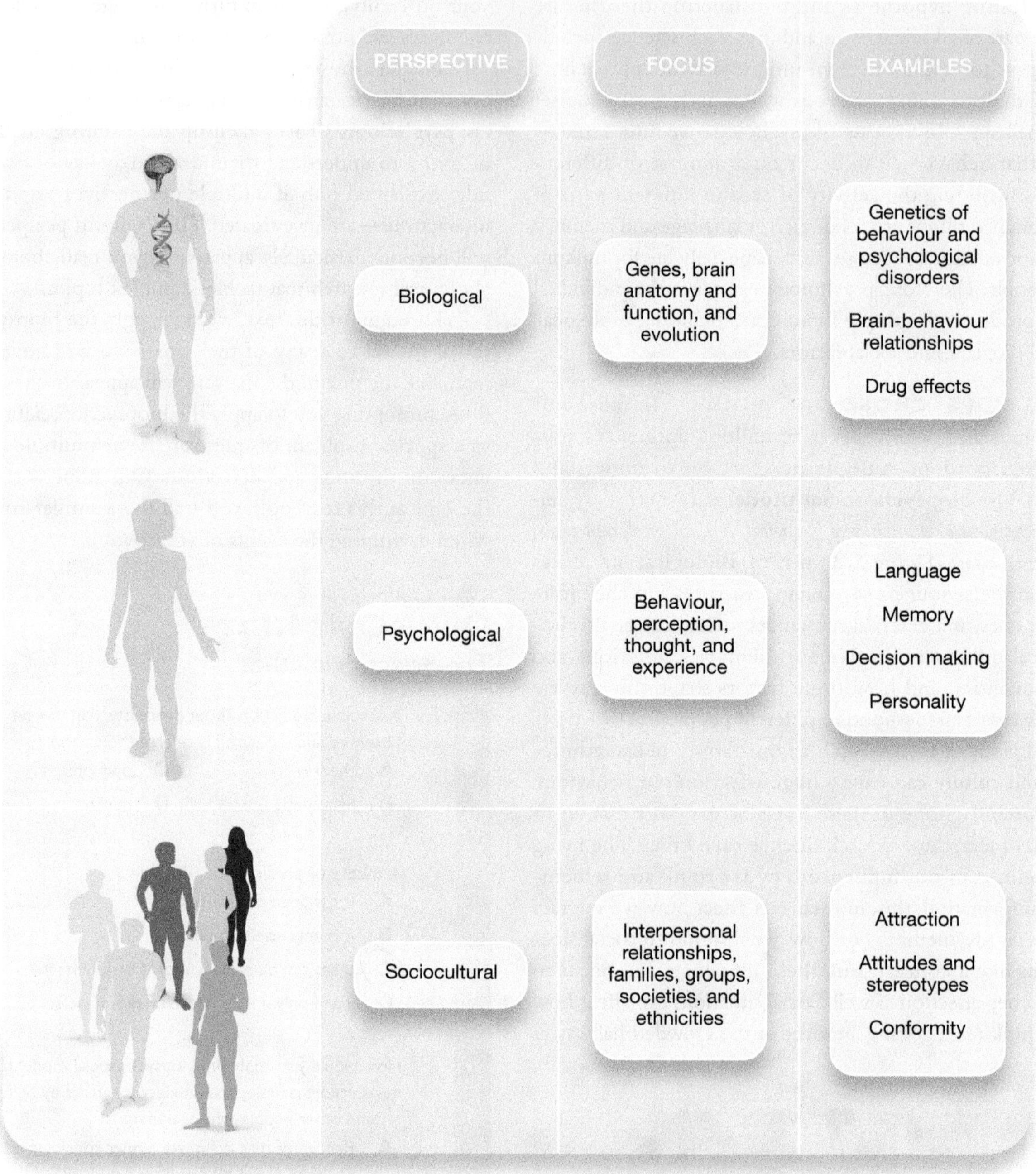

PERSPECTIVE	FOCUS	EXAMPLES
Biological	Genes, brain anatomy and function, and evolution	Genetics of behaviour and psychological disorders Brain-behaviour relationships Drug effects
Psychological	Behaviour, perception, thought, and experience	Language Memory Decision making Personality
Sociocultural	Interpersonal relationships, families, groups, societies, and ethnicities	Attraction Attitudes and stereotypes Conformity

{FIG. 1.2} **The Biopsychosocial Model** Psychologists view behaviour from multiple perspectives. A full understanding of human behaviour comes from analyzing biological, psychological, and sociocultural factors.

Building Scientific Literacy

A major aim of this book is to teach you the theoretical foundations, concepts, and applicable skills that are central to the field of psychology. This book is also designed to help you develop **scientific literacy**, *the ability to understand, analyze, and apply scientific information*. As you can see in Figure 1.3, scientific literacy has several key components, starting with the ability to learn new information. Certainly this text will provide you with new terminology and concepts, but you will continue to encounter psychological and scientific terminology long after you have completed this course. Being scientifically literate means that you will be able to read and interpret new terminology, or know where to go to find out more.

Simulate Survey: What Do You Know about Psychology?

But, memorizing different terms is not enough to make someone scientifically literate. We also

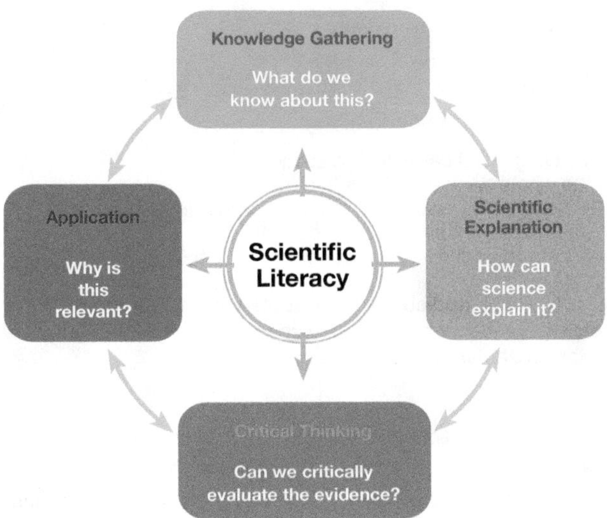

{FIG. 1.3} **A Model for Scientific Literacy** Scientific literacy involves four different skills: gathering knowledge about the world, explaining it using scientific terms and concepts, using critical thinking, and applying and using information.

have to examine whether the ideas being presented were scientifically tested, and whether those studies were designed properly. It is absolutely essential that we ask such questions. Doing so allows us to separate the information that we *should* find convincing from the information that we should view with caution. It will also allow you to better analyze the information presented to you by politicians, corporations, and the media; this will make it more difficult for these groups to influence your behaviour. Finally, we want to be able to apply the results of scientific studies to different situations; in other words, to *generalize* the results. Generalization shows us that the studies conducted in universities and hospitals can provide insight into behaviours that extend far beyond the confines of the lab.

WORKING THE SCIENTIFIC LITERACY MODEL

How We Learn and Remember

To develop your scientific literacy skills, in every module (beginning with Chapter 2) we will revisit this model and its four components as they apply to a specific psychological topic—a process we call *working the model.* This will help you to move beyond simply learning the vocabulary of psychological research toward *understanding* scientific explanations, thinking critically, and discovering applications of the material. In order to demonstrate how these sections of the book will work, let's use an example that will be familiar to many: planning study times for your different classes.

What do we know about effective studying techniques?

In the first stage of the Scientific Literary Model, we attempt to gather the available knowledge about the topic that we're investigating, in this case massed vs. distributed study techniques. As you've likely noticed, many high school and university courses, including your psychology course, require you to learn definitions and factual information such as the names of famous psychologists. However, students differ on how they attempt to remember this information for exams (and, we hope, beyond that time). Many students use what is called *massed learning*—they perform all of their studying for an exam in one lengthy session. Another approach is *spaced* or *distributed learning*—having shorter study sessions, but spreading them over several days. Which technique do you prefer? If you use the massed learning technique (most students prefer it . . . or end up using it because they've left studying until the last minute), it is likely because it *seems* easier and it may even give you the sense that it is more effective than distributed learning. Actually, the two strategies are not equally effective; distributed learning is the better of the two.

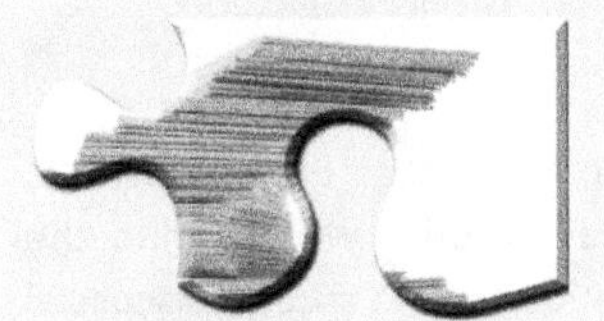

How can science explain this difference?

In the second stage of the Scientific Literacy Model, we examine whether the information that is available about a topic has been tested in scientific studies. In our example, massed and distributed learning have been studied by psychologists for almost a century (Cepeda et al., 2006; Edwards, 1917). In a typical study, experimental participants read a list of words or a passage of text and then complete a test assessing their memory for what they read. In some cases, the participants read the same list of words repeatedly (massed learning) whereas in other cases there are delays in between the participants' reading of the lists. The results of such studies have consistently shown that memory is better when you spread out your study sessions (Terry, 1982).

For example, in one study conducted by Nate Kornell (2009), a group of 20 student volunteers learned pairs of synonyms (e.g., *effulgent – brilliant*) by using flashcards, a common study tool. All participants completed one test in which they used massed learning and one test in which they used distributed or spaced learning. Each pair of synonyms was presented four

You have a total of 20 terms to learn.

Massing: Studying a deck of five cards four times in a row. This masses study for an individual card, such as card A in the drawing above.

You have a total of 20 terms to learn.

Spacing: Leaving all 20 cards in one stack and studying the whole deck four times in a row. This spaces the studying for each card, such as card A in the drawing above. However, in both conditions, card A will be studied the same number of times (four).

{FIG. 1.4} **Massed Versus Spaced Practice** In both conditions, volunteers studied each vocabulary word four times. In the massed condition, shown at left, the individual cards were studied closer together whereas in the spaced condition, at right, they were studied further apart. Spaced learning results in better memory for vocabulary terms.

times; however, the amount of time between each of these presentations was manipulated by the experimenter. In the distributed condition, participants went through a large stack of 20 synonyms. Thus, there were 20 trials separating one exposure to the synonym from the next. In contrast, in the massed condition, participants were given small stacks of five synonyms. After going through a stack four times, they were then given the next stack of five synonyms. Therefore, there were only five trials separating one exposure to the synonym from the next. At the end of the study period, the researcher administered a memory test and discovered that the volunteers could remember significantly more words from the spaced condition than from the massed condition (see Figure 1.4). Interestingly, the participants *thought* they had performed better in the massed learning session. From these results, he concluded that it is better to study by using spaced or distributed practice.

Can we critically evaluate alternative explanations?

In the third stage of the Scientific Literacy Model, we examine the limitations of the studies discussed earlier; we also look for alternative explanations for the results. The studies discussed above do not provide evidence that spacing works for all kinds of learning. The terms the students studied were common words that would likely be found on a standardized, general vocabulary test. Would distributed learning improve performance in other situations? Data from a number of research areas suggests that it would. Studies of motor (movement) skills ranging from moving a computer mouse to following an object on the screen to learning new basketball shots all indicate that distributed practice leads to better performance (Lee & Genovese, 1988; Singer, 1965). A recent brain-imaging study has also shown that distributed learning leads to increased activity in areas related to memory representations (Takashima et al., 2007; memory and the brain is discussed more in Module 7.1). Thus, there appears to be *converging evidence* from other research areas in support of the claim that distributed learning is superior to massed learning.

However, one thing that is missing from the existing research studies is pressure. When students "cram" for exams using massed learning, they are likely experiencing a lot of stress caused by the situation they find themselves in (see Module 14.2 for a discussion of stress). In contrast, the experiments mentioned here involve primarily laboratory-based studies that are not meaningful to the participants. Future research is needed to determine whether stress and self-relevance alter the difference between massed and distributed learning scores.

Why is this finding relevant?

In the final stage of the the Scientific Literacy Model, we attempt to apply the results to situations outside of the laboratory. For instance, you would ideally apply this knowledge about massed and distributed learning to your own experiences as a student. Each chapter you read in this text includes definitions, and there is a set of flashcards available with the online tools accompanying this text at MyPsychLab. Perhaps you will consider the distributed-learning method when studying key terms for each module. This technique would probably also be useful in other courses, such as history, where you may need to match dates and major historical events, or in a foreign language course, where you are learning new vocabulary and verb conjugations. Distributed learning has also proven useful in many clinical contexts, such as helping people improve their memory abilities after suffering a traumatic brain injury (Hillary et al., 2003). Sometimes simple experiments can have widespread implications; that's something to remember.

TayaCho/iStockphoto

Now that you have read this feature, we hope you understand how scientific information fits into the four components of the model. But there is still much to learn about working the model: In the next section, we will describe critical thinking skills and how to use them.

CRITICAL THINKING, CURIOSITY, AND A DOSE OF HEALTHY SKEPTICISM People are confronted with more information on a daily basis than at any other point in our history. Some of it is credible and can be used to help guide your decisions or behaviour. But, we also must deal with claims—often, but not always, made by people trying to sell you things—that are not always true.

> "This political party will not base its positions on public opinion polls."
>
> "These remedies were developed by ancient cultures and have been used for centuries."
>
> "Join now and find your soul mate."

Misinformation can sometimes seem far more abundant than accurate information, which is why it is important to develop critical thinking skills.

Refer back to Figure 1.3. As the model shows, critical thinking is an important element of scientific literacy. **Critical thinking** *involves exercising curiosity and skepticism when evaluating the claims of others, and with our own assumptions and beliefs*. The ability to think critically can be learned and developed, but most of us need to make a conscious effort to do so (Halpern, 1996). Research points to a core set of habits and skills for developing critical thinking:

1. Be curious. Simple answers are sometimes too simple, and common sense is not always correct (or even close to it). For example, giving your brain some time to rest after having a stroke (a form of brain damage) *hinders* rather than helps your recovery (see Module 3.3).
2. Examine the nature and source of the evidence; not all research is of equal quality. For example, you will likely find a more accurate account of prejudiced attitudes if you use a subtle, experimental technique than if you directly ask people whether they have these attitudes (see Module 13.2).
3. Examine assumptions and biases. This includes your own assumptions as well as the assumptions of those making claims. Research examining the impact of human behaviour on climate change may be biased if it is funded by oil companies (see Module 2.2).
4. Avoid overly emotional thinking. Emotions can tell us what we value, but they are not always helpful when it comes to making critical decisions. For example, you may have strong responses when hearing about differences in the cognitive abilities of males and females (see Module 3.1); however, it is important to put those aside to examine the studies themselves.
5. Tolerate ambiguity. Most complex issues do not have clear-cut answers. Psychologists have identified a number of factors leading to depression, but no single factor *guarantees* that a person will suffer from this condition (see Module 15.3).
6. Consider alternative viewpoints and alternative interpretations of the evidence. For example, it is clear that we require sleep in order to function properly; however, there are several theories that can explain the functions that sleep serves (see Module 5.1).

If you follow these steps, you will be well on your way to developing critical thinking habits and skills. However, determining what does *not* constitute critical thinking is important as well. Critical thinking is not a philosophy, a belief, or a faith, nor is it meant to make everyone arrive at the same answer. Complex issues often remain ambiguous, and at times a question may have several plausible answers. Although critical thinking cannot guarantee a correct answer—and sometimes it even delivers unpleasant ones—it will help find and justify good answers.

Critical thinking means considering other viewpoints, but it also means that some ideas can be incorrect. In many cases, one answer emerges as the best one because a large body of evidence converges upon it. Critical thinking does not mean being negative or arbitrarily critical; it simply means that you intentionally examine knowledge, beliefs, and the means by which conclusions were obtained.

Put another way, critical thinking involves cautious skepticism. We are constantly being told about amazing products that help us control body weight, improve thinking and memory, enhance sexual performance, and so on. As consumers, there are always going to be claims we really hope to be true. But as critical thinkers, we meet these claims with a good dose of skepticism (*e.g., Is there sound evidence that this diet helps people to achieve and maintain a healthy weight?*). Being skeptical can be challenging, especially when it means asking for evidence that we may not want to find. Often the great products or the miracle cures that we have always hoped for really *are* "too good to be true." Being curious *and* skeptical leads you to ask important questions about the science underlying such claims. Doing so leads us to search for and evaluate evidence, which is never a bad thing.

Simulate
The Pseudoscience of Astrology

Listen
Science and Pseudoscience

Explore
Accelerated Learning

Watch
John Cacioppo: What Is Important to Learn from an Intro to Psychology Course?

Watch
IT Video: How Much Do You Know About Psychology?

Explore
How to Be a Critical Thinker

Shiva/Shutterstock.com

Independent reports of alien abductions often resemble events and characters depicted in science fiction movies.

MYTHS IN MIND

Abducted by Aliens!

Occasionally we hear claims of alien abductions, ghost sightings, and other paranormal activity. Countless television shows and movies, both fictional and documentary based, reinforce the idea that these types of events can and do occur. Alien abductions are probably the most far-fetched stories, yet many people believe they occur or at least regard them as a real possibility. What is even more interesting are the extremely detailed accounts given by purported alien abductees. However, physical evidence of an abduction is always lacking. So what can we make of the validity of alien abduction stories?

Scientific and critical thinking involve the use of the *principle of parsimony*, which means that the simplest of all competing explanations (the most "parsimonious") of a phenomenon should be the one we accept. Is there a simpler explanation for alien abductions? Probably so. Psychologists who study alien abduction cases have discovered some interesting patterns. First, historical reports of abductions typically spike just after the release of science fiction movies featuring space aliens. Details of the reports often follow specific details seen in these movies (Clancy, 2005). Second, it probably would not be too surprising to learn that people who report being abducted are prone to fantasizing and having false memories (vivid recollection and belief in something that did not happen; Lynn & Kirsch, 1996; Spanos et al., 1994). Finally, people who claim to have been abducted are likely to experience sleep paralysis (waking up and becoming aware of being unable to move—a temporary state that is not unusual) and hallucinations while in the paralyzed state (McNally et al., 2004). You can likely see how these three factors could explain reports of alien abductions. Following the principle of parsimony typically leads to real, though sometimes less spectacular, answers—although these answers might leave the so-called "abductees" feeling alienated.

Quick Quiz 1.1b Building Scientific Literacy

KNOW ...

1 Someone who exercises curiosity and skepticism about assumptions and beliefs is using _______.

- **A** critical thinking
- **B** a hypothesis
- **C** pseudoscience
- **D** the biopsychosocial model

UNDERSTAND ...

2 Scientific literacy does *not* include _______.

- **A** gathering knowledge
- **B** accepting common sense explanations
- **C** critical thinking
- **D** applying scientific information to everyday problems

APPLY ...

3 Paul is considering whether to take a cholesterol-reducing medicine that has been recommended by his physician. He goes to the library and learns that the government agency that oversees medications—Health Canada—has approved the medication after dozens of studies had been conducted on its usefulness. Which aspect of critical thinking does this *best* represent?

- **A** Paul has examined the nature and source of the evidence.
- **B** Paul was simply curious.
- **C** Paul did not consider alternative viewpoints.
- **D** Paul was avoiding overly emotional thinking.

Answers can be found on page ANS-1.

Module Summary

Now that you have read this module you should

KNOW ...

- ***The key terminology of the scientific method*:**

biopsychosocial model (p. 5)
critical thinking (p. 9)
hypothesis (p. 3)
pseudoscience (p. 4)
psychology (p. 3)
scientific literacy (p. 6)
scientific method (p. 3)
theory (p. 4)

UNDERSTAND ...

- ***The steps of the scientific method.*** The basic model in **Figure 1.1 (p. 3)** guides us through the steps of the scientific method. Scientific theories generate hypotheses, which are specific and testable predictions. If a hypothesis is confirmed, new hypotheses may stem from it, and the original theory receives added support. If a hypothesis is rejected, the original hypothesis may be modified and retested, or the original theory may be modified or rejected.
- ***The concept of scientific literacy.*** *Scientific literacy* refers to the process of how we think about and understand scientific information. The model for scientific literacy was summarized in **Figure 1.3 (p. 7)**. Working the model involves answering a set of questions:

  What do we know about a phenomenon?

  How can science explain it?

  Can we critically evaluate the evidence?

  Why is this relevant?

  You will see this model applied to concepts in each chapter of this text. This includes gathering knowledge, explaining phenomena in scientific terms, engaging in critical thinking, and knowing how to apply and use your knowledge.

FotosearchRF/Glow Images

APPLY ...

- ***The biopsychosocial model to behaviour.*** This is a model we will use throughout the text. As you consider each topic, think about how biological factors (e.g., the brain and genetics) are influential. Also consider how psychological factors such as thinking, learning, emotion, and memory are relevant. Social and cultural factors complete the model. These three interacting factors influence our behaviour.
- ***The steps in critical thinking.*** To be useful, critical thinking is something not just to memorize, but rather to use and apply. Remember, critical thinking involves (1) being curious, (2) examining evidence, (3) examining assumptions and biases, (4) avoiding emotional thinking, (5) tolerating ambiguity, and (6) considering alternative viewpoints. Try applying these steps below in **Table 1.1** and check your answers on page ANS-1.

ANALYZE ...

- ***The use of the term scientific theory.*** As you read in this module, the term *theory* is often used very casually in the English language, sometimes synonymously with *opinion*. Thus it is important to analyze the scientific meaning of the term and contrast it with the alternatives. A scientific theory is an explanation for a broad range of observations, integrating numerous findings into a coherent whole. Remember, theories are not the same thing as opinions or beliefs, all theories are not equally plausible, and, strange as it may sound, a measure of a good scientific theory is not determined by the number of people who believe it to be true.

Table 1.1 :: Critical Thinking

Practise applying critical thinking skills to the scenario below:

Magic Mileage is a high-tech fuel additive that actually increases the distance you can drive for every litre by 20%, while costing only a fraction of the gasoline itself!! Wouldn't you like to cut your fuel expenses by one-fifth? Magic Mileage is a blend of complex engine-cleaning agents and patented "octane-booster" that not only packs in extra kilometres per litre but also leaves your engine cleaner and running smooth while reducing emissions!

1. How might this appeal lead to overly emotional thinking?
2. Can you identify assumptions or biases the manufacturer might have?
3. Do you have enough evidence to make a judgment about this product?

nagib/Shutterstock

Module **1.2**

How Psychology Became a Science

Learning Objectives

After reading this module you should

KNOW ...	UNDERSTAND ...	APPLY ...	ANALYZE ...
The key terminology of psychology's history	How various philosophical and scientific fields became major influences on psychology	Your knowledge to distinguish among the different specializations in psychology	How the philosophical ideas of empiricism and determinism are applied to human behaviour

When we try to imagine the earliest investigations of human behaviour, we rarely think about axe wounds to the head. As it turns out, we should. The ancient Egyptians were a fierce military force for several centuries. The wealth accumulated during these military campaigns filled the palaces of the pharaohs with gold and jewels and allowed them to construct massive monuments like the pyramids. But one side effect of having many battles was that members of the Egyptian army also suffered many injuries, including some to the head. Although the primitive medical knowledge of the time condemned most brain-injured patients to death, some did in fact survive and attempted to return to their normal lives. However, as one might expect when someone has suffered an axe (*khopesh*) wound to the head, such attempts were not always successful. Similar problems had likely occurred in earlier times. What makes ancient Egypt stand out is that military doctors noticed—and documented—*patterns* that emerged in their patients. As noted in the Edwin Smith papyrus (obviously named after the American discoverer, not the Egyptian authors), damage to different parts of the brain resulted in different types of impairments ranging from problems with vision to problems with higher-order cognitive abilities. Although primitive by modern standards, this initial attempt to link a brain-based injury to a change in behaviour marked the first step toward our modern study of psychology.

Focus Questions

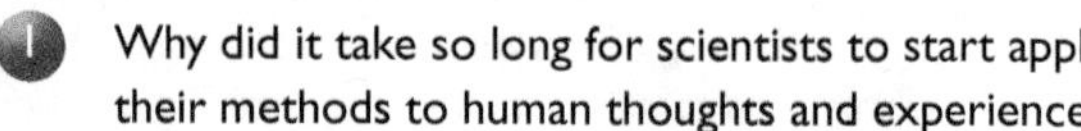

1. Why did it take so long for scientists to start applying their methods to human thoughts and experience?
2. What has resulted from the application of scientific methods to human behaviour?

Psychology has long dealt with some major questions and issues that span philosophical inquiry and scientific study. For example, psychologists have questioned how environmental, genetic, and physiological processes influence behaviour. They have wrestled with the issue of whether our behaviour is determined by external events, or if we have free will to act. Psychology's search for answers to these and other questions continues, and in this module we put this search into historical context and see how these questions have influenced the field of psychology as it exists today.

Ljupco Smokovski/Shutterstock.com

Most people believe that the behaviour of billiard balls will be *determined* by the laws of physics. They roll where the energy directs them, not where they want to go. Could human behaviour be determined by natural laws as well?

Psychology's Philosophical and Scientific Origins

Science is more than a body of facts to memorize or a set of subjects to study. Science is actually a philosophy of knowledge that stems from two fundamental beliefs: empiricism and determinism.

Empiricism *is a philosophical tenet that knowledge comes through experience.* In everyday language, you might hear the phrase "Seeing is believing," but in the scientific sense, empiricism means that knowledge about the world is based on careful observation, not on common sense or speculation. Whatever we see or measure should be observable by anyone else who follows the same methods. In addition, scientific theories must be logical explanations of how the observations fit together. Thus, although the empiricist might say, "Seeing is believing," thinking and reasoning about observations are just as important.

Determinism *is the belief that all events are governed by lawful, cause-and-effect relationships.* This is easy enough when we discuss natural laws such as gravity—we probably all agree that if you drop an object, it will fall (unless it is a helium balloon). But does the lawfulness of nature apply to the way we think and act? Does it mean that we do not have control over our own actions? This interesting philosophical debate is often referred to as *free will versus determinism.* While we certainly feel as if we are in control of our own behaviours—that is, we sense that we have free will—there are compelling reasons (discussed later in this book) to believe that some of our behaviours are determined. The level of determinism or free will psychologists attribute to humans is certainly debated, and to be a psychologist, you do not have to believe that every single thought, behaviour, or experience is determined by natural laws. But psychologists certainly do recognize that behaviour is determined by both internal (e.g., genes, brain chemistry) and external influences.

Psychological science is both empirical and deterministic. We now know that behaviour can only be understood by making observations and testing hypotheses. We also know that behaviour occurs at several different levels ranging from cells to societies. However, this modern knowledge did not appear overnight. Instead, our understanding of why we behave the way we do is built upon the hard work, creativity, and astute observational powers of scientists throughout history dating (at least) as far back as the ancient Mediterranean societies of Egypt, Greece, and Rome.

Explore
History of Psychology Timeline

INFLUENCES FROM THE ANCIENTS: PHILOSOPHICAL INSIGHTS INTO BEHAVIOUR As you read in the opening section of this module, ancient Egyptian doctors noticed that damage to different brain areas led to vastly different impairments. While such an observation marked the first recorded linking of biology and behaviour, it was not the only important insight to come out of ancient societies.

In ancient Greece, the physician Hippocrates (460–370 BCE) developed the world's first personality classification scheme. The ancient Greeks believed that four *humours* or fluids flowed throughout the body and influenced both health and personality. These four humours included blood, yellow bile, black bile, and phlegm (theories were a bit gross in ancient times). Different combinations of these four humours were thought to lead to specific moods and behaviours. Galen of Pergamon (127–217), arguably the greatest of the ancient Roman physicians, refined Hippocrates' more general work and suggested that the four humours combined to create *temperaments,* or emotional and personality characteristics that remained stable throughout the lifetime. Galen's four temperaments (each related to a humour) included:

> *Sanguine* (blood), a tendency to be impulsive, pleasure-seeking, and charismatic;
>
> *Choleric* (yellow bile), a tendency to be ambitious, energetic, and a bit aggressive;
>
> *Melancholic* (black bile), a tendency to be independent, perfectionistic, and a bit introverted; and
>
> *Phlegmatic* (phlegm), a tendency to be quiet, relaxed, and content with life.

Like Hippocrates, Galen recognized that the temperaments of most people would be a combination of these extremes. He went on to provide detailed descriptions of how different temperaments could be combined in his book *De Temperamentis*. Although such a classification system is primitive by modern standards, the work of Hippocrates and Galen moved the understanding of human behaviour forward by attempting to categorize different types of personalities; we will see much more scientifically rigorous attempts to do the same thing later in this book (see Module 12.1). Roman, and later Persian, physicians also attempted to link different foods with different humours (e.g., cold foods led to an increase in the phlegm humour); so, if a person's humours were out of balance (leading to a physical or emotional problem), a dietary adjustment was sometimes advised to help him or her return to a balanced state.

However, the golden age of Greek and Roman thought came to a crashing halt in the latter parts of the fourth century; this was the beginning of the Dark Ages, a time in which few medical or scientific advances were made. In fact, some of Galen's medical teachings were suppressed, often being replaced by religious texts or philosophy that was consistent with the views of religious leaders (Gross, 1998). Indeed, although some discoveries were made about human anatomy during this period, few notable advances in the study of behaviour were made over the next one thousand years.

Psychology also did not immediately benefit from the scientific revolution of the 1500s and 1600s. Once the scientific method started to take hold around 1600, physics, astronomy, physiology, biology, and chemistry all experienced unprecedented growth in knowledge and technology. But it took psychology until the late 1800s to become scientific. Why was this the case? One of the main reasons was *zeitgeist*, a German word meaning "spirit of the times." **Zeitgeist** *refers to a general set of beliefs of a particular culture at a specific time in history.* It can be used to understand why some ideas take off immediately, whereas other perfectly good ideas may go unnoticed for years.

The power of zeitgeist can be very strong, and there are several ways it prevented psychological science from emerging in the 1600s. Perhaps most important is that people were not ready to accept a science that could be applied to human behaviour and thought. To the average person of the 1600s, viewing human behaviour as the result of predictable physical laws was troubling. Doing so would seem to imply the philosophy of **materialism**: *the belief that humans, and other living beings, are composed exclusively of physical matter.* Accepting this idea would mean that we are nothing more than complex machines that lack a self-conscious, self-controlling soul. The opposing belief, that there are properties of humans that are not material (a mind or soul separate from the body), is called *dualism*.

Although most early thinking about the mind and behaviour remained philosophical in nature, scientific methods were generating great discoveries for the natural sciences of physics, biology, and physiology. This meant that the early influences on psychology came from the natural and physical sciences. (Figure 1.5 provides a timeline that summarizes some of the major events in the history of psychology.)

INFLUENCES FROM PHYSICS: EXPERIMENTING WITH THE MIND The initial forays into scientific psychology were conducted by physicists and physiologists. One of the earliest explorations was made by Gustav Fechner (1801–1887), who studied sensation and perception (see Module 4.1). As a physicist, Fechner was interested in the natural world of moving objects and energy. He turned his knowledge to psychological questions about how the physical and mental worlds interact. Fechner coined the term **psychophysics**, *which is the study of the relationship between the physical world and the mental representation of that world.*

As an example of psychophysical research, imagine you are holding a one-pound (.45 kg) weight in your right hand and a five-pound (2.27 kg) weight in your left hand. Obviously, your left hand will feel the heavier weight, but that is not what interested Fechner. What if a researcher places a quarter-pound weight (113 g) in each hand, resting on top of the weight that is already there? Fechner wanted to know which of the quarter-pound weights would be perceived as heavier. Oddly enough, although both weigh the same amount, the quarter-pound weight in your right hand will be more noticeable than the quarter-pound weight added to your left hand, almost as if it were heavier (see Figure 1.6 on p. 16). Through experiments like these, Fechner demonstrated basic principles of how the physical and mental worlds interact. In fact, he developed an equation to precisely calculate the *perceived* change in weight, and then extended

ca. 1500 BCE: Ancient Egyptian doctors describe behavioural impairments caused by brain damage.

ca. 430 BCE–216 AD: Greek and Roman physicians develop the four humours and four temperaments theories of personality and behaviour.

Late 1700s: Franz Mesmer develops techniques to treat mental illness, including the use of hypnosis.

Around 1850: Gustav Fechner pioneers the study of psychophysics.

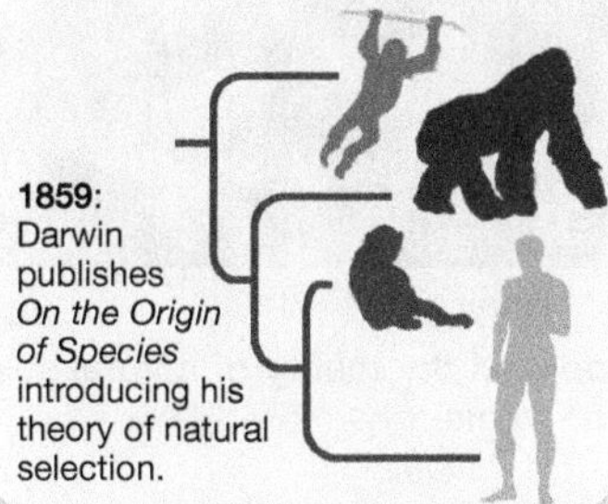

1859: Darwin publishes *On the Origin of Species* introducing his theory of natural selection.

1861: Physician Paul Broca discovers a brain area associated with the production of speech, now known as Broca's area, establishing that regions of the brain are specialized to serve different functions.

1879: Wilhelm Wundt establishes the first psychological laboratory in Leipzig, Germany, and two years later he establishes the first journal in psychology.

1880s: Francis Galton introduces and develops the study of anthropometrics.

1885: Hermann Ebbinghaus begins his scientific study of memory.

1890: William James, founder of the functionalist approach, publishes *Principles of Psychology*.

1891: James Mark Baldwin founds the first psychology laboratory in the British Commonwealth at the University of Toronto.

1892: The American Psychological Association (APA) is established.

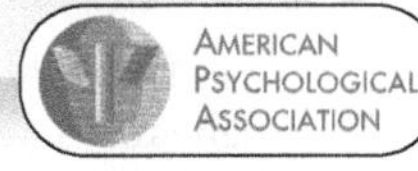

1900: Sigmund Freud writes *The Interpretation of Dreams*, a key book in the development of psychoanalysis.

Early 1900s: Ivan Pavlov demonstrates the basic principles of classical conditioning.

1905: Alfred Binet develops the first intelligence test.

1911: Edward Thorndike demonstrates the basic principles of instrumental learning, forming the basis for the study of operant conditioning.

1912: Max Wertheimer establishes the field of gestalt psychology.

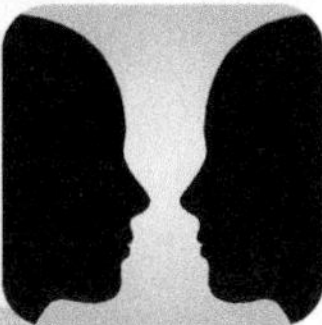

1913: John B. Watson writes "Psychology as the Behaviorist Views It," establishing behaviourism as the primary school of thought in American psychology.

1934: Wilder Penfield founds McGill University's Montreal Neurological Institute. While there, Penfield uses electrical stimulation to map out the neural underpinnings of movement and touch.

1936: Kurt Lewin authors *Principles of Topological Psychology*, which introduces the social psychological formulation that the behaviour of individuals is influenced by their social environment.

1938: B. F. Skinner writes the *Behavior of Organisms*, which furthers the cause of behaviourism.

1939: The Canadian Psychological Association is founded.

1949: Donald Hebb publishes *The Organization of Behavior*, focusing research into the mechanisms of memory.

1951: Carl Rogers writes *Client-Centered Therapy*, which helps establish humanistic psychology.

1952: The first *Diagnostic and Statistical Manual of Mental Disorders*, now in its fifth edition, is published by the American Psychiatric Association.

1967: Ulrich Neisser publishes *Cognitive Psychology*, which introduces a major new subfield of psychology.

1971: B. F. Skinner publishes *Beyond Freedom and Dignity*, stirring controversy over radical behaviourism.

1978: Herbert Simon wins the Nobel Prize in economics for research in cognitive psychology (there is no Nobel Prize dedicated to psychology).

1980s–early 1990s: Brain-imaging techniques such as magnetic resonance imaging become mainstream methods for studying brain anatomy and function in human subjects.

1990: The Canadian Society for Brain, Behaviour, and Cognitive Science is established.

CSBBCS
SCSCCC

1990s: U.S. President George H. W. Bush proclaims the 1990s to be "The Decade of the Brain," and there is unprecedented growth in neuroscience and biological psychology.

2003: The Human Genome Project is completed.

Left, centre: Bettmann/Corbis; left bottom: The APA logo is a trademark of the American Psychological Association. Reproduced with permission. No further reproduction or distribution is permitted without written permission from the American Psychological Association; centre: pio3/Shutterstock.com; right, centre right: AP Images; right, centre left: Science and Society/SuperStock; right, bottom: The Canadian Society for Brain, Behaviour, and Cognitive Science

{FIG. 1.5} **Major Events in the History of Psychology**

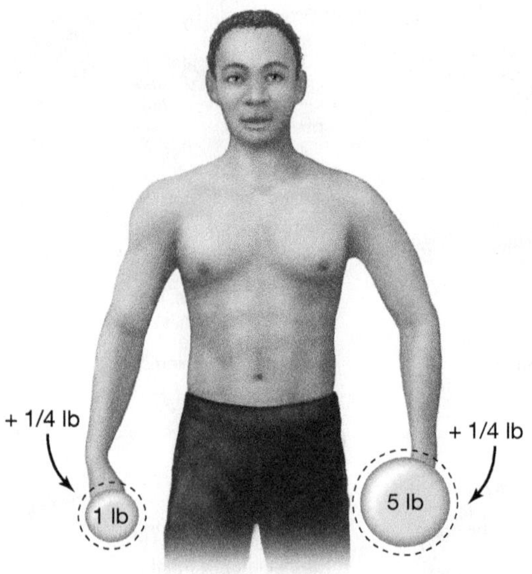

{FIG. 1.6} **The Study of Psychophysics** Gustav Fechner studied relationships between the physical world and our mental representations of that world. For example, Fechner tested how people detect changes in physical stimuli.

Pictorial Press Ltd/Alamy

Charles Darwin proposed the theory of natural selection to explain how evolution works.

this formula to apply to changes in brightness, loudness, and other perceptual experiences. This work served as the foundation for the modern study of perception.

INFLUENCES FROM EVOLUTIONARY THEORY: THE ADAPTIVE FUNCTIONS OF BEHAVIOUR

Around the same time Fechner was doing his experiments, Charles Darwin (1809–1882) was studying the many varieties of plants and animals found around the world. Darwin noticed that animal groups that were isolated from one another often differed by only minor variations in physical features. These variations seemed to fine-tune the species according to the particular environment in which they lived, making them better equipped for survival and reproduction. Darwin's theory of evolution by *natural selection* was based on his observations that the genetically inherited traits that contribute to survival and reproductive success are more likely to flourish within the breeding population (i.e., useful traits will be passed on to future generations). These specific traits differ across locations because different traits will prove beneficial in different environments. This theory explains why there is such a diversity of life on Earth.

Darwin's theory also helps to explain human (and animal) behaviour. As Darwin pointed out in *The Expression of the Emotions in Man and Animals* (1872), behaviour is shaped by natural selection, just as physical traits are (see Module 3.1). Over the course of millions of years of evolution, a certain range of behaviours helped people survive and reproduce. For example, having *some* aggressive impulses allowed our ancestors to hunt as well as to defend themselves when threatened. However, individuals who were too aggressive would be more likely to be killed in an unnecessary fight; likewise, an individual who was not aggressive enough might not have killed animals to survive or might have hesitated when defending him- or herself. Therefore, having a level of aggressiveness that fell within a particular range increased the likelihood that the individual would reproduce. The modern behaviours that we engage in every day—memory, emotions, forming social bonds, and so on—were the same behaviours that allowed our ancestors to flourish over the course of our species' history. The same principle applies to other species as well. Darwin's recognition that behaviours, like physical traits, are subject to hereditary influences and natural selection was a major contribution to psychology.

INFLUENCES FROM MEDICINE: DIAGNOSES AND TREATMENTS Medicine contributed a great deal to the biological perspective in psychology. It also had a considerable influence on the development of **clinical psychology**, *the field of psychology that concentrates on the diagnosis and treatment of psychological disorders.* A research topic that impacted both fields was the study of *brain localization*, the idea that certain parts of the brain control specific mental abilities and personality characteristics.

In the mid-1800s, localization was studied in two different ways. The first was *phrenology*, which gained considerable popularity for more than 100 years thanks to physicians Franz Gall (1758–1828) and Johann

Spurzheim (1776–1832). Gall, Spurzheim, and their followers believed that the brain consisted of 27 "organs," corresponding to mental traits and dispositions that could be detected by examining the surface of the skull. Although it seems silly now, there was a logic behind phrenology. Its supporters believed that different traits and abilities were distributed across different regions of the brain (e.g., "combativeness" was located at the back of the brain behind the ears). If a person possessed a particular trait or ability, then the brain area related to that characteristic would be larger in the same way that your arms would be larger if your job required you to lift things. Larger brain areas would cause bumps on a person's head in the same way that a muscular arm could cause the fabric of a shirt to stretch. So, by measuring the bumps on a person's head, proponents of phrenology believed that it would be possible to identify the different traits that an individual possessed. Phrenology continued to gather supporters for nearly a century before being abandoned by serious scientists. You might have encountered images of the phrenological map of the skull (see Figure 1.7).

The other approach to localization entailed the study of brain injuries and the ways in which they affect behaviour. This work had a scientific grounding that phrenology lacked. There were many intriguing cases described

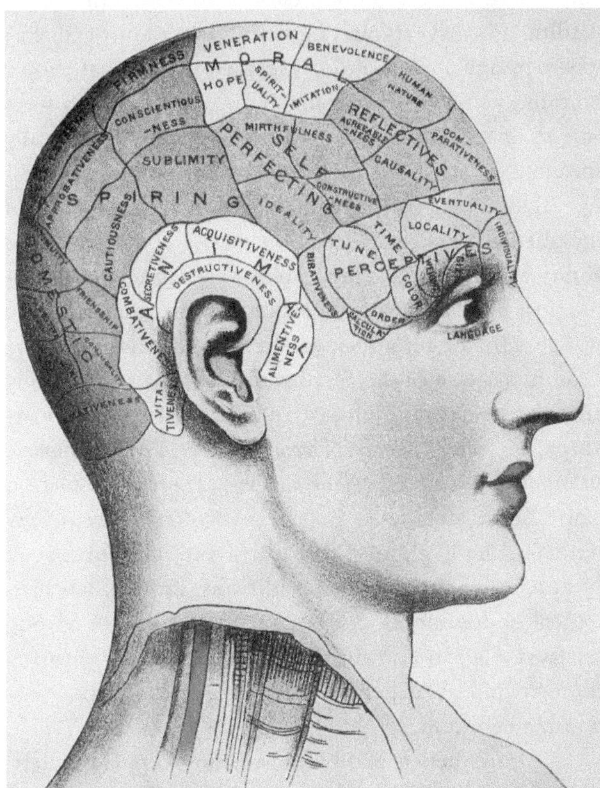

Classic Image/Alamy

{FIG. 1.7} **A Phrenology Map** Early scholars of the brain believed that mental capacities and personalities could be measured by the contours, bumps, and ridges distributed across the surface of the skull.

by physicians of the 1800s, including these two well-known examples that we will return to in Module 8.3:

- Physician Paul Broca studied a patient named Tan. Tan received this name because it was the only word he could speak, despite the fact that he could hear and understand perfectly well. Broca identified an area of the left side of Tan's brain that was damaged, and claimed to have found where speech production was localized; that area of the brain is now known as *Broca's area*. (Oddly, a physician named Marc Dax presented a similar finding 25 years before Broca's landmark paper; however, it received little attention [Roe & Finger, 1996]. Perhaps the zeitgeist was not yet ready for this type of result.)
- Motivated by Broca's work, Karl Wernicke identified *Wernicke's area* in 1874. Patients with damage to Wernicke's area could speak in sentences that sounded normal, but with unusual or made-up words. Patients who regained some of their speech later reported that, although they could hear just fine, no speech—not even their own—made sense during the recovery period. Thus, Wernicke's area appears to be critical for language comprehension.

Of course, the influence of the medical perspective was not isolated to studies of brain localization. Additional medical influences on psychology came from outside of mainstream practices. Franz Mesmer, an 18th-century Austrian physician practising in Paris, believed that prolonged exposure to magnets could redirect the flow of metallic fluids in the body, thereby curing disease and insanity. Although his claim was rejected outright by the medical and scientific communities in France, some of his patients seemed to be cured after being lulled into a trance. Modern physicians and scientists attribute these "cures" to the patients' belief in the treatment—what we now call *psychosomatic medicine*.

The medical establishment eventually grew more intrigued by the trances Mesmer produced in his patients, naming the phenomenon *hypnosis* (see Module 5.1). This practice also caught the attention of an Austrian physician named Sigmund Freud (1856–1939), who began to use hypnosis to treat his own patients. Freud was particularly interested in how hypnosis seemed to have cured several patients of *hysterical paralysis*—a condition in which an individual loses feeling and control in a specific body part, despite the lack of any known neurological damage or disease. These experiences led Freud to develop his famous theory and technique called *psychoanalysis*.

Psychoanalysis *is a psychological approach that attempts to explain how behaviour and personality are influenced by unconscious processes.* Freud acknowledged that

Mary Evans/SIGMUND FREUD COPYRIGHTS/Alamy

Sigmund Freud developed the concept of an unconscious mind and its underlying processes in his theory of psychoanalysis.

conscious experience includes perceptions, thoughts, a sense of self, and the sense that we are in control of ourselves. However, he also believed in an unconscious mind that contained forgotten episodes from early childhood and urges to fulfill self-serving sexual and aggressive impulses. Freud proposed that because these urges were unconscious, they could exert influence in strange ways, such as restricting the use of a body part (psychosomatic or hysterical paralysis). Freud believed hypnosis played a valuable role in his work. When a person is hypnotized, dreaming, or perhaps medicated into a trancelike state, he thought, the psychoanalyst could have more direct access into the individual's unconscious mind. Once Freud gained access, he could attempt to determine and correct any desires or emotions he believed were causing the unconscious to create the psychosomatic conditions.

Although Freud did not conduct scientific experiments, his legacy can be seen in some key elements of scientific psychology. First, many modern psychologists make inferences about unconscious mental activity, just as Freud had advocated (although not all of them agree with the specific theories proposed by Freud). Second, the use of medical ideas to treat disorders of emotions, thought, and behaviour—an approach known as the *medical model*—can be traced to Freud's influence. Third, Freud incorporated evolutionary thinking into his work; he emphasized how physiological needs and urges relating to survival and reproduction can influence our behaviour. Finally, Freud placed great emphasis on how early life experiences influence our behaviour as adults—a perspective that comes up many times in this text. So, although people often mock some of his theories, Freud's impact on modern psychology is deserving of respect.

THE INFLUENCE OF SOCIAL SCIENCES: MEASURING AND COMPARING HUMANS A fifth influential force came out of the social sciences of economics, sociology, and anthropology. These disciplines developed statistical methods for measuring human traits, which soon became relevant to the emerging field of psychology. An early pioneer in measuring perception and in applying statistical analyses to the study of behaviour was Sir Francis Galton. Galton was probably most inspired by his cousin, Charles Darwin, who had just published his theory of evolution by natural selection. Galton believed that heredity (genetics) explained psychological differences among people. The idea of hereditary psychology fit Galton's beliefs about social class. For example, he noticed that great achievement tended to run in families. After all, Galton's cousin was a great naturalist, his uncle Erasmus was a celebrated physician and writer, and Galton himself was no slouch (he began reading as a 2-year-old child, and was a fan of Shakespeare by age 6). To Galton, it seemed natural that people who did better in scholarship, business, and wealth were able to do so because they were *better* people (genetically speaking).

To support his beliefs, Galton developed ways of measuring what he called *eminence*—a combination of ability, morality, and achievement. One observation supporting his claim for a hereditary basis for eminence was that the closer a relative, the more similar the traits. Galton was one of the first investigators to scientifically take on the question of **nature and nurture relationships**, *the inquiry into how heredity (nature) and environment (nurture) influence behaviour and mental processes.* Galton came down decidedly on the nature side, seemingly ignoring the likelihood that nurturing influences such as upbringing and family traditions, rather than biological endowments, could explain similarities among relatives. Galton also supported his beliefs by ignoring the fact that great people can and do come from very humble beginnings.

Galton's beliefs and biases led him to pursue scientific justification for *eugenics*, which literally translates as "good genes." He promoted the belief that social programs should encourage intelligent, talented individuals to have children, whereas criminals, those with physical or mental disability, and non-White races should be

Science and Society/SuperStock

Francis Galton set up his anthropometric (literally "human measurement") laboratory at the International Health Exhibition in London in 1885.

kept out of the English gene pool. The eugenics movement was based largely on what the researchers wanted to believe was true, not on quality research methods. It ultimately led to the mistreatment of many individuals, particularly immigrants and the descendants of slaves who were not of Galton's own demographic group. It also influenced the thinking of Adolf Hitler, with chilling consequences.

In modern times, biological and genetic approaches to explaining behaviour are thriving (and, thankfully, eugenics has vanished). Indeed, U.S. President George H. W. Bush declared the 1990s to be "The Decade of the Brain." With the advent of new brain-imaging techniques (see Module 3.4), this area of psychology—*biological psychology*—is poised to provide new and important insights into the underlying causes of our behaviour.

Quick Quiz 1.2a
Psychology's Philosophical and Scientific Origins

KNOW ...

1 In philosophical terms, a materialist is someone who might believe that

- **A** money buys happiness.
- **B** species evolve through natural selection.
- **C** personality can be measured by feeling for bumps on the surface of the skull.
- **D** everything that exists, including human beings, are composed exclusively of physical matter.

UNDERSTAND ...

2 According to Sigmund Freud, which of the following would be the most likely explanation for why someone is behaving aggressively?

- **A** They are acting according to psychophysics.
- **B** There is something going on at the unconscious level that is causing them to behave this way.
- **C** Their cigars are missing and someone's got to pay.
- **D** The environment is determining their behavioural response.

APPLY ...

3 Jan believes that all knowledge is acquired through experience with the world. Jan is probably _______.

- **A** an empiricist
- **B** a supporter of eugenics
- **C** a clinical psychologist
- **D** a phrenologist

ANALYZE ...

4 Francis Galton made a significant contribution to psychology by introducing methods for studying how heredity contributes to human behaviour. Which alternative explanation was Galton overlooking when he argued that heredity accounts for these similarities?

- **A** The primary importance of the nature side of the nature-versus-nurture debate
- **B** The fact that people who share genes live together in families, so they tend to share environmental privileges or disadvantages
- **C** A materialistic account of behaviour
- **D** The concept of dualism, which states that the mind is separate from the body

Answers can be found on page ANS-1.

The Beginnings of Contemporary Psychology

Watch Basics: Diverse Perspectives

As you now know, before psychology became its own discipline, there were scientists working across different fields who were converging on a study of human behaviour. By modern standards, Darwin, Fechner, and others had produced psychological research but it was not referred to as such because the field had not yet fully formed. Nevertheless, progress toward a distinct discipline of psychology was beginning.

By the late 1800s, the zeitgeist had changed so that the study of human behaviour was acceptable. Ideas flourished. Most importantly, researchers began to investigate behaviour in a number of different ways. You will see this breadth as you read the rest of this module. We will include references to other modules (e.g., see Module 6.1) to illustrate that the history that you are reading in this module had a direct effect on the modern understanding of behaviour that you will read about in the rest of this textbook.

STRUCTURALISM AND FUNCTIONALISM: THE BEGINNINGS OF PSYCHOLOGY Most contemporary psychologists agree that Wilhelm Wundt (1832–1920) was largely responsible for establishing psychology as an independent scientific field. Wundt established the first laboratory dedicated to studying human behaviour in 1879 at the University of Leipzig, where he conducted numerous experiments on how people sense and perceive. His primary research method was *introspection*, meaning "to look within." Introspection required a trained volunteer to experience a stimulus and then report each individual sensation he or she could identify. For example, if the volunteer was given a steel ball to hold in one hand, he would likely report the sensations of cold, hard, smooth, and heavy. To Wundt, these basic sensations were the mental "atoms" that combined to form the molecules of experience. Wundt also developed *reaction time* methods as a way of measuring mental effort. In one such study, volunteers watched an apparatus in which two metal balls swung into each other to make a clicking sound. The volunteers required about one-eighth of a second to react to the sound, leading Wundt to conclude that mental activity is not instantaneous, but rather requires a small amount of effort measured by the amount of time it takes to react. What made Wundt's work distinctly psychological was his focus on measuring mental events and examining how they were affected by his experimental manipulations. Wundt's ideas made their way to the United States and Canada through students who worked with him. However, whereas Wundt's research often attempted to link a person's perceptions with concepts such as free will (a philosophy known as *voluntarism*), many of his students wanted to move psychological research in a different direction (Rieber et al., 1980). One student, Edward Titchener, adopted the same method of introspection used by Wundt to devise an organized map of the structure of human consciousness. His line of research, **structuralism**, *was an attempt to analyze conscious experience by breaking it down into basic elements, and to understand how these elements work together.* Titchener chose the term *elements* deliberately as an analogy with the periodic table in the physical sciences. He believed that mental experiences were made up of a limited number of sensations, which were analogous to elements in physics and chemistry. According to Titchener, different sensations can form and create complex compounds, just like hydrogen and water can combine to form water—H_2O—or the hydroxide ion—OH^-.

The same year Wundt set up his first laboratory, an American scholar named William James (1842–1910) set out to write the first textbook in psychology, *The Principles of Psychology*, which was eventually published in 1890. Trained as a physician, James combined his knowledge of

akg-images/Newscom

German scientist Wilhelm Wundt is widely credited as the "father" of experimental psychology.

Mary Evans Picture Library/Alamy

William James was a highly influential American psychologist who took a functionalist approach to explaining behaviour.

physiology with his interest in the philosophy of mental activity. Among his many interests, he sought to understand how the mind functions. In contrast to structuralism, which looks for permanent, unchanging elements of thought, James was influenced by Darwin's evolutionary principles; he preferred to examine behaviour in context, and explain how our thoughts and actions help us adapt to our environment. **Functionalism** *is the study of the purpose and function of behaviour and conscious experience.* According to functionalists, in order to fully understand a behaviour, one must try to figure out what purpose it may have served over the course of our evolution. These principles are found today in the modern field of *evolutionary psychology*, an approach that interprets and explains modern human behaviour in terms of forces acting upon our distant ancestors (see Module 3.1). According to this approach, our brains and behaviours have been shaped by the physical and social environment that our ancestors encountered. Over the next century, this idea was extended to a number of subfields in psychology ranging from the study of brain structures to the study of social groups. Indeed, regardless of their research area, most psychologists are still fascinated by the question, *What function does the behaviour we're investigating serve?* In other words, *why* do we behave the way we do?

During the early years of psychology, the pioneers of this field were trying to find a way to use the methods and instruments of the natural sciences to understand behaviour. Although some of their techniques fell out of favour, by the beginning of the 20th century it was clear that the discipline of psychology was here to stay. With that sense of permanence in place, the second generation of psychologists could focus on refining the subject matter and the methods, and on turning psychology into a widely accepted scientific field.

THE RISE OF BEHAVIOURISM Early in the 20th century, biologists became interested in how organisms learn to anticipate their bodily functions. One of the first to do so was Professor Edwin Twitmyer (1873–1943), an American psychologist interested in reflexes. His work involved a contraption with a rubber mallet that would regularly tap the patellar tendon just below the kneecap; this, of course, causes a kicking reflex in most individuals. To make sure his volunteers were not startled by the mallet, the contraption would ring a bell right before the mallet struck the tendon. As is often the case in experiments, the technology failed after a number of these bell-ringing and hammer-tapping combinations: The machine rang the bell, but the hammer did not come down on the volunteer's knee. But the real surprise was this—the volunteer's leg kicked anyway! How did that happen? Because the sound of the bell successfully predicted the hammer, the ringing soon had the effect of the hammer itself, a process now called *classical conditioning* (see Module 6.1). The study of conditioning would soon become a focus of **behaviourism**, *an approach that dominated the first half of the 20th century of North American psychology and had a singular focus on studying only observable behaviour, with little to no reference to mental events or instincts as possible influences on behaviour.*

Mansell/Time Life Pictures/Getty Images

Ivan Pavlov (on the right) explained classical conditioning through his studies of salivary reflexes in dogs.

Twitmyer's research was coolly received when he announced his findings at the American Psychological Association meeting. Not a single colleague bothered to ask him a question. The credit for discovering classical conditioning typically goes to a Russian physiologist named Ivan Pavlov (1849–1936). Pavlov, who won the 1904 Nobel Prize for his research on the digestive system, noticed that the dogs in his laboratory learned to salivate to a tone if the tone had a history of sounding just prior to the delivery of food. This observation quickly led to more focused research on mechanisms of learning; the principles of learning that Pavlov and others identified provided a foundation for the behaviourist movement.

In North America, behaviourism was championed by John B. Watson, a researcher at Johns Hopkins University in Baltimore (1878–1958). As research accumulated on the breadth of behaviours that could be conditioned, Watson began to believe that all behaviour could ultimately be explained through conditioning. This emphasis on learning also came with stipulations about what could and could not be studied in psychology. Watson was adamant that only observable changes in the environment and behaviour were appropriate for scientific study. Methods such as Wundt's introspection, he said, were too subjective to even consider:

> *Psychology as the behaviorist views it is a purely objective natural science. Its theoretical goal is the prediction and control of behavior. Introspection forms no essential part of its methods. (Watson, 1913, p. 158)*

In the diplomatic world of science, this statement was akin to carving "Wundt sucks!" in a park bench. Watson believed so much in the power of experience (and so little in the power of genetics) that he was certain he could engineer a personality however he wished, if given enough control over the environment. Perhaps his most famous statement sums it up:

> *Give me a dozen healthy infants, well-formed, and my own specified world to bring them up in and I'll guarantee to take any one at random and train him to become any type of specialist I might select—doctor, lawyer, artist, merchant-chief and, yes, even beggar-man and thief, regardless of his talents, penchants, tendencies, abilities, vocations, and race of his ancestors. (Watson, 1930, p. 82)*

After a rather public indiscretion involving a female graduate student (due to his wife's social status, his extramarital affair appeared on the front page of the Baltimore newspapers; Fancher, 1990), Watson was dismissed from his university job. But, he quickly found his new career—as well as his fortune—in advertising. Most advertisers at the time just assumed they should inform people about the merits of a product. Watson and his colleagues applied a scientific approach to advertising and discovered a consumer's knowledge about the product really was not that important, so long as he or she had positive emotions associated with it. Thus, Watson's company developed ads that employed behaviourist principles to form associations between a product's brand image and positive emotions. If Pavlov's dogs could be conditioned to salivate when they heard a tone, what possibilities might there be for conditioning humans in a similar way? Modern advertisers want the logos for their brands of snacks or the trademark signs for their restaurants to bring on a specific craving, and some salivation along the way. And so, from beer commercials with scantily clad women dancing at parties, to car commercials with high intensity music and vistas of the Cabot Trail, and from impossibly cute kittens playing with toilet paper rolls to giant billboards of bunnies and hippos pitching telecommunications products, the influence of John B. Watson and his colleagues on modern advertising is felt every day.

Watch The Complexity of Humans: Phil Zimbardo

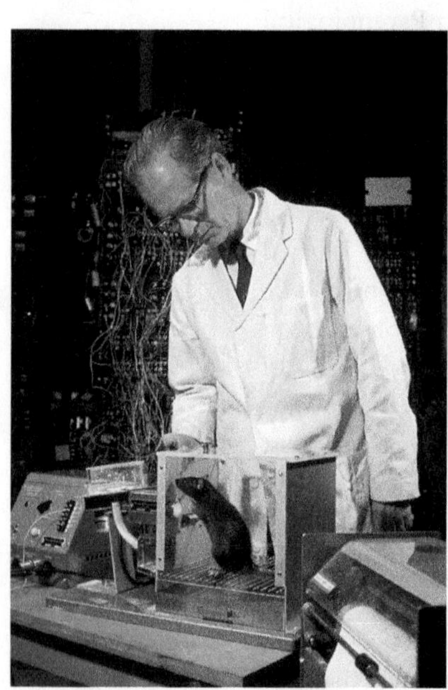
Nina Leen/Time Life Pictures/Getty Images

B. F. Skinner revealed how rewards affect behaviour by conducting laboratory studies on animals. **Click on this photo in your eText to see more details.**

Taking up the reins from Watson was B. F. Skinner (1904–1990), another behaviourist who had considerable influence over North American psychology for several decades (see Module 6.2). Much like Watson, Skinner believed that psychology was the study of behaviour and *not* of the unobservable mind. In Skinner's view, the foundation of behaviour was how an organism responded to rewards and punishments. This theory is logical in many ways—we tend to repeat actions that are rewarded (e.g., studying for exams leads to better grades, so we study for other exams) and avoid actions that lead to punishment (e.g., if you vomit after eating a 2-L container of ice cream, you will be unlikely to do so again . . . for a while). In order to identify the principles of reward and punishment, Skinner opted to use a tightly controlled experimental setup involving animals such as rats and pigeons. Typically, these studies occurred with animals held in small chambers in which they could manipulate a lever to receive rewards. The experimenter would control when rewards were available, and would observe the effects that changing the reward schedule had on the animals' behaviour. You might ask what this work had to do with human behaviour. The behaviourists believed that the principles of reward and punishment could apply to all organisms, both human and nonhuman. Indeed, Watson explicitly stated that behaviourist psychology "recognizes no line between man and brute" (Watson, 1913, p. 158).

Watson's and Skinner's concept of behaviourism met with resistance from many psychologists. If our behaviour is controlled by external rewards and the satisfaction of motivational drives, then this leaves little room for free will—the notion that we are free to make choices and guide our own behaviour without external influence. Many of those who resisted believed that humans could rise above their reward-based motivations and could choose between behaviours based on their own beliefs and interpretations of a situation.

HUMANISTIC PSYCHOLOGY EMERGES Psychology, by the mid-20th century, was dominated by two perspectives, behaviourism and Freudian psychoanalytic approaches, which had almost entirely removed free will from the understanding of human behaviour. To the behaviourists, human experience was the product of a lifetime of rewards, punishments, and learned associations. To the psychoanalysts, human experience was the result of unconscious forces at work deep in the human psyche. From both perspectives, the individual person was merely a product of forces that operated *on* her, and she had little if any control over her own destiny or indeed, even her own choices, beliefs, and feelings.

In contrast to these radically disempowering perspectives, a new movement of psychologists arose, which emphasized personal responsibility, free will, the universal longing for growth, meaning and connection, and which highlighted the power that individuals possessed to shape their own consciousness and choose their own path through life. This new perspective, **humanistic psychology**, *focuses on the unique aspects of each individual human, each person's freedom to act, his or her rational thought, and the belief that humans are fundamentally different from other animals.* Among the many major figures of humanistic psychology were Carl Rogers (1902–1987) and Abraham Maslow (1908–1970). Both psychologists focused on the positive aspects of humanity and the factors that lead to a productive and fulfilling life. Humanistic psychologists sought to understand the *meaning* of personal experience. They believed that people could attain mental well-being and satisfaction through gaining a greater understanding of themselves, rather than by being diagnosed with a disorder or having their problems labelled. Both Rogers and Maslow believed that humans strive to develop a sense of self and are motivated to personally grow and fulfill their potential (see Module 12.3). This view stands in particular contrast to the psychoanalytic tradition, which originated from a medical model and, therefore, focused on illnesses of the body and brain. The humanistic perspective also contrasted with behaviourism in proposing that humans had the freedom to act and a rational mind to guide the process.

Michael Rougier/Time & Life Pictures/Getty Images

Carl Rogers helped develop the humanistic psychology movement, which emphasized human strengths and free will.

THE BRAIN AND BEHAVIOUR The behaviourists and humanists were not the only researchers attempting to understand human abilities. Many neurologists, surgeons, and brain scientists were also focused on these questions. Notable among them was Karl Lashley (1890–1958), a professor at Harvard University and the director of the Yerkes Laboratories of Primate Biology in Florida. Lashley was interested in locating the *engram,* the place in the brain where a memory trace was stored. Using rats, Lashley systematically examined how the size and location of brain damage affected performance on tasks such as maze navigation. His studies, which extended over several years, produced two main findings. One was that the exact location of the damage did not affect performance; long-term memories are stored throughout many parts of the brain (i.e., they are not localized to specific regions like some aspects of language). The second, known as the *principle of mass action,* stated that the size of the damage did have an effect, with larger lesions causing a greater impairment in performance. The fact that Lashley was unable to identify the precise location of learning was disheartening for him. At the end of his career in 1950, he wrote, "It is difficult to conceive of a mechanism that can satisfy the conditions set for [the localization of the memory trace]. Nevertheless, in spite of such evidence against it, learning sometimes does occur."

One such mechanism explaining how learning occurs was discovered by Canadian neuroscientist Donald Hebb (1904–1985) at the Montreal Neurological Institute. Hebb, a former student of Lashley's, conducted numerous studies examining how cells in the brain change over the course of learning. He observed that when a brain cell consistently stimulates another cell, metabolic and physical changes occur to strengthen this relationship. In other words, cells that fire together wire together (Hebb, 1949; see Module 7.1). This theory, now known as Hebb's Law, demonstrated that memory—a behaviour that we can measure and that affects so many parts of our lives—is actually related to activity occurring at the cellular level (Brown & Milner, 2003; Cooper, 2005). It also reinforced the notion that behaviour can be studied at a number of different levels ranging from neurons (brain cells) to the entire brain. (Later research, discussed in Module 7.3, notes that memory is related to social factors as well.)

Further evidence for the relationship between the brain and everyday behaviours came from the stimulating work of Wilder Penfield (1891–1976), founder and original director of the Montreal Neurological Institute.

The Canadian Press Images/Montreal Gazette

Donald Hebb made significant contributions to our understanding of memory and the brain.

Montreal Gazette/The Canadian Press Images

Wilder Penfield, founder of the world-famous Montreal Neurological Institute, used electrical stimulation of the brain to discover how movement and touch were represented in the brain. Like Hebb's, many of his discoveries are still taught in psychology and neuroscience classes throughout the world.

Along with his colleague, Herbert Jasper, Penfield developed a surgical procedure to help patients with epilepsy. This procedure involved removing cells from the brain regions where the seizures began; doing so would prevent the seizures from spreading to other areas of the brain. However, before operating, Penfield needed to find a way to map out the functions of the surrounding brain regions so that he could try to avoid damaging areas that performed important functions such as language. To do this, Penfield electrically stimulated each patient's brain while the patient was under local anesthetic (i.e., was awake, and therefore conscious). The patient was then able to report the sensations he experienced after each burst of electricity. Based on several patients' reports, Penfield was able to create precise maps of the sensory and motor (movement) cortices in the brain (Penfield & Jasper, 1951; Todman, 2008). Importantly, his work also showed that people's subjective experiences can be represented in the brain (see Module 3.3). This insight suggested that the simple stimulus-response model put forth by the behaviourists was not a complete representation of our complex mental world.

Simulate How Good Is Your Memory for Stories?

THE COGNITIVE REVOLUTION Although behaviourism dominated psychology in the United States and Canada throughout the first half of the 20th century, the view that observable behaviours were more important than thoughts and mental imagery was not universal. In Europe, psychologists retained an emphasis on thinking, and ignored the North Americans' cries to study only what could be directly observed. The European focus on thought flourished through the early 1900s, long before psychologists in North America began to take seriously the idea that they could study mental processes, even if they could not directly see them. Thus, it was the work of European psychologists that formed the basis of the cognitive perspective. Early evidence of an emerging cognitive perspective concerned the study of memory. The German psychologist Hermann Ebbinghaus (1850–1909) collected reams of data on remembering and forgetting. The results of his studies produced numerous "forgetting curves." These curves showed that most of what a person learns will be forgotten rapidly, but that the rate of forgetting will then slow down, enabling us to remember *some* of the information that we have learned. Not only is the forgetting curve a staple of modern psychology, but some of Ebbinghaus's methods are also still applied to memory research today (see Module 7.2).

British psychologist Frederick Bartlett (1886–1969) also used experiments to better understand human memory. Bartlett found that our memory was not like a photograph, but was instead influenced by a number of outside factors including a person's cultural knowledge and experiences. Think about the last film or television show you saw. Do you remember the exact words in the script? Do you remember what the characters were wearing? Bartlett's work demonstrated that we are more likely to remember the general storyline than any of these other details, and that our cultural knowledge shapes what elements of a storyline we find important enough to remember (Bartlett, 1932).

Another precursor to cognitive psychology can be seen in the early to mid-1900s movement of **gestalt psychology**, *an approach emphasizing that psychologists need to focus on the whole of perception and experience, rather than its parts* (see Module 4.1). (*Gestalt* is a German word that refers to the complete form of an object; see Figure 1.8.) This contrasts with the structuralist goal of breaking experience into its individual parts. For example, if Wundt or Titchener were to hand you an apple, you would not think, "Round, red, has a stem . . ."; you would simply think to yourself, "This is an apple." Gestalt psychologists argued that much of our thinking and experience occur at a higher, more organized level than Wundt emphasized; they believed that Wundt's approach to understanding experience made about as much sense as understanding water only by studying its hydrogen and oxygen atoms.

In the 1950s—around the time that there was increasing interest in humanistic psychology—the scientific study of cognition was becoming accepted practice in North American psychology. The invention of the computer gave psychologists a useful analogy for understanding and talking about the mind (the *software* of the brain). Linguists argued that grammar and vocabulary were far too complex to be explained in behaviourist terms; the alternative was to propose abstract mental processes. There was a great deal of interest in memory and perception as well, but it was not until 1968 that these areas of research were given the name "cognitive psychology" by Ulrich Neisser (1928–2012). *Cognitive psychology* is a modern psychological perspective that focuses on processes such as memory, thinking, and language. Thus, much of what cognitive psychologists study consists of mental processes that are inferred through rigorous experimentation.

{FIG. 1.8} **The Whole Is Greater Than the Sum of Its Parts** The Gestalt psychologists emphasized humans' ability to see whole forms. For example, you probably perceive a sphere in the centre of this figure, even though it does not exist on the page.

In the 1970s and 1980s, the boundary between cognitive psychology and biopsychology slowly began to fade. As brain-imaging tools became more sophisticated, cognitive psychologists began working with brain researchers to identify the neural areas involved with complex abilities like memory, emotions, and decision making. This new field became known as *cognitive neuroscience,* a specialized field that is growing faster than any other area of psychology. It is also expanding into new topics of investigation, with researchers now using cognitive and brain-imaging techniques to examine issues related to social behaviour, laying the groundwork for the integrative field known as *social-cognitive neuroscience.*

SOCIAL AND CULTURAL INFLUENCES The vast majority of behaviourist and cognitive psychology research focuses on an individual's responses to some sort of stimulus. Missing from this equation, however, is that fact that people often have to respond to stimuli or events in the presence of other people. The effects of other people on one's behaviour have not been lost on psychologists; indeed, the recognition of this influence can be found in the very early years of psychology. An American psychologist, Norman Triplett (1861–1931), conducted one of the first formal experiments in this area, observing that cyclists ride faster in the presence of other people than when riding alone. Triplett published the first social psychology research in 1898, and a few social psychology textbooks appeared in 1908.

Despite the early interest in this field, studies of how people influence the behaviour of others did not take off until the 1940s. The events in Nazi-controlled Germany that led up to World War II contributed to the development of this new perspective in psychology in at least two ways. First, Adolf Hitler's political machine was explicitly anti-Jewish and anti-intellectual. To escape persecution by the German government, a significant number of German professors and scientists from a range of disciplines fled to North America (and some, including Freud, to the United Kingdom). These psychologists brought with them the influence of gestalt psychology. The exchange of ideas between these researchers and the mostly behaviourist North American psychologists allowed psychology to grow in new directions. Second, research on social influences began as a result of collaborations between sociologists (who study populations of

Watch
Frank Manis: How Is Research Applied in the Classroom?

humans) and psychologists (who were studying individuals at that time). Together, they attempted to understand how normal individuals could be transformed into brutal prison camp guards, how political propaganda affected people, and how society might address issues of stereotyping and prejudice (see Module 13.1). This research evolved into what is now known as *social psychology*, the study of the influence of other people on our behaviour.

However, psychologists also noted that not *all* people responded to social groups or the presence of others in the same way. While some people were transformed into prison camp guards in World War II, others objected and joined resistance movements. These individual differences were observable in normal, everyday life as well: Some people are talkative and outgoing while others are quiet. These observations led to the development of *personality psychology,* the study of how different personality characteristics can influence how we think and act.

Although it's easy to think of social psychology and personality psychology as being distinct, in reality, your personality and the social situations you are in interact. This relationship was most eloquently described by Kurt Lewin (1890–1947), the founder of modern social psychology. Lewin suggested that behaviour is a function of the individual and the environment, or, if you're a fan of formulas (and who isn't?), B = f{I,E}. What Lewin meant was that all behaviours could be predicted and explained through understanding how an individual with a specific set of traits would respond in a context that involved a specific set of conditions. Take two individuals as an example: One tends to be quiet and engages in solitary activities such as reading, whereas the other is talkative and enjoys being where the action is. Now put them in a social situation, such as a large party at a university dorm or a small get-together at a friend's house. How will the two behave? Given the disparity between the individuals and between the two environments, we would suspect very different behaviours would emerge for these two individuals in the different settings. The outgoing person may have a wonderful time at the big party, while the quiet person desperately tries to find someone to talk to or pretends to be fascinated by something on his phone. But, at the smaller get-together, the quieter person will likely be much more relaxed, while the outgoing person might be bored. Neither behaviour is *better*, but they *are* different. This outcome illustrates the essence of Lewin's formulation of social psychology.

On a broader but related scale, *cross-cultural psychology* is the field that draws comparisons about individual and group behaviour among cultures; it helps us understand the role of society in shaping behaviour, beliefs, and values. Many cross-cultural studies compare the responses of North American research participants (generally psychology students like you) to those of individuals in non-Western countries such as China or Japan. However, Western countries with high immigration rates like Canada and the U.S. also provide researchers with the opportunity to compare the responses and experiences of first- and second-generation Canadians (Abouguendia & Noels, 2001; Gaudet et al., 2005). This type of research therefore allows us to examine how people respond when being pulled in different directions by family history and the culture of their current country of residence. Such comparisons are also being performed using brain-imaging, demonstrating that our social and cultural experiences can also be embedded in our brain tissue (Losin et al., 2010).

In conclusion, the trends that emerged during the formative years of psychology laid the foundation for the modern perspectives and theories we see today. Psychology is now a clearly established discipline—there are established venues such as professional organizations and journals to disseminate the results of psychological research. However, it is important to remember that what you encounter in the upcoming modules will still reflect psychology's early influences. Although modern technology, such as brain scans and computing, would likely baffle psychology's founders, it is likely that they would find the results of modern research absolutely relevant to their own interests. It is also likely that they would be enthusiastic about the increasing levels of collaboration between the different areas of psychology, and about the current zeitgeist of treating human behaviour as a complex system with biological, psychological, and sociocultural components.

Monkey Business Images/Shutterstock.com

The study of first- and second-generation Canadians allows psychologists to better understand the (sometimes conflicting) influences of family traditions and modern society.

Quick Quiz 1.2b The Beginnings of Contemporary Psychology

KNOW ...

1. ______ was the study of the basic components of the mind, while ______ was the study of how they work.
   - **A** Structuralism; functionalism
   - **B** Behaviourism; functionalism
   - **C** Functionalism; structuralism
   - **D** Humanism; structuralism

UNDERSTAND ...

2. A distinct feature of behaviourism is its
   - **A** search for the deeper meaning of human existence.
   - **B** search for patterns that create a whole that is greater than its parts.
   - **C** use of introspection.
   - **D** exclusive emphasis on observable behaviour.

APPLY ...

3. Gwen is in search of the deeper meaning of her life, and would like to learn more about her potential as a human being. Which of the following types of psychologists would likely be most useful to her?
   - **A** Humanistic
   - **B** Gestalt
   - **C** Behaviourist
   - **D** Social

4. The gestalt psychologists, with their focus on perception and experience, are closely linked to modern-day ________ psychologists.
   - **A** developmental
   - **B** social
   - **C** cognitive
   - **D** evolutionary

Answers can be found on page ANS-1.

Module Summary

Module 1.2

Now that you have read this module you should

KNOW ...

- ***The key terminology of psychology's history:***

behaviourism (p. 21)
clinical psychology (p. 16)
determinism (p. 13)
empiricism (p. 13)
functionalism (p. 21)
gestalt psychology (p. 25)
humanistic psychology (p. 23)
materialism (p. 14)
nature and nurture relationships (p. 18)
psychoanalysis (p. 17)
psychophysics (p. 14)
structuralism (p. 20)
zeitgeist (p. 14)

UNDERSTAND ...

- ***How various philosophical and scientific fields became major influences on psychology.*** The philosophical schools of determinism, empiricism, and materialism provided a background for a scientific study of human behaviour. The first psychologists were trained as physicists and physiologists. Fechner, for example, developed psychophysics, whereas Titchener looked for the elements of thought. Darwin's theory of natural selection influenced psychologist William James's idea of functionalism—the search for how behaviours may aid the survival and reproduction of the organism.

nagib/Shutterstock

APPLY ...

- ***Your knowledge to distinguish among the different specializations in psychology.*** Try the activity in **Table 1.2** and check your answers on page ANS-1.

ANALYZE ...

- ***How the philosophical ideas of empiricism and determinism are applied to human behaviour.*** Psychology is based on empiricism, the belief that all knowledge—including knowledge about human behaviour—is acquired through the senses. All sciences, including psychology, require a deterministic viewpoint. Determinism is the philosophical tenet that all events in the world, including human actions, have a physical cause. The deterministic view is also essential to the sciences. Applying determinism to human behaviour has been met with resistance by many because it appears to deny a place for free will.

Table 1.2 :: Areas of Specialization within Psychology

Apply your knowledge to distinguish among different specializations in psychology. You should be able to read a description of a psychologist on the left and match her or his work to a specialization on the right. Check your answers on page ANS-1.

Explore
Psychologists at Work

1. I am an academic psychologist who studies various methods for improving study habits. I hope to help people increase memory performance and become better students. I am a(n) __________.
2. My work focuses on how the presence of other people influences an individual's acceptance of and willingness to express various stereotypes. I am a(n) __________.
3. I have been studying how childrearing practices in Guatemala, Canada, and Cambodia all share some common elements, as well as how they differ. I am a(n) __________.
4. I am interested in behaviours that are genetically influenced to help animals adapt to their changing environments. I am a(n) __________.
5. I help individuals identify problem areas of their lives and ways to correct them, and guide them to live up to their full potential. I am a(n) __________.

a. social psychologist
b. cross-cultural psychologist
c. cognitive psychologist
d. humanistic psychologist
e. evolutionary psychologist

Work the Scientific Literacy Model :: Understanding the Scientific Origins of Psychology

1 What do we know about psychological science?

Figure 1.5 on **page 15** outlined the movement of psychology toward a scientific study of human behaviour, including influences from fields such as medicine and physics. Refresh your memory of contemporary psychology, including the rise of behaviourism, humanistic psychology, social psychology, biological psychology, and cognitive psychology, by reviewing the discussion on **pages 19–26.** Psychologists today often use multiple, unique perspectives to study a topic, but they share with other scientists a common set of methods for understanding our world. **Figure 1.1** on **page 3** offers a reminder of how psychologists use the scientific method to study human behaviour. Of course, approaching any subject scientifically requires that we understand some key concepts. Review the discussion of determinism and empiricism on **page 13**. Psychologists assume that a multitude of factors cause our behaviour (determinism), and that our understanding of behaviour comes from observing what we can see and measure (empiricism). Here is a tip:

Remember that an **Empirical** approach means knowledge is gained through **Experience**, often by conducting **Experiments**.

2 How can science explain behaviour?

Regardless of their theoretical approach, psychologists rely on the scientific method to gather data. Testing hypotheses and constructing theories are key parts of all scientific endeavours, and the scientific method involves a dynamic interaction between these two tasks. Recall from **page 21** that the proponents of behaviourism, for example, relied almost exclusively on studying observable behaviour. Classic studies by Watson and Skinner make up the foundation of our knowledge in those areas today, and you can see the results of Watson's research on behavioural conditioning in the evolution of modern advertising. Moreover, the rise of cognitive psychology eventually allowed the application of the scientific method to phenomena that behaviourists of the time thought were unobservable, such as memory and thought processes.

Sarah2/Shutterstock

4 Why is this relevant?

Watch the accompanying video excerpt on the different psychological perspectives. You can access the video at MyPsychLab or by clicking the play button in the centre of your eText. If your instructor assigns this video as a homework activity, you will find additional content to help you in MyPsychLab. You can also view the video by using your smart phone and the QR code below, or you can go to the YouTube link provided.

After you have read this chapter and watched the video, imagine your friend Jake has become very anxious ever since he started taking harder classes in his major. The university's counsellor diagnosed him with an anxiety disorder. Compare and contrast how the behavioural, humanistic, biological, and cognitive approaches would view the origins and treatment of Jake's anxiety. Then, describe how each of the four approaches is viewed by psychologists today.

3 Can we critically evaluate scientific claims?

As outlined on **page 6**, scientific literacy consists of abilities to understand, analyze, and apply scientific information. A key component of scientific literacy—critical thinking—involves exercising curiosity and skepticism when evaluating the claims of others, and when assessing our own assumptions and beliefs. For instance, the alien abductions **Myths in Mind** on **page 10** reminds us that seeking the simplest of all explanations, also known as applying the principle of parsimony, will generally put you on the path to thinking scientifically and critically. Recall that a key characteristic of a scientific hypothesis is its ability to be tested. We mention astrology as an example because its predictions are typically so general that they cannot be falsified. It is a good idea to be skeptical of any claims that are based on assumptions that cannot be proved or disproved; many times they are couched in pseudoscientific terminology.

MyPsychLab **Your turn to Work the Scientific Literacy Model:** Watch the accompanying video on YouTube, or on your phone (using the Layar app or QR code). If your instructor has assigned this as a homework activity, you can find the video clip and additional content at MyPsychLab. Answer the questions that accompany the video clip to test your understanding.

youtube.com/workthemodel

SCAN WITH LAYAR
See page xxiv for instructions

2

Reading and Evaluating Scientific Research

Ryan Jorgensen-Jorgo/Shutterstock

Photosindia/Getty Images

Module 2.1

Principles of Scientific Research

Learning Objectives

After reading this module you should

KNOW ...	UNDERSTAND ...	APPLY ...	ANALYZE ...
The key terminology related to the principles of scientific research	The five characteristics of quality scientific research How biases might influence the outcome of a study	The concepts of reliability and validity to examples	Whether anecdotes, authority figures, and common sense are reliably truthful sources of information

Does listening to classical music make you smarter? In January 1998, Governor Zell Miller of Georgia placed a $105 000 line in his state budget dedicated to purchasing classical music (Sack, 1998). He even paid the conductor of the Atlanta Symphony to select optimal pieces for this CD. Apparently, Georgia's well-meaning governor and state legislature believed that providing young children with classical music would make them smarter. There were many reasons to believe this assumption might be true, starting with the observation that most people we know who listen to classical music seem intelligent and sophisticated. At around the same time that Georgia took this step, consumers were being bombarded with advertisements about "the Mozart effect." Suddenly the classical sections at music stores were dusted off and moved to the front of the store, with signs drawing customers' attention to the intelligence-boosting effects of the CDs. Parents were told that it was never too early to start their children on a Mozart program, even as fetuses residing in the womb. In fact, part of the Georgia budget, as well as the budget in some other U.S. states, was dedicated to handing out classical CDs along with hospital birth certificates. Eventually, the enthusiasm toward the Mozart effect died down—after other scientists were unable to replicate the results. It turns out that the hype surrounding the Mozart effect was based on the results of *one* study (Rauscher et al., 1993). In this study, the twelve adult participants who listened to Mozart performed better than other adults on a test of spatial ability. These (temporary) differences in spatial intelligence were then inflated by the popular press to mean intelligence *in general* (a big difference!). Based on a single study, companies created a multi-million dollar industry, and the state of Georgia spent an extra $105 000.

This example is not meant to demonize the media or to mock Governor Miller. Rather, it highlights the need for greater scientific literacy in our society. The researchers did not make any unethical claims, the media were trying to present an interesting science-based story to their audience, and Governor Miller wanted to improve the well-being of the children in his state. But, because of a lack of scientific literacy and critical thinking, these events have now become a cautionary tale.

Focus Questions

1. We hear claims from marketers and politicians every day, but how can we evaluate them?
2. Can we evaluate evidence even if we are not scientists?

Watch
Music as a Universal Language

Research methods don't initially inspire much passion in students. However, this chapter might be the most important one in the book in many ways. This chapter will give you the training to become a critical consumer of scientific claims that are made by the media, corporations, politicians, and even scientists. Every time you open a news website, you encounter scientific topics such as how certain foods are linked with cancer risks or psychological issues, or you read about wonder drugs that will improve your grades. Some of this research is fantastic, but some is not. The goal of this chapter is to help you separate the good from the questionable, and to show you that asking tough questions about how research was designed and conducted is never a bad thing. Doing so prevents you from being tricked and manipulated . . . and from spending $105 000 on Mozart CDs.

Watch
What's in It for Me? How Am I Being Influenced?

Watch
Thinking Like a Psychologist: Thinking Critically

What makes science such a powerful technique for examining behaviour? Perhaps the single most important aspect of scientific research is that it strives for objectivity. *Objectivity* assumes that certain facts about the world can be observed and tested independently from the individual who describes them (e.g., the scientist). Everyone—not just the experts—should be able to agree on these facts given the same tools, the same methods, and the same context. Achieving objectivity is not a simple task, however.

As soon as people observe an event, their interpretation of it becomes *subjective*, meaning that their knowledge of the event is shaped by prior beliefs, expectations, experiences, and even their mood. A scientific, objective approach to answering questions differs greatly from a subjective one. Most individuals tend to regard a scientific approach as one that is rigorous and demands proof. Although these are not inaccurate characterizations of scientific thinking and research, there is more to explore.

Five Characteristics of Quality Scientific Research

During the past few centuries, scientists have developed methods to help bring us to an objective understanding of the world. The drive for objectivity influences how scientific research is conducted in at least five ways. Quality scientific research meets the following criteria:

1. It is based on measurements that are *objective, valid,* and *reliable.*
2. It can be *generalized.*
3. It uses techniques that reduce *bias.*
4. It is made *public.*
5. It can be *replicated.*

As you will soon read, these five characteristics of good research overlap in many ways, and they will apply to any of the methods of conducting research that you will read about in this textbook.

SCIENTIFIC MEASUREMENT: OBJECTIVITY, RELIABILITY, AND VALIDITY The foundation of scientific methodology is the use of **objective measurements**, *the measure of an entity or behaviour that, within an allowed margin of error, is consistent across instruments and observers.* In other words, the way that a quality or a behaviour is measured must be the same regardless of who is doing the measuring and the exact tool they are using. For example, weight is measured in pounds or kilograms. One kilogram in St. John's is the same as one kilogram in Victoria—researchers don't get to choose how much mass a kilogram is worth. Similarly, your weight will be the same regardless of whether you're using the scale in your bathroom or the scale in the change room at the gym. However, your weight *will* vary slightly from scale to scale—this is the margin of error

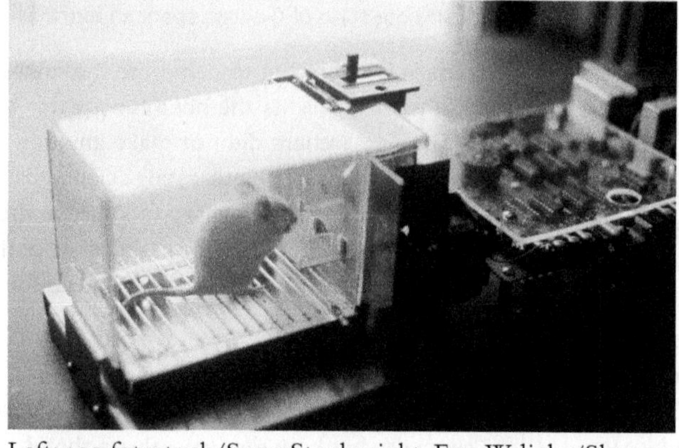

Left: age fotostock/SuperStock; right: Ewa Walicka/Shutterstock.com

Psychologists make observations using a variety of methods. They might observe and record behavioural responses such as lever pressing for a reward by laboratory animals, or ask people to complete questionnaires that measure thoughts, preferences, emotions, and other variables.

mentioned in the definition. Scientists in a given field have to agree upon how much variability is allowable. Most people will be comfortable if their weight differs by one or two kilograms depending on the scale being used. But, if you weigh 70 kg on one scale and 95 kg on the other, then you know one of your measurement tools is inaccurate.

In this example, weight would be considered a **variable**, *the object, concept, or event being measured.* Variables are a key part of the research described in all of the chapters in this book ranging from perceptual processes, to learning and memory, to how we interact with each other, and so on. Each of these variables can be described and measured. For most of psychology's history, measurements involved observations of behaviour in different situations or examinations of how participants responded on a questionnaire or to stimuli presented on a computer. However, as technology advanced, so did the ability to ask psychological questions in new and interesting ways. High-tech equipment, such as functional magnetic resonance imaging (fMRI), allows researchers to view the brain and see which areas are activated while you perform different tasks such as remembering words or viewing emotional pictures. Other physiological measures might involve gathering samples of blood or saliva, which can then be analyzed for enzymes, hormones, and other biological variables that relate to behaviour and mental functioning. With this greater number of measurement options, it's now possible to examine the same variable (e.g., anxiety) using a number of different techniques. Doing so strengthens our ability to understand the different elements of behaviour.

Regardless of the specific experimental question being asked, any method used by a researcher to measure a variable needs to include carefully defined terms. This isn't always as easy as it sounds. How would you define personality, shyness, or cognitive ability? This is the type of question a researcher would want to answer very carefully, not only for planning and conducting a study, but also when sharing the results of that research. In order to do so, researchers must decide upon a precise definition that other researchers could understand. These **operational definitions** *are statements that describe the procedures (or operations) and specific measures that are used to record observations* (Figure 2.1). For example, depression could be operationally defined as "a score of 21 or higher on the Beck Depression Inventory" (Beck & Steer, 1977), with the measure being a common and widely accepted clinical questionnaire.

The concept of operational definitions would have been helpful when the Georgia legislators considered implementing a state-wide program based on the Mozart

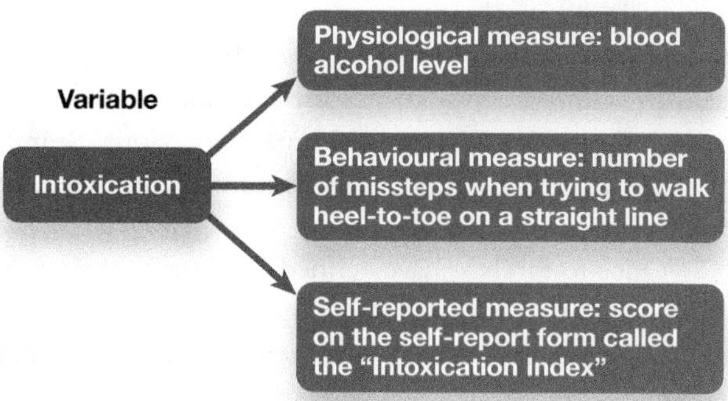

{FIG. 2.1} **Operational Definitions** A variable, such as the level of intoxication, can be operationally defined in multiple ways. This figure shows operational definitions based on physiology, behaviour, and self-report measures. **Click on this figure in your eText to see more details.**

effect. They should have asked, "How do the researchers define the outcome of their study? Do they mean listening to classical music makes you *smarter*, or just that you remember better? Do they claim the effect is permanent, or does it occur only while listening to Mozart?" Here is what the legislators would have found if they had looked up the answers in the scientific reports before spending over \$100 000, which was a lot of money in 1998 (Steele et al., 1999):

- Researchers have used several different objective measures of thinking and reasoning in studies of listening to classical music, including objective behavioural measures.
- Based on these measures, the only improvement seems to be in one specific type of thinking called spatial reasoning—that is, the ability to look at objects and mentally manipulate them.
- Researchers have also found that, averaged across a number of studies including 714 individuals, the average increase in spatial reasoning from listening to classical music is only 1½ points on an "IQ"-style intelligence test. (That gain is very small, given the fact that if you took the test twice in a week, it would be perfectly normal for your score to change by as much as 9 points.) In addition, this improvement is short-lived—it disappears after approximately 10 minutes.
- Initially researchers attributed the improvement to classical music (especially piano concertos) because the same result was not found with other types of music or with silence. Subsequently, however, researchers found the same type and size of effect after participants listened to a recording of a Stephen King horror novel, a result that companies producing Mozart-effect CDs did not take a shining to.

These conclusions make a very strong argument against investing the time, money, and effort in writing policy that relies so heavily on the Mozart effect. They also provide an important lesson to anyone making policy decisions that involve human behaviour: Search through the existing research literature *before* you make any decisions.

Once researchers have defined their terms, they then turn their attention toward the tools they plan to use to measure their variable(s) of interest. The behavioural measurements that psychologists make must be valid and reliable. **Validity** refers to *the degree to which an instrument or procedure actually measures what it claims to measure.* This seems like a simple task, but creating valid measures of complex behaviours is quite challenging. To go back to the depression example, researchers cannot simply ask people a few questions and then randomly decide that one score qualifies as depressed while another does not. Instead, for the measure to be valid, a particular score would have to differentiate depressed and non-depressed people in a way that accurately maps on to how these people actually feel (i.e., a depressed person would score differently than a non-depressed person). The creation of valid measures is therefore quite time-consuming and requires a great deal of testing and revising before the final product is ready for use.

In addition to being valid, a measurement tool must also be reliable. A measure demonstrates **reliability** *when it provides consistent and stable answers across multiple observations and points in time.* There are actually a number of different types of reliability that affect psychological research. *Test-retest reliability* examines whether scores on a given measure of behaviour are consistent across test sessions. If your scores on a test of depression vary widely each time you take the test, then it is unlikely that your test is reliable. *Alternate-forms reliability* is a bit more complicated. This form of reliability examines whether different forms of the same test produce the same results. Why would you need multiple forms of a test? In many situations, a person will be tested on multiple occasions. For instance, individuals with brain damage might have their memory tested soon after they arrive at the hospital and then at one or more points during their rehabilitation. If you give these individuals the exact same test, it is possible that any improvement is simply due to practice. By having multiple versions of a test that produce the same results (e.g., two equally difficult lists of words as stimuli for memory tests), researchers and hospital workers can test individuals on multiple occasions and know that their measurement tools are equivalent.

Explore
Diversity in Psychological Inquiry

A third type of reliability takes place when observers have to score or rate a behaviour or response. For example, psychologists might be interested in the effects of nonverbal behaviour when people interact, so they might videotape participants solving a problem and then have trained raters count the number of touches or the amount of eye contact that occurred during the experiment. As another example, participants might write down lengthy, open-ended responses to an experimenter's questions; these responses would then be rated on different variables by laboratory personnel. The catch is that more than one person must do the rating; otherwise it is impossible to determine if the responses were accurately measured or if the results were due to the single rater. Having more than one rater allows you to have *inter-rater reliability,* meaning that the raters agree on the measurements that were taken. If you design an experiment with clear operational definitions and criteria for the raters, then it is likely that you will have high inter-rater reliability.

Reliability and validity are essential components of scientific research. In addition, it is usually very important that your results are not limited to a small group of people in a single laboratory. Instead, it is ideal for these results to relate to other groups and situations—in other words, to be generalizable.

GENERALIZABILITY OF RESULTS Although personal testimony can be persuasive and (sometimes) interesting, psychologists are primarily interested in understanding behaviour *in general.* This involves examining trends and patterns that will allow us to predict how *most people* will respond to different stimuli and situations. **Generalizability** *refers to the degree to which one set of results can be applied to other situations, individuals, or events.* For example, imagine that one person you know claimed that a memory-improvement course helped her raise her grades. How useful is the course? Based on this information, you would initially view the course favourably. However, upon further reflection, you'd realize that a number of other factors could have influenced your friend's improvement, not the least of which is that she is suddenly paying more attention to her grades! At this point, you would wisely decide to wait until you've heard more about the course before investing your hard-earned money. But, if you found out that several hundred people in your city had taken the same course and had experienced similar benefits, then these results will appear more likely to predict what would happen if you or other people took the course. They are generalizable.

As you can see from this example, one way to increase the possibility that research results will generalize is to study a large group of participants. By examining and reporting an average effect for that group, psychologists can get a much better sense of how individuals are *likely* to behave. But how large of a group is it possible to study? Ideally, it would be best to study an entire **population**, *the group that researchers want to generalize about*. In reality, the task of finding all population members, persuading them to participate, and measuring their behaviour is impossible in most cases. Instead, psychologists typically study a **sample**, *a select group of population members*. Once the sample has been studied, then the results may be generalized to the population as a whole.

It is important to note that how a sample is selected will determine whether your results are generalizable. If your sample for the memory-improvement course was limited to middle-aged male doctors in Edmonton, it would be difficult to generalize those results to all Canadians. Instead, researchers try to use a **random sample**, *a sampling technique in which every individual of a population has an equal chance of being included*. If you wanted to study the population of students at your school, for example, the best way to obtain a true random sample would be to have a computer generate a list of names from the entire student body. Your random sample—a subset of this population—would then be identified, with each member of the population having an equal chance of being selected regardless of class standing, gender, major, living situation, and other factors. Of course, it isn't always possible to use random sampling. This is particularly true if you are hoping that your results generalize to a large population or to all of humanity. In these cases, researchers often have to settle for **convenience samples**, *samples of individuals who are the most readily available*—for example, Introductory Psychology students.

In addition to generalizing across individuals, psychological research should generalize across time and location. Research should ideally have high **ecological validity**, *meaning that the results of a laboratory study can be applied to or repeated in the natural environment*. Sometimes this connection doesn't seem obvious, such as computer-based studies testing your ability to pay attention to different stimuli on a computer screen, but such seemingly artificial situations are assessing human abilities that are used in very common situations such as driving or finding a friend in a crowded classroom.

Although generalizability and ecological validity are important qualities of good research, we need to be careful not to *over-generalize*. For example, results from a convenience sample of university students might not predict how a group of elderly people would do on the same task. Conversely, in the Mozart effect example that began this module, most of the studies involved adults, yet companies and politicians assumed—with very little evidence—that the results would generalize to children, including infants. Therefore, scientific literacy also involves thinking critically about when it is *appropriate* to generalize results to other groups, times, and locations.

SOURCES OF BIAS IN PSYCHOLOGICAL RESEARCH Of course, generalizability is only important if the experiment itself were conducted without bias. While creating objective, reliable, and valid measures is important in quality research, various types of bias can be unintentionally introduced by the researchers; this is known as a *researcher bias*. For instance, the experimenter may treat participants in different experimental conditions differently, thus making it impossible to know if any differences were due to the experimental manipulation being tested or were instead due to the experimenter's behaviour. It is also possible for the participants, including animals, to introduce their own bias; these effects are known as *subject biases* or *participant biases*. Sometimes this bias will involve a participant trying to figure out what the experimenters are testing or trying to predict the responses that the researchers are hoping to find.

Watch
Women, Health, and Stress: Florence Denmark

Bias can also be introduced by the act of observation itself. A wonderful example of this tendency was provided by workers at the Western Electric Company's Hawthorne Works, a Chicago-area factory in the 1920s. Researchers went to the factory to study the relationship between productivity and working conditions. When the researchers introduced some minor change in working conditions, such as an adjustment to the lighting, the workers were more productive for a period of time. When they changed another variable in a different study—such as having fewer but longer breaks—productivity increased again. What was not obvious to the researchers was that *any* change in factory conditions brought about increased productivity, presumably because the changes were always followed by close attention from the factory supervisors (Adair, 1984; Parsons, 1974). The results were due to the participants noticing that they were being observed rather than to the variables being manipulated. In honour of these observations, a *behaviour change that occurs as a result of being observed* is now known as the **Hawthorne effect**.

In most psychological research, the participants are aware that they are being observed. The challenge for the experimenters is to limit the effect that they have on the results of their own study so that the results are due to the variables being studied rather than to the participants responding to cues from the researcher.

Engineering and drafting school, ca. 1925. Western Electric Company photograph album. Baker Library Historical Collections. Harvard Business School. (olvwork278414)

The Hawthorne Effect, named after the Western Electric Company's Hawthorne Works in Chicago, states that individuals sometimes change their behaviour when they think they are being observed.

WORKING THE SCIENTIFIC LITERACY MODEL

Demand Characteristics and Participant Behaviour

Results of psychological studies *should* provide uncontaminated views of behaviour. In reality, however, people who participate in psychological studies typically enter the research environment with a curiosity about the subject of the study. Researchers need to withhold as much detail as possible (while still being ethical) to get the best, least biased results possible.

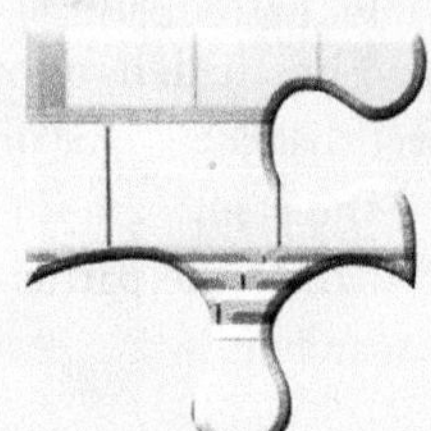

What do we know about how bias affects research participants?

When studying human behaviour, a major concern is **demand characteristics**, *inadvertent cues given off by the experimenter or the experimental context that provide information about how participants are expected to behave.* Demand characteristics can range from very subtle to obvious influences on the behaviour of research participants (Orne, 1962). They can take the form of responding based on **social desirability** (also known as *socially desirable responding*), *which means that research participants respond in ways that increase the chances that they will be viewed favourably.* This type of bias is particularly relevant when the study involves an interview in which the researcher has face-to-face contact with the volunteers.

Demand characteristics may also be a problem in laboratory studies, where participants often try to figure out the purpose of the experiment. Subtle and even obvious cues by the researcher or the experimental context can give away the purpose of the study. For example, imagine you walk into a laboratory and a psychologist asks you to put on a heavy backpack. She then shows you a ramp and asks you to estimate how steep the ramp is. It certainly seems plausible that the experimenter wants to know whether wearing the backpack will affect your judgment about the steepness of the ramp. Research has shown that even in this simple example there looms the possibility of demand characteristics that can affect performance.

How can science test the effects of demand characteristics on behaviour?

One explanation for demand effects is that people are generally searching for a reason for their behaviour. When there is no explanation for performing a given set of actions, such as putting on a backpack and climbing a ramp, people tend to draw their own conclusions (e.g., assuming that the purpose of the study is to see if wearing a backpack affects steepness judgments). Durgin and colleagues (2009) tested this possibility by performing a study in which participants wore no backpack, wore a 25-pound (11-kg) backpack with no explanation given, or wore the same backpack and were told that it contained electrical equipment that would be used to measure muscle activity in participants' ankles. To increase the believability of this procedure, actual electrodes with wires running to the backpack were attached to the ankles of members of the third group. The participants were taken separately to a room that contained a ramp and were asked to judge how steep they thought it was before and after they stepped onto it. After completing the procedure, the participants sat at a computer and took a survey that included questions in which they guessed the purpose of the study. The researchers found that the participants who wore the backpack but did not receive an explanation for doing so judged the ramp to be steeper than did the other two groups. This group difference occurred both before and after the participants actually used the ramp. Importantly, when questioned at the end of the study, the no-explanation group stated that they believed that the purpose of the experiment was to determine how wearing a backpack affects steepness judgments. Students who did not wear a backpack or, most importantly, who wore one with recording equipment they assumed was critical to the study, did not report this belief. The participants who did not have an explanation for the study attempted to guess what it was, leading to demand characteristics that affected perceptual judgments about the ramp's slope (Durgin et al., 2009).

Demand characteristics can also be explained by researchers and observers introducing biases and unwittingly drawing out the responses they desire. Some classic examples of how expectations can influence results come from the research of Rosenthal and colleagues. In one study, researchers told teachers in 18 different classrooms that a group of children had an "unusual" potential for learning, when in reality they were just a random selection of students (Rosenthal & Jacobson, 1966). After eight months of schooling, the children singled out as especially promising showed significant gains not just in grades, but in intelligence test scores, which are believed to be relatively stable. Why would this occur if the students were randomly selected? The best explanation is that the observers (i.e., teachers) assumed those students would do well, and were therefore more likely to pay attention to those students and to give them positive and encouraging feedback. These positive experiences with the teachers likely motivated these students to improve themselves. In other words, the students changed their behaviour patterns in order to match up with the expectations of the teachers. It is easy to see how similar experimenter effects could occur in psychological research studies.

Experimenter bias can even be found when people work with animals. When research assistants were told they were handling "bright" rats, it appeared that the animals learned significantly faster than when the assistants were told they were handling "dull" rats. Because it is unlikely that the rats were influenced by demand characteristics—they were not trying to give the researchers what they wanted—the most likely explanation for this difference is that researchers made subtle changes in how they treated the animals, and in how they observed and recorded behaviour (Rosenthal & Fode, 1963).

How can we critically evaluate the issue of bias in research?

This issue of bias in research is very difficult to overcome. Very few researchers intentionally manipulate their participants; however, as you have read, many times these influences are subtle and accidental. In most cases, experimenters (often graduate students and undergraduate research assistants) complete rigorous training and follow careful scripts when explaining experimental procedures to participants. These precautions help reduce experimenter effects.

One way to evaluate whether participants' expectations are influencing the results is to create an additional manipulation in which the researchers give different groups of participants different expectations of the results. If the groups then differ when performing the same task, then some form of demand characteristic, in this case from the participant, might be influencing performance. For instance, one study asked participants to detect any changes that might occur between two different, alternating driving scenes (e.g., part of the scene might disappear in one of the scenes). Some of the participants were told that the ability to detect these changes was important for driving; other participants were told that it wasn't important for driving. The group told that detecting changes was not important for successful driving performed significantly worse than the other group (Pearson & Schaefer, 2005). Manipulating participants' expectations is an effective way of testing whether demand characteristics could be playing a role in the results of experiments. Of course, it is not always practical to include an additional group in a study, and, when doing clinical research, manipulating expectations might not be ethical. But when researchers begin performing research on new topics or with new research methods, testing for demand characteristics would be a wise decision.

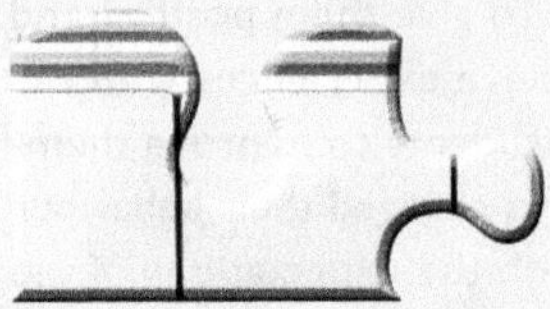

Why is this relevant?

Demand characteristics and other sources of bias all have the potential to compromise research studies. Given the time, energy, and monetary cost of conducting research, it is critical that results are as free from contamination as possible. The science of psychology involves the study of a number of very sensitive topics; the results are often used to allow policymakers to make better-informed decisions. Producing biased results will therefore have negative effects upon society as a whole. Demand effects are particularly problematic when studying clinical populations or when performing experiments with different types of clinical treatments. The results of these studies affect what we know about different patient populations and how we can help them recover from their different conditions. Biased results could therefore affect the health care of vulnerable members of our society.

kkgas/iStockphoto

The fact that demand characteristics can alter results is of particular importance for researchers investigating new drug treatments for different conditions. Patients enter treatment programs (and experiments) with a number of expectations. It turns out these expectations can produce their own unique effects.

TECHNIQUES THAT REDUCE BIAS Although biases can be a threat to the validity and reliability of psychological research, experimenters have established a number of techniques that can reduce the impact of subject and researcher biases. One of the best techniques for reducing subject bias is to provide anonymity and confidentiality to the volunteers. *Anonymity* means that each individual's responses are recorded without any name or other personal information that could link a particular individual to specific results. *Confidentiality* means that the results will be seen only by the researcher. Ensuring anonymity and confidentiality are important steps toward gathering honest responses from research participants. Participants are much more likely to provide information about sensitive issues like their sexual

PSYCH @

The Hospital: The Placebo Effect

The demand effect that we know the most about is the **placebo effect,** *a measurable and experienced improvement in health or behaviour that cannot be attributable to a medication or treatment.* This term comes from drug studies, in which it is standard procedure for a group, unbeknownst to them, to be given an inactive substance (the placebo) so that this group can be compared to a group given the active drug. What often happens is that people in the placebo group report feeling better because they have the expectation that the drug will have an effect on their brain and body. This effect has been reported time and again—not just with drugs, but with other medical and surgical treatments as well. Why do people receiving a placebo claim to feel better? The initial explanation was that the patients' expectations caused them to simply convince themselves they feel better (i.e., it is "all in their head"). Other research noted that many people who are given a placebo show physiological evidence of relief from pain and nausea (Hrobjartsson & Gotzsche, 2010). Research conducted at the Rotman Research Institute in Toronto suggests that both of these explanations have merit. Helen Mayberg and colleagues (2002) found that people responding to placebos showed increased activity in several regions of the frontal lobes. This activity *may* relate to the participants creating a new "mental set" of their current state; in other words, creating the belief that their pain was going to decrease. Interestingly, these researchers also noted a decrease in activity in a number of other brain regions that might represent changes in the sensitivity of pain pathways. These results suggest that there are multiple ways for placebos to affect our responses to pain. Placebos are an important part of experimental research in psychology and related fields, so it is important to recognize their potential influence on how research participants respond.

history, drug use, or emotional state if they can do so confidentially and anonymously.

In a related issue, participant anxiety about the experiment—which often leads to changes in how people respond to questions—can be reduced if researchers provide full information about how they will eventually use the data. Many people assume that psychologists are "analyzing them"; in fact, if you mention at your next family gathering that you're taking psychology, it is almost certain that someone will make a joke about this. If volunteers know that the data will *not* be used to diagnose psychiatric problems, affect their grades, or harm them in some other way, then their concerns about the study will be less likely to affect their performance.

Another source of bias in psychological research involves participants' expectations of the effects of a treatment or manipulation. We saw this tendency in the discussion of the placebo effect discussed earlier. The critical element of the placebo effect is that the participants believe the pill or liquid they are consuming is actually a drug. If they knew that they were receiving a sugar pill instead of a pain medication, they would not experience any pain relief. Therefore, it is important that experiments involving drugs (recreational or therapeutic) utilize what are known as *blind* procedures. In a **single-blind study**, *the participants do not know the true purpose of the study, or else do not know which type of treatment they are receiving (for example, a placebo or a drug)*. In this case, the subjects are "blind" to the purpose of the study. Of course, a researcher can introduce bias as well. This bias is not going to be overt. It is unlikely that a researcher will laugh and call the placebo group "suckers" and then play Pink Floyd albums and Spongebob cartoons for the people in the drug condition. But the researcher might unintentionally treat individuals in the two conditions differently, thus biasing the results. In order to eliminate this possibility, researchers often use a technique known as a **double-blind study**, *a study in which neither the participant nor the experimenter knows the exact treatment for any individual.* To carry out a double-blind procedure, the researcher must arrange for an assistant to conduct the observations or, at the very least, the researcher must not be told which type of treatment a person is receiving until after the study is completed.

Double-blind procedures are also sometimes used when researchers are testing groups that differ on variables such as personality characteristics or subtle demographic factors such as sexual orientation. If the experimenter knows that a participant has scored high on a test of psychopathy, she might treat him differently than she treated a person who scored low on the same test. Keeping the experimenter (and participants) blind to these results allows the research to remain objective. Therefore, researchers should use these techniques whenever possible.

CandyBox Images/Shutterstock

In a single-blind study, the nurse would know whether the patient was in the placebo or treatment condition, but the patient would not. In a double-blind study, neither the nurse nor the patient would know which condition the patient was in. A double-blind study is less likely to be biased by the experimenter.

SHARING THE RESULTS Once a group of researchers has designed and conducted an objective experiment that is free of bias, it is important to communicate their findings to other scientists. Psychology's primary mode of communication is through academic journals. Academic journals resemble magazines in that they are usually softbound periodicals with a number of articles by different authors (online formats are typically available as well). Unlike magazines, however, journal articles represent primary research or reviews of multiple studies on a single topic. When scientists complete a piece of research, they may write a detailed description of the theory, hypotheses, measures, and results and submit the article for possible publication. You will not find journals or research books in your average mall bookstore because they are too technical and specialized for the general market (and are not exactly page-turners), but you will find thousands of them in your university library.

However, only a fraction of the journal articles that are written eventually get published. Rather, before research findings can be published, they must go through **peer review**, *a process in which papers submitted for publication in scholarly journals are read and critiqued by experts in the specific field of study.* In the field of psychology, peer review involves two main tasks. First, an editor receives the manuscript from the researcher and determines whether it is appropriate subject matter for the journal (for example, an article on 17th-century Italian sculpture would not be appropriate for publication in the *Journal of Cognitive Neuroscience*, which is focused on biological explanations for memory, thinking, language, and decision making). Second, the editor sends copies of the manuscript to a select group of peer reviewers—"peer" in this case refers to another professional working within the same field of study. These reviewers critique the methods and results of the research and make recommendations to the editor regarding the merits of the research. In this process, the editors and reviewers serve as gatekeepers for the discipline, which helps increase the likelihood that the best research is made public.

REPLICATION Once research findings have been published, it is then possible for other researchers to build upon the knowledge that you have created; it is also possible for researchers to double check whether or not your results simply occurred by chance (which does happen). Science is an ongoing and self-correcting process. The finest, most interesting published research study can quickly become obsolete if it cannot be replicated. **Replication** *is the process of repeating a study and finding a similar outcome each time.* As long as an experiment uses sufficiently objective measurements and techniques, and if the original hypothesis was correct, then similar results *should* be achieved by later researchers who perform the same types of studies. Results are not always replicated in subsequent investigations, however.

One familiar example is that of the purported Mozart effect that was featured in the story at the beginning of this module. Although the general idea that listening to classical music could make a person smarter had been around for years, one of the first scientific studies of this hypothesis was conducted in 1993 (Rauscher et al., 1993). Other researchers were skeptical of the results and examined the study through partial replications, meaning they employed highly similar methods (e.g., Steele et al., 1997). The original researchers responded by critiquing the replications and recommending a number of changes (Rauscher & Shaw, 1998). Another partial replication was conducted following this advice, but it still did not yield the same results as the original study (Steele et al., 1999). This failure to replicate the original findings does not mean that the authors of the original study were dishonest. It could mean they unintentionally introduced researcher bias, or perhaps the sampling was biased, or perhaps the results were just a fluke. But certainly this example emphasizes the value of replication: Correct hypotheses and sound methods should produce repeatable results.

In the big picture, peer review and replication are self-corrective measures for all disciplines, because they ensure that published results did not occur through carelessness, dishonesty, or coincidence.

Quick Quiz 2.1a

Five Characteristics of Quality Scientific Research

KNOW ...

1 The degree to which an instrument measures what it is intended to measure is known as ________.

A validity **C** verifiability
B generalizability **D** reliability

2 When psychologists question how well the results of a study apply to other samples or perhaps other situations, they are inquiring about the ________ of the study.

A validity **C** verifiability
B generalizability **D** reliability

UNDERSTAND ...

3 In a single-blind study, the participants do not know the purpose of the study or the condition to which they are assigned. What is the difference in a double-blind study?

A The researcher tells the participants the purpose and their assigned conditions in the study.
B The participants also do not know when the actual study begins or ends.
C The researcher also does not know which condition the participants are in.
D The participants know the condition to which they have been assigned, but the researcher does not.

APPLY ...

4 Dr. Rose gives a standardized personality test to a group of psychology majors in January and again in March. Each individual's score remains nearly the same over the two-month period. From this, Dr. Rose can infer that the test is ________.

A reliable **C** objective
B generalizable **D** verified

Answers can be found on page ANS-1.

Five Characteristics of Poor Research

In the preceding section, you read about what makes for quality research; it is generally safe to assume that the opposite characteristics detract from the quality of research. Good research uses valid, objective measures; poor research uses measures that are less valid, less reliable, and, therefore, less likely to be replicable. However, other issues must also be scrutinized if you hear someone make a scientific-sounding claim. Most claims are accompanied by what might sound like evidence, but evidence can come in many forms. How can we differentiate between weak versus strong evidence? Poor evidence comes most often in one of five varieties: untestable hypotheses, anecdotes, a biased selection of available data, appeals to authority, and appeals to (so-called) common sense.

Perhaps the most important characteristic of science is that its hypotheses are testable. For a hypothesis to be testable, it must be **falsifiable**, meaning that *the hypothesis is precise enough that it could be proven false.* If a hypothesis is not falsifiable, that means that there is no pattern of data that could possibly prove that this view is wrong; instead, there is always a way to reinterpret the results to make the hypothesis match the data. If you cannot disconfirm a hypothesis, then there is no point in testing it. There are very few examples of unfalsifiable hypotheses in modern psychology. However, early personality work by Freud did suffer from this problem (see Module 12.3). Briefly, Freud believed that the personality consisted of three components: the id (which was focused on pleasure), the superego (which was based on following rules), and the ego (which attempted to balance the two opposing forces). Although this theory provided wonderful metaphors for behaviour, it is impossible to test. If a person does not behave in the predicted fashion, the analyst can simply say that the other personality component (e.g., the id) was more involved at that moment. There would be no way to prove him wrong. Luckily, researchers have built upon Freud's pioneering work and have created much more scientific (and falsifiable) theories of personality, a topic discussed later in this book.

A second characteristic of poor research is the use of **anecdotal evidence**, *an individual's story or testimony about an observation or event that is used to make a claim as evidence.* For example, a personal testimonial on a product's webpage might claim that a man used subliminal weight-loss CDs to lose 50 pounds in six months. But there is no way of knowing whether the CDs were responsible for the person's weight loss; the outcome could have been due to any number of things, such as a separate physical problem or changes in food intake and lifestyle that had nothing to do with the subliminal messages. In fact, you do not even know if the anecdote itself is true: The "before" and "after" photos could easily be doctored. Therefore, we must be wary of such anecdotal claims; if they are not backed up by a peer-reviewed scientific study, then we should view the claims with caution.

However, we still need to be careful even if a scientific claim is backed up by published data. It is possible that some individuals—particularly politicians and corporations—might present only the data that support their views. A beautiful example of this *data selection bias* is shown in the debate over whether human behaviour is a major cause of climate change. A climate-change denier could point out that 24 peer-reviewed scientific studies cast doubt on whether human behaviour is a cause of global warming. Twenty-four sounds like a large body of research. However, James Powell, a member of the U.S. National Science Board, carefully examined all of the climate-change data and found 13 926 papers supporting this view (see Figure 2.2). Therefore, a very selective slice of the data would present one (biased) result, but a thorough and scientific representation of the data would present an entirely different view of the same issue.

The fourth kind of questionable evidence is the **appeal to authority**—*the belief in an "expert's" claim even when no supporting data or scientific evidence is present.* Expertise is not actually evidence; "expert" describes the person making the claim, not the claim itself. It is entirely possible that the expert is mistaken, dishonest, overpaid, or misquoted. True experts are good at developing evidence, so if a claim cites someone's expertise as evidence, then you should see whether the expert offers the corresponding data to support the claim. It is not unusual for people to find that an expert's claim

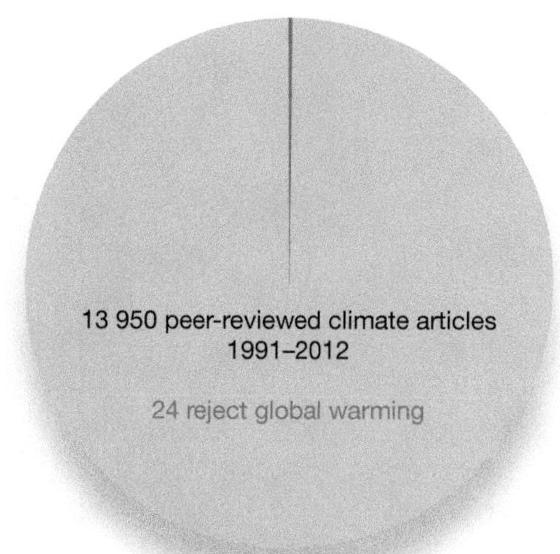

{FIG. 2.2} **Data Selection Bias** People with a particular political or economic agenda can still make claims that appear scientific if they perform a biased selection of the available data. Groups opposed to the idea that human activity is playing a role in global warming often point to published research supporting their view. However, when one examines *all* of the data on global warming, it appears that negative findings make up less than 1% of the results, suggesting that these individuals are full of hot air.

actually has no evidence backing it, but rather that it is simply an opinion. In other cases, it turns out that the experts have a hidden agenda or a "conflict of interest." It is important to look at what the expert stands to gain by lending his or her name to a product or scientific theory.

Finally, the evidence may consist of an **appeal to common sense**, *a claim that appears to be sound, but lacks supporting scientific evidence.* For example, many people throughout history assumed the world was the stationary centre of the universe. The idea that the Earth could orbit the sun at blinding speeds was deemed nonsense—the force generated would seemingly cause all the people and objects to be flung into space!

In addition to common sense, beliefs can originate from other potentially unreliable sources. For example, *appeals to tradition* ("We have always done it this way!") as well as their opposite, *appeals to novelty* ("It is the latest thing!"), can lead people to believe the wrong things. Claims based on common sense, tradition, or novelty may be worthy of consideration, but whether something is true cannot be evaluated by these standards alone. Instead, what we need is careful and objective testing. What we need is science.

Quick Quiz 2.1b

Five Characteristics of Poor Research

KNOW ...

1 Claiming that something is true because "it should be obvious" is really just ________.

- **A** anecdotal evidence
- **B** an appeal to common sense
- **C** an appeal to authority
- **D** generalizability

UNDERSTAND ...

2 Appeals to authority do not qualify as good evidence because

- **A** they always lack common sense.
- **B** authority figures are likely to distort the truth.
- **C** authority does not mean that there is sound, scientific evidence.
- **D** authority is typically based on anecdotal evidence.

APPLY ...

3 Ann is convinced that corporal punishment (e.g., spanking) is a good idea because she knows a child whose behaviour improved because of it. Whether or not you agree with her, Ann is using a flawed argument. Which type of evidence is she using?

- **A** Anecdotal
- **B** Objective
- **C** Generalizable
- **D** An appeal to authority

Answers can be found on page ANS-1.

Module Summary

Module 2.1

Now that you have read this module you should

KNOW ...

- ***The key terminology related to the principles of scientific research*:**

anecdotal evidence (p. 41)	peer review (p. 39)
appeal to authority (p. 41)	placebo effect (p. 38)
appeal to common sense (p. 42)	population (p. 35)
convenience samples (p. 35)	random sample (p. 35)
demand characteristics (p. 36)	reliability (p. 34)
double-blind study (p. 39)	replication (p. 40)
ecological validity (p. 35)	sample (p. 35)
falsifiable (p. 41)	single-blind study (p. 39)
generalizability (p. 34)	social desirability (p. 36)
Hawthorne effect (p. 35)	validity (p. 34)
objective measurements (p. 32)	variable (p. 33)
operational definitions (p. 33)	

UNDERSTAND ...

- ***The five characteristics of quality scientific research.*** These characteristics include that (1) measurements are objective, valid, and reliable; (2) the research can be generalized; (3) it uses techniques that reduce bias; (4) the findings are made public; and (5) the results can be replicated. For example, objective, valid, and reliable measurements make it possible for other scientists to test whether they could come up with the same results if they followed the same procedures. Psychologists mostly study samples of individuals, but usually they are more concerned about describing principles that generalize to a broader population. Single- and double-blind procedures are standard ways of reducing bias. Finally, the process of publishing results is what allows scientists to share information, evaluate hypotheses that have been confirmed or refuted, and, if needed, replicate other researchers' work.
- ***How biases might influence the outcome of a study.*** Demand characteristics affect how participants respond in research studies—understandably, they often attempt to portray themselves in a positive light, even if that means not answering questions or behaving in a fully truthful manner. Researchers can also influence the outcomes of their own studies, even unintentionally.

APPLY ...

- ***The concepts of reliability and validity to examples.*** Try this activity to see how well you can apply these concepts. Read the following descriptions, and determine whether each scenario involves an issue with reliability or validity. Check your answers on page ANS-1.

Photosindia/Getty Images

1. Dr. Tatum is doing very standard physiological recording techniques on human participants. Each morning she checks whether the instruments are calibrated and ready for use. One day she discovered that the instrumentation was way off the mark, and would surely give very inconsistent readings compared to previous days. *Would this affect the reliability or validity of her research? Explain.*
2. Dr. Nielson uses a behavioural checklist to measure happiness in the children he studies at an elementary school. Every time he and his associates observe the children, they reach near-perfect agreement on what they observed. Another group of psychologists observes the same children in an attempt to identify which children are energetic and which seem tired and lethargic. It turns out that the same children whom Dr. Nielson identifies as happy, using his checklist, are also the children whom the second group of psychologists identify as energetic. *It appears there may be a problem with Dr. Nielson's measure of happiness. Do you think it is a problem of reliability or validity? Explain.*

ANALYZE ...

- ***Whether anecdotes, authority figures, and common sense are reliably truthful sources of information.*** To evaluate evidence, you should ask several questions. First, is someone supplying anecdotal evidence? As convincing as a personal testimony may be, anecdotal evidence is not sufficient for backing any claim that can be scientifically tested. Second, is support for the claim based on the words or endorsement of an authority figure? Endorsement by an authority figure is not necessarily a bad thing, as someone who is an authority at something should be able to back up the claim. But the authority of the individual alone is not satisfactory, especially if data gathered through good scientific methods do not support the claim. Finally, common sense also has its place in daily life, but by itself is insufficient as a final explanation for anything. Explanations based on good scientific research should override those based on common sense.

Blend Images/Alamy

Module 2.2

Scientific Research Designs

Learning Objectives

After reading this module you should

KNOW ...	UNDERSTAND ...	APPLY ...	ANALYZE ...
The key terminology related to research designs	What it means when variables are positively or negatively correlated How experiments help demonstrate cause-and-effect relationships	The terms and concepts of experimental methods to research examples	The pros and cons of descriptive, correlational, and experimental research designs

Can your attitude affect your health? This is the old question of "mind over matter," and psychologist Rod Martin thinks the answer is definitely yes. He says that if you can laugh in the face of stress, your psychological and physical health will benefit. Martin has found several interesting ways to build evidence for this argument (Martin, 2002, 2007). For example, he developed a self-report instrument that measures sense of humour. People who score high on this measure—those who enjoy a good laugh on a regular basis—appear to be healthier in a number of ways. As interesting as this evidence is, it simply illustrates that humour and health are *related*—there is no guarantee that one *causes* the other. To make such a claim, researchers would have to use the experimental method, one of the many research designs discussed in this module.

Focus Questions

 What are some of the ways researchers make observations?

 Do some research techniques provide stronger evidence than others?

Psychologists always begin their research with a *research question*, such as "What is the most effective way to study?", "What causes us to feel hungry?", or "How does attitude affect health?" In most cases, they also make a prediction about the outcome they expect—the hypothesis. Psychologists then create a *research design*, a set of methods that allows a hypothesis to be tested. Research designs influence how investigators (1) organize the stimuli used to test the hypothesis, (2) make observations, and (3) evaluate the results. Because several types of designs are available, psychologists must choose the one that best addresses the research question and that is most suitable to the subject of their research. Before we examine different research designs, we should quickly review the characteristics that all of them have in common.

- *Variables.* A variable is a property of an object, organism, event, or something else that can take on different values. How frequently you laugh is a variable that could be measured and analyzed.
- *Operational definitions.* Operational definitions are the details that define the variables for the purposes of a specific study. For sense of humour, this definition might be "the score on the Coping Humour Scale."
- *Data.* When scientists collect observations about the variables of interest, the information they record is called data. For example, data might consist of the collection of scores on the Coping Humour Scale from each individual in the sample.

These characteristics of research designs are important regardless of the design that is used. However, a number of other factors will guide the researchers as they select the appropriate research design for their topic of interest.

Descriptive Research

The beginning of any new line of research must involve descriptive data. Descriptive research answers the question of "what" a phenomenon is; it describes its characteristics. Once these observations have been performed and the data examined, they can be used to inform more sophisticated future studies that ask "why" and "how" that phenomenon occurs.

Here are a few examples of descriptive research questions:

- How many words can the average two-year-old speak?
- How many hours per week does the typical university student spend on homework?
- What proportion of the population will experience depression or an anxiety disorder at some point in their lives?

As you can see, research questions address the appearance of a behaviour, its duration or frequency, its prevalence in a population, and so on. To answer those questions, researchers usually gather data using one or more of the following designs: *case studies, naturalistic observation,* and *surveys and questionnaires.*

CASE STUDIES A **case study** *is an in-depth report about the details of a specific case.* Rather than developing a hypothesis and then objectively testing it on a number of different individuals, scientists performing a case study describe an individual's history and behaviour in great detail. Of course, case studies are not performed on just anyone. They are generally reserved for individuals who have a very uncommon characteristic or have lived through a very unusual experience.

Watch
Humour and Brains

Watch
The Big Picture: How to Answer Psychological Questions

Perhaps the most famous case study in psychology (and neurology) is that of Phineas Gage (1823–1860). Gage was a foreman working for the Rutland and Burlington Railroad Company in the northeastern U.S. state of Vermont. On September 13, 1848, 25-year-old Gage was helping his crew blast through a rocky outcrop near the town of Cavendish. As part of this job, holes were drilled into the rock; blasting powder, a fuse, and sand were added; and then this mixture was squished down with a large tamping iron, an iron rod that was 109 cm in length and just over 3 cm in diameter. Late that afternoon, Gage got distracted and likely began tamping before the sand had been added to the mixture (Macmillan, 2008). The result was that the tamping iron caused a spark which set off the blast powder. This caused the iron rod to be

Jack & Beverly Wilgus/The Past Tense of Picture/Brightbytes.com

Phineas Gage proudly holding the tamping iron that nearly killed him, and that made him one of the most famous names in the history of psychology and neuroscience. The information learned from case studies of Gage led to hundreds of subsequent scientific studies that have helped researchers learn a great deal about the frontal lobes of the brain. Interestingly, over the course of a few years, Gage slowly recovered enough of his self-control to hold down different jobs, including one as a long-distance stagecoach driver in South America (Macmillan, 2008); however, he never did recover all of his self-control. Had doctors paid more attention to this partial recovery, it would have been one of the first reported cases of the brain's ability to compensate and repair itself after injury.

propelled upwards underneath Gage's eye and through his head. According to the original medical report of the incident (Harlow, 1848; available online for interested readers), it was found 25 m away, suggesting that it was travelling very quickly as it tore through Gage's brain.

Amazingly, Gage survived the accident, although his physical recovery took most of a year (Bigelow, 1850; Harlow, 1849). However, it quickly became apparent that Gage's injuries were not limited to physical damage; his mental state had also been affected. Reports indicate that while he had been a reputable citizen prior to the accident, afterward he became much more impulsive, inconsiderate, indecisive, and impatient. Harlow (1868) reported that Gage's friends claimed that the changes were so pronounced that he "was no longer Gage." The doctors treating Gage rightfully concluded that these sudden changes were due to the brain damage that he had suffered. Examination at the time of the accident—which involved Dr. Harlow sticking his finger into the hole in Gage's head—suggested that this damage was located in the frontal lobes of the brain, a region now known to be involved in a number of complex behaviours including decision making and emotional regulation (see Modules 8.2 and 11.4). Because Gage's case was documented in a series of detailed case-study reports, it was possible for future doctors and researchers to use this information to gain a better understanding of the role of the frontal lobes and the problems that emerge when this brain area is damaged.

The case of Phineas Gage is obviously quite striking. However, although case studies tell us a lot about an individual's condition, is it really science? Different researchers have different opinions about the merit of such reports, with some viewing them as important scientific contributions and others viewing them as simply interesting stories.

WORKING THE SCIENTIFIC LITERACY MODEL

Case Studies as a Form of Scientific Research

Case studies allow the clinician or researcher to present more details about an individual than would be possible in a research report involving a number of participants; however, this detail comes at a price. Is a thorough description of a single individual still a form of science or is it simply an example of anecdotal evidence?

What do we know about using case studies as a form of scientific research?

Case studies have been a form of psychological research for over a century. Freud used case studies of unique patients when he initially described many of his theories of personality and development. Case studies have also been critical for our understanding of the brain. Phineas Gage was just one of many unique neurological patients that have taught us how different areas of the brain influence particular behaviours. In each situation, the researchers described their patient in great detail so the case study could improve the treatment of similar patients in the future.

Case studies can also be useful in describing symptoms of psychological disorders and detailed descriptions about specific successes or failures in treatment. One recently published example of a case study did both (Elkins & Moore, 2011). The authors of this study described the experience of a certain type of anxiety disorder and the steps used in therapy to treat the anxiety over a 16-week period. They were able to document how and when changes occurred and the effects of the treatment on other aspects of the individual's life. This level of detail would not be available if the authors had not focused on a single case. However, as case studies only describe a single individual, there is no guarantee that the findings can be generalized to other individuals and situations.

How can science test the usefulness of case studies?

Although it is tempting to view case studies as simply being descriptions of an individual, they can also serve another important scientific function: They can be used to test an existing hypothesis. For example, until a couple of years ago, researchers thought that the amygdala—a fear centre in the brain—was essential for emotional information to grab our attention (e.g., the way your attention is almost always drawn to a spider walking across your ceiling). It made sense that a fear centre would be a necessary part of a fear response. Brain-imaging studies showed that this structure was active when these types of images were displayed to healthy participants. But, what would happen if someone with no amygdala on either side of her brain was put in this situation? A case study with one such patient (there are fewer than 300 worldwide) found that her attention was still grabbed by emotional stimuli (Tsuchiya et al., 2009). This told researchers that their models of how emotion and attention work together were too simplistic, and forced them to look at other brain structures that could be influencing these processes. In other words, the case study was used not to generate hypotheses, but to actually test an existing scientific theory.

Case studies can also be used to find similarities between different concepts. For example, a number of computer-based studies have shown that healthy individuals can be taught to associate everyday objects with emotional responses such as fear

(Van Damme et al., 2004). These previously neutral objects will then capture attention in the same way as a spider walking across a ceiling (Smith et al., 2006). Research has indicated that this ability to link emotional responses to previously unemotional objects may play a role in the development of posttraumatic stress disorder (PTSD), a condition in which specific stimuli trigger intense emotional responses due to a previous traumatic event (Shin et al., 2003). In fact, in one case study, a PTSD patient with a fear of cars (after being hit by one) showed the exact same results on an emotion-and-attention test as healthy participants who had been taught to associate cars with a loud noise earlier in the experiment (Smith et al., 2008). Without this case study, it would be difficult to show the link between this cognitive mechanism and this clinical condition.

How can we critically evaluate the role of case studies in research?

Although at first glance it would appear that case studies would have limited generalizability, the above section demonstrates that they can help guide our understanding of existing scientific theories (Flyvbjerg, 2006). Case studies can also spawn a large amount of other research. Take Phineas Gage, for example. Although there are very few, if any, other reports of individuals experiencing a tamping rod shooting through their frontal lobes, other studies have examined whether the physiological effects of such an injury can be mimicked in other ways, and whether this damage leads to similar impairments. A number of studies of patients who suffered damage to the frontal lobes after car accidents and strokes have noted that these individuals become more impulsive and risk-prone than they had been before their accident (Bechara et al., 1994; Damasio, 1994). Researchers have also created lesions similar to Phineas Gage's in animal subjects (e.g., laboratory rats) and observed similar tendencies (Quirk & Beer, 2006).

Finally, researchers can use computer simulations to model the effects of this form of brain damage. In one study—cheekily entitled *Spiking Phineas Gage*—Brandon Wagar and Paul Thagard (2004) created a computerized neural network that used both cognitive and emotional information to produce simple decisions. After the network "learned" the task, the researchers altered its parameters so that the frontal lobe node of the network did not function properly. As predicted, this network's responses quickly became more dependent upon emotional impulses, just like patients with frontal-lobe damage such as Phineas Gage. The important point here is that all of these different research projects examined the role of the frontal lobes in a different way, thus providing us with a more thorough understanding of this brain region. Therefore, the case study of a single patient who somehow survived a terrifying brain injury has stimulated hundreds of scientific research papers leading to improvements in our understanding of how the brain works. Fittingly, such information will be essential in the treatment of any modern-day Phineas Gages.

Why is this relevant?

These studies demonstrate that case studies are not simply anecdotes that scientists tell each other when they sit around the campfire. Instead, single cases serve as an inspiration for many future studies that attempt to test whether the observed result can be generalized to more individuals, perhaps even to humans in general. Indeed, as you continue reading this textbook, you'll be introduced to a number of unique individuals whose stories have informed and guided psychological science for over a century. Without them, our understanding of topics ranging from vision to memory to language to emotions would not be as sophisticated as it has become. These topics would also lack the story-like narratives that make psychology so compelling.

Of course, case studies are often limited to individuals with unique conditions or experiences. They cannot be used to answer all types of research questions. For instance, there are times when a researcher might be interested in how groups of people or animals behave in environments outside of the controlled laboratory setting or interview room. In these situations, an entirely different form of descriptive research is necessary to examine psychological behaviours.

i4lcocl2/Fotolia

NATURALISTIC OBSERVATION An alternative form of descriptive research is to observe people (or animals) in their natural settings. When psychologists engage in such **naturalistic observations**, *they unobtrusively observe and record behaviour as it occurs in the subject's natural environment.* The key word here is "unobtrusively"; in other words, the individuals being observed shouldn't know that they are being observed. Otherwise, the mere act of observation could change the participants' behaviours (imagine how your conversations with friends would change if you knew a psychologist were listening and taking notes). Most students have seen television programs about scientists in search of chimpanzees in a rainforest or driving a Range Rover in pursuit of a herd of elephants. This certainly is a form of observation, but there is more to it than just watching animals in the wild. When a scientist conducts naturalistic observation research, she is making systematic observations of specific variables according to operational definitions. By having a very precise definition of what a variable is and how it will be measured, researchers using naturalistic observations can ensure that their results are objective and that different people observing the same environment would score the behaviours in the same way (e.g., two observers would both call the same movement by a chimpanzee a grooming behaviour).

Although it may appear that naturalistic observation is only useful for animal studies or nature programs on TV, there have been a number of interesting human-focused naturalistic observation studies conducted as well. For example, a study conducted by psychologists at Carleton University in Ottawa measured the behaviour of spectators at youth hockey games (Bowker et al., 2009). These researchers were specifically interested in the types of comments made by spectators—the intensity of the remarks, who made them (male vs. female), and who they were directed toward (players, other spectators, or everyone's favourite target, the referees), among other variables. They also examined whether the observed trends changed depending upon whether the game was in a highly competitive or a more recreational league. The researchers found that females made more comments than males; these comments were largely positive and directed toward the players. Males tended to make more negative comments as well as directions on how to improve play (e.g., "Skate faster!"). Both female and male spectators made more negative comments when watching competitive, as opposed to recreational, leagues; these comments were largely directed toward the referees. Based on these observations, which involved five observers attending 69 hockey games, the authors concluded that the behaviour of spectators is not as negative and unsettling as is often reported in the media (Bowker et al., 2009).

CREATISTA/Shutterstock.Com

Researchers who use naturalistic observation record behaviour in natural, non-laboratory settings and do so as unobtrusively as possible.

Thus, naturalistic observations can occur anywhere that behaviours occur, be it in "nature," in a hockey rink, or even in a bar (Graham & Wells, 2004). The key point is that the researchers must pay attention to specific variables and use operational definitions. However, naturalistic observations may not always provide researchers with the specific types of information they are after. In these cases, researchers may need to adopt a different research strategy in order to describe a given behaviour.

SURVEYS AND QUESTIONNAIRES Another common method of descriptive research used by psychologists is **self-reporting**, *a method in which responses are provided directly by the people who are being studied, typically through face-to-face interviews, phone surveys, paper and pencil tests, and web-based questionnaires*. These methods allow researchers to assess attitudes, opinions, beliefs, and abilities. Despite the range in topics and techniques, their common element is that the individuals speak for themselves. Surveys and questionnaires are still a method of observation, but the observations are provided by the people who are being studied rather than by the psychologist.

Although this method initially sounds simple, the creation of objective survey and questionnaire items is extremely challenging. Care must be taken not to create biased questions that could affect the results one way or another. If you're interested in studying emotional sensitivity, you can't ask, "Given that men are drooling pigs, how likely are they to notice someone is unhappy?" Similarly, if you're studying a subject that some individuals might not want to openly discuss, it is important to develop questions that touch on the issue without being too off-putting. For example, asking people, "How depressed are you?" and giving them a 7-point scale might not work, as some respondents might not want to state that they are depressed. But, questionnaires can tap into the symptoms of depression by asking questions about energy levels, problems with sleeping, problems concentrating, and changes in one's mood. The researchers could then use the responses for these questions to determine if a respondent was depressed.

This leads to an important question: How do researchers figure out if their questions are valid? For clinical questionnaires, the researchers can compare results to a participant's clinical diagnosis. For questionnaires examining other phenomena, researchers perform a large amount of pretesting in order to calculate *norms*, or average patterns of data. Almost all of the questionnaires that you will encounter as a psychology student will have undergone prior testing to establish norms and to confirm that the research tool is both valid and reliable. This testing will involve hundreds or even thousands of participants; their efforts help ensure that self-report measures such as questionnaires are a useful tool in psychology's quest to understand different behaviours.

Quick Quiz 2.2a

Descriptive Research

KNOW ...

1 When psychologists observe behaviour and record data in the environment where it normally occurs, they are using ________.

- **A** case studies
- **B** naturalistic observation
- **C** the supervisory method
- **D** artificial observation

2 Any property of an organism, event, or something else that can take on different values is called _______.

- **A** an operational definition
- **B** data
- **C** a variable
- **D** a case study

APPLY ...

3 A psychologist is completing a naturalistic observation study of children's aggressive behaviour on a playground. She says that aggression is "any verbal or physical act that appears to be intended to hurt or control another child." She then goes on to list specific examples. It appears that the psychologist is attempting to establish a(n)

- **A** good relationship with the children.
- **B** variable.
- **C** observational definition.
- **D** operational definition.

Answers can be found on page ANS-1.

Correlational Research

Psychologists performing descriptive research almost always record information about more than one variable when they are collecting data. In these situations, the researchers may look for an association among the variables. They will ask whether the variables tend to occur together in some pattern, or if they tend to occur at opposite times. **Correlational research** *involves measuring the degree of association between two or more variables.* For example, consider these two questions:

- What is the average education level of people in every country in the world?
- What is the average family income in every country of the world?

These two questions ask for very different types of information, but their answers may be related. Is it likely that countries with higher education levels also tend to have higher income levels? By asking two or more questions—perhaps through a survey—researchers can start to understand the associations among variables.

Explore Correlations Do Not Show Causation

Correlations can be visualized when presented in a graph called a *scatterplot*, as shown in Figure 2.3.

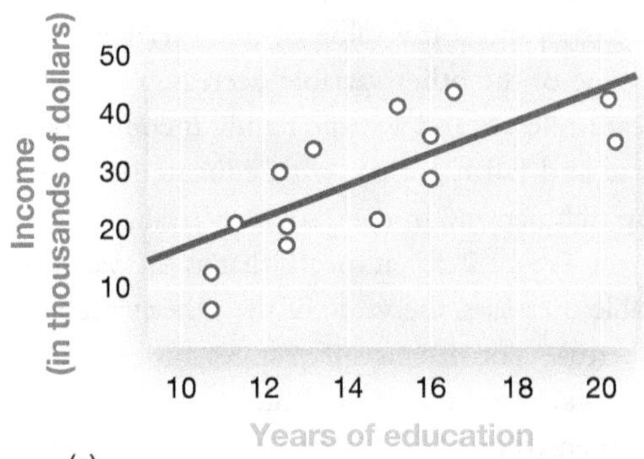

(a)

Irritability
Hours of sleep

(b)

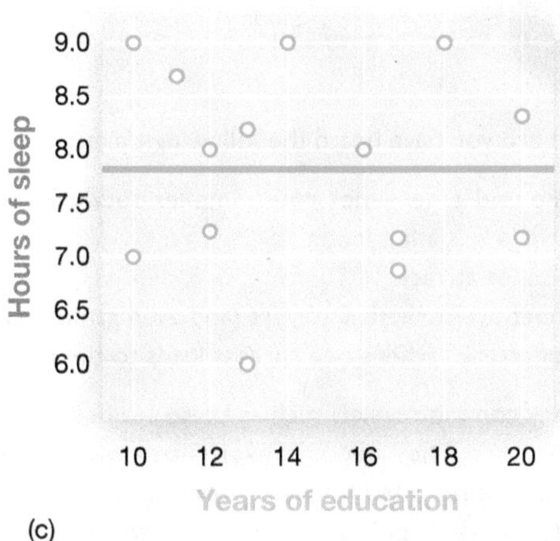

(c)

{FIG. 2.3} **Correlations Are Depicted in Scatterplots** Here we see two variables that are positively correlated (a) and negatively correlated (b). In the example of a zero correlation (c), there is no relationship between the two variables.

Research Methods

In scatterplot (a), you can see the data for education and income. Each dot represents one participant's (or in this example, one country's) data; when you enter dots for all of the participants, you often see a pattern emerge. In this case, the dots show a pattern that slopes upward and to the right, indicating that countries with higher education levels tend to have a higher average income. That correlation is not surprising, but it illustrates one of the two main characteristics that describe correlations:

- Correlations take a *direction*. If correlations are positive (see Figure 2.3a), it means that the two variables change values in the same direction. So, if the value of one variable increases, the value of the other variable also tends to increase, and if the value of one variable decreases, the value of the other variable decreases. For example, education levels and average family income both tend to rise and fall together, with educated nations also being rich nations. In contrast, if correlations are negative (see Figure 2.3b), it means that as the value of one variable increases, the value of the other variable tends to decrease. For instance, if you get a lot of sleep, you are less likely to be irritable; but, if you don't get much sleep, then you will be more likely to be irritable.
- Correlations have a *magnitude* or *strength*. This refers to how closely the changes in one variable are linked to changes in another variable (e.g., if variable A goes up one unit, will variable B also go up one unit). This magnitude is described in terms of a mathematical measure called the *correlation coefficient*. A correlation coefficient of zero means that there is no relationship between the two variables (see Figure 2.3c). A coefficient of +1.0 means that there is a very strong positive correlation between the variables. A coefficient of −1.0 means that there is a very strong negative correlation between the variables. Importantly, +1.0 and −1.0 coefficients have an equal magnitude or strength; however, they have a different direction.

You will encounter many correlations in this text, and it will be important to keep in mind the direction of the relationship—whether the variables are positively or negatively associated. One key point to remember is that the correlation coefficient is a measure of association only—*it is not a measure of causality*. In other words, correlation does not equal causation. This is an extremely important point!

In many cases, a correlation gives the *impression* that one variable causes the other, but that relationship cannot be determined from correlational research. For example, we noted in the beginning of the module that a sense of humour is associated with good health—this is a positive correlation. But that does not mean that humour *is responsible for* the good health. Perhaps good health leads to a better sense of humour. Or perhaps neither causes the other, but rather a third variable causes both good health and good sense of humour. This possibility is known as the **third variable problem**, *the possibility that a third, unmeasured variable is actually responsible for a well-established correlation between two variables.* Consider the negative correlation between sleep and irritability shown in scatterplot (b) of Figure 2.3. Numerous third variables could account for this relationship. Stress, depression, diet, and workload could *cause* both increased irritability and lost sleep. As you can see, correlations must be interpreted with caution.

MYTHS IN MIND

Beware of Illusory Correlations

Chances are you have heard the following claims:

- Crime and emergency room intakes suddenly increase when there is a full moon.
- Opposites attract.
- Competitive basketball players (and even gamblers) get on a "hot streak" where one success leads to the next.

Many common beliefs such as these are deeply ingrained in our culture. They become even more widely accepted when they are repeated frequently. It is difficult to argue with a hospital nurse or police officer who *swears* that full-moon nights are the busiest and craziest of all. The conventional, reserved, and studious man who dates a carefree and spirited woman *confirms* that opposites attract. And, after Steve Nash has hit a few amazing three-point shots, of course his chances of success just get better and better as the game wears on.

But do they? Each of these three scenarios is an example of what are called *illusory correlations*—relationships that really exist only in the mind, rather than in reality. It turns out that well-designed studies have found no evidence that a full moon leads to, or is even related to, bizarre or violent behaviour (Lilienfeld & Arkowitz, 2009). People who are attracted to each other are typically very similar (Buston & Emlen, 2003). Also, although some games may be better than others, overall the notion of a "hot streak" is not a reality in basketball or in blackjack (Caruso et al., 2010; Gilovich et al., 1985).

Why do these illusory correlations exist? Instances of them come to mind easily and are more memorable than humdrum examples of "normal" nights in the ER, perfectly matched couples, and all of the times Steve Nash misses a shot, even in his best games. However, just because examples are easy to imagine, it does not mean that this is what typically occurs.

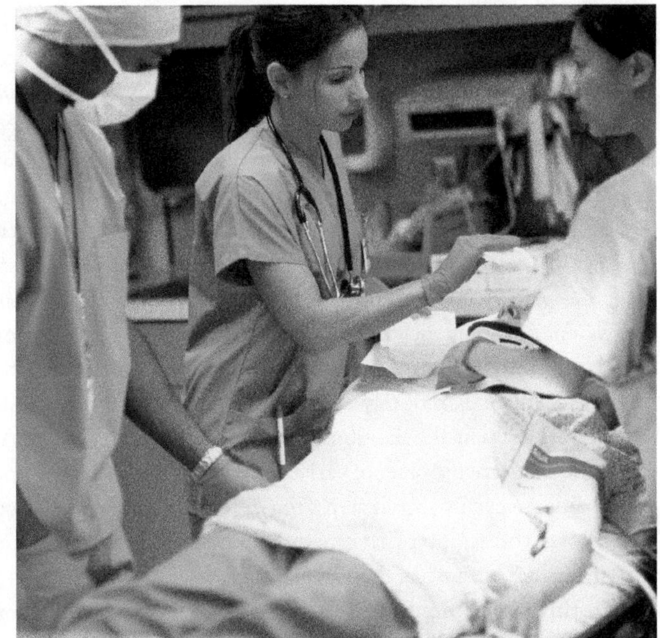

Left: Gary yim/Shutterstock; right: Fancy/Glow Images

Contrary to *very* popular belief, a full moon is statistically unrelated to unusual events or increased emergency room visits.

Quick Quiz 2.2b

Correlational Research

KNOW …

1 Which of the following correlation coefficients shows the strongest relationship between two variables?

A +.54

B −.72

C +1.1

D +.10

UNDERSTAND …

2 What does it mean to say that two variables are negatively correlated?

A An increase in one variable is associated with a decrease in the other.

B An increase in one variable is associated with an increase in the other.

C A decrease in one variable is associated with a decrease in the other.

D The two variables have no relationship.

ANALYZE …

3 Imagine Dr. Martin finds that sense of humour is positively correlated with psychological well-being. From this, we can conclude that

A humour causes people to be healthier.

B health causes people to be funnier.

C people who have a good sense of humour tend to be healthier.

D people who have a good sense of humour tend to be less healthy.

Answers can be found on page ANS-1.

Experimental Research

Watch Basics: Scientific Research Methods

Experimental designs improve on descriptive and correlational studies because they are the only designs that can provide strong evidence for cause-and-effect relationships. Like correlational research, experiments have a minimum of two variables, but there are two key differences between correlational research and experiments: the random assignment of the participants and the experimenter's control over the variables being studied. As you will see, these unique features are what make experimental designs so powerful.

THE EXPERIMENTAL METHOD Imagine you were conducting an experiment testing whether seeing photographs of nature scenes would reduce people's responses to stressful events. You carefully created two sets of images—one of peaceful images of the B.C. coastline, Lake Louise, Algonquin Park in Ontario, and rugged Maritime coastlines—and another of neutral images such as houses. When the first two participants arrive at the laboratory for your study, one is wearing a t-shirt supporting a local environmental organization and the other is wearing a t-shirt emblazoned with an oil sands company logo. Which participant gets assigned to the nature scene condition and which gets assigned to the neutral condition? If you are conducting an objective, unbiased study, the answer to this question is that either participant is equally likely to be assigned to either condition. Indeed, a critical element of experiments is **random assignment**, *a technique for dividing samples into two or more groups in which participants are equally likely to be placed in any condition of the* *experiment*. Random assignment allows us to assume the two groups will be roughly equal (Figure 2.4).

If we assigned anyone who looked like they were nature lovers to the nature scene condition, then our experiment might not be telling us about the effects of the images. Instead, some other **confounding variable**—*a variable outside of the researcher's control that might affect or provide an alternative explanation for the results*—could potentially enter the picture. In our example, the variables of political awareness or tendency to be "outdoorsy" might play an even larger role in the study than the stimuli you worked so hard to create. Randomly assigning participants to the different experimental conditions also allows the researcher to assume that other sources of variability such as mood and personality are evenly spread across the different conditions. This allows you to infer that any differences between the two groups are because of the variable you are testing.

In this experiment, we are manipulating one variable (the types of images being viewed) and measuring another variable (stress response). *The variable that the experimenter manipulates to distinguish between two or more groups* is known as the **independent variable.** The participants cannot alter these variables, as they are controlled by the researcher. In contrast, the **dependent variable** *is the observation or measurement that is recorded during the experiment and subsequently compared across all groups*. The levels of this variable are dependent upon the participants' responses or performance. In our example, the type of images being viewed is the independent variable and the participants' stress response is the dependent variable.

Simulate Distinguishing Independent and Dependent Variables

This experiment is an example of a **between-subjects design**, *an experimental design in which we compare the performance of participants who are in different groups*. One of these groups, the **experimental group**, *is the group in the experiment that receives a treatment or the stimuli targeting a specific behaviour*, which in this specific example would be exposure to nature scenes. The experimental group always receives the treatment. In contrast, the **control group** *is the group that does not receive the treatment or stimuli targeting a specific behaviour; this group therefore serves as a baseline to which the experimental group is compared*. In our example, the control group would not be exposed to nature photographs. What if the experimental group showed reduced stress compared to the control group? Assuming that the experiment was well designed and all possible confounds were accounted for,, the researchers could conclude that the independent variable—exposure to images of nature—is responsible for the difference.

Hypothesis: Nature causes a reduction in stress.

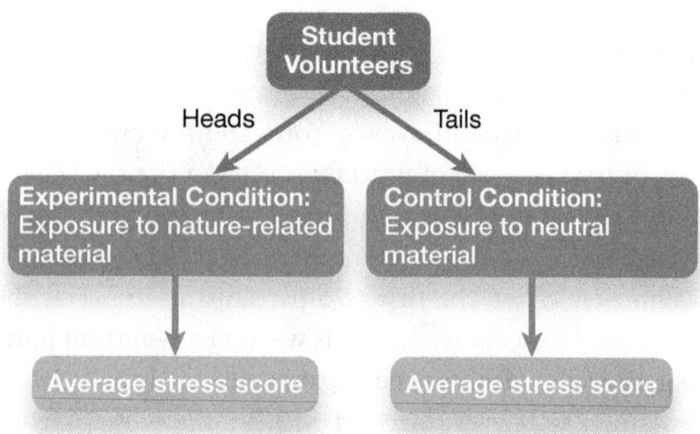

{FIG. 2.4} **Elements of an Experiment** If we wanted to test whether exposure to nature-related images causes a reduction in stress (as is assumed by people who have nature scenes as their computer's wallpaper), we would first need to randomly assign people in our sample to either the experimental or control condition. The dependent variable, the stress levels, would be measured following exposure to either nature-related or neutral material. To test whether the hypothesis is true the average stress scores in both groups would be compared. **Click on this figure in your eText to see more details.**

A between-subjects design allows the researcher to examine differences between groups; however, it is also open to criticism. What if the two groups were different from each other simply by chance? That would make it more difficult to detect any differences caused by your independent variable. In order to reduce this possibility, researchers often use **within-subjects designs**, *an experimental design in which the same participants respond to all types of stimuli or experience all experimental conditions*. In the experiment we've discussed in this section, a within-subjects design would have involved participants viewing all of the images from one condition (e.g., nature photographs) before being tested, and then viewing all of the images from the other condition (e.g., neutral photographs) before being tested again. In this case, the order of the conditions would be randomly assigned for each participant.

As you can see, designing an experiment requires the experimenter to make many decisions. However, in some cases, some of these decisions are taken out of the researchers' hands.

THE QUASI-EXPERIMENTAL METHOD Random assignment and manipulation of a variable are required for experiments. They allow researchers to make the case that differences between the groups originate from the independent variable. In some cases, though, random assignment is not possible. **Quasi-experimental research** *is a research technique in which the two or more groups that are compared are selected based on predetermined characteristics, rather than random assignment*. For example, you will read about many studies in this text that compare men and women. Obviously, in this case one cannot flip a coin to randomly assign people to one group or the other. Also, if you gather one sample of men and one sample of women, they could differ in any number of ways that are not necessarily relevant to the questions you are studying. As a result, all sorts of causes could account for any differences that would appear: genetics, gender roles, family history, and

Table 2.1 :: Strengths and Limitations of Different Research Designs

METHOD	STRENGTHS	LIMITATIONS
Naturalistic observation	Allows for detailed descriptions of subjects in environments where behaviour normally occurs	Poor control over possibly influential variables
Surveys/questionnaires	Quick and often convenient way of gathering large quantities of self-report data	Poor control; participants may not answer honestly, written responses may not be truly representative of actual behaviour
Case studies	Yields detailed information, often of rare conditions or observations	Focus on a single subject limits generalizability
Correlational study	Shows strength of relationships between variables	Does not allow researcher to determine cause-and-effect relationships
Experiment	Tests for cause-and-effect relationships; offers good control over influential variables	Risk of being artificial with limited generalization to real-world situations

so on. Thus, quasi-experiments can point out relationships among preexisting groups, but they cannot determine what it is about those groups that lead to the differences.

CONVERGING OPERATIONS An underlying theme of this module has been that each method of studying behaviour has benefits as well as limitations (see Table 2.1). For example, naturalistic observation research allows psychologists to see behaviour as it normally occurs, but it makes experimental control very difficult—some would argue impossible. Conversely, to achieve true random assignment while controlling for any number of confounding variables and outside influences, the situation may be made so artificial that the results of an experiment do not apply to natural behaviour. Luckily, psychologists do not have to settle on only one method of studying behaviour. Most interesting topics have been studied using a variety of possible designs, measures, and samples. In fact, when a theory's predictions hold up to dozens of tests using a variety of designs—a perspective known as *converging operations*—we can be much more confident of its accuracy, and are one step closer to understanding the many mysteries of human (and animal) behaviour.

Quick Quiz 2.2c Experimental Research

KNOW ...

1. The process of setting up two or more groups in an experiment is called _______.
   - **A** correlation
   - **B** observation
   - **C** random assignment
   - **D** experimental selection

UNDERSTAND ...

2. A researcher sets up an experiment to test a new antidepressant medication. One group receives the treatment, and the other receives a placebo. The researcher then measures depression using a standardized self-report measure. What is the independent variable in this case?
   - **A** Whether the individuals scored high or low on the depression measure
   - **B** Whether the individuals received the treatment or a placebo
   - **C** Whether the individuals were experiencing depression before the study began
   - **D** Whether the individuals' depression decreased or increased during the study period

APPLY ...

3. A researcher compares a group of Conservatives and Liberals on a measure of beliefs about poverty. What makes this a quasi-experimental design?
   - **A** The researcher is comparing pre-existing groups, rather than randomly assigning people to them.
   - **B** You cannot be both a Conservative and a Liberal at the same time.
   - **C** There are two independent variables.
   - **D** There is no operational definition for the dependent variable.

ANALYZE ...

4. A researcher is able to conduct an experiment on study habits in his laboratory and finds some exciting results. What is one possible shortcoming of using this method?
   - **A** Results from laboratory experiments do not always generalize to real-world situations.
   - **B** Experiments do not provide evidence about cause-and-effect relationships.
   - **C** It is not possible to conduct experiments on issues such as study habits.
   - **D** Laboratory experiments do not control for confounding variables.

Answers can be found on page ANS-1.

Module Summary

Module
2.2

Now that you have read this module you should

KNOW …

- ***The key terminology related to research designs:***

between-subjects design (p. 52)
case study (p. 45)
confounding variable (p. 52)
control group (p. 52)
correlational research (p. 49)
dependent variable (p. 52)
experimental group (p. 52)
independent variable (p. 52)
naturalistic observation (p. 47)
quasi-experimental research (p. 52)
random assignment (p. 51)
self-reporting (p. 48)
third variable problem (p. 50)
within-subjects design (p. 52)

UNDERSTAND …

- ***What it means when variables are positively or negatively correlated.*** When two or more variables are positively correlated, their relationship is direct—they increase or decrease together. For example, income and education level are positively correlated. Negatively correlated variables are inversely related—as one increases, the other decreases. Substance abuse may be inversely related to cognitive performance—higher levels of substance abuse are often associated with lower cognitive ability.
- ***How experiments help demonstrate cause-and-effect relationships.*** Experiments rely on randomization and the manipulation of an independent variable to show cause and effect. At the beginning of an experiment, two or more groups are randomly assigned—a process that helps ensure that the two groups are roughly equivalent. Then, researchers manipulate an independent variable; perhaps they give one group a drug and the other group a placebo. At the end of the study, if one group turns out to be different, that difference is most likely due to the effects of the independent variable.

APPLY …

- ***The terms and concepts of experimental methods to research examples.*** Here are two examples for practice. Check your answers on page ANS-1.
  1. Dr. Vincent randomly assigns participants in a study to exercise versus no exercise conditions and, after 30 minutes, measures mood levels. In this case, exercise level is the ________ variable and mood is the ________ variable.

Blend Images/Alamy

  2. Dr. Harrington surveyed students on multiple lifestyle measures. He discovered that as the number of semesters that university students complete increases, their anxiety level increases. If number of semesters and anxiety increase together, this is an example of a(n) ________ correlation. Dr. Harrington also found that the more time students spent socializing, the less likely they were to become depressed. The increase in socializing and decrease in depression is an example of a(n) ________ correlation.

ANALYZE …

- ***The pros and cons of descriptive, correlational, and experimental research designs.*** Descriptive methods have many advantages, including observing naturally occurring behaviour and providing detailed observations of individuals. In addition, when correlational methods are used in descriptive research, we can see how key variables are related. Experimental methods can be used to test for cause-and-effect relationships. One drawback is that laboratory experiments may be limited in how far their results may generalize to real-world situations.

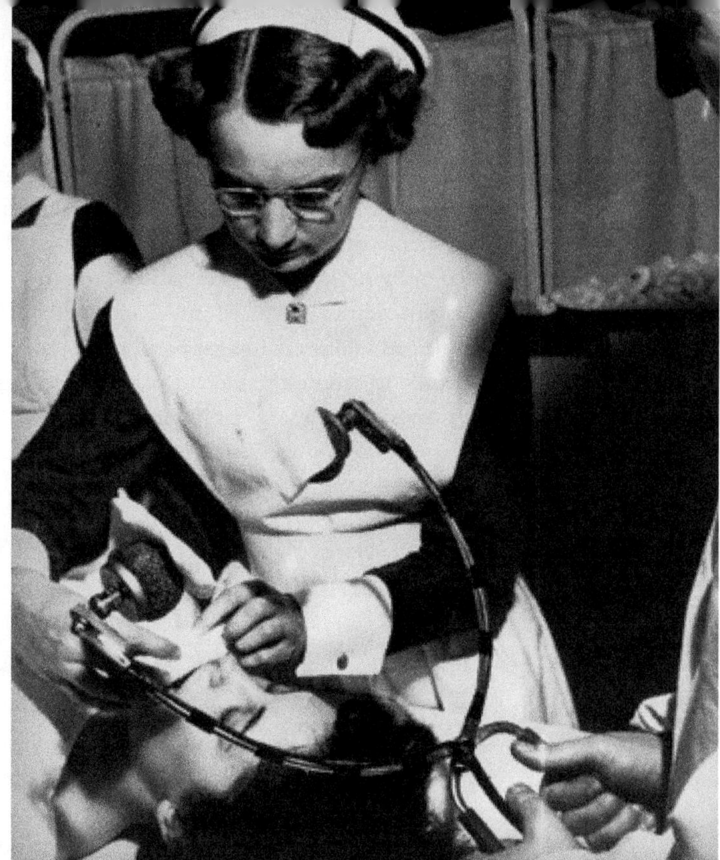

Bettmann/CORBIS

Module 2.3

Ethics in Psychological Research

Learning Objectives

After reading this module you should

KNOW ...	UNDERSTAND ...	APPLY ...	ANALYZE ...
The key terminology of research ethics	The importance of reporting and storing data Why animals are often used in scientific research	The ethical principles of scientific research to examples	The role of using deception in psychological research

In the early 1950s, the United States' Central Intelligence Agency (CIA) became involved in the field of psychology. After hearing that their enemies in the Soviet Union, China, and North Korea had tried to use mind-control techniques—including mind-altering drugs—on U.S. prisoners of war, the CIA felt it had no choice but to research these techniques themselves. Project MKUltra had begun. After recruiting former Nazi scientists who had studied torture and "brainwashing" during World War II (and who had been prosecuted as war criminals), the CIA secretly poured tens of millions of dollars into research laboratories at hospitals and universities in order to study mind-control techniques that would alter people's personalities, memories, and ability to control themselves while being interrogated. At least one of these institutions was in Canada.

Scottish psychiatrist Donald Ewen Cameron used CIA funds (as well as $500 000 from the Canadian government) to perform terrifying experiments at the Allan Memorial Institute of McGill University from 1957 to 1964. Patients who were admitted to the institute for fairly minor problems such as anxiety disorders or depression were—without giving proper consent or being informed of the reason for the "treatment"—subjected to manipulations that can only be called torture. These patients received drugs that caused temporary paralysis or even coma, electroconvulsive therapy set at more than 30 times the recommended strength, constant noises, and even looped tapes repeating messages (Klein, 2007). These treatments led to amnesia, confusion, and anxiety; participants in these programs were never the same (Collins, 1988).

Project MKUltra was officially ended in 1973. The experiments are now generally accepted as being among the most unethical studies in the history of science. In the 1980s, the Canadian government paid $100 000 to each of the 127 victims of Cameron's unauthorized research program. For several decades, the CIA's interrogation manual referred to "studies at McGill University" (McCoy, 2006).

Focus Questions

 Which institutional safeguards are now in place to protect the well-being of research participants?

 Does all research today require that people be informed of risks and consent to participate in a study?

The topics that psychologists study deal with living, sensing organisms, which raises a number of ethical issues that must be addressed before any study begins. These concerns include protecting the physical and mental well-being of participants, obtaining consent from them, and ensuring that their responses remain confidential. The procedures discussed in the next section have been developed as protections for participants; they are critical not only to ensure the individual well-being of the study participants, but also to maintain a positive and trustworthy image of the scientists who conduct research.

Promoting the Welfare of Research Participants

The CIA mind-control research program certainly is an extreme case—extreme in the harm done to the volunteers, the disregard for their well-being, and its secretive nature. Today, most research with human participants involves short-term, low-risk methods, and there are now ethical guidelines and procedures for ensuring the safety and well-being of all individuals involved in research. In Canada, all institutions that engage in research with humans, including colleges and universities, are required to have a **research ethics board (REB)**, *a committee of researchers and officials at an institution charged with the protection of human research participants.* (If you read a research report from an American institution, they will refer to Institutional Review Boards [IRBs]; these are the same thing as REBs.) REBs help ensure that researchers abide by the ethical rules set out in the *Tri-Council Policy Statement: Ethical Conduct for Research Involving Humans (2nd edition)*, a set of requirements created by the Government of Canada's Panel of Research Ethics. The REBs are intended to protect individuals in two main ways: (1) The committee weighs potential risks to the volunteers against the possible benefits of the research, and (2) it requires that volunteers agree to participate in the research (i.e., they give informed consent).

Watch
Special Topics: Ethics and Psychological Research

WEIGHING THE RISKS AND BENEFITS OF RESEARCH The majority of psychological research involves minimal exposure to physical or mental stress such as computer-based studies of perception or questionnaires studying personality traits. Even so, great care is taken to protect participants. However, some research is slightly riskier such as exposing individuals to brief periods of stress, inducing a negative mood, asking about sensitive topics, or even asking participants to engage in brief periods of exercise. Some studies have even exposed humans to the virus that causes the common cold, or made small cuts to the skin to study factors that affect healing. The benefits that this type of research provides in promoting health and well-being must be weighed against the short-term risks to the people who consent to participate in these studies.

It must be stressed that physical risks are rare in psychological research. More common are measures that involve possible cognitive and emotional stress. Here are a couple of examples:

- *Mortality salience.* In this situation participants are made more aware of death, which can be done in a number of ways. For example, participants may be asked to read or write about what happens to a human body after death.
- *Writing about upsetting or traumatic experiences.* People who have experienced recent trauma such as the death of a loved one or being laid off from a long-term job might be asked to write about that experience in great detail, sometimes repeatedly.

Another source of risk is related to the fact that some studies ask participants to provide the experimenter with sensitive and/or personal information. Think about all the topics in psychology that people might want to keep to themselves: opinions about teachers or supervisors, a history of substance abuse, criminal records, medical records, and so on. Disclosing this information is a potential threat to a person's reputation, friends, and family. Psychologists must find ways to minimize these risks so that participants do not suffer any unintended consequences of participating in psychological research.

Indeed, everyone involved in the research process—the researcher, the REB, and the potential volunteer—must determine whether the study's inherent risks are worth what can potentially be learned if the research goes forward. Consider again the stressors mentioned previously:

- *Mortality salience.* The stress tends to be short term, and psychologists learn how decisions are influenced by recent events in a person's life, such as the loss of a loved one or experiencing a major natural disaster. These decisions range from making charitable donations to voting for or against going to war.
- *Writing about upsetting experiences.* Although revisiting a stressful experience can be difficult, researchers learn how coping through expression can help emotional adjustment and physical health. In fact, participants who write about stress tend to be healthier—emotionally and physically—than those who write about everyday topics (such as describing their dorms or apartments).

These stressful situations have potential benefits that can be applied to other people. The psychologists who undertake such research tend to be motivated by several factors—including the desire to help others, the drive to satisfy their intellectual curiosity, and even their own livelihood and employment. The REB serves as a third party that weighs the risks and benefits of research without being personally invested in the outcome. Under today's standards, there is no chance that the CIA mind-control studies would have been initiated, except in secrecy outside of the public process of science. The danger to the participants in that study—*victims* might be a better term—far outweighed any scientific benefit gained from these experiments, even if the participants had known what they were getting into. Today, it is mandatory that research participants be informed of any risks to which they may be exposed and willfully volunteer to take part in a study.

OBTAINING INFORMED CONSENT In addition to weighing the risks versus the benefits of a study, researchers must ensure that human volunteers truly are *volunteers*. This may seem redundant, but it is actually a tricky issue. Recall that the human subjects in the CIA mind-control studies were volunteers only in the sense that they voluntarily sought treatment from the researchers. But did they volunteer to undergo procedures that were very close to being torture? Had the men and women known the true nature of the study, it is doubtful that any would have continued to participate. Currently, participants and patients have much more protection than they did in the 1950s and 1960s. Before any experimental procedures begin, all participants must provide **informed consent**: *A potential volunteer must be informed (know the purpose, tasks, and risks involved in the study) and give consent (agree to participate based on the information provided) without pressure.*

To be truly informed about the study, volunteers should be told, at minimum, the following details (see also Figure 2.5):

- The topic of the study
- The nature of any stimuli (e.g., images, sounds, smells) to which they will be exposed
- The nature of any tasks (e.g., tests, puzzles) they will complete
- The approximate duration of the study
- Any potential physical, psychological, or social risks involved
- The steps that the researchers have taken to minimize those risks

Ethical practices often involve resolving conflicting interests, and in psychological research the main conflict is between the need for informed consent and the need for "blinded" volunteers. (Recall from Module 2.1 that in the best experimental designs the participants do not know exactly what the study is about, because such information may lead to subject bias.) Consider the mortality salience example. If a researcher told a participant, "We are going to test how a recent stressor you have experienced has affected your behaviour," then the experiment probably would not work. In these cases, researchers use **deception**—*misleading or only partially informing participants of the true topic or hypothesis under investigation.* In psychological research, this typically amounts to a "white lie" of sorts. The participants are given enough information to evaluate their own risks. In medical research situations, however, deception can be much more serious. For example, patients who are being tested with an experimental drug may be randomly chosen to receive a placebo. Importantly, in both cases, the deception is only short-term; once the experiment is over, the participants are informed of the true nature of the study and why deception was necessary.

Once participants are informed, they must also be able to give consent. Again, meeting this standard is trickier than it sounds. To revisit the mind-control studies, the patients were emotionally vulnerable people seeking help from a noted psychiatrist (Dr. Cameron was the President of both the Canadian and American

Informed Consent Statement

You are invited to participate in a research study assessing your attitudes and behaviours related to alcohol. We ask that you read this document before agreeing to participate in this study. Although the legal drinking age is 19, participants do not need to be of age, nor do they need to be regular drinkers. Participants must be at least 18 years of age and be willing to anonymously share opinions about alcohol. The study takes 30 minutes to complete. There are no risks associated with this study.

If you agree to be in this study, you will be asked to complete a survey and rate 40 statements about alcohol and alcohol use in your life. You may refuse to answer any questions and may withdraw from the study without penalty at any time. This research project has been reviewed and approved by the Research Ethics Board.

Thank you for your time.

__ I give consent to participate in this study

Participant Signature: ________________ Date: ________

__ I do not wish to participate in this study

{FIG. 2.5} **Informed Consent** Research participants must provide informed consent before taking part in any study. As shown here, the participant must be made aware of the basic topic of the study as well as any possible risks.

Watch
Before Informed Consent: Robert Guthrie

Psychiatric Associations) at a world-class university. They were not told of the treatments they would receive; in some cases, the patients were not informed that they were part of a study at all! Clearly, informed consent was not provided by these research participants. Based on the ethical issues arising from this and many other disturbing studies, modern psychological (and psychiatric and neurological) research includes the following elements in determining whether full consent is given:

- *Freedom to choose.* Individuals should not be at risk for financial loss, physical harm, or damage to their reputation if they choose not to participate.
- *Equal opportunities.* Volunteers should have choices. For example, if the volunteers are introductory psychology students seeking course credit, they must have nonresearch alternatives available to them for credit should they choose not to participate in a study.
- *The right to withdraw.* Volunteers should have the right to withdraw from the study, at any time, without penalty. The right to give informed consent stays with the participants throughout the entire study.
- *The right to withhold responses.* Volunteers responding to surveys or interviews should not have to answer any question that they feel uncomfortable answering.

Usually, these criteria are sufficient for ensuring full consent. Sometimes, however, psychologists are interested in participants who cannot give their consent that easily. If researchers are studying children or individuals with mental disabilities, some severe psychiatric disorders, or certain neurological conditions, then a third party must give consent on behalf of the participant. This usually amounts to a parent or next-of-kin and, of course, all the rules of informed consent still apply.

After participating in the research study, participants must undergo a full **debriefing**, *meaning that the researchers should explain the true nature of the study, and especially the nature of and reason for the deception*. The debriefing of subjects is an important part of the scientific process. You've already read how it is used when deception (or a placebo) is part of a study. But, even in more straightforward experiments, debriefing is necessary to ensure that the participants understand why their time and effort was necessary. This results in the participants leaving the experiment better-informed about your topic of study as well as about the many considerations involved in creating a psychology experiment.

Mona Lisa Production/Science Source

Many psychologists use animals in their research, so ethical codes have been extended to cover nonhuman species. **Click on this photo in your eText to see more details.**

THE RIGHT TO ANONYMITY AND CONFIDENTIALITY A final measure of protection involves anonymity and confidentiality. *Anonymity* means that the data collected during a research study cannot be connected to individual participants. In many cases, volunteers can respond on a survey or through a computer-based experimental task without recording their name. This setup is ideal because it reduces both methodological problems (socially desirable responding) and the social risks to participants. If pure anonymity is not possible—for example, when a researcher must watch the participant perform a task—then confidentiality is a reasonable substitute. *Confidentiality* includes at least two parts. First, researchers cannot share specific data or observations that can be connected with an individual. Second, all records must be kept secure (for example, in a password-protected database or locked filing cabinet) so that identities cannot be revealed unintentionally.

THE WELFARE OF ANIMALS IN RESEARCH Many people who have never taken a psychology course view psychology as the study of *human* behaviour, possibly because most psychological research does involve humans. But research with animals is just as important to psychological science for a number of reasons. The simplest and perhaps most obvious is that the study of psychology *does include* the behaviour of animals. However, the most significant reason is that scientists can administer treatments to animals that could never be applied to humans, such as lesioning (damaging) specific areas of the brain in order to examine the resulting behavioural impairments. In addition, genetic research requires species with much shorter life spans than our own so that several successive generations can be observed. Finally, scientists can manipulate the breeding of laboratory animals to meet the needs of their experimental procedures. Selective breeding allows researchers to study highly similar groups of subjects, which helps control for individual differences based on genetic factors.

These forms of animal-based experimentation have improved our understanding of a number of different areas of behaviour. The research area that has benefited most from the use of animal subjects is the study of different brain-related diseases. This leads to an ethical dilemma, however: Is it ethically acceptable to create disease-like symptoms in animals if it could lead to discoveries that could help thousands—or sometimes millions—of people?

WORKING THE SCIENTIFIC LITERACY MODEL

Animal Models of Disease

MPTP (1-methyl-4-phenyl-1,2,3,6-tetrahydropyridine) was accidentally discovered in 1976 by a 23-year-old chemistry graduate student who was attempting to create MPPP, a synthetic drug that produces morphine-like effects. Three days after injecting himself with what he thought would be a pleasure-inducing drug, he began to show symptoms of Parkinson's disease, including tremors and difficulties initiating movements. Six years later, seven young people in Santa Clara County, California, were diagnosed with Parkinson's disease, which typically develops in older adults. Again, these individuals had injected doses of MPPP that were contaminated with MPTP. Based on these cases, neurologists quickly realized that the compound MPTP could prove useful as a model of Parkinson's disease (Langston et al., 1983). Animals receiving injections of MPTP quickly develop Parkinsonian symptoms; it is therefore possible to use these animals to test possible treatments of this disorder. MPTP is now the toxin most frequently used for animal models of Parkinson's disease (Blesa et al., 2012). This leads to interesting questions, however. Are animal models valid and useful tools for researchers trying to find treatments and cures for diseases? And, is this process ethical?

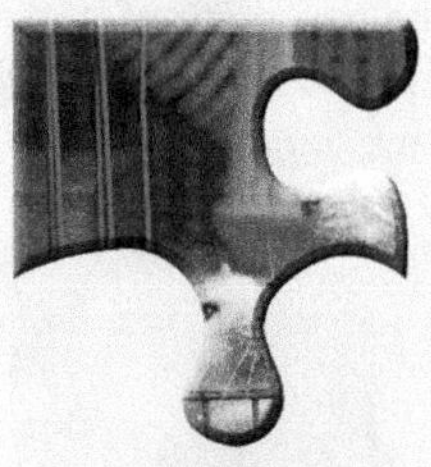

What do we know about animal models of diseases?

MPTP is just one of hundreds of techniques for modelling different diseases. There are animal models for Alzheimer's disease, depression, schizophrenia, autism, stroke, Huntington's disease, epilepsy, and drug addiction, among many others (Nestler & Hyman, 2010; Virdee et al., 2012). Not all diseases or conditions can be modelled in the same way, however. Depending upon the underlying cause of the disorder and the brain areas that are likely involved, there are at least four methods scientists can use to create an animal model. First, if a disease is associated with a specific brain area, researchers could anesthetize an animal and remove or damage that part of its brain. Brain damage could also occur by introducing a toxic substance, as occurred in the MPTP patients. Second, scientists could introduce a substance that increased or decreased the levels of certain brain chemicals known as *neurotransmitters* in the brain. Parkinson's disease is caused by a loss of the neurotransmitter dopamine; therefore, a drug that reduced dopamine levels could simulate the symptoms of Parkinson's. Third, researchers could create animal models of certain disorders by altering the environments of the animals. For instance, placing animals in an environment that is physically or socially stressful can cause them to behave similarly to individuals with anxiety disorders (Willner et al., 1987). Finally, scientists can manipulate the genetic make-up of animals. While earlier research was limited to selectively breeding animals so that they became more prone to a disease, it is now possible to directly alter the genetic codes of animals so that particular traits and physical structures are altered (Spires-Jones & Knafo, 2012). However, despite the enormous possibilities associated with animal models, these techniques are only as good as the scientists who use them.

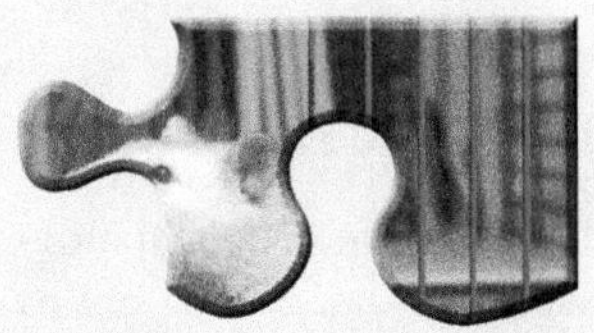

How can science test animal models of diseases?

The primary goal of developing animal models of a neurological condition, such as the MPTP model of Parkinson's disease, is to simulate the characteristics of a disease so that researchers can test possible treatments without harming humans. Although this may sound unethical at first, there is a logic behind the use of animal models. In order to find treatments for a disease, scientists need a very large number of individuals with the disease to use as test subjects. Any given treatment that is currently available to humans underwent testing with thousands—sometimes tens of thousands—of animals in order to test different chemical compounds and doses to ensure that the side effects of the treatment did not outweigh its benefits. There are simply not enough people with some diseases for this type of trial-and-error testing to occur. Any study that could take place would require the cooperation of universities and hospitals across the world. And, if that single attempt did not work, it would be difficult to find patients who had not already been tested to use in subsequent treatment attempts. Therefore, the use of animal models was a product of necessity.

Importantly, animal models are not developed in a random fashion. Instead, each animal model of a disease must have the following three characteristics (Dzirasa & Covington III, 2012). First, it must share the same physiological and behavioural features of the disease as appear in humans. An animal model of depression would not be accepted if the animals were energetic and playful; instead, the animals' behaviours must resemble the behaviours of humans with depression. Additionally, both the animal model and the "real" disorder must involve similar brain structures; otherwise, you are comparing apples and oranges. Second, the tests used to measure the behaviours must be valid. For depressed humans, laboratory tests often involve questionnaires or computer-based tests; these are obviously not useful research methods when testing rats or mice. Instead, the researcher must use an indirect test to try to tap into the same underlying symptom. So, if a depressed human seemed to get less pleasure out of life than she did previously (known as *anhedonia*), an animal researcher would have to find a way to measure a similar behaviour in rats. In this case, scientists use a sucrose preference test, a task in which rats have the opportunity to seek out a pleasurable taste (sugar!) if they are motivated to do so. The assumption is that "depressed" rats, just like depressed humans, would be less likely to seek out such stimuli (Cryan et al., 2002). Finally, the subjects in animal models (e.g., mice) must respond to treatments in the same way that humans would. So, animals that are genetically altered to be prone to depression-like behaviours should respond to anti-depressants. If they don't, then the animal model is not valid.

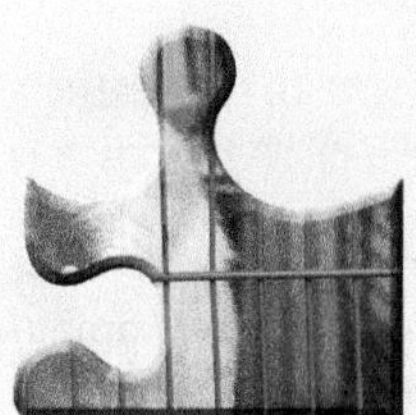

How can we critically evaluate these models?

The easiest criticism of animal models of disease is that animal brains are not human brains. Human brains are obviously more complex; therefore, how valid is it to assume that treatments that change an animal's behaviour will benefit humans? And, if this isn't guaranteed, is it ethical to use animal subjects in this way? A second criticism is that researchers are only beginning to understand the specific brain areas involved with a number of different conditions. Oftentimes, a large number of interacting brain areas are involved with a disorder. So, if we are unclear of the biology involved in the human version of the disease, how accurate can the resulting animal models really be? Additionally, it is fairly easy to test the validity of animal models of neurological diseases that have clear, observable symptoms (e.g., Parkinson's disease and epilepsy); animals modelling epilepsy will have seizures that you can see. However, models of psychological conditions like depression and schizophrenia present a greater challenge, as the symptoms are often thought-based and subjective. The rat can't explain what he is seeing or feeling. Instead, the researchers must infer that these mental states are occurring (in one form or another) in the animal subjects being tested. Finally, is an animal with limited cognitive abilities even capable of serving as a model for a disorder that involves impairments of higher-order cognitive abilities (Nestler & Hyman, 2010)? For example, how can you tell if a laboratory rat is having a hallucination?

These are all valid criticisms of the use of animal models of diseases. Although there are no perfect counterarguments, there are points that researchers can make in defence of animal models. First, if the conditions of a good model discussed in the previous section are met, then we can assume that the animal model is a fairly close approximation of the disorder it is being used to study. So, if the animals' behaviours resemble those of the human patients, if the tasks being used to test the animals are valid measures, and if the animals respond to the same treatments as humans (if treatments are available), then we can be confident in our animal model. The confidence will increase if other lines of research produce results similar to those found with the animal model. So, if brain-imaging tests in humans find problems in the same brain areas being manipulated in an animal model, that model becomes more valid. Through the use of converging operations—using multiple research methods to analyze the same question—it is possible to create effective animal models.

Why is this relevant?

Anyone who has watched an elderly relative become a shadow of his or her former self as a result of a neurological disease such as Alzheimer's or Parkinson's disease can understand the usefulness of animal models. It is impossible to perform large-scale research investigating these disorders and their possible treatment without the use of these experiments. Therefore, the animals used in these studies are helping to reduce the suffering of millions of people around the world. Whether you agree that it is appropriate to use animals in this fashion is a personal decision that you will have to make on your own. It is important to note that the researchers who perform this type of research also think about these issues. They certainly don't take their ethical responsibilities lightly; every university and research hospital has extremely strict requirements for the treatment of laboratory animals and the well-being of all animals is monitored by laboratory technicians and veterinarians. Importantly, all of these activities are closely monitored by the institution's REB.

Maslov Dmitry/Fotolia

REBS FOR ANIMAL-BASED RESEARCH Many ethical standards for animal research were developed at the same time as those for human research. In fact, hospitals and universities have established committees responsible for the ethical treatment of animals, which are in some ways similar to REBs that monitor human research. To be sure, there are differences in standards applied to human research and animal research. For example, we obviously do not ask for informed consent from animals. Nevertheless, similar procedures have been put in place to ensure that risk and discomfort are managed in a humane way, and that the pain or stress an animal may experience can be justified by the potential scientific value of the research.

Three main areas of ethical treatment are emphasized by researchers and animal welfare committees. The first is the basic care of laboratory animals—that is, providing appropriate housing, feeding, and sanitation for the species. The second is minimization of any pain or discomfort experienced by the animals. Third, although it is rare for a study to *require* discomfort, when it is necessary, the researchers must ensure that the pain can be justified by the potential benefits of the research. The same standards apply if animals are to be sacrificed for the research.

Quick Quiz 2.3a

Promoting the Welfare of Research Participants

KNOW ...

1 The Research Ethics Board (REB) is the group that determines

A whether a hypothesis is valid.

B whether the benefits of a proposed study outweigh its potential risks.

C whether a study should be published in a scientific journal.

D whether animal research is overall an ethical practice.

UNDERSTAND ...

2 Which of the following is *not* a requirement for informed consent?

A Participants need to know the nature of the stimuli to which they will be exposed.

B Participants need to understand any potential physical, psychological, or social risks involved in the research.

C Participants need to have a face-to-face meeting with the researcher before volunteering.

D Participants need to know the approximate duration of the study.

ANALYZE ...

3 In a memory study, researchers have participants study a list of words, and then tell them it was the wrong list and that they should forget it. This deception is meant to see how effectively participants can forget something they have already studied. If the researchers plan to debrief the participants afterward, would this design meet the standards of an ethical study?

A No, it is not okay to mislead individuals during the course of a study.

B Yes, given that the participants are not at risk and that they will be debriefed, this seems to be an ethical study.

C No, because the researchers should not debrief the participants.

D Yes, because participants fully understood all aspects of the study.

Answers can be found on page ANS-1.

Ethical Collection, Storage, and Reporting of Data

Ethical research does not end when the volunteers go home. Researchers have continuing commitments to the participants, such as the requirement to maintain the anonymity, confidentiality, and security of the data. Once data are reported in a journal or at a conference, they should be kept for a reasonable amount of time—generally, three to five years is acceptable. The purpose of keeping data for a lengthy period relates to the public nature of good research. Other researchers may request access to the data to reinterpret it, or perhaps examine the data before attempting to replicate the findings. It might seem as though the confidentiality requirement conflicts with the need to make data public, but this is not necessarily true. For example, if the data are anonymous, then none of the participants will be affected if and when the data are shared.

In addition to keeping data safe, scientists must be honest with their data. Some researchers experience great external pressure to obtain certain results. These pressures may relate to receiving tenure at a university; gaining funding from a governmental, industrial, or non-profit agency; or providing evidence that a product (for example, a medical treatment for depression) is effective.

Unfortunately, cases of *scientific misconduct* sometimes arise when individuals fabricate or manipulate their data to fit their desired results. For instance, in 1998, British researcher Andrew Wakefield and his colleagues published a paper in the highly influential medical journal *The Lancet* describing a link between the vaccine for measles, mumps, and rubella and the incidence rate of autism (Wakefield et al., 1998; see Module 10.1). The response was immediate—many concerned parents stopped having their children vaccinated out of fear that their kids would then develop autism. Panic was increased by sensationalistic media reports of the study as well as by an anti-vaccine media campaign launched by former *Playboy* centrefold (and, apparently, amateur developmental neurobiologist) Jenny McCarthy. Vaccine rates plummeted. However, autism rates did not change; what did change were the incidence rates of the diseases the vaccines would have prevented. Hundreds of preventable deaths occurred because children were not vaccinated. Then something interesting happened: Numerous institutions in several different countries reported that they were unable to replicate Wakefield's results. As his data received more attention, it became clear that some of it had been manipulated to fit his theory. Additional investigations uncovered the fact that Wakefield planned to develop screening kits to test for stomach problems associated with the vaccine; in other words, he had a financial motivation for creating a controversy related to the vaccine. Luckily, such cases of misconduct seem to be rare and, as occurred in this instance, other scientists are likely to find that the study cannot be replicated in such instances.

The chances of fraudulent data being published can also be decreased by requiring researchers to acknowledge any potential conflicts of interest, which might include personal financial gain from an institution or company that funded the work. If you look at most published journal articles, you will see a footnote indicating which agency or organization provided the funds for the study. This annotation is not just a goodwill gesture; it also informs the public when there is the *potential* for a company or government agency to influence research. Incidentally, the CIA was not mentioned in any published work resulting from the mind-control studies discussed at the beginning of this module. Dr. Cameron's family destroyed all of his papers upon his death in 1967.

Quick Quiz 2.3b Ethical Collection, Storage, and Reporting of Data

UNDERSTAND ...

1 Researchers should store their data after they present or publish it because

- **A** other researchers may want to examine the data before conducting a replication study.
- **B** other researchers may want to reinterpret the data using different techniques.
- **C** the process of informed consent requires it.
- **D** both a and b are true.

APPLY ...

2 After completing a naturalistic observation study, a researcher does not have quite enough evidence to support her hypothesis. If she decides to go back to her records and slightly alters a few of the observations to fit her hypothesis, she is engaged in ________.

- **A** scientific forgery
- **B** scientific misconduct
- **C** correcting the data
- **D** ethical behaviour

Answers can be found on page ANS-1.

Module Summary

Module 2.3

Now that you have read this module you should

KNOW ...

- ***The key terminology of research ethics:***

debriefing (p. 58)
deception (p. 57)
informed consent (p. 57)
research ethics board (REB) (p. 56)

UNDERSTAND ...

- ***The importance of reporting and storing data.*** Making data public allows scientific peers as well as the general public to have access to the details of research studies. This information includes details about participants, the procedures they experienced, and the outcome of the study. Furthermore, the requirement that data be stored allows fellow researchers to verify reports as well as to examine the study for any possible misconduct. Fortunately, such cases are rare.
- ***Why animals are often used in scientific research.*** First, many research questions that affect medical and public health cannot be answered without animal testing. Second, obvious ethical considerations may not allow such research to be conducted on human subjects. Third, by working with animal models, scientists can control genetic and environmental variables that cannot be controlled with humans.

APPLY ...

- ***The ethical principles of scientific research to examples.*** For practice, read the following two scenarios and identify why they may fail to meet ethical standards. Check your answers on page ANS-1.

1. Dr. Nguyen wants to expose individuals first to a virus that causes people to experience colds, and then to varying levels of exercise to test whether exercise either facilitates or inhibits recovery. She is concerned that people will not volunteer if they know they may experience a cold, so she wants to give them the informed consent after completing the study.

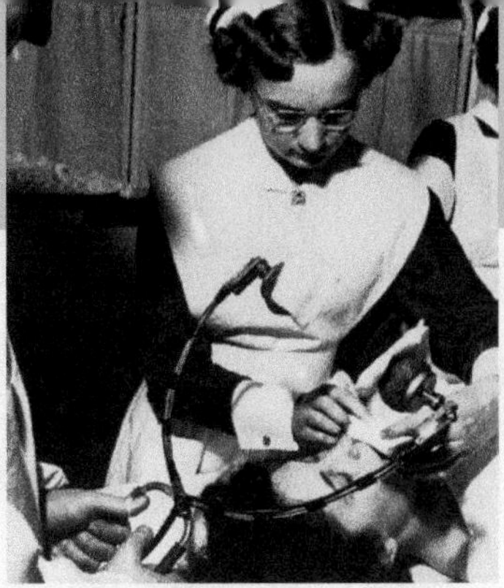

Bettmann/CORBIS

2. Researchers set up a study on sexuality that involves answering a series of questions in an online survey. At the end of each page of the survey, the software checks whether all of the questions are answered; it will not continue if any questions are left blank. Students cannot advance to the end of the survey and receive credit for participation until they answer all the questions.

ANALYZE ...

- ***The role of using deception in psychological research.*** It is often the case that fully disclosing the purpose of a study before people participate in it would render the results useless. Thus, specific details of the study are not provided during informed consent (although all potential risks are disclosed). When deception of any kind is used, researchers must justify that the benefits of doing so outweigh the costs.

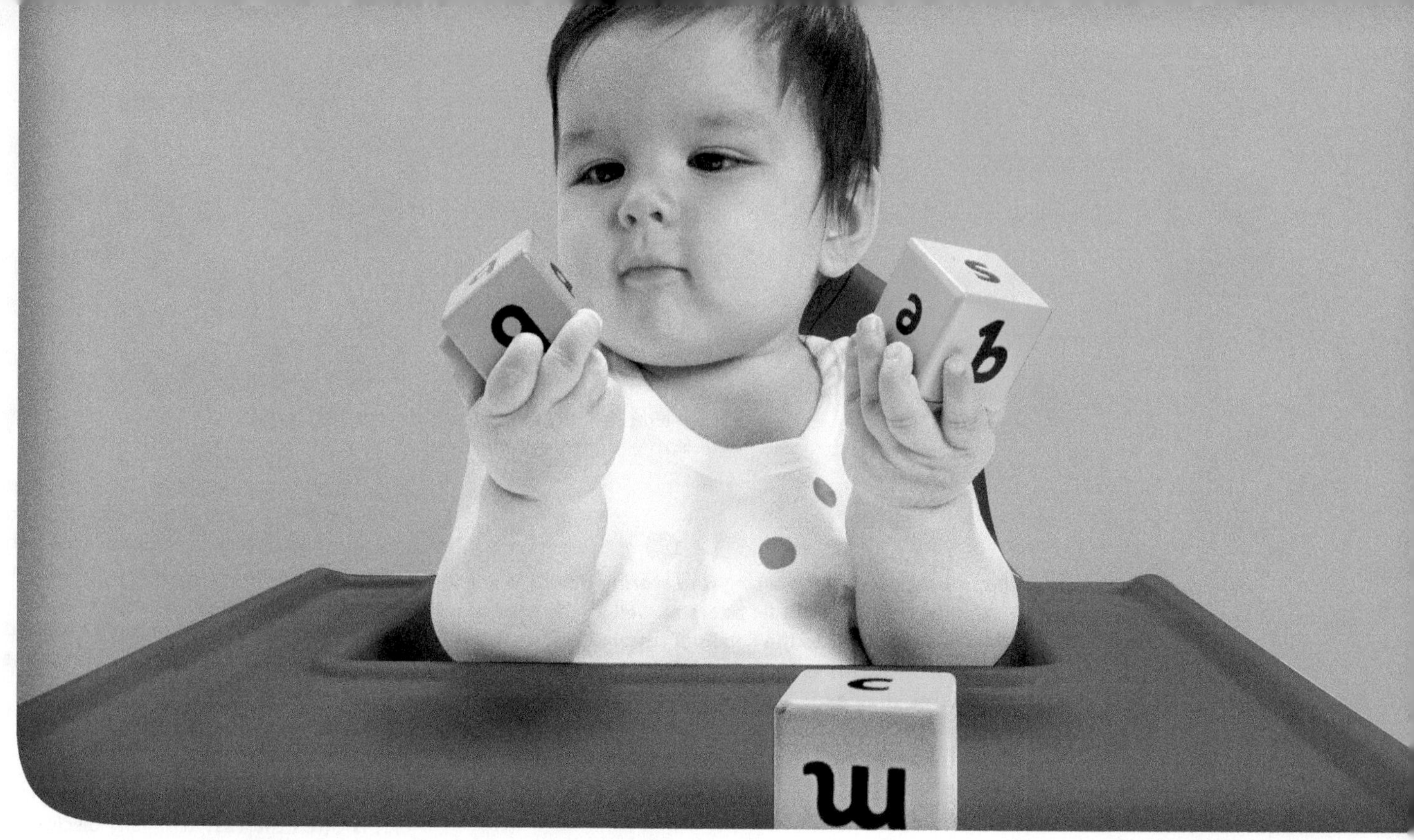

Imagesource/Glow Images

Module 2.4

A Statistical Primer

Learning Objectives

After reading this module you should

KNOW ...	UNDERSTAND ...	APPLY ...	ANALYZE ...
The key terminology of statistics	How and why psychologists use significance tests	Your knowledge to interpret the most frequently used types of graphs	The choice of central tendency statistics based on the shape of the distribution

Would you be surprised to learn that even infants and toddlers can think about probability, the foundation of statistics? Dr. Allison Gopnik (2010) writes about some interesting experiments showing just how statistically minded young children are. For example, consider the illustration below. If a researcher reached in and randomly selected five balls, would you be more surprised if they were all red or all white? Given that the white balls outnumber the red, you would be much more surprised if the researcher pulled out five red balls. Interestingly, infants show the same response. In another experiment, Gopnik's research team placed blue or yellow blocks into a fancy contraption. Yellow blocks appeared to make the machine light up two out of three times (67% of the time), whereas the blue blocks only seemed to work two out of six times (33% of the time). When asked to "make the machine light up," preschoolers selected the yellow blocks, which had a higher probability of working. If eight-month-olds and preschoolers can think statistically, adults should also be able to do so!

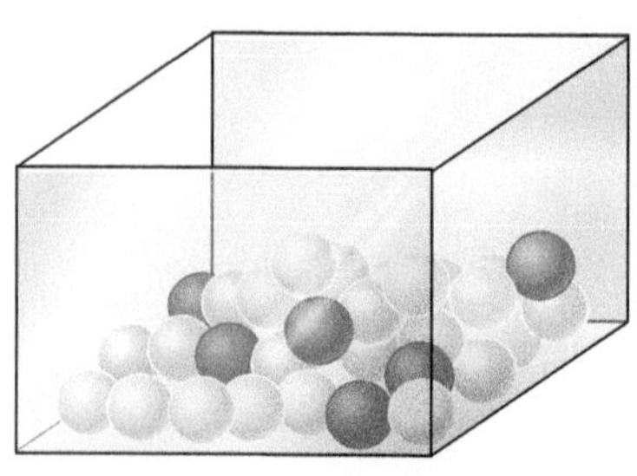

Focus Questions

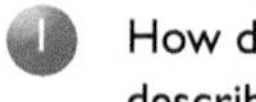

1. How do psychologists use statistics to describe their observations?

2. How are statistics useful in testing the results of experiments?

Statistics initially seem scary to a lot of people. But, they don't have to be. Statistics can be boiled down to two general steps. First, we need to organize the numbers so that we can get a "big picture" view of the results; this process is helped by the creation of tables or graphs. Second, we want to test to see if any differences between groups or between experimental conditions are meaningful. Once these steps have been completed, it is possible to determine whether the data supported or refuted our hypothesis. In order to keep statistics simple, this module is organized around these two general steps.

Descriptive Statistics

Once research data have been collected, psychologists use **descriptive statistics**, *a set of techniques used to organize, summarize, and interpret data.* This gives you the "big picture" of the results. In most research, the statistics used to describe and understand the data are of three types: *frequency*, *central tendency*, and *variability*.

FREQUENCY Imagine that you asked a group of students who had just taken the Graduate Record Exam (GRE), a standardized test taken by people who want to go to graduate school, how well they did on the exam. Assuming they were honest, you would likely find scores ranging from the 300s up to the high 600s. What you would want to know is (1) whether some scores occurred more often than others and (2) whether all of the scores were clumped in the middle or more evenly spaced across the whole range. These two pieces of information make up the data's *distribution;* the examination of the distribution is a useful first step when analyzing data. Figure 2.6 depicts these data in the form of a *histogram,* a type of *bar graph.* As with most bar graphs, the vertical axis of this graph shows the **frequency**, *the number of observations that fall within a certain category or range of scores.* These graphs are generally very easy to interpret: The higher the bar, the more scores that fall into the specific range. For example, if you look on the horizontal axis in Figure 2.6, you will see a column of test scores corresponding to people who scored around 500 on the test. Looking over to the vertical axis, you will see there were four individuals in that range. It is usually easy to describe the distribution of scores from a histogram. By examining changes in frequency across the horizontal axis—basically by describing the heights of the bars—we can learn something about the variable.

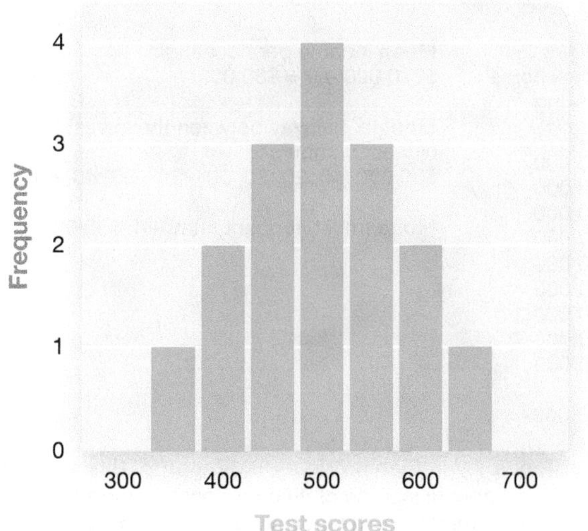

{FIG. 2.6} **Graphing Psychological Data** The frequency of standardized test scores forming a normal curve.

Histograms are a nice and simple way to present data and are excellent for providing researchers and students with an initial idea of what the data look like. But, they are not the only way to depict results of an experiment. Sometimes it is easier to answer questions about the distribution of the data if we present the same information using a smooth line called a *curve.* Sometimes a distribution is a symmetrical *curve*, as it is with our GRE scores. In this case, the left half is the mirror image of the right half. This is known as a **normal distribution** (sometimes called *the bell curve*), *a symmetrical distribution with values clustered around a central, mean value.*

Many variables wind up in a normal distribution, such as the scores on most standardized tests. Other variables have what is known as a skewed distribution, like the ones shown in Figure 2.7. You've likely encountered skewed distributions in your own life. Imagine a situation in which the grades on a school assignment were incredibly high, with only a few people performing poorly. In this case, the curve would show a **negatively skewed distribution**, *a distribution in which the curve has an extended tail to the left of the cluster.* However, what if the test were extremely difficult, like a calculus exam written by an angry professor with a broken coffee maker? In this case, most people in the course would have low scores, with only a few stellar students getting As. These results would produce a **positively skewed distribution**, *a distribution in which the long tail is on the right of the cluster.* Although researchers generally prefer to have normally distributed data, skewed results are quite common. Most of the time, skews occur because there is an upper or lower limit to the data. For example, a person cannot take less than 0 minutes to complete a quiz, so a curve depicting times to complete a quiz cannot continue indefinitely to the left, beyond the zero point. In contrast, just one person could take a very long time to complete a quiz, causing the right side of the curve to extend far to the right. Which type of skew would that be?

CENTRAL TENDENCY When examining data, it is often useful to look at where the scores seem to cluster together. When we do this, we are estimating **central tendency**, *a measure of the central point of a distribution.*

Simulate Doing Simple Statistics

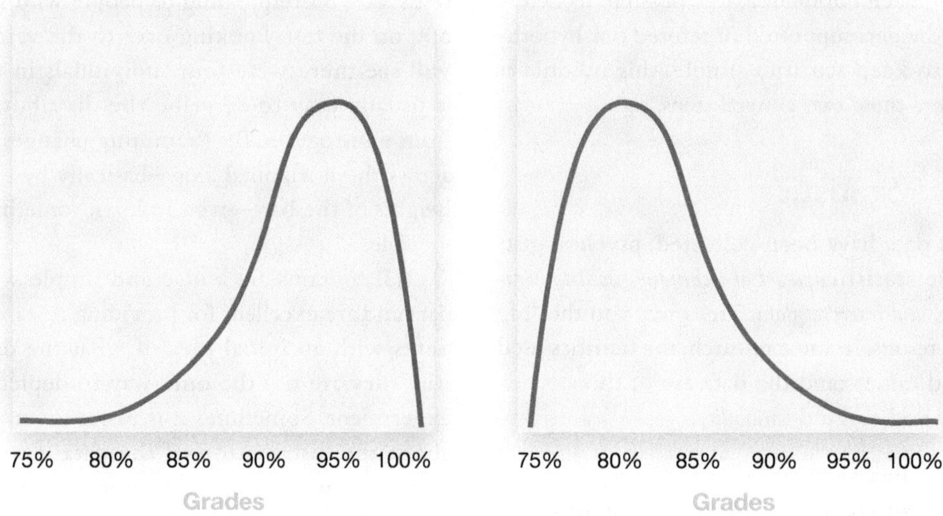

{FIG. 2.7} **Skewed Distributions** Negatively skewed distributions have an extended tail to the left (as in the left graph above). Positively skewed distributions have an extended tail to the right (as in the right graph above).

Although we naturally assume that the central tendency is "the average," there are actually three different measures of central tendency used in psychology. The first measure is known as the **mean**, *the arithmetic average of a set of numbers*. This is the measure of central tendency that we are most familiar with as it is used for class averages and in most sports (e.g., batting average in baseball or goals-against average in hockey). A second measure of central tendency is the **median**, *the 50th percentile—the point on the horizontal axis at which 50% of all observations are lower, and 50% of all observations are higher.* The third and final measure of central tendency is the **mode**, *which is the category with the highest frequency (that is, the category with the most observations).*

At first glance, it might seem silly to have three different methods of measuring the central tendency of your data. Indeed, when the data are normally distributed as they are in Figure 2.8, the mean, median, and mode are identical. The mean is $30 000, which is exactly in the centre of the histogram. The same can be said for the median; again, it is $30 000, with half of the incomes less than $30 000 and half more than

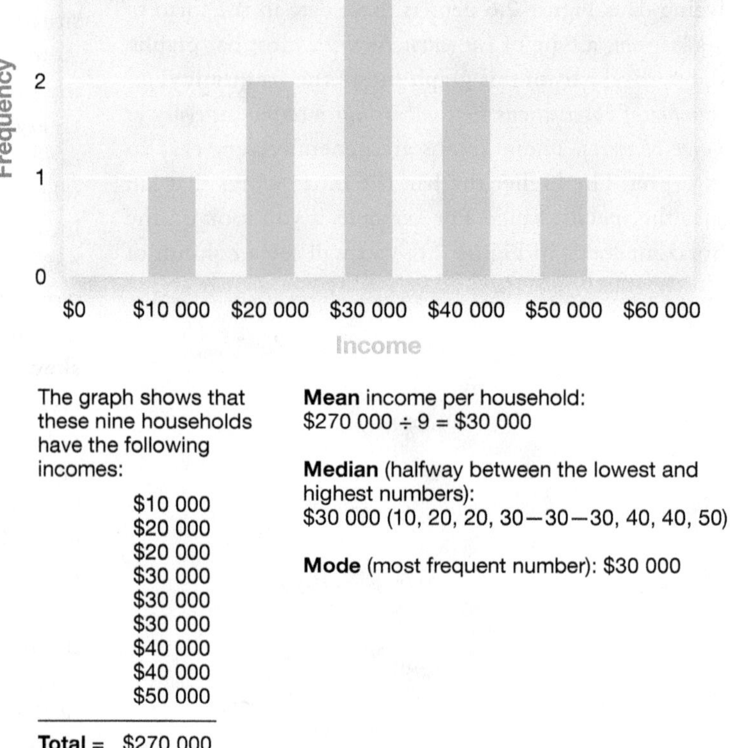

{FIG. 2.8} **Central Tendency in Symmetrical Distributions** This symmetrical histogram shows the annual income of nine randomly sampled households. Notice that the mean, median, and mode are all in the same spot—this is characteristic of normal distributions.

$30 000. Likewise, the mode is the same as the mean and median—$30 000 has the highest frequency, which, as seen in Figure 2.8, is 3. So, if the three measures of central tendency are equal, which do we use? If the data are normally distributed, researchers generally use the mean. But, if the data are skewed in some way, then researchers need to think about which measure is best. The measure used *least* is the mode. Because it provides less information than the mean or the median, the mode is typically only used when dealing with categories of data. For example, when you vote for a candidate, the mode represents the candidate with the most votes, and (in most cases) that person wins.

When the data are not a perfectly symmetrical curve, the mean, median, and mode produce different values. If the histogram spreads out in one direction—in Figure 2.9, it is positively skewed—we are usually better off calculating central tendency by using the median. This is because extreme values (positive or negative) will have a large effect on the mean, but will not affect the median. In other words, when you start to add extremely wealthy households to the data set, the tail extends to the right and the mean is pulled in that direction. The longer the tail, the more the mean is pulled away from the centre of the curve. By comparison, the median stays relatively stable, so it is a better choice for describing central tendency when dealing with skewed data. For instance, if you added Bill Gates' annual income (approximately $3.71 billion dollars) to the list of nine incomes listed in Figure 2.9, the mean income becomes just over $371 million. If you take the median of those ten incomes, the central tendency is $30 000. Looking at those data, which measure seems most consistent with the "big picture" of the results?

VARIABILITY Measures of central tendency help us summarize a group of individual cases with a single number by identifying a cluster of scores. However, this information only tells us part of the story. As you can see in Figure 2.10, scores can differ in terms of their **variability**, *the degree to which scores are dispersed in a distribution*. In other words, some scores are quite spread out while others are more clustered. High variability means that there are a larger number of cases that are closer to the extreme ends of the continuum for that set of data (e.g., a lot of excellent students *and* a lot of poor students in a class). Low variability means that most of the scores are similar (e.g., a class filled with "B" students). Variability can be caused by measurement errors, imperfect measurement tools, differences between participants in the study, or characteristics of participants on that given day (e.g., mood, fatigue levels). All data sets have some variability. But, if information about variability is not provided by the researcher, it is impossible to understand how well the measure of central tendency—the single

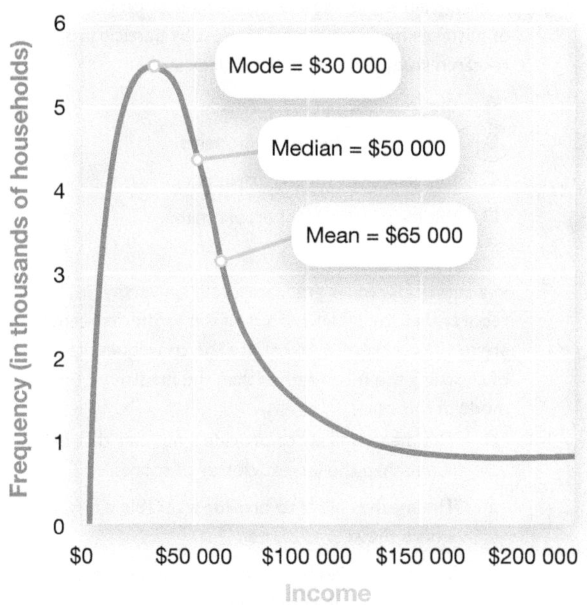

{FIG. 2.9} **Central Tendency in a Skewed Distribution** The mean is not always the ideal measure of central tendency. In this example, the mode and the median are actually more indicative of how much money most people make.

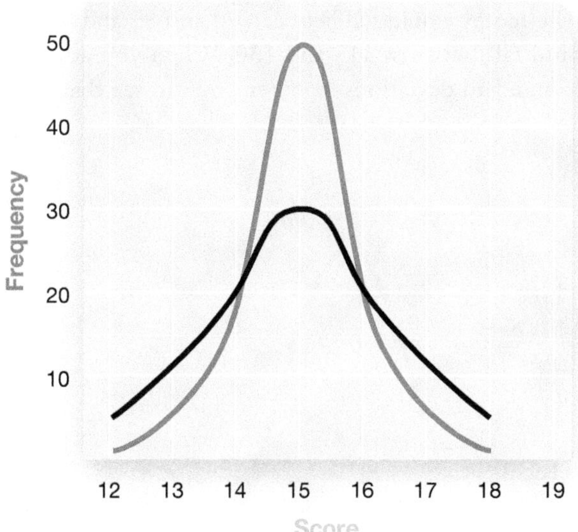

{FIG. 2.10} **Visualizing Variability** Imagine that these curves show how two classes fared on a 20-point quiz. Both classes averaged scores of 15 points. However, the students in one class (depicted in red) scored much more similarly to one another compared to students in another class (depicted in black), whose scores showed greater variability. The class represented by the black line would have a higher standard deviation.

score representing the data—reflects the entire data set. Therefore, whenever psychologists report data from their research, their measures of central tendency are virtually always accompanied by measures of variability.

One calculation that allows researchers to link central tendency and variability is known as the **standard deviation**, *a measure of variability around the mean.* Think of it as an estimate of the *average distance from the mean*. Perhaps the best way to understand the standard deviation is by working through an example. In a standard intelligence test, there is a normal distribution (a bell curve) with a mean of 100 and a standard deviation of 15 (see Module 9.1). Based on what you've read in this module, you would infer that 100 is the mid-point of the curve when these data are graphed. But, how much of the data is included in each standard deviation? As you can see in Figure 2.11, researchers have found that approximately 68% of the data are found within one standard deviation of the mean—34% above the mean (between 100 and 115) and 34% below the mean (between 85 and 100). This makes intuitive sense—we would expect a fairly large proportion of the scores to be grouped near the average score. As we move further away from the average score, each standard deviation would make up less and less of the data, because really high or really low scores are relatively rare. So, the next standard deviation in our example makes up roughly 27% of the data—13.5% of the scores would fall between 70 and 85 and 13.5% would fall between 115 and 130. When you add the two standard deviations together, you can see that they include over 95% of the IQ scores in the population. Therefore, when you hear about people like the physicist Stephen Hawking, whose IQ is estimated to be around 160, you can see that these are rare individuals indeed (comprising less than one-tenth of a percent of the population).

This section of the module demonstrates that by making a graph and reporting two numbers—the measure of central tendency and the standard deviation—you can provide a "big picture" summary of your data that almost anyone can understand. That's Step 1 of statistics. Step 2 uses these measures to test whether or not your hypothesis is supported by your data—in other words, whether your project worked.

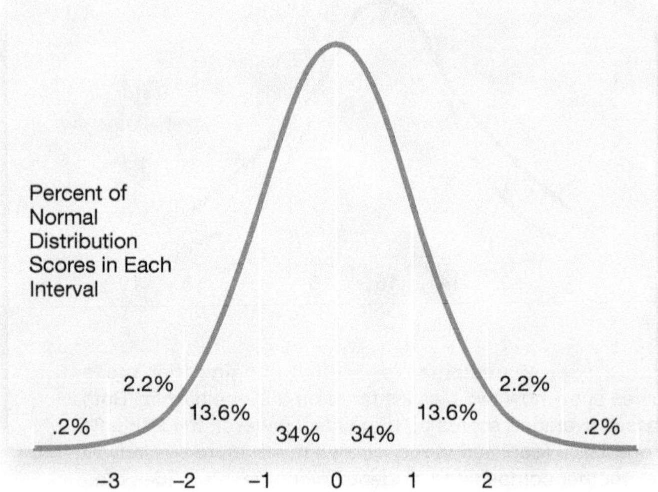

{FIG. 2.11} **Standard Deviations in a Normal Distribution** In a normal curve, most of the data are clustered within one standard deviation of the mean. Over 95% of the data in a normal distribution are found within two standard deviations of the mean.

Quick Quiz 2.4a

Descriptive Statistics

KNOW ...

1 The ________ always marks the 50th percentile of the distribution.

- **A** mean
- **B** median
- **C** mode
- **D** standard deviation

2 The ________ is a measure of variability around the mean of a distribution.

- **A** mean deviation
- **B** median
- **C** mode
- **D** standard deviation

APPLY ...

3 A histogram is created that presents data on the number of mistakes made on a memory test by participants in a research study. The vertical axis indicates

- **A** the frequency of errors made.
- **B** the total number of participants.
- **C** the gender of the participants.
- **D** the mean number of errors made.

ANALYZE ...

4 In a survey of recent graduates, your university reports that the mean salaries of the former students are positively skewed. What are the consequences of choosing the mean rather than the median or the mode in this case?

- **A** The mean is likely to provide a number that is lower than the largest cluster of scores.
- **B** The mean is likely to provide a reliable estimate of where the scores cluster.
- **C** The mean is likely to provide a number that is higher than the largest cluster of scores.
- **D** The mean provides the 50th percentile of the distribution, making it the best choice to depict this cluster of scores.

Answers can be found on page ANS-1.

Hypothesis Testing: Evaluating the Outcome of the Study

After researchers have described their data, the next step is to test whether the data support their hypothesis. In order to do this, researchers analyze data using a **hypothesis test**—*a statistical method of evaluating whether differences among groups are meaningful, or could have been arrived at by chance alone.* What scientists are essentially trying to do is determine if their experimental manipulation is the cause of any difference between groups or between conditions. However, the ability to tease out these differences is affected by the concepts discussed earlier in this module—specifically, the measure of central tendency for the groups being measured as well as the variability of data in each of the groups. The difference in the central tendency for the two groups represents a "signal" that we are trying to detect, similar to a voice in a loud room. The variability represents the "noise," the outside forces that are making it difficult to detect the signal.

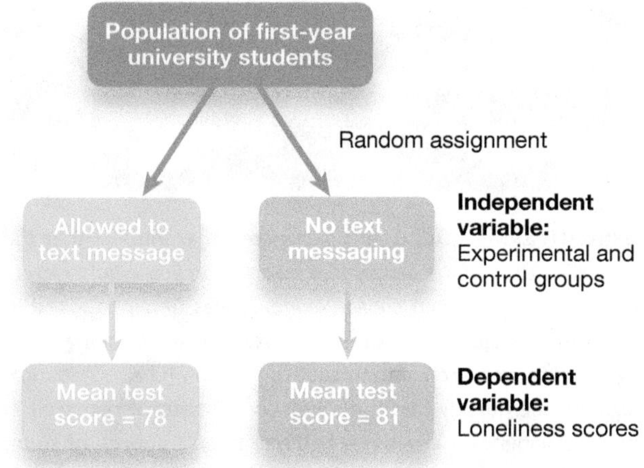

{FIG. 2.12} **Testing a Simple Hypothesis** To conduct an experiment on whether texting reduces loneliness, students would be randomly assigned to either text-messaging or no-text-messaging groups. Their average scores on a loneliness scale would then be compared.

To make this discussion more concrete, let's use an example of a behaviour that almost everyone performs: texting. Let's say that we wanted to test whether text messaging reduces feelings of loneliness in first-year university students. For three days, randomly selected students who regularly send text messages are assigned to one of two groups: those who can text and those who cannot. After three days, the students fill out a survey measuring how lonely they have felt. The diagram in Figure 2.12 shows us the key elements of such an experiment. Individuals are sampled from the population and randomly assigned to either the experimental or control group. The independent variable consists of the two groups, which includes texting or no texting. The dependent variable is the outcome—in this case, loneliness (as measured by a valid questionnaire), with larger scores indicating greater loneliness. As you can see, the mean loneliness score of the group who could text message is three points below the mean of the group who did not text message (78 vs. 81, respectively). So, based on this information, are you willing to say that texting causes people to feel less lonely? Or have we left something out?

What we do not know from the diagram is the variability of test scores. On the one hand, it is quite possible that the scores of the two groups look like the graphs on the left in Figure 2.13. In that situation, the means are three points apart and the standard deviation is very small, so the curves have very little overlap. In this case, it is fairly easy to detect differences between the groups; the "signal" is easy to pick out from the "noise." On the other hand, the scores of each group could have a broad range and therefore look like the graphs on the right. In that case, the group means are three points apart, but the groups overlap so much—the standard deviations are very high—that they seem virtually identical. In this case, the "noise"—the variability within each of the two groups—is so large that it is difficult to detect the "signal," the differences between the two groups.

How, then, would researchers know if the difference in scores is meaningful? "Meaningful" seems like a vague term; as we have already discussed, science requires precise definitions. In order to address this problem, psychologists perform analyses that rely on the concept of *statistical significance.*

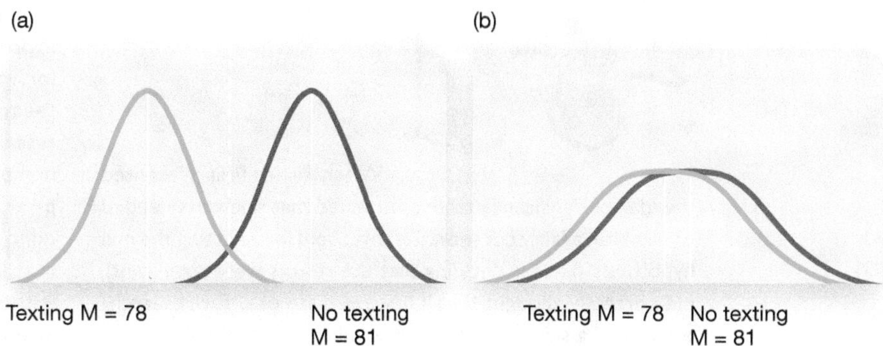

{FIG. 2.13} **How Variability Affects Hypothesis Testing** (a) The means (represented by M) differ between the two groups, and there is little overlap in the distribution of scores. When this occurs, the groups are much more likely to be significantly different. (b) Even though the means differ, there is much overlap between the distributions of scores. It is unlikely that these two means would be significantly different.

WORKING THE SCIENTIFIC LITERACY MODEL

Statistical Significance

Statistical significance is a concept that implies that *the means of the groups are farther apart than you would expect them to be by random chance alone*. It was first proposed in 1925 by Ronald Fisher, an English statistician working at an agricultural research station east of London (U.K.). Statistical significance quickly became a key component of research in many disciplines. However, it has also been a source of some surprisingly intense arguments (Cohen, 1994).

What do we know about statistical significance?

Statistical significance testing is based on the researcher making two hypotheses. The *null hypothesis* assumes that any differences between groups (or conditions) are due to chance. The *experimental hypothesis* assumes that any differences are due to a variable controlled by the experimenter. The goal of researchers is to find differences between groups that are so large that it is virtually impossible for the null hypothesis to be true; in other words, they are not due to chance. The probability of the results being due to chance is known as a *p-value*. Lower *p*-values indicate a decreased likelihood that your results were a fluke, and therefore an increased likelihood that you had a great idea and designed a good experiment.

So, how do we find the *p*-value? The specific formulas used for these calculations will vary according to how the experiment is set up. But, they all involve a measure of central tendency (usually the mean) and a measure of variability (usually the standard deviation). These numbers are then used in statistical tests that will produce a *p*-value.

What can science tell us about statistical significance?

When Fisher first presented the idea of significance testing, he noted that scientists needed to establish a fairly conservative threshold for rejecting the null hypothesis (i.e., for deciding that the results were significant). He correctly thought that if it were quite easy for researchers to find a significant result, it would increase the likelihood that results labelled as being significant were actually due to chance. If enough of these false positives occurred, then the entire idea of significance would soon become meaningless. Fisher therefore recommended that researchers use $p < 0.05$ as the cut-off point (this value was consistent with earlier statistical techniques, so his decision was likely an attempt to compromise with other statisticians; Stigler, 2008). If a *p*-value were less than 0.05, then there was less than a 5% chance that the results were due to chance. This *p*-value quickly became the standard in a number of fields, including psychology.

Of course, just because a particular value is widely accepted does not mean that scientists can stop using their critical thinking skills. Sometimes the consequences of having a false positive are quite severe, as in the case of testing new medicines for a disease. It would be tragic to make claims about a wonder drug only to find out that the results were due to a chance result that could not be reproduced. In such cases, researchers sometimes use an even more conservative *p*-value, such as requiring results to be less than 0.01 (i.e., $p < 0.01$).

It is also worth noting that when testing small sample sizes, it is difficult for the results to reach significance. But, some types of research, such as studies of rare brain-damaged patients, have a limited number of potential participants. It therefore becomes more difficult to detect statistically significant differences in these studies despite the fact that the groups do appear to differ when you look at graphs of the data (Bezeau & Graves, 2001). In these cases, significant testing might not be the best statistical tool for analyzing the data. Luckily, significance testing is not the only technique available.

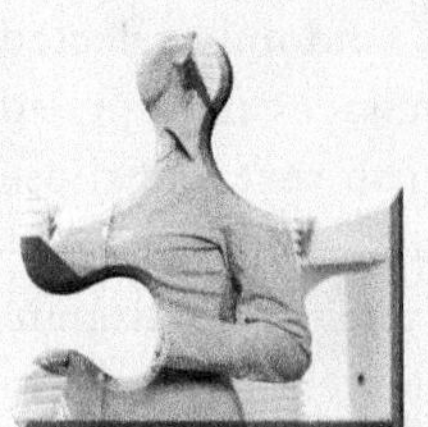

Can we critically evaluate the use of statistical significance testing in research?

Although significance testing has been a potent tool for researchers in the social sciences for almost a century, it does have some detractors. American psychologist Paul Meehl (1967) subtly described significance testing as "a potent but sterile intellectual rake who leaves in his merry path a long train of ravished maidens but no viable scientific offspring" (p. 265). Although this description may be a touch dramatic, there *are* at least two concerns related to significance testing. The first is the problem of multiple comparisons. If a "fluke" result can occur approximately 5% of the time, the more tests you perform for your experiment, the greater the likelihood that one of them is due to chance. In order to cope with this problem, researchers generally use a stricter acceptable *p*-value; as the number of comparisons increases, researchers decrease the *p*-value (i.e., make it more conservative). This makes it more difficult to produce significant results, but does help ensure that the results are not due to chance. A second problem is the fact that as you increase the number of participants in your study, it becomes easier to find significant effects. At first blush, this doesn't seem like a valid concern. Having more participants means that you are sampling a larger portion of the population of interest. Isn't that a good thing? The answer is yes, of course it is. But, if you sample thousands of people—as often happens in medical studies tracking potential lifestyle causes of diseases—extremely small differences will still be statistically significant. The media provides almost daily reports of different foods increasing or decreasing the risk of particular diseases. Before totally altering your lifestyle, it is best to look up the original report to see if the difference was large, or was simply due to the fact that the sample size was in the thousands.

As an alternative to significance testing, Jacob Cohen (1988) developed a technique known as *power analysis,* whose goal is to calculate *effect sizes.* Rather than saying that a difference is significant, which is essentially a yes–no decision, effect sizes tell the researcher whether the difference is statistically small or large. So, instead of an experiment supporting or disproving a theory, effect sizes allow the researcher to adjust how much they believe that their hypothesis is true (Cohen, 1994).

Why is this relevant?

Statistical significance gives psychology researchers a useful standard for deciding if the differences between groups (or experimental conditions) are meaningful. Having established criteria for deciding if an effect is significant is important, because it means that all researchers are using standardized tools. If different research groups were using different criteria for deciding that effects were "real," then it would be nearly impossible for that research area to move forward—people would be speaking different languages. Significance testing makes sure that everyone is on the same page, statistically speaking. However, as noted above, there are alternative methods for examining data. Effect sizes are becoming commonplace in many areas of psychology; an increasing number of academic journals now require researchers to calculate *both* statistical significance *and* effect sizes, thus giving readers an even more detailed picture of the data.

pressmaster/Fotolia

A final point is that, although statistical significance tells us that results are meaningful, there is still a possibility that the results were due to chance. It is only through replication—having other laboratories repeat the experiments and produce similar results—that we can become confident that a difference is meaningful. Many scientists now make their stimuli and data available to other researchers in order to encourage this process. This move toward openness and replication is itself quite significant.

Quick Quiz 2.4b Hypothesis Testing: Evaluating the Outcome of the Study

UNDERSTAND ...

1. A hypothesis test is conducted after an experiment to
   - **A** determine whether the two groups in the study are exactly the same.
   - **B** determine how well the two groups are correlated.
   - **C** see if the groups are significantly different, as opposed to being different due to chance.
   - **D** summarize the distribution using a single score.

ANALYZE ...

2. Imagine an experiment where the mean of the experimental group is 50 and the mean of the control group is 40. Given that the two means are obviously different, is it still possible for a researcher to say that the two groups are not significantly different?
   - **A** Yes, the two groups could overlap so much that the difference was not significant.
   - **B** Yes, if the difference was not predicted by the hypothesis.
   - **C** No, because the two groups are so far apart that the difference must be significant.
   - **D** No, in statistics a difference of 10 points is just enough to be significant.

Answers can be found on page ANS-1.

Module Summary

Module 2.4

Now that you have read this module you should

KNOW ...

- ***The key terminology of statistics:***

central tendency (p. 65)
descriptive statistics (p. 65)
frequency (p. 65)
hypothesis test (p. 69)
mean (p. 66)
median (p. 66)
mode (p. 66)
negatively skewed distribution (p. 65)
normal distribution (p. 65)
positively skewed distribution (p. 65)
standard deviation (p. 68)
statistical significance (p. 70)
variability (p. 67)

UNDERSTAND ...

- ***How and why psychologists use significance tests.*** Significance tests are statistics that tell us whether differences between groups or distributions are meaningful. For example, the averages of two groups being compared may be very different. However, how much variability there is among individuals within each of the groups will determine whether the averages are significantly different. In some cases, the averages of the two groups may be different, yet not statistically different because the groups overlap so much. This possibility explains why psychologists use significance tests—to test whether groups really are different from one another.

APPLY ...

- ***Your knowledge to interpret the most frequently used types of graphs.*** Take a look at Figure 2.14, a histogram showing the grades from a quiz in a statistics course, at the top of the next column and then answer the following questions and check your answers on page ANS-1.

1. What is the shape of this distribution? Normal, negatively skewed, or positively skewed?
2. What grade range is the mode for this class?
3. How many people earned a grade in the "B" range (between 80 and 89)?

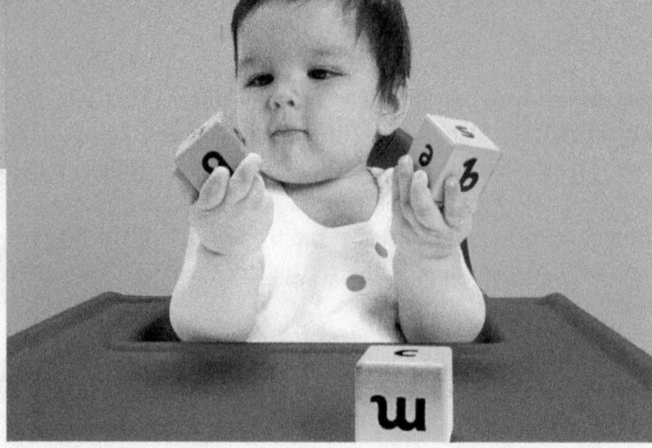

Imagesource/Glow Images

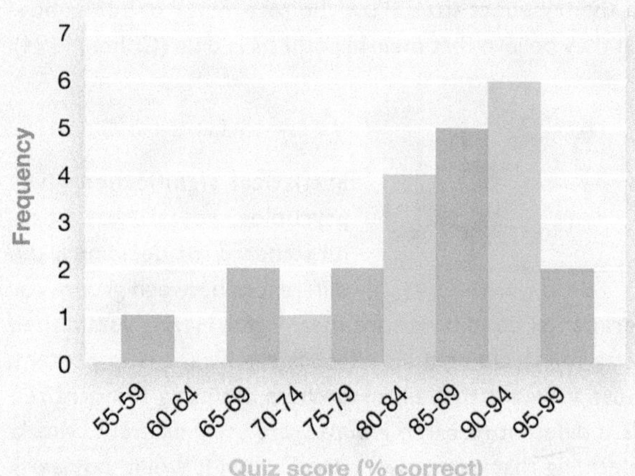

{FIG. 2.14} Application Activity

ANALYZE ...

- ***The choice of central tendency statistics based on the shape of the distribution.*** Although the mean is the most commonly used measure of central tendency, it is not always the best method for describing a set of data. For example, incomes are positively skewed. Suppose one politician claims the mean income level is \$40 000, while the other claims that the median income level is \$25 000. Which politician is giving the more representative measure? It would seem that the median would be a more representative statistic because it is not overly influenced by extremely high scores.

Work the Scientific Literacy Model :: Understanding Research Design

1 What do we know about scientific research?

On **page 50** we discussed the difference between correlation and causation. Imagine reading a study that states that aggressive people tend to have red bedrooms. Will painting your bedroom red cause you to act aggressively? It simply means that the variables of room colour and aggressive acts are statistically related. Only an experiment can show causality, so turn to **Figure 2.4 on page 52** for a review of its elements.

To understand scientific experiments, you should know the difference between a dependent variable, which is the variable that is measured during the experiment and compared across all of the groups, and the independent variable, which is the variable that the researcher manipulates.

To make sure you have correctly labelled the variables in an experiment, insert the variable names into the following phrase.

How ________ affects ________.
(*i.v.*) (*d.v.*)

In this case, the room colour is the independent variable and aggressiveness is the dependent variable.

2 How can science help differentiate between different kinds of research designs?

Conducting sound research means not only knowing which questions to ask, but also how to ask them correctly. Early psychological research in North America was based almost exclusively on observations of behaviour and self-reports, but over time new technologies such as functional magnetic resonance imaging (fMRI) expanded the number of variables psychologists can study. In the past few centuries, scientists have developed a variety of research designs suited to answer many new research questions; **Table 2.1 on page 53** offers a snapshot of the strengths and limitations of each. Regardless of the design used, scientific research must be based on objective, reliable measurements; it should generalize to a population from which the sample was drawn; it should avoid bias; and it should be made public so that others can learn from it, evaluate it, and replicate it.

Ryan Jorgensen-Jorgo/Shutterstock

3 Can we critically evaluate scientific research designs?

Understanding the characteristics of different scientific methods can help you evaluate the claims you encounter in everyday life. Think back to what you know about correlation and causation. The news media in particular often perpetuate the idea that an association, or correlation, between two variables is the same as a cause-and-effect relationship. For example, "Happiness Makes You Live Longer" is more dramatic than the headline "There Is a Positive Correlation between Happiness and Longevity." When evaluating research, notice qualifying words such as "might increase" and "could have an effect," both of which suggest correlation. Similarly, in **Myths in Mind on page 50**, we explored the idea that many common beliefs are actually illusory correlations. When two relatively rare events happen simultaneously, such as a full moon and an uncommonly busy night in the emergency room, then we might overestimate their relationship. That your staunchly conservative friend is dating an equally passionate liberal is more memorable than the fact that most of your coupled friends support the same political candidates.

4 Why is this relevant?

Watch the accompanying video excerpt about the scientific method. You can access the video at MyPsychLab or by clicking the play button in the centre of your eText. If your instructor assigns this video as a homework activity, you will find additional content to help you in MyPsychLab. You can also view the video by using your smart phone and the QR code below, or you can go to the YouTube link provided.

After you have read this chapter and watched the video, imagine you have been asked to create an experimental design to test the hypothesis that talking on a cell phone impairs driving skills. Explain why a control condition would be important to include in testing this hypothesis. How should participants be assigned to conditions? How can the researchers design the experiment so that the only difference between both conditions is the use of a cell phone?

MyPsychLab **Your turn to Work the Scientific Literacy Model:** Watch the accompanying video on YouTube, or on your phone (using the Layar app or QR code). If your instructor has assigned this as a homework activity, you can find the video clip and additional content at MyPsychLab. Answer the questions that accompany the video clip to test your understanding.

youtube.com/workthemodel

SCAN WITH LAYAR

3

Biological Psychology

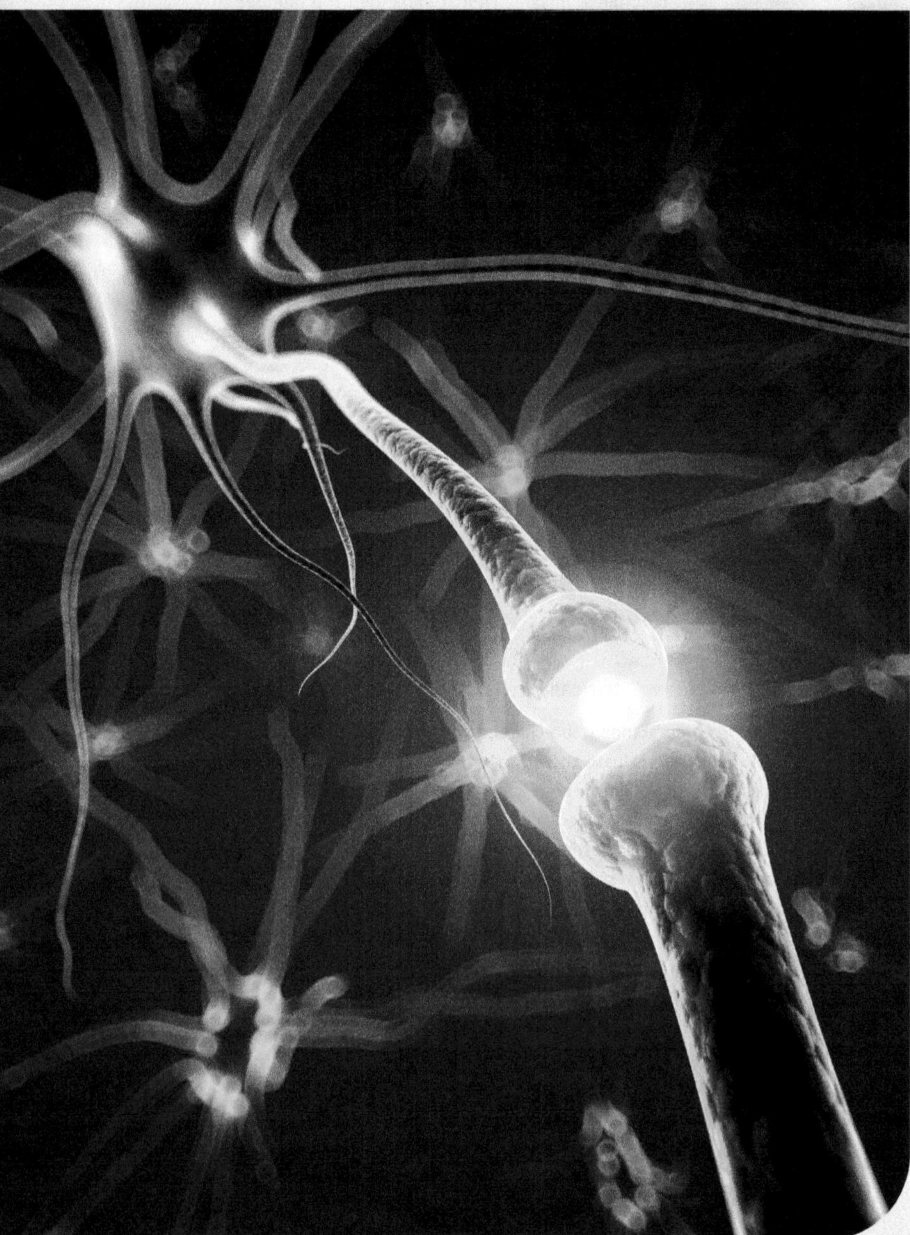
Sebastian Kaulitzki/Shutterstock

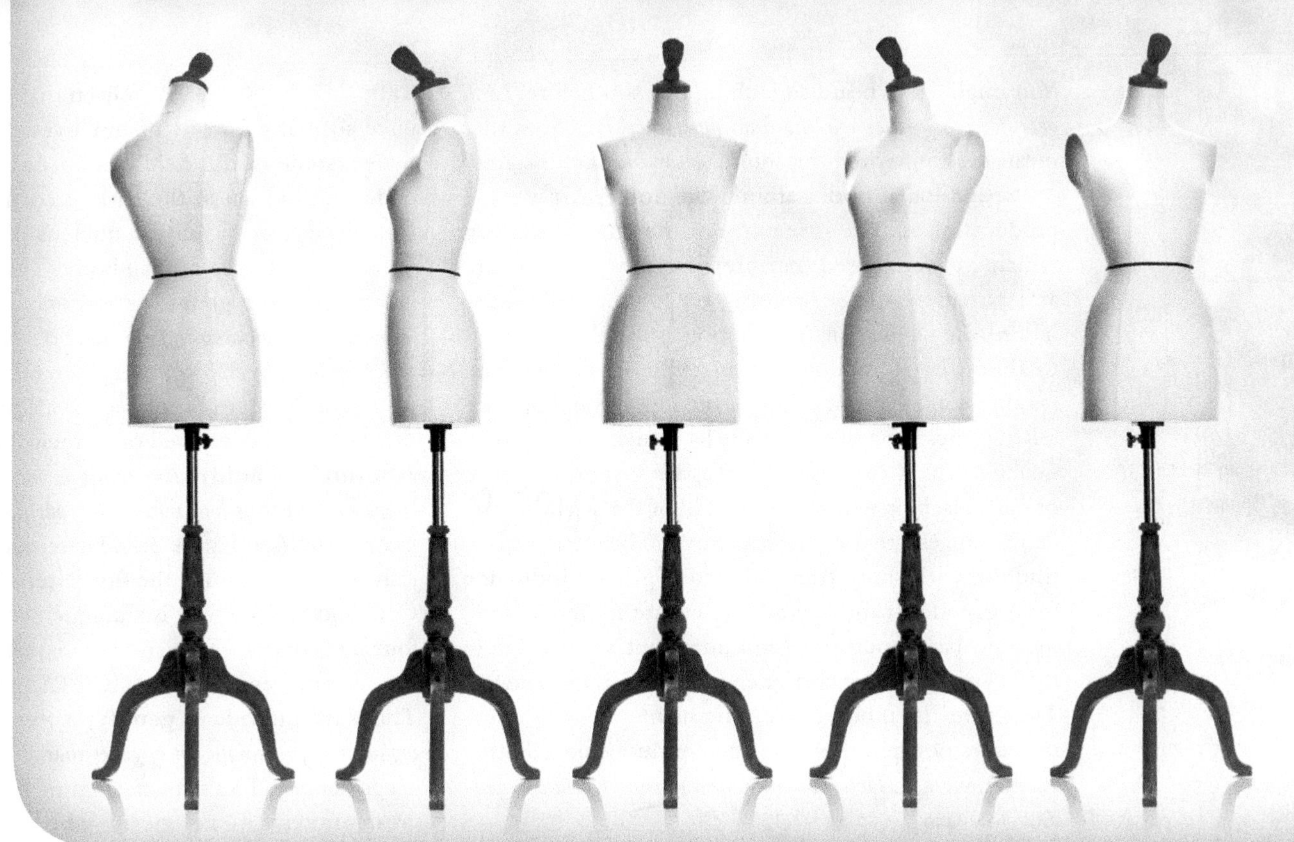

Roberto A Sanchez/iStockphoto

Module 3.1

Genetic and Evolutionary Perspectives on Behaviour

Learning Objectives

After reading this module you should

KNOW ...	UNDERSTAND ...	APPLY ...	ANALYZE ...
The key terminology related to genes, inheritance, and evolutionary psychology	How twin and adoption studies reveal relationships between genes and behaviour	Your knowledge of genes and behaviour to hypothesize why a trait might be adaptive	Claims that scientists have located a specific gene that controls a single trait or behaviour Explanations for cognitive gender differences that are rooted in genetics

Psychologist Martie Haselton has given new meaning to the phrase *dress for success*. She is not talking about professional advancement, however; rather, she is referring to success in attracting a mate. Dr. Haselton is an evolutionary psychologist—she studies how human behaviour has evolved to solve problems that relate to survival and reproductive success. As part of her work, she has discovered that the clothes people choose are related to sexual motivation in some subtle ways.

In one project, Dr. Haselton and her colleagues invited female volunteers to the laboratory to participate in a study about personality, sexuality, and health. The young women were not given any specific directions about what to wear and during their visit to the laboratory they agreed to be photographed. Later, male and female volunteers viewed the photographs to judge whether they thought the women in the photos had dressed to look attractive. It turns out that women were rated as having dressed more attractively when they were in their peak level of fertility of the menstrual cycle (Durante et al., 2008; Haselton et al., 2007). The researchers suggested that wearing such clothing during the fertile phase of the menstrual cycle was an attempt to be noticed by a potential mate (although the women in the study might disagree).

Of course, evolutionary psychologists are quick to point out that females are not alone in "signalling" their receptiveness for sexual activity. Males provide numerous—if not more obvious—examples. Evolutionary psychologists might point out that body building, flaunting material assets, and other public displays of strength and status are common male strategies for attracting mates. Researchers must ask themselves this question: Is this behaviour just a coincidence? Or is this how the evolutionary forces that allowed our species to survive for hundreds of thousands of years are influencing our behaviour in the modern world? Evolutionary psychologists like Dr. Haselton are building evidence to argue that how we dress and how we send many other signals can be explained by evolutionary principles, a topic we explore in this module.

Focus Questions

1. How is human behaviour influenced by genetic factors?
2. How has evolution played a role in modern-day human behaviour?

You might have heard something like this before: *Leah gets her passion for reading from her father*. But does that mean Leah inherited this interest? Or did she just grow up with a lot of books around the home? Are we the products of our genes (nature) or the environment in which we were raised (nurture)? Debates about nature and nurture have been going on for many decades; indeed, the nature-nurture question can easily be applied to almost every module in this textbook. Perhaps one reason people have so often debated nature and nurture relationships is because humans have such a strong tendency to think in either/or categories: yes or no, true or false, black or white. In reality, all of the available evidence suggests that nature and nurture lie along a continuum, with some traits subject to greater influence from genetics (nature) while others are more environmentally based (nurture). Most important, we now know that genetics and experience are never independent. Therefore, the modern scientific nature–nurture question does not split them into two exclusive possibilities. Rather, we ask, *How do nature and nurture interact to produce behaviour?*

Explore
Building Blocks of Genetics

Heredity and Behaviour

Examples of genetic influences on physical traits easily come to mind because we tend to share our eye colour, facial characteristics, stature, and skin colouration with our parents. But research has made it clear that behaviours are influenced by genes just as physical characteristics are; indeed, the two are often related. Genetics has an influence on the brain, just as it has an influence on eye colour, and changes in brain functions lead to changes in behaviour. Therefore, although a discussion of genetics may seem unrelated to how you think or feel, the work of genes—both during development and during everyday life—has a dramatic effect on your behaviour.

THE GENETIC CODE Given that genetics can influence so many aspects of our lives, it is important to review some of this field's basic concepts. Our genetic code isn't hidden in the darkest corners of our brains. Instead, it is found in the nucleus of most of the billions of cells in the human body. This genetic material is organized into **genes**, *the basic units of heredity; genes are responsible for guiding the process of creating the proteins that make up our physical structures and regulate development and physiological processes throughout the lifespan.*

Genes are composed of segments of **DNA (deoxyribonucleic acid)**, *a molecule formed in a double-helix shape that contains four nucleotides: adenine, cytosine, guanine, and thymine* (see Figure 3.1). These nucleotides are typically abbreviated using the first letter of their names—A, C, G, and T. Each gene is a unique combination of these four nucleotides. For example, a sequence of nucleotides on a certain gene may be AGCCTAATCG . . . and so on. This is the individual's **genotype**, *the genetic makeup of an organism—the unique set of genes that comprise that individual's genetic code.* This sequence represents the code used to create proteins. Genes specify which types of molecules a cell should produce and when to produce them. The result of these instructions is an organism's **phenotype**, *the physical traits or behavioural characteristics that show genetic variation, such as eye colour, the shape and size of facial features, and even personality.* This phenotype develops because of differences in the nucleotide sequencing of A, C, G, and T, as well as through interactions with the environment.

Genes are organized in pairs along **chromosomes**, *structures in the cellular nucleus that are lined with all of the genes an individual inherits*. Humans have approximately 20 000–25 000 genes distributed across 23 pairs of chromosomes, half contributed by the mother and half by the father (see Figure 3.2). (In some cases, an extra chromosome—a *trisomy*—is present, thus altering the genetic make-up as well as the phenotype of the

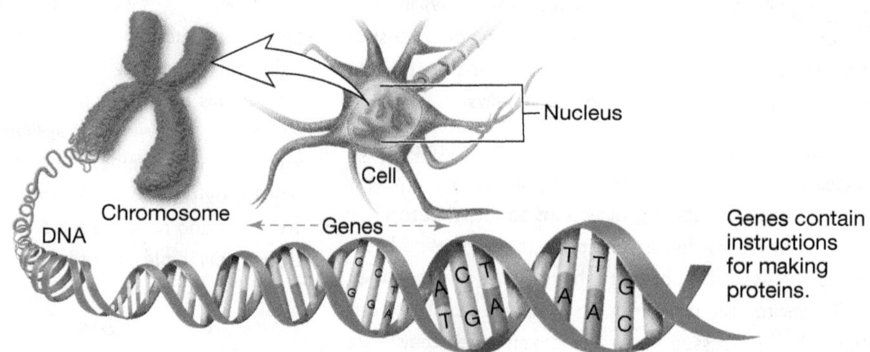

{FIG. 3.1} **DNA Molecules** The nucleus of a cell contains copies of each chromosome. Chromosomes are composed of the genes arranged in the familiar double helix—a long strand of DNA molecules. **Click on this figure in your eText to see more details.**

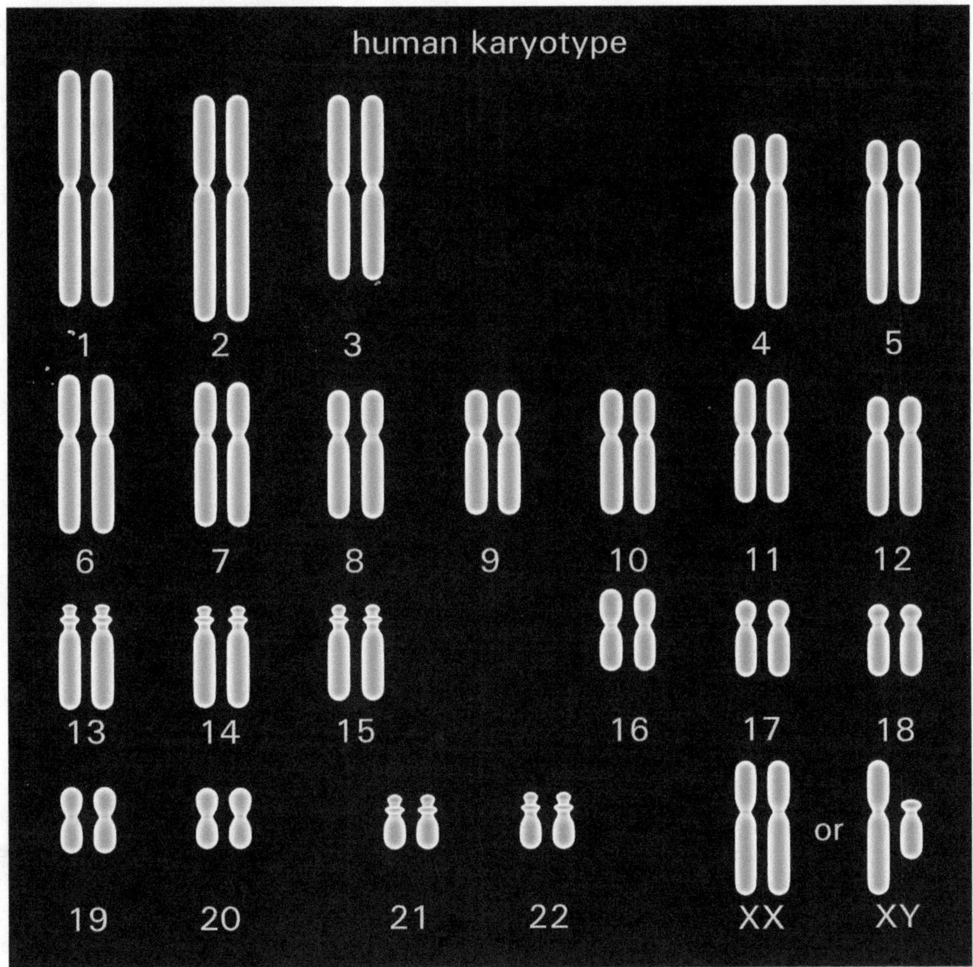

somersault1824/Shutterstock

{FIG. 3.2} **Human Chromosomes** Human DNA is aligned along 23 paired chromosomes. Numbers 1–22 are common to both males and females. Chromosome 23 is sex linked, with males having the XY pattern and females the XX pattern.

individual. The most common chromosomal abnormality is Down Syndrome, a trisomy on the 21st chromosome, although many others exist.)

If two corresponding genes at a given location on a pair of chromosomes are the same, they are referred to as *homozygous*. If the two genes differ, they are *heterozygous*. Whether a trait is expressed depends on which combination of pairs is inherited. In order to make these abstract concepts more concrete, let's look at an example that affects everyone: our sense of taste. Researchers have shown that the ability to taste a very bitter substance called phenylthiocarbamide (PTC) is based on which combination of genes we inherit from either parent (the genotype; see Figure 3.3). The test for whether you can taste PTC (the phenotype) is typically performed by placing a small tab of paper soaked in the substance on the tongue. Some people are "tasters"; they cringe at the bitter taste of PTC. Others—the "nontasters"—cannot taste anything other than the tab of paper. Those who are tasters inherit at least one copy of the *dominant* gene for tasting (abbreviated capital "T") from either parent. People can also inherit a *recessive* copy of this gene (t). Those who report tasting PTC are either homozygous dominant (TT) or heterozygous (Tt). Nontasters are homozygous recessive (tt)—they inherited a recessive copy of the gene from both parents. Those who are tasters may find foods such as Brussels sprouts, cauliflower, and cabbage to be unpleasant, or at least too bitter to eat, as these foods contain PTC.

In this example, the genotype represents what was inherited (i.e., tt, Tt, or TT). The phenotype represents the physical and behavioural manifestation of that genotype that occurs through interactions with the environment (i.e., being a taster or a nontaster for this *specific* sensation—note that nontasters in this context might have normal responses to other tastes). As you will see, this attempt to link genes to behaviour is a rapidly growing area of research in psychology and medicine.

As geneticists continue to unravel different parts of the entire human genome, it is becoming increasingly clear that simple examples like the taster-nontaster trait provide only a glimpse of what knowledge might soon

Explore
Dominant and Recessive Traits

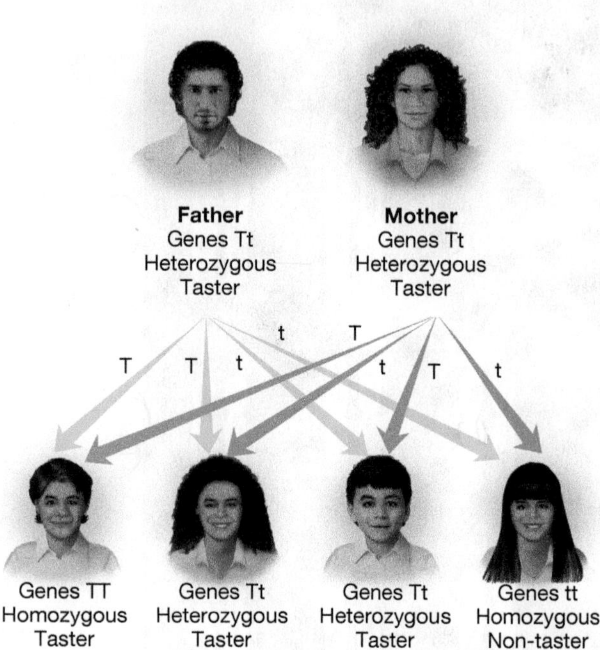

{FIG. 3.3} **Genetic Inheritance** Whether someone tastes the bitter compound PTC depends on which copies of the gene he or she inherits. Shown here is the statistically probable outcome of two heterozygous (Tt) parents with four children.

be available to us. Indeed, in recent years, an entirely new field has developed that attempts to identify the genes involved with specific behaviours: behavioural genomics.

BEHAVIOURAL GENOMICS: THE MOLECULAR APPROACH Although researchers have suggested that genetics play a role in many abilities and behaviours, until recently it has not been possible to determine *how* traits are inherited. To make this determination, researchers now go straight to the source of genetic influence—to the genes themselves. **Behavioural genomics** *is the study of DNA and the ways in which specific genes are related to behaviour.* The technology supporting behavioural genomics is relatively new, but once it became available, researchers initiated a massive effort to identify the components of the entire human genome—the *Human Genome Project*. This project, which was completed in 2003, resulted in the identification of approximately 20 000–25 000 genes. Imagine the undertaking: determining the sequences of the billions of A, C, G, and T nucleotides making up the genes, including where each gene begins and ends, and how they are all arranged on the chromosomes. The Human Genome Project itself did not directly provide a cure for a disease or an understanding of any particular behaviour. Instead, it has led to an abundance of new techniques and information about where genes are located, and it opened the door for an entirely new era of research (Plomin & Crabbe, 2000). Indeed, researchers can now compare the genotypes of different groups of people (e.g., depressed and non-depressed individuals) to look for differences that might shed light on the cause of different conditions. For example, in 1997, researchers identified a gene that was found in families prone to Parkinson's disease (Polymeropoulos et al., 1997). Since then, a number of mutations that are linked to Parkinson's have been identified including *SNCA*, *Parkin*, *PINK1*, *DJ1*, and *LRRK2* (Klein & Schlossmacher, 2006).

Watch
Genetic Predisposition to Alcoholism

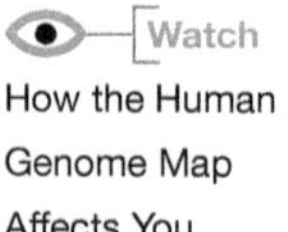
Watch
How the Human Genome Map Affects You

However, we must be cautious in our interpretation of such discoveries. Like any approach to answering scientific questions, behavioural genomic research does have its limitations. For example, although a single gene has been identified as a risk factor for Alzheimer's disease, not everyone who inherits it develops the disease. The same is true for many other conditions. This brings us to a common misconception about genes and behaviour.

MYTHS IN MIND

Single Genes and Behaviour

Enter the phrase "scientists find the gene for" into your favourite Internet search engine and you will wind up with more hits than you would ever have time to sift through. Although it is true that behaviour, both normal and abnormal, can be traced to individual genes, typically *combinations* of genes influence behaviour. When it comes to complex characteristics such as personality or disorders like Alzheimer's disease and schizophrenia, there is very little chance that any single gene could be responsible for them (Duan et al., 2010). A person's intelligence and his predisposition to alcoholism, anxiety, shyness, and depression are all examples of traits and conditions with genetic links, but they all involve multiple genes.

Another misconception is that a single gene can affect only one trait. In reality, the discovery that a particular gene predisposes someone to alcoholism does not mean that this gene is *only* relevant to alcohol addiction; it most likely affects other traits as well. For example, genes that are present in people who abuse alcohol are also more likely to be found in individuals who have a history of other problems such as additional forms of drug dependence and antisocial behaviour. In other words, these different behaviours may share some characteristics, and the gene may be related to that "shared genetic liability" (Dick, 2007).

When you encounter a headline beginning "Scientists find gene for . . . ," don't read it as "Scientists found THE gene for. . . ." It would be wise to carefully read on to fully understand what is being reported. It is likely that the news describes the work of scientists who found another one of the many genes involved in a disorder or, in the case of Alzheimer's disease, a gene that is a risk factor and not the sole cause.

BEHAVIOURAL GENETICS: TWIN AND ADOPTION STUDIES People have long observed that behavioural characteristics can be inherited. For many centuries, the clearest evidence of this possibility came from animal breeding, where animals such as dogs have been reared to be hunters, herders, protectors, or companions. Because we cannot use the methods of dog breeders to study humans, some alternatives are required. This desire to understand the degree to which genetics can explain individual differences in abilities and behaviours spawned a new field of research. **Behavioural genetics** *is the study of how genes and the environment influence behaviour.* Behavioural genetic methods applied to humans typically involve comparing people of different levels of relatedness, such as parents and their offspring, siblings, and unrelated individuals, and measuring resemblances for a specific trait of interest. However, the group that has provided the most insight into the genetic effects on behaviour is twins.

Twins present an amazing opportunity to conduct natural experiments on how genes influence behaviour. One method commonly used in twin studies involves comparing identical and fraternal twins. **Monozygotic twins** *come from a single ovum (egg), which makes them genetically identical (almost 100% genetic similarity).* An ideal comparison group, **dizygotic twins** (fraternal twins) *come from two separate eggs fertilized by two different sperm cells that share the same womb; these twins have approximately 50% of their genetics in common.* Researchers around the world have studied the genetic and environmental bases of behaviour by comparing monozygotic twins, dizygotic twins, non-twin siblings, and unrelated individuals. The assumption underlying these studies is that if a trait is genetically determined, then individuals with a greater genetic similarity will also have a greater similarity for that trait. Researchers have also examined these different groups in *longitudinal studies,* studies that follow the same individuals for many years, often decades. For example, one twin study determined the degree to which anxiety and depression are influenced by genetics in children and adolescents. It was far more likely for both monozygotic twins to show anxiety or depressive symptoms than for both dizygotic twins to do so; thus, these results demonstrate the influential role that genes play in depression (Boomsma et al., 2005).

Behavioural geneticists use twin studies to calculate **heritability**—*a statistic, expressed as a number between zero and one, that represents the degree to which genetic differences between individuals contribute to individual differences in a behaviour or trait found in a population.* A heritability of 0 means that genes do not contribute to individual differences in a trait, whereas a heritability of 1.0 indicates that genes account for all individual differences in a trait. It is important to point out that heritability scores do

Monozygotic?

Dizygotic

Top: Creatas Images/Getty Images/Thinkstock; bottom: Martin Harvey/Alamy

Identical twins are genetically the same, whereas fraternal twins are no more closely related than full siblings from different pregnancies. However, fraternal twins do share much of the same prenatal and postnatal environment if they are reared together. Researchers assume, then, that if the identical twins are more similar on a given trait than fraternal twins, this difference is due to genetics. But, it is *possible* that identical twins are treated more similarly than are fraternal twins (so they have more nature *and* more nurture in common). How would this affect your interpretation of twin studies?

Watch
Basics: Genetic Mechanisms and Behavioural Genetics

not simply reflect how much genetics contributes to the trait itself. Rather, heritability scores tell us the degree to which genetics explain *differences* between people with that trait. For instance, the heritability of having a mouth

Comstock Images/Getty Images/Thinkstock

There is heritable variation in body height—although environmental factors contribute to variation in height among family members.

is 0. This is not to say that genetics has nothing to do with us having mouths, but we all have mouths, so there aren't many individual differences to deal with on this trait. But, as you read earlier, there *are* individual differences in the ability to taste certain flavours. Some of this will be genetic (as you read), and some of this will be due to the foods you are exposed to while growing up. Therefore, the heritability for tasting different flavours would be between 0 and 1.

Heritability estimates are rarely, if ever, an extreme value of 0 or 1.0. Instead, genetics and environmental influences (e.g., family life) both account for some of the differences in our behaviour. For instance, the estimated heritability found in the study on depression and anxiety described earlier was approximately .76 for 3-year-old identical twin pairs (Boomsma et al., 2005). This tells us that 76% of individual differences in depression and anxiety at age 3 can be attributed to genetic factors in the population that was studied. However, depression and anxiety can also obviously be influenced by our different life experiences. It should not be a surprise to learn that heritability estimates for these behaviours change as we age. In the Boomsma et al. (2005) study, the heritability of anxiety and depression went from .76 at age 3 to .48 at age 12 for the identical twin pairs. This change is likely due to the fact that an individual's peer group and social life can have a larger effect on one's emotional well-being during the "tween" and teen-aged years than they would during the toddler years (when family is the main non-genetic factor). This finding should serve as a reminder that the environment never stops interacting with genes.

Watch
In the Real World: Taking Control of Our Genes

Behavioural geneticists also study adopted children to estimate genetic contributions to behaviour. The adopted family represents the *nurture* side of the continuum, whereas the biological family represents the *nature* side. On the one hand, if adopted children are more like their biological parents than their adoptive parents on measures of traits such as personality and intelligence, we might conclude that these traits have a strong genetic component. On the other hand, if the children are more like their adoptive, genetically unrelated parents, a strong case can be made that environmental factors outweigh the biological predispositions. Interestingly, young adopted children are more similar to their adoptive parents in intelligence levels than they are to their biological parents. By the time they reach 16 years, however, adopted adolescents score more similarly to their biological parents than their adoptive parents in tests of intelligence, suggesting that some genes related to intelligence do not exert their influence(s) on behaviour until later on in development (Plomin et al., 1997). Compare this finding to that from the study described in the preceding paragraphs: For intelligence, heritability seems to increase with age, whereas the opposite is true for depression and anxiety.

Although heritability estimates provide important information about the different effects of "nature" and "nurture" on different behaviours, we have to be cautious about how we generalize this information. Heritability estimates are limited to the population being studied. We cannot make definitive statements about the heritability of depression in Egypt based on the results of a study conducted in Canada (although we can use the Canadian study to generate hypotheses about what we *think* we would find if we performed the same study in Egypt). This is because any estimate of heritability is affected by (1) the amount of genetic variability within the group being studied and (2) the variability in the environments that members of that group might be exposed to. For example, people from an isolated village in the Amazon rainforest would likely not have much variability in their genetics because they would not have a lot of contact with outside groups. In contrast, many Canadians have diverse genetic backgrounds. The isolated Amazon villagers would also spend most of their lives in the same village and its surrounding areas, thus leading to less variability in their environments than people in a city like Vancouver might experience. This is not to say that one way of life is better than another—but we need to be mindful of these differences in genetic and environmental variability so that we don't incorrectly assume that North American genetic studies generalize to the entire world.

GENE EXPRESSION AND BEHAVIOUR The fact that heritability estimates change over time based on our different experiences shows us that nature and nurture interact to produce behaviour. What these estimates don't tell us is *how* that interaction occurs in our bodies and brains. Recent advances in our understanding of genetics and the human genome have begun to shed light on some of these relationships.

Almost every cell in our bodies contains the same genes, the basic unit of heredity. But, only some of these genes are active, leading to the production of proteins (or other gene products like ribosomal RNA); the other genes are inactive and do not influence protein production. Of the approximately 20 000-25 000 genes in the human genome, between 6000 and 7000 are active in the human brain. These genes influence the development of different brain structures, the production of chemicals that allow brain cells to communicate with each other, and the refinement of connections between cells that allow large-scale brain networks to form (French & Pavlidis, 2011). The expression of these genes is influenced by genetics, environmental factors that influence the chemical make-up of the cells, or a combination of the two.

If some genes fail to be activated (or *expressed*) properly, people may be at a greater risk for developing brain-related disorders. For example, Dan Geschwind and colleagues (2011) found that children with autism had less gene expression in several regions of the brain. This decrease in gene expression was linked to problems with language, decision making, and understanding other people's emotions. Researchers are now investigating ways to alter gene expression in order to treat different brain disorders such as Parkinson's disease and Alzheimer's disease.

Importantly, gene expression is a life-long process (Champagne, 2010). Factors such as diet, stress level, and sleep can influence whether genes are turned on or off. This study of *changes in gene expression that occur as a result of experience and that do not alter the genetic code* is known as **epigenetics.** Studies with mice have shown that increased maternal licking and grooming (the rodent equivalent of cuddling) led to an increase in the expression of the *GR* gene in the hippocampus (Francis et al., 1999). This gene influences stress responses and can affect how well (or poorly) individuals respond to novel situations. Low levels of licking and grooming led to decreased *GR* expression and a larger stress response (Weaver et al., 2004). Similar effects have been observed in humans. Decreased GR expression was noted in a recent study of childhood abuse victims who later committed suicide, demonstrating the power of these gene–environment interactions. Indeed, there is increasing evidence that epigenetics plays a role in a number of psychological disorders (Labrie et al., 2012).

This process is evident in long-term studies of the relationship between genes, stress, and depression. The brain chemical known as serotonin is related to mood, and imbalances of it are associated with depression (see Module 3.2 and Module 13.3). Recently, researchers have identified a gene related to the release of serotonin. There are two versions of this gene—short and long (referring to length of the DNA strands). Researchers have found that people who inherit two copies of the short version are at greater *risk* for developing depression, whereas those who inherit two long copies are at a far lower risk (Caspi et al., 2003; Caspi et al., 2010). But what is critical here is not just which genes are inherited, but also how much stress people experience. Figure 3.4 shows how this relationship works. As the number of major stressful life events increases, those who inherit two copies of the short version of this gene are far more likely to develop depression, whereas those who inherit two long copies are buffered from depression. People who inherit one copy of each gene (are heterozygous) show intermediate responses to stressful events. Notice that the type of serotonin gene inherited has no effect on depression after only one or two major stressful events. The gene–environment interaction becomes apparent after an *accumulation* of events. This interaction between a genetic predisposition for a disorder and life stress is known as the *diathesis-stress model* of psychological disorders (*diathesis* is Greek for "disposition" or "vulnerability"). It is just one of many examples of how nature and nurture interact.

The fact that gene expression can be influenced by the environment is an example of the *social* part of the *biopsychosocial model* of behaviour discussed throughout this textbook—nurture can influence nature. Some researchers have speculated that gene expression could also be influenced by the culture in which one lives. Culture, family, and other social bonds all influence how we respond—both psychologically *and* biologically—to different situations and stimuli. Therefore, these sociocultural factors have the potential to influence whether or not certain genes are expressed (Richardson & Boyd, 2005).

Watch Special Topics: Epigenetics—A Revolutionary Science

Although many of the changes in gene expression do not alter the genetic code, some do get passed on from generation to generation. Chemically-induced changes in the expression of genes in the amygdala and hippocampus—structures related to emotion and memory—have been shown to influence anxiety-related behaviours for *three generations* of rats (Skinner et al., 2008)! Licking and grooming have similarly been shown to affect both gene expression and maternal behaviours across three generations (Champagne et al., 2003). Therefore, how you behave now could have lasting effects on the genetic codes of your grandchildren.

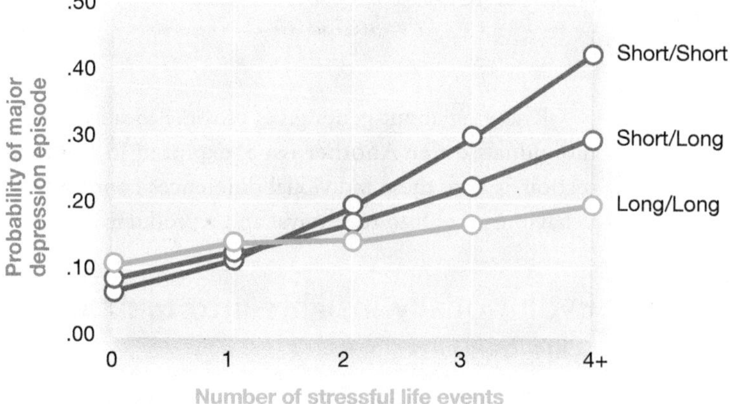

{FIG. 3.4} **Gene and Environment Interactions** Stress interacts with genes and influences whether someone becomes depressed. People who inherit two copies of the short version of a gene that codes for serotonin activity in nerve cells are at an increased risk for becoming depressed in response to major life stressors. Those who inherit two long copies are buffered from becoming depressed as life stressors accumulate.

Quick Quiz 3.1a

Heredity and Behaviour

KNOW ...

1 The chemical units that provide instructions on how specific proteins are to be produced are called ________.

A chromosomes
B genes
C genomic
D autosomes

UNDERSTAND ...

2 A person who is homozygous for a trait

A always has two dominant copies of a gene.
B always has two recessive copies of a gene.
C has identical copies of the gene.
D has different copies of the gene.

APPLY ...

3 If a researcher wanted to identify how someone's life experiences could affect the expression of different genes and thus put that person at risk for developing depression, she would most likely use which of the following methods?

A Behavioural genomics
B A comparison of monozygotic and dizygotic twins in different parts of the world
C An adoption study
D Epigenetics

ANALYZE ...

4 Imagine you hear a report about a heritability study that claims trait X is "50% genetic." Which of the following is a more accurate way of stating this?

A Fifty percent of individual differences of trait X within a population are due to genetic factors.
B Only half of a population has the trait.
C The trait is homozygous.
D More than 50% of similarities of trait X within a population are due to genetic factors.

Answers can be found on page ANS-1.

Watch
The Big Picture: Genes, Evolution, and Human Behaviour

Knowing about genes gives us some idea as to why individuals differ. Another issue, explored in the next section, is how these individual differences contribute to behaviours that lead to survival and reproductive success.

Evolutionary Insights into Human Behaviour

On December 27, 1831, a young Charles Darwin began his voyage on the HMS *Beagle,* a ship tasked to survey the coastline of South America. Darwin's (self-funded) position was to act as a naturalist, examining the wildlife, flora, and geology of the areas the ship visited. This five-year voyage, which included additional stops in Australia and South Africa, exposed Darwin to a vast number of species and eventually led to him developing one of the most important (and controversial) theories in human history.

While travelling among the different Galápagos Islands (900 km west of modern-day Ecuador), Darwin noticed small differences between members of the same species of birds and turtles. These differences meshed quite well with the particular environments the animals lived in. He also identified fossils from a number of extinct species. Based on these observations, Darwin deduced that some members of a species were more "fit" for a particular environment than others, and that the fittest individuals would be more likely to prosper and reproduce. Individuals that were not well-matched to their environment would not reproduce. If an entire species was not fit for its environment, it could go extinct. These observations were later described as Darwin's theory of **natural selection**, *the process by which favourable traits become increasingly common in a population of interbreeding individuals, while traits that are unfavourable become less common* (see Figure 3.5).

Of course, individual animals could not control whether or not they were fit for a given environment. Instead, the genes of some animals would combine in such a way to produce traits favourable to that setting (i.e., they were adaptive) and the genes of other animals would combine in less useful ways. Because the adaptive or fit animals were more likely to survive and reproduce, these traits would then be more likely to be passed on to future generations. Darwin termed this process **evolution**, *the change in the frequency of genes occurring in an interbreeding population over generations.*

Evolution is not a continuous process, however. If an animal is perfectly adapted for its environment, then there is no evolutionary pressure for change to occur. Let's call that version 1.0 of the animal. But what if some pressure such as a change in the climate or the availability of food occurs? In this case, a given trait might be advantageous in that specific environment and specific point in time. Through natural selection, this trait would eventually become common within that species and may in the future serve other functions and interact with the environment in novel ways. Let's call this version 2.0 of the animal. When the next environmental pressure occurred, a subset of version 2.0 of the animal would possess traits that makes them more evolutionarily fit than the other version 2.0 animals. This subset would survive and reproduce, eventually leading to version 3.0 of the animal. While this description is oversimplified, it does illustrate a key point: Any modern species is based upon version after version after version of species that were fit for their particular environment and time.

{FIG. 3.5} **How Traits Evolve** Evolution through natural selection requires both that a trait be heritable (i.e., be passed down through reproductive means) and that certain individuals within a breeding population have a reproductive advantage for having the trait.

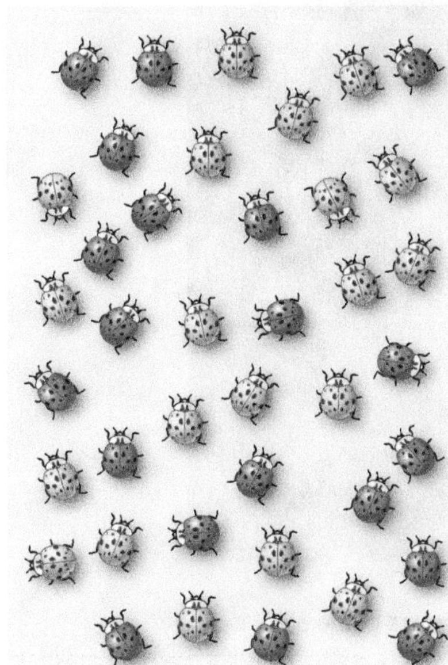

Suppose colouration is a genetically inherited trait in lady bugs.

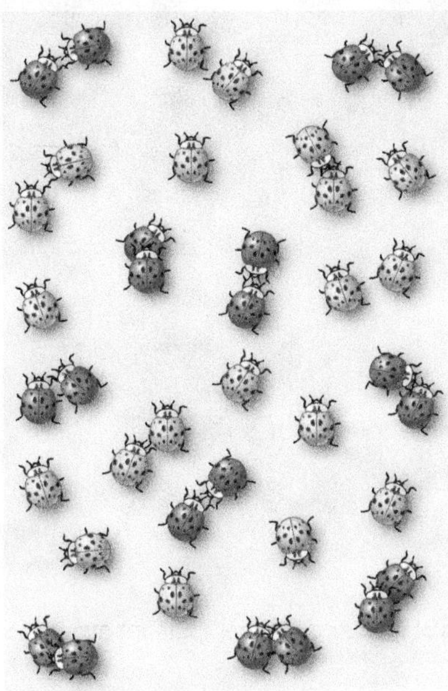

Suppose a bird that preys on these lady bugs can see the yellow ones better. This brings about a survival and reproductive advantage to red lady bugs that have red-coloured offspring.

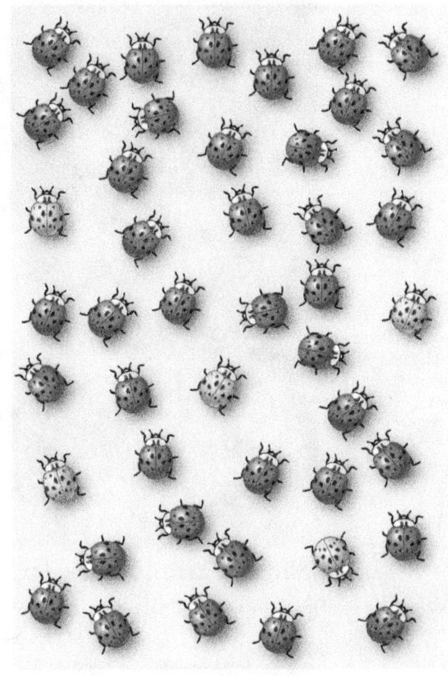

Genes for red colouration should spread through the population because natural selection favours red lady bugs over yellow lady bugs.

EVOLUTIONARY PSYCHOLOGY How do Darwin's theories of evolution and natural selection relate to human behaviour? Part of the answer is that humans are animals too. Just as turtles and birds faced numerous evolutionary challenges over the last few hundred years, so too did modern humanity's ancestors. There is fossil evidence showing that many branches of our ancestral family tree died out, likely because their physical and mental characteristics were not fit for their environment. A second part of the answer is that the development of traits that improve survival is based on the shuffling of the genetic material that you read about earlier in this module. Although DNA had not been discovered yet, Darwin's theory can be directly linked to the fact that cytosine, adenine, guanine, and thymine can be reordered to produce different combinations of genes.

Darwin's theories met with considerable opposition. By stating that animals evolved over time based on environmental pressures, Darwin was challenging the view that animals had been created "as is" by an all-knowing deity. By stating that all humans had common ancestors that evolved into modern people, Darwin was demonstrating that all people—regardless of ethnicity or economic status—were essentially equal. This view was not popular in Victorian England, where the aristocracy looked at the working class with disdain and where the English felt that they had the right to colonize non-Caucasian countries such as India. However, over time, Darwin's ideas became accepted in almost all scientific circles. Today, a modern branch of psychology known as *evolutionary psychology* attempts to explain human behaviours based on the beneficial function(s) they may have served in our species' development.

Watch: Thinking Like a Psychologist: Evolutionary Psychology

INTRA- AND INTERSEXUAL SELECTION Of all the evolutionary pressures that an individual faces, perhaps the most pressing is the need to pass on our genetic material to future generations. This challenge occurs even when there are no environmental pressures, as individual members of a species will each be motivated to reproduce. It should come as no surprise, then, that adaptations have evolved to help some individuals increase their chances of mating (Darwin, 1871).

Of course, having the opportunity to mate is not always simple. In some species, members of one sex (usually males) compete for access to the other sex (usually females). For instance, some deer and caribou literally lock horns in violent fights known as *rutting*. The winner of the fight is much more likely to mate with females than is the loser. Similar examples occur in many primate species. Here, a dominant male—often referred to as the *alpha male*—intimidates other males and is more likely to mate with multiple females than are the subordinate males. These are examples of **intrasexual selection**, *a situation in which members of the same sex compete in order to win the opportunity to mate with members of the opposite sex.*

Watch: Evolution and Sex: Michael Bailey

John E Marriott/Glow Images

In intrasexual selection, members of the same sex compete for access to members of the other sex.

Intrasexual selection is evolutionarily advantageous because the animals most likely to become dominant are the strongest and/or smartest, and therefore the most fit for that time and place.

A second form of sexual selection is known as **intersexual selection**, *a situation in which members of one sex select a mating partner based on their desirable traits.* Some of these traits are a result of genetics. For instance, a number of experiments have shown that people rate symmetrical faces as being more attractive than asymmetrical faces (Gangestad et al., 1994; Rhodes et al., 2006). Women prefer men who are taller (6'0 or 1.83 m), with good posture, and not very hairy (Buss, 2003; Dixson et al., 2010). Men prefer women who are slightly shorter than them, have full lips, high cheekbones, and a small chin. Researchers at the University of Toronto found that participants preferred female faces in which the distance between the eyes was 46% of the width of the face from ear to ear, and in which the distance between the eyes and the mouth was 36% of the length of the face (Pallett et al., 2010). (In case you're curious, the actress Jessica Alba's face perfectly matches this geometry.) However, not all elements of intersexual selection are the gift (or curse) of our genes. Men often present cues that highlight their masculinity, such as wearing clothes that display their muscles. They also attempt to appear large and athletic, particularly when around potential mates. For example, if an attractive woman walks by a group of men, they tend to stand up straight to appear taller and healthier, and thus more attractive (this makes for wonderful people-watching at bars). Women also attempt to highlight attractive elements of their physique. The multibillion-dollar cosmetics industry provides tools for women to change their skin tone, skin texture, hair colour, fragrance, eyelash colour and thickness, and lip colour. Clothing is also used to increase attractiveness. At the beginning of this module, you learned that women dress more attractively when they are ovulating. Recently, a group of researchers have suggested that some of these clothing selections might actually be tapping into primal impulses that are hard-wired into our genetic code.

Simulate Perceptions of Attractiveness

Left: Shawn Hempel/Shutterstock.com; centre: BrazilPhotos.com/Alamy; right: MartiniDry/Shutterstock.com

Animals of many species use colouration as a way to attract the attention of potential mates, and those who are most colourful are often preferred. This does not include men who paint their chests at football games.

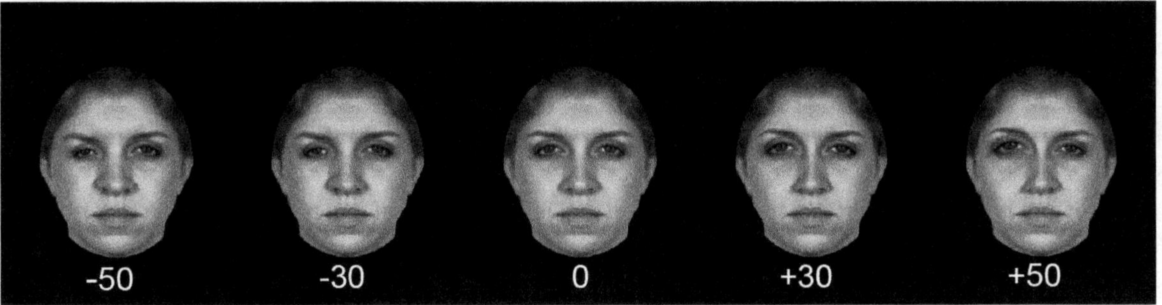

University of Western Australia

Facial Symmetry and Attraction Which face do you prefer of these five? You likely chose the middle face because it has the highest level of symmetry. People can detect this quality without even having to study the faces very closely.

WORKING THE SCIENTIFIC LITERACY MODEL

Ruby Red Lipstick and That Sexy Red Dress

We have all had the experience of seeing a woman in a red dress walk into a room and turn everyone's head. We have also all seen women with striking red lipstick that makes her lips the focus of attention. As an observer, what do you think when you see these women? A number of studies suggest that people assume that these women are highlighting their sex appeal, a result that surprises no one.

What do we know about the colour red and sexual attraction?

Several studies in different countries have found that men respond differently to the colour red than to other colours. Lipstick is generally some shade of red and serves to make the lips fuller and more vibrant. Women in red dresses seem to attract more attention from heterosexual males than other women in the room. These observations are not simply anecdotes; a growing body of research has shown that the colour red changes men's responses to women. For instance, when black-and-white photographs of women are presented on a red background, these women are rated as being more attractive than when the same images are presented on a white background (Elliot & Niesta, 2008). Researchers in France have found that males tip waitresses more generously when the women are wearing a red shirt (Guéguen & Jacob, 2012a), have a red ornament in their hair (Jacob et al., 2012), or are wearing red (rather than pink or brown) lipstick (Guéguen & Jacob, 2012b). People are also more likely to pick up female hitchhikers if they are wearing red (Guéguen, 2010). So why does the colour red have these effects? This question has a one-word answer: SEX.

How can science provide evidence that the colour red is sexually advantageous?

Women who are wearing red clothes are perceived to be more interested in having sex than women wearing other colours. This perception occurs even when the same woman is shown in identical t-shirts whose colour has been digitally altered (Guéguen, 2012); it is not affected by the attractiveness of the female model. Not surprisingly, the assumption that women in red were more sexually available also made them more attractive to heterosexual males (Pazda et al., 2012). Although these assumptions seem crude, they are consistent with trends found in photographs appearing on dating websites. Elliot and Pazda (2012) found that women who displayed red were more likely to be interested in casual sex than were women who displayed any other colour on their website profile picture (see Figure 3.6). A follow-up study found that women displayed red more prominently when posting photographs to websites

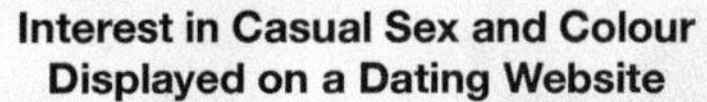

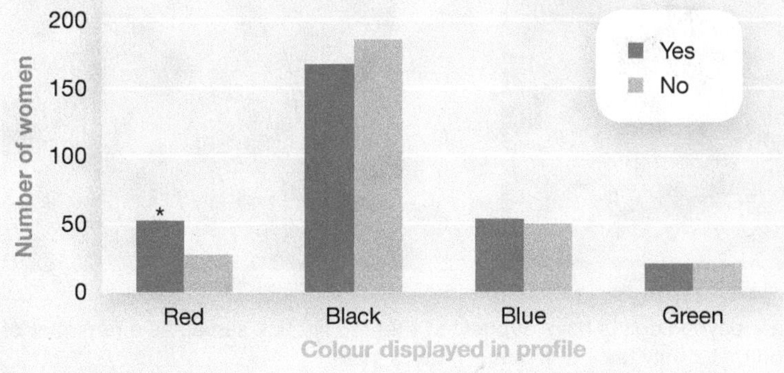

{FIG. 3.6} **Red and Sexuality** Women were more likely to display red when attempting to meet a casual sex partner than when attempting to meet a potential spouse.

dedicated to facilitating casual sex "hook ups" than to websites dedicated to meeting a future spouse. These researchers have also found that women were more likely to choose a red than a green or blue shirt when they expected to converse with an attractive man. There was no colour difference when the women expected to meet another woman or an unattractive man (Elliot et al., 2013). So why is red associated with sex?

Evolutionary psychologists are quick to point out that red is associated with sexual receptivity in many animals, including humans. Female baboons and chimpanzees—species that are evolutionarily close to humans—have redder chests and genitals when they are near ovulation than at other times of their cycles (Deschner et al., 2004; Dixson, 1983). This blushing appears to be linked to estrogen levels, which open up the blood vessels of these regions (Setchell & Wickings, 2004). In these species, males respond to the red swellings with copulation attempts and, if unsuccessful, self-stimulation (Waitt et al., 2006). These researchers also found that male rhesus monkeys (*Macaca mulatta)* spend more time looking at red-enhanced photographs of female anogenital regions than at other images.

In humans, sexual interest is associated with flushing in the face, neck, and upper chest (Changizi, 2009). Anthropological research has shown that women have used lipstick and rouge to mimic these vascular changes (and thus appear more attractive to men) for over 10 000 years (Low, 1979). Some researchers have even suggested that red lipstick is used by women to make their mouths resemble aroused female genitals (Morris, 2005; Stephen et al., 2009). While it is doubtful that women are *consciously* wearing red lipstick to mimic primate reproductive organs, evolutionary psychologists would suggest that they are definitely interested in some form of monkey business.

Left: Theo Allofs/Corbis; right: Subbotina Anna/Fotolia

Evolutionary psychologists have suggested that red lipstick serves as a reminder of genitals and that it may tap into a primal urge to mate.

Can we critically evaluate this evidence?

Evolutionary psychology explanations are often difficult to definitively prove, and the red dress and lipstick explanations are no different. It is difficult to separate the evolutionary forces of the colour red from learned associations, such as the linking of red with brothels ("red-light district") or images from literature or the entertainment world (e.g., "the lady in red"). One critical point about mating is that males are more likely to invest more resources in attempting to mate with someone who is younger and more likely to bear offspring. So, would the red-dress effect (as it is now known) be age-specific? One experiment has tested this possibility, and its results are consistent with the evolutionary explanation. In a study similar to the tipping experiment discussed earlier, the colour red had a much larger effect on the tips given to younger waitresses than to older, post-menopausal waitresses (Schwarz & Singer, 2012).

There is also the possibility that red's continued association with sex in society has created a self-fulfilling prophecy in which women now wear red to highlight their sexuality because that is how this message is conveyed in our culture (as opposed to wearing white or blue). If this is the case, then would red imply sexual receptivity in other cultures? To test this hypothesis, Elliot and colleagues (2013) tested individuals in a remote village in Burkina Faso (in Western Africa); care was taken to select participants with little exposure to Western people and values. Importantly, in this village, the colour red had negative associations—death, bad luck, and sickness—and no sexual connotations. The participants viewed black-and-white photographs of women surrounded by either a red or a blue border. Consistent with North American and European studies—and contrary to their cultural norms—the women with the red borders were rated as being more attractive. (Due to cultural prohibitions, it was not possible to discuss whether the women were viewed as being sexually available.) This study suggests that the findings are more universal than previously thought, although obviously other explanations are still possible.

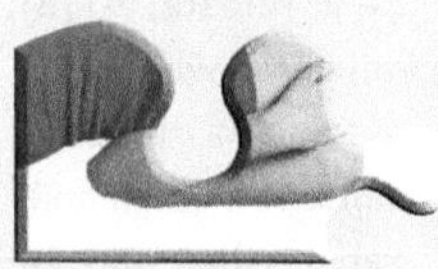

Why is this relevant?

The so-called "red-dress effect" demonstrates that people can be sending subtle messages about themselves to others, sometimes without meaning to (or having any desire to) do so. Whether or not you believe the evolutionary psychology explanation for this effect, it is tough to argue with the data indicating that people associate the colour red with sexuality, particularly for females. (Red is also associated with higher status in males; Elliot et al., 2010.) Interestingly, another staple of the female wardrobe, the little *black* dress, is not associated with sexual availability. Instead, females in such an outfit are judged as being attractive because they are fashionable (Pazda et al., 2013), thus suggesting that there are multiple cognitive processes involved with judgments of attractiveness.

Of course, it is important to point out that women wearing red are *not* necessarily indicating their willingness to have sex! These data are trends across the population and do not predict individual people's behaviour. Sometimes a woman in a red dress is evidence of nothing more than the fact that her other clothes are in the laundry.

Deklofenak/Shutterstock.com

Of course, there are other qualities we look for in a potential partner, particularly when it comes to long-term mates. But what are these qualities, and do members of other cultures value similar characteristics? Buss (1989) conducted a survey of more than 10 000 people from 37 different cultures to discover what they most valued in a long-term partner. Across this broad sample, both men and women agreed that love, kindness, commitment, character, and emotional maturity were important. However, there were some interesting differences. Women valued men with strong financial prospects, status, and good health whereas men placed a greater emphasis on physical beauty, youth, and other characteristics that relate to reproduction. Other researchers have found similar sex differences (see Figure 3.7). Researchers in the United States showed yearbook photographs to heterosexual male and female research participants. Along with the photographs, participants were provided with information about each individual's socioeconomic status (SES), a measure of their financial status. SES had a much greater effect on females' willingness to enter relationships with these individuals than it did for males (Townsend & Levy, 1990a). In a subsequent study, these researchers clothed the same models in outfits that implied high, medium, or low SES. Participants were asked to rate their willingness to engage in different types of relationships with this person ranging from "Coffee and conversation" to "Sex only" to "Marriage." Clothing, the indicator of SES, had a much larger effect on females than males, particularly when the model was not physically attractive. Men were much more willing to engage in "Sex only" relationships regardless of SES or attractiveness (Townsend & Levy, 1990b).

How can we explain this difference? According to evolutionary psychologists, this difference might be due to the resources required to raise offspring. Females have a limited number of eggs, and thus a finite number of opportunities to pass on their genes to another generation. If a female became pregnant and had a baby, she would require resources to help raise the child, particularly when the child is quite young and it is difficult for the woman to bring in her own resources. Therefore, it would make sense that females would be attracted to males who can provide these resources; this sometimes means mating with someone who is older and more established in life (Trivers, 1972). In contrast, men have a seemingly infinite amount of sperm and have fewer limits on the number of people they could theoretically impregnate. Given that their evolutionary impulse is to pass on their genes to as many offspring as possible, it makes sense for them to be attracted to young, healthy women who are likely able to reproduce (Buss, 1989). Oddly, these motivations don't appear in many love songs.

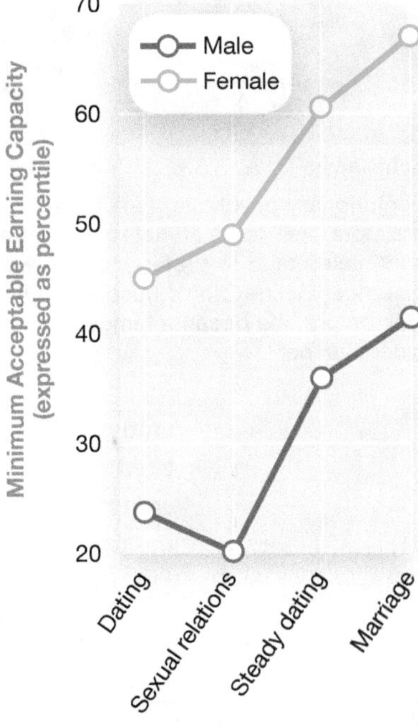

{FIG. 3.7} **Sex Differences in the Minimum Acceptable Earning Level for Different Types of Relationships** Females place a much higher value on economic stability than do males, particularly for long-term relationships. This result may be due to the fact that females can produce a limited number of offspring and therefore need to ensure that a mate has enough resources to ensure their survival. Evolutionary psychology is not necessarily romantic.

EVOLUTION, THE BRAIN, AND BEHAVIOUR

Evolutionary forces have obviously shaped more than just our mating preferences. They have shaped our bodies and

Schroewig/DPA/ABACA/Newscom

Evolutionary psychology explains why females are more likely to be attracted to older males and why males tend to prefer younger women. For instance, Céline Dion's husband (who she met well before she became famous) is significantly older than her.

our brains. The first member of the genus from whom modern humans developed, *Homo habilis* ("handy man"), appeared roughly 2.5 million years ago (Harris, 1983). Its brain was 50% larger than its ancestors' (Hofman, 1983); it was also the first of our ancestors to use stone tools. This was a monumental cognitive leap—this species could now actively shape its environment to suit its needs rather than passively responding to the forces of nature. This ability allowed *Homo habilis* to thrive for roughly 800 000 years. At that point, a new member of the *Homo* genus emerged: *Homo erectus* ("erect man," based on its ability to walk upright). *Homo erectus* had a brain that was approximately one-third larger than that of *Homo habilis*. This increased brain power allowed them to harness the use of fire and to make much more precise hunting tools than their ancestors. Importantly, each advance in the quality of their tools stimulated further advances (similar to how each version of a computer program is, theoretically, an improvement on the previous version).

Homo erectus was able to adapt to different environmental conditions for over two million years. Around 200 000 years ago, however, a new member of the *Homo* genus arrived on the scene: *Homo sapiens* ("wise men"). *Homo sapiens* arose in Africa and quickly spread throughout the world. Their brains were slightly larger than *Homo erectus'*, and this small difference in brain size led to large differences in their ability to shape their world. Early *Homo sapiens* had sophisticated stone tools, sharp spear points for hunting, and long blades (Wynn, 2002). They were also the first of our ancestors to produce symbolic representations of objects and ideas, as shown in carvings and cave paintings (Chase & Dibble, 1987). This ability to think in the abstract and to communicate ideas ensured that knowledge could be passed on from generation to generation, a key factor in the development of modern human society.

When reading about this progression in cognitive power and brain size, it's easy to fall into the logical trap that more brain equals more intelligence. While there is definitely a relationship, it's not quite that simple. Large animals have large brains; elephants and blue whales have brains that are substantially larger than ours. However, although these species are intelligent, theirs are no match for the human brain.

There are at least three reasons that human brains are more powerful than any other on the planet. First, human brains have more folds and grooves on the outer surface of the brain than any other species. This tissue is the *cerebral cortex*, the location of billions of cell bodies and the site of most of our advanced cognitive abilities (see Module 3.3). Second, the front third of the human brain is more developed than that of any other species (see Figure 3.8). This large neural area, known as the *frontal lobes,* is critical for our ability to form plans, solve problems, make decisions, and control our attention and actions, among many other functions (Stuss, 2011). We therefore have more processing power at our disposal than any other species. Finally, humans and a few other species have found a way to "cheat" some of the biological restrictions on brain and head size. In many species, a newborn infant is able to function to some degree soon after being born. Baby deer struggle to their feet within minutes. Humans do not. This is because the human brain has not finished developing at birth. Instead, the sections of the skull are not fully fused, thus allowing more brain growth to occur. This process is known as *neotony,* and allows humans to develop large brains while limiting (to some degree) the physical dangers associated with the baby exiting the narrow birth canal. Without neotony, humans would either have smaller brains, or females would need to change their body shape.

EVOLUTION AND COGNITION Changes in the size of different brain structures have also been shaped by evolutionary forces. Some of these differences allow researchers to link behaviours that were performed by our ancestors with modern cognitive abilities. The best-known example of this line of thinking is the hunter-gatherer theory of sex differences in cognition (Silverman & Eals, 1992). Many studies have examined sex differences (and similarities) on a number of variables (Kimura, 1999; Rogers, 1999). However, the hunter-gatherer theory explicitly links performance on specific tasks to the different roles performed by males and females over the course of our evolutionary history.

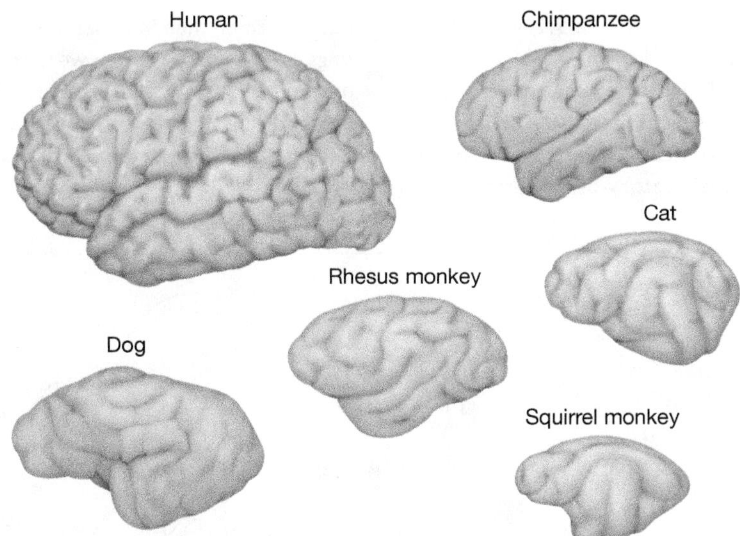

{FIG. 3.8} **The Prefrontal Cortex in Different Species** Human brains have much more space dedicated to the frontal lobes, particularly the prefrontal cortex, than any other species. This brain area is related to many of our higher cognitive functions like problem solving and decision making.

BIOPSYCHOSOCIAL PERSPECTIVES

Hunters and Gatherers: Men, Women, and Spatial Memory

Evolutionary psychologists claim that the brain consists of a set of cognitive adaptations for solving problems related to survival and reproductive fitness. They also hypothesize that male and female brains will differ in some ways because males and females have had to solve a different set of problems in order to survive and reproduce. Specifically, due to their size and strength, males were traditionally responsible for tracking and killing animals. These responsibilities would require males to travel over long distances without becoming lost. Females, due to the fact that they cared for children, remained closer to home and instead spent time foraging for berries and edible plants. Males' responsibilities would favour individuals with good spatial skills; females' responsibilities would favour memory for the location of objects (e.g., plants). The question, then, is whether the abilities that were adaptive for males and females over the course of our species' evolution are still present today. Put another way, will modern males and females show performance differences on different tests of spatial abilities that are consistent with their historic roles as hunter (males) and gatherer (females)?

One sex difference that has been reported involves solving the mental rotation task seen in Figure 3.9.

Instructions

1. Take a close look at standard object #1 in Figure 3.9. One of the three objects to the right of it is the same. Which one matches the standard? Repeat this with standard object #2 and the three comparison shapes to the right of it.
2. Many researchers find that, on average, males and females differ in their ability to perform this task. Do you think that

{FIG. 3.9} **Mental Rotation Task**

Answers: 1. A; 2. B

- Males perform better than females?
- Females perform better than males?

Research shows that males are generally able to perform this task more quickly than females, and with greater accuracy. In fact, researchers have found that males with high testosterone levels were better at solving the task than males with low levels of testosterone (Hooven et al., 2004). The male advantage in this task has been observed across 40 different countries, suggesting that the finding is not restricted to Canadian universities (Silverman et al., 2007). Overall, evidence from many studies suggests that there is a biological and evolutionary explanation for the male advantage in

Explore Virtual Brain: Hormones and Sex

performing this specific task. (In Module 9.2, we examine these claims in more detail.)

Researchers have also found that females outperform males on different types of spatial tasks, specifically, tests involving memory for the spatial *location* of objects (see Figure 3.10). In addition to laboratory-based tests, females outperformed men in experiments conducted in natural settings. In one study, women were able to locate specific plants more quickly than were men and also made fewer mistakes in identifying them (New et al., 2007). This advantage *may* be due to females' evolutionary role as a gatherer rather than as a hunter.

{FIG. 3.10} **Spatial Location Memory Task** In this task, participants are asked to remember the location of specific items.

Before concluding this module, it is worth adding a note of caution. Although evolutionary explanations for cognitive behaviour are fascinating, it is important to be careful about over-interpreting the findings. For instance, although males and females differ on some skills, the differences are generally quite small, with many females outperforming males on spatial tasks. You should also remember that there are often alternative explanations for the results. Therefore, while evolutionary psychology presents possible explanations, it is more likely that they are only *one of many* factors influencing your behaviour.

Quick Quiz 3.1b Evolutionary Insights into Human Behaviour

KNOW ...

1 For a trait to evolve, it must have a(n) _________ basis.

A learned

B adaptive

C heritable

D developmental

APPLY ...

2 Evolution is best defined as

A a gradual increase in complexity.

B a change in gene frequency over generations.

C solving the challenge of survival by adapting.

D a progression toward a complex human brain.

ANALYZE ...

3 Evolutionary psychologists have made some claims that sex differences in cognitive abilities are genetically determined. Which of the following is *not* an alternative explanation for such claims?

A Hormone levels affect performance.

B Sociocultural history affects performance.

C Different educational experiences affect performance.

D Technological limitations prevent the accurate study of sex differences.

Answers can be found on page ANS-1.

Module Summary

Module 3.1

Now that you have read this module you should

KNOW ...

- ***The key terminology related to genes, inheritance, and evolutionary psychology:***

behavioural genetics (p. 79)
behavioural genomics (p. 78)
chromosomes (p. 76)
dizygotic twins (p. 79)
DNA (deoxyribonucleic acid) (p. 76)
epigenetics (p. 81)
evolution (p. 82)
genes (p. 76)
genotype (p. 76)
heritability (p. 79)
intersexual selection (p. 84)
intrasexual selection (p. 83)
monozygotic twins (p. 79)
natural selection (p. 82)
phenotype (p. 76)

UNDERSTAND ...

- ***How twin and adoption studies reveal relationships between genes and behaviour.*** Both methods measure genetic, environmental, and interactive contributions to behaviour. Twin studies typically compare monozygotic twins (genetically identical) and dizygotic twins (full siblings sharing the prenatal environment) to estimate heritability. Adoption studies compare adopted children to their adoptive and biological parents. These designs allow researchers to determine heritability, a number between 0 and 1 that estimates the degree to which individual differences in a trait (in a given population) are due to genetic factors. A heritability of 1.0 would mean that genes contribute to 100% of individual differences. Many human characteristics, including intelligence and personality, have heritability estimates typically ranging between .40 and .70.

APPLY ...

- ***Your knowledge of genes and behaviour to develop hypotheses about why a trait may be adaptive.*** Try putting yourself in an evolutionary psychologist's position and answer the following two questions (check your answers on page ANS-1):

1. Many evolutionary psychologists claim that men are more interested in a mate's physical attractiveness and youth, whereas women are more interested in qualities that contribute to childrearing success, such as intelligence and wealth. If this is the case, then who do you think would express more jealousy over sexual infidelity—men or women?
2. Researchers (Cramer et al., 2008) asked volunteers to rate how upset they would be by sexual infidelity in a mate and then they plotted the results in the graph shown in Figure 3.11. Do their results confirm your hypothesis?

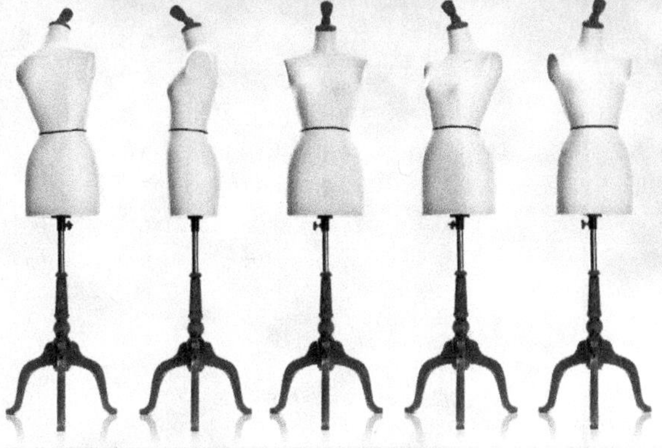

Roberto A Sanchez/iStockphoto

ANALYZE ...

- ***Claims that scientists have located a specific gene that controls a single trait or behaviour.*** As you learned in this module, most psychological traits, as well as disorders such as Alzheimer's disease, involve multiple genes, some of which may not even yet be discovered. (See the Myths in Mind feature on page 78.)
- ***Explanations for cognitive sex differences that are rooted in genetics.*** The Biopsychosocial Perspectives feature on page 89 summarized research showing that males have an advantage when it comes to a specific mental rotation task. Given that this is a relatively consistent sex difference, high testosterone levels are associated with better performance on the task, and the male advantage has been found cross-culturally, it seems plausible that this difference has a genetic basis. In future chapters we will return to issues and discussion of sex-based differences in cognitive abilities (see Module 9.3).

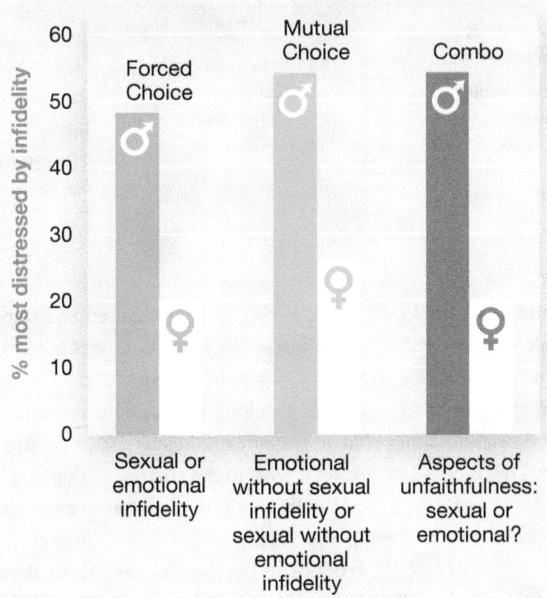

{FIG. 3.11} **Men's and Women's Reactions to Infidelity** Men find sexual infidelity more distressing than do women, regardless of how a question is framed.

Rod Williams/naturepl.com

Module 3.2

How the Nervous System Works: Cells and Neurotransmitters

Learning Objectives

After reading this module you should

KNOW ...	UNDERSTAND ...	APPLY ...	ANALYZE ...
The key terminology associated with nerve cells, hormones, and their functioning	How nerve cells communicate The ways that drugs and other substances affect the brain The roles that hormones play in our behaviour	Your knowledge of neurotransmitters to form hypotheses about drug actions	The claim that we are born with all the nerve cells we will ever have

A bite from an Australian species of snake called the taipan can kill an adult human within 30 minutes. In fact, it is recognized as the most lethally venomous species of snake in the world (50 times more potent than the also fatal venom of the king cobra). The venom of the taipan is neurotoxic, meaning that it specifically attacks cells of the nervous system. These cells are involved with more than just "thinking"—in fact, networks of nervous system cells working together are critical for basic life functions like breathing and having a heartbeat. A direct attack on these cells, therefore, spells trouble. In the case of the taipan, its bite first leads to drowsiness followed by difficulties controlling one's head and neck muscles. Victims then experience progressive difficulty with swallowing, followed by tightness of the chest and paralysis of breathing. If enough venom was injected and treatment is not available, coma and death occur. All of this happens because of damage to the cells that will be discussed in this module—cells that work together to produce the complex human behaviours we engage in every day.

Incidentally, not all snake venom attacks the nervous system. The venom found in most rattlesnakes in North America is not neurotoxic (although you still shouldn't hug one). Instead, it damages tissue in the vicinity of the bite as well as those tissues it reaches within the bloodstream, particularly the heart. Although this is not exactly comforting news, it should at least allow you to enjoy nature without being afraid that a snake will attack your nervous system's cells. That's what spiders are for ...

Focus Questions

 Which normal processes of nerve cells are disrupted by a substance like snake venom?

 What roles do chemicals play in normal nerve cell functioning?

When we think of cells, we often imagine looking at plants or earthworms through a microscope in high-school biology class. Although thrilling, this activity likely seems to be the furthest thing from the study of behaviour. However, cells—particularly cells in the nervous system—play an incredibly important role in absolutely everything you do, from moving and sensing to thinking and feeling. Understanding how cells function and communicate with each other as part of networks will help you better understand topics discussed in later modules, such as how we learn (Modules 6.1, 6.2, and 7.1), how different drugs (both clinical and recreational) work (Modules 5.3 and 16.3), and how stress affects our bodies and brains (Module 14.2). This module therefore serves as a building block that will deepen your understanding of almost all of the behaviours that make you "you."

Neural Communication

The human body is composed of many different types of cells. Psychologists are most interested in **neurons**, *one of the major types of cells found in the nervous system, that are responsible for sending and receiving messages throughout the body*. Billions of these cells receive and transmit messages every day, including while you are asleep. Millions of them are firing as a result of you reading these words. In order to understand how this particular type of cell can produce complex behaviours, it is necessary to take a closer look at the structure and function of the neuron.

THE NEURON The primary purpose of neurons is to "fire," to receive input from one group of neurons and to then transmit that information to other neurons. Doing so allows single neurons to work together as part of networks involving thousands (and sometimes millions) of other cells; this will eventually lead to some form of behaviour. To that end, neurons are designed in such a way that there are parts of the cell specialized for receiving incoming information *from* other neurons and parts of the cell specialized for transmitting information *to* other neurons.

Watch
The Basics: How the Brain Works, Part 1

Explore
Structure of a Neuron

All neurons have a **cell body** (also known as the *soma*), *the part of a neuron that contains the nucleus that houses the cell's genetic material* (see Figure 3.12). Genes in the cell body synthesize proteins that form the chemicals and structures that allow the neuron to function. The activity of these genes can be influenced by the input coming from other cells. This input is received by **dendrites**, *small*

Explore
Dendritic Spreading

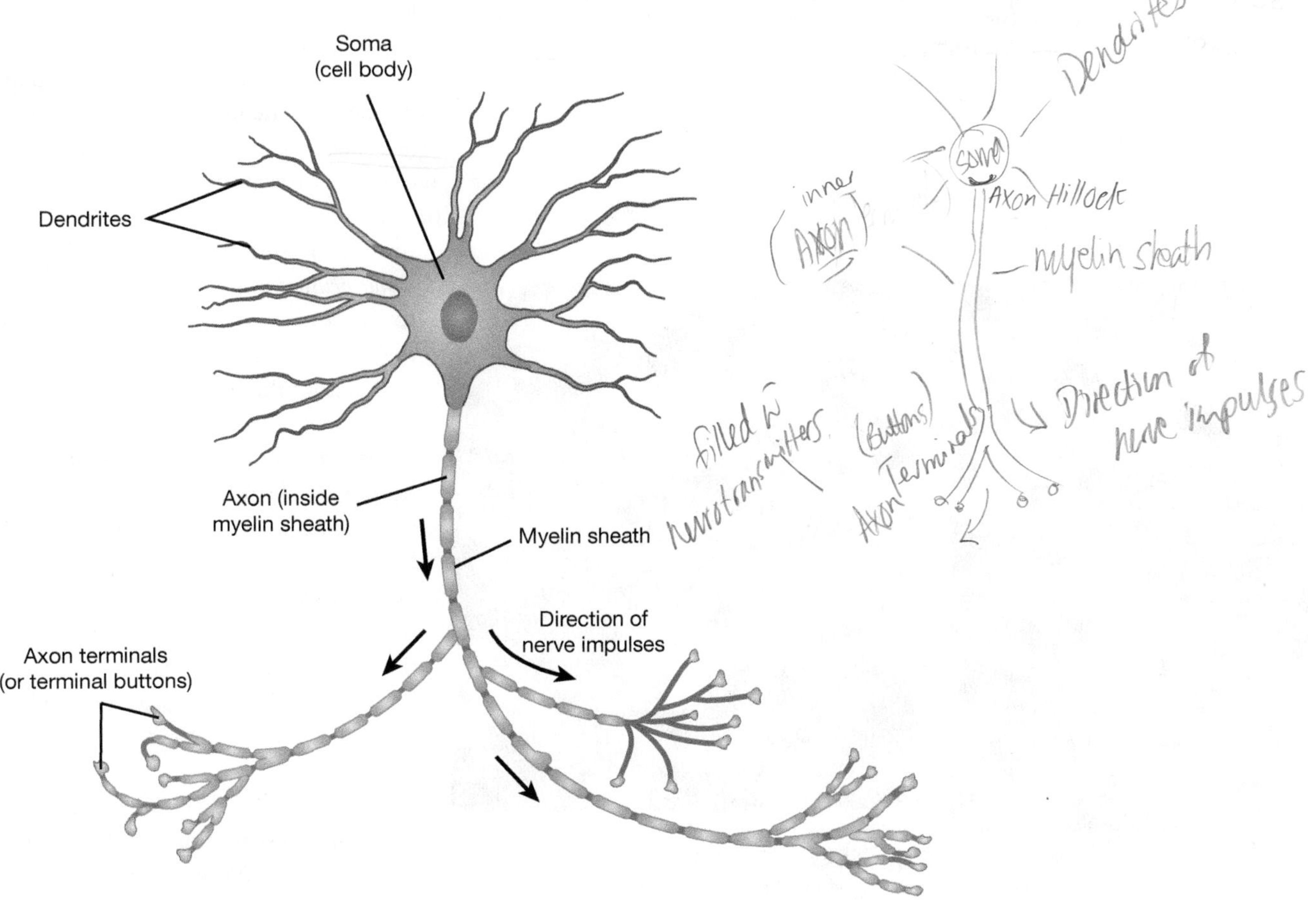

{FIG. 3.12} **A Neuron and Its Key Components** Each part of a nerve cell is specialized for a specific task.

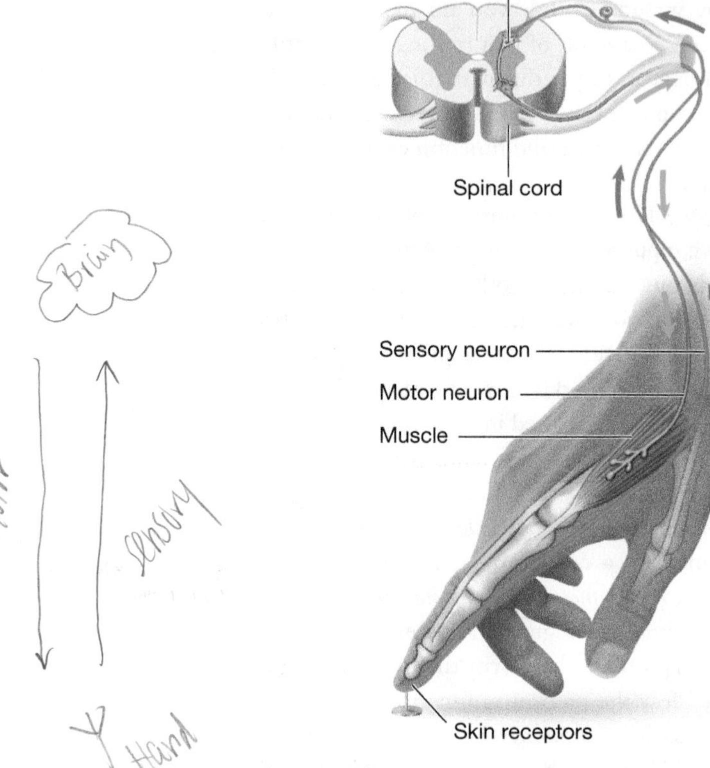

{FIG. 3.13} **Sensory and Motor Neurons** Sensory neurons carry information toward the spinal cord and the brain, whereas motor neurons send messages to muscles of the body. The interneuron links the sensory and motor neurons. This is the pathway of a simple withdrawal response to a painful stimulus.

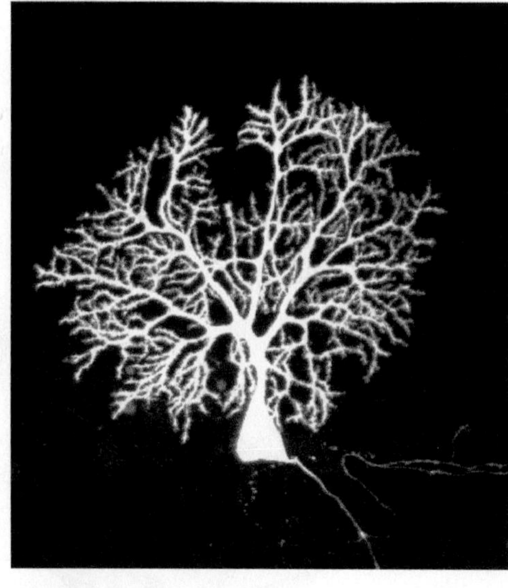

Left: Ralph Jr/Getty Images; right: David Becker/Getty Images

Many sensory neurons (left image) are quite simple and have few dendrites. Neurons in the cerebellum (right image) have large dendritic branches. These structural differences are related to the different functions served by these different neurons.

branches radiating from the cell body that receive messages from other cells and transmit those messages toward the rest of the cell. At any given point in time, a neuron will receive input from several other neurons (sometimes over 1000 other neurons!). These impulses from other cells will travel across the neuron to the base of the cell body known as the *axon hillock*. If the axon hillock receives enough stimulation from other neurons, it will initiate a chemical reaction that will flow down the rest of the neuron.

This chemical reaction is the initial step in a neuron communicating with other cells (i.e., influencing whether other cells will fire or not). The activity will travel from the axon hillock along a tail-like structure that protrudes from the cell body. This structure, the **axon**, *transports information in the form of electrochemical reactions from the cell body to the end of the neuron.* When the activity reaches the end of the axon, it will arrive at *axon terminals*, bulb-like extensions filled with vesicles (little bags of molecules). These vesicles contain **neurotransmitters**, *the chemicals that function as messengers allowing neurons to communicate with each other.* The impulse travelling down the axon will stimulate the release of these neurotransmitters, thus allowing neural communication to take place. Many different types of neurotransmitters exist, and each can have a number of different functions—something we will explore in more detail later in this module.

Although all neurons are designed to transmit information, not all neurons perform the same function. *Sensory neurons* receive information from the bodily senses and bring it toward the brain. Neurons that respond to touch or pain sensations of the skin bring the message toward the spinal cord and to the brain. In contrast, *motor neurons* carry messages away from the brain and spinal cord and toward muscles in order to control their flexion and extension (see Figure 3.13).

Within the brain itself, the structure and function of neurons varies considerably. Some cells have few if any dendrites extending from the cell body; these cells do not perform tasks requiring a lot of interactions with other neurons. In contrast, some neurons have huge branches of dendrites. Obviously, these latter neurons will perform functions involving more communication between neurons. The key point is that these differences between neurons are not simply due to chance—they have a purpose. The physical structure of a neuron is related to the function it performs.

GLIAL CELLS Although neurons are essential for our ability to sense, move, and think, they cannot function without support from other cells. This support comes from different types of cells collectively known as *glia* (Greek for "glue"). **Glial cells** *are specialized cells*

MYTHS IN MIND

We Are Born with All the Brain Cells We Will Ever Have

For decades, neuroscience taught us that nerves do not regenerate; in other words, scientists believed that we are born with all of the brain cells we will ever have. This conclusion made perfect sense because no one had ever seen new neurons form in adults, and severe neurological damage is often permanent.

In the past 15 years or so, however, advances in brain science have challenged this belief (Wojtowicz, 2012). Researchers have observed *neurogenesis*—the formation of new neurons—in a limited number of brain regions, particularly in a region critical for learning and memory (Eriksson et al., 1998; Tashiro et al., 2007). The growth of a new cell, including neurons, starts with *stem cells*—a unique type of cell that does not have a predestined function. When a stem cell divides, the resulting cells can become part of just about anything—bone, kidney, or brain tissue. The deciding factor seems to be the stem cell's chemical environment (Abematsu et al., 2006).

Our increased understanding of neurogenesis has raised some exciting possibilities—perhaps scientists can discover how to trigger the neural growth in other parts of the nervous system. Doing so might allow scientists to repair damaged brain structures or to add cells to brain areas affected by degenerative diseases like Parkinson's disease and Alzheimer's disease. When this technology is developed, there may finally be hope for recovery from injury and disease in all nerve cells.

of the nervous system that are involved in mounting immune responses in the brain, removing waste, and synchronizing the activity of the billions of neurons that constitute the nervous system. Given that glial cells perform so many different support functions, it should come as no surprise to learn that they outnumber neurons in the brain by a ratio of approximately 10 to 1.

A critical function served by certain glial cells is to insulate the axon of a neuron. These glial cells form a white substance called **myelin**, *a fatty sheath that insulates axons from one another, resulting in increased speed and efficiency of neural communication.* In an unmyelinated axon, the neural impulse decays quickly and needs to be regenerated along the axon; the myelin protects the impulse from this decay, thus reducing how often the impulse needs to be regenerated. The speed difference between axons with and without myelin is substantial. Axons without myelin transmit information at speeds ranging from 0.5 to 10 m/s (metres per second); myelinated axons transmit information at speeds of up to 150 m/s (Hartline & Coleman, 2007; Hursh, 1939). For obvious reasons, most neurons in the brain have myelin.

When the myelin sheath is damaged, the efficiency of the axon decreases substantially. For instance, *multiple sclerosis* is a disease in which the immune system does not recognize myelin and attacks it—a process that can devastate the structural and functional integrity of the nervous system. When myelin breaks down in multiple sclerosis, it impairs the ability of the affected neurons to transmit information along their axons. As a result, groups of brain structures that normally fire together to produce a behaviour can no longer work as a functional network (Rocca et al., 2010; Shu et al., 2011). It would be similar to trying to drive a car that is missing a wheel. The specific symptoms associated with multiple sclerosis differ depending upon where in the brain the myelin damage occurred. Numbness or tingling sensations could be caused by the disruption of sensory nerve cell signals that should otherwise reach the brain. Problems with voluntary, coordinated movement could be due to the breakdown of myelin that supports motor nerves. The important point is that damage to a small group of axons can lead to impairments in the functioning of large networks of brain areas (Rocca et al., 2012).

Listen
Stem Cells

As you can see, each part of an individual neuron and glial cell performs an important function. Ultimately, however, it is the activity of networks of nerve cells that allows messages to be transmitted within the brain and the rest of the body. This activity involves the most important function a neuron can perform: to fire.

THE NEURON'S ELECTRICAL SYSTEM: RESTING AND ACTION POTENTIALS Neural activity is based on changes in the concentrations of charged atoms called *ions*. When a neuron is not transmitting information, the outside of the neuron has a relatively high concentration of positively charged ions, particularly sodium and potassium, while the interior of the axon has fewer positively charged ions as well as a relatively high concentration of negatively charged chloride ions. This difference in charge between the inside and outside of the cell leaves the inside of the axon with a negative charge of approximately −70 millivolts (−70 mV; see the first panel of Figure 3.14). This *relatively stable state during which the cell is not transmitting messages* is known as its **resting potential**.

Explore
Virtual Brain: Neural Conduction

Importantly, this seemingly stable resting state involves a great deal of tension. This is because of two forces, the *electrostatic gradient* and the *concentration gradient*. Don't let these technical terms scare you: the electrostatic gradient just means that the inside and outside of the cell have different charges (negative and positive, respectively), and the concentration gradient just means that different types of ions are more densely packed on one side of the membrane than on the other (e.g., there

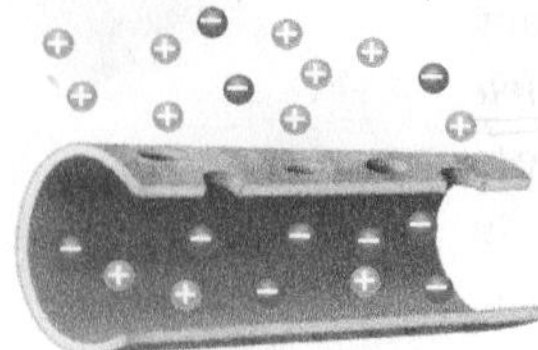

Resting potential.

Positively charged ions rush into the cell during an action potential.

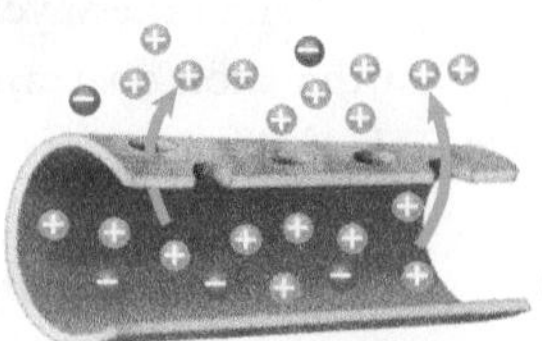

After the nerve has fired, the positively charged ions are pumped back out of the cell.

{FIG. 3.14} **Electrical Charges of the Inner and Outer Regions of Nerve Cells** The inner and outer environments of a nerve cell at rest differ in terms of their electrical charge. During the resting potential, there is a net negative charge. When a nerve cell is stimulated, generating an action potential, positively charged ions rush inside the cell membrane. After the cell has fired, the positively charged ions are channelled back outside the nerve cell as it returns to a resting state. **Click on this figure in your eText to see more details.**

Simulate
How Synapses Work

Explore
The Synapse

Simulate
Membrane Transport

Explore
The Action Potential

Simulate
Closer Look: Action Potential

are more sodium ions outside the cell than inside the cell). However, most substances have a tendency to move from areas of high concentration to areas of low concentration whenever possible; in other words, substances spread out whenever they can so that they are evenly distributed. So, if small pores (known as *ion channels*) opened up in the neuron's cell membrane, there would be a natural tendency for positively charged sodium ions to rush into the cell.

This is what happens when a neuron is stimulated. The surge of positive ions into the cell changes the potential of the neuron (e.g., changing from –70 mV to –68 mV). These charges flow down the dendrites and cross the cell body to the axon hillock, where the cell body meets the axon. If enough positively charged ions reach the axon hillock to push its charge past that cell's firing threshold (e.g., –55 mV), the neuron will then initiate an **action potential**, *a wave of electrical activity that originates at the base of the axon and rapidly travels down its length* (see the middle panel of Figure 3.14). When an action potential occurs, the charge of that part of the axon changes from approximately –70 mV to approximately +35 mV; in other words, the cell changes from being negatively to positively charged (see Figure 3.15). This change does not occur along the entire axon at once. Rather, as one part of the axon becomes depolarized, it forces open the ion channels ahead of it, thus causing the action potential to move down the length of the axon as positively charged ions rush through the membrane pores (Hodgkin, 1937). This pattern continues until the action potential reaches the axon terminal.

Of course, if this were the entire story, then all of our neurons would fire once and never fire again because the ion channels would remain open. Luckily for us, there are mechanisms in place to help our neurons return to their resting state (–70 mV) so that they can fire again. At each point of the axon, the ion channels slam shut as soon as the action potential occurs. The sodium ions that had rushed into the axon are then rapidly pumped back out of the cell, returning it to a resting state. This process of removing the sodium ions from the cell often causes the neuron to become *hyperpolarized;* this means that the cell is more negative than its normal resting potential (e.g., –72 mV instead of –70 mV). This additional negativity makes the cell *less* likely to fire. It normally takes 2–3 milliseconds for the membrane to adjust back to its normal resting potential. This *brief period in which a neuron cannot fire is known as a* **refractory period**.

When the action potential reaches the axon terminal, it triggers the release of that cell's neurotransmitters into the **synapses**, *the microscopically small spaces that separate individual nerve cells*. The cell that releases these chemicals is known as the *presynaptic cell* ("before the synapse") whereas the cell that receives this input is known as the *postsynaptic cell* (or "after the synapse"). The dendrites of the postsynaptic cell contain specialized receptors that are designed to hold specific molecules, including neurotransmitters. Then, this process of neural communication will begin again.

Although this description of an action potential explains how a neuron fires, it does not explain how the nervous system differentiates between a weak and a strong neural response. It would make intuitive sense for a stronger stimulus (e.g., a loud noise) to produce a larger action potential than a weak stimulus (e.g., someone

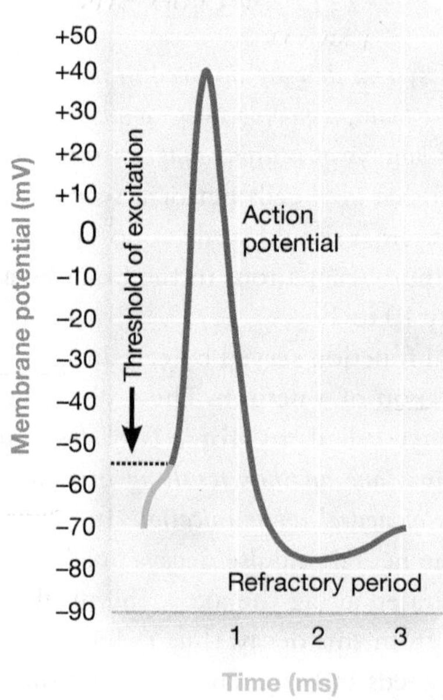

{FIG. 3.15} **Time Course and Phases of a Nerve Cell Going from a Resting Potential to an Action Potential** Nerve cells fire once the threshold of excitation is reached. During the action potential, positively charged ions rush inside the cell membrane, creating a net positive charge within the cell. Positively charged ions are then forced out of the cell as it returns to its resting potential.

whispering); however, this is not the case. When stimulated, a given neuron always fires at the same intensity and speed. This activity adheres to the **all-or-none principle**: *Individual nerve cells fire at the same strength every time an action potential occurs.* Neurons do not "sort of" fire, or "overfire"—they just fire. Instead, the strength of a sensation is determined by the *rate* at which nerve cells fire as well as by the number of nerve cells that are stimulated. A stimulus is experienced intensely because a greater number of cells are stimulated, and the firing of each cell occurs repeatedly.

Quick Quiz 3.2a

Neural Communication

KNOW ...

1 A positive electrical charge that is carried away from the cell body and down the length of the axon is a(n) ______.

- **A** refractory period
- **B** resting potential
- **C** action potential
- **D** dendrite

2 Which of the following is a function of glial cells?

- **A** Glial cells slow down the activity of nerve cells.
- **B** Glial cells help form myelin.
- **C** Glial cells suppress the immune system response.
- **D** Glial cells contain the nucleus that houses the cell's genetic material.

UNDERSTAND ...

3 A neuron will fire when the ions inside the cell body are

- **A** in the resting potential.
- **B** shifted to a threshold more positive than the resting potential.
- **C** shifted to a threshold more negative than the resting potential.
- **D** in the refractory period.

4 Sensory and motor nerves differ in that

- **A** only sensory neurons have dendrites.
- **B** only motor neurons have axons.
- **C** sensory neurons carry messages toward the brain, and motor neurons carry information away from the brain.
- **D** sensory neurons carry messages away from the brain, and motor neurons carry information toward the brain.

Answers can be found on page ANS-1.

The Chemical Messengers: Neurotransmitters and Hormones

As you read in the first part of this module, the *presynaptic neuron* releases neurotransmitters into the synapse; a fraction of these neurotransmitters will bind to receptors on the *postsynaptic neuron*. This binding can have one of two effects on the postsynaptic cell. If the actions of a neurotransmitter cause the neuron's membrane potential to become less negative (e.g., changing from −70 mV to −68 mV), it is referred to as *excitatory* because it has increased the probability that an action potential will occur in a given period of time. In contrast, if the actions of a neurotransmitter cause the membrane potential to become more negative (e.g., changing from −70 mV to −72 mV), it is referred to as *inhibitory* because it has decreased the likelihood that an action potential will occur. An important factor in determining whether a postsynaptic neuron is excited or inhibited is the type of neurotransmitter(s) binding with its receptors.

{FIG. 3.16} **The Lock-and-Key Analogy for Matching of Neurotransmitters and Receptors** The molecular structures of different neurotransmitters must have specific shapes in order to bind with the receptors on a neuron.

Many different types of neurotransmitters have been identified, although most neurons send and receive a limited number of neurotransmitters. Each neurotransmitter typically has its own unique molecular shape. A lock-and-key analogy is sometimes used to explain how neurotransmitters and their receptors work: When neurotransmitters are released at the axon terminal, they cross the synapse and fit in a particular receptor of the dendrite like a key in a lock (see Figure 3.16).

After neurotransmitter molecules have bound to postsynaptic receptors of a neighbouring cell, they are released back into the **synaptic cleft**, *the minute space between the axon terminal (terminal button) and the dendrite.* This process is almost as important as the action potential itself. Prolonged stimulation of the receptors makes it more difficult for the cell to return to its resting potential; this is obviously necessary for the neuron to be able to fire again. Therefore, if a neurotransmitter remained latched onto a receptor for long periods of time, it would decrease the number of times that the neurons could fire (i.e., it would make your brain less powerful).

Once neurotransmitters have detached from the receptors and float back into the synapse, they are either broken down by enzymes or go through **reuptake**, *a process whereby neurotransmitter molecules that have been released into the synapse are reabsorbed into the axon terminals of the presynaptic neuron* (see Figure 3.17). Reuptake serves as a sort of natural recycling system for neurotransmitters. It is also a process that is modified by many commonly used drugs. For example, the class of antidepressant drugs known as selective serotonin reuptake inhibitors (SSRIs), not surprisingly, inhibits reuptake of the neurotransmitter serotonin; in this way, SSRIs such as fluoxetine (Prozac)

Simulate Neurotransmitters: Communicators between Neurons

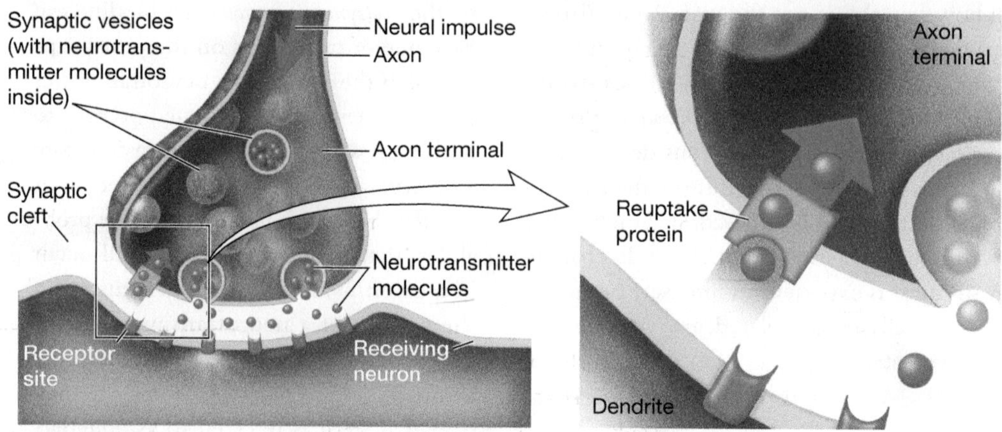

{FIG. 3.17} **Major Events at the Synapse** As the action potential reaches the axon terminals, neurotransmitters (packed into spherically shaped vesicles) are released across the synaptic cleft. The neurotransmitters bind to the postsynaptic (receiving) neuron. In the process of reuptake, some neurotransmitters are returned to the presynaptic neuron via reuptake proteins. These neurotransmitters are then repackaged into synaptic vesicles.

eventually increase the amount of serotonin available at the synapse. The result is a decrease in depression and anxiety. The process of reuptake occurs for a number of different neurotransmitters released throughout the nervous system.

Watch
In the Real World: Neurotransmitters

TYPES OF NEUROTRANSMITTERS There are literally dozens of neurotransmitters influencing the functioning of your brain as you read this module. The various neurotransmitters listed in Table 3.1 are only a small sample of the chemicals that produce your behaviour. As noted in the previous section of this module, each of these neurotransmitters has a molecular structure and is designed to match particular types of receptors, similar to how different keys will fit into different locks. These substances also differ in terms of the specific brain areas they target. As a result, different neurotransmitters will have different effects on our behaviour.

The most common neurotransmitters in the brain are *glutamate* and *GABA*. **Glutamate** *is the most common excitatory neurotransmitter in the brains of vertebrates* (Dingledine et al., 1999; Meldrum, 2000). It is involved in a number of processes, including our ability to form new memories (Bliss & Collingridge, 1993; Peng et al., 2011). Abnormal functioning of glutamate-releasing neurons has also been implicated in a number of brain disorders including the triggering of seizures in epilepsy (During & Spencer, 1993) and damage caused by strokes (Hazell, 2007; McCulloch et al., 1991). In contrast, **GABA** (**gamma-amino butyric acid**, for those of you enraged by acronyms) *is the primary inhibitory neurotransmitter of the nervous system, meaning that it prevents neurons from generating action potentials.* It accomplishes this feat by reducing the negative charge of neighbouring neurons even further than their resting state of −70 mV. When GABA binds to receptors, it causes an influx of negatively charged chloride ions to enter the cell, which is the opposite net effect of what happens when a neuron is stimulated. As an inhibitor, GABA facilitates sleep (Tobler et al., 2001) and reduces arousal of the nervous system. Low levels of GABA have been linked to epilepsy, likely because there is an imbalance between inhibitory GABA and excitatory glutamate (Upton, 1994).

Table 3.1 :: Major Neurotransmitters and Their Functions

NEUROTRANSMITTER	SOME MAJOR FUNCTIONS
Glutamate	Excites nervous system; memory and autonomic nervous system reactions
GABA (gamma-amino butyric acid)	Inhibits brain activity; lowers arousal, anxiety, and excitation; facilitates sleep
Acetylcholine	Movement; attention
Dopamine	Control of movement; reward-seeking behaviour; cognition and attention
Norepinephrine	Memory; attention to new or important stimuli; regulation of sleep and mood
Serotonin	Regulation of sleep, appetite, mood

Another common neurotransmitter is acetylcholine. **Acetylcholine** *is one of the most widespread neurotransmitters within the body, found at the junctions between nerve cells and skeletal muscles; it is very important for voluntary movement.* Acetylcholine released from neurons connected to the spinal cord binds to receptors on muscles. The change in the electrical properties of the muscle fibres leads to a contraction of that muscle. This link between the nervous system and muscles is known as *a neuromuscular junction*. A number of animals release venom that influences the release of acetylcholine, including the black widow spider (Diaz, 2004) and a number of snakes. Recall the neurotoxic snake venom discussed at the beginning of this module: This toxin disrupts the activity of acetylcholine transmission at the neuromuscular junctions. Different snakes carry slightly different types of neurotoxic venom. Some types of venom block acetylcholine release at the presynaptic terminals, preventing its release into the synapse. Another type of venom blocks the receptors on the postsynaptic cell, preventing acetylcholine from binding to them (Lewis & Gutmann, 2004). Either way, the effects are devastating.

In addition to these effects in neuromuscular junctions, acetylcholine activity in the brain is associated with attention and memory (Drachman & Leavitt, 1974; Himmelheber et al., 2000). Altered levels of this neurotransmitter have also been linked to cognitive deficits associated with aging and Alzheimer's disease (Bartus et al., 1982; Craig et al., 2011). Indeed, several drugs used to reduce the progression of Alzheimer's disease are designed to slow the removal of acetylcholine from the synapse, thus allowing it to have a larger effect on postsynaptic cells (Darvesh et al., 2003). The fact that acetylcholine can influence functions ranging from movement to memory shows us that *where* in the nervous system a neurotransmitter is released can have a dramatic influence on *what* roles that neurotransmitter will serve.

This point is particularly noticeable when one discusses a class of neurotransmitters known as the *monoamines.* This group of brain chemicals includes the well-known neurotransmitters dopamine, norepinephrine, and serotonin. **Dopamine** *is a monoamine neurotransmitter involved in such varied functions as mood, control of voluntary movement, and processing of rewarding experiences.* When reading this definition, you can't help but be stunned by the variety of processes influenced by dopamine. This breadth is due to the fact that dopamine is released by neurons in (at least) three pathways extending to different parts of the brain including areas in the centre of the brain related to movement and to reward responses (Koob & Volkow, 2010; Martinez & Narendren, 2010; see Module 5.3) and areas in the front third of the brain involved with controlling our attention (Robbins, 2000).

Attention is also influenced by our overall alertness or arousal, a characteristic that is affected by the neurotransmitter norepinephrine. **Norepinephrine** (also known as *noradrenaline*) *is a monoamine synthesized from dopamine molecules that is involved in regulating stress responses, including increasing arousal, attention, and heart rate.* Norepinephrine is formed in specialized nuclei in the bottom of the brain (known as the *brain stem*) and projects throughout the cortex, influencing the activity of a number of different systems ranging from wakefulness to attention (Berridge & Waterhouse, 2003). It also projects down the spinal cord and serves as part of the "fight-or-flight" response to threatening stimuli (Zimmerman et al., 2012). Norepinephrine often works alongside *epinephrine* (also known as *adrenaline*), a hormone and neurotransmitter created in the adrenal gland on the kidneys. Both norepinephrine and epinephrine energize individuals to help them become more engaged with a given activity. (Interesting trivia: Epinephrine has its name because the name *adrenaline* was trademarked by a drug company.)

Finally, **serotonin** *is a monoamine involved in regulating mood, sleep, aggression, and appetite* (Cappadocia et al., 2009; Young & Leyton, 2002). It is formed in the brain stem and projects throughout the brain and spinal cord. Serotonin is the neurotransmitter that you are most likely to have heard of due to its critical role in depression. As discussed earlier in this module, many antidepressant medications block the reuptake of serotonin, thus ensuring that this substance remains in the synapse for longer durations. The result is an elevation of mood and a decrease in symptoms of depression and anxiety. Research also indicates that serotonin is related to the perception of pain. For instance, individuals prone to migraine headaches are also more likely to have lower levels of serotonin in the brain (Hamel, 2007; Sicuteri & Testi, 1961). Additionally, altered levels of serotonin have been found in patients with chronic pain conditions such as fibromyalgia; indeed, reviews of the research indicate that different medications promoting the activity of serotonin decrease reports of pain by 50% (Bardin, 2011; Häuser et al., 2013). However, we must be careful not to assume that a complex process like pain can be explained by the activity of a single neurotransmitter. In fact, a number of different substances have been linked to these unpleasant experiences.

WORKING THE SCIENTIFIC LITERACY MODEL

Pain and Substance P

Pain is not a simple process. Instead, there are a number of different neural systems and neurotransmitters involved with our responses to painful stimuli (see Module 4.4). In fact, serotonin, norepinephrine, and dopamine have all been implicated in some part of the pain response. One neurotransmitter that hasn't been discussed yet, however, is known as **Substance P**, *a neurotransmitter involved in the experience of pain.*

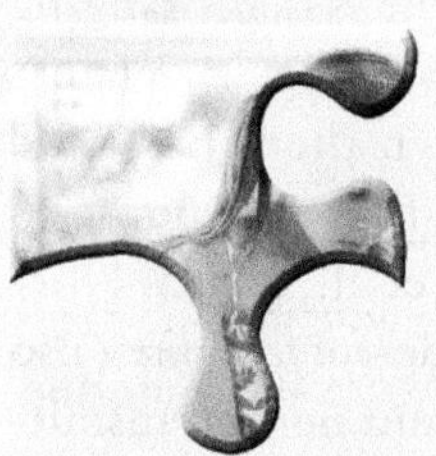

What do we know about Substance P?

Substance P was first discovered in 1931 when a paste made from the brain and intestine of a horse was found to cause muscles to contract (Von Euler & Gaddum, 1931); that was one heck of a party. It was named Substance P because the paste became powdery (Gaddum & Schild, 1934). Twenty years later, Austrian physiologist Fred Lembeck determined that this substance was associated with the transmission of pain (Harrison & Geppetti, 2001; Lembeck, 1953). Lembeck and others noted that Substance P was found in the dorsal root of the spinal cord, an area that transmits pain information back to the brain (Otsuka et al., 1972), as well as in several different brain areas related to the pain response (Mantyh, 2002). So, when tissue on the skin surface is damaged, sensory nerves carry messages to the spinal cord and then up to the brain. In turn, these CNS structures release Substance P, giving rise to the perception of pain.

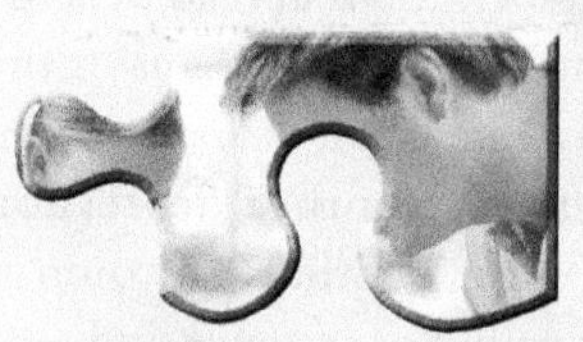

How can science explain what Substance P does?

From an evolutionary standpoint, it makes sense to have pathways specialized for the perception of pain. Pain is an important messenger telling you to stop doing something that is harming your body. Compelling evidence for the role of Substance P comes from an examination of the brain areas containing Substance P receptors. These receptors are densely packed in a structure in the middle of the brain called the *periaqueductal grey* (Yip & Chahl, 2001). This brain region receives pain- and temperature-related input from the spinal cord and sends it to different areas of the *cerebral cortex*, the wrinkled outer surface of the brain involved with many sophisticated processes. It also receives input from the cortex and transmits it through the spinal cord to the rest of the body. The fact that a neural area known to be associated with pain perception also contains receptors for Substance P suggests that this neurotransmitter is likely involved with pain responses.

However, this is not the only part of the brain containing Substance P receptors. They are also found in the amygdala (which responds to fear and arousal) and the hypothalamus (which is related to fight-or-flight responses and the release of different hormones). Why would this be the case? One possibility is that pain is not simply a physical sensation. A large body of research now suggests that when we feel pain, it is a combination of *both* sensation and an emotional response. Sometimes the tears that fall after we stub our toe are due not only to being hurt, but to being frustrated (among many other emotions).

Can we critically evaluate this research?

Evidence in favour of the role of Substance P in pain perception comes from a group of patients with a rare condition called *congenital insensitivity to pain*. These individuals lack the ability to perceive pain, and even in early childhood acquire significant damage to the skin, joints, eyes, and other body regions. Because they lack a pain response, these individuals do not take action to prevent physical damage to the body. Research in the U.K. (ironically conducted by someone named Dr. Misery) found that some individuals with this disorder lack Substance P receptors in the peripheral nerves (Misery et al., 1999). Studies such as this provide strong evidence for this neurotransmitter's role in pain perception.

More contentious is the issue of pain and emotion. There is a great deal of evidence linking emotion and pain. For instance, social "pain" resulting from being rejected activates similar brain areas as physical pain (Eisenberger, 2012; Eisenberger et al., 2003). There is also evidence that patients with chronic pain conditions are also more likely to suffer from depression (Dunne & Dunne, 2012). Interestingly, some investigators have found that drugs that influence the levels of Substance P in the brain have antidepressant properties (Adell, 2004). However, these researchers are quick to note that such drugs could also potentially influence other neurotransmitter systems. Therefore, more research is needed to clarify this issue.

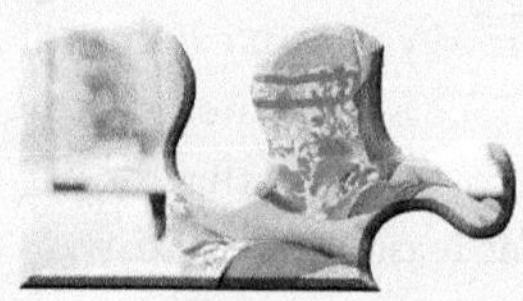

Why is this relevant?

Millions of people suffer from chronic pain. In addition to compromising the well-being of affected individuals, problems with pain translate into reduced work productivity, increased health care costs, and, for some people, an increased risk of developing dependence on or addiction to prescription painkillers (Baumeister et al., 2012). By better understanding the physiological basis of pain, including how brain areas related to pain and emotion interact, researchers may be able to develop more effective drugs and other techniques to help alleviate pain. Thus, the study of neurotransmitters like Substance P could eventually improve the lives of millions of patients and their families. That's research of substance!

Martin Barraud/OJO Images/Getty Images

DRUG EFFECTS ON NEUROTRANSMISSION

Drugs of all varieties, from prescription to recreational, affect the chemical signalling that takes place between nerve cells. **Agonists** *are drugs that enhance or mimic the effects of a neurotransmitter's action.* The well-known drug nicotine is an acetylcholine agonist, meaning that it stimulates the receptor sites for this neurotransmitter. The antianxiety drug alprazolam (Xanax) is a GABA agonist—it causes relaxation by increasing the activity of this inhibitory neurotransmitter. Drugs can behave as agonists either directly or indirectly. A drug that behaves as a *direct agonist* physically binds to that neurotransmitter's receptors at the postsynaptic cells (e.g., nicotine molecules attach themselves to receptors that acetylcholine molecules would normally stimulate). A drug that acts as an *indirect agonist* facilitates the effects of a neurotransmitter, but does not physically bind to the same part of the receptor as the neurotransmitter. For example, a drug that blocks the process of reuptake would be an indirect agonist. A drug that attaches to another binding site on a receptor but does not interfere with the neurotransmitter's binding would also be an indirect agonist.

Drugs classified as **antagonists** *inhibit neurotransmitter activity by blocking receptors or preventing synthesis of a neurotransmitter* (see Figure 3.18). You may have heard of the cosmetic medical procedure known as a Botox injection. Botox, which is derived from the nerve-paralyzing bacterium that causes botulism, blocks the action of acetylcholine by binding to its postsynaptic receptor sites (Dastoor et al., 2007). Blocking acetylcholine could lead to paralysis of the heart and lungs; however, when very small amounts are injected into tissue around the eyes, the antagonist simply paralyzes the muscles that lead to wrinkles. When muscles are not used, they cannot stretch the skin—hence the reduction in wrinkling when acetylcholine activity is blocked. Because Botox directly binds with acetylcholine receptors and thus prevents acetylcholine from doing so, it is considered a *direct antagonist.* If a chemical reduces the influence of a neurotransmitter *without* physically blocking the receptor, it would be classified as an *indirect antagonist.*

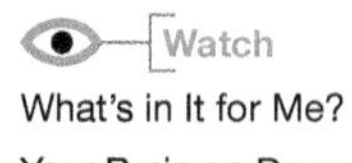

Watch
What's in It for Me? Your Brain on Drugs

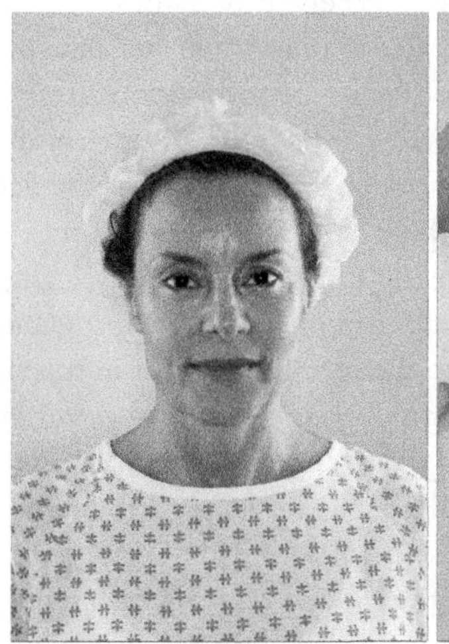

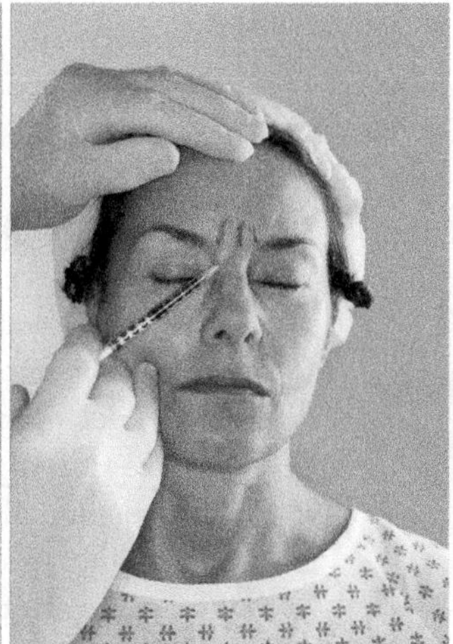

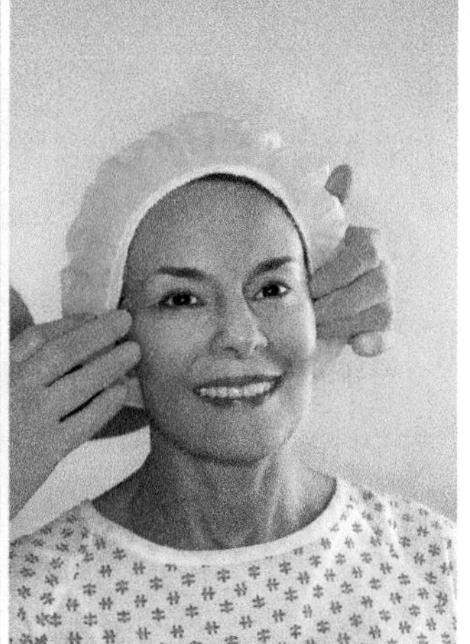

Thinkstock/Getty Images

Botox injections paralyze muscles, which can increase youthful appearance in areas such as the face.

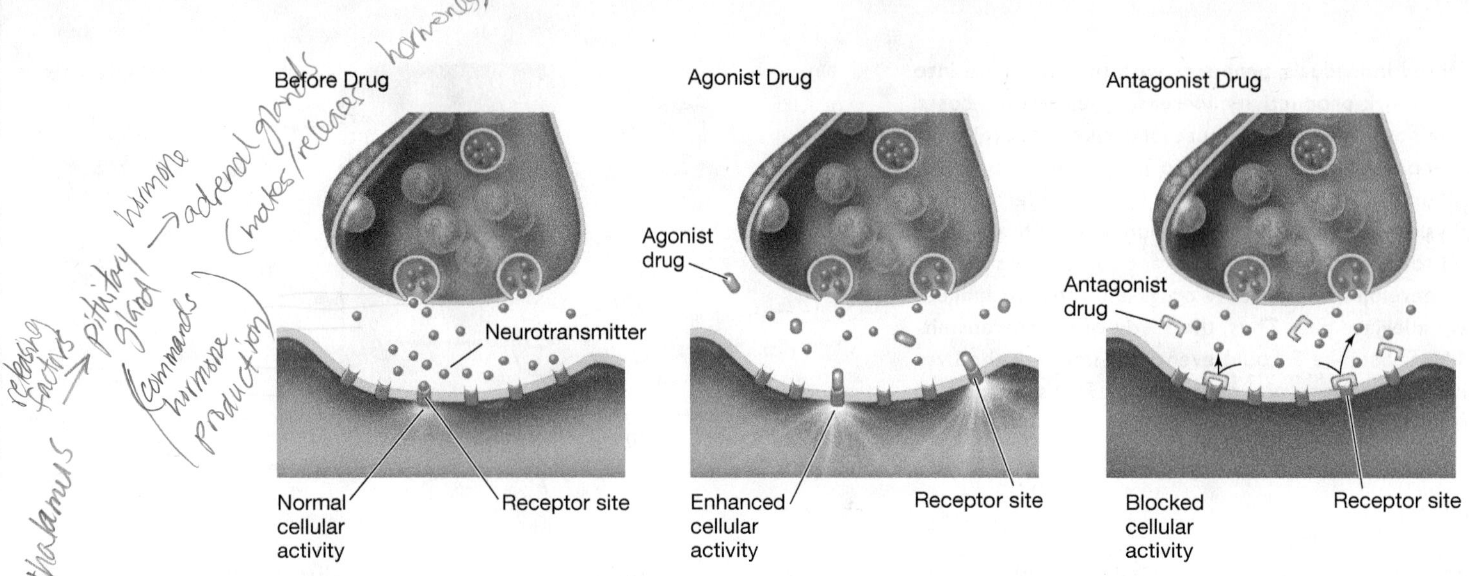

{FIG. 3.18} **Drug Effects at the Synapses** Drugs can act as agonists by facilitating the effects of a neurotransmitter, or as antagonists by blocking these effects. **Click on this figure in your eText to see more details.**

Explore The Endocrine System

Watch The Endocrine System

HORMONES AND THE ENDOCRINE SYSTEM

Neurotransmitters are not the body's only chemical messenger system. **Hormones** *are chemicals secreted by the glands of the endocrine system.* Generally, neurotransmitters work almost immediately within the microscopic space of the synapse, whereas hormones are secreted into the bloodstream and travel throughout the body. Thus, the effects of hormones are much slower than those of neurotransmitters. With help from the nervous system, the endocrine system contributes to *homeostasis*—the balance of energy, metabolism, body temperature, and other basic functions that keeps the body working properly (see Figure 3.19; see

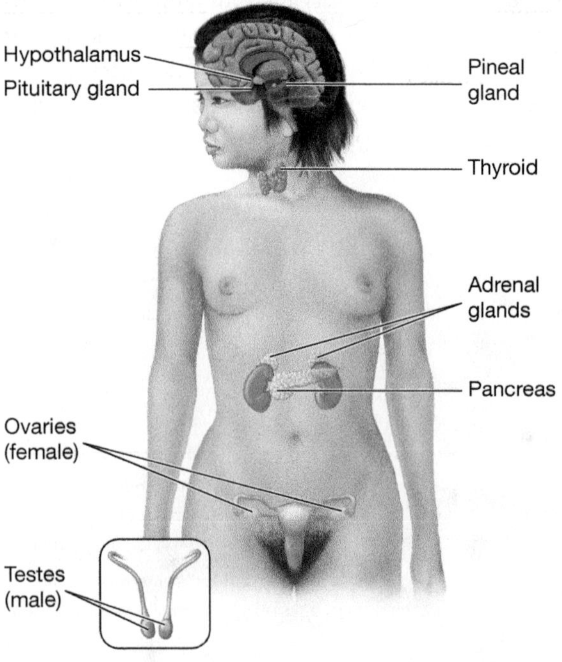

{FIG. 3.19} **The Endocrine System** Glands throughout the body release and exchange hormones. The hypothalamus interacts with the endocrine system to regulate hormonal processes.

Module 11.1). In other words, the brain triggers activity in the endocrine system which then influences the brain's activity via hormones. This cycle continues as our brain and body attempt to maintain the appropriate energy levels for dealing with the environment.

The brain area that is critical for this brain-endocrine relationship is the **hypothalamus**, *a brain structure that regulates basic biological needs and motivational systems.* The hypothalamus releases specialized chemicals called releasing factors that stimulate the **pituitary gland**—*the master gland of the endocrine system that produces hormones and sends commands about hormone production to the other glands of the endocrine system.* These hormones can be released by glands throughout the body before finding their way to the brain via the bloodstream.

How we respond to stress illustrates nicely how the nervous and endocrine systems influence each other. In psychological terms, stress is loosely defined as an imbalance between perceived demands and the perceived resources available to meet those demands. Such an imbalance might occur if you suddenly realize your midterm exam is tomorrow at 8:00 A.M. Your resources—time and energy—may not be enough to meet the demand of succeeding on the exam. The hypothalamus, however, sets chemical events in motion that physically prepare the body for stress. It signals the pituitary gland to release a hormone into the bloodstream that in turn stimulates the **adrenal glands**, *a pair of endocrine glands located adjacent to the kidneys that release stress hormones, such as cortisol and epinephrine.* Cortisol and epinephrine help mobilize the body during stress, thus providing enough energy for you to deal with the sudden increase in activity necessary to respond to the stress-inducing situation (see Module 14.2).

Another important chemical is **endorphin**, *a hormone produced by the pituitary gland and the hypothalamus* *that functions to reduce pain and induce feelings of pleasure.* Endorphins are released into the bloodstream during events such as strenuous exercise, sexual activity, or injury. They act on portions of the brain that are attuned to reward, reinforcement, and pleasure, inhibiting the perception of pain and increasing feelings of euphoria (extreme pleasantness and relaxation). Morphine—a drug derived from the poppy plant—binds to endorphin receptors (the term *endorphin* translates to *endogenous [internal] morphine*). Morphine molecules fit into the same receptor sites as endorphins and, therefore, produce the same painkilling and euphoric effects.

Testosterone is a hormone that serves multiple functions, including driving physical and sexual development over the long term, and surging during sexual activity and in response to threats. This hormone is often cited as an explanation for behaviour. It can be tempting to conclude that if a behaviour has a biological explanation, then the behaviour cannot change—and testosterone provides a great example. Because it is related to male sexual development and functioning, this hormone was traditionally targeted as an explanation for why men tend to be more physically aggressive than women. In other words, there was an assumption that testosterone *causes* aggression. (For the record, women have testosterone and it serves many of the same functions in them as it does in men.) In fact, the data do show that the highest levels of violence, aggression, and homicide occur among young males against other young males—that is, within the group whose members tend to have the highest levels of testosterone (Archer, 2004; O'Connor et al., 2004). But, the truth is much more complicated than simply attributing aggression to testosterone. Testosterone is *correlated* with more aggressive thoughts and feelings, but if aggressive behaviour is defined as physical violence, then the relationship between testosterone and aggression is actually rather weak (Archer et al., 2005; Book et al., 2001). In other words, testosterone levels are related to how we think and feel, but not necessarily to how we act.

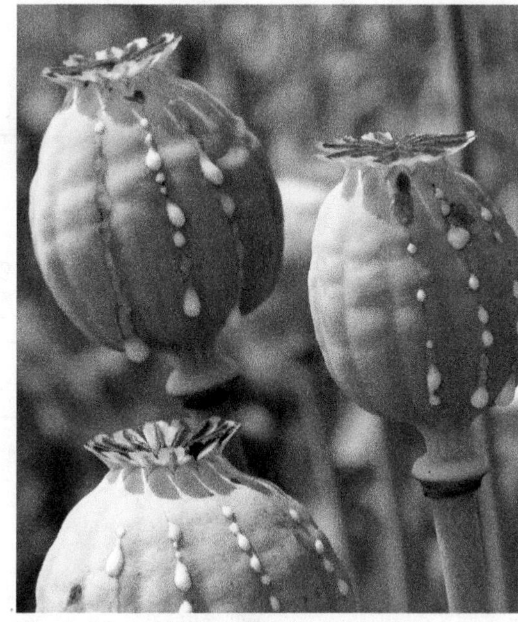

Martin Nemec/Shutterstock.com

Extracts from the seeds of some poppy flowers contain opium. Morphine and one of its derivatives, heroin, can be synthesized from these seeds.

NEURONS IN CONTEXT When reading about neuronal structures, neurotransmitters, and hormones, it is easy to lose sight of how these cells and molecules fit together with discussions of genetics (Module 3.1) and larger brain structures (Module 3.3). In the last few years, a number of genes related to different neurotransmitters have been identified. These genes can influence how the neurotransmitters are formed as well as processes such as reuptake. These seemingly minor differences in genes can affect neurotransmitter levels and thus how neurons communicate with each other. This alters the networks of neurons firing together in the brain; these networks of structures produce your thoughts, movements, and sensations. So, while a discussion of brain cells seems far removed from the science of behaviour, these brain cells are, in fact, what makes you "you."

Quick Quiz 3.2b The Chemical Messengers: Neurotransmitters and Hormones

KNOW ...

1 A(n) ________ is a drug that blocks the actions of a neurotransmitter.

A agonist
B antagonist
C stop agent
D endorphin

UNDERSTAND ...

2 To reverse the effects of neurotoxic venom from a snakebite, which of the following actions would likely be most effective?

A Give the patient a high dose of dopamine.
B Give the patient a substance that would allow the body to resume transmission of acetylcholine.
C Give the patient a drug that would increase GABA transmission.
D Give the patient an acetylcholine antagonist.

APPLY ...

3 People who experience a *loss* of pain sensation in the middle of exercise are likely having a rush of ________.

A adrenaline
B norepinephrine
C pituitary
D endorphin

ANALYZE ...

4 People often attribute male aggression to high levels of testosterone. Which of the following statements is an important consideration regarding this claim?

A High testosterone levels may be correlated with aggression, but may not necessarily be the cause of it.
B Testosterone is found exclusively in males and, therefore, is a likely cause of male aggression.
C Cultural factors are unrelated to testosterone levels.
D Testosterone does not affect aggressive behaviours.

Answers can be found on page ANS-1.

Module Summary

Module 3.2

Now that you have read this module you should

KNOW ...

- ***The key terminology associated with nerve cells, hormones, and their functioning:***

acetylcholine (p. 99)
action potential (p. 96)
adrenal glands (p. 102)
agonists (p. 101)
all-or-none principle (p. 97)
antagonists (p. 101)
axon (p. 94)
cell body (p. 93)
dendrites (p. 93)
dopamine (p. 99)
endorphin (p. 102)
GABA (gamma-amino butyric acid) (p. 98)
glial cells (p. 94)
glutamate (p. 98)
hormones (p. 102)
hypothalamus (p. 102)
myelin (p. 95)
neuron (p. 93)
neurotransmitters (p. 94)
norepinephrine (p. 99)
pituitary gland (p. 102)
refractory period (p. 96)
resting potential (p. 95)
reuptake (p. 97)
serotonin (p. 99)
Substance P (p. 100)
synapses (p. 96)
synaptic cleft (p. 97)

UNDERSTAND ...

- ***How nerve cells communicate.*** Nerve cells fire because of processes involving both electrical and chemical factors. A stimulated nerve cell goes from resting potential to action potential following an influx of positively charged ions inside the membrane of the cell. As the message reaches the end of the nerve cell, neurotransmitters are released into synapses and bind to neighbouring postsynaptic cells. Depending on the type of neurotransmitter, the effect can be either inhibitory or excitatory.
- ***The ways that drugs and other substances affect the brain.*** Drugs can be agonists or antagonists. A drug is an agonist if it enhances the effects of a neurotransmitter. This outcome occurs if the drug increases the release of a neurotransmitter, blocks reuptake, or mimics the neurotransmitter by binding to the postsynaptic cell. A drug is an antagonist if it blocks the effects of a neurotransmitter. Antagonists block neurotransmitter release, break down neurotransmitters in the synapse, or block neurotransmitters by binding to postsynaptic receptors.
- ***The roles that hormones play in our behaviour.*** Hormones have multiple influences on behaviour. The nervous system—in particular, the hypothalamus—interacts with the endocrine system in controlling the release of hormones. A few of humans' many hormonally controlled responses include reactions to stress and pain as well as sexual responses. Some hormones are associated with, though not necessarily a primary cause of, aggressive behaviour.

Rod Williams/naturepl.com

APPLY ...

- ***Your knowledge of neurotransmitters to form hypotheses about drug actions.*** In this module you read about how SSRIs slow down the reuptake process to increase the amount of serotonin at the synapse. Consider another drug—a monoamine oxidase inhibitor (MAOI).

1. Based on its name, *monoamine oxidase inhibitor,* which neurotransmitters would be affected by such a drug? (See page 98.)
2. If monoamine oxidase is an enzyme that breaks down monoamine transmitters, what would happen if a drug inhibits the enzyme? What effect would this action have on levels of the neurotransmitters (i.e., an overall increase or decrease)?
3. Would the effects of an MAOI resemble those of an SSRI? (SSRIs are discussed on page 97.) Check your answers on page ANS-1.

ANALYZE ...

- ***The claim that we are born with all the nerve cells we will ever have.*** Earlier in this module, a Myths in Mind feature (page 95) addressed the question of whether we are born with all of the nerve cells we will ever have. Although scientists once believed this to be true, we now know that neurogenesis—the growth of new neurons—takes place in several parts of the brain. One of these regions is the hippocampus, which is involved in learning and memory (see Module 7.1). In many other areas of the brain, neurogenesis has not been observed. Nevertheless, during normal development, neurons make new connections with neighbouring cells.

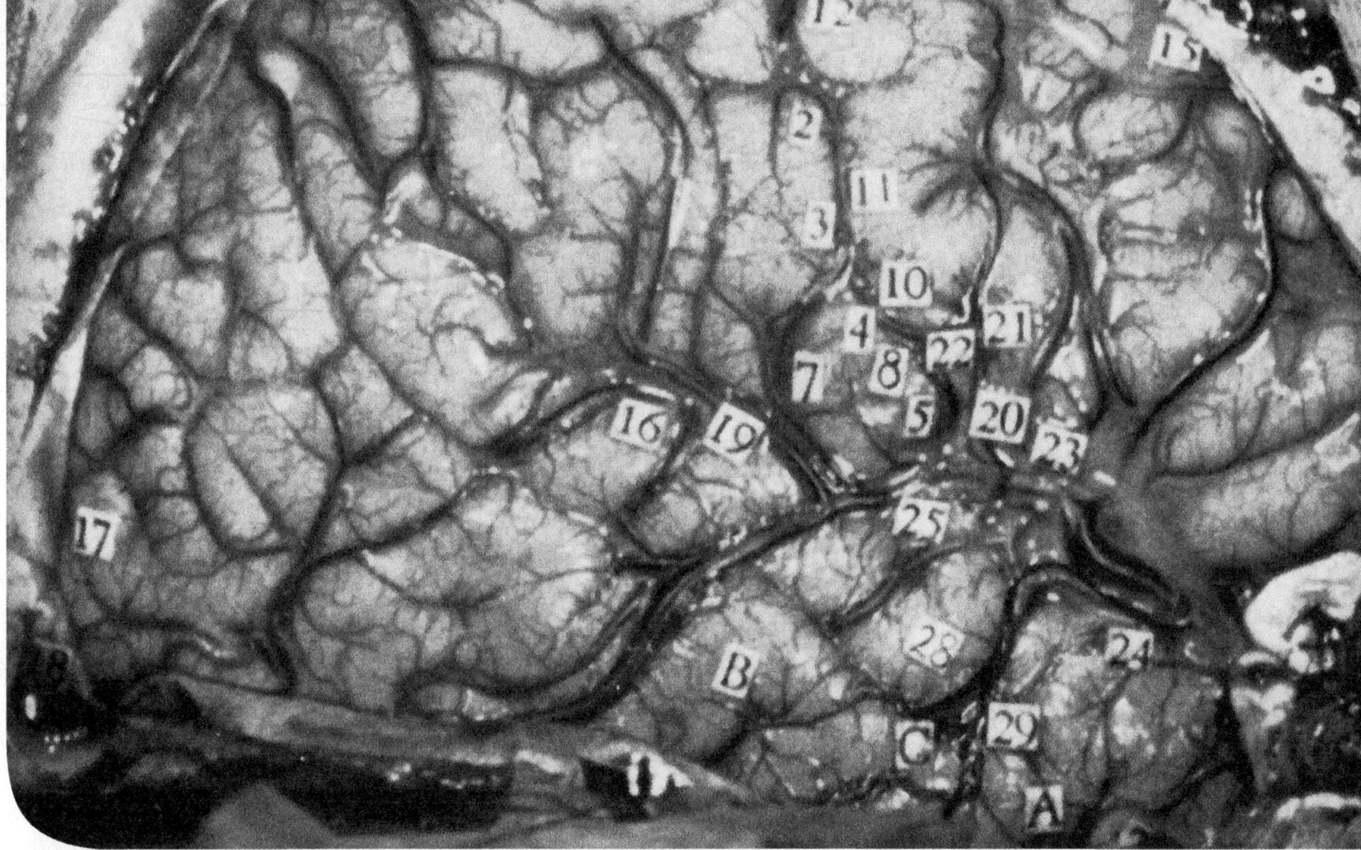

Montreal Neurological Hospital and Institute

Module 3.3

Structure and Organization of the Nervous System

Learning Objectives

After reading this module you should

KNOW ...	UNDERSTAND ...	APPLY ...	ANALYZE ...
The key terminology associated with the structure and organization of the nervous system	How studies of split-brain patients reveal the workings of the brain	Your knowledge of brain regions to predict which abilities might be affected when a specific area is injured or diseased	Whether neuroplasticity will help people with brain damage

Some of you may have seen this Canadian Heritage Moment on television: A woman smells toast burning and then collapses to the ground while having a seizure. The scene then changes to a surgical suite. Dr. Wilder Penfield, a doctor at the Montreal Neurological Institute, is electrically stimulating different parts of the woman's brain prior to her surgery to remove the brain tissue causing her seizures. In one scene, she reports that she sees "the most wonderful lights." After another electrical burst, she asks, "Did you pour cold water on my hand, Dr. Penfield?" Then, in the scene's climax, the patient says, "Dr. Penfield! I can smell burnt toast!" By locating the sensation that immediately preceded the woman's seizure, Dr. Penfield was able to deduce the probable source of the woman's seizures.

In addition to showing us that early brain researchers were part scientist and part detective, this Canadian Heritage Moment also makes an important point about the organization of the brain: Different parts of the brain will be related to different functions, including sensations, memories, and emotions. In this module, we will discuss many of the important brain regions related to the biology of behaviour. (Note: If you haven't seen the video mentioned in this section, you can find it online here: http://www.youtube.com/watch?v=kNdM9JhTPJw.)

Focus Questions

 How do the different divisions of the nervous system work together when you are startled?

 How does the brain control movement?

In this module, we translate our knowledge of nerve cells into an understanding of how they work as an integrated system. This section of the textbook is rich with terminology and can be

Watch
Nervous System

Watch
The Big Picture: My Brain Made Me Do It

Watch
The Basics: How the Brain Works, Part 2

challenging. As you read through it, try to think about how the different parts of the nervous system apply to your own behaviour and experiences. Doing so will help you remember the terms, and will also show you that many different parts of your nervous system interact when you perform even the simplest of behaviours.

Divisions of the Nervous System

Think about it: billions of cells work together to let you have a personality, feel emotions, dance, enjoy music, and remember all of the ups and downs you experience in life. In addition to these voluntary activities, the nervous system is also involved in a number of involuntary processes like controlling your heart rate, blinking, and breathing. Given these diverse functions, it shouldn't be surprising to hear that the nervous system has a number of divisions that allow these processes to seamlessly take place. We begin our exploration of the nervous system by examining the most basic of these distinctions—the difference between the central and peripheral nervous systems.

THE CENTRAL NERVOUS SYSTEM Look up from this page and examine the objects around you. What are they? Can you use words to describe them? How would you use them? Your ability to think up answers to these questions involves different parts of your central nervous system. The **central nervous system (CNS)** *consists of the brain and the spinal cord* (see Figure 3.20). The human brain is perhaps the most complex entity known. Its capacity to store information is almost limitless. Your personality, preferences, memories, and conscious awareness are all packed into this three-pound structure made up of approximately 100 billion individual neurons. The other part of the CNS, the spinal cord, runs from your neck down to the base of your spine. The spinal cord receives information from the brain and stimulates nerves that extend out into the body; this stimulation produces movements. It also receives information from sensory nerves in the body and transmits it back to the brain (or, in the case of reflexes, organizes rapid movements *without* the help of the brain). These two structures are critical for our survival. But, our ability to move and to sense the outside world would be impossible without another major division of the nervous system.

THE PERIPHERAL NERVOUS SYSTEM Wiggle your fingers. Now feel the edges of this book (or the edge of your computer if you're reading an eText). In both cases, you are sending information from your central nervous system to the nerves in the rest of your body that control movement. You are also receiving sensory input from your body as you interact with your environment. These processes are performed by the **peripheral nervous system (PNS)**, a *division of the nervous system that transmits signals between the brain and the rest of the body and is divided into*

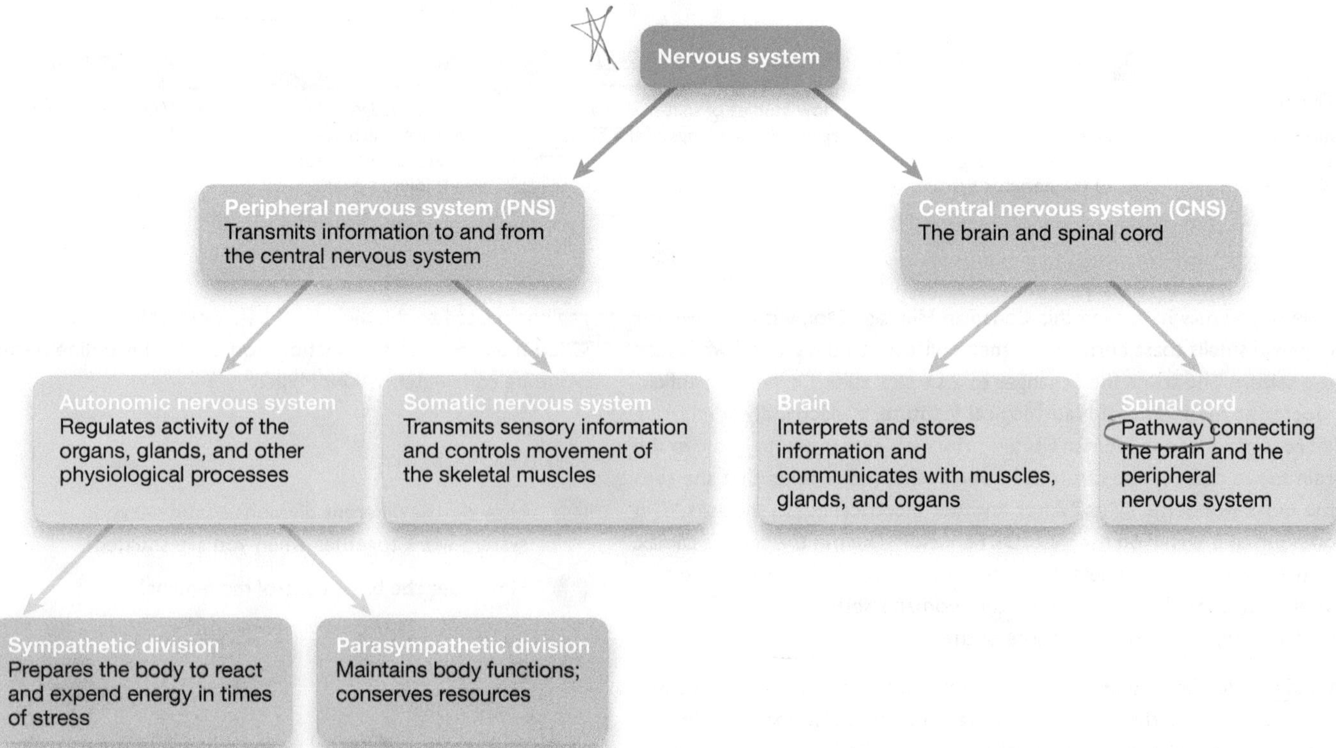

{FIG. 3.20} **The Organization of the Nervous System** The nervous system can be divided into several different components, each with a specific set of structures and functions. **Click on this figure in your eText to see more details.**

two subcomponents, the somatic system and the autonomic system (see Figure 3.20). The **somatic nervous system** *consists of nerves that control skeletal muscles, which are responsible for voluntary and reflexive movement; it also consists of nerves that receive sensory input from the body.* This would be the division of the PNS that is active when you wiggle your fingers or feel the edge of a book. Any voluntary behaviour, such as coordinating the movements needed to reach, walk, or move a computer mouse, makes use of the somatic nervous system.

But, not all behaviours are voluntary. For example, it is unlikely that you can make your heart race or your palms sweat. Responses such as these are often automatic, occurring outside of our conscious control. These behaviours are performed by the **autonomic nervous system**, *the portion of the peripheral nervous system responsible for regulating the activity of organs and glands.* This system includes two subcomponents, one that increases our ability to make rapid responses, and one that helps us return back to normal levels of emotional arousal. The **sympathetic nervous system** *is responsible for the fight-or-flight response of an increased heart rate, dilated pupils, and decreased salivary flow—responses that prepare the body for action.* If you hear footsteps behind you as you are walking alone or if you barely avoid an accident while driving, then you will experience *sympathetic* arousal. In this process, blood is directed toward your skeletal muscles, heart rate and perspiration increase, and digestive processes are slowed; each of these responses helps to direct energy where it is most needed in case you need to respond. However, if you remained in this heightened state of emotional arousal, you would quickly run out of energy resources. It is therefore important for you to have a system in place that allows your body to quickly return to normal levels of energy use. The **parasympathetic nervous system** *helps maintain homeostatic balance in the presence of change; following sympathetic arousal, it works to return the body to a baseline, nonemergency state.* Generally speaking, the parasympathetic nervous system does the opposite of what the sympathetic nervous system does (see Figure 3.21).

Simulate Muscle Contraction

Explore The Autonomic Nervous System

So, if you thought you saw a snake beside your foot, you would have a sympathetic nervous system response that

Simulate Do You Fly or Fight?

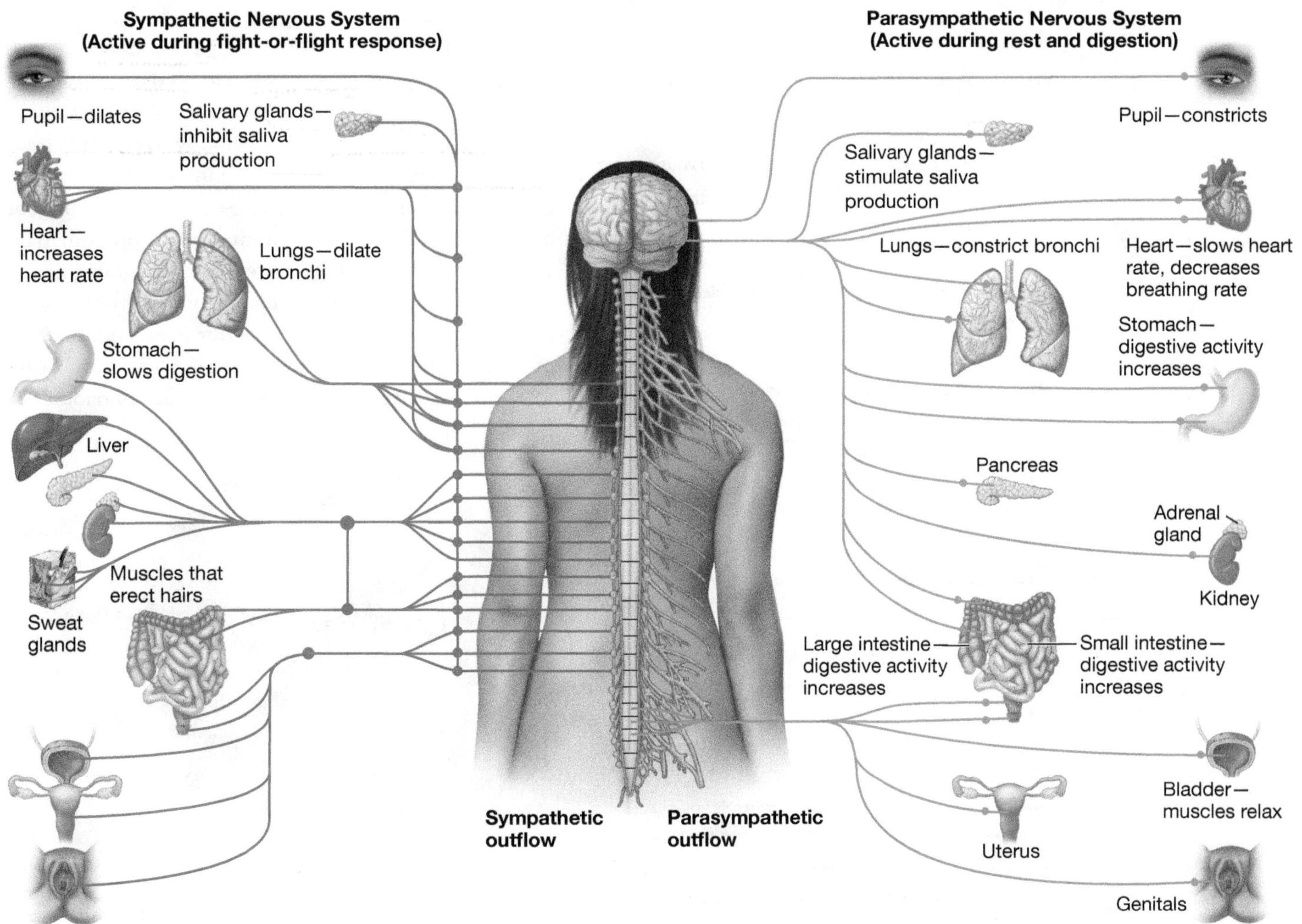

{FIG. 3.21} **The Autonomic Nervous System** The sympathetic and parasympathetic divisions of the autonomic nervous system control and regulate responses by the glands and organs of the body.

Simulate The Human Cerebrum

would increase your heart rate and would send blood toward your leg muscles. Your brain (CNS) would initiate a movement and send that order down the spinal cord (CNS) where it would project out from spinal nerves (PNS) that influence the activity of muscles. Sensory feedback (PNS) from the skin and muscles would travel back to the spinal cord (CNS) and up to the brain (CNS). After some time had passed and you realized that it was actually a stick, not a snake, your parasympathetic nervous system (PNS) would help you calm down so that you were no longer frightened and no longer using up all of your energy responding to this stimulus.

Although these different parts of the PNS and CNS clearly influence a number of our responses, most of these activities are biologically simple. An exception is the activity that occurs in the brain, a stunningly complex structure made up of hundreds of smaller parts. As most of our behaviour is directed by brain activity, the rest of this module will focus on explaining how the different parts of this biological marvel function, alone and in larger networks.

Quick Quiz 3.3a

Divisions of the Nervous System

KNOW ...

1 Which division of the peripheral nervous system is responsible for countering much of the activity associated with the sympathetic nervous system?

A Somatic nervous system
B Spinal cord
C Central nervous system
D Parasympathetic nervous system

2 The central nervous system consists of which of the following?

A The brain and the spinal cord
B The brain and the voluntary muscles
C The brain and the nerves controlling digestion and other automatic functions
D The somatic and autonomic systems

UNDERSTAND ...

3 A major difference between the somatic and autonomic branches of the nervous system is that

A the somatic nervous system controls involuntary responses, and the autonomic nervous system controls voluntary movement.
B the somatic nervous system is located in the brain, and the autonomic nervous system is located peripherally.
C the somatic nervous system controls voluntary movement, and the autonomic nervous system controls involuntary responses.
D the somatic nervous system controls sensation, and the autonomic nervous system controls movement.

Answers can be found on page ANS-1.

The Brain and Its Structures

When you look at the brain, you will immediately notice that it appears to be divided into two symmetrical halves known as *cerebral hemispheres*. Each hemisphere contains the same structures, although there are some small differences in the size of these brain areas (Springer & Deutsch, 1998). Within each hemisphere, the structures of the brain are organized in a hierarchical fashion. The human brain, as well as that of other animals, can be subdivided into three main regions: the hindbrain, the midbrain, and the forebrain (Table 3.2). This system of dividing the brain may tempt you to view it as a mass of separate compartments. Keep in mind that the entire brain is composed of highly integrated circuitry and feedback loops. In other words, although the forebrain may perform complex thinking processes like decision making, its activity is influenced by (and influences) structures in the midbrain and the hindbrain.

THE HINDBRAIN: SUSTAINING THE BODY The hindbrain consists of structures that are critical to controlling basic, life-sustaining processes. At the top of the spinal cord is a region called the **brain stem**, *which is the "stem" or bottom of the brain and consists of two structures: the medulla and the pons* (Figure 3.22). Nerve cells in the medulla connect with the body to perform basic functions such as regulating breathing, heart rate, sneezing, salivating, and even vomiting—all those actions your body does with little conscious control on your part. The fact that the medulla can control all of these activities without us consciously controlling our responses is important—without this ability, our lives would consist of nothing more than sending signals to various organs to ensure that we stayed alive. The pons contributes to

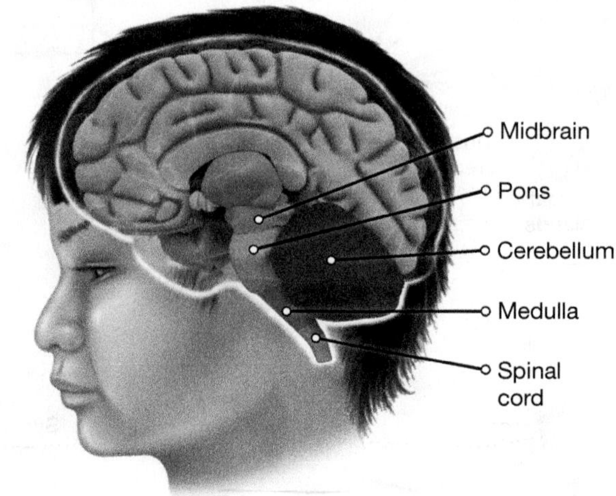

{FIG. 3.22} **The Hindbrain and Midbrain** Structures in the hindbrain are responsible for basic functions that sustain the body. The midbrain includes structures that control basic sensory responses and voluntary movement.

Table 3.2 :: Major Brain Regions, Structures, and Their Functions

REGIONS AND STRUCTURES	FUNCTIONS
Hindbrain	
Brain stem (medulla and pons)	Breathing, heart rate, sleep, and wakefulness
Cerebellum	Balance, coordination and timing of movements; attention and emotion
Midbrain	
Superior colliculus	Orienting visual attention
Inferior colliculus	Orienting auditory attention
Forebrain	
Basal ganglia	Movement, reward processing
Amygdala	Emotion
Hippocampus	Memory
Hypothalamus	Temperature regulation, motivation (hunger, thirst, sex)
Thalamus	Sensory relay station
Cerebral Cortex	
Frontal lobe	Thought, planning, language, movement
Parietal lobe	Sensory processing, bodily awareness
Occipital lobe	Visual processing
Temporal lobe	Hearing, object recognition, language, emotion

general levels of wakefulness, and also appears to have a role in dreaming (see Module 5.1). Due to its connections to other structures in the brain and spinal cord, the pons is also part of a number of networks including those that control balance, eye movements, and swallowing (Nolte, 1999).

An additional hindbrain structure, the *reticular formation* extends from the medulla upwards to the midbrain, a higher brain region that will be described shortly. The reticular formation influences attention and alertness. When you wake up in the morning, you can thank (in part) your reticular formation. This structure also communicates with cells in the spinal cord involved with movements related to walking and posture.

The structures in the hindbrain are able to influence a number of different behaviours through their connections to other parts of the brain and spinal cord. They also have dense connections with another hindbrain structure, the cerebellum. The **cerebellum** (Latin for "little brain") *is the lobe-like structure at the base of the brain that is involved in the monitoring of movement, maintaining balance, attention, and emotional responses*. The cerebellum's role in movement has been known for almost two centuries (Flourens, 1824; Schmahmann, 2004). Damage to this structure leads to uncoordinated and jerky movements that interfere with walking, posture, and most limb movements. These symptoms suggest that the cerebellum is involved with coordinating and timing ongoing movements rather than with generating responses on its own (Yamazaki & Tanaka, 2009). However, recent research indicates that these timing functions extend beyond movement. Patients with damage to the cerebellum have difficulty controlling their attention (Schweizer et al., 2007a, b). They also have problems with emotional control, including personality changes and impulsivity, a set of symptoms now known as the *cognitive affective behavioural syndrome* (Schmahmann & Sherman, 1998). The cerebellum is likely able to influence this wide variety of functions because it has dense connections to a number of areas in the forebrain as well as to evolutionarily older structures in the base of the brain like the hypothalamus, a structure related to the autonomic nervous system (Stoodley & Schmahmann, 2010; Zhu et al., 2006). Through these connections, the so-called "little brain" is able to have a big effect on behaviour.

THE MIDBRAIN: SENSATION AND ACTION The cerebellum is not the only neural region involved with both movement and attention. The **midbrain**, which *resides just above the hindbrain, primarily functions as a relay station between sensory and motor areas* (Figure 3.22). For example, have you ever detected a sudden movement out of the corner of your eye? This ability to capture your visual attention is influenced by the *superior colliculus* (plural *colliculi*). Of course, your ability to orient your attention is not limited to visual stimuli. How do you respond when someone's cell phone rings in class? You, quite naturally, pay attention to that new sound and turn

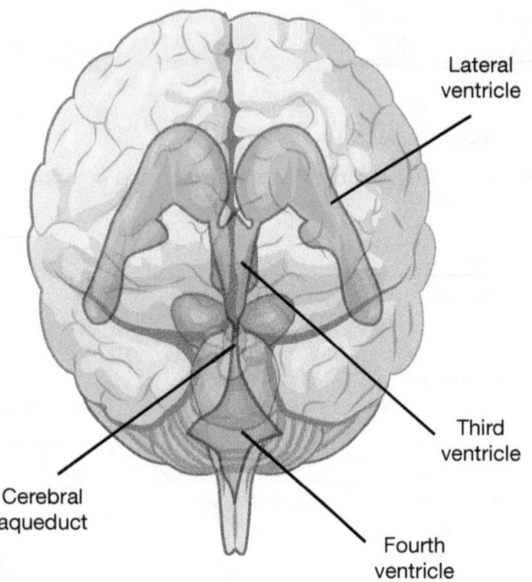

{FIG. 3.23} **The Cerebral Ventricles** Four ventricles in the brain contain cerebrospinal fluid. This provides nutrition and cushioning for many parts of the brain.

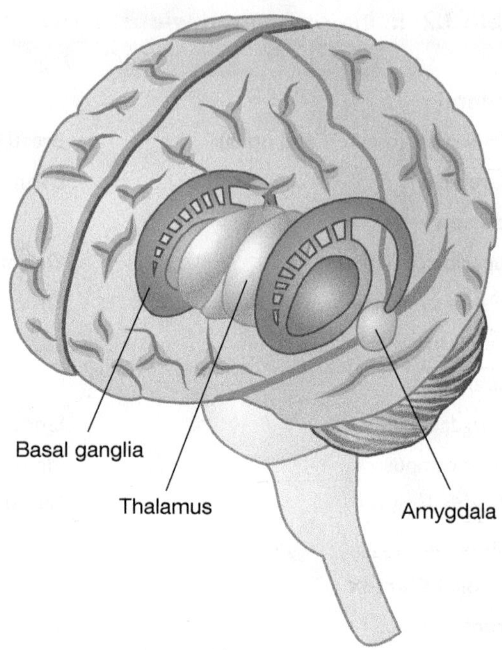

{FIG. 3.24} **The Basal Ganglia** The basal ganglia function in both voluntary movement and responses to rewarding stimuli. **Click on this figure in your eText to see more details.**

your head toward its source (while mentally judging the person's ringtone). This ability to move your auditory attention is influenced by another midbrain structure, the *inferior colliculus* (plural *colliculi*).

Like the hindbrain, structures in the midbrain do not act as independent units; rather, they are part of much larger networks. This concept is powerfully illustrated by the *substantia nigra*. This midbrain area has connections to structures in the forebrain (discussed below); this network of dopamine-releasing cells is involved with the control of movements. Parkinson's disease—a condition marked by major impairments in voluntary movement—is caused by a loss of the dopamine-producing cells in this network.

THE FOREBRAIN: EMOTION, MEMORY, AND THOUGHT The **forebrain**, *the most visibly obvious region of the brain, consists of all of the neural structures that are located above the midbrain, including all of the folds and grooves on the outer surface of the brain; the multiple interconnected structures in the forebrain are critical to such complex processes as emotion, memory, thinking, and reasoning.* The forebrain also contains spaces called *ventricles* (Figure 3.23). Although the ventricles appear hollow, they are filled with cerebrospinal fluid, a solution that helps to eliminate wastes and provides nutrition and hormones to the brain and spinal cord. Cerebrospinal fluid also cushions the brain from impact against the skull.

Sitting next to the ventricles are the **basal ganglia**, *a group of three structures that are involved in facilitating planned movements, skill learning, and integrating sensory and movement information with the brain's reward system* (Figure 3.24; Conn et al., 2005). The basal ganglia form networks that promote and inhibit movements. These two networks interact to allow us to have our different muscles work together in the correct sequence rather than having them "flex" at random times. People who are very practised at a specific motor skill, such as playing an instrument or riding a bicycle, have actually modified their basal ganglia through practice to better coordinate engaging in the activity. Damage to the basal ganglia can lead to movement disorders like Parkinson's disease—involving resting tremors and problems initiating and coordinating movements—and Huntington's disease—involving uncontrollable movements of the body, head, and face. The basal ganglia are also affected in people who have Tourette's syndrome—a condition marked by erratic and repetitive facial and muscle movements (called *tics*), heavy eye blinking, and frequent noise making such as grunting, snorting, or sniffing. The excess dopamine that appears to be transmitted within the basal ganglia contributes to many of the classic Tourette's symptoms (Baym et al., 2008). Incidentally, contrary to popular belief, the shouting of obscenities (*coprolalia*) is actually relatively uncommon in people with Tourette's syndrome.

Some parts of the basal ganglia are also involved in emotion, particularly experiences of pleasure and reward (Berridge et al., 2009). These structures respond to several different types of rewards including tasty foods like chocolate (Small et al., 2003) and monetary rewards (Elliot et al., 2003; Zald et al., 2004). They also form a network with a nearby structure—the *nucleus accumbens*—whose activity accompanies many kinds of pleasurable experiences, including sexual excitement and satisfying a food craving (Avena et al., 2008). As you will read in Module 5.3, this basal ganglia–nucleus accumbens network is also related to the pleasurable effects caused by some drugs (Uchimura & North, 1990).

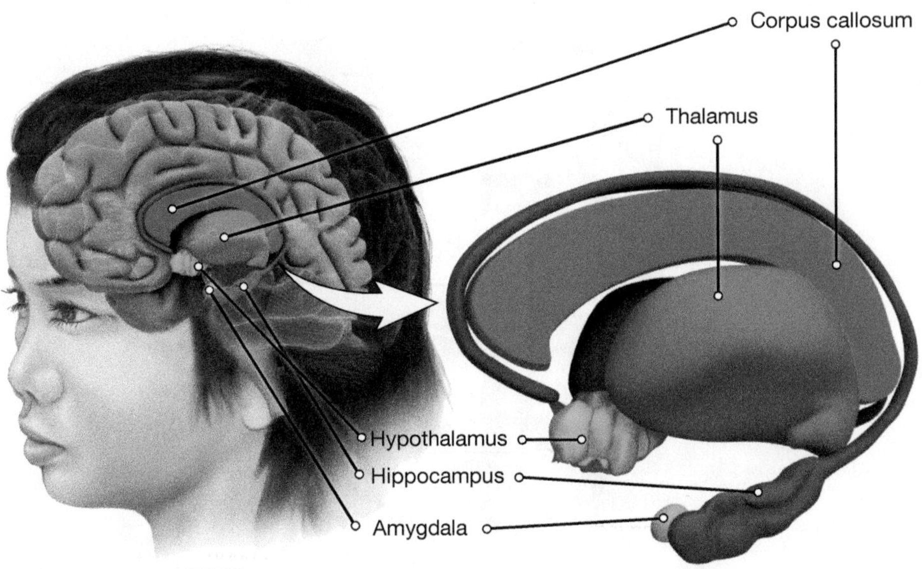

{FIG. 3.25} **The Limbic System** Structures in the limbic system include the hypothalamus, hippocampus, and amygdala, which play roles in regulating motivation, memory, and emotion. **Click on this figure in your eText to see more details.**

Another major set of forebrain structures comprises the **limbic system**, *an integrated network involved in emotion and memory* (Maclean, 1952; see Figure 3.25). One key structure in the limbic system is the **amygdala**, *which facilitates memory formation for emotional events, mediates fear responses, and appears to play a role in recognizing and interpreting emotional stimuli, including facial expressions.* In addition, the amygdala connects with structures in the nervous system that are responsible for adaptive fear responses such as freezing in position when a possible threat is detected; it is also connected to areas responsible for attention, which is why you usually notice when a spider is on your wall. Just below the amygdala is another limbic structure called the hippocampus (Greek for "seahorse"—something it physically resembles if you've had a few drinks). The **hippocampus** *is critical for learning and memory, particularly the formation of new memories* (Squire et al., 2007; see Module 7.1).

You have already encountered the *hypothalamus* in Module 3.2 when you read about its relationship to the endocrine system, and you will encounter it again in Module 11.1 when you read about its influence on the regulation of hunger and thirst. The hypothalamus serves as a sort of thermostat, maintaining the appropriate body temperature, and it regulates drives such as aggression and sex by interacting with the endocrine system. In fact, regions of the hypothalamus trigger orgasm for both females and males (Meston et al., 2004; Peeters & Giuliano, 2007). Direct electrical stimulation of parts of the hypothalamus can produce intense physical pleasure. In a classic set of studies in the 1950s, Olds (1958) found that rats who could press a lever to stimulate the lateral (outside part) of the hypothalamus did so for hours on end, often forgoing food and sleep in order to repeatedly press the lever. In fact, the rats were willing to cross a painful electrical grid in order to reach the lever so that they could return to stimulating themselves.

Another important, albeit less arousing, forebrain structure is the **thalamus**, *a set of nuclei involved in relaying sensory information to different regions of the brain.* Most of the incoming sensory information, including what we see and hear, is routed through specific nuclei in the thalamus. Different types of information are processed by different nuclei before being sent to more specialized regions of the brain for further processing (Sherman, 2007; Sherman & Guillery, 1996). Many of these regions are found in the outer layer known as the cerebral cortex.

{Explore} The Limbic System

THE CEREBRAL CORTEX The **cerebral cortex** *is the convoluted, wrinkled outer layer of the brain that is involved in multiple higher functions, such as thought, language, and personality.* This highly advanced, complex structure has increased dramatically in size as the primate brain has evolved (Kouprina et al., 2002; see Module 3.1). The wrinkled surface of the brain seems to have solved a biological problem endured by our species, as well as by many other mammals: how to pack more cells (i.e., more computing power) into the same amount of space. Because the skull can only be so large, the brain has countered this constraint by forming a wrinkled surface—thereby increasing the surface area of the cortex. More surface area means more neurons and, likely, greater cognitive complexity.

The cerebral cortex consists primarily of the cell bodies and dendrites of neurons; these parts of the neuron give the outer part of the brain a grey-brown colour. The axons of these neurons extend throughout the brain and allow communication between different neural regions to occur. Most of these axons are wrapped in a white, fatty substance called myelin (see Module 3.2) which helps speed up the transmission of neural impulses. Figure 3.26 shows a slice of the brain revealing contrasting light and dark regions, known as *white matter* and *grey*

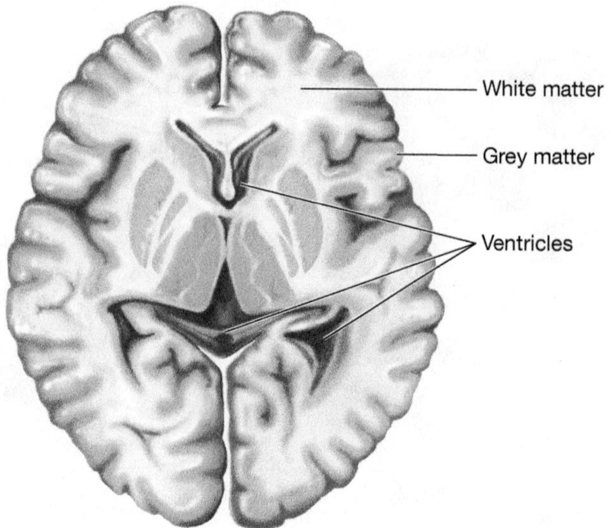

{FIG. 3.26} **Grey and White Matter of the Brain** The cerebral cortex includes both grey matter and white matter, which consist of myelinated axons. Also seen here are the ventricles of the brain. These cavities within the brain are filled with cerebrospinal fluid that provides nourishment and exchange of chemicals with the brain as well as its protective structure.

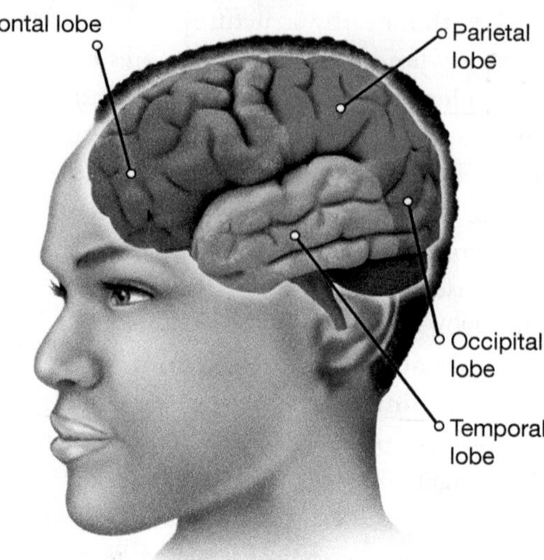

{FIG. 3.27} **The Four Lobes of the Cerebral Cortex** The cerebral cortex is divided into the frontal, parietal, occipital, and temporal lobes. **Click on this figure in your eText to see more details.**

matter. When you see an image like Figure 3.26, it is easy to underestimate the complexity of the brain and its connections. Just to put this image into perspective:

- The grey matter of the brain consists of approximately 100 billion neurons (Drachman, 2005).
- The white matter of a 20-year-old male brain would extend approximately 176 000 km; for a 20-year-old female brain, it would extend approximately 149 000 km (Marner et al., 2003).
- Healthy adults have between 100 and 500 trillion synapses, or connections between cells (Drachman, 2005). Each of these synapses can fire several times a second.

That is a considerable amount of computing power.

THE FOUR LOBES In each cerebral hemisphere, the cortex forms the outer surface of four major areas known as *lobes*: the occipital, parietal, temporal, and frontal lobes (Figure 3.27). Each of the cerebral lobes has a particular set of functions. Nerve cells from each of the four lobes are interconnected, however, and are also networked with regions of the midbrain and hindbrain already described.

The **occipital lobes** *are located at the rear of the brain and are where visual information is processed* (see Module 4.2). The occipital lobes receive visual information from the thalamus. After processing this information, they send it out along two different visual pathways, one that projects to the temporal lobes and is involved with object recognition and one that projects to the parietal lobes and is involved with using vision to guide our movements (Milner & Goodale, 2006).

The **parietal lobes** *are involved in our experiences of touch as well our bodily awareness* (see Module 4.4). At the anterior (front) edge of the parietal lobe is the *somatosensory cortex*—a band of densely packed nerve cells that register touch sensations. The amount of neural tissue dedicated to a given body part in this region is roughly based on the number of sensory receptors present at each respective body region. For instance, the volume of nerve cells in the somatosensory cortex corresponding to the face and hands is proportionally greater than the volume of cells devoted to less sensitive regions like the torso and legs. This is because we acquire more sensory information from our face and hands than we do from most other body parts; very few people use their stomach when trying to identify objects by touch. This difference in the amount of space in the somatosensory cortex allocated to different parts of the body is depicted in Figure 3.28; figures such as this are referred to as a *homunculus* or "little man."

Regions within the parietal lobes also function in performing mathematical, visuospatial, and attention tasks. Damage to different regions of the parietal lobe can lead to specific impairments. For instance, right parietal lobe damage can lead to *neglect,* a situation in which the patient does not attend to anything that appears in the left half of his or her visual field (Heilman & Valenstein, 1979; Hughlings Jackson, 1876/1932); neglect can even occur for the left half of the patient's *imagined* visual images (Bisiach & Luzatti, 1978)!

The **temporal lobes** *are located at the sides of the brain near the ears and are involved in hearing* (see Module 4.3), *language* (see Module 8.3), *and some higher-level aspects of vision such as object and face recognition* (see Module 4.2).

Patients with damage to the right parietal lobe sometimes show evidence of neglect, a failure to attend to the left half of their visual field.

Different sections of the temporal cortex perform different roles. The anterior (front) part of this region is involved with memory for semantic knowledge, basic facts like Victoria is the capital of B.C. Damage to this region can lead to semantic dementia, a disorder in which patients have difficulty remembering information about concepts. For instance, patients might have problems answering questions about whether pine trees or palm trees are more likely to be found on a tropical island (Hodges & Graham, 2001). The superior (top) part of the temporal cortex is known as the *auditory cortex*—it is essential for our ability to hear. Damage to this region leads to problems with hearing despite the fact that the patient's ears work perfectly; this condition is known as *cortical deafness* (Mott, 1907). Slightly behind this region, near the back of the temporal lobe, is *Wernicke's area,* which is related to understanding language (Wernicke, 1874). The close proximity of the hearing and language-comprehension areas makes sense, as these two functions are closely related (see Module 8.3 for a detailed discussion of language).

Some of the structures on the bottom surface of the temporal lobes have a key role in memory. These brain areas send information about the objects being viewed and their location or context to the hippocampus, a forebrain structure discussed above (Diana et al., 2007; Eichenbaum et al., 2007). The hippocampus—which is found in the medial or middle portions of the temporal lobes—then sends output to different brain areas, particularly regions of the frontal lobes, showing again that many different areas of the brain work together to produce almost every behaviour we perform.

The **frontal lobes** *are important in numerous higher cognitive functions, such as planning, regulating impulses and emotion, language production, and voluntary movement* (Goldman-Rakic, 1996). The frontal lobes also allow you to deliberately guide and reflect on your own thought processes. Like the temporal lobes, the frontal lobes can be divided into a number of subsections with specific functions (Miller & Cummings, 2007). A key distinction is between areas related to movement and areas related to the control of our mental lives.

Toward the rear of the frontal lobes is a thick band of neurons that form the *primary motor cortex,* which is involved in the control of voluntary movement. Like the somatosensory cortex discussed above, the primary motor cortex is organized in a homunculus, with different body areas requiring different amounts of space (see Figure 3.28). Body parts such as the fingers that perform fine-motor control will require more space in the motor cortex than areas like the upper thigh, which does

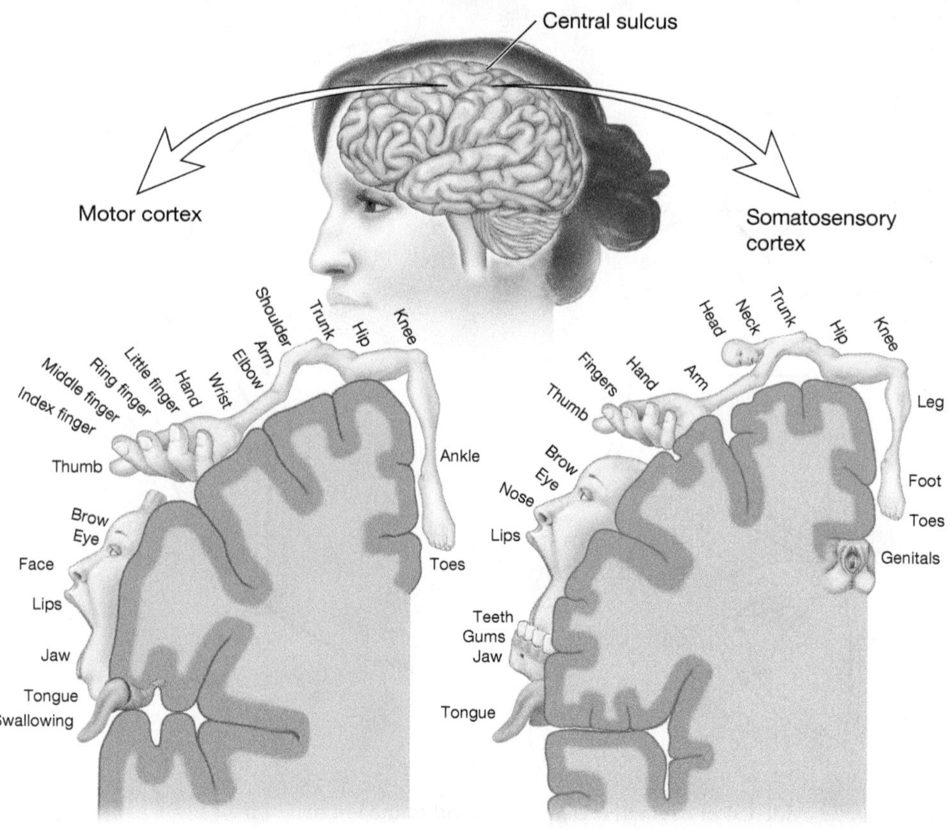

{FIG. 3.28} **The Body as Mapped on the Motor Cortex and Somatosensory Cortex** The regions of the motor cortex are involved in controlling specific body parts. The somatosensory cortex registers touch and other sensations that correspond to the body region depicted. Why do you think it is evolutionarily useful to have these two cortices next to each other in the brain?

not perform many intricate movements. Importantly, motor areas in the frontal lobes are active not just when moving the corresponding body part, but also when planning a movement. This ability to prepare movements before they are needed would clearly be useful when dealing with threats and likely contributed to our species' survival.

The front two-thirds of the frontal lobes are known as the *prefrontal cortex*. This region, which itself can be divided into a number of subsections, performs many of our higher-order cognitive functions such as decision making and controlling our attention. The prefrontal cortex has connections to many of the other brain areas discussed in this module, and appears to help regulate their activity; these control processes are known as *executive functions*. Such functions are not always necessary; however, when we encounter new situations or need to override our normal responses, the prefrontal cortex is almost always involved (Milner, 1963; Stuss & Knight, 2002).

Given their importance, we would obviously like to find ways to strengthen our executive functions. Recently, researchers have found a surprising way to do so: exercise.

Watch
Thinking Like a Psychologist: The Prefrontal Cortex: The Good, the Bad, and the Criminal

Explore
Healthy versus Bad Habits and Brain Functioning

PSYCH @
The Gym

Somehow, physical exertion, pain, and breaking down and rebuilding muscle end up making people feel better. But the benefits of exercise do not apply just to mood: Exercise also affects cognitive activities such as learning and memory. But how?

In recent years, neuroscientists have begun unravelling the mystery of how exercise benefits brain health. Brain imaging studies have revealed that people who engage in regular exercise show improved functioning of the prefrontal cortex compared to non-exercisers. In addition, people who exercise perform better than non-exercisers on tasks involving planning, scheduling, and multitasking (see Davis et al., 2011; Hillman et al., 2008). Animal studies have shown that exercise increases the number of cells in the hippocampus, which is critical for memory, and increases the quantity of brain chemicals that are responsible for promoting cell growth and functioning (Cotman & Berchtold, 2002). But animals are not the only beneficiaries of an exercise program; similar findings have been reported for elderly people who regularly engage in aerobic exercise (Erickson et al., 2011).

Despite the clear benefits associated with exercise, many school curricula have dropped physical education in favour of spending more time on preparation for standardized testing. It is not clear that time away from the gym and the playground is having much benefit. A review of 14 studies—12 conducted in the U.S., one in British Columbia (Ahmed et al., 2007), and one in South Africa—found a "significant positive relationship" between physical activity and academic performance (Singh et al., 2012). This effect may be due to changes in blood flow to the brain, a reduction in stress due to time away from schoolwork, a positive emotional experience associated with play, or, more likely, a combination of several factors. Science is clearly demonstrating that exercise affects the brain basis of learning and memory (Cotman & Berchtold, 2002; Hillman et al., 2008). These results suggest that provincial governments should *increase*, not *decrease*, funding for physical education in schools. Hopefully these studies will help get that ball rolling.

The four lobes of the brain are found in both of our cerebral hemispheres. It is therefore important to have some way for these brain regions to communicate with each other. This prevents us from having our left and right hemispheres working against each other. In Figure 3.29, you can see that crossing the midline of the brain is a densely concentrated bundle of nerve cells called the **corpus callosum**, *a collection of neural fibres connecting the two hemispheres.* This thick band of fibres allows the right and left hemispheres to communicate with each other. This communication has an added benefit: It allows the two hemispheres to work together to produce some of our behaviours. It also opens up the possibility that each hemisphere will become specialized for performing certain functions.

LEFT BRAIN, RIGHT BRAIN: HEMISPHERIC SPECIALIZATION Although they appear to be mirror images of each other, the two sides of the cortex often perform very different functions, a phenomenon called *hemispheric specialization.* Speaking in very general terms, the right hemisphere is specialized for cognitive tasks that involve visual and spatial skills, recognition of visual stimuli, and musical processing. In contrast, the left hemisphere is more specialized for language and math (Corballis, 1993; Gazzaniga, 1967, 2000). However, although some hemispheric differences are quite pronounced, many are a matter of degree (Springer & Deutsch, 1998).

Our understanding of hemispheric specialization expanded greatly through work with *split-brain patients.* In the 1960s, physicians hoping to curtail severe epileptic seizures in their patients used a surgical procedure to treat individuals who were not responding to other therapies. The surgeon would sever the corpus callosum, leaving a patient with two separate cerebral hemispheres. This surgery is not as drastic as it might sound. Patients were remarkably normal after the operation, but several interesting observations were made. One was that split-brain patients responded quite differently to visual input that was presented to either hemisphere alone (Sperry, 1982).

To see how this works, take a look at Figure 3.30. Imagine the person pictured has a split brain. On the one hand, she is able to match the two objects to her right, and can verbalize the match, because the left side of her visual system perceives the objects and language is processed in the left hemisphere of the brain. On the other hand, a visual stimulus presented on the left side of the body is processed on the right side of the brain. As you can see from Figure 3.30, when the object is

Watch
IT-Video: Balancing

Simulate
Hemispheric Experiments

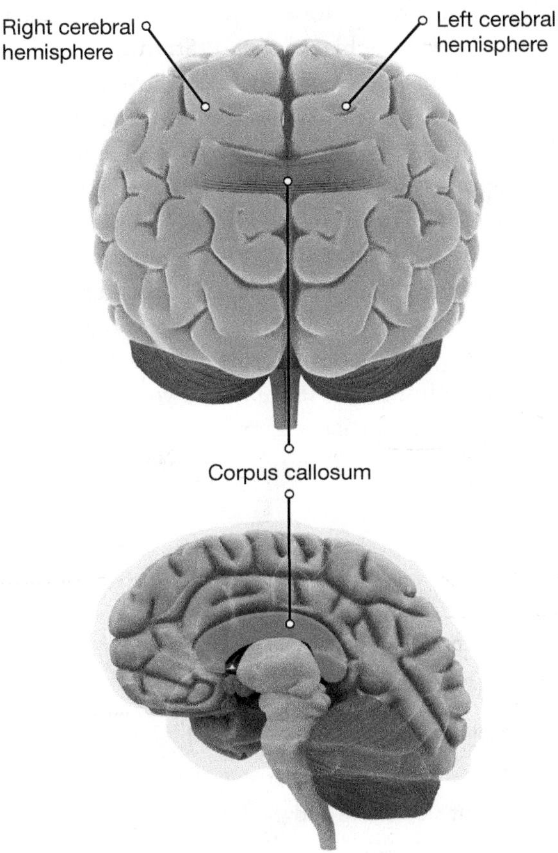

{FIG. 3.29} **The Corpus Callosum** The left and right hemispheres of the brain are connected by a thick band of axons called the corpus callosum.

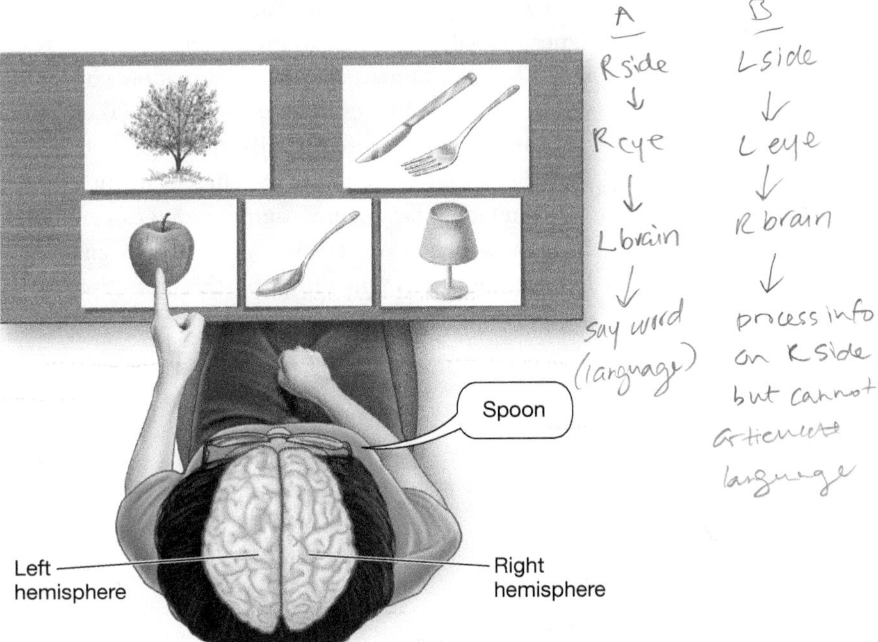

{FIG. 3.30} **A Split-Brain Experiment** This woman has had a split-brain operation. She is able to verbalize which objects match when they are placed to her right side, because language is processed in the left hemisphere. She cannot verbalize the matching objects at left, but can identify them by pointing.

Simulate
Split-Brain

presented to the left side of the split-brain patient, the individual does not verbalize which of the objects match, because her right hemisphere is not specialized for language and cannot label the object. If asked to point at the matching object, however, she is able to do so (but only with her left hand, which is controlled by the right hemisphere). Thus, she is able to process the information using her right hemisphere, but cannot articulate it with language.

Watch Special Topics: The Plastic Brain

Today, split-brain studies are extremely rare, as modern epilepsy medications are often sufficient to treat the symptoms of these patients without the need to sever the corpus callosum. However, the insights gained from these patients still inform our understanding of the brain. It must be stressed, however, that many of these differences are a matter of degree rather than being an absolute one-hemisphere-or-the-other distinction. Indeed, the reality is that most cognitive functions are spread throughout multiple brain regions, with one hemisphere sometimes being superior to the other hemisphere (see Table 3.3).

Watch Brain Building

Before finishing a discussion of the hemispheres, it is also important to point out that the media often misrepresents how hemispheric specialization works. Terms like "left-brained" and "right-brained" are used quite frequently, with the assumption that left-brained people are rigid-thinking accountants who spend hours counting their grey suits and right-brained people are creative Bohemian artists who flamboyantly wander from experimental art exhibits to melodramatic poetry readings. There are numerous websites that allow you to test yourself on this dimension. However, while these types of characters undoubtedly exist, the degree to which these personalities are linked to different hemispheres is very limited. In fact, neuroimaging studies of personality traits show that characteristics similar to left- and right-brained people (as measured by the pseudoscientific tests) are distributed across both hemispheres (De Young et al., 2010).

THE CHANGING BRAIN: NEUROPLASTICITY

In Module 3.2, you read about *stem cells,* immature cells whose final role—be it a neuron or a kidney cell—is based on the chemical environment in which it develops. In other words, the cell's experience (its environment) influenced its physical structure. While fully formed neurons will never have this type of flexibility, brain cells do have a remarkable property called **neuroplasticity**—*the capacity of the brain to change and rewire itself based on individual experience.* For example, numerous studies have shown that the occipital lobes of people who are blind are used for non-visual purposes (Pascual-Leone et al., 2005). This plasticity was beautifully demonstrated in a brain-imaging study using healthy individuals. All participants underwent brain imaging to determine the areas that became active when they performed tasks related to hearing and touch; during this initial phase, the occipital lobes—a region associated with vision—was not active. These participants were then blindfolded for five days before being scanned again. During the second scan session, brain areas normally dedicated to vision became active during touch and hearing tasks (Pascual-Leone & Hamilton, 2001).

There are numerous other examples of neuroplasticity. For example, experienced musicians develop a greater density of grey matter in the areas of the motor cortex of the frontal lobe as well as in the auditory cortex (Gaser & Schlaug, 2003). Studies of children have found that individuals who practised an instrument regularly for over two years had a thicker corpus callosum in areas connecting the left and right frontal and temporal lobes (Schlaug et al., 2009). Even a seemingly silly skill like learning to juggle can influence the thickness of white-matter pathways connecting different brain areas (Scholz et al., 2009). The key point in all of these studies is that although genetics controls *some* of your brain's characteristics, your brain's connections are not set in stone. What you *do* with (and to) your brain can have a dramatic effect on your brain's connections and thus how your brain functions.

Table 3.3 :: Examples of Hemispheric Asymmetries

LEFT HEMISPHERE	RIGHT HEMISPHERE
Language production	Visuospatial skills
Language comprehension	Prosody (emotional intonation)
Word recognition	Face recognition
Arithmetic	Attention (rapid orienting to new stimuli)
Moving the right side of the body	Moving the left side of the body

WORKING THE SCIENTIFIC LITERACY MODEL

Neuroplasticity and Recovery from Brain Injury

The fact that neuroplasticity exists makes it seem like recovery from brain damage should be easy—the remaining brain areas should simply rewire themselves to take over the functions of the damaged brain areas. However, it's not that simple—and we're lucky it isn't.

What do we know about neuroplasticity?

Some animals with relatively simple brains and spinal cords, such as fish and some amphibians, have a lifelong ability to regenerate damaged areas of their central nervous system. If members of these species suffer a brain or spinal cord injury, they will automatically create new tissue to replace the damaged nerves (Sperry, 1951, 1956, 1963, 1968). Humans can do this to a limited degree in the peripheral nervous system as well. This is because chemicals called *trophic factors* (growth factors) can stimulate the growth of new dendrites and axons. However, the ability of the human brain to recover from damage is more limited. New neurons can form in adulthood, but only in a few regions such as part of the hippocampus (Eriksson et al., 1998). That means we can't simply grow a new brain part whenever we're injured.

Our ability to repair our brains is also limited by the presence of chemicals that actually *inhibit* the growth of new axons around an injured area (Yang & Schnarr, 2008). Why would this occur? Researchers suggest that these inhibitory chemicals prevent the brain from forming incorrect connections between brain areas, a result that might produce even larger behavioural problems than the initial damage itself (Berlucchi, 2011; Kolb et al., 2010). So, if our central nervous system is protecting us against neuroplasticity, how can neuroplasticity be the key to recovering from brain damage?

How can science explain how neuroplasticity contributes to recovery from brain damage?

Although it seems like the brain is preventing its own recovery, there are actually a number of ways that neuroplasticity can work to help patients with brain damage. One possibility is that the same area in the opposite hemisphere will take over some of the functions of the damaged region. Stunning evidence of this phenomenon has been found in studies of Melodic Intonation Therapy (MIT; Norton et al., 2009). Researchers have found that some patients with damage to Broca's area—a part of the left frontal lobe involved with the production of speech—can actually sing using fluent, articulated words, even though they cannot speak those same words (see Figure 3.31). In a study of this technique, patients who had suffered strokes affecting Broca's area underwent intensive MIT sessions. During these sessions the patients would sing long strings of words using just two pitches, while rhythmically tapping their left hand to the melody. You can try this out with the help of Figure 3.32. The patients underwent 80 or more sessions lasting 1.5 hours each day, 5 days per week. Remarkably, this therapy has worked for multiple patients—after these intensive therapy sessions, they typically regain significant language function (Schlaug et al., 2009). The therapy does not "heal"

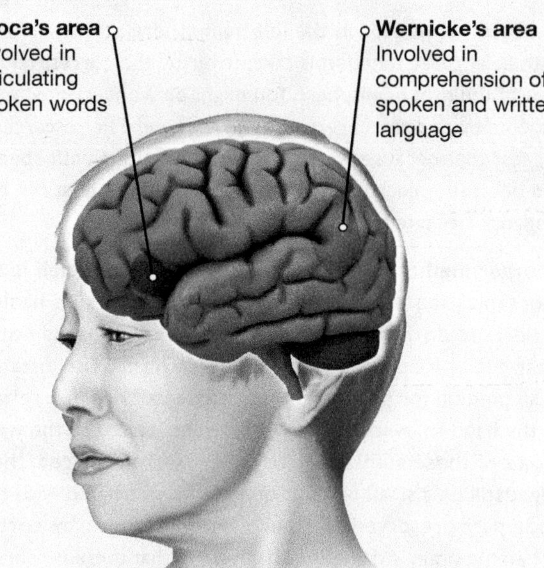

{FIG. 3.31} **Brain Specialization** Broca's area and Wernicke's area are associated with different aspects of language function. Damage to Broca's area produces difficulties in generating speech known as *Broca's aphasia.*

Explore: Virtual Brain: Brain Damage and Neuroplasticity

Simulate: Mechanisms of Evolution

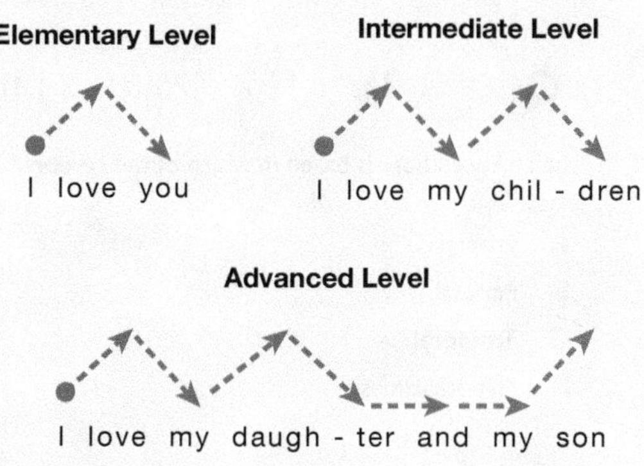

{FIG. 3.32} **Musical Intonation Therapy** During musical intonation therapy, patients are asked to sing phrases of increasing complexity.

damaged nerve cells in the left hemisphere at Broca's area. Rather, language function is taken over by the corresponding area of the *right* hemisphere. You might be wondering why the patients tapped the fingers of their left hand. The researchers suggest that because we typically gesture along with speech, and because speech itself involves motor movements, the tapping may facilitate the recovery process.

Another method that the brain uses to repair itself is the reorganization of neighbouring neural regions. In healthy brains, the distinction between most brain areas is not as clear-cut as it appears on textbook diagrams. For instance, it is common for parts of the somatosensory cortex related to the hand to overlap a bit with regions related to the wrist. If one of those somatosensory areas were damaged, there might still be a small number of neurons associated with that body part preserved in other parts of the nearby cortex. When the brain is damaged, it is thought that these preserved neurons attempt to form new connections. Doing so would allow some sensation to return. This process is enhanced if the doctors force the patient to use the affected brain area as much as possible during rehabilitation (Mark et al., 2006). Although it seems cruel, patients must remember to "use it or lose it." Indeed, research has shown that improvements in a patient's recovery are linked to the reorganization of the affected brain area (Pulvermüller & Berthier, 2008).

Can we critically evaluate this research?

There are obviously limits to the effects of neuroplasticity. If a patient has damage to large amount of her brain, it will not be possible for her to return to her normal level of functioning. Additionally, plasticity is more likely to be effective in younger people, particularly children, than in older adults (Kennard, 1942). Plasticity is most effective when the child is in a developmental stage that is already associated with the formation of new synapses (Kolb & Gibb, 2008; Kolb et al., 2010). Therefore, it is important not to over-generalize the results just discussed. It is also possible that results that seem to be due to neuroplasticity are actually due to some other factor, such as changes in hormone levels, the brain's metabolism, or growth factor levels (Knaepen et al., 2010; Sperry, 1968). Although all of these alternative explanations have been tested to some degree in animal studies, it is sometimes difficult to generalize those findings to the human brain (Kolb et al., 2010). Therefore, much more research is needed before researchers can make any definitive statements about how neuroplasticity helps brain-damaged patients recover.

Why is this relevant?

Each year, 40 000–50 000 Canadians suffer strokes (Heart and Stroke Foundation of Canada, 2013) and over 150 000 suffer traumatic brain injuries (e.g., car accidents; Brain Injury Society of Toronto, 2013). Over 55 000 Canadians are living with brain tumours (Brain Tumour Foundation of Canada, 2013). Neuroplasticity will occur, to some degree, in the majority of these individuals. It is what will help people regain some of their abilities and some of their independence. Understanding neuroplasticity will improve the care given to patients. It will also inspire new research and innovative techniques designed to help the brain heal itself (Kim et al., 2010). This research may affect your grandparents or your parents. And eventually, this research may affect you.

Tony Hutchings/Getty Images

Quick Quiz 3.3b The Brain and Its Structures

KNOW ...

1 The ability to hear is based in which of the cerebral lobes?

A Frontal
B Parietal
C Temporal
D Hypothalamus

UNDERSTAND ...

2 Why would a person who has undergone a split-brain operation be unable to name an object presented to his left visual field, yet be able to correctly point to the same object from an array of choices?

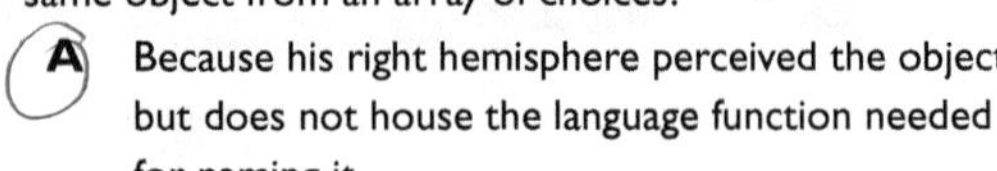

A Because his right hemisphere perceived the object, but does not house the language function needed for naming it
B Because the image was processed on his left hemisphere, which is required for naming objects
C Because pointing is something done with the right hand
D Because the right hemisphere of the brain is where objects are seen

APPLY ...

3 Damage to the somatosensory cortex would most likely result in which of the following impairments?

- **A** Inability to point at an object
- **B** Impaired vision
- **C** Impaired mathematical ability
- **D** Lost or distorted sensations in the region of the body corresponding to the damaged area

ANALYZE ...

4 Which of the following statements best summarizes the results of experiments on exercise and brain functioning?

- **A** Both human and animal studies show cognitive benefits of exercise.
- **B** Animal studies show benefits from exercise, but the results of human studies are unclear.
- **C** Exercise benefits mood but not thinking.
- **D** Exercise only benefits older people.

Answers can be found on page ANS-1.

Module Summary

Module 3.3

Now that you have read this module you should

KNOW ...

- ***The key terminology associated with the structure and organization of the nervous system:***

amygdala (p. 111)
autonomic nervous system (p. 107)
basal ganglia (p. 110)
brain stem (p. 108)
central nervous system (CNS) (p. 106)
cerebellum (p. 109)
cerebral cortex (p. 111)
corpus callosum (p. 115)
forebrain (p. 110)
frontal lobes (p. 113)
hippocampus (p. 111)
limbic system (p. 111)
midbrain (p. 109)
neuroplasticity (p. 116)
occipital lobes (p. 112)
parasympathetic nervous system (p. 107)
parietal lobes (p. 112)
peripheral nervous system (PNS) (p. 106)
somatic nervous system (p. 107)
sympathetic nervous system (p. 107)
temporal lobes (p. 112)
thalamus (p. 111)

UNDERSTAND ...

- ***How studies of split-brain patients reveal the workings of the brain.*** Studies of split-brain patients were important in that they revealed that the two hemispheres of the brain are specialized for certain cognitive tasks. For example, studies of split-brain patients showed that the left hemisphere was specialized for language. These studies were carried out before other brain-imaging techniques (see Module 3.4) became available.

APPLY ...

- ***Your knowledge of brain regions to predict which abilities might be affected when a specific area is injured or diseased.*** Review **Table 3.2**, which summarizes each of the major brain regions described in this module. Then try to answer these questions (check your answers on page ANS-1):

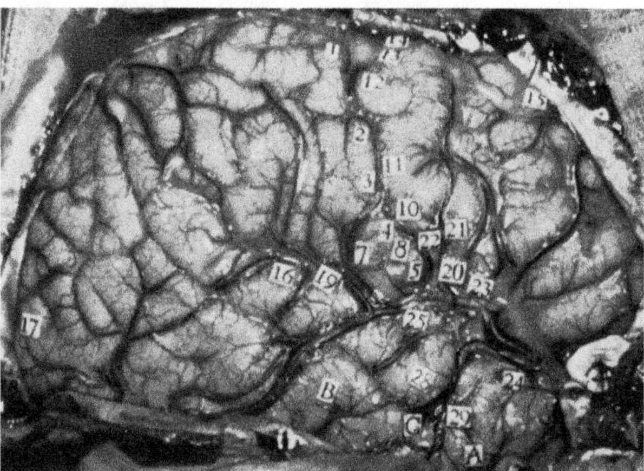

Montreal Neurological Hospital and Institute

1. While at work, a woman suffers a severe blow to the back of her head and then experiences visual problems. Which part of her brain has most likely been affected?
2. If an individual has a stroke and loses the ability to speak in clear sentences, what part of the brain is most likely to have been damaged?
3. If an individual develops a tumour that affects the basal ganglia, which types of behaviours or abilities are likely to be affected?
4. A man suffers a gunshot wound that slightly damages his cerebellum. Which problems might he experience (aside from repeatedly asking himself why someone shot him in the head)?

ANALYZE ...

- ***Whether neuroplasticity will help patients with brain damage.*** There are many examples of experience changing the structure of the brain. Research suggests that neuroplasticity can also help people recover from brain damage. If the damage is isolated to one cerebral hemisphere, cells in the same region of the opposite hemisphere may be able to take over some of the impaired functions. Additionally, it is possible that some of the cells involved with a function (e.g., sensation of the hand) were undamaged; these remaining cells may form new, stronger connections over the course of rehabilitation.

Sun Media/Splash News/Newscom

Module 3.4

Windows to the Brain: Measuring and Observing Brain Activity

Learning Objectives

After reading this module you should

KNOW . . .	UNDERSTAND . . .	APPLY . . .	ANALYZE . . .
The key terminology associated with measuring and observing brain activity	How studies of animals with brain lesions can inform us about the workings of the brain	Your knowledge of neuroimaging techniques to see which ones would be most useful in answering a specific research question	Whether neuroimaging can be used to diagnose brain injuries

On March 8, 2011, Boston Bruins' (giant) defenceman Zdeno Chara dangerously bodychecked Montreal Canadiens' forward Max Pacioretty into the boards; Pacioretty hit the "stanchion," the location where the plexiglass begins next to the players' bench. Pacioretty lay motionless on the ice for several minutes with many people in the audience concerned for his life. He was taken off the ice on a stretcher while still unconscious and was rushed to the hospital for a neurological exam. He was diagnosed with a fracture of the 4th cervical vertebra (a bone in the neck) but, luckily, no spinal cord damage; he also had a severe concussion, also known as a mild traumatic brain injury. Injuries such as Pacioretty's lead to a number of questions for people interested in the biology of behaviour: How can psychologists and medical personnel acquire clear images of a person's brain for medical or research purposes? Is it possible to map out which brain areas are firing when people are performing a specific task like viewing photographs or memorizing a list of words? And, can scientists learn anything about the healthy brain by studying patients who have suffered brain damage? These topics will be addressed in the current module.

For those interested, Pacioretty made a full recovery, scoring 33 goals for the Canadiens over the course of the next season. Later that year, he won the Bill Masterton Trophy, handed out by the National Hockey League to the player who provides the best example of perseverance, team spirit, and dedication to hockey. He was very, very lucky.

Focus Questions

 How can lesions help us learn about the brain?

 How can we make sense of brain activity as it is actually occurring?

In Module 3.3, you read about different brain areas and their functions. This leads to an obvious question: How did researchers find out what these brains areas do? In this module, we will examine the different methods and tools available to physicians and researchers in their quest to map out the functions of different brain areas.

Insights from Brain Damage

Early studies of the brain often involved case studies. A doctor would note a patient's unique set of symptoms and would then ghoulishly wait for him or her to die so that an autopsy could be performed in order to identify the damaged area. As medical knowledge improved, surgeons began to routinely operate on the brains of patients with neurological problems. This allowed researchers to examine patients before and after brain surgery to see the effect that removing tissue would have on behaviour. However, in each of these cases, insights into the brain were based on individuals who had suffered some sort of trauma or illness. There was no way to test how healthy brains function. In the last four decades, advances in brain imaging have changed this, and have allowed researchers to safely measure the brain's activity.

This is not to say that studying patients with brain damage is not scientifically useful. In fact, quite the opposite is true. The only way researchers can truly hope to understand how the brain works is by using a number of different methods to assess its function.

LESIONING AND BRAIN STIMULATION Studies of patients who have suffered brain damage will appear in a number of modules in this book. The logic of this method is that if a person has part of his or her brain damaged and is unable to perform a particular task (e.g., form new memories), then it is assumed that the damaged structure plays a role in that behaviour. One drawback of studying human patients, however, is that the researcher has no control over where the damage occurs. A stroke generally produces widespread damage; rarely will it harm a single area while leaving the rest of the brain totally unaffected. This diffuse damage makes it difficult for brain researchers to perform controlled studies of patients—each patient will have a unique pattern of damage. It is also difficult to isolate the effects of damage to one brain area when several are damaged.

In order to gain more experimental control (and a much larger number of subjects), scientists often create brain damage in animals. This process is known as **lesioning**, *a technique in which researchers intentionally damage an area in the brain* (a *lesion* is abnormal or damaged brain tissue). Creating lesions allows the researcher to isolate single brain structures. He or she can then study animals with and without lesions to see how specific behaviours are changed by the removal of that brain tissue. The control subjects are often part of *a sham group*, a set of animals that go through all of the surgical procedures aside from the lesion itself in order to control for the effects of stress, anesthesia, and the annoyance of stitches. An example of the lesion method is found in studies of spatial learning. Researchers hypothesized that the hippocampus was vital for this ability. In order to test this hypothesis, the researchers lesioned the hippocampus on both sides of the brains of one group of rats and performed sham surgery on the other rats. Each rat was then put into the Morris Water Maze (Morris, 1981); this device consists of a container filled with an opaque (non-transparent) fluid. The rat is placed in the water and must swim around until it finds a small platform hidden under the fluid. At first, the rat finds the platform by chance; over time, the rat learns the location of the platform and swims to it immediately. However, rats with lesions to the hippocampus show a marked impairment in learning the location of the platform, presumably because the hippocampus is critical for many spatial abilities (Morris et al., 1982). This

akg-images/Newscom

Before brain imaging technology became available, neurosurgeons had to do quite a bit of guesswork. Dr. Harvey Cushing was one of the world's first neurosurgeons. Dr. Cushing, who operated on patients with brain tumours, had to rely on behavioural symptoms to determine where to target his attempts at removing the tumours.

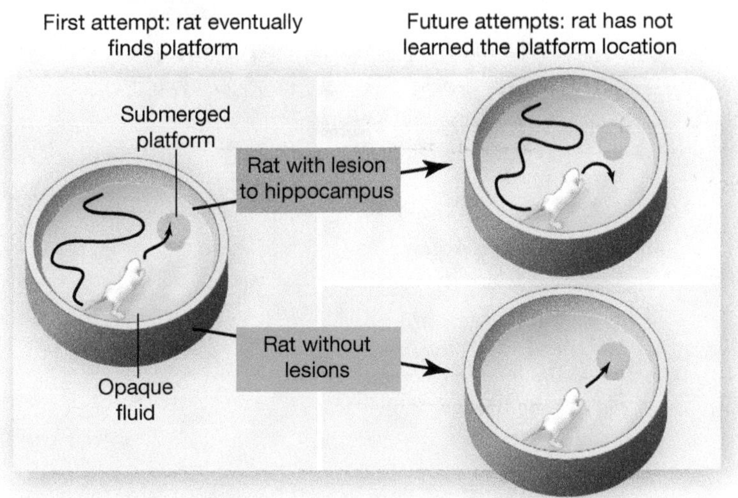

Tools like the Morris Water Maze allow researchers to test the effects of brain lesions on behaviours such as spatial memory.

example demonstrates the power of the lesion method to determine the roles played by specific brain areas.

Less drastic techniques impair brain activity only temporarily; in fact, some can be safely applied to humans. For instance, researchers can study brain functions using **transcranial magnetic stimulation (TMS)**, *a procedure in which an electromagnetic pulse is delivered to a targeted region of the brain* (Bestmann, 2008; Terao & Ugawa, 2002). This pulse interacts with the flow of ions around the neurons of the affected area. The result is a temporary disruption of brain activity, similar to the permanent disruption caused by a brain lesion. This procedure has the advantage that healthy human volunteers can be studied (as opposed to animals or brain-damaged people, many of whom are elderly). TMS has been used to investigate a number of cognitive processes ranging from visual perception (Perini et al., 2012) to arithmetic abilities (Andres et al., 2011) to memory for words and abstract shapes (Floel et al., 2004). In each case, impairments in performance after receiving the TMS "temporary lesion" tell the researcher that the stimulated brain area is likely involved in that cognitive process.

Interestingly, if a weaker electromagnetic pulse is delivered, TMS can also be used to stimulate, rather than temporarily impair, a brain region (Figure 3.33). For example, TMS has been used to increase the activity in the frontal lobes—an area related to planning and inhibiting behaviour—when people were performing a gambling task. This change led the participants to behave in a more cautious, risk-averse manner than when they performed the task without this stimulation (Fecteau et al., 2007). TMS has also been used to stimulate under-active areas associated with depression, suggesting that this tool has clinical applications as well (Kluger & Triggs, 2007). In fact, researchers have used this technique to help patients deal with symptoms of disorders ranging from Parkinson's disease (Degardin et al., 2012) to movement problems caused by strokes (Corti et al., 2012; Schlaug et al., 2008).

Although lesion work and TMS allow researchers to understand what happens to the brain when certain regions are removed or inactive, these methods don't provide a picture of the brain's structures or its patterns of activity. Luckily, there have been astonishing advances in structural and functional neuroimaging over the past forty years.

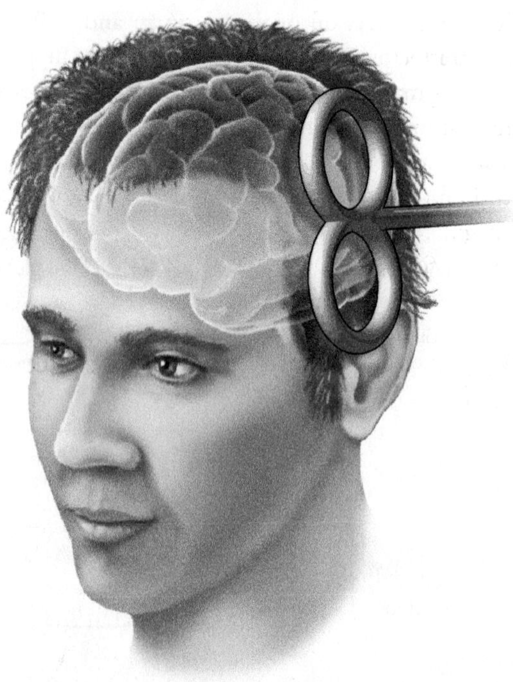

{FIG. 3.33} **Brain Stimulation** Transcranial magnetic stimulation involves targeting a magnetic field to a very specific region of the brain. Depending on the amount of stimulation, researchers can either temporarily stimulate or disable the region.

Watch
Brain Imaging

Quick Quiz 3.4a

Insights from Brain Damage

KNOW ...

1 The control group in a typical lesion study is called the

- **A** metacranial group.
- **B** pseudo-incision group.
- **C** sham group.
- **D** static group.

UNDERSTAND ...

2 Why do researchers often use the lesion method instead of studying humans with brain damage?

- **A** It is possible to test more subjects using the lesion method.
- **B** Brain damage usually differs between patients.
- **C** The patients usually only have damage in one specific area.
- **D** Both (A) and (B) are true.

ANALYZE ...

3 Dr. Cerveau performed a TMS lesion study in her lab. She found that applying a pulse to the parietal lobes prevented people from pressing a keypad in response to a suddenly appearing image. She concluded that the lesion affected attention. Why should we be cautious of her claim?

- **A** TMS is not a valid method of lesioning brain areas.
- **B** The TMS lesion covered a large area and may have affected other functions that might have slowed participants' responses.
- **C** Response times are not a valid measure of how people pay attention.
- **D** All of the above are valid concerns.

Answers can be found on page ANS-1.

Structural and Functional Neuroimaging

Neuroimaging (or brain imaging) is becoming increasingly important for many fields, particularly for psychology. Being able to examine the brains of living people and to measure neural activity while participants perform different tasks provides an astonishing window into the mind. Neuroimaging has also revolutionized medicine, allowing doctors to see with great precision the size and location of brain injuries. The remainder of this module will focus on the two types of brain scanning: structural and functional neuroimaging.

STRUCTURAL NEUROIMAGING At the beginning of this module, you read about Montreal Canadiens' forward Max Pacioretty's scary injury and his surprising return to the National Hockey League. When Pacioretty first arrived at the hospital, the doctors would obviously have wanted to determine the extent of the damage to his brain. In order to get this information, it was necessary to use **structural neuroimaging**, *a type of brain scanning that produces images of the different structures of the brain*. This type of neuroimaging is used to measure the size of different brain areas and to determine whether any brain injury has occurred.

There are three commonly used types of structural neuroimaging. **Computerized tomography** (or **CT scan**) *is a structural neuroimaging technique in which x-rays are sent through the brain by a tube that rotates around the head*. The x-rays will pass through dense tissue (e.g., grey matter) at a different speed than they will pass through less dense tissue, like the fluid in the ventricles (Hounsfield, 1980). A computer then calculates these differences for each image that is taken as the tube moves around the head and combines that information into a three-dimensional image (see Figure 3.34). As an interesting historical aside, the first commercial CT scanner was created by EMI in the early 1970s (and was called the EMI-Scanner), a company also involved in the music industry. This company had enough money to pay for four years of medical-imaging research because they were also the record label of a band known as The Beatles (Filler, 2009).

CT scans were considered state of the art for over a decade. However, in the 1970s and early 1980s, a new form of structural neuroimaging emerged. **Magnetic resonance imaging** (or **MRI**) *is a structural imaging technique in which clear images of the brain are created based on how different neural regions absorb and release energy while in a magnetic field*. Although this sounds confusing, understanding MRIs involves three steps. First, a brain (or other body part) is placed inside a strong magnetic field; this causes the protons of the brain's hydrogen atoms to spin in the same direction. Second, a pulse of radio waves is sent through the brain; the energy of this pulse is absorbed by the atoms in the brain and knocks them out of their previous position (aligned with the magnetic field). Finally, the pulse of radio waves is turned off. At this point, the atoms again become aligned with the magnetic field. But, as they do so, they release the energy they absorbed during the pulse. Different types of tissue—grey matter, white matter, and fluid—release different amounts of energy and return to their magnetic alignment at different speeds. Computers are used to calculate these differences and provide a very detailed three-dimensional image of the brain (Huettel et al., 2009).

As you can see from Figure 3.34, MRIs produce much clearer images than CT scans and are more accurate at detecting many forms of damage including concussions like that suffered by Max Pacioretty (Bazarian et al., 2007). So, why are CT scanners still used? Let's go back to Pacioretty's injury. He was hit into a structure that consisted of a thin pad covering metal and plexiglass, so the chances of him having metal in his brain were quite slim. But what if a person entered the hospital after a car accident? He might have fragments of metal in his body; these would not react well to a powerful magnet. Therefore, CT scans, aside from being cheap, are a safe first-assessment tool for brain injuries. When the doctors have more information about the patient

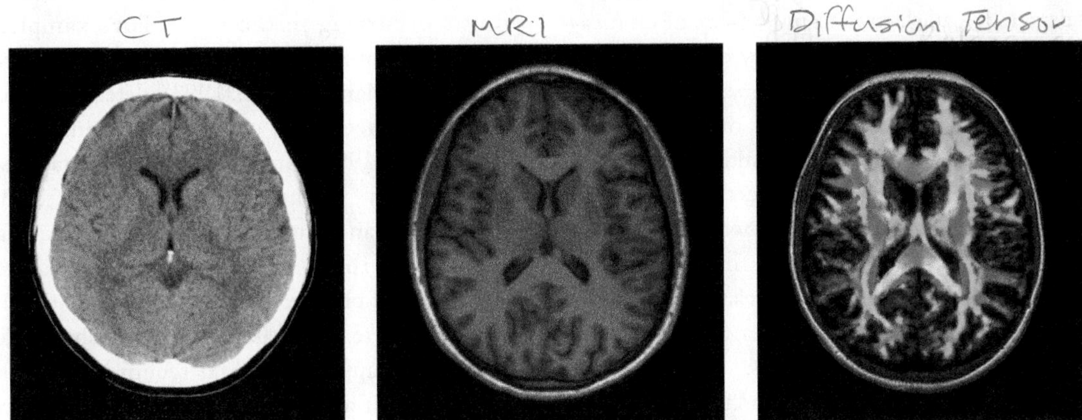

Left: Guy Croft SciTech/Alamy; centre: Mark Krause; right: Zephyr/Science Source

{FIG. 3.34} **Structural Neuroimaging** Three different types of structural neuroimaging: (a) a CT scan, (b) an MRI scan, and (c) a diffusion tensor imaging scan.

and his injury, then it is possible that the more accurate MRI will be used.

A final type of structural neuroimaging technique is also the newest. **Diffusion tensor imaging** (or **DTI**) *is a form of structural neuroimaging allowing researchers or medical personnel to measure white-matter pathways in the brain.* Although it is natural to assume that the grey matter—the cell bodies—is the most sensitive part of the brain, white-matter damage has been found in an increasing number of brain disorders (Shenton et al., 2012). This is because most head injuries cause the brain to twist around in the skull. The result is that some of the white-matter pathways connecting different brain areas are torn. A large number of studies have shown that these pathways are damaged in individuals who have suffered concussions (Niogi & Mukherjee, 2010), although it is unclear whether professional and collegiate/university sports leagues are using this technology when making return-to-play decisions for injured athletes (Johnson et al., 2012).

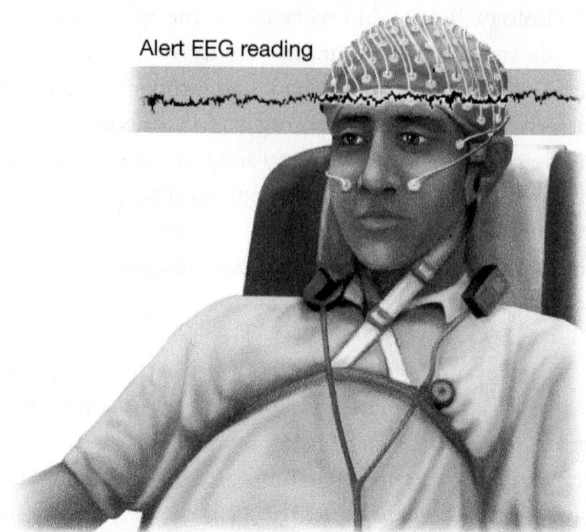

{FIG. 3.35} **Measuring Brain Activity** The electroencephalogram measures electrical activity of the brain by way of electrodes that amplify the signals emitted by active regions.

FUNCTIONAL NEUROIMAGING Although structural images provide useful information about the brain's anatomy, they do not tell us much about the functions of those brain areas. This information is gathered using **functional neuroimaging**, *a type of brain scanning that provides information about which areas of the brain are active when a person performs a particular behaviour.* There are a number of different functional neuroimaging methods available to researchers and physicians. A common trade-off is between *temporal resolution* (how brief a period of time can be accurately measured) and *spatial resolution* (a clear picture of the brain). Which tool is used depends upon the type of question being asked.

A neuroimaging method with fantastic temporal resolution is an **electroencephalogram** (or **EEG**), *which measures patterns of brain activity with the use of multiple electrodes attached to the scalp.* The neural firing of the billions of cells in the brain can be detected with these electrodes, amplified, and depicted in an electroencephalogram. EEGs measure this activity every millisecond. They can tell us a lot about general brain activity during sleep (see Module 5.1), during wakefulness, and while patients or research participants are engaged in a particular cognitive activity (see Figure 3.35). EEGs are also used to detect when patients with epilepsy are having a seizure; this would be shown by a sudden spike in activity (neuronal firing) in one or more brain areas. The convenience and relatively inexpensive nature of EEGs, compared to other modern methods, make them very appealing to researchers.

But, how can EEG be used to further our understanding of human behaviour? In most studies, researchers would be interested in how brain responses differ for different types of stimuli, such as happy or fearful faces. EEGs have perfect temporal resolution for this task, but they have a problem: How do you link the EEG output (a bunch of squiggly lines) with your stimuli? To do this, researchers have developed a technique known as *event-related potentials* (or ERPs). ERPs use the same sensors as EEGs; however, a computer takes note of exactly when a given stimulus (e.g., a smiling face) was presented to the participant. The experimenter can then examine the EEG readout for a brief period of time (usually 1–2 seconds) following the appearance of that stimulus. Importantly, the experiment can collect the average brain responses for different types of experimental trials; so, if an experiment contained 50 separate stimulus presentations—25 happy faces and 25 fearful faces—the experimenter could collect the *average* pattern of data after each type of stimulus (i.e., there would be one set of squiggly lines for happy faces and one for fearful faces).

Critically, the peaks and valleys of these *waveforms* are not random—each is associated with some sort of process occurring in the brain. For example, initial detection of some sort of visual image could occur after 80–120 ms (Mangun et al., 1993); determining that the image was a face might occur at approximately 170 ms (Bötzel et al., 1995). And, identifying that face as someone you know might occur sometime after 300 ms. Researchers can then look at the size of the peaks and valleys to determine whether there was a difference in the amount of brain activity in response to the different stimulus types (e.g., a peak at 200 ms was higher for fearful than for happy faces). This technique can also have clinical uses. If a patient (e.g., someone with multiple sclerosis) was missing an expected waveform, the neurologist could conclude that a particular region of her brain was not functioning normally (Ruseckaite et al., 2005).

Although ERPs are very useful for measuring *when* brain activity is occurring, they are much less effective at identifying exactly *where* that activity is taking place. Part of this problem is due to the fact that the skull disrupts the electrical signal from the neurons' firing; this reduces the accuracy of ERP measurements. In order to get around this, some researchers measure the magnetic activity associated with cells firing. This is accomplished by using **magnetoencephalography** (or **MEG**), *a neuroimaging technique that measures the tiny magnetic fields created by the electrical activity of nerve cells in the brain.* Like EEG, MEG records the electrical activity of nerve cells just a few milliseconds after it occurs, which allows researchers to record brain activity at nearly the instant a stimulus is presented (Hamalainen et al., 1993). So, in a study with happy and fearful faces, MEG could measure when an image was detected and when it was recognized as being a face (Halgren et al., 2000). However, like ERPs, this speed comes with a trade-off; namely, MEGs do not provide a detailed picture of the activity of specific brain areas, so it is difficult to isolate *where* in the brain the activity occurred.

A functional imaging method that *can* show activity of the whole brain is **positron emission tomography** (or **PET**), *a type of scan in which a low level of a radioactive isotope is injected into the blood, and its movement to regions of the brain engaged in a particular task is measured.* This method works under the assumption that active nerve cells use up energy at a faster rate than do cells that are less active. As a result, more blood will need to flow into those active areas in order to bring more oxygen and glucose to the cells. If the blood contains a radioactive isotope (as in a PET study), more radioactivity will be detected in areas of the brain that were active during that period of time. In most studies, participants will complete separate blocks of trials or even separate scanning sessions for different types of experimental trials. The activity from these sessions is then compared to see which brain areas are more (or less) active in response to different types of stimuli. For instance, researchers at McGill University provided the first evidence that the ventral (bottom) portions of the right hemisphere of the brain were involved with recognizing faces (Sergent et al., 1992).

The greatest strength of PET scans is that they show metabolic activity of the brain. PET also allows researchers to measure the involvement of specific types of receptors (e.g., types of dopamine receptors) in different brain regions while people perform an experimental task (e.g., Woodward et al., 2009). A drawback is that PET scans take a long time to acquire—at least two minutes—which is a problem when you want to see moment-by-moment activity of the brain. The radioactivity of PET also generally limits the participants to men because it is possible that female participants could be in the early stages of pregnancy. In that case, the risks of participating would far outweigh the rewards. Instead, researchers are increasingly turning to a powerful neuroimaging technique with excellent spatial resolution.

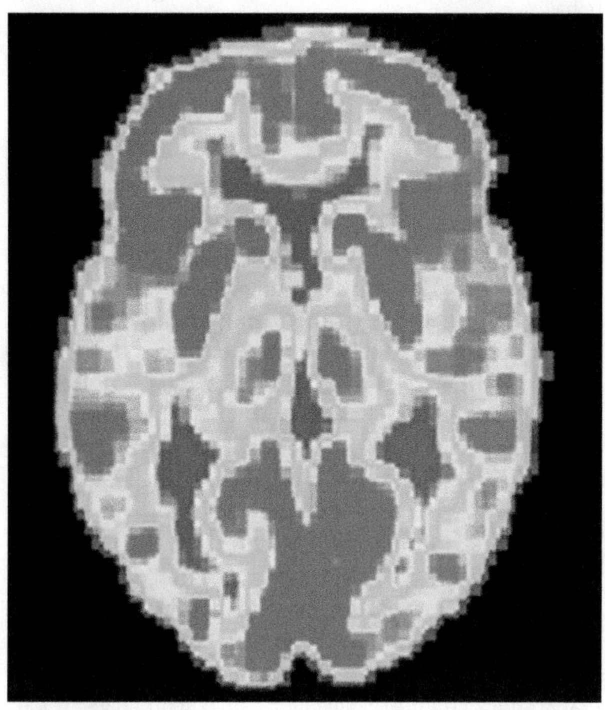

Science Source

PET scans use radioactive isotopes to help identify which areas of the brain were most active.

WORKING THE SCIENTIFIC LITERACY MODEL

Functional MRI and Behaviour

Functional magnetic resonance imaging (or fMRI) *measures brain activity by detecting the influx of oxygen-rich blood into neural areas that were just active* (Kwong et al., 1992; Ogawa et al., 1992). Like PET scanning, fMRI can produce an accurate image of the functional brain. However, its ease of use (and lack of radioactivity) has quickly made it one of the most influential research tools in modern psychology.

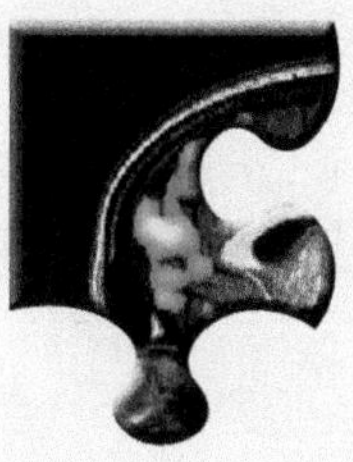

What do we know about fMRI and Behaviour?

If you type in "functional MRI" into the PubMed.gov research database, you will see that there have been over 5500 papers published since this technology was developed just over 20 years ago. The growth in this field is staggering—there are literally hundreds of fMRI research papers published each year. Researchers are using fMRI to study almost every topic discussed in this book ranging from sensory processes (Chapter 4) to memory (Chapter 7) to social behaviours (Chapter 13). Importantly, fMRI is also being used to examine clinical issues including psychological disorders (Chapter 15) and disorders of consciousness (e.g., vegetative states, Module 5.3). It is also being used to examine brain activity in neurological patients like Max Pacioretty—psychologists and medical personnel can look at what areas of the brain are active when a person is performing different tasks such as remembering lists of words. If the patterns of activity deviate from normal patterns, then there may be cause for concern. With this surge in fMRI research and clinical use, it is important to examine *how* fMRI links blood flow to descriptions of behaviour.

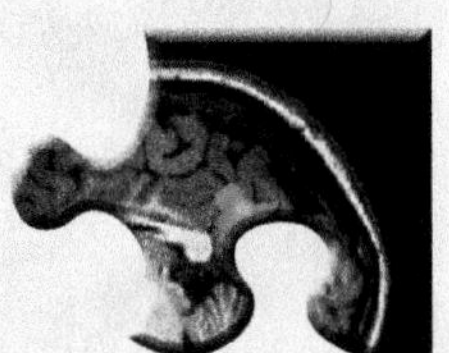

How can science explain how fMRI is used to examine behaviour?

When a brain area is involved with a particular function, it will use up oxygen. The result is that blood in these areas will be deoxygenated (without oxygen molecules). The body responds by sending in more oxygen-rich blood to replace the deoxygenated blood. Critically, these two types of blood have different magnetic properties. So, by measuring the changing magnetic properties of the blood in different brain areas, it is possible to see which areas were active when the person performed a particular task (Huettel et al., 2009; Magri et al., 2012). When you see pictures of different brain areas "lit up," those colourful areas indicate that more activity occurred in that location during one experimental condition than during another (see Figure 3.36). To continue our example of perceiving faces, researchers could present happy or fearful faces to participants while they were in the fMRI scanner (which is the same machine used for structural MRI scans). After the study, the researchers could look at the average amount of brain activity that occurred when each participant viewed each type of face. In this case, seeing faces would activate a region in the bottom of the right hemisphere known as the *fusiform gyrus* (Kanwisher et al., 1997; see Module 4.2). Faces expressing fear would activate the amygdala (see Module 3.3), and faces expressing happiness activate a wide network of structures in the frontal lobes (Phillips et al., 1998). Thus, fMRI provides very detailed images of *where* brain activity is occurring. Unfortunately, it can only measure activity at the level of seconds rather than milliseconds; therefore, it lacks the temporal resolution of ERP and MEG (see Table 3.4).

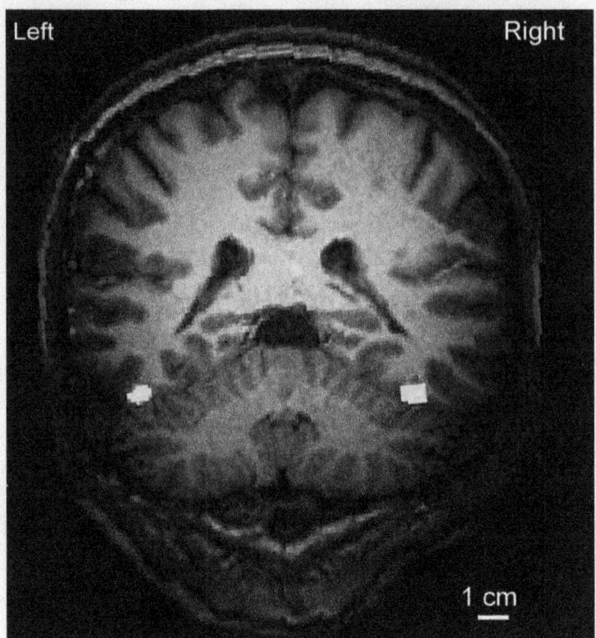

DORIS TSAO/MCT/Landov

{FIG. 3.36} **Functional Magnetic Resonance Imaging** Functional MRI technology allows researchers to determine how blood flow, and hence brain activity, changes as study participants or patients perform different tasks. In this image, the coloured areas depict increases in blood flow to the left and right temporal lobes, relative to the rest of the brain, during a cognitive task.

Can we critically evaluate this research?

Although researchers have shown that the activity that we see in fMRI images is actually linked to the firing of neurons (Logothetis et al., 2001), we still need to be cautious when interpreting fMRI data. One reason is that it is correlational in nature. Activity increases or decreases at the same time as different stimuli are perceived; however, we can't definitely show that the activity was *caused* by the stimuli. We simply take a leap of faith (of sorts) that it was. Also, just because a brain area is *active* while we perform a task does not mean that it is *necessary* for that task. It is possible that a given area that "lights up" on fMRI is a small part of a larger network, or performs a supporting role. Therefore, it is useful to look at research using other methods (if available) to see if similar brain areas were implicated in a given behaviour.

There is an additional reason to be cautious of fMRI data. There is a growing trend for neuroimaging, particularly fMRI, to be used to explain or justify phenomena that are not easily measured (Satel & Lilienfeld, 2013). Images of brains with areas lit up can be found on almost every major online news site. The problem is that many of the claims made in these stories are overstated (more likely, but not always, by the media than by the scientists). Given the massive connections between brain areas, headlines that suggest that scientists have discovered the "hate centre" or *the* neural structure associated with how someone will vote are misleading. Most brain areas are activated by *many* different situations and stimuli. So, just as you would raise your skeptical eyebrows in response to reports of scientists finding the single gene for a given behaviour (see Module 3.2), you should apply your critical-thinking skills toward claims about scientists identifying the single brain area for any complex process.

Why is this relevant?

It is difficult to overstate how important fMRI has been to psychological science. It has allowed researchers to map out the networks associated with every topic discussed in this book, thus providing most of the "bio" components of the biopsychosocial model of behaviour. Recently, researchers at Queen's University and the University of Manitoba have found ways to perform fMRI on neurons in the spinal cord (Kornelsen et al., 2013; Stroman, 2005); in fact, there is even evidence of spinal cord activity in response to making emotional faces (Smith et al., 2013). Thus, it will soon be possible to measure how the *entire* central nervous system responds to different stimuli, an ability that will allow us to gain a more complete understanding of human behaviour.

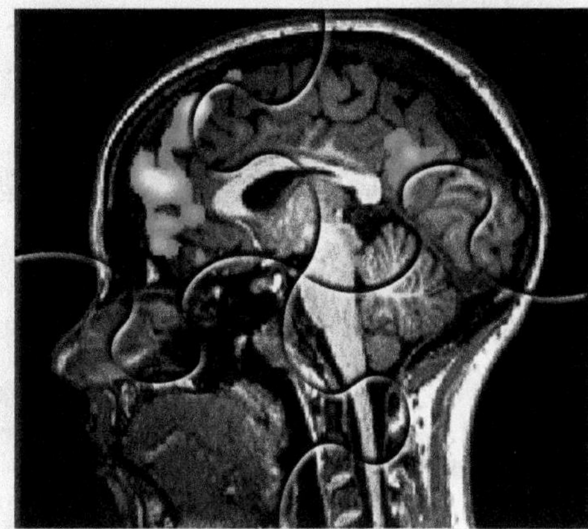

Dr. Jen Kornelsen

Table 3.4 :: Common Methods of Functional Neuroimaging

NEUROIMAGING METHOD	ADVANTAGES	DISADVANTAGES
EEG/ERP	Excellent temporal resolution (measures activity at the millisecond level); inexpensive	Poor spatial resolution (does not give a picture of individual brain structures)
MEG	Excellent temporal resolution (measures activity at the millisecond level)	Poor spatial resolution (does not give a picture of individual brain structures)
PET	Provides a picture of the whole brain (although not as clear as fMRI); allows researchers to examine activity related to specific neurotransmitters (e.g., dopamine)	Very poor temporal resolution (takes at least 2 minutes to scan the brain, often longer); involves radioactive isotopes that limit possible participants; very expensive
fMRI	Excellent spatial resolution (clear images of brain structures)	Temporal resolution is not as good as ERP or MEG (it takes approximately two seconds to scan the whole brain)

Quick Quiz 3.4b Structural and Functional Neuroimaging

KNOW ...

1 The brain-imaging technique that involves measuring blood flow in active regions of the brain is called

- **A** magnetic resonance imaging.
- **B** MEG scan.
- **C** PET scan.
- **D** transcranial magnetic stimulation.

UNDERSTAND ...

2 Which of the following techniques does not provide an actual picture of the brain?

- **A** PET scan
- **B** MRI
- **C** Electroencephalogram (EEG)
- **D** fMRI

APPLY ...

3 A neuroscientist was interested in identifying the brain areas involved when women see photographs of their loved ones. Which functional neuroimaging technique would be the most useful in identifying these regions?

- **A** fMRI
- **B** MRI
- **C** Transcranial magnetic stimulation (TMS)
- **D** CT scan

ANALYZE ...

4 A drawback of PET scans compared to newer techniques, such as magnetoencephalography, is that

- **A** PET is slower, which means it is more difficult to measure moment-to-moment changes in brain activity.
- **B** PET is faster, which makes it difficult to figure out how brain activity relates to what someone sees or hears.
- **C** PET is too expensive for research use.
- **D** PET is slower, and it does not provide a picture of the brain.

Answers can be found on page ANS-1.

Module 3.4

Module Summary

Sun Media/Splash News/Newscom

Now that you have read this module you should

KNOW ...

- ***The key terminology associated with measuring and observing brain activity:***

computerized tomography (CT) scan (p. 123)
diffusion tensor imaging (DTI) (p. 124)
electroencephalogram (EEG) (p. 124)
functional magnetic resonance imaging (fMRI) (p. 125)
functional neuroimaging (p. 124)
lesioning (p. 121)
magnetic resonance imaging (MRI) (p. 123)
magnetoencephalography (MEG) (p. 125)
positron emission tomography (PET) (p. 125)
structural neuroimaging (p. 123)
transcranial magnetic stimulation (TMS) (p. 122)

UNDERSTAND ...

- ***How studies of animals with brain lesions can inform us about the workings of the brain.*** Researchers have learned a great deal from studies of neurological patients; however, because most accidental brain damage is spread out across many structures, it is difficult to determine the effect of damage to *a particular structure*. Lesion studies with animals allow researchers to address this type of question by intentionally damaging a very specific region of the brain. These studies also allow researchers to test far more subjects than they could if they were testing humans with brain damage; therefore, animal lesion studies allow researchers to answer more questions than would otherwise be possible.

APPLY ...

- ***Your knowledge of neuroimaging techniques to see which ones would be most useful in answering a specific research question.*** Review **Table 3.4**, which summarizes each of the major types of functional neuroimaging. Then decide which one should be used to answer each of the following research questions (check your answers on page ANS-1):

1. Lynn was an epilepsy patient seeking treatment. Her seizures did not involve the muscle twitches typical of grand mal seizures. Instead, she would stop talking and stare blankly into the distance for 20–30 seconds (this is known as a petit mal seizure). Her neurologist wanted to use a neuroimaging method to detect when she was having a seizure. Which one should she use?
2. Neil was interested in how dopamine neurons in the brain responded when participants were given rewarding foods like jelly beans versus bland foods. Which functional neuroimaging method should he use to answer his question?
3. Jen wanted to measure the precise brain areas that were active when people experienced pain. Which neuroimaging method would give her this information?
4. Jason was interested in how people pay attention to more than one stimulus at the same time. He wanted to measure brain responses within the first half second after images were flashed on a computer screen. Which method(s) would allow him to answer his research question?

ANALYZE ...

- ***Whether neuroimaging can be used to diagnose brain injuries.*** Several methods for measuring brain activity were covered in this module. A CT scan can provide an initial picture of the brain; this is used most often when a patient first enters the hospital. If a more detailed image is necessary and the patient does not have metal fragments in his body, then MRI is used. If researchers are particularly interested in diagnosing white-matter damage, diffusion tensor imaging (DTI) may be used as well. Additionally, any of the functional imaging methods discussed in this module could show different patterns of activity for individuals with and without brain damage, depending upon the task being performed and the location of the injury.

Work the Scientific Literacy Model :: Understanding Brain Functions

1 What do we know about structures of the brain?

See **Table 3.2** for a list of the major brain regions, structures, and their functions. As you review this material, try to come up with strategies to distinguish these terms. For example, two brain structures commonly confused with each other are the hypothalamus and the hippocampus. Although the hypothalamus and the hippocampus are both part of the limbic system, they have very different functions. The hypothalamus serves as a sort of thermostat, maintaining the appropriate body temperature, and it can affect drives such as aggression and sex. The hippocampus is critical for learning and memory, particularly the formation of new memories. Can you think of a memory device that might help you keep these two brain structures separate? One suggestion: For the hippocampus, think of the last part of the word—"campus." To successfully navigate your university's campus, you need to keep in mind where certain buildings are located. This area is exactly the type of task that involves a functioning hippocampus. As you study, try to come up with your own memory devices to help recall the different brain structures and their functions.

2 How can science help explain brain structure and function?

As discussed on **page 121**, in the very early days of brain research, scientists had to rely almost exclusively on case studies to gather data. There was no way to image the brain of a living, breathing patient or research participant. Today, through neuroimaging technology, researchers are able to take detailed pictures of the brain and can examine the actual activity of major structures such as the hypothalamus and the hippocampus while that activity is occurring. Researchers have developed a variety of methods for studying the brain, each of which offers some advantage over the others. See **pages 121–125** for detailed descriptions of methods for measuring and observing brain activity: electroencephalogram (EEG), positron emission tomography (PET) scans, magnetic resonance imaging (MRI), functional MRI (fMRI), magnetoencephalography (MEG), brain lesioning, and transcranial magnetic stimulation (TMS).

Sebastian Kaulitzki/Shutterstock

4 Why is this relevant?

Watch the accompanying video excerpt on brain functions. You can access the video at MyPsychLab or by clicking the play button in the centre of your eText. If your instructor assigns this video as a homework activity, you will find additional content to help you in MyPsychLab. You can also view the video by using your smart phone and the QR code below, or you can go to the YouTube link provided.

After you have read this chapter and watched the video, imagine that your best friends invite you over for pizza and a friendly game of cards. Describe how the following parts of the brain are involved during your evening of eating pizza, socializing, and playing cards: Broca's area, hippocampus, hypothalamus, and occipital lobe.

3 Can we critically evaluate claims about brain function?

Modern methods have helped us understand a great deal about brain structures and functions, but many misunderstandings persist. In **Myths in Mind on page 95**, we addressed the question of whether humans are born with all of the nerve cells we will ever have. In the past 15 years or so, advances in brain science have challenged this traditionally held belief. Researchers have observed neurogenesis in a limited number of brain regions, particularly in the hippocampus. Some areas within the hippocampus have the capacity to generate new cells long after birth.

Also, in our discussion of hemispheric specialization on **page 115**, we discussed how the degree to which people are "right-brained" or "left-brained" is often exaggerated in the popular media. Creative artists are often described as "right-brained," whereas logical and analytical types are supposedly "left-brained." In reality, most cognitive functions are spread throughout multiple brain regions.

It is easy to get caught up in thinking about these kinds of generalities as absolutes. Whenever you encounter "scientific claims" in the popular media, it is important to properly evaluate the information before embracing it as truth.

MyPsychLab **Your turn to Work the Scientific Literacy Model:** Watch the accompanying video on YouTube, or on your phone (using the Layar app or QR code). If your instructor has assigned this as a homework activity, you can find the video clip and additional content at MyPsychLab. Answer the questions that accompany the video clip to test your understanding.

youtube.com/workthemodel

SCAN WITH LAYAR

4

Sensation and Perception

SERHAT AKAVCI/Shutterstock

Martin Philbey/Redferns/Getty Images

Module 4.1

Sensation and Perception at a Glance

Learning Objectives

After reading this module you should

KNOW ...	UNDERSTAND ...	APPLY ...	ANALYZE ...
The key terminology of sensation and perception	What stimulus thresholds are The methods of signal detection theory	Your knowledge of signal detection theory to identify hits, misses, and correct responses in examples	Claims that subliminal advertising and backward messages can influence your behaviour

In December 1985, 18-year-old Ray Belknap shot himself to death in Reno, Nevada. His friend, James Vance, attempted to do the same but survived, his face forever scarred by the shotgun blast. Vance later claimed that his actions were influenced by "subliminal messages" found in the heavy metal music of the band Judas Priest. His family sued the band for damages. The prosecution claimed that when played backwards, the song "Better by You, Better Than Me" contained the phrase "do it." This phrase was allegedly perceived by the two youths, prompting them to attempt suicide. Although this claim seems outlandish, it led to lengthy legal proceedings and received heavy media coverage. It took the work of two Canadian psychologists to demonstrate that these allegations were unfounded. Their research, described later in this module, demonstrates the importance of scientific literacy and provides interesting insights about the abilities—and limitations—of our perceptual systems.

Focus Questions

 What is the difference between sensation and perception?

 What are the principles that guide perception?

Sensation and perception are different, yet integrated processes. To illustrate this point, take a look at the Necker cube in Figure 4.1. After staring at it for several seconds, you likely noticed that the perspective changed: The cube seemingly flipped its orientation on the page. Although the cube remains constant on the page and in the way it is reflected in the eye, it can be perceived in different

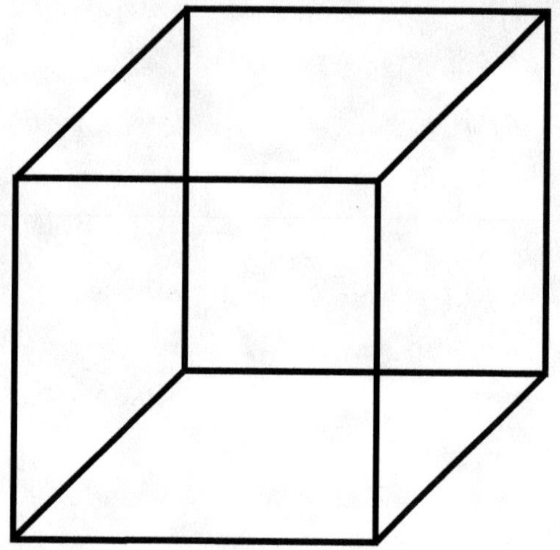

{FIG. 4.1} **The Necker Cube** Stare at this object for several seconds until it changes perspectives.

ways. The switching of perspectives is a perceptual phenomenon that takes place in the brain.

Sensing the World Around Us

The world outside of the human body is full of light, sound vibrations, and objects we can touch. A walk through campus can be filled with the moving shadows of towering elm trees, the sounds of birds chirping, and the cool crisp air of an autumn morning. In order to make sense of all this information, the body has developed an amazing array of specialized processes for sensing and perceiving the world around us. The process of detecting and then translating the complexity of the world into meaningful experiences occurs in two stages.

Watch
The Big Picture: Taking in the World Around Us

The first step is **sensation**, *the process of detecting external events by sense organs and turning those stimuli into neural signals.* At the sensory level, the sound of someone's voice is simply noise, and the sight of a person is merely a combination of colour and motion. All of this raw sensory information is then relayed to the brain, where perception occurs. **Perception** *involves attending to, organizing, and interpreting stimuli that we sense.* Perception includes recognizing the sounds as a human voice and understanding that certain colours, shapes, and motion together make up the image of a human being walking toward you.

The raw sensations detected by the sensory organs are turned into information that the brain can process through **transduction**, *when specialized receptors transform the physical energy of the outside world into neural impulses.* These neural impulses travel into the brain and influence the activity of different brain structures, which ultimately gives rise to our *internal representation* of the world.

The sensory receptors involved in transduction are different for the different senses (summarized in Table 4.1). The transduction of light occurs when it reaches receptors at the back of the eye; light-sensitive chemicals in the retina then convert this energy into nerve impulses that travel to numerous brain centres where colour and motion are perceived and objects are identified (see Figure 4.2). The transduction of sound takes place in a specialized structure called the cochlea, where sound energy is converted into neural impulses that travel to the hearing centres of the brain.

The brain's ability to organize our sensations into coherent perceptions is remarkable. All of our senses use the same mechanism for transmitting information in the brain: the action potential (see Module 3.2). As a result, the brain is continually bombarded by waves of neural impulses representing the world in all its complexity; yet, somehow, it must be able to separate different sensory signals from one another so that we can experience distinct sensations—sight, sound, touch, smell, and taste. It accomplishes this feat by sending signals from different sensory organs to different parts of the brain. Therefore, it is not the original sensory input that is most important for generating our perceptions; rather, it is the brain area that processes this information. We see because visual information gets sent to the occipital lobes, which

Table 4.1 :: Stimuli Affecting Our Major Senses and Corresponding Receptors

SENSE	STIMULI	TYPE OF RECEPTOR
Vision (Module 4.2)	Light waves	Light-sensitive structures at the back of the eye
Hearing (Module 4.3)	Sound waves	Hair cells that respond to pressure changes in the ear
Touch (Module 4.4)	Pressure, stretching, or piercing of the skin surface	Different types of nerve endings that respond to pressure, temperature changes, and pain
Taste (Module 4.4)	Chemicals on the tongue and in the mouth	Cells lining the taste buds of the tongue
Smell (Module 4.4)	Chemicals contacting mucus-lined membranes of the nose	Nerve endings that respond selectively to different compounds

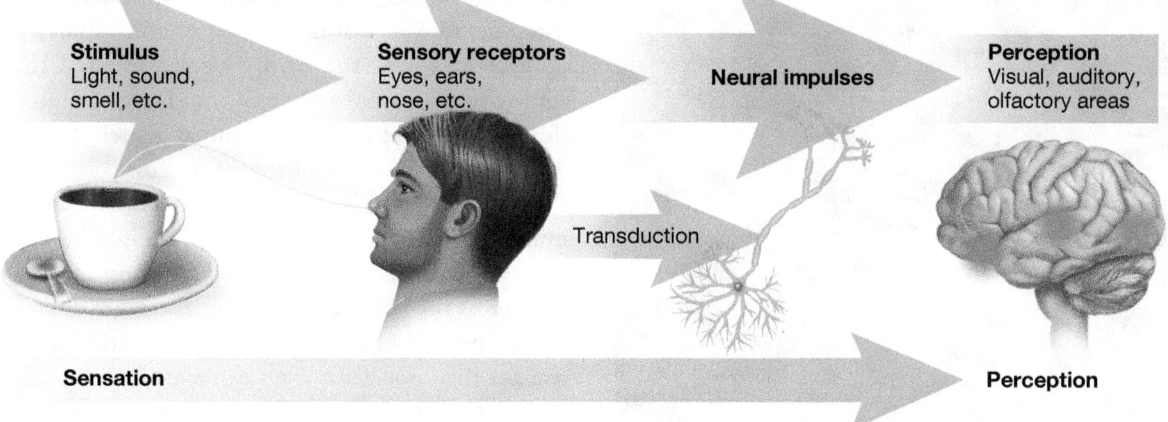

{FIG. 4.2} **From Stimulus to Perception** Sensing and perceiving begin with the detection of a stimulus by one of our senses. Receptors convert the stimulus into a neural impulse, a process called transduction. Our perception of the stimulus takes place in higher, specialized regions of the brain. **Click on this figure in your eText to see more details.**

generates our experience of vision. We hear because auditory information gets sent to our temporal lobes, which generates our experience of hearing. This idea, that *the different senses are separated in the brain,* was first proposed in 1826 by the German physiologist Johannes Müller and is known as the **doctrine of specific nerve energies.**

Although this separation seems perfectly logical, it requires that distinct pathways connect sensory organs to the appropriate brain structures. Interestingly, these pathways are not fully distinct in the developing brain. Researchers at McMaster University have demonstrated that infants have a number of overlapping sensations (Maurer & Maurer, 1988; Spector & Maurer, 2009). For instance, spoken language elicits activity in areas of the brain related to hearing, but also in brain areas related to vision. This effect does not disappear until age three (Neville, 1995). As children age, the pathways in their brains become more distinct, with less useful connections being pruned away. Thus, perception is a skill that our brains learn through experience.

Experience also influences how we adapt to sensory stimuli in our everyday lives. Generally speaking, our sensory receptors are most responsive upon initial exposure to a stimulus. For example, when you first walk into a crowded restaurant or when you exit a dark movie theatre after a matinee, the sound and light you encounter initially seem intense. This feeling occurs because both the sensory receptors and brain areas related to perception are extremely sensitive to change. A change in the environment provides new information for the brain, and the processing of new information is useful for survival. Thus, from an evolutionary perspective, our brains evolved to be highly selective to signals of danger and to rapidly recognize opportunities for useful resources in the environment. The *orienting response* describes how we quickly shift our attention to stimuli that signal a change in our sensory world.

The flip side of this ability is that we allocate progressively less attention to stimuli that remain the same over time; these unchanging stimuli elicit less activity in the nervous system and are perceived as being less intense over time. So, the sound of traffic outside your room will seem less annoying after a few minutes than it did when you first started studying. This process is known as **sensory adaptation**, *the reduction of activity in sensory receptors with repeated exposure to a stimulus.* Sensory adaptation provides the benefit of allowing us to adjust to our surroundings and shift our focus to other events that may be important.

There is a real-world example of sensory adaptation that most of us experience every day. Watch television for 5–10 minutes; but, rather than follow the plot of the show, pay attention to how many times the camera angle changes. Directors change the camera angle (and thus your sensation and perception) every few seconds in order to prevent you from experiencing sensory adaptation. The image on the screen will change from wide-angle shots to close-ups of different actors, and that change stimulates your orienting response, making it difficult for you to look away. Whether this over-exposure to rapidly changing stimuli is having a permanent effect on our brains—particularly the developing brains of children—is a hotly debated issue in current psychological research (Bavelier et al., 2010; Healy, 2004).

Flashon Studio/Shutterstock.com

Sensory adaptation is one process that accounts for why we respond less to a repeated stimulus—even to something that initially seems impossible to ignore.

STIMULUS THRESHOLDS How loud does someone have to whisper for you to hear that person? If you touch a railroad track, how sensitive are your fingers to vibrations from a distant train? One early researcher, physicist and philosopher William Gustav Fechner (1801–1887), coined the term *psychophysics*: *the field of study that explores how physical energy such as light and sound and their intensity relate to psychological experience.* Fechner and other early psychophysicists were interested in some basic questions about perceptual experience and sought to understand general principles of perception. A popular approach was to measure the minimum amount of a stimulus needed for detection, and the degree to which a stimulus must change in strength for the change to be perceptible.

Simulate Weber's Law

See if you can estimate human sensory abilities in the following situations (based on Galanter, 1962):

- If you were standing atop a mountain on a dark, clear night, how far away do you think you could detect the flame from a single candle?
- How much perfume would need to be spilled in a three-room apartment for you to detect the odour?

On a clear night, a candle flame can be detected 50 km away. One drop of perfume is all that is needed for detection in a three-room apartment. Although these examples might seem a bit odd, each of these values represents an **absolute threshold**—that is, *the minimum amount of energy or quantity of a stimulus required for it to be reliably detected at least 50% of the time it is presented* (Figure 4.3). For example, imagine an experimenter asked you to put on headphones and listen for spoken words; however, she manipulated the volume at which the words were presented so that some could be heard and some could not. Your absolute threshold would be the volume at which you could detect the words 50% of the time. But, your absolute threshold might differ from the person beside you—the minimum amount of pressure, sound, light, or chemical required for detection varies among individuals and across the life span. There are also large differences across species. The family dog may startle, bark, and tear for the door before you can even detect a visitor's approach, and a cat can detect changes in shadows and light that go unnoticed by humans. There is no magic or mystery in either example: These animals simply have lower absolute thresholds for detecting sound and light.

Another measure of perception refers to how well an individual can detect whether a stimulus has changed. A **difference threshold** *is the smallest difference between stimuli that can be reliably detected at least 50% of the time.* When you add salt to your food, for example, you are attempting to cross a difference threshold that your taste receptors can register. Whether you actually detect a difference, known as a *just noticeable difference*, depends primarily on the intensity of the original stimulus. The more intense the original stimulus, the larger the amount of it that must be added for the difference threshold to be reached. For example, if you add one pinch of salt to a plate of french fries that already had one pinch sprinkled on them, you can probably detect the difference. However, if you add one pinch of salt to fries that already had four pinches applied, you probably will not detect much of a difference. Apparently, to your senses, a single pinch of salt does not always equal one pinch.

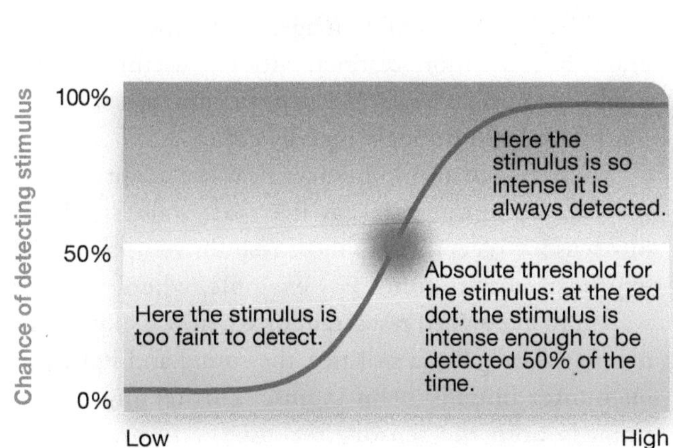

{FIG. 4.3} **Absolute Thresholds** The absolute threshold is the level at which a stimulus can be detected 50% of the time.

Jostein Hauge/Shutterstock.com

Compared to people, dogs have amazingly low thresholds for detecting smells. Dogs have even been trained to detect tumours in people with various types of cancer.

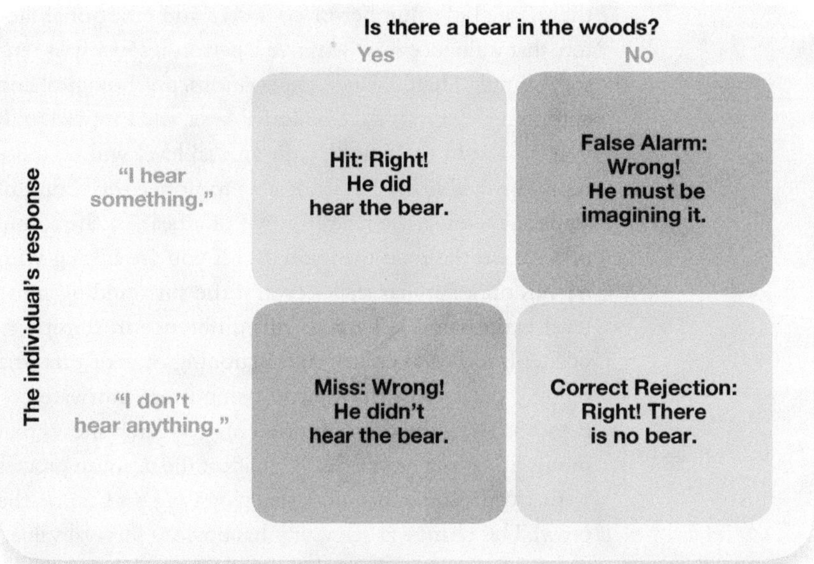

{FIG. 4.4} **Signal Detection Theory** Signal detection theory recognizes that a stimulus is either present or absent (by relying on the sensory process) and that the individual either reports detecting the stimulus or does not (the decision process). The cells represent the four possible outcomes of this situation. Here we apply signal detection theory to a man alone in the woods.

The study of stimulus thresholds has its limitations. Whether someone perceives a stimulus is determined by self-report—that is, by an individual reporting that she either did or did not detect a stimulus. But, not all people are equally willing to say they sensed a weak stimulus. Some people may wait until they are 100% certain that a candle was viewed whereas other people may claim to see a faint candlelight just because they expect to see it. This concept has real-world implications. Think of a radiologist trying to detect tumours in a set of images: If there are differences in the absolute threshold of different radiologists, then one might miss tumours that the other would have detected. But, this scenario is even more complex—different radiologists might be more or less likely to report seeing a tumour when they are unsure of what they have seen. How do we confirm whether these stimuli were truly perceived, or whether the individuals were just guessing?

SIGNAL DETECTION If you are certain that a stimulus exists (e.g., you were hit in the face with a soccer ball), then there is no reason to worry about whether you did or did not perceive something. However, there are many instances in which we must make decisions about sensory input that is uncertain, as in the previous example of a radiologist. It is in these ambiguous situations that signal detection theory can be a powerful tool for the study of our sensory systems. **Signal detection theory** *states that whether a stimulus is perceived depends on both sensory experience and judgment made by the subject.* Thus, the theory requires us to examine two processes: a sensory process and a decision process. In a typical signal detection experiment conducted in the laboratory, the experimenter presents either a faint stimulus or no stimulus at all; this is the *sensory process.* The subject is then asked to report whether or not a stimulus was actually presented; this is the *decision process.*

In developing signal detection theory, psychologists realized that there are four possible outcomes (see Figure 4.4). For example, you may be correct that you heard a sound (a *hit*), or correct that you did not hear a sound (known as a *correct rejection*). Of course, you will not always be correct in your judgments. Sometimes you will think you heard something that is not there; psychologists refer to this type of error as a *false alarm.* On other occasions you may fail to detect that a stimulus was presented (a *miss*). By analyzing how often a person's responses fall into each of these four categories, psychologists can accurately measure the sensitivity of that person's sensory systems.

Studies using signal detection theory have shown that whether a person can accurately detect a weak stimulus appears to depend on a number of factors. First among these is the sensitivity of a person's sensory organs. For instance, some people can detect tiny differences in the tastes of spicy foods, whereas other people experience them all as "hot." But, in addition to these objective differences, there are also a number of cognitive and emotional factors that influence how sensitive a person is to various sensory stimuli. These include expectations, psychological and autonomic-nervous-system arousal level, and motivation. If you are lost in the woods, your arousal level will be quite high. You will likely be better able to notice the sound of someone's voice, the far-off growl of a bear, or the sound of a car on the road than you will if you are hiking with friends on a familiar trail—even if the surrounding noise level is the same. Why does this difference in sensitivity occur? Is it due to enhanced functioning of your ears (the sensory process) or due to you being more motivated to detect sounds (the decision process)? Research shows that motivational changes are likely to affect the decision process so that you assume that every snapping twig is a bear on the prowl. This change in sensitivity has obvious survival value.

So far, we have been describing research about stimuli that individuals have consciously perceived. But, what is the fate of information that stimulated the sensory organs but was too weak to reach conscious awareness? Could such a weak stimulus still influence our behaviour, thoughts, and feelings? And, how could we accurately assess such a phenomenon? These questions abound when discussing the myths—and the realities—of subliminal perception.

MYTHS IN MIND

Setting the Record Straight on Subliminal Messaging

Do you think that messages presented to you so rapidly that you couldn't consciously see them would still influence your behaviour? In the 1950s, a marketing researcher named James Vicary suggested such persuasion can indeed occur. Vicary claimed that by presenting the messages "eat popcorn" and "drink Coca-Cola" on a movie screen, he was able to increase the sales of popcorn and Coke at that theatre. Although later exposed as a hoax, Vicary's claims received a great deal of attention from both the public and the CIA and spawned a huge subliminal self-help industry. But, does *subliminal perception*—meaning perception below the threshold of conscious awareness—really exist? And if so, can it really control our motivations, beliefs, and behaviours?

The answer to the first question is *yes*, we can perceive subliminal stimuli *under strict laboratory conditions*. This phenomenon has been demonstrated time and again in cognitive psychology experiments (Van den Bussche et al., 2009). In this type of study, experimenters often present a word or an image for a fraction of a second. This presentation is then immediately followed by another image, known as a *mask*, which is displayed for a longer period of time. The mask interferes with the conscious perception of the "subliminal" stimulus—indeed, the perceivers are often unaware that any stimulus appeared before the mask (e.g., Cheesman & Merikle, 1986). Yet, a number of brain imaging studies have shown that these rapidly presented stimuli do in fact influence patterns of brain activity (Critchley et al., 2000). Thus it appears that subliminal perception can occur, and it can produce small effects in the nervous system.

However, can subliminal perception influence behaviours? Numerous companies selling subliminal self-help products would like you to believe so. However, research by Canadian psychologists suggests that these claims may be inaccurate. For example, Merikle and Skanes (1992) tested the usefulness of subliminal weight-loss tapes. Female participants were randomly assigned to one of three experimental conditions: (1) subliminal weight-loss tapes, (2) subliminal tapes for the reduction of dental anxiety, and (3) a wait list (no tapes). The women were weighed before and after a six-week period to see if the tapes affected weight loss. The researchers found no difference between the three groups, suggesting that the tapes were entirely ineffective.

A similar study by American researchers suggests that even if some improvement *were* to occur after participants heard subliminal tapes, these effects may be due to the participants' expectations (Greenwald et al., 1991). In this study, participants were given subliminal cassettes that supposedly improved memory or improved self-esteem. Importantly, the labels on the tapes varied such that half of the participants received the correct cassette-label pairing (e.g., a memory cassette with a memory label) and half received the opposite (e.g., a memory cassette with a self-esteem label). Testing conducted after one month of use showed no effects based on the content of the cassettes. However, there was a general overall improvement in all conditions, suggesting that simply being in an experiment helped both self-esteem and memory. Importantly, there was also a trend for participants to believe that the cassettes had produced the desired effect—but this perceived improvement was for the ability that was on the cassette's *label*, not necessarily what the participants *actually heard*. In other words, their expectations led them to believe that they had improved an ability even though they hadn't received any subliminal help for that ability.

Research also demonstrates that subliminal messages are unlikely to create motivations that hadn't previous existed, a grave concern of many people in the 1950s and 1960s. At best, such messages might enhance a motivation or goal that we already have. Erin Strahan and her colleagues at the University of Waterloo examined whether subliminal stimuli related to thirst would differentially affect thirsty and non-thirsty viewers (Strahan et al., 2002). They found that after viewing thirst-related subliminal stimuli (the words "thirst" and "dry"), thirsty participants drank more of a beverage and rated it more positively than did non-thirsty participants (who were not influenced by the subliminal words). No group difference was found when the subliminally presented words were not thirst-related. These results demonstrate that although subliminal perception can activate an *already existing* motivational state, it cannot create a *new* motivational state. Therefore, it is definitely *not* a form of "mind control."

DG Photography/Alamy

Do you see a cigarette advertisement in this photo? There is not an obvious one, but you may be reminded of Marlboro cigarettes as you look at this race car. Critics have accused sponsors of this Formula One car of using the barcode design to create an image similar to Marlboro Red cigarettes. Inquiries into attempts at subliminal advertising over this issue ensued.

Quick Quiz 4.1a

Sensing the World Around Us

KNOW ...

1 __________ is the study of how physical events relate to psychological perceptions of those events.

- **A** Sensation
- **B** Sensory adaptation
- **C** Perception
- **D** Psychophysics

UNDERSTAND ...

2 The minimum stimulation required to detect a stimulus is a(n) ______, whereas the minimum required to detect the difference between two stimuli is a(n) ______.

- **A** just noticeable difference; difference threshold
- **B** absolute threshold; difference threshold
- **C** difference threshold; absolute threshold
- **D** just noticeable difference; absolute threshold

3 Signal detection theory improves on simple thresholds by including the influence of

- **A** psychological factors, such as expectations.
- **B** engineering factors, such as how well a set of speakers is designed.
- **C** whether an individual has hearing or visual impairments.
- **D** the actual intensity of the stimulus.

APPLY ...

4 Walking on a crowded downtown sidewalk, Ben thinks he hears his name called, but when he turns around, he cannot find anyone who might be speaking to him. In terms of signal detection theory, mistakenly believing he heard his name is an example of a ______.

- **A** hit
- **B** miss
- **C** bogus hit
- **D** false alarm

ANALYZE ...

5 Is it reasonable to conclude that subliminal messages have a *strong* effect on behaviour?

- **A** No, research shows that they have no effect whatsoever.
- **B** No, although research shows they might have mild effects.

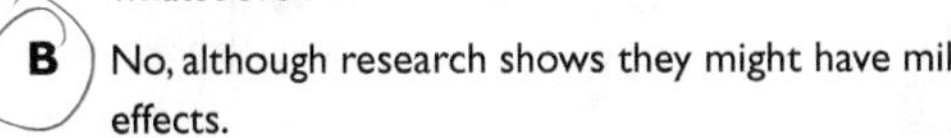

- **C** Yes, the research shows that subliminal ads are powerful.
- **D** Conclusions about subliminal messages have not been reached by psychologists.

Answers can be found on page ANS-2.

Perceiving the World Around Us

The study of thresholds, signal detection, and subliminal perception has given us answers to many basic questions about how we sense and perceive our environment. But, how do we actually form perceptions from all of this sensory information? The attempt to answer this question has a rich history in psychology, taking us back to the first half of the 20th century.

GESTALT PRINCIPLES OF PERCEPTION In 1910, Max Wertheimer was riding on a train from Vienna, Austria, to Frankfurt, Germany. As he stared out the window at the Central European countryside, he noticed that the buildings in the distance appeared to be moving backwards. Wertheimer was intrigued by this obvious illusion, and decided to investigate the experience when he arrived in Frankfurt later that day. That evening, he bought himself a stroboscope, a toy that displayed pictures in rapid succession. He noticed that individual pictures did not move; but, when presented within a fraction of a second of each other, the individual images created the perception of movement. This simple observation had an astounding impact on the study of perception, and led to the development of the Gestalt school of psychology.

Gestalt psychology is an approach to perception that emphasizes that "the whole is greater than the sum of its parts." In other words, the individual parts of an image may have little meaning on their own, but when combined together, the whole takes on a significant perceived form. Gestalt psychologists identified several key principles to describe how we organize features that we perceive.

One basic Gestalt principle is that objects or "figures" in our environment tend to stand out against a background. Gestalt psychologists refer to this basic perceptual rule as the *figure–ground* principle. The text in front of you is a figure set against a background, but you may also consider the individual letters you see to be figures against the background of the page. This perceptual tendency is particularly apparent when the distinction between figure and ground

Simulate
Distinguishing Figure-Ground Relationships

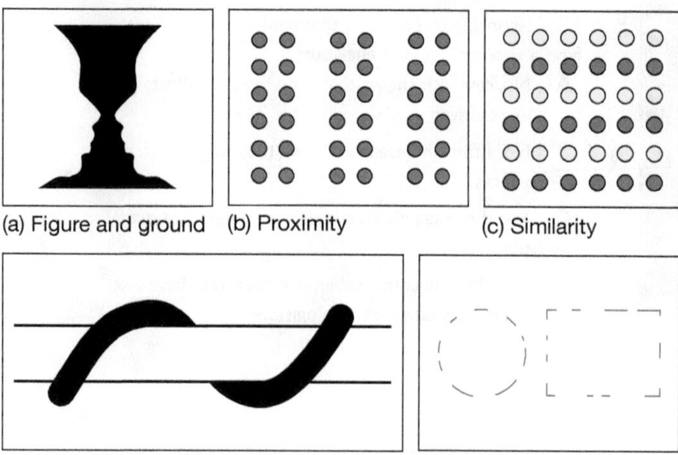

{FIG. 4.5} **Gestalt Principles of Form Perception** (a) Figure and ground. (b) Proximity helps us group items together so that we see three columns instead of six rows. (c) Similarity occurs when we perceive the similar dots as forming alternating rows of yellow and red, not as columns of alternating colours. (d) Continuity is the tendency to view items as whole figures even if the image is broken into multiple segments. (e) Closure is the tendency to fill in gaps so as to see a whole object. **Click on this figure in your eText to see more details.**

Simulate Gestalt Laws of Perception

Simulate Ambiguous Figures

is ambiguous, as can be seen in the face–vase illusion in Figure 4.5(a). Do you see a vase or two faces in profile? At the level of sensation, there is neither a vase nor two faces—there is just a pattern. What makes it a perceptual illusion is the recognition that there are two objects, but there is some ambiguity as to which is figure and which is ground. The figure–ground principle applies to hearing as well. When you are holding a conversation with one individual in a crowded party, you are attending to the figure (the voice of the individual) against the background noise (the ground). If the person you are speaking with is dull, you may attend to the music instead of what he or she is saying to you. In this case, the music would become the figure and the droning voice would become the ground. Exactly which object is the figure and which is the ground in any given moment therefore depends on many factors, including what you are motivated to pay attention to.

Proximity and *similarity* are two additional Gestalt principles that influence perception. We tend to treat two or more objects that are in close proximity to each other as a group. Because of their proximity, a dozen eggs in a carton looks like two rows of six eggs, rather than six rows of two eggs. Similarity can be experienced by viewing groups of people in uniform, such as at the opening ceremony of the Vancouver Olympics. We tend to group together individuals wearing the same uniform based on their visual similarity.

Some other key Gestalt principles can also be seen in Figure 4.5. *Continuity*, or "good continuation," refers to the perceptual rule that lines and other objects tend to be continuous, rather than abruptly changing direction. The black object snaking its way around the white object is viewed as one continuous object rather than two separate ones. A related principle, called *closure*, refers to the tendency to fill in gaps to complete a whole object.

It is important to note that Gestalt concepts are not simply a collection of isolated examples. Rather, when put together, they demonstrate an incredibly important characteristic of the perceptual system: we create our own organized perceptions out of the different sensory inputs that we experience. The next time you go outside, look at how we create organized perceptions of architecture, interior design, fashion, and even corporate logos. All of these examples show how much of "you" is in your perceptual experience the world.

The illusions and figures you have viewed in this section reveal some common principles that guide how we perceive the world. We can take this exploration a step further by discussing the cognitive processes that underlie these principles, a topic that brings us back to the controversial court case discussed at the beginning of this module.

Dr. Morley Read/Shutterstock.com

Animals and insects take advantage of figure–ground ambiguity to camouflage themselves from predators. Can you see the walking stick insect in this photo?

Shen Hong/Xinhua/Photoshot/Newscom

The principle of similarity in action. We perceive groups of sports fans based on the colour of their clothing, as seen here at the Opening Ceremonies of the Vancouver 2010 Olympics.

WORKING THE SCIENTIFIC LITERACY MODEL

Backward Messages in Music

Humans are experts at pattern recognition. This ability to detect patterns is the basis for our ability to understand speech. To newborn babies, speech is a series of nonsense sounds. But, with experience, we are able to group together different sounds, which leads to the perception of spoken words. But, how sophisticated are these pattern-recognition abilities? This question is central to the issue of backward messages in music.

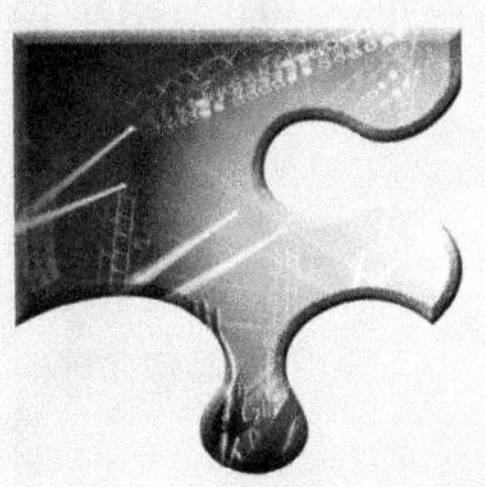

What do we know about backward messages in music?

The idea that music can contain backward messages has a long history. Fans have reported finding evidence of these messages in a few songs from The Beatles. "Messages" have also been found in 1970s songs by Led Zeppelin and Queen. For example, when Queen's song "Another One Bites the Dust" is played backwards, some listeners claim to hear "It's fun to smoke marijuana." However, most examples of backward messages are due to *phonetic reversal,* where a word pronounced backwards sounds like another word (e.g., dog and god). Indeed, in most cases, the bands claim to be unaware that any backward messages exist.

Importantly, until the 1980s, few people believed that these messages could be *perceived* when the music was played forward (i.e., properly), let alone that these messages could *influence people's behaviour.* This changed with the Judas Priest lawsuit discussed at the beginning of this module. In that case, the prosecution claimed that "backward messages" in the music caused two boys to attempt suicide. Could psychology research explain whether these claims were valid?

How can science explain backward messages?

John Vokey and Don Read (1985) from the University of Lethbridge conducted a series of studies that related to the backward messages controversy. These researchers recorded a number of passages onto audio cassettes and then played the cassettes backwards for participants. They found that people could make superficial judgments about the gender of the speaker (98.9% correct), about whether two speakers were the same (78.5% correct), and about the language being spoken—English, French, or German (46.7% correct, where chance performance is 33.3%). However, when asked to make judgments about the *content* of the backward messages, performance fell to chance levels. Participants were unable to distinguish between nursery rhymes, Christian, satanic, pornographic, or advertising messages (19.1% correct, where chance performance is 20%).

But, what if the participants knew what patterns to listen for? It is a common experience that when a backward message is identified in a song and people are told the message in advance, they are able to identify it. To test whether such expectations could influence perception, Vokey and Read asked participants to listen for specific phrases in the backward messages (these were "phrases" that the researchers had picked out after repeatedly listening to the backward stimuli). When asked to listen for "Saw a girl with a weasel in her mouth" and "I saw Satan," 84.6% of the participants agreed that the phrases were perceivable.

Can we critically evaluate this research?

Our perceptions of the world are influenced both by the stimuli themselves as well as by our own mindset. For example, the centre of Figure 4.6 can be perceived as either the number 13 or the letter B depending upon whether you're reading numbers (12 and 14) or letters (A and C). This is an example of **top-down processing**, *when our perceptions are influenced by our expectations or by our prior knowledge.* Reading "12" and "14" gives us the expectation that the ambiguous stimulus in between them must be "13." In the backward messages experiment, participants used top-down processing to perceive specific phrases.

If the participants were not given any directions from the experimenters and instead simply listened to the music backwards and tried to detect messages based on the different sounds that could be heard, they would be engaging in a different type of processing. **Bottom-up processing** *occurs when we perceive individual bits of sensory information (e.g., sounds) and use them to construct a more complex perception (e.g., a message).* As you might expect, bottom-up processing would occur when you encounter something that is unfamiliar or difficult to recognize.

A

12 B 14

C

{FIG. 4.6} **Top-Down Processing** Is the centre the letter B or the number 13?

{FIG. 4.7} **Expectations Influence Perception** Is this a rat or a man's face? People who look at pictures of animals before seeing this image see a rat, whereas those looking at pictures of faces see the image as a man's face.

Explore
Perceptual Set

Top-down and bottom-up processing can be studied using some interesting stimuli, such as the image in Figure 4.7. When you initially looked at this image, you might have seen either a rat or a man. Unless you are currently surrounded by animals or a lot of people, there was very little to guide your perception of the image—you were using bottom-up processing and were just as likely to have thought the image was a rat or a man. However, when people first look at pictures of animals, they tend to see the rat first; if they look at pictures of people, the man is perceived first. Thus, top-down processes can influence the perception of the image as well. In short, the way we perceive the world is a combination of both top-down and bottom-up processing (Beck & Kastner, 2009).

Incidentally, Vokey and Read were asked to testify in the Judas Priest case in order to explain how their psychology experiments related to the legal proceedings. Judas Priest was found not guilty.

Why is this relevant?

These results suggest that we interpret patterns of stimuli in ways that are consistent with our expectations. Several researchers have demonstrated that it is possible to form a *perceptual set*—a filter that influences what aspects of a scene we perceive or pay attention to. But, focusing on particular patterns of stimuli also means that we are *not* focusing on other patterns; in some cases, we ignore pieces of information that don't fit with our expectations. In the backward messages study, participants had to ignore many different sounds in order to detect the sounds that resembled "Saw a girl with a weasel in her mouth." As we'll see in the next section, sometimes our perceptual sets are so fixed that we fail to notice unexpected objects that are clearly visible . . . and very interesting.

Anna Omelchenko/Shutterstock

ATTENTION AND PERCEPTION The example of backward messages shows us that what we pay attention to can affect what we perceive. In fact, in many cases, we are *paying attention to more than one stimulus or task at the same time*, a phenomenon known as **divided attention**. Simultaneously playing a video game and holding a conversation involves divided attention; so does using Facebook and Twitter while you are listening to your charming professor lecture. Although we often feel that dividing our attention is not affecting our performance, there is substantial evidence from both laboratory and real-world studies telling us otherwise (Pashler, 1998; Stevenson et al., 2013).

Simulate
Selective Attention

In contrast, **selective attention** *involves focusing on one particular event or task*, such as focused studying, driving without distraction, or attentively listening to music or watching a movie. In this case, you are paying more attention to one part of your environment so that you can accurately sense and perceive the information it might provide (e.g., watching the road while driving). While useful, this process comes at a cost—your perception of other parts of your environment suffers (e.g., you don't notice the birds in the trees). Most of the time, selective attention is quite beneficial; however, there are times when this focus is so powerful that we fail to perceive some very obvious things.

Imagine you are watching your favourite team play basketball. You're a big fan of a particular player and are intently watching his every move. Would you notice if a person in a gorilla suit ran onto the court for a few seconds? Most people would say "yes." However, psychological research suggests otherwise. Missing the obvious can be surprisingly easy—especially if you are focused on just one particular aspect of your environment. For example, researchers asked undergraduate students to watch a video of students dressed in white t-shirts actively moving around while passing a ball to one another. The participants' task was to count the number of times the ball was passed. To complicate matters, there were also students in black t-shirts doing the same thing with another ball; however, the participants were instructed to ignore them. This is a top-down task because the participants selectively attended to a single set of events. The participants in this study found the task very easy; most were able to accurately count the number of passes, give or take a few.

But what if a student wearing a gorilla suit walked through the video, stopped, pounded her chest, and walked off screen? Who could miss that? Surprisingly, about half the participants failed to even notice the gorilla (Simons & Chabris, 1999). This number was even higher in elderly populations (Graham & Burke, 2011). This result is an example of **inattentional blindness**, *a failure to notice clearly visible events or objects because attention is directed elsewhere* (Mack & Rock, 1998). You can imagine how shocked the participants were when they watched the film again without selectively attending to one thing and realized they had completely missed the gorilla. Inattentional blindness shows that when we focus on a limited number of features, we might not pay much attention to anything else.

Inattentional blindness accounts for many common phenomena. For example, people who witness automobile accidents or criminal behaviour may offer faulty or incomplete testimony. In sports, athletes and referees often miss aspects of a game because they are focusing on one area of action (Memmert & Furley, 2007); inattentional blindness decreases as expertise with the game increases (Furley et al., 2010). Interestingly, research conducted at Dalhousie University has shown that stimuli that were not perceived in an inattentional blindness study still influenced performance on later memory tasks, suggesting that these stimuli did in fact influence our perceptual system (Butler & Klein, 2009). Although this doesn't necessarily mean that referees will be haunted by missed calls, it does mean that the refs weren't blind—just inattentionally blind.

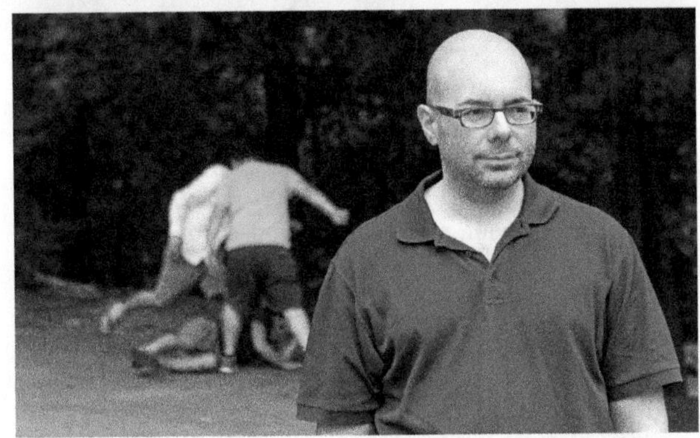

Top: Simons, D. J., & Chabris, C. F. (1999). Gorillas in our midst: Sustained inattentional blindness for dynamic events. *Perception, 28*, 1059–1074. Figure provided by Daniel Simons; bottom: Courtesy of Chris Chabris. Photo by Matt Milless

Do you think you would fail to notice the student in the gorilla suit at a basketball game (top photo, Simons & Chabris, 1999)? In another study of inattentional blindness, researchers discovered that when participants were focused on running after a confederate at night, only 35% of the subjects noticed a staged fight going on right in their pathway, and during the day only 56% noticed (Chabris et al., 2011).

Quick Quiz 4.1b Perceiving the World Around Us

KNOW ...

1 Which gestalt principle refers to the perceptual rule that lines and other objects tend to be continuous, rather than abruptly changing direction?

A Figure–ground
B Continuity
C Proximity and similarity
D Psychophysics

UNDERSTAND ...

2 Failure to notice particular stimuli when paying close attention to others is known as ________.

A misattention
B divided attention
C multitasking
D intentional blindness

ANALYZE ...

3 While watching television, you see a report about a group of parents complaining that backward messages in music are making their children misbehave. According to research, you would tell these parents that

A only backward messages containing emotional information can influence people.
B there is no evidence that backward messages can be perceived unless people are told what to listen for.
C previous research has shown that backward messages can influence behaviour.
D researchers have not come to a definitive conclusion about the effects of backward messages.

Answers can be found on page ANS-2.

Module Summary

Module **4.1**

Now that you have read this module you should

KNOW ...

- ***The key terminology of sensation and perception*:**

absolute threshold (p. 134)
bottom-up processing (p. 139)
difference threshold (p. 134)
divided attention (p. 140)
doctrine of specific nerve energies (p. 133)
inattentional blindness (p. 141)
perception (p. 132)
selective attention (p. 140)
sensation (p. 132)
sensory adaptation (p. 133)
signal detection theory (p. 135)
top-down processing (p. 139)
transduction (p. 132)

UNDERSTAND ...

- ***What stimulus thresholds are.*** Stimulus thresholds can be either *absolute* (the minimum amount of energy to notice a stimulus) or based on *difference* (the minimum change between stimuli required to notice they are different).
- ***The methods of signal detection theory.*** Signal detection theory involves testing whether a participant perceives stimuli by measuring hits (stimulus was presented and detected), misses (stimulus was presented and undetected), false alarms (stimulus was not presented and reported as present), and correct rejections (stimulus was not presented and not reported as present).

APPLY ...

- ***Your knowledge of signal detection theory to identify hits, misses, and correct responses in examples.*** For practice, consider **Figure 4.4 (p. 135)**, along with this example: Imagine a girl who has seen a scary television program and now, while trying to go to sleep, worries about monsters in the closet. Identify which of the four events (A–D) goes within the correct box; that is, identify it as a hit, a miss, a false alarm, or a correct rejection. Warning: For half of these events, you may have to assume there really are monsters in the closet. You can find the answers on page ANS-2.

Martin Philbey/Redferns/Getty Images

Hit:	False alarm:
Miss:	Correct rejection:

A. There is no monster in the closet, and the girl is confident that she has not heard anything.

B. There really are monsters in the closet, but the girl has not heard them.

C. There really is a monster in the closet and she hears it.

D. There is no monster in the closet, but the girl insists that she heard something.

ANALYZE ...

- ***Claims that subliminal advertising and backward messages can influence your behaviour.*** As you read in the Myths in Mind feature, we certainly can perceive stimuli below the level of conscious awareness, and this perception can affect our behaviour in some ways. However, research suggests that subliminal advertising has little effect on one's consumer behaviour. Similarly, studies of backward messages in music have shown that individuals *cannot* perceive the meaning of these messages *unless they are specifically told what they should listen for*, suggesting that the Devil in heavy metal music is really just top-down processing.

Stephen Smith

Module 4.2

The Visual System

Learning Objectives

After reading this module you should

KNOW ...	UNDERSTAND ...	APPLY ...	ANALYZE ...
The key terminology relating to the eye and vision	How visual information travels from the eye through the brain to give us the experience of sight The theories of colour vision	Your knowledge to explain how we perceive depth in our visual field	How we perceive objects and faces

A man stood on a wooden footbridge with his two-year-old son staring at a beautiful pond filled with lily pads. Vibrant pink tropical flowers thrust their green stalks out of the water, appearing to dance in the sunlight reflecting off tiny waves rippling from a small grey fountain in the middle of the pond. Amidst the lily pads, the man and his son could see reflections of palm trees, a blue sky, and the powerful Caribbean sun. However, despite the fact that both individuals were processing the same sensory stimuli, their perceptions of those stimuli were dramatically different. The man's experience with different environments allowed him to recognize that there were a variety of plant species in the pond (even if he had no idea what they were called). The toddler, on the other hand, saw different colours and objects, but likely didn't notice the diversity of plant species. They were just "green things." A member of the gardening staff who worked in that environment every day would have had a much more intricate and detailed perception of the visual scene than either the man or his son ... even though they all *sensed* the same thing. Vision—and the cognition that goes with it—is something we finetune with experience.

Focus Questions

1. Which brain areas are involved with identifying your coffee cup versus reaching for your coffee cup?
2. What tricks can artists use to make two-dimensional paintings appear three dimensional?

The world is a visual place to most humans. We use vision to navigate through beautiful landscapes, city centres, and the interiors of buildings. We also use vision to communicate via facial expressions and the written word (such as this textbook, which you undoubtedly photocopy and tape to your bedroom walls). In this module, we explore how vision works—starting out as patterns of light entering the eye, and ending up as a complex, perceptual

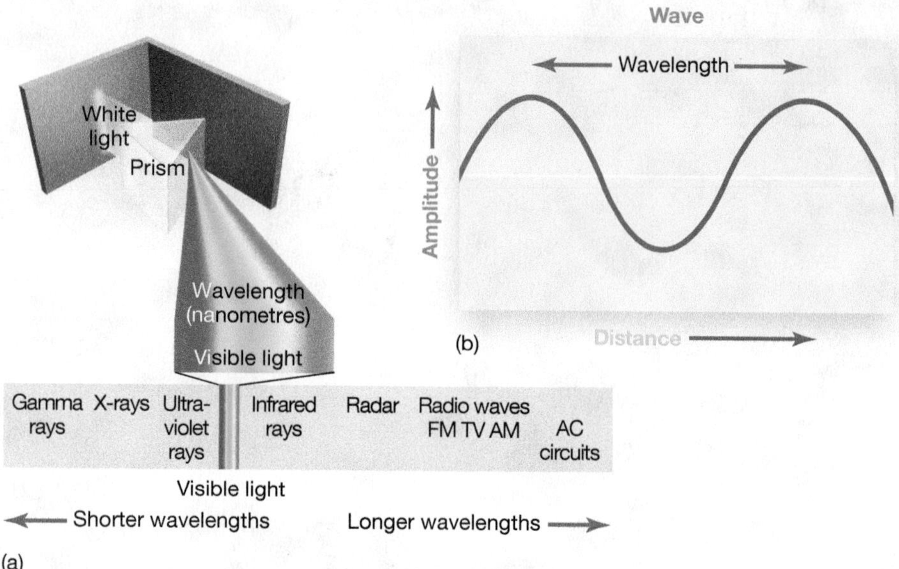

{FIG. 4.8} **Light Waves in the Electromagnetic Spectrum** (a) The electromagnetic spectrum: When white light is shined through a prism, the bending of the light reveals the visible light spectrum. The visible spectrum falls within a continuum of other waves of the electromagnetic spectrum. (b) Wavelength is measured by amplitude and distance.

experience. We begin with an overview of the basic physical structures of the eye and brain that make vision possible, and then discuss the *experience* of seeing.

The Human Eye

The eye is one of the most remarkable of the human body's physical structures. It senses an amazing array of information, translates that information into neural impulses, and transfers it to the brain for complex, perceptual processing. To ensure that this sequence of events begins correctly, the eye needs specialized structures that allow us to regulate how much light comes in, to start decoding the various colours, to maintain a focus on the most important objects in a scene, and to turn physical energy into action potentials, the method by which information is transmitted in the brain.

HOW THE EYE GATHERS LIGHT The primary function of the eye is to gather light and change it into an action potential. But, "light" itself is quite complex. Although physicists have written vast tomes on the topic of light, for the purposes of human perception, "light" actually refers to radiation that occupies a relatively narrow band of the electromagnetic spectrum, shown in Figure 4.8a. Light travels in waves that vary in terms of two different properties: length and amplitude. The term *wavelength* refers to the distance between peaks of a wave—differences in wavelength correspond to different colours on the electromagnetic spectrum. As you can see from Figure 4.8a, long wavelengths correspond to our perception of reddish colours and short wavelengths correspond to our perception of bluish colours. Interestingly, some organisms, such as bees, can see in ultraviolet and some reptiles can see in infrared light. These interspecies differences are likely due to the different evolutionary demands the different species have faced. What pressures do you think led humans to develop their specific visual system? Although no one can answer this question with absolute certainty, some researchers have suggested that our red-green vision allowed us to distinguish between types of edible vegetation (Regan et al., 2001). Others have suggested that our vision developed to allow us to take advantage of pigment-related social cues such as blushing (Changizi et al., 2006).

Wavelength is not the only characteristic that is important for vision. *Amplitude* refers to the height of a wave (see Figure 4.8b). Low-amplitude waves are seen as dim colours, whereas high-amplitude waves are seen as bright colours. Light waves can also differ in terms of how many different wavelengths are being viewed at once. When you look at a clear blue sky, you are viewing many different wavelengths of light at the same time—but the blue wavelengths are more prevalent and therefore dominate your impression. If a large proportion of the light waves are clustered around one wavelength, you will see an intense, vivid colour. If there are a large variety of wavelengths being viewed at the same time, the colour will appear to be "washed out." Figure 4.9 depicts these

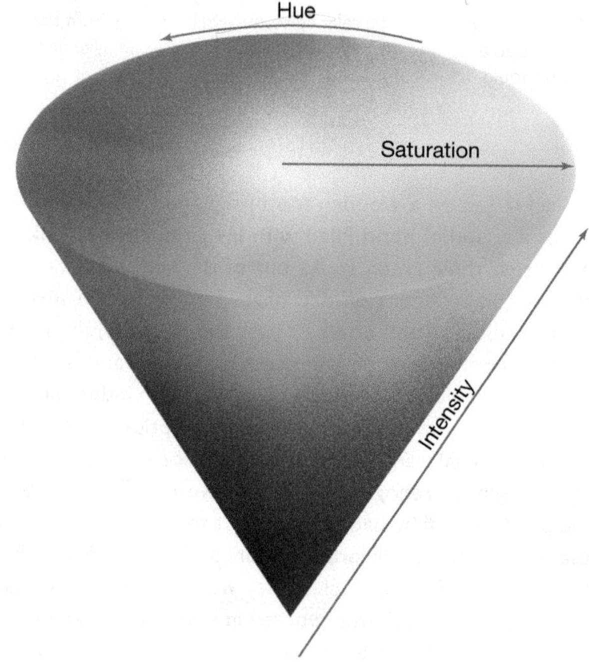

{FIG. 4.9} **Hue, Intensity, and Saturation** Colours vary by hue (colour), intensity (brightness), and saturation (colourfulness or "density").

different characteristics of light—wavelength, amplitude, and purity—as we generally perceive them. These characteristics of light will be experienced by us as *hue* (colour of the spectrum), *intensity* (brightness), and *saturation* (colourfulness or density). It is in the eye that this transformation from sensation to perception takes place.

THE STRUCTURE OF THE EYE The eye consists of specialized structures that regulate the amount of light that enters the eye and organizes it into a pattern that the brain can interpret (see Figure 4.10). The **sclera** *is the white, outer surface of the eye* and the **cornea** *is the clear layer that covers the front portion of the eye and also contributes to the eye's ability to focus.* Light enters the eye through the cornea and passes through an opening called the pupil. The **pupil** *regulates the amount of light that enters by changing its size; it dilates (expands) to allow more light to enter and constricts (shrinks) to allow less light into the eye.* The changes in the pupil's size are performed by the **iris**, *a round muscle that adjusts the size of the pupil; it also gives the eyes their characteristic colour.* Behind the pupil is the **lens**, *a clear structure that focuses light onto the back of the eye.* The lens can change its shape to ensure that the light entering the eye is refracted in such a way that it is focused when it reaches the back of the eye. This process is known as *accommodation*. When the light reaches the back of the eye, it will stimulate a layer of specialized receptors that convert light into a message that the brain can then interpret, a process known as *transduction*. These receptors are part of a complex structure known as the retina.

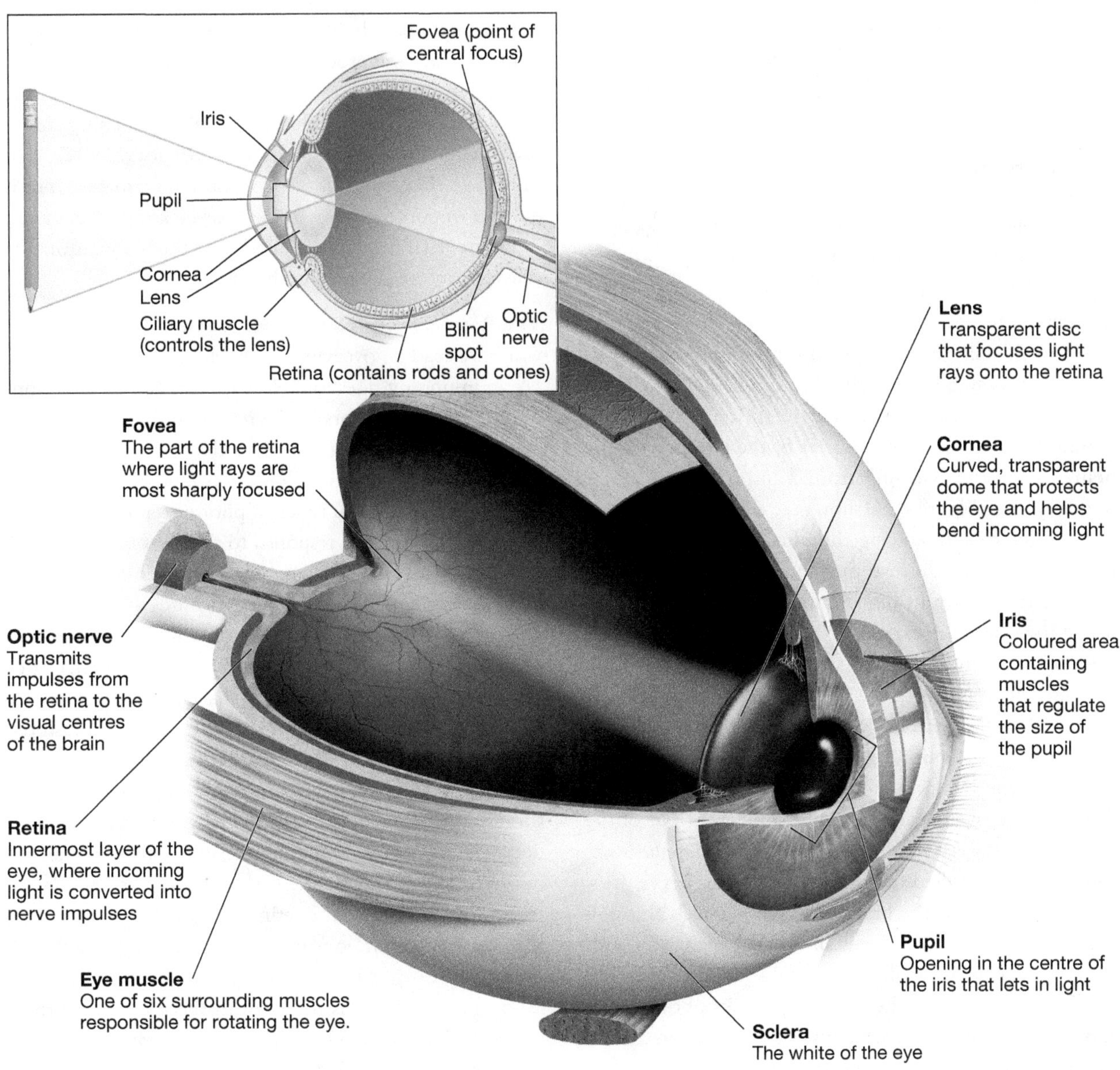

{FIG. 4.10} **The Human Eye and Its Structures** Notice how the lens inverts the image that appears on the retina (see inset). The visual centres of the brain correct the inversion.

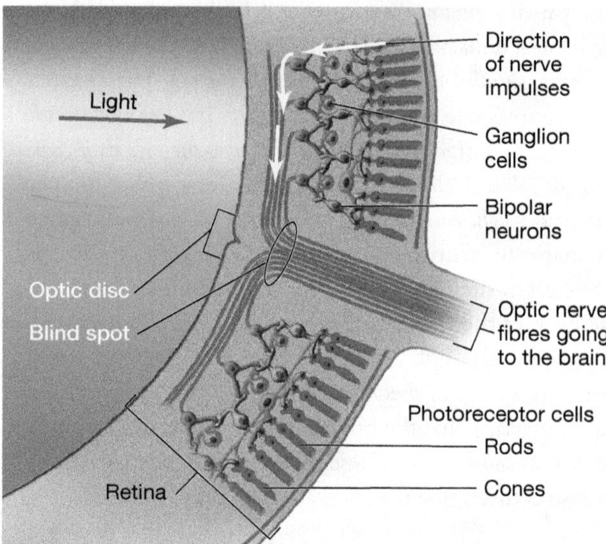

{FIG. 4.11} **Arrangement of Photoreceptors in the Retina** Bipolar and ganglion cells collect messages from the light-sensitive photoreceptors and converge on the optic nerve, which then carries the messages to the brain.

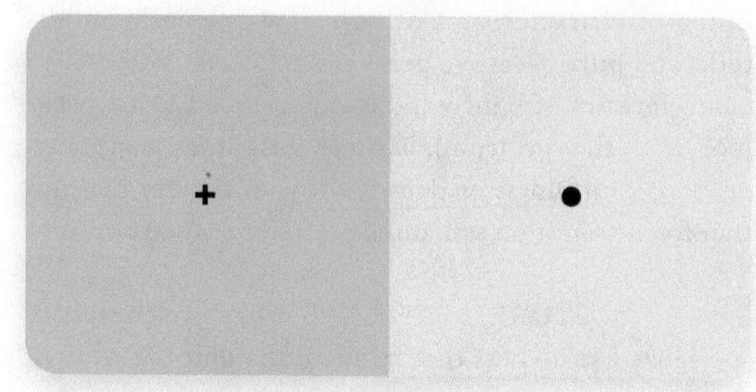

{FIG. 4.12} **Finding Your Blind Spot** To find your blind spot, close your left eye and, with your right eye, fix your gaze on the + in the green square. Slowly move the page toward you. When the page is approximately 6 inches away, you will notice that the black dot on the right disappears because of your blind spot. Not only does the black dot disappear, but its vacancy is replaced by yellow: The brain "fills it in" for you.

Explore
Receptive Fields

The **retina** *lines the inner surface of the eye and consists of specialized receptors that absorb light and send signals related to the properties of light to the brain.* The retina contains a number of different layers, each performing a slightly different function. At the back of the retina are specialized receptors called *photoreceptors.* These receptors, which will be discussed in more depth below, are where light will be transformed into a neural signal that the brain can understand. It may seem strange that light would stimulate the deepest layer of the retina, with the neural signal then turning around and moving forward in the eye (see Figure 4.11); however, there is a reason for this strange design. Having the photoreceptors wedged into the back of the eye protects them and provides them with a constant blood supply, both of which are useful to your ability to see.

Information from the photoreceptors at the back of the retina is transmitted to the ganglion cells closer to the front of the eye. The ganglion cells gather up information from the photoreceptors; this information will then alter the rate at which the ganglion cells fire. The activity of all of the ganglion cells is then sent out of the eye through *a dense bundle of fibres that connect to the brain;* this structure is called the **optic nerve**. This nerve presents a challenge to the brain. Because it travels through the back of the eye, it creates an area on the retina with no photoreceptors, called the *optic disc.* The result is a *blind spot*—a space in the retina that lacks photoreceptors. You can discover your own blind spot by performing the activity described in Figure 4.12.

Explore
Light and the Optic Nerve

Watch
IT Video: Blindspot

The blind spot illustrates just how distinct the processes of sensation and perception are. Why do we fail to notice a completely blank area of our visual field? If we consider only the process of sensation, we cannot answer this question. We have to invoke perception: The visual areas of the brain are able to "fill in" the missing information for us (Ramachandran & Gregory, 1991). Not only does the brain fill in the missing information, but it does so in context. Thus, once the black dot at the right of Figure 4.12 reaches the blind spot, the brain automatically fills in the vacancy with yellow.

The Retina: From Light to Nerve Impulse Now that you have read an overview of the eye's structures, we can ask an important question: How can the firing of millions of little photoreceptors in the retina produce vivid visual experiences like seeing sunlight reflect off of a pond? The simple answer is that not all photoreceptors are the same. There are two general types of photoreceptors—*rods* and *cones*—each of which responds to different characteristics of light. **Rods** *are photoreceptors that occupy peripheral regions of the retina; they are highly sensitive under low light levels* (see Figure 4.13). This type of sensitivity makes rods particularly responsive to black and grey. In contrast, **cones** *are photoreceptors that are sensitive to the different wavelengths of light that we perceive as colour.* Cones tend to be clustered around the **fovea**, *the central region of the retina.*

When the rods and cones are stimulated by light, their physical structure briefly changes. This change decreases the amount of the neurotransmitter glutamate being released, which alters the activity of neurons in the different layers of the retina. The final layer to receive this changed input consists of ganglion cells, which will eventually output to the optic nerve. Interestingly, the ratio of ganglion cells to cones in the fovea is approximately one to one; in contrast, there are roughly 10 rods for every ganglion cell. So, all of the input from a cone is clearly transmitted to a ganglion cell whereas the input from a rod must compete with input from other rods

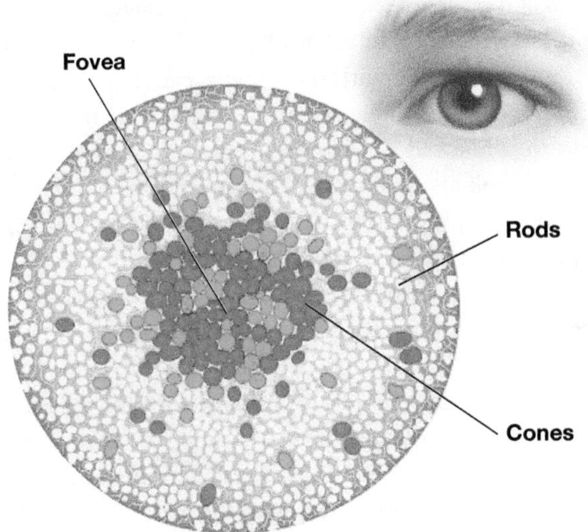

{FIG. 4.13} **Distribution of Rods and Cones on the Retina** Cones are concentrated at the fovea, the centre of the retina, while rods are more abundant in the periphery. There are approximately 120 million rods and approximately 6 to 8 million cones in the adult retina.

(similar to ten people talking at you at the same time). So, cones are clustered in the fovea (i.e., are the centre of our visual field) and have a one-to-one ratio with ganglion cells while rods are limited to the periphery of the retina and have a ten-to-one ratio with ganglion cells. These differences help explain why colourful stimuli are often perceived as sharp images while shadowy grey images are perceived as being hazy or unclear.

In daylight or under artificial light, the cones in the retina are more active than rods—they help us to detect differences in the colour of objects and to discriminate the fine details of them. In contrast, if the lights suddenly go out or if you enter a dark room, at first you see next to nothing. Over time, however, you gradually begin to see your surroundings more clearly. **Dark adaptation** *is the process by which the rods and cones become increasingly sensitive to light under low levels of illumination.* What is actually happening during dark adaptation is that the photoreceptors are slowly becoming regenerated after having been exposed to light. The complete process of dark adaptation typically takes approximately 20 minutes, although most of the changes occur within the first 10 minutes of darkness. We do not see colour at night or in darkness because rods are more active than cones under low light levels.

The phenomenon of dark adaptation explains why we can find our friends in a dark movie theatre. It does not, however, explain why we perceive the sky as being blue or a stop sign as being red. Luckily, 200 years of vision research has provided answers to such questions.

The Retina and the Perception of Colours Our experience of colour is based on how our visual system interprets different wavelengths on the electromagnetic spectrum (refer back to Figure 4.8). Colour is not actually a characteristic of the objects themselves, but is rather an interpretation of these wavelengths by the visual system. As you learned earlier, the cones of the retina are specialized for responding to different wavelengths of light that correspond to different colours. However, the subjective experience of colour occurs in the brain. Currently, two theories exist to explain how neurons in the eye can produce these colourful experiences.

One theory suggests that three different types of cones exist, each of which is sensitive to a different range of wavelengths on the electromagnetic spectrum. These three types of cones were initially identified in the 18th century by physicist Thomas Young and then independently rediscovered in the 19th century by Hermann von Helmholtz. The resulting **trichromatic theory** (or **Young-Helmholtz theory**) *maintains that colour vision is determined by three different cone types that are sensitive to short, medium, and long wavelengths of light.* These cones respond to wavelengths associated with the colours blue, green, and red. The relative responses of the three types of cones allow us to perceive many different colours on the spectrum (see Figure 4.14) and allow us to experience

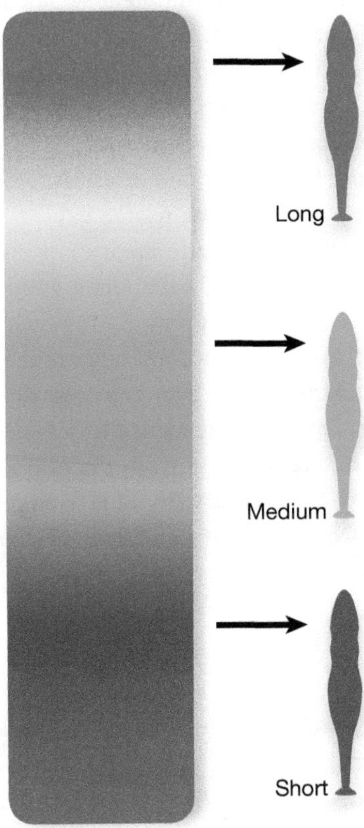

{FIG. 4.14} **The Trichromatic Theory of Colour Vision** According to this theory, humans have three types of cones that respond maximally to different regions of the colour spectrum. Colour is experienced by the combined activity of cones sensitive to short, medium, and long wavelengths.

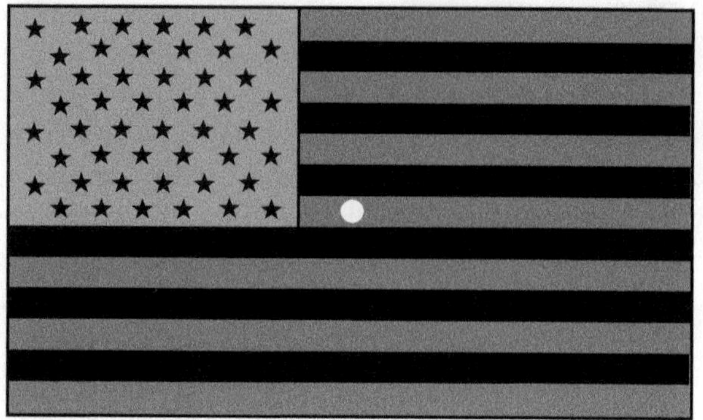

{FIG. 4.15} **The Negative Afterimage: Experiencing Opponent-Process Theory** Stare directly at the white dot within the flag above and avoid looking away. After about a minute, immediately shift your focus to a white background. What do you see?

the vast array of colours seen in environments like that discussed at the beginning of this module. For example, yellow is perceived by combining the stimulation of red- and green-sensitive cones, whereas light that stimulates all cones equally is perceived as white. (Note: mixing different wavelengths of light produces different colours than when you mix different colours of paint.) Modern technology has been used to measure the amount of light that can be absorbed in cones and has confirmed that each type responds to different wavelengths. Additionally, different types of colour blindness have been linked to (relatively common) genetic anomalies that impair the functioning of particular types of cones. Thus, *some* aspects of our colour vision can be explained by the characteristics of the cones in our retinas.

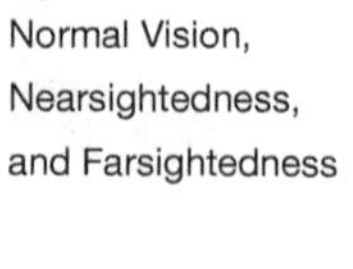

Explore Normal Vision, Nearsightedness, and Farsightedness

However, not all colour-related experiences can be explained by the trichromatic theory. For instance, stare at the image in Figure 4.15 for about a minute and then look toward a white background. After switching your gaze to a white background, you will see the colours of red, white, and blue rather than green, black, and yellow. How can we explain this tendency to see such a *negative afterimage*, a different colour from the one you actually viewed? In the 19th century, Ewald Hering proposed the **opponent-process theory** of colour perception, *which states that we perceive colour in terms of opposing pairs: red to green, yellow to blue, and white to black*. This type of perception is consistent with the activity patterns of retinal ganglion cells. A cell that is stimulated by red is inhibited by green; when red is no longer perceived (as when you suddenly look at a white wall), a "rebound" effect occurs. Suddenly, the previously inhibited cells that fire during the perception of green are free to fire, whereas the previously active cells related to red no longer do so. The same relationship occurs for yellow and blue as well as for white and black.

The trichromatic and opponent-process theories are said to be complementary because both are required to explain how we see colour. The trichromatic theory explains colour vision in terms of the activity of cones. The opponent-process theory of colour vision explains what happens when ganglion cells process signals from a number of different cones at the same time. Together, they allow us to see the intense world of colours that we experience every day.

COMMON VISUAL DISORDERS Of course, not everyone can see colours. In fact, many people reading this book will have some form of *colour blindness*. Most forms of colour blindness affect the ability to distinguish between red and green. In people who have normal colour vision, some cones contain proteins that are sensitive to red and some contain proteins that are sensitive to green. However, in most forms of colour blindness, one of these types of cones does not contain the correct protein (e.g., a "green cone" contains proteins that are sensitive to wavelengths of light that produce the colour red). Most forms of colour blindness are genetic in origin.

There are also visual disorders caused by the shape of the eye itself. Changes to the shape of the eye sometimes prevent a focused image from reaching the photoreceptors in the retina. *Nearsightedness*, or *myopia*, occurs when the eyeball is slightly elongated, causing the image that the cornea and lens focus on to fall short of the retina (see Figure 4.16). People who are nearsighted can see objects that are relatively close up but have difficulty

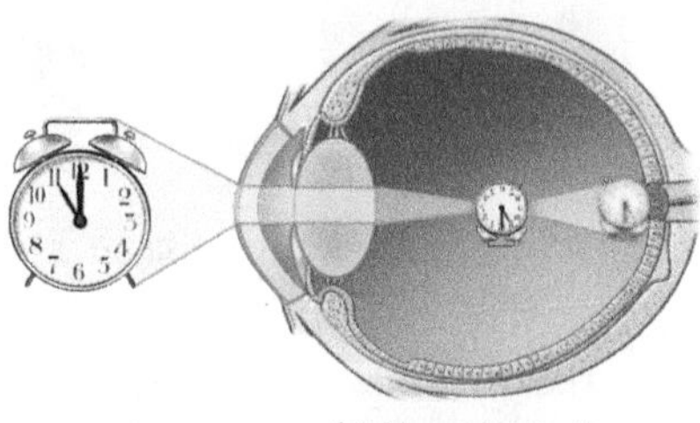

(a) Nearsighted eye

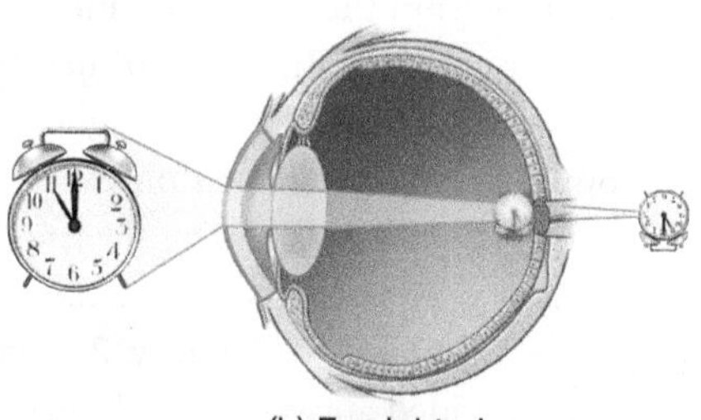

(b) Farsighted eye

{FIG. 4.16} **Nearsightedness and Farsightedness** Nearsightedness and farsightedness result from misshapen eyes. If the eye is elongated, or too short, images are not centred on the retina. **Click on this figure in your eText to see more details.**

focusing on distant objects. Alternatively, if the length of the eye is shorter than normal, the result is *farsightedness* or *hyperopia*. In this case, the image is focused *behind* the retina. Farsighted people can see distant objects clearly but not those that are close by. Both types of impairments can be corrected with contact lenses or glasses, thus allowing a focused visual image to stimulate the *retina* at the back of the eye, where light energy is converted into neural impulses.

In the last 20 years, an increasing number of people have undergone laser eye surgery in order to correct near- or farsightedness. In this type of surgery, surgeons use a laser to reshape the cornea so that incoming light focuses on the retina, which produces close to perfect vision. In nearsighted patients, the doctors attempt to flatten the cornea, whereas in farsighted patients the doctors attempt to make the cornea steeper. Although the idea of having a laser fire into your eyes sounds frightening, approximately 95% of the patients who undergo these surgeries report being satisfied with the results (Solomon et al., 2009). Seeing is believing.

It is important to remember that the initial sensations of light that are processed in the eye itself provide very specific information about the environment that we are viewing. But, in order for this raw sensory information to be perceived by the person, this information needs to exit the eye and enter the brain.

Visual Perception and the Brain

Information from the optic nerve travels to numerous areas of the brain. The first major destination is the *optic chiasm*, the point at which the optic nerves cross at the midline of the brain (see Figure 4.17). For each optic nerve, about half of the nerve fibres travel to the same side of the brain (ipsilateral), and half of them travel to the opposite side of the brain (contralateral). As can be seen in Figure 4.17, the outside half of the retina (closest to your temples) sends its optic nerve projections ipsilaterally. In contrast, the inside half of the retina (closest to your nose) sends its optic nerve projections contralaterally. The result of this distribution is that the left half of your visual field is initially processed by

Quick Quiz 4.2a

The Human Eye

KNOW ...

1 Cones are predominantly gathered in a central part of the retina known as the ________.

A fovea
B photoreceptor
C blind spot
D optic chiasm

2 Which of the following conditions occurs when the eye becomes elongated, causing the image to fall short of the retina?

A Prosopagnosia
B Motion parallax
C Farsightedness
D Nearsightedness

UNDERSTAND ...

3 Crystal was at a modern art gallery. After staring at a large, red square (that was somehow worth $20 million), she looked at the wall and briefly saw the colour green. Which theory can explain Crystal's experience?

A Opponent process theory
B Hyperopia
C Trichromatic theory
D Motion parallax

APPLY ...

4 Jacob cannot distinguish between the colours red and green. What structure(s) of the eye is/are most likely not functioning properly?

A Rods
B Cornea
C Cones
D Lens

Answers can be found on page ANS-2.

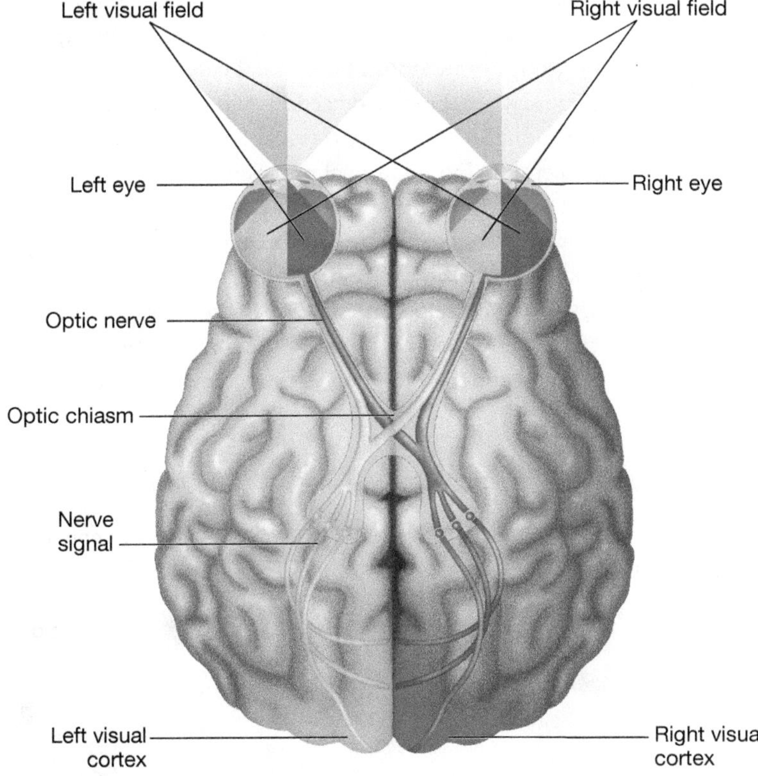

{FIG. 4.17} **Pathways of the Visual System in the Brain** The optic nerves route messages to the visual cortex. At the optic chiasm, some of the cells remain on the same side and some cross to the opposite side of the brain. This organization results in images appearing in the left visual field being processed on the right side of the brain, and images appearing in the right visual field being processed on the left side of the brain. **Click on this figure in your eText to see more details.**

the right hemisphere of your brain, whereas the right half of your visual field is initially processed by the left hemisphere of your brain. Although this system seems like it was designed by a confused person pushing a shopping cart full of stray cats, this system serves important functions, particularly if a person's brain is damaged. In this case, having both eyes send *some* information to both hemispheres increases the likelihood that *some* visual abilities will be preserved.

Fibres from the optic nerve first connect with the thalamus, the brain's "sensory relay station." The thalamus is made up of over 20 different nuclei with specialized functions. The *lateral geniculate nucleus (LGN)* is specialized for processing visual information. Fibres from this nucleus send messages to the visual cortex, located in the occipital lobe, where the complex processes of visual perception begin.

How does the visual cortex make sense of all this incoming information? It starts with a division of labour among specialized cells. One set of cells in the visual cortex—first discovered by Canadian David Hubel and his colleague Torsten Wiesel in 1959—are referred to as *feature detection cells*; these cells respond selectively to simple and specific aspects of a stimulus, such as angles and edges (Hubel & Wiesel, 1962). Researchers have been able to map which feature detection cells respond to specific aspects of an image by measuring the firing rates of groups of neurons in the visual cortex in lab animals (Figure 4.18). Feature detection cells of the visual cortex are thought to be where visual input is organized for perception, but additional processing is required as well and involves additional neural pathways. From the primary visual cortex, information about different features is sent for further processing in the surrounding secondary visual cortex. This area consists of a number of specialized regions that perform specific functions such as the perception of colour and movement. These regions begin the process of putting together primitive visual information into a bigger picture.

These specialized areas are the beginning of two streams of vision, each of which performs different visual functions (see Figure 4.19). The *ventral stream* extends from the visual cortex to the lower part of the temporal lobe. The *dorsal stream*, on the other hand, extends from the visual cortex to the parietal lobe. Both streams are essential for our ability to function normally in our visual world.

THE VENTRAL STREAM The ventral stream of vision extends from the visual cortex in the occipital lobe to the anterior (front) portions of the temporal lobe. This division of our visual system performs a critical function: object recognition. Groups of neurons in the temporal lobe gather shape and colour information from different regions of the secondary visual cortex and combine it into a neural representation of an object. This region also gives that representation a name, such as "cat" or "dog." Brain imaging experiments have shown that damage to this stream of vision causes dramatic impairments in object recognition (James et al., 2003). Other studies have noted that different categories of objects such as tools and instruments are represented in distinct areas of the anterior temporal lobes (Tranel et al., 1997). Indeed, researchers have identified rare cases where brain-damaged individuals show a striking inability to name items from one category while being unimpaired at naming other categories (e.g., Dixon et al., 1997); this deficit only affects the visual perception of those objects (e.g., a guitar), not the knowledge about those objects (e.g., that a guitar has six strings). But tools, animals, and musical instruments are not the only categories that are represented in distinct areas of the ventral stream of vision. One group of stimuli—possibly the most evolutionarily important one in our visual world—may have an entire region of the brain dedicated to its perception.

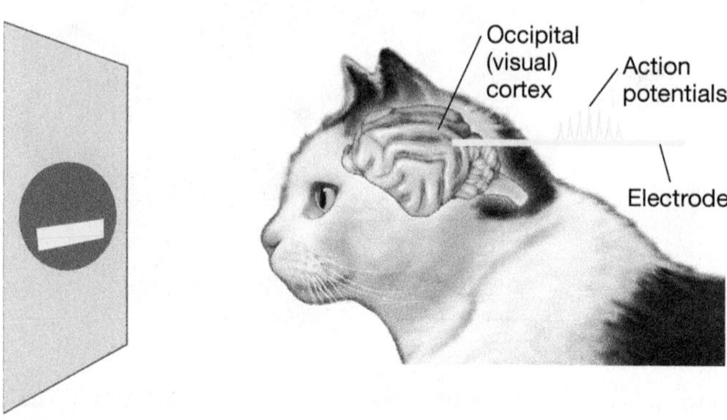

{FIG. 4.18} **Measuring the Activity of Feature Detection Cells** Scientists can measure the activity of individual feature detector cells by inserting a microscopic electrode into the visual cortex of an animal. The activity level will peak when the animal is shown the specific feature corresponding to that specific cell.

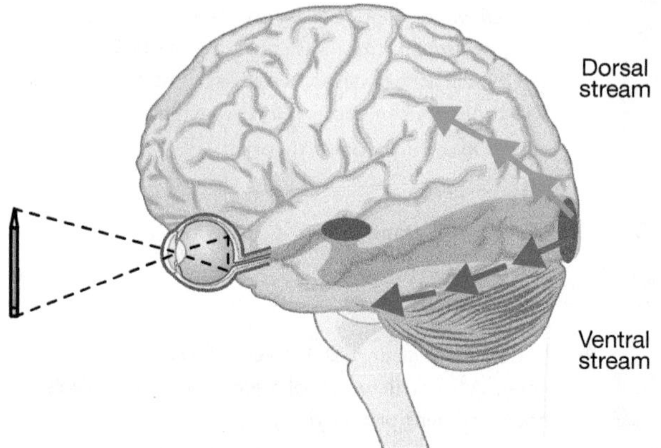

{FIG. 4.19} **The Two Streams of Vision** Neural impulses leave the visual centres in the occipital lobe along two different pathways. The ventral (bottom) stream extends to the temporal lobe and the dorsal (top) stream extends to the parietal lobe.

WORKING THE SCIENTIFIC LITERACY MODEL

Are Faces Special?

Faces provide us with an incredible amount of social information. In addition to using faces to identify specific other people, we can use them as a source of important social information such as someone's emotional state. Other people's faces could therefore give you hints as to how you respond to them, or to the situation you are both in. Given their importance, it seems logical that faces would be processed differently than many less important types of visual stimuli.

What do we know about face perception?

Look at the painting in Figure 4.20. What do you see? When you look at the image on the left, you will likely see a somewhat dreary bowl filled with vegetables. However, when most people see the image on the right, they perceive a face. They can obviously tell that the "face" is just the bowl of vegetables turned upside down, but the different items in the bowl do resemble the general shape of a face. The Italian artist Guiseppe Archimboldo produced a number of similar paintings in which "faces" could be perceived within other structures. What Archimboldo was highlighting was the fact that faces appear to stand out relative to other objects in our visual world.

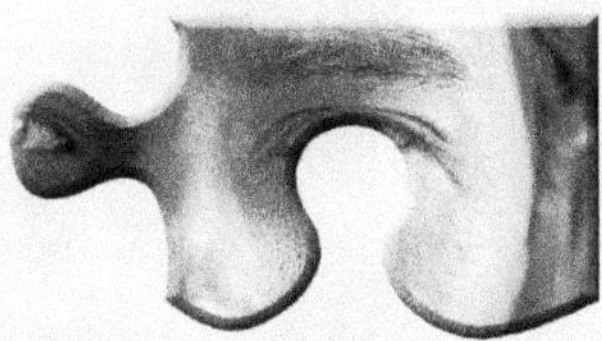

How can science explain how we perceive faces?

Not everyone sees the faces in Archimboldo's painting, however; in fact, some neurological patients don't see faces at all. Specific genetic problems or damage to this area can lead to an inability to recognize faces, a condition known as *prosopagnosia,* or face blindness. People with face blindness are able to recognize voices and other defining features of individuals (e.g., Angelina Jolie's lips), but not faces. Importantly, these patients tend to have damage or dysfunction in the same general area of the brain: the bottom of the right temporal lobe. So, although prosopagnosia is a rare clinical condition, it does help us understand some basic processes that are involved in perceiving faces.

Brain-imaging studies have corroborated the location of the "face area" of the brain (Kanwisher et al., 1997). Using fMRI, researchers have consistently detected activity in this region, now known as the *fusiform face area (FFA).* This area appears to be specialized for recognizing upright faces. When faces are inverted, they become less "face-like" and responses in this brain region decrease. (Figure 4.21 provides an interesting visual phenomenon related to inverted faces). Additionally, the FFA responds more strongly to the entire face than to individual features; unlike other types of stimuli, faces are processed holistically rather than as a nose, eyes, ears, chin, and so on (Tanaka & Farah, 1993).

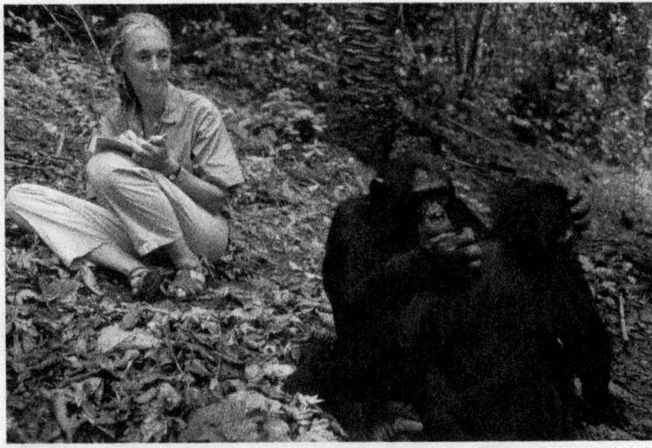

Michael Nichols/National Geographic/Getty Images

World-renowned chimpanzee researcher Jane Goodall has face blindness (prosopagnosia). Her sister also has it—there appear to be genetic links to the condition. Despite being face blind, Dr. Goodall and others with this condition use nonfacial characteristics to recognize people, or, in her case, hundreds of individual chimpanzees (Goodall & Berman, 1999).

Importantly, like many other sensory functions, the ability to perceive faces is dependent upon experience. Researchers at McMaster and Brock Universities have found that early visual input to the right, but not left, hemisphere of the brain is essential for the development of normal face perception (Le Grand et al., 2004, 2005). Our face perception skills also develop as we grow up—adults out-perform children on

Special Topics: Recognizing Faces

Museo Civico Ala Ponzone, Cremona, Italy/The Bridgeman Art Library International

{FIG. 4.20} **Seeing Faces** At left is a painting of turnips and other vegetables by the Italian artist Giuseppe Archimboldo. The image at right is the same image rotated 180 degrees—does it resemble a human face?

PA Photos/Landov

{FIG. 4.21} **The Face Inversion Effect** After viewing both upside-down faces, you probably noticed a difference between the two pictures. Now turn your book upside down and notice how the distortion of one of the faces is amplified when viewed from this perspective.

tests of face recognition (Mondloch et al., 2006) and the fusiform face area does not show special sensitivity to faces until approximately age 10 (Aylward et al., 2005).

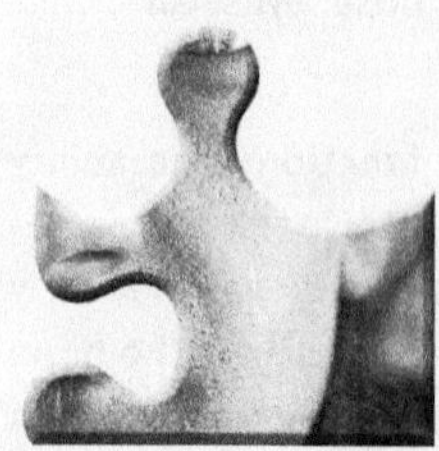

Can we critically evaluate this evidence?

Although no one doubts that faces are processed by the fusiform face area, there are alternative explanations for these effects. One possibility is that the FFA is being activated by one of the perceptual processes involved with perceiving faces rather than by the faces themselves. One such process is expertise. We are all experts at recognizing faces. Think of all of the people that you've gone to school with over the years. Think of all of the entertainers, athletes, and politicians you could recognize. You have the ability to distinguish between thousands of different faces. Canadian psychologist Isabel Gauthier and her colleagues suggested that maybe face recognition isn't all that special. Instead, maybe the fusiform face area is simply an area related to processing stimuli that we have become experts at recognizing. To test this hypothesis, she trained undergraduate students to recognize different types of a novel group of objects called Greebles (see Figure 4.22). Before training, these stimuli did not trigger activity in the fusiform face area; however, after training, this area did become active (Gauthier et al., 1999). Further support for this expertise hypothesis comes from studies of bird and car experts (Gauthier et al., 2000). Both groups showed greater levels of brain activity in the fusiform face area in response to stimuli related to their area of expertise (e.g., cars for car enthusiasts). Although this research doesn't negate the studies showing face-specific processing in this area, it does suggest that more research is necessary to see just how specialized this region of the ventral stream of vision really is.

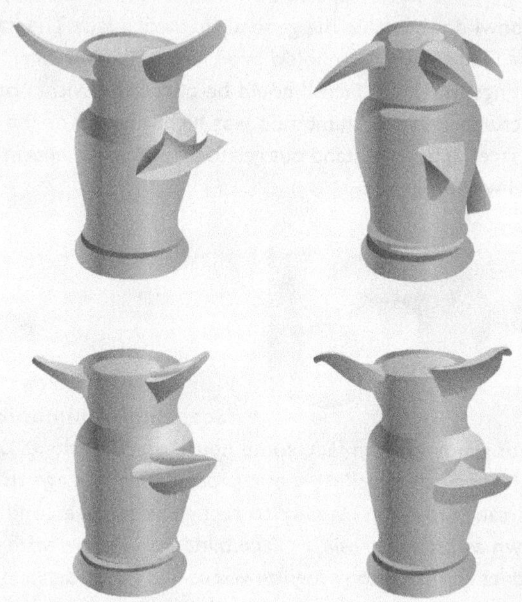

{FIG. 4.22} **Expertise for Faces and "Greebles"** The above images are Greebles, faceless stimuli used to test whether the fusiform face area responds only to faces (Gauthier & Tarr, 1997). Participants in these studies are taught to classify the Greebles on a number of characteristics such as sex ("male" and "female"). Although this task seems difficult, after several training sessions participants can rapidly make such a decision. These "Greeble experts" also show increased activity in the region of the brain associated with processing faces.

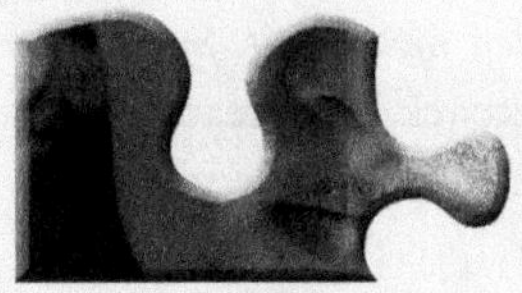

Why is this relevant?

The fact that a specific brain region is linked with the perception of faces is very useful information for neurologists and emergency room physicians. If a patient has trouble recognizing people, it could be a sign that he has damage to the bottom of the right temporal lobe. Indeed, based on studies of prosopagnosia, tests of face memory are now part of most assessment tools used by doctors and researchers. The fact that fMRI studies corroborate the location of the FFA increases our confidence that such tools are in fact valid.

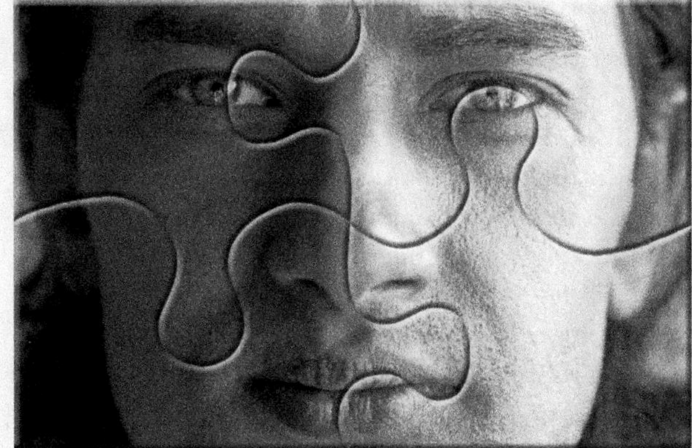

Inga Dudkina/Shutterstock.com

At this point in the module, we have looked at how we sense visual information and how this information is constructed by our brain-based perceptual system into objects that can influence our behaviour, such as a face or an animal. But, our visual system has even more tricks for us. Somehow, we can identify objects even when they are viewed in different lighting conditions or at different angles—your cat is still your cat, regardless of whether it is noon or midnight. This observation is an example of what is called **perceptual constancy**, *the ability to perceive objects as having constant shape, size, and colour despite changes in perspective.* What makes perceptual constancy possible is our ability to make relative judgments about shape, size, and lightness. For *shape constancy*, we judge the angle of the object relative to our position (see Figure 4.23). *Colour constancy* allows us to recognize an object's colour under varying levels of illumination. For example, a bright red car is recognized as bright red whether in the shade or in full sunlight. *Size constancy* is based on judgments of how close an object is relative to one's position as well as to the positions of other objects. In each of these cases, the constancy is aided by our experience with the objects as well as by the presence of other objects that can serve as comparisons. In other words, constancies are affected by top-down processing (see Module 4.1) when our perceptions are influenced by expectations and prior knowledge. This processing becomes even more important when we have to decide how we plan to interact with the objects we are perceiving, a function performed by the second stream of our visual system.

THE DORSAL STREAM The dorsal stream of vision extends from the visual cortex in our occipital lobe upwards to the parietal lobe. Its function is less intuitive than that of the ventral stream, but is just as important.

(a)

(b)

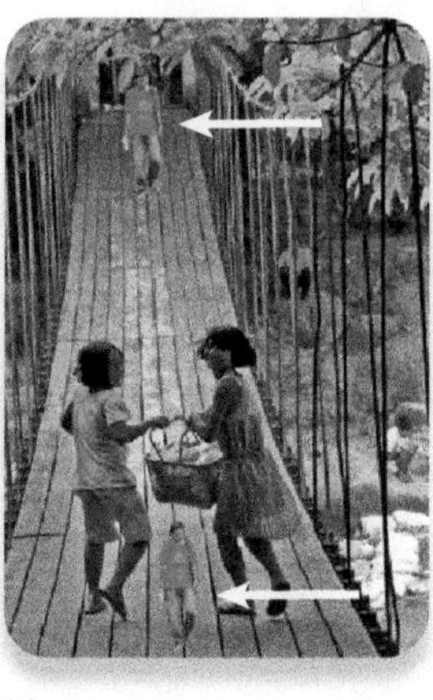

(c)

Centre: Brian Prawl/Shutterstock; right: Forget Patrick/Sagaphoto.Com/Alamy

{FIG. 4.23} **Perceptual Constancies** (a) We perceive the door to be a rectangle despite the fact that the two-dimensional outline of the image on the retina is not always rectangular. (b) Colour constancy: We perceive colours to be constant despite changing levels of illumination. (c) Size constancy: the person in the red shirt appears normal in size when in the background. A replica of this individual placed in the foreground appears unusually small because of size constancy.

Imagine looking at your morning cup of coffee sitting on the table you're working at. You immediately recognize that the object is a cup, and that the liquid inside of it is coffee, something you drink. You also decide that it is time to have a sip, thus requiring your arm to move so that your hand can grasp the mug of caffeinated goodness. Someone with a healthy brain can do this effortlessly. However, someone with damage to the dorsal stream of vision would have great difficulty performing this simple function. How can we explain this impairment?

Leslie Ungerleider and Mortimer Mishkin (1982) suggested that the ventral and dorsal stream of vision could be referred to as the "what" and "where" pathways. The ventral stream identifies the object, and the dorsal stream locates it in space and allows you to interact with it. Although this description is accurate, researchers at Western University (formerly the University of Western Ontario) have suggested that the function of the "where" pathway is more specific (Goodale et al., 1991; Milner & Goodale, 2006). Their initial research was based on studies involving a patient known as "D.F." (in order to preserve patients' anonymity, their names are never provided in research papers). D.F. was a healthy middle-aged woman who suffered damage to her temporal lobe, interfering with the ventral stream of vision. As a result, her ability to recognize objects was severely impaired; indeed, she could not recognize letters or line drawings. However, she could still reach for objects as though she had perfect vision. For instance, when asked to put a letter in a mailbox, she was able to do so, even if the angle of the mail slot was changed by a sneaky researcher (see Figure 4.24). Goodale and colleagues correctly hypothesized that D.F.'s dorsal stream was preserved, and that this pathway was involved with *visually guided movement*. So, when you reach out to grab your backpack after reading this module, remember that the "simple" ability to recognize and reach for the object requires multiple pathways in the brain.

DEPTH PERCEPTION Our ability to use vision to guide our actions is dependent on our depth perception. We need to be able to gauge the distances between different objects as well as to determine where different objects are located relative to each other. This type of information can be detected in a number of ways.

Binocular depth cues *are distance cues that are based on the differing perspectives of both eyes.* One type of binocular depth cue, called **convergence**, *occurs when the eye muscles contract so that both eyes focus on a single object.* Convergence typically occurs for objects that are relatively close to you. For example, if you move your fingertip toward your nose, your eyes will move inward and will turn toward each other. The sensations that occur as these muscles contract to focus on a single object provide the brain with additional information used to create the perception of depth.

One reason humans have such a fine-tuned ability to see in three dimensions is that both of our eyes face forward. This arrangement means that we perceive objects from slightly different angles, which in turn enhances depth perception. For example, choose an object in front of you, such as a pen held at arm's length from your body, and focus on that object with one eye while keeping the other eye closed. Then open your other eye to look at the object (and close the eye you were just using). You will notice that the position of your pen appears to change. This effect demonstrates **retinal disparity** (also called binocular disparity), *the difference*

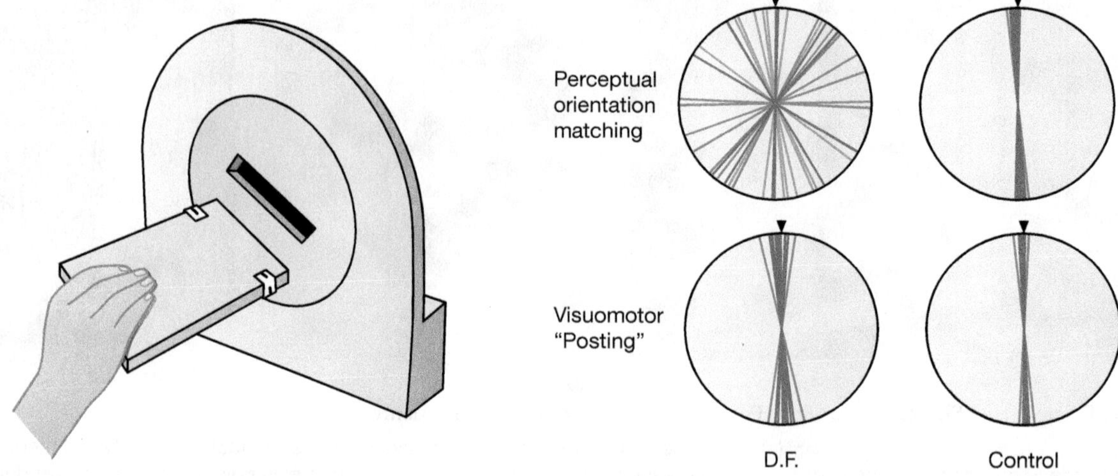

{FIG. 4.24} **Testing the Dorsal Stream** Patient D.F. was able to rotate her hand to fit an envelope into a mail slot despite having difficulties identifying either object. Her preserved dorsal stream of vision allowed her to use vision to guide her arm's motions.

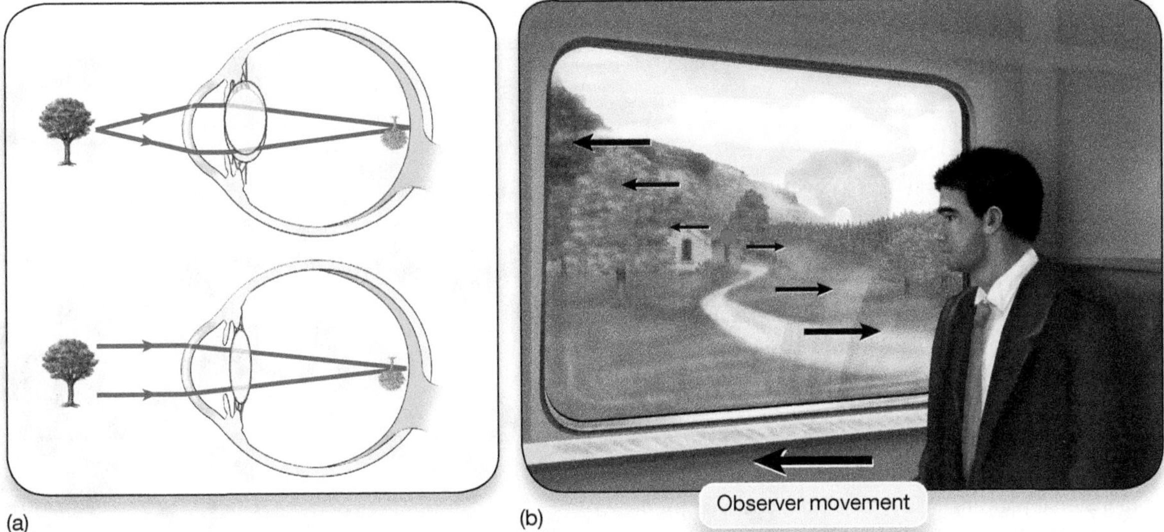

{FIG. 4.25} **Two Monocular Depth Cues** (a) Accommodation. From the top left image light comes from a distant object, and the lens focuses the light on the retina. From the bottom left image the lens changes shape to *accommodate* the light when the same object is moved closer. (b) Motion parallax. Looking out the train window, objects close to you race past quickly and in the opposite direction that you are headed. At the same time, distant objects appear to move slowly and in the same direction that you are travelling.

in relative position of an object as seen by both eyes, which provides information to the brain about depth. Your brain relies on cues from each eye individually and from both eyes working in concert—that is, in stereo. Most primates, including humans, have *stereoscopic vision*, which results from overlapping visual fields. The brain can use the difference between the information provided by the left and right eye to make a judgment about the distance of the objects being viewed. Species that have eyes with no overlap in their visual field, such as some fish, likely do not require as much depth information in order to survive in their particular environment. These species might also be able to make use of depth information perceived by each eye individually.

Monocular cues *are depth cues that we can perceive with only one eye.* We have already discussed one such cue, called *accommodation,* earlier in this module. During accommodation, the lens of your eye curves to allow you to focus on nearby objects. Close one eye and focus on a nearby object, and then slightly change your focus to an object that is farther away; the lens changes shape again so the next object comes into focus (see Figure 4.25a). The brain receives feedback about this movement which it can then use to help make judgments about depth. Another monocular cue is *motion parallax*; it is used when you or your surroundings are in motion. For example, as you sit in a moving vehicle and look out of the passenger window, you will notice objects closer to you, such as the roadside, parked cars, and nearby buildings, appear to move rapidly in the opposite direction of your travel. By comparison, far-off objects such as foothills and mountains in the distance appear to move much more slowly, and in the same direction as your vehicle. The disparity in the directions travelled by near and far-off objects provides a monocular cue about depth.

Left: photofriday/Shutterstock.com; right: David Davis/Shutterstock.com

The parakeet on the left, lacking stereoscopic vision, must turn its head to the side to view images directly. In contrast, owls have stereoscopic vision, as indicated by their forward-facing eyes. This gives owls superior depth perception—not to mention outstanding predatory skills.

PSYCH @

The Artist's Studio

Watch
What's in It for Me? Perceptual Magic in Art

Although we often think of painters as being eccentric people prone to cutting off their ears, they are actually very clever amateur vision scientists. Rembrandt (1606–1669) varied the texture and colour details of different parts of portraits in order to guide the viewer's gaze toward the clearest object. The result is that more detailed regions of a painting attract attention and receive more eye fixations than less detailed regions (DiPaola, Riebe, & Enns, 2011).

In addition to manipulating a viewer's eye movements, painters also use a variety of depth cues to transform their two-dimensional painting into a three-dimensional perception. This use of *pictorial depth cues* is quite challenging, which is why some paintings seem vibrant and multilayered (like nature) while others seem flat and artificial. So what are some strategies that artists use to influence our visual perception?

Explore
Five Well-Known Illusions

To understand how artists work, view the painting by Gustave Caillebottein shown in Figure 4.26. In this painting, you will notice that the artist used numerous cues to depict depth:

- *Linear perspective:* Parallel lines stretching to the horizon appear to move closer together as they travel farther away. This effect can be seen in the narrowing of the streets and the converging lines of the sidewalks and the top of the building in the distance. This effect is nicely demonstrated by the illusion in Figure 4.27.
- *Interposition:* Nearby objects block our view of far-off objects, such as the umbrellas blocking the view of buildings behind them.
- *Light and shadow:* The shadow cast by an object allows us to detect both the size of the object and the relative locations of objects. In addition, closer objects reflect more light than far-away objects.
- *Texture gradient:* Objects that are coarse and distinct at close range become fine and grainy at greater distances. In the painting, for example, the texture of the brick street varies from clear to blurred as distance increases.
- *Height in plane:* Objects that are higher in our visual field are perceived as farther away than objects low in our visual field. The base of the main building in the background of the painting is at about the same level as the man's shoulder, but we interpret this effect as distance, not as height.
- *Relative size:* If two objects in an image are known to be of the same actual size, the larger of the two must be closer. This can be seen in the various sizes of the pedestrians.

The Art Gallery Collection /Alamy

{FIG. 4.26} **Pictorial Depth Cues** Artists make use of cues such as linear perspective, texture gradient, relative size, and others to create the sense of depth.

Interestingly, Harvard neurobiologists recently speculated that Rembrandt suffered from "stereo blindness," an inability to form binocular images (Livingstone & Conway, 2004). He would therefore have had to rely on monocular cues to form the perceptions that led to his innovative depictions of the visual world.

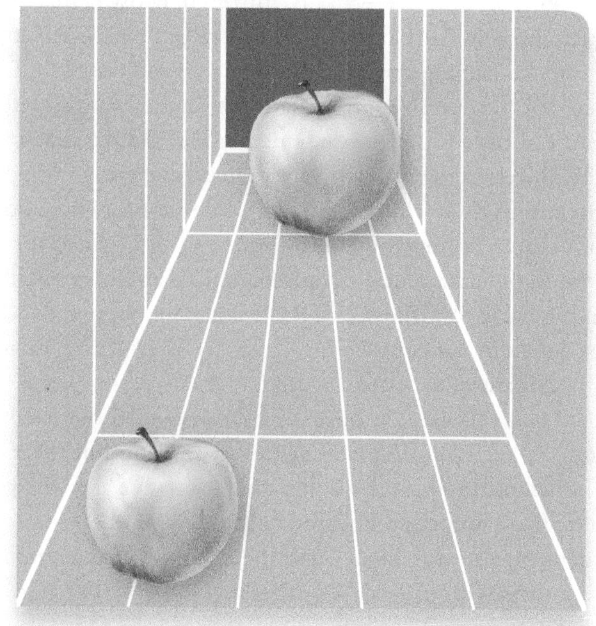

{FIG. 4.27} **The Corridor Illusion** Linear perspective and height in plane create the perception of depth here. The result is that the object at the "back" of the drawing appears to be larger than the one in the foreground; in reality, they are identical in size.

Quick Quiz 4.2b Perception and the Brain

KNOW ...

1 Also called face-blindness, which of the following conditions is the inability to recognize faces?

A Prosopagnosia
B Farsightedness
C Trichromatism
D Astigmatism

2 The ________ in the thalamus is where the optic nerves from the left and right eyes converge.

A fovea
B occipital lobe
C lateral geniculate nucleus
D retina

UNDERSTAND ...

3 A familiar person walks into the room. Which of the following choices places the structures in the appropriate sequence required to recognize the individual?

A Optic chiasm, visual cortex, photoreceptors, optic nerve
B Visual cortex, optic chiasm, photoreceptors, optic nerve
C Photoreceptors, optic nerve, optic chiasm, visual cortex
D Photoreceptors, optic chiasm, optic nerve, visual cortex

APPLY ...

4 A patient with brain damage can recognize different objects but is unable to reach out to grasp the object that she sees. This impairment is best explained by the difference between the

A primary and secondary visual cortices.
B rods and cones.
C temporal lobe and the frontal lobes.
D ventral and dorsal streams.

ANALYZE ...

5 Some people claim that there is a brain area dedicated to the perception of faces. Although there is a great deal of evidence in favour of this claim, what is the best evidence *against* it?

A Doctors have yet to find a brain-damaged patient who cannot recognize faces.
B The neuroimaging studies of face perception do not show consistent results.
C The brain area related to face processing is also active when people see images from categories in which they have expertise.
D The brain area related to face processing is equally sensitive to faces that are upright or upside down.

Answers can be found on page ANS-2.

Module Summary

Module 4.2

Now that you have read this module you should

KNOW . . .

- ***The key terminology relating to the eye and vision*:**

binocular depth cues (p. 154)	opponent-process theory (p. 148)
cones (p. 146)	optic nerve (p. 146)
convergence (p. 154)	perceptual constancy (p. 153)
cornea (p. 145)	pupil (p. 145)
dark adaptation (p. 147)	retina (p. 146)
fovea (p. 146)	retinal disparity (p. 154)
iris (p. 145)	rods (p. 146)
lens (p. 145)	sclera (p. 145)
monocular cues (p. 155)	trichromatic theory (p. 147)

UNDERSTAND . . .

- ***How visual information travels from the eye through the brain to give us the experience of sight.*** Light is transformed into a neural signal by photoreceptors in the retina. This information is then relayed via the optic nerve through the thalamus and then to the occipital lobe of the cortex. From this location in the brain, neural circuits travel to other regions for specific levels of processing. These include the temporal lobe for object recognition and the parietal lobe for visually guided movement.
- ***The theories of colour vision.*** The two theories reviewed in this module are the trichromatic and opponent-process theories. According to trichromatic theory, the retina contains three different types of cones that are sensitive to different wavelengths of light. Colour is experienced as the net combined stimulation of these receptors. The trichromatic theory is not supported by phenomena such as the negative afterimage. Opponent-process theory, which emphasizes how colour perception is based on excitation and inhibition of opposing colours (e.g., red–green, blue–yellow, white–black), explains this phenomenon. Taken together, both theories help explain how we perceive colour.

Stephen Smith

APPLY . . .

- ***Your knowledge to explain how we perceive depth in our visual field.*** For practice, take a look at the accompanying photo. Can you identify at least four monocular depth cues that are present in the image below? Check out our answers on page ANS-2.

Getty Images/Thinkstock

ANALYZE . . .

- ***How we perceive objects and faces.*** Object perception is accomplished by specialized perceptual regions of the temporal lobe (the ventral stream of vision). Perceptual constancies allow us to recognize objects even though their shape, size, and colour may appear to change because their orientation, distance, and lightness in relation to us are not always the same. Facial recognition is a specialized perceptual process, which is supported by evidence from people who are face blind but are otherwise successful at recognizing objects.

IGphotography/iStockphoto

Module 4.3

The Auditory System

Learning Objectives
After reading this module you should

KNOW ...	UNDERSTAND ...	APPLY ...	ANALYZE ...
The key terminology relating to the ear and hearing	Different characteristics of sound and how they correspond to perception How technology is used to restore hearing	Your knowledge of sound localization	How the emotional characteristics of music can be used by advertisers

What would the soundtrack to your life sound like? Although each of us has our own musical preferences, some songs have the power to evoke similar emotions in large groups. Stadiums pump out songs that unite and energize fans, DJs at dance clubs select songs that fit the mood of excitement and sexual energy, and even in the workplace certain types of music can harmonize people focusing on a common goal (or can unite the workers in a common dislike of Nickelback). Daniel Levitin, a McGill psychologist, musician, and author of *This Is Your Brain on Music*, believes that we are hard-wired not just to hear music, but to *feel* a significant emotional connection to it. Each of our lives' soundtracks would probably be different, but Dr. Levitin argues that human identity has music at its core, and that common themes in music include love, friendship, knowledge, religion, relationships, and joy (Levitin, 2006). Music is perceived both at a basic level of sound and at a much deeper emotional level.

Focus Questions

 1. How does the auditory system sense and perceive something complex like music?

 2. How do we localize sounds in our environment?

In this module we will explore characteristics of sound, the physical structures that support the sensation of sound, and the pathways involved in its perceptual processing. We will also examine how music affects memory and emotion, and how this relationship can influence our behaviour.

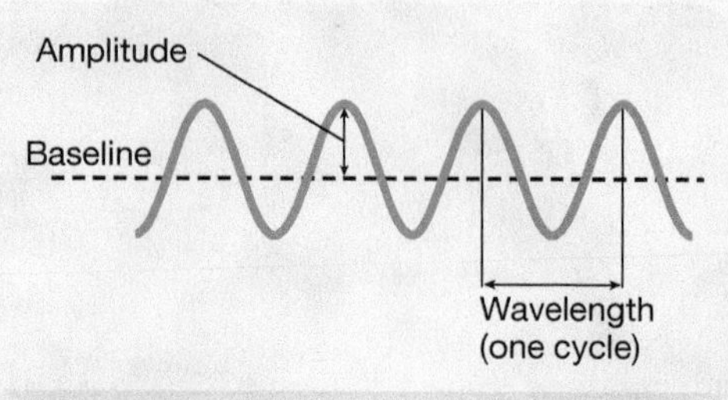

(a) Long-wavelength (low-frequency) sound

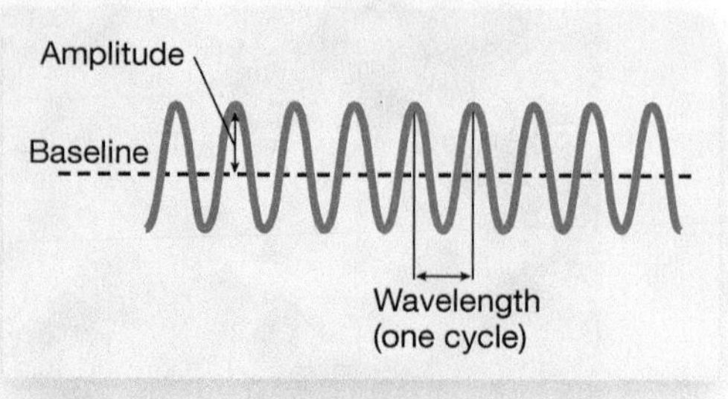

(b) Short-wavelength (high-frequency) sound

{FIG. 4.28} **Characteristics of Sound: Frequency and Amplitude** The frequency of a sound wave (cycles per second) is associated with pitch, while amplitude (the height of the sound wave) is associated with loudness.

Explore
Virtual Brain: Mechanisms of Perception

Explore
Frequency and Amplitude of Sound Waves

Watch
Ear Ringing

Watch
IT Video: Mosquito

Sound and the Structures of the Ear

The function of the ear is to gather sound waves. The function of *hearing* is to extract some sort of meaning from those sound waves; this meaning informs you about the nature of the sound source, such as someone calling your name, a referee's whistle, or a vehicle coming toward you. How do people gain so much information from invisible waves that travel through the air?

SOUND The function of that remarkably sensitive and delicate device, the human ear, is to detect *sound waves* and to transform that information into neural signals. Sound waves are simply changes in mechanical pressure transmitted through solids, liquids, or gases. Sound waves have two important characteristics: frequency and amplitude (see Figure 4.28). *Frequency* refers to wavelength and is measured in hertz (Hz), the number of cycles a sound wave travels per second. **Pitch** *is the perceptual experience of sound wave frequencies.* High-frequency sounds, such as tires screeching on the road, have short wavelengths and a high pitch. Low-frequency sounds, such as those produced by a bass guitar, have long wavelengths and a low pitch. The *amplitude* of a sound wave determines its loudness: High-amplitude sound waves are louder than low-amplitude waves. Both types of information are gathered and analyzed by our ears.

Humans are able to detect sounds in the frequency range from 20 Hz to 20 000 Hz. Figure 4.29 compares the hearing ranges of several different species. Look closely at the scale of the figure—the differences are of a much greater magnitude than could possibly fit on this page using a standard scale. The comparisons show that mice, for example, can hear frequencies close to five times greater than humans, but have difficulty hearing lower frequencies that we can easily detect.

Loudness—a function of sound wave amplitude—is typically expressed in units called decibels (dB). Table 4.2 compares decibel levels ranging from nearly inaudible to injury inducing. Although we doubt you spend much time beside jet engines, we do suggest wearing earplugs to concerts to protect your ears, even if they don't match your always-stylish "I'm a Belieber" t-shirt.

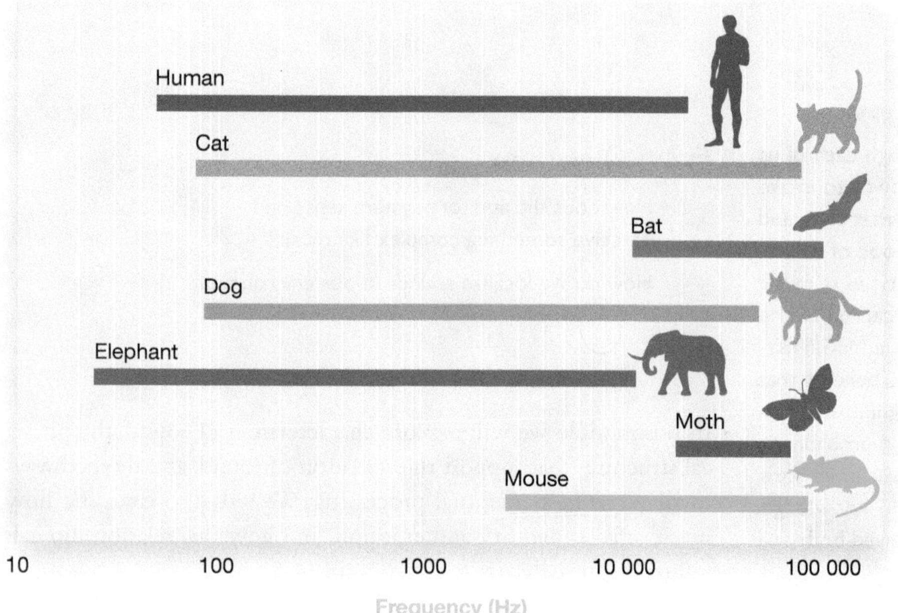

{FIG. 4.29} **A Comparison of Hearing Ranges in Different Species**

THE HUMAN EAR The human ear is divided into outer, middle, and inner regions (see Figure 4.30). The most noticeable part of your ear is the *pinna*, the outer region that helps channel sound waves to the ear and allows you to determine the source or location of a sound. The *auditory canal* extends from the pinna to the eardrum. Sound waves reaching the eardrum cause it to vibrate. Even very soft sounds, such as a faint whisper, produce vibrations of the eardrum. The middle ear consists of three tiny moveable bones called *ossicles*, known individually as the malleus (hammer), incus (anvil), and stapes (stirrup). The eardrum is attached to these bones, so any movement of the eardrum due to sound vibrations results in movement of the ossicles.

Table 4.2 :: Decibel Levels for Some Familiar Sounds

SOUND	NOISE LEVEL (dB)	EFFECT
Jet engines (near) Rock concerts (varies)	140 110–140	We begin to feel pain at about 125 dB
Thunderclap (near) Power saw (chainsaw)	120 110	Regular exposure to sound over 100 dB for more than one minute risks permanent hearing loss
Garbage truck/Cement mixer	100	No more than 15 minutes of unprotected exposure is recommended for sounds between 90 and 100 dB
Motorcycle (25 ft) Lawn mower	88 85–90	85 dB is the level at which hearing damage (after eight hours) begins
Average city traffic Vacuum cleaner Normal conversation	80 70 50–65	Annoying; interferes with conversation; constant exposure may cause damage Intrusive; interferes with telephone conversation Comfortable hearing levels are under 60 dB
Whisper Rustling leaves	30 20	Very quiet Just audible

The ossicles attach to an inner ear structure called the **cochlea**—*a fluid-filled membrane that is coiled in a snail-like shape and contains the structures that convert sound into neural impulses.* Converting sound vibrations to neural impulses is possible because of hair-like projections that line the *basilar membrane* of the cochlea. The pressing and pulling action of the ossicles causes parts of the basilar membrane to flex. This causes the fluid within the cochlea to move, displacing these tiny hair cells. When hair cells move, they stimulate the cells that comprise

Watch
Noise and the Brain

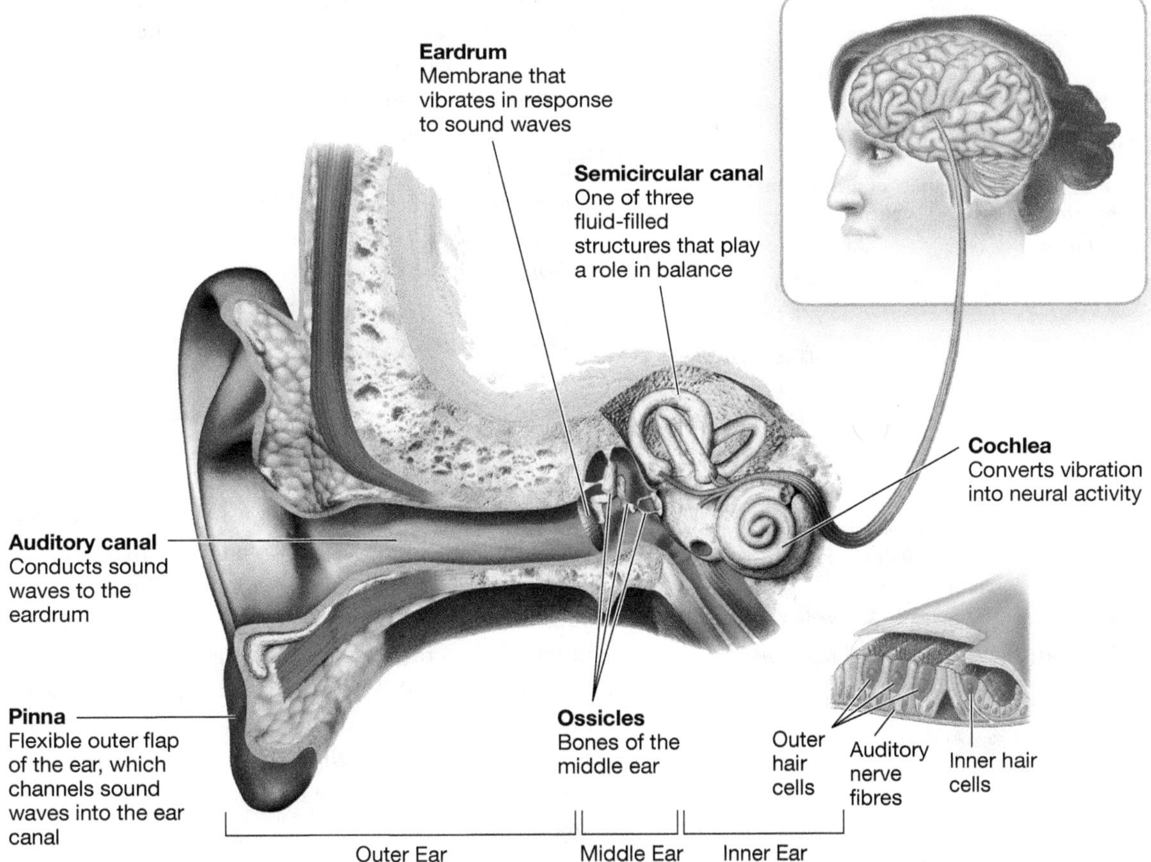

{FIG. 4.30} **The Human Ear** Sound waves travel from the outer ear to the eardrum and middle ear, and then through the inner ear. The cochlea of the inner ear is the site at which transduction takes place through movement of the tiny hair cells lining the basilar membrane. The auditory cortex of the brain is a primary brain region where sound is perceived. **Click on this figure in your eText to see more details.**

Explore
Major Structures of the Ear

the auditory nerves. The auditory nerves are composed of bundles of neurons that fire as a result of hair cell movements. These auditory nerves send signals to the thalamus—the sensory relay station of the brain—and then to the auditory cortex, located within the temporal lobes.

As you might expect, damage to any part of the auditory system will result in hearing impairments. However, recent technological advances are allowing individuals to compensate for this hearing loss. *Cochlear implants* are now quite common and have been used to help tens of thousands of individuals regain some of their hearing. These devices typically consist of a small microphone that detects sounds from the outside world and electronically stimulates parts of the membranes in the cochlea (see Figure 4.31). Although these devices are not a perfect substitute for a normally functioning auditory system, they do allow individuals to hear low-frequency sounds such as those used in human speech. These devices are particularly useful for young children (Fitzpatrick et al., 2011; Peterson et al., 2010), as the brains of children more easily form new pathways in response to the stimulation from the implants.

Listen
Psychology in the News: Cochlear Implants

Watch
Cochlear Implants

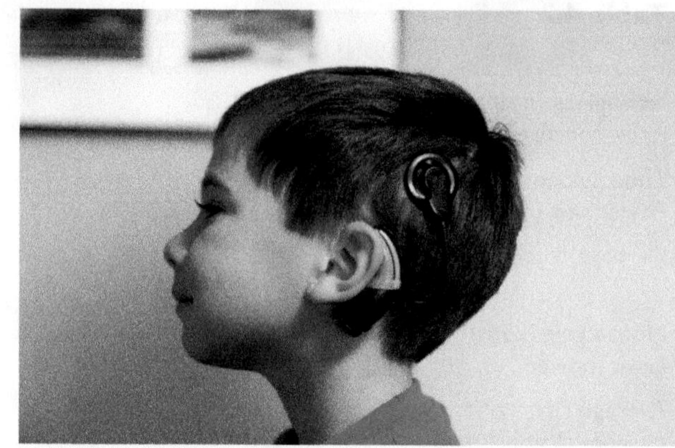

Carlos Osorio/Toronto Star/Getty Images

{FIG. 4.31} **A Cochlear Implant** The speech processor and microphone are located just above the pinna. A wire with tiny electrodes attached is routed through the cochlea.

Quick Quiz 4.3a

Sound and Structures of the Ear

KNOW ...

1 The ________ is the quality of sound waves that is associated with changes in pitch.

A frequency
B amplitude
C pinna
D decibel

2 The ________ is a snail-shaped, fluid-filled organ that converts sound waves into a neural signal.

A ossicle
B pinna
C cochlea
D outer ear

UNDERSTAND ...

3 The amplitude of a sound wave determines its loudness; ________-amplitude sound waves are louder than ________-amplitude waves.

A low; high
B short; tall
C wide; narrow
D high; low

Answers can be found on page ANS-2.

The Perception of Sound

It is quite remarkable that we are able to determine what makes a sound and where the sound comes from by simply registering and processing sound waves. In this section we examine how the auditory system accomplishes these two tasks, starting with the ability to locate a sound in the environment.

SOUND LOCALIZATION: FINDING THE SOURCE Accurately identifying and orienting oneself toward a sound source has some obvious adaptive benefits. Over the course of evolution, failure to do so could result in an organism becoming someone else's dinner, or failing to catch dinner of one's own. Thus, auditory systems have developed to allow organisms, including humans, to orient toward sounds in the environment. This **sound localization**, *the process of identifying where sound comes from,* is handled by parts of the brain stem as well as by a midbrain structure called the *inferior colliculus*.

There are two ways that we localize sound. First, we take advantage of the slight time difference between a sound hitting both ears to estimate the direction of the source. If your friend shouts your name from your left side, the left ear will receive the information a fraction of a second before the right ear. Second, we localize sound by using differences in the intensity in which sound is heard by both ears—a phenomenon known as a *sound shadow* (Figure 4.32). If the source of the sound is to your left, the left ear will experience the sound more intensely than the right because the right ear will be in the sound shadow. The inferior colliculi (plural) detect differences in the times when sound reaches the left versus the right ear, as well as the intensity of the sound between one side and the other, allowing us to identify where it is coming from.

THEORIES OF PITCH PERCEPTION To explain how we perceive pitch, we will begin in the cochlea and work toward brain centres that are specialized for hearing. How does the cochlea pave the way for pitch

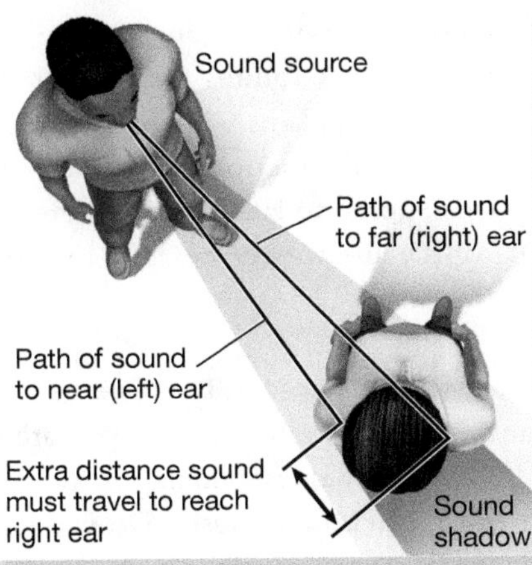

{FIG. 4.32} **How We Localize Sound** To localize sound, the brain computes the small difference in time at which the sound reaches each of the ears. The brain also registers differences in loudness that reach both ears.

perception? One explanation involves the specific arrangement of hair cells along the basilar membrane. Not all hair cells along the basilar membrane are equally responsive to sounds within the 20 to 20 000 Hz range of human hearing. High-frequency sounds stimulate hair cells closest to the ossicles, whereas lower-frequency sounds stimulate hair cells toward the end of the cochlea (see Figure 4.33). Thus, *how we perceive pitch is based on the location (place) along the basilar membrane that sound stimulates,* a tendency known as the **place theory of hearing.** As it turns out, place theory works well to explain hearing at higher frequencies, but hair cells for detecting lower frequencies are not so conveniently laid out at the end the cochlea.

Another determinant of how and what we hear is the rate at which the ossicles press into the cochlea, sending a wave of activity down the basilar membrane. According to **frequency theory**, *the perception of pitch is related to the frequency at which the basilar membrane vibrates.* A 70-Hz sound stimulates the hair cells 70 times per second. Thus, 70 nerve impulses per second travel from the auditory nerves to the brain, which interprets the sound frequency in terms of pitch (Figure 4.33). However, we quickly reach an upper limit on the capacity of the auditory nerves to send signals to the brain: Neurons cannot fire more than 1000 times per second. Given this limit, how can we hear sounds exceeding 1000 Hz?

The answer lies in the *volley principle*. A single neuron cannot fire more than 1000 times per second, but a group of neurons could certainly accomplish this feat. According to the volley principle, groups of neurons fire in alternating (hence the term "volley") fashion. A sound measuring 5000 Hz can be perceived because groups of neurons fire in rapid succession.

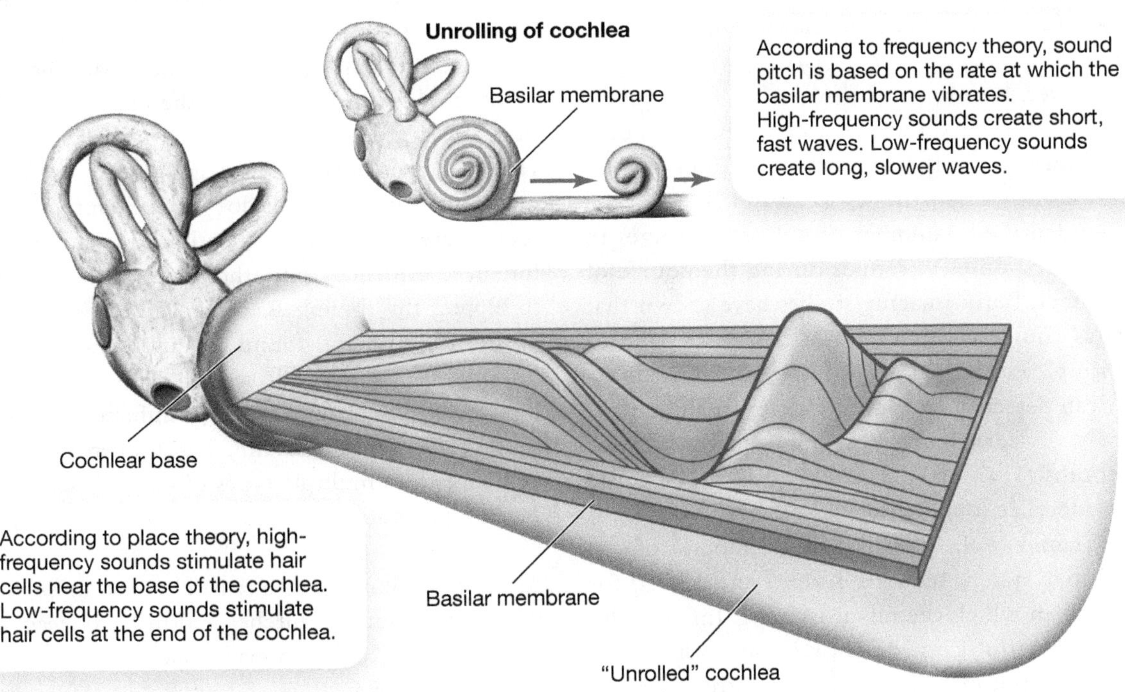

{FIG. 4.33} **The Basilar Membrane of the Cochlea and Theories of Hearing**

Currently, the place, frequency, and volley theories are all needed to explain our experience of hearing. Place theory is most applicable to high-pitched noises. Frequency theory, in combination with the volley principle, better explains how we hear low-pitched noises. When we hear complex stimuli, such as music, the place, frequency, and volley principles are likely all functioning at the sensory level. However, turning this sensory information into the perception of music, voices, and other important sounds occurs in specialized regions of the brain.

AUDITORY PERCEPTION AND THE BRAIN The **primary auditory cortex** *is a major perceptual centre of the brain involved in perceiving what we hear.* The auditory cortex is organized in very similar fashion to the cochlea. Cells within different areas across the auditory cortex respond to specific frequencies. For example, high musical notes are processed at one end of the auditory cortex, and progressively lower notes are heard as you move to the opposite end (Wang et al., 2005). As in the visual system, the primary auditory cortex is surrounded by brain regions that provide additional sensory processing. This *secondary auditory* cortex helps us to interpret complex sounds, including those found in speech and music. Interestingly, the auditory cortices in the two hemispheres of the brain are not equally sensitive. In most individuals the right hemisphere is able to detect smaller changes in pitch than the left hemisphere (Hyde et al., 2007). Given this fact, it is not surprising that the right hemisphere is also superior at detecting sarcasm, as this type of humour is linked to the tone of voice used (Voyer et al., 2008).

However, we are not born with a fully developed auditory cortex. In order to perceive our complex auditory world, the auditory cortices must *learn* to analyze different patterns of sounds. Researchers have identified a number of different changes in the brain's responses to sounds during the course of development. Brain-imaging studies have shown that infants as young as three months of age are able to detect simple changes in pitch (He et al., 2007, 2009). Infants can detect silent gaps in a tone (an ability that may help us learn languages) between the ages of 4–6 months (Trainor et al., 2003), and develop the ability to localize sound at approximately eight months of age (Trainor et al., 2010). By twelve months of age, the auditory system starts to become specialized for the culture in which the infant is living. Infants who are 10–12 months of age do not recognize sound patterns that are not meaningful in their native language or culture (Werker & Lalonde, 1988; see Module 8.3); indeed, children in this age group show different patterns of brain activity when hearing culturally familiar and unfamiliar sounds (Fujioka et al., 2011). This brain plasticity explains why many of us have difficulty hearing fine distinctions in the sounds of languages we are exposed to later in life. Interestingly, this fine-tuning of the auditory cortex also influences how we perceive music.

THE PERCEPTION OF MUSIC The next time you listen to music, concentrate on what you are thinking and on how your body is responding. Do you find yourself subtly moving with the music? Do you notice that you are moving your fingers to the beat? Do you sing (or hum) along to the music? Are you able to stay in tune? Most people are able to perform some or all of these musical responses, even if they have no musical training. Because our auditory systems have evolved to be able to distinguish between different rapidly changing pitches that are important for understanding speech, we also have a brain that is nicely designed for perceiving different elements of music (Levitin, 2008). However, music perception has evolved out of more than our linguistic capabilities; mysteriously, the brain areas involved in the perception of some elements of music are also involved in coordinating movements.

For example, researchers at the Montreal Neurological Institute have found that areas of the frontal lobes and cerebellum related to the planning of movements increase their activity levels when people are perceiving rhythms (Chen et al., 2008). Other researchers have shown that individual differences in the ability to detect musical beats are linked to differences in activity in the basal ganglia (Grahn & McAuley, 2009), a group of brain structures in the centre of the brain that are related to the coordination of movement. However, brain-imaging experiments show which areas of the brain are *active*; this does not guarantee that these regions are *necessary* for a function to occur. We therefore need evidence from other types of research studies to support this finding. Recently, Jessica Grahn (now at Western University) found that individuals with Parkinson's disease—who have damage to structures that input to the basal ganglia—have difficulty picking out subtle musical beats (Grahn, 2009). Therefore, there is evidence from multiple types of research studies linking the perception of music to brain areas related to movement.

But, it is important to remember that music is more than just a bunch of pitches and beats. Instead, music adds its own "texture" to many aspects of our lives, even if we're not paying attention to it. It does this by tapping into our more primal brain areas, namely those related to the experience of emotions.

WORKING THE SCIENTIFIC LITERACY MODEL

Music, Emotion, and Advertising

At the beginning of this module, we discussed the important emotional information conveyed by music. The fact that music influences our emotions is not new—politicians always have music playing before their speeches, many churches include music as part of their ceremonies, and sports teams blast music during stoppages of play. However, as with many areas of psychology, the pioneers of using music's emotional characteristics were people trying to sell products. Advertisers have been using catchy jingles and mood music in radio ads for almost 100 years (O'Reilly & Tennant, 2009) and some webpages now have music as part of the banner ads. So, what do we know about music and emotion, and how do marketing companies use this knowledge to influence which products we buy?

What do we know about music and advertising?

Music perception involves the emotional brain centres, such as those found in the limbic system (Bhatara et al., 2011; Gosselin et al., 2005). Indeed, in a novel study, researchers at the Université de Montréal and Concordia University found that patients with damage to the amygdala, an area of the brain related to the experience of fear, were impaired in their ability to recognize that particular pieces of music, such as the theme to *Jaws*, were scary. Studies such as this imply that in healthy brains, the emotion centres respond during the perception of music in order to help us understand its meaning.

In addition to influencing our feelings, the emotional aspects of music also allow us to structure our other perceptions (Cohen, 2002). Try watching a horror movie with no sound—without the music "telling you" when to become tense and when to relax, your experience of the film will be as muted as the volume. This influence of music on our thinking extends beyond the movie theatre, however. Advertisers have been aware of music's powerful effects for decades.

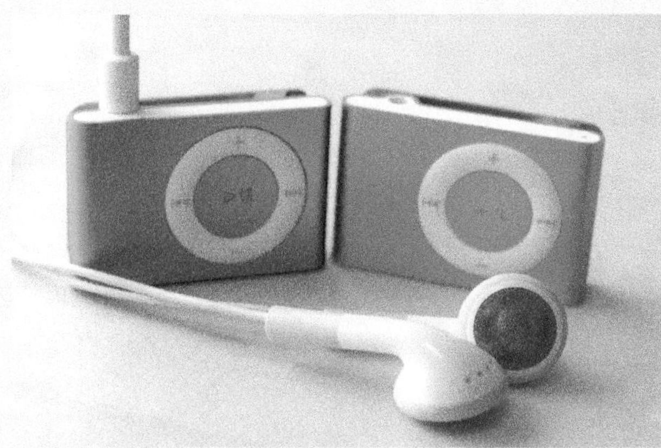

Ulrich Niehoff/imagebroker/Alamy

What song comes to mind when you see an iPod? For many people, it is Feist's "1-2-3-4." Can you think of other examples of music and products becoming strongly linked?

How can science be used to explain the influence of music on advertising success?

A key factor in mixing music and advertising is finding the correct balance. Music should be emotionally arousing, but not overwhelming. We have all had the experience of thinking, "What a cool commercial! What were they selling again?" That's bad news for a company paying tens of thousands of dollars for a 30-second commercial on Hockey Night in Canada. Researchers have found that some musical characteristics are useful in improving memory for a commercial's product. Music with meaningful lyrics had a more positive effect on memory for product information than instrumental music or nonsense lyrics (Olsen, 2002). Additionally, people tend to prefer popular songs to new music, likely because popular songs already have positive memories associated with them (Hébert & Peretz, 1997). Sometimes, an ad will be so successful that the song and product are permanently linked, such as Feist's "1-2-3-4" and Apple's iPod. So, what about the lyrics themselves? We all know that music helps us recall lyrics; researchers have found that musical jingles in commercials greatly enhance memory if the jingle contains the brand's name (Yalch, 1991).

Can we critically evaluate this information?

One explanation for the positive effects of music on attitudes toward products relates to the vast number of associations we have with songs and melodies. Music evokes visual images, and images have been shown to improve performance on memory tests. So, if music is paired with a commercial (or, better yet, in a jingle with the product's name in it), it is easier for the consumer to remember and feel positively toward that particular product (Stewart & Punj, 1998). Recent studies of the brain provide one possible explanation for the effectiveness of jingles. Using EEG, researchers found that people learning verbal material that was sung (like a jingle) showed more coherent patterns of firing in the network of neurons in the frontal lobes than did people who heard the same material spoken normally. Thus, music provides structure, and structure aids memory.

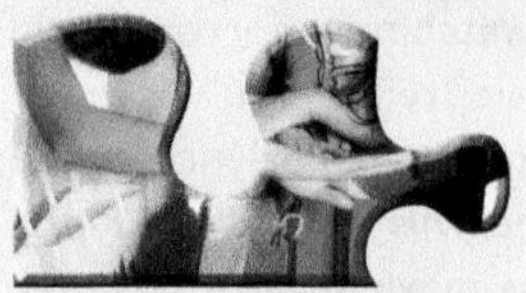

Why is this relevant?

The fact that an auditory stimulus—music—can influence what products we purchase at the mall is astounding. It is also a wonderful example of how different areas of our brain interact to produce complex behaviours. It is easy to forget how interconnected these seemingly distinct behaviours really are. People often view psychology as consisting of independent ideas (or modules), yet no part of human behaviour is truly independent—everything is interconnected in some way.

Incidentally, if you go to a shopping mall, you'll notice that music is used for an additional purpose in stores. Stores whose images are based on being "cool" and youth-oriented will blast modern music in an attempt to show that they are trendy. Although one goal of this action is to draw in young customers in the same way that commercials do, there is an extra goal at work. These stores also need to *repel* older people who might harm the store's youthful image. Admittedly, given that many of these old folks are parents with credit cards, these retailers might soon be singing a different tune.

argo74/Shutterstock

Quick Quiz 4.3b The Perception of Sound

KNOW ...

1 The primary auditory cortex is found in which lobe of the brain?

A Frontal
B Temporal
C Occipital
D Parietal

UNDERSTAND ...

2 ________ explains pitch perception when hair cells are stimulated at the same rate that a sound wave cycles.

A Place theory
B Frequency theory
C The volley principle
D Switch theory

3 Neurons cannot fire fast enough to keep up with high-pitched sound waves. Therefore, they alternate firing according to the ________.

A place theory
B frequency theory
C volley principle
D switch theory

APPLY ...

4 While crossing the street, you know a car is approaching on your left side because

A the left ear got the information just a fraction of a second before the right ear.
B the right ear got the information just a fraction of a second before the left ear.
C the right ear experienced the sound more intensely than the left ear.
D both ears experienced the sound at the same intensity.

Answers can be found on page ANS-2.

Module Summary

Module 4.3

Now that you have read this module you should

KNOW ...

- ***The key terminology relating to the ear and hearing***:

cochlea (p. 161)
frequency theory (p. 163)
pitch (p. 160)
place theory of hearing (p. 163)
primary auditory cortex (p. 164)
sound localization (p. 162)

UNDERSTAND ...

- ***Different characteristics of sound and how they correspond to perception.*** Sound can be analyzed based on its frequency (the number of cycles a sound wave travels per second) as well as on its amplitude (the height of a sound wave). Our experience of pitch is based on sound wave frequencies. Amplitude corresponds to loudness: The higher the amplitude, the louder the sound.
- ***How technology is used to restore hearing.*** Cochlear implants are remarkable devices that can restore much of a person's hearing. However, this technology works best for young children because their brains are more adaptable than the brains of adults.

APPLY ...

- ***Your knowledge of sound localization.*** Get a friend to participate in a quick localization demonstration. Have her sit with her eyes closed, covering her right ear with her hand. Now walk quietly in a circle around your friend, stopping occasionally to snap your fingers. When you do this, your friend should point to where you are standing, based solely on the sound. If her right ear is covered, at which points will she be most accurate? At which points will she have the most errors? Use the principles of sound localization to make your predictions.

IGphotography/iStockphoto

ANALYZE ...

- ***How the emotional characteristics of music can be used by advertisers.*** Music is an important part of television and radio commercials. They can capture our attention and can influence how we perceive different products. Researchers have found that musical "jingles" that mention the product's name are quite effective in making that product more memorable. Using popular songs is also an effective method of influencing consumers. But, now that you know how marketers are using music to persuade you, you can be aware of this manipulation. You might still buy their products, but the knowledge of advertisers' techniques will allow you to make an informed decision when making your purchase, or to march to a different drummer.

tuja66/iStockphoto

Module 4.4

Touch and the Chemical Senses

Learning Objectives

After reading this module you should

KNOW ...	UNDERSTAND ...	APPLY ...	ANALYZE ...
The key terminology of touch and chemical senses	How pain messages travel to the brain The relationship between smell, taste, and food flavour experience	Your knowledge about touch to describe the acuity of different areas of skin Your knowledge to determine whether you or someone you know is a "supertaster"	How different senses are combined together

Would you ever describe your breakfast cereal as tasting pointy or round? Probably not. Touch, taste, and smell combine together to make your favourite foods, yet most of us can still identify the separate components associated with what is felt, tasted, and smelled. Individuals with a condition called *synesthesia* experience blended perceptions, such that affected individuals might actually hear colours or feel sounds (Cytowic, 1993). For the individuals who experience this condition, even letters or numbers may have a colour associated with them. To illustrate this effect, find the number 2 below:

5555555555555555555555
5555555555555555555555
5555555555555525555555
5555555555555555555555

People who have a type of synesthesia in which words or numbers have unique colours associated with them find the 2 faster than people without synesthesia because the colours cause the 2s to "pop out" (Blake et al., 2005). In some individuals, even the *idea* of a number can elicit a colourful response (Dixon et al., 2000). Synesthesia can also involve blending taste and touch, which certainly can influence dining experiences. People may avoid oatmeal because it tastes bland, but can you imagine avoiding a food because it tastes "pointy," or relishing another food because of its delicate hints of corduroy? Synesthesia occurs in an estimated 1 in 500 people. For the 499 others, touch, taste, and smell are distinct senses.

Focus Questions

1. How are our experiences of touch, taste, and smell distinct?
2. What are the different types of sensations that are detected by our sense of touch?

Generally speaking, vision and hearing are the senses that we seem to be aware of the most and, therefore, have received the most attention from researchers. In this module, we will explore the senses of touch, taste, and smell. Putting them together in a single module is not meant to diminish their importance, however. Our quality of life, and possibly our survival, would be severely compromised without these senses. We will also examine how we combine information from our different senses into vibrant *multimodal* experiences, such as when taste and smell are combined to create a perception of flavour.

The Sense of Touch

The sense of touch allows us to actively investigate our environment and the objects that are in it (Lederman & Klatzky, 2004; Lederman et al., 2007). Using touch, we can acquire information about texture, temperature, and pressure upon the skin. These different forms of stimulation are combined to give us a vivid physical sense of every moment. Imagine you're at a concert. You don't just hear music. You *feel* the vibrations of the bass rippling through you. You *feel* the heat of the crowd. You *feel* other people brushing up against you. And, you *feel* your own body moving to the rhythm of the music. These sensual experiences—which seem so social and so distant from the nervous system—are dependent on the actions of several types of receptors located just beneath the surface of the skin, and also in the muscles, joints, and tendons. These receptors send information to the *somatosensory cortex* in the parietal lobes of the brain, the neural region associated with your sense of touch.

Sensitivity to touch varies across different regions of the body. One simple method of testing sensitivity, or *acuity*, is to use the two-point threshold test shown in Figure 4.34. Regions with high acuity, such as the fingertips, can detect the two separate, but closely spaced, pressure points of the device, whereas less sensitive regions such as the lower back will perceive the same stimuli as only one pressure point. Body parts such as the fingertips, palms, and lips are highly sensitive to touch compared to regions such as the calves and forearm. Research has shown that women have a slightly more refined sense of touch than men, precisely because their fingers (and therefore their receptors) are smaller (Peters et al., 2009). Importantly, the sensitivity of different parts of the body also influences how much space in the somatosensory cortex is dedicated to analyzing each body part's sensations. Regions of the body that send a lot of sensory input to the brain such as the lips have taken over large portions of the somatosensory cortex while less sensitive regions like the thigh use much less neural space.

Like vision and hearing, touch is very sensitive to change. Merely laying your hand on the surface of an object does little to help identify it. What we need is an active exploration that stimulates receptors in the hand. **Haptics** *is the active, exploratory aspect of touch sensation and perception.* Active touch involves feedback. For example, as you handle an object, such as a piece of fruit, you move your fingers over its surface to identify whether any faults may be present. Your fingertips can help you determine whether the object is the appropriate shape and can detect bruising or abnormalities that may make it unsuitable. Haptics allows us not only to identify objects, but also to avoid damaging or dropping them. Fingers and hands coordinate their movements using a complementary body sense called **kinesthesis**, *the sense of bodily motion and position.* Receptors for kinesthesis reside in the muscles, joints, and tendons. These receptors transmit information about movement and the position of your

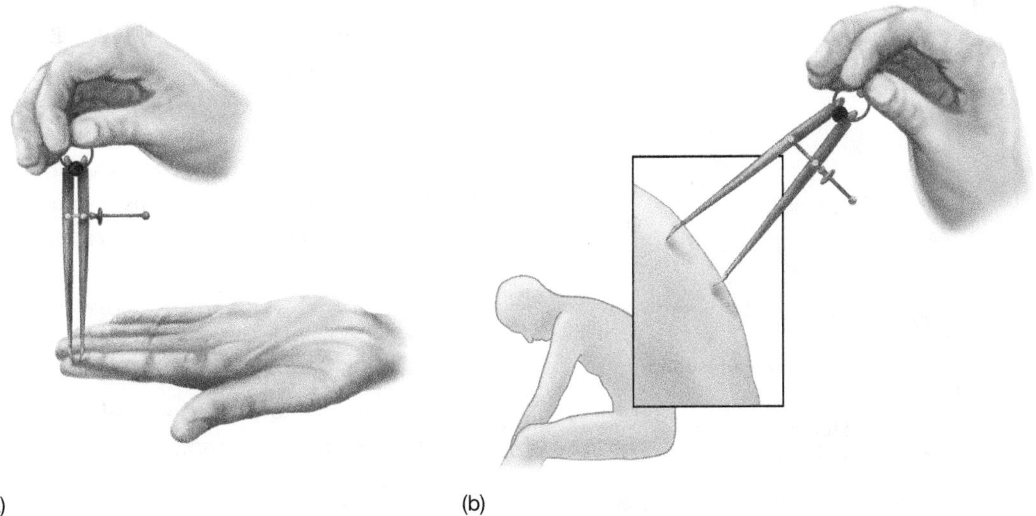

{FIG. 4.34} **Two-Point Threshold Device for Measuring Touch Acuity** The more sensitive regions of the body can detect two points even when they are spaced very close together. Less sensitive parts of the body have much larger two-point thresholds.

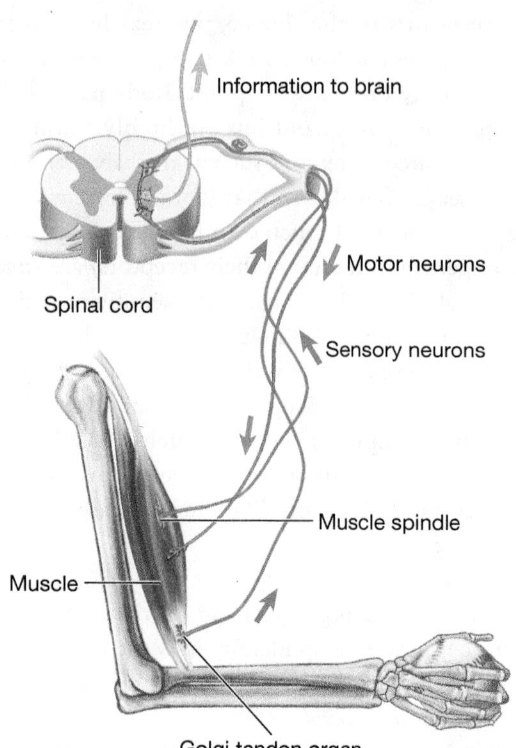

{FIG. 4.35} **The Sense of Kinesthesis** Receptors in muscles and at the joints send sensory messages to the brain, helping us maintain awareness and control of our movements. Muscle spindles and Golgi tendon organs are sensory receptors that provide information about changes in muscle length and tension.

Watch
In the Real World: Managing Pain

Watch
Brain Pain

muscles, limbs, and joints to the brain (Figure 4.35). As you handle an object, your kinesthetic sense allows you to hold it with enough resistance to avoid dropping it, and to keep your hands and fingers set in such a way as to avoid letting it roll out of your hands. Touch, therefore, provides us with a great deal of information about our bodies and the world around them.

FEELING PAIN Of course, not all of the information we receive from our sense of touch is pleasant. **Nociception** *is the activity of nerve pathways that respond to uncomfortable stimulation.* Our skin, teeth, corneas, and internal organs contain nerve endings called *nociceptors*, which are receptors that initiate pain messages that travel to the central nervous system (see Figure 4.36). Nociceptors come in varieties that respond to various types of stimuli—for example, to sharp stimulation, such as a pin prick, or to extreme heat or cold (Julius & Basbaum, 2001).

Two types of nerve fibres transmit pain messages. Fast fibres register sharp, immediate pain, such as the pain felt when your skin is scraped or cut. Slow fibres register chronic, dull pain, such as the lingering feelings of bumping your knee into the coffee table. Although both slow and fast fibres eventually send input to the brain, these impulses first must travel to cells in the spinal cord; the firing of neurons within the spinal cord will influence how this pain is experienced.

Pain varies from mild to severe and from acute (brief) to chronic. How do we explain differences in pain experiences? One long-held theory of pain perception is the **gate-control theory**, *which explains our experience of pain as an interaction between nerves that transmit pain messages and those that inhibit these messages.* According to this theory, cells in the spinal cord regulate how much pain signalling reaches the brain. The spinal cord serves as a "neural gate" that pain messages must pass through (Melzack & Wall, 1965, 1982). The spinal cord contains small nerve fibres that conduct pain messages and larger nerve fibres that conduct other sensory signals such as those associated with rubbing, pinching, and tickling sensations. Stimulation of the small pain fibres results in the experience of pain, whereas the larger fibres inhibit pain signals. Thus, the large fibres close the gate that is opened by the smaller fibres. According to gate-control theory, if you stub your bare toe, rubbing the area around the toe may alleviate some of the pain, because the large fibres carrying the message about touch inhibit the firing of smaller fibres carrying pain signals. Likewise, putting ice on a wound reduces pain by overriding the signals transmitted by the small fibres.

{FIG. 4.36} **Cross-Section of Skin and Free Nerve Endings That Respond to Pain** The nerve endings that respond to pain reside very close to the surface of the skin and, as you are likely aware, are very sensitive to stimulation. **Click on this figure in your eText to see more details.**

Input from both the large and small fibres will be sent from the spinal cord to the brain. There, the sensory information will branch off to (at least) two different areas of the brain. One region, the somatosensory cortex, registers the pain sensations occurring over the entire surface of the body. The other region, the anterior cingulate gyrus, influences our attentional and emotional responses to the pain; this brain region is found on the medial (middle) surface of the brain immediately above the corpus callosum. Although you might not immediately think of pain as an emotional experience, you can likely think of situations in which you were quite upset and frustrated after hurting yourself. These feelings are due, in part, to activity of the anterior cingulate gyrus, which forms networks with many structures within the limbic system.

Our discussion thus far has focused on how we perceive pain when it affects our own body. But, how do you feel when you see *someone else* in pain? And, does the pain of other people affect how your own pain feels? Psychology researchers have begun to address these complicated—and fascinating—questions.

WORKING THE SCIENTIFIC LITERACY MODEL

Empathy and Pain

A running theme of this chapter has been that sensation and perception involve an interaction with your environment. While the term *environment* often makes people think of birds, trees, and buildings, a key part of our environment is other people. Is it possible for one person's somatosensory experiences to influence those of another person?

What do we know about empathy and pain?

We've all seen someone in pain. Sometimes it's a friend stubbing his toe on a chair, other times it's a hockey player crushed against the boards in front of thousands of spectators. Our experience of those situations differs a great deal. If we see someone we care about in pain, we experience negative emotions and sometimes even feel pain ourselves. If it is a stranger or someone we don't like (e.g., an opposing hockey team's player), we might not have as intense a reaction. This leads to several interesting questions. Are you able to feel the pain of others? Under what conditions? And how does the presence of another person influence how you experience pain?

How does science explain the influence of empathy on pain perception?

The power of emotion in the experience of pain is profound. In one study, researchers at McGill University asked participants to immerse their right hand in hot water while viewing emotionally negative videos (disaster scenes) and neutral videos (cityscape scenes). Participants rated the unpleasantness of the pain as being higher when they watched disaster scenes (Loggia et al., 2008a). These results suggest that the emotional component of pain can influence our physical sensations, particularly when it involves seeing the suffering of others.

In another study, these researchers asked participants to either feel high or low levels of empathy for an actor in a video. The researchers then measured the participants' sensitivity to painful heat stimuli while they watched the actor experience similar stimulation. Participants who felt empathy for the actor reported experiencing higher levels of pain than did low-empathy participants. This result suggests that emotionally connecting with someone else in pain can influence our own sensitivity (Loggia et al., 2008b).

Can we critically evaluate the research?

An obvious criticism of research studies involving emotion and the experience of pain is that the participants may simply be reporting what they think the experimenters want to hear. If you were in a study in which someone was manipulating your mood, you would likely be able to predict the hypotheses being tested in that study. It is therefore necessary to find additional support for these self-report experiments. Numerous neuroimaging studies have found that activity in a brain structure called the insula (near the junction of the frontal lobes and the top of the temporal lobes) is related to the awareness of bodily sensations (Wiens, 2007). Activity in the insula also increases when people are performing empathy-related tasks (Fukushima et al., 2011). Thus, there might be a biological link between feeling pain and feeling empathy.

Stronger support comes from studies that show an effect of empathy on pain perception in individuals that are much less likely to be influenced by the experimenter's expectations: mice! When injected with a pain-inducing substance, mice that were tested in pairs showed more pain-related behaviours than did mice that were tested alone. But, this effect only occurred when the mice were cagemates with their test partner (i.e., they knew the other mouse)! Additionally, observing a cagemate in pain altered the mouse's own pain sensitivity, suggesting that these animals are capable of some form of empathy (Langford et al., 2006). Even more remarkable, some male mice refused to show pain responses in the presence of mice they didn't know (a mouse version of the male tendency to act macho); this effect, not surprisingly, appears to be dependent upon the hormone testosterone (Langford et al., 2011). Taken together, these neuroimaging and animal-based studies suggest that our own pain can be dramatically influenced by the pain of those around us.

Why is this relevant?

These studies demonstrate that our sensations, particularly pain, can be influenced by the experiences of other people. Feeling negative emotions or seeing someone else feel pain makes our own pain more unpleasant. Although these studies might seem a bit morbid, they do offer an incredibly important insight that could affect the well-being of many people. If people can influence each other's negative sensations, then it should be possible to influence each other's positive sensations. Just as pain can be "contagious," so too might happiness and well-being.

blickwinkel/Alamy

Studies conducted at McGill University provide evidence that mice can feel empathy.

Vuk Vukmirovic/Shutterstock

PHANTOM LIMB PAIN Astonishingly, it is possible for people to feel pain in body parts that no longer exist. *Phantom limb sensations* are frequently experienced by amputees, who report pain and other sensations coming from the absent limb. Amputees describe such sensations as itching, muscle contractions, and, most unfortunately, pain. One explanation for phantom pain suggests that rewiring occurs in the brain following the loss of the limb. After limb amputation, the area of the somatosensory cortex formerly associated with that area is no longer stimulated by the lost limb. Thus, if someone has her left arm amputated, the right somatosensory cortex that registers sensations from the left arm no longer has any input from this limb. Healthy nerve cells become hypersensitive when they lose connections. The phantom sensations, including pain, may occur because the nerve cells in the cortex continue to be active, despite the absence of any input from the body.

One ingenious treatment for phantom pain involves the mirror box (Figure 4.37). This apparatus uses the

{FIG. 4.37} **A Mirror Box Used in Therapy for People with Limb Amputation** In this case, a woman who has lost her left arm can experience some relief from phantom pain by moving her intact hand, such as by unclenching her fist. In turn, she will experience relief from phantom pain corresponding to her left side.

reflection of the amputee's existing limb, such as an arm and hand, to create the visual appearance of having both limbs. Amputees often find that watching themselves move and stretch the phantom hand, which is actually the mirror image of the real hand, results in a significant decrease in phantom pain and in both physical and emotional discomfort (Ramachandran & Altschuler, 2009).

Researchers have conducted experiments to determine how well mirror box therapy works compared both to a control condition and to mentally visualizing the presence of a phantom hand. Over the course of four weeks of regular testing, the people who used the mirror box had significantly reduced pain compared to a control group who used the same mirror apparatus, except the mirror was covered, as well as compared to the group who used mental visualization (Figure 4.38; Chan et al., 2007). Notice in Figure 4.38 that everyone was given mirror therapy after the fourth week of the study, and that the procedure seems to have lasting, positive benefits. No one is sure why mirror box therapy works, but evidence suggests that the short-term benefits are due to how compelling the illusion is; in the long term, this therapy may actually result in reorganization of the somatosensory cortex (Ramachandran & Altschuler, 2009).

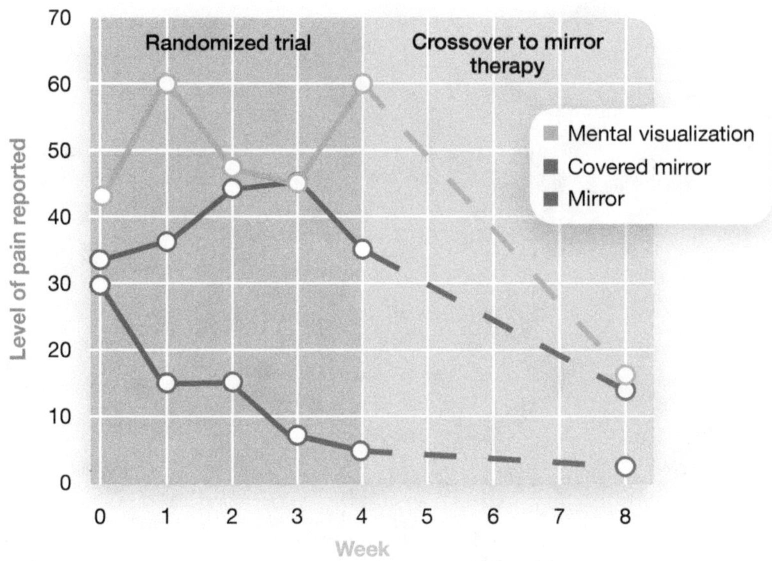

{FIG. 4.38} **Mirror Box Therapy Compared to Mental Visualization and a Control Condition**

Quick Quiz 4.4a

The Sense of Touch

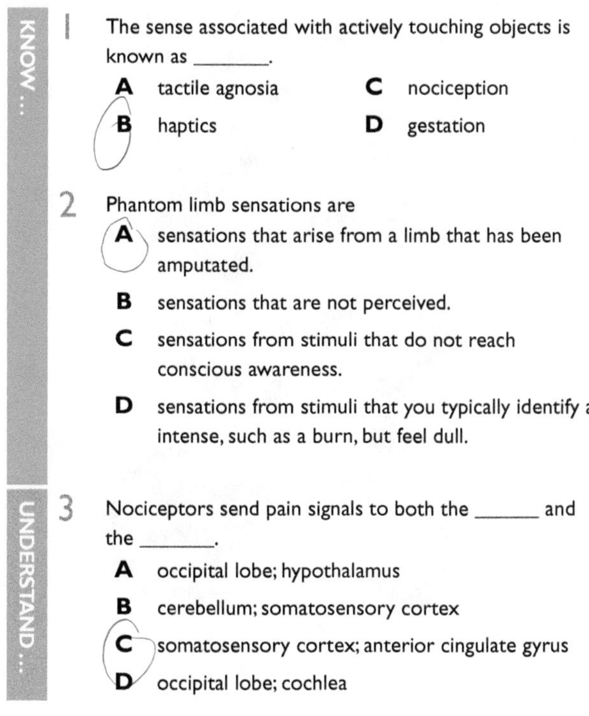

KNOW ...

1 The sense associated with actively touching objects is known as _______.

A tactile agnosia **C** nociception

B haptics **D** gestation

2 Phantom limb sensations are

A sensations that arise from a limb that has been amputated.

B sensations that are not perceived.

C sensations from stimuli that do not reach conscious awareness.

D sensations from stimuli that you typically identify as intense, such as a burn, but feel dull.

UNDERSTAND ...

3 Nociceptors send pain signals to both the ______ and the _______.

A occipital lobe; hypothalamus

B cerebellum; somatosensory cortex

C somatosensory cortex; anterior cingulate gyrus

D occipital lobe; cochlea

APPLY ...

4 A student gently touches a staple to her fingertip and to the back of her arm near her elbow. How are these sensations likely to differ? Or would they feel similar?

A The sensation would feel like two points on the fingertip but is likely to feel like only one point on the arm.

B The sensations would feel identical because the same object touches both locations.

C The sensation would feel like touch on the fingertips but like pain on the elbow.

D The sensation would feel like two points on the arm but is likely to feel like only one point on the fingertip.

Answers can be found on page ANS-2.

The Chemical Senses: Taste and Smell

The chemical senses comprise a combination of both taste and smell. Although they are distinct sensory systems, both begin the sensory process with chemicals activating receptors on the tongue and mouth, as well as in the nose.

THE GUSTATORY SYSTEM: TASTE The **gustatory system** *functions in the sensation and perception of taste.* But, what exactly is this system tasting? Approximately 2500 identifiable chemical compounds are found in the food we eat (Taylor & Hort, 2004). When combined, these compounds give us an enormous diversity of taste

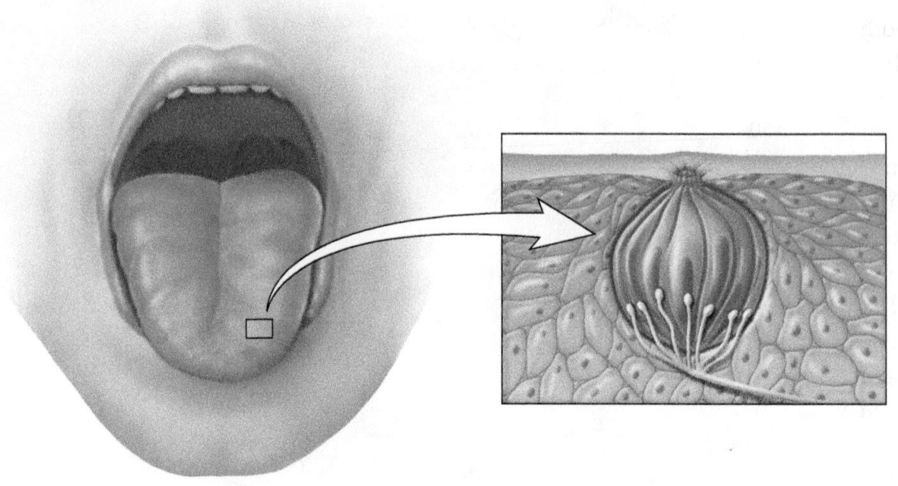

{FIG. 4.39} **Papillae and Taste Buds** The tongue is lined with papillae (the bumpy surfaces). Within these papillae are your taste buds, the tiny receptors to which chemicals bind.

sensations. The *primary tastes* include salty, sweet, bitter, and sour. In addition, a fifth taste, called *umami*, has been identified (Chaudhari et al., 2000). Umami, sometimes referred to as "savouriness," is a Japanese word that refers to tastes associated with seaweed, the seasoning monosodium glutamate (MSG), and protein-rich foods such as milk and aged cheese.

Taste is registered primarily on the tongue, where roughly 9000 taste buds reside. On average, approximately 1000 taste buds are also found throughout the sides and roof of the mouth (Miller & Reedy, 1990). Sensory neurons that transmit signals from the taste buds respond to different types of stimuli, but most tend to respond best to a particular taste. Our experience of taste reflects an overall pattern of activity across many neurons, and generally comes from stimulation of the entire tongue rather than just specific, localized regions. The middle of the tongue has very few taste receptors, giving it a similar character to the blind spot on the retina (Module 4.2). We do not feel or sense the blind spot of the tongue because the sensory information is filled in, just as we find with vision. Taste receptors replenish themselves every 10 days throughout the life span—the only type of sensory receptor to do so.

Receptors for taste are located in the visible, small bumps (*papillae*) that are distributed over the surface of the tongue. The papillae are lined with taste buds. Figure 4.39 shows papillae, taste buds, and an enlarged view of an individual taste bud and a sensory neuron that sends a message to the brain. The bundles of nerves that register taste at the taste buds send the signal through the thalamus and on to higher-level regions of the brain, including the *gustatory cortex*; this region is located in the back of the frontal lobes and extends inward to the insula (near the top of the temporal lobe). Another region, the *secondary gustatory cortex*, processes the pleasurable experiences associated with food.

Why do some people experience tastes vividly while other people do not? One reason is that the number of taste buds present on the tongue influences the psychological experience of taste. Although approximately 10 000 taste buds is the average number found in humans, there is wide variation among individuals. Some people may have many times this number. *Supertasters,* who account for approximately 25% of the population, are especially sensitive to bitter tastes such as those of broccoli and black coffee. They typically have lower rates of obesity and cardiovascular disease, possibly because they tend not to prefer fatty and sweet foods. Figure 4.40 shows the number of papillae, and hence taste buds, possessed by a supertaster compared to those without this ability.

How much of our taste preferences are learned and how much is innate? Like most of our behaviours, there is no simple answer. Human infants tend to prefer the foods consumed by their mothers during gestation (Beauchamp & Mennella, 2009). Soon after starting solid foods, children begin to acquire a taste for the foods prevalent in their culture. Would you eat a piece of bread smeared with a sticky brown paste that was processed from wasted yeast used to make beer in

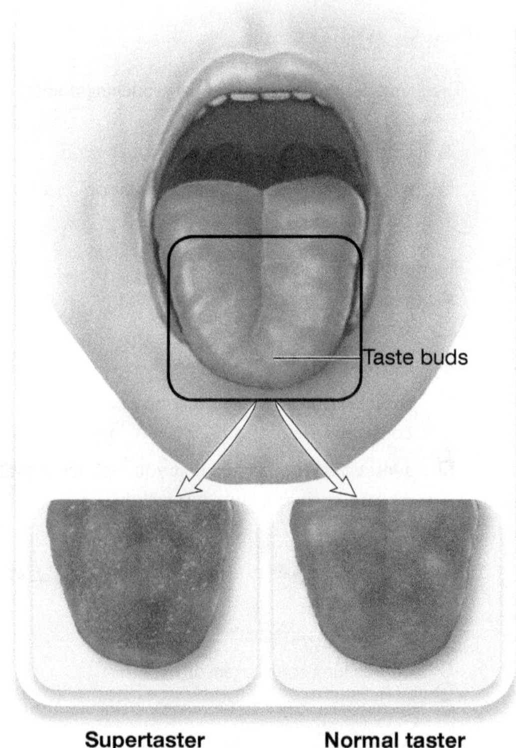

{FIG. 4.40} **Density of Papillae, and Hence Taste Buds, in a Supertaster and in a Normal Taster**

a brewery? This product, called vegemite, is actually quite popular among people in Switzerland, Australia, and New Zealand. People brought up eating vegemite may love it, while most others find it tastes like death. The Masai people of Kenya and Tanzania enjoy eating a coagulated mixture of cow's blood and milk. These foods may sound unappetizing to you. Of course, non-Canadians are often repulsed by poutine, a decadent mixture of French fries, cheese curds, and gravy, so we should be careful not to judge . . . too much.

Closely related to taste is our sense of smell, which senses the chemical environment via a different mode than does taste.

THE OLFACTORY SYSTEM: SMELL The **olfactory system** *is involved in smell—the detection of airborne particles with specialized receptors located in the nose.* Our sensation of smell begins with nasal air flow bringing in molecules that bind with receptors at the top of the nasal cavity. (So, when you smell something, you are actually taking in part of the environment—including other people—into your body.) Within the nasal cavity is the **olfactory epithelium**, *a thin layer of cells that are lined by sensory receptors called cilia*—tiny hair-like projections that contain specialized proteins that bind with the airborne molecules that enter the *nasal cavity* (Figure 4.41). Humans have roughly 1000 different types of odour receptors in their olfactory system. If this is the case, then how it is possible for us to detect approximately 10 000 different smells? The answer is that it is the *pattern* of the stimulation, involving more than one receptor, which gives rise to the experience of a particular smell (Buck & Axel, 1991). Different combinations of cilia are stimulated in response to different odours.

These groups of cilia then transmit messages to neurons that converge on the *olfactory bulb* (on the bottom surface of the frontal lobes), which serves as the brain's central region for processing smell. The olfactory bulb connects with several regions of the brain through the olfactory tract, including the limbic system (emotion) as well as regions of the cortex where the subjective experience of pleasure (or disgust) occurs.

MULTIMODAL INTEGRATION Modules 4.2–4.4 have described our five different sensory systems. After reading about them, it is quite tempting to view the five systems as being distinct from one another. After all, our brains are set up in such a way that it is simple to separate the different senses. Indeed, the Doctrine of Specific Energies stated *in 1826* that our senses are separated in the brain (see Module 4.1). However, this view is at odds with some of our sensory experiences. Many of these experiences are actually combinations of multiple types of sensations, just as they are in individuals with synesthesia, the condition discussed at the beginning of this module. For example, the perceptual experience of flavour combines taste and smell (Small et al., 1997). You have probably noticed that when you have nasal congestion, your experience of flavour is diminished. This loss of taste occurs because approximately 80% of our information about food comes from olfaction (Murphy et al., 1977). This link between taste and smell is a perfect example of **multimodal integration**, *the ability to combine sensation from different modalities such as vision and hearing into a single integrated perception.*

Watch Alzheimer's Smell Test

Watch Basics: In Full Appreciation of the Cookie

Watch Aromatherapy

Watch Thinking Like a Psychologist: Can Smells Alter Mood and Behavior?

Simulate Which Senses Do You Use?

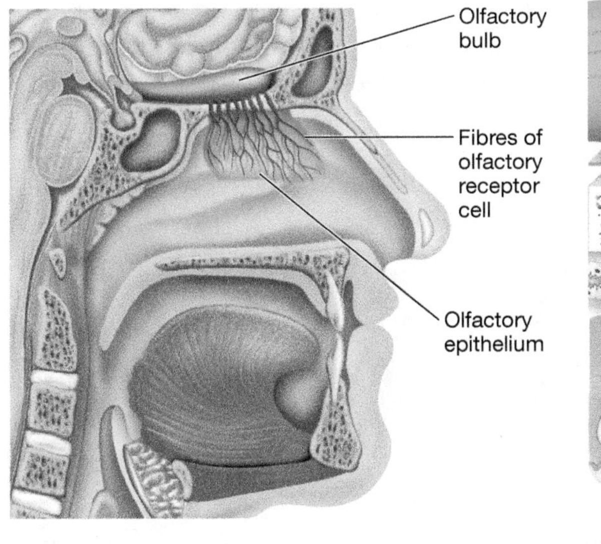

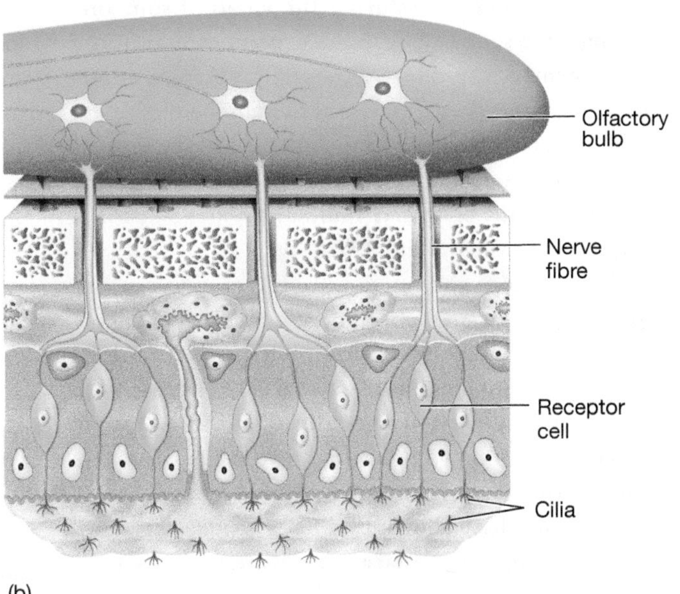

{FIG. 4.41} **The Olfactory System** Lining the olfactory epithelium are tiny cilia that collect airborne chemicals, sending sensory messages to the nerve fibres that make up the olfactory bulb. **Click on this figure in your eText to see more details.**

Multimodal integration is so much more than simply combining different senses. In fact, it's a form of problem-solving performed by your brain hundreds of times each day. We must decide, almost instantaneously, if two types of sensation should be integrated into a multimodal perception. How do we do this? One factor is whether the different sensations are in a similar location. If you hear a "meow" and see a cat with its mouth open, you infer that the movements of the cat's mouth and the "meow" sound were linked together. We also make use of temporal information. Sensations that occur in roughly the same time period are more likely to be linked than those that are not. If you hear a "meow" five seconds before the cat's mouth moved, you will not likely combine the sound with the sight of the cat (unless you know your cat is a ventriloquist).

Multimodal integration occurs quite naturally—we're often unaware of these perceptions until some outside force interferes with it. We've all had the experience of watching a television show or youtube.com clip in which the movement of the characters' lips didn't match up with the sound of their voices. These perceptions are often annoying because the lag between the image and the sound makes it difficult to combine the two into the expected multimodal perception. In fact, sometimes this mismatch can interfere with perception, even to the point of producing new perceptions that did not actually occur.

This result occurred by accident in a study conducted by Harry McGurk and John MacDonald in 1976. These researchers were investigating language perception in infants and had videos of different actors speaking sounds such as /ba-ba/. However, when the sound /ba-ba/ was presented during the video of someone mouthing the sound /ga-ga/, the experimenters noticed that it seemed to produce an entirely different multimodal stimulus: /da-da/. It was as though the movement of the speaker's lips provided the viewer with the expectation of a particular sound; this expectation biased the perception of the presented sounds. This phenomenon is now known as the *McGurk Effect*.

Expectations and multimodal integration can also influence our social interactions. We routinely integrate visual and auditory information when we are speaking with someone. Researchers have found that both woman and men rated masculine faces (i.e., tough, rugged faces) as being more attractive when they were matched with a masculine voice (Feinberg et al., 2008). Other studies have shown that heterosexual men preferred viewing female faces that were paired with a high-pitched than a low-pitched voice (Feinberg et al., 2005). Facial expressions of a singer also influence judgments of the emotional content of songs (Thompson, Russo, & Quinto, 2008). These studies show us that we naturally form auditory expectations when we visually perceive a face.

So, if our brains are set up to perceive our senses separately and then combine them only when it seems appropriate (due to location, time, and expectations), how can we explain synesthesia, the condition discussed in the opening of this module? These blended multimodal associations (e.g., chicken that tastes "pointy") do not come and go. Rather, they occur automatically and are consistent over time (Ramachandran & Hubbard, 2003). Why does synesthesia occur?

This question has puzzled scientists since the first reported case of synesthesia in 1812 (Sachs, 1812; Jewanski et al., 2009). To date, there is still no clear answer. Researchers have noted that synesthesia does run in families (Baron-Cohen, 1996). However, the exact genes involved with this condition are still unknown. In fact, researchers at the University of Waterloo found a pair of identical twins, only one of whom had synesthesia (Smilek et al., 2001)!

Neuroimaging studies have provided some insight into this condition. For instance, one research group tested synesthetes who have specific colour perceptions appear whenever they read a number (e.g., every time they see "2", it appears with a yellow border). These researchers found activity in areas of the brain related to colour perception in synesthetes, but not non-synesthetes (Nunn et al., 2002). Studies such as this suggest that the brains of people with synesthesia may contain networks that link different sensory areas in ways not found in other people.

This finding demonstrates a point made repeatedly in this book: Our experiences involve groups of brain areas working together. This point holds for all five of our senses, as well as for their multimodal integration.

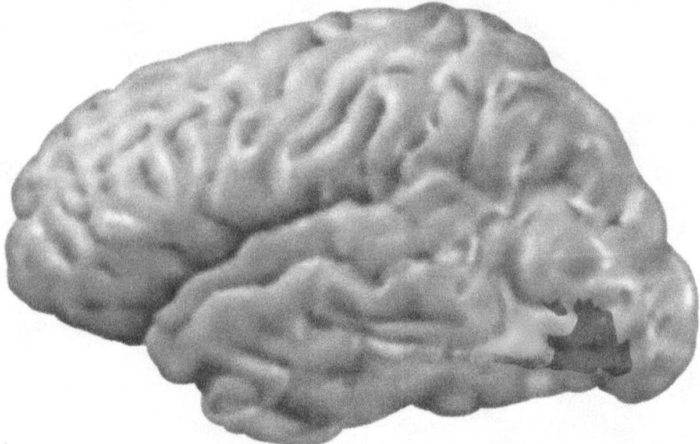

Synesthetes who experience colours when they see letters or numbers have stronger connections between brain areas related to colour (red) and letters/numbers (green).

Quick Quiz 4.4b The Chemical Senses: Taste and Smell

KNOW ...

1 The bumps that line the tongue surface and house our taste buds are called ______.

A epithelia
B gustates
C the gustatory cortex
D papillae

2 Where are the receptor cells for smell located?

A The papillae
B The olfactory epithelium
C The olfactory bulb
D The odour buds

UNDERSTAND ...

3 The perceptual experience of flavour originates from:

A taste cues alone.
B olfactory cues alone.
C olfactory and taste cues together.
D haptic and olfactory cues together.

APPLY ...

4 After eating grape lollipops, you and a friend notice that your tongues have turned purple. With the change in colour, it is easy to notice that there are many more papillae on your friend's tongue. Who is more likely to be a supertaster?

A You are, because you have fewer, and therefore more distinct, papillae.
B Your friend is, because she has many more papillae to taste with.
C You are, because less dye stuck to your tongue, allowing you to taste more.
D It could be either of you because supertasting is unrelated to the number of papillae.

ANALYZE ...

5 An exchange student at your school dislikes root beer but often craves seaweed. What is the best explanation for her taste preferences?

A She grew up drinking root beer and is sick of it.
B She grew up consuming seaweed.
C Seaweed is a culturally universal preference.
D These are most likely individual preferences that are unrelated to culture and experience.

Answers can be found on page ANS-2.

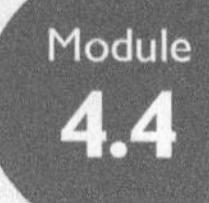

Module Summary

Module 4.4

tuja66/iStockphoto

Now that you have read this module you should

KNOW ...

- ***The key terminology of touch and chemical senses:***

gate-control theory (p. 170)	multimodal integration (p. 175)
gustatory system (p. 173)	nociception (p. 170)
haptics (p. 169)	olfactory epithelium (p. 175)
kinesthesis (p. 169)	olfactory system (p. 175)

UNDERSTAND ...

- ***How pain messages travel to the brain.*** According to gate-control theory, small nerve fibres carry pain messages from their source to the spinal cord, and then up to, among other regions, the anterior cingulate gyrus and somatosensory cortex. However, large nerve cells that register other types of touch sensations (such as rubbing) can override signals sent by small pain fibres.
- ***The relationship between smell, taste, and food flavour experience.*** Both senses combine to give us flavour experiences. Contact with food activates patterns of neural activity among nerve cells connected to the taste buds, and food's odours activate patterns of nerve activity in the olfactory epithelium. The primary and secondary gustatory cortex and the olfactory bulb are involved in the perceptual experience of flavour.

APPLY ...

- ***Your knowledge about touch to describe the acuity of different areas of skin.*** You can try this yourself by creating a two-point threshold device like the one shown earlier in **Figure 4.34 (page 169)**. You can fashion one out of a straightened paper clip that you could hold up to a ruler. Set the two points about 5 mm apart and gently apply them to different parts of the body—your fingertips, your elbow, your cheek. Which parts of your body are sensitive enough to feel both points, and on which parts does it feel like a single object is touching you? Now try the experiment again with the two points closer together. Can you detect a change in acuity?
- ***Your knowledge to determine whether you or someone you know is a "supertaster."*** Scientists use a very precise measurement system to identify supertasters, but one less complicated way to do so is to dye your tongue by placing a drop of food colouring on it, or by eating or drinking something dark blue or purple. Next, count the number of papillae you can see in a 4-mm circle. You can accomplish this by viewing the dyed portion of your tongue through the punched hole in a sheet of loose-leaf notebook paper. If you can count more than 30 papillae, then chances are you are a supertaster. Of course, if you already know that you do not like bitter vegetables like broccoli or asparagus, then perhaps you would expect to find a high number of papillae.

ANALYZE ...

- ***How different senses are combined together.*** Humans have five distinct types of senses. However, that does not mean that these senses always operate independently—they often interact to form more vivid experiences. The flavour of food is an experience that involves both taste *and* smell. Numerous other studies have shown that our visual perception interacts with our auditory system, leading us to be surprised when sounds such as the pitch of someone's voice don't match the visual image of his or her face.

Work the Scientific Literacy Model :: Understanding Visual Perception

1 What do we know about the process of perception?

Review **Figure 4.2** on **page 133** for a reminder of the complex processes of sensation and perception. But what about the cognitive processes that guide this perception? As mentioned on **page 139**, depending on the information available, we process information, or stimuli, in either a top-down or bottom-up direction. Remember that top-down processing happens when our perception of an object is shaped by our existing knowledge or prior information, and bottom-up processing happens when our perception is based only on the information available from the stimulus. Think of it this way: Bottom-up processing occurs when perception starts at the most basic (bottom) level—the stimulus. Top-down processing occurs at a higher (top) level, as you are approaching the stimulus armed with previous knowledge.

Consider a baby's toy giraffe. You are familiar with giraffes and children's toys, so you would process the object from the top down. But giraffes, and even the concept of toys, are new to an infant. Perceiving this stimulus would consist of taking in all of its elements, including its shape, size, and texture. Thus, this brand-new object is perceived from the bottom up—from its most basic elements.

2 How can science help explain how visual perception works?

See **pages 139–140** for a discussion of studies that show how top-down and bottom-up processing often work together to help us categorize and identify stimuli. Research has also revealed that our brains have limited resources and, consequently, sometimes make errors in perception. For example, inattentional blindness prevents us from seeing one stimulus if we are focused on another. This was demonstrated in a classic study when subjects viewing a video were asked to attend to one cognitive task (counting the number of times a ball was passed back and forth) and didn't notice a person in a gorilla suit strolling across the screen. This is an example of how processing information in a top-down manner can impede our ability to notice events that, in hindsight, should have been obvious.

3 Can we critically evaluate claims about perception?

If the frequency with which we encounter objects influences our ability to perceive them, and concentrating on one stimulus can make us blind to another, then is it possible to trick our perceptions through exposure to subliminal stimuli? **Myths in Mind** on **page 136** notes that while the brain exhibits a small response to subliminal stimuli, the key word is *small*. Your behaviour is unlikely to be drastically influenced, either positively or negatively, by subliminal messaging. There is also no evidence that backward messages in music will influence your behaviour. Also keep in mind how the concept of inattentional blindness can be important when it comes to critically evaluating the value of eyewitness testimony. For example, can a person who witnesses a hit-and-run accident, even from a close range, accurately recall the model and colour of the car if, at the time of the accident, her attention was focused on a cell phone conversation?

4 Why is this relevant?

Watch the accompanying video excerpt on sensation and perception. You can access the video at MyPsychLab or by clicking the play button in the centre of your eText. If your instructor assigns this video as a homework activity, you will find additional content to help you in MyPsychLab. You can also view the video by using your smart phone and the QR code below, or you can go to the YouTube link provided.

Once you have read this chapter and watched the video, consider what you know about the processes of perception. The Gestalt psychologists maintained that when people perceive sensory elements, their tendency is to see things in terms of the entire form or pattern rather than as individual parts. Identify and describe each of the basic principles of perceptual organization from the Gestalt perspective, including figure–ground, similarity, proximity, continuity, closure, and symmetry.

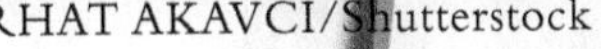

SERHAT AKAVCI/Shutterstock

MyPsychLab **Your turn to Work the Scientific Literacy Model:** Watch the accompanying video on YouTube, or on your phone (using the Layar app or QR code). If your instructor has assigned this as a homework activity, you can find the video clip and additional content at MyPsychLab. Answer the questions that accompany the video clip to test your understanding.

youtube.com/workthemodel

SCAN WITH LAYAR

5

Consciousness

Lava 4 images/Shutterstock

Sylvia Serrado/Glow Images

Module 5.1

Biological Rhythms of Consciousness: Wakefulness and Sleep

Learning Objectives

After reading this module you should

KNOW ...	UNDERSTAND ...	APPLY ...	ANALYZE ...
The key terminology associated with sleep, dreams, and sleep disorders	How the sleep cycle works Theories of why we sleep	Your knowledge to identify and practise good sleep habits	Different theories about why we dream

Smashing through a window in your sleep seems perfectly plausible if it occurs as part of a dream. Mike Birbiglia did just this—but in his case, it was both dream and reality. Birbiglia is a comedian whose show, *Sleepwalk with Me*, is full of stories of personal and embarrassing moments, which include jumping through a second-storey window of his hotel room while he was asleep. He awoke upon landing; picked his bloodied, half-naked self up; and went to the hotel front desk to notify personnel of what happened. Perhaps his comedy is just his way of dealing with an otherwise troubling sleep problem—a serious condition called REM behaviour disorder. People with REM behaviour disorder act out their dreams, which clearly has the potential to be very dangerous. In Mike's case, the injury was self-inflicted. Other people with the condition, however, have been known to hit or choke their bed partner. As it turns out, jumping through windows is not entirely uncommon for people with REM behaviour disorder (Schenck et al., 2009). In this module, we explore how normal sleep works, and we explain how and why sleep disorders, such as Mike Birbiglia's, occur.

Focus Questions

1. How do body rhythms affect memory and thinking?
2. What is REM and how is it related to dreaming?

Consciousness *is a person's subjective awareness, including thoughts, perceptions, experiences of the world, and self-awareness.* Every day we go through many changes in consciousness—our thoughts and perceptions are constantly adapting to new situations. In some cases, when we are paying close attention to something, we seem to be more in control of conscious experiences. In other situations, such as when we are daydreaming, consciousness seems to wander. These changes in our subjective experiences, and the difficulty in defining them, make consciousness one of the most challenging areas of psychological study. We will begin this module by exploring the alternating cycles of consciousness—sleeping and waking.

What Is Sleep?

It makes perfect sense to devote a module to a behaviour that humans spend approximately one-third of their lives doing. What happens during sleep can be just as fascinating as what happens during wakefulness. Psychologists and non-psychologists alike have long pondered some basic questions about sleep, such as "Why do we need sleep?" and "Why do we dream?" But perhaps we should begin with the most basic question: "What is sleep?"

Listen
Brain Time

BIOLOGICAL RHYTHMS Life involves patterns—patterns that cycle within days, weeks, months, or years. Organisms have evolved *biological rhythms* that are neatly adapted to the cycles in their environment. For example, bears are well known for hibernating during the cold winter months. Because this behaviour happens on a yearly basis, it is part of a *circannual rhythm* (a term that literally means "a yearly cycle"). This type of rhythm is an example of an *infradian rhythm,* which is any rhythm that occurs over a period of time longer than a day. In humans, the best-known infradian rhythm is the menstrual cycle. However, most biological rhythms occur with a much greater frequency than once a month. For instance, heart rate, urination, and some hormonal activity occur in 90–120-minute cycles. These more frequent biological rhythms are referred to as *ultradian rhythms.*

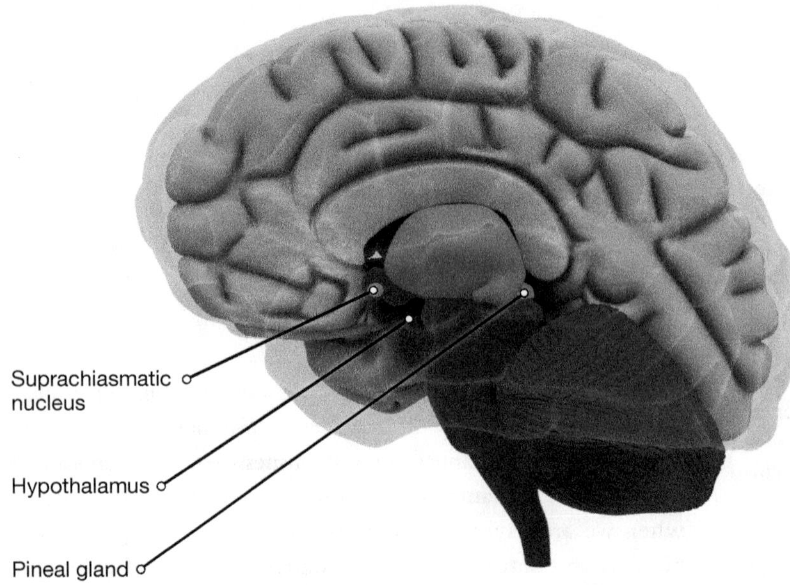

{FIG. 5.1} **Pathways Involved in Circadian Rhythms** Cells in the retina send messages about light levels to the suprachiasmatic nucleus, which in turn relays the information to the pineal gland, which secretes melatonin.

However, the biological rhythm that appears to have the most obvious impact upon our lives is a cycle that occurs over the course of a day. **Circadian rhythms** *are internally driven daily cycles of approximately 24 hours affecting physiological and behavioural processes* (Halberg et al., 1959). They involve the tendency to be asleep or awake at specific times, to feel hungrier during some parts of the day, and even the ability to concentrate better at certain times than at others (Lavie, 2001; Verwey & Amir, 2009).

Think about your own circadian rhythms: When are you most alert? At which times of day do you feel the most tired? Night shift workers and night owls aside, we tend to get most of our sleep when it is dark outside because our circadian rhythms are regulated by daylight interacting with our nervous and endocrine (hormonal) systems. One key brain structure in this process is the *suprachiasmatic nucleus* (SCN) of the hypothalamus. Cells in the retina of the eye relay messages about light levels in the environment to the SCN (Hendrickson et al., 1972; Morin, 2013). The SCN, in turn, communicates signals about light levels with the pineal gland (see Figure 5.1). The pineal gland releases a hormone called *melatonin,* which peaks in concentration at nighttime and is reduced during wakefulness. Information about melatonin levels feeds back to the hypothalamus (i.e., they influence each other); our sleep–wake cycle is controlled by these interactions.

But what actually causes us to adopt these circadian rhythms? Why don't we stay awake for days and then sleep all weekend? There are two explanations for our 24-hour rhythms. One is **entrainment**, *when biological rhythms become synchronized to external cues such as light, temperature, or even a clock.* Because of its effects on the SCN-melatonin system, light is the primary entrainment mechanism for most mammals (Wever et al., 1983). We tend to be awake during daylight and asleep during darkness. We're also influenced by the time on our clocks. If you're tired at 8 P.M., you normally try to fight your fatigue until a "normal" bed time such as 10 P.M. Why? Because we've been trained to believe that some times of day are associated with sleep and others are not.

However, not all of our body rhythms are a product of entrainment. Instead, some are **endogenous rhythms**, *biological rhythms that are generated by our body independent of external cues such as light.* Studying endogenous rhythms is tricky because it is difficult to remove all of the external cues from a person's world. To overcome this problem, researchers in the 1960s and 1970s asked motivated volunteers to spend extended periods of time (months) in caves or in isolation chambers. For instance, Jürgen Aschoff (1965; Aschoff et al., 1967;

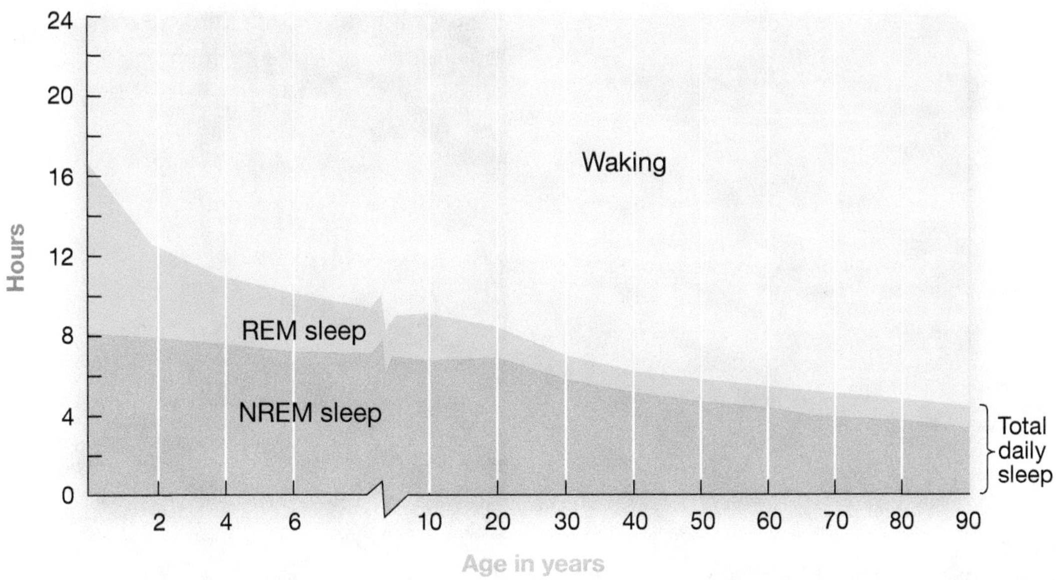

{FIG. 5.2} **Sleep Requirements Change with Age** People tend to spend progressively less time sleeping as they age. The amount of a certain type of sleep, REM sleep, declines the most.

Aschoff & Wever, 1962) had participants stay in an underground chamber for four weeks. These researchers noted that individuals tended to adopt a 25-hour day. Michel Siffre, a French cave expert, remained by himself in a dark cave for much longer durations than Aschoff's participants: two months in 1962 and six months in 1972 (Foer & Siffre, 2008). Whenever he woke up or intended to go to sleep, he called his support team who were stationed at the entrance to the cave. Data from Siffre and a number of his subsequent participants indicated that most people fell into a 24.5-hour circadian rhythm. Although a few participants would briefly enter longer cycles—sometimes as long as 48-hour days—most people possess an endogenous circadian rhythm that is 24–25 hours in length (Lavie, 2001; Mills, 1964).

Although our sleep–wake cycle remains relatively close to 24 hours in length throughout our lives, some patterns within our circadian rhythms do change with age (Caci et al., 2009). As shown in Figure 5.2, researchers have found that we need much less sleep—especially a type called REM sleep—as we move from infancy and early childhood into adulthood. Moreover, people generally experience a change in when they prefer to sleep. In your teens and 20s, many of you will become night owls who prefer to stay up late and sleep in. When given the choice, those of you in this age range prefer to work, study, and play late in the day. Later in adulthood, many of you will find yourselves going to bed earlier and getting up earlier, and you may begin to prefer working or exercising before teenagers even begin to stir. In fact, research shows that these patterns are more than just preferences: People actually do show higher alertness and cognitive functioning during their preferred time of day (Cavallera & Giudici, 2008; Hahn et al., 2012). For instance, researchers at the University of Toronto have found that when older adults (approximately 60–80 years of age) are tested later in the day as opposed to early in the morning, they have a greater difficulty separating new from old information (Hasher et al., 2002) and have a larger variability in their reaction times on a test in which they learned to pair together a digit and a symbol (Hogan et al., 2009). These results have implications for the cognitive testing older patients receive in hospitals; clearly, these individuals will appear healthier if tested in the morning as opposed to later in the day, when their bodies are preparing to go to sleep.

THE STAGES OF SLEEP We have already seen how sleep fits into the daily rhythm, but if we take a closer look, we will see that sleep itself has rhythms. In order to measure these rhythms, scientists use **polysomnography**, *a set of objective measurements used to examine physiological variables during sleep*. Some of the devices used in this type of study are familiar, such as one to measure respiration and a thermometer to measure body temperature. In addition, electrical sensors attached to the skin measure muscle activity around the eyes and other parts of the body. However, sleep cycles themselves are most often defined by the *electroencephalogram (EEG)*, a device that measures brain waves using sensors attached to the scalp (see Module 3.4).

Watch
Basics: Rhythms of Consciousness

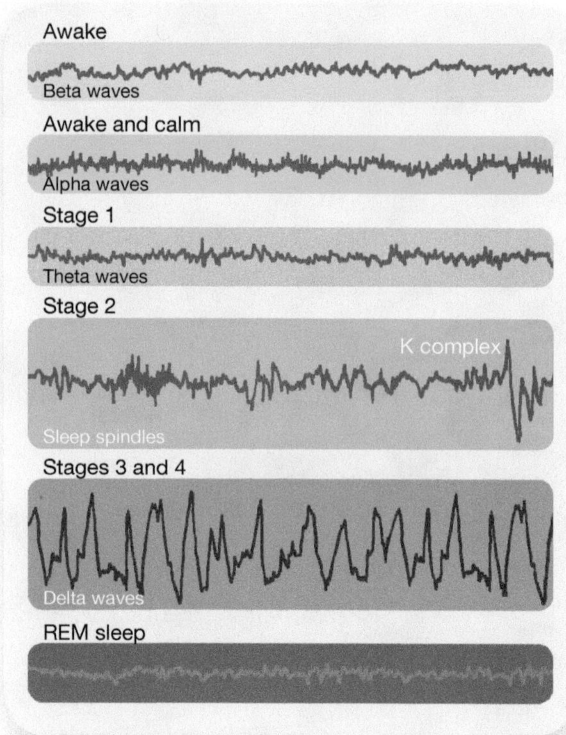

{FIG. 5.3} **EEG Recordings during Wakefulness and Sleep** Brain waves, as measured by the frequency and amplitude of electrical activity, change over the course of the normal circadian rhythm. Beta waves are predominant during wakefulness, but give way to alpha waves during periods of calm and as we drift into sleep. Theta waves are characteristic of stage 1 sleep. As we reach stage 2 sleep, the amplitude (height) of brain waves increases. During deep sleep (stages 3 and 4), the brain waves are at their highest amplitude. During REM sleep, they appear similar to the brain waves occurring when we are awake. **Click on this figure in your eText to see more details**.

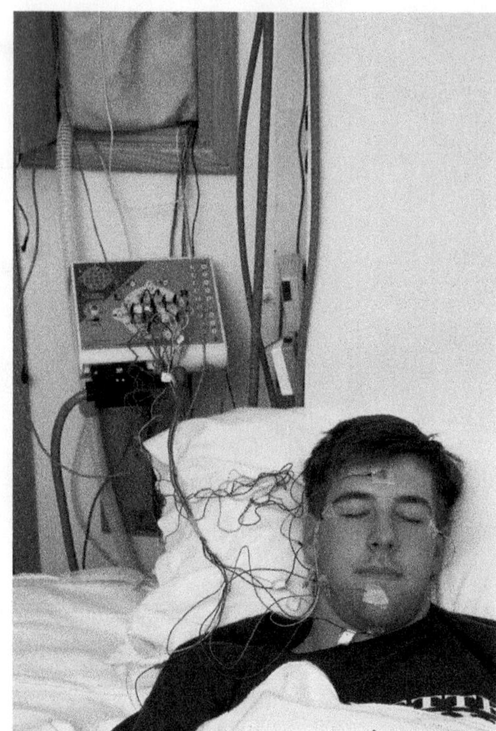

Hank Morgan/Science Source

Using physiological recording devices, sleep researchers and doctors can monitor eye movements, brain waves, and other physiological processes.

The output of an EEG is a waveform, like that shown in Figure 5.3. These waves can be described by their *frequency*—the number of up-down cycles every second—and their *amplitude*—the height and depth of the up-down cycle. *Beta waves*—high-frequency, low-amplitude waves—are characteristic of wakefulness. Their irregular nature reflects the bursts of activity in different regions of the cortex, and they are often interpreted as a sign that a person is alert. As the individual begins to shift into sleep, the waves start to become slower, larger, and more predictable; these *alpha waves* signal that a person may be daydreaming, meditating, or starting to fall asleep. These changes in the characteristics of the waves continue as we enter deeper and deeper stages of sleep.

The EEG signals during sleep move through four different stages. In stage 1, brain waves slow down and become higher in amplitude—these are known as *theta waves*. Breathing, blood pressure, and heart rate all decrease slightly as an individual begins to sleep. However, at this stage of sleep, you are still sensitive to noises such as the television in the next room. After approximately 10 to 15 minutes, the sleeper enters stage 2, during which brain waves continue to slow. As shown in Figure 5.3, stage 2 includes *sleep spindles* (clusters of high-frequency but low-amplitude waves) and *K complexes* (small groups of larger amplitude waves), which are detected as periodic bursts of EEG activity. What these bursts in brain activity mean is not completely understood, but evidence suggests they may play a role in helping maintain a state of sleep and in the process of memory storage (Fogel et al., 2007; Gais et al., 2002)—a topic we cover more fully later on.

As stage 2 sleep progresses, we respond to fewer and fewer external stimuli, such as lights and sounds. Approximately 20 minutes later, we enter stage 3 sleep, in which brain waves continue to slow down and assume a new form called *delta waves* (large, looping waves that are high-amplitude and low-frequency). The process continues with the deepest stage of sleep, stage 4, during which time the sleeper will be difficult to awaken.

About an hour after falling asleep, we reach the end of our first stage 4 sleep phase. At this point, the sleep cycle goes in reverse and we move back toward stage 1. However, we do not remain in stage 1 sleep for long; instead, we move into a unique stage of **REM sleep**—*a stage of sleep characterized by quickening brain waves, inhibited body movement, and rapid eye movements (REM)*. This stage is sometimes known as *paradoxical sleep* because the EEG waves appear to represent a state of wakefulness, despite the fact that we remain asleep. The REM pattern is so distinct that the first four stages are known collectively as *non-REM (NREM) sleep*. At the end of the first REM phase, we cycle back toward deep sleep stages and back into REM sleep again every 90 to 100 minutes. (Think back to the beginning of this module: What type of biological rhythm would a 90–100-minute cycle represent?)

The sleep cycle through a typical night of sleep is summarized in Figure 5.4. As shown in the figure, the deeper stages of sleep (3 and 4) predominate during the earlier portions of the sleep cycle, but gradually give way to longer REM periods.

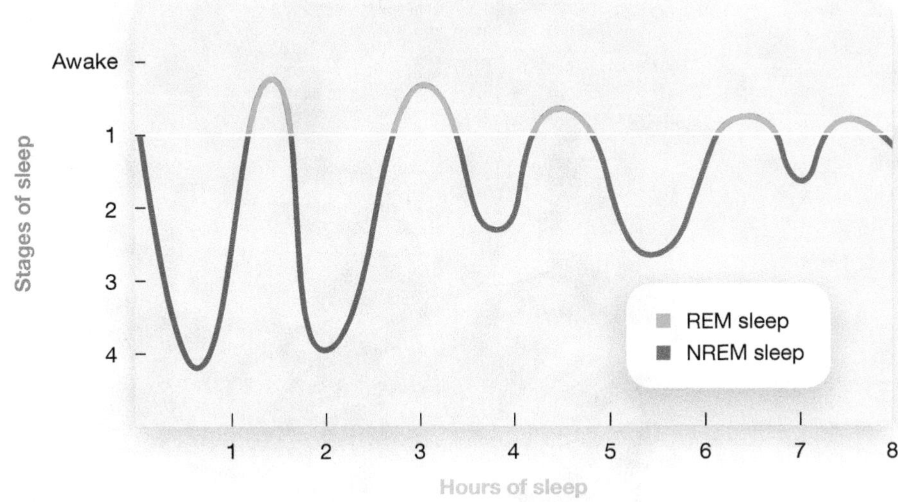

{FIG. 5.4} **Order and Duration of Sleep Stages through a Typical Night** Our sleep stages progress through a characteristic pattern. The first half of a normal night of sleep is dominated by deep, slow-wave sleep. REM sleep increases in duration relative to deep sleep during the second half of the night. **Click on this figure in your eText to see more details.**

Quick Quiz 5.1a

What Is Sleep?

KNOW ...

1 Large, periodic bursts of brain activity that occur during stage 2 sleep are known as ________.

- **A** beta waves
- **B** sleep spindles
- **C** delta waves
- **D** alpha waves

UNDERSTAND ...

2 Why is REM sleep known as paradoxical sleep?

- **A** The brain waves appear to be those of an awake person, but the individual seems to be in a deep sleep.
- **B** The brain waves resemble those of a sleeping individual, but the person behaves as if he is nearly awake.
- **C** The brain wave patterns in REM sleep are totally unlike those produced by brain activity at any other time.
- **D** The brain waves resemble those of a sleeping individual, and the person seems to be in a very deep sleep.

APPLY ...

3 Which of the following is the most likely order of sleep stages during the first 90 minutes of a night of rest?

- **A** Stages 1-2-3-4-1-2-3-4-REM
- **B** Stages 1-2-3-4-REM-1-2-3-4
- **C** Stages 1-2-3-4-3-2-1-REM
- **D** Stages REM-4-3-2-1

Answers can be found on page ANS-2.

Why We Need Sleep

Sleep is such a natural part of life that it is difficult to imagine what the world would be like if there were no such thing. It raises another question: Why do humans and other animals need to sleep in the first place?

THEORIES OF SLEEP The most intuitive explanation for why we sleep is probably the **restore and repair hypothesis**, *the idea that the body needs to restore energy levels and repair any wear and tear experienced during the day's activities*. Research on sleep deprivation clearly shows that sleep is a physical and psychological necessity, not just a pleasant way to relax. A lack of sleep eventually leads to cognitive decline, emotional disturbances, and impaired functioning of the immune system (Born et al., 1997). For some species, sleep deprivation can be more detrimental—even fatal—than food deprivation (Rechtschaffen, 1998).

Although there is good evidence supporting the restore and repair hypothesis, it does not account for all the reasons why we sleep. Imagine you have had an unusually active day on Saturday and then spend all day Sunday relaxing. Research shows that you are likely to feel sleepier on Saturday night, but you will need only slightly more sleep after the high-activity day, despite what the restore and repair hypothesis would suggest (Horne & Minard, 1985). The same is true for days filled with mentally challenging activities (De Bruin et al., 2002). Rather than requiring more sleep, it could be that sleep is more efficient after an exhausting day (Montgomery et al., 1987); in other words, more restoring and repairing may go on in the same amount of time.

Kurhan/Fotolia

The restore and repair hypothesis suggests that people will need more sleep after a physically demanding day.

Watch
Virtual Brain: Sleep and Dreaming

A second explanation for sleep, the **preserve and protect hypothesis**, *suggests that two more adaptive functions of sleep are preserving energy and protecting the organism from harm* (Berger & Philips, 1995; Siegel, 2005). To support this hypothesis, researchers note that the animals most vulnerable to predators sleep in safe hideaways and during the time of day when their predators are most likely to hunt (Siegel, 1995). Because humans are quite dependent upon our vision, it made sense for us to sleep at night, when we would be at a disadvantage compared to nocturnal predators. Quantity of sleep differs between animal species as well. Hoofed species like antelope (the species you always see getting killed in nature programs) sleep less than four hours per day, primarily because they have to remain alert in case a predator attacks. Conversely, animals such as lions and bears rarely fall victim to predators and can therefore afford a luxurious 15 hours of sleep per day. (The sleepiest animal appears to be the brown bat. It sleeps an average of 19.9 hours out of each 24 hours . . . because really, who would eat a bat?) The underlying message from this theory is that each species' sleep patterns have evolved to match their sensory abilities and their environment.

Thus, there are complementary theories that answer the question of why we sleep. The amount that any animal sleeps is a combination of its need for restoration and repair along with its need for preservation and protection. Each theory explains part of our reasons for drifting off each night. Importantly, both theories would produce sleep patterns that would improve a species' evolutionary fitness. Of course, this discussion of the reasons for sleep leads to an equally important discussion, particularly for students: What happens when we don't get enough sleep?

SLEEP DEPRIVATION AND SLEEP DISPLACEMENT

Chances are you have experienced disruptions to your sleep due to jet lag or to an "occasional late night" (i.e., life as a student). And, we've all had that awful feeling in the spring when we are robbed of a precious hour of slumber by Daylight Savings Time. We don't usually think of time shifts as being anything more than an annoyance. However, researchers have found that, over a 20-year period, switching to Daylight Savings Time in the spring costs workers an average of 40 minutes of sleep and significantly increases work-related injuries on the Monday following the time change (Barnes & Wagner, 2009). The same analysis showed that returning to standard time in the fall produces no significant changes in sleep or injuries. Similar results have been noted for traffic accidents. Stanley Coren at the University of British Columbia found that there was a significant increase in the number of accidents immediately following the "spring forward," but not after the "fall back" (1996a; see Figure 5.5). Coren also looked at accidental deaths unrelated to car accidents (Coren, 1996b). Using U.S. data from 1986–1988, he found a 6.6% increase in accidental deaths in the four days following the "spring forward" of Daylight Savings Time. Importantly, the effects of disrupted sleep aren't limited to clumsiness; a substantial amount of research has shown that it can affect our thinking and decision making as well (Lavie, 2001).

Sleep deprivation *occurs when an individual cannot or does not sleep*. In other words, it can be due to some external factor that is out of your control (e.g., noisy neighbours) or to some self-inflicted factor (e.g., studying, staying up to watch the late hockey game on TV, etc.). Exactly how sleep deprivation affects daily functioning has been the subject of scientific inquiry since 1896, when researchers examined cognitive abilities in people kept awake for 90 consecutive hours (Patrick & Gilbert, 1896). In almost all of the studies in the past century, the strength of the circadian rhythms was evident; the volunteers generally went through cycles of extreme sleepiness at night, with normal levels of wakefulness in the daytime (especially the afternoon). However, each night saw an increasing level of sleepiness, likely as an attempt by the body to preserve and protect the health of the individual. In addition to feelings of fatigue, researchers have discovered a number of specific impairments resulting from being deprived of sleep. These include difficulties with multitasking, maintaining attention for long periods of time, assessing risks, incorporating new information into a strategy (i.e., "thinking on the fly"), working memory (i.e., keeping information in conscious awareness), inhibiting responses, and keeping information in the correct temporal order (Durmer & Dinges, 2005; Lavie, 2001; Wimmer et al., 1992). Importantly, these deficits also appear after partial sleep deprivation, such as when you don't get enough sleep (Cote et al., 2008). In fact, cognitive deficits typically appear when individuals have less than seven hours of sleep for a few nights in a row (Dinges, 2006; Dinges et al., 2005).

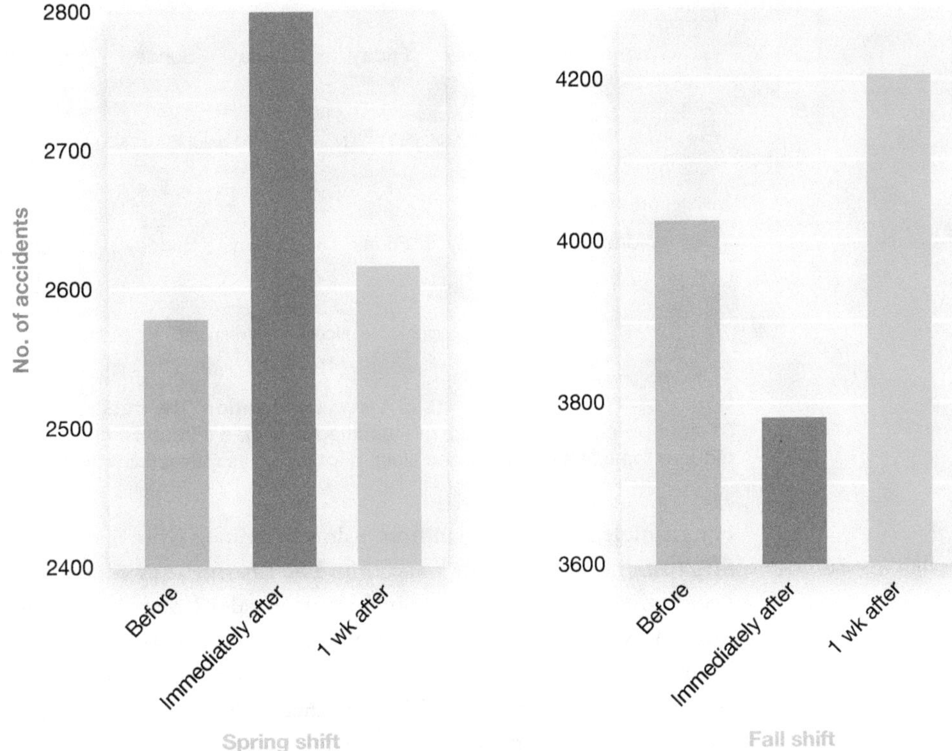

{FIG. 5.5} **Car Accident Statistics for the Years 1991 and 1992** These data represent the number of car accidents on the Monday before, the Monday immediately after, and the Monday one week after the spring and fall time changes. Note the dramatic increase in accidents immediately following the spring time change, when we lose one hour of sleep. Astute observers will also note that, overall, there were still more accidents in the fall than in the spring (the *y*-axes are different in the two graphs); this is likely due to the inclement weather found in many parts of Canada in October. These data are from the Canadian Ministry of Transport (and exclude Saskatchewan, which doesn't observe Daylight Savings Time).

The problems associated with sleep deprivation aren't limited to your ability to think. Research with adolescents shows that for every hour of sleep deprivation, predictable increases in physical illness, family problems, substance abuse, and academic problems occur (Roberts et al., 2009). Issues also arise with your coordination, a problem best seen in studies of driving ability. Using a driving simulator, researchers found that participants who had gone a night without sleeping performed at the same level as people who had a blood-alcohol level of 0.07 (Fairclough & Graham, 1999). A study of professional truck drivers accustomed to long shifts found that going 28 hours without sleep produced driving abilities similar to someone with a blood-alcohol level of 0.1, which is above the legal limit throughout North America (Williamson & Feyer, 2000). Given that sleep deprivation is as dangerous as driving while mildly intoxicated (Dawson & Reid, 1997; Maruff et al., 2005), it is not surprising that it is one of the most prevalent causes of fatal traffic accidents (Lyznicki et al., 1998; Sagberg, 1999).

Sleep deprivation has led to some serious errors in the medical field as well. Medical residents and attending physicians often work through the night at hospitals; in some fields such as Internal Medicine, the doctors often don't even have time for naps. From what you've read in the preceding paragraphs, you can see that this is obviously a recipe for disaster. For instance, researchers at Harvard noted a number of critical errors by medical interns who were tired, including draining the wrong lung, prescribing a medication dose 10 times higher than it should have been, and causing an accidental overdose of benzodiazepines (Landrigan et al., 2004). Exhausted medical interns were also more likely to crash their cars on the way home (Barger et al., 2005) and suffer from job stress and burnout (Chen et al., 2008). These findings have motivated some researchers to investigate potential benefits of alternative work schedules; by limiting the length of shifts and reducing the number of hours worked per week, the number of medical errors decreased by 36% (Figure 5.6; Landrigan et al., 2004). Recently, Canadian medical residents ("residency" is the 2- to 5-year internship performed after completing medical school that precedes becoming a licensed, independent physician) were granted limits on the length of their shifts and on the number of nights they can be "on call" per month. Perhaps someone was reading psychology research . . . or listening to the lawyers.

Watch
In the Real World: Sleep, Memory, and Learning

Cognitive and coordination errors are not limited to situations involving full or partial sleep deprivation. They can also occur when *the timing* of our sleep is altered. This phenomenon, **sleep displacement**, *occurs when an individual is prevented from sleeping at the normal time although she may be able to sleep earlier or later in the day than usual.*

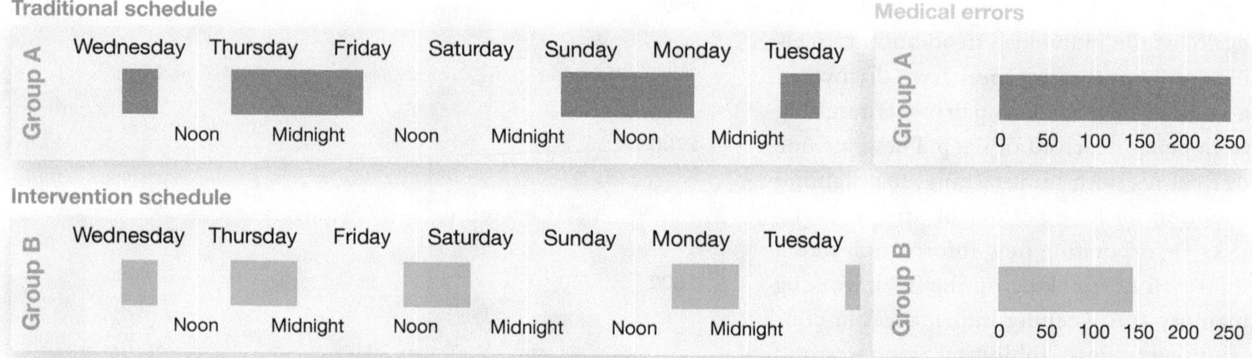

{FIG. 5.6} **The Costly Effects of Sleep Deprivation** The traditional schedule of a medical intern (Group A) requires up to a 31-hour on-call shift, whereas the modified schedule (Group B) divides the 31 hours into two shorter shifts. The latter schedule reduces the effects of prolonged sleep deprivation as measured in terms of medical errors.

For example, consider a man from balmy Winnipeg who flies to London (U.K.) for a vacation. The first night in London, he may try to go to bed at his usual 12 A.M. time. However, his body's rhythms will be operating six hours earlier—they are still at 6 P.M. Winnipeg time. If he is like most travellers, this individual will experience sleep displacement for three or four days until he can get his internal rhythms to synchronize with the external day–night cycles. **Jet lag** *is the discomfort a person feels when sleep cycles are out of synchronization with light and darkness* (Arendt, 2009). How much jet lag people experience is related to how many time zones they cross, and how quickly they do so (e.g., driving versus flying). Also, it is typically easier to adjust when travelling west. When travelling east, a person must try to fall asleep earlier than usual, which is difficult to do. Most people find it easier to stay up longer than usual, which is what westward travel requires.

For someone on a long vacation, jet lag may not be too much of an inconvenience. But imagine an athlete who has to be at her physical best, or a business executive who must remain sharp through an afternoon meeting. For these individuals, it is wise to arrive a week early if possible, or to try to adapt to the new time zone before leaving.

Although jet lag has limited implications for our lives (unless you happen to be a pilot or a flight attendant who crosses oceans several times a month), many of you will at some point in your lives have jobs that require shift work. In many hospitals, nurses and support staff rotate across three different 8-hour shifts over the course of a month (e.g., midnight–8 A.M., 8 A.M.–4 P.M., 4 P.M.–midnight). Switching shifts requires a transition similar to jet lag; your day is suddenly altered by several hours. In order to better adapt to these changes, companies and hospitals are increasingly scheduling the shift rotations so that workers are able to stay up later (similar to travelling westward in the jet lag example). This reduces the negative effects on a worker's sleep patterns, which reduces the symptoms of sleep deprivation, thus giving the employer a more alert (and friendlier) employee.

Tyler Olson/Shutterstock.com

How can you reduce jet lag? A person who is used to sleeping from midnight until 8 A.M. should go to bed an hour earlier each night and stay in bed for eight hours. Five hours before bedtime, he should take a melatonin supplement and, upon waking, should turn on bright lights. Following these steps should reduce the effects of jetlag and will allow him to enjoy his first day in Europe (as opposed to sleeping through it).

Quick Quiz 5.1b

Why We Need Sleep

KNOW ...

1 When does sleep displacement occur?

A When an individual tries to sleep in a new location

B When an individual is allowed to sleep only at night

C When an individual is allowed to sleep, but not at his normal time

D When an individual is not allowed to sleep during a controlled laboratory experiment

UNDERSTAND ...

2 Sleep may help animals stay safe and conserve energy for when it is needed most. This is known as the ________.

A preserve and protect hypothesis

B restore and repair hypothesis

C REM rebound hypothesis

D preserve and repair hypothesis

APPLY ...

3 Jamie reports that it is easier for her to adjust to a new time zone when flying west than when flying east. This occurs because

A it is easier to get to sleep earlier than dictated by your circadian rhythms.

B it is easier to stay up later than your circadian rhythms expect.

C there is more sunlight when you travel west.

D there is less sunlight when you travel west.

Answers can be found on page ANS-2.

Theories of Dreaming

It is very difficult to think about sleeping without thinking about dreaming. Dreams are mysterious, and have captured our imaginations for most of human history. A study of 1348 Canadian university students found that some patterns emerge when we analyze the *content* of our dreams. Using a statistical technique called factor analysis, these researchers found that students' dreams can be reduced to 16 different factors or subtypes. Females tended to have a larger number of negative dreams related to failures, loss of control, and frightening animals. Males, on the other hand, had more positive dreams including those related to magical abilities and encounters with alien life (Nielsen et al., 2003). However, studies such as this one, despite being conducted properly, do not provide insight into the purpose(s) dreams serve in our lives.

THE PSYCHOANALYTIC APPROACH One of the earliest and most influential theories of dreams was developed by Sigmund Freud in 1899. His classic work, *The Interpretation of Dreams,* dramatically transformed the Western world's view of both the function and meaning of dreams. Freud viewed dreams as an unconscious expression of *wish fulfillment.* He believed that humans are motivated by primal urges, with sex and aggression being the most dominant. Because giving in to these urges is impractical most of the time (not to mention potentially immoral and illegal), we learn ways of keeping these urges suppressed and outside of our conscious awareness. When we sleep, however, we lose the power to suppress our urges. Without this active suppression, these drives are free to create the vivid imagery found in our dreams. This imagery can take two forms. **Manifest content** involves *the images and storylines that we dream about.* In many of our dreams, the manifest content involves sexuality and aggression, consistent with the view that dreams are a form of wish fulfillment. However, in other cases, the manifest content of dreams might seem like random, bizarre images and events. Freud would argue that these images are anything but random; instead, he believed they have a hidden meaning. This **latent content** is *the actual symbolic meaning of a dream built on suppressed sexual or aggressive urges.* Because the true meaning of the dream is latent, Freud advocated *dream work,* the recording and interpreting of dreams. Through such work, Freudian analysis would allow you to bring the previously hidden sexual and aggressive elements of your dreams into the forefront, although it might mean you'd never look at the CN Tower the same way again.

Simulate
Are Dreams Meaningful?

It is difficult to overstate the influence that Freud's ideas have had on our culture's beliefs about dreaming. There is an abundance of books offering insight into interpreting dreams including dictionaries that claim to define certain symbols found in a dream's latent content. However, it is important to note that the scientific support for Freud's work is quite limited. Although his theories are based on extensive interviews with patients, many of these theories are difficult to test in a scientific manner because they cannot be falsified (i.e., there is no way to prove them wrong). Moreover, dream work requires a subjective interpreter to understand dreams rather than using objective measures. Therefore, the analysis of your dream might have more to do with the mindset of the analyst than it does your own hidden demons. Not surprisingly modern dream research focuses much more on the biological activity of dreaming. These studies focus primarily on REM sleep, when dreams are most common and complex.

THE ACTIVATION–SYNTHESIS HYPOTHESIS

Freud saw deep psychological meaning in the latent content of dreams. In contrast, the **activation–synthesis hypothesis** *suggests that dreams arise from brain activity originating from bursts of excitatory messages from the pons, a part of the brain stem* (Hobson & McCarley, 1977). This electrical activity produces the telltale signs of eye movements and

Listen
Lucid Dreaming

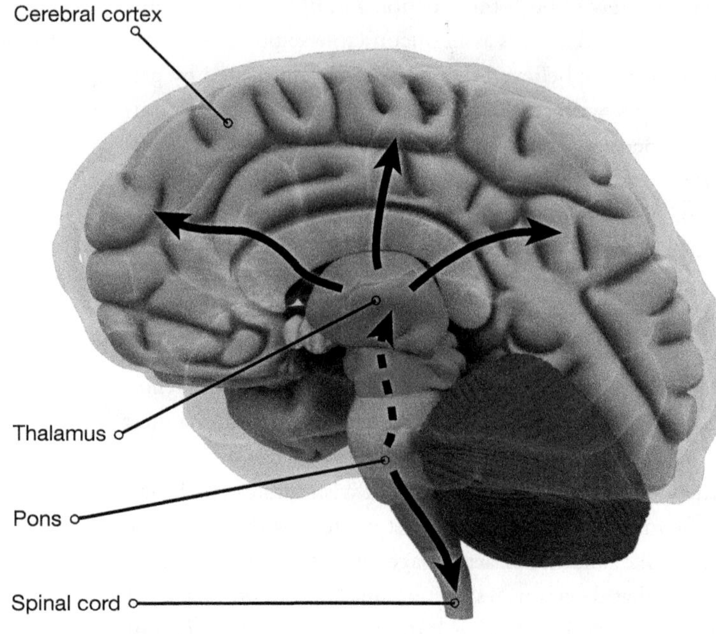

{FIG. 5.7} **The Activation–Synthesis Hypothesis of Dreaming** The pons, located in the brain stem, sends excitatory messages through the thalamus to the sensory and emotional areas of the cortex. The images and emotions that arise from this activity are then woven into a story. Inhibitory signals are also relayed from the pons down the spinal cord, which prevents movement during dreaming.

the EEG activity during REM sleep; moreover, the burst of activity stimulates the occipital and temporal lobes of the brain, producing imaginary sights and sounds, as well as numerous other regions of the cortex (see Figure 5.7). Thus, the brain stem initiates the *activation* component of the model. The *synthesis* component arises as different areas of the cortex of the brain try to make sense of all the images, sounds, and memories (Hobson et al., 2000). Imagine having a dozen different people each provide you with one randomly selected word, with your task being to organize these words to look like a single message; this is essentially what your cortex is doing every time you dream. Because we are often able to turn these random messages into a coherent story, researchers assume that the frontal lobes—the region of the brain associated with forming narratives—play a key role in the synthesis process (Eiser, 2005).

The activation–synthesis model, although important in its own right, has some interesting implications. If the cortex is able to provide (temporary) structure to input from the brain stem and other regions of the brain, then that means the brain is able to work with and restructure information while we dream. If that is the case, then is it possible that dreaming is part of our ability to learn or think?

WORKING THE SCIENTIFIC LITERACY MODEL

Dreams, REM Sleep, and Learning

The activation–synthesis model of dreaming suggests that our dreams result from random brain stem activity that is organized—to some degree—by the cortex. Although this theory is widely accepted, it doesn't provide many specifics about the *purpose* of dreams. *Why* do we have these processes occurring and what functions do they serve? Dream researcher Rosalind Cartwright (Cartwright et al., 2006; Webb & Cartwright, 1978) proposed the **problem-solving theory**—*the theory that thoughts and concerns are continuous from waking to sleeping, and that dreams may function to facilitate finding solutions to problems encountered while awake.* This theory suggests that many of the images and thoughts we have during our dreams are relevant to the problems that we face when we are awake. For instance, researchers have found that individuals who are in poor physical health have more dreams about pain, injuries, illnesses, and medical themes than do healthy individuals (King & DeCicco, 2007). Another study showed that the number of threatening images in participants' dreams increased immediately following the September 11 terrorist attacks (Propper et al., 2007). However, although no one doubts that our daily concerns find their way into our dreams, the problem-solving theory does not explain if (or how) any specific cognitive mechanisms are influenced by dreaming. In contrast, increasing evidence suggests that REM sleep, the sleep stage involved with dreaming, is essential for a number of cognitive functions.

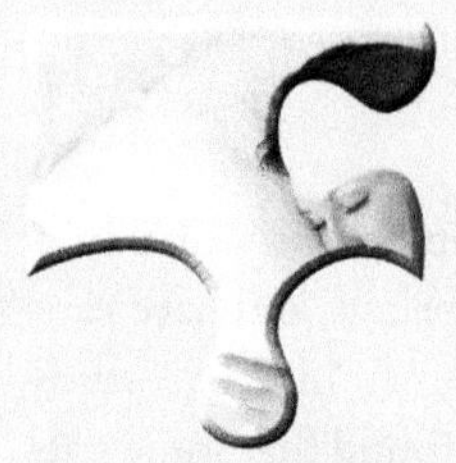

What do we know about dreams, REM sleep, and learning?

Approximately 20–25% of our total sleep time is taken up by REM, or rapid eye movement, sleep. When we are deprived of REM sleep, we typically experience a phenomenon called *REM rebound*—our brains spend an increased time in REM-phase sleep when given the chance. If you usually sleep 8 hours but get only 3 hours of sleep on a particular night, you can recover from the sleep deficit the next time you sleep with only the normal 8 hours; however, your time in REM sleep will increase considerably. The fact that our bodies actively try to catch up on missed REM sleep suggests that it may serve an important function.

As discussed earlier in this module, REM sleep produces brainwaves similar to being awake, yet we are asleep (Aserinsky & Kleitman, 1953). This similarity suggests that the types of functions being performed by the brain are likely similar during the two states. Studies with animals have shown that REM sleep is associated with a number of different neurotransmitter systems, all of which influence activity of the brain stem. Projections from the brain stem can then affect a number of different functions, including movement (which is inhibited), emotional regulation (through connections to the amygdala and frontal lobes), and learning (Brown et al., 2012). Clearly REM is not simply about twitching eyes! The challenge for psychologists is to determine the specific functions that are, and are not, affected by REM.

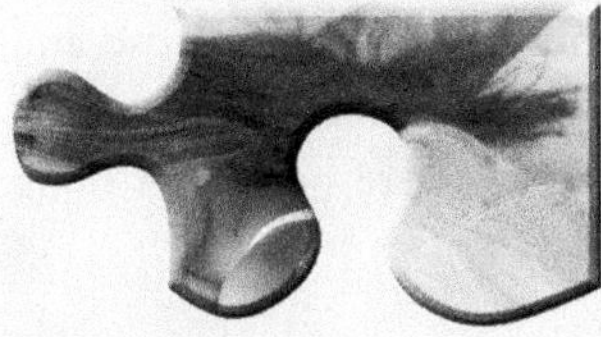

How can science explain the effects of dreams and REM sleep on learning?

In the last 25 years, scientists have performed an extraordinary number of experiments in their attempt to understand how REM sleep (and possibly dreaming) influences our thinking. The results of these studies show that REM sleep affects some, but not all, types of memory. If someone were to give you a list of words to remember and then tested you later, this would be an example of declarative memory. The effect of REM sleep disruption on declarative memory was tested in a study conducted by Carlyle Smith at Trent University. Different groups of participants had only their REM sleep disrupted, only their non-REM sleep disrupted, or all of their sleep disrupted. When their memory for the words was tested, there were no differences between the groups, suggesting that REM sleep is not critical for this simple type of memory. However, when researchers gave participants tests that involved a larger number of steps or procedures, a different pattern of results emerged: Being deprived of REM sleep produced large deficits in performance (Smith, 2001).

Several studies have shown that the amount of REM sleep people experience increases the night after learning a new task (Smith et al., 2004). For instance, Mandai and colleagues (1989) found increases in REM sleep in individuals the night following a Morse-code learning task. There was a high correlation between retention levels for the Morse code signals, the number of REM episodes, and the density of the REM activity (i.e., the frequency of eye movements made during REM episodes). In a study directly related to students' lives, Smith and Lapp (1991) measured REM sleep 3–5 days after senior undergraduate students had completed their fall semester final exams. These students had more REM sleep episodes and a greater REM sleep density than they had when they were tested in the summer, when less learning was taking place. They also had higher values than age-matched participants who were not in university. These results suggest that REM sleep may help us consolidate or maintain newly learned information.

Several studies have demonstrated that REM sleep and dreaming also influence our ability to problem solve. Depriving people of REM sleep reduces their ability to perform a complex logic task (Smith, 1993). This may be due to the fact that our ability to form new associations increases during REM sleep (Stickgold et al., 1999; Walker et al., 2002). REM sleep appears to be involved with linking together steps in the formation of new memories and in reorganizing information in novel ways.

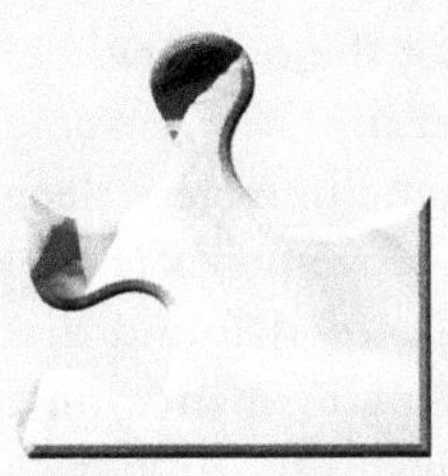

Can we critically evaluate this evidence?

We have to be cautious when we consider the different effects that REM sleep, and perhaps dreaming, have on memory and problem solving. Although there is a great deal of evidence that REM sleep does influence a number of different abilities, most of this research is correlational. As you've undoubtedly heard before, correlation does not equal causation. Therefore, we can't guarantee that REM sleep is *causing* the improvements in memory—just that its disruption *is related to* poor performance on a number of tasks. It is also unclear whether the observed effects are due to dreaming or to some other REM-related function.

In addition to these questions, it is also worth noting that the effects from these studies are not occurring during every period of REM sleep. When it comes to memory, not all REM sleep is created equally. The final few REM periods in the early morning appear to be critical for learning (Smith, 2001). Stickgold and colleagues (2000) found that performance on a visual search task (in which you try to find a particular target image that is hidden amongst distracter images, similar to "Where's Waldo?") correlated with the amount of *non*-REM sleep a person had in the early part of the night and the amount of REM sleep in the early morning. Therefore, to say that REM sleep, in general, improves some types of learning is an oversimplification. Further research is needed to understand what makes these early morning windows of REM special.

Why is this relevant?

Studies of REM sleep and learning show us that the benefits of sleep go beyond restoring and repairing the body. Rather, the effect(s) of REM sleep on our ability to learn new tasks should serve as a wake-up call to all of us. Almost everyone in a university setting is working on a less-than-optimal amount of sleep despite the fact that REM sleep is clearly an important part of our ability to learn. This seems counterproductive. Studying and sleeping every night is a much more effective way to retain information than pulling a frantic all-nighter just before the exam, even if we all feel like we're out of time.

Deklofenak/Fotolia

Interestingly, REM sleep is not the only stage of sleep that affects our ability to learn. There is some evidence that the sleep spindles found in stage 2 sleep are involved with learning new movements (Fogel et al., 2007). Smith and MacNeil (1994) found that disrupting stage 2 sleep impaired performance on a pursuit-rotor task in which participants try to move a computer mouse so that the cursor follows an object on the computer screen. However, when participants were asked to move as though the image was in a mirror (so that an object farther away on the screen was closer to their body), REM, and not stage 2 sleep, became essential. The only difference between the two tasks was the cognitive difficulty associated with figuring out which movement to perform (Aubrey et al., 1999). This suggests that the brain has different systems for processing simple and complex movements and that these systems are influenced by different stages of sleep (Smith, 2001).

Watch
Special Topics: Sleep Disorders

Watch
IT Video: Night Sleep

Quick Quiz 5.1c
Theories of Dreaming

KNOW ...

1 The problem-solving theory of dreaming proposes that

A dreams create more problems than they solve.

B the problems and concerns we face in our waking life also appear in our dreams.

C the symbols in our dreams represent unconscious urges related to sex and aggression.

D we cannot solve complex moral or interpersonal problems until we have dreamed about them.

UNDERSTAND ...

2 The *synthesis* part of the activation–synthesis hypothesis suggests that

A the brain interprets the meaning of symbolic images.

B the brain stem activates the cortex to produce random images.

C the cortex stimulates the brain stem to produce interpretations of dreams.

D the brain tries to link together, or make sense of, randomly activated images.

ANALYZE ...

3 Scientists are skeptical about the psychoanalytic theory of dreaming because the ________ of a dream is entirely subject to interpretation.

A latent content

B sleep stage

C activation

D manifest content

Answers can be found on page ANS-2.

Disorders and Problems with Sleep

Throughout this module, we have seen that sleep is an essential biological and psychological process; without sleep, individuals are vulnerable to cognitive, emotional, and physical symptoms. Given these widespread effects, it should come as no surprise that a lot of research has been directed at improving our ability to diagnose and treat sleep disorders. In the final section of this module, we will discuss some of the more common sleep disorders.

INSOMNIA The most widely recognized sleeping problem is **insomnia**, *a disorder characterized by an extreme lack of sleep*. According to a 2002 Canadian Community Health Survey from Statistics Canada, one in seven Canadian adults (3.3 million people) suffer from insomnia. This number was lowest in the 18–25 age bracket (10%) and highest in individuals 75 years of age and older (20%). Although the average adult may need 7 to 8 hours of sleep to feel rested, substantial individual differences exist. For this reason, insomnia is defined not in terms of the hours of sleep, but rather in terms of the degree to which a person feels rested during the day. If a person feels that her sleep disturbance is affecting her schoolwork, her job, or her family and social life, then it is indeed a problem. However, for this condition to be thought of as a sleep *disorder*, it would have to be present for three months or more—one or two "bad nights" is unpleasant, but is not technically insomnia.

Although insomnia is often thought of as a single disorder, it may be more appropriate to refer to *insomnias* in the plural. *Onset insomnia* occurs when a person has difficulty falling asleep (30 minutes or more), *maintenance insomnia* occurs when an individual cannot easily return to sleep after waking in the night, and *terminal insomnia* or *early morning insomnia* is a situation in which a person wakes up too early—sometimes hours too early—and cannot return to sleep (Pallesen et al., 2001).

It is important to remember that for a sleep disorder to be labelled insomnia, the problems with sleeping must be due to some internal cause; not sleeping because your roommate snores does not count as insomnia. Sometimes insomnia occurs as part of another problem, such as depression, pain, too much caffeine, or various drugs (Schierenbeck et al., 2008); in these cases, the sleep disorder is referred to as a *secondary insomnia*. In cases in which insomnia is the only symptom that a person is showing, and other causes can be ruled out, physicians would label the sleep disorder as *insomnia disorder*. If you think back to our earlier discussion of sleep deprivation, you can see

Steve Prezant/Glow Images

Insomnia can arise from worrying about sleep. It is among the most common of all sleep disorders.

why insomnia—despite not seeming serious—can have a profound effect on a person's ability to function in our demanding world. However, it isn't the only disorder that can affect our ability to sleep a full eight hours each night.

NIGHTMARES AND NIGHT TERRORS Although most of our dreams are interesting and often bizarre, some of our dreams really scare us. **Nightmares** *are particularly vivid and disturbing dreams that occur during REM sleep.* They can be so emotionally charged that they awaken the individual (Levin & Nielsen, 2007). Almost everyone—as many as 85% to 95% of adults—can remember having bad dreams that have negative emotional content, such as feeling lost, sad, or angry, within a one-year period (Levin, 1994; Schredl, 2003). Data from numerous studies indicate that nightmares are correlated with psychological distress including anxiety (Nielsen et al., 2000; Zadra & Donderi, 2000), negative emotionality (Berquier & Ashton, 1992; Levin & Fireman, 2002), and emotional reactivity (Kramer et al., 1984). They are more common in females (Nielsen et al., 2006), likely because women tend to have higher levels of depression and emotional disturbances. Indeed, in individuals with emotional disorders, the "synthesis" part of dreaming appears to reorganize information in a way consistent with their mental state, with a focus on negative emotion.

Tore Nielsen from the Université de Montréal and his colleagues have suggested that nightmares are due to problems with our brains' emotion networks (Nielsen & Levin, 2007). When we dream, several brain structures related to emotion are activated (Maquet et al., 1996). Although the thought of these emotional systems firing when you are asleep seems frightening, it appears that they are serving an adaptive function (Levin & Nielsen, 2007). When we are awake and we experience negative events, we tend to link the event with our emotional response (fear, anger, etc.). During dreaming, however, recollection of the negative event is paired with a number of random images and memories due to the random firing of the brain stem. As a result, the event-emotion link becomes less prominent. So, these emotional brain areas are *reducing* our emotional responses to negative thoughts and experiences (Fisher et al., 1970; Nielsen & Zadra, 2005). During nightmares, however, this process does not occur properly, leading to an emotionally unpleasant dream. Individuals with emotional disorders have a greater likelihood of having dysfunctions with this emotional regulation system because different emotional brain structures—particularly the amygdala—tend to be overactive in these individuals (Kellett & Kokkinidis, 2004; Shin et al., 2006).

Nightmares, although unpleasant, are a normal part of life. In contrast, 1–6% of children and 1% of adults experience **night terrors**—*intense bouts of panic and arousal that awaken the individual, typically in a heightened emotional state.* A person experiencing a night terror may call out or scream, fight back against imaginary attackers, or leap from the bed and start to flee before waking up. Unlike nightmares, night terrors are not dreams. These episodes occur during NREM sleep, and the majority of people who experience them typically do not recall any specific dream content. Night terrors increase in frequency during stressful periods, such as when parents are separating or divorcing (Schredl, 2001). There is also some evidence linking them to feelings of anxiety, which suggests that for some sufferers, counselling and other means for reducing anxiety may help reduce the symptoms (Kales et al., 1980; Szelenberger et al., 2005).

MOVEMENT DISTURBANCES To sleep well, an individual needs to remain still. During REM sleep, the brain prevents movement by sending inhibitory signals down the spinal cord. A number of sleep disturbances, however, involve movement and related sensations. For example, **restless legs syndrome** *is a persistent feeling of discomfort in the legs and the urge to continuously shift them into different positions* (Smith & Tolson, 2008). This disorder affects approximately 5% to 10% of the population (generally older adults), and occurs at varying levels of severity. For those individuals who are in constant motion, sleep becomes very difficult. They awake periodically at night to reposition their legs, although they often have no memory of doing so. The mechanism causing RLS is unclear; however, there is some evidence that it is linked to the dopamine system and to an iron deficiency (Allen, 2004). Therefore, current treatments are focused on keeping dopamine and iron at normal levels in these patients.

A more common movement disturbance is **somnambulism**, or *sleepwalking, a disorder that involves wandering and performing other activities while asleep*. It occurs during NREM sleep, stages 3 and 4, and is more prevalent during childhood. Sleepwalking is not necessarily indicative of any type of sleep or emotional disturbance, although it may put people in harm's way. People who sleepwalk are not acting out dreams, and they typically do not remember the episode. (For the record, it is not dangerous to wake up a sleepwalker, as is commonly thought. At worst, he or she will be disoriented.) There is no reliable medicine that curbs sleepwalking; instead, it is important to add safety measures to the person's environment so that the sleepwalker doesn't get hurt.

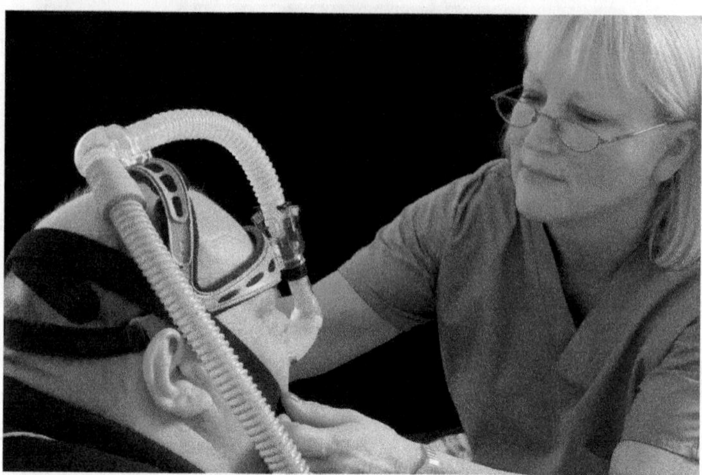
Custom Medical Stock Photo/Alamy
This CPAP device treats apnea by maintaining pressure in the airway.

A similar, but more adult, disorder is *sexomnia* or *sleep sex*. Individuals with this condition engage in sexual activity such as the touching of the self or others, vocalizations, and sex-themed talk while in stages 3 and 4 sleep (Shapiro et al., 2003). In the original case report of this disorder (Motet, 1897, described in Thoinot, 1913), a man exposed his genitals to a policeman (that's bad). He was unable to recall the incident afterwards and was sentenced to three months in jail. Other reports are more extreme, including sex with strangers and unwanted contact with sleeping partners (Béjot et al., 2010). The exact cause of sexomnia is unknown, although stress, fatigue, and a history of trauma have all been mentioned as possible factors (Schenck et al., 2007).

Another potentially dangerous condition is *REM behaviour disorder*, which was introduced in the beginning of this module. People with this condition do not show the typical restriction of movement during REM sleep; in fact, they appear to be acting out the content of their dreams (Schenck & Mahowald, 2002). Imagine what happens when an individual dreams of being attacked—the dreamed response of defending oneself or even fighting back can be acted out. Not surprisingly, this action can awaken some individuals. Because it occurs during REM sleep, however, some individuals do not awaken until they have hurt themselves or someone else, as occurred with Mike Birbiglia (Schenck et al., 1989). Unlike sleep-walking and restless legs syndrome, REM behaviour disorder can be treated with medication; benzodiazepines, which inhibit the central nervous system, have proven effective in reducing some of the symptoms associated with this condition (Paparrigopoulos, 2005). However, given the potential side effects of this class of drug, this option should only be taken if the person is a threat to himself or others.

SLEEP APNEA The disorders discussed thus far have focused on changes in the brain that lead to altered thinking patterns (nightmares and night terrors) and movements. In contrast, **sleep apnea** *is a disorder characterized by the temporary inability to breathe during sleep* (*apnea* literally translates to "without breathing"). Although a variety of factors contribute to sleep apnea, this condition appears to be most common among overweight and obese individuals, and it is roughly twice as prevalent among men as among women (Lin et al., 2008; McDaid et al., 2009). In most cases of apnea, the airway becomes physically obstructed, at a point anywhere from the back of the nose and mouth to the neck (Figure 5.8). Therefore, treatment for mild apnea generally involves dental devices that hold the mouth in a specific position during sleep. Weight-loss efforts should accompany this treatment in cases in which it is a contributing factor. In moderate to severe cases, a continuous positive airway pressure (CPAP) device can be used to force air through the nose, keeping the airway open through increased air pressure (McDaid et al., 2009).

In rare but more serious cases, sleep apnea can also be caused by the brain's failure to regulate breathing. This failure can happen for many reasons, including

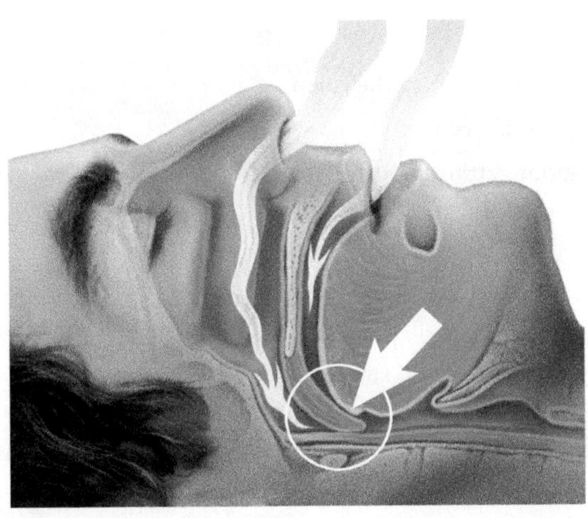

{FIG. 5.8} **Sleep Apnea** One cause of sleep apnea is the obstruction of air flow, which can seriously disrupt the sleep cycle.

damage to or deterioration of the medulla of the brain stem, which is responsible for controlling the chest muscles during breathing.

You might wonder if disorders that stop breathing during sleep can be fatal. They can be, but rarely are. As breathing slows too much or stops altogether, oxygen levels in the blood rapidly decline, resulting in a gasping reflex and resumed oxygen flow. Actually, gasping may not even result in waking up. A person with sleep apnea may not be aware that he is constantly cycling through oxygen loss and gasping as he sleeps, although it would certainly be noticed by anyone sharing a bed with him. It is often the case that affected individuals discover that they have sleep apnea only after visiting their physician.

Although sleep apnea is serious in its own right, it also leads to a number of other problems. Repeatedly waking up during the night reduces the quality of an individual's sleep and can lead to a mild form of sleep deprivation (Naelgele et al., 1995). In fact, individuals who suffer from sleep apnea often perform more poorly on tests requiring mental flexibility, the control of attention, and memory (Fulda & Schulz, 2003). Treating sleep apnea will therefore not only improve a person's physical safety and fatigue levels, but also the person's ability to think.

NARCOLEPSY While movement disorders, sleep apnea, and night terrors can all lead to insomnia, another condition is characterized by nearly the opposite effect. **Narcolepsy** *is a disorder in which a person experiences extreme daytime sleepiness and even sleep attacks.* These bouts of sleep may last only a few seconds, especially if the person is standing or driving when she falls asleep and is jarred awake by falling, a nodding head, or swerving of the car. Even without such disturbances, the sleep may last only a few minutes or more, so it is not the same as falling asleep for a night's rest.

Narcolepsy differs from more typical sleep in a number of other ways. People with a normal sleep pattern generally reach the REM stage after more than an hour of sleep, but a person experiencing narcolepsy is likely to go almost immediately from waking to REM sleep. Also, because REM sleep is associated with dreaming, people with narcolepsy often report vivid dream-like images even if they did not fully fall asleep.

Why does narcolepsy occur? Scientists have investigated a hormone called *orexin* that functions to maintain wakefulness. Individuals with narcolepsy have fewer brain cells that produce orexin, resulting in greater difficulty maintaining wakefulness (Nakamura et al., 2011). Luckily, medications are available to treat this condition, thus allowing these individuals to function relatively normally (Mayer, 2012).

OVERCOMING SLEEP PROBLEMS Everyone has difficulty sleeping at some point, and there are many myths and anecdotes about what will help. For some people, relief can be as simple as a snack or a warm glass of milk; it can certainly be difficult to sleep if you are hungry. Others might have a nightcap—a drink of alcohol—in hopes of inducing sleep, although the effects can be misleading. Alcohol may make you sleepy, but it disrupts the quality of sleep, especially the REM cycle, and may leave you feeling unrested the next day. Fortunately, most people respond very well to psychological interventions. By practising good *sleep hygiene*—healthy sleep-related habits—they can typically overcome sleep disturbances in a matter of a few weeks (Morin et al., 2006; Murtagh & Greenwood, 1995). The techniques shown in Table 5.1 are effective for many people who prefer self-help methods, but effective help is also available from psychologists, physicians, and even (sometimes) over the Internet (Ritterband et al., 2009; van Straten & Cuijpers, 2009).

Although research supports the use of cognitive and behavioural techniques, people often turn to drugs to help them sleep. A number of sleep aids are available on an over-the-counter basis, and several varieties of prescription drugs have been developed as well. For most of the 20th century, drugs prescribed for insomnia included sedatives such as barbiturates (Phenobarbital) and benzodiazepines (e.g., Valium). Although these drugs managed to put people to sleep, several problems with their use were quickly observed. Notably, people quickly developed tolerance to these agents, meaning they required increasingly higher doses to get the same effect, and many soon came to depend on the drugs so much that they could not sleep without them (Pallesen et al.,

Table 5.1 :: **Nonpharmacological Techniques for Improving Sleep**

1. Use your bed for sleeping only, not for working or studying. (Sexual activity is an appropriate exception to the rule.)
2. Do not turn sleep into work. Putting effort into falling asleep generally leads to arousal instead of sleep.
3. Keep your clock out of sight. Watching the clock increases pressure to sleep and worries about getting enough sleep.
4. Get exercise early during the day. Exercise may not increase the amount of sleep, but it may help you sleep better. Exercising late in the day, however, may leave you restless and aroused at bedtime.
5. Avoid substances that disrupt sleep. Such substances include caffeine (in coffee, tea, many soft drinks, and other sources), nicotine, and alcohol. Illicit drugs such as cocaine, marijuana, and ecstasy also disrupt healthy sleep.
6. If you lie in bed worrying at night, schedule evening time to deal with stress. Write down your worries and stressors for approximately 30 minutes prior to bedtime.
7. If you continue to lie in bed without sleeping for 30 minutes, get up and do something else until you are about to fall asleep, and then return to bed.
8. Get up at the same time every morning. Although this practice may lead to sleepiness the first day or two, eventually it helps set the daily rhythm.
9. If you still have problems sleeping after four weeks, consider seeing a sleep specialist to get tested for sleep apnea, restless legs syndrome, or other sleep problems that may require more specific interventions.

Source: Based on recommendations from the American Psychological Association, 2004.

2001). Even though benzodiazepines are generally safer than barbiturates, the risk of dependence and worsening sleep problems makes them suitable only for short-term use—generally for a week or two—and only after sleep hygiene efforts have failed.

Modern sleep drugs are generally thought to be much safer in the short term, and many have been approved for long-term use as well. However, few modern drugs have been studied in placebo-controlled experiments, and even fewer have actually been studied for long-term use (e.g., for more than a month; Krystal, 2009). So, it is safer to change your sleep hygiene (sleeping routines) than to directly alter your brain chemistry if you want to put your sleeping problems to rest.

Quick Quiz 5.1d Disorders and Problems with Sleep

KNOW ...

1 When people do not show the typical restriction of movement during REM sleep, despite physical evidence to the contrary, they are experiencing ____________.

A somnambulism

B REM behaviour disorder

C insomnia

D restless legs syndrome

2 ____________ is(are) a condition in which a person's breathing becomes obstructed or stops during sleep.

A Somnambulism

B Night terrors

C Narcolepsy

D Sleep apnea

APPLY ...

3 Which of the following is *not* good advice for improving your quality of sleep?

A Use your bed for sleeping only—not homework or watching TV.

B Exercise late in the day to make sure you are tired when it is time to sleep.

C Avoid drinking caffeine, especially late in the day.

D Get up at the same time every morning to make sure you develop a reliable pattern of sleep and wakefulness.

Answers can be found on page ANS-2.

Module Summary

Sylvia Serrado/Glow Images

Now that you have read this module you should

KNOW . . .

- ***The key terminology associated with sleep, dreams, and sleep disorders*:**

activation–synthesis hypothesis (p. 189)
circadian rhythms (p. 182)
consciousness (p. 181)
endogenous rhythms (p. 182)
entrainment (p. 182)
insomnia (p. 192)
jet lag (p. 188)
latent content (p. 189)
manifest content (p. 189)
narcolepsy (p. 195)
night terrors (p. 193)
nightmares (p. 193)
polysomnography (p. 183)
preserve and protect hypothesis (p. 186)
problem-solving theory (p. 190)
REM sleep (p. 185)
restless legs syndrome (p. 193)
restore and repair hypothesis (p. 185)
sleep apnea (p. 194)
sleep deprivation (p. 186)
sleep displacement (p. 187)
somnambulism (p. 194)

UNDERSTAND . . .

- ***How the sleep cycle works.*** The sleep cycle consists of a series of stages going from stage 1 through stage 4, cycles back down again, and is followed by a REM phase. The first sleep cycle lasts approximately 90 minutes. Deep sleep (stages 3 and 4) is longest during the first half of the sleep cycle, whereas REM phases increase in duration during the second half of the sleep cycle.
- ***Theories of why we sleep.*** Sleep theories include the restore and repair hypothesis and the preserve and protect hypothesis. According to the restore and repair hypothesis, we sleep so that the body can recover from the stress and strain on the body that occurs during waking. According to the preserve and protect hypothesis, sleep has evolved as a way to reduce activity and provide protection from potential threats, and to reduce the amount of energy intake required. Evidence supports both theories, so it is likely that there is more than one reason for sleep.

APPLY . . .

- ***Your knowledge to identify and practise good sleep habits.*** Try completing the Epworth Sleepiness Scale to make sure you are getting enough sleep **(Table 5.2)**. If you score 10 points or higher, you are probably not getting enough sleep. You can always refer to **Table 5.1** for tips on improving your sleep.

ANALYZE . . .

- ***Different theories about why we dream.*** Dreams have fascinated psychologists since Freud's time. From his psychoanalytic perspective, Freud believed that the manifest content of dreams could be used to uncover their symbolic, latent content. Contemporary scientists are skeptical about the validity of this approach given the lack of empirical evidence to support it. The activation–synthesis theory eliminates the meaning of dream content, suggesting instead that dreams are just interpretations of haphazard electrical activity in the sleeping brain that are then organized to some degree by the cortex. Increasing evidence suggests that REM sleep, the sleep stage associated with dreaming, improves our ability to form new procedural (step-by-step) memories and to find solutions to problems.

Table 5.2 :: Epworth Sleepiness Scale

Use the following scale to choose the most appropriate number for each situation:
0 = would *never* doze or sleep 1 = *slight* chance of dozing or sleeping
2 = *moderate* chance of dozing or sleeping 3 = *high* chance of dozing or sleeping

SITUATION	CHANCES OF FALLING ASLEEP
Sitting and reading	0 1 2 3
Watching TV	0 1 2 3
Sitting inactive in a public place	0 1 2 3
Being a passenger in a motor vehicle for an hour or more	0 1 2 3
Lying down in the afternoon	0 1 2 3
Sitting and talking to someone	0 1 2 3
Sitting quietly after lunch (no alcohol)	0 1 2 3
Stopped for a few minutes in traffic while driving	0 1 2 3
Your total score	

Source: Johns (1991)

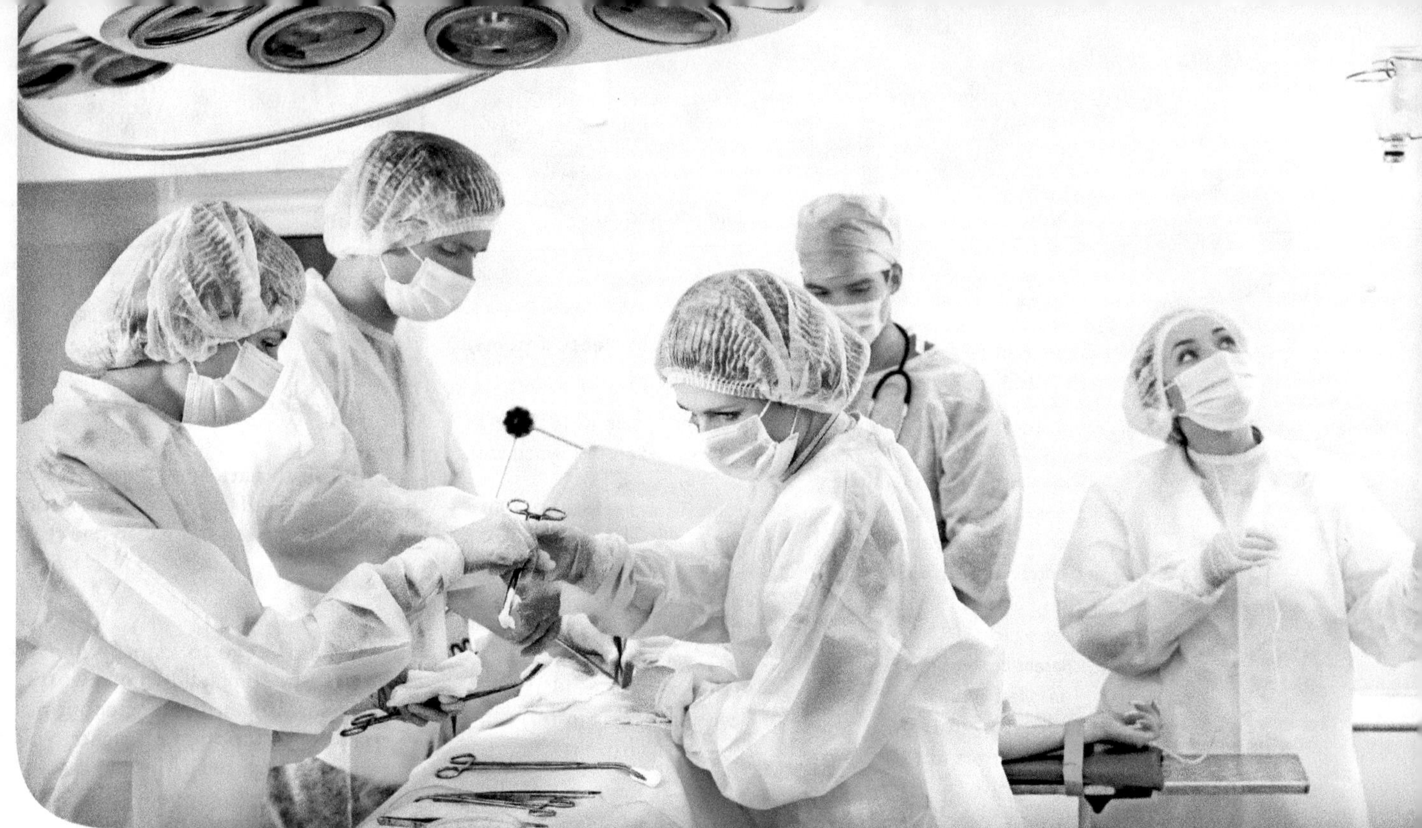

Gennadiy Poznyakov/Fotolia

Module 5.2

Altered States of Consciousness: Hypnosis, Meditation, and Disorders of Consciousness

Learning Objectives After reading this module you should	KNOW ...	UNDERSTAND ...	APPLY ...	ANALYZE ...
	The key terminology associated with hypnosis, meditation, and disorders of consciousness	The competing theories of hypnosis	Your knowledge of hypnosis to identify what it can and cannot do	The effectiveness of meditation for use in therapy The ability of researchers to detect consciousness in brain-damaged patients

"Just a moment! I don't like the patient's colour. Much too blue. Her lips are very blue. I'm going to give a little more oxygen. . . . There, that's better now. You can carry on with the operation" (Levinson, 1965, p. 544). If you were undergoing surgery with a local anesthetic and heard this, you would certainly be worried . . . if not panicking. But, what if you had been given general anesthetic so that you were "unconscious"? Presumably, you should be blissfully unaware of the fact that you were turning blue. However, when prompted by an experimenter one month later, 8 of the 10 patients who heard these statements—which were a script read during real surgeries as part of an experiment—were able to report back some elements of the fake crisis. Four of the patients were able to give an almost verbatim account of what the experimenter said. In other studies, post-operative patients were able to fill in word stems (e.g., H O - - -) with words presented under anesthesia (e.g., HORSE, not HOUSE) at levels far above chance (Bonebakker et al., 1996; Merikle & Daneman, 1996). How is this possible? At present, no one knows exactly how someone who is anesthetized can still recall some of the information presented to them while they were unconscious. What these studies do illustrate, however, is that consciousness is not a simple on-off switch. Instead, there are a number of possible states of consciousness, each with its own abilities and limitations.

Focus Questions

 How is information perceived in different states of consciousness?

 Is information processed in the background of our awareness?

Consciousness varies by degree—much lies between being awake versus being asleep. Humans have a remarkable ability to alter where on this continuum they want to reach. Techniques such as hypnosis and meditation are ways of inducing what many regard as an altered state of consciousness. Also, injury or illness can temporarily or permanently change a person's level of consciousness. In this module, we examine each of these topics related to consciousness.

Hypnosis

The caricature of a hypnotist as an intense-looking bearded man swinging his glistening pocket watch back and forth before an increasingly subdued subject will probably always be around, though it promotes just one of many misunderstandings about hypnosis. **Hypnosis** is actually *a procedure of inducing a heightened state of suggestibility*. According to this definition, hypnosis is *not* a trance, as is often portrayed in the popular media (Kirsch & Lynn, 1998). Instead, the hypnotist simply suggests changes, and the subject is more likely (but not certain) to comply as a result of the suggestion.

Although one could conceivably make suggestions about almost anything, hypnotic suggestions generally are most effective when they fall into one of three categories:

- *Ideomotor suggestions* are related to specific actions that could be performed, such as adopting a specific position.
- *Challenge suggestions* indicate actions that are not to be performed, so that the subject appears to lose the ability to perform an action.
- *Cognitive-perceptual suggestions* involve a subject remembering or forgetting specific information, or experiencing altered perceptions such as reduced pain sensations (Kirsch & Lynn, 1998).

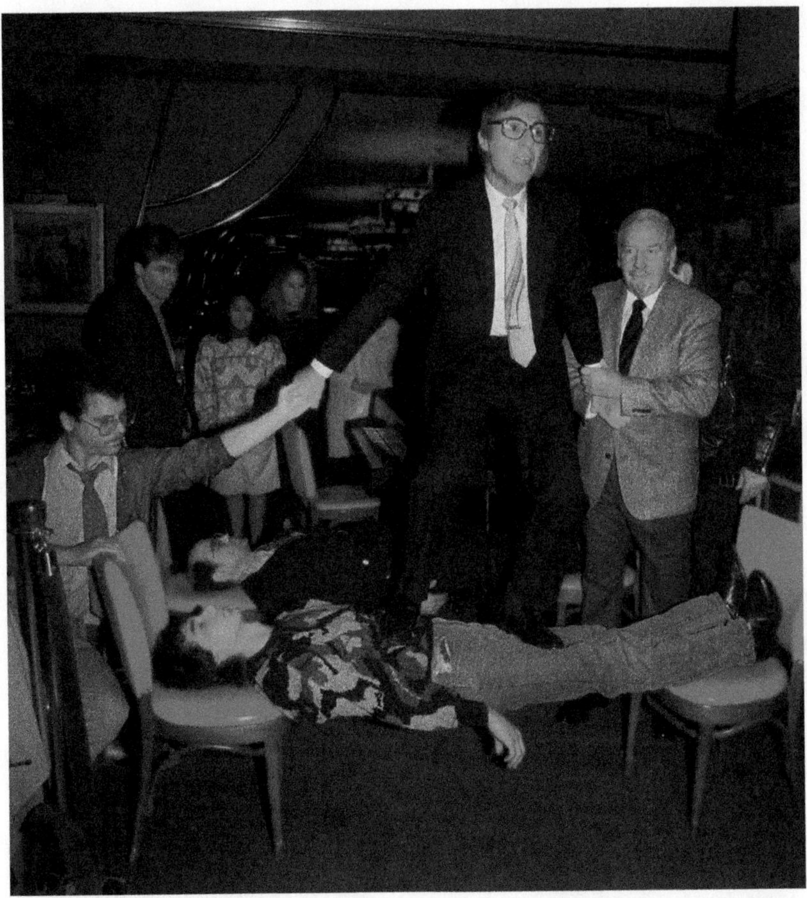

Bookstaver/AP Images

Stage hypnotists often use the human plank demonstration with their subjects. They support an audience volunteer on three chairs. To the audience's amazement, when the chair supporting the mid-body is removed, the hypnotized subject does not fall (even when weight is added, as shown in the photo). However, nonhypnotized subjects also do not fall. (Please do not try this at home—there is a trick behind it!)

People who have not encountered scientific information about hypnosis are often skeptical that hypnosis can actually occur or are very reluctant to be hypnotized themselves (Capafons et al., 2008; Molina & Mendoza, 2006). It is important to note that hypnotists cannot make someone do something against their will. For example, the hypnotist could not suggest that an honest person rob a bank and expect the subject to comply. Instead, the hypnotist can increase the likelihood that subjects will perform simple behaviours that they have performed or have thought of before, and would be willing to do (in some contexts) when in a normal conscious state.

THEORIES OF HYPNOSIS In the previous section, we discussed the types of behaviours that can and cannot be influenced by hypnosis; in this section, we attempt to uncover how this process actually works. The word *hypnosis* comes from the Greek *hypno,* meaning "sleep." In reality, scientific research tells us that hypnosis is nothing like sleep. Instead, hypnosis is based on an interaction between (1) automatic (unconscious) thoughts and behaviours and (2) a supervisory system (Norman & Shallice, 1986), sometimes referred to as *executive processing.* The roles played by these two pieces of the puzzle differ across theories of hypnosis.

Dissociation theory *explains hypnosis as a unique state in which consciousness is divided into two parts: an observer and a hidden observer* (Hilgard, 1977, 1986). It may sound magical, but this kind of divided state is actually quite common. Take any skill that you have mastered, such as driving a car or playing an instrument. When you began, it took every bit of your conscious awareness to focus on the correct movements—you were a single, highly focused observer of your actions. In this case, your behaviour required a lot of executive processing. After a few years of practice, you could do it automatically while you observed and paid attention to something else. In this case, you required much less executive processing. Although we call the familiar behaviour automatic, there is still a hidden observer—that is, a part of you that is paying attention to the task. During hypnosis, a similar split occurs between automatic (observer) and executive

Simulate What Altered States Have You Experienced?

Watch The Big Picture: States of Consciousness

Watch Hypnosis

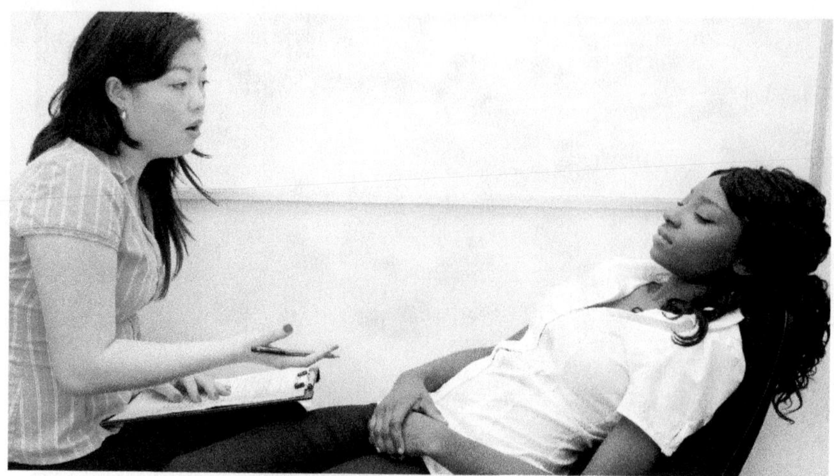
Paula Connelly/iStockphoto
Hypnotherapy involves a trained therapist giving hypnotic suggestions to a client.

Watch
Thinking Like a Psychologist: The Uses and Limitations of Hypnosis

(hidden observer) processing. Susceptible individuals will experience *less* input from the executive (Jamieson & Sheehan, 2004; Woody & Bowers, 1994). Instead, the suggestion from the hypnotist will act as an executive, guiding the behaviours that feel automatic. In support of this view, neuroimaging studies have found reduced activity in the anterior cingulate cortex, a region of the frontal lobe related to executive functions, in hypnotized subjects (Raz et al., 2005).

A second approach, **social-cognitive theory**, *explains hypnosis by emphasizing the degree to which beliefs and expectations contribute to increased suggestibility*. This perspective is supported by experiments in which individuals are told either that they will be able to resist ideomotor suggestions or that they will not be able to resist them. In these studies, people tend to conform to what they have been told to expect—a result that cannot be easily explained by dissociation theory (Lynn et al., 1984; Spanos et al., 1985). Similarly, research on hypnosis as a treatment for pain shows that *response expectancy*—whether the individual believes the treatment will work—plays a large role in the actual pain relief experienced (Milling, 2009). The idea that expectations influence hypnotic responses implies that some form of executive processing is influencing the experiences of an individual. Consistent with this view, researchers have found that different brain areas related to executive functions have stronger connections (fire at the same time more frequently) in highly hypnotizable than in less hypnotizable individuals (Hoeft et al., 2012). Hypnotizable subjects also show larger changes from "baseline levels" of activity in the frontal lobes when they view images while hypnotized, suggesting that they are more engaged with external stimuli (e.g., the voice of a hypnotist) than are less hypnotizable individuals (McGeown et al., 2009).

At this point, there appears to be some evidence in favour of both hypotheses. This lack of clarity is due to the fact that hypnosis did not receive much scientific attention for most of the 20th century. However, despite the fact that there is not a clear answer as to how hypnosis works, most scientists agree that for *some* individuals hypnosis can be a powerful therapeutic tool.

APPLICATIONS OF HYPNOSIS Although it is used far less frequently than medications or talk-based therapies, hypnosis has been used to treat a number of different physical and psychological conditions. Hypnosis is often used in conjunction with other psychotherapies such as cognitive-behavioural therapy (CBT) rather than as a stand-alone treatment. The resulting *cognitive hypnotherapy* has been used as an effective treatment for depression (Alladin & Alibhai, 2007), anxiety (Abramowitz et al., 2008; Schoenberger et al., 1997), eating disorders (Barabasz, 2007), hot flashes of cancer survivors (Elkins et al., 2008), and irritable bowel syndrome (Golden, 2007), among many others (Nash et al., 2009). Hypnosis is far from a cure-all, however. For example, researchers found that hypnotherapy combined with a nicotine patch is more effective as a smoking cessation intervention than the patch alone. Nonetheless, only one-fifth of the individuals receiving this kind of therapy managed to remain smoke-free for a year (Carmody et al., 2008). Moreover, the individuals receiving hypnotherapy for depression improved only 5% to 8% more on several measures of depressive symptoms than those who received traditional therapy. The best conclusion regarding hypnosis in therapy is that it shows promise, especially when used in conjunction with other evidence-based psychological or medical treatments.

Perhaps the most practical use for hypnosis is in the treatment of pain. If researchers can demonstrate its effectiveness in this application, it may be a preferred method of pain control given painkillers' potential side effects and risk of addiction. What does the scientific evidence say about the use of hypnosis in treating pain? A review of 18 individual studies found that approximately 75% of all individuals experienced adequate pain relief with this approach beyond that provided by traditional analgesics or no treatment (Montgomery et al., 2000). What happened to the other 25%? Perhaps the failure of the treatment in this group is attributable to the fact that some people are more readily hypnotized than others. In addition, to truly understand pain control, researchers must distinguish among different types of pain. Research has shown that hypnosis generally works as well as drug treatments for *acute pain*, which is the intense, temporary pain associated with a medical or dental procedure (Patterson & Jenson, 2003). The effect of hypnosis on chronic pain is more complicated, as some conditions are due to purely physical causes whereas others are more psychological in nature. For these latter conditions, it is likely that the patient will expect to continue to feel pain regardless of the treatment, thus reducing the effectiveness of hypnosis.

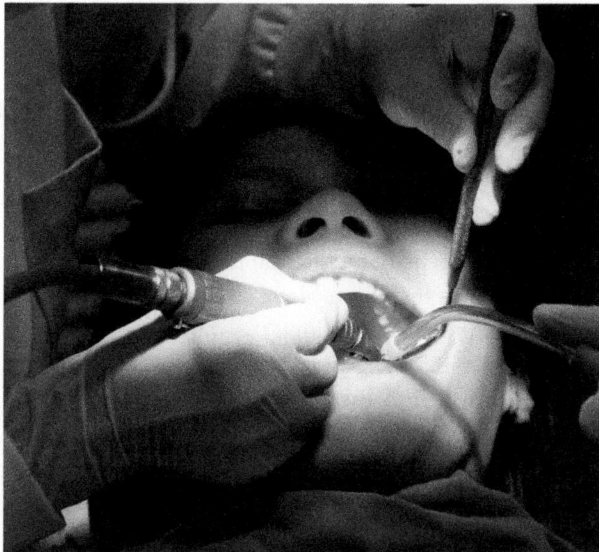

susaro/iStockphoto.com

Under hypnosis, people can withstand higher levels of pain for longer periods of time, including the discomfort associated with dental procedures.

MYTHS IN MIND

Recovering Lost Memories through Hypnosis

Before the limitations of hypnosis were fully understood, professionals working in the fields of psychology and law regularly used this technique for uncovering lost memories. What a powerful tool this would be for a psychologist—if a patient could remember specifics about trauma or abuse it *could* greatly help the individual's recovery. Similarly, law enforcement and legal professionals could benefit by learning the details of a crime recovered through hypnosis—or so many assumed.

As you have read, hypnosis puts the subject into a highly suggestible state. This condition leaves the individual vulnerable to prompts and suggestions by the hypnotist. A cooperative person could certainly comply with suggestions and create a story that, in the end, was entirely false. This has happened time and again. In reality, hypnosis does not improve memory (Kihlstrom, 1997; Loftus & Davis, 2006). Today, responsible psychologists do not use hypnotherapy to uncover or reconstruct lost memories. Police officers have also largely given up this practice. In 2007, the Supreme Court of Canada ruled that testimony based on hypnosis sessions alone cannot be submitted as evidence (*R. v. Trochy,* 2007, 1 S.C.R. 239, 2007 SCC6).

Quick Quiz 5.2a

Hypnosis

KNOW ...

1 ____________ suggestions specify that certain actions cannot be performed while hypnotized.

- **A** Ideomotor
- **B** Challenge
- **C** Cognitive-perceptual
- **D** Disassociation

UNDERSTAND ...

2 Dr. Johnson claims that hypnosis is a distinct state of consciousness in which there is a "hidden" observer. It appears that she is endorsing the ____________ theory of hypnosis.

- **A** social-cognitive
- **B** psychoanalytic
- **C** dissociation
- **D** hypnotherapy

APPLY ...

3 Hypnosis has been shown to be moderately successful as a therapy for all of the following *except*

- **A** addiction.
- **B** pain therapy.
- **C** causing long-term personality changes.
- **D** depression and anxiety.

ANALYZE ...

4 Which of the following statements best describes the scientific consensus about recovering memories with hypnosis?

- **A** Memories "recovered" through hypnosis are highly unreliable and should never be used as evidence in court.
- **B** If the memory is recovered by a trained psychologist, then it may be used as evidence in court.
- **C** Recovering memories through hypnosis is a simple procedure and, therefore, the findings should be a regular part of court hearings.
- **D** Memories can be recovered only in individuals who are highly hypnotizable.

Answers can be found on page ANS-2.

Meditation

During hypnosis, an individual enters an altered state of consciousness in which he or she is more suggestible than at other times. In many ways, hypnosis seems like a reduced state of awareness. In contrast, there are some instances in which individuals feel as though they have a greater-than-normal awareness of some elements of their world. One such instance is meditation.

TYPES OF MEDITATION We have all seen people meditating, be it in person, on television, or on the Internet. Some people lie down; others sit cross-legged

Watch
What's in It for Me? Altered States of Consciousness

or on their knees. Some people close their eyes. Some chant a word or phrase repeatedly while others focus on a point in space or on their body. Regardless of the differences in meditation techniques, almost all meditators go through similar experiences—noticing their racing thoughts, experiencing boredom or doubt that meditating is worthwhile, and perhaps, as they concentrate on their bodily sensations, some negativity. However, as they gain experience, most meditators report feeling happy and more relaxed. These reports lead to a number of scientific questions. What *is* meditation? And, how would you go about *testing* its effect?

Meditation *is any procedure that involves a shift in consciousness to a state in which an individual is highly focused, aware, and in control of mental processes.* However, to say "meditation" is a bit simplistic, as meditation has many different techniques and is practised, in some form, in almost every known culture. You may be familiar with some of these practices, or at least their associated names, such as transcendental meditation and Zen Buddhist meditation.

In some types of meditation, the individual focuses his or her attention on a chosen object, such as a point on the wall or a physical sensation like the feeling related to breathing. This technique is known as *focused attention (FA) meditation.* When distracting or negative thoughts enter into one's awareness and interfere with meditation, people are taught to accept these thoughts in a non-judgmental manner, and to then nudge their attention back to its original focus (Lutz et al., 2008). Although this technique is initially quite difficult, over time people become quite good at maintaining their attention on their chosen object. This increase in expertise is also reflected in how the brains of FA meditators function. In an fMRI study, expert meditators (more than 19 000 hours of meditation) produced greater levels of activity in the dorsal (top) part of the frontal lobes as well as in the parietal lobes, areas related to the control of attention (Brefczynski-Lewis et al., 2007). Interestingly, individuals with an extraordinary number of meditation hours—44 000!—had *lower* levels of activation in most of these areas. This may reflect the fact that less effort is required to control the focus of attention as people reach this level of expertise with meditation (Lutz et al., 2008).

A second type of meditation is *open monitoring (OM) meditation*. This technique also uses focused attention to train the mind and to reduce the influence of distractions. After initial training with FA, however, people can then transition into the use of OM styles of meditating. Here, meditators pay attention to the moment-by-moment sensations without focusing on any particular object (Lutz et al., 2008). A key feature of OM is to attempt to experience each sensation intensely, examining its rich sensory properties and emotional characteristics in great depth; however, these sensations should not become the sole focus of attention, preventing the meditator from responding to other sensations. Not surprisingly, OM meditation uses different brain areas than FA meditation. Rather than using neural regions related to focusing attention, it activates structures involved with *disengaging* attention (i.e., letting go) and on awareness of bodily states (Farb et al., 2007).

BOISVIEUX Christophe/hemis.fr/Alamy

The neural activity of expert meditators differs from that of novices. This difference demonstrates how the patterns of activity in your brain change as a result of your life experiences.

MEDITATION, COGNITION, AND EMOTION

Regardless of the specific meditation technique used, most meditators report that they have greater emotional control than they did prior to meditation training. Their reports are supported by neuroimaging studies showing reduced activity in emotion-related structures such as the amygdala and emotional regions of the frontal lobes of meditators (Brefczynski-Lewis et al., 2007; Taylor et al., 2011).

Computer-based studies of meditators have shown that meditating also enhances our ability to control what we pay attention to (Tang et al., 2007). Additionally, improvements in our ability to inhibit responses (e.g., stopping yourself when you are about to press the wrong button) that occur as a result of meditation training predict improvements in emotional well-being (Sahdra et al., 2011). Presumably, focusing attention on specific objects or ideas during meditation takes attention *away from* more negative thoughts about the self. In other words, it allows meditators to pay less attention to their own emotions and narratives about their lives.

The idea that the feelings of happiness and relaxation associated with meditation are due, in part, to us becoming more attentive to the present moment and less attentive to our own "stories" has found some support in research performed at the University of Toronto. Norm Farb and colleagues (2007) used fMRI to examine brain activity in trained meditators and a control group of non-meditators. Participants were asked to take one of two perspectives while reading lists of positive (e.g., charming) and negative (e.g., greedy) words. During half of the experiment, participants were asked to use a Narrative Focus, which required them to think about what each word meant and how it related to him or her. During the other half of the experiment, participants were asked to use an Experiential Focus, which required them to pay attention to their thoughts and bodily reactions to the words as they happened, but without any judgment or elaboration. If they found themselves distracted by any memories or thoughts inspired by a word, they were to calmly return their attention to the present moment. The results were intriguing: During the Experiential Focus condition (which is quite similar to a meditative state), trained meditators showed a larger decrease in activity in areas of the frontal lobes related to "the self" (the medial prefrontal cortex) than did novices. They also showed increased activity in areas related to the perception of one's bodily states. These results suggest that meditation does in fact help us separate ourselves from our own narratives and live in the present moment. Given that numerous other studies have shown that meditation leads to decreased levels of anxiety (Chen et al., 2012; Hoffman et al., 2011), it is possible that redirecting attention away from our own self-focused thoughts might improve our ability to be happy.

Meditation (in its different forms) has become a part of a number of different clinical treatment programs. For example, *mindfulness-based stress reduction* programs have been developed to teach and promote mindfulness meditation as a way of improving well-being and reducing negative experiences (see Module 14.3). These programs are generally well received by patients and can significantly reduce everyday levels of stress, depression, and anxiety, as well as more chronic psychiatric disorders (Chiesa & Serretti, 2011; Olivo et al., 2009). Additionally, meditation programs have been used to help people reduce pain, in both short-term experiments (e.g., Zeidan et al., 2010) and in long-term studies with chronic pain patients (Grant & Rainville, 2009; McCracken et al., 2007). Thus, meditation appears to affect attention, sensation, and emotional well-being.

Quick Quiz 5.2b

Meditation

KNOW ...

1 What function is *not* affected by meditation?

A Visual perception

B The control of attention

C Emotional well-being

D Awareness of bodily sensation

ANALYZE ...

2 What is known about the effects of meditation on pain perception?

A Beliefs about meditation are mostly superstition.

B All forms of meditation have proven effective at reducing pain.

C Some forms of meditation such as MBSR are effective in controlling chronic pain.

D Meditation is not an effective method for controlling pain.

Answers can be found on page ANS-2.

Disorders of Consciousness

In 1990, a Florida woman named Terri Schiavo collapsed to the ground. She had suffered a full cardiac arrest, resulting in massive brain damage due to a lack of oxygen. She would never regain consciousness. After she had been in a coma for almost three months, her diagnosis was changed to a persistent vegetative state. In 1998, her husband asked the hospital to remove her feeding tube because he was sure she wouldn't want to live this way. Her parents fought the decision, claiming part of Terri was still conscious. The ethical and legal battles continued for seven years, and included President George W. Bush cutting his vacation short in order to return to Washington to sign a legal order keeping her alive (Cranford, 2005). Eventually, after the U.S. Supreme Court refused to hear an appeal, her feeding tube was removed for the last time. Terri Schiavo died on March 31, 2005.

The Terri Schiavo case highlights the importance of consciousness in medical decision making. As you have already seen in this module, consciousness can take many forms, all of which vary in terms of how aware a person is of his or her environment. In patients with brain damage, the degree to which a patient is conscious of her surroundings can influence the diagnosis that she receives. Neurologists distinguish between six types of consciousness, ranging from little-to-no

Watch In the Real World: Managing Pain

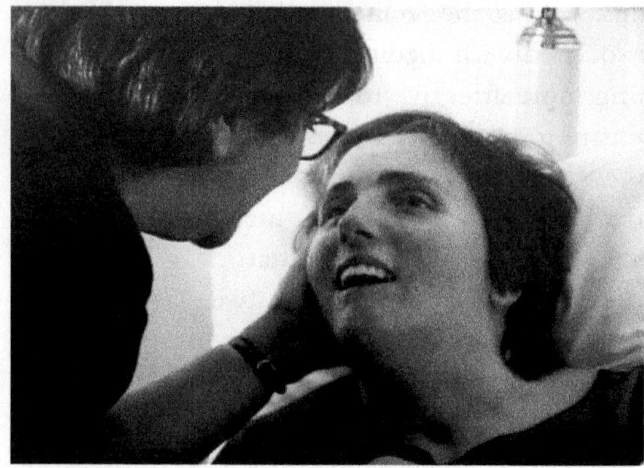

Left: Schindler Family Photo/AP Images; right: Reuters/Landov

Terri Schiavo suffered severe brain damage after going into cardiac arrest. She was diagnosed as being in a persistent vegetative state and subsequently taken off of life support in 2005.

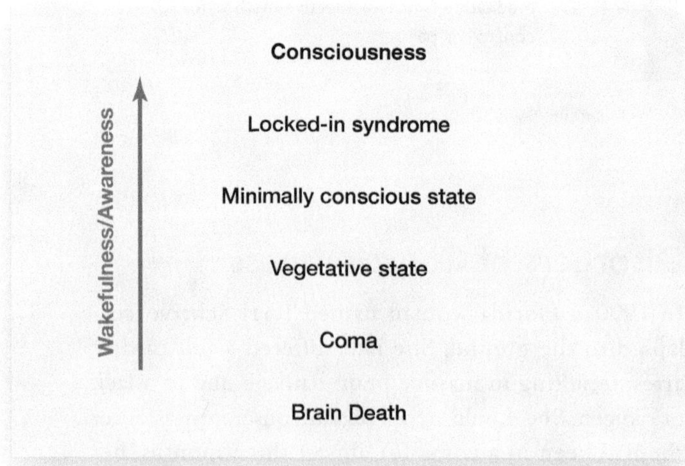

{FIG. 5.9} **Disorders of Consciousness** Although more nuanced diagnoses exist, this diagram depicts six key levels of consciousness used in the diagnosis of brain-damaged individuals.

brain function up to normal levels of awareness (see Figure 5.9).

The lowest level of consciousness in a person who is still technically alive is known as **brain death**, *a condition in which the brain, specifically including the brain stem, no longer functions* (American Academy of Neurology, 1995). Individuals who are brain dead have no hope of recovery because the brain stem regions responsible for maintaining basic life functions like breathing and maintaining the heartbeat do not function (see Figure 5.10).

In contrast to brain death, a **coma** *is a state marked by a complete loss of consciousness.* It is generally due to damage to the brain stem or to widespread damage to both hemispheres of the brain (Bateman, 2001). Patients who are in a coma have an absence of both wakefulness and awareness of themselves or their surroundings (Gawryluk et al., 2010). Some of the patient's brain stem reflexes will be suppressed, including pupil dilation and constriction in response to changes in brightness. Typically, patients who survive this stage begin to recover to higher levels of consciousness within 2–4 weeks, although there is no guarantee that the patient will make a full recovery.

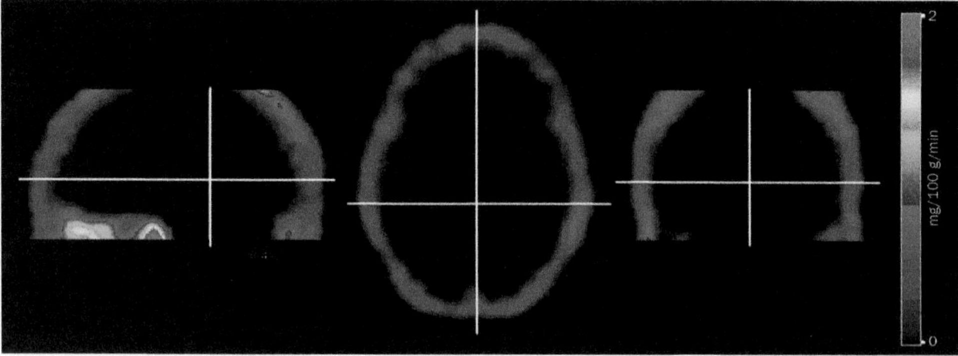

{FIG. 5.10} **Neuroimaging of Brain Death** This positron emission tomography (PET) scan shows the amount of glucose being used by the brain. In a healthy brain, most of the image would be yellow, green, or red, indicating activity. Here, only the tissue surrounding the brain is using glucose, giving the image the appearance of being an empty skull; functionally speaking, it is one.

If a patient in a coma improves slightly, the individual may enter a **persistent vegetative state**, *a state of minimal to no consciousness in which the patient's eyes may be open, and the individual will develop sleep–wake cycles without clear signs of consciousness*. For example, vegetative state patients do not appear to focus on objects in their visual field, nor do they track movement. These patients generally do not have damage to the brain stem. Instead, they have extensive brain damage to the grey matter and white matter of both hemispheres, leading to impairments of most functions (Laureys et al., 2004; Owen & Coleman, 2008). The likelihood of recovery from a vegetative state is time dependent. If a patient emerges from this state within the first few months, he or she could regain some form of consciousness. In contrast, if symptoms do not improve after three months, the patient is classified as being in a *permanent vegetative state;* the chances of recovery from that diagnosis decrease sharply (Wijdicks, 2006).

Thus far, we have discussed disorders of consciousness as though there were a quick-and-easy tool for diagnoses. While this is definitely true for brain death, distinguishing between other conditions is much more difficult. In fact, misdiagnosis of these disorders is estimated to be as high as 43% (Gawryluk et al., 2010; Schnakers et al., 2009). The challenge, therefore, is to develop or adapt tools that will help neurologists more accurately diagnose these mysterious conditions.

WORKING THE SCIENTIFIC LITERACY MODEL

Assessing Consciousness in the Vegetative State

Determining a brain-damaged patient's level of consciousness is quite challenging. It also has important implications for the patient's treatment. If she is shown to have some degree of awareness of her situation and/or her environment, then it seems reasonable to get her opinion on matters affecting her treatment. In contrast, if she is unresponsive, then such decisions should be made entirely by the family and the medical team. Everyone wants what is best for the patient, but the tools used to assess consciousness are still a work in progress.

What do we know about the assessment of consciousness in vegetative patients?

The initial assessment of consciousness in severely brain-damaged patients is generally performed at the patient's bedside. Doctors will perform tests of a patient's reflexes (e.g., pupil responses, which involve the brain stem) and examine other simple responses. The most common assessment tool is the Glasgow Coma Scale (GSC), a 15-item checklist for the physician. The GCS measures eye movements—whether they can open at all, open in response to pain, open in response to speech, or open spontaneously without any reason. The next five items on this checklist assess language abilities (e.g., does she use incorrect words?). The final six items measure movement abilities such as whether the patient responds to pain and whether she can obey commands. Scores of 9 or below reflect a severe disturbance of consciousness. (For comparison, individuals suffering from a concussion tend to score between 13 and 15, which is labelled as a mild disturbance.)

Checklists such as the GSC provide a useful initial indicator of a brain-damaged patient's abilities. However, many of the behaviours measured by this and similar assessment tools focus more on overt behaviours (i.e., movements) than on questions of awareness. A patient's inability to move may imply a greater disturbance of consciousness than actually exists, thus leading to potential misdiagnoses. Improvements in brain-imaging techniques may prove to be a more sensitive tool for investigating consciousness.

How can science explain consciousness in vegetative patients?

Researchers have argued for some time that *some* patients in a persistent vegetative state can show *some* signs of consciousness. For example, some patients have shown rudimentary responses to language. There have been cases of neurological changes in response to one's name (Staffen et al., 2006) as well as the emotional tone of a speaker's voice (Kotchoubey et al., 2009). However, the most stunning example of consciousness in this patient group was shown by Adrian Owen (now at Western University) and his colleagues (Owen et al., 2006). In their study, a 23-year-old patient in a vegetative state was asked to perform two different mental imagery tasks during an fMRI scan. In one task, she was asked to imagine playing tennis, an activity involving a specific set of movements. In the other task, she was asked to imagine visiting all of the rooms in her house, starting at the front door (this required her to develop a spatial map of her house). Despite not being able to respond to any questions verbally, this patient's brain showed clear evidence of understanding the commands. Imagining playing tennis activated brain areas related to movement; imagining walking through her house activated a spatial network including the parahippocampal gyrus, and the parietal lobe. This result provided stunning evidence that the patient did, in fact, have some degree of consciousness.

Owen and his colleagues have performed several subsequent studies with larger groups of patients. However, not all patients are able to modify their own brain activity. In a study including 54 patients, only five were able to perform the tennis–house task (Monti et al., 2010). But, one of these patients was able to do something remarkable: He was able to learn to use the tennis–house imagery task to communicate! The experimenters asked him simple questions and told him to imagine playing tennis if he wanted to respond "yes" and to imagine walking through his house if he wanted to respond "no" (see Figure 5.11). Using this technique, he was able to demonstrate that some of his cognitive abilities were preserved. Of course, we must be cautious and remember that this is only one patient among dozens who were tested. The ongoing challenge for researchers is to determine what made the five "fMRI responders" different from the 49 non-responders, and to use that information to help identify other patients who might still retain some degree of consciousness.

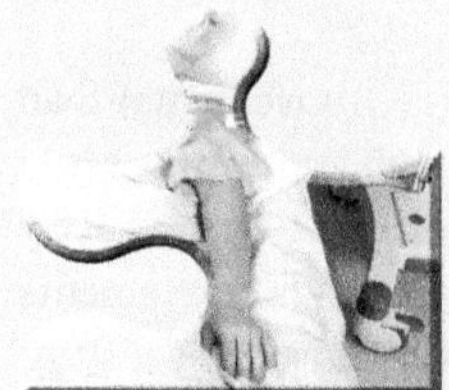

Can we critically evaluate this evidence?

The initial neuroimaging studies of consciousness in vegetative state patients are indeed promising. However, there are some important issues that need to be dealt with. First, we mentioned above that up to 43% of patients with disorders of consciousness are misdiagnosed. Given that only a small subset of the vegetative state patients were able to modify their brain activity, it is possible that they were not actually in a vegetative state, but instead had a less severe condition. Second, the researchers are equating language abilities with consciousness; yet, consciousness could take the form of responses to other, non-linguistic stimuli (Overgaard & Overgaard, 2011). This criticism would be particularly important if a vegetative state patient had damage to brain areas related to language comprehension.

We also have to be cautious about the use of PET and fMRI scans in patients with widespread brain damage. Both types of neuroimaging measure characteristics of blood flow in the brain. But, damage to the brain will alter how the blood flows (Rossini et al., 2004); therefore, we need to be careful when

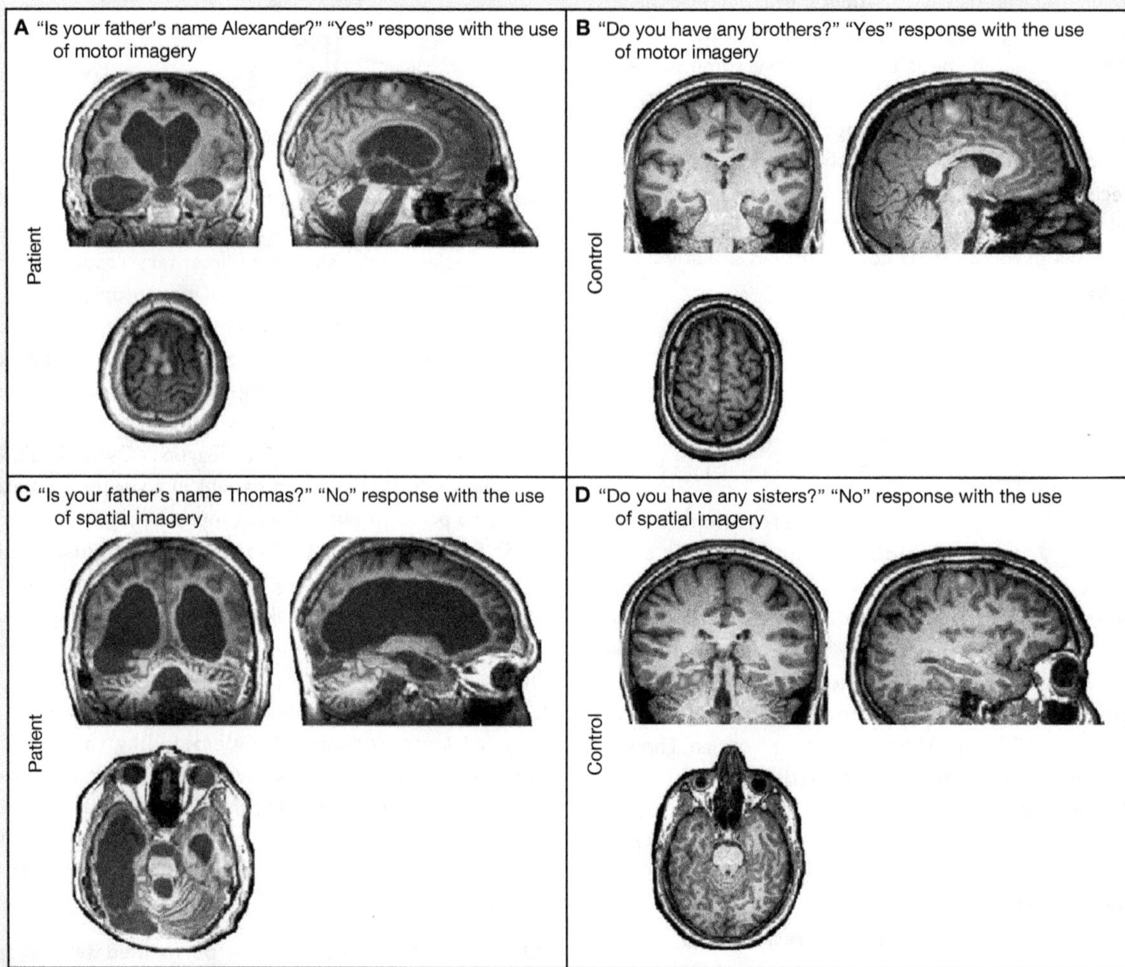

New England Journal of Medicine, 362(7), p. 587

{FIG. 5.11} **Using fMRI to Communicate with a Vegetative Patient** Results of two sample communication scans obtained from Patient 23 (Panels A and C) and a healthy control subject (Panels B and D) during functional MRI are shown. In Panels A and B, the observed activity pattern (orange) was very similar to that observed in the motor-imagery localizer scan (i.e., activity in the supplementary motor area alone), indicating a "yes" response. In Panels C and D, the observed activity pattern (blue) was very similar to that observed in the spatial-imagery localizer scan (i.e., activity in both the parahippocampal gyrus and the supplementary motor area), indicating a "no" response. This figure depicts the results of this vegetative patient (Panels A and C) and a healthy control participant (Panels B and D); the names used in the questions have been changed to protect the privacy of the patient.

comparing patients with healthy controls. One way around this latter concern is to use multiple methods of neuroimaging (Gawryluk et al., 2010). Increasing numbers of research groups are using EEG, which measures neural activity using electrodes attached to the scalp, to search for brain function in vegetative patients (Cruse et al., 2011; Wijnen et al., 2007). Given that distinct brain waves have been identified for sensory detection of a stimulus, the detection of unexpected auditory stimuli, higher-level analysis of stimuli, and semantic (meaning) analysis of language, this technology could provide important insights into the inner worlds of vegetative state patients. Indeed, Canadian researchers have developed the EEG-based Halifax Consciousness Scanner for this specific purpose (http://mindfulscientific.ca/hcs/).

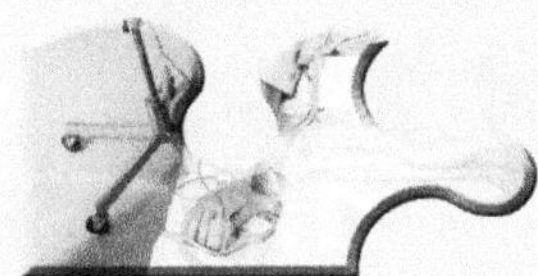

Why is this relevant?

Neuroimaging investigations of consciousness in vegetative state patients could literally have life-and-death implications. Currently, doctors have a very difficult time determining a patient's level of consciousness if they cannot move or make some sort of response. However, this information influences the decision about whether to remove that patient from life support. If brain imaging could provide insight into the inner world of patients (or, in some cases, lack thereof), it would provide doctors and family members with valuable information that would help them make the right decision for the patient.

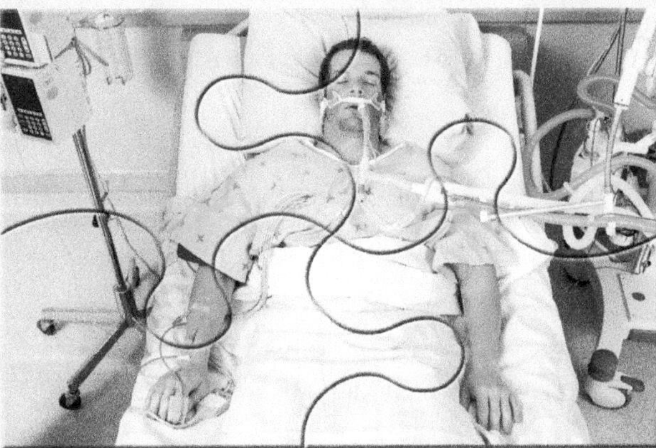

Tyler Olson/Shutterstock.com

There are two other disorders of consciousness that are often diagnosed by neurologists. One is the **minimally conscious state (MCS)**, *a disordered state of consciousness marked by the ability to show some behaviours that suggest at least partial consciousness, even if on an inconsistent basis.* A minimally conscious patient must show *some* awareness of himself or his environment, and be able to reproduce this behaviour. Examples of some behaviours that are tested are following simple commands, making gestures or yes/no responses to questions, and producing movements or emotional reactions in response to some person or object in their environment. When neuroimaging is used, minimally conscious patients show more activity than vegetative patients (see Figure 5.12), including activity in some higher-order sensory and cognitive regions (Boly et al., 2004).

The disorder of consciousness that most resembles the healthy, awake state—at least in terms of awareness—is **locked-in syndrome**, *a disorder in which the patient is aware and awake but, because of an inability to move his or her body, appears unconscious* (Smith & Delargy, 2005). Locked-in syndrome was brought to the attention of most people by the movie *The Diving Bell and the Butterfly*, which depicted Jean-Dominique Bauby's attempts to communicate to the outside world using eye movements. This disorder is caused by damage to part of the pons, the region of the brain stem that sticks out like an Adam's apple. Most patients with locked-in syndrome remain paralyzed. Luckily, new technology is making it easier for these patients to communicate with the outside world.

The final stage of consciousness is the healthy, conscious brain. That's you. Be grateful.

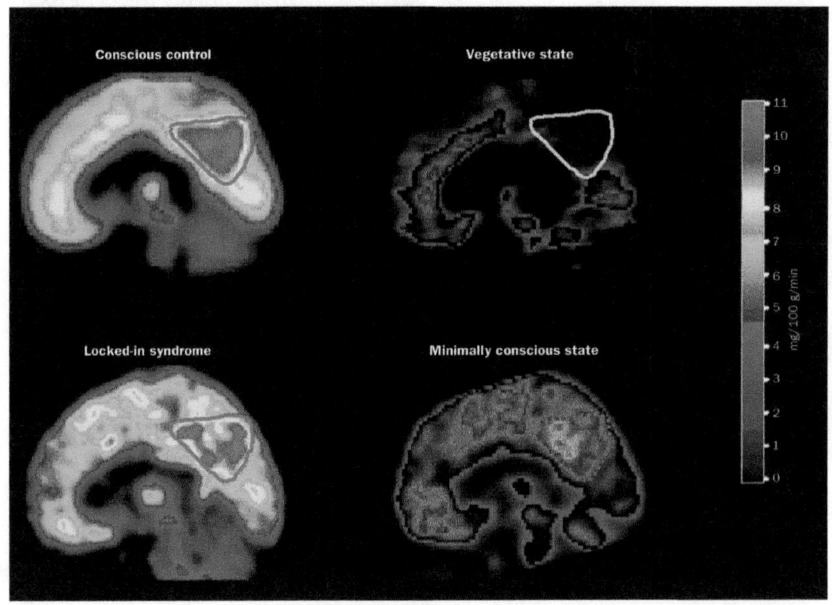

{FIG. 5.12} **Brain Activity in Four Levels of Consciousness** PET images of brain activity found in a healthy conscious brain and the brains of three patients with different types of brain damage. The highlighted red area near the back of the brain (along the midline) is the precuneus and the posterior cingulate cortex; these areas are involved in a number of different functions and use the most energy in the brain.

Quick Quiz 5.2c Disorders of Consciousness

KNOW ...

1 ________ is a disorder of consciousness in which an individual may open the eyes and exhibit sleep–wake cycles but show no specific signs of consciousness.

A A coma

B A persistent vegetative state

C Brain death

D A minimally conscious state

UNDERSTAND ...

2 What is the difference between a persistent vegetative state (PVS) and a minimally conscious state (MCS)?

A Nothing—they are both names for the same state.

B Someone in an MCS can have conversations, unlike someone in a PVS.

C Someone in an MCS has sleep–wake cycles, unlike someone in a PVS.

D People in an MCS show at least some behaviours that indicate consciousness, even if on an irregular basis.

Answers can be found on page ANS-2.

Module Summary

Module **5.2**

Now that you have read this module you should

KNOW ...

- ***The key terminology associated with hypnosis, meditation, and disorders of consciousness:***

brain death (p. 204)
coma (p. 204)
dissociation theory (p. 199)
hypnosis (p. 199)
locked-in syndrome (p. 207)
meditation (p. 202)
minimally conscious state (MCS) (p. 207)
persistent vegetative state (p. 204)
social-cognitive theory (p. 200)

UNDERSTAND ...

- ***The competing theories of hypnosis.*** Dissociation theory states that hypnosis involves a division between observer and hidden observer, whereas social-cognitive theory states that hypnosis is a process in which the beliefs and expectations about the process heighten the subject's willingness to follow suggestions.

APPLY ...

- ***Your knowledge of hypnosis to identify what it can and cannot do.*** Answer the following statements with true or false and check your answers on page ANS-2.

True or False?

Hypnosis could *potentially* work in the following scenarios:

1. Temporarily increasing physical strength
2. Helping someone quit smoking
3. Inducing a hallucination
4. Remembering details of a crime scene

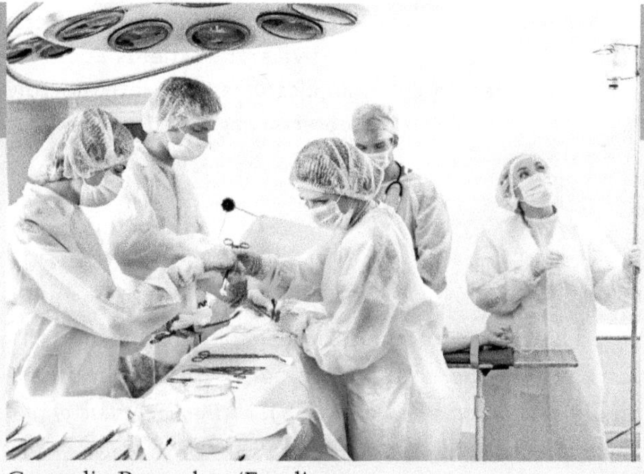

Gennadiy Poznyakov/Fotolia

5. Recovering a traumatic memory
6. Helping someone relax
7. Reducing pain sensation

ANALYZE ...

- ***The effectiveness of meditation for use in therapy.*** People who meditate often find that this practice helps reduce symptoms of depression, stress, and anxiety, and provides pain relief. For serious conditions, meditation typically needs to be accompanied by additional therapies or treatments to provide relief.
- ***The ability of researchers to detect consciousness in brain-damaged patients.*** Consciousness is difficult to detect using traditional bedside testing because many of these testing tools require movement. Using neuroimaging (specifically fMRI), it has been possible to detect conscious awareness in some patients who are in a vegetative state, as well as in patients who are in a minimally conscious state and those with locked-in syndrome.

Benne Ochs/Glow Images

Module 5.3

Drugs and Conscious Experience

Learning Objectives

After reading this module you should

KNOW ...	UNDERSTAND ...	APPLY ...	ANALYZE ...
The key terminology related to different categories of drugs and their effects on the nervous system and behaviour	Drug tolerance and dependence	Your knowledge to better understand your own beliefs about drug use	The difference between spiritual and recreational drug use The short- and long-term effects of drug use

Could taking a drug-induced trip be a way to cope with traumatic stress or a life-threatening illness? A variety of medications for reducing anxiety or alleviating depression are readily available. However, a few doctors and psychologists have suggested that perhaps a 6-hour trip on psychedelic "magic" mushrooms (called psilocybin) could be helpful to people dealing with difficult psychological and life problems. (It would also help them communicate with the sparkling trilingual dragon sighing in the bathtub.)

In the 1960s, a fringe group of psychologists insisted that psychedelic drugs were the answer to all the world's problems. The outcast nature of this group and the ensuing "war on drugs" prompted mainstream psychologists to shelve any ideas that a psychedelic drug or something similar could be used in a therapeutic setting. This perception appears to be changing, however. Recently, Roland Griffiths from Johns Hopkins University in Maryland has been conducting studies on the possible therapeutic benefits of psilocybin mushrooms. Cancer patients who were experiencing depression volunteered to take psilocybin as a part of Dr. Griffiths' study. Both at the end of their experience and 14 months later, they reported having personally meaningful, spiritually significant experiences that improved their overall outlook on life (Griffiths et al., 2008). This study would best be described as preliminary, as additional experiments involving controls and follow-up evaluations are needed. It is likely that such investigations will be forthcoming, as Griffiths is one of several researchers who are now exploring the possibility that mushrooms and similar drugs could be used in therapy.

Focus Questions

 How do we distinguish between recreationally abused drugs and therapeutic usage?

 Which other motives underlie drug use?

Every human culture uses drugs. It could even be argued that every *human* uses drugs, depending on your definition of the term. Many of the foods that we eat contain the same types of compounds found in mind-altering drugs. For example, nutmeg contains compounds similar to those found in some psychedelic substances, and chocolate contains small amounts of the same compounds found in amphetamines and marijuana (Wenk, 2010). Of course, caffeine and alcohol—both of which are mainstream parts of our culture—are also drugs. The difference between a drug and a nondrug compound seems to be that drugs are taken because the user has an intended effect in mind. Regardless of why we use them, drugs influence the activity of some elements of our central nervous system, affecting us both physically and psychologically. In this module, we will discuss these physical and psychological effects of drug use. We will then examine how these processes are affected by different classes of drugs.

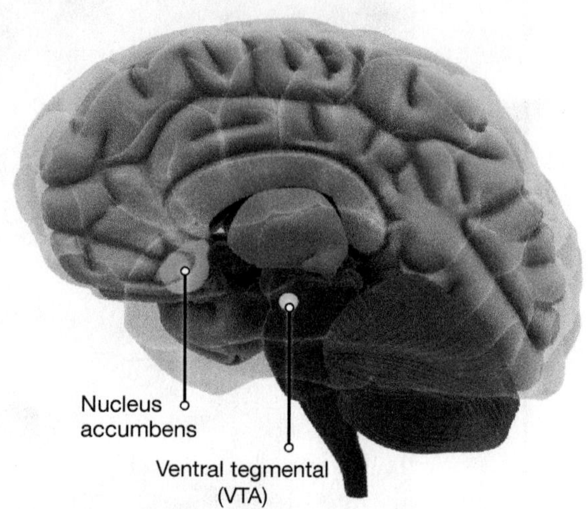

{FIG. 5.13} **Brain Regions Associated with the Effects of Drugs** The nucleus accumbens and ventral tegmental area are associated with reward responses to many different drugs.

Physical and Psychological Effects of Drugs

Although we often think of drugs as having a simple effect such as relieving pain or "getting someone high," the reality is actually much more complicated. To truly understand the impact of a drug on how people act and feel, we have to look at both the short-term and the long-term effects of drugs.

SHORT-TERM EFFECTS As you've already learned elsewhere in this book, your brain contains a number of different chemical messengers called neurotransmitters. These brain chemicals are released by a neuron (the pre-synaptic neuron) into the synapse, the space between the cells. They then bind to receptors on the surface of other neurons (the post-synaptic neurons), thus making these neurons more or less likely to fire. Drugs influence the amount of activity occurring in the synapse. Thus, they can serve as an *agonist* (which enhances or mimics the activity of a neurotransmitter) or an *antagonist* (which blocks or inhibits the activity of a neurotransmitter).

The short-term effects of drugs can be caused by a number of different brain mechanisms including (1) altering the amount of the neurotransmitter being released into the synapse, (2) preventing the reuptake (i.e., reabsorption back into the cell that released it) of the neurotransmitter once it has been released, thereby allowing it to have a longer influence on neurons, (3) blocking the receptor that the neurotransmitter would normally bind to, or (4) binding to the receptor in place of the neurotransmitter. In all of these scenarios, the likelihood of the postsynaptic neurons firing is changed, resulting in changes to how we think, act, and feel.

Different drugs will influence different neurotransmitter systems. For instance, the "club drug" ecstasy primarily affects serotonin levels whereas painkillers like OxyContin™ affect opioid receptors. However, the brain chemical that is most often influenced by drugs is dopamine, a neurotransmitter that is involved in responses to rewarding, pleasurable feelings (Volkow et al., 2009). Dopamine release in two brain areas, the *nucleus accumbens* and the *ventral tegmental area*, is likely related to the "high" associated with many drugs (Koob, 1992; see Figure 5.13). These positive feelings serve an important, and potentially dangerous, function: They reinforce the drug-taking behaviour. This reinforcing effect is so powerful that, for someone who has experience with a particular drug, even the *anticipation* of taking the drug is pleasurable and involves the release of dopamine (Schultz, 2000).

But, the drug–neurotransmitter relationship is not as simple as it would seem. This is because the effects of drugs involve biological, psychological, and social mechanisms. Think about the effects of alcohol. Drinking half a bottle of wine at a party often leads people to be more outgoing, whereas drinking half a bottle at home might cause them to fall asleep on the couch. In each case, the drug was the same: alcohol. But the effects of the drug differed because the situations in which the drug was consumed changed. The setting in which drugs are consumed can also have a more sinister effect: Overdoses of some drugs are more common when they are taken in new environments than when they are taken in a setting that the person often uses for drug consumption (Siegel et al., 1982). When people enter an environment that is associated with drug use, their bodies prepare to metabolize

Kzenon/Shutterstock

Expectations and the environment both play a large role in the effects that a drug will have on a person's behaviour.

drugs even before they are consumed (i.e., their bodies become braced for the drug's effects). Similar preparations do not occur in new environments, which leads to larger, and potentially fatal, drug effects (see Module 6.1). Another psychological factor that influences drug effects is the person's experience with a drug. It takes time for people to learn to associate taking the drug with the drug's effects on the body and brain. Therefore, a drug might have a much more potent effect on a person the third or fourth time he took it than it did the first time, which is very common with some drugs, such as marijuana. Finally, a person's expectations about the drug can dramatically influence its effects. If a person believes that alcohol will make him less shy, then it is likely that a few glasses of wine will have that effect.

How can we reconcile these psychological effects with the physiological effects discussed above? To do so, we have to remember that the psychological states mentioned above also influence the activity of brain areas. For instance, dealing with novel or stressful situations (e.g., being surrounded by strangers, or your parents arriving home early) often requires input from the frontal lobes; this activity might reduce the impact that drugs are having on a person's behaviour. A similar result can occur when a person has expectations about a drug. This mental set can itself change the activity of different brain areas and can alter the effects of a drug. Thus, the effects of drugs are yet another example of how our biology and psychology interact to create our conscious experiences.

LONG-TERM EFFECTS Importantly, the effects that different drugs will have on us change as we become frequent users. Think about a drug that most of you use: caffeine (found in coffee, tea, and some soft drinks). The first time you had a cup of coffee, you were likely wired and unable to sleep. But, veteran coffee drinkers rarely experience such a large burst of energy; some can even drink coffee before going to bed. This is an example of **tolerance**, *when repeated use of a drug results in a need for a higher dose to get the intended effect.* While tolerance might seem annoying, it is actually the brain's attempt to keep the level of neurotransmitters at stable levels. When receptors are overstimulated by neurotransmitters, as often happens during drug use, the neurons fire at a higher rate than normal. In order to counteract this effect and return the firing rate to normal, some of the receptors move further away from the synapse so that they are more difficult to stimulate, a process known as *down-regulation*.

Tolerance is not the only effect that can result from long-term use of legal or illegal drugs. Another is **physical dependence**, *the need to take a drug to ward off unpleasant physical withdrawal symptoms.* The characteristics of dependence and withdrawal symptoms differ from drug to drug. Caffeine withdrawal can involve head and muscle aches and impaired concentration. Withdrawal from long-term alcohol abuse is much more serious. A person who is dependent on alcohol can experience extremely severe, even life-threatening, withdrawal symptoms including nausea, increased heart rate and blood pressure, and hallucinations and delirium. However, drug dependence is not limited to physical symptoms. **Psychological dependence** *occurs when addiction develops without any physical symptoms of withdrawal.* Many people use drugs in order to ward off negative emotions. When they no longer have this defence mechanism, they experience stress, depression, and anxiety. Therefore, treatment programs for addiction often include some form of therapy that will allow users to learn to cope with these emotional symptoms while they are attempting to deal with the physical symptoms of withdrawal.

There is no single cause of drug dependence; instead, researchers believe that numerous factors—biological, psychological, and social—influence whether someone will become dependent upon a drug as well as the severity of that dependence. Increasing evidence suggests that genetics play a role in addiction (Foroud et al., 2010). Currently, researchers are attempting to identify the specific genes—or groups of genes—that make someone prone to becoming addicted to different drugs such as alcohol. However, genes are obviously not the only cause of drug dependence. Early experiences with different drugs can shape our attitudes toward them and influence how we consume those drugs later in life (Zucker et al., 2008). If someone tries wine in a family setting, it will feel much less like a "cool" part of teenage rebellion than if that person tries the same drink at a high school house party. That initial introduction can alter how that person views alcohol for years to come. Dependence is also influenced by the fact that drugs are often taken in the same situations, such as a cup of coffee to start your day or alcohol whenever you see particular friends. Eventually, taking the drug becomes linked in your memory to that setting or that group of people. When you next see those people or enter that environment, thoughts of the drug will often resurface, making it more likely that you will use, or at least crave, that drug. Addiction rates are also affected by the culture in which the person lives; for instance, alcoholism rates are lower in religious and social groups that prohibit drinking even though these groups are genetically similar to the rest of the population (Chentsova-Dutton & Tsai, 2007; Haber & Jacob, 2007). Finally, all of these variables interact with a person's personality; individuals with impulsive personality traits are more likely to become addicted to drugs regardless of their early experiences or cultural setting (Lejuez et al., 2010; Perry & Carroll, 2008). Thus, drug dependence does not have a single, simple cause, but is instead influenced by a number of interacting factors, as would be expected by the biopsychosocial model of behaviour.

Quick Quiz 5.3a

Physical and Psychological Effects of Drugs

KNOW ...

1 Dependence occurs when

A an individual will die if he does not continue to use the drug.

B an individual desires a drug for its pleasant effects.

C an individual has to take the drug to prevent or stop unpleasant withdrawal symptoms.

D an individual requires increasingly larger amounts of a substance to experience its effects.

UNDERSTAND ...

2 When does drug tolerance occur?

A When an individual needs increasingly larger amounts of a drug to achieve the same desired effect

B When individuals do not pass judgment on drug abusers

C When an individual experiences withdrawal symptoms

D When an individual starts taking a new drug for recreational purposes

APPLY ...

3 Which is NOT a way in which drugs affect neurotransmitter levels?

A Binding to receptors that would normally receive the neurotransmitters

B Stimulating the release of excess neurotransmitters

C Preventing down-regulation from occurring

D Preventing neurotransmitters from being reabsorbed into the cell that released them

Answers can be found on page ANS-2.

Table 5.3 :: The Major Categories of Drugs

DRUGS	PSYCHOLOGICAL EFFECTS	CHEMICAL EFFECTS	TOLERANCE	LIKELIHOOD OF DEPENDENCE
Stimulants: cocaine, amphetamine, ecstasy	Euphoria, increased energy, lowered inhibitions	Increase dopamine, serotonin, norepinephrine activity	Develops quickly	High
Marijuana	Euphoria, relaxation, distorted sensory experiences, paranoia	Stimulates cannabinoid receptors	Develops slowly	Low
Hallucinogens: LSD, psilocybin, DMT, ketamine	Major distortion of sensory and perceptual experiences. Fear, panic, paranoia	Increase serotonin activity Block glutamate receptors	Develops slowly	Very low
Opiates: heroin	Intense euphoria, pain relief	Stimulate endorphin receptors	Develops quickly	Very high
Sedatives: barbiturates, benzodiazepines	Drowsiness, relaxation, sleep	Increase GABA activity	Develops quickly	High
Alcohol	Euphoria, relaxation, lowered inhibitions	Primarily facilitates GABA activity; also stimulates endorphin and dopamine receptors	Develops gradually	Moderate to high

Commonly Abused Illegal Drugs

Thus far, we have discussed some of the ways in which drugs can affect our brain and our behaviour. These drugs are categorized based on their effects on the nervous system. Drugs can speed up the nervous system, slow it down, stimulate its pleasure centres, or distort how it processes the world. Table 5.3 provides an overview of some of the better-known drugs.

Almost all of the drugs discussed in this chapter are known as **psychoactive drugs**, *substances that affect thinking, behaviour, perception, and emotion*. However, not all of them are legal. As you will see, the boundary between illicit recreational drugs and legal prescription drugs can be razor-thin at times. Many common prescription medications are chemically similar, albeit safer, versions of illicit drugs; additionally, many legal prescription drugs are purchased illegally and used in ways not intended by the manufacturer.

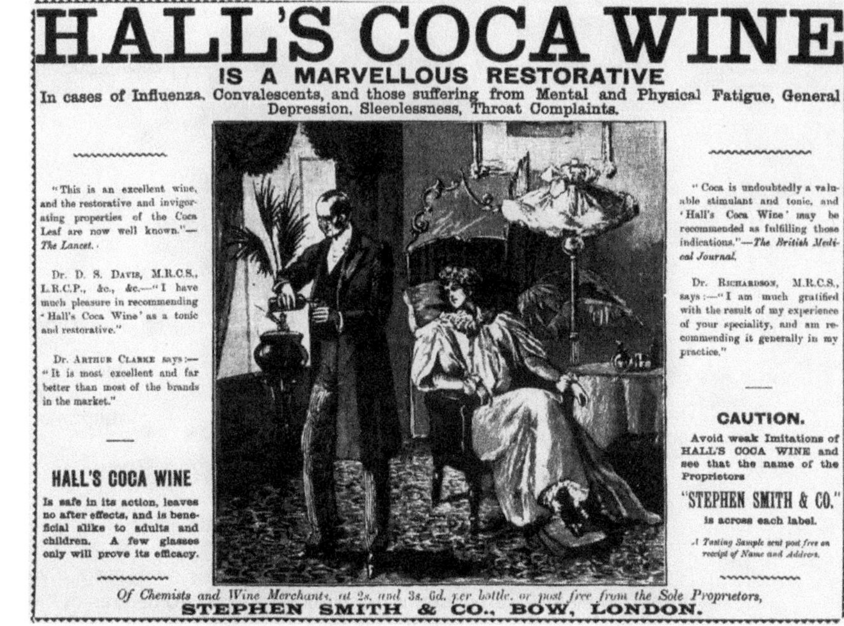

Advertising Archive/Courtesy Everett Collection

It often comes as a surprise to learn that the very substances that people can become addicted to, or whose possession and use can even land them in prison today, were once ingredients in everyday products. Cocaine was once used as an inexpensive, over-the-counter pain remedy. A concoction of wine and cocaine was popular, and the drug was also added to cough syrups and drops for treating toothaches. Coca-Cola used to contain nine milligrams of cocaine per glass; this practice ceased in 1903 (Liebowitz, 1983).

STIMULANTS **Stimulants** *are a category of drugs that speed up the nervous system, typically enhancing wakefulness and alertness*. There are a number of different types of stimulant drugs, ranging from naturally occurring substances such as leaves (cocaine) and beans (coffee) to drugs produced in a laboratory (crystal meth). Additionally, each drug has its own unique effect on the nervous system, influencing the levels of specific neurotransmitters in one of the four ways discussed earlier in this module.

Cocaine, one of the most commonly abused stimulants, is synthesized from coca leaves, most often grown in South American countries such as Colombia, Peru, and Bolivia. The people who harvest these plants often take the drug in its simplest form—they chew on the leaves and experience a mild increase in energy. However, by the time it reaches Canadian markets, it has been processed into powder form. It is typically snorted and absorbed into the bloodstream through the nasal passages or, if prepared as crack cocaine, smoked in a pipe. Cocaine influences the nervous system by blocking the reuptake of dopamine in reward centres of the brain, although it can also influence serotonin and norepinephrine levels as well (see Figure 5.14). By preventing dopamine from being reabsorbed by the neuron that released it, cocaine increases the amount of dopamine in the synapse between the cells, thus making the postsynaptic cell more likely to fire. The result is an increase in energy levels and a feeling of euphoria.

Amphetamines, another group of stimulants, come in a variety of forms. Some are prescription drugs, such as methylphenidate (Ritalin) and modafinil (Provigil), which are typically prescribed for attention-deficit/hyperactivity disorder (ADHD) and narcolepsy, respectively. When used as prescribed, these drugs can have beneficial effects; oftentimes, however, these drugs are used recreationally. Other stimulants, such as methamphetamine, are not prescribed drugs. Methamphetamine, which stimulates the release of dopamine in presynaptic cells (see Figure 5.14), may be even more potent than cocaine when it comes to addictive potential. It is also notorious for causing

Simulate
What Drugs Have You Used?

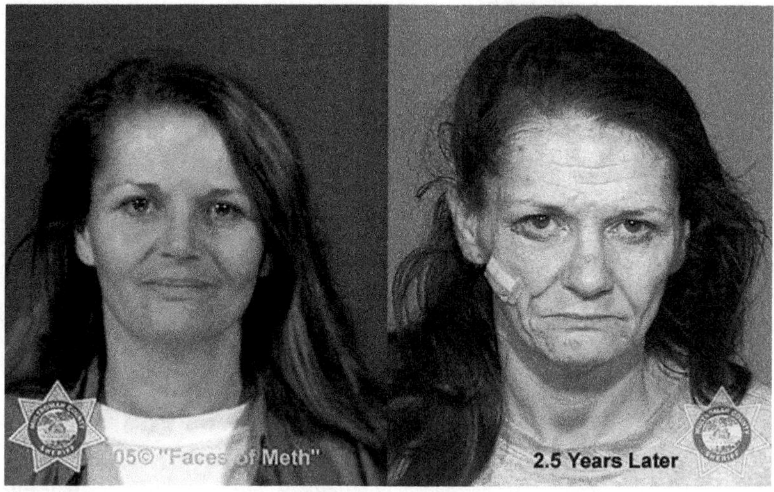

Multnomah County Sheriff/Splash/Newscom

Theresa Baxter was 42 when the picture on the left was taken. The photo on the right was taken 2½ years later; the effects of methamphetamine are obvious and striking.

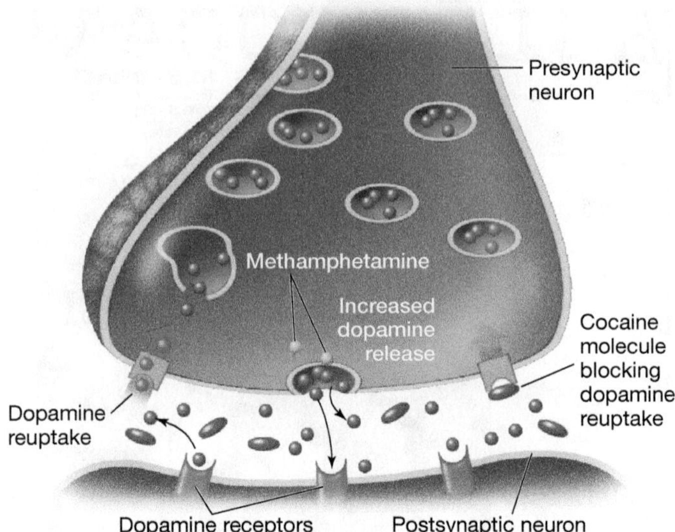

{FIG. 5.14} **Stimulant Effects on the Brain** Like many addictive drugs, cocaine and amphetamines stimulate the reward centres of the brain, including the nucleus accumbens and ventral tegmental area. Cocaine works by blocking reuptake of dopamine, and methamphetamine works by increasing the release of dopamine at presynaptic neurons. **Click on this figure in your eText to see more details.**

BLUE	GREEN	YELLOW
PINK	RED	ORANGE
GREY	BLACK	PURPLE
TAN	WHITE	BROWN

{FIG. 5.15} **The Stroop Test** The Stroop test requires you to read aloud the colour of the letters of these sample words. The task measures your ability to inhibit a natural tendency to read the word, rather than identify the colour. Chronic methamphetamine users have greater difficulty with this task than do non-users. **Click on this figure in your eText to see more details.**

Simulate Virtual Brain: Drug Addiction and Brain Reward Circuits

significant neurological as well as external physical problems. For example, chronic methamphetamine abusers often experience deterioration of their facial features, teeth, and gums, owing to a combination of factors. First, methamphetamine addiction can lead to neglect of basic dietary and hygienic care. Second, the drug is often manufactured from a potent cocktail of substances including hydrochloric acid and farm fertilizer—it is probably not surprising that these components can have serious side effects on appearance and health.

Long-term use of potent stimulants like methamphetamines can actually alter the structure of the user's brain. Compared to non-users, people who have a history of abusing methamphetamine have been shown to have structural abnormalities of cells in the frontal lobes, which reduces the brain's ability to inhibit irrelevant thoughts (Tobias et al., 2010). This ability can be measured through the Stroop task (Figure 5.15), which challenges a person's ability to inhibit reading a word in favour of identifying its colour. Methamphetamine abusers had greater difficulty with this task than non-users, and they also had reduced activity in the frontal lobes, likely because of the damage described previously (Salo et al., 2010).

Changes in brain structure have also been noted in chronic users of **ecstasy (3,4-methylenedioxy-*N*-methylamphetamine or MDMA)**, *a drug that is typically classified as a stimulant, but also has hallucinogenic effects* (Cowan et al., 2008). MDMA was developed in the early 1900s as a possible prescription drug. Many decades later, in the 1980s, it was labelled a "club drug" because of its frequent appearance at nightclub and rave parties. Ecstasy exerts its influence on the brain by stimulating the release of massive amounts of the neurotransmitter serotonin; it also blocks its reuptake, thereby ensuring that neurons containing serotonin receptors will fire at levels much greater than normal. Ecstasy heightens physical sensations and is known to increase social bonding and compassion among those who are under its influence. Unfortunately, this drug has also been linked to a number of preventable deaths. Heat stroke and dehydration are major risks associated with ecstasy use, especially when the drug is taken in a rave where there is a high level of physical exertion from dancing in an overheated environment.

The long-term effects of ecstasy use are difficult to identify because most users of this drug also abuse other illegal substances. That said, studies using animals show that MDMA damages some of the brain's serotonin-producing cells (Lyles & Cadet, 2003). Additionally, recent neuroimaging data show that using ecstasy can produce unique damage (independent of the effects of other drugs) in several areas of the cortex in the left hemisphere (Cowan et al., 2003). Given that the left hemisphere is also critical for language abilities, it should come as no surprise that ecstasy users show slight impairments on language-based tests of memory (e.g., lists of words; Laws & Kokkalis, 2007).

HALLUCINOGENS **Hallucinogenic drugs** *are substances that produce perceptual distortions*. Depending on the type of hallucinogen consumed, these distortions may be visual, auditory, and sometimes tactile in nature, such as the experience of crawling sensations against the skin. Hallucinogens also alter how people perceive their own thinking. For example, deep significance may be attached to what are normally mundane objects, events, or thoughts. One commonly used hallucinogen is LSD (lysergic acid diethylamide), which is a laboratory-made (synthetic) drug. Hallucinogenic substances also occur in nature, such as psilocybin (a mushroom) and mescaline (derived from the peyote cactus). Hallucinogens can have very long-lasting effects—more than 12 hours for LSD, for example. These drugs may also elicit powerful emotional experiences that range from extreme euphoria to fear, panic, and paranoia. The two most common hallucinogens, LSD and psilocybin, both act on the transmission of serotonin.

Short-acting hallucinogens have become increasingly popular for recreational use. The effects of two of these hallucinogens, ketamine and DMT (dimethyltryptamine), last for about an hour. Ketamine (street names include "Special K" and "Vitamin K") was originally developed as a surgical anesthetic to be used in cases where a gaseous anesthetic could not be applied, such as on the battlefield. It has been gaining popularity among university students as well as among people who frequent dance clubs and raves. Ketamine induces dream-like states, memory loss, dizziness, confusion, and a distorted sense of body ownership (i.e., feeling like your body and voice don't belong to you; Fu et al., 2005; Morgan et al., 2010). This synthetic drug blocks receptors for glutamate, which is an excitatory neurotransmitter that is important for, among other things, memory.

The short-acting hallucinogen known as DMT occurs naturally in such different places as the bark from trees native to Central and South America and on the skin surface of certain toads. DMT is even found in very small, naturally produced amounts in the human nervous system (Fontanilla et al., 2009). The function of DMT in the brain remains unclear, although some researchers have speculated that it plays a role in sleep and dreaming, and even out-of-body experiences (Barbanoj et al., 2008; Strassman, 2001). DMT is used in Canada primarily for recreational purposes. Users frequently report having intense "spiritual" experiences, such as feeling connected to or communicating with divine beings (as well as aliens, plant spirits, and other beings that aren't part of most modern people's version of reality). In fact, its ability to apparently enhance spiritual experiences has been well known in South American indigenous cultures. DMT is the primary psychoactive ingredient in ayahuasca, which plays a central role in shamanistic rituals involving contact with the spirit world. An increasing number of Canadians have used another drug, *salvia divinorum*, for similar purposes.

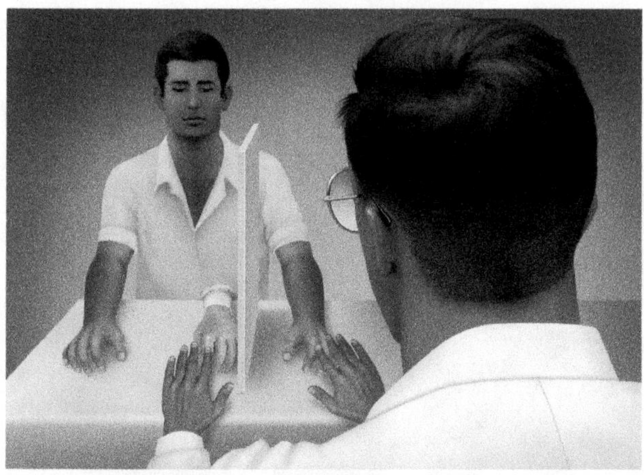

The rubber hand illusion occurs when a volunteer places a hand out of view behind a panel, with the rubber hand in plain view. When a researcher brushes the hidden and rubber hands at the same time, the rubber hand appears real to the volunteer. Sober individuals experience this phenomenon, but people under the influence of ketamine have magnified illusory experiences (Morgan et al., 2010).

BIOPSYCHOSOCIAL PERSPECTIVES

Recreational and Spiritual Uses of *Salvia divinorum*

Salvia divinorum is an herb that grows in Central and South America. When smoked or chewed, salvia induces highly intense but short-lived hallucinations. Use of this drug also leads to *dissociative experiences*—a detachment between self and body (Sumnall et al., 2011).

Test what you know about this drug:

True or False?

1. Sale, possession, and use of salvia are prohibited by the Canadian government.
2. Very few young people in Canada who use drugs have tried salvia.
3. Salvia has profound healing properties.

An exploration of salvia reveals a great deal about how cultural views affect how drugs are perceived. A single drug could be described as recreational, addictive, and a scourge to society in one culture, yet highly valued and spiritually significant to another.

Answers

1. True. It is illegal to sell salvia because it has not been approved as a natural product by Health Canada. However, enforcement of this regulation is under the control of Health Canada's Health Products and Food Branch Inspectorate (which does relatively little to enforce it), not the RCMP. There are plans to place salvia on Schedule III of the *Controlled Drugs and Substances Act*, a move that would criminalize the possession of all forms of the herb.

2. False. The use of salvia is on the rise among North Americans and Europeans, particularly among younger people (Nyi et al., 2010). Approximately 7.3% of Canadians aged 15–24 have tried it (Canadian Alcohol and Drug Use Survey, Health Canada, 2010).
3. False. There is no scientific evidence that salvia has healing properties. Whether one agrees with this statement, however, depends on who is asked. Among the Mazateca people of Mexico, salvia is used in divine rituals in which an individual communicates with the spiritual world. Shamans of the Mazateca people use salvia for spiritual healing sessions. They believe the drug has profound medicinal properties.

Drugs such as salvia and ayahuasca raise important questions about the effects of drugs and our view toward them. Although a given drug usually has standard, reliable effects on brain chemistry, the subjective experience it provides, the purposes it is used for, and people's attitudes toward the drug may vary widely, depending on the cultural context.

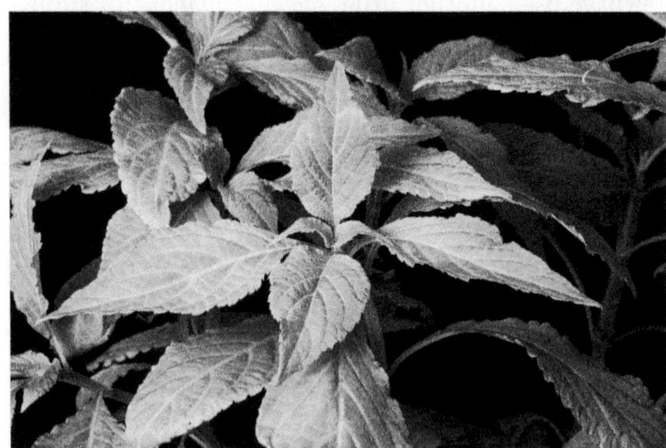

Ted Kinsman/Science Source

Salvia divinorum is a type of sage plant that grows naturally in Central and South America. Users of the herb combine juices from the leaves with tea for drinking, or the leaves are chewed or smoked.

Don Ryan/AP Images

Head shops in Canada sell salvia in packets for immediate consumption, despite the fact that it is technically illegal to do so. This practice may not occur for much longer if the drug is reclassified under the *Controlled Drugs and Substances Act*.

MARIJUANA Thus far, we have discussed drugs that stimulate the central nervous system and drugs that lead to altered states of consciousness. However, not all drugs neatly fit into these distinct categories. For instance, **marijuana** is *a drug comprising the leaves and buds of the* Cannabis *plant that produces a combination of hallucinogenic, stimulant, and relaxing (narcotic) effects*. These buds contain a high concentration of a compound called tetrahydrocannabinol (THC). THC mimics *anandamide,* a brain chemical that occurs naturally in the brain and the peripheral nerves. Both anandamide and THC bind to cannabinoid receptors and induce feelings of euphoria, relaxation, reduced pain, and heightened and sometimes distorted sensory experiences (Edwards et al., 2012; Ware et al., 2010). They also stimulate one's appetite (Kirkham, 2009). Although "having the munchies" might seem like a funny side effect for recreational users, it is an incredibly important benefit for cancer sufferers who use medicinal marijuana to counteract the nausea and lack of appetite that occurs following chemotherapy (Machado Rocha et al., 2008).

From the above list, it is clear that marijuana use can affect a number of different behaviours. Missing from this list, however, are the effects that this drug can have on our cognitive abilities.

JeremyNathan/Shutterstock

THC, the active ingredient in marijuana, has been shown to have a number of effects, including stimulating hunger, reducing pain, altering sensory experiences, inducing euphoria, and altering memory and cognition.

WORKING THE SCIENTIFIC LITERACY MODEL

Marijuana, Memory, and Cognition

No one doubts that marijuana affects a person's thinking and behaviour. That said, descriptions of the exact nature of these effects are often more anecdotal than scientific. The earliest reference to marijuana is found in the ancient Hindu text *Raja Nirghanta*, which translates the drug as "promoter of success," "the cause of the reeling gait," and "the laughter moving" (see Chopra & Chopra, 1957). Indeed. More recent descriptions have noted that marijuana's effects on your ability to think are both widespread and testable.

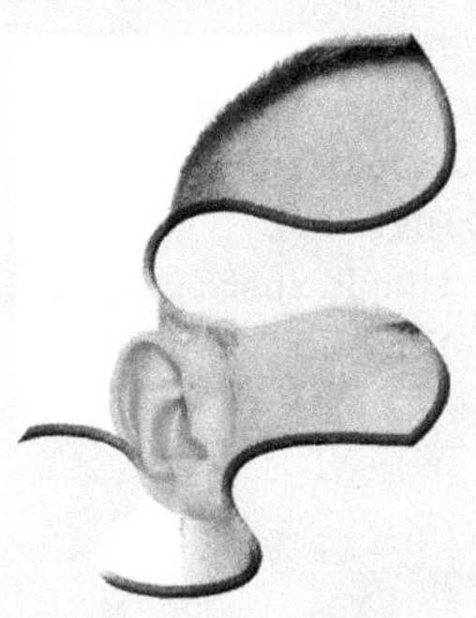

What do we know about the effects of marijuana on memory and cognition?

Studies of people under the influence of marijuana have demonstrated a number of different impairments to memory processes (Crean et al., 2011). Several researchers have confirmed that marijuana disrupts short-term memory (Ranganathan & D'Souza, 2006). Studies of long-term memory indicate that people under the influence of marijuana have difficulty recalling words from lists, but are still able to recognize items that they have seen before (Miller & Cornett, 1978). They also show a reduced ability to recall information from prose passages (Miller et al., 1977). Importantly, there was a tendency for people who were "high" to commit intrusion errors—adding in words that were not actually on a list of to-be-remembered items—and to inaccurately believe that they recognized an item that was not previously presented (i.e., a "false positive"; Hooker & Jones, 1987; Pfefferbaum et al., 1977).

Marijuana also affects a number of cognitive abilities. Executive functions, such as decision making and the control of attention, are critical for dealing with novel situations, and for changing or inhibiting responses to stimuli in the environment. Many executive functions are impaired by THC. For instance, marijuana slows the decision-making process (Vadhan et al., 2007) and can also reduce its accuracy (Ramaekers et al., 2006). It also impairs people's ability to problem solve and to change their strategies while performing a task (Bolla et al., 2002; Pope et al., 2003). Additionally, research suggests that recreational marijuana users have poorer attentional abilities (Hermann et al., 2007), although the evidence for this latter claim is mixed (Crean et al., 2011).

How can science explain these effects?

Neuroimaging results indicate that the memory and cognitive difficulties experienced by people who smoke marijuana are likely related to changes in how these people's brains function. Numerous studies have noted that reduced performance on memory tests is related to decreases in brain activity in the right frontal lobe (Block et al., 2002; Jager et al., 2007). Interestingly, some researchers have found that even when marijuana users and healthy control participants produce the same results on a memory test, their brains generate different patterns of activity. For instance, Kanayama and colleagues (2004) found that participants who had recently smoked marijuana (< 24 hours ago) were able to perform a spatial memory task; but doing so recruited a much more widespread network of brain regions, including several that are not typically associated with memory. This suggests that the brains of marijuana users need to work harder to reach the same level of performance, oftentimes relying on additional brain structures to help out (Jager et al., 2006).

Problems with executive functions can also be explained, at least in part, by differing patterns of brain activity. The inability to inhibit responses on a Stroop task (which was discussed earlier in this module) was related to the fact that marijuana users had less activity than healthy controls in a number of frontal-lobe regions (Eldreth et al., 2004; Gruber & Yurgelun-Todd, 2005). These studies also demonstrated that, similar to the memory studies, the brains of marijuana users had additional activity in brain regions not typically associated with the task they were performing. In other words, these brains had to find alternative networks to allow them to compensate for the marijuana so that they could still perform the task (Martín-Santos et al., 2010).

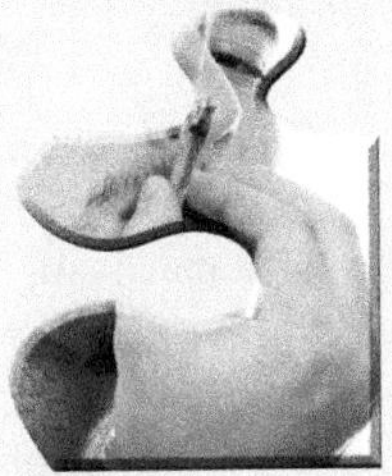

Can we critically evaluate this information?

When we look at these data, we have to remember that fMRI activity is correlational. The orange and yellow "lights" in the brain pictures represent areas that are activated at the same time that a person is performing a task; but, it doesn't mean that those areas are causing the person's behaviour. More importantly, we have to think of the participants in drug studies. Many of the people involved in these studies use more than one drug (e.g., marijuana plus alcohol, tobacco, and possibly other drugs). It is therefore difficult to isolate the effects of marijuana *by itself* on cognition. In order to support the claims that marijuana does impair memory and executive functions, we can look at which areas of the brain

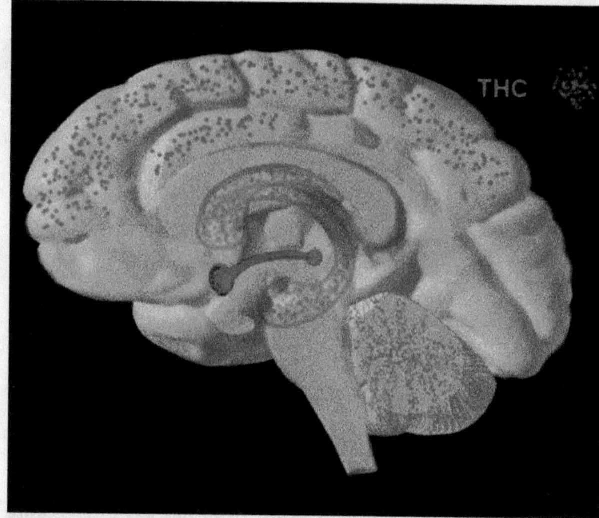

National Institute of Drug Abuse

The locations of the CB1 receptors, which bind to the active ingredient in marijuana, help explain the diverse effects users often experience. CB1 receptors are found in the frontal lobes (executive functions), hippocampus (memory), and cerebellum (coordination of movement). They are also found in the nucleus accumbens, an area related to the rewarding feeling associated with many drugs.

are involved with these abilities and then see if marijuana targets those areas. Memory involves the hippocampus and the frontal lobes (among other areas). Executive functions use the frontal lobes, particularly in the medial (middle) regions of the brain. As it turns out, a receptor sensitive to THC, the cannabinoid (CB1) receptor, is found throughout the hippocampus (Heyser et al., 1993) and in the medial region of the frontal lobes (Pertwee & Ross, 2002). Further research has shown that stimulating the CB1 receptor influences dopamine levels in the frontal lobes (Chen et al., 1990; Pistis et al., 2001), which results in impairments in short-term memory and higher-level thinking (Ranganathan & D'Souza, 2006). Thus, there is a cellular-level mechanism that can explain (some of) the odd behaviours that you see when people are smoking up.

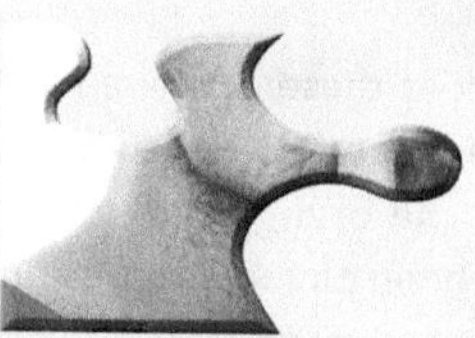

Why is this relevant?

Individuals who have marijuana-related problems with executive functions have trouble learning and using the skills necessary for recovering from their drug addiction; this difficulty makes it more likely that they will relapse and begin using marijuana again (Crean et al., 2011). This is problematic given that heavy long-term use of marijuana is related to a four-point decline in IQ scores (a number that isn't huge, but is still something to think about; Fried et al., 2002). More importantly, the data we've discussed indicate that the frontal lobes, which are not fully developed until the late teens, are sensitive to marijuana. This is a cause for concern. The brain develops in a step-by-step fashion, with higher-order cognitive areas (i.e., the frontal lobes) developing after other areas have fully matured (Gogtay et al., 2004). Using marijuana during an earlier stage of development can therefore have a much larger effect on a person's future than if the same dose were to be consumed or smoked later in life (Squeglia et al., 2009). Unfortunately for teenage pot smokers, data support this assertion. Increasing evidence indicates that the effects of marijuana on memory and executive functions are much larger in people who started taking the drug before the age of 17 (Brook et al., 2008; Pope et al., 2003). These data therefore suggest that prevention programs should specifically target teens to ensure that their cognitive abilities don't go up in smoke.

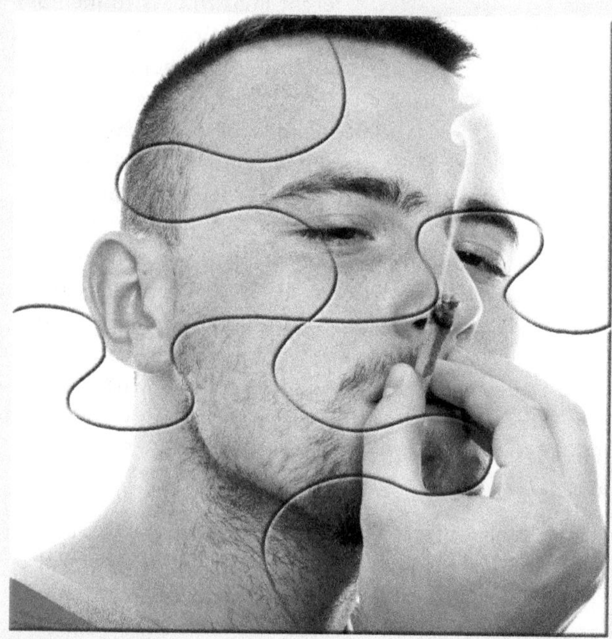

JanMika/Fotolia

Currently, marijuana is the most commonly used illegal drug in Canada. Indeed, the prevalence of marijuana use in the past year for people 15–24 was 21.6% (Canadian Alcohol and Drug Use Monitoring Survey, Health Canada, 2012). This high usage rate reflects, in part, the fact that this drug is so readily available. A similar issue is emerging for another class of drugs, opiates, which includes well-known narcotics such as heroin, as well as many commonly abused prescription drugs.

Opiates **Opiates** (*also called narcotics*) *are drugs such as heroin and morphine that reduce pain and induce extremely intense feelings of euphoria.* These drugs bind to endorphin receptors in the nervous system. Endorphins ("endogenous morphine") are neurotransmitters that reduce pain and produce pleasurable sensations—effects magnified by opiates. Naturally occurring opiates are derived from certain species of poppy plants that are primarily grown in Asia and the Middle East. Opiate drugs are very common in medical and emergency room settings. For example, the drug fentanyl is used in emergency rooms to treat people in extreme pain. A street version of fentanyl, known as "China White," can be more than 20 times the strength of more commonly sold doses of heroin.

Treating opiate addiction can be incredibly challenging. People who are addicted to opiates and other highly addictive drugs enter a negative cycle of having to use these drugs simply to ward off withdrawal effects, rather than to actually achieve the sense of euphoria they may have experienced when they started using them. Methadone is an *opioid* (a synthetic opiate) that binds to opiate receptors but does not give the same kind of high that heroin does. A regimen of daily methadone treatment can help people who are addicted to opiates avoid painful withdrawal symptoms as they learn to cope without the drug. In recent years, newer alternatives to methadone have been found to be more effective and need to be taken only a few times per week.

Another opioid, oxycodone (OxyContin®), has helped many people reduce severe pain while having relatively few side effects. Unfortunately, this drug, along with a similar product, Percocet®, has very high abuse potential. It is often misused, especially by those who have obtained it through illegal means (i.e., without a prescription). Indeed, the abuse of prescription opiates is a growing problem in Canada, particularly among high school students and the elderly (Sproule et al., 2009); this topic will be discussed in more detail later in this module.

Quick Quiz 5.3b
Commonly Abused Illegal Drugs

KNOW ...

1 ________ are drugs that increase nervous system activity.

A Hallucinogens

B Narcotics

C Psychoactive drugs

D Stimulants

2 Drugs that are best known for their ability to alter normal visual and auditory perceptions are called ________.

A hallucinogens

B narcotics

C psychoactive drugs

D stimulants

ANALYZE ...

3 Which statement best illustrates the relationship between spiritual and recreational uses of drugs?

A Drugs that are treated as illegal in Canada are generally considered illegal everywhere.

B Drugs have different effects on brain chemistry depending on the culture.

C Drugs can provide different subjective experiences depending on the culture.

D Drugs that are legal in Canada are usually illegal and considered dangerous in other cultures.

Answers can be found on page ANS-2.

Legal Drugs and Their Effects on Consciousness

So far we have covered drugs that are, for the most part, produced and distributed illegally. Some prescription drugs can also have profound effects on consciousness and, as a consequence, are targets for misuse.

SEDATIVES **Sedative drugs**, *sometimes referred to as "downers," depress activity of the central nervous system. Barbiturates* were an early form of medication used to treat anxiety and promote sleep. High doses of these drugs can shut down the brain stem regions that regulate breathing, so their medical use has largely been discontinued in favour of safer drugs. Barbiturates have a high potential for abuse, typically by people who want to lower inhibitions, relax, and try to improve their sleep. (Incidentally, these agents do not really improve sleep. Barbiturates actually reduce the amount of REM sleep.)

Newer forms of sedative drugs, called *benzodiazepines,* include prescription drugs such as Xanax, Ativan, and Valium. These drugs increase the effects of gamma-aminobutyric acid (GABA), an inhibitory neurotransmitter that helps reduce feelings of anxiety or panic. The major advantage of benzodiazepine drugs over barbiturates is that they do not specifically target the brain regions responsible for breathing and, even at high doses, are unlikely to be fatal. However, people under the influence of any kind of sedative are at greater risk for injury or death due to accidents caused by their diminished attention, reaction time, and motor control.

PRESCRIPTION DRUG ABUSE Prescription drugs are commonly abused by illicit users; over 15% of Canadian high school students have reported abusing prescription drugs at some point in their lives (Hammond et al., 2010; Figure 5.16). The prevalence of prescription drug abuse becomes even more extreme when these students enter university. Surveys have shown that as many as 31% of university students sampled have abused Ritalin, the stimulant commonly prescribed as a treatment for ADHD (Bogle &

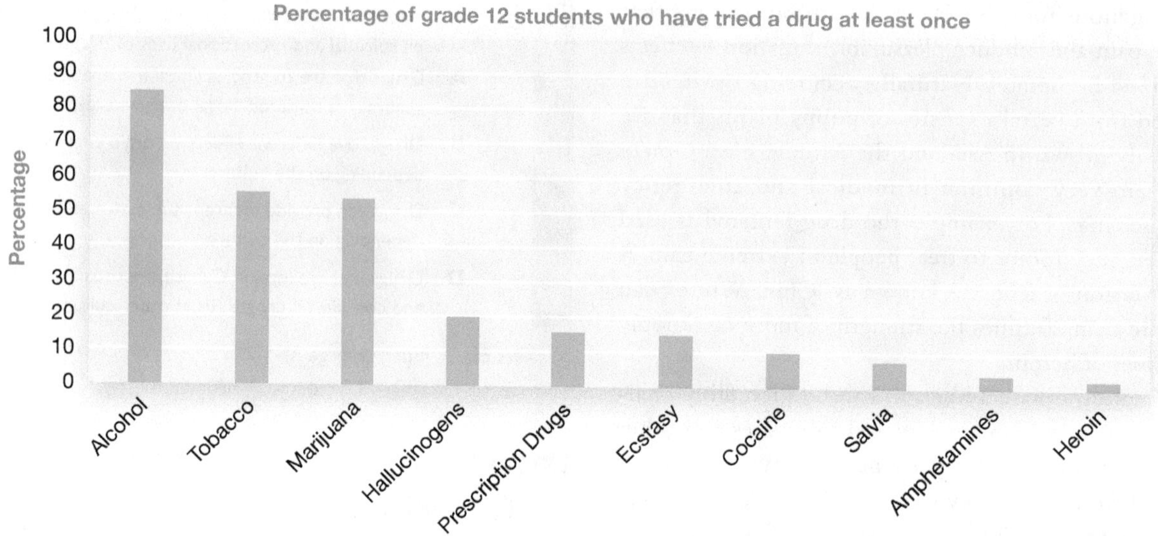

{FIG. 5.16} **Frequency of Drug Use among Grade 12 Students** The abuse of prescription and over-the-counter drugs is becoming increasingly common in Canada. In a 2008 nationwide survey, over 15% of Grade 12 students admitted to illegally using these drugs at least once. This figure illustrates how the prevalence of prescription drug abuse compares to that of other frequently abused substances (adapted from Hammond et al., 2010).

Smith, 2009). A massive number of prescription drugs are available on the market, including stimulants, opiates, and sedatives. In 2011, 3.2% of Canadians (approximately 1.1 *million* people) used prescription drugs for nonmedical reasons within the year prior to the survey (Health Canada, 2012). Users typically opt for prescription drugs as their drugs of choice because they are legal (when used as prescribed), pure (i.e., not contaminated or diluted), and relatively easy to get. Prescription drugs are typically taken at large doses, and administered in such a way to get a quicker, more intense effect—for example, by crushing and snorting stimulants such as Ritalin (see Figure 5.17).

Some of the most commonly abused prescription drugs in Canada are painkillers such as OxyContin®. When used normally, OxyContin is a pain-reliever that slowly releases an opioid over the course of approximately 12 hours, thus making it a relatively safe product (Roth et al., 2000). However, crushing the OxyContin tablet frees its opioid component oxycodone from the slow-release mechanism; it can then be inhaled or dissolved in liquid and injected to provide a rapid "high" (Carise et al., 2007). Almost 80% of people entering treatment programs for OxyContin abuse admitted that the drug was not prescribed to them, suggesting that there is a flourishing trade in this drug. Indeed, a recent study of drug users in Vancouver found that OxyContin is quite easy to illegally purchase in Canada (Nosyk et al., 2012); not surprisingly, the number of people entering drug rehabilitation programs for oxycodone abuse is also increasing (Sproule et al., 2009). In order to counteract this trend, Purdue Pharma Canada, the company that makes the drug, has replaced it with a similar substance, OxyNeo®, that is more difficult to grind up into a powder. However, this action will likely have little effect on addiction rates—in April 2013, the federal government allowed *six* pharmaceutical companies to begin manufacturing generic (cheaper) versions of the drug.

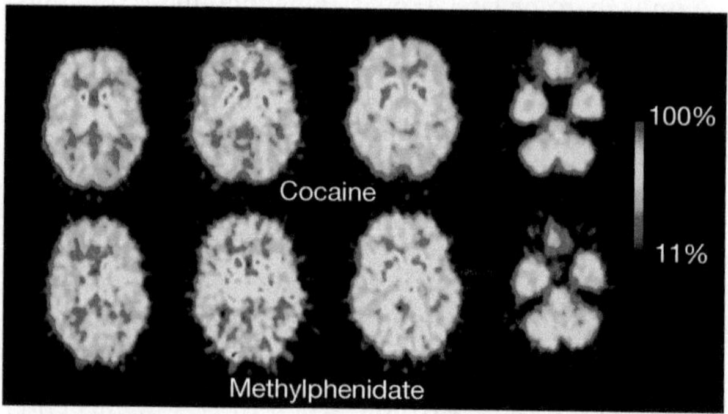

The National Institute on Drug Abuse

{FIG. 5.17} **Ritalin and Cocaine** Stimulants like methylphenidate (Ritalin) affect the same areas of the brain as cocaine, albeit with different speed and intensity.

Curbing prescription drug abuse poses quite a challenge. Approaches to reducing this problem include efforts to develop pain medications that do not act on pleasure and reward centres of the brain. For example, pain can be reduced by the administration of compounds that stimulate cannabinoid receptors in peripheral regions of the nervous system, thereby avoiding the high associated with stimulation of receptors within the brain. Many communities offer prescription drug disposal opportunities, which helps remove unused drugs from actual or potential circulation. In addition, doctors and other health care professionals are becoming increasingly aware that some individuals seeking prescription drugs are doing so because they are addicted to them.

ALCOHOL Alcohol can be found in nearly every culture, although some frown on its use more than others. Alcohol use is a part of cherished social and spiritual rituals, but is also associated with violence and accidents. It has the power to change societies, in some cases for the worse. Several decades ago, "problem drinking" was not an issue for the Carib people of Venezuela, for example. During specific yearly festivals, alcohol was brewed and consumed in limited amounts. In more recent years, the influence of Western civilization has led to the emergence of problems with alcohol abuse and alcoholism in this group of people (Seale et al., 2002). Most societies regard alcohol as an acceptable form of drug use, though they may attempt to limit and regulate its use through legal means. Customs and social expectations also affect usage. For example, drinking—especially heavy drinking—is considered more socially acceptable for men than for women.

Alcohol has a number of effects on the brain. It initially targets GABA receptors, and subsequently affects opiate and dopamine receptors. The stimulation of opiate and dopamine receptors accounts for the euphoria associated with lower doses as well its rewarding effects. The release of GABA, an inhibitory neurotransmitter, reduces the activity of the central nervous system, which helps explain the impairments in balance and coordination associated with consumption of alcohol. But if alcohol increases the release of an inhibitory brain chemical, why do people become *less* inhibited when they drink? The reason for this behaviour is that alcohol inhibits the frontal lobes of the brain. One function of the frontal lobes is to inhibit behaviour and impulses, and alcohol appears to impair the frontal lobe's ability to do so—in other words, it inhibits an inhibitor.

The lowered inhibitions associated with alcohol may help people muster the courage to perform a toast at a wedding, but many socially unacceptable consequences are also associated with alcohol use. Alcohol abuse has been linked to health problems, sexual and physical assault, automobile accidents, missing work or school, unplanned pregnancies, and contracting sexually transmitted diseases (Griffin et al., 2010). These effects are primarily associated with heavy consumption, which can often lead to *alcohol myopia* (Steele & Josephs, 1990). When intoxicated, people often pay more attention to cues related to their desires and impulses (e.g., good-looking people) and less attention to cues related to inhibiting those desires (e.g., friends, condom machines). This tendency to focus on short-term rewards rather than long-term consequences is particularly noticeable in underage drinkers whose frontal lobes (which help inhibit behaviour) are not fully developed. Alcohol myopia is also more likely to occur in people with low self-esteem; these individuals may focus on their fear of social rejection and will respond by engaging in risky behaviours that they feel will lead to social acceptance (MacDonald & Martineau, 2002).

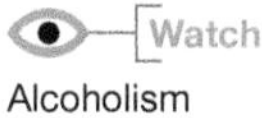
Watch
Alcoholism

PSYCH @

University Parties

Researchers have determined that university students drink significantly more than their peers who do not attend university (Carter et al., 2010). In one study, nearly half of the university student participants binge-drank, one-third drove under the influence, 10% to 12% sustained an injury or were assaulted while intoxicated, and 2% were victims of date rape while drinking (Hingson et al., 2009). Alcohol abuse in our society is widespread, especially during times of celebration (Glindemann et al., 2007), so it might seem as if universities have few options at their disposal to reduce reckless drinking on campus. Psychologists Kent Glindemann, Scott Geller, and their associates, however, have conducted some interesting field studies in fraternity houses at their U.S. university. For example, in two separate studies, these researchers measured the typical blood-alcohol level at fraternity parties. They then offered monetary awards or entry into a raffle for fraternities that could keep their average blood-alcohol level below 0.05 at their next party. The interventions proved to be successful in both studies, with blood-alcohol levels being significantly reduced from the baseline (Fournier et al., 2004; Glindemann et al., 2007).

Kzenon/Shutterstock.com

Holidays, birthdays, and other celebrations are associated with higher than normal levels of intoxication. For instance, researchers found that birthdays and St. Patrick's Day were associated with a 0.02 increase in the average blood-alcohol level of U.S. fraternity members (Glindemann et al., 2007).

WHY ARE SOME DRUGS LEGAL AND OTHERS ILLEGAL? In the November 2012 U.S. election, Colorado and Washington (the state, *not* Washington, D.C.) voted to legalize marijuana. Colorado Governor John Hickenlooper cautioned users by noting that, "[F]ederal law still says marijuana is an illegal drug, so don't break out the Cheetos or Goldfish too quickly." That caveat aside, these votes do suggest that attitudes toward certain drugs are changing in the U.S., which has traditionally been much more conservative than Canada. They also force us to more carefully examine why some drugs are labelled as being legal or illegal.

It makes sense for drugs with intense effects such as opium to be illegal but for chemically similar drugs with weaker effects such as OxyContin to be legal (with prescriptions). But, some distinctions are less clear. Nicotine is more addictive than THC, the active ingredient in marijuana, yet the selling of tobacco products is legal and marijuana is not. As you read earlier in this module, alcohol can lead to violence and many risky behaviours; marijuana's most dangerous effects are to the lungs and to short-term memory (and perhaps the waistline). Yet, it is legal to buy alcohol in Canada (and even at gas stations in the U.S.!), while marijuana is bought and sold illegally, with users risking criminal records every time they light up. A counter-argument is that police can use a breathalyzer to test if people are drinking and driving whereas no such test is available for marijuana, a drug known to interfere with coordination. As you can see, the decision to legalize or criminalize a drug is not a simple one.

The purpose of this section is not to promote one drug or another! But, it *is* to promote critical thinking and the use of science when making decisions. Your generation will likely be asked to make legal decisions about a number of drugs ranging from marijuana to several often-abused prescription drugs. Using rigorously controlled experiments to test the physiological and psychological effects of different drugs will allow you to make informed decisions about whether or not that substance should be banned.

Quick Quiz 5.3c Legal Drugs and Their Effects on Consciousness

KNOW ...

1 Drugs that depress the activity of the central nervous system are known as __________.

A stimulants
B sedatives
C hallucinogens
D GABAs

APPLY ...

2 Research shows that one effective way to decrease problem drinking on a college or university campus is to

A hold informative lectures that illustrate the dangers of drinking.
B give up—there is little hope for reducing drinking on campus.
C provide monetary incentives for student groups to maintain a low average blood-alcohol level.
D threaten student groups with fines if they are caught drinking.

ANALYZE ...

3 Why are benzodiazepines believed to be safer than barbiturates?

A Barbiturates can inhibit the brain's control of breathing.
B Benzodiazepines can be prescribed legally, but barbiturates cannot.
C No one misuses benzodiazepines.
D Both benzodiazepines and barbiturates are viewed as equally dangerous.

Answers can be found on page ANS-2.

Module Summary

Module **5.3**

Now that you have read this module you should

Benne Ochs/Glow Images

KNOW ...

- ***The key terminology related to different categories of drugs and their effects on the nervous system and behaviour:***

ecstasy (MDMA) (p. 214)
hallucinogenic drugs (p. 214)
marijuana (p. 216)
opiates (p. 218)
physical dependence (p. 211)
psychoactive drugs (p. 213)
psychological dependence (p. 211)
sedative drugs (p. 219)
stimulants (p. 213)
tolerance (p. 211)

UNDERSTAND ...

- ***Drug tolerance and dependence.*** Tolerance is a physiological process in which repeated exposure to a drug leads to a need for increasingly larger dosages to experience the intended effect. Physical dependence occurs when the user takes a drug to avoid withdrawal symptoms. Psychological dependence occurs when people feel addicted to a drug despite the absence of physical withdrawal symptoms; this form of dependence is often related to a person's emotional reasons for using a drug (e.g., dealing with stress or negative emotions).

APPLY ...

- ***Your knowledge to better understand your own beliefs about drug use.*** One tool that might help you in this regard is the scale in **Table 5.4**. For each item on the left, circle the number in the column that represents your level of agreement.

ANALYZE ...

- ***The difference between spiritual and recreational drug use.*** The difference, such as in the case of salvia, is dependent upon cultural factors, the setting in which the drug is used, and the expectations of the user.
- ***The short- and long-term effects of drug use.*** Review **Table 5.3** (page 212) for a summary of short-term effects of the major drug categories. Long-term effects of drug use include tolerance, physical dependence, and psychological dependence. Additionally, long-term use of a number of drugs can change the structure of the brain, leading to permanent deficits in a number of different cognitive and physical abilities.

Table 5.4 :: What Are Your Beliefs About Drug Use?

After you have circled an answer for each item, add up all the circled numbers to find your final score.

	STRONGLY DISAGREE	DISAGREE	NEUTRAL	AGREE	STRONGLY AGREE
Marijuana should be legalized.	1	2	3	4	5
Marijuana use among teachers can be just healthy experimentation.	1	2	3	4	5
Personal use of drugs should be legal in the confines of one's own home.	1	2	3	4	5
Daily use of one marijuana cigarette is not necessarily harmful.	1	2	3	4	5
Tobacco smoking should be allowed in high schools.	1	2	3	4	5
It can be normal for a teenager to experiment with drugs.	1	2	3	4	5
Persons convicted for the sale of illicit drugs should not be eligible for parole.	5	4	3	2	1
Lifelong abstinence is a necessary goal in the treatment of alcoholism.	5	4	3	2	1
Once a person becomes drug-free through treatment he can never become a social user.	5	4	3	2	1
Parents should teach their children how to use alcohol.	5	4	3	2	1
Total					

Source: Chappel, Veach, & Krug, 1985.

Note: This scale measures permissive attitudes toward substance use and abuse. Higher scores indicate more permissive attitudes.

Work the Scientific Literacy Model :: Understanding the Rhythms of Sleep

1 What do we know about the stages of sleep?

As part of our circadian rhythm (see **page 182** for a broad overview), sleep follows a relatively predictable pattern. Review **Figure 5.3 on page 184** for a snapshot of the various sleep stages and the brain wavelength activity that characterizes each stage. To get to know your brain waves, review the discussion on **page 184**. As noted there, beta waves are characteristic of wakefulness. Hint: Beta starts with a **b** for "busy"—the activity level of your brain while you are awake. Other wavelengths include alpha (characteristic of a relaxed state), theta (early stages of sleep), and delta (deep sleep). The first four stages of sleep are collectively known as non-REM sleep. REM sleep occurs after the last stage of non-REM sleep and is the stage in which we do most of our dreaming. If you're having trouble remembering the difference between non-REM and REM sleep, note that REM sleep is also called *paradoxical sleep*. During the restorative REM sleep stage, brain activity increases to the point where it resembles wakefulness (beta waves), but your body is paradoxically in a state of sleep and temporary loss of muscle tone. While our need for REM sleep might change from infancy to older adulthood, the stages of sleep we cycle through remain constant.

2 How can science help explain the importance of sleep?

Devices such as the electroencephalogram (EEG) have allowed modern sleep researchers to isolate sleep stages, differentiate between REM and non-REM sleep, and explore the consequences of sleep deprivation. New information like the suggested link between stage 2 sleep spindles and memory formation is a result of research taking advantage of this kind of technology. Research also shows that even minor sleep disturbances, such as turning the clock forward for Daylight Savings Time or experiencing jetlag, can affect natural sleep rhythms. The negative effects of sleep deprivation are also well documented by research; **page 187** describes a study reporting a correlation between teenagers' lack of sleep and an increase in illness, family problems, and even substance abuse. Researchers have also shown that driving while sleepy can be as dangerous as driving under the influence of alcohol, and that the long, demanding work shifts that deprive doctors and nurses of needed rest can lead to job stress, burnout, and potentially tragic errors in medical care.

Lava 4 images/Shutterstock

4 Why is this relevant?

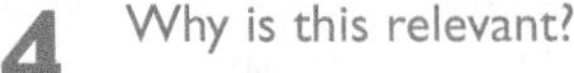

Watch the accompanying video excerpt on the rhythms of consciousness. You can access the video at MyPsychLab or by clicking the play button in the centre of your eText. If your instructor assigns this video as a homework activity, you will find additional content to help you in MyPsychLab. You can also view the video by using your smart phone and the QR code below, or you can go to the YouTube link provided.

After you have read this chapter and watched the video, imagine that your roommate has been coming back to the dorm at all hours of the night, disrupting your sleep. Describe a typical night's sleep cycle and then describe how your sleep is affected when you are woken up during each of the different stages of sleep. Be sure to differentiate the impact in all the stages.

3 Can we critically evaluate claims about sleep?

Many people worry that they are not getting enough sleep. Consider what you know about the available research. Do we all need a solid 8 hours of sleep nightly to be functioning members of society? Because we are all unique individuals, our bodies may require more or less sleep. A better rule of thumb than just counting your number of hours slept is to think about how well rested you may feel during the day. When it comes to shift workers and schedules, adjusting the distribution of hours worked (see **Figure 5.6 on page 188**) has a positive effect on cognitive functioning. Also, if you're not feeling well rested, before turning to sleep-aid drugs, consider improving your sleep hygiene by following some of the methods in **Table 5.1 on page 196**.

MyPsychLab **Your turn to Work the Scientific Literacy Model:** Watch the accompanying video on YouTube, or on your phone (using the Layar app or QR code). If your instructor has assigned this as a homework activity, you can find the video clip and additional content at MyPsychLab. Answer the questions that accompany the video clip to test your understanding.

youtube.com/workthemodel

SCAN WITH LAYAR

6

Learning

lculig/Shutterstock

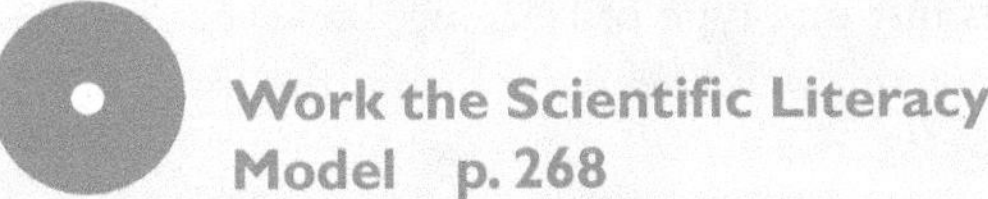

Brenda Carson/Fotolia

Module 6.1

Classical Conditioning: Learning by Association

Learning Objectives

After reading this module you should

KNOW ...	UNDERSTAND ...	APPLY ...	ANALYZE ...
The key terminology involved in classical conditioning	How responses learned through classical conditioning can be acquired and lost The role of biological and evolutionary factors in classical conditioning	The concepts and terms of classical conditioning to new examples	Claims that artificially sweetened beverages are a healthier choice

What do you think of when you smell freshly baked cookies? Chances are you associate the smell of cookies with your mother or grandmother, and immediately experience a flood of memories associated with them. These associations form naturally. It is quite unlikely that your grandmother shoved a chocolate chip cookie under your nose and screamed, "Remember me!" Instead, you linked these two stimuli together in your mind; now, the smell of cookies is associated with the idea of grandmother. This ability to associate stimuli provides important evolutionary advantages: It means that you can use one stimulus to predict the appearance of another, and that your body can initiate its response to the second stimulus before it even appears. Although the link between your grandmother and the smell of cookies does not seem related to your survival, similar associations such as the smell of a food that made you sick and a feeling of revulsion just might. Interestingly, we are not the only species with this ability—even the simplest animals such as the earthworm can learn by association, suggesting that these associations are in fact critical for survival. In this module, we will explore the different processes that influence how these associations form.

Focus Questions

 Which types of behaviours can be learned?

 Do all instances of classical conditioning go undetected by the individual?

Learning *is a process by which behaviour or knowledge changes as a result of experience.* To many people, the term "learning" signifies the activities that students do—reading, listening, and taking tests in order to acquire new information. This process, which is known as *cognitive learning*, is just one type of learning, however. Another way that we learn is by *associative learning*, which is the focus of this module.

Pavlov's Dogs: Classical Conditioning of Salivation

Research on associative learning has a long history in psychology, dating back to Ivan Pavlov (1849–1936), a Russian physiologist and the 1904 Nobel laureate in medicine (for work on digestion, *not* his now-famous conditioning research). Pavlov studied digestion, using dogs as a model species for his experiments. As a part of his normal research procedure, he collected saliva and other gastric secretions from the dogs when they were presented with meat powder. Pavlov and his assistants noticed that as they prepared dogs for procedures, even before any meat powder was presented, the dogs would start salivating. This curious observation led Pavlov to consider the possibility that digestive responses were more than just simple reflexes in response to food. If dogs salivate in anticipation of food, then perhaps the salivary response can also be learned (Pavlov's lab assistants referred to them as "psychic secretions"). Pavlov began conducting experiments in which he first presented a sound from a metronome, a device that produces ticking sounds at set intervals, and then presented meat powder to the dogs. After pairing the sound with the food several times, Pavlov discovered that the metronome by itself could elicit salivation (see Figure 6.1).

{FIG. 6.1} **Associative Learning** Although much information may pass through the dog's brain, in Pavlov's experiments on classical conditioning an association was made between the tone and the food. (Pavlov used a metronome as well as other devices for presenting sounds. In this module, the term "tone" represents the stimulus that was paired with food in his experiments.)

Pavlov's discovery began a long tradition of inquiry into what is now called **classical conditioning**—*learning that occurs when a neutral stimulus elicits a response that was originally caused by another stimulus.* In Pavlov's experiments, the neutral stimulus was the sound of the tone, which was paired with meat powder that could by itself elicit salivation (Figure 6.2). After repeated pairings, the dogs learned that the tone predicted meat powder. Eventually, just hearing the tone alone could elicit salivation. Classical conditioning, also referred to as *Pavlovian conditioning*, influences many other responses as well and occurs in a variety of settings. Indeed, Pavlov's work inspired thousands of future studies and served as one of the foundations of *behaviourism,* a line of inquiry focused on observable behaviours rather than unobservable mental events (see Module 1.2).

You can think about classical conditioning in mechanical terms—that is, one event causes another. A *stimulus* is an external event or cue that elicits a response. Stimuli (plural), such as food, water, pain, or sexual contact, elicit different types of responses. An **unconditioned stimulus (US)** *is a stimulus that elicits a reflexive response without learning.* In each context, the terms "conditioning" and "learning" are synonymous. Thus the "unconditioned" part of the unconditioned stimulus refers to the fact that it can elicit a response in the absence of any learning. An **unconditioned response (UR)** *is a reflexive, unlearned reaction to an unconditioned stimulus.* In Pavlov's experiment, meat powder elicited unconditioned salivation in his dogs (see the top panel of Figure 6.2). The link between the US and the UR is, by definition, unlearned. The dog's parents did not have to teach it to salivate when food appeared; this response occurs naturally. In addition to food eliciting salivation, other unconditioned stimulus and response relationships include flinching (a UR) in response to a loud sound (US), and blinking (UR) in response to a puff of air to the eye (US).

Watch
The Big Picture: What Does It Mean to Learn?

Watch
Basics: Classical Conditioning: An Involuntary Response

Recall that a defining characteristic of classical conditioning is that a neutral stimulus comes to elicit a response. It does so because the neutral stimulus is

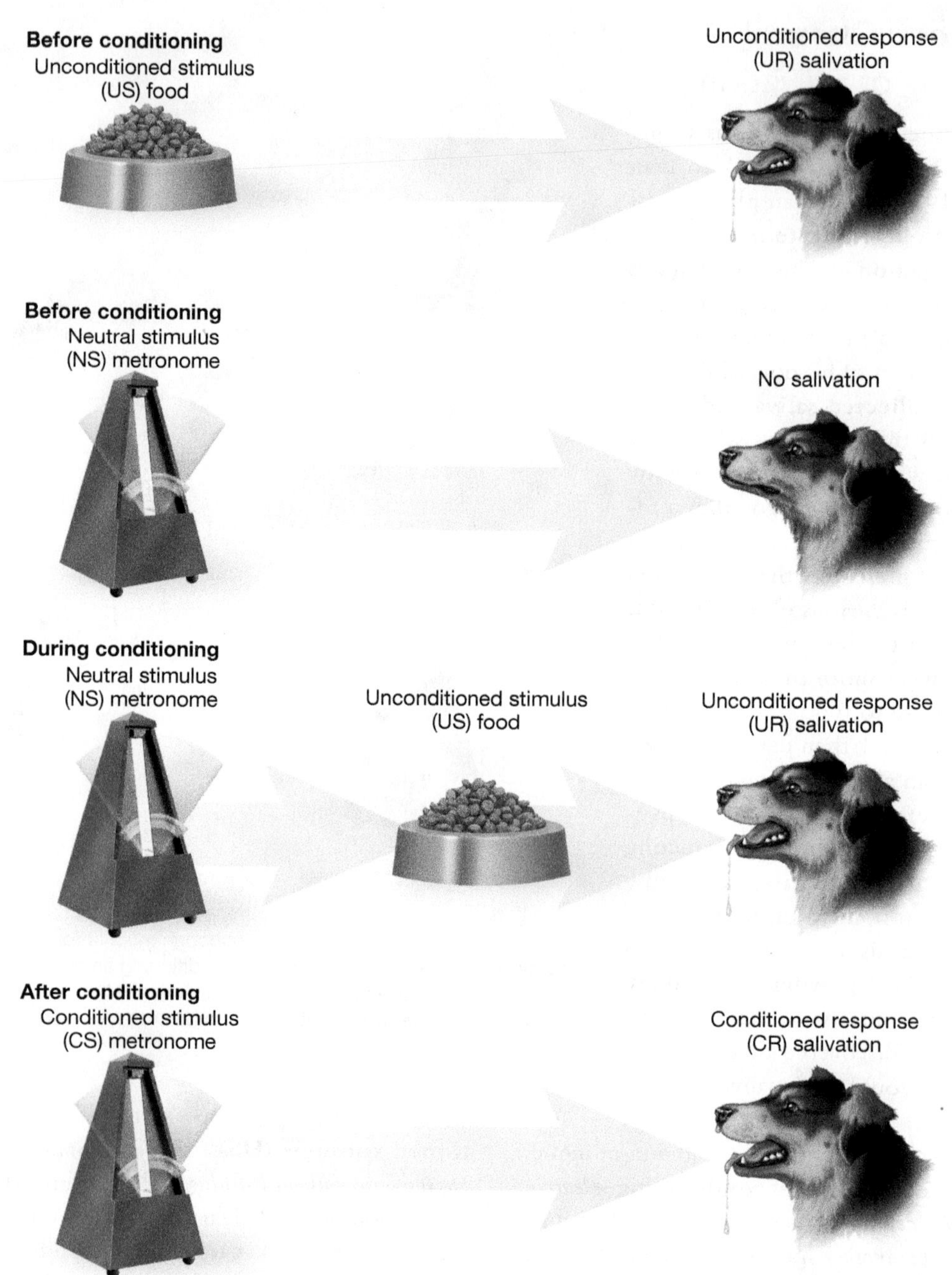

Explore
Three Stages of Classical Conditioning

{FIG. 6.2} **Pavlov's Salivary Conditioning Experiment** Food elicits the unconditioned response of salivation. Before conditioning, the tone elicits no response by the dog. During conditioning, the tone repeatedly precedes the food. After conditioning, the tone alone elicits salivation. **Click on this figure in your eText to see more details.**

paired with, and therefore predicts, an unconditioned stimulus. In Pavlov's experiment, the tone was *originally* a neutral stimulus because it did not elicit a response, least of all salivation (see Figure 6.2); however, over time, the tone began to influence the dogs' responses because of its association with food. In this case, the tone became a **conditioned stimulus (CS)**, *a once-neutral stimulus that later elicits a conditioned response because it has a history of being paired with an unconditioned stimulus.* A **conditioned response (CR)** *is the learned response that occurs to the conditioned stimulus.* After being repeatedly paired with the US, the once neutral tone in Pavlov's experiment became a conditioned stimulus (CS) because it elicited the conditioned response of salivation. To establish that conditioning has taken place, the tone (CS) must elicit salivation in the *absence* of food (US; see the bottom panel of Figure 6.2).

A common point of confusion is the difference between a conditioned response and an unconditioned response—in Pavlov's experiment, they are both salivation. What distinguishes the UR from the CR is the stimulus that elicits them. Salivation is a UR if it occurs in response to a US (food). Salivation is a CR if it occurs in response to a CS (the tone). A CS can have this effect only if it becomes *associated* with a US. In other words, UR is a naturally occurring response whereas a CR must be *learned*.

CLASSICAL CONDITIONING AND THE BRAIN As noted above, classical conditioning can occur in extremely simple organisms such as *Aplysia*, a type of sea slug (Hawkins, 1984; Pinsker et al., 1970). Of course, the number of possible conditioned responses is more limited in the sea slug than in humans. But, the fact that both of these species can be classically conditioned suggests that at its heart, classical conditioning is a simple biological process. The connections between specific groups of neurons (or specific axon terminals and receptors sites on neurons) become strengthened during each instance of classical conditioning (Murphy & Glanzman, 1997).

In most conditioning experiments, the US reliably triggers the UR; this relationship is thought to be represented by strong neural connections between groups of neurons in the temporal lobes of the brain. But, what happens when the CS is presented at approximately the same time as the US? According to the Hebb Rule (named after Canadian neurologist Donald Hebb; see Module 7.1), when a weak connection between neurons is stimulated at the same time as a strong connection, the weak connection becomes strengthened. So, before conditioning, there may be a strong connection between a puff of air and a blinking response and a weak connection between a tone and the blinking response. But, if both networks are stimulated at the same time, the link between the tone and the blinking response would be strengthened. Over repeated conditioning trials, this connection would become strong enough that the tone itself would trigger an eyeblink (see Figure 6.3).

When reading these examples, it's quite easy to think of conditioning as something unrelated to your life. Not many of us undergo eyeblink conditioning. But these principles still apply to your everyday existence. For instance, some of you may live in an old house; if someone flushes the toilet while you're in the shower, the water turns scalding hot for a few seconds. Over time, the sound of the toilet flushing in your house would likely make you jump back slightly. What do you think the US, UR, CS, and CR would be in this situation? The shriek-inducing hot water would be the US and your response—jumping back out of the water—would be the UR. Over time, the sound of the toilet flushing would be the CS, because it would trigger CR, which would again be the jumping response. Importantly, as you will read in the next section of this module, the strength of these networks—and thus of the conditioning—will vary depending upon how often and how consistently the CS and the US appear together.

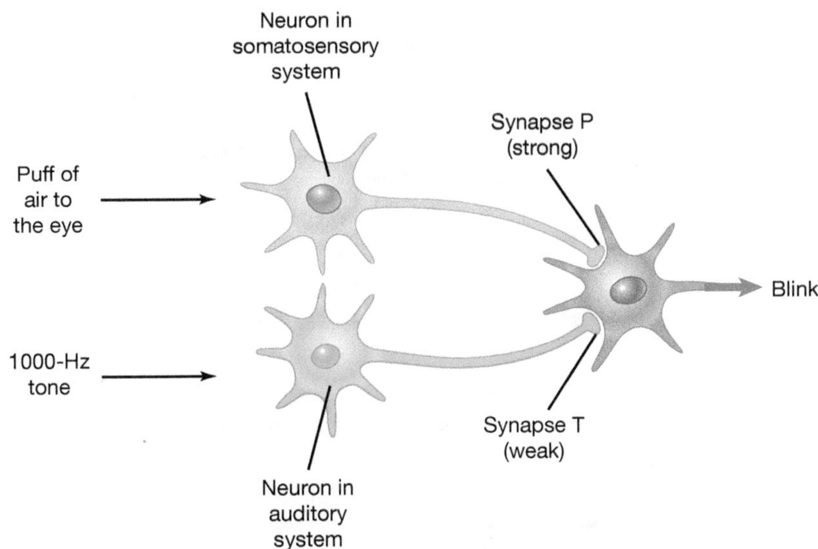

{FIG. 6.3} **Conditioning and Synapses** During conditioning, weak synapses fire at the same time as related strong synapses. The simultaneous activity strengthens the connections in the weaker synapse.

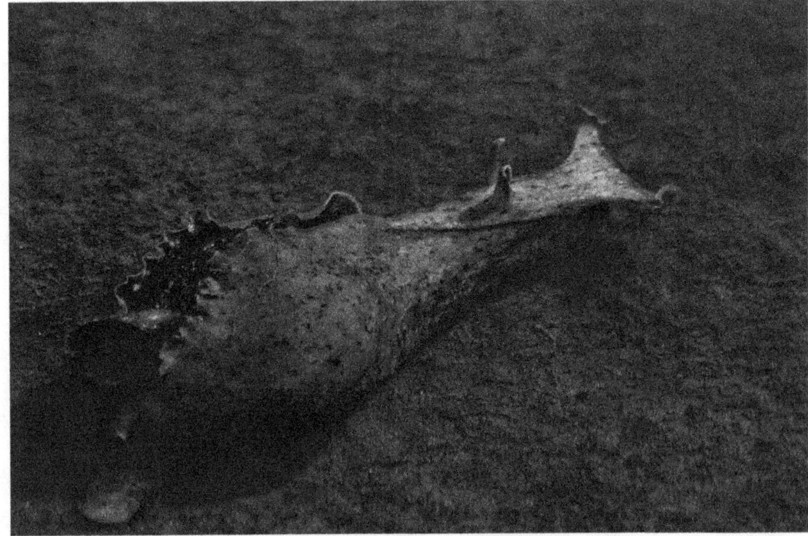

Elliotte Rusty Harold/Shutterstock

Even neurologically simple organisms like the *Aplysia* can be classically conditioned.

Quick Quiz 6.1a

Pavlov's Dogs: Classical Conditioning of Salivation

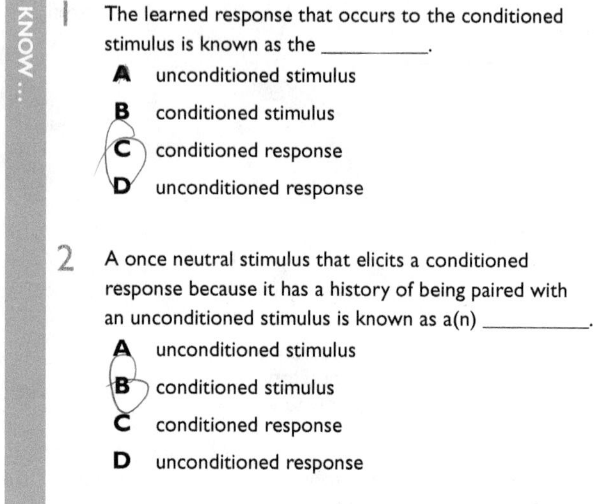

KNOW ...

1 The learned response that occurs to the conditioned stimulus is known as the ________.

- **A** unconditioned stimulus
- **B** conditioned stimulus
- **C** conditioned response
- **D** unconditioned response

2 A once neutral stimulus that elicits a conditioned response because it has a history of being paired with an unconditioned stimulus is known as a(n) ________.

- **A** unconditioned stimulus
- **B** conditioned stimulus
- **C** conditioned response
- **D** unconditioned response

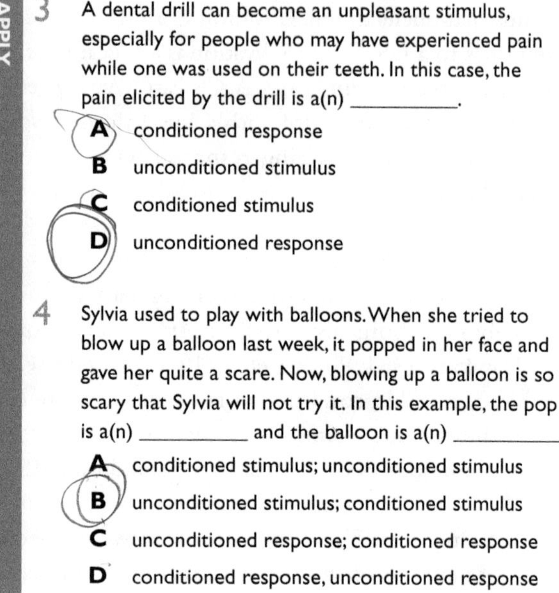

APPLY ...

3 A dental drill can become an unpleasant stimulus, especially for people who may have experienced pain while one was used on their teeth. In this case, the pain elicited by the drill is a(n) ________.

- **A** conditioned response
- **B** unconditioned stimulus
- **C** conditioned stimulus
- **D** unconditioned response

4 Sylvia used to play with balloons. When she tried to blow up a balloon last week, it popped in her face and gave her quite a scare. Now, blowing up a balloon is so scary that Sylvia will not try it. In this example, the pop is a(n) ________ and the balloon is a(n) ________.

- **A** conditioned stimulus; unconditioned stimulus
- **B** unconditioned stimulus; conditioned stimulus
- **C** unconditioned response; conditioned response
- **D** conditioned response, unconditioned response

Answers can be found on page ANS-2.

Processes of Classical Conditioning

Although classically conditioned responses typically involve reflexive actions, there is still a great deal of flexibility in how long they will last and how specific they will be. Conditioned responses may be very strong and reliable, which is likely if the CS and the US have a long history of being paired together. Conditioned responding may diminish over time, or it may occur with new stimuli with which the response has never been paired. We now turn to some processes that account for the flexibility of classically conditioned responses.

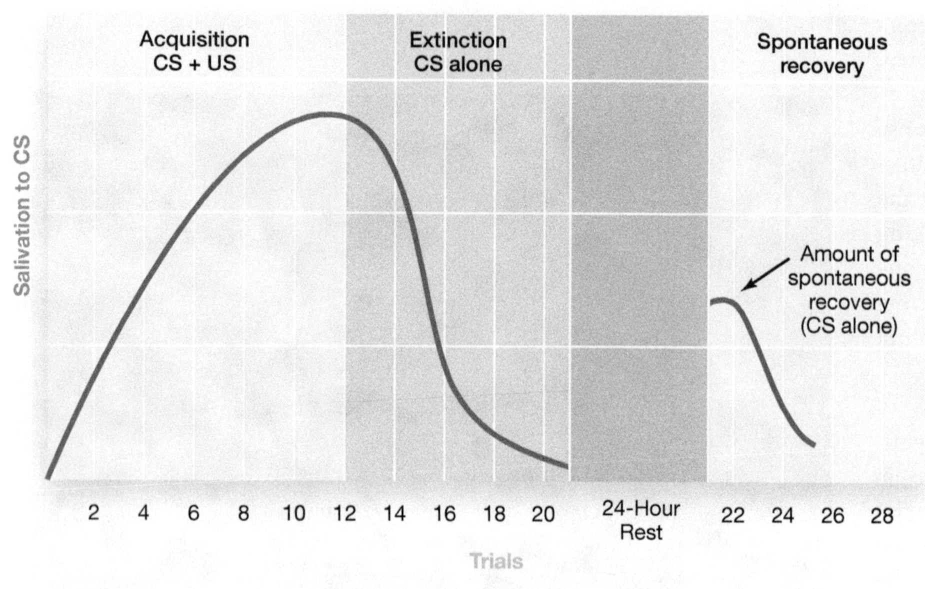

{FIG. 6.4} **Acquisition, Extinction, and Spontaneous Recovery** *Acquisition* of a conditioned response occurs over repeated pairings of the CS and the US. If the US no longer occurs, conditioned responding diminishes—a process called *extinction*. Often, following a time interval in which the CS does not occur, conditioned responding rebounds when the CS is presented again—a phenomenon called *spontaneous recovery*.

ACQUISITION, EXTINCTION, AND SPONTANEOUS RECOVERY Learning involves a change in behaviour due to experience, which can include acquiring a new response. **Acquisition** *is the initial phase of learning in which a response is established*; thus, in classical conditioning, acquisition is the phase in which a neutral stimulus is repeatedly paired with the US. In Pavlov's experiment, the conditioned salivary response was *acquired* with numerous tone–food pairings (see Figure 6.4). A critical part of acquisition is the predictability with which the CS and the US occur together. In Pavlov's experiment, conditioning either would not occur or would be very weak if food was delivered only sometimes (i.e., inconsistently) when the tone was sounded. There may be a neural explanation for this phenomenon; synapses are strengthened when neurons (or groups of neurons) fire at the same time, as in conditioning. For instance, the activity of cells in the amygdala steadily increases as animals are conditioned with either an electrical shock (Quirk et al., 1995) or food (Gallagher et al., 1990) serving as the US. But, this simultaneous firing would be less frequent if the CS and US were not always paired together; and, the synapses that are related to this conditioning would therefore be weaker than if the pairing occurred more frequently.

Of course, even if a conditioned response is fully acquired, there is no guarantee it will persist forever. **Extinction** *is the loss or weakening of a conditioned response when a conditioned stimulus and unconditioned stimulus no longer occur together.* For the dogs in Pavlov's experiment, if a tone is presented repeatedly and no food follows, then salivation should occur less and less, until eventually it may not occur at all (Figure 6.4). This trend probably makes sense from a biological perspective: If the tone is no longer a reliable predictor of food, then salivation becomes unnecessary. At the neural level, the rate of firing in brain areas related to the learned association decreases over the course of extinction (Robleto et al., 2004). However, even after extinction occurs, a previously established conditioned response can return.

A number of studies have shown that classically conditioned behaviours that had disappeared due to extinction could quickly reappear if the CS was paired with the US again. This tendency suggests that the networks of brain areas related to conditioning were preserved in some form (Schreurs, 1993; Schreurs et al., 1998). Additionally, some animals (and humans) show **spontaneous recovery**, *or the reoccurrence of a previously extinguished conditioned response, typically after some time has passed since extinction.* Pavlov and his assistants noticed that salivation would reappear when the dogs were later returned to the experimental testing room where acquisition and extinction trials had been conducted. The dogs would also salivate again in response to a tone, albeit less so than at the end of acquisition (Figure 6.4). Why would salivation spontaneously return after the response had supposedly extinguished? One possibility is that extinction also involves learning something new (Bouton, 1994). In this case, Pavlov's dogs would be learning that a tone indicates that food will *not* appear. It is possible that spontaneous recovery is a case of the animal not being able to retrieve the memory of extinction and thus reverting back to the original memory, the classically conditioned response (Bouton, 2002; Brooks et al., 1999).

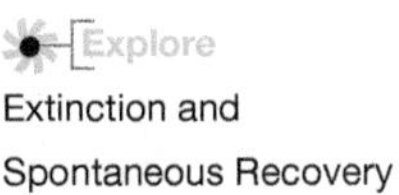

Extinction and Spontaneous Recovery

Extinction and spontaneous recovery are evidence that classically conditioned responses can change once they are acquired. Further evidence of flexibility of conditioned responding can be seen in some other processes of classical conditioning, including generalization and discrimination learning.

STIMULUS GENERALIZATION AND DISCRIMINATION Stimulus **generalization** *is a process in which a response that originally occurs to a specific stimulus also occurs to different, though similar, stimuli.* In Pavlov's experiment, dogs salivated not just to the original tone (CS), but also to very similar tones (see Figure 6.5). At the cellular level, generalization may be explained, at least in part, by the Hebb rule discussed above. When we perceive a

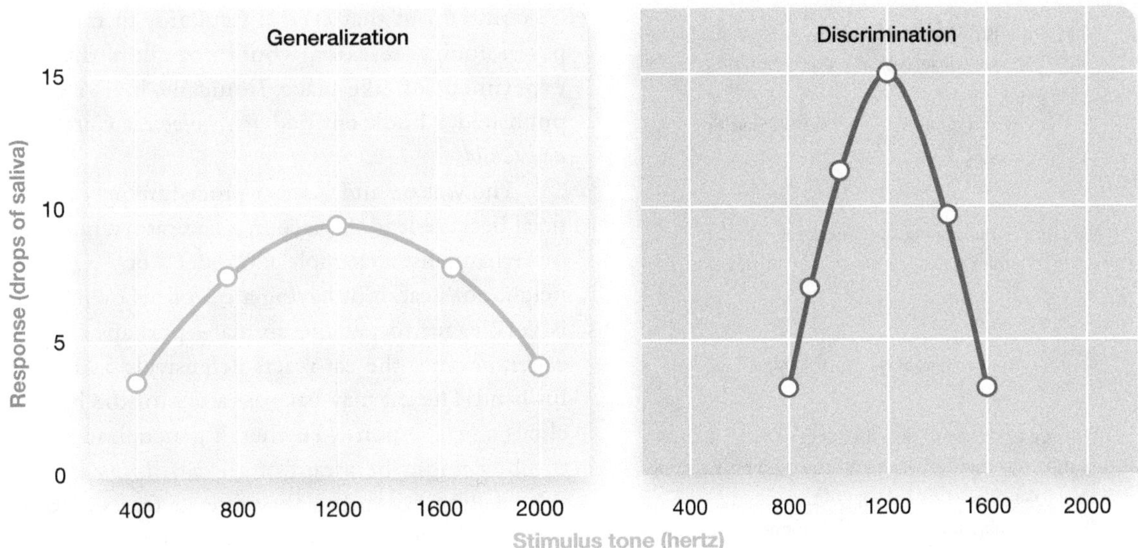

{FIG. 6.5} **Stimulus Generalization and Discrimination** A conditioned response may generalize to other similar stimuli. In this case, salivation occurs not just to the 1200-Hz tone used during conditioning, but to other tones as well. Discrimination learning has occurred when responding is elicited by the original training stimulus, but much less so, if at all, to other stimuli.

stimulus, it activates not only our brain's representation of that item, but also our representations of related items. Some of these additional representations (e.g., a tone that has a slightly higher or lower pitch than the conditioned stimulus) may become activated at the same time as the synapses involved in conditioned responses. If this did occur, according to the Hebb rule, the additional synapse would become strengthened and would therefore be more likely to fire along with the other cells in the future.

Generalization allows for flexibility in learned behaviours, although it is certainly possible for behaviour to be *too* flexible. Salivating in response to *any* sound would be wasteful because not every sound correctly predicts food. Thus Pavlov's dogs also showed **discrimination**, *which occurs when an organism learns to respond to one original stimulus but not to new stimuli that may be similar to the original stimulus.* In salivary conditioning, the CS might be a 1200-hertz tone, which is the only sound that is paired with food. The experimenter might produce tones of 1100 or 1300 hertz as well, but not pair these with food. This point is critical: If stimuli that are similar to the CS are presented *without* a US, then it becomes *less* likely that these stimuli will lead to stimulus generalization. Instead, these other tones would have their own memory representation in the brain—in which they did *not* receive food. So, stimulus discrimination would occur if salivation was triggered by the target 1200-hertz tone, but much less so, if at all, by other tones (Figure 6.5).

Explore
Stimulus Generalization and Stimulus Discrimination in Classical Conditioning

Explore
Stimulus Generalization and Stimulus Discrimination in Operant Conditioning

Quick Quiz 6.1b
Processes of Classical Conditioning

KNOW ...

1 What is the reoccurrence of a previously extinguished conditioned response, typically after some time has passed since extinction?

A Extinction
B Spontaneous recovery
C Acquisition
D Discrimination

UNDERSTAND ...

2 In classical conditioning, the process during which a neutral stimulus becomes a conditioned stimulus is known as _________.

A extinction
B spontaneous recovery
C acquisition
D discrimination

APPLY ...

3 Your dog barks every time a stranger's car pulls into the driveway, but not when you come home. Reacting to your car differently is a sign of _________.

A discrimination
B generalization
C spontaneous recovery
D acquisition

Answers can be found on page ANS-2.

Explore
Classical Conditioning of Little Albert

Watch
Special Topics: Learning to Overcome Phobias

Applications of Classical Conditioning

Now that you are familiar with the basic processes of classical conditioning, we can begin to explore its many applications. Classical conditioning is a common phenomenon that applies to many different situations, including emotional learning, aversions to certain foods, advertising, and sexual responses.

CONDITIONED EMOTIONAL RESPONSES Psychologists dating back to John Watson in the 1920s recognized that our emotional responses could be influenced by classical conditioning (Paul & Blumenthal, 1989; Watson & Rayner, 1920). These **conditioned emotional responses** *consist of emotional and physiological responses that develop to a specific object or situation.* In one of the earliest, and most diabolical, studies of conditioned emotional responses, Watson and Rayner conditioned an 11-month-old child known as Albert B. (also referred to as "Little Albert") to fear white rats. When they presented Albert with a white rat, he showed no fear at first, and even reached out for the animal. Then, while Albert was in the vicinity of the rat, they startled him by striking a steel bar with a hammer. Watson and Rayner reported that Albert quickly associated the rat with the startling sound; the child soon showed a conditioned emotional response just to the rat. In this situation, the loud noise would be the US and fear would be the UR; over time, the white rat became the CS with fear being the CR. Little Albert not only developed a fear of rats, the emotional conditioning generalized to other white furry objects including a rabbit and a Santa Claus mask. It should be pointed out that ethical standards in modern-day psychological research would not allow this type of experiment to take place. Ironically, in 1928, Watson published a book entitled *Psychological Care of Infant and Child.*

The Watson and Rayner procedure may seem artificial because it took place in a laboratory, but here is a more naturalistic example. Consider a boy who sees his neighbour's cat. Not having a cat of his own, the child is very eager to pet the animal—perhaps a little too eager, because the cat reacts defensively and scratches his hand. The cat may become a CS for the boy, which elicits a fear response. Further, if generalization occurs, the boy might be afraid of all cats. Now imagine if this reaction becomes a very intense fear: Conditioned emotional responses like these offer a possible explanation for many phobias, which are intense, irrational fears of specific objects or situations (discussed in detail in Module 15.2).

Archives of the History of American Psychology, The Center for the History of Psychology-The University of Akron

Watson and Rayner generalized Albert's fear of white rats to other furry, white objects. Shown here, Watson tests Albert's reaction to a Santa Claus mask. For those interested, Little Albert passed away as a result of a brain illness (i.e., for reasons unrelated to this study) at the age of 5 (Beck et al., 2009; Fridlund et al., 2012). **Click on this image in your eText to see video footage of Little Albert.**

During the past two decades, researchers have made great strides in identifying the brain regions responsible for such conditioned emotional responses. When an organism learns a fear-related association such as a tone predicting the onset of a startling noise, activity occurs in the amygdala, a brain area related to fear (LeDoux, 1995; Maren, 2001; see Modules 3.3 and 11.4). If an organism learns to fear a particular location, such as learning that a certain cage is associated with an electrical shock, then context-related activity in the hippocampus will interact with fear-related activity in the amygdala to produce *contextual fear conditioning* (Kim & Fanselow, 1992; Phillips & LeDoux, 1992).

Fear conditioning procedures have also been used to examine learning and emotional processes in a number of clinical populations. Often, these procedures are combined with neuroimaging techniques (see Module 3.4) to examine both the cognitive and the biological components of these behaviours. For example, scientists have conducted some fascinating experiments on people diagnosed with psychopathy (the diagnosis of "psychopathy" is very similar to antisocial personality disorder, a topic we discuss later in other chapters of this textbook). People with this disorder are notorious for disregarding the feelings of others. In one study, a sample of people diagnosed with psychopathy looked at brief presentations of human faces (the CS) followed by a painful stimulus (the US). The painful stimulus would then trigger a negative emotional response (the UR). What *should* have happened is that, over repeated pairings,

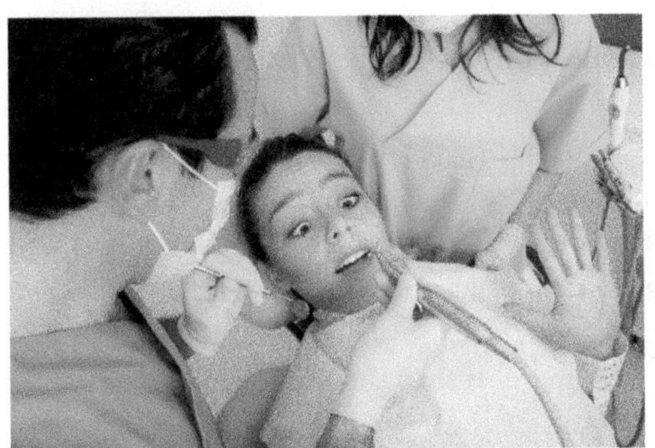

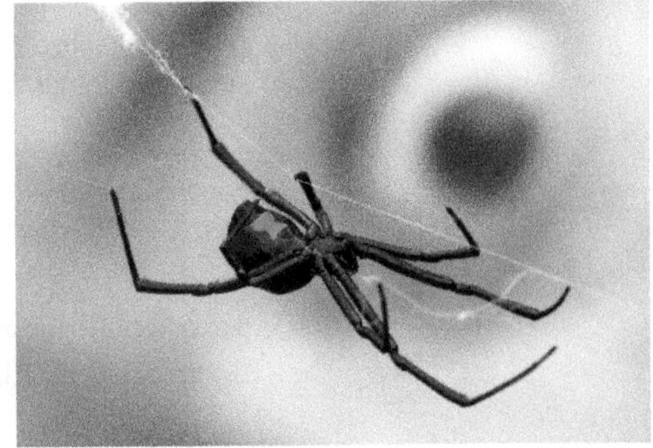

Left: Özgür Donmaz/iStockphoto.com; centre: Silvia Boratti/iStockphoto.com; right: Mark Kostich/iStockphoto.com

Some commonly feared objects and situations. Psychologists are finding that we are predisposed to fear specific objects that have posed threats over our evolutionary history.

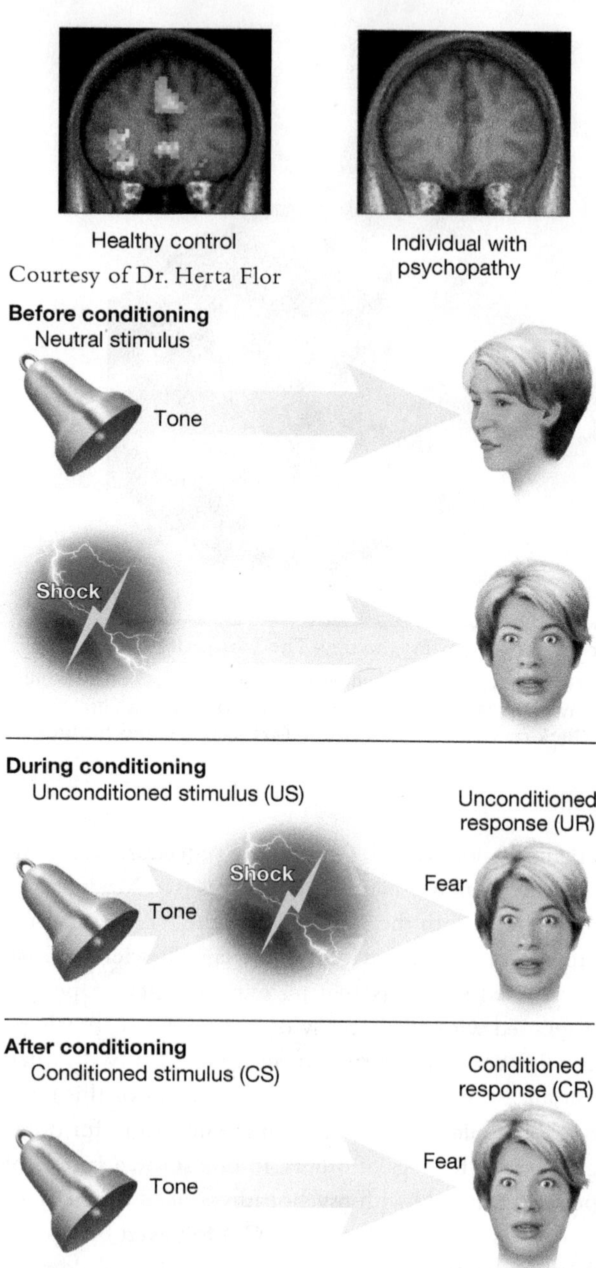

{FIG. 6.6} **Fear Conditioning and the Brain** During fear conditioning, a neutral stimulus (NS) such as a tone or a picture of a human face is briefly presented followed by an unconditioned stimulus (US), such as a mild electric shock. The result is a conditioned fear response to the CS. A procedure like this has been used to compare fear responses in people diagnosed with psychopathy with control participants. The brain images above show that those with psychopathy (right image) show very little responding in their emotional brain circuitry when presented with the CS. In contrast, control participants show strong activation in their emotional brain centres (left image) (Birbaumer et al., 2005).

participants would acquire a negative emotional reaction (the CR) to the faces (the CS); but, this particular sample did not react this way. Instead, these individuals showed very little physiological arousal, their emotional brain centres remained quiet, and overall they did not seem to mind looking at pictures of faces that had been paired with pain (see Figure 6.6; Birbaumer et al., 2005). People who showed no signs of psychopathy did not enjoy this experience. In fact, following several pairings between CS and US, the control group showed increased physiological arousal and activity of the emotion centres of the brain, and understandably reported disliking the experience of the experiment.

EVOLUTIONARY ROLE FOR FEAR CONDITIONING A healthy fear response is important for survival, but not all situations or objects are equally dangerous. Snakes and heights probably elicit more fear and caution than butterflies or freshly mown grass. In fact, fearing snakes is very common, which makes it tempting to conclude that we have an *instinct* to fear them. In reality, young primates (both human children and young monkeys, for example) tend to be quite curious about, or at least indifferent to, snakes, so this fear is most likely the product of learning rather than instinct.

Psychologists have conducted some ingenious experiments to address how learning is involved in snake fear. For instance, photographs of snakes (the CS) were paired with a mild electric shock (the US). One unconditioned response that a shock elicits is increased palm sweat—known as the skin conductance response. This reaction, part of the fight-or-flight response generated by the autonomic nervous system (Module 3.3), occurs when our bodies are aroused by a threatening or uncomfortable stimulus. Following several pairings between snake photos and shock in an experimental setting, the snake photos alone (the CS) elicited a strong increase in skin conductance response (the CR). For comparison, participants were also shown nonthreatening pictures of flowers, paired with the shock. Much less intense conditioned responding developed in response to pictures of flowers, even though the pictures had been paired with the shock just as many times as the snake pictures had been paired with the shock (Figure 6.7; Öhman & Mineka, 2001). Thus, it appears we are predisposed to acquire a fear of snakes, but not flowers.

This finding may not be too surprising, but what about other potentially dangerous objects such as guns? In modern times, guns are far more often associated with death or injury than snakes, and certainly flowers. When the researchers paired pictures of guns (the CS) with the shock (US), they found that conditioned arousal to guns among participants was less than that to snake photos, and comparable to that of harmless flowers. In addition, the conditioned arousal to snake photos proved longer lasting and slower to extinguish than the conditioned responding to pictures of guns or flowers (Öhman & Mineka, 2001). However, before completely accepting this finding, it is important to point out that the participants in this study were from Stockholm, Sweden, a city that has relatively little gun violence. It is unclear whether similar results would be found in participants who lived in a location where gun violence was more prevalent.

This caveat aside, given that guns and snakes both have the potential to be dangerous, why is it so much easier to learn a fear of snakes than a fear of guns? One possibility is that over time, humans have evolved a strong predisposition to fear an animal that has a long history of causing severe injury or death (Cook et al., 1986; Öhman & Mineka, 2001). The survival advantage has gone to those who quickly learned to avoid animals such as snakes. The same is not true for flowers (which do not attack humans) or guns (which are relatively new in our species' history). This explanation is known as **preparedness**, *the biological predisposition to rapidly learn a response to a particular class of stimuli* (Seligman, 1971). Preparedness helps make sense of these research findings from an evolutionary perspective.

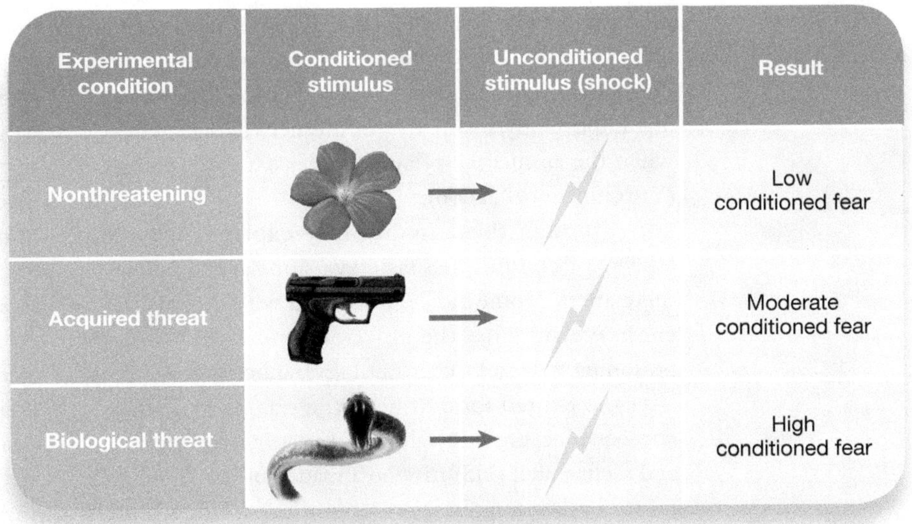

{FIG. 6.7} **Biologically Prepared Fear** Physiological measures of fear are highest in response to photos of snakes after the photos are paired with an electric shock—even higher than the responses to photos of guns. Flowers—something that humans generally do not need to fear in nature—are least effective when it comes to conditioning fear responses.

CONDITIONED TASTE AVERSIONS Another example of an evolutionarily useful conditioned fear response comes from food aversions. Chances are there is a food that you cannot stand to even look at because it once made you ill. This new aversion isn't due to chance; rather, your brain and body have linked the taste, sight, and smell of that food to the feeling of nausea. In this situation, the taste (and often the sight and smell) of the food or fluid serves as the CS. The US is the experience of feeling sick; this, in turn, leads to behavioural responses related to aversion (the UR). Aversion is not simply a case of "feeling gross." Instead, it involves both a feeling (and in some species, a facial expression) of disgust *and* a withdrawal or avoidance response. When the CS and US are linked, the taste of the food or fluid soon produces aversion responses, even in the absence of physical illness. (the CR; see Figure 6.8). This *acquired dislike or disgust of a food or drink because it was paired with illness is known as* **conditioned taste aversion** (Garcia et al., 1966).

Conditioned taste aversions may develop in a variety of ways, such as through illness associated with food poisoning, the flu, medical procedures, or excessive intoxication. Importantly, these conditioned aversions only occur for the flavour of a particular food rather than to other stimuli that may have been present when you became ill. For example, if you were listening to a particular song while you got sick from eating tainted spinach or a two-week-old tuna sandwich, your aversion would develop to the taste of spinach, but not to the song that was playing. Thus, humans (and many other animals) are biologically prepared to associate food, but not sound, with illness (Garcia et al., 1966).

Neuroimaging studies provide us with additional insights into conditioned taste aversions. These studies show responses in brain areas related to disgust and emotional arousal (Yamamoto, 2007) as well as in brain stem regions related to vomiting (Reilly & Bornovalova, 2005; Yamamoto & Fujimoto, 1991). Additionally, neurons in reward centres in the brain show altered patterns of activity to the food associated with illness (Yamamoto et al., 1989). These different brain responses suggest that

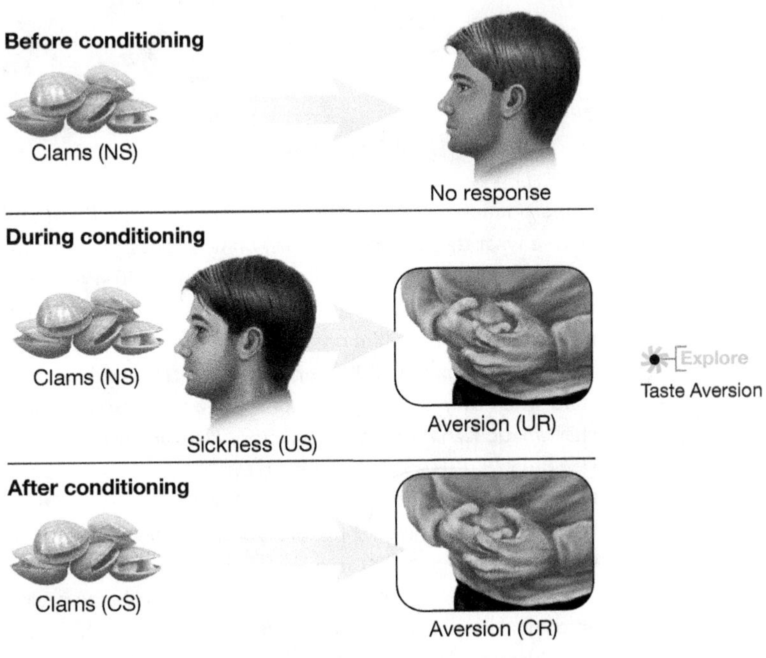

{FIG. 6.8} **Conditioned Taste Aversions** Classical conditioning can account for the development of taste aversions. Falling ill after eating a particular food can result in conditioned feelings of disgust as well as withdrawal responses when you are later re-exposed to the taste, smell, or texture of the food.

Explore
Taste Aversion

illness triggers a strong emotional response that causes the reward centres to update their representation of the illness-causing food, thus making that food less rewarding. Importantly, many parts of this network are activated when the animal (or person) is later exposed to the CS (Yasoshima et al., 2006).

Although these studies may explain how some aspects of conditioned taste aversions are maintained, there are still some riddles associated with this phenomenon. For instance, the onset of symptoms from food poisoning may not occur until several hours have passed after the tainted food or beverage was consumed. As a consequence, the interval between tasting the food (CS) and feeling sick (US) may be a matter of hours, whereas most conditioning happens only if the CS and the US occur very closely to each other in time. Another peculiarity is that taste aversions are learned very quickly—a single CS-US pairing is typically sufficient. These special characteristics of taste aversions are extremely important for survival. The flexibility offered by a long window of time separating CS and US, as well as the requirement for only a single exposure, raises the chances of acquiring an important aversion to the offending substance.

One potential explanation for these characteristics involves the food stimuli themselves. Usually, a conditioned taste aversion develops to something we have ingested that has an unfamiliar flavour. If you have eaten the same ham and Swiss cheese sandwich at lunch for years, and you become ill one afternoon after eating it, you will be less prone to develop a conditioned taste aversion. This scenario can be explained by *latent inhibition*, which occurs when frequent experience with a stimulus before it is paired with a US makes it less likely that conditioning will occur after a single episode of illness (Lubow & Moore, 1959). Latent inhibition applies to many instances in which classical conditioning can occur—not just to conditioned taste aversions. For example, a child who is clawed by the family cat after years of otherwise friendly interactions is less likely to develop a fear of cats than a child who is scratched during her very first encounter with a cat. The unfamiliarity of foods that trigger conditioned taste aversions likely makes it easier for these conditioned responses to occur. Such foods stick out when they are experienced for the first time and are therefore much easier to remember, even after considerable time has passed.

Conditioned taste aversions are a naturally occurring experience. However, conditioned emotional responses are also being created by advertisers to influence our responses. As you will read in the next section, food is not the only stimulus that can make you feel sick.

WORKING THE SCIENTIFIC LITERACY MODEL

Conditioning and Negative Political Advertising

Some politicians have charisma; you want to like them and believe what they say. Examples fall on both sides of the political spectrum. U.S. President Ronald Reagan (1980–1988) was so beloved that some journalists were instructed not to say negative things about him on camera. Bill Clinton (1992–2000) and Barack Obama (2009–present) are treated like rock stars when they travel internationally. We have also had fairly charismatic Canadian politicians. Both Liberal Pierre Trudeau (1968–1979, 1980–1984) and Progressive Conservative Brian Mulroney (1984–1993) seemed quite likeable for most of their time as Prime Minister. Not everyone has this type of charisma, however. In these cases, politicians need to use advertising and carefully constructed "photo ops" in order to create emotional responses that might influence voting behaviours. In an ideal world, these advertisements would focus on issues and would highlight the candidates' positive qualities. Unfortunately, the last few decades have seen a dramatic upsurge in a different form of advertising: negative attack ads. As you will see, many aspects of these advertisements rely on the principles of classical conditioning and, in the process, treat you, the voter, like one of Pavlov's dogs.

What do we know about classical conditioning in negative political advertising?

Negative political advertisements routinely include unflattering images. In the next federal or provincial election, pay attention to the commercials that are sponsored by each party. You will see a few tricks. First, many images of opponents will be black-and-white and of a grainy quality; this trick is designed to make viewers feel mildly frustrated when viewing the slightly unclear photographs. Second, the images of the attacked politicians will include them expressing a negative emotion. In some, they will be yelling (angry faces trigger a physiological response in people). In others, they will have facial expressions that appear smug, or that make it seem as though they feel contempt toward the person they're looking at (which, in this case, would appear to be *you*). The assumption underlying these attack ads is that if you pair a party leader with imagery that generates unpleasant emotions, then viewers will associate that leader with negative feelings and be less likely to vote for that party.

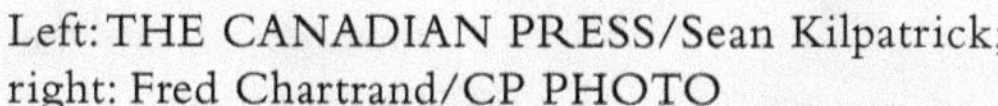
Left: THE CANADIAN PRESS/Sean Kilpatrick; right: Fred Chartrand/CP PHOTO

Most attack ads use grainy, black-and-white images of the opponent in the hope that the frustration associated with seeing an unclear image will become associated with the person depicted in that photograph.

In this case, the CS would be the attacked politician. The US would be the negative imagery. The UR would be the negative emotional response to the imagery (or unflattering photograph). Eventually, the individuals who constructed the ad would hope that simply seeing the attacked person would produce a negative emotional response (CS) along with the thought, "I will not vote for him or her."

The question, then, is "Does this work?"

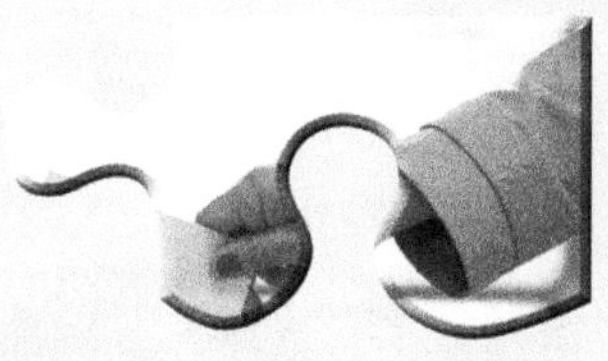

How can science help explain the role of classical conditioning in negative political advertising?

An attempt to use negative emotions to alter people's opinions of political candidates is similar to a psychology research technique known as *evaluative conditioning*. In an evaluative conditioning study, experimenters pair a stimulus (e.g., a shape) with either positive or negative stimuli (e.g., an angry face). The repeated association of a stimulus with an emotion leads participants to develop a positive or negative feeling toward that stimulus (depending upon the emotional pairing). This is precisely what political strategists are attempting to do when they show unpleasant pictures of an opponent and pair it with angry narrators and emotional labels. And, in the laboratory, evaluative conditioning works. This phenomenon has been found with visual, auditory, olfactory (smell), taste, and tactile (touch) stimuli. It has been used to alter feelings toward objects ranging from snack foods (Lebens et al., 2011) to consumer brands (Walther & Grigoriadis, 2004) to novel shapes (Olson & Fazio, 2001).

A number of studies have specifically attempted to use conditioning to create negative attitudes toward products or behaviours (Moore et al., 1982; Zanna et al., 1970), a goal similar to the attack ads you see each election. For instance, Stuart and colleagues (1990) found that associating a new brand of toothpaste with negative pictures decreased evaluations of that product. Other research has shown that undesirable music has similar effects. In research conducted at the University of British Columbia, Gerald Gorn (1982) paired a CS, a pen, with either positively evaluated music (from the film *Grease*) or undesirable music (in this case, classical East Indian music). Participants were later given a choice of one of two pens, one of which was from their earlier positive or negative conditioning experience. Only 30% of the participants who had associated a particular pen with the undesirable music selected that pen, suggesting that the pen had become a CS. Although these studies aren't directly testing ways to manipulate your like or dislike of particular leaders, they *are* demonstrating that conditioning can be used to influence attitudes and behaviours.

Can we critically evaluate this information?

A major question, both with negative political advertising and with the Gorn (1982) study, is whether producing a negative opinion of one option (be it a pen or a candidate) automatically means that you are producing a positive opinion of the other option. In the Gorn study, there were only two options, so we can't tell if the results are due to liking one option or disliking the other option. The same issue arises with regard to studies of U.S. politics—there are only two parties. However, with five political parties running in the next federal election in Canada, there is a danger that attack ads might produce negative opinions of the target, but still not boost opinions of the party running the ads.

We also need to consider the fact that Canada is a vastly multicultural country, particularly in large urban centres like Toronto and Vancouver. Research has shown that different cultures will respond to negative advertising in different ways (Chuang, 2006). Additionally, people with different education levels or who differ in terms of socioeconomic status might also vary in how they respond to these types of ads (Chou & Lien, 2011). These concerns are not lost on politicians, however. In fact, many of the ads that you are exposed to are not targeted at you. Instead, they have been carefully crafted to influence the opinions of specific groups, such as undecided voters, students, and so on (Pinkleton, 1997). Doing so increases the likelihood that viewers will have the emotional reaction that makes up the US and CR in the conditioned emotional response.

Of course, politicians also need to be careful not to overstep certain boundaries that might create sympathy for the target of the negative ads. In October 1993, the ruling Progressive Conservative Party broadcast two television commercials that highlighted the partial facial paralysis of Liberal leader (and future Prime Minister) Jean Chrétien. One ad asked, "Is this a Prime Minister?" Another had a female narrator stating, "I personally would be embarrassed if he were to become the Prime Minister of Canada." The goal of the commercials was not to attack Chrétien's political credentials or experience, which far surpassed those of the other party leaders (who were relatively inexperienced). Instead, the ads were designed to link the negative emotion associated with physical deformities, and any stigma associated with those injuries, to the Liberal party so that people would feel uneasy about voting for this party. It didn't work. The public outcry in response to the commercials caused the Conservatives to withdraw the ads after a day; indeed, people who saw the ads were likely to sympathize with Chrétien and feel anger toward Conservative leader Kim Campbell (Haddock & Zanna, 1997). The Liberals won the election handily, with the Conservatives being reduced to three seats in the House of Commons.

Allstar Picture Library/Alamy

Negative ads can backfire if the public views them as overly personal or insensitive. Mocking Jean Chrétien's facial paralysis led to a disastrous outcome for the Progressive Conservative party in the 1993 election.

Why is this relevant?

Dozens of studies indicate that people are prone to a *third-person effect* whereby they assume that other people are more affected by advertising and mass media messages than they themselves are (Cheng & Riffe, 2008; Perloff, 2002). Thus, there appears to be a disconnect between the power of negative advertising and people's awareness of its effects. It is important to realize that conditioning often occurs without our conscious awareness. Our brains are designed to make associations; it's how we learn. So, by becoming aware of how marketing companies and politicians are using classical conditioning to influence how you vote, you can try to reduce the effect of their manipulation. That way, when you cast your vote, it will hopefully be because of issues you care about and not because of conditioned emotional responses.

Christian Schwier/Fotolia

Quick Quiz 6.1c
Applications of Classical Conditioning

KNOW ...

1 Conditioning a response can take longer if the subject experiences the conditioned stimulus repeatedly before it is actually paired with a US. This phenomenon is known as ______.

A preparedness
B extinction
C latent inhibition
D acquisition

UNDERSTAND ...

2 Why are humans biologically *prepared* to fear snakes and not guns?

A Guns kill fewer people than do snakes.
B Guns are a more recent addition to our evolutionary history.
C Snakes are more predictable than guns.
D Guns are not a natural phenomenon, whereas snakes do occur in nature.

APPLY ...

3 A television advertisement for beer shows young people at the beach drinking and having fun. Based on classical conditioning principles, the advertisers are hoping you will buy the beer because the commercial elicits

A a conditioned emotional response of pleasure.
B a conditioned emotional response of fear.
C humans' natural preparedness toward alcohol consumption.
D a taste aversion to other companies' beers.

Answers can be found on page ANS-2.

Learning without Awareness

Many forms of learning involve a person or animal actively responding to a stimulus. However, as you have read in this module, many instances of classical conditioning can occur without any effort—or even awareness—on the part of the individual. The final section of this module provides some real-world examples of how classical conditioning can affect a person's behaviour without he or she being aware of this influence. Specifically, you will read about how classical conditioning is involved in physiological reactions that occur during drug taking, sexual arousal, and the consumption of diet beverages. Of course, this list isn't exhaustive; there are many other examples of classical conditioning affecting behaviour (Domjan, 2004). But, by seeing the breadth of activities that *are* influenced by conditioning, you may be inspired to examine whether these processes are influencing other areas of your life.

DRUG USE AND TOLERANCE Classical conditioning accounts for some drug-related phenomena, such as cravings and tolerance (see Module 5.3). Cues that accompany drug use can become conditioned stimuli that elicit cravings (Sinha, 2009). For example, a cigarette lighter, the smell of tobacco smoke, or the presence of another smoker can elicit cravings in people who smoke.

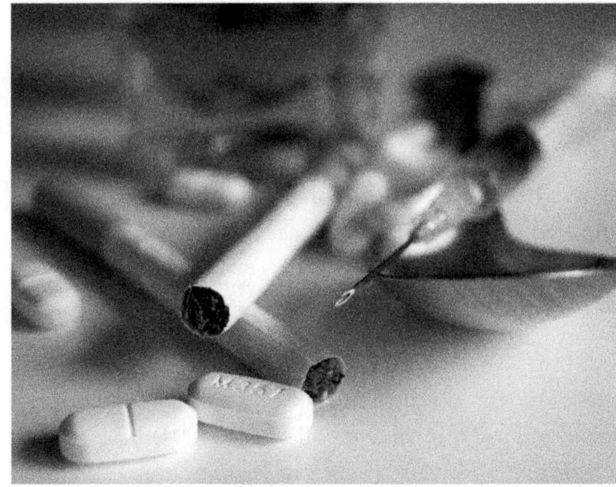

Lee O'Dell/Shutterstock.com
Physiological reactions to drugs are influenced by stimuli that are associated with administration of the drug.

Conditioning can also influence drug tolerance, or a decreased reaction that occurs with repeated use of the drug (Siegel et al., 2000). When a person takes a drug, his or her body attempts to metabolize that substance. Over time, the setting and paraphernalia associated with the drug-taking begin to serve as cues (a CS) that a drug (US) will soon be processed by the body (UR). As a result of this association, the physiological processes involved with metabolizing the drug will begin with the appearance of the CS rather than when the drug is actually consumed. In other words, because of conditioning, the body is already braced for the drug before the drug has been snorted, smoked, or injected. This response means that, over time, more of the drug will be needed to override these preparatory responses so that the desired effect can be obtained; this change is referred to as *conditioned drug tolerance*.

This phenomenon can have fatal consequences for drug abusers. Shepard Siegel (1984), a psychologist at McMaster University, conducted interviews with patients who were hospitalized for overdosing on heroin. Over the course of his interviews, a pattern among the patients emerged. Several individuals reported that they were in situations unlike those that typically preceded their heroin injections—for example, in a different environment or even using an injection site (i.e., part of the body) that differed from the usual ritual. As a result of these differences, the CSs that were normally paired with delivery of the drug changed, leaving their bodies unprepared for delivery of the drug. Without a conditioned preparatory response bracing the body for the drug's effects, delivery of even a *normal* dose of the drug can be lethal. This finding has been confirmed in animal studies: Siegel and his associates (1982) found that conditioned drug tolerance and overdosing can also occur with rats. When rats received heroin in an environment different from where they experienced the drug previously, mortality was double that in control rats that received the same dose of heroin in their normal surroundings (64% versus 32%).

SEXUAL AROUSAL Sexual arousal and reproductive physiology can also be influenced by classical conditioning. For example, Domjan and colleagues (2004) have studied conditioned sexual responses in Japanese quail. Males of this species will vigorously copulate with an artificial model (the CS) that has a history of being paired with a female quail (the US). These birds become highly persistent when it comes to copulating with these models—they continue to do so even when actual sexual opportunities have long since vanished. That is, the responses resist the process of extinction described previously. Some have argued that this persistent copulation with an inanimate object mirrors the sexual fetishism found in some humans (Köksal et al., 2004), a comparison that may ruffle some feathers.

Michael Domijan, University of Texas at Austin

Classically conditioned sexual behaviour in a male quail. After this object (the CS) is paired with a live female quail (the US), the male quail will direct its sexual responses to the CS alone.

A fetish involves sexual attraction and fixation on an object. Some common fetishes involve leather, lace, shoes, boots, and undergarments, none of which elicit unconditioned sexual responses (Lalumière & Quinsey, 1998). A conditioned sexual fetish can form if there is an association between the object (the CS) and sexual encounters (the US). As you can probably imagine, this phenomenon is not often studied in the laboratory. In one rare study, however, male volunteers were conditioned to experience sexual arousal when shown photos of shoes alone after such photos had been paired with sexually explicit photos (Rachman, 1966). Several explanations have been proposed for how sexual fetishes might develop, and classical conditioning certainly appears to play a role (Lowenstein, 2002). Nevertheless, in the case of sexual fetishism (and unlike the case of the Japanese quail), the conditioning does not seem to function in a way that is conducive to actual reproductive success, given that the fixation on the desired object detracts many affected individuals from normal sexual functioning.

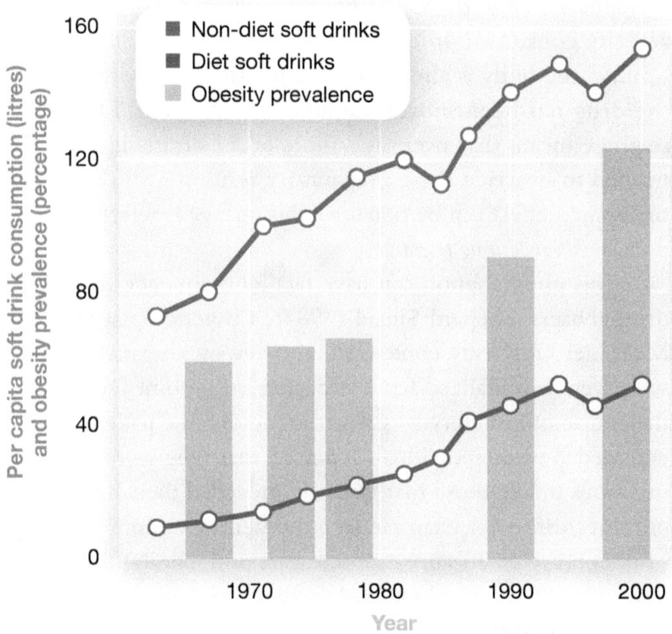

{FIG. 6.9} **Diet Soda Consumption's Association with Increased (Not Decreased) Prevalence of Obesity**

THE PARADOX OF "DIET" BEVERAGES Finally, classical conditioning may help explain why diet drinks are seemingly ineffective in helping people lose weight (Swithers et al., 2009; Swithers & Davidson, 2005). As you can see in Figure 6.9, the consumption of diet beverages has risen over the last several decades. Given that these drinks contain no calories, one would expect that obesity levels should have decreased over this time. In fact, the opposite has occurred, and this counterintuitive trend can be explained with classical conditioning.

Through neural mechanisms linking the brain and digestive system, humans actually become conditioned to the foods and drinks that they consume, including those that contain real sugar. Sweet tastes send a message to the body that a high dose of calories is on the way. For example, the taste of a candy bar is a conditioned stimulus (CS) that tells the body that a large amount of calories (the US) is soon to arrive in the gut. This relationship is an important one for the body to learn, as it helps maintain an energy balance—eventually your body tells you it is time to stop eating sweets and switch to something else, perhaps with fewer calories. Artificially sweetened beverages disrupt this relationship between the sugary sweet CS and high-calorie food US. The artificially sweetened taste of a diet soda is not followed by a high dose of calories that your body "expects." So how does the body respond? It continues to send out hunger messages: Your gut "tells" you to make up for the calories by opening up a bag of cookies or potato chips. This linkage may very well help explain why, overall, artificially sweetened beverages do not promote weight loss. It also shows us how far-reaching the concepts of classical conditioning have become. Pavlov's observations of his salivating dogs were really just a drop in the bucket.

Quick Quiz 6.1d Learning without Awareness

KNOW ...

1 When a heroin user develops a routine, the needle can become the ______, whereas the body's preparation for the drug in response to the presence of the needle is the ______.

A CS; CR
B US; UR
C US; CR
D CS; US

ANALYZE ...

2 Which is the *best* explanation for why diet beverages do not prevent people from gaining weight?

A Diet beverages actually have more calories than regular beverages.
B The artificially sweetened beverages seem to stimulate hunger for high-calorie foods.
C People who drink diet beverages typically eat more food than those who drink only water.
D Diet drinks elicit conditioned emotional reactions that lead people to overeat.

Answers can be found on page ANS-2.

Module Summary

Module 6.1

Brenda Carson/Fotolia

Now that you have read this module you should

KNOW ...

- ***The key terminology involved in classical conditioning:***

acquisition (p. 230)
classical conditioning (p. 227)
conditioned emotional response (p. 232)
conditioned response (CR) (p. 228)
conditioned stimulus (CS) (p. 228)
conditioned taste aversion (p. 235)
discrimination (p. 232)
extinction (p. 231)
generalization (p. 231)
learning (p. 226)
preparedness (p. 235)
spontaneous recovery (p. 231)
unconditioned response (UR) (p. 227)
unconditioned stimulus (US) (p. 227)

UNDERSTAND ...

- ***How responses learned through classical conditioning can be acquired and lost.*** Acquisition of a conditioned response occurs with repeated pairings of the CS and the US. Once a response is acquired, it can be extinguished if the CS and the US no longer occur together. During extinction, the CR diminishes, although it may reappear under some circumstances. For example, if enough time passes following extinction, the CR may spontaneously recover when the organism encounters the CS again.
- ***The role of biological and evolutionary factors in classical conditioning.*** Not all stimuli have the same potential to become a strong CS. Responses to biologically relevant stimuli, such as snakes, are more easily conditioned than are responses to stimuli such as flowers or guns, for example. Similarly, avoidance of potentially harmful foods is critical to survival, so organisms can develop a conditioned taste aversion quickly (in a single trial) and even when ingestion and illness are separated by a relatively long time interval.

APPLY ...

- ***The concepts and terms of classical conditioning to new examples.*** Read the three scenarios that follow and identify the conditioned stimulus (CS), the unconditioned stimulus (US), the conditioned response (CR), and the unconditioned response (UR) in each case. [*Hint:* When you apply the terms CS, US, CR, and UR, a good strategy is to identify whether something is a stimulus (something that elicits) or a response (a behaviour). Next, identify whether the stimulus automatically elicits a response (the US) or does so only after being paired with a US (a CS). Finally, identify whether the response occurs in response to the US alone (the UR) or the CS alone (the CR).] Check your answers on page ANS-2.

1. Cameron and Tia went to the prom together, and during their last slow dance the DJ played the theme song for the event. During the song, the couple kissed. Now, several years later, whenever Cameron and Tia hear the song, they feel a rush of excitement.
2. Harry has visited his eye doctor several times due to problems with his vision. One test involves blowing a puff of air into his eye. After repeated visits to the eye doctor, Harry starts blinking as soon as the instrument is being applied.
3. Sarah went to a new restaurant and experienced the most delicious meal she has ever tasted. The restaurant starts advertising on the radio, and now every time an ad comes on, Sarah finds herself craving the meal she had enjoyed so much.

ANALYZE ...

- ***Claims that artificially sweetened beverages are a healthier choice.*** Because of classical conditioning, the digestive system responds to the flavour of the artificially sweetened (CS) beverage as though a high-calorie food source (the US) is on the way. When the low-calorie beverage reaches the digestive system, the gut has already prepared itself for something high in calories (the CR). As a consequence, hunger messages continue to be sent to the brain. Because the "diet" beverage does not deliver on the promise of high calories, the person experiences an increased level of hunger.

Mike Mergen/Bloomberg via Getty Images

Module 6.2

Operant Conditioning: Learning through Consequences

Learning Objectives

After reading this module you should

KNOW ...	UNDERSTAND ...	APPLY ...	ANALYZE ...
The key terminology associated with operant conditioning	The role that consequences play in increasing or decreasing behaviour How schedules of reinforcement affect behaviour	Your knowledge of operant conditioning to examples	The effectiveness of punishment on changing behaviour

Gambling is a multibillion-dollar industry in Canada. According to Statistics Canada, the net revenue from lotteries, video-lottery terminals (VLTs), and casinos was $13.74 billion in 2011. That's an average of $515 per person. Given these huge sums, it is clear that some individuals are spending more than they should on this habit. Psychologists and government officials have invested a considerable amount of time into the development of prevention and treatment programs for gambling addictions. Although these programs have led to addiction rates levelling off in recent years, compulsive gambling *is* still a problem in Canada. So, what compels people to keep pulling the lever on a slot machine or pressing buttons on a VLT screen when logic would tell them to stop and go home?

Although the answer to this question is complicated (Hodgins et al., 2011), it is clear that reinforcement plays a role in these behaviours. As you will read in this module, rewarding a behaviour—which happens when someone wins money after pressing the button on a VLT—makes that behaviour more likely to occur again in the future. These effects are larger when the reward doesn't happen every time and isn't predictable—qualities that perfectly describe gambling. The machines aren't the only ones having their buttons pushed.

Focus Questions

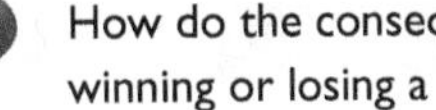

1. How do the consequences of our actions—such as winning or losing a bet—affect subsequent behaviour?
2. Many behaviours, including gambling, are reinforced only part of the time. How do the odds of being reinforced affect how often a behaviour occurs?

Table 6.1 :: Major Differences between Classical and Operant Conditioning

	CLASSICAL CONDITIONING	OPERANT CONDITIONING
Target response is ...	Automatic	Voluntary
Reinforcement is ...	Present regardless of whether a response occurs	A consequence of the behaviour
Behaviour mostly depends on ...	Reflexive and physiological responses	Skeletal muscles

Very few of our behaviours are random. Instead, people tend to repeat actions that previously led to positive or rewarding outcomes. If you try a new food and like it, you will eat that food again. Conversely, if a behaviour previously led to a negative outcome, people are less likely to perform that action again. If you try a new food and gag, then you will likely not eat that food again. These types of stimulus-response relationships are known as **operant conditioning**, *a type of learning in which behaviour is influenced by consequences.* The term *operant* is used because the individual *operates* on the environment before consequences can occur. In contrast to classical conditioning, which typically affects *reflexive* responses, operant conditioning involves *voluntary* actions such as speaking or listening, starting and stopping an activity, and moving toward or away from something. Whether and when we engage in these types of behaviours depend on how our unique collection of previous experiences has influenced what we do, and do not, find rewarding.

Initially the difference between classical and operant conditioning may seem unclear. One useful way of telling the difference is that in classical conditioning a response is *not* required for a reward (or unconditioned stimulus) to be presented; to return to Pavlov's dogs, meat powder is presented regardless of whether salivation occurs. Learning has taken place if a conditioned response develops following pairings between the conditioned stimulus and the unconditioned stimulus. In other words, the dogs learned the association between a tone and food (as shown by their salivation), but they didn't have to actually *do* anything. In operant conditioning, a response and a consequence are required for learning to take place. Without a response of some kind, there can be no consequences (see Table 6.1 for a summary of differences between operant and classical conditioning).

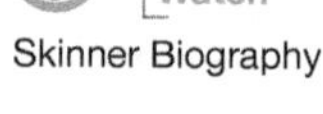

Skinner Biography

Processes of Operant Conditioning

The concept of *contingency* is important to understanding operant conditioning; it simply means that a consequence depends upon an action. Earning good grades is generally contingent upon studying effectively. Excelling at athletics is contingent upon training and practice. The consequences of a particular behaviour can be either reinforcing or punishing (see Figure 6.10).

REINFORCEMENT AND PUNISHMENT **Reinforcement** *is a process in which an event or reward that follows a response increases the likelihood of that response occurring again.* We can trace the scientific study of reinforcement's effects on behaviour back to Edward Thorndike, who conducted experiments in which he measured the time it took cats to learn how to escape from puzzle boxes (see Figure 6.11). Thorndike (1905) observed that over repeated trials, cats were able to escape more rapidly because they learned which responses worked (such as pressing a pedal on the floor of the box). From his experiments, Thorndike proposed the *law of effect*—the idea that responses followed by satisfaction will occur again and those that are not followed by satisfaction become less likely. In this definition, "satisfaction" implies either that the animal's desired goal was achieved (e.g., escaping the puzzle box) or it received some form of reward for the behaviour (e.g., food).

Within a few decades of the publication of Thorndike's work, the famous behaviourist B. F. Skinner began conducting his own studies on the systematic relationship between reinforcement and

Reinforcement increases behaviour.

Behaviour: Try the new café on 2nd Avenue.

Consequence: The meal and service were fantastic!

Effect: The behaviour is reinforced. You'll go there again.

Punishment decreases behaviour.

Behaviour: Try listening to the new radio station in town.

Consequence: The music is terrible!

Effect: You won't listen to that station again.

{FIG. 6.10} **Reinforcement and Punishment** The key distinction between reinforcement and punishment is that reinforcers, no matter what they are, increase behaviour. Punishment involves a decrease in behaviour, regardless of what the specific punisher may be. Thus both reinforcement and punishment are defined based on their effects on behaviour. **Click on this figure in your eText to see more details.**

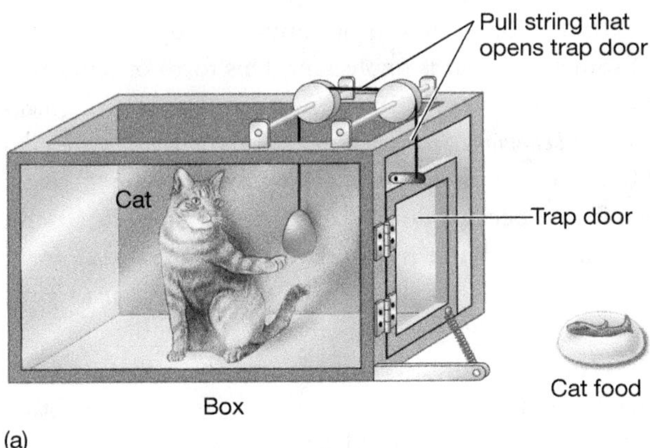

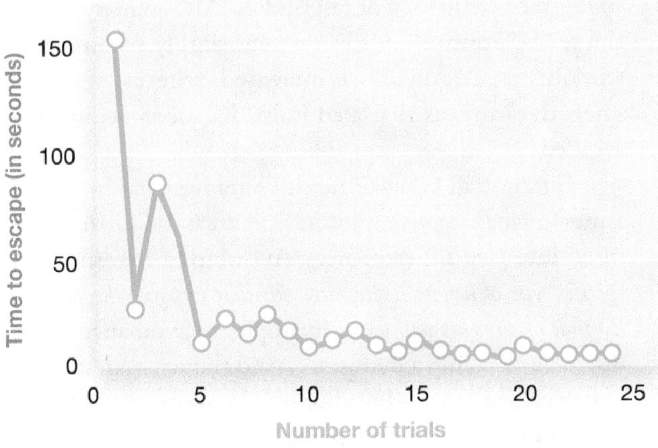

{FIG. 6.11} **Thorndike's Puzzle Box and the Law of Effect** Thorndike conducted experiments in which cats learned an operant response that was reinforced with escape from the box and access to a food reward (a). Over repeated trials, the cats took progressively less time to escape, as shown in this learning curve (b).

behaviour. Although operant conditioning can explain many human behaviours, most of its basic principles stem from laboratory studies conducted on nonhuman species such as pigeons or rats, which were placed in an apparatus such as the one pictured in Figure 6.12. *These operant chambers*, sometimes referred to as *Skinner boxes*, include a lever or key that the subject can manipulate. Pushing the lever may result in the delivery of a reinforcer such as food. In operant conditioning terms, a **reinforcer** *is a stimulus that is contingent upon a response, and that increases the probability of that response occurring again.* (So, a reinforcer would be a stimulus like food, whereas reinforcement would be the changes in the frequency of a behaviour like lever-pressing that occur *as a result of* the food reward.) Using operant chambers, researchers record the animal's rate of responding over time (a measure of learning), and typically set a criterion for the number of responses that must be made before a reinforcer becomes available. As you will read later in this module, animals and humans are quite sensitive to how many responses they must make, or how long they must wait, before they will receive a reward.

Watch
Pigeon in Skinner Box

After studying Figure 6.12, you might wonder whether observations made with this apparatus could possibly apply to real-world situations. In fact, similar machinery can be found in all sorts of real-world settings. People pull levers on slot machines, press buttons on vending machines, and click on Internet links. Researchers use machinery such as operant chambers to help them control and quantify learning, but the general principles of operant conditioning apply to life outside and away from such machines.

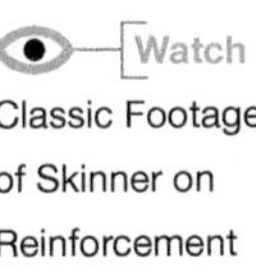

Classic Footage of Skinner on Reinforcement

The discussion thus far has focused on how reinforcement can lead to increased responding; but, decreased responding is also a possible outcome of an encounter with a stimulus. **Punishment** *is a process that decreases the future probability of a response.* Thus, a **punisher** *is a stimulus that is contingent upon a response, and that results in a decrease in behaviour.* Like reinforcers, punishers are defined not based on the stimuli themselves, but rather on their effects on behaviour. In all cases, a punisher—be it yelling, losing money, or

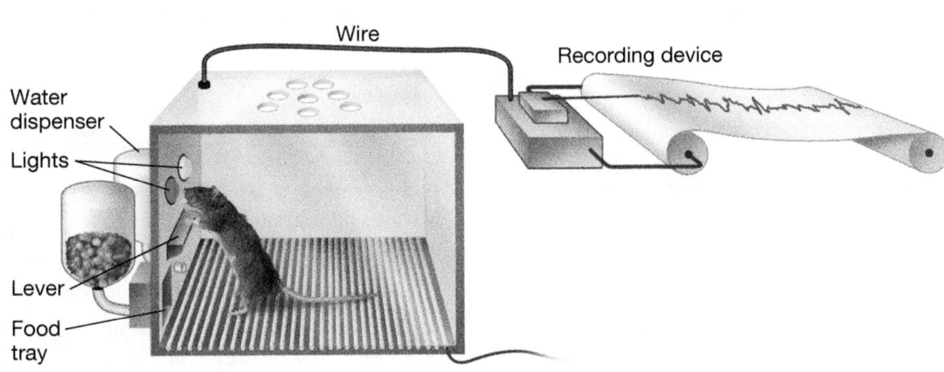

{FIG. 6.12} **An Operant Chamber** The operant chamber is a standard laboratory apparatus for studying operant conditioning. The rat can press the lever to receive a reinforcer such as food or water. The lights can be used to indicate when lever pressing will be rewarded. The recording device measures cumulative responses (lever presses) over time.

going to jail—will make it less likely that a particular response will occur again.

Watch
What's in It for Me? How to Make Healthier Choices

POSITIVE AND NEGATIVE REINFORCEMENT AND PUNISHMENT Thus far, we have differentiated between reinforcement (when a response increases the likelihood that a behaviour will occur again) and punishment (when a response decreases the likelihood that a behaviour will occur again). In both of these cases, it is natural to think of the responses as something that is added to the situation. For instance, a behaviour could be reinforced by giving the animal food. Or, it could be punished by shocking the animal. But, both reinforcement and punishment can be accomplished by *removing* a stimulus as well. In the descriptions that follow, try to remember the following four terms as they are used in operant conditioning:

- Reinforcement: this *increases* the chances of a behaviour occurring again
- Punishment: this *decreases* the chances of a behaviour occurring again
- Positive: this means that a stimulus is *added* to a situation; positive can refer to reinforcement or punishment
- Negative: this means that a stimulus is *removed* from a situation; negative can refer to reinforcement or punishment

These terms can be combined to produce four different subtypes of operant conditioning. For instance, a response can be strengthened because it brings a reward. This form of reinforcement, **positive reinforcement**, *is the strengthening of behaviour after potential reinforcers such as praise, money, or nourishment follow that behaviour* (see Table 6.2). For example, if you laugh at your professor's jokes, the praise will serve as a reward; this will increase the likelihood that he will tell more jokes. (Remember: the "positive" in positive reinforcement indicates the *addition* of a reward.) Positive reinforcement can be a highly effective method of rewarding desired behaviours among humans and other species.

Behaviour can also be reinforced by the removal of something that is unpleasant. This form of reinforcement, **negative reinforcement**, *involves the strengthening of a behaviour because it removes or diminishes a stimulus* (Table 6.2). For instance, taking aspirin is negatively reinforced because doing so removes a painful headache. Similarly, studying in order to prevent nagging from your parents is also a form of reinforcement as your behaviour, studying, will increase.

Negative reinforcement is a concept that students frequently find confusing because it seems unusual that something aversive could be involved in the context of reinforcement. Recall that reinforcement (whether positive or negative) always involves an increase in the strength or frequency of responding. Also remember that the term "positive" in this context simply means that a stimulus is introduced or increased, whereas the term "negative" means that a stimulus has been reduced or avoided.

But, not all types of negative reinforcement are the same; in fact, negative reinforcement can be further classified into two subcategories. **Avoidance learning** *is a specific type of negative reinforcement that removes the possibility that a stimulus will occur.* Examples of avoidance learning include taking a detour to avoid traffic congestion on a particular road, and paying bills on time to avoid late fees. In these cases, negative situations are avoided. Interestingly, scientists have used brain-imaging techniques to show that a region of the frontal lobes, the orbitofrontal cortex (just above your eyes), shows increased activity when people successfully avoid a negative outcome (in this case, losing money). This same area was active when participants received a monetary reward, thus suggesting that avoidance learning (negative reinforcement) uses some of the same brain networks as positive reinforcement (Kim et al., 2006).

Another form of negative reinforcement, **escape learning**, *occurs if a response removes a stimulus that is already present.* Covering your ears upon hearing overwhelmingly loud music is one example. You cannot

Table 6.2 :: Distinguishing Types of Reinforcement and Punishment

	CONSEQUENCE	EFFECT ON BEHAVIOUR	EXAMPLE
Positive reinforcement	Stimulus is added or increased.	Increases the response	A child gets an allowance for making her bed, so she is likely to do it again in the future.
Negative reinforcement	Stimulus is removed or decreased.	Increases the response	The rain no longer falls on you after opening your umbrella, so you are likely to do it again in the future.
Positive punishment	Stimulus is added or increased.	Decreases the response	A pet owner scolds his dog for jumping up on a house guest, and now the dog is less likely to do it again.
Negative punishment	Stimulus is removed or decreased.	Decreases the response	A parent takes away TV privileges to stop the children from fighting.

Mike Clarke/iStockphoto.com

Avoidance and escape learning. Getting caught in road construction is typically an aversive event. Avoidance learning might involve taking precautionary measures, such as starting the trip on an alternative route so you do not encounter the construction at all. Escape responses, such as pulling out of the traffic jam to take a shortcut, occur after the stimulus is already encountered. Either response would be negatively reinforced, as it removes the aversive stimulus of being stuck.

avoid the music, because it is already present, so you escape the aversive stimulus instead. The responses of taking a detour and covering your ears both increase in frequency because they have effectively removed the offending stimuli. In the laboratory, operant chambers such as the one pictured in Figure 6.12 (p. 245) often come equipped with a grid metal floor that can be used to deliver a mild electric shock; responses that remove (escape learning) or prevent (avoidance learning) the shock are negatively reinforced. This highly controlled environment allows researchers to carefully monitor all aspects of an animal's environment while investigating the different contingencies that will cause a behaviour to increase or decrease in frequency.

As with reinforcement, various types of punishment are possible. **Positive punishment** *is a process in which a behaviour decreases in frequency because it was followed by a particular, usually unpleasant, stimulus* (Table 6.2). For example, some cat owners use a spray bottle to squirt water when the cat hops on the kitchen counter or scratches the furniture. Remember that the term "positive" simply means that a stimulus is added to the situation (i.e., no one is claiming that spraying a cat with water is an emotionally positive experience). In these cases, the stimuli are punishers because they decrease the frequency of a behaviour.

Finally, **negative punishment** *occurs when a behaviour decreases because it removes or diminishes a particular stimulus* (Table 6.2). Withholding someone's privileges as a result of an undesirable behaviour is an example of negative punishment. A parent who "grounds" a child does so because this action removes something of value to the child. If effective, the outcome of the grounding will be to decrease the behaviour that got the child into trouble.

Based on this section, you can see how the frequency of a behaviour can be increased (reinforcement) or decreased (punishment) by a number of different stimuli or responses. The obvious question, then, is why do some stimuli affect behaviour while others have no influence whatsoever? Is there a biological explanation for this difference?

PRIMARY AND SECONDARY REINFORCERS

Reinforcers can come in two main forms. **Primary reinforcers** *consist of reinforcing stimuli that satisfy basic motivational needs—needs that affect an individual's ability to survive (and, if possible, reproduce).* Examples of these inherently reinforcing stimuli include food, water, shelter, and sexual contact. In contrast, **secondary reinforcers** *consist of stimuli that acquire their reinforcing effects only after we learn that they have value.* Money and praise are both examples of secondary reinforcers. They are more abstract and do not *directly* influence survival-related behaviours.

Top: Lana Sundman/Alamy; bottom: Richard Goldberg/Shutterstock.com

Animals pressing levers in operant chambers to receive rewards may seem artificial. However, if you look around you will see that our environment is full of devices that influence our operant responses.

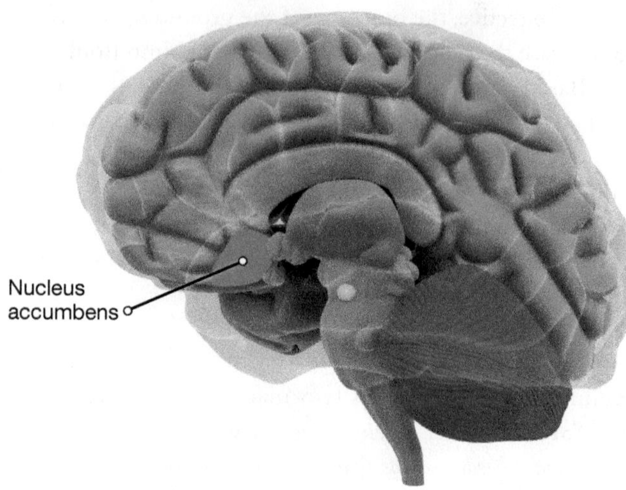

{FIG. 6.13} **Reward Processing in the Brain** The nucleus accumbens is one of the brain's primary reward centres.

Both primary and secondary reinforcers satisfy our drives, but what underlies the motivation to seek out these reinforcers? The answer is complex, but research points to a specific brain circuit including a structure called the *nucleus accumbens* (see Figure 6.13). The nucleus accumbens becomes activated during the processing of all kinds of rewards, including primary ones such as eating and having sex (see Modules 11.1 and 11.2), as well as "artificial" rewards such as using cocaine and smoking a cigarette (see Module 5.3). Variations in this area might also account for why individuals differ so much in their drive for reinforcers. For example, scientists have discovered that people who are prone to risky behaviours such as gambling and alcohol abuse are more likely to have inherited particular copies of genes that code for dopamine and other reward-based chemicals of the brain (Comings & Blum, 2000). Researchers have also found that individuals who are impulsive, and therefore vulnerable to gambling and drug abuse, release more dopamine in brain areas related to reward; dopamine is also not efficiently removed from the synapses in these areas (Buckholtz et al., 2010).

Secondary reinforcers also trigger the release of dopamine in reward areas of the brain. A number of neuroimaging experiments have shown that monetary rewards cause dopamine to be released in parts of the basal ganglia (Elliott et al., 2000) as well as in the medial regions of the frontal lobes (Knutson et al., 2003). Some of these areas directly overlap with those involved with primary reinforcers (Valentin & O'Doherty, 2009).

How can dopamine be related to operant conditioning? When a behaviour is rewarded for the first time, dopamine is released (Schultz & Dickinson, 2000); this reinforces these new, reward-producing behaviours so that they will be performed again (Morris et al., 2006; Schultz, 1998). These dopamine-releasing neurons in the nucleus accumbens and surrounding areas help maintain a record of which behaviours are, and are not, associated with a reward. Interestingly, these neurons increase their rate of firing when you have to update your understanding of which actions lead to rewards; so, they are involved with *learning* new behaviour-reward associations as well as with reinforcement itself.

Once a response has been learned, the individual may soon learn that reinforcement or punishment will occur under only certain conditions and circumstances. A pigeon in an operant chamber may learn that pecking is reinforced only when the chamber's light is switched on, so there is no need to continue pecking when the light is turned off. This illustrates the concept of a **discriminative stimulus**—*a cue or event that indicates that a response, if made, will be reinforced.* Our lives are filled with discriminative stimuli. Before we pour a cup of coffee, we might check whether the light on the coffee pot is on—a discriminative stimulus that tells us the beverage will be hot and, presumably, reinforcing. There are also numerous social examples of discriminative stimuli. For instance, you might only ask to borrow your parents' car when they show signs of being in a good mood. In this case, your parents' mood (smiling, laughing, etc.) will dictate whether you perform

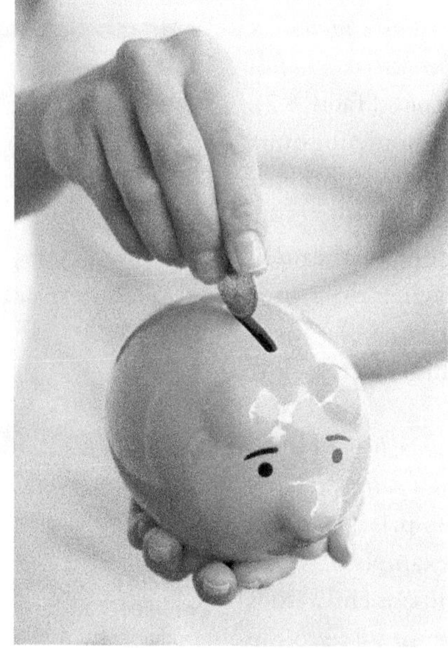

Left: Iurii Konoval/Shutterstock.com; right: Morgan Lane Photography/Shutterstock.com

Primary reinforcers satisfy basic biological needs, such as hunger or thirst. Secondary reinforcers, such as money, acquire their value and are typically associated with access to primary reinforcers.

a behaviour (asking to borrow the car). Discriminative stimuli demonstrate that we (and animal subjects) can use cues from our environment to help us decide whether to perform a conditioned behaviour.

DISCRIMINATION AND GENERALIZATION The idea of a discriminative stimulus should not be confused with the concept of *discrimination*. Discrimination occurs when an operant response is made to one stimulus but not to another, even if they are similar. For example, a pigeon may learn that he will receive a reward if he pecks at a key after a 1000-Hz tone, but not if he performs the same action following a 2000-Hz tone. As a result, he won't peck at the key after a 2000-Hz tone. Or, to extend our earlier example, you may quickly learn that your father will lend you the car whereas your mother will not. In this case, the process of discrimination would lead you to perform a behaviour (asking to borrow the car) when you are with your father but not when you are with your mother.

In contrast to discrimination, *generalization* occurs when an operant response takes place to a new stimulus that is similar to the stimulus present during original learning. In this case, a pigeon who learned to peck a key after hearing a 1000-Hz tone may attempt to peck the key whenever *any* tone is presented. If petting a neighbour's border collie (a type of dog) led to a child laughing and playing with the animal, then he might be more likely to pet other dogs or even other furry animals. In this instance, a specific reinforcement related to an action (petting a *specific* dog) led to a similar behaviour (petting) occurring in other instances (petting *other* dogs).

If you've noticed similarities between discrimination and generalization in operant conditioning and the same processes in classical conditioning, you are not mistaken. The same general logic underlies these concepts in both types of conditioning. However, while discrimination and generalization in classical conditioning were due to the strengthening of synapses as a result of simultaneous firing, in operant conditioning, the mechanism appears to be dopamine-secreting neurons. Research has shown that dopamine neurons can discriminate between rewarding and neutral stimuli as long as the two stimuli are visually or auditorily distinct (Ljungberg et al., 1992). However, if stimuli closely resemble reward-predicting items, dopamine neurons will fire (Schultz, 1998), although the amount of activity is smaller than it is following the expected reward-predicting item (Schultz & Romo, 1987, 1990).

DELAYED REINFORCEMENT AND EXTINCTION The focus of this module thus far has been on behavioural and biological responses to reinforcement and punishment. In most of these studies, the reward or punishment occurred immediately following the behaviour. This allows individuals to predict when a reward will occur (Schultz & Dickinson, 2000). But, you know from your own life that rewards are not always immediate. What happens if the reward is delayed, or doesn't occur at all? As early as 1911, Thorndike noted that reinforcement was more effective if there was very little time between the action and the consequence. Indeed, in a study with pigeons, researchers found that the frequency of responses (pecking a button) decreased as the amount of time between the pecking and the reward (a food pellet) increased (Chung & Herrnstein, 1967). Interestingly, neuroscientists have found that neural activity decreases during this time as well. In fact, delays of as little as half a second decrease the amount of neural activity in dopamine-releasing neurons (Hollerman & Schultz, 1996).

This effect of *delayed reinforcement* influences a number of human behaviours as well. For instance, drugs that have their effect (i.e., produce their rewarding feeling) soon after they are taken are generally more addictive than drugs whose effects occur several minutes or hours after being taken (see Module 5.3). This difference is due, in part, to the greater difficulty in mentally associating the reinforcement from the drug (the consequence) with drug-taking (the action).

Sometimes, however, a reinforcer is not just delayed; it doesn't occur at all. A pigeon may find that pressing a key in its operant chamber no longer leads to a food reward. You may find that your parents no longer let you borrow the car no matter how nicely you ask. Although both you and the pigeon may persist in your behaviour for a while, eventually you'll stop. This change is known as **extinction**, *the weakening of an operant response when reinforcement is no longer available.* If you lose your Internet connection, for example, you will probably stop trying to refresh your web browser because there is no reinforcement for doing so—the behaviour will no longer be performed. Extinction, like most of the observable behaviours you've read about in this module, is related to dopamine. If you expect a reward for your behaviour and none comes, the amount of dopamine being released decreases (Schultz, 1998). Dopamine release will increase again when there is a new behaviour-reward relationship to learn.

Table 6.3 differentiates among the processes of extinction, generalization, and discrimination in classical and operant conditioning.

REWARD DEVALUATION In all of these examples of operant conditioning, the value of the reinforcement remained the same. But, if you think about your own

Table 6.3 :: Comparing Discrimination, Generalization, and Extinction in Classical and Operant Conditioning

PROCESS	CLASSICAL CONDITIONING	OPERANT CONDITIONING
Discrimination	A CR does not occur in response to a different CS that resembles the original CS.	There is no response to a stimulus that resembles the original discriminative stimulus used during learning.
Generalization	A different CS that resembles the original CS used during acquisition elicits a CR.	Responding occurs to a stimulus that resembles the original discriminative stimulus used during learning.
Extinction	A CS is presented without a US until the CR no longer occurs.	Responding gradually ceases if reinforcement is no longer available.

life it quickly becomes apparent that this is not always the case. Food is incredibly rewarding when you are hungry but becomes less so after you have eaten a large meal (see Module 11.1). Similarly, $100 seems like a lot of money when you are a starving student, but will seem less important when you are a doctor with a high income. If a behaviour is more likely to occur because of reward, what happens when the reward becomes less rewarding?

Scientists have found that behaviours do change when the reinforcer loses some of its appeal (Colwill & Rescorla, 1985, 1990). In a typical experiment, rats are trained to press two different levers, each associated with a different reward (e.g., two different rewarding tastes). If the experimenters pre-feed the animal with one of these two tastes, they will crave it less than the other; in other words, its reward will be devalued compared to the other taste. Researchers consistently find a decrease in the response rate for the "devalued" reward, whereas the other reward remains largely unaffected.

Reward devaluation can also occur by making one of the rewards less appealing. In this version of reward devaluation, one of the reinforcing tastes is paired with a toxin that made the rats feel ill; this obviously reduces its value! (Ideally, this pairing would occur outside of the operant chamber so that the toxin didn't serve as a positive punishment.) The rats would then have the choice of two levers to press, one associated with a rewarding taste and the other associated with the taste that is now less rewarding than before. When these rats were later given the opportunity to choose between the two operant learning tasks, they showed a strong preference for the task whose reward had not been devalued (Colwill & Rescorla, 1985, 1990).

How would this phenomenon apply to *your* behaviour? One example is eating behaviour. If you are really hungry, then food will be very rewarding. In fact, you'd likely walk across campus to get some pizza, even in the dead of winter. But, if you've already eaten pizza today, you would be significantly less motivated to take that same walk because the pizza seems less rewarding. Neuroimaging studies have confirmed this assumption—when participants were given several pieces of a chocolate, it became less appealing than it had been when they received their first piece. This change in reported value was related to decreased activation in the brain's reward centres (Small et al., 2001).

Quick Quiz 6.2a

Processes of Operant Conditioning

KNOW ...

1 ________ removes the immediate effects of an aversive stimulus, whereas ________ removes the possibility of an aversive stimulus from occurring in the first place.

A Avoidance learning; escape learning

B Positive reinforcement; positive punishment

C Negative reinforcement; negative punishment

D Escape learning; avoidance learning

2 A basic need such as food may be used as a ________ reinforcer, whereas a stimulus whose value must be learned is a ________ reinforcer.

A primary; continuous

B secondary; shaping

C primary; secondary

D continuous; secondary

UNDERSTAND ...

3 As a consequence for misbehaving, many teachers use "time out." How does this consequence affect students' behaviour?

A It adds a stimulus to decrease bad behaviour.

B It takes away a stimulus to decrease bad behaviour.

C It adds a stimulus to increase bad behaviour.

D It takes away a stimulus to increase bad behaviour.

APPLY ...

4 Lucy hands all of her homework in to her psychology professor on time because she does not want to lose points for late work. This is an example of ________.

A avoidance learning

B positive reinforcement

C escape learning

D positive punishment

Answers can be found on page ANS-2.

Applications of Operant Conditioning

Now that you have learned the basic processes of operant conditioning, you should have a sense of how much our behaviour is influenced by rewards and punishments. In this section, the focus is on some specific applications of operant conditioning.

SHAPING Rats placed in operant chambers do not automatically go straight for the lever and begin pressing it to obtain food rewards. Instead, they must first learn that lever pressing accomplishes something. Getting a rat to press a lever can be done by reinforcing behaviours that *approximate* lever pressing, such as standing up, facing the lever, standing while facing the lever, placing paws upon the lever, and pressing downward. **Shaping** *is a procedure in which a specific operant response is created by reinforcing successive approximations of that response.* Shaping is done in a step-by-step fashion until the desired response—in this case, lever pressing—is learned. These techniques can also be used to help people develop specific skill sets (e.g., toilet training). A similar process, *chaining,* involves linking together two or more shaped behaviours into a more complex action or sequence of actions. When you see an animal "acting" in a movie, its behaviours were almost certainly learned through lengthy shaping and chaining procedures.

Bork/Shutterstock.com

Applications of shaping. Reinforcement can be used to shape complex chains of behaviour in animals and humans. (Later attempts to teach the cat to use a bidet were less successful.)

PSYCH @

The Special Needs Classroom

Operant conditioning is the basis for an educational method called *applied behaviour analysis* (ABA), which involves using close observation, prompting, and reinforcement to teach behaviours, often to people who experience difficulties and challenges owing to a developmental condition such as autism (Granpeesheh et al., 2009). People with autism are typically nonresponsive to normal social cues from a very early age. This impairment can lead to a deficit in developing many skills, ranging from basic, everyday ones to complex skills such as language. For example, explaining how to clear dishes from the dinner table to a child with autism could prove difficult. Psychologists who specialize in ABA often shape the desired behaviour using prompts (such as asking the child to stand up, gather silverware, stack plates, and so on) and verbal rewards as each step is completed. These and more elaborate ABA techniques can be used to shape a remarkable variety of behaviours to improve the independence and quality of life for people with autism.

Explore The Shaping Process

Explore Shaping

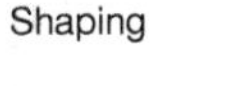

Explore Dolphins at Sea World

SCHEDULES OF REINFORCEMENT Operant conditioning is used, intentionally or unintentionally, in many different areas of our lives. However, the exact timing of the action and reinforcement (or punishment) differs across situations. Typically, a given behaviour is rewarded according to some kind of schedule. These **schedules of reinforcement**—*rules that determine when reinforcement is available*—can have a dramatic effect on both the learning and unlearning of responses (Ferster & Skinner, 1957). Reinforcement may be available at highly predictable or very irregular times. Also, reinforcement may be based on how often someone engages in a behaviour, or on the passage of time.

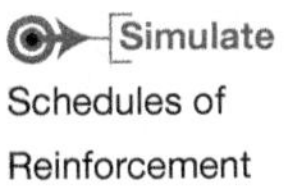

Simulate Schedules of Reinforcement

During **continuous reinforcement**, *every response made results in reinforcement*, and learning initially occurs rapidly. For example, vending machines (should) deliver a snack every time the correct amount of money is deposited. In other situations, not every action will lead to reinforcement; we also encounter situations where reinforcement is available only some of the time. For example, telephoning a friend may not always get you an actual person on the other end of the call. In this kind of **partial (intermittent) reinforcement**, *only a certain number of responses are rewarded, or a certain amount of time must pass before reinforcement is available.* Four types of partial reinforcement schedules are possible (see Figure 6.14). These schedules have different effects on rates of responding.

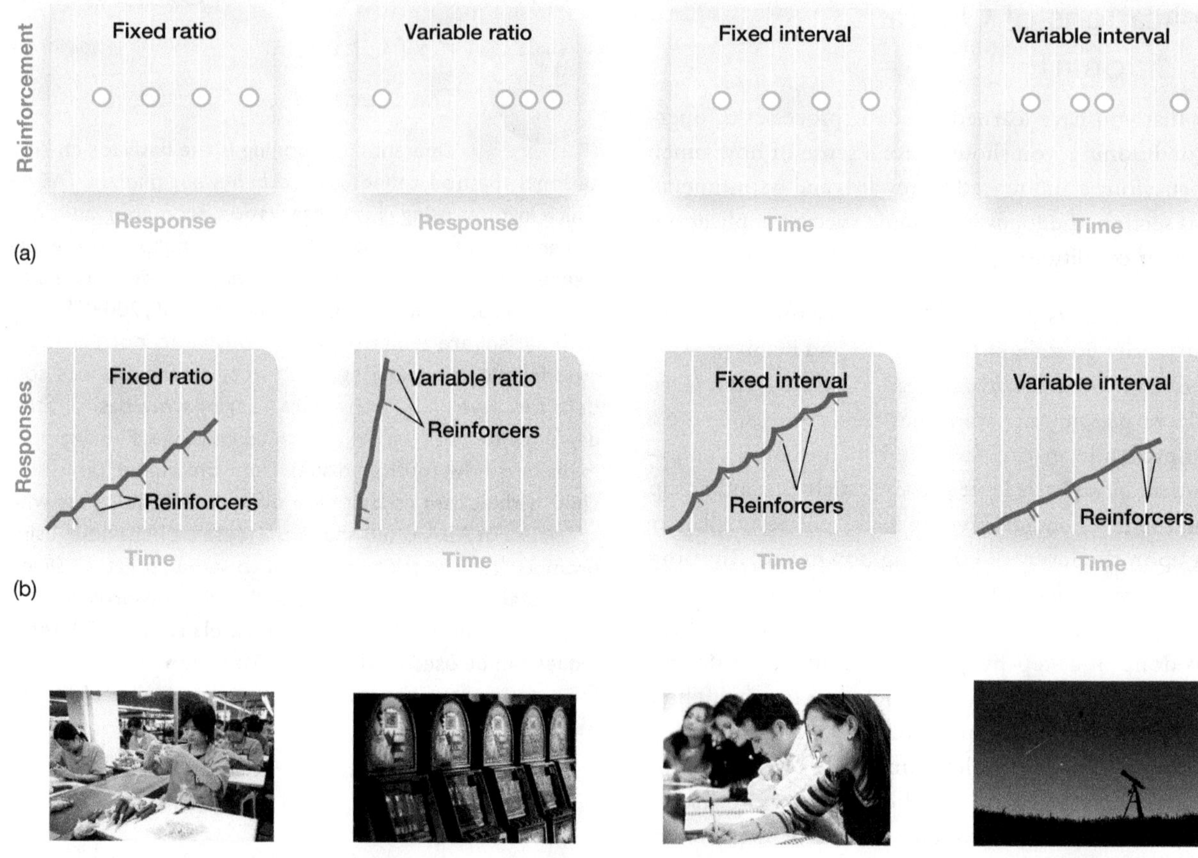

Bottom, left: Imaginechina via AP Images; bottom, centre left: LIGHTREIGN/Alamy; bottom, centre right: Andresr/Shutterstock; bottom, right: Bill Fehr/Shutterstock.com

{FIG. 6.14} **Schedules of Reinforcement** (a) Four types of reinforcement schedule are shown here: fixed ratio, variable ratio, fixed interval, and variable interval. Notice how each schedule differs based on when reinforcement is available (interval schedules) and on how many responses are required for reinforcement (ratio schedules). (b) These schedules of reinforcement affect responding in different ways. For example, notice the vigorous responding that is characteristic of the variable ratio schedule, as indicated by the steep upward trajectory of responding. (c) Real-world examples of the four types of reinforcement schedules. **Click on this figure in your eText to see more details.**

An important distinction for these schedules of reinforcement is the difference between *ratio* and *interval* schedules. Ratio schedules mean that the reinforcements are based on the *amount of responding*. In contrast, interval schedules are based on the *amount of time between reinforcements*, not the number of responses an animal (or human) makes. A second distinction is between *fixed* and *variable* schedules. A fixed schedule means that the schedule of reinforcement remains the same over time. A variable schedule means that the schedule of reinforcement, although linked to an average (e.g., 10 lever presses), varies from reinforcement to reinforcement. Keeping these two distinctions in mind should help you make sense of the four different reinforcement schedules discussed below.

In a **fixed-ratio schedule**, *reinforcement is delivered after a specific number of responses have been completed.* For example, a rat may be required to press a lever 10 times to receive food. Similarly, a worker in a factory may get paid based on how many items he worked on (e.g., receiving $1 for every five items produced). In both cases, a certain number of responses are required before a reward is given.

In a **variable-ratio schedule**, *the number of responses required to receive reinforcement varies according to an average.* A VR5 (variable ratio with an average of five trials between reinforcements) could include trials that require seven lever presses for a reward to occur, followed by four, then six, then three, and so on. But, the average at the end of the experiment would be five. Slot machines at casinos operate on variable-ratio reinforcement schedules. The odds are that the slot machine will not give anything back, but sometimes a player will get a modest winning. Of course, hitting the jackpot is very infrequent. The variable nature of the reward structure for playing slot machines helps explain why responding on this schedule can be vigorous and persistent. Slot machines and other games of chance hold out the *possibility* that at some point players will be rewarded, but it is unclear how many responses will be required before the reward occurs. The fact that the reinforcement *is* due to the number of times a player responds promotes strong response levels (i.e., more money spent on gambling). In animal studies, variable-ratio schedules lead to the highest rate of responding of the four types of reinforcement schedules.

In contrast to ratio schedules, interval schedules are based on the passage of time, not the number of responses. A **fixed-interval schedule** *reinforces the first response occurring after a set amount of time passes.* If your charming psychology professor gives you an exam every three weeks, your reinforcement for studying is on a fixed-interval schedule. In Figure 6.14, notice how the fixed-interval schedule shows that responding drops off after each reinforcement is delivered (as indicated by the tick marks). However, responding increases because reinforcement is soon available again. This schedule may reflect how you devote time to studying for your next exam—studying time tends to decrease after an exam, and then builds up again as another test looms.

The final reinforcement schedule is the **variable-interval schedule**, *in which the first response is reinforced following a variable amount of time.* The time interval varies around an average. For example, if you were watching the nighttime sky during a meteor shower, you would be rewarded for looking upward at irregular times. A meteor may fall on average every 5 minutes, but there will be times of inactivity for a minute, 10 minutes, 8 minutes, and so on.

As you can see from Figure 6.14, ratio schedules tend to generate relatively high rates of responding. This outcome makes sense in light of the fact that in ratio schedules, reinforcement is based on how often you engage in the behaviour (something you have some control over) versus how much time has passed (something you do not control). For example, looking up with greater frequency does not *cause* more meteor activity because a variable-interval schedule is in effect. In contrast, a salesperson is on a variable-ratio schedule because approaching more customers increases the chances of making a sale.

One general characteristic of schedules of reinforcement is that partially reinforced responses tend to be very persistent. For example, although people are only intermittently reinforced for putting money into a slot machine, a high rate of responding is maintained and may not decrease until after a great many losses in a row (or the individual runs out of money). The effect of partial reinforcement on responding is especially evident during extinction. The **partial reinforcement effect** *refers to a phenomenon in which organisms that have been conditioned under partial reinforcement resist extinction longer than those conditioned under continuous reinforcement.* This effect is likely due to the fact that the individual is accustomed to not receiving reinforcement for every response; therefore, a lack of reinforcement is not surprising and does not alter the motivation to produce the response, even if reinforcement is no longer available. We see this effect in many situations ranging from gambling to cheesy pick-up lines in bars to the numerous superstitions developed by professional and amateur athletes.

WORKING THE SCIENTIFIC LITERACY MODEL

Reinforcement and Superstition

It is clear that reinforcement can appear in multiple forms and according to various schedules. What all forms have in common is the notion that the behaviour that brought about the reinforcement will be strengthened. But what happens if the organism is mistaken about what caused the reinforcement to occur—will it experience reinforcement anyway? This raises the topic of superstition.

What do we know about superstition and reinforcement?

Reinforcement is often systematic and predictable. If it is not, then behaviour is eventually extinguished. In some cases, however, it is not perfectly clear what brings about the reinforcement. Imagine a baseball player who tries to be consistent in how he pitches. After a short losing streak, the pitcher suddenly wins a big game. If he is playing the same way, then what happened to change his luck? Did an alteration in his pre-game ritual lead to the victory? Humans the world over are prone to believing that some ritual or lucky charm will somehow improve their chances of success or survival. Psychologists believe these superstitions can be explained by operant conditioning.

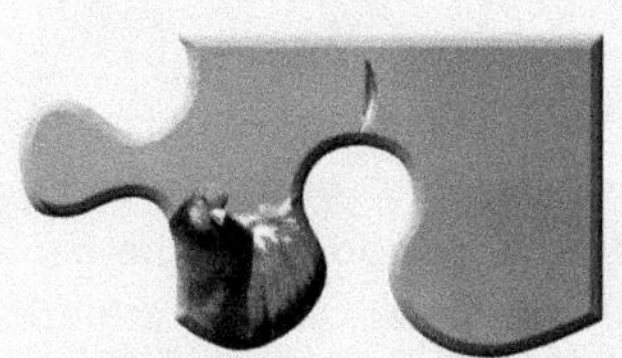

How can science explain superstition?

Decades ago, B. F. Skinner (1948) attempted to create superstitious behaviour in pigeons. Food was delivered every 15 seconds, regardless of what the pigeons were doing. Over time, the birds started engaging in "superstitious" behaviours. The pigeons repeated the behaviour occurring just before reinforcement, even if the behaviour was scratching, head-bobbing, or standing on one foot. A pigeon that happened to be turning in a counterclockwise direction when reinforcement was delivered repeated this seemingly senseless behaviour.

Humans are similarly superstitious. For example, in a laboratory study involving humans, psychologists constructed a doll that could spit marbles (Wagner & Morris, 1987). Children were told that the doll would sometimes spit marbles at them and that these marbles could be collected and traded for toys. The marbles were ejected at random intervals, leading several of the children to develop superstitious behaviours such as sucking their thumbs or kissing the doll on the nose.

Psychologists have conducted controlled studies to see whether superstitious behaviours have any effect on performance outcomes. In one investigation, college students, 80% of whom believed in the idea of "good luck," were asked to participate in a golf putting contest in which members of one group were told they were playing with "the lucky ball," and others were told they would be using "the ball everyone has used so far." Those who were told they were using the lucky ball performed significantly better than those who used the ball that was not blessed with good luck (Damisch et al., 2010). These effects also occurred in other tasks, such as memory and anagram games, and participants also showed better performance at tasks if allowed to bring a good luck charm.

Robert Beck/Newscom

Former NHL goaltender Patrick Roy appears on almost every sports magazine's list of "most superstitious athletes." Some of these behaviours are likely due to the partial reinforcement effect.

Can we critically evaluate these findings?

Superstitious beliefs, though irrational on the surface, may enhance individuals' belief that they can perform successfully at a task. Sometimes these beliefs can even enhance performance, as the golf putting experiment revealed. These findings, however, are best applied to situations where the participant has some control over an outcome, such as taking an exam or playing a sport. People who spend a lot of time and money gambling are known to be quite superstitious, but it is important to distinguish between games of chance versus skill in this setting. "Success" at most gambling games is due entirely, or predominantly, to chance. Thus, the outcomes are immune to the superstitious beliefs of the players.

Superstitions are also prone to the confirmation bias, the tendency to seek out evidence in favour of your existing views and ignore inconsistent information, and the partial reinforcement effect discussed above. If an athlete believes that a superstitious behaviour leads to success, then he or she will notice when the behaviour *does* lead to success. However, given that losing is generally part of being an athlete, there will be times when the behaviour is not reinforced. Given what you've read about the partial reinforcement effect, it is easy to see how a superstitious behaviour could be difficult to change. For instance, former NHL goaltender Patrick Roy was as famous for his many superstitions as he was for his playoff heroics. During every game he would (1) skate backwards toward his net before spinning around at the last minute (which made it appear smaller), (2) talk to his goalposts, (3) thank his goalposts when the puck hit one of them, and (4) avoid touching the blue line and red line when skating off the ice. Roy has the second-highest total of wins for NHL goalies and the most playoff wins in history (151). But, in addition to his 702 reinforcers, he also lost over 400 games in his impressive career.

Why is this relevant?

Between Skinner's original work with pigeons, and more contemporary experiments with people, it appears that operant conditioning plays a role in the development of some superstitions. Perhaps you have a good-luck charm or a ritual you must complete before a game or even before taking a test. Think about what brings you luck, and then try to identify why you believe in this relationship. Can you identify a specific instance when you were first reinforced for this behaviour? Then remember that the superstition is a form of reinforcement, a linking of a behaviour and a response that is formed *in your mind.* Whether a superstition affects your performance is based on whether or not you allow it to.

G Tipene/Shutterstock

APPLYING PUNISHMENT People tend to be more sensitive to the unpleasantness of punishment than they are to the pleasures of reward. Psychologists have demonstrated this asymmetry in laboratory studies with university students who play a computerized game in which they can choose a response that can bring either a monetary reward or a monetary loss. It turns out that the participants found losing money to be about three times as punishing as being rewarded with money was pleasurable. In other words, losing $100 is three times more punishing than gaining $100 is reinforcing (Rasmussen & Newland, 2008).

The use of punishment raises some ethical concerns—especially when it comes to physical means. A major issue that is debated all over the world is whether corporal punishment (e.g., spanking) is acceptable to use with children. In fact, more than 20 countries, including Sweden, Austria, Finland, Denmark, and Israel, have banned the practice. It is technically legal to spank a child aged 2–12 in Canada; in a contentious decision, the Supreme Court of Canada (in a 6–3 vote) upheld Section 43 of the *Criminal Code* allowing spanking (*Canadian Foundation for Children, Youth and the Law* v. *Canada (Attorney General)*, 2004). Some parents use this tactic because it works: Spanking is generally a very effective punisher when it is used for immediately stopping a behaviour (Gershoff, 2002). However, one reason so few psychologists advocate spanking is because it is associated with some major side effects (Gershoff, 2002; Gershoff & Bitensky, 2007). In a recent review of this research published in the *Canadian Medical Association Journal*, investigators at the University of Manitoba noted that spanking has been associated with poorer parent–child relationships, poorer mental health for both adults and children, delinquency in children, and increased chances of children becoming victims or perpetrators of physical abuse in adulthood (Durrant & Ensom, 2012).

Watch Thinking Like a Psychologist: Physical Punishment—You Decide!

It is also important to note that, while punishment may suppress an unwanted behaviour temporarily, by itself it does not teach which behaviours are appropriate. As a general rule, punishment of any kind is most effective when combined with reinforcement of an alternative, suitable response. Table 6.4 offers some general guidelines for maximizing the effects of punishment and minimizing negative side effects.

Table 6.4 :: Punishment Tends to Be Most Effective when Certain Principles Are Followed

PRINCIPLE	DESCRIPTION AND EXPLANATION
Severity	Should be proportional to offence. A small fine is suitable for parking illegally or littering, but inappropriate for someone who commits assault.
Initial punishment level	The initial level of punishment needs to be sufficiently strong to reduce the likelihood of the offence occurring again.
Contiguity	Punishment is most effective when it occurs immediately after the behaviour. Many convicted criminals are not sentenced until many months after they have committed an offence. Children are given detention that may not begin until hours later. Long delays in punishment are known to reduce its effectiveness.
Consistency	Punishment should be administered consistently. A parent who only occasionally punishes a teenager for breaking her curfew will probably have less success in curbing the behaviour than a parent who uses punishment consistently.
Show alternatives	Punishment is more successful, and side effects are reduced, if the individual is clear on how reinforcement can be obtained by engaging in appropriate behaviours.

ARE CLASSICAL AND OPERANT LEARNING DISTINCT EVENTS? It is tempting to think of behaviour as being due to *either* classical conditioning *or* operant conditioning. However, it is possible, even likely, that a complex behaviour is influenced by both types of learning, each influencing behaviour in slightly different ways. Consider gambling with video lottery terminals (VLTs), the topic of the opening story in this module. As discussed above, slot machines and VLTs use a variable-ratio schedule of reinforcement, a type of operant conditioning that leads to a high response rate. But, the flashy lights, the dinging sounds coming from the machine, and even the chair all serve as conditioned stimuli for the unconditioned response of excitement associated with gambling. So, classical conditioning produces an emotional response and operant conditioning maintains the behaviour. Given these forces, should we really be surprised that VLTs are so alluring to people, particular those prone to problem gambling (Clarke et al., 2012; Nicki et al., 2007)?

Quick Quiz 6.2b Applications of Operant Conditioning

KNOW ...

1 Shaping is the process of

- **A** reinforcing a series of responses that approximate the desired behaviour.
- **B** decreasing the likelihood of a behaviour.
- **C** reinforcing the basic motivational needs of a subject.
- **D** punishing a series of responses that you want to increase.

UNDERSTAND ...

2 Pete cannot seem to stop checking the change slots of vending machines. Although he usually does not find any money, occasionally he finds a quarter. Despite the low levels of reinforcement, this behaviour is likely to persist due to __________.

- **A** escape learning
- **B** the partial reinforcement effect
- **C** positive punishment
- **D** generalization

APPLY ...

3 Frederick trained his parrot to open the door to his cage by pecking at a lever three times. Frederick used a __________ schedule of reinforcement to encourage the desired behaviour.

- **A** variable-interval
- **B** variable-ratio
- **C** fixed-interval
- **D** fixed-ratio

ANALYZE ...

4 A friend regularly spanks his children to decrease their misbehaviour. Which statement is most accurate in regard to this type of corporal punishment?

- **A** Spanking is an effective method of punishment and should always be used.
- **B** Spanking can be an effective method of punishment but carries risks of additional negative outcomes.
- **C** Spanking is not an effective method of punishment, so it should never be used.
- **D** The effects of spanking have not been well researched, so it should not be used.

Answers can be found on page ANS-2.

Module Summary

Module 6.2

Mike Mergen/Bloomberg via Getty Images

Now that you have read this module you should

KNOW ...

- ***The key terminology associated with operant conditioning:***

avoidance learning (p. 246)
continuous reinforcement (p. 251)
discriminative stimulus (p. 248)
escape learning (p. 246)
extinction (p. 249)
fixed-interval schedule (p. 253)
fixed-ratio schedule (p. 252)
negative punishment (p. 247)
negative reinforcement (p. 246)
operant conditioning (p. 244)
partial (intermittent) reinforcement (p. 251)
partial reinforcement effect (p. 253)
positive punishment (p. 247)
positive reinforcement (p. 246)
primary reinforcer (p. 247)
punisher (p. 245)
punishment (p. 245)
reinforcement (p. 244)
reinforcer (p. 245)
schedules of reinforcement (p. 251)
secondary reinforcer (p. 247)
shaping (p. 251)
variable-interval schedule (p. 253)
variable-ratio schedule (p. 252)

UNDERSTAND ...

- ***The role that consequences play in increasing or decreasing behaviour.*** Positive and negative reinforcement increase the likelihood of a behaviour, whereas positive and negative punishment decrease the likelihood of a behaviour. Positive reinforcement and punishment involve adding a stimulus to the situation, whereas negative reinforcement and punishment involve removal of a stimulus.
- ***How schedules of reinforcement affect behaviour.*** Schedules of reinforcement can be fixed or variable, and can be based on intervals (time) or ratios (the number of responses). In contrast to continuous reinforcement, intermittent schedules tend to elicit vigorous responding. Our tendency to link our behaviour to reinforcement is particularly evident when it comes to superstition—where a ritual is *believed* to bring about reinforcement, regardless of whether it actually does.

APPLY ...

- ***Your knowledge of operant conditioning to examples.*** The concepts of positive and negative reinforcement and punishment are often the most challenging when it comes to this material. Read the following scenarios and determine whether positive reinforcement, negative reinforcement, positive punishment, or negative punishment explains the change in behaviour. Check your answers on page ANS-2.

1. Bill is caught for cheating on multiple examinations. As a consequence, the school principal suspends him for a three-day period. Bill likes being at school and, when he returns from his suspension, he no longer cheats on exams. Which process explains the change in Bill's behaviour? Why?
2. Ericka earns As in all of her math classes. Throughout her schooling, she finds that the personal and social rewards for excelling at math continue to motivate her. She eventually completes a graduate degree and teaches math. Which process explains her passion for math? Why?
3. Automobile makers install sound equipment that produces annoying sounds when a door is not shut properly, lights are left on, or a seat belt is not fastened. The purpose is to increase proper door shutting, turning off of lights, and seat belt fastening behaviour. Which process explains the behavioural change these sounds are attempting to make?
4. Hernan bites his fingernails and cuticles to the point of bleeding and discomfort. To reduce this behaviour, he applies a terrible-tasting topical lotion to his fingertips; the behaviour stops. Which process explains Hernan's behavioural change?

ANALYZE ...

- ***The effectiveness of punishment on changing behaviour.*** Many psychologists recommend that people rely on reinforcement to teach new or appropriate behaviours. The issue here is not that punishment does not work, but rather that there are some notable drawbacks to using punishment as a means to change behaviour. For example, punishment may teach individuals to engage in avoidance or aggression, rather than developing an appropriate alternative behaviour that can be reinforced.

Courtesy of Victoria Horner and the Chimpanzee Sanctuary and Wildlife Conservation Trust, Ngamba Island, Uganda

Module 6.3

Cognitive and Observational Learning

Learning Objectives

After reading this module you should

KNOW ...	UNDERSTAND ...	APPLY ...	ANALYZE ...
The key terminology associated with cognitive and observational learning	The concept of latent learning and its relevance to cognitive aspects of learning	Principles of observational learning outside of the laboratory	The claim that viewing violent media increases violent behaviour

Are you smarter than a chimpanzee? For years psychologists have asked this question, but in a more nuanced way. More specifically, they have tested the problem-solving and imitative abilities of chimpanzees and humans to help us better understand what sets us apart from, and what makes us similar to, other animals. Chimps and humans both acquire many behaviours from observing others, but imagine if you pitted a typical human preschooler against a chimpanzee. Who do you think would be the best at learning a new skill just by watching someone else perform it? Researchers Victoria Horner and Andrew Whiten asked this question by showing 3- and 4-year-old children how to retrieve a treat by opening a puzzle box, and then they demonstrated the task to chimpanzees as well. But there was one trick thrown in: As they demonstrated the process, the researchers added in some steps that were unnecessary to opening the box. The children and chimps both figured out how to open it, but the children imitated all the steps—even the unnecessary ones—while the chimps skipped the useless steps and went straight for the treat (Horner & Whiten, 2005).

What can we conclude from these results? Maybe it is true that both humans and chimps are excellent imitators, although it appears the children imitated a little too well, while the chimps imitated in a smarter manner. Clearly, we both share a motivation to imitate—which is a complex cognitive ability and one of the keys to learning new skills.

Focus Questions

 What role do cognitive factors play in learning?

 Which processes are required for imitation to occur?

The first two modules of this chapter focused on relatively basic ways of learning. Classical conditioning occurs through the formation of associations (Module 6.1), and operant conditioning involves

changes in behaviour due to rewarding or punishing consequences (Module 6.2). Both types of learning emphasize relationships between stimuli and responses and avoid making reference to an organism that does the *thinking* part of the learning process. However, since the 1950s, psychologists have recognized that cognitive processes such as thinking and remembering are useful to theories and explanations of how we learn.

Cognitive Perspectives on Learning

Cognitive psychologists have contributed a great deal to psychology's understanding of learning. In some cases, they have presented a very different view from behaviourism by addressing unobservable mental phenomena. In other cases, their work has simply complemented behaviourism by integrating cognitive accounts into even the seemingly simplest of learned behaviours, such as classical and operant conditioning.

LATENT LEARNING Much of human learning involves absorbing information and then demonstrating what we have learned by performing a task, such as taking a quiz or exam. Learning, and reinforcement for learning, may not be expressed until there is an opportunity to do so. In other words, learning may be occurring even if there is no behavioural evidence of it taking place.

Psychologist Edward Tolman proposed that humans, and even rats, express **latent learning**—*learning that is not immediately expressed by a response until the organism is reinforced for doing so.* Tolman and Honzik (1930) demonstrated latent learning in rats running a maze (see Figure 6.15). The first group of rats could obtain food if they navigated the correct route through the maze. They were given 10 trials to figure out an efficient route to the end of the maze, where food was always waiting. A second group was allowed to explore the maze, but did not have food available at the other end until the 11th trial. A third group (a control) never received food while in the maze. It might seem that only the first group—the one that was reinforced on all trials—would learn how to best shuttle from the start of the maze to the end. After all, it was the only group that was consistently reinforced. This is, in fact, what happened—at least for the first 10 trials. Tolman and Honzik discovered that rats that were finally rewarded on the 11th trial quickly performed as well as the rats that were rewarded on every trial (see Figure 6.15). It appears that this second group of rats was learning after all, but only demonstrated their knowledge when they received reinforcement worthy of quickly running through the maze.

If you put yourself in the rat's shoes—or perhaps paws would be more appropriate—you will realize that humans experience latent learning as well. Consider a familiar path you take to work or school. There is probably a spot along that route that you have never stopped at, simply because there is no reason to—perhaps it is a vacant storefront. But imagine you discover one day that a fantastic and inexpensive new restaurant opened up in that spot. You would have no trouble finding it in the

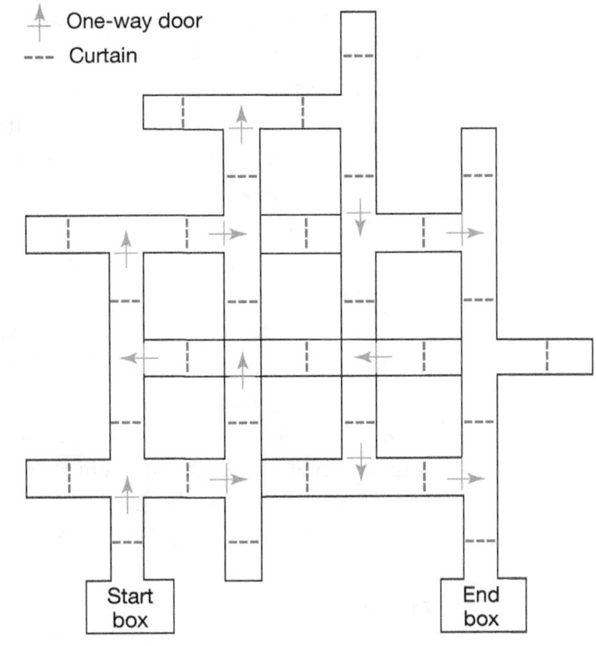

(a)

Average number of errors
Days of experience in maze
Never reinforced
Latent learning evident once reinforcement begins, on day 11
Always reinforced

(b)

{FIG. 6.15} **Learning without Reinforcement** Tolman and Honzik (1930) placed rats in the start box and measured the number of errors they made en route to the end box. Rats that were reinforced during the first 10 days of the experiment made fewer errors. Rats that were reinforced on day 11 immediately made far fewer errors, which indicated that they had learned some spatial details of the maze even though food reinforcement was not available during the first 10 trials for this group.

Simulate What Learning Techniques Do You Use?

Simulate Latent Learning

future because you have an understanding of the general area. Tolman and Honzik assumed that this process held true for their rats, and they further hypothesized that rats possess a *cognitive map* of their environment, much like our own cognitive map of our surroundings. This classic study is important because it illustrates that humans (and rats) acquire information in the absence of immediate reinforcement and that we can use that information when circumstances allow.

It is important to point out that latent learning did not disprove the operant learning research that highlighted the importance of reinforcement (Module 6.2). Instead, most of the controversy centred on the idea of cognitive maps and the statement that *no* reinforcement had occurred during the first 10 trials. Later research suggested that the rats may have been learning where different parts of the maze were located *in relation* to each other rather than forming a *complete* map of the environment (Whishaw, 1991). Additionally, there is no guarantee that the rats didn't find exploring the maze on the first 10 trials to be rewarding in some way, as rats are naturally curious about their environment. Because it is experimentally difficult, if not impossible, to answer some of these questions, much of the debate about the mechanisms underlying latent learning remains unresolved (Jensen, 2006).

S-O-R THEORY OF LEARNING Latent learning suggests that individuals engage in more "thinking" than is shown by operant conditioning studies, which focus on the relationship between a stimulus and a response (S–R). Instead, cognitive theories of learning suggest that the individual is actively processing and analyzing information; this activity influences observable behaviours as well as our internal mental lives. Because of the essential role played by the individual, this early view of cognitive learning was referred to as the *S-O-R theory* (*stimulus-organism-response theory*; Woodworth, 1929).

Simulate The Experiment: Learning

S–R and S–O–R theorists both agreed that thinking took place; however, they disagreed about the contents and causes of the thoughts. S–R psychologists assumed that thoughts were based on the S–R contingencies that an organism had learned throughout its life; in other words, thinking was a form of behaviour. Individual differences in responding would therefore be explained by the different learning histories of the individuals. S–O–R psychologists, on the other hand, assumed that individual differences were based on people's (or animals') cognitive *interpretation* of that situation—in other words, what that stimulus meant to them. In this view, the same stimulus in the same situation could theoretically produce different responses based on a variety of factors including an individual's mood, fatigue, the presence of other organisms, and so on. For example, the same comment to two coworkers might lead to an angry response from one person and laughter from another. The explanation for these differences is the *O* in the S–O–R theory; each person or organism will think about or interpret a situation in a slightly different way.

Quick Quiz 6.3a
Cognitive Perspectives on Learning

KNOW ...

1 A theory of learning that highlights the role played by an individual's interpretation of a situation is (the)
- **A** classical conditioning theory.
- **B** operant conditioning theory.
- **C** stimulus-organism-response theory.
- **D** individualist theory.

UNDERSTAND ...

2 Contrary to some early behaviourist views, ________ suggests that learning can occur without any immediate behavioural evidence.
- **A** latent learning
- **B** operant conditioning
- **C** classical conditioning
- **D** desirable difficulties

Answers can be found on page ANS-2.

Observational Learning

The first two modules in this chapter focused on aspects of learning that require direct experience. Pavlov's dogs experienced the tone and the food one right after the other, and learning occurred. Rats in an operant chamber experienced the reinforcing consequences of pressing a lever, and learning occurred. However, not all learning requires direct experience, and this is a good thing. Can you imagine if surgeons had to learn by trial and error? Who on earth would volunteer to be the first patient?

Luckily, many species, including humans, are able to learn new skills and new associations without directly experiencing them. **Observational learning** *involves changes in behaviour and knowledge that result from watching others.* Humans have elaborate cultural customs and rituals that spread through observation. The cultural differences we find in dietary preferences, clothing styles, athletic events, holiday rituals, music tastes, and so many other customs exist because of observational learning. Socially transmitting behaviour is an efficient approach. Indeed, it is the primary way that adaptive behaviour spreads so rapidly within a population, even in nonhuman species (Heyes & Galef, 1996). For example, cats that observe others being trained to leap over a hurdle to avoid a foot shock

Cathy Keifer/Shutterstock.com

Even rats have a special way of socially transmitting information. Without directly observing what other rats have eaten, rats will smell the food on the breath of other rats and then preferentially search for this food.

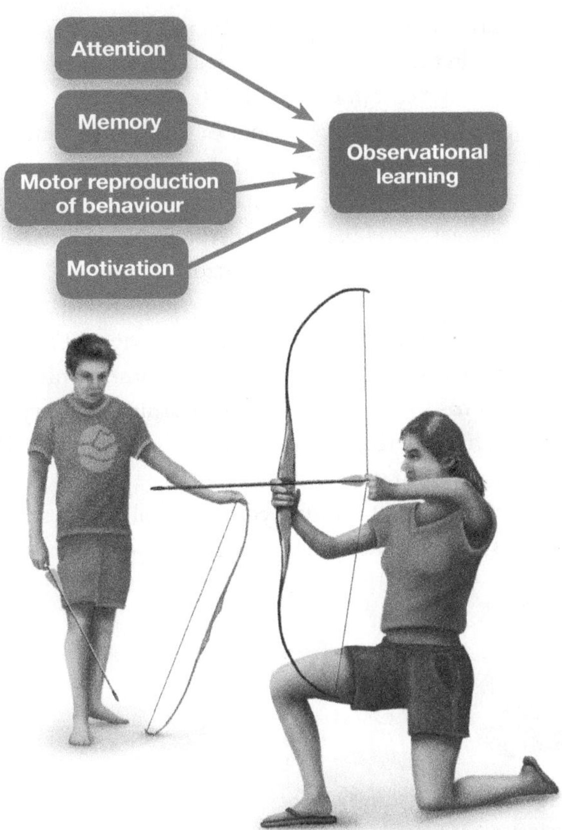

{FIG. 6.16} **Processes Involved in Observational Learning** For observational learning to occur, several processes are required: attention, memory, the ability to reproduce the behaviour, and the motivation to do so.

learn the same trick faster than cats who did not observe this training (John et al., 1968). A less shocking example involves rats' foraging behaviour. Before setting off in search of food, rats smell the breath of other rats. They will then search preferentially for food that matches the odour of their fellow rats' breath. To humans, this practice may not seem very appealing—but for rats, using breath as a source of information about food may help them survive. By definition, a breathing rat is a living rat, so clearly the food the animal ate did not kill it. Living rats are worth copying. Human children are also very sensitive to social cues about what they should avoid. Curious as they may be, even young children will avoid food if they witness their parents reacting with disgust toward it (Stevenson et al., 2010). However, for observational learning to occur, some key processes need to be in place if the behaviour is to be successfully transmitted from one person to the next.

PROCESSES SUPPORTING OBSERVATIONAL LEARNING Albert Bandura (Bandura, 1973; Bandura & Walters, 1973) identified four processes involved in observational learning: *attention* to the act or behaviour, *memory* for it, the *ability to reproduce it*, and the *motivation* to do so (see Figure 6.16). Without any one of these processes, observational learning would be unlikely—or at least would result in a poor rendition.

First, consider the importance of attention. Seeing someone react with a classically conditioned fear to snakes or spiders can result in acquiring a similar fear—even in the absence of any direct experience with snakes or spiders (LoBue et al., 2010). As an example, are you afraid of sharks? It is likely that many of you have this fear, even if you live thousands of kilometres away from shark-infested waters. The fear you see on the faces of people in horror movies and in "Shark Week" documentaries is enough for you to learn this experience. Observational learning can extend to operant conditioning as well. Observing someone being rewarded for a behaviour facilitates imitation of the same behaviours that bring about rewards.

Second, memory is an important facet of observational learning. When we learn a new behaviour, there is often a delay before the opportunity to perform it arises. If you tuned in to a cooking show, for example, you would need to recreate the steps and processes required to prepare the dish at a later time. Recent brain-imaging research also indicates that memory is a key component of observational learning. Using fMRI, scientists found that receiving money is associated with activity in parts of the basal ganglia and the orbitofrontal cortex, areas related to processing rewards (see Module 6.2).

In contrast, observing someone else receive money leads to activity in the hippocampus, an area related to memory formation (Bellebaum et al., 2012). Interestingly, memory for how to reproduce a behaviour or skill can be found at a very early age (Huang, 2012). Infants just nine months of age can reproduce a new behaviour, even if there is up to a one-week delay between observing the act and having the opportunity to do so (Meltzoff, 1988).

Third, observational learning requires that the observer can actually reproduce the behaviour. This can be very challenging, depending on the task. Unless an individual has a physical impairment, learning an everyday task—such as operating a can opener—is not difficult. By comparison, hitting a baseball thrown by a Toronto Blue Jays pitcher requires a very specialized skill set. Research indicates that observational learning is most effective when we first observe, practise immediately, and continue practising soon after acquiring the response. For example, one study found that the optimal way to develop and maintain motor skills is by repeated observation before and during the initial stages of practising (Weeks & Anderson, 2000). It appears that watching someone else helps us practise effectively, and allows us to see how errors are made. When we see a model making a mistake, we know to examine our own behaviour for similar mistakes (Blandin & Proteau, 2000; Hodges et al., 2007).

Finally, motivation is clearly an important component of observational learning. On the one hand, being hungry or thirsty will motivate an individual to find out where others are going to find food and drink. On the other hand, a child who has no aspirations to ever play the piano will be less motivated to observe his teacher

MYTHS IN MIND

Teaching Is Uniquely Human

Teaching is a significant component of human culture and a primary means by which information is learned in classrooms, at home, and many other settings. But are humans the only species with the ability to teach others? Some intriguing examples of teaching-like behaviour have been observed in nonhuman species (Thornton & Raihani, 2010). Prepare to be humbled.

Teaching behaviour was recently discovered in ants (Franks & Richardson, 2006)—probably the last species we might suspect would demonstrate this complex ability. For example, a "teacher" ant gives a "pupil" ant feedback on how to locate a source of food.

Field researchers studying primates discovered the rapid spread of potato-washing behaviour in Japanese macaque monkeys (Kawai, 1965). Imo—perhaps one of the more ingenious monkeys of the troop—discovered that potatoes could be washed in salt water, which also may have given them a more appealing taste. Potato-washing behaviour subsequently spread through the population, especially among the monkeys that observed the behaviour in Imo and her followers.

Transmission of new and unique behaviours typically occurs between mothers and their young (Huffman, 1996). Chimpanzee mothers, for example, actively demonstrate to their young the special skills required to crack nuts open (Boesch, 1991). Also, mother killer whales appear to show their offspring how to beach themselves (Rendell & Whitehead, 2001), a behaviour that is needed for the type of killer whale that feeds on seals that congregate along the shoreline.

In each of these examples, it is possible that the observer animals are imitating the individual who is demonstrating a behaviour. These observations raise the possibility that teaching may not be a uniquely human endeavour.

Miles Barton/Naturepl.com

Primate researchers have documented the spread of potato washing in Japanese macaque monkeys across multiple generations. Monkeys appear to learn how to do this by observing experienced monkeys from their troop.

Danita Delimont Creative/Alamy

Is this killer whale teaching her offspring to hunt for seals? Researchers have found evidence of teaching in killer whales and a variety of other nonhuman species.

during lessons. He will also be less likely to practise the observed behaviour that he is trying to learn.

Observational punishment is also possible, but appears to be less effective at changing behaviour than reinforcement. Witnessing others experience negative consequences may decrease your chances of copying someone else's behaviour. Even so, we are sometimes surprisingly bad at learning from observational punishment. Seeing the consequences of smoking, drug abuse, and other risky behaviours does not seem to prevent many people from engaging in the same activities.

IMITATION AND OBSERVATIONAL LEARNING

One of the primary mechanisms that allows observational learning to take place is **imitation**—*recreating someone else's motor behaviour or expression, often to accomplish a specific goal.* From a very young age, infants imitate the facial expressions of adults (Meltzoff & Moore, 1977). Later, as they mature physically, children readily imitate motor acts produced by a model, such as a parent, teacher, or friend. This ability seems to be something very common among humans. However, it is currently unclear what imitation actually is, although a number of theories exist. Some researchers suggest that children receive positive reinforcement when they properly imitate the behaviour of an adult and that imitation is a form of operant learning (Horne & Erjavec, 2007). Others suggest that imitation allows children to gain a better understanding of their own body parts versus the "observed" body parts of others (Mitchell, 1987). Finally, imitation might involve a more cognitive representation of one's own actions as well as the observed actions of someone else (Whiten, 2000). It is likely that all three processes are involved with imitation at different points in human (and some animal) development (Zentall, 2012).

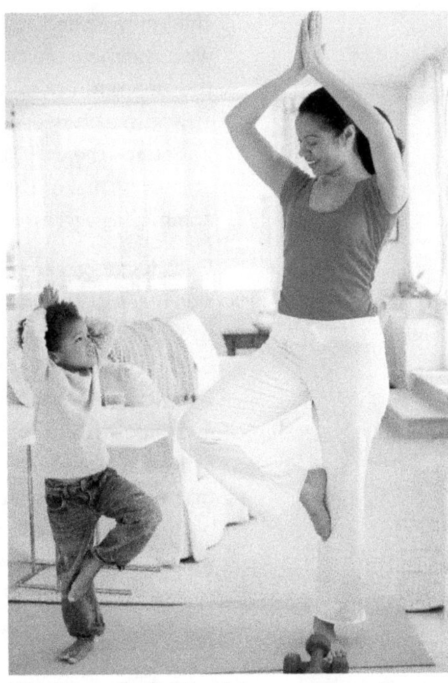

JGI/Jamie Grill/Blend Images/Getty Images

Infants and children actively imitate others, particularly adults.

At the beginning of this module, we raised the topic of human imitation—namely, how children, in contrast to chimpanzees, may imitate *beyond* what is necessary. Psychologists have found that both children from industrialized regions of Australia and children from remote nonindustrialized communities in Africa over-imitate the actions of adults who model how to open a contraption using a variety of sticks, switches, and knobs. The adult demonstrating the actions involved in opening the box added irrelevant steps to the process—many of which the children were compelled to imitate (Nielsen & Tomaselli, 2010). Perhaps humans are so wired and motivated to learn from others that evolution has given us, but not nonhumans, the tendency to over-imitate.

WORKING THE SCIENTIFIC LITERACY MODEL

Linking Media Exposure to Behaviour

Over-imitating behaviours such as opening contraptions with sticks is fairly harmless. However, not all of the behaviours children see are this innocent. Children (and adults) are exposed to dozens of violent actions in the media, on the Internet, and in computer games every day. If kids are imitating the behaviours they see in other contexts, does this mean that the media are creating a generation of potentially violent people?

What do we know about media effects on behaviour?

In some cases, learning from the media involves direct imitation; in other cases, what we observe shapes what we view as normal or acceptable behaviour. Either way, the actions people observe in the media can raise concerns, especially when children are watching. Given that North American children now spend an average of five hours per day interacting with electronic media, it is no wonder that one of the most discussed and researched topics in observational learning is the role of media violence in developing aggressive behaviours and desensitizing individuals to the effects of violence (Anderson et al., 2003; Huesmann, 2007). So how have researchers tackled the issue?

How can science explain the effect of media exposure on children's behaviour?

Simulate: Media Violence and Societal Aggression

One of the first experimental attempts to test whether exposure to violence begets violent behaviour in children was made by Albert Bandura and colleagues (1961, 1963). In a series of studies, groups of children watched an adult or cartoon character attack a "Bobo" doll, while another group of

Simulate: Bandura's Study on Observation Learning

children watched adults who did not attack the doll. Children who watched adults attack the doll did likewise when given the opportunity, in some cases even imitating the specific attack methods used by the adults. The other children did not attack the doll. This provided initial evidence that viewing aggression makes children at least temporarily more prone to committing aggressive acts toward an inanimate object.

Decades of research has since confirmed that viewing aggression is associated with increased aggression and desensitization to violence (Bushman & Anderson, 2007). In one beautifully Canadian study, Wendy Josephson (1987) had children aged 7–9 view a violent or nonviolent film before playing a game of floor hockey. Not surprisingly, children who viewed the violent film were more likely to act aggressively (i.e., to commit an act that would be penalized in a real hockey game). As an added twist, in some of the floor hockey games, a referee carried a walkie-talkie that had appeared in the violent film and thus served as a reminder of the violence. This movie-associated cue stimulated more violence, particularly in children who the teachers had indicated were prone to aggression.

Visual images are not the only source of media violence, however. Music, particularly hip hop and rap music (Herd, 2009), has become increasingly graphic in its depictions of violence over the last few decades. Psychologists have found that songs with violent lyrics can lead to an increase in aggressive and hostile thoughts in a manner similar to violent movies (Anderson et al., 2003). In one study, German researchers asked male and female participants to listen to songs with sexually aggressive lyrics that were degrading to women. After listening to this music, the participants were asked to help out with a (staged) taste-preference study by pouring hot chili sauce into a plastic cup for another participant (who was actually a confederate of the experimenters). The researchers found that after listening to aggressive music that degraded women, males poured more hot sauce for a female than for a male confederate; this difference did not occur after listening to neutral music. Female participants did not show this effect. Male participants also recalled more negative and aggressive thoughts. Interestingly, when women listened to lyrics that were demeaning to men, they too recalled more negative and hostile information (Fischer & Greitmeyer, 2006). Thus, the effects of media violence are not limited to the visual domain and can affect both males and females.

Can we critically evaluate this research?

Exposure to violent media and aggressive behaviour and thinking are certainly related to each other. However, at least two very important questions remain. First, does exposure to violence *cause* violent behaviour or desensitization to violence? Second, does early exposure to violence turn children into violent adolescents or adults? Unfortunately, there are no simple answers to either question, due in large part to investigators' reliance on correlational designs,

Albert Bandura

In Albert Bandura's experiment, children who watched adults behave violently toward the Bobo doll were aggressive toward the same doll when given the chance—often imitating specific acts that they viewed. **Click on this image in your eText to watch video footage of this experiment**.

Watch
Classic Footage of Bandura's Bobo Doll Experiment

which are typically used for studying long-term effects. Recall that correlational studies can establish only that variables are related, but cannot determine that one variable (media) causes another one (violent behaviour). What is very clear from decades of research is that a positive correlation exists between exposure to violent media and aggressive behaviour in individuals, and that this correlation is stronger than those between aggression and peer influence, abusive parenting, or intelligence (Bushman & Anderson, 2007).

Another concern with these studies is that they aren't really examining *why* people respond aggressively when they see violent imagery. Although there is clearly a role for observational learning, a number of researchers have also suggested that people become desensitized to the violence and thus less likely to inhibit their own violent impulses. Recent brain-imaging studies support this view. In one study, activity in parts of the frontal and parietal lobes showed reductions in activity as people became less sensitive to aggression shown in videos (Strenziok et al., 2011). In another experiment, participants with a low history of exposure to media violence showed more activity in frontal-lobe regions related to inhibiting responses than did participants who had more exposure to media violence and who had a history of aggressive behaviour. These differences were particularly strong when participants had to inhibit responses related to aggression-related words (Kalnin et al., 2011). Although these studies don't definitively explain why media violence affects behaviour, they do point to at least one potential cause.

Why is this relevant?

Clearly then, media violence is a significant risk factor for future aggressiveness. Many organizations have stepped in to help parents make decisions about which type of media their children will be exposed to. The Motion Picture Association of America has been rating movies, with violence as a criterion, since 1968. (Canada does not have a national ratings system; individual provinces each rate movies.) Violence on television was being monitored and debated even before the film industry took this step. Since the 1980s, parental advisory stickers have been appearing on music with lyrics that are sexually explicit, reference drug use, or depict violence. Even more recently, due to a drastic upsurge in their popularity and sophistication, video games have been labelled with parental advisory stickers. Of course, as you know, these precautions have little effect on what children watch, listen to, and play. Kids will always find a way to access this type of material. But, providing parents with more information about how these depictions of violence can affect children will hopefully highlight some of the dangers of these images and lyrics, and may inspire them to *talk to* their kids about how violence can be real. Doing so might teach children and adolescents to be better at examining how media violence could be affecting their own behaviour.

Watch
In the Real World: Learning Aggression

Christopher T Stein/Digital Vision/Getty Images

Dwayne Newton/PhotoEdit

Graphic violence in video games has become commonplace.

Watch
Violence and Video Games: Douglas Gentile

MIRROR NEURONS Neuroscientists have provided additional insight into the functions of imitation. In the 1990s, Italian researchers discovered that groups of neurons in parts of the frontal lobes associated with planning movements became active both when a monkey performed an action *and* when it observed another monkey perform an action (di Pellegrino et al., 1992). These cells, now known as *mirror neurons,* are also found in several areas in the human brain and have been linked to many different functions ranging from understanding other people's emotional states to observational learning (Rizzolatti et al., 1996; Rizzolatti & Craighero, 2004). Additionally, groups of neurons appear to be sensitive to the context of an action. In one study, participants viewed a scene of a table covered in a plate of cookies, a teapot, and a cup. In one photo of these items, the setting is untouched. In this case, reaching for the cup of tea would indicate that the person intended to have a sip. In another photo, many of the cookies are gone and the milk container has been knocked over. In this case, reaching for the cup of tea—the identical action as in the previous photo—would indicate that the person was cleaning up the mess. Incredibly, different groups of mirror neurons fired in response to the two images, despite the fact that the identical movement was being viewed (Iacoboni et al., 2005).

It remains unclear whether mirror neurons are related to media depictions of violence. However, given that goal-directed movements are the focus of attention in violent movies and video games, it is reasonable to expect that mirror neurons will be responding as well.

BIOPSYCHOSOCIAL PERSPECTIVES

Violence, Video Games, and Culture

Can pixilated, fictional characters controlled by your own hands make you more aggressive or even violent? Adolescents, university students, and even a lot of adults in their thirties and forties play hours of video games each day, many of which are very violent. Also, because video games are becoming so widespread, concerns have been raised about whether the correlations between media violence and aggression are found across different cultures. What do you think: Do these games increase aggression and violent acts by players? First, test your knowledge and assumptions and then see what research tells us.

True or False?

1. **A regular pattern of playing violent video games *causes* violent behaviour.**
2. **Gamers who play violent video games are less likely to behave aggressively if they are able to personalize their own character.**
3. **Playing violent video games reduces a person's sensitivity to others' suffering and need for help.**
4. **Gamers from Eastern cultures, who play violent video games as much as Westerners, are less prone to video game–induced aggression.**
5. **Physiological arousal is not affected by violent video games.**
6. **Male gamers are more likely to become aggressive by playing video games than female gamers.**

Answers

1. *True.* **Playing violent video games has both short- and long-term effects on violent thinking and behaviour.**
2. *False.* **Personalizing a character seems to increase aggressive behaviour.**
3. *True.* **People who play violent video games often become less sensitive to the feelings and well-being of others.**
4. *False.* **Gamers from both Eastern and Western cultures show the same effects.**
5. *False.* **Players of violent video games show increased physiological arousal during play.**
6. *False.* **There are no overall gender differences in aggression displayed by gamers.**

(These data are from Anderson et al., 2010; Carnagey et al., 2007; and Fischer et al., 2010.)

Of course, these data don't mean that you should never watch a violent movie or violent video game. And, you don't need to delete your gangsta rap songs and replace them with a steady diet of Taylor Swift. Rather, these data show you that the media *can* influence your behavior. As you read in Modules 6.1 and 6.2, we can learn associations even without conscious awareness. It's up to you to become aware of how media violence can lead to (unintentional) observational learning. Doing so will help ensure that your actions are, in fact, your own.

Quick Quiz 6.3b Observational Learning

KNOW ...

1 Observational learning

A is the same thing as teaching.

B involves a change in behaviour as a result of watching others.

C is limited to humans.

D is not effective for long-term retention.

2 ________ is the replication of a motor behaviour or expression, often to accomplish a specific goal.

A Observational learning

B Latent learning

C Imitation

D Cognitive mapping

APPLY ...

3 Nancy is trying to learn a new yoga pose. To obtain the optimal results, research indicates she should

A observe, practise immediately, and continue to practise.

B observe and practise one time.

C just closely observe the behaviour.

D observe the behaviour just one time and then practise on her own.

ANALYZE ...

4 Which is the most accurate conclusion from the large body of research that exists on the effects of viewing media violence?

A Viewing aggression directly causes increased aggression and desensitization to violence.

B Viewing aggression does not cause increased aggression and desensitization to violence.

C Viewing aggression is related to increased aggression and desensitization to violence.

D Viewing aggression is not related to increased aggression and desensitization to violence.

Answers can be found on page ANS-2.

Module Summary

Module 6.3

Now that you have read this module you should

KNOW ...

- ***The key terminology associated with cognitive and observational learning:***

imitation (p. 263)
latent learning (p. 259)
observational learning (p. 260)

UNDERSTAND ...

- ***The concept of latent learning and its relevance to cognitive aspects of learning.*** Without being able to observe learning directly, it might seem as if no learning occurs. However, Tolman and Honzik showed that rats can form "cognitive maps" of their environment. They found that, even when no immediate reward was available, rats still learned about their environment.

APPLY ...

- ***Principles of observational learning outside of the laboratory.*** Based on what you read about in this module, how would you use observational learning in each of these settings? Check your answers on page ANS-2.

  1. Teaching children how to kick a soccer ball
  2. Improving efficiency in a busy office

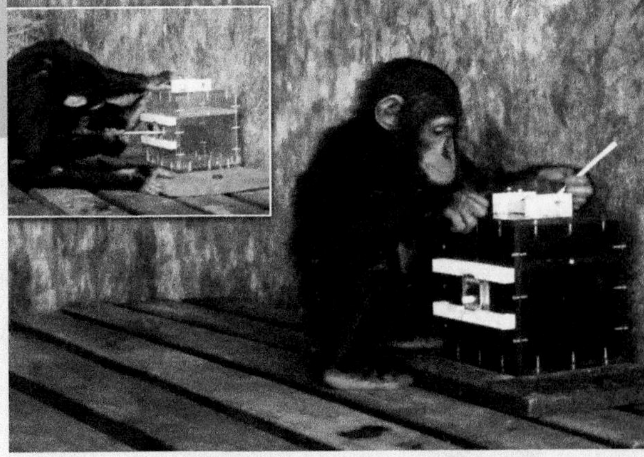

Courtesy of Victoria Horner and the Chimpanzee Sanctuary and Wildlife Conservation Trust, Ngamba Island, Uganda

  3. Improving environmental sustainability in your university

Are you simply letting people observe your behaviour, or does your plan involve elements learned in other modules in this chapter (e.g., shaping)?

ANALYZE ...

- ***The claim that viewing violent media increases violent behaviour.*** Psychologists agree that observational learning occurs and that media can influence behaviour. Many studies show a correlational (noncausal) relationship between violent media exposure and aggressive behaviour. Also, experimental studies, going all the way back to Albert Bandura's work of several decades ago, indicate that exposure to violent media can at least temporarily increase aggressive behaviour.

Work the Scientific Literacy Model :: Understanding Reinforcement and Punishment

1 What do we know about reinforcement and punishment?

Review **Figure 6.10 on page 244** and **Table 6.2 on page 246** for help distinguishing between reinforcement and punishment. As you review this material, think about how you could mentally organize these concepts. If you are positively reinforced, then some external incentive is given to you. If you are negatively reinforced, then your behaviour has resulted in something aversive being removed. For example, the child in line at the grocery store who whines until his dad gives him candy is positively reinforced for whining: He receives something he wants (candy), so the next time the child is at the store, his behaviour (whining) is likely to increase. The father is negatively reinforced, because he gives his son the candy and the whining (something he finds aversive) stops. Both father and son were reinforced because each is likely to repeat the behaviour that got them what they wanted.

While the father was negatively reinforced in this scenario, no one was *punished.* If you are confused about the difference between negative reinforcement and punishment, consider this: Most people find the outcome of negative reinforcement to be desirable but are upset about being punished.

2 How can science help explain how reinforcement and punishment work?

Page 244 included a discussion of how early research with animal subjects proved that systematic reinforcement can shape behaviours in both animals and humans. Also, on **page 248**, we mentioned how modern researchers have identified a specific region of the brain, the nucleus accumbens, that becomes activated during the processing of rewarding activities such as eating (see **Figure 6.13**). Individual differences in this area of the brain might account for why some people can easily modify their behaviour through reinforcement or punishment, whereas others struggle to do so. Research has also revealed that people tend to react more strongly to the unpleasantness of punishment than they do to the pleasures of reward, which raises questions about the effectiveness of punishment versus reinforcement. For example, parents who spank their children often see short-term results when a child stops her undesirable behaviour, but studies have found that spanking has several negative side effects. Research also suggests that the negative side effects increase or decrease depending on the severity of the physical punishment.

lculig/Shutterstock

4 Why is this relevant?

Watch the accompanying video excerpt on operant conditioning. You can access the video at MyPsychLab or by clicking the play button in the centre of your eText. If your instructor assigns this video as a homework activity, you will find additional content to help you in MyPsychLab. You can also view the video by using your smart phone and the QR code below, or you can go to the YouTube link provided.

After you have read this chapter and watched the video, imagine that you are asked by a roommate to help him devise a weight-loss program to increase his chances of making the football team. Create a one-month behaviour modification program based on the principles of operant conditioning which will help him get started toward his goal.

3 Can we critically evaluate claims about reinforcement and punishment?

Do these findings suggest that all punishment is ineffective and that reinforcement is the only way to successfully modify behaviour? The discussion of punishment on **page 255** explained that while punishment may temporarily stop an unwanted behaviour, it does not teach appropriate behaviours. For example, if the latest fad diet severely restricts the amount and kind of food you can eat, you may lose pounds in the short term, but once the diet is over, you will probably go back to your unhealthy ways and gain back the weight. Generally, punishment of any kind is most effective when it is combined with reinforcing alternative responses. See the guidelines in **Table 6.4 on page 255** for tips on using punishment and minimizing its negative side effects.

MyPsychLab **Your turn to Work the Scientific Literacy Model:** Watch the accompanying video on YouTube, or on your phone (using the Layar app or QR code). If your instructor has assigned this as a homework activity, you can find the video clip and additional content at MyPsychLab. Answer the questions that accompany the video clip to test your understanding.

youtube.com/workthemodel

SCAN WITH LAYAR

7

Memory

Andreka/Shutterstock

Jsemeniuk/E+/Getty Images

Module 7.1

Memory Systems

Learning Objectives

After reading this module you should

KNOW...	UNDERSTAND...	APPLY...	ANALYZE...
The key terminology of memory systems	Which structures of the brain are associated with specific memory tasks and how the brain changes as new memories form	Your knowledge of the brain basis of memory to predict what types of damage or disease would result in which types of memory loss	The claim that humans have multiple memory systems

In October 1981, an Ontario man lost control of his motorcycle and flew off an exit ramp west of Toronto. He suffered a severe head injury and required immediate brain surgery in order to treat the swelling caused by the impact. Brain scans conducted after the accident showed extensive damage to the medial temporal lobes (including the hippocampus) as well as to both frontal lobes and the left occipital lobe. When the man, now known as patient K.C., recovered consciousness, doctors quickly noted that he had severe memory impairments. However, when psychologists from the University of Toronto dug deeper into K.C.'s condition, it became clear that he had retained some memory for general knowledge, but that he had lost his *episodic memory,* the memory of his specific experiences (Tulving et al., 1988). Strikingly, K.C. could recall the facts about his life (e.g., where he lived) but could not recall his personal experiences or feelings relating to those facts (e.g., sitting on the steps with friends).

K.C.'s devastating experience helped researchers prove that we have several different types of memory, each involving different networks of brain areas (Rosenbaum et al., 2005). His case also hearkens back to a philosophical question posed by William James (1890/1950) over a century ago: If an individual were to awaken one day with his or her personal memories erased, would he or she still be the same person?

Focus Questions

 How is it possible to remember just long enough to have normal conversations and activities but then to forget them almost immediately?

 How would damage to different brain areas affect different types of memory?

You have probably heard people talk about memory as if it were a single ability:

- I have a terrible memory!
- Isn't there some way I could improve my memory?

But have you ever heard people talk about memory as if it were several abilities?

- One of my memories works well, but the other is not so hot.

Probably not. However, as you will learn in this module, *memory* is actually a collection of several systems that store information in different forms for differing amounts of time (Atkinson & Shiffrin, 1968). The path that information takes as it is stored in memory can be seen in Figure 7.1.

The Atkinson-Shiffrin Model

In the 1960s, Richard Atkinson and Richard Shiffrin reviewed what psychologists knew about memory at that time and constructed the memory model that bears their name (see Figure 7.1). The first thing to notice about the Atkinson-Shiffrin model is that it includes three memory stores (Atkinson & Shiffrin, 1968). **Stores** *retain information in memory without using it for any specific purpose*; they essentially serve the same purpose as hard drives serve for a computer. The three stores include sensory memory, short-term memory (STM), and long-term memory (LTM), which we will investigate in more detail later. In addition, **control processes** *shift information from one memory store to another*; they are represented by the arrows in the model. Information enters the

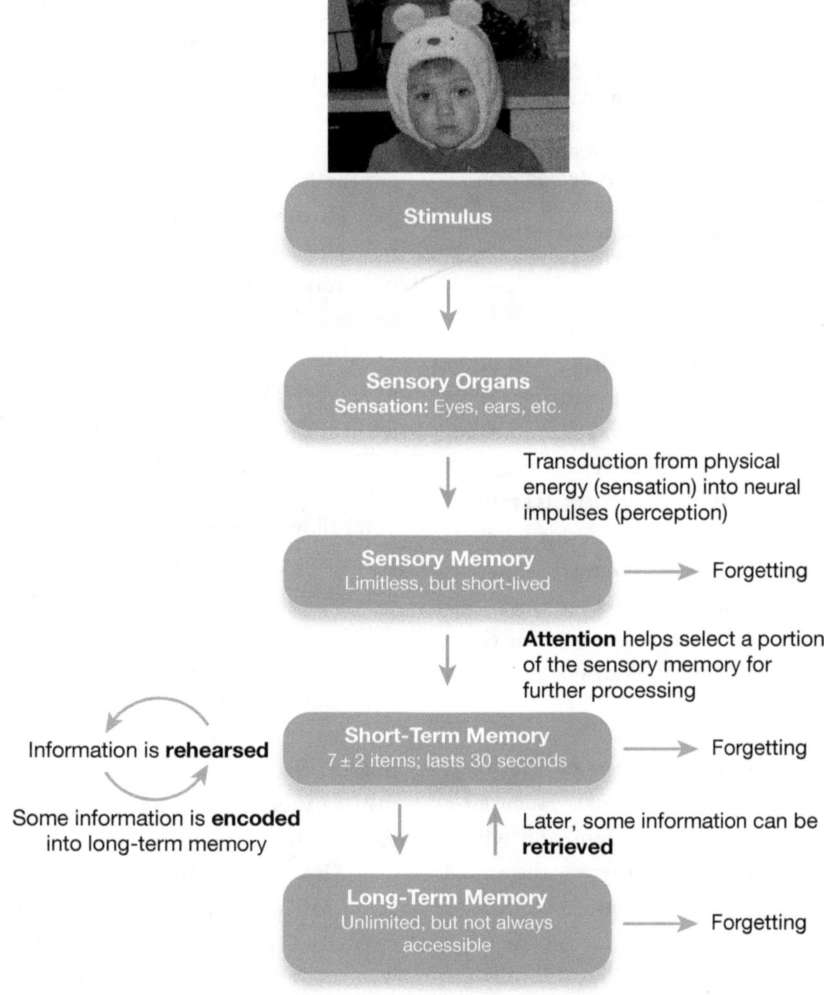

{FIG. 7.1} **The Atkinson-Shiffrin Model** Memory is a multistage process. Information flows through a brief sensory memory store into short-term memory, where rehearsal encodes it into long-term memory for permanent storage. Memories are retrieved from long-term memory and brought into short-term storage for further processing. **Click on this figure in your eText to see more details.**

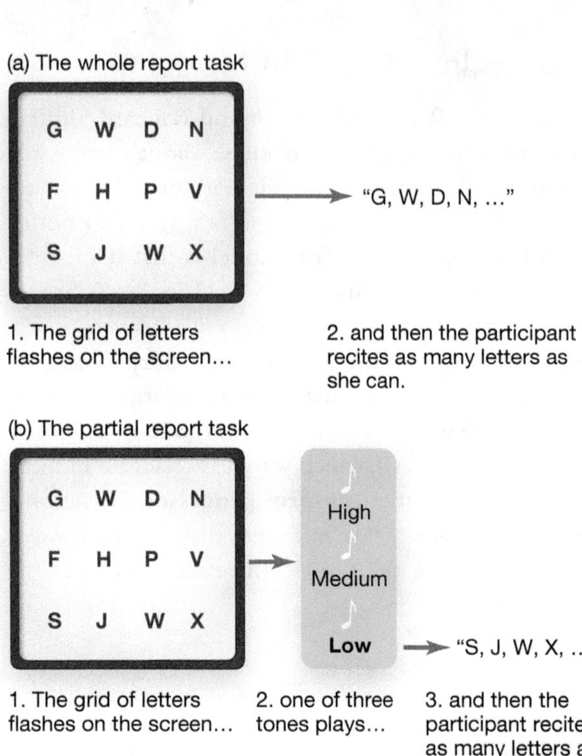

{FIG. 7.2} **A Test of Iconic Sensory Memory** Sperling's participants viewed a grid of letters flashed on a screen for a split second, then attempted to recall as many of the letters as possible. In the whole report condition (a), they averaged approximately four items, usually from a single row. By comparison, as Sperling demonstrated, they could remember more than four items in the partial report condition (b). In these trials, participants could usually name *any* row of four items, depending on the row they were cued to recite.

sensory memory store through vision, hearing, and other senses, and the control process we call **attention** *selects which information will be passed on to STM*. Some (but not all) information in STM goes through **encoding**, *the process of storing information in the LTM system*. **Retrieval** *brings information from LTM back into STM*; this happens when you become aware of existing memories, such as remembering the movie you saw last week. In this module, we are primarily concerned with the various types of memory stores, so next we will examine each one in detail.

Explore Key Processes in Stages of Memory

Explore Encoding, Storage, and Retrieval in Memory

SENSORY MEMORY **Sensory memory** *is a memory store that accurately holds perceptual information for a very brief amount of time*—how brief depends on which sensory system we talk about. *Iconic memory,* the visual form of sensory memory, is held for about one-half to one second. *Echoic memory*, the auditory form of sensory memory, is held for considerably longer, but still only for about five seconds (Cowan et al., 1990).

How much information can be held in sensory memory? This important question was very difficult to answer, because sensory memories disappear faster than an individual can report them. George Sperling devised a brilliant method for testing the storage capacity of iconic memory. In his experiment, researchers flashed a grid of letters on a screen for a split second (Figure 7.2a), and participants had to report what they saw. In the *whole report* condition, participants attempted to recall as many of the letters as possible—the *whole* screen. Participants were generally able to report only three or four of the letters, and these would all be in the same line. But does this mean that the iconic sensory memory system can only store three or four bits of information at a time? Sperling thought that it likely had a larger capacity, but hypothesized that the memory of the letters actually faded faster than participants could report them. To test this, in the *partial report* condition, participants were again flashed a set of letters on the screen, but the display was followed immediately by a tone that was randomly chosen to be low, medium, or high (Figure 7.2b). After hearing the tone, participants were to report the corresponding line of letters—bottom, middle, or top. Under these conditions, participants still reported only three or four of the letters, but they could report them from any randomly selected line. Because the tone came after the screen went blank, the only way the participants could get the letters right is if they recalled them from memory. Thus Sperling argued that iconic memory could hold all 12 letters as a mental image, but that they would only remain in sensory memory long enough for a few letters to be reported.

But if information in our sensory memory disappears after half a second, then how can we have any continuous perceptions? How can you stare meaningfully into someone's eyes without that person fading away from memory half a second later? Or, how can you follow the spider crawling across your wall without it continually disappearing like the letters in Sperling's experiment? The answer is attention. Attention allows us to move a small amount of the information from our sensory memory into STM for further processing. This information is often referred to as being within the "spotlight of attention" (Pashler, 1999). Information that is outside of this spotlight of attention is not transferred into STM and is quite unlikely to be remembered.

The relationship between sensory memory and attention is beautifully illustrated by a phenomenon known as *change blindness* (Rensink et al., 1997, 2000; Simons & Levin, 1997). In a typical change blindness experiment, participants view two nearly identical versions of a photograph (or some other stimulus); these stimuli will have only one difference between them

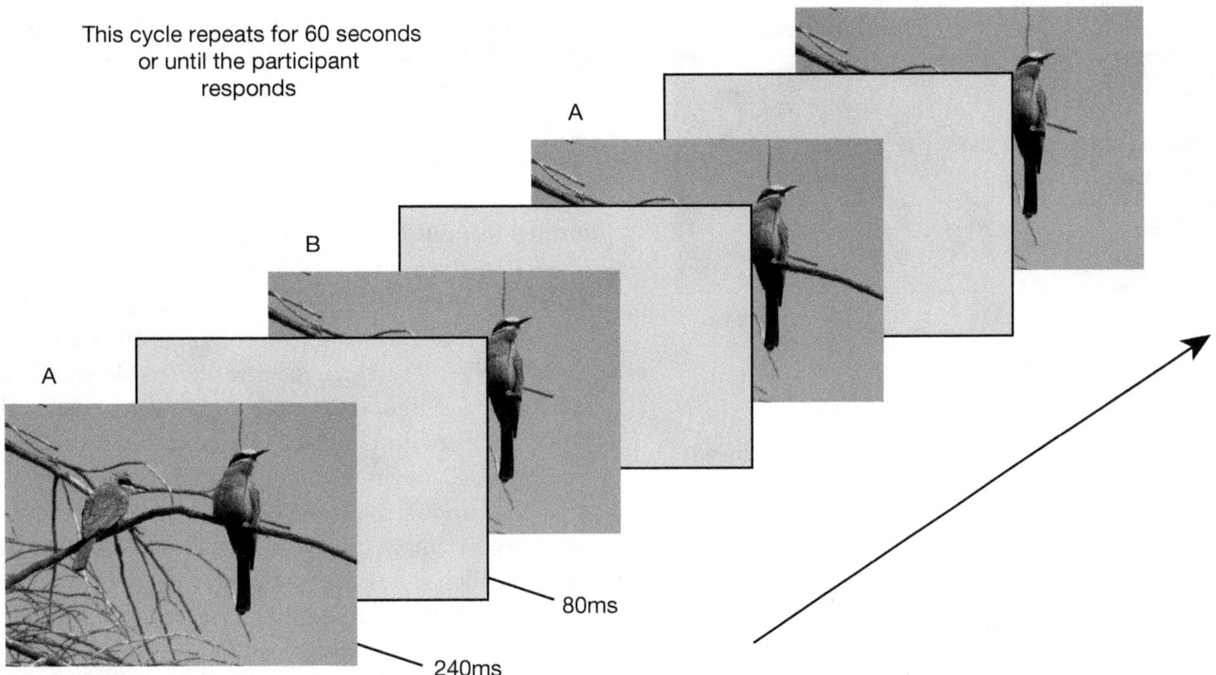

{FIG. 7.3} **Change Blindness, Attention, and Sensory Memory** In change blindness, the sensory memory of photograph A disappears before the onset of photograph B, making it difficult to identify the difference between the two pictures. However, if a person is paying attention to the area that differs between the two photographs, then the representation of that part of the first photograph will still be in short-term memory when the second photograph appears, thus making it relatively easy to spot the change. In this example, part of a tree branch disappears in photograph B.

(e.g., a car is different colours in the two photographs). The goal on each trial of the experiment is to locate the difference. However, the way in which the images are displayed presents quite a challenge. The two versions of the photograph are alternately presented for 240 ms each, with a blank screen in between them. So, a participant would see Photograph 1, blank screen, Photograph 2, blank screen, Photograph 1, blank screen, and so on. If the difference item within the two photographs (e.g., the car) is not the focus of attention, people generally fail to notice the change (hence the term *change blindness*). This is because one version of the changing item fades from sensory memory just as the next version appears (see Figure 7.3). However, if the participant is paying attention to that changing element, the image of the first version of that item will be transferred into STM when the second, changed version appears on the screen. The difference between the two photographs then becomes apparent.

An obvious question that arises is: Why don't people quickly move their spotlight of attention around so that they can transfer all of their sensory memory into short-term memory? Unfortunately, there is a limit to how much information can be transferred at once (Marois & Ivanoff, 2005).

SHORT-TERM MEMORY AND THE MAGICAL NUMBER 7 Although transferring information from sensory into short-term memory increases the chances that this information will be remembered later, it is not guaranteed. This is because **short-term memory (STM)** is *a memory store with limited capacity and duration (less than a minute).* The capacity of STM was summed up by one psychologist as *The Magical Number 7 ± 2* (Miller, 1956). In his review, Miller found study after study in which participants were able to remember seven units of information, give or take a couple. One researcher made the analogy between STM and a juggler who can keep seven balls in the air before dropping any of them. Similarly, STM can rehearse only seven units of information at once before forgetting something (Nairne, 1996).

This point leads to an important question: What, exactly, is "a unit of information"? The answer varies from situation to situation. It turns out that, whenever possible, we expand our memory capacity with **chunking**, *organizing smaller units of information into larger, more meaningful units.* Consider these examples:

1. O B T N C H C V N T C N S N C
2. C B C H B O C T V T S N C N N

(a)

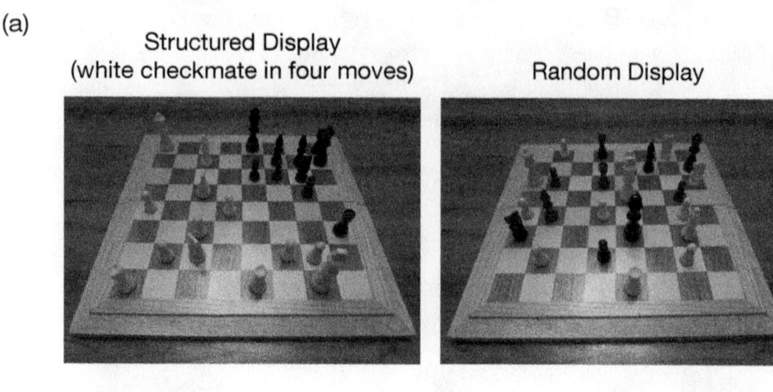

(b)

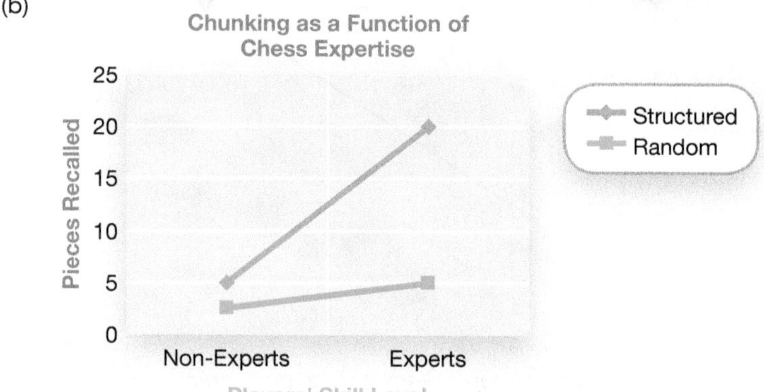

{FIG. 7.4} **Chunking in Chess Experts** Chess experts have superior STM for the locations of pieces on a chess board due to their ability to create STM chunks. This advantage only occurs when the pieces are placed in a meaningful way, as they would appear in a game. (a) A depiction of a board with the pieces placed as they would appear in a game (left) and pieces placed in random locations (right). (b) The difference in STM for meaningful vs. randomly placed pieces increased as a function of the test subject's chess experience.

If we randomly assigned one group of volunteers to remember the first list, and another group to remember the second list, how would you expect the two groups to compare? Look carefully at both lists. List 2 is easier to remember than list 1. Volunteers reading list 2 have the advantage of being able to apply patterns that fit their background knowledge; specifically, they can chunk these letters into five groups based on popular television networks:

CBC HBO CTV TSN CNN

In this case, chunking reduces 15 bits of information to a mere five. We do the same thing with phone numbers. We turn the area code (403) into one chunk, the first three numbers (555) into another chunk, and then the final four numbers into one or two chunks depending upon the numbers (e.g., 1867 might be one chunk because it can be remembered as the year Canada became a country, while 8761 could be remembered as two chunks representing the jersey numbers for hockey players Sidney Crosby and Rick Nash or, if you're not a hockey addict, some other meaningful pattern).

The ability to chunk material varies from situation to situation. If you had never watched television, then the five chunks of information in the example above wouldn't be very meaningful to you. This suggests that experience or expertise plays a role in our ability to chunk large amounts of information so that it fits into our STM. Studies of chess experts have confirmed that this is the case. Whereas most people would memorize the positions of chess pieces on a board individually, chess masters perceive it as a single unit, like a photograph of a scene (Chase & Simon, 1973; Gobet & Simon, 1998). Therefore, they are able to remember the positions of significantly more chess pieces than could novices. Of course, chunking only works when the chess pieces are aligned in meaningful chess positions; when they are randomly placed on the board, the experts' memory advantage disappears (see Figure 7.4). Chunking also allows the chess masters to envision what the board will look like after future moves, again providing them an edge over novices.

Importantly, this expertise is not necessarily based on some innate talent; it can be learned through intensive practice. The most stunning confirmation of this view comes from the Polgár sisters of Budapest, Hungary (Flora, 2005). Their father, Lázló Polgár, decided before they were born that he was going to raise them to become chess grandmasters. Doing so would confirm his belief that anyone could be trained to become a world-class expert in any field if he or she worked hard enough (he was not a grandmaster himself). Polgár trained his daughters in the basics of chess, and had them memorize games so that they could visualize each move on the board. After thousands of hours of what amounts to "chunking training," the girls (who, luckily, enjoyed chess) rose to the top of the chess world. The eldest daughter, Susan, became the first female to earn the title of Grandmaster through tournament play. The youngest daughter, Sofia, is an International Master. The middle daughter, Judit, is generally thought of as the best female chess player in history.

LONG-TERM MEMORY Not all of the information that enters STM is retained. A large proportion of it is lost forever. This isn't necessarily a bad thing, however. Imagine if every piece of information you thought about remained accessible in your memory. Your mind would be filled with phone numbers, details from text messages, images from billboards and ads on buses, as well as an incredible amount of trivial information from other people (e.g., overhearing the coffee order of the person in front of you). Instead, only a small amount of information from STM is encoded or transformed into memory traces. Encoding allows information to enter the final memory store in the Atkinson-Shiffrin model. This store, **long-term memory (LTM)**, *holds information for extended periods of time, if not permanently.* Unlike short-term memory, long-term memory has no capacity limitations. All of the information that undergoes encoding will be entered into LTM.

Once entered into LTM, the information needs to be organized. Researchers have identified at least two ways in which this organization occurs. One way is based on the semantic categories that the items belong to (Collins & Loftus, 1975). The mental representation of *cat* would be connected to and stored near the mental representation of other animals such as *dog* and *mouse*. This tendency was nicely illustrated in an experiment from the 1950s. Participants were asked to remember a list of 60 words that were drawn from four different categories. Although the words were randomly presented, participants recalled them in semantically related groups (e.g., lion, tiger, cheetah . . . guitar, violin, cello, etc.). This tendency suggests that semantically related items are stored near each other in LTM (see Module 8.1). Additional support for this view comes from a unique patient with brain damage. Patient M.D. had a selective impairment for naming fruits and vegetables; he could name photographs of other items quite well (Hart et al., 1985).

LTM is also organized based on the sounds of the word and on how the word looks. This explains part of the *tip of the tongue (TOT) phenomenon,* when you are able to retrieve similar sounding words or words that start with the same letter but can't quite retrieve the word you actually want (Brown & McNeill, 1966). What appears to be happening in these situations is that nearby items, or nodes, in your neural network are activated.

Of course, having the information in LTM doesn't necessarily mean that you can access it when you want to. If that were the case, then everyone would have a perfect grade-point average and no one would be impressed by your knowledge of trivial information, such as the last name of The Count from the children's program *Sesame Street* (Answer: von Count). Instead, the likelihood that a given piece of information will undergo retrieval—the process of accessing memorized information and returning it to short-term memory—is influenced by a number of different factors including the quality of the original encoding and the strategies used to retrieve the information. These important processes are described in depth later in this chapter.

WORKING THE SCIENTIFIC LITERACY MODEL

Distinguishing Short-Term from Long-Term Memory Stores

The Atkinson-Shiffrin model of memory is very neat and tidy, with different memory stores contained in separate boxes. The problem is that the real world rarely involves 30-second blocks of time filled with 7 ± 2 pieces of information followed by a short break to encode them. Instead, we are often required to use both STM and LTM at the same time. Without this ability, we wouldn't be able to have conversations nor would we be able to understand paragraphs of text like this one. So, if both STM and LTM are constantly working together, how do we isolate the functions of each memory store?

What do we know about short-term and long-term memory stores?

As you'll recall (thanks to your LTM), STM lasts for approximately 30–60 seconds and usually contains 7 ± 2 units of information; LTM has no fixed time limits or capacity. The distinction between STM and LTM can be revealed with a simple experiment. Imagine everyone in your psychology class studied a list of 15 words and then immediately tried to recall the words in the list. The serial position curve—the U-shaped graph in Figure 7.5—shows what the results would look like according to the **serial position effect**: *In general, most*

Simulate
The Serial Position Curve

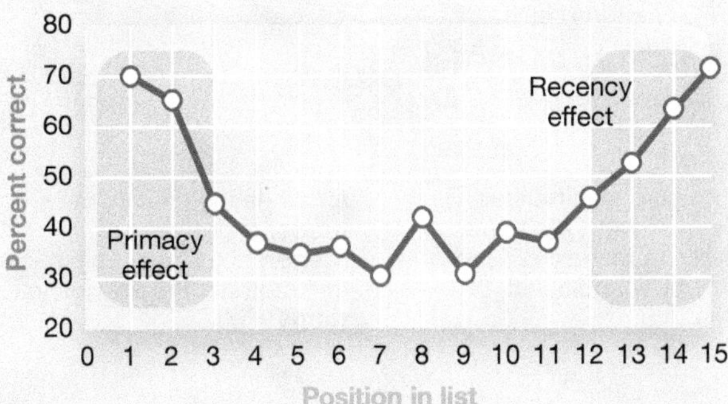

{FIG. 7.5} **The Serial Position Effect** Memory for the order of events is often superior for original items (the primacy effect) and later items (the recency effect). The serial position effect provides evidence of distinct short-term and long-term memory stores. **Click on this figure in your eText to see more details.**

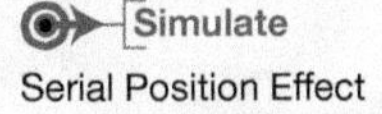

people will recall the first few items from a list and the last few items, but only an item or two from the middle (Ebbinghaus, 1885/1913). This finding holds true for many types of information, ranging from simple strings of letters to the ads you might recall after watching the Super Bowl (Laming, 2010; Li, 2010).

The first few items are remembered relatively easily (known as the *primacy effect*) because they have begun the process of entering LTM. The last few items are also remembered well (known as the *recency effect*); however, this is because those items are still within our STM (Deese & Kaufman, 1957). The fate of the items in the middle of the test is more difficult to determine, as they would be in the process of being encoded into LTM. As you have already read, some information is lost during this stage.

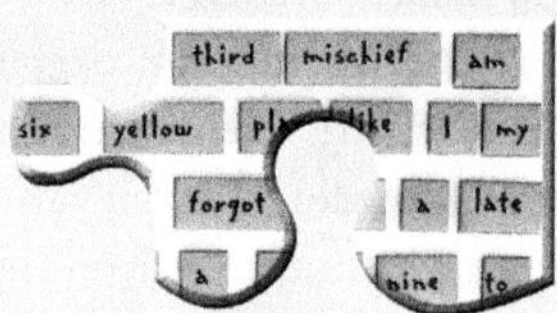

How can science explain the difference between STM and LTM stores?

The shape of the serial position effect (see Figure 7.5) suggests that there are two different processes at work. But, how do we explain the dip in the middle of the curve? Memory researchers suggest that this dip in performance is caused by two different mechanisms. First, the items that were at the beginning of the list produce **proactive interference**, *a process in which the first information learned (e.g., in a list of words) occupies memory, leaving fewer resources left to remember the newer information.* The last few items on the list create **retroactive interference**—that is, *the most recently learned information overshadows some older memories that have not yet made it into long-term memory* (see Figure 7.6). Together, these two types of interference would result in poorer memory performance for items in the middle of a list.

Sam was asked to remember a list of 10 words:
happy, train, carrot, water, bus, sky, cat, candy, hike, telephone.

Happy, Train, Carrot, Water

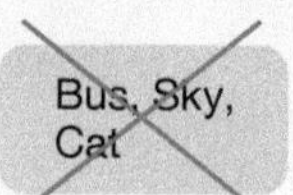

Candy, Hike, Telephone

After hearing the first four words on the list, *proactive interference* made it difficult to remember additional information.

After hearing the last three words, *retroactive interference* made it difficult to remember the preceding words.

As a result, Sam could not recall the words in the middle of the list.

{FIG. 7.6} **Proactive and Retroactive Interference Contribute to the Serial Position Effect**

In addition to demonstrating behavioural differences between STM and LTM, scientists have also used neuroimaging to attempt to identify the different brain regions responsible for each form of memory. Deborah Talmi and colleagues (2005) performed an fMRI experiment in which they asked ten volunteers to study a list of 12 words presented one at a time on a computer screen. Next, the computer screen flashed a word and the participants had to determine whether the word was from their study list. The researchers were mostly concerned about the brain activity that occurred when the volunteers correctly recognized words. When volunteers remembered information from early in the serial position curve, the hippocampus was active (this area is associated with the formation of LTM, as you will read about later). By comparison, the brain areas associated with sensory information—hearing or seeing the words—were more active when people recalled items at the end of the serial position curve. Thus, the researchers believed they had isolated the effects of two different neural systems which, working simultaneously, produce the serial position curve.

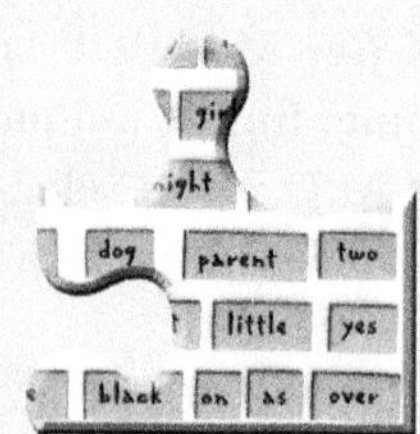

Can we critically evaluate the distinction between STM and LTM?

In order to evaluate the idea that the serial-position effect is caused by two interacting memory systems, we need at least two types of tests. First, we need to find evidence that it is possible to change the performance on one test but not the other. Then we need to find medical cases in which brain damage affected one system, but not the other. Together, these findings would support the view that STM and LTM stores can be distinguished from each other.

The fact that it is possible to separately affect the primacy and recency effects was demonstrated in the 1950s and 1960s. When items on a list are presented quickly, it becomes more difficult to completely encode those items into long-term memory. The result is a reduction in the primacy effect; however, STM will still contain the most recently presented items, thus leaving the recency effect unchanged (Murdock, 1962). The recency effect can be reduced by inserting a delay between the presentation of the list and the test. This delay will allow other information to fill up STM; LTM, as shown by the primacy effect, will be unaffected (Bjork & Whitten, 1974).

Evidence from neurological patients also supports the distinction between STM and LTM. STM deficits can occur after damage to the lower portions of the temporal and parietal lobes, as well as to lateral (outside) areas of the frontal lobes (Müller & Knight, 2006). In contrast, damage to the hippocampus will prevent the transfer of memories from STM to

LTM (Scoville & Milner, 1957). These patients will have relatively preserved memories of their past, but will be unable to add to them with new information from short-term memory.

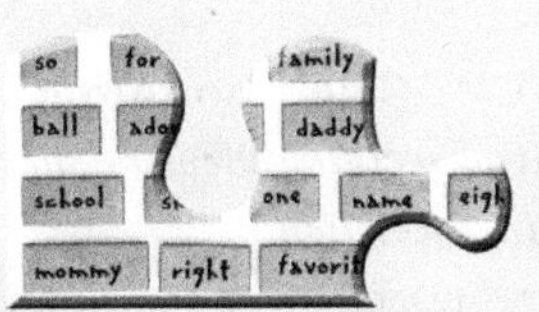

Why is this relevant?

The idea of multiple memory stores is theoretically interesting and can explain some of the minor memory problems we all experience (e.g., forgetting parts of a phone number). But, being able to distinguish between STM and LTM has more wide-reaching implications. The fact that it is possible to separate STM and LTM—and that these stores are driven by different brain systems—suggests that you could use simple tests like the serial-position effect to predict where a neurological patient's brain damage had occurred. Many common assessment tools such as the Wechsler Memory Scales include tests of both types of memory in order to do just that. Clues uncovered by these initial assessment tests can be used by emergency room physicians and neurologists to assist with their diagnosis and may lead them to request a brain scan for a patient (to look for damage) when they might not otherwise have done so.

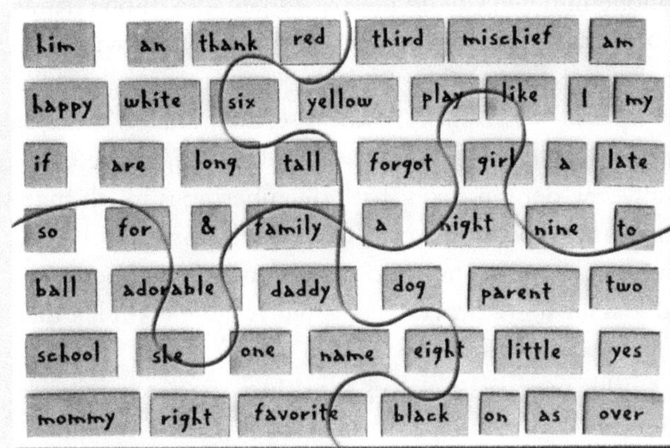

Clayton Hansen/iStockphoto

The Atkinson-Shiffrin Model provides a very good introduction to the different stages of memory formation. However, as we will see later in this module, memory is much more complex than is implied by this box-and-arrow diagram. In the next section, we will discuss working memory, a form of STM that involves a number of different, complementary, pieces.

Quick Quiz 7.1a

The Atkinson-Shiffrin Model

KNOW...

1 Which elements of memory do not actually store information, but instead describe how information may be shifted from one type of memory to another?

A Serial position effects

B Recency effects

C Primacy effects

D Control processes

2 ________ lasts less than a minute, whereas ________ holds information for extended periods of time, if not permanently.

A Long-term memory; short-term memory

B Short-term memory; sensory memory

C Short-term memory; long-term memory

D Long-term memory; process memory

APPLY...

3 Chris forgot about his quiz, so he had only 5 minutes to learn 20 vocabulary words. He went through the list once, waited a minute, and then went through the list again in the same order. Although he was confident, his grade indicated that he missed approximately half of the words. Which words on the list did he most likely miss, and why?

A According to the primacy effect, he would have missed the first few words on the list.

B According to the recency effect, he would have missed the last few words on the list.

C According to the serial position effect, most of the items he missed were probably in the middle of the list.

D According to the primacy effect, he would have missed all of the words on the list.

ANALYZE...

4 Brain scans show that recently encountered items are processed in one area of the brain, whereas older items are stored in a different area. Which concept does this evidence support?

A Multiple memory stores

B A single memory store

C Complex control processes

D Retrieval

Answers can be found on page ANS-2.

The Working Memory Model: An Active STM System

Imagine you are driving a car when you hear the announcement for a radio contest—*the 98th caller at 1-800-555-HITS will win $98!* As the DJ shouts out the phone number, you do not have a pen or a phone handy, and traffic is swarming, so what do you do? You will probably try to remember the number by using **rehearsal**, *or repeating information* (in this case, the number) *until you do not need to remember it anymore.* Psychological research, however, demonstrates that remembering is much more than just repeating words to yourself. Instead, keeping information like the radio station's phone number available is an active process that is much more complex than one would expect.

This process involves **working memory**, *a model of short-term remembering that includes a combination of memory components that can temporarily store small amounts of information for a short period of time.* This includes new information such as the specific phone number that will win $98 for you, as well as keeping track of the traffic patterns. Working memory can also draw from older information that is stored in a relatively stable way—the fact that you know what a phone is and how to operate one, and that $98 translates into roughly 25 iced cappuccinos.

A key feature of working memory is that it recognizes that stimuli are encoded simultaneously in a number of different ways (e.g., with vision and hearing) rather than simply as a single unit of information. Indeed, the classic working memory model for short-term remembering can be subdivided into three storage components (Figure 7.7), each of which has a specialized role (Baddeley, 2001; Jonides et al., 2005): the phonological loop, the visuospatial sketchpad, and the episodic buffer. These storage components are then coordinated by a control centre known as the central executive. Each component will be discussed in more detail below.

{FIG. 7.7} **Components of Working Memory Work Together to Manage Complex Tasks**

THE PHONOLOGICAL LOOP The **phonological loop** *is a storage component of working memory that relies on rehearsal and that stores information as sounds, or an auditory code.* It engages some portions of the brain that specialize in speech and hearing, and it can be very active without affecting memory for visual and spatial information. While the magical number 7 provides a good estimate of STM capacity in general, to focus more precisely on phonological memories, we must examine how long it takes to pronounce those items. Based on the *word-length effect*, we know that people remember more one-syllable words (*sum, pay, bar,* ...) than four- or five-syllable words (*helicopter, university, alligator,* ...) in a short-term-memory task (Baddeley et al., 1975). Despite the fact that both *bar* and *alligator* are single chunks, you remember more chunks if they are single syllables. Research indicates that working memory can store as many syllables as can be rehearsed in about two seconds, and that this information is retained for approximately 15 seconds (Brown, 1958; Peterson & Peterson, 1959). So, in the radio-contest example, you would likely be able to remember the phone number (it can be spoken in under two seconds unless you talk like you're from Texas), but you would need to pull over to use your phone fairly quickly, before the information started to fade away.

THE VISUOSPATIAL SKETCHPAD The **visuospatial sketchpad** *is a storage component of working memory that maintains visual images and spatial layouts in a visuospatial code.* It keeps you up to date on where objects are around you and where you intend to go. To do so, the visuospatial sketchpad engages portions of the brain related to perception of vision and space and does not affect memory for sounds. Just as the phonological store can be gauged at several levels—that is, in terms of the number of syllables, the number of words, or the number of chunks—items stored in visuospatial memory can be counted based on shapes, colours, and textures. This leads to an important question: Can a smooth, square-shaped, red block count as one chunk? Or do texture, shape, and colour of the block act as three separate units of information? Research has consistently shown that a square-shaped block painted in two colours is just as easy to recognize as the same-shaped block painted in one colour (Vogel et al., 2001). Therefore, visuospatial working memory may use a form of chunking. This process of combining visual features into a single unit goes by a different name, however: *feature binding* (see Figure 7.8).

After visual feature binding, visuospatial memory can accurately retain approximately four whole objects, regardless of how many individual features one can find on those objects. Perhaps this is evidence for the existence of a second magical number—four (Awh et al., 2007; Vogel et al., 2001).

To put feature binding into perspective, consider the amount of visual information available to you when you are driving a car as in the story that started this section. If you are at the wheel, watching traffic, you probably would not look at a car in front of you and remember images of red, shiny, and smooth. Instead, you would simply have these features bound together in the image of the car, and you would be able to keep track of three or four such images without much problem as you glance at the speedometer and then back to the traffic around you.

THE EPISODIC BUFFER Recent research suggests that working memory also includes an **episodic buffer**—that is, *a storage component of working memory that combines the images and sounds from the other two components into coherent, story-like episodes.* These episodes include the relevant information that will allow you to make sense of the images and sounds, such as "I was driving to a friend's house when I heard the radio DJ give a number to call."

The episodic buffer is the most recently hypothesized working memory system (Baddeley, 2001). The episodic buffer seems to hold 7 to 10 pieces of information, which may be combined with other memory stores. This aspect of its operation can be demonstrated by comparing memory for prose (words strung into sentences) to memory for unrelated words. When people are asked to read and remember meaningful prose, they usually remember 7 to 10 *more* words than when reading a random list of unrelated words. Some portion of working memory is able to connect the prose with information found in LTM ("knowledge") to increase memory capacity.

THE CENTRAL EXECUTIVE Finally, working memory includes one component that is not primarily used for storing information. Instead, the **central executive** *is the control centre of working memory; it coordinates attention and the exchange of information among the three*

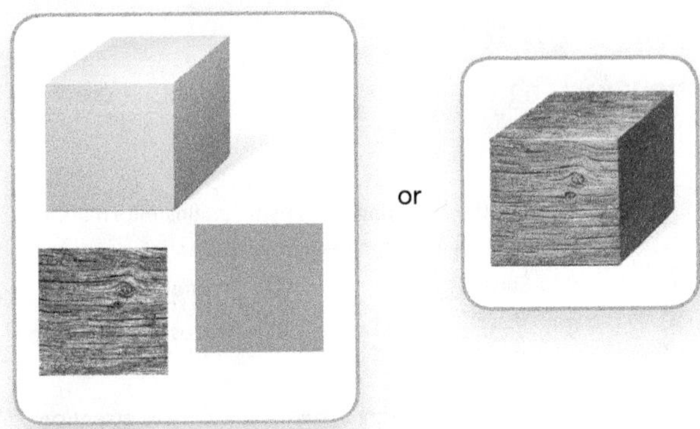

{FIG. 7.8} **Working Memory Binds Visual Features into a Single Chunk** Working memory sometimes stores information such as shape, colour, and texture as three separate chunks, like the three pieces of information on the left. For most objects, however, it stores information as a single chunk, like the box on the right.

storage components. It does so by examining what information is relevant to the person's goals, interests, and prior knowledge and then focusing attention on the working memory component whose information will be most useful in that situation. For example, when you see a series of letters from a familiar alphabet, it is easy to remember the letters by rehearsing them in the phonological loop. In contrast, if you were to look at letters or characters from a foreign language—perhaps you are visiting Seoul and you do not know Korean—you may not be able to convert them to sounds; thus you would assign them to the visuospatial sketchpad instead (Paulesu et al., 1993). Regions within the frontal lobes of the brain are responsible for carrying out these tasks for the central executive.

So how do these four components of the working-memory system work for you when you cannot pull your car over immediately to place the 98th call? Most of us would rely on our phonological loop, repeating the number 1-800-555-HITS to ourselves until we can call. Meanwhile, our visuospatial sketchpad is remembering where other drivers are in relation to our car, even as we look away to check the speedometer, the rearview mirror, or the volume knob. Finally, the episodic buffer binds together all this information into episodes, which might include information such as "I was driving to school," "the DJ announced a contest," and "I wanted to pull over and call the station." In the middle of all this activity is the central executive, which guides attention and ensures that each component is working on the appropriate task. Thus, although your memories often seem almost automatic, there is actually a lot of work going on in your working memory.

Quick Quiz 7.1b

The Working Memory Model: An Active STM System

KNOW...

1 Which of the following systems maintains information in memory by repeating words and sounds?

A Episodic buffer
B Central executive
C Phonological loop
D Visuospatial sketchpad

2 Which of the following systems coordinates attention and the exchange of information among memory storage components?

A Episodic buffer
B Central executive
C Phonological loop
D Visuospatial sketchpad

UNDERSTAND...

3 When psychologists ask research participants to remember combinations of letters (such as TJD), why might they have participants engage in distracting tasks such as counting backward by threes?

A Counting backward prevents rehearsal, so researchers can see how long an unrehearsed memory trace will last.
B Researchers try to make the participants forget.
C Counting backward can facilitate episodic binding.
D Researchers are actually interested in backward-counting ability.

APPLY...

4 When Nick looks for his friend's motorcycle in a parking lot, he sees a single object, not two wheels, a seat, and a red body. This is an example of _______.

A a phonological loop
B feature binding
C buffering
D proactive interference

Answers can be found on page ANS-2.

Long-Term Memory Systems: Declarative and Nondeclarative Memories

Figure 7.1 at the beginning of this module suggests that humans have just one type of long-term memory (LTM). However, as you read in the story about the neurological patient K.C., LTM has a number of different components. K.C. could learn new skills, draw maps, and remember basic facts. Yet, he was unable to recall specific episodes in his own life (Tulving & Markowitsch, 1998). What do cases like K.C.'s tell us about the organization of LTM?

One way to categorize LTM is based on whether or not we are conscious of a given memory (see Figure 7.9). Specifically, **declarative memories** (or **explicit memories**) *are memories that we are consciously aware of and that can be verbalized, including facts about the world and one's own personal experiences.* In contrast, **nondeclarative memories** (or **implicit memories**) *include actions or behaviours that you can remember and perform without awareness.* But, this initial division only scratches the surface of LTM's complexity. Both declarative and nondeclarative memories have multiple subtypes, each with its own characteristics and brain networks.

DECLARATIVE MEMORY Declarative memory comes in two varieties (Tulving, 1972). **Episodic memories** *are declarative memories for personal experiences that seem to be organized around "episodes" and are recalled from a first-person ("I" or "my") perspective.* Examples of episodic memories would be your first day of university, the party you went to last month, and watching the Olympics on TV. **Semantic memories,** on the other hand, are *declarative memories that include facts about the world.* Examples of semantic memories would include knowing that Halifax is the capital of Nova Scotia, remembering that Sean Connery was the first actor to play James Bond, and that bananas are (generally) yellow. The two types of memory can be contrasted in an example: Your semantic memory is your knowledge of what a bike is, whereas episodic memory is the memory of a specific time when you rode a bike.

The case of K.C. provides compelling evidence that semantic and episodic memories are distinct forms of declarative memory. Although K.C. had no specific memories of events that took place in his high school or his house, he did understand that he had

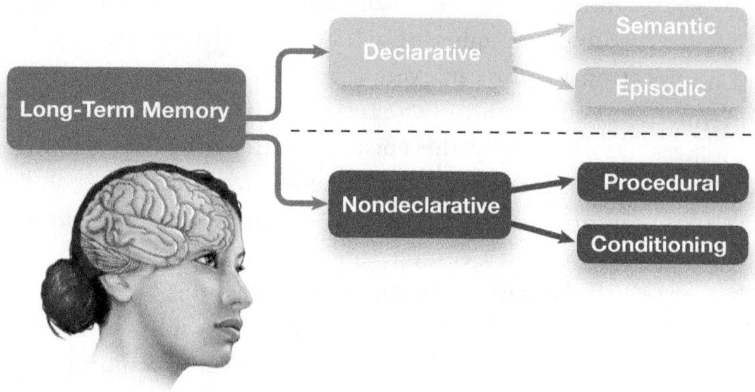

{FIG. 7.9} **Varieties of Long-Term Memory** Long-term memory can be divided into different systems based on the type of information that is stored. **Click on this figure in your eText to see more details.**

Monkey Business Images/Shutterstock.com

This child may have episodic memories of specific piano lessons, semantic memories about what a piano is and how it works, and procedural memories about how to play a few songs.

attended high school and that he lived in a specific home in Mississauga, ON. However, K.C. is not the only example of the distinction between these types of memory. Studies of older adults have noted that they show similar (but much less severe) impairments to K.C. on memory tests. As people get older, their episodic memory declines more rapidly than their semantic memory (Luo & Craik, 2008). Older people are more likely to forget where they went on vacation five years ago than they are to forget something like the names of provincial capitals (Levine et al., 2002). Interestingly, they also show normal performance on a number of tests related to nondeclarative memories.

NONDECLARATIVE MEMORY Nondeclarative memory occurs when previous experiences influence performance on a task that does not require the person to intentionally remember those experiences (Graf & Schacter, 1985). The earliest published report of this form of memory came in 1845 when a British physician named Robert Dunn described the details of a woman with amnesia (Schacter, 1985). This woman learned how to make dresses following her injury, but had no conscious memory of learning to do so. A more pointed example was published in the early 20th century by Claparède (1911/1951). He reported on an amnesic woman who learned not to shake his hand because he had previously stuck her with a pin attached to his palm. In both cases, the behaviours of patients with no conscious memories were altered because of previous experiences, thus suggesting that this previous information was encoded into LTM in some form.

But, nondeclarative memories are not isolated to cases of amnesia. You have thousands of nondeclarative memories in your brain right now. These memories can take many different forms. **Procedural memories** are *patterns of muscle movements (motor memory)* such as how to walk, play piano, or drive a car. We often don't think of the individual steps involved in these behaviours, yet we execute them flawlessly most of the time. This is the type of nondeclarative memory demonstrated by the amnesic woman who learned how to make dresses. Another form of nondeclarative memory is *classical conditioning,* when a previously neutral stimulus (e.g., a bell) produces a new response (e.g., salivating) because it has a history of being paired with another stimulus that produces that response (e.g., food). Although these associations can sometimes be consciously recalled, this recollection is not necessary for conditioning to successfully take place (see Module 6.1).

One method of testing nondeclarative memory (without poking participants with pins) is through a laboratory technique known as *priming.* Priming is based on the idea that previous exposure to a stimulus will affect an individual's later responses, either to that same stimulus or to something related to it. For instance, if the word "chase" were flashed on a computer screen and you were later asked to complete the word stem "cha–" with the first word that came to mind, you would likely complete it with "chase" despite the fact that there are more common completions for that stem (e.g., chair). Importantly, this effect can occur regardless of whether the primed stimulus was consciously perceived or attended to (Merikle & Joordens, 1997). Although this seems like a phenomenon that would be isolated to the laboratory, priming actually occurs all the time in the real world. We are constantly being influenced by previous exposure to advertisements, people, and a host of environmental cues such as temperature (Gawronski et al., 2005; Strick et al., 2009). Even if we don't consciously recall some of these previous experiences, they do bias our behaviours. For example, advertisements for trucks often show them performing rugged, "manly" activities such as hauling large piles of wood down a bumpy dirt road (it's what men do). We aren't expected to remember the road or any other details of the commercials; in fact, we might not remember having seen the commercial at all. But, the next time we see that brand of truck, we immediately remember that it is strong and reliable, just like our nondeclarative memories.

It is important to remember that distinctions between different types of memories do not mean that those memories work in isolation. Many day-to-day tasks involve both declarative and nondeclarative memory. You might know how to ride a bike, which is an example of a nondeclarative procedural memory; but, knowing that bikes are two-wheeled vehicles is a declarative semantic memory. Each type of memory adds its own unique contribution to the events we experience—and the new memories we form—every day.

Watch
The Basics: Do You Remember When?

Quick Quiz 7.1c
Long-Term Memory Systems: Declarative and Nondeclarative Memories

KNOW...

1 Memories for information that was learned without our being aware of it are known as __________.
- A semantic memories
- B episodic memories
- C nondeclarative memories
- D declarative memories

2 Memories that can be verbalized, whether they are about your own experiences or your knowledge about the world, are called __________.
- A nondeclarative memories
- B procedural memories
- C conditioned memories
- D declarative memories

Watch
Neurological Basis of Memory: Howard Eichenbaum

APPLY...

3 Mary suffered a head injury during an automobile accident and was knocked unconscious. When she woke up in a hospital the next day, she could tell that she was in a hospital room, and she immediately recognized her sister, but she had no idea why she was in the hospital or how she got there. Which memory system seems to be affected in Mary's case?
- A Semantic memories
- B Episodic memories
- C Nondeclarative memories
- D Working memories

Answers can be found on page ANS-2.

Explore
Virtual Brain: Learning and Memory

The Cognitive Neuroscience of Memory

So far, we have primarily discussed the behavioural and cognitive aspects of memory; but, the *biopsychosocial model* reminds us that everything involves a biological component as well. Therefore, psychologists also look at how the nervous system changes with the formation of new memories. To explore the cognitive neuroscience of memory, we will take a brief look at the neuronal changes that occur as memories are forming and strengthening, and will then examine the brain structures involved in long-term storage. Finally, we will use examples from studies of amnesia and other forms of memory loss to understand how our memory models fit with biological data.

MEMORY AT THE NEURAL LEVEL Memory at the cellular level can be summed up in the following way: Cells that fire together, wire together. This idea was proposed in the 1940s by Canadian neuroscientist Donald Hebb. Specifically, he suggested that when neurons fire at the same time, it leads to chemical and physical changes in the neurons, making them more likely to fire together again in the future (Hebb, 1949). Later research proved Hebb correct, and demonstrated that changes occur across numerous brain cells as memories are forming, strengthening, and being stored (Lømo, 1966). This process, **long-term potentiation (LTP)**, *demonstrated that there is an enduring increase in connectivity and transmission of neural signals between nerve cells that fire together.*

The discovery of LTP occurred when researchers electrically stimulated two neurons in a rabbit's hippocampus—a key memory structure of the brain located in an area called the medial temporal lobes (see Figure 7.10). Stimulation to the hippocampus increased the number of electrical potentials from one neuron to the other. Soon, the neurons began to generate *stronger* signals than before, a change that could last up to a few hours (Bliss & Lømo, 1973). This finding does not mean that LTP *is* memory—no one has linked the strengthening of a particular synapse with a specific memory like your first day of university. In fact, no one has seen LTP outside of a laboratory. But, the strengthening of synapses shown in LTP studies may be one of the underlying mechanisms that allow memories to form.

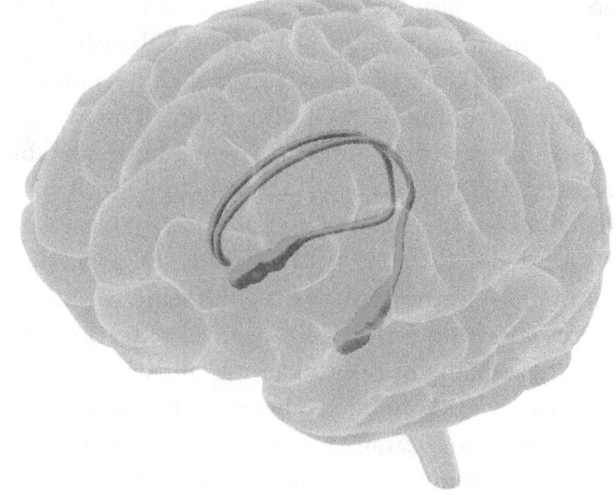

{FIG. 7.10} **The Hippocampus** The hippocampus resides within the temporal lobe and is critical for memory processes.

To see how such microscopic detail relates to memory, consider the very simple case of learning and remembering discussed in a previous module: eye-blink conditioning. Imagine you hear a simple tone right before a puff of air is blown in your eye; you will reflexively blink. After two or three pairings, just the tone will be enough to cause an eye blink—this is an example of classical conditioning (see Module 6.1). At the neural level, the tone causes a series of neurons to respond, and the puff of air causes another series of neurons to respond. With repeated tone and air puff pairings, the neurons that are involved in hearing the tone, and those that control the blinking response, develop a history of firing together. This simultaneous activation provides the opportunity for synapses to become strengthened, representing the first stages of memory.

This relationship is not permanent, however. Lasting memories require **consolidation**, *the process of converting short-term memories into long-term memories in the brain*, which may happen at the level of small neuronal groups or across the cortex (Abraham, 2006). When neurons fire together a number of times, they will adapt and make the changes more permanent—a process called *cellular consolidation*. This process involves physical changes to the synapse between the cells so that the presynaptic cell is more likely to stimulate a *specific* postsynaptic cell (or group of cells). Without the consolidation process, the initial changes to the synapse eventually fade away, and presumably so does the memory. (This process can therefore be summed up with the saying: Use it or lose it.) To demonstrate the distinction between the initial learning and longer-term consolidation, researchers administered laboratory rats a drug that allowed LTP, but prevented consolidation from occurring (by blocking biochemical actions). The animals were able to learn a task for a brief period, but they were not able to form long-term memories. By comparison, rats in the placebo group, whose brains were able to consolidate the information, went through the same tasks and formed long-term memories without any apparent problems (Squire, 1986).

The initial strengthening of synapses and longer-term consolidation of these connections allow us to form new memories, thus providing us with an ability to learn and to adapt our behaviour based on previous experiences. However, these processes are not performed in all areas of the brain. Instead, specific structures and regions serve essential roles in allowing us to form and maintain our memories, a fact powerfully demonstrated by the memory deficits of patients with amnesia.

MEMORY, THE BRAIN, AND AMNESIA On August 31, 1953, Henry Molaison was a 27-year-old man with intractable epilepsy. Because his seizures could not be controlled by medications, Mr. Molaison had been referred to Dr. William Scoville, a respected Hartford-based neurosurgeon, for treatment. Dr. Scoville and his colleagues had suggested that removing the areas of Molaison's brain that triggered the seizures would cure, or at least tame, his epilepsy. On September 1, 1953, Henry Molaison underwent a resection (removal) of his medial temporal lobes—including the hippocampus—on both sides of his brain. After that day, he became known to the world as neurological patient H.M.

H.M.'s surgery was successful in that he no longer had seizures. However, as he recovered from his surgery, it became apparent that the procedure had produced some unintended consequences. The doctors quickly determined that H.M. had **amnesia**—*a profound loss of at least one form of memory*. However, not all of his memories were lost; in fact, numerous studies conducted by Brenda Milner of McGill University demonstrated that H.M. retained many forms of memory (Milner, 1962; Scoville & Milner, 1957). He was able to recall aspects of his childhood. He could also remember the names of the nurses who had treated him before the surgery, although he was unable to learn the names of nurses who he met afterward. Indeed, H.M. appeared unable to encode new information at all. Therefore, H.M. was experiencing a specific subtype of amnesia known as **anterograde amnesia**, *the inability to form new memories for events occurring after a brain injury*.

Watch Special Topics: When Memory Fails

H.M.'s anterograde amnesia was not due to problems with his sensory memory or his STM. Both abilities remained normal throughout his life (Corkin, 2002). He was also able to recall details of his past, such as incidents from his school years and from jobs he had held; this demonstrates that his LTM was largely intact (Milner et al., 1968). He was also able to form new implicit memories. He was able to learn new skills such as drawing a picture by looking at its reflection in the mirror despite the fact that he had no memory for learning this skill (Milner, 1962). Similar improvements were found for solving puzzles (Cohen et al., 1985). After extensive testing, researchers concluded that H.M.'s amnesia was not due to problems with a particular memory store, but was instead due to problems with one of the control processes associated with those stores. Specifically, H.M. could not transfer declarative memories from STM into LTM.

The fact that H.M.'s brain damage was due to a precise surgical procedure (rather than to widespread damage from an accident like patient K.C.) allowed

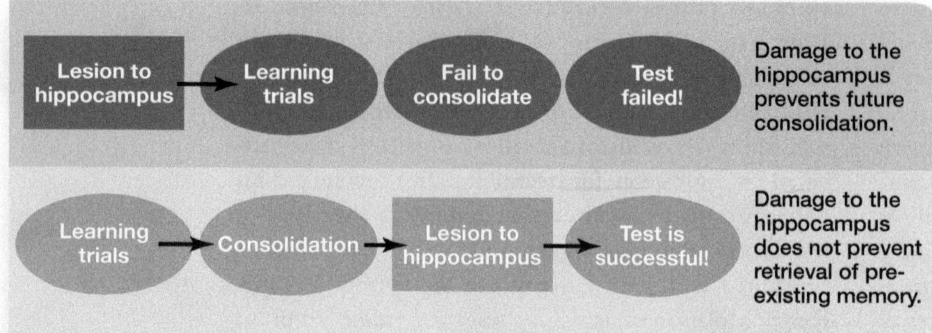

{FIG. 7.11} **Damage to the Hippocampus: Disruption of Consolidation** When the hippocampus is damaged, the injury interferes with consolidation, the formation of long-term memories. Such damage does not prevent recall of preexisting memories, however.

researchers to pinpoint the area of the brain responsible for this specific memory problem. H.M. was missing the medial temporal lobes of both hemispheres. This damage included the hippocampus and surrounding cortex as well as the amygdala. Based on H.M. and several similar cases, researchers concluded that this region of the brain must be involved with consolidating memories, enabling information from STM to enter and remain in LTM, a process that most of us take for granted.

Indeed, studies of hippocampal cells have demonstrated that this structure is critical for the process of consolidation discussed above. Although the hippocampus is not where most declarative memories are actually stored, it does maintain LTP networks until the acquired behaviour can form more connections throughout the brain. Eventually, the to-be-remembered behaviour will form networks involving the cortex. At this point, the hippocampus will not be necessary for the memory to be retrieved. However, without the hippocampus, as in the case of H.M., these new cortical networks will never be formed because the original LTP and consolidation processes would not have been completed (see Figure 7.11).

The hippocampus also appears to be essential for spatial memories such as remembering the layout of your house or recalling the route you would take to get to a friend's house. This function might also be linked to consolidation—remembering spatial information often involves updating a memory with new information such as learning alternative routes to get to your destination (i.e., "filling in" your map of an area). Remarkably, brain-imaging studies suggest that the size of a person's hippocampus can vary with the amount of spatial information that people are asked to consolidate. Researchers at Kings College London (U.K.) examined the brains of taxi drivers in that maze-like city and compared them to the brains of age-matched control participants. The taxi drivers, who were required to undergo extensive training and to memorize most of London, had substantially larger hippocampi than did the control participants (Maguire et al., 2000). This result implies that the demanding memory requirements of that job altered the structure of brain areas related to memory consolidation and spatial memory.

It is important to note that our long-term memories do not just collect dust after they have formed. They can be updated regularly, such as when someone reminds you of an event from years ago, or when you are reminded of information you learned as a child. In this way, memories undergo a process called *reconsolidation*, in which the hippocampus functions to update, strengthen, or modify existing long-term memories (Lee, 2010; Söderlund et al., 2012). These memories then form networks in different regions of the cortex, where they can (sometimes) be retrieved when necessary. These long-term declarative memories are distributed throughout the cortex of the brain, rather than being localized in one region—a phenomenon known as *cross-cortical storage* (Paller, 2004). Interestingly, with enough use, some of the memory networks will no longer need input from the hippocampus. The cortical networks themselves will become self-sustaining. The more that memory is retrieved, the larger and more distributed that network will become.

Newer memories, because they haven't had as much time to form extensive networks using cross-cortical storage, are much more likely to be lost following brain damage than are older memories. This brain damage

Lana Rastro/Alamy

Researchers in London found that the hippocampi of taxi drivers, who navigate the complex maze of the city, are larger than the hippocampi of non-taxi drivers (Maguire et al., 2000). What other careers do you think would produce changes in the structure of the brain?

disrupts the consolidation of recently experienced memories, causing them to fade away (Brown, 2002). This type of memory loss is known as **retrograde amnesia**, *a condition in which memory for the events preceding trauma or injury is lost* (see Figure 7.12). It can be caused by damage to the medial temporal lobes (as in patient K.C.) or to the cortex of the frontal lobes. This type of amnesia is quite common following head injuries, including minor ones such as concussions. However, the "lost time" is generally limited to the seconds or minutes leading up to the injury. The loss of extensive periods of time, as seen in K.C., is quite rare (despite what you see on soap operas).

The fact that memories can be lost after even minor brain damage shows us that our memory systems are quite delicate. Each of the boxes and arrows in the Atkinson-Shiffrin model (Figure 7.1) can be disrupted in some way; but, the formation and storage of long-term memories seems to be particularly sensitive to injuries. K.C.'s devastating injury shows us that when we lose our memories, we lose an important part of ourselves. So be careful.

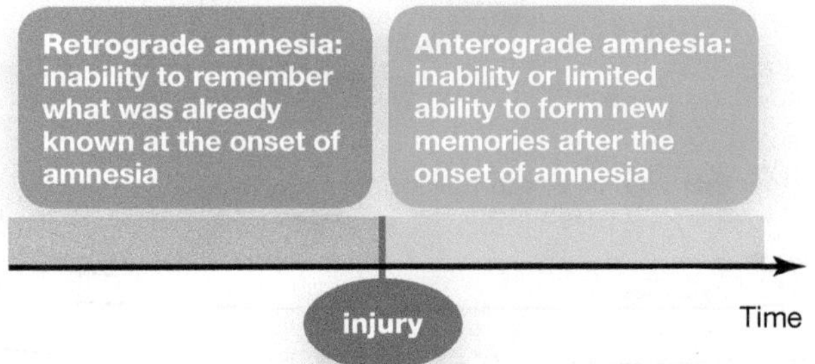

{FIG. 7.12} **Retrograde and Anterograde Amnesia** The term *amnesia* can apply to memory problems in both directions. It can wipe out old memories, and it can prevent consolidation of new memories.

Quick Quiz 7.1d The Cognitive Neuroscience of Memory

KNOW...

1 _________ is a process that all memories must undergo to become long-term memories.

- **A** Consolidation
- **B** Retrograde remembering
- **C** Anterograde remembering
- **D** Chunking

UNDERSTAND...

2 Long-term potentiation can be described as

- **A** a decrease in a neuron's electrical signalling.
- **B** neurons generating stronger signals than before, which then persist.
- **C** neural networking.
- **D** an example of working memory.

APPLY...

3 Damage to the hippocampus is most likely to produce _________.

- **A** retrograde amnesia
- **B** consolidation
- **C** anterograde amnesia
- **D** seizures

Answers can be found on page ANS-2.

Module Summary

Module **7.1**

Now that you have read this module you should

KNOW...

- ***The key terminology of memory systems*:**

amnesia (p. 283)
anterograde amnesia (p. 283)
attention (p. 272)
central executive (p. 279)
chunking (p. 273)
consolidation (p. 283)
control process (p. 271)
declarative memory (p. 280)
encoding (p. 272)
episodic buffer (p. 279)
episodic memory (p. 280)
long-term memory (LTM) (p. 275)
long-term potentiation (LTP) (p. 282)
nondeclarative memory (p. 280)
phonological loop (p. 278)
proactive interference (p. 276)
procedural memory (p. 281)
rehearsal (p. 278)
retrieval (p. 272)
retroactive interference (p. 276)
retrograde amnesia (p. 285)
semantic memory (p. 280)
sensory memory (p. 272)
serial position effect (p. 275)
short-term memory (STM) (p. 273)
stores (p. 271)
visuospatial sketchpad (p. 278)
working memory (p. 278)

UNDERSTAND...

- ***Which structures of the brain are associated with specific memory tasks and how the brain changes as new memories form.*** The hippocampus is critical to the formation of new declarative memories. Long-term potentiation at the level of individual nerve cells is the basic mechanism underlying this process. Long-term memory stores are distributed across the cortex. Working memory utilizes the parts of the brain associated with visual and auditory perception, as well as the frontal lobes (for functioning of the central executive).

APPLY...

- ***Your knowledge of the brain basis of memory to predict what types of damage or disease would result in which types of memory loss.*** Try responding to these questions for practice (check your answers on page ANS-2):

1. Dr. Richard trains a rat to navigate a maze, and then administers a drug that blocks the biochemical activity involved in long-term potentiation. What will happen to the rat's memory? Will it become stronger? Weaker? Or is it likely the rat will not remember the maze at all?

Jsemeniuk/E+/Getty Images

2. In another study, Dr. Richard removes a portion of the rat's hippocampus the day after it learns to navigate a maze. What will happen to the rat's memory? Will it become stronger? Weaker? Or will it be unaffected by the procedure?

ANALYZE...

- ***The claim that humans have multiple memory systems.*** Consider all the evidence from biological and behavioural research, not to mention the evidence from amnesia. Data related to the serial position effect indicate that information at the beginning and end of a list is remembered differently, and even processed and stored differently in the brain. Also, evidence from amnesia studies suggests that LTM and STM can be affected separately by brain damage or disease. Most psychologists agree that these investigations provide evidence supporting the existence of multiple storage systems and control processes.

Tkreykes/Fotolia

Module 7.2

Encoding and Retrieving Memories

Learning Objectives

After reading this module you should

KNOW...	UNDERSTAND...	APPLY...	ANALYZE...
The key terminology related to forgetting, encoding, and retrieval	How the type of cognitive processing employed can affect the chances of remembering what you encounter	What you have learned to improve your ability to memorize information	Whether emotional memories are more accurate than non-emotional ones

According to legend, the first person to develop methods of improving memory was the Greek poet Simonides of Ceos (556–468 BCE). After presenting one of his lyric poems at a dinner party in northern Greece, the host, Scopas, told him that he was only going to pay half of the cost of the poem (he clearly wasn't impressed by the work). Soon after this exchange, a grumpy Simonides was told that two men on horses wanted to talk to him outside. While talking to the horsemen, the roof of Scopas' house collapsed, killing everyone inside (Greek legends are not happy places…). When relatives wanted to bury the family, they were unable to figure out who the remains belonged to; none of the guests could recall where the family members had been sitting. Simonides had encoded the information differently than the rest of the guests; he was able to assist the family by creating a visual image of the dinner party and listing who was sitting in each chair. His story demonstrates one of the key points to be discussed in this module—that how you encode information affects the likelihood of you remembering that information later.

Focus Questions

 1. What causes some memories to be strong, while others are weak?

 2. How can we improve our memory abilities?

Why are some memories easier to recall than others? Why do we forget things? How can you use memory research to improve your performance at school and at work? These questions are addressed in this module, where we focus on factors that influence the encoding and retrieval of memories.

Encoding and Retrieval

In its simplest form, memory consists of encoding new information, storing that information, and then retrieving that stored information at a later time. As you have read elsewhere in this book, *encoding* is the process of transforming sensory and perceptual information into memory traces, and *retrieval* is the process of accessing memorized information and returning it to short-term memory. In between these two processes is the concept of **storage**, *which refers to the time and manner in which information is retained between encoding and retrieval.* Over the past fifty years, researchers have uncovered a number of factors that influence how our memory systems work, and also how we can improve our chances of remembering information. The most important of these factors appears to be how the information was encoded in the first place.

Explore
Encoding, Storage, and Retrieval in Memory

REHEARSAL: THE BASICS OF ENCODING What would you do if someone gave you the address for a house party but you didn't have a pen or your phone around? How would you keep the address in mind until you had a chance to run to your car to write it down? If you're like most people, you will recite the address over and over again until you can write it down. This type of memorization is known as rehearsal to psychologists (although your teachers may have called it *learning by rote*), and it is something probably all of us have tried (see Module 7.1). Indeed, students often try to learn vocabulary terms by reading flashcards with key terms and definitions over and over. But, is this strategy effective?

Certainly this approach works some of the time, but is it really *the most* effective way to remember? The answer is a resounding "no" (Craik & Watkins, 1973). The limitations of this form of rehearsal were shown in a sneaky experiment performed in the 1970s (see Figure 7.13); in this study, participants were asked to remember a four-digit number. After seeing the number, they were asked to repeat a single word until being prompted to report the number. The delay between the presentation of the number and the participants' responses varied from 2–18 seconds; this meant that the amount of time each word was repeated also varied. Because participants were trying to remember the digits, they barely paid attention to the word they repeated. Later, when the researchers surprised the participants by asking them to recall the distracting word they had repeated, they found virtually no relationship between the duration of rehearsal (between 2 and 18 seconds) and the proportion of individuals who could recall the word (Glenberg, Smith, & Green, 1977). In other words, longer rehearsal did not lead to better recall. This is not to say that repeating the word had no effect at all; rather, this study demonstrated that repeating information only had a small benefit, and that this benefit was not increased with longer rehearsal times.

It turns out that it is not *how long* we rehearse information, but rather *how* we rehearse it that determines the effectiveness of memory. Individuals in the study just described were engaged in **maintenance rehearsal**—*prolonging exposure to information by repeating it*—which does relatively little to facilitate encoding that leads to

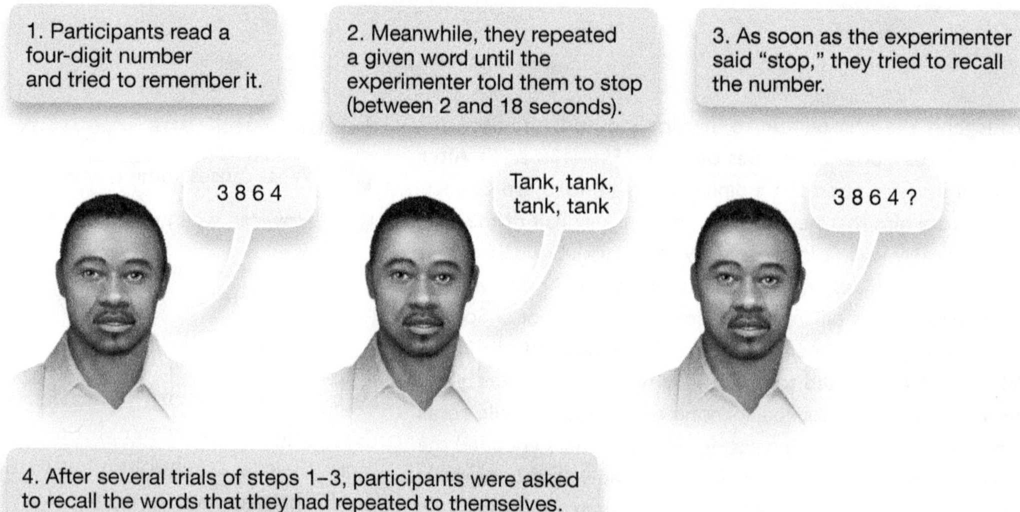

{FIG. 7.13} **Rote Rehearsal Has Limited Effects on Long-Term Memory** After participants completed the procedure depicted in this figure, they were given a surprise test of their memory for the words that they had recited. There was no difference in the recall of words rehearsed for 2 or 18 seconds. This result suggests that simply repeating the word—maintenance rehearsal—has a limited effect on our memory.

the formation of long-term memories (although it is better than nothing). By comparison, **elaborative rehearsal**—*prolonging exposure to information by thinking about its meaning*—significantly improves the process of encoding (Craik & Tulving, 1975). For example, repeating the word *bottle*, and then imagining what a bottle looks like and how it is used, is an elaborative technique. In the story that began this module, Simonides used a form of elaborative rehearsal by not only memorizing a list of people at a table (Scopus, Constantine, Helena, etc.), but actively imagining the dinner table and thinking about where people were relative to each other. Although maintenance rehearsal helps us remember for a very short time, elaborative rehearsal improves long-term learning and remembering. This is likely a topic that is important to you as a student. In virtually every class you take, you have key terms to learn and exams to test your progress. You should see how the two types of rehearsal come into play in these processes. Students who simply repeat key terms and their definitions are employing maintenance rehearsal, and are less likely to do well on an exam. The wise strategy is to try to elaborate on the material rather than simply repeating it.

LEVELS OF PROCESSING Although we often find ourselves using maintenance rehearsal "in a pinch," we rarely use that strategy for information that we intend to remember much later. Instead, we focus on elaborative encoding, where additional sensory or semantic (meaning) information is associated with the to-be-remembered item. But, not all elaborative encoding is created equal. Instead, different types of elaborative encoding can produce markedly different levels of recall. The details surrounding this variability were first described by researchers at the University of Toronto, and led to a framework for memory known as *levels of processing* (LOP).

The LOP framework begins with the understanding that our ability to recall information is most directly related to how that information was initially processed (Craik & Lockhart, 1972). Differences in processing can be described as a continuum ranging from shallow to deep processing. *Shallow processing*, as you might guess, involves more superficial properties of a stimulus, such as the sound or spelling of a word. *Deep processing*, on the other hand, is generally related to an item's meaning or its function. It should come as no surprise that deep processing is associated with better retention and retrieval. The superiority of deep processing was demonstrated in a study in which participants encoded words using shallow processing (e.g., "Does this word rhyme with *dust?... TRUST*") or deep processing (e.g., "Is this word a synonym for *locomotive?... TRAIN*"). When given a surprise memory test for the words, the differences ranged from recalling as few as 14% of the shallow words to 96% of the deeply processed words (Craik & Tulving, 1975). In essence, they were almost seven times more likely to recall a deep-processed word than one that was processed at only a shallow level. Importantly, such effects are limited to LTM; STM memory rates are unaffected by shallow or deep processing (Rose et al., 2010; Figure 7.14).

Simulate Depth of Processing

Similar effects have been found for two other forms of deep processing. The *self-reference effect* occurs when you think about information in terms of how it relates to you or how it is useful to you; this type of encoding will lead to you remembering that information better than you otherwise would have (Symons & Johnson, 1997). That outcome is not terribly surprising, but it is still helpful to think about when learning material that you might not be interested in at first. Perhaps less intuitive is *survival processing*. Researchers have found that when items are processed as they relate to survival, they are more likely to be recalled (Butler, Kang, & Roediger, 2009). Thus, if you find yourself wanting to remember something, see if you can relate it to your own experiences or identify ways in which the information may aid survival.

Although encoding strategies clearly influence our ability to remember information later, they only tell

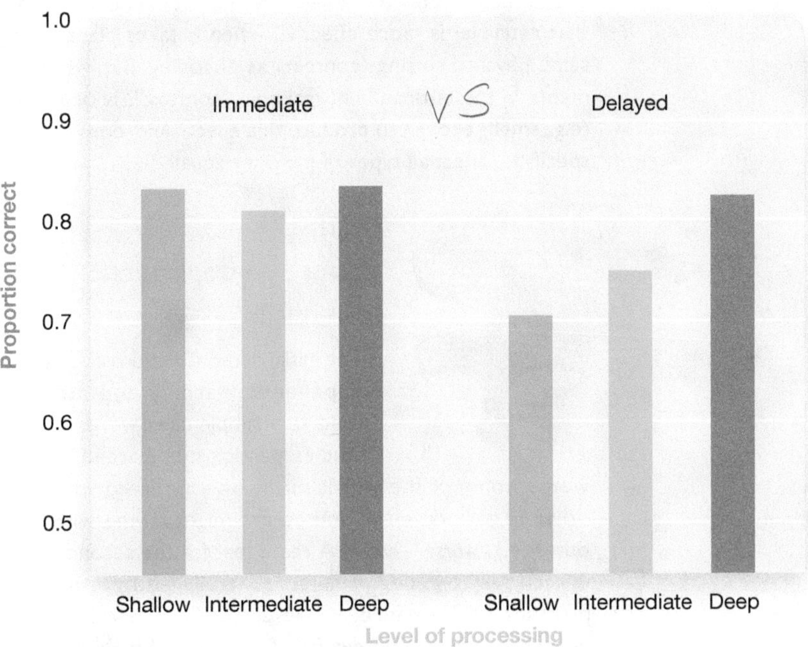

{FIG. 7.14} **Levels of Processing Affect Long-Term Memory, but Not Working Memory** When tested immediately after studying words, levels of processing do not seem to affect memory. In contrast, when there is a gap between studying words and being tested, levels of processing are important. When words are encoded based on their meaning (semantics), they are better retained in long-term memory (Rose et al., 2010).

part of the story. The conditions in which we attempt to retrieve information from memory can also affect whether or not that information will be recalled.

RETRIEVAL Once information is encoded—be it in a deep or shallow fashion—and stored in memory, the challenge is then to be able to retrieve that information when it is needed. There are two forms of intentional memory retrieval, both of which are familiar to long-suffering students like the readers of this textbook. *Recognition* involves identifying a stimulus or piece of information when it is presented to you. Examples of recognition memory would be identifying someone you know on the bus (or in a police lineup) or multiple-choice test questions. *Recall* involves retrieving information when asked, but without that information being present during the retrieval process. Examples of this would be describing a friend's appearance to someone else or short-answer questions on an exam.

Simulate Recall

Recall is helped substantially when there are hints, or *retrieval cues*, that help prompt our memory. The more detailed the retrieval cue, the easier it is for us to produce the memory. For instance, if you were given a list of 30 words to remember, it is unlikely that you would be able to recall all of the words. But, if you were given a hint for a "forgotten" word, such as "gr—" for the word "grape," you would be likely to retrieve that information. The hint "grap-" would provide even more information than "gr—" and would lead to even better retrieval (Tulving & Watkins, 1975). However, life is not a series of word lists. Instead, retrieval cues in the real world often involve places, people, sights, and sounds—in other words, the environment or context in which you are trying to retrieve a memory. Researchers have found that *retrieval is most effective when it occurs in the same context as encoding*, a tendency known as the **encoding specificity principle** (Tulving & Thompson, 1973).

WORKING THE SCIENTIFIC LITERACY MODEL

Context-Dependent Memory

The encoding specificity principle can take many forms. One of the most intuitive is *context-dependent memory*, the idea that retrieval is more effective when it takes place in the same physical setting (context) as encoding. But, what elements of the environment make up "context"? Is one sense (e.g., smell) enough to produce this effect? And, does context specificity affect all types of memory equally?

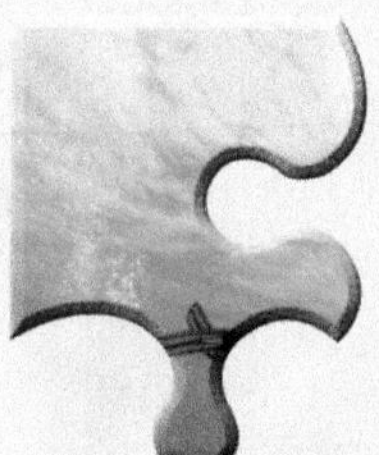

What do we know about context–dependent memory?

The initial demonstrations of context-dependent learning and memory used very simple cues: words. In such studies, participants learned pairs of words; some of the words might be associated with each other (e.g., *bark – dog*) and others might rhyme with each other (e.g., *worse – nurse*). A recall test for the second words in each pair (e.g., dog or nurse) generally led to respectable memory performance. However, performance improved when the original context (the first word of the word pair) was reinstated and could serve as a retrieval cue; the more information from the original context that was included, the better the level of retrieval (Tulving & Watkins, 1975).

Subsequent studies have focused on the role of environmental contexts on memory. In a classic study, members of a scuba club volunteered to memorize word lists—half of the test participants did so while diving 20 feet (6.7 m) underwater, and half did so while on land (Godden & Baddeley, 1975). After a short delay, the divers were tested again; however, some of the experimental participants had switched locations. This led to four test groups: trained and tested underwater, trained and tested on dry land, trained underwater but tested on land, and trained on land but tested underwater. As you can see in Figure 7.15, the results demonstrated that context affects memory. Those who were tested in the same context as where encoding took place (i.e., land–land or underwater–underwater) remembered approximately 40% more items than those who switched locations (i.e., land–underwater or underwater–land). Thus, both controlled laboratory studies and studies involving dramatic environmental manipulations have shown that matching the encoding and retrieval contexts leads to better recall of studied material.

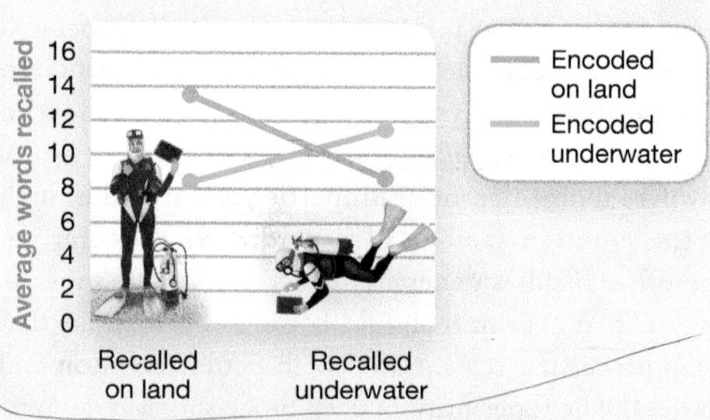

{FIG. 7.15} **Context-Dependent Learning** Divers who encoded information on land had better recall on land than underwater. Divers who encoded information underwater had the reverse experience, demonstrating better recall underwater than when on land.

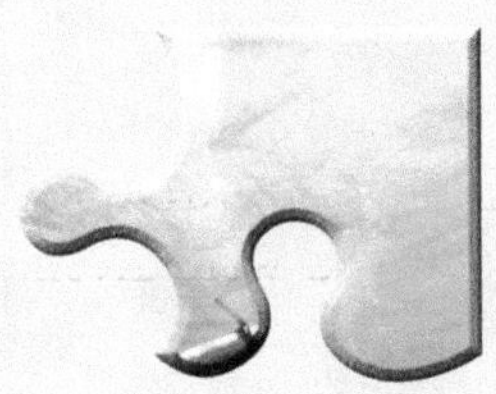

How can science explain context-dependent memory?

Context-dependent memory clearly demonstrates that the characteristics of the environment can serve as retrieval cues for memory. In the Godden and Baddeley (1975) study above, the primary cue was likely the feeling of being underwater; however, diving also involves a change of lighting as well as the sounds of the breathing apparatus. In other words, when we encode information, we are also encoding information from a number of different senses (vision, hearing, touch, etc.). Presumably, each of these senses can help trigger memories. For instance, most of you have had the experience where an odour (e.g., cookies) instantly brings back memories (e.g., your grandmother's kitchen). This common phenomenon was tested in a clever experiment by researchers in the U.K. In this study, researchers tested whether memory for a Viking museum in York, U.K., could be enhanced if the memory test occurred in a room with a similar distinctive set of smells as the museum (burned wood, apples, garbage, beef, fish, rope/tar, and earth ... which was the Viking equivalent of Axe® body spray). The researchers found that participants produced more accurate memories for the museum when the smell of the test room matched the smell of the museum (Aggleton & Waskett, 1999). Similar results have been found for the effect of smells on memory for word lists (Stafford et al., 2009). Context-dependent memory has also been found for the flavour of gum being chewed during encoding and retrieval (Baker et al., 2004) as well as for the amount of background noise when students are studying and taking a test (Grant et al., 1998). These results suggest that matching the physical and sensory characteristics of the encoding and retrieval environments affect memory, likely due to the retrieval cues provided by these attributes.

Brain-imaging studies have also provided evidence in favour of context-dependent memory. Studies using fMRI have found increased activity in the hippocampus and parts of the prefrontal cortex (part of the frontal lobes) when the retrieval conditions match the context in which the memory was encoded (Kalisch et al., 2006; Wagner et al., 1998). Activity in the right frontal lobes is particularly sensitive to context, likely because this region is known to be critical for the retrieval process (Tulving et al., 1994). Indeed, the precise size and area of the frontal lobes that is activated varies depending upon the context in which retrieval occurs, suggesting that environmental context can influence the firing of brain networks.

Can we critically evaluate this evidence?

Although there is evidence that context-dependent memory exists, there are some important limitations to these effects. First, not all types of memory are equally enhanced by returning a person to the context in which he or she encoded the to-be-remembered information. Recognition memory (e.g., multiple-choice questions) is not significantly helped by context; this is likely due to the fact that the presence of the item (e.g., a photograph or one of the options on a test question) serves as a very strong retrieval cue. Context does not add much above and beyond this cue (Fernández & Alonso, 2001). Recall, on the other hand, requires you to generate the to-be-remembered information without any external cues. In this case, returning to the encoding context could help prompt a memory. A second, and related, limitation of context-dependent memory is that not all types of information are equally affected. Information that is central to a memory episode (e.g., a person's face in a photograph or in a conversation) is generally unaffected by context. Peripheral information (e.g., the faces of people who were nearby when you were having a conversation) does seem to be enhanced when a person returns to the original context (Brown, 2003; Sutherland & Hayne, 2001). As a rule, when memory for information is quite good, context will have little effect on accuracy; however, when memory is relatively poor, then returning to the encoding context can improve recall.

But, there is one additional issue related to context-dependent memory. Researchers at Simon Fraser University have noted that returning a person to the context in which he encoded information can improve recall *and* increase the number of false positives (i.e., saying "I remember" to stimuli that were never seen). Wong and Read (2011) showed participants a video of a staged crime; viewing took place in either a large testing room or a small study room. Participants returned one week later for a follow-up test in which they were asked to identify the culprit from a photo lineup. This test took place either in the same room as the initial viewing of the video or in the opposite room. The catch was that for half of the participants, the photo lineup did not include the person from the original video (the "target absent condition"). The results of the test demonstrated the effect of context: Performance was much higher when the testing took place in the same room as the initial encoding. However, participants who took the test in the same context as they saw the video were also more likely to claim that a photo looked familiar *even in the target-absent condition* (see Figure 7.16). Returning to the encoding context may therefore alter a person's threshold for saying "I remember." This trend is likely due to the retrieval cues associated with the environment leading to a feeling of familiarity that is mistakenly attributed to the to-be-remembered information (Leboe & Whittlesea, 2002), in this case the face of a criminal. This study has clear implications for police procedures, as many police departments encourage returning witnesses to the scene of a crime in order to improve their memories (Hershkowitz et al., 1998; Kebbel et al., 1999).

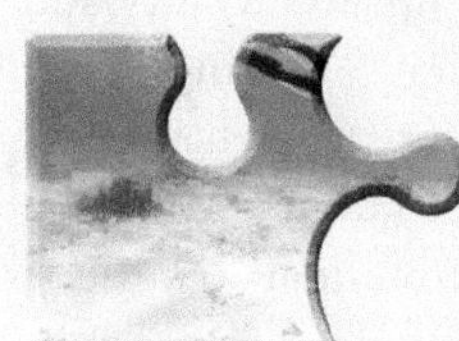

Why is this relevant?

One the most interesting implications of context-dependent memory research is that it implies that some forgotten information is not

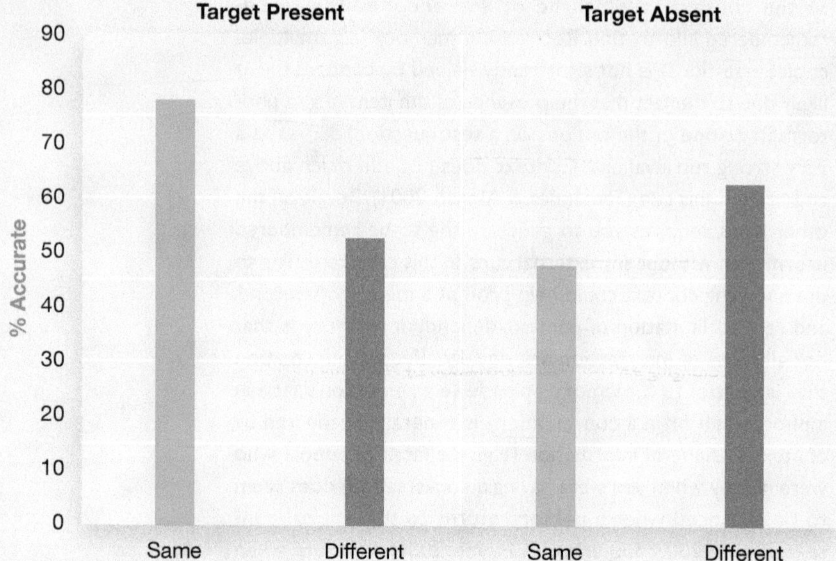

{FIG. 7.16} **False Familiarity and Context-Dependent Memory** In a study involving the identification of a thief in a staged robbery, participants viewed a robbery and then later selected the thief from a lineup of photographs. If both stages of the study were performed in the same room (i.e., the context had been reinstated, CR), identification of the thief increased. However, we should also keep in mind that participants were also more likely to rate an incorrect face as being familiar; this is shown by the *lower* accuracy score for the Same than for the Different contexts in the Target Absent condition on the right (Wong & Read, 2011).

Rostislav Ageev/Fotolia

gone forever, but is instead simply inaccessible because the proper cues have not been provided (Tulving, 1974). This is the assumption made by police investigators who return witnesses to the scene of the crime. It's also similar to some memory-improvement strategies such as the mental imagery technique used by Simonides in the story at the beginning of this module. However, the results of the Wong and Read (2011) photo lineup story do suggest that we need to be cautious in our interpretation of context-dependent memory, as the retrieval cues associated with the context could actually lead to false feelings of familiarity that could have devastating effects on people's lives.

It is usually not difficult to spot these context effects while they are occurring. Almost everyone has had the experience of walking into a room to retrieve something—maybe a specific piece of mail or a roll of tape—only to find that they have no idea what they intended to pick up. We might call this phenomenon *context-dependent forgetting*, if we believe the change in the environment influenced the forgetting. It is certainly frustrating, but can be reversed by the *context reinstatement effect*, which occurs when you return to the original location and the memory suddenly comes back. But, research also shows that these effects are not isolated to external contexts; your *internal* environment can serve as a retrieval cue for your memory as well.

STATE-DEPENDENT LEARNING Many of you will have had the experience of waking up after a party and realizing that pockets of time are now "missing." Your memory for those periods of time appears to have vanished. But, is that information gone forever, or can it be accessed in the same way that environmental cues can help you access some context-dependent memories? Research suggests that retrieval is more effective when your internal state matches the state you were in during encoding. In the first demonstration of this *state-dependent memory*, Goodwin and colleagues (1969) got half of their participants extremely drunk (their blood-alcohol level was three times the legal limit); the other half were sober. Participants encoded information and completed several memory tests; they were then instructed to return 24 hours later for additional testing (and a new liver). On Day 2 of testing, half of participants were again put into a state of severe intoxication; half of these participants had also been drunk on Day 1, and the other half had been sober. Thus, there were four groups: drunk on Day 1 and Day 2 (drunk-drunk), drunk-sober, sober-drunk, and sober-sober. Not surprisingly, the sober-sober group outperformed all of the others. However, tests of recall showed that the drunk-drunk group outperformed the groups in which participants were intoxicated during only one of the two test sessions. The state of intoxication served as a retrieval cue for the participants' memory. As with context-dependent memory, this effect appears to be strongest for declarative memory (e.g., recall), the form of memory that requires the participant to generate the response on her own (Duka et al., 2001).

Similar effects have been found for other substances. For instance, marijuana researchers have found that "experienced smokers" who learned (encoded) information while under the effects of marijuana performed better if they received marijuana before subsequent tests than if they were sober (Hill et al., 1973; Stillman et al., 1974). This group also outperformed participants who encoded information while sober, but were given marijuana before the testing on Day 2. However, the experimenters, in a beautiful example of an understatement, did note that "marihuana did produce some overall impairment in performance" (Stillman et al., 1974, p. 81). State-dependent memory has also been observed for caffeine (Kelemen & Creeley, 2003), a finding that might influence how some of you study and take exams. However, it is important to remember that, like context-dependent memory, the effects of state-dependent memory are fairly small and limited to artificial stimuli such as word lists. There is therefore no guarantee that drinking yourself silly will fill in the gaps of your memory for your previous wild night.

MOOD-DEPENDENT LEARNING Just as similar contexts and chemical states can improve memory, people remember better if their mood at retrieval matches their mood during encoding (Bower, 1981; Eich & Metcalfe, 1989). Volunteers in one study generated words while in a pleasant or unpleasant mood, and then attempted to remember them in either the same or a different mood. The results indicated that if the type of mood at encoding and retrieval matched, then memory was superior. However, changes in the intensity of the mood did not seem to have an effect (Balch et al., 1999).

As with context- and state-dependent memory, mood-dependent memory has some limitations (Eich et al., 1994). Mood has a very small effect on recognition memory; it has much larger effects on recall-based tests. Additionally, it produces larger effects when the participant must generate both the to-be-remembered information (e.g., "an example of a musical instrument is a g________") than if the stimuli are externally generated (e.g., "remember this word: guitar"). In the first example, the participant must put more of his own cognition into the encoding process; therefore, those cognitive processes become important retrieval cues later on.

Although its effects are limited, mood-dependent memory does show that a person's emotional state can have an effect on encoding and retrieval. As we shall see, the influence of emotion can be even more dramatic when the stimuli themselves are emotional in nature.

Quick Quiz 7.2a

Encoding and Retrieval

KNOW...

1 The time and manner in which information is retained between encoding and retrieval is __________.

- **A** maintenance rehearsal
- **B** storage
- **C** elaborative rehearsal
- **D** recall

2 Prolonging exposure to information by repeating it to oneself is referred to as ________.

- **A** maintenance rehearsal
- **B** storage
- **C** elaborative rehearsal
- **D** recall

UNDERSTAND...

3 According to the levels of processing approach to memory, thinking about synonyms is one method of _______ processing that should _______ memory for that term.

- **A** shallow; decrease
- **B** deep; increase
- **C** maintenance; increase
- **D** dualistic; decrease

APPLY...

4 If you are learning vocabulary for a psychology exam, you are better off using a(n) ________ technique.

- **A** maintenance rehearsal
- **B** elaborative rehearsal
- **C** serial processing
- **D** consolidation

5 When taking a math exam, the concept of ________ would indicate that you would do best if you took the exam in the same physical setting as the setting where you learned the material.

- **A** context-dependent learning
- **B** state-dependent learning
- **C** mood congruence
- **D** elaborative rehearsal

Answers can be found on page ANS-2.

Emotional Memories

Do you remember what you ate for lunch last Tuesday? Is that event imprinted on your memory forever? Unless your lunch was spectacularly good or bad, it's unlikely that the memory of your sandwich will be very vivid. But what if you saw police arrest people who were fighting in the cafeteria? Or what if you got food poisoning from your tuna sandwich? Suddenly, that lunch became much more memorable. Indeed, when you think

Simulate What Do You Remember?

back to different times in your life, the events that first come to mind are often emotional in nature such as a wonderful birthday party or the fear of starting at a new school. Emotion seems to act as a highlighter for memories, making them easier to retrieve than neutral memories. This is because emotional stimuli and events are generally self-relevant and are associated with arousal responses such as an increase in heart rate and sweating. In linking emotion and memory back to topics discussed earlier in this module, it seems reasonable to assume that emotion leads to deep processing of stimuli.

The tendency for emotion to enhance our memory for events has been demonstrated in a number of studies (LaBar & Cabeza, 2006). For instance, in one experiment, two groups of volunteers viewed the same slideshow depicting a woman's daily activities, with the final slide showing a bunch of friends gathered outside her door. If that was all the experiment entailed, the two groups would have about an equal chance of remembering the details—but, psychologists are sneaky, so there was obviously some sort of experimental manipulation involved. In this case, one group was told that they were watching the woman on the way to her birthday party, whereas the other group was told that the woman was severely depressed and had thoughts of suicide. Thus, one group received a mildly positive narrative for the scene whereas the other group received a strongly negative narrative. The volunteers who had been given the sad scenario actually remembered more details from the slideshow (Laney et al., 2003). Because the two groups were randomly assigned, we assume that the only thing that could have led to the stronger memories was the level of emotion tied to the photos for one of the groups.

Research has shown that this beneficial effect of emotion is strongest after long (one hour or more) rather than short delays (LaBar & Phelps, 1998; Sharot & Phelps, 2004). This suggests that emotion's largest influence is on the process of consolidation, when information that has recently been transferred from short-term memory (STM) into long-term memory (LTM) is strengthened and made somewhat permanent. Emotion has less of an effect on STM and on recognition memory; these types of memory have much less variability than LTM, thus leaving less room for emotion to influence accuracy levels.

Emotion also changes the type of information that is encoded. Specifically, central information about the gist of a scene (e.g., a snake) receives extra attention and is more likely to be remembered than peripheral information (e.g., the flowers near the snake). This phenomenon can take a more sinister turn in the courtroom. Many eyewitnesses to crimes have shown reductions in memory accuracy due to *weapon focus,* or the tendency to focus on the weapon at the expense of peripheral information including the identity of the person holding the weapon (Kramer et al., 1990; Loftus et al., 1987). Interestingly, damage to the amygdala eliminates these effects, suggesting that this emotion-related structure plays a key role in the formation of emotional memories (Adolphs et al., 2005).

creestee/Shutterstock.com

Emotional items, particularly if they are threatening, capture attention and are more likely to be retained in memory. An example of this is the phenomenon of *weapon focus* in which people recall the central element of the scene (the weapon) but quickly forget the peripheral details.

The above studies suggest that emotional material received deeper (rather than shallow) processing. However, levels of processing is not the only factor influencing memory and emotions. Emotion can influence memory consolidation even if the stimuli themselves are not emotional in nature. For example, in one study, participants studied a list of words and were then randomly assigned to view a tape of oral surgery (the emotional condition) or the way to brush your teeth effectively (presumably *not* the emotional condition). After the slideshow, the group members who viewed the surgery tape remembered more of the words (see Figure 7.17) (Nielson et al., 2005). Thus, emotions can lead to stronger memory

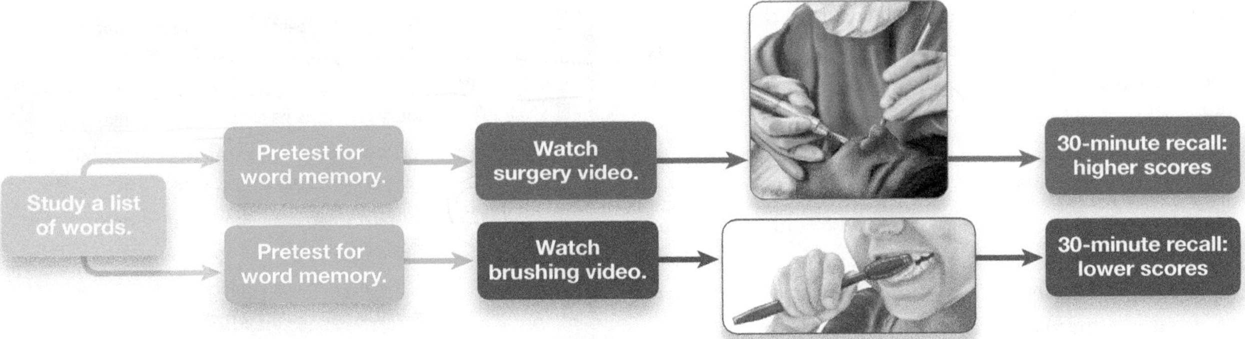

{FIG. 7.17} **Does Emotion Improve Memory?** Both groups remembered approximately the same percentage of words at pretest, and then watched dentistry videos unrelated to the word lists. The group whose members watched the more emotional video recalled more of the words in the end (Nielson et al., 2005).

formation, even if the information is not directly related to the emotional event.

Researchers have identified many of the biological mechanisms that allow emotion to influence memory (Phelps, 2004). Much of this relationship involves structures in the temporal lobe of the brain, the hippocampus (the structure associated with the encoding of long-term memories) and the amygdala (the structure involved in emotional processing and responding). Brain imaging shows that emotional memories often activate the amygdala, whereas non-emotional memories generated at the same time do not (Sharot et al., 2007). Activity in the amygdala then influences the firing patterns of other temporal-lobe structures, including the hippocampus; this link is a major part of the emotion-memory relationship (Dolcos et al., 2004). It is also quite time-sensitive—amygdala responses to individual stimuli predict later memory accuracy for those items (Canli et al., 2000). Of course, this association does not guarantee that all of the details of an experience will be remembered with complete accuracy.

FLASHBULB MEMORIES Can you remember where you were when Sidney Crosby scored "the golden goal" against Team USA in the Olympic hockey final? Unless your celebration led to alcohol-induced amnesia, it's likely that you have some mental image of that scene. What type of details are part of that image? Can you remember what you were wearing? Who was with you? For non-hockey fans, that afternoon was simply a fun time with friends. But for others, the memory of that event might take on an almost photographic quality. This phenomenon led researchers to label such an intense and unique memory as being a **flashbulb memory**—*an extremely vivid and detailed memory about an event and the conditions surrounding how one learned about the event* (Brown & Kulik, 1977). (The term *flashbulb* refers to the flash of a camera.) These highly charged emotional memories typically involve recollections of location, what was happening at the time of the event, and the emotional reactions of self and others (Brown & Kulik, 1977).

Top: Beth Dixson/Alamy; bottom: John Lok/MCT/Newscom

Many people have flashbulb memories of the September 11, 2001, terrorist attacks. However, not all flashbulb memories are negative. According to TSN, 80% of Canadians watched Sidney Crosby crush the dreams of the American hockey team in the Vancouver Olympics. Do you remember that moment? Are you sure?

Some may be personal memories, such as the memory of an automobile accident. Other events are so widely felt that they seem to form flashbulb memories for an entire society, such as the assassination of U.S. President Kennedy in 1963 (Brown & Kulik, 1977), the explosion of the space shuttles *Challenger* or *Columbia* (Kershaw et al., 2009; Neisser & Harsch, 1992), and the terrorist attacks of September 11, 2001 (Hirst et al., 2009; Paradis et al., 2004). One defining feature of flashbulb memories is that people are highly confident that their recollections are accurate. But is this confidence warranted?

MYTHS IN MIND

The Accuracy of Flashbulb Memories

Although flashbulb memories are very detailed and individuals reciting the details are very confident of their accuracy, it might surprise you to learn that they are not necessarily more accurate than any other memories. For example, researchers examined how university students remembered the September 11, 2001, attacks in comparison to an emotional but more mundane event (Talarico & Rubin, 2003). On September 12, 2001, they asked students to describe the events surrounding the moment they heard about the attacks. For a comparison event, they asked students to describe something memorable from the preceding weekend, just two or three days before the attacks. Over several months, the students were asked to recall details of both events, and the researchers compared the accuracy of the two memories. Although their memory for both events was fading at the same rate and they were equal in accuracy, the students acknowledged the decline in memory only for the mundane events. They continued to feel highly confident in their memories surrounding the September 11 attacks, when, in fact, those memories were not any more accurate. The same pattern has been found for other major flashbulb events, such as the 1986 space shuttle *Challenger* explosion and the verdict in the O. J. Simpson murder trial (Neisser & Harsch, 1992; Schmolk et al., 2000).

Watch: The Big Picture: The Woman Who Cannot Forget

Watch: In the Real World: The Memories We Don't Want

Quick Quiz 7.2b

Emotional Memories

KNOW...

1 ________ are extremely vivid and detailed memories about an event.

A Flashbulb memories
B Deep memories
C Rehearsal memories
D Semantic memories

UNDERSTAND...

2 One study had participants view tapes of dental surgery after studying a word list. This study concluded that

A emotional videos have no effect on memory.
B emotional videos can enhance memory, but only for material related to the video itself.
C emotional videos can enhance memory even for unrelated material.
D emotional videos can enhance memory for related material, while reducing memory for unrelated material.

ANALYZE...

3 Which statement best sums up the status of flashbulb memories?

A Due to the emotional strain of the event, flashbulb memories are largely inaccurate.
B Recall for only physical details is highly accurate.
C Both emotion and physical details are remembered very accurately.
D Over time, memory for details decays, similar to what happens with nonflashbulb memories.

Answers can be found on page ANS-2.

Forgetting and Remembering

Have you ever had the experience of studying intensely for an exam, writing it, and then forgetting almost everything as soon as you walked out of the exam room? This phenomenon is quite common, particularly if you did all of your studying the night before (or morning of) the exam. Forgetting information is probably a good thing, at least if it occurs in moderation. We don't need to remember every detail about each bus ride into school. Instead, we want to have some control over what we do remember, thus allowing us to keep the useful information (e.g., terms for an exam) and deleting the less useful information (e.g., the name of whatever creature of the deep Lindsay Lohan is dating). Of course, if we had that type of control, there would be no need to study the intricacies of why we remember and forget things. As you will see, this issue has been researched extensively.

THE FORGETTING CURVE: HOW SOON WE FORGET . . . It might seem odd that the first research on remembering was actually a documentation of how quickly people forget. However, this approach does make sense: Without knowledge of forgetting, it is difficult to ascertain how well we can remember. This early work was conducted by Hermann Ebbinghaus, whom many psychologists consider the founder of memory research. Ebbinghaus (1885) was his own research participant in his studies; these experiments involved him studying hundreds of nonsense syllables for later memory tests. His rationale was that because none of the syllables had any meaning, none of them should have been easier to remember based on past experiences. Ebbinghaus studied lists of these syllables until he could repeat them twice (which is the worst pick-up line ever). He then tested himself repeatedly—this is where his persistence really shows—day after day.

How soon do we forget? The data indicated that Ebbinghaus forgot about half of a list in an hour. If Ebbinghaus had continued to forget at that rate, the rest of the list should be lost after two hours. In reality, that was not the case. After a day, he could generally remember one-third of the material, and he could still recall between one-fifth and one-fourth of the words after a week. The graph in Figure 7.18 shows the basic pattern in his test results, which has come to be known as a *forgetting curve*. It clearly shows that most forgetting occurs right away, and that the rate of forgetting eventually slows to the point where one does not seem to forget at all. These results have stood the test of time. In fact, in the century after Ebbinghaus conducted his research, more than 200 articles were published in psychological journals that fit Ebbinghaus's forgetting curve (Rubin & Wenzel, 1996). In fact, one study demonstrated that this forgetting curve applies to information learned over 50 years before (see Figure 7.19; Bahrick, 1984).

Given that the forgetting curve has been documented in hundreds of experiments, it seems inevitable that we will forget most of the information that we attempt to encode. However, as you have undoubtedly learned over the course of your studies, there are techniques that will allow you to improve your memory so that the forgetting curve is not as steep.

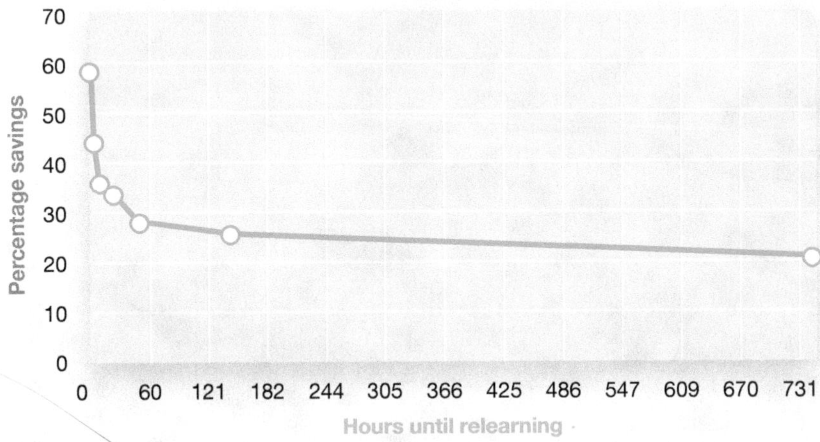

{FIG. 7.18} **Ebbinghaus's Forgetting Curve** This graph reveals Ebbinghaus's results showing the rate at which he forgot a series of nonsense syllables. You can see that there is a steep decline in performance within the first day and that the rate of forgetting levels off over time.

MNEMONICS: IMPROVING YOUR MEMORY SKILLS

At the beginning of this module, you read about the poet Simonides and his ability to use mental imagery to improve his memory, thus allowing him to identify the remains of people crushed under a collapsed roof. Simonides was using a primitive type of **mnemonic**—*a technique intended to improve memory for specific information*. As you will see in this section, there are a number of different mnemonics that could be used to improve memory, something that might be of interest to overwhelmed students.

The technique that Simonides was using is known as the **method of loci** (pronounced "LOW-sigh"), *a mnemonic that connects words to be remembered to locations along a familiar path*. To use the method of loci, one must first imagine a route that has landmarks or easily identifiable spaces—for example, the things you pass on your way from your home to a friend's house or the seats around a dinner table. Once the path is identified, the learner takes a moment to visually relate the first word on the list to the first location encountered. For example, if you need to remember to pick up noodles, milk, and soap from the store and the first thing you pass on the way to your friend's house is an intersection with a stop sign, you might picture the intersection littered with noodles, and so on down the list. The image doesn't need to be cool—it just needs to be distinct enough to be memorable. When it is time to recall the items, the learner simply imagines the familiar drive, identifying the items to be purchased as they relate to each location along the path.

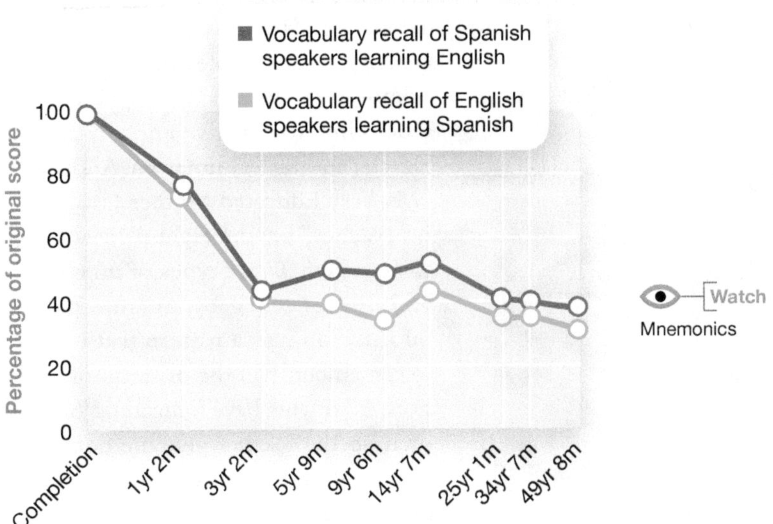

{FIG. 7.19} **Bahrick's Long-Term Forgetting Curve** This forgetting curve indicates the rate at which adults forgot the foreign language they took in high school. Compared to new graduates, those tested two to three years later forgot much of what they learned. After that, however, test scores stabilized, just as Ebbinghaus's did a century earlier (Bahrick, 1984).

Watch Mnemonics

Lori Howard/Shutterstock.com

The method of loci relies on mental imagery of a familiar location or path, like this path that students take to class three times a week.

Andersen Ross/Iconica/Gettyimages

Restaurant staff often rely on mnemonic devices to remember which diner receives each item.

However, the method of loci can become a bit cumbersome when a person has to remember hundreds of different facts, as occurs for university exams. A more practical mnemonic is the use of **acronyms**, *pronounceable words whose letters represent the initials of an important phrase or set of items.* For example, the word "scuba" came into being with the invention of the self-contained underwater breathing apparatus. "Roy G. Biv" gives you the colours of the rainbow: red, orange, yellow, green, blue, indigo, and violet. A related mnemonic, the **first-letter technique**, *uses the first letters of a set of items to spell out words that form a sentence.* It is like an acronym, but it tends to be used when the first letters do not spell a pronounceable word (see Figure 7.20). One well-known example is "Every Good Boy Does Fine" for the five lines on the treble clef in musical notation. Another is "My Very Educated Mother Just Served Us Nachos" for the eight planets in the solar system. These types of mnemonic techniques work by organizing the information into a pattern that is easier to remember than the original information. Acronyms have a meaning of their own, so the learner gets the benefit of both elaborative rehearsal and deeper processing.

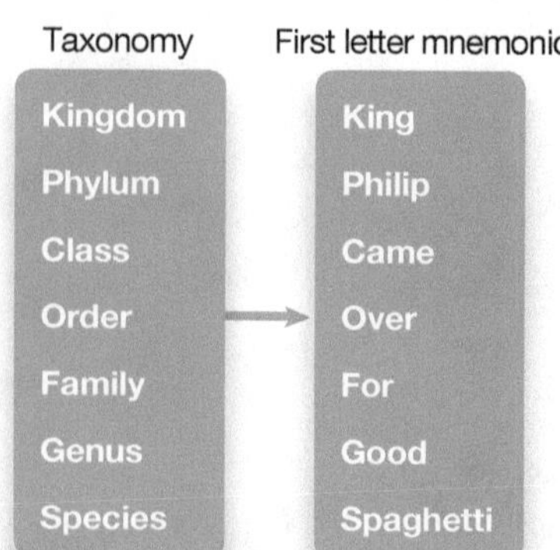

{FIG. 7.20} **The First-Letter Technique** Students of biology often use mnemonics, such as this example of the first letter technique, which helps students remember the taxonomic system.

A number of mnemonic devices are based on the premise of dual coding. **Dual coding** *occurs when information is stored in more than one form*—such as a verbal description and a visual image, or a description and a sound—and it regularly produces stronger memories than the use of one form alone (Clark & Paivio, 1991). Dual coding leads to the information receiving deeper, as opposed to shallow, processing; this is because the additional sensory representations create a larger number of memory associations. This leads to a greater number of potential retrieval cues that can be accessed later. For example, most children growing up in North America learned the alphabet with the help of a song. In fact, even adults find themselves humming portions of that song when alphabetizing documents in a file cabinet (you'll do it too if asked which letter comes after "k"). Both the visual "A-B-C-D" and the musical "eh-bee-see-dee" are encoded together, making memory easier than if you were simply given visual information to remember (e.g., "☛✍☞☚", which is ABCD in the meaningless "wingdings2" font). The simplest explanation for the dual-coding advantage is that twice as much information is stored.

The application of mnemonic strategies can be found in restaurants where waiters are not allowed to write out orders. These waiters use a variety of the techniques discussed in this chapter. Some use chunking strategies, such as remembering soft drinks for a group of three customers, and cocktails for the other four. Waiters also use the method of loci to link faces with positions at the table. In one study, a waiter was able to recall as many as 20 dinner orders (Ericsson & Polson, 1988). He used the method of loci by linking food type (starch, beef, or fish) with a table location, and he used acronyms to help with encoding salad dressing choices. Thus RaVoSe for a party of three would be ranch, vinegar and oil, and sesame. Waiters, as well as memory researchers, will tell you that the worst thing restaurant patrons can do is switch seats, as it completely disrupts the mnemonic devices used by the waiter (Bekinschtein et al., 2008).

While these mnemonic devices can help with rote memorization, they may not necessarily improve your understanding of material. Researchers have begun to examine other memory boosters that may offer more benefits to you as a student as you prepare for exams. For example, some research has shown that *desirable difficulties* can aid learning. These techniques make studying slower and more effortful, but result in better overall remembering. They include spacing out your studying rather than cramming, and studying material in varying orders.

Another popular approach to studying is to use flashcards. Although psychologists have begun to understand how this process benefits students, they also have identified a few pitfalls that can hinder its effects. First is the spacing effect. When studying with flashcards, it is better to use one big stack rather than several smaller stacks; using the entire deck helps take advantage of the effect of spacing the cards. A second potential problem is the fact that students become overconfident and drop flashcards as soon as they believe they learn the material. In reality, doing so seems to reduce the benefits of overlearning the material (making it more difficult to forget) and spacing out cards in the deck (Kornell, 2009; Kornell & Bjork, 2007). No matter how you study, you should take advantage of the **testing effect,** *the finding that taking practice tests can improve exam performance, even without additional studying*. In fact, researchers have directly compared testing to additional studying and have found that, in some cases, testing actually improves memory more (Roediger et al., 2010). That's why psychology textbooks such as this one include "Quick Quizzes" and online tests—to help you improve your memory. . . .

Quick Quiz 7.2c

Forgetting and Remembering

KNOW...

1 Dual coding seems to help memory by

- **A** allowing for maintenance rehearsal.
- **B** ensuring that the information is encoded in multiple ways.
- **C** ensuring that the information is encoded on two separate occasions.
- **D** duplicating the rehearsal effect.

APPLY...

2 If you are preparing for an exam by using flashcards, you will probably find that you are more confident about some of the items than others. To improve your exam performance, you should

- **A** drop the cards you already know.
- **B** keep the cards in the deck even if you feel like you know them.
- **C** use elaborative rehearsal.
- **D** use the method of loci.

3 If you wanted to remember a grocery list using the method of loci, you should

- **A** imagine the items on the list on your path through the grocery store.
- **B** match rhyming words to each item on your list.
- **C** repeat the list to yourself over and over again.
- **D** tell a story using the items from the list.

Answers can be found on page ANS-2.

Watch
IT Video: Cramming

Watch
What's in It for Me? Making It Stick

Module Summary

Module 7.2

Tkreykes/Fotolia

Now that you have read this module you should

KNOW...

- ***The key terminology related to forgetting, encoding, and retrieval*:**

acronym (p. 298)
dual coding (p. 298)
elaborative rehearsal (p. 289)
encoding specificity principle (p. 290)
first-letter technique (p. 298)
flashbulb memory (p. 295)
maintenance rehearsal (p. 288)
method of loci (p. 297)
mnemonic (p. 297)
storage (p. 288)
testing effect (p. 299)

UNDERSTAND...

- ***How the type of cognitive processing employed can affect the chances of remembering what you encounter.*** Generally speaking, the deeper the processing, the more likely something is to be remembered. Greater depth of processing may be achieved by elaborating on the meaning of the information, through increased emotional content, and through coding in images and sounds simultaneously.

APPLY...

- ***What you have learned to improve your ability to memorize information.*** The best way to do so is to give it a try. One mnemonic device that might be helpful is the method of loci. Have someone create a shopping list for you while you prepare yourself by imagining a familiar path (perhaps the route you take to class). When you are ready to learn the list, read a single item on the list and imagine it at some point on the path. Feel free to exaggerate the images in your memory—each item could become the size of a stop sign or might take on the appearance of a particular building or tree that you pass by. Continue this pattern for each individual item until you have learned the list. Then try what Ebbinghaus did: Test your memory over the course of a few days. How do you think you will do?

ANALYZE...

- ***Whether emotional memories are more accurate than non-emotional ones.*** Both personal experiences and controlled laboratory studies demonstrate that emotion enhances memory. However, as we learned in the case of flashbulb memories, even memories for details of significant events decline over time, although confidence in memory accuracy typically remains very high.

RiceWithSugar/Shutterstock.com

Module 7.3

Constructing and Reconstructing Memories

Learning Objectives

After reading this module you should

KNOW...	UNDERSTAND...	APPLY...	ANALYZE...
The key terminology used in discussing how memories are organized and constructed	How schemas serve as frameworks for encoding and constructing memories How psychologists can produce false memories in the laboratory	What you have learned to judge the reliability of eyewitness testimony	The arguments in the "recovered memory" debate

In 1992, the Saskatchewan town of Martensville was rocked by a sex abuse scandal. A complaint about a suspicious diaper rash from a parent of a toddler attending a local daycare led to a police investigation. After repeated and extensive interviewing, the children claimed to remember astonishing things including extensive sexual abuse, human sacrifice, a "Devil Church," and a Satanic cult known as The Brotherhood of the Ram. The owners of the daycare along with several other individuals—including five police officers—were eventually arrested. However, a closer examination of the police investigation identified some serious problems. Expert witnesses noted that the questions used in the interviews were leading and suggestive. While certainly well-meaning, the investigators—who were not trained to interview child witnesses—forgot a critical piece of information: Memories are not like photographs perfectly depicting an event from our past. Instead, they are reconstructed each time we retrieve them, and can therefore be altered by a number of different factors.

Focus Questions

 How is it possible to remember events that never happened?

 Do these false memories represent memory problems, or are they just a normal part of remembering?

The true story that opened this module demonstrates that memories for past events can change over time. In a less disturbing example, cognitive psychologist and renowned memory researcher Ulric Neisser once recounted what he was doing on December 7, 1941, the day Japan attacked Pearl Harbor. Neisser was sitting in the living room listening to a baseball game on the radio when the program was interrupted with the news (Neisser, 2000). Or was he? He had certainly constructed a very distinct memory for this emotional event, but something must have gone wrong. Baseball season does not last through December. As this example demonstrates, even memory researchers are prone to misremembering. In this module we will examine how such misremembering occurs and what it says about how memories are constructed . . . and reconstructed.

How Memories Are Organized and Constructed

Think about the last time you read a novel or watched a film. What do you recall about the story? If you have a typical memory, you will forget the proper names of locations and characters quickly, but you will be able to remember the basic plot for a very long time (Squire, 1989; Stanhope et al., 1993). The plot may be referred to as the *gist* of the story and it impacts us much more than characters' names, which are often just details. As it turns out, much of the way we store memories depends on our tendency to remember the gist of things.

Watch
IT Video: Penny Test

Explore
Schema

THE SCHEMA: AN ACTIVE ORGANIZATION PROCESS The gist of a story gives us "the big picture," or a general structure for the memory; details can be added around that structure. Gist is often influenced by **schemas**, *organized clusters of memories that constitute one's knowledge about events, objects, and ideas.* Whenever we encounter familiar events or objects, these schemas become active, and they affect what we expect, what we pay attention to, and what we remember. Because we use these patterns automatically, it may be difficult to understand what they are, even though you have been using them your whole life. Here is an example; read the following passage through one time:

> *The procedure is quite simple. First, you arrange things into different groups. Of course, one pile may be sufficient, depending on how much there is to do. If you have to go somewhere else due to lack of facilities, that is the next step; otherwise, you are pretty well set. It is important not to overdo things. That is, it is better to do too few things at once than too many. At first the whole procedure will seem complicated. Soon, however, it will become just another facet of life. After the procedure is completed, one arranges the materials into different groups again. Then they can be put into their appropriate places. Eventually they will be used once more, and the whole cycle will have to be repeated (Bransford & Johnson, 1973).*

At this point, if you were to write down the details of the paragraph solely from memory, how well do you think you would do? Most people do not have high expectations for themselves, but they would blame it on how vague the paragraph seems. Now, what if we tell you the passage is about doing laundry? If you read the paragraph a second time, you should see that it is easier to understand, as well as to remember.

WORKING THE SCIENTIFIC LITERACY MODEL

How Schemas Influence Memory

Although schemas are used to explain memory, they can be used to explain many other phenomena as well, such as the way we perceive, remember, and think about people and situations. In each case, schemas provide a ready-made structure that allows us to process new information more quickly than we could without this mental shortcut. This makes schemas extremely useful. But, are they accurate?

What do we know about schemas?

The laundry demonstration tells us quite a bit about schemas and memory. First, most of us have our own personal schema about the process of doing laundry. Refer back to the definition of schema—a cluster of memories that constitutes your knowledge about an event (gathering clothes, going to the laundromat), object (what clothes are, what detergent is), or idea (why clean clothes are desirable). When you read the paragraph the first time, you probably did not know what the objects and events were. However, when you were told it was about doing laundry, it *activated* your laundry schema—your personal collection of concepts and memories. Once your schema was activated, you were prepared to make sense of the story and could likely fill in the gaps of your memory for the passage with stored knowledge from your schema in long-term memory (LTM). Second, we should point out that schemas are involved in all three stages of memory: They guide what we attend to during encoding, organize stored memories, and serve as cues when it comes time to retrieve information.

How can science explain schemas?

Where do schemas come from? They appear to be

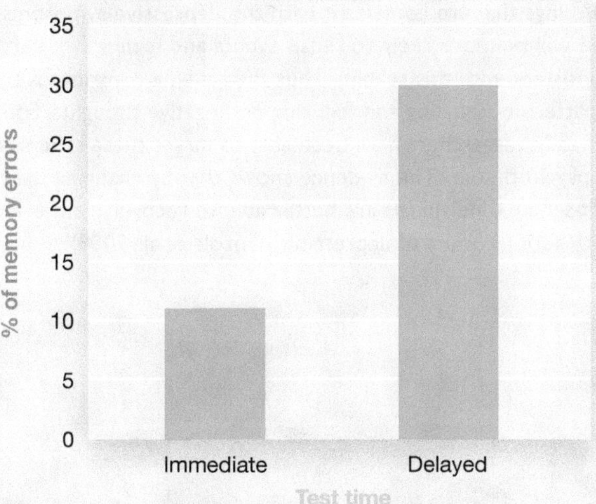

{FIG. 7.21} **Schemas Affect How We Encode and Remember** In this study, memory was accurate when tested immediately, as shown by the small proportion of errors on the "immediate" side of the graph. After two days, however, participants misremembered seeing the schema-inconsistent tasks in line with stereotypes. For example, they misremembered the homemaker stirring cake batter even if they had actually seen the handyman do it (Kleider et al., 2008). **Click on this figure in your eText to see more details.**

products of culture and experience (e.g., Ross & Wang, 2010). For example, individuals within a culture tend to have schemas related to gender roles—men and women are each assumed to engage in certain jobs and to behave in certain ways. Even if an individual realizes that these schemas are not 100% accurate (in fact, they can be far from accurate in some cases), he or she is likely to engage in schematic processing when having difficulty remembering something specific.

A study by Heather Kleider and her associates (2008) demonstrates how schemas influence memory quite well. These investigators had research participants view photographs of a handyman engaged in schema-consistent behaviour (e.g., working on plumbing) as well as a few schema-inconsistent tasks (e.g., folding a baby's clothing). Mixed in with these photos were images of a stay-at-home mother doing chores, including the same tasks. Immediately after viewing the photographs, participants were quite successful at remembering correctly who had performed what actions. However, after two days, what types of memory mistakes do you think the researchers found? As you can see from Figure 7.21, individuals began making mistakes, and these mistakes are consistent with gender schemas.

Research indicates that we remember events using **constructive memory**, *a process by which we first recall a generalized schema and then add in specific details* (Scoboria et al., 2006; Silva et al., 2006). To this end, schemas can affect our memory in two ways:

1. *Organization.* When we encounter a new situation, some objects and events will undoubtedly fit our schemas (i.e., our expectations) better than others. When the new information makes sense—that is, when it fits our schema—it can be easier to recall, yet it may be more difficult to recognize or report the exact details.
2. *Distinctiveness.* When we encounter new information, some of it will not fit our schemas. If the new information stands out as weird or unusual, it will be easy to recall. If it does not fit our schema, but is not all that unusual, it will likely be forgotten (Silva et al., 2006). Information that does not fit into our schemas but is also not terribly interesting (e.g., a muscular man with tattoos driving a minivan) will be more difficult to remember.

Can we critically evaluate the concept of a schema?

The concept of a schema is certainly useful in describing our methods of mental organization, but some psychologists remain skeptical of its validity. After all, you cannot record brain activity and expect to see a *particular* schema, and individuals generally are not aware that they are using schematic processing. It may even be the case that what we assume are schemas about laundry, gender, or ourselves are different every time we think about these topics. If that is the case, then describing this tendency as a schema might even be misleading.

However, recent brain-imaging studies suggest that schemas do exist and likely help with the process of memory consolidation (Wang & Morris, 2010). Both encoding and retrieving information that was consistent with a schema learned during the experiment led to greater activity in a network involving

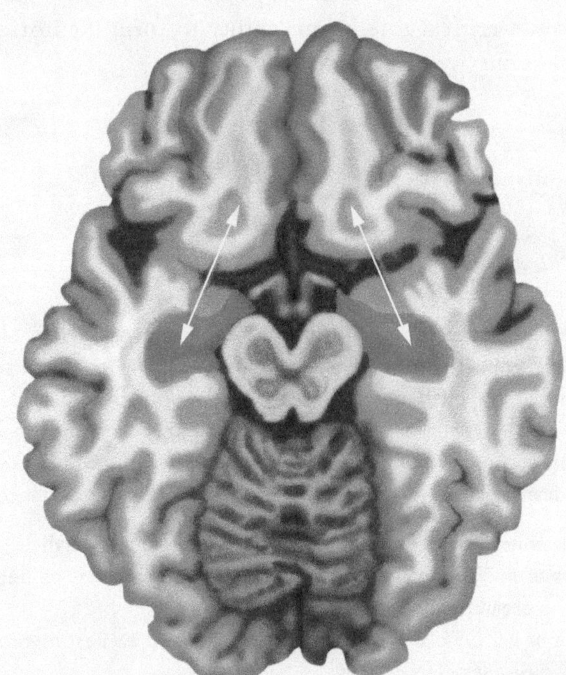

Brain-imaging data suggest that encoding information consistent with a schema activates a network involving structures in the medial temporal lobe (including our friend, the hippocampus) and parts of the frontal lobes.

parts of the medial temporal lobes (including the hippocampus) and the frontal lobes (van Kesteren et al., 2010a, 2010b). Additionally, adding new information to an existing schema actually changes the expression of genes in the frontal lobes; so, you are essentially rewriting parts of your brain when you add to a schema (Tse et al., 2011). Thus, while we cannot identify the neural correlates for a *specific* schema like that for doing laundry, it *is* possible to see how schemas influence brain activity while new information is encoded and entered into the structure of our LTM.

Why is this relevant?

Schemas are not limited to memories for other people; in fact, we all have schemas about ourselves. Clinical psychology researchers have become particularly concerned with the ways in which these *self-schemas* may contribute to psychological problems. Consider a person with clinical depression—a condition that involves negative emotion, lack of energy, self-doubt, and self-blame. An individual with depression is likely to have a very negative self-schema, which means that he will pay attention to things that are consistent with the depressive symptoms, and will be more likely to recall events and feelings that are consistent with this schema. Thus the schema contributes to a pattern of thinking and focusing on negative thoughts. Fortunately, researchers have been able to target these schemas in psychotherapy. The evidence shows that by changing their self-schema, individuals are better able to recover from even very serious bouts of depression (Dozois et al., 2009).

Glow Images

Schemas about the self are based on past experiences and are used to organize the encoding of self-relevant information in a way that can influence our responses (Markus, 1977). But self-schemas may serve an additional role during development. Some evidence suggests that the ability to form schemas, particularly self-schemas, plays a critical role in our ability to form memories about our lives.

BIOPSYCHOSOCIAL PERSPECTIVES

Your Earliest Memories

Watch Learning and Memory in Infants: Kimberley Cuevas

Think back to the earliest memory you can recall: How old were you? It is likely that you do not have any personal or autobiographical memories from before your third birthday. Psychologists have been trying to explain this phenomenon—sometimes called *infantile amnesia*. Which of the following explanations do you think are supported by scientific evidence?

Yes or no? The nervous system is still developing at birth.

Yes or no? Young children need to develop schemas to help organize and store memories.

Yes or no? Different cultures tend to develop earliest memories at different ages.

Did you say yes to all of these? If so, you are in agreement with what scientific research shows. For example, cross-cultural cognitive research indicates that self-schemas begin to develop around the ages of 18 to 24 months (Howe, 2003). Without these schemas, it is difficult and maybe even impossible to organize and encode memories about the self. This is not a universal phenomenon, however. Other researchers taking a cross-cultural perspective have found that a sense of self emerges earlier among European Americans than among people living in eastern Asia, which correlates with earlier ages of first memories among European Americans (Fivush & Nelson, 2004; Ross & Wang, 2010). Why might this difference arise? The European American emphasis on developing a sense of self encourages thinking about personal experiences, which increases the likelihood that personal events—such as your third birthday party with that scary drunken clown who showed up, or getting chased by a dog—will be remembered. In contrast, Asian cultures tend to emphasize social harmony and collectiveness over individualism, resulting in a schema that is more socially integrated than in Westerners. This may explain the slightly later onset of autobiographical memory in Asian children. It will be interesting to see if this cultural difference changes as Asian cultures become more "Americanized."

Do these findings mean that we could get infants to remember early life events by teaching them to talk about themselves at an early age? It is not likely. The most plausible reason why we do not have memories that exist before age three years is because the nervous system, including key memory regions, continues to develop through infancy and toddlerhood. Its immaturity limits the degree to which a young person can think, reflect on, and remember personal experiences (Newcombe et al., 2000).

Quick Quiz 7.3a

How Memories Are Organized and Constructed

KNOW...

1 Schemas appear to affect which of the following stages of memory?

A Encoding
B Storage
C Retrieval
D All of these stages

2 The act of remembering through recalling a framework and then adding specific details is known as ________.

A constructive memory
B confabulation
C schematic interpretation
D distinctiveness

UNDERSTAND...

3 Information that does not fit our expectations for a specific context is likely to be forgotten if

A it is extremely unusual.
B it only fits our expectations for another completely different context.
C it is unexpected, but really not that unusual.
D it is schema consistent.

Answers can be found on page ANS-2.

Memory Reconstruction

You've all heard the cliché, "You are what you eat." But, it's also becoming increasingly clear to psychologists that "You are what you remember" (Wilson & Ross, 2003). As you read earlier in this module, our memories are organized to a large degree by our schemas, including self-schemas. There is no guarantee, however, that these schemas are 100% accurate. In fact, a growing body of research is showing that our memories of our past are influenced by our motivation to view ourselves in particular ways. In other words, the past that we remember is influenced by our mental state and our view of ourselves in the present (Albert, 1977).

This bias was nicely demonstrated in a study conducted by researchers at Concordia University and the University of Waterloo (Conway & Ross, 1984). The researchers had one group of participants complete a study skills course while another group remained on a waiting list. The course itself proved completely ineffective, at least in terms of improving study skills. The course did have an interesting effect on memory, however. Participants who completed the study course rated their previous study skills lower than they had rated them prior to taking the course; participants on the waiting list rated their study skills as being unchanged. Therefore, the study course participants revised their memories of their past abilities in a way that allowed them to feel as though they benefited from the course. This memory bias allowed them to feel as though they were improving over time, a bias that almost all of us have about ourselves (Ross & Wilson, 2000).

The results of such studies demonstrate that our memories are not stable, but instead change over time. Indeed, we have all experienced a **false memory**, *remembering events that did not occur, or incorrectly recalling details of an event.* It is important to remember that these incorrect memories do not necessarily indicate a dysfunction of memory, but rather reflect normal memory processes—which are very much imperfect. As you read in the discussion of schemas, the elements of a memory must be reconstructed each time that memory is retrieved. This reconstruction is influenced by the demands of the current situation. Indeed, psychologists have identified several ways in which our memories can be biased; they have also noted how these biases can affect a number of real-world situations, particularly in the legal system.

THE PERILS OF EYEWITNESS TESTIMONY Have you ever witnessed a crime, or even a minor traffic accident? When asked later about what you witnessed, how accurate were your reports? Most of us feel quite confident in our ability to retrieve this type of information. However, psychologists have shown that a number of minor factors can dramatically influence the details of our "memories."

In one classic study, Elizabeth Loftus and John Palmer (1974) showed undergraduate research participants film clips of traffic accidents. Participants were asked to write down a description of what they had seen, and were then asked a specific question: "About how fast were the cars going when they smashed into each other?" However, the exact wording of this question varied across experimental conditions. For some participants, the word "smashed" was replaced by "collided," "bumped," "contacted," or "hit." The results of the study were stunning—simply changing one verb in the sentence produced large differences in the estimated speed of the vehicles (see Figure 7.22). At one extreme, the word "smashed" led to an estimate of 65.2 km/h. At the low end of the spectrum, the word "contacted" led to estimates of 51.2 km/h. So, changing the verb altered the remembered speed of the vehicles by 14 km/h. In a follow-up study, Loftus and Palmer also found that participants in the "smashed" condition were more likely to insert false details such as the presence of broken glass into their accident reports. This study was a powerful demonstration of the effect of question wording on memory retrieval and provided police with

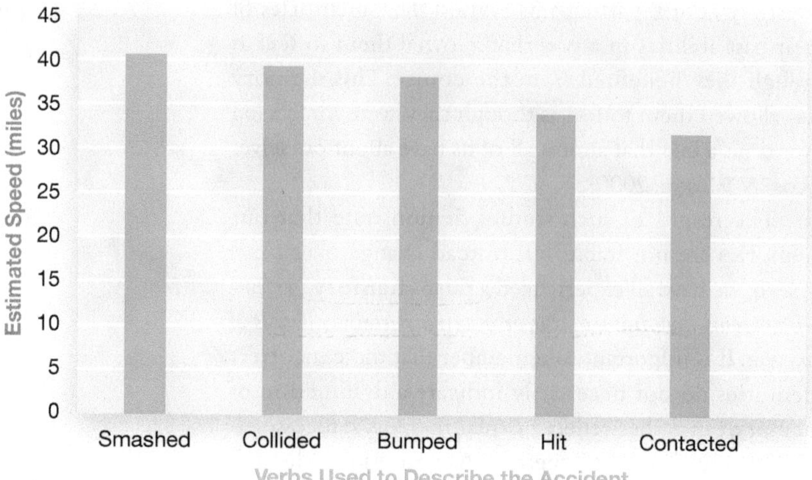

{FIG. 7.22} **The Power of a Word** Simply changing the wording of a question altered participants' recollections of a filmed traffic accident. All participants viewed the same filmed traffic accidents and all participants received the identical question with the exception of one key verb: smashed, collided, bumped, hit, or contacted.

Source: Based on data from Table 1 from Loftus and Palmer (1974), p. 586.

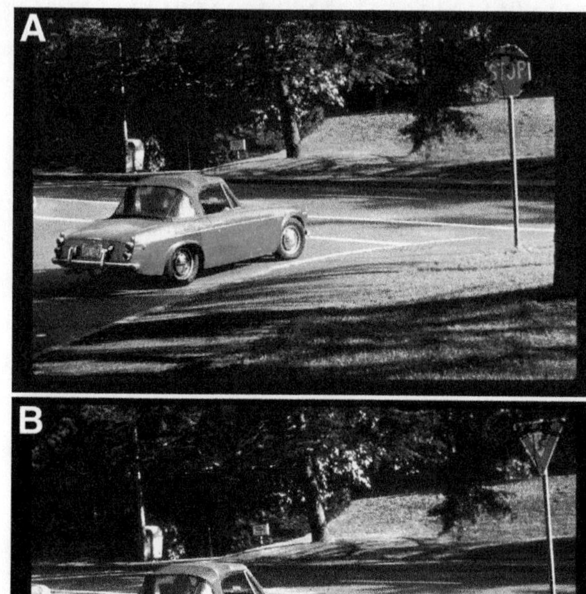

Courtesy of Elizabeth Loftus

Participants in one study viewed the top photo and later were asked about the "yield sign," even though they saw a stop sign. This small bit of misinformation was enough to get many participants to falsely remember seeing a yield sign. Similarly, participants who first viewed the bottom photo could be led to misremember seeing a stop sign with a single misleading question.

important information about the need for caution when questioning witnesses.

Another factor that can alter memories of an event—and that has implications for the legal system—is the information that is encoded after the event has occurred. When accurate, such information could theoretically improve people's memories; however, this type of information is not always accurate, which explains why jury members are asked to avoid reading about or watching TV reports related to the case with which they are involved. Psychologists have shown that this legal procedure is a wise one, as a number of studies have proven the existence of the **misinformation effect**, *when information occurring after an event becomes part of the memory for that event.* In the original studies of this topic (Loftus, 1975), researchers attempted to use the misinformation effect to change the details of people's memories. For example, in one study, students viewed a videotape of a staged car crash. In the experimental conditions, participants were asked about an object that was not in the video. One such question was about the yield sign in the car crash video, even though the scene had contained a stop sign, not a yield sign. Later, when asked if they had seen a yield sign, participants in the experimental group were likely to say yes. As this experiment demonstrates, one can change the details of a memory by asking a leading question.

Children are particularly susceptible to misinformation effects and to the effects of a question's wording (Bruck & Ceci, 1999). In one study, five- and six-year-old children watched a janitor (really an actor) named Chester as he cleaned some dolls and other toys in a playroom. For half of the children, his behaviour was innocent and simply involved him cleaning the toys. For the other children, Chester's behaviour seemed abusive and involved him treating the toys roughly. The children were later questioned by two interviewers who were (1) accusatory (implying that Chester had been playing with the dolls when he should have been working), (2) innocent (implying that Chester was simply cleaning the dolls), or (3) neutral (not implying anything about Chester's behaviour). When the interviewer's tone matched what the children saw, such as innocent questioning about Chester when he treated the toys nicely or accusatory questioning when Chester was rough with the toys, the children's reports of the behaviour were quite accurate. However, when the interview technique did not match the observed behaviour (e.g., accusatory questioning when Chester had simply cleaned the toys), the children's responses matched the interviewer's tone. In other words, the tone of the interviewer altered the details of the information that the children retrieved and reported (Thompson et al., 1997).

Children are also as dependent as adults on schemas. For example, researchers told children about their clumsy friend Sam Stone. On numerous occasions, they told funny stories about Sam's life, including the times he broke a Barbie doll and tore a sweater. Later, the children met "Sam Stone." During his time in the classroom, he did not perform a single clumsy act. The following day, the teacher showed the children a torn book and a dirty teddy bear, but did not link Sam to these damaged items. When questioned a few weeks later, however, many of the three- and four-year-old children reported that Sam Stone had ruined these objects. Some even claimed to have witnessed these acts themselves (Leichtman & Ceci, 1995). These findings should not lead us to ignore the eyewitness testimony of children; but, they should also remind us (and investigators) that memories—particularly those of children—are not stable and unchanging like a photograph.

PSYCH @

Court: Is Eyewitness Testimony Reliable?

In the United States, more than 220 individuals convicted of crimes have been exonerated based on DNA evidence; more than 75% of the original convictions were the result of mistaken eyewitness testimony (Innocence Project, 2010; Wells & Quinlivan, 2009). Although Canada lags far behind the U.S. in the re-examination of questionable convictions, there have been a number of recent cases in which people wrongfully convicted of murder were released. Considering that many cases do not have DNA evidence available (it has been lost or destroyed, or the quality of DNA samples has deteriorated), there are likely to be many more wrongful convictions that we will never know about.

While trying to pinpoint the individual responsible for a crime, investigators often present a lineup of a series of individuals (either in person or in photographs) and ask the eyewitness to identify the suspect. Given the constructive nature of memory, it should come as no surprise to hear that an eyewitness gets it wrong from time to time. The consequences of this kind of wrongful conviction are dire: An innocent person goes to jail while a potentially dangerous person stays free.

How can the science of memory improve this process? Here are the six main suggestions for reforming procedures:

1. *Employ double-blind procedures*. Elsewhere in this book, we discussed how double-blind procedures help reduce experimenter bias. Similarly, a double-blind lineup can prevent an investigator from biasing an eyewitness, either intentionally or accidentally.
2. *Use appropriate instructions*. For example, the investigator should include the statement, "The suspect might not be present in the lineup." Eyewitnesses often assume the guilty person is in the lineup, so they are likely to choose a close match. This risk can be greatly reduced by instructing the eyewitness that the correct answer may be "none of the above."
3. *Compose the lineup carefully*. The lineup should include individuals who match the eyewitness's description of the perpetrator, not the investigator's beliefs about the suspect.
4. *Use sequential lineups*. When an entire lineup is shown simultaneously, the witness may assume one of the people is guilty and settle on the best candidate. If the people in the lineup are presented one at a time, witnesses are less likely to pick out an incorrect suspect because they are willing to consider the next person in the sequence.
5. *Require confidence statements*. Eyewitness confidence can change as a result of an investigator's response, or simply by seeing the same suspect in multiple lineups, neither of which make the testimony any more accurate. Therefore, confidence statements should be taken in the witness's own words after an identification is made.
6. *Record the procedures*. Eyewitness researchers have identified at least a dozen specific things that can go wrong during identification procedures. By recording these procedures, expert witnesses can evaluate the reliability of testimony during hearings.

Recently, Canadian legal experts produced the *2011 Report of the Federal/Provincial/Territorial Heads of Prosecutions Subcommittee on the Prevention of Wrongful Convictions*. This 233-page document presents recommendations to the legal community for the use of eyewitness testimony, among other investigative practices, and highlights the need for testimony from experts including psychologists.

IMAGINATION AND FALSE MEMORIES Because our memories are not always as accurate as we would like them to be, people use a number of techniques to try to help themselves retrieve information. One of these techniques is to imagine the situation that you are trying, but failing, to remember. However, although this strategy seems logical at first, the results of several studies suggest that the retrieved memories may not be very accurate. Research indicates that repeatedly imagining an action such as breaking a toothpick makes it very difficult for people to remember whether or not they performed that imagined action (Goff & Roediger, 1998). In fact, imagining events can often lead to **imagination inflation**, *the increased confidence in a false memory of an event following repeated imagination of the event*. The more readily and clearly we can imagine events, the more certain we are that the memories are accurate.

Watch Thinking Like a Psychologist: Police Lineup

To study this effect, researchers created a list of events that may or may not have happened to the individuals in their study (e.g., got in trouble for calling 911, found a $10 bill in a parking lot). The volunteers were first asked to rate their confidence that the event happened. In sessions held over a period of days, participants were asked to imagine these events, until finally they were asked to rate their confidence again. For each item they were asked to imagine, repeated imagination *inflated* their confidence in the memory of the event (Garry et al., 1996; Garry & Polaschek, 2000). Importantly, imagination inflation is very similar to *guided imagery*, a technique used by some clinicians (and some police investigators) to help people recover details of events that they are unable to remember. It involves a guide giving instructions to participants to imagine certain events. Like the misinformation effect, guided imagery can be used to alter memories for actual events, but it can also create entirely false memories. For example, in one experiment, volunteers were asked to imagine a procedure in which a nurse removed a sample of skin from a finger. Despite the fact that this is not a medical procedure and that it almost certainly never occurred, individuals in the experimental group reported more often that this event had actually happened to them than their peers in the control condition reported (Mazzoni & Memon, 2003). In other words, attempting to imagine an event can implant new—and false—events into a person's memory.

Simulate Creating False Memories

CREATING FALSE MEMORIES IN THE LABORATORY Given that several research studies have shown that false memories are fairly easy to create, and given that such memories can have dramatic and tragic consequences when they appear in clinical or legal settings, it became important for researchers to develop techniques that would allow them to study false memories in more detail. The first of these techniques to be used is the Deese-Roediger-McDermott (DRM) paradigm (see Figure 7.23). In the **DRM procedure,** *participants study a list of highly related words called semantic associates* (which means they are associated by meaning). The word that would be the most obvious member of the list just happens to be missing. This missing word is called the *critical lure*. What happens when the participants are given a memory test? A significant proportion of participants remember the critical lure, even though it never appeared on the list (Deese, 1959; Roediger & McDermott, 1995). When individuals recall the critical lure, it is called an *intrusion*, because a false memory is sneaking into an existing memory.

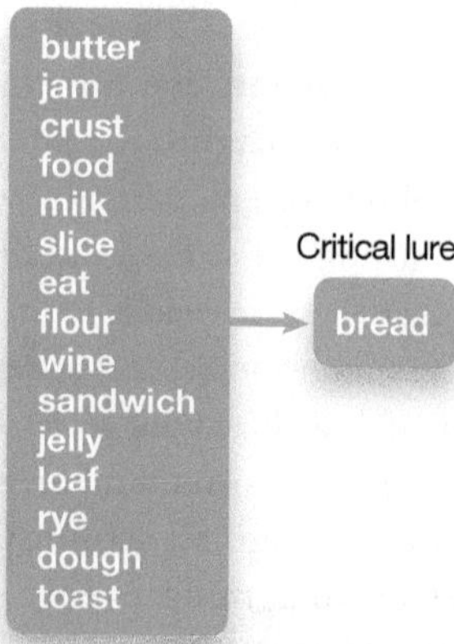

{FIG. 7.23} **A Sample Word List and Its Critical Lure for the DRM Procedure** The words on the left side are all closely related to the word "bread"—but "bread" does not actually appear on the list. People who study this list of words are very likely to misremember that "bread" was present.

The fact that people make intrusion errors is not particularly surprising. However, the strength of the effect is astonishing. In routine studies, the DRM lures as many as 70% of the participants. The most obvious way to reduce this effect would be to simply explain the DRM procedure and warn participants that intrusions may occur. Although this approach has proved effective in reducing intrusions, false memories still occur (Gallo et al., 1997). Obviously, intrusions are very difficult to prevent, but not because memory is prone to mistakes. In fact, memory is generally accurate and extremely efficient, given the millions of bits of information we encounter every day. Instead, the DRM effect reflects the fact that normal memory processes are constructive.

A second method of creating false memories in the laboratory comes from doctored photographs. For instance, researchers at the University of Victoria and their colleagues exposed undergraduate research participants to altered photographs showing the participant and his or her parent taking a ride on a hot-air balloon, an event that did not actually occur (Wade et al., 2002). For this type of experiment to work, the volunteers in the study had to recruit the help of their family. Their parents provided pictures of the participant from early childhood, along with an explanation of the event, the location, and the people and objects in the photo. The researchers took one of the pictures and digitally cut and pasted it into a balloon ride. On three occasions the participants went through the set of pictures, the true originals plus the doctored photo, in a structured interview process (the kind designed to help police get more details from eyewitnesses). By the end of the third session, half the participants had some memory for the balloon ride event, even though it never occurred (Wade et al., 2002).

Photographic images such as the ones used in the hot-air balloon study leave it to the participant to fill in the gaps as to what "happened" on their balloon ride. Other researchers have gone so far as to create false

Courtesy of Wade, K., Garry, M., Read, J., & Lindsay, S

In one study of false memory, true photos were obtained from volunteers' families (left), and were edited to look like a balloon ride (right). About half of the volunteers in this study came to recall some details of an event that never happened to them.

videotaped evidence of an event (Nash et al., 2009). For this method, a volunteer was videotaped watching a graduate student perform an action. Then, researchers videotaped a researcher performing an additional action. Then the videos were spliced together to show the volunteer watching an event that she, in reality, did not actually see. Now imagine you were shown a video of yourself watching an action you had not seen before—would you believe it? In fact, a significant portion of the individuals did form memories of the events they had never witnessed. This type of false memory retrieval mirrors that created in the guided imagery exercises used in some clinical settings, a trend that sparked a very contentious debate in both the scientific and legal communities.

THE DANGER OF FALSE REMEMBERING In the early 1990s, Beth Rutherford sought the help of her church counsellor to deal with personal issues. During their sessions, the counsellor managed to convince her that her father, a minister, had raped her. The memory was further elaborated so that she remembered becoming pregnant and that her father had forced her to undergo an abortion using a coat hanger. You can imagine what kind of effects this had on the family. Her father had little choice but to resign from his position, and his reputation was left in shambles. Although it can be difficult to prove some false memories, this incident is particularly disturbing because it *could* have been supported by medical evidence. When a medical investigation was finally conducted, absolutely no evidence was found that Beth had ever been raped or that she had ever been pregnant (Loftus, 1997).

Beth's story is an example of a false **recovered memory**, *a memory of a traumatic event that is suddenly recovered after blocking the memory of that event for a long period of time,* often many years. This idea that we suppress traumatic memories is popularly known as *repression* from Freudian psychoanalysis; however, a repressed memory can still affect other psychological processes, leading people to suffer in other ways such as experiencing depression. This school of thought suggests that if a repressed memory can be recovered, then a patient can find ways to cope with the trauma. Some therapists espouse this view and use techniques such as hypnosis and guided imagery to try to unearth repressed memories.

Simulate Memory Experiment

Can we suppress our memories of traumatic life events? As it turns out, it is *possible* although not very common. In one survey study, researchers examined the testimony of people who had been imprisoned in Camp Erika, a Nazi concentration camp in The Netherlands, in the early 1940s (Wagenaar & Groeneweg, 1990). Most of the prisoners were able to provide detailed information about their time in the concentration camp, but a minority of prisoners did not remember many emotional events during their imprisonment including the names and appearances of people who tortured them and the fact that they had witnessed murders! But, being able to suppress a horrific memory is very different from then recovering that memory years later.

Recovered memories, like many other types of long-term memory, are difficult to study because one can rarely determine if they are true or false. This uncertainty has led to the **recovered memory controversy**, *a heated debate among psychologists about the validity of recovered memories* (Davis & Loftus, 2009). On one side of the controversy are some clinical mental health workers (although certainly not the majority) who regularly attempt to recover memories they suspect have been repressed. On the opposing side are the many psychologists who point out that the techniques that might help "recover" a memory bear a striking resemblance to those that are used to create false memories in laboratory research; they often involve instructions to remember, attempts to form images, and social reinforcement for reporting memories (Spanos et al., 1994). How can this disagreement be resolved?

One method is to use brain imaging to differentiate true and false memories. Psychologists have found that when people recount information that is true, the visual and other sensory areas of the brain become more active. When revealing falsely remembered information, these same individuals have much less activity in the sensory regions—the brain is not drawing on mental imagery because it was not there in the first place (Dennis et al., 2012; Stark et al., 2010). Interestingly, these brain results do not always map onto the participants' conscious memories of what they had seen. So, this method might be able to distinguish between true and false memories better than the participant himself (Johnson et al., 2012). However, although these neuroimaging results are promising, these studies did not use stimuli that were as emotional as the recovered memories patients report. Therefore, as with most areas of psychology, much more research will be needed in this controversial area.

Although this module provides some frightening examples of how malleable our memories are, there is actually something inspirational about these results. We construct our own memories and, as a result, our own reality. Therefore, we have the power to focus our memories on the positive experiences of our lives, or on the negative ones. It's up to you—remember that.

Quick Quiz 7.3b Memory Reconstruction

KNOW...

1 If you are presented with a list of 15 words, all of which have something in common, you are most likely participating in a study focusing on __________.

A misinformation effects
B the DRM procedure
C imagination inflation
D repression

2 Which of the following effects demonstrates that one can change the details of a memory just by how a question is phrased?

A Misinformation effects
B The DRM procedure
C Imagination inflation
D Repression

UNDERSTAND...

3 What might happen if a study participant viewed a doctored photograph of an event that did not actually occur?

A The person could develop a memory for the event and he would *not* recognize that it was a false memory.
B The person would be unable to form memories of the event.
C The person could develop a memory for the event, but he would clearly recognize that it was a false memory.
D We cannot make any predictions about what might or might not happen.

APPLY...

4 Jonathan witnessed a robbery. The police then asked him to select the perpetrator from a lineup. You can be most confident in his selection if

A the authorities smiled after Jonathan's response so that he would feel comfortable during the lineup procedure
B the authorities had the lineup presented all at the same time so Jonathan could compare the individuals.
C the lineup included individuals of different races and ethnicities.
D Jonathan was given the option to not choose any of the people from the lineup if no one fit his memory.

ANALYZE...

5 Psychologists who study false memories have engaged in a debate over the validity of recovered memories. Why are they skeptical about claims of recovered memories?

A They have never experienced recovered memories themselves.
B Many of the techniques used to recover memories in therapy bear a striking similarity to the techniques used to create false memories in research.
C Brain scans can easily distinguish between true and false memories.
D Scientists have proved that it is impossible to remember something that you have once forgotten.

Answers can be found on page ANS-2.

Module Summary

Module 7.3

Now that you have read this module you should

RiceWithSugar/Shutterstock.com

KNOW...

- ***The key terminology used in discussing how memories are organized and constructed*:**

constructive memory (p. 303)
DRM procedure (p. 308)
false memory (p. 305)
imagination inflation (p. 307)
misinformation effect (p. 306)
recovered memory (p. 309)
recovered memory controversy (p. 310)
schema (p. 302)

UNDERSTAND...

- ***How schemas serve as frameworks for encoding and constructing memories.*** Schemas guide our attention, telling us what to expect in certain circumstances. They organize long-term memories and provide us with cues when it comes time to retrieve those memories.
- ***How psychologists can produce false memories in the laboratory.*** Psychologists have found that a number of factors contribute to the construction of false memories, including misinformation, imagination inflation, and the semantic similarities used in the DRM procedure.

APPLY...

- ***What you have learned to judge the reliability of eyewitness testimony.*** Eyewitness testimony is absolutely crucial to the operation of most legal systems, but how reliable is it? Since 1989, 225 U.S.-based cases of exonerations (convictions that have been overturned due to new evidence after the trial) have been made possible thanks to the help of The Innocence Project. In these cases, the original convictions were based on the following information (some cases included multiple sources):

  Eyewitness misidentification (173 cases)
  Improper or unvalidated forensics (116 cases)
  False confessions (51 cases)
  Questionable information from informants (36 cases)

  What percentage of the exonerations involve eyewitness mistakes? What do these data suggest about research on eyewitness testimony? (See our answers on page ANS-3.)

ANALYZE...

- ***The arguments in the "recovered memory" debate.*** You should first understand the premise behind the idea of recovered memories: Some people believe that if a memory is too painful, it might be blocked from conscious recollection, only to be recovered later through therapeutic techniques. Others argue that it is difficult to prove that a "recovered" memory is actually recovered. Given how easy it is to create false memories, they argue, any memory believed to be recovered should be viewed with skepticism.

Work the Scientific Literacy Model :: Understanding How We Remember and Forget

1 What do we know about the basic processes of memory?

Review **pages 288–289** for the processes involved in memory acquisition and recall. Then review **Figure 7.1 on page 271** for the Atkinson-Shiffrin model of memory storage. Both are important concepts in the chapter, but the details of how they work together can be confusing. Encoding is the process of transforming sensory information into memory, whereas retrieval is the process of accessing and using memory. In addition, there is storage, or how memory is retained after it is encoded. The Atkinson-Shiffrin model organizes these processes as they relate to different types of memory storage—sensory memory, short-term memory (STM), and long-term memory (LTM). Recall that the process of converting short-term memories to lasting memories in the brain is called consolidation; without it, memories cannot become permanent. For example, if an image is encoded to sensory memory, it is stored for a very short time, and then is either forgotten or converted to STM. After it is encoded to STM, the image is stored by way of rehearsal, and then either forgotten or encoded to LTM. Once the image is in long-term memory, the brain will consolidate it and then store the memory for years—maybe even permanently.

2

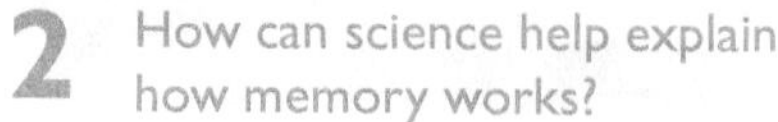

Research shows that the hippocampus is crucial to consolidating long-term memories. Support for this idea also comes from outside the laboratory: Binge-drinking has noticeable effects on the hippocampus, which can result in memory loss or blackouts. On **page 283**, we discussed the example of H.M., a man who was unable to form new memories after his hippocampus was surgically removed.

When the structures of the brain are in good working order, the right strategies help us create lasting memories. **Figure 7.14 on page 289** shows us that simple repetition is not as effective as more involved types of rehearsal in creating such memories, and research on levels of processing reveals that it is not so much how *long* we try to memorize something, but rather *how* we do so. If thinking about information in a certain way helps us remember something, can feelings about the information do the same? On **page 294**, we mentioned studies that suggest a link between emotions and the quality of memories.

Of course, our memories are not perfect—a point supported by research on the misinformation effect and the DRM paradigm, two procedures used in false memory research.

3 Can we critically evaluate claims about memory?

If emotions enhance processing of information, can we completely trust our most vivid and emotional memories? **Myths in Mind on page 296** explored the idea of flashbulb memories. Researchers have found that despite the level of detail involved in memories tied to emotional events, they are ultimately no more accurate than any other type of memories. Similarly, the controversy around recovered memories continues, both because of the difficulty of proving or disproving them and because methods of recovering "lost" memories bear a striking similarity to laboratory experiments that produce false memories.

On a more positive note, **Psych @ Court on page 307** discussed how we can use what we know about the science of memory to improve accuracy in police lineups. A practical application of this chapter's concepts included using what you know about the forgetting curve (**Figure 7.18, p. 297**) to strategize ways to consolidate memories for easy retrieval when you need them, such as at test time. Using dual-coding in mnemonic strategies, like the method of loci, can aid learning, as can taking your studying beyond basic repetition of information. Finally, on **page 299** we suggested over-learning and creating desirable difficulties to develop a deeper understanding and memory for the material.

4

Andreka/Shutterstock

Watch the accompanying video excerpt on remembering. You can access the video at MyPsychLab or by clicking the play button in the centre of your eText. If your instructor assigns this video as a homework activity, you will find additional content to help you in MyPsychLab. You can also view the video by using your smart phone and the QR code below, or you can go to the YouTube link provided.

After you have read the chapter and watched the video, imagine you are reading your textbook and studying for an upcoming exam in psychology. Identify and describe each step in the process required for remembering information from your textbook in order to do well on the exam. Discuss two strategies for improving memory and provide examples of how each could help you on the exam.

MyPsychLab **Your turn to Work the Scientific Literacy Model:** Watch the accompanying video on YouTube, or on your phone (using the Layar app or QR code). If your instructor has assigned this as a homework activity, you can find the video clip and additional content at MyPsychLab. Answer the questions that accompany the video clip to test your understanding.

youtube.com/workthemodel

SCAN WITH LAYAR

8

Thought and Language

ICP/incamerastock/Alamy

Dmitry Vereshchagin/Fotolia

Module 8.1

The Organization of Knowledge

Learning Objectives

After reading this module you should

KNOW ...	UNDERSTAND ...	APPLY ...	ANALYZE ...
The key terminology associated with concepts and categories	Theories of how people organize their knowledge about the world How experience and culture can shape the way we organize our knowledge	Your knowledge to identify prototypical examples	The claim that the language we speak determines how we think

When Edward regained consciousness in the hospital, his family immediately noticed that something was wrong. The most obvious problem was that he had difficulty recognizing faces, a relatively common disorder known as *prosopagnosia*. As the doctors performed more testing, it became apparent that Edward had other cognitive problems as well. Edward had difficulty recognizing objects—but not *all* objects. Instead, he couldn't distinguish between different types of instruments and different types of animals even though he could use language to describe their appearance. His ability to recognize most other types of objects seemed normal.

Neurological patients like Edward may seem unrelated to your own life. However, for specific categories of visual information to be lost, they must have been stored in similar areas of the brain before brain damage occurred. Therefore, these cases give us some insight into how the brain stores and organizes the information that we have encoded into memory.

Focus Questions

 How do people form easily recognizable categories from complex information?

 How does culture influence the ways in which we categorize information?

Each of us has amassed a tremendous amount of knowledge in the course of our lifetime. Indeed, it is impossible to put a number on just how many facts each of us knows. Imagine trying to record everything you ever learned about the world—how many books could you fill? Instead of asking how much we know, psychologists are interested in how we keep track of it all. In this module, we will explore what those processes are like and how they work. We will start by learning about the key terminology before presenting theories about how knowledge is stored over the long term.

Concepts and Categories

A **concept** *is the mental representation of an object, event, or idea.* Although it seems as though different concepts should be distinct from each other, there are actually very few independent concepts. You do not have just one concept for *chair*, one for *table*, and one for *sofa*. Instead, each of these concepts can be divided into smaller groups with more precise labels, such as *arm chair* or *coffee table.* Similarly, all of these items can be lumped together under the single label, *furniture*. Psychologists use the term **categories** to refer to *these clusters of interrelated concepts.* We form these groups using a process called *categorization.*

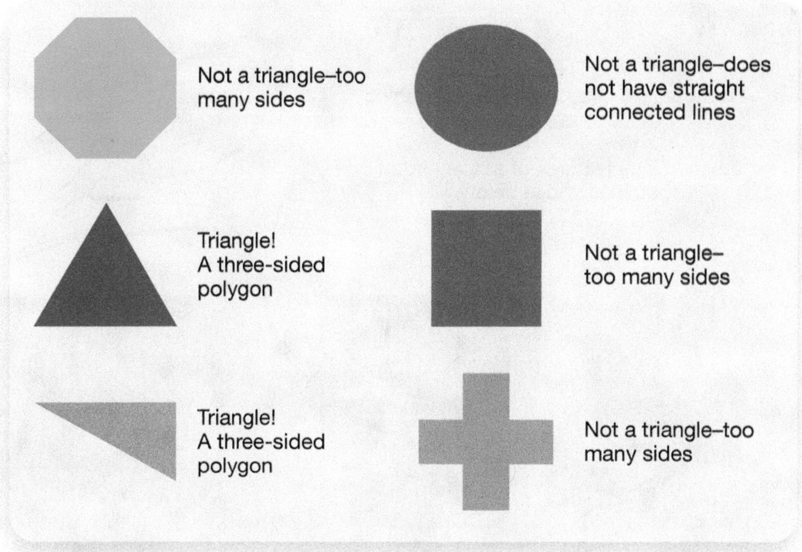

{FIG. 8.1} **Using the Definition of a Triangle to Categorize Shapes**

CLASSICAL CATEGORIES: DEFINITIONS AND RULES Categorization is difficult to define in that it involves elements of perception (Chapter 4), memory (Chapter 7), and "higher-order" processes like decision making (Module 8.2) and language (Module 8.3). The earliest approach to the study of categories is referred to as **classical categorization**; *this theory claims that objects or events are categorized according to a certain set of rules or by a specific set of features*—something similar to a dictionary definition (Lakoff & Johnson, 1999; Rouder & Ratcliffe, 2006). Definitions do a fine job of explaining how people categorize items in certain situations. For example, a triangle can be defined as "a figure (usually, a plane rectilinear figure) having three angles and three sides" (*Oxford English Dictionary,* 2011). Using that definition, you should find it easy to categorize the triangles in Figure 8.1.

Classical categorization does not tell the full story of how categorization works, however. We use a variety of cognitive processes in determining which objects fit which category. One of the major problems we confront in this process is **graded membership**—*the observation that some concepts appear to make better category members than others.* For example, see if the definition in Table 8.1 fits your definition of *bird* and then categorize the items in the table.

Watch: Basics: The Mind Is What the Brain Does

Ideally, you said yes to the sparrow and penguin, and no to the apple. But did you notice any difference in how you responded to the sparrow and penguin? Psychologists have researched classical categorization using a behavioural measure known as the *sentence-verification technique*, in which volunteers wait for a sentence to appear in front of them on a computer screen and respond as fast as they can with a yes or no answer to statements such as *A sparrow is a bird*, or, *A penguin is a bird.* The choice the subject makes, as well as her reaction time to respond, is measured by the researcher. Sentence-verification shows us that some members of a category are recognized faster than others (Olson et al., 2004; Rosch & Mervis, 1975). In other words, subjects almost always answer "yes" faster to sparrow than to penguin. This seems to go against a classical, rule-based categorization system because both sparrows and penguins are equally good fits for the definition, but sparrows are somehow perceived as being more bird-like than penguins. Thus, a modern approach to categorization must explain how "best examples" influence how we categorize items.

Table 8.1 :: Categorizing Objects According to the Definition of *Bird*

Definition: Any of the class Aves of warm-blooded, egg-laying, feathered vertebrates with forelimbs modified to form wings. (American Heritage Dictionary, 2007)

Now categorize a set of items by answering *yes* or *no* regarding the truth of the following sentences.

1. A sparrow is a bird.
2. An apple is a bird.
3. A penguin is a bird.

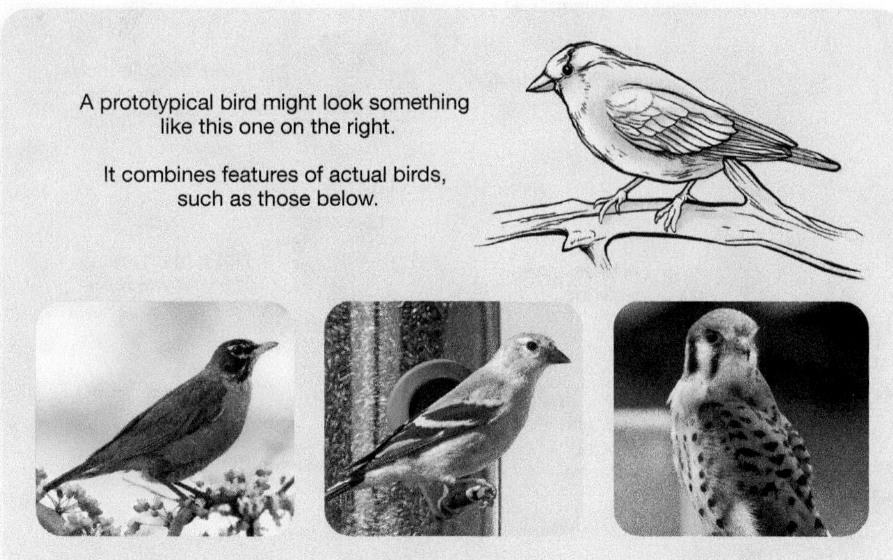

Left: chatursunil/Shutterstock.com; centre: Al Mueller/Shutterstock.com; right: Leo/Shutterstock.com

{FIG. 8.2} **A Prototypical Bird** Click on this figure in your eText to see more details.

PROTOTYPES: CATEGORIZATION BY COMPARISON When you hear the word *bird*, what mental image comes to mind? Does it resemble an ostrich? Or is your image closer to a robin, sparrow, or blue jay? The likely image that comes to mind when you imagine a bird is what psychologists call a prototype (see Figure 8.2). **Prototypes** *are mental representations of an average category member* (Rosch, 1973). If you took an average of the three most familiar birds, you would get a prototypical bird.

Prototypes allow for classification by resemblance. When you encounter a little creature you have never seen before, its basic shape—maybe just its silhouette—can be compared to your prototype of a bird. A match will then be made and you can classify the creature as a bird. Notice how different this process is from classical categorization: No rules or definitions are involved, just a set of similarities in overall shape and function.

The main advantage of prototypes is that they help explain why some category members make better examples than others. Ostriches are birds just as much as blue jays are, but they do not resemble the rest of the family very well. In other words, blue jays are closer to the prototypical bird.

Now that you have read about categories based on a set of rules or characteristics (classical categories) and as a general comparison based on resemblances (prototypes), you might wonder which approach is correct. Research says that we can follow either approach—the choice really depends on how complicated a category or a specific example might be. If there are a few major distinctions between items, we use resemblance; if there are complications, we switch to rules (Feldman, 2003; Rouder & Ratcliff, 2004, 2006). For example, in the case of seeing a bat dart by, your first impression might be "bird" because it resembles a bird. But if you investigated further, you will see that a bat fits the classical description of a mammal, not a bird. In other words, it has hair, gives live birth rather than lays eggs, and so on.

NETWORKS AND HIERARCHIES Classical categorization and prototypes only explain part of how we organize information. Each concept that we learn has similarities to other concepts. A sparrow has physical similarities to a bat (e.g., size and shape); a sparrow will have even more in common with a robin because they are both birds (e.g., size, shape, laying eggs, etc.). These connections among ideas can be represented in a network diagram known as a **semantic network**, *an interconnected set of nodes (or concepts) and the links that join them to form a category* (see Figure 8.3). *Nodes* are circles that represent concepts, and *links* connect them together

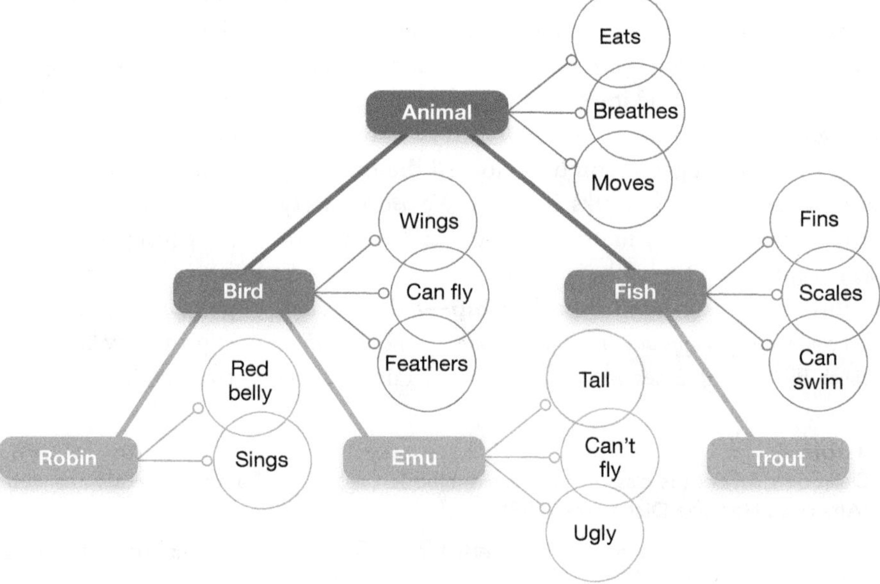

{FIG. 8.3} **A Semantic Network Diagram for the Category "Animal"** The nodes include the basic-level categories, *Birds* and *Fish*. Another node represents the broader category of *Animals*, while the lowest three nodes represent the more specific categories of *Robins*, *Emus*, and *Trout*.

to represent the structure of a category as well as the relationships among different categories (Collins & Loftus, 1975). In these networks, similar items have more, and stronger, connections than unrelated items. These connections explain why it is easier to identify one member of a category (e.g., oranges, from the category "fruit") after seeing another word from that category (e.g., apple) than after seeing an unrelated word (e.g., elephant). Activating the individual concept for "apple" makes connected nodes in the network more likely to become activated, a phenomenon known as *priming*.

Something you may notice about Figure 8.3 is that it is arranged in a *hierarchy*—that is, it consists of a structure moving from general to very specific. This organization is important because different levels of the category are useful in different situations. The most frequently used level, in both thought and language, is the *basic-level category,* which is located in the middle row of the diagram (where birds and fish are) (Johnson & Mervis, 1997; Rosch et al., 1976). A number of qualities make the basic-level category unique:

- Basic-level categories are the terms used most often in conversation.
- They are the easiest to pronounce.
- They are the level at which prototypes exist.
- They are the level at which most thinking occurs.

To get a sense for how different category levels influence our thinking, we can compare sentences referring to an object at different levels. Consider what would happen if someone approached you and made any one of the following statements:

- "There's an *animal* in your yard."
- "There's a *bird* in your yard."
- "There's a *robin* in your yard."

The second sentence—"There's a bird in your yard"—is probably the one you are most likely to hear, and it makes reference to a basic level of a category (birds). Many people would respond that the choice of *animal* as a label indicates confusion, claiming that if the speaker knew it was a *bird*, he should have said so; otherwise, it sounds like he is trying to figure out which kind of animal he is looking at. Indeed, *superordinate categories* like "animal" are generally used when someone is uncertain about an object or when he or she wishes to group together a number of different examples from the basic-level category (e.g., birds, cats, dogs). In contrast, when the speaker identifies a *subordinate-level category* like *robin*, it suggests that there is something special about this particular type of bird. It may also indicate that the speaker has expert-level knowledge of the basic category and that using the more specific level is necessary to get her point across in the intended way.

In order to demonstrate the usefulness of semantic networks in our attempt to explain how we organize knowledge, complete this easy test generated by the animal network in Figure 8.3. If you were asked to react to dozens of sentences, and the following two sentences were included among them, which do you think you would mark as "true" the fastest?

- *A robin is a bird.*
- *A robin is an animal.*

As you can see in the network diagram, *robin* and *bird* are closer together; in fact, to connect *robin* to *animal*, you must first go through *bird*. Sure enough, people regard the sentence "A robin is a bird" as a true statement faster than "A robin is an animal."

Now consider another set of examples. Which trait do you think you would verify faster?

- *A robin has wings.*
- *A robin eats.*

Using the connecting lines as we did before, we can predict that it would be the first statement about wings. As research shows, our guess would be correct. The next question scientists must ask is *why?* Research involving brain-damaged patients suggests that many of our categorization abilities are due to the manner in which this information is organized in the brain.

Simulate The Mind's Organization of Conceptual Knowledge

WORKING THE SCIENTIFIC LITERACY MODEL

Categories and the Brain

When we see an object, we attempt to retrieve its name from memory; this is part of the process of recognizing the things around us. Identifying the object also activates the semantic network that is associated with it. How is this possible? Some researchers suggest that our brain stores items from the same category in the same general area. This organization would help explain phenomena like semantic priming. But, is this really how our brain organizes the objects we see?

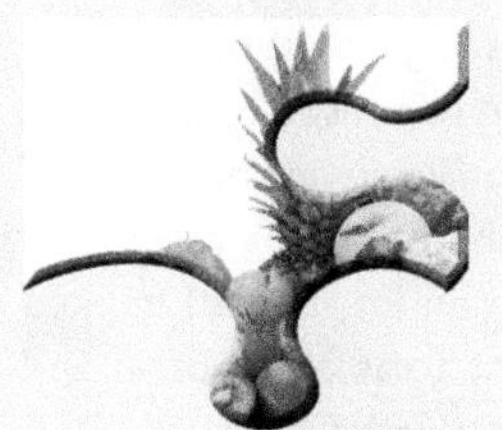

What do we know about categories and the brain?

Initial attempts to understand how information is organized in the brain relied on patients with

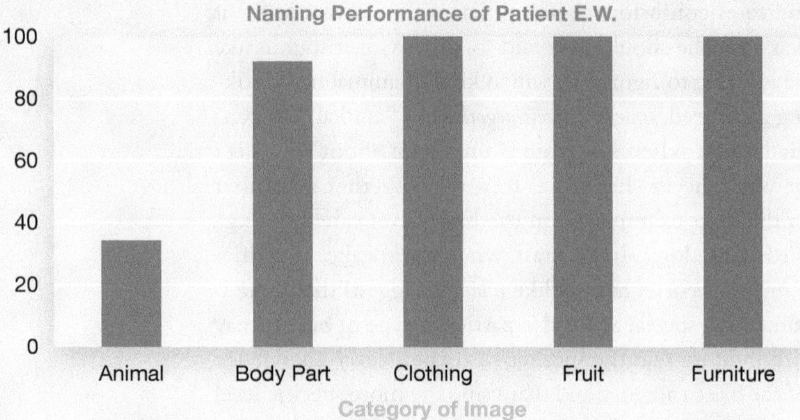

{FIG. 8.4} **Naming Errors for a CSVA Patient** Patients with CSVA have problems identifying members of specific categories. When asked to identify the object depicted by different line drawings, patient E.W. showed a marked impairment for the recognition of animals. Her ability to name items from other categories demonstrated that her overall perceptual abilities were preserved. Data from Caramazza and Shelton (1998).

damage to the temporal lobes who displayed a very specific set of symptoms. These patients had trouble identifying objects such as pictures of animals or vegetables despite the fact that they were able to describe the different shapes that made up those objects (i.e., they could still see). The fact that these deficits were for particular categories of objects was intriguing, as it suggested that damaging certain parts of the brain could affect the ability to recognize some categories while leaving others unaffected (Warrington & McCarthy, 1983; Warrington & Shallice, 1979). Because these problems were isolated to certain categories, these patients were diagnosed as having a disorder known as *category specific visual agnosia* (or *CSVA*). An example of such a patient was described at the opening of this module.

Early attempts to find a pattern in these patients' deficits focused on the distinction between living and non-living categories (see Figure 8.4). Several patients with CSVA had difficulties identifying fruits, vegetables, and/or animals; however, these patients were still able to accurately identify members of categories such as tools and furniture (Arguin et al., 1996; Bunn et al., 1998). A smaller group of patients showed the opposite pattern of results, with deficits for non-living categories (Cappa et al., 1998; Saffran & Schwartz, 1994). Based on these patterns of data, scientists suggested that different categories are organized in the brain based on their sensory (visual, touch, etc.) and functional features (i.e., what they are used for) (Warrington & Shallice, 1984). Members of the same living categories (e.g., birds) have a number of sensory features in common, such as shape, the presence of feathers, and skinny legs. Members of the same non-living categories (e.g., tools) have a number of functional features in common (e.g., used to fix things, associated with repetitive movements like sawing or hammering). Therefore, the fact that living and non-living categories relied on different types of information (in general) implied that they would be stored in different areas of the brain, and would explain the symptoms of patients with CSVA.

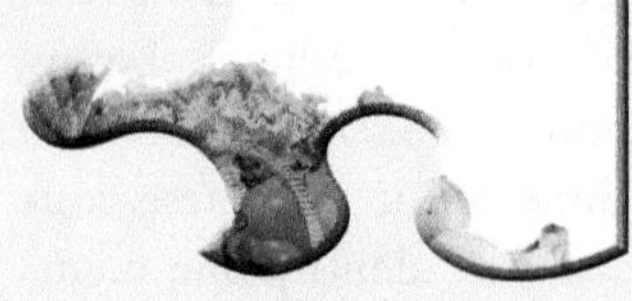

How can science explain how categories are organized in the brain?

As scientists began to look more closely at the deficits of these patients, it became clear that the living vs. non-living distinction was a bit too simplistic. First, some patients had problems with very specific categories *within the larger category of living items*. So, a patient could identify animals but not fruits and vegetables (Samson & Pillon, 2003). The second problem was that there are so many possible categories of living and non-living things that it became unlikely that each could be fit into its own unique part of the brain. In reaction to these and other problems, researchers developed new theories that better fit the data. In one popular view, known as the *domain-specific hypothesis*, researchers proposed that evolutionary pressures led to the development of specialized circuits in the brain for a *small group of categories* that were important for our survival. These categories included animals, fruits and vegetables, members of our own species, and possibly tools (Caramazza & Mahon, 2003). This theory can explain most, but not all, of the problems observed in the patients tested thus far.

One weakness of this view is that it doesn't take into account people's different experiences with each category. If you are a chef at a vegetarian restaurant, you would obviously spend more time learning about different fruits and vegetables than the average person. As a result, you would form more connections in your semantic network for vegetables. You would also form more brain connections for this category because you would have memories of learning to cook different dishes. The question, then, is whether these large networks in the brain would provide some back-up systems so that your knowledge of vegetables would be preserved even after brain damage. Research by Canadian scientists suggests that it would. Their patient, known by the initials E.L.M., played the bugle in a military band when he was younger. Over time, he became an expert with brass instruments. When tested after his stroke, the researchers found that he was impaired at naming stringed instruments but was still able to name different types of brass instruments (Dixon et al., 2002). This result doesn't mean that the domain-specific hypothesis is incorrect; but, it does show that our experiences influence how we categorize objects and information.

Can we critically evaluate this information?

Although these different case studies are compelling, we must be cautious about assuming these results apply to how the healthy brain organizes information (Bukach et al., 2004). An important concern is that the damage associated with CSVA differs slightly from patient to patient, making it difficult to say with any certainty that damage to a particular area will definitely result in a deficit related to a specific category. Also, the causes of this damage vary from patient to patient (e.g., stroke, car accident, etc.), as do their personal experiences. Additionally, testing procedures and stimuli differ across laboratories; therefore, there is no guarantee that problems related to a particular category are being assessed in the same way for different patients. Finally, these studies cannot tell us if the deficits are due to damage to a specific brain region or if that damage instead disrupted a pathway that just happened to *cross through* that brain region.

In order to address some of these concerns, it was necessary for researchers to conduct studies with healthy-brained individuals. Researchers have used brain imaging to show that different parts of the temporal lobes are active when people view items from different categories including animals, tools, and people (Martin et al., 1996). Thus, although different people will vary in terms of the exact location that these categories are stored, it does appear that some categories are stored separately from others.

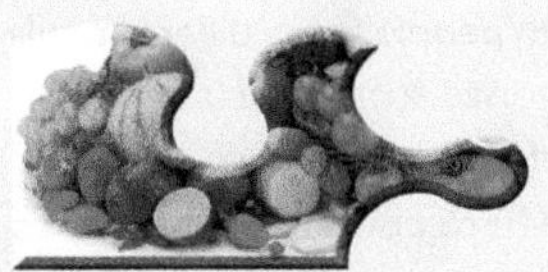

Why is this relevant?

Knowledge of how our brain organizes and stores information can have an obvious impact upon medical treatments. Understanding where important categories of objects are stored in memory will allow surgeons to avoid those regions during surgery. It will also provide health-care workers with useful information when they are making initial assessments of patients. If a patient appears to have problems naming objects, a nurse or doctor informed about categorization research would begin to look for patterns in the patient's errors to see if some categories are more affected than others. Additionally, the fact that a patient's life experiences can alter how categories are distributed in the brain suggests that doctors need to learn more about a patient's history before making a diagnosis. As you will read below, experience doesn't just alter how existing concepts are categorized—it can also influence how *new* items are incorporated into existing semantic networks.

M.studio/Fotolia

CATEGORIZATION AND EXPERIENCE Our ability to form categories is based on our experiences. As we are exposed to new stimuli, we instinctively try to organize them into groups based on similar physical and semantic features. But, this process doesn't end in childhood. Instead, researchers have noted that adults integrate new stimuli into categories based on what they have experienced before (Jacoby & Brooks, 1984). When encountering a new item, people will select its category by retrieving the item(s) that are most similar to it from memory (Brooks, 1978). In fact, recent studies have found that we sometimes retrieve individual features (e.g., a beaver's tail) rather than an entire object from memory (Brooks & Hannah, 2006; Hannah, 2005). Normally, these procedures lead to fast and accurate categorization. If you see an animal with wings and a beak, you can easily retrieve from memory a bird that you previously saw; doing so will lead you to infer that this new object is a bird, even if it is a type of bird that you might not have encountered before.

However, there are also times when our reliance on previously experienced items can lead us astray. In a series of studies with medical students and practising physicians, Geoffrey Norman and colleagues at McMaster University found that recent exposure to an example from one category can bias how people diagnose new cases (Leblanc et al., 2001; Norman et al., 1989a, 1989b). In one experiment, medical students were taught to diagnose different skin conditions using written rules as well as photographs of these diseases. Some of the photographs were typical examples of that disorder whereas other photographs were unusual cases that resembled other disorders. When tested later, the participants were more likely to rely on the previously viewed photographs than they were on the rules (a fact that would surprise most medical schools); in fact, the unusual photographs viewed during training even led to wrong diagnoses for test items that were textbook examples of that disorder (Allen et al., 1992)! This shows the power that our memory can have on how we take in and organize new information. As an aside, expert physicians were accurate over 90% of the time in most studies, so you can still trust your doctor.

Quick Quiz 8.1a

Concepts and Categories

KNOW ...

1 A ______ is a mental representation of an average member of a category.

A basic-level category **C** similarity principle
B prototype **D** network

2 ______ refer to mental representations of objects, events, or ideas.

A Categories **C** Primings
B Concepts **D** Networks

UNDERSTAND ...

3 Classical categorization approaches do not account for ______, a type of categorization that notes some items make better category members than others.

A basic-level categorization
B prototyping
C priming
D graded membership

APPLY ...

4 Janice, a medical school student, looked at her grandmother's hospital chart. Although her grandmother appeared to have problems with her intestines, Janice thought the pattern of the lab results resembled those of a patient with lupus who Janet had seen in the clinic earlier that week. Janice is showing an example of

A how memory for a previous example can influence categorization decisions.
B how people rely on prototypes to categorize objects and events.
C how we rely on a set of rules to categorize objects.
D how we are able to quickly categorize examples from specific categories.

Answers can be found on page ANS-3.

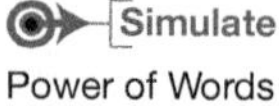
Simulate
Power of Words

Culture and Categories

The human brain is wired to perceive similarities and differences and, as we learned from prototypes, the end result of this tendency is to categorize items based on these comparisons as well as on our previous experiences with members of different categories. However, our natural tendency to do so interacts with our cultural experiences; how we categorize objects depends to a great extent on what we have learned about those objects from others in our culture.

Various researchers have explored the relationships between culture and categorization by studying basic-level categories among people from different cultural backgrounds. For example, researchers have asked individuals from traditional villages in Central America to identify a variety of plants and animals that are extremely relevant to their diet, medicine, safety, and other aspects of their lives. Not surprisingly, these individuals referred to plants and animals at a more specific level than North American university students would (Bailenson et al., 2002; Berlin, 1974). Thus, categorization is based—at least to some extent—on cultural learning. Psychologists have also discovered that cultural factors influence not just how we categorize individual objects, but also how objects in our world relate to one another.

BIOPSYCHOSOCIAL PERSPECTIVES

Culture and Categorical Thinking

Animals, relatives, household appliances, colours, and other entities all fall into categories. However, people from different cultures might differ in how they categorize such objects. In North America, cows are sometimes referred to as "livestock" or "food animals," whereas in India, where cows are regarded as sacred, neither category would apply.

In addition, how objects are *related* to each other differs considerably across cultures. Which of the two photos in Figure 8.5a do you think someone from North America took? Researchers asked both American and Japanese university students to take a picture of someone, from whatever angle or degree of focus they chose. American students were more likely to take close-up pictures, whereas Japanese students typically included surrounding objects (Nisbett & Masuda, 2003). When asked which two objects go together in Figure 8.5b, American college students tend to group cows with chickens—because both are animals. In contrast, Japanese students coupled cows with grass, because grass is what cows eat (Gutchess et al., 2010; Nisbett & Masuda, 2003). These examples demonstrate cross-cultural differences in perceiving how objects are related to their environments. People raised in North America tend to focus on a single characteristic, whereas Japanese people tend to view objects in relation to their environment.

Researchers have even found differences in brain function when people of different cultural backgrounds view and categorize objects (Park & Huang, 2010). Figure 8.6 reveals differences in brain activity when Westerners and East Asians view photos of objects, such as an animal, against a background of grass and trees. Areas of the brain devoted to processing both objects (lateral parts of the occipital lobes) and background (the parahippocampal gyrus, an area underneath the hippocampus) become activated when Westerners view these photos, whereas only areas devoted to background processes become activated in East Asians (Goh et al., 2007). These findings demonstrate that a complete understanding of how humans categorize objects requires application of the biopsychosocial model.

(a)

(b)

Top: Nisbett & Masuda (2003, PNAS)

{FIG. 8.5} **Your Culture and Your Point of View** (a) Which of these two pictures do you think a North American would be more likely to take? (b) Which two go together?

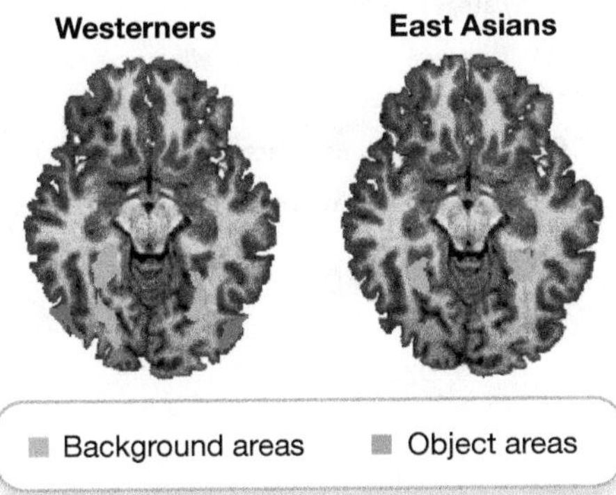

Park et al. Culture Wires the Brain: A Cognitive Neuroscience Perspective. *Perspectives on Psychological Science,* 2010; 5 (4): 391. Reprinted by Permission of SAGE Publications.

{FIG. 8.6} **Brain Activity Varies by Culture** Brain regions that are involved in object recognition and processing are activated differently in people from Western and Eastern cultures. Brain regions that are involved in processing individual objects are more highly activated when Westerners view focal objects against background scenery, whereas people from East Asian countries appear to attend to background scenery more closely than focal objects.

Cultural differences in how people think and categorize items have also led to the idea of **linguistic relativity** (or the **Whorfian hypothesis**)—*the theory that the language we use determines how we understand the world.* For example, the English language has several colour names, such as *black, white, red, blue, green, yellow, purple, orange,* and *pink.* If speakers want to be more specific, they use some combination of other terms, such as *blue-green* or *sky-blue.* By comparison, some cultures have fewer dedicated colour words; the Dani people of New Guinea, for example, have one word for blue-green, but no words to distinguish what English speakers consider to be prototypically blue or prototypically green. Do these language differences affect the way individuals perceive, categorize, and remember colours?

The results of research in this area are mixed. When dividing colour samples, similar to what you would find when shopping for paint, English speakers set aside different stacks of cards for samples that seemed more blue and those that seemed more green. In contrast, the Dani included those same samples in one larger blue-green category (Roberson et al., 2000). However, subsequent research has not been able to clarify whether this effect occurred because the language differences led the subjects to actually perceive colour differently (true linguistic relativity) or if they were just using language as a means to complete the sorting task. For example, when individuals were asked to use a verbal distracter (producing irrelevant speech), it prevented them from using the colour terms for the sorting task. In that case, there are no differences between cultures (Roberson & Davidoff, 2000). Therefore, although many of these studies are compelling and receive attention in the media, more research needs to be performed to rule out alternative explanations and to prevent us from drawing incorrect conclusions like the one discussed below.

MYTHS IN MIND

How Many Words for Snow?

From time to time, people repeat a bit of "wisdom" about how language relates to thinking. One often-cited example is about the Inuit in Canada's Arctic regions, who are thought to have many words for snow, each with a different meaning. For example, *aput* means snow that is on the ground, and *gana* means falling snow. This observation, which was made in the early 19th century by anthropologist Franz Boas, was often repeated and exaggerated, with claims that Inuit people had dozens of words for different types of snow. With so many words for snow, it was thought that perhaps the Inuit people perceive snow differently than someone who does not live near it almost year-round. Scholars used the example to argue that language determines how people categorize the world.

Research tells us that we must be careful in over-generalizing the influence of language on categorization. The reality is that the Inuit seem to categorize snow the same way a person from the rest of Canada does. Someone from balmy Winnipeg can tell the difference between falling snow, blowing snow, sticky snow, drifting snow, and "oh-sweet-God-it's-snowing-in-May-snow," just as well as an Inuit who lives with snow almost year-round (Martin, 1986). Therefore, we see that the linguistic relativity hypothesis is incorrect in this case: The difference in vocabulary for snow does not lead to differences in perception.

Ton Koene/age fotostock/SuperStock

The Inuit do have multiple words for snow, but so do a lot of other cultures.

Quick Quiz 8.1b Culture and Categories

KNOW ...

1 The idea that our language influences how we understand the world is referred to as ________.

- **A** the context specificity hypothesis
- **B** sentence verification
- **C** the Whorfian hypothesis
- **D** priming

ANALYZE ...

2 Research on linguistic relativity suggests that

- **A** language has a complete control over how people categorize the world.
- **B** language can have some effects on categorization, but the effects are limited.
- **C** language has no effect on categorization.
- **D** researchers have not addressed this question.

Answers can be found on page ANS-3.

Module Summary

Module **8.1**

Now that you have read this module you should

KNOW ...

- ***The key terminology associated with concepts and categories***:

categories (p. 315)
classical categorization (p. 315)
concept (p. 315)
graded membership (p. 315)
linguistic relativity (Whorfian hypothesis) (p. 321)
prototypes (p. 316)
semantic network (p. 316)

UNDERSTAND ...

- ***Theories of how people organize their knowledge about the world.*** First, certain objects and events are more likely to be associated in clusters. The priming effect demonstrates this phenomenon; for example, hearing the word "fruit" makes it more likely that you will think of "apple" than, say, "table." More specifically, we organize our knowledge about the world through semantic networks, which arrange categories from general to specific levels. Usually we think in terms of basic-level categories, but under some circumstances we can be either more or less specific. Studies of people with brain damage suggest that the neural representations of members of evolutionarily important categories are stored together in the brain. These studies also show us that our previous experience with a category can influence how we categorize new stimuli and how it is stored in the brain.
- ***How experience and culture can shape the way we organize our knowledge.*** One of many possible examples of this influence was discussed. Specifically, ideas of how objects relate to one another differ between people from North America and people from Eastern Asia. People from North America (and Westerners in general) tend to focus on individual, focal objects in a scene, whereas people from Japan tend to focus on how objects are interrelated.

Dmitry Vereshchagin/Fotolia

APPLY ...

- ***Your knowledge to identify prototypical examples.*** Try the following questions for practice (check your answers on page ANS-3):
  1. What is the best example for the category of fish: a hammerhead shark, a trout, or an eel?
  2. What do you consider to be a prototypical sport? Why?
  3. Some categories are created spontaneously, yet still have prototypes. For example, what might be a prototypical object for the category "what to save if your house is on fire"?

ANALYZE ...

- ***The claim that the language we speak determines how we think.*** Researchers have shown that language can influence the way we think, but it cannot entirely shape how we perceive the world. For example, people can categorize colours even if they do not have specific words for them.

NEW YORK POST Page Six

TUESDAY, DECEMBER 4, 2012 LATE CITY FINAL www.nypost.com $1.00

Pushed on the subway track, this man is about to die

DOOMED

Polaris/Newscom

Module 8.2

Problem Solving, Judgment, and Decision Making

Learning Objectives After reading this module you should	KNOW ...	UNDERSTAND ...	APPLY ...	ANALYZE ...
	The key terminology of problem solving and decision making	The characteristics that problems have in common How obstacles to problem solving are often self-imposed	Your knowledge to determine if you tend to be a maximizer or a satisficer	Whether human thought is primarily logical or intuitive

Ki-Suck Han was about to die. He had just been shoved onto the subway's tracks and was desperately scrambling to climb back onto the station's platform as the subway train rushed toward him. If you were a few metres away from Mr. Han, what would you have done? What factors would have influenced your actions?

In this case, the person on the platform was R. Umar Abbasi, a freelance photographer working for *The New York Post.* Mr. Abbasi did not put down his camera and run to help Mr. Han. Instead, he took a well-framed photograph that captured the terrifying scene. The photograph was published on the front page of the *Post* and was immediately condemned by people who were upset that the photographer didn't try to save Mr. Han's life (and that the *Post* used the photograph to make money). In a statement released to other media outlets, the *Post* claimed that Mr. Abbasi felt that he wasn't strong enough to lift the man and instead tried to use his camera's flash to signal the driver. According to this explanation, Mr. Abbasi analyzed the situation and selected a course of action that he felt would be most helpful. Regardless of whether you believe this account, it does illustrate an important point: Reasoning and decision making can be performed in a number of ways and can be influenced by a number of factors. That is why we don't all respond the same way to the same situation.

Focus Questions

1. How do people make decisions and solve problems?

2. How can having multiple options lead people to be dissatisfied with their decisions?

In other modules of this text, you have read about how we learn and remember new information (Modules 7.1 and 7.2) and how we organize our knowledge of different concepts (Module 8.1).

This module will focus on how we *use* this information to help us solve problems and make decisions. Although it may seem like such "higher-order cognitive abilities" are distinct from memory and categorization, they are actually a wonderful example of how the different topics within the field of psychology relate to each other. When we try to solve a problem or decide between alternatives, we are actually drawing on our knowledge of different concepts and using that information to try to imagine different possible outcomes (Green et al., 2006). How well we perform these tasks depends on a number of factors including our problem-solving strategies and the type of information available to us.

Defining and Solving Problems

You are certainly familiar with the general concept of a problem, but in psychological terminology, **problem solving** *means accomplishing a goal when the solution or the path to the solution is not clear* (Leighton & Sternberg, 2003; Robertson, 2001). Indeed, many of the problems that we face in life contain *obstacles* that interfere with our ability to reach our goals. The challenge, then, is to find a technique or strategy that will allow us to overcome these obstacles. As you will see, there are a number of options that people use for this purpose—although none of them are perfect.

PROBLEM-SOLVING STRATEGIES AND TECHNIQUES Each of us will face an incredible number of problems in our lives. Some of these problems will be straightforward and easy to solve; however, others will be quite complex and will require us to come up with a novel solution. How do we remember the strategies we can use for routine problems? And, how do we develop new strategies for nonroutine problems? Although these questions *appear* as if they could have an infinite number of answers, there seem to be two common techniques that we use time and again.

One type of strategy is more objective, logical, and slower, whereas the other is more subjective, intuitive, and quicker (Gilovich & Griffin, 2002; Holyoak & Morrison, 2005). The difference between them can be illustrated with an example. Suppose you are trying to figure out where you have left your phone. You've tried the trick of calling yourself using a landline phone, but you couldn't hear it ringing. So, it's not in your house. A *logical* approach might involve making of list of the places you've been in the last 24 hours and then retracing your steps until you (hopefully) find your phone. An *intuitive* approach might involve thinking about previous times you've lost your phone or wallet and using these experiences to guide your search (e.g., "I'm always forgetting my phone at Dan's place, so I should look there first").

When we think logically, we rely on **algorithms**, *problem-solving strategies based on a series of rules.* As such, they are very logical and follow a set of steps, usually in a preset order. Computers are very good at using algorithms because they can follow a preprogrammed set of steps and perform thousands of operations every second. People, however, are not always so careful. We tend to rely on intuition to find strategies and solutions that seem like a good fit for the problem. These are called **heuristics**, *problem-solving strategies that stem from prior experiences and provide an educated guess as to what is the most likely solution.* Heuristics are often quite efficient; these "rules of thumb" are usually accurate and allow us to find solutions and to make decisions quickly. In the example of trying to figure out where you left your phone, you are more likely to put your phone down at a friend's house than on the bus, so that increases the likelihood that your phone is still sitting on his coffee table. Calling your friend to ask about your phone is much simpler than retracing your steps from class to the gym to the grocery store, and so on.

Of course, different problems call for different approaches. In fact, in some cases, it might be useful to start off with one type of problem-solving and then switch to another. Think about how you might play the children's word-game known as hangman, shown in Figure 8.7. Here, the goal state is to spell a word. In the initial state, you have none of the letters or other clues to guide you. So your obstacles are to overcome (i.e., fill in) blanks without guessing the wrong letters. How would you go about achieving this goal?

On one hand, an algorithm might go like this: Guess the letter *A*, then *B*, then *C*, and so on through the alphabet until you lose or until the word is spelled. However, this would not be a very successful approach. An alternative algorithm would be to find out how frequently each letter occurs in the alphabet and then guess the letters in that order until the game ends with you

Watch
The Big Picture: I Am, Therefore I Think

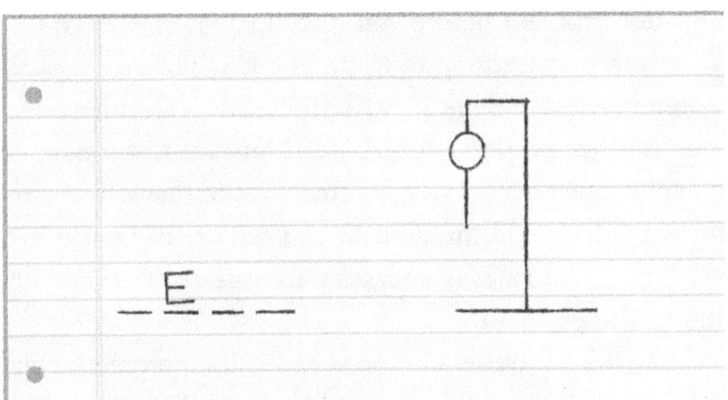

{FIG. 8.7} **Problem Solving in Hangman** In a game of hangman, your job is to guess the letters in the word represented by the four blanks to the left. If you get a letter right, your opponent will put it in the correct blank. If you guess an incorrect letter, your opponent will draw a body part on the stick figure. The goal is to guess the word before the entire body is drawn.

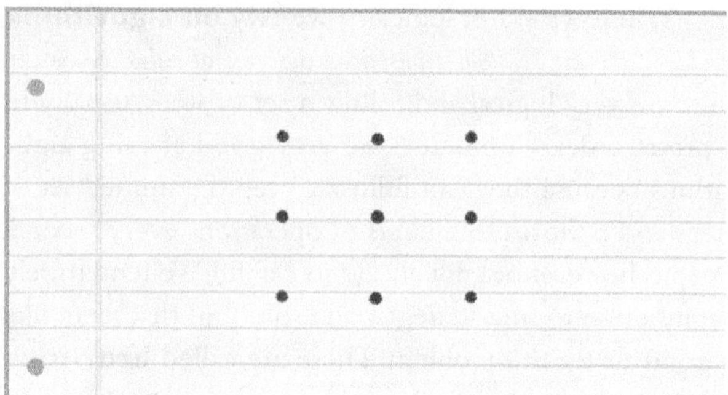

{FIG. 8.8} **The Nine-Dot Problem** Connect all nine dots using only four straight lines and without lifting your pen or pencil (Maier, 1930). The solution to the problem can be seen on page 327 (Figure 8.9).

winning or losing. So, you would start out by selecting *E,* then *A,* and so on. On the other hand, a heuristic might be useful. For example, if you discover the last letter is *G,* you might guess that the next-to-last letter is *N,* because you know that many words end with *-ing.*

As you can see, some problems (such as the hangman game) can be approached with either algorithms or heuristics. In other words, most people start out a game like hangman with an algorithm: Guess the most frequent letters until a recognizable pattern emerges, such as *-ing,* or the letters *-oug* (which are often followed by *h,* as in *tough* or *cough*) appear. At that point, you might switch to heuristics and guess which words would be most likely to fit in the spaces.

COGNITIVE OBSTACLES Using algorithms or heuristics will often allow you to eventually solve a problem; however, there are times when the problem-solving rules and strategies that you have established might actually get in the way of problem solving. The nine-dot problem (Figure 8.8; Maier, 1930) is a good example of such *a cognitive obstacle.* The goal of this problem is to connect all nine dots using only four straight lines and without lifting your pen or pencil off the paper. Try solving the nine-dot problem before you read further.

Here is something to think about when solving this problem: Most people impose limitations on where the lines can go, even though those limits are not a part of the rules. Specifically, people often assume that a line cannot extend beyond the dots. As you can see in Figure 8.9, breaking these rules is necessary in order to find a solution to the problem.

Having a routine solution available for a problem generally allows us to solve that problem with less effort than we would use if we encountered it for the first time. This efficiency saves us time and effort. Sometimes, however, routines may impose cognitive barriers that impede solving a problem if circumstances change so that the routine solution no longer works. A **mental set** *is a cognitive obstacle that occurs when an individual attempts to apply a routine solution to what is actually a new type of problem.* Sometimes a mental set occurs when an individual applies the routine solution when a much easier solution is possible. Figure 8.10 presents a problem that often elicits a mental set. The answer appears at the bottom of the page, but make your guess before you check it. Did you get it right? If not, then you probably succumbed to a mental set.

Mental sets can occur in many different situations. For instance, a person may experience **functional fixedness,** *which occurs when an individual identifies an object or technique that could potentially solve a problem, but can think of only its most obvious function.* Functional fixedness can be illustrated with a classic thought problem: Figure 8.11 shows two strings hanging from a ceiling. Imagine you are asked to tie the strings together. However, once you grab a string, you cannot let go of it until both are tied together. The problem is, unless you have extraordinarily long arms, you cannot reach the second string while you are holding on to the first one (Maier, 1931). So how would you solve the problem? Figure 8.13 on p. 328 offers one possible answer and an explanation of what makes this problem challenging.

Problem solving occurs in every aspect of life, but as you can see, there are basic cognitive processes that appear no matter what the context. We identify the goal we want to achieve, try to determine the best strategy to do so, and hope that we do not get caught by unexpected obstacles—especially those we create in our own minds.

Quick Quiz 8.2a
Defining and Solving Problems

KNOW ...

1 ________ are problem-solving strategies that provide a reasonable guess for the solution.

A Algorithms **C** Operators

B Heuristics **D** Subgoals

UNDERSTAND ...

2 Javier was attempting to teach his daughter how to tie her shoes. The strategy that would prove most effective in this situation would be a(n) ________.

A heuristic **C** obstacle

B algorithm **D** mental set

3 Jennifer was trying to put together her new bookshelf in her bedroom. Unfortunately, she didn't have a hammer. Frustrated, she went outside and sat down beside some bricks that were left over from a gardening project. Her inability to see that the bricks could be used to hammer in nails is an example of a(n) ________.

A mental set **C** algorithm

B functional fixedness **D** heuristic

Answers can be found on page ANS-3.

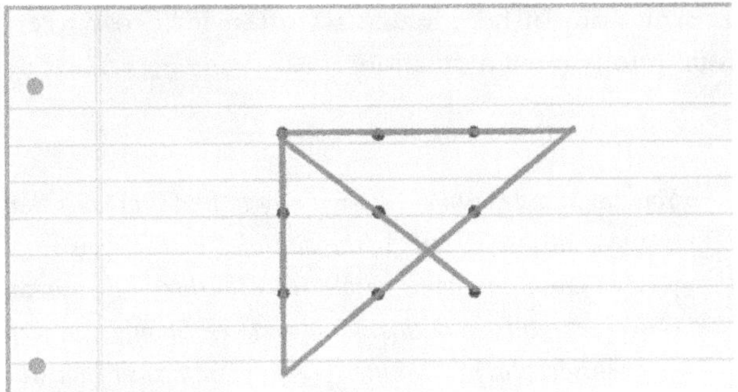

{FIG. 8.9} **One Solution to the Nine-Dot Problem** In this case, the tendency is to see the outer edge of dots as a boundary, and to assume that one cannot go past that boundary. However, if you are willing to extend some of the lines beyond the dots, it is actually quite a simple puzzle to complete.

{FIG. 8.10} **The Five-Daughter Problem** Maria's father has five daughters: Lala, Lela, Lila, and Lola. What is the fifth daughter's name?

The fifth daughter's name is Maria.

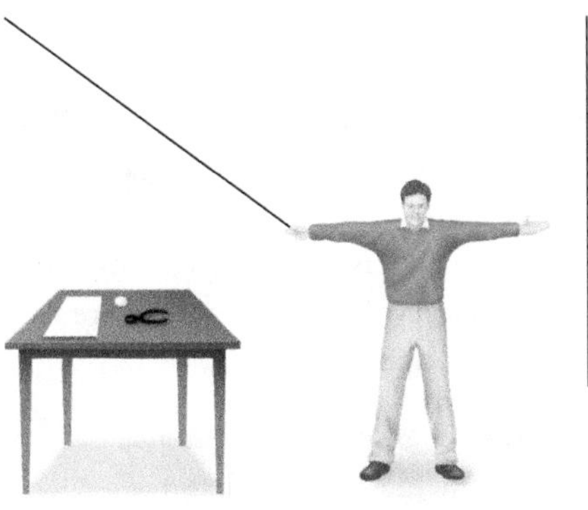

{FIG. 8.11} **The Two-String Problem** Imagine you are standing between two strings and need to tie them together. The only problem is that you cannot reach both strings at the same time (Maier, 1931). In the room with you is a table, a piece of paper, a pair of pliers, and a ball of cotton. What do you do? For a solution, see Figure 8.13 on page 328. **Click on this figure in your eText to see more details.**

Judgment and Decision Making

Like problem solving, judgments and decisions can be based on logical algorithms, intuitive heuristics, or a combination of the two types of thought (Gilovich & Griffin, 2002; Holyoak & Morrison, 2005). We tend to use heuristics more often than we realize, even those of us who consider ourselves to be logical thinkers. In this section of the module, we will examine specific types of heuristics and consider how they influence how we make and evaluate decisions.

Watch
In the Real World: Changing Your Mind

REPRESENTATIVENESS AND AVAILABILITY

Please read the following scenario:

Linda is 31 years old, single, outspoken, and very bright. She majored in philosophy. As a student, she was deeply concerned with issues of discrimination and social justice, and also participated in antinuclear demonstrations. Which is more likely?

(A) *Linda is a bank teller.*
(B) *Linda is a bank teller and is active in the feminist movement.*

Which answer did you choose? In a study that presented this problem to participants, the researchers reported that (B) was chosen more than 80% of the time. Most respondents stated that option (B) seemed more correct even though option (A) is actually much more likely and would be the correct choice based on the question asked (Tversky & Kahneman, 1982).

So how is the correct answer (A)? Individuals who approach this problem from the stance of probability theory would apply some simple logical steps. The world has a certain number of (A) bank tellers; this number would be considered the *base rate*, or the rate at which you would find a bank teller in the world's population just asking random people on the street if they are a bank teller. Among the base group, there will be a certain number of (B) bank tellers who are feminists, as shown in Figure 8.12. In other words, the number of bank tellers who are feminists will always be a fraction of (i.e., less than) the total number of bank tellers. But, because many of Linda's qualities could relate to a "feminist," the idea that Linda is a bank teller *and* a feminist feels correct. This type of error, known as the *conjunction fallacy*, reflects the mistaken belief that finding a specific member in two overlapping categories (i.e., a member of the *conjunction* of two categories) is more likely than finding any member of one of the larger, general categories.

Explore
The Two-String Problem

The conjunction fallacy demonstrates the use of the **representativeness heuristic**: *making judgments of likelihood based on how well an example represents a specific*

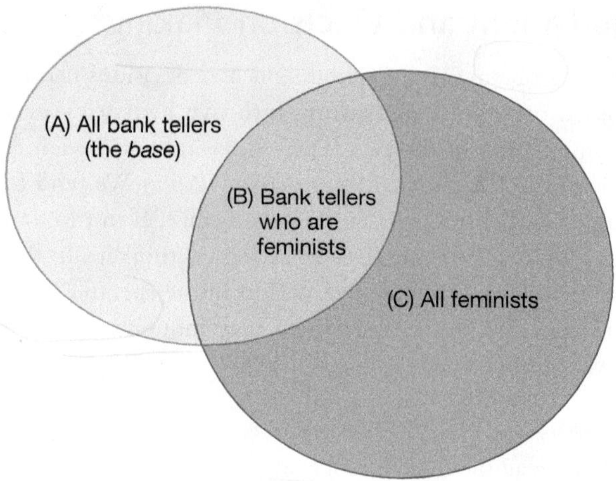

{FIG. 8.12} **The Conjunction Fallacy** There are more bank tellers in the world than there are bank tellers who are feminists, so there is a greater chance that Linda comes from either (A) or (B) than just (B) alone.

category. In the bank teller example, we cannot identify any traits that seem like a typical bank teller. At the same time, the traits of social activism really do seem to represent a feminist. Thus, the judgment was biased by the fact that Linda seemed representative of a feminist, even though a feminist bank teller will always be rarer than bank tellers in general (i.e., the representativeness heuristic influenced the decision more than logic or mathematical probabilities).

Seeing this type of problem has led many people to question what is wrong with people's ability to use logic: Why is it so easy to get 80% of the people in a study to give the wrong answer? In fact, there is nothing inherently *wrong* with using heuristics; they simply allow individuals to obtain quick answers based on readily available information. In fact, heuristics often lead to correct assumptions about a situation.

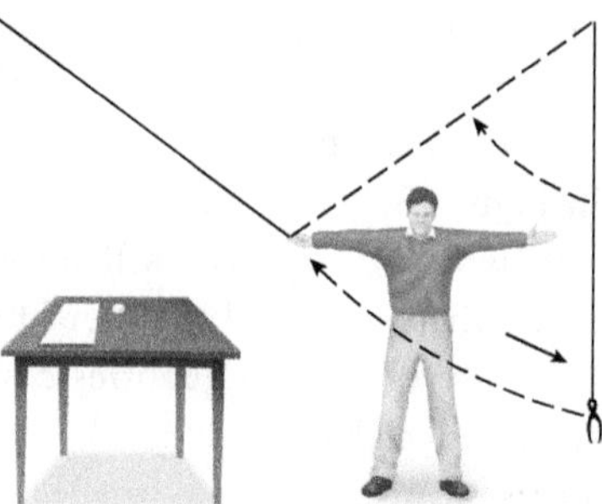

{FIG. 8.13} **A Solution to the Two-String Problem** One solution to the two-string problem from page 327 is to take the pliers off the table and tie them to one string. This provides enough weight to swing one string back and forth while you grab the other. Many people demonstrate functional fixedness when they approach this problem—they do not think of using the pliers as a weight because its normal function is as a grasping tool.

Consider this scenario:

You are in a department store trying to find a product that is apparently sold out. At the end of the aisle, you see a young man in tan pants with a red polo shirt—the typical employee's uniform of this chain of stores. Should you stop and consider the probabilities yielding an answer that was technically most correct?

(A) *A young male of this age would wear tan pants and a red polo shirt.*
(B) *A young male of this age would wear tan pants and a red polo shirt and work at this store.*

Or does it make sense to just assume (B) is correct, and to simply ask the young man for help (Shepperd & Koch, 2005)? In this case, it would make perfect sense to assume (B) is correct and not spend time wondering about the best logical way to approach the situation. In other words, heuristics often work and, in the process, save us time and effort. However, there are many situations in which these mental short cuts can lead to biased or incorrect conclusions.

The **availability heuristic** *entails estimating the frequency of an event based on how easily examples of it come to mind.* In other words, we assume that if examples are readily *available,* then they must be very frequent. For example, researchers asked volunteers which was more frequent in the English language:

(A) *Words that begin with the letter K*
(B) *Words that have K as the third letter*

Most subjects chose (A) even though it is not the correct choice. The same thing happened with the consonants *L, N, R,* and *V,* all of which appear as the third letter in a word more often than they appear as the first letter (Tversky & Kahneman, 1973). This outcome reflects the application of the availability heuristic: People base judgments on the information most readily available.

Of course, heuristics often do produce correct answers. Subjects in the same study were asked which was more common in English:

(A) Words that begin with the letter *K*
(B) Words that begin with the letter *T*

In this case, more subjects found that words beginning with T were readily available to memory, and they were correct. The heuristic helped provide a quick intuitive answer.

There are numerous real-world examples of the availability heuristic. In the year following the September 11, 2001, terrorist attacks, people were much more likely to overestimate the likelihood that planes could crash and/or be hijacked. As a result, fewer people flew that year than in the year prior to the attacks, opting instead to travel by car when possible. The availability of the image of planes crashing into the World Trade Center was so vivid and easily retrieved from memory that it influenced decision making. Ironically, this shift proved to be dangerous, particularly given that driving is statistically *much* more dangerous than flying. Gerd Gigerenzer, a German psychologist at the Max Planck Institute in Berlin, examined traffic fatalities on U.S. roads in the years before and after 2001. He found that in the calendar year following these terrorist attacks, there were more than 1500 additional deaths on American roads (when compared to the average of the previous years). Within a year of the attacks, the number of people using planes returned to approximately pre-9/11 levels; so did the number of road fatalities (Gigerenzer, 2004). In other words, for almost a year, people overestimated the risks of flying because it was easier to think of examples of 9/11 than to think of all of the times hijackings and plane crashes did *not* occur; and, they underestimated the risks associated with driving because these images were less available to many people. This example shows us that heuristics, although often useful, can cause us to incorrectly judge the risks associated with many elements of our lives (Gardner, 2008).

Marcio Jose Sanchez/AP Images

The availability of extreme events like 9/11 and plane crashes leads people to overestimate the likelihood of experiencing these events.

ANCHORING EFFECTS While the representativeness and availability heuristics involve our ability to remember examples that are similar to the current situation, other heuristics influence our responses based on the way that information is presented. Issues such as the wording of a problem, the variety of multiple-choice options, and the problem's frames of reference can have a profound impact on judgments. One such effect, known as the **anchoring effect**, *occurs when an individual attempts to solve a problem involving numbers and uses previous knowledge to keep (i.e.,* anchor*) the response within a limited range.* Sometimes this previous knowledge consists of facts that we can retrieve from memory. For example, imagine that you are asked to name the year that British Columbia became part of Canada. Although most of you would, of course, excitedly jump from your chair and shout, "1871!" the rest might assume that if Canada became a country in 1867, then B.C. likely joined a few years after that. In this latter case, the birth of our country in 1867 served as an anchor for the judgment about when B.C. joined Confederation.

The anchoring heuristic has also been produced experimentally. In these cases, questions worded in different ways can produce vastly different responses (Epley & Gilovich, 2006; Kahneman & Miller, 1986). For example, consider what might happen if researchers asked the same question to two different groups, using a different anchor each time:

(A) What percentage of countries in the United Nations are from Africa? Is it greater than or less than 10%? What do you think the exact percentage is?

(B) What percentage of countries in the United Nations are from Africa? Is it greater than or less than 65%? What do you think the exact percentage is?

Researchers conducted a study using similar methods and found that individuals in group (A), who received the 10% anchor, estimated the number to be approximately 25%. Individuals in group (B), who received the 65% anchor, estimated the percentage at approximately 45%. In this case, the anchor obviously had a significant effect on the estimates.

The anchoring heuristic can have a large effect on your life. For example, have you ever had to bargain with someone while travelling? Or have you ever negotiated the price of a car? If you are able to establish a low anchor during bargaining, the final price is likely to be much lower than if you let the salesperson dictate the terms. So don't be passive—use what you learn in this course to save yourself some money.

FRAMING EFFECTS Decision making can also be influenced by how a problem is worded or *framed.* Consider the following dilemma: Imagine that you are a selfless doctor volunteering in a village in a disease-plagued part of Africa. You have two treatment options. Vaccine A has been used before; you know that it will save 200 of the 600 villagers. Vaccine B is untested; it has a 33% chance of saving all 600 people and a 67% chance of saving no one. Which option would you choose?

Now let's suppose that you are given two different treatment options for the villagers. Treatment C has been used before and will definitely kill 67% of the villagers. Treatment D is untested; it has a 33% chance of killing none of the villagers and a 67% chance of killing them all. Which option would you choose?

Most people choose the vaccine that will definitely save 200 people (Vaccine A) and the treatment that has a chance of killing no one (Treatment D). This tendency is interesting because options A and C are identical as are options B and D. As you can see by looking at Figure 8.14, the only difference between them is that one is framed in terms of saving people and the other is framed in terms of killing people. Yet, people become much more risk-averse when the question is framed in terms of potential losses (or deaths). Interestingly, when people don't follow the typical pattern of framed responses (e.g., selecting Treatment C rather than being risk-averse and selecting Treatment D), there is an increase in activity in regions of the prefrontal cortex associated with learning new rules (de Martino et al., 2006). This activity suggests that the brain may be attempting to incorporate this response into a new set of mental rules that can be used to guide similar decisions in the future.

BELIEF PERSEVERANCE AND CONFIRMATION BIAS Whenever we solve a problem or make a decision, we have an opportunity to evaluate the outcome to make sure we got it right and to judge how satisfied we are with the decision. However, feeling satisfied does not necessarily mean we are correct.

Imagine you and several friends sit down for a poker match with an old deck of cards. The dealer removes

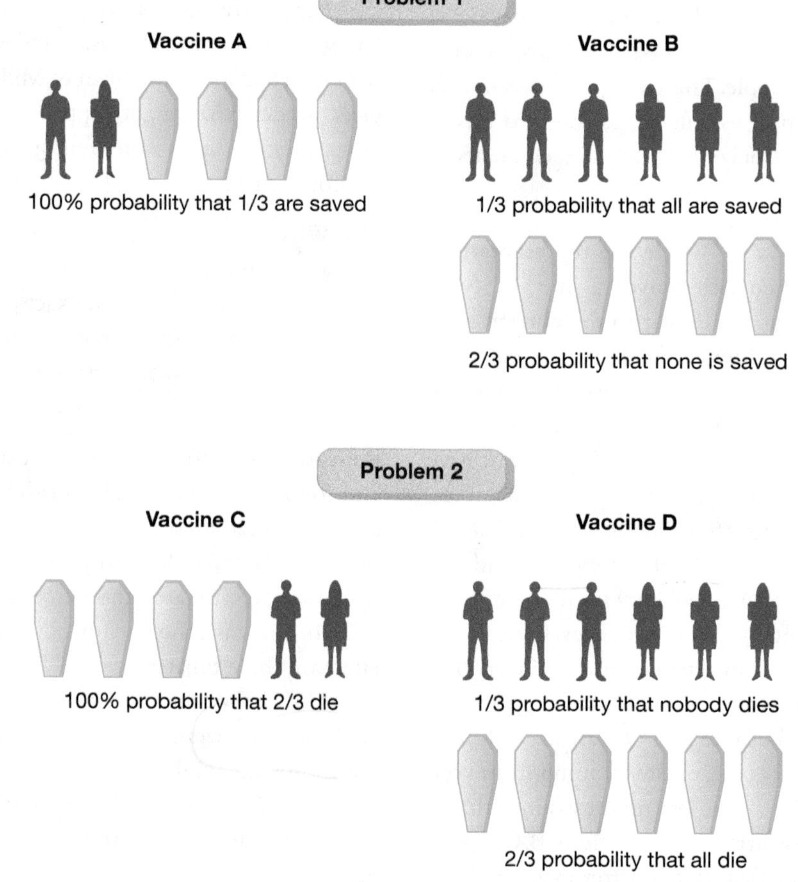

{FIG. 8.14} **Framing Effects** When people are asked which vaccine or treatment they would use to help a hypothetical group of villagers, the option they select is influenced by how the question is worded or framed. If the question is worded in terms of saving villagers, most people choose Vaccine A. If the question is worded in terms of killing villagers, most people choose Treatment D.

the cards from the box and counts to make sure they are all present. At first, he comes up with 51 cards—one short. On the second try, he gets 52 cards—the correct amount. Now that he has reached the expected number, he goes on to deal the first round. What is wrong with his reasoning in this case?

The most obvious problem is that the dealer assumed that he had counted correctly when he counted 52 cards (the expected number) without entertaining the possibility that he was correct when he counted 51 cards (an unexpected number). This is an example of **belief perseverance**, *when an individual believes he or she has the solution to the problem or the correct answer for a question* (e.g., How many cards are in this deck?), *and accepts only evidence that will confirm those beliefs.* Our dealer knew the correct number of cards would be 52. He exhibited the belief perseverance by ignoring the count that gave him 51 as some sort of mistake; meanwhile, the count that confirmed his idea that there should be 52 cards was considered to be correct.

Along the same general lines, the **confirmation bias** *occurs when an individual searches for only evidence that will confirm his or her beliefs instead of evidence that might disconfirm them.* This differs from belief perseverance in that the confirmation bias is the *search* for a particular type of evidence, not a way of *evaluating* evidence that already exists. In the case of our dealer, he could have laid out all 13 cards from each suit to ensure that he had a full deck—that would have been a logical way to identify if any cards were missing. Instead, he exhibited the confirmation bias by seeking out only confirmatory evidence.

Confirmation bias and belief perseverance together can dramatically influence a person's beliefs, especially in relation to complex, emotionally charged areas such as religion and politics. In fact, much of the research on these biases shows that people treat evidence in ways that minimize negative or uncomfortable feelings while maximizing positive feelings (Westen et al., 2006). For example, one American study examined the brain regions and self-reported feelings involved in interpreting information about presidential candidates during the 2004 campaign. The participants were all deeply committed to either the Republican (George "Dubya" Bush) or Democratic (John Kerry) candidate, and they all encountered information that was threatening toward each candidate. As you can see from the results in Figure 8.15, participants had strong emotional reactions to threatening (self-contradictory) information about their own candidate, but not to the alternative candidate, or a relatively neutral person, such as a retired network news anchor. Analyses of the brain scans demonstrated that very different neural processes were at work in each condition. When the threat was directed at the participant's own candidate, brain areas associated with ignoring or suppressing information were more active, whereas few of the regions associated with logical thinking were activated (Westen et al., 2006).

Explore Confirmation Bias

These data demonstrate that a person's beliefs can influence their observable behavioural responses to information as well as the brain activity underlying these behaviours. As we shall see, decision making—and our happiness with those decisions—can also be influenced by a person's personality.

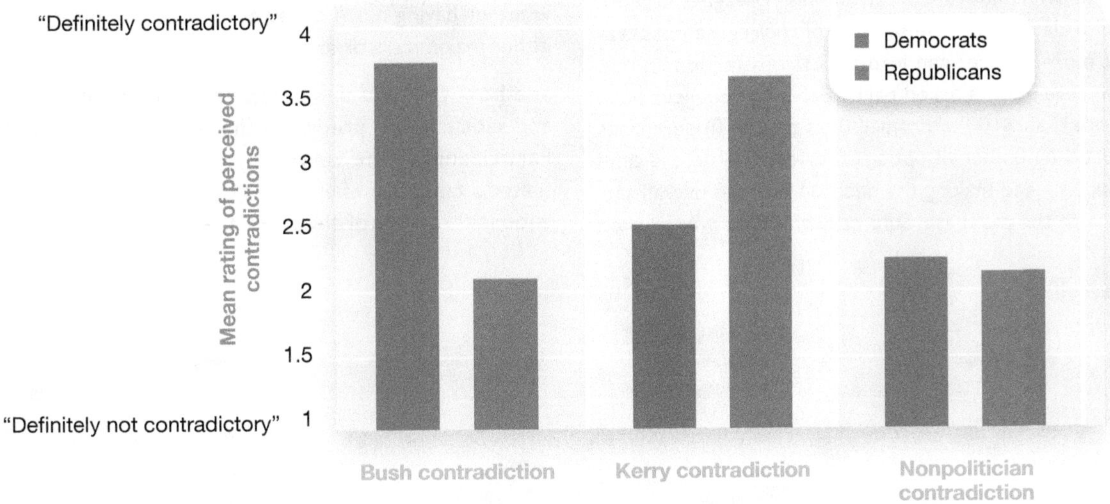

{FIG. 8.15} **Ratings of Perceived Contradictions in Political Statements** Democrats and Republicans reached very different conclusions about candidates' contradictory statements. Democrats readily identified the opponent's contradictions but were less likely to do so for their own candidate; the same was true for Republican responders.

WORKING THE SCIENTIFIC LITERACY MODEL

Maximizing and Satisficing in Complex Decisions

One privilege of living in a technologically advanced, democratic society is that we get to make many decisions for ourselves. However, for each decision there can be more choices than we can possibly consider. As a result, two types of consumers have emerged in our society. *Satisficers* are individuals who seek to make decisions that are, simply put, "good enough." In contrast, *maximizers* are individuals who attempt to evaluate every option for every choice until they find the perfect fit. Most people exhibit some of both behaviours, satisficing at times and maximizing at other times. However, if you consider all the people you know, you can probably identify at least one person who is an extreme maximizer—he or she will always be comparing products, jobs, classes, and so on, to find out who has made the best decisions. At the same time, you can probably identify an extreme satisficer—the person who will be satisfied with his or her choices as long as they are "good enough."

What do we know about maximizing and satisficing?

If one person settles for the good-enough option while another searches until he finds the best possible option, which individual do you think will be happier with the decision in the end? Most people believe the maximizer will be happier, but this is not always the case. In fact, researchers such as Barry Schwartz of Swarthmore College and his colleagues have no shortage of data about the *paradox of choice*, the observation that more choices can lead to less satisfaction. In one study, the researchers asked participants to recollect both large (more than $100) and small (less than $10) purchases and report the number of options they considered, the time spent shopping and making the decision, and the overall satisfaction with the purchase. Sure enough, those who ranked high on a test of maximization invested more time and effort, but were actually less pleased with the outcome (Schwartz et al., 2002).

Watch What's in It for Me? Making Choices

In another study, researchers questioned recent university graduates about their job search process. Believe it or not, maximizers averaged 20% higher salaries, but were less happy about their jobs than satisficers (Iyengar et al., 2006). This outcome occurred despite the fact that the opposite would seem to be true—*if* humans were perfectly logical decision makers.

So now we know that just the presence of alternative choices can drive down satisfaction—but how can that be?

How can science explain maximizing and satisficing?

To answer this question, researchers asked participants to read vignettes that included a trade-off between number of choices and effort (Dar-Nimrod et al., 2009). Try this example for yourself:

> *Your cleaning supplies (e.g., laundry detergent, rags, carpet cleaner, dish soap, toilet paper, glass cleaner) are running low. You have the option of going to the nearest grocery store (5 minutes away), which offers 4 alternatives for each of the items you need, or you can drive to the grand cleaning superstore (25 minutes away), which offers 25 different alternatives for each of the items (for approximately the same price). Which store would you go to?*

In the actual study, maximizers were much more likely to spend the extra time and effort to have more choices. Thus, if you decided to go to the store with more options, you are probably a maximizer. What this scenario does not tell us is whether having more or fewer choices was pleasurable for either maximizers or satisficers.

See how well you understand the nature of maximizers and satisficers by predicting the results of the next study: Participants at the University of British Columbia completed a taste test of *one* piece of chocolate, but they could choose this piece of chocolate from an array of 6 pieces or

Table 8.2 :: Satisfaction of Maximizers and Satisficers

	6 ALTERNATIVES	30 ALTERNATIVES
Maximizers	5.64	4.73
Satisficers	5.44	6.00

Source: Adapted from Dar-Nimrod et al. (2009). The Maximization Paradox: The costs of seeking alternatives. *Personality and Individual Differences, 46*, 631–635, Figure 1 and Table 1.

an array of 30 pieces. When there were 6 pieces, who was happier—maximizers or satisficers? What happened when there were 30 pieces to choose from? As you can see in Table 8.2, the maximizers were happier when there were fewer options. On a satisfaction scale indicating how much they enjoyed the piece of chocolate that they selected, the maximizers scored higher in the 6-piece condition (5.64 out of 7) than in the 30-piece condition (4.73 out of 7; Dar-Nimrod et al., 2009). In contrast, satisficers did not show a statistical difference between the conditions (5.44 and 6.00 for the 6-piece and 30-piece conditions, respectively).

Can we critically evaluate this information?

One hypothesis that seeks to explain the dissatisfaction of maximizers suggests that they invest more in the decision, so they expect more from the outcome. Imagine that a satisficer and a maximizer purchase the same digital camera for $175. The maximizer may have invested significantly more time and effort into the decision so, in effect, she *feels like* she paid considerably more for the camera.

Regardless of the explanation, we should keep in mind that maximizers and satisficers are preexisting categories. People cannot be randomly assigned to be in one category or another, so these findings represent the outcomes of quasi-experimental research (see Module 2.2). We cannot be sure that the act of maximizing leads to dissatisfaction based on these data. Perhaps maximizers are the people who are generally less satisfied, which in turn leads to maximizing behaviour.

Why is this relevant?

Although we described maximizing and satisficing in terms of purchasing decisions, you might also notice that these styles of decision making can be applied to other situations, such as multiple-choice exams. Do you select the first response that sounds reasonable (satisficing), or do you carefully review each of the responses and compare them to one another before marking your choice (maximizing)? Once you make your choice, do you stick with it, believing it is good enough (satisficing), or are you willing to change your answer to make the best possible choice (maximizing)? Despite the popular wisdom that you should never change your first response, there may be an advantage to maximizing on exams. Research focusing on more than 1500 individual examinations showed that when people changed their answers, they changed them from incorrect to correct 51% of the time, from correct to incorrect 25% of the time, and from incorrect to another incorrect option 23% of the time (Kruger et al., 2005).

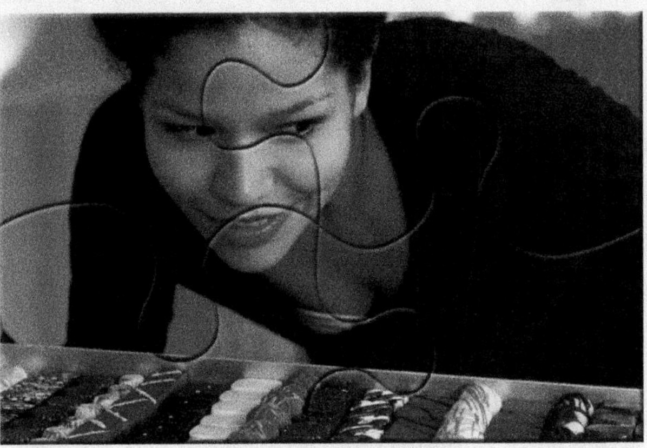

Gogo Images/Glow Images

The research discussed above suggests that there are some aspects of our consumer-based society that might actually be making us less happy. This seems counterintuitive given that the overwhelming number of product options available to us almost guarantees that we will get exactly what we want (or *think* we want). Recently, brain-imaging researchers began studying consumer behaviour in an attempt to understand what makes us like (and buy) particular products. As you read the following section, think about whether the results of these, and future, studies will increase or decrease people's happiness. No one knows for sure—what do *you* think?

PSYCH @

Decision Making and Neuromarketing

Psychology and marketing have been linked for over a century. In fact, Freud's nephew, Edward Bernays, was one of the first advertising executives to appeal to consumers' desires as opposed to simply providing information about a product (Ewen, 1996). In these early years, advertisers would study psychological theories and then test their new-and-improved ad campaigns on focus groups, small groups of individuals from the demographic that their product was aimed at (e.g., white males, aged 40–65). In the last 10 years, however, the psychological tools used by marketers have become much more advanced, and potentially worrisome.

With advances in brain-imaging techniques (see Module 3.4), it is now possible to examine how the brain responds to different stimuli, including different consumer products. This new field, *neuromarketing,* triggered fears that big corporations could use techniques like functional magnetic resonance imaging (fMRI) and event-related potentials (ERPs) to unlock our secret motivations for wanting and buying products (e.g., Lindstrom & Underhill, 2010). Indeed, early books in this area made strong claims suggesting that people had "buy buttons" in their brains; in other words, these authors were claiming that if a product triggered activity in a particular brain area, it would indicate that the person was going to buy that product (Renvoise & Morin, 2007).

In reality, there is no buy button in your brain. However, neuroscientists have been able to identify several regions of the brain involved with the decision to buy a product. In one study, researchers found the nucleus accumbens, part of a reward centre in the brain, is active when we view products that we like. When the price attached to the product was deemed to be too high, activity was detected in the insula (a brain area related to disgust); decreased activity was found in the medial parts of the prefrontal cortex (a brain area that responds to an item's reward value). Astonishingly, the researchers were able to link particular patterns of brain activity to a person's intent to buy the presented item (Knutson et al., 2007). This activity occurred *before* the participant indicated that she was going to make the purchase!

Companies are now using neuromarketing during the design phase of product development to predict whether consumers will like different features and packaging (Ariely & Berns, 2011). These companies claim that in a decade, marketers will be able to predict your consumer preferences as accurately, or better, than you can. It remains to be seen, however, whether neuromarketing studies reliably predict behaviour in the real world and whether they provide any insights that can't be uncovered through traditional—and cheaper—marketing techniques.

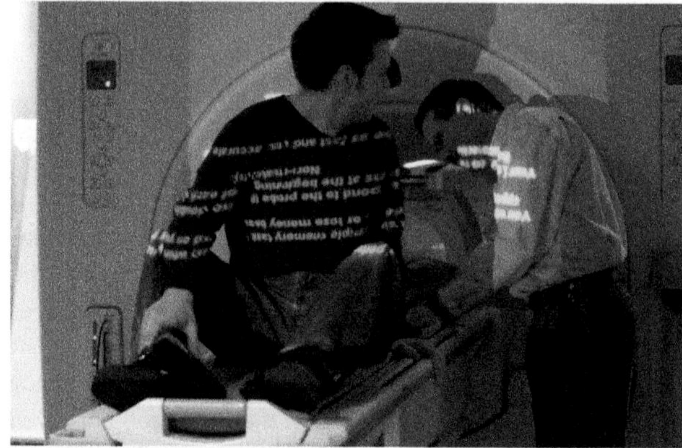

Hector Amezcua/ZUMA Press/Newscom

Quick Quiz 8.2b

Judgment and Decision Making

KNOW ...

1 Based on ________, people judge something as more likely if it strongly represents a specific category.

A anchoring
B priming
C loss aversion
D representativeness

2 When an individual makes judgments based on how easily things come to mind, he or she is employing the ________ heuristic.

A confirmation
B representativeness
C availability
D belief perseverance

UNDERSTAND ...

3 Belief perseverance seems to function by

A maximizing positive feelings.
B minimizing negative feelings.
C maximizing negative feelings while minimizing positive feelings.
D minimizing negative feelings while maximizing positive feelings.

ANALYZE ...

4 Why do psychologists assert that heuristics are beneficial for problem solving?

A Heuristics increase the amount of time we spend arriving at good solutions to problems.
B Heuristics decrease our chances of errors dramatically.
C Heuristics help us make decisions efficiently.
D Heuristics are considered the most logical thought pattern for problem solving.

5 The fact that humans so often rely on heuristics is evidence that

A humans are not always rational thinkers.
B it is impossible for humans to think logically.
C it is impossible for humans to use algorithms.
D humans will always succumb to the confirmation bias.

Answers can be found on page ANS-3.

Module Summary

Module 8.2

Now that you have read this module you should

KNOW ...

- ***The key terminology of problem solving and decision making*:**

algorithms (p. 325)
anchoring effect (p. 329)
availability heuristic (p. 328)
belief perseverance (p. 331)
confirmation bias (p. 331)
functional fixedness (p. 326)
heuristics (p. 325)
mental set (p. 326)
problem solving (p. 325)
representativeness heuristic (p. 327)

UNDERSTAND ...

- ***The characteristics that problems have in common.*** All problems involve people attempting to reach some sort of goal; this goal can be an observable behaviour like learning to serve a tennis ball or a cognitive behaviour like learning Canada's ten provincial capitals. This process involves forming strategies that will allow the person to reach the goal. It may also require a person to overcome one or more obstacles along the way.
- ***How obstacles to problem solving are often self-imposed.*** Many obstacles arise from the individual's mental set, which occurs when a person focuses on only one known solution and does not consider alternatives. Similarly, functional fixedness can arise when an individual does not consider alternative uses for familiar objects.

APPLY ...

- ***Your knowledge to determine if you tend to be a maximizer or a satisficer.*** To do so, rate the following items on a scale from 1 (completely disagree) to 7 (completely agree), with 4 being a neutral response.
    1. Whenever I'm faced with a choice, I try to imagine what all the other possibilities are, even ones that aren't present at the moment.
    2. No matter how satisfied I am with my job, it's only right for me to be on the lookout for better opportunities.
    3. When I am in the car listening to the radio, I often check other stations to see whether something better is playing, even if I am relatively satisfied with what I'm listening to.

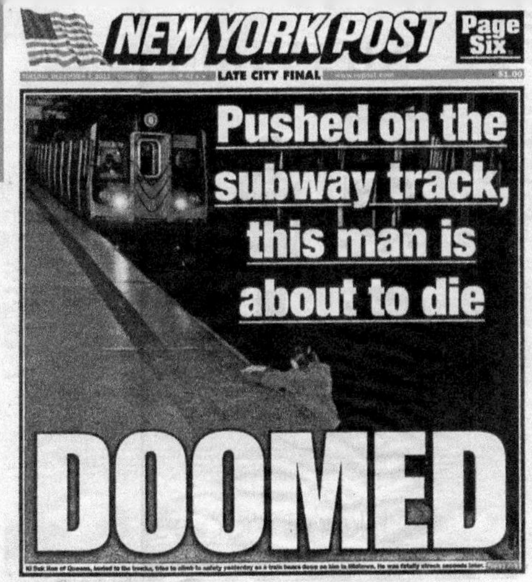

NEW YORK POST
Page Six
LATE CITY FINAL

Pushed on the subway track, this man is about to die

DOOMED

Polaris/Newscom

4. When I watch TV, I channel surf, often scanning through the available options even while attempting to watch one program.
5. I treat relationships like clothing: I expect to try a lot on before finding the perfect fit.
6. I often find it difficult to shop for a gift for a friend.
7. When shopping, I have a difficult time finding clothing that I really love.
8. No matter what I do, I have the highest standards for myself.
9. I find that writing is very difficult, even if it's just writing to a friend, because it's so difficult to word things just right. I often do several drafts of even simple things.
10. I never settle for second best.

When you are finished, average your ratings together to find your overall score. Scores greater than 4 indicate maximizers; scores less than 4 indicate satisficers. Approximately one-third of the population scores below 3.25 and approximately one-third scores above 4.75. Where does your score place you?

ANALYZE ...

- ***Whether human thought is primarily logical or intuitive.*** This module provides ample evidence that humans are not always logical. Heuristics are helpful decision-making and problem-solving tools, but they do not follow logical principles. Even so, the abundance of heuristics does not mean that humans are never logical; instead, they simply point to the limits of our rationality.

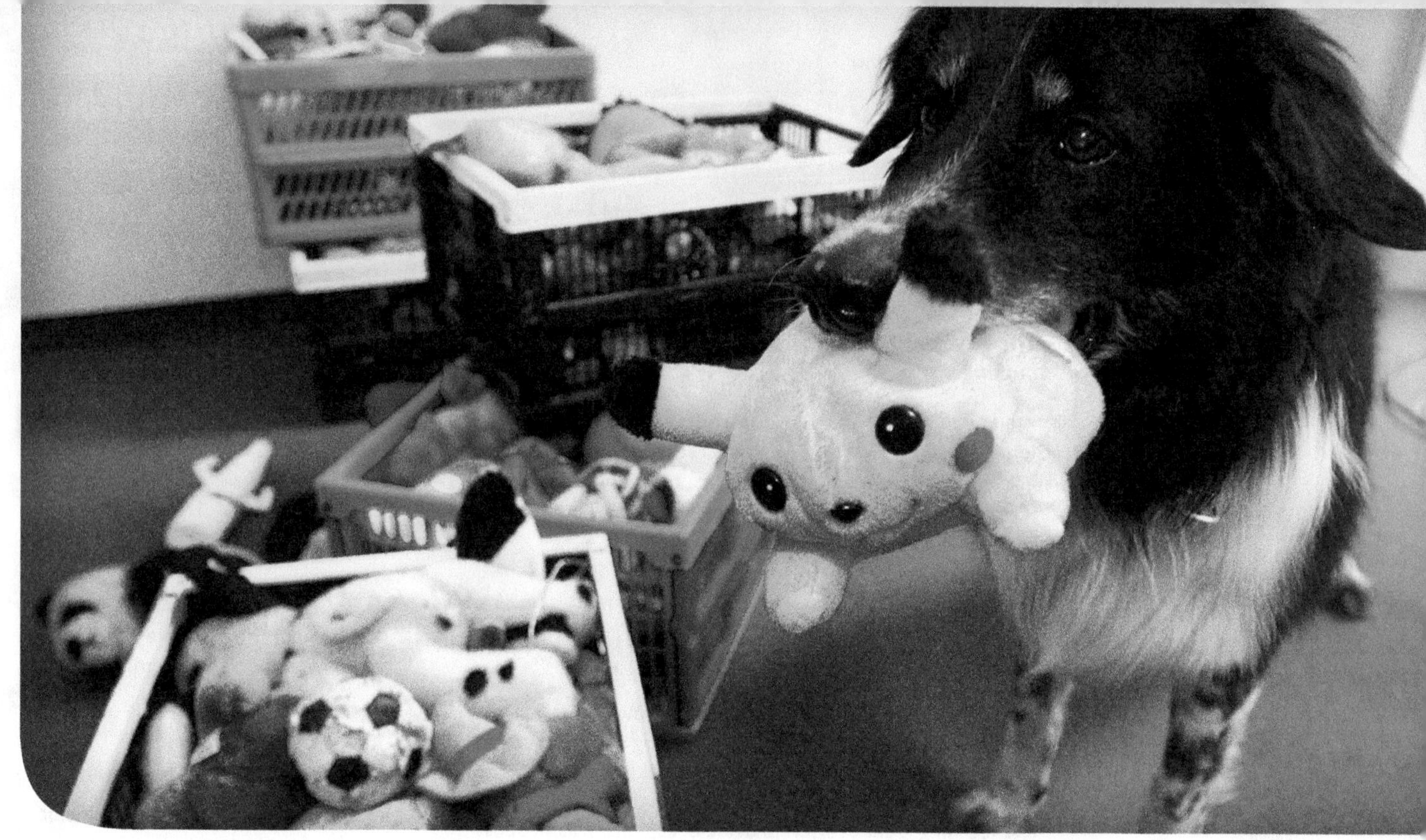

Reuters

Module 8.3

Language and Communication

Learning Objectives

After reading this module you should

KNOW ...	UNDERSTAND ...	APPLY ...	ANALYZE ...
The key terminology from the study of language	How language is structured How genes and the brain are involved in language use	Your knowledge to distinguish between units of language such as phonemes and morphemes	Whether species other than humans are able to use language

Dog owners are known for attributing a lot of intelligence, emotion, and "humanness" to their canine pals. Sometimes they may appear to go overboard—such as Rico's owners, who claimed their border collie understood 200 words, most of which refer to different toys and objects he likes to play with. His owners claimed that they could show Rico a toy, repeat its name a few times, and toss the toy into a pile of other objects; Rico would then retrieve the object upon verbal command. Rico's ability appeared to go well beyond the usual "sit," "stay," "heel," and perhaps a few other words that dog owners expect their companions to understand.

Claims about Rico's language talents soon drew the attention of scientists, who skeptically questioned whether the dog was just responding to cues by the owners, such as their possible looks or gestures toward the object they asked their pet to retrieve. The scientists set up a carefully controlled experiment in which no one present in the room knew the location of the object that was requested. Rico correctly retrieved 37 out of 40 objects. The experimenters then tested the owners' claim that Rico could learn object names in just one trial. Rico again confirmed his owners' claims, and the researchers concluded that his ability to understand new words was comparable to that of a three-year-old child (Kaminski et al., 2004).

However, as you will see in this module, Rico's abilities, while impressive, are dwarfed by those of humans. Our ability to reorganize words into complex thoughts is unique in the animal kingdom and may even have aided our survival as a species.

Focus Questions

 1 What is the difference between language and other forms of communication?

 2 Might other species, such as chimpanzees, also be capable of learning human language?

Communication happens just about anywhere you can find life. Dogs bark, cats meow, monkeys chatter, and mice can emit sounds undetectable to the human ear when communicating. Honeybees perform an elaborate dance to communicate the direction, distance, and quality of food sources (von Frisch, 1967). Animals even communicate by marking their territories with their distinct scent, much to the chagrin of the world's fire hydrants. Language is among the ways that humans communicate. It is quite unlike the examples of animal communication mentioned previously. So what differentiates language from these other forms of communication? And, what is it about our brains that allows us to turn different sounds and lines into the sophisticated languages found across different human cultures?

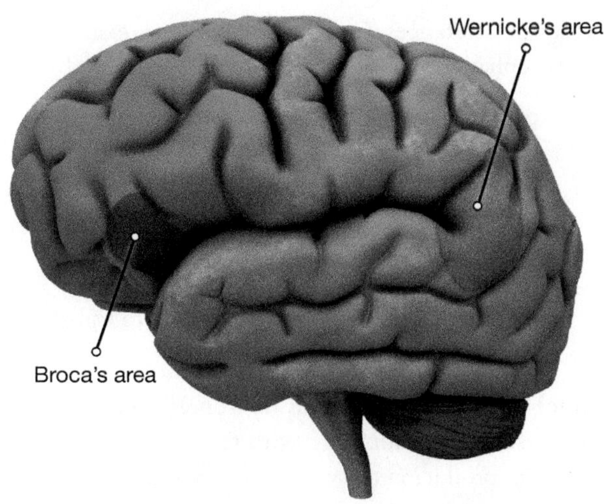

{FIG. 8.16} **Two Language Centres of the Brain** Broca's and Wernicke's areas of the cerebral cortex are critical to language function. **Click on this figure in your eText to see more details.**

What Is Language?

Language is one of the most intensively studied areas in all of psychology. Thousands of experiments have been performed to identify different characteristics of language as well as the brain regions associated with them. But, all fields of study have a birthplace. In the case of the scientific study of language, it began with an interesting case study of a patient in Paris in the early 1860s.

EARLY STUDIES OF LANGUAGE In 1861, Paul Broca, a physician and founder of the Society of Anthropology of Paris, heard of an interesting medical case. The patient appeared to show a very specific impairment resulting from a stroke suffered 21 years earlier. He could understand speech and had fairly normal mental abilities; however, he had great difficulty *producing* speech and often found himself uttering single words separated by pauses (uh, er . . .). In fact, this patient acquired the nickname "Tan" because it was one of the only sounds that he could reliably produce. Tan had what is known as **aphasia**, *a language disorder caused by damage to the brain structures that support using and understanding language.*

Tan died a few days after being examined by Broca. During the autopsy, Broca noted that the brain damage appeared primarily near the back of the frontal lobes in the left hemisphere. Over the next couple of years, Broca found 12 other patients with similar symptoms and similar brain damage, indicating that "Tan" was not a unique case. This *region of the left frontal lobe that controls our ability to articulate speech sounds that compose words* is now known as **Broca's area** (see Figure 8.16). The symptoms associated with this damage, as seen in Tan, are known as *Broca's aphasia.*

The fact that a brain injury could affect one part of language while leaving others preserved suggested that the ability to use language involves a number of different processes using different areas of the brain. In the years following the publication of Broca's research, other isolated language impairments were discovered. In 1874, a young Prussian (German) physician named Carl Wernicke published a short book detailing his study of different types of aphasia. Wernicke noted that some of his patients had trouble with language *comprehension* rather than language *production.* These patients typically had damage to the posterior superior temporal gyrus (the back and top part of the temporal lobe). This region, now known as **Wernicke's area**, *is the area of the brain most associated with finding the meaning of words* (see Figure 8.16). Damage to this area results in *Wernicke's aphasia*, a language disorder in which a person has difficulty understanding the words he or she hears. These patients are also unable to produce speech that other people can understand—the words are spoken fluently and with a normal intonation and accent, but these words seem randomly thrown together (i.e., what is being said does not make sense). Consider the following example:

> Examiner: I'd like to have you tell me something about your problem.
>
> Person with Wernicke's aphasia: Yes, I, ugh, cannot hill all of my way. I cannot talk all of the things I do, and part of the part I can go alright, but I cannot tell from the other people. I usually most of my things. I know what can I talk and know what they are, but I cannot always come back even though I know they should be in, and I know should something eely I should know what I'm doing . . .

The important thing to look for in this sample of speech is how the wrong words appear in an otherwise fluent stream of utterances. Contrast this with an example of Broca's aphasia:

> Examiner: Tell me, what did you do before you retired?
>
> Person with Broca's aphasia: Uh, uh, uh, pub, par, partender, no.
>
> Examiner: Carpenter?
>
> Person with Broca's aphasia: (Nodding to signal yes) Carpenter, tuh, tuh, twenty year.

Notice that the individual has no trouble understanding the question or coming up with the answer. His difficulty is in producing the word *carpenter* and then putting it into an appropriate phrase. Did you also notice the missing morpheme /-s/ from *twenty year*? This is another characteristic of Broca's aphasia: The individual words are often produced without normal grammatical flair: no articles, suffixes, or prefixes.

Broca's aphasia can include some difficulties in comprehending language as well. In general, the more complex the syntax, the more difficult it will be to understand. Compare these two sentences:

> The girl played the piano.
>
> The piano was played by the girl.

These are two grammatically correct sentences (although the second is somewhat awkward) that have the same meaning but are structured differently. Patients with damage to Broca's area would find it much more difficult to understand the second sentence than the first. This impairment suggests that the distinction between speech production and comprehension is not as simple as was first thought. Indeed, as language became a central topic of research in psychology, researchers quickly realized that this ability—or set of abilities—is among the most complex processes humans perform.

PROPERTIES OF LANGUAGE Language, like many other cognitive abilities, flows so automatically that we often overlook how complicated it really is. However, cases like those described above show us that language is indeed a complex set of skills. Researchers define **language** *as a form of communication that involves the use of spoken, written, or gestural symbols that are combined in a rule-based form.* With this definition in mind, we can distinguish which features of language make it a unique form of communication.

- Language can involve communication about objects and events that are not in the present time and place. We can use language to talk about events happening on another planet or that are happening within atoms. We can also use different tenses to indicate that the topic of the sentence occurred or will occur at a different time. For instance, you can say to your roommate, "I'm going to order pizza tonight," without her thinking the pizza is already there.
- Languages can produce entirely new meanings. It is possible to produce a sentence that has never been uttered before in the history of humankind, simply by reorganizing words in different ways. As long as you select English words and use correct grammar, others who know the language should be able to understand it. You can also use words in novel ways. Imagine the tabloid newspaper headline: *Bat Boy Found in Cave!* In North American culture, "bat boys" are regular kids who keep track of the baseball bats for ball players. In this particular tabloid, the story concerned a completely novel creature that was part bat and part boy. Both meanings could be correct, depending upon the context in which the term *bat boy* is used.
- Language is passed down from parents to children. As we will discuss later in this module, children learn to pay attention to the particular sounds of their native language(s) at the expense of other sounds (Werker, 2003). Children also learn words and grammatical rules from parents, teachers, and peers. In other words, even if we have a natural inclination to learn *a* language, experience dictates *which* language(s) we will speak.

Language requires us to link different sounds (or gestures) with different meanings in order to understand and communicate with other people. Therefore, understanding more about these seemingly simple elements

Weekly World News

Words can be arranged or combined in novel ways to produce ideas that have never been expressed before.

of language is essential for understanding language as a whole.

PHONEMES AND MORPHEMES: THE BASIC INGREDIENTS OF LANGUAGE Languages contain discrete units that exist at differing levels of complexity. When people speak, they assemble these units into larger and more complex units. Some psychologists have used a cooking analogy to explain this phenomenon: We all start with the same basic language ingredients, but they can be mixed together in an unlimited number of ways (Pinker, 1999).

Phonemes *are the most basic of units of speech sounds.* You can identify phonemes rather easily; the phoneme associated with the letter *t* (which is written as /t/, where the two forward slashes indicate a phoneme) is found at the end of the word *pot* or near the beginning of the word *stop*. If you pay close attention to the way you use your tongue, lips, and vocal cords, you will see that phonemes have slight variations depending on the other letters around them. Pay attention to how you pronounce the /t/ phoneme in *stop, stash, stink,* and *stoke.* Your mouth will move in slightly different ways each time, and there will be very slight variations in sound, but they are still the same basic phoneme. Individual phonemes typically do not have any meaning by themselves; if you want someone to stop doing something, asking him to /t/ will not suffice.

Morphemes *are the smallest meaningful units of a language.* Some morphemes are simple words, whereas others may be suffixes or prefixes. For example, the word *pig* is a morpheme—it cannot be broken down into smaller units of meaning. You can combine morphemes, however, if you follow the rules of the language. If you want to pluralize *pig*, you can add the morpheme /-s/, which will give you *pigs*. If you want to describe a person as a pig, you can add the morpheme /-ish/ to get *piggish*. In fact, you can add all kinds of morphemes to a word as long as you follow the rules. You could even say *piggable* (able to be pigged) or *piggify* (to turn into a pig). These words do not make much literal sense, but they combine morphemes according to the rules; thus we can make a reasonable guess as to the speaker's intended meaning. Our ability to combine morphemes into words is one distinguishing feature of language that sets it apart from other forms of communication (e.g., we don't produce a lengthy series of facial expressions to communicate a new idea). In essence, language gives us *productivity*—the ability to combine units of sound into an infinite number of meanings.

Finally, there are the words that make up a language. **Semantics** *is the study of how people come to understand meaning from words.* Humans have a knack for this kind of interpretation, and each of us has an extensive mental dictionary to prove it. Not only do normal speakers know tens of thousands of words, but they can often understand new words they have never heard before based on their understanding of morphemes.

Although phonemes, morphemes, and semantics have an obvious role in spoken language, they also play a surprising role in our ability to read. When you recognize a word, you effortlessly translate the word's visual form (known as its *orthography*) into the sounds that make up that word (known as its *phonology* or *phonological code*). These sounds are combined into a word, at which point you can access its meaning or semantics. However, not all people are able to translate orthography into sounds. Individuals with *dyslexia* have difficulties translating words into speech sounds. Indeed, children with dyslexia show less activity in the left fusiform cortex (near the back and bottom of the temporal lobe), a brain area involved with word recognition and with linking word and sound representations (Desroches et al., 2010). This difficulty linking letters with phonemes leads to unusually slow reading in both children and adults despite the fact that these people have normal hearing and are cognitively and neurologically healthy (Desroches & Joanisse, 2009; Shaywitz, 1998).

This research into the specific impairments associated with dyslexia allows scientists and educators to develop treatment programs to help children improve their reading and language abilities. One of the most successful programs has been developed by Maureen Lovett and her colleagues at Sick Kids Hospital in Toronto and Brock University. Their Phonological and Strategy Training (PHAST) program (now marketed as Empower™ Reading to earn research money for the hospital) has been used to assist over 6000 students with reading disabilities. Rather than focusing on only one aspect of language, this program teaches children new word-identification and reading-comprehension strategies while also educating them about how words and phrases are structured (so that they know what to expect when they see new words or groups of words). Children who completed these programs showed improvements on a number of measures of reading and passage comprehension (Frijters et al., 2013; Lovett et al., 2012). Given that 5–15% of the population has some form of reading impairment, treatment programs like the PHAST could have a dramatic effect on our educational system.

As you can see, languages derive their complexity from several elements, including phonemes, morphemes, and semantics. And, when these systems are not functioning properly, language abilities suffer. But phonemes, morphemes, and semantics are just the list of the ingredients of language—we still need to figure out how to mix these ingredients together.

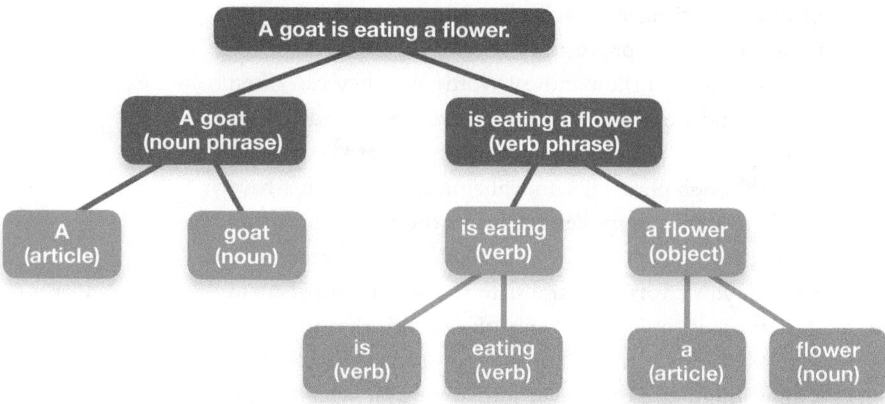

{FIG. 8.17} **Syntax Allows Us to Understand Language by the Organization of the Words** The rules of syntax help us divide a sentence into noun phrases, verb phrases, and other parts of speech.

SYNTAX: THE LANGUAGE RECIPE Perhaps the most remarkable aspect of language is **syntax**, *the rules for combining words and morphemes into meaningful phrases and sentences*—the recipe for language. Children master the syntax of their native language before they leave elementary school. They can string together morphemes and words when they speak, and they can easily distinguish between well-formed *and* ill-formed sentences. But despite mastering those rules, most speakers cannot tell you what the rules are; syntax just seems to come naturally. It might seem odd that people can do so much with language without a full understanding of its inner workings. Of course, people can also learn how to walk without any understanding of the biochemistry that allows their leg muscles to contract and relax.

Watch Susan Goldwin-Meadow: The Role of Gesture in Thinking

The most basic units of syntax are nouns and verbs. They are all that is required to construct a well-formed sentence, such as *Goats eat.* Noun–verb sentences are perfectly adequate, if a bit limited, so we build phrases out of nouns and verbs, as the diagram in Figure 8.17 demonstrates.

Syntax also helps explain why the order of words in a sentence has such a strong effect on what the sentence means. For example, how would you make a question out of this statement?

(A) *A goat is in the garden.*
(B) IS *a goat* ______ *in the garden?*

This example demonstrates that a statement (A) can be turned into a well-formed question (B) just by moving the verb "is" to the beginning of the sentence. Perhaps that is one of the hidden rules of syntax. Try it again:

(A) *A goat that is eating a flower is in the garden.*
(B) IS *a goat that* ______ *eating a flower is in the garden?*

As you can see, the rule "move *is* to the beginning of the sentence" does not apply in this case. Do you know why? It is because we moved the wrong *is.* The phrase *that is eating a flower* is a part of the noun phrase because it describes the goat. We should have moved the *is* from the verb phrase. Try it again:

(A) *A goat that is eating a flower is in the garden.*
(B) IS *a goat that is eating a flower* ______ *in the garden?*

This is a well-formed sentence. It may be grammatically awkward, but the syntax is understandable (Pinker, 1994).

As you can see from these examples, the order of words in a sentence helps determine what the sentence means, and syntax is the set of rules we use to determine that order.

PRAGMATICS: THE FINISHING TOUCHES If syntax is the recipe for language, pragmatics is the icing on the cake. Unlike syntax, which takes place in your brain, **pragmatics** *is the study of nonlinguistic elements of language use.* It places heavy emphasis on the speaker's behaviours and the social situation (Carston, 2002).

Pragmatics reminds us that sometimes *what* is said is not as important as *how* it is said. For example, a student who says, "I ate a 50-pound cheeseburger," is most likely stretching the truth, but you probably would not call him a liar. Pragmatics helps us understand what he implied. The voracious student was actually *flouting*—or blatantly disobeying—a rule of language in a way that is obvious (Grice, 1975; Horn & Ward, 2004). There are all sorts of ways in which flouting the rules can lead to implied, not literal meanings; a sample of those are shown in Table 8.3.

Table 8.3 :: Pragmatic Rules Guiding Language Use

THE RULE	FLOUTING THE RULE	THE IMPLICATION
Say what you believe is true.	My roommate is a *giraffe*.	He does not *really* live with a giraffe. Maybe his roommate is very tall?
Say only what is relevant.	Is my blind date good-looking? *He's got a great personality.*	She didn't answer my question. He's probably not good-looking.
Say only as much as you need to.	I like my lab partner, but he's no *Einstein*.	Of course he's not Einstein. Why is she bothering to tell me this? She probably means that her partner is not very smart.

Importantly, pragmatics depends upon both the speaker (or writer) and listener (or reader) understanding that rules are being flouted in order to produce a desired meaning. If you speak with visitors from a different country, you may find that they don't understand what you mean when you flout the rules of Canadian English or use slang (shortened language). When we say "The goalie stood on his head," most hockey-mad Canadians understand that we are commenting on a goaltender's amazing game; however, someone new to hockey would be baffled by this expression. This is another example of how experience—in this case with a culture—influences how we use and interpret language.

Quick Quiz 8.3a

What Is Language?

KNOW ...

1 What are the rules that govern how words are strung together into meaningful sentences?

A Semantics **C** Morphemics
B Pragmatics **D** Syntax

2 The study of how people extract meaning from words is called ________.

A syntax **C** semantics
B pragmatics **D** flouting

UNDERSTAND ...

3 Besides being based in a different region of the brain, a major distinction between Broca's aphasia and Wernicke's aphasia is that

A words from people with Broca's aphasia are strung together fluently, but often make little sense.
B Broca's aphasia is due to a FOXP2 mutation.
C Wernicke's aphasia results in extreme stuttering.
D words from people with Wernicke's aphasia are strung together fluently, but often make little sense.

APPLY ...

4 ________ is an example of a morpheme, while ________ is a phoneme.

A /dis/; /ta/ **C** /da/; /ah/
B /a/; /like/ **D** /non/; /able/

Answers can be found on page ANS-3.

The Development of Language

Human vocal tracts are capable of producing approximately 200 different phonemes. However, no language uses all of these sounds. Jul'hoan, one of the "clicking languages" of Botswana, contains almost 100 sounds (including over 80 different consonant sounds). In contrast, English contains about 40 sounds. But, if Canadians are genetically identical to people in southern Africa, why are our languages different? And, why can't we produce and distinguish between some of the sounds of these other languages? It turns out that experience plays a major role in your ability to speak the language, or languages, that you do.

Watch Thinking Like a Psychologist: Multilingualism: Speaking One's Mind

INFANTS, SOUND PERCEPTION, AND LANGUAGE ACQUISITION Say the following phrase out loud: "Your doll." Now, say this phrase: "This doll." Did you notice a difference in how you pronounced *doll* in these two situations? If English is your first language, it is quite likely that you didn't notice the slight change in how the letter "d" was expressed. But, Hindi speakers would have no problem making this distinction. To them, the two instances of the word *doll* would be pronounced differently and would mean *lentils* and *branch,* respectively.

Janet Werker of the University of British Columbia and her colleagues have found that very young English-learning infants are able to distinguish between these two "d" sounds. But, by 10 months of age, the infants began hearing sounds in a way that is consistent with their native language; because English has only one "d" sound, English-learning infants no longer detected the difference between these two sounds (Werker & Tees, 1984; Werker et al., 2012). This change is not a weakness on the part of English-learning infants. Rather, it is evidence that they are learning the statistical principles of their language. Infants who hear only English words will group different pronunciations of the letter "d" into one category because that is how this sound is used in English. Hindi-learning children will learn to separate different types of "d" sounds because this distinction is important. A related study using two "k" sounds from an Interior Salish (First Nations) language from British Columbia produced similar results—English-learning infants showed a significant drop-off in hearing sounds for the non-English language after 8–10 months (Werker & Tees, 1984).

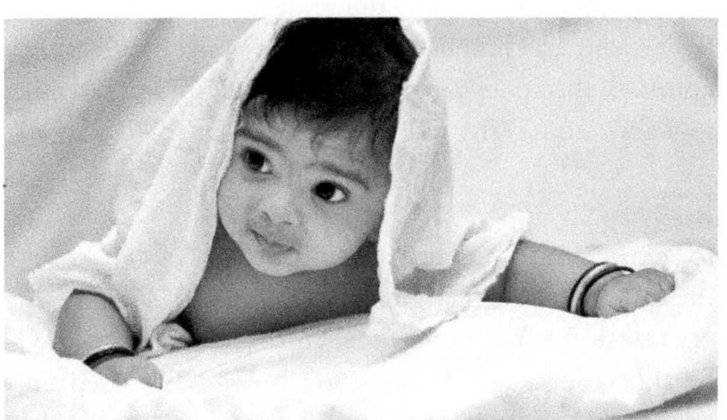

CVR/Flickr/Getty Images

Infants are able to distinguish between almost all of the phonemes humans can produce; however, by 8–10 months of age, infants show superior perception of phonemes from their own language.

Watch
Stimulating Language Development

In addition to becoming experts at identifying the sounds of their own language, infants also learn how to separate a string of sounds into meaningful groups (i.e., into words). Infants as young as two months old show a preference for speech sounds over perceptually similar non-speech sounds (Vouloumanos & Werker, 2004). And, when presented with pronounceable non-words (e.g., *strak*), infants prefer to hear words that follow the rules of their language. An English-learning baby would prefer non-words beginning in "str" to those beginning in "rst" because there are a large number of English words that begin with "str" (Jusczyk et al., 1993). Additionally, newborn infants can distinguish between function words (e.g., prepositions) and content words (e.g., nouns and verbs) based on their sound properties (Shi et al., 1999). By six months of age, infants prefer the content words (Shi & Werker, 2001), thus showing that they are learning which sounds are most useful for understanding the meaning of a statement.

By the age of 20 months, the children are able to use the perceptual categories that they developed in order to rapidly learn new words. In some cases, children can perform **fast mapping**—*the ability to map words onto concepts or objects after only a single exposure.* Human children seem to have a fast-mapping capacity that is superior to any other organism on the planet. This skill is one potential explanation for the *naming explosion*, a rapid increase in vocabulary size that occurs at this stage of development.

The naming explosion has two biological explanations as well. First, at this stage of development, the brain begins to perform language-related functions in the left hemisphere, similar to the highly efficient adult brain; prior to this stage, this information was stored and analyzed by both hemispheres (Mills et al., 1997). Second, the naming explosion has also been linked to an increase in the amount of myelin on the brain's axons, a change that would increase the speed of communication between neurons (Pujol et al., 2006). These changes would influence not only the understanding of language, but also how a child uses language to convey increasingly complex thoughts such as "How does Spiderman stick to walls?" and "Why did Dad's hair fall out?"

Watch
Language Development

PRODUCING SPOKEN LANGUAGE Learning to identify and organize speech sounds is obviously an important part of language development. An equally critical skill is producing speech that other people will be able to understand. Early psychologists focused only on behavioural approaches to language learning. They believed that language was learned through imitating sounds and being reinforced for pronouncing and using words correctly (Skinner, 1985). Although it is certainly true that imitation and reinforcement are involved in language acquisition, they are only one part of this complex process (Messer, 2000). Here are a few examples that illustrate how learning through imitation and reinforcement is just one component of language development:

- Children often produce phrases that include incorrect grammar or word forms. Because adults do not (often) use these phrases, it is highly unlikely that such phrases are imitations.
- Children learn irregular verbs and pluralizations on a word-by-word basis. At first, they will use "ran" and "geese" correctly. However, when children begin to use grammar on their own, they over-generalize the rules. A child who learns the /-ed/ morpheme for past tense will start saying *runned* instead of *ran*. When she learns that /-s/ means more than one, she will begin to say *gooses* instead of *geese*. It is also unlikely that children would produce these forms by imitating.
- When children use poor grammar, or when they over-generalize their rules, parents may try to correct them. Although children will acknowledge their parents' attempts at instruction, this method does not seem to work. Instead, children go right back to over-generalizing.

In light of these and many other examples, it seems clear that an exclusively behaviourist approach falls short in explaining how language is learned. After all, there are profound differences in the success of children and adults in learning a new language: Whereas adults typically struggle, children seem to learn the language effortlessly. If reinforcement and imitation were the primary means by which language was acquired, then adults should be able to learn just as well as children.

The fact that children seem to learn language differently than adults has led psychologists to use the term *language acquisition* when referring to children instead of *language learning.* The study of language acquisition has revealed remarkable similarities among children from all over the world. Regardless of the language, children seem to develop this capability in stages, as shown in Table 8.4.

SENSITIVE PERIODS FOR LANGUAGE The phases of language development described above suggest that younger brains are particularly well-suited to acquiring languages; this is not the case for older brains. Imagine a family with two young children who immigrated to Canada from a remote Russian village where no one spoke English. The parents would struggle with English courses, while the children would attend English-speaking schools. Within a few years, the parents would have accumulated some vocabulary but they would likely still have difficulty with pronunciation and

Table 8.4 :: Milestones in Language Acquisition and Speech

AVERAGE TIME OF ONSET (MONTHS)	MILESTONE	EXAMPLE
1–2	Cooing	Ahhh, ai-ai-ai
4–10	Babbling (consonants start)	Ab-ah-da-ba
8–16	Single-word stage	Up, mama, papa
24	Two-word stage	Go potty
24+	Complete, meaningful phrases strung together	I want to talk to Grandpa.

grammar (Russian-speaking people often omit articles such as *the*). Meanwhile, their children would likely pick up English without much effort and have language skills equivalent to those of their classmates; they would have roughly the same vocabulary, the same accents, and even the same slang.

Why do children pick up a language so much more easily than adults? Most psychologists agree that there is a *sensitive period* for language—a time during childhood in which children's brains are primed to develop language skills (see also Module 10.1). Children can absorb language almost effortlessly, but this ability seems to fade away starting around the seventh year. Thus, when families immigrate to a country that uses a different language, the children are able to pick up this language much more quickly than their parents (Hakuta et al., 2003; Hernandez & Li, 2007).

A stunning example of critical periods comes from Nicaragua. Until 1979, there was no sign language in this Central American country because there were no schools for people with hearing impairments and therefore no (perceived) need for a common sign language. When the first schools for the deaf were established, adults and teenaged students attempted to learn to read lips. While few mastered this skill, these students did do something even more astonishing: They developed their own primitive sign language. This language, *Lenguaje de Signos Nicaragüese (LSN)*, involves a number of elaborate gestures similar to a game of charades and does not have a consistent set of grammatical rules. But, it was a start. Children who attended these schools at an early age (i.e., during the sensitive period for language acquisition) used this language as the basis for a more fluent version of sign language: *Idioma de Signos Nicaragüese (ISN)*. ISN has grammatical rules and can be used to express a number of complicated, abstract ideas (Pinker, 1994). It is now the standard sign language in Nicaragua. The difference between LSN and ISN is similar to the difference between adults and children learning a new language. If you acquire the new language during childhood, you will be much more fluent than if you try to acquire it during adulthood (Senghas, 2003; Senghas et al., 2004).

Left: Stephen McBrady/PhotoEdit; right: Kayte Deioma/PhotoEdit

Signed languages share the same characteristics of spoken languages. They have a rich vocabulary, syntax, and set of pragmatic rules.

THE BILINGUAL BRAIN Let's go back to the example of the Russian-speaking family who immigrated to balmy Canada. The young children learning English would also be speaking Russian at home with their parents. As a result, they would be learning two languages essentially at the same time. What effect would this situation have on their ability to learn each language?

Although bilingualism leads to many benefits (see below), there are some costs to learning more than one language. Bilingual children tend to have a smaller vocabulary in each language than unilingual children (Mahon & Crutchley, 2006). In adulthood, this difference is shown not by vocabulary size, but by how easily bilinguals can access words. Compared to unilingual adults, bilingual adults are slower at naming pictures (Roberts et al., 2002), have more difficulty on tests that ask them to list words starting with a particular letter (Rosselli et al., 2000), have more tip-of-the-tongue experiences in which they can't quite retrieve a word (Gollan & Acenas, 2004), and are slower and less accurate when making word/non-word judgments (Ransdell & Fischler, 1987). These problems with accessing words may be due to the fact that they use each language less than a unilingual person would use their single language (Michael & Gollan, 2005).

The benefits of bilingualism, however, appear to far outweigh the costs. One difference that has been repeatedly observed is that bilingual individuals are much better than their unilingual counterparts on tests that require them to control their attention or their thoughts. These abilities, known as *executive functions* (or *executive control*), enable people who speak more than one language to inhibit one language while speaking and listening to another (or to limit the interference across languages). If they didn't, they would produce confusing sentences like *The chien is tres sick.* Although most of you can figure out this person is talking about a sick dog, you can see how such sentences would make communication challenging. Researchers have found that bilinguals score better than unilinguals on tests of executive control throughout the lifespan, beginning in infancy (Kovacs & Mehler, 2009) and the toddler years (Poulin-Dubois et al., 2011) and continuing throughout adulthood (Costa et al., 2008) and into old age (Bialystok et al., 2004). Bilingualism has also recently been shown to have important health benefits. Because the executive control involved with bilingualism uses areas in the frontal lobes, these regions may form more connections in bilinguals than unilinguals (Bialystok, 2009, 2011a, 2011b). As a result, these brains likely have more back-up systems if damage occurs. Indeed, Ellen Bialystok at York University and her colleagues have shown that being bilingual helps protect against the onset of dementia and Alzheimer's disease (Bialystok et al., 2007; Schweizer et al., 2012), a finding that leaves many at a loss for words.

Quick Quiz 8.3b

The Development of Language

KNOW ...

1 What is fast mapping?

A The rapid rate at which chimpanzees learn sign language

B The ability of children to map concepts to words with only a single example

C The very short period of time that language input can be useful for language development

D A major difficulty that people face when affected by Broca's aphasia

UNDERSTAND ...

2 The term "sensitive period" is relevant to language acquisition because

A exposure to language is needed during this time for language abilities to develop normally.

B Broca's area is active only during this period.

C it is what distinguishes humans from the apes.

D it indicates that language is an instinct.

ANALYZE ...

3 What is the most accurate conclusion from studies of bilingualism and the brain?

A Being bilingual causes the brain to form a larger number of connections than it normally would.

B Being bilingual reduces the firing rate of the frontal lobes.

C Only knowing one language allows people to improve their executive functioning.

D Being bilingual makes it more likely that a person will have language problems if they suffer brain damage.

Answers can be found on page ANS-3.

Genes, Evolution, and Language

This module began with a discussion of two brain areas that are critical for language production and comprehension: Broca's area and Wernicke's area, respectively. But, these brain areas didn't appear out of nowhere. Rather, genetics and evolutionary pressures led to the development of our language-friendly brains. Given recent advances in our understanding of the human genome (see Module 3.1), it should come as no surprise that researchers are actively searching for the genes involved with language abilities.

WORKING THE SCIENTIFIC LITERACY MODEL

Genes and Language

Given that language is a universal trait of the human species, it likely involves a number of different genes. These genes would, of course, also interact with the environment. In this section we examine whether it is possible that specific genes are related to language.

What do we know about genes and language?

Many scientists believe that the evidence is overwhelming that language is a unique feature of the human species, and that language evolved to solve problems related to survival and reproductive fitness. Language adds greater efficiency to thought, allows us to transmit information without requiring us to have direct experience with potentially dangerous situations, and, ultimately, facilitates communicating social needs and desires. Claims that language promotes survival and reproductive success are difficult to test directly with scientific experimentation, but there is a soundness to the logic of the speculation. We can also move beyond speculation and actually examine how genes play a role in human language. As with all complex psychological traits, there are likely many genes associated with language. Nevertheless, amid all of these myriad possibilities, one gene has been identified that is of particular importance.

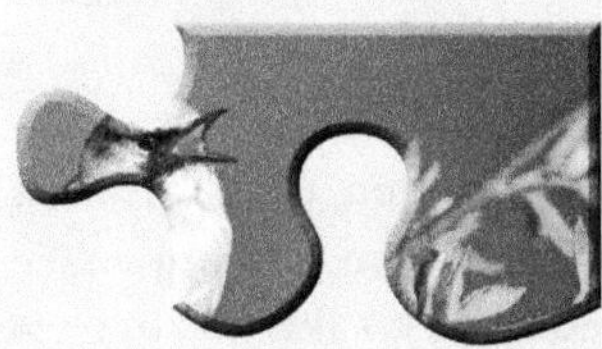

How can science explain a genetic basis of language?

Studies of this gene have primarily focused on the KE family (their name is abbreviated to maintain their confidentiality). Many members of this family have inherited a mutated version of a gene on chromosome 7 (see Figure 8.18; Vargha-Khadem et al., 2005). Each gene has a name—and this one is called FOXP2. All humans carry a copy of the FOXP2 gene, but the KE family passes down a mutated copy. Those who inherit the mutated copy have great difficulty putting thoughts into words (Tomblin et al., 2009). Thus, it appears that the physical and chemical processes that FOXP2 codes for are related to language function.

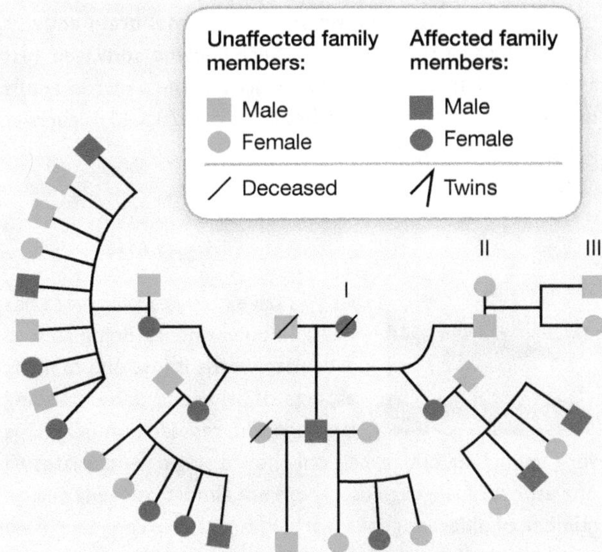

{FIG. 8.18} **Inheritance Pattern for the Mutated FOXP2 Gene in the KE Family** Family members who are "affected" have inherited a mutated form of the FOXP2 gene, which results in difficulty with articulating words. As you can see from the centre of the figure, the mutated gene is traced to a female family member, and has been passed on to the individuals of the next two generations.

What evidence indicates that this gene is specifically involved in language? If you were to ask the members of the family who inherited the mutant form of the gene to speak about how to change the batteries in a flashlight, they would be at a loss. A rather jumbled mixture of sounds and words might come out, but nothing that could be easily understood. However, these same individuals have no problem actually performing the task. Their challenges with using language are primarily restricted to the use of words, not with their ability to *think*.

Scientists have used brain-imaging methods to further test whether the FOXP2 mutation affects language. One group of researchers compared brain activity of family members who inherited the mutation of FOXP2 with those who did not (Liégeois et al., 2003). During the brain scans, the participants were asked to generate words themselves, and also to repeat words back to the experimenters. As you can see from Figure 8.19, the members of the family who were

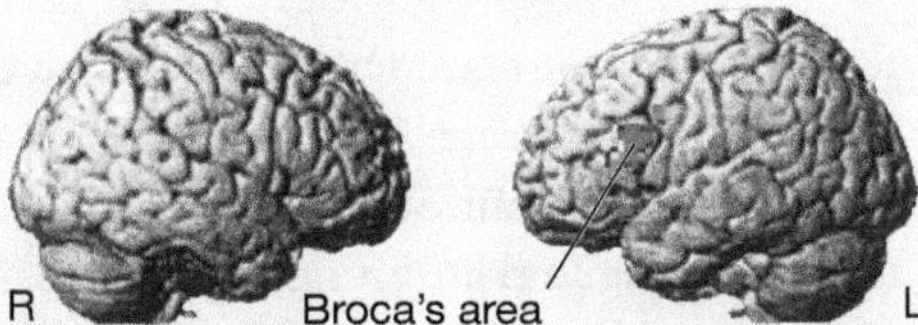

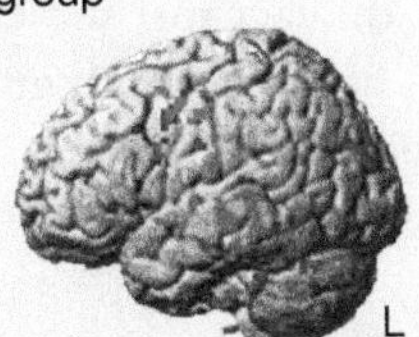

Liégeois, F., Badeweg, T., Connelly, A., Gadian, D.G., Mishkin, M., & Vargha-Khadem, F. (2003). Language fMRI abnormalities associated with FOXP2 gene mutation. *Nature Neuroscience, 6*, 1230–1237.

{FIG. 8.19} **Brain Scans Taken while Members of the KE Family Completed a Speech Task** The unaffected group shows a normal pattern of activity in Broca's area, while the affected group shows an unusual pattern.

unaffected by the mutation showed normal brain activity: Broca's area of the left hemisphere became activated, just as expected. In contrast, Broca's area in the affected family members was silent, and the brain activity that did occur was unusual for this type of task.

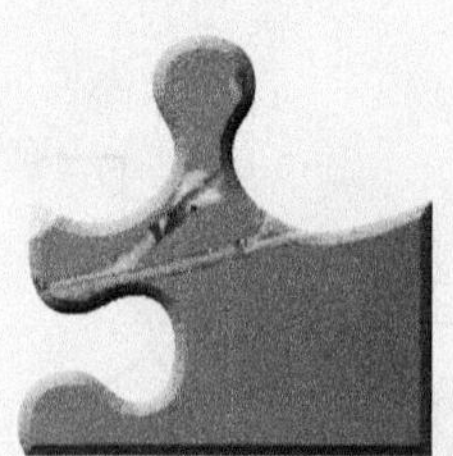

Can we critically evaluate this evidence?

As you have now read, language has multiple components. Being able to articulate words is just one of many aspects of using and understanding language. The research on FOXP2 is very important, but reveals only how a single gene relates to one aspect of language use. There are almost certainly a large number of different genes working together to produce *each* component of language. To their credit, FOXP2 researchers are quick to point out that many other genes will need to be identified before we can claim to understand the genetic basis of language; FOXP2 is just the beginning.

It is also worth noting that although the FOXP2 gene affects human speech production, it does occur in other species that do not produce sophisticated language. This gene is found in both mice and birds as well as in humans, and the human version shares a very similar molecular structure to the versions observed in these other species. Interestingly, the molecular structure and activity of the FOXP2 gene in songbirds (unlike non-songbirds) is similar to that in humans, again highlighting its possible role in producing meaningful sounds (Vargha-Khadem et al., 2005).

Why is this relevant?

This work illuminates at least part of the complex relationship between genes and language. Other individual genes that have direct links to language function will likely be discovered someday as well. It is possible that this information could be used to help us further understand the genetic basis of language disorders. The fact that the FOXP2 gene is found in many other species suggests that it may play a role in one of the components of language rather than being *the* gene for language. Thus, researchers will have to search elsewhere in their quest to understand why and how human language became so much more complex than that of any other species.

Glenn Bartley/All Canada Photos/Glow Images

The fact that animals such as songbirds have some of the same language-related genes as humans suggests that other species may have *some* language abilities. As it turns out, many monkey species have areas in their brains that are similar to Broca's and Wernicke's area. As in humans, these regions are connected by white-matter pathways, thus allowing them to communicate with each other (Galaburda & Pandya, 1982). These areas appear to be involved with the control of facial and throat muscles and with identifying when other monkeys have made a vocalization. This is, of course, a far cry from human language. But, the fact that some monkey species have similar "neural hardware" to humans does lead to some interesting speculations about language abilities in the animal kingdom.

CAN ANIMALS USE LANGUAGE? Psychologists have been studying whether nonhuman species can acquire human language for many decades. Formal studies of language learning in nonhuman species gained momentum in the mid-1950s when psychologists attempted to teach spoken English to a chimpanzee named Viki (Hayes & Hayes, 1951). Viki was **cross-fostered**, *meaning that she was raised as a member of a family that was not of the same species.* Like humans, chimps come into the world dependent on adults for care, so the humans who raised Viki were basically foster parents. Although the psychologists learned a lot about how smart chimpanzees can be, they did not learn that Viki was capable of language—she managed to whisper only about four words after as many years of trying.

Psychologists who followed in these researchers' footsteps did not consider the case to be closed. Perhaps Viki's failure to learn spoken English was a limitation not of the brain, but of physical differences in the vocal tract and tongue that distinguish humans and chimpanzees. One project that began in the mid-1960s involved teaching chimpanzees to use American Sign Language (ASL). The first chimpanzee involved in this project was named Washoe. The psychologists immersed Washoe in

Photo permission granted by Friends of Washoe

Washoe was the first chimpanzee taught to use some of the signs of American Sign Language. Washoe died in 2007 at age 42 and throughout her life challenged many to examine their beliefs about human uniqueness.

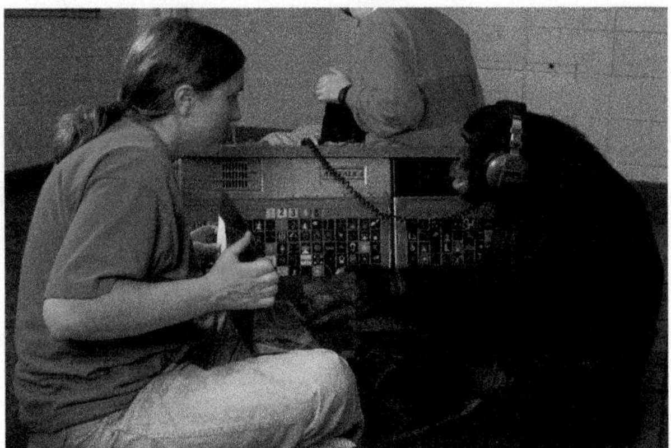

MICHAEL NICHOLS/National Geographic Stock

Kanzi is a bonobo chimpanzee that has learned to use an artificial language consisting of graphical symbols that correspond to words. Kanzi can type out responses by pushing buttons with these symbols, shown in this photo. Researchers are also interested in Kanzi's ability to understand spoken English (which is transmitted to the headphones by an experimenter who is not in the room).

an environment rich with ASL, using signs instead of speaking and keeping at least one adult present and communicating with her throughout the day. By the time she turned two years old, Washoe had acquired about 35 signs through imitation and direct guidance of how to configure and move her hands. Eventually, she learned approximately 200 signs. She was able to generalize signs from one context to another and to use a sign to represent entire categories of objects, not just specific examples. For example, while Washoe learned the sign for the word "open" on a limited number of doors and cupboards, she subsequently signed "open" to many different doors, cupboards, and even her pop bottles. The findings with Washoe were later replicated with other chimps (Gardner et al., 1989).

Instead of using sign language, some researchers have developed a completely artificial language to teach to apes. This language consists of symbols called *lexigrams*—small keys on a computerized board that represent words and, therefore, can be combined to form complex ideas and phrases. One subject of the research using this language is a bonobo named Kanzi (bonobos are another species of chimpanzee). Kanzi has learned approximately 350 symbols through training, but he learned his first symbols simply by watching as researchers attempted to teach his mother how to use the language. In addition to the lexigrams he produces, Kanzi seems to recognize about 3000 spoken words. His trainers claim that Kanzi's skills constitute language (Savage-Rumbaugh & Lewin, 1994). They argue that he can understand symbols and at least some syntax; that he acquired symbols simply by being around others who used them; and that he produced symbols without specific training or reinforcement. Those who work with Kanzi conclude that his communication skills are quite similar to those of a young human in terms of both the elements of language (semantics and syntax) and the acquisition of language (natural and without effortful training).

Findings with apes have inspired psychologists to see if other intelligent, large-brained animals might be able to acquire language. Dolphin trainers have long marvelled at how adept their pupils are at responding to gestures. Dolphins can learn that unique gestures can refer to specific objects as well as directions such as right and left (Herman, 2002). Do the dolphins simply associate a single gesture with a response that, if made, is rewarded with food? As it turns out, the dolphins can respond appropriately when given gestural commands such as one meaning "put the ball on the left into the basket on the right." Thus, they may not merely associate a gesture with an action and a reward, but rather understand the use of gestures as symbols (Herman et al., 1993).

Watch
Classic Footage of Chimpanzees and Sign Language

Despite their ability to communicate in complex ways, debate continues to swirl about whether these animals are using language. Returning to chimpanzees, many language researchers point out that their signing and artificial language use is very different from how humans use language. Is the vastness of the difference important? Is using 200 signs different in some critical way from being able to use 4000 signs, roughly the number found in the ASL dictionary (Stokoe et al., 1976)? If our only criterion for whether a communication system constitutes language is the number of words used, then we can say that nonhuman species acquire some language skills after extensive training. But as you have learned in this module, human language involves more than just using words. In particular, our manipulation of phonemes, morphemes, and syntax allow us to utter an infinite number of words and sentences, thereby conveying an infinite number of thoughts.

Some researchers who have worked closely with language-trained apes observed too many critical differences between humans and chimps to conclude that language extends beyond our species (Seidenberg & Pettito, 1979). For example:

- One major argument is that apes are communicating only with symbols, not with the phrase-based syntax used by humans. Although some evidence of syntax has been reported, the majority of their "utterances" consist of single signs, a couple of signs strung together, or apparently random sequences.
- There is little reputable experimental evidence showing that apes pass their language skills to other apes.
- Productivity—creating new words (gestures) and using existing gestures to name new objects or events—is rare, if it occurs at all.
- Some of the researchers become very engaged in the lives of these animals and talk about them as friends and family members (Fouts, 1997; Savage-Rumbaugh & Lewin, 1994). This tendency has left critics to wonder the extent to which personal attachments to the animals might interfere with the objectivity of the data.

It must be pointed out that the communication systems of different animals have their own adaptive functions. It is possible that these species simply didn't have a need to develop a complex form of language. However, in the case of chimpanzees, this point doesn't hold true. Both humans and chimpanzees evolved in small groups in (for the most part) similar parts of the world; thus, chimpanzees would have faced many of the same social and environmental pressures as humans. However, their brains, although quite sophisticated, are not as large or well-developed as those of humans. It seems, therefore, that a major factor in humanity's unique language abilities is the wonderful complexity and plasticity of the brain.

Quick Quiz 8.3c Genes, Evolution, and Language

KNOW ...

1 Which nonhuman species has had the greatest success at learning a human language?

A Border collies
B Bonobo chimpanzees
C Dolphins
D Rhesus monkeys

UNDERSTAND ...

2 Studies of the KE family and the FOXP2 gene indicate that

A language is controlled entirely by a single gene found on chromosome 7.
B language is still fluent despite a mutation to this gene.
C this particular gene is related to one specific aspect of language.
D mutations affecting this gene lead to highly expressive language skills.

ANALYZE ...

3 What is the most accurate conclusion from research conducted on primate language abilities?

A Primates can learn some aspects of human language, though many differences remain.
B Primates can learn human language in full.
C Primates cannot learn human language in any way.
D There are not enough research data to reach reliable conclusions on this topic.

Answers can be found on page ANS-3.

Module Summary

Module 8.3

Reuters

Now that you have read this module you should

KNOW ...

- ***The key terminology from the study of language*:**

aphasias (p. 337)
Broca's area (p. 337)
cross-foster (p. 346)
fast mapping (p. 342)
language (p. 338)
morpheme (p. 339)
phoneme (p. 339)
pragmatics (p. 340)
semantics (p. 339)
syntax (p. 340)
Wernicke's area (p. 337)

UNDERSTAND ...

- ***How language is structured.*** Sentences are broken down into words that are arranged according to grammatical rules (syntax). The relationship between words and their meaning is referred to as semantics. Words can be broken down into morphemes, the smallest meaningful units of speech, and phonemes, the smallest sound units that make up speech.
- ***How genes and the brain are involved in language use.*** Studies of the KE family show that the FOXP2 gene is involved in our ability to speak. However, mutation to this gene does not necessarily impair people's ability to think. Thus, the FOXP2 gene seems to be important for just one of many aspects of human language. Multiple brain areas are involved in language—two particularly important ones are Broca's and Wernicke's areas.

APPLY ...

- ***Your knowledge to distinguish between units of language such as phonemes and morphemes.*** Which of these represent a single phoneme and which represent a morpheme? Do any of them represent both? Check your answers on page ANS-3.
  1. /dis/
  2. /s/
  3. /k/

ANALYZE ...

- ***Whether species other than humans are able to use language.*** Nonhuman species certainly seem capable of acquiring certain aspects of human language. Studies with apes have shown that they can learn and use some sign language or, in the case of Kanzi, an artificial language system involving arbitrary symbols. Critics have pointed out that many differences between human and nonhuman language use remain.

Work the Scientific Literacy Model :: Understanding Cognitive Obstacles

1 What do we know about problem solving and decision making?

We generally approach problems either logically (with an algorithm) or intuitively (with a heuristic), and usually with some combination of both. For example, suppose you are moving to university, and your car is fully packed except for one last box that does not seem to fit. If you took an algorithmic approach to this problem, you might go online to find a physics website. After entering the dimensions of your car's trunk as well as those of each box, you would print out the optimal placement of each box and repack your car according to the step-by-step directions. If you took a heuristic approach, you might remember that your mother always told you to pack the big items first and then squeeze the smaller ones in. Using this general rule of thumb, you would reorganize the trunk.

Now review the idea of cognitive obstacles on **page 326**. Imagine you are thinking ahead to future moves, and shopping for a bigger car. Despite its documented record of poor gas mileage, you decide to buy the model that first comes to mind, being persuaded by all the ads for the car you have recently seen. In this instance, you are displaying the availability heuristic, or making a decision based only on information that is readily available.

2 How can science help explain the cognitive obstacles to problem solving and decision making?

As mentioned in the discussion on **pages 325–333**, research shows that people often treat evidence in ways that minimize their own discomfort and maximize their positive feelings. Called *confirmation bias,* this situation occurs when we filter information through our existing belief systems and perspectives. We are even more likely to exhibit this bias when the information relates to highly charged issues such as politics or religion.

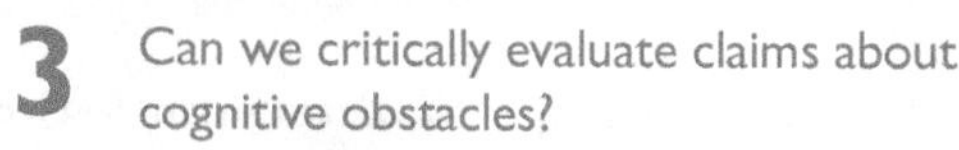

ICP/incamerastock/Alamy

4 Why is this relevant?

Watch the accompanying video excerpt about making choices. You can access the video at MyPsychLab or by clicking the play button in the centre of your eText. If your instructor assigns this video as a homework activity, you will find additional content to help you in MyPsychLab. You can also view the video by using your smart phone and the QR code below, or you can go to the YouTube link provided.

Consider what you know about cognitive shortcuts and obstacles. After you have read this chapter and watched the video, imagine that Maria's method of studying worked effectively throughout high school until she took her first foreign language course. In this course, her grades were much lower than usual. How might a mental set have played a role in Maria's academic problem?

3 Can we critically evaluate claims about cognitive obstacles?

The fact that people consistently make decisions based on representativeness or availability, and make biased judgments so that they can maintain their sense of comfort in the world, leads many people to wonder what is wrong with human thought processes. Surely they must be flawed! In reality, there is nothing inherently wrong with using heuristics; in fact, they can sometimes be valuable and useful. Heuristics allow people to make quick decisions based on readily available information. While the use of cognitive shortcuts can also open us up to mistakes and biases, being aware that we are fallible encourages us to be more effective critical thinkers and to spend more time evaluating our decisions.

MyPsychLab **Your turn to Work the Scientific Literacy Model:** Watch the accompanying video on YouTube, or on your phone (using the Layar app or QR code). If your instructor has assigned this as a homework activity, you can find the video clip and additional content at MyPsychLab. Answer the questions that accompany the video clip to test your understanding.

youtube.com/workthemodel

SCAN WITH LAYAR

9

Intelligence Testing

Mihai Simonia/Shutterstock

LesPalenik/Shutterstock.com

Module 9.1

Measuring Intelligence

Learning Objectives

After reading this module you should

KNOW ...	UNDERSTAND ...	APPLY ...	ANALYZE ...
The key terminology associated with intelligence and intelligence testing	The reasoning behind the eugenics movements and its use of intelligence tests	The concepts of entity theory and incremental theory to help kids stay in school	Why it is difficult to remove all cultural bias from intelligence testing

Leilani Muir kept trying to get pregnant, but to no avail. Finally, frustrated, she went to her doctor to see if there was a medical explanation. It turned out that there was, but not one that she expected; the doctors found that her fallopian tubes had been surgically destroyed, permanently sterilizing her.

How could someone's fallopian tubes be destroyed without them knowing? Unfortunately, Leilani is one of the tens of thousands of victims of the misguided application of intelligence tests. Born into a poor farming family near Calgary, Alberta, Leilani was entered by her parents into the Provincial Training School for Mental Defectives when she was 11. A few years later, she was given an intelligence test, and she scored 64, which was below the 70 point cutoff required by law for forced sterilization.

You may not have heard of forced sterilization, but it was a not uncommon practice in the United States and parts of Canada for almost half of the 20th century. In 1928, Alberta passed the Sexual Sterilization Act, giving doctors the power to sterilize people deemed to be "genetically unfit," without their consent. One of the criteria that could qualify a person for being genetically unfit was getting a low score on an IQ test.

In Leilani's case, when she was 14, she was told by doctors she needed to have her appendix removed, so trusting the good doctors, she went under the knife, changing her life forever. She was never told of the fallopian tube surgery, and had to find out on her own after her many attempts to get pregnant. Later in her life, Leilani had her IQ re-tested. She scored 89, which is close to average and well above the cutoff for forced sterilization.

In 1996, Leilani received some measure of justice. She sued the government of Alberta and won her case, becoming the first person to receive compensation for injustices committed under the Sexual Sterilization Act. For her lifetime of not being able to have children, she received almost $750 000 in damages.

Focus Questions

1. How have intelligence tests been misused in modern society?

2. Why do we have the types of intelligence tests that we have?

The Canadian Press Images/*Edmonton Journal*

Mary Evans Picture Library/Alamy

Sir Francis Galton believed that intelligence was something people inherit. Thus, he believed that an individual's relatives were a better predictor of intelligence than practice and effort.

What happened to Leilani Muir was terrible and should never have happened. But this story also serves to drive home an extremely important truth about psychology, and science more generally—*it is important to measure things properly*. Leilani's life-altering misfortune was the result of both inhumane policies as well as the failure to accurately measure her intelligence. Her initially low score was the result of an error in a single measurement. Intelligence is not something like length or mass; there is no objective standard to which we can compare our measures to see if they are accurate. Instead, we have to rely upon rigorous testing of our methodologies. If this testing is not done well then, as this story attests, horrible consequences can ensue.

So, how *can* we measure intelligence accurately? What does the science say? As you will see in this module, this question is not easy to answer. Intelligence measures have a very chequered past, making the whole notion of intelligence one of the most hotly contested areas in all of psychology.

Different Approaches to Intelligence Testing

Intelligence is a surprisingly difficult concept to define. You undoubtedly know people who earn similar grades even though one seems to be smarter than the other. What characteristics make one person seem more intelligent than the other? Is that characteristic really intelligence, or is it some other quality such as maturity or poise? As you can see, defining intelligence is not a simple matter. The history of psychology has seen dozens of attempts to do so, and dozens of methods for measuring this very complex entity. We will begin this module by examining attempts at measuring intelligence, and will then review some of the social consequences of intelligence testing.

Watch

Special Topics: Intelligence Testing, Then and Now

INTELLIGENCE AND PERCEPTION: GALTON'S ANTHROPOMETRIC APPROACH The systematic attempt to measure intelligence in the modern era began with Sir Francis Galton (1822–1911). Galton believed that because people learn about the world through their senses, those with superior sensory abilities would be more sensitively attuned to the world, and able to learn more about it. Thus, sensory abilities should be an indicator of a person's intelligence. In 1884, Galton created a set of 17 sensory tests, such as the highest and lowest sounds people could hear or their ability to tell the difference between objects of slightly different weights, and began testing people's abilities in his *anthropometric* laboratory. **Anthropometrics** (literally, "the measurement of people") referred to *methods of measuring physical and mental variation in humans.* Galton's lab attracted many visitors, allowing him to measure the sensory abilities of thousands of people in England (Gillham, 2001).

One of Galton's colleagues, James McKeen Cattell, took his tests to the United States and began measuring the abilities of university students. This research revealed, however, that people's abilities on different sensory tests were not correlated with each other, or only very weakly. For example, having exceptional eyesight seemed to signify little about whether one would have exceptional hearing. Clearly, this was a problem, because if two measures don't correlate well with each other, then they can't both be indicators of the same thing, in this case Galton's sensory definition of intelligence. Cattell also found that students' scores on the sensory tests did not predict their grades, which one would expect would also be an indicator of intelligence. As a result, Galton's approach to measuring intelligence was generally abandoned.

INTELLIGENCE AND THINKING: THE STANFORD–BINET TEST In contrast to Galton, a prominent French psychologist, Alfred Binet, argued that intelligence should be indicated by more complex thinking processes, such as memory, attention, and comprehension. This view has influenced most intelligence researchers up to the present day; they define **intelligence** as *the ability to think, understand, reason, and adapt to or overcome obstacles* (Neisser et al., 1996). From this perspective, intelligence reflects how well people are able to reason and solve problems, plus their accumulated knowledge.

In 1904, Binet and his colleague, Theodore Simon, were hired by the French government to develop a test to measure intelligence. At the end of the 19th century, institutional reforms in France had made primary school education available to all children. As a result, French educators struggled to deliver a curriculum to students ranging from the very bright to those who found school exceptionally challenging. To respond to this problem, the French government wanted an objective way of identifying "retarded" children who would benefit from specialized education (Siegler, 1992).

Watch
Language Assessment Portions of Stanford-Binet Intelligence Scale

Binet and Simon experimented with a wide variety of tasks, trying to capture the complex thinking processes that Binet believed comprised intelligence. They settled on thirty tasks, arranged in order of increasing difficulty. For example, simple tasks included repeating sentences and defining common words like "house." More difficult tasks included constructing sentences using combinations of certain words (e.g., Paris, river, fortune), reproducing drawings from memory, and being able to explain how two things differed from each other. Very difficult tasks included being able to define abstract concepts and to logically reason through a problem (Fancher, 1985).

Watch
Classic Footage of Assessment of Memory with the Stanford-Binet Intelligence Scale

Binet and Simon gave their test to samples of children from different age groups to establish the average test score for each age. Binet argued that a child's test score measured her **mental age**, *the average intellectual ability score for children of a specific age*. For example, if a 7-year-old's score was the same as the average score for 7-year-olds, she would have a mental age of 7, whereas if it was the same as the average score for 10-year-olds, she would have a mental age of 10, even though her chronological age would be 7 in both cases. A child with a mental age lower than her chronological age would be expected to struggle in school and to require remedial education.

The practicality of Binet and Simon's test was apparent to others, and soon researchers in the United States began to adapt it for their own use. Lewis Terman at Stanford University adapted the test for American children and established average scores for each age level by administering the test to thousands of children. In 1916, he published the first version of his adapted test, and named it the Stanford-Binet Intelligence Scale (Siegler, 1992).

Terman and others almost immediately began describing the **Stanford-Binet test** as *a test intended to measure innate levels of intelligence*. This differed substantially from Binet, who had viewed his test as a measure of a child's current abilities, not as a measure of an innate capacity. There is a crucial difference between believing that test scores reflect a changeable ability or an innate capacity that is presumably fixed. The interpretation of intelligence as a fixed, innate ability set the stage for the incredibly misguided use of intelligence tests in the decades that followed, as we discuss later in this module.

To better reflect people's presumably innate and fixed levels of intelligence, Terman adopted William Stern's concept of the **intelligence quotient**, or **IQ**, a label that has stuck to the present day. *IQ is calculated by taking a person's mental age, dividing it by his chronological age, and then multiplying by 100*. For example, a 10-year-old child with a mental age of 7 would have an IQ of $7/10 \times 100 = 70$. On the other hand, if a child's mental and chronological ages were the same, the IQ score would always be 100, regardless of the age of the child; thus, 100 became the standard IQ for the "average child."

To see the conceptual difference implied by these two ways of reporting intelligence, consider the following two statements. Does either one sound more optimistic than the other?

- He has a mental age of 7, so he is 3 years behind.
- He has an IQ of 70, so he is 30 points below average.

To many people, being 3 years behind in mental age seems changeable; with sufficient work and assistance, such a child should be able to catch back up to his peers.

On the other hand, having an IQ that's 30 points below average sounds like the diagnosis of a permanent condition; such a person seems doomed to be "unintelligent" forever.

One other odd feature of both Binet's mental age concept and Stern's IQ was that they didn't make much sense when you applied them to adults. For example, is a person with the mental age of 45 not as smart as someone with the mental age of 70? Similarly, imagine a 30-year-old with a mental age of 30; her IQ would be 100. But in 10 years, when she was 40, if her mental age stayed at 30, she would have an IQ of only 75. Given that IQ scores remain constant after about age 16 (Eysenck, 1994), this would mean that adults get progressively less smart with every year that they age.

To adjust for this problem, psychologists began to use a different measure, *deviation IQ,* for calculating the IQ of adults (Wechsler, 1939). The deviation IQ is calculated by comparing the person's test score with the average score for people of the same age. In order to calculate deviation IQs, one must first establish the norm, or average, for a population. To do so, psychologists administer tests to huge numbers of people, and use these scores to estimate the average for people of different ages. These averages are then used as baselines against which to compare the person. Because "average" is defined to be 100, a deviation IQ of 100 means that the person is average, whereas an IQ of 115 would mean that the person's IQ is above average (see Figure 9.1). One advantage of using deviation IQ scores is that, because they are calculated relative to others of the same age, it avoids the problem of IQ scores that consistently decline with age.

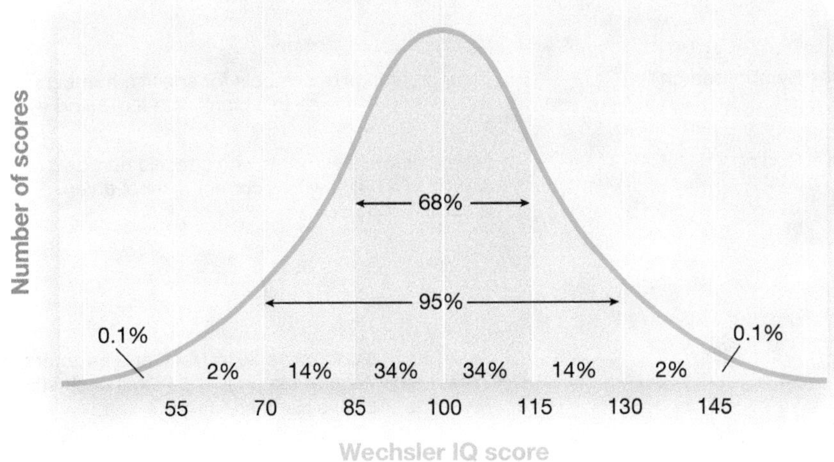

{FIG. 9.1} **The Normal Distribution of Scores for a Standardized Intelligence Test**

THE WECHSLER ADULT INTELLIGENCE SCALE

David Wechsler developed an IQ test that was specialized for adult populations. After much research, this evolved into the **Wechsler Adult Intelligence Scale (WAIS)**, which remains the most common intelligence test in use today for adolescents and adults. The WAIS is currently in its fourth edition. (In an ironic twist, Wechsler himself was classified as having mild intellectual disabilities—"feeble minded" was the term used at the time—as a nine-year-old child when his family immigrated to the United States from Romania.)

The *WAIS* provides a single IQ score for each test taker—the *Full Scale IQ*—but also breaks intelligence into a General Ability Index (GAI) and a Cognitive Proficiency Index (CPI), as shown in Figure 9.2. The GAI is computed from scores on the Verbal Comprehension and Perceptual Reasoning indices. These measures tap into an individual's intellectual abilities, but without placing much emphasis on how fast he can solve problems and make decisions. The CPI, in contrast, is based on the Working Memory and Processing Speed subtests. It is included in the Full Scale IQ category because greater working memory capacity and processing speed allow more cognitive resources to be devoted to reasoning and solving problems. Figure 9.3 shows some sample test items from the WAIS.

RAVEN'S PROGRESSIVE MATRICES

Although the Stanford-Binet test and the WAIS have been widely used across North America, they have also been criticized by a number of researchers. One of the key problems with many intelligence tests is that questions often require knowledge of the test developer's culture and language. This cultural bias puts people from different cultures and social classes at an immediate disadvantage. However, clearly a person's intelligence should not be affected by whether they are fluent in English or familiar with Western culture. In response to this problem, psychologists have tried to develop more valid, "culture-free" tests.

Cultural Influences on Intelligence: Robert Sternberg

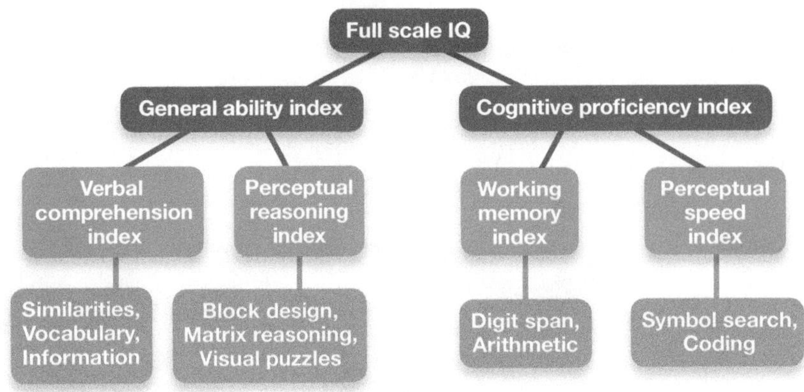

{FIG. 9.2} **Subscales of the Wechsler Adult Intelligence Scale**

Processing Speed Index	
Symbol search	View groupings of symbols for specific numbers of each symbol, and fill in a blank with a missing symbol.
Coding	Match different symbols with specific numbers, and fill in a blank with a correct symbol given a certain number.

Working Memory Index	
Arithmetic	Jack has $16 and owes $8 to Hank and $4 to Frank. What percentage of the original $16 will Jack still have after he pays Hank and Frank?
Digit span	Recall the order of number strings in both forward and reverse directions.

Perceptual Reasoning Index	
Matrix reasoning	View the pattern in the top two rows and fill in the blank of the third row. 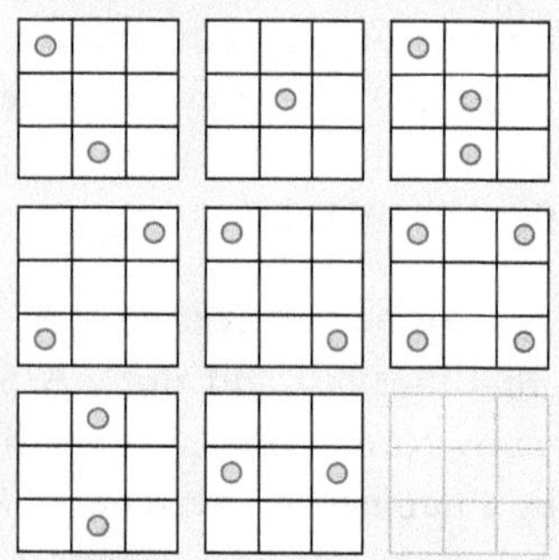

Block Design

Which three pieces are needed to make this puzzle?

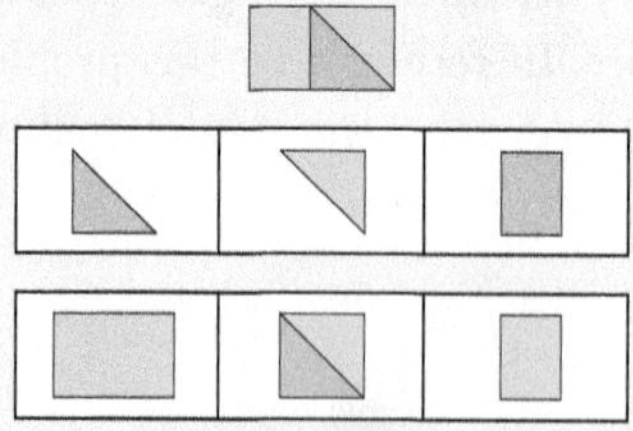

Verbal Comprehension Index	
Vocabulary	What does *profligate* mean?
Similarities	In what way are a bicycle and a car alike?
Information	On which continent is Japan located?

{FIG. 9.3} **Types of Problems Used to Measure Intelligence** These hypothetical problems are consistent with the types seen on the Wechsler Adult Intelligence Scale.

In the 1930s, John Raven developed **Raven's Progressive Matrices**, *an intelligence test that is based on pictures, not words, thus making it relatively unaffected by language or cultural background.* The main set of tasks found in Raven's Progressive Matrices measure the extent to which test takers can see patterns in the shapes and colours within a matrix and then determine which shape or colour would complete the pattern (see Figure 9.4). Note how this type of problem does not require knowledge of a specific language, culture, or human-made object or custom.

Quick Quiz 9.1a

Different Approaches to Intelligence Testing

KNOW ...

1 Galton developed anthropometrics as a means to measure intelligence based on ________.

- **A** creativity
- **B** perceptual abilities
- **C** physical size and body type
- **D** brain convolution

UNDERSTAND ...

2 The deviation IQ is calculated by comparing an individual's test score

- **A** at one point in time to that same person's test score at a different point in time.
- **B** to that same person's test score from a different IQ test; the "deviation" between the tests is a measure of whether either test is inaccurate.
- **C** to that same individual's school grades.
- **D** to the average score for other people who are the same age.

3 In an attempt to be culturally unbiased, Raven's Progressive Matrices relies upon what types of questions?

- **A** Verbal analogies
- **B** Spatial calculations
- **C** Visual patterns
- **D** Practical problems that are encountered in every culture

APPLY ...

4 If someone's mental age is double her chronological age, what would her IQ be?

- **A** 100
- **B** 50
- **C** 200
- **D** Cannot be determined with this information

Answers can be found on page ANS-3.

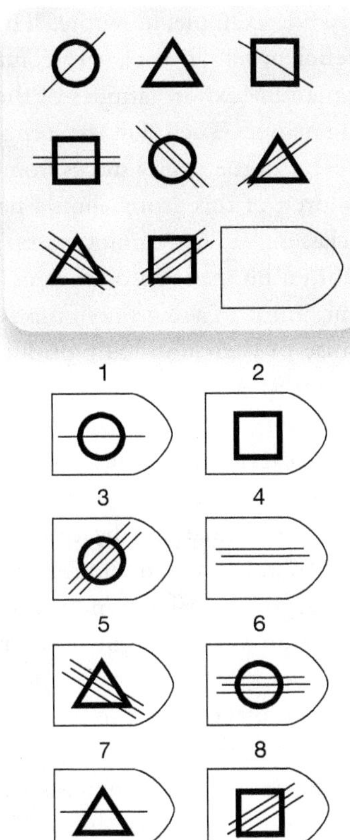

{FIG. 9.4} **Sample Problem from Raven's Progressive Matrices** Which possible pattern (1–8) should go in the blank space? Check your answer at the bottom of the page.

The Chequered Past of Intelligence Testing

IQ testing in North America got a significant boost during World War I. Lewis Terman, developer of the Stanford-Binet test, worked with the United States military to develop a set of intelligence tests that could be used to identify which military recruits had the potential to become officers and which should be streamed into non-officer roles. The intention was to make the officer selection process more objective, thereby increasing the efficiency and effectiveness of officer training programs. Following World War I, Terman argued for the use of intelligence tests in schools for similar purposes—identifying students who should be channelled into more "advanced" academic topics that would prepare them for higher education, and others who should be channelled into more skill-based topics that would prepare them for direct entry into the skilled trades and the general workforce. Armed with his purportedly objective IQ tests, he was a man on a mission to improve society. However, the way he went about doing so was rife with problems.

Answer to Figure 9.4: Pattern 6.

IQ TESTING AND THE EUGENICS MOVEMENT

In order to understand the logic of Terman and his followers, it is important to examine the larger societal context in which his theories were developed. The end of the 19th and beginning of the 20th centuries was a remarkable time in human history. A few centuries of European colonialism had spread Western influence through much of the world. The Industrial Revolution, which was concentrated in the West, compounded this, making Western nations more powerful militarily, technologically, and economically. And in the sciences, Darwin's paradigm-shattering work on the origin of species firmly established the idea of evolution by natural selection (see Module 3.1), permanently transforming our scientific understanding of the living world.

Although an exciting time for the advancement of human knowledge, this confluence of events also had some very unfortunate outcomes, especially in terms of how colonialism affected non-Western cultures and people of non-Caucasian ethnicities. In particular, the stage was set for social "visionaries" to apply Darwin's ideas to human culture, and to explain the military–economic–technological dominance of Western cultures by assuming that Westerners (and especially Caucasians) were genetically superior. This explanation served as a handy justification for the colonial powers' imposition of Western-European values on other cultures; in fact, it was often viewed that the colonizers were actually doing other cultures a favour, helping to "civilize" them by assimilating them into a "superior" cultural system.

The "social Darwinism" that emerged gave rise to one of the more ugly social movements of recent times—*eugenics*, which means "good genes" (Gillham, 2001). The history of eugenics is intimately intertwined with the history of intelligence testing. In fact, Francis Galton himself, a cousin of Charles Darwin, made an extensive study of the heritability of intelligence, and it was he who coined the term eugenics.

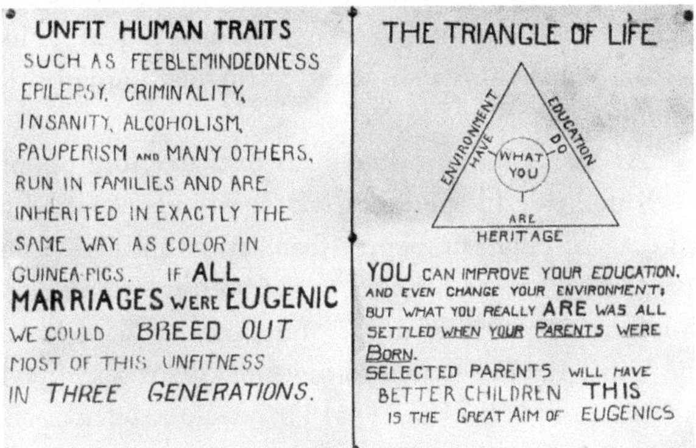

American Philosophical Society

Many people viewed eugenics as a way to "improve" the human gene pool. Their definition of "improve" is certainly up for debate.

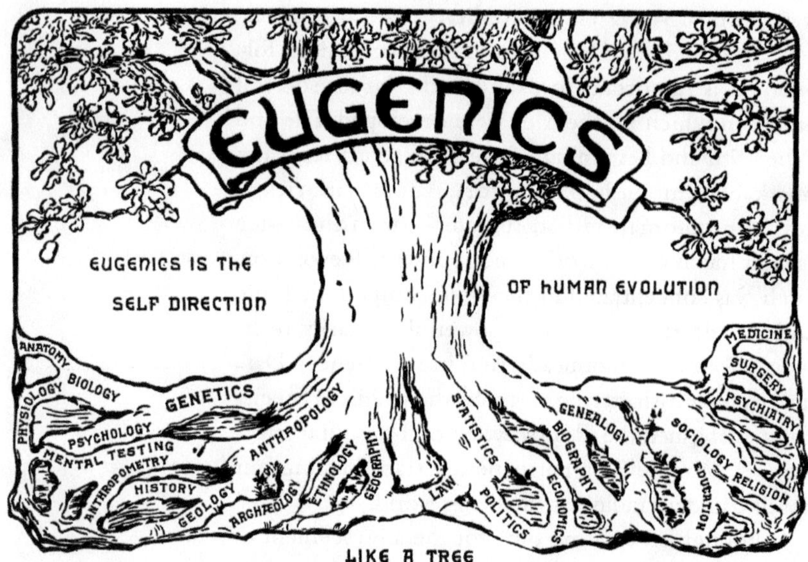

American Philosophical Society

Supporters of eugenics often noted that its logic was based on research and philosophy from many different fields. Doing so put the focus on the abstract intellectual characteristics of eugenics rather than on some of its disturbing, real-world implications.

Galton noticed that many members of his own family were successful businessmen and some, like Charles Darwin, eminent scientists. He studied other families and concluded that eminence ran in families, which he believed was due to "good breeding." Although families share more than genes, such as wealth, privilege, and social status, Galton believed that genes were the basis of the family patterns he observed (Fancher, 2009).

Galton's views influenced Lewis Terman, who promoted an explicitly eugenic philosophy; he argued for the superiority of his own "race," and in the interest of "improving" society, believed that his IQ tests provided a strong empirical justification for eugenic practices. One such practice was the forced sterilization of people like Leilani Muir who we discussed at the beginning of this module.

As Terman administered his tests to more people, it seemed like his race-based beliefs were verified by his data. Simply put, people from other cultures didn't score as highly on his tests as did Western Caucasians. For example, 40% of new immigrants to Canada and the United States scored so low they were classified as "feebleminded" (Kevles, 1985). He concluded that people from non-Western cultures and non-White ethnicities did not, in general, have as high IQs, and he therefore argued that it was appropriate, even desirable, to stream them into less challenging academic pursuits and jobs of lower status. For example, he wrote, "High-grade or border-line deficiency . . . is very, very common among Spanish-Indian and Mexican families of the Southwest and also among negroes. Their dullness seems to be racial, or at least inherent in the family stocks from which they come. . . . Children of this group should be segregated into separate classes. . . . They cannot master abstractions but they can often be made into efficient workers . . . from a eugenic point of view they constitute a grave problem because of their unusually prolific breeding" (Terman, 1916, pp. 91–92).

Such ideas gained enough popularity that forced sterilization was carried out in at least 30 states and two Canadian provinces, lasting for almost half a century. In Alberta, the Sexual Sterilization Act remained in force until 1972, by which time more than 2800 people had undergone sterilization procedures in that province alone. And as you might have guessed, new immigrants, the poor, Native people, and Blacks were sterilized far more often than the White middle and upper classes.

Although the actions of eugenicists were horribly misguided and inflicted irreparable suffering on so many, it is a disturbing lesson to realize that they were, initially, motivated by arguably "good" humanitarian values. Eugenicists like Terman genuinely believed that they were making the world a better place. Just like a farmer would breed undesirable characteristics out of his livestock, they believed they were doing the same for society. It's easy, and comforting, to simply demonize the eugenicists, assuming only "evil" people would do such a thing. It's far more challenging to accept that people with good intentions can, if guided by questionable science, end up inflicting great harm.

THE RACE AND IQ CONTROVERSY One of the reasons intelligence tests played so well into the agendas of eugenicists is that, from Terman onwards, researchers over the last century have consistently found differences in the IQ scores of people from different ethnic groups. Before we go any further, we want to acknowledge that this is a difficult, and potentially upsetting, set of research findings. However, it's important to take a close look at this research, and to understand the controversy that surrounds it, because these findings are well known in the world of intelligence testing and could be easily misused by those who want to spread prejudiced views. As you will see, when you take a close look at the science, the story is not nearly as clear as it may appear at first glance.

The root of this issue about "race and IQ" is that there is a clear and reliable hierarchy of IQ scores across different ethnic groups. This was first discovered in the early 1900s, and by the 1920s, the United States passed legislation making it standard to administer intelligence tests to new immigrants arriving at Ellis Island for entry into the country. The result was that overwhelming numbers of immigrants were officially classified as "morons" and "feebleminded." Some psychologists suspected that these tests were unfair, and that the low scores of these minority groups might be due to language barriers and a lack of knowledge of American culture. Nevertheless, as intelligence tests were developed that were increasingly culturally sensitive—such as Raven's Progressive Matrices—these differences persisted. Specifically, Asian people tended to score the highest, followed by Whites, followed by Latinos and Blacks; this has been found in samples in several parts of the world, including Canada (Rushton & Jensen, 2005). Other researchers have found that Native people in Canada score lower as a group than Canadians with European ancestry (e.g., Beiser & Gotowiec, 2000).

The race-IQ research hit the general public in 1994 with the publication of *The Bell Curve* (Herrnstein & Murray, 1994), which became a best-seller. This book focused on over two decades of research that replicated the race differences in IQ that we mentioned earlier. Herrnstein and Murray also argued that human intelligence is a strong predictor of many different personal and social outcomes, such as workplace performance, income, and the likelihood of being involved in criminal activities. Additionally, *The Bell Curve* argued that those of high intelligence were reproducing less than those of low intelligence, leading to a dangerous population trend in the United States. They believed that America was becoming an increasingly divided society, populated by a small class of "cognitive elite," and a large underclass with lower intelligence. They argued therefore that a healthy society would be a *meritocracy,* in which people who had the most ability and worked the hardest would receive the most wealth, power, and status. Those who didn't have what it took to rise to the top, such as those with low IQs, should be allowed to live out their fates, and should not therefore be helped by programs such as Head Start, affirmative action programs, or scholarships for members of visible minorities. Instead, the system should simply allow people with the most merit to rise to the top, even if they ended being disproportionately of certain cultural or ethnic backgrounds.

As you can imagine, this research sparked a bitter controversy. Within the academic world, some researchers have claimed that these findings are valid (e.g., Gottfredson, 2005), whereas others have argued that these results are based on flawed methodologies and poor measurements (e.g., Lieberman, 2001; Nisbett, 2005). Others have sought to discredit Herrnstein and Murray's conclusions, in particular their argument that the differences in IQ scores between ethnic groups means that there are inherent, genetic differences in intelligence between the groups. Within the general public, reaction was similarly mixed, with many people seizing upon it to justify policies such as limiting immigration, discontinuing affirmative action programs, and otherwise working to overturn decades of progress made in the fight for civil rights and equality.

PROBLEMS WITH THE RACIAL SUPERIORITY INTERPRETATION In many ways, the simplest critique of the racial superiority interpretation of these test score differences is that the tests themselves are culturally biased. This critique was lodged against intelligence tests from the time of Terman and, as we discussed earlier, a considerable amount of research focused on creating tests that were not biased due to language and culture. But in spite of all this work, the test score differences between ethnic groups remained.

Watch
Cultural Biases: Robert Guthrie

A more subtle critique was that it wasn't necessarily the tests that were biased, but the very process of testing itself. If people in minority groups are less familiar with standardized tests, if they are less motivated to do well on the tests, or if they are less able to focus on performing well during the testing sessions, they will be more likely to produce lower test scores. This indeed seems to be the case; researchers have found that cultural background affects many aspects of the testing process including how comfortable people are in a formal testing environment, how motivated they are to perform well on such tests, and their ability to establish rapport with the test administrators (Anastasi & Urbina, 1996).

Research has also indicated that the IQ differences may be due to a process known as **stereotype threat**, *which occurs when negative stereotypes about a group cause group members to underperform on ability tests* (Steele, 1997). In other words, if a Black person is reminded of the stereotype that Black people perform more poorly than White people on intelligence tests, she may end up scoring lower on that test because she was afraid of living up to that stereotype. Researchers have identified at least three reasons why this happens. First, stereotype threat increases arousal due to the fact that individuals are aware of the negative stereotype about their group, and are concerned that a poor performance may reflect poorly on their group; this arousal then undermines their test performance. Second, stereotype threat causes people to become more self-focused, paying more attention to how well they are performing, thus leaving fewer cognitive resources for them to focus on the test itself. Third, stereotype threat increases the tendency for people to

Watch
In the Real World: Intelligence Tests and Stereotypes

Watch
Joshua Aronson: Can Technology Help People Overcome Stereotype Threat?

Andresr/Shutterstock.com

Stereotype threat: Just being reminded of a stereotype can reduce performance on mental tasks.

Watch
Demographics and Intelligence Testing: Robert Guthrie

actively try to inhibit negative thoughts they may have, which also reduces the cognitive resources that could otherwise be used to focus on the test (Schmader et al., 2008). There have now been more than 200 studies on stereotype threat (Nisbett et al., 2012), establishing it as a reliable phenomenon that regularly suppresses the test scores of many stereotyped groups in a variety of settings.

These concerns cast doubt on the *validity* of IQ scores for members of non-White ethnic and cultural groups, suggesting that a test score reflects not merely IQ but also other factors, such as linguistic or cultural bias in the testing situation. Other researchers have taken issue with the *genetic interpretation* of the findings, arguing that even if one accepts that the tests are valid and there really are intelligence differences between groups in society, this may not reflect innate, genetic differences. For example, consider the circumstances that poor people and ethnic minorities face in countries like Canada or the United States. People from such groups tend to experience a host of factors that contribute to poorer cognitive and neurological development, such as poorer nutrition, greater stress, lower-quality schools, worse medical treatment, higher rates of illness (Acevedo-Garcia et al., 2008), and greater exposure to industrial toxins such as lead (Dilworth-Bart & Moore, 2006). Given the accumulation of these factors, it seems highly likely (although the controversy continues in the literature) that the race-IQ gap is explained not by genetic differences, but by differences in environments, stereotype threat effects, and responses to the process of testing itself.

These disadvantages can also make people from economically poorer backgrounds and some ethnic minorities feel like their efforts to succeed are futile. In other words, initial difficulties in school or on achievement tests may lead individuals to believe that they are not intelligent and that, due to their difficult lives, there is no hope for improvement. However, recent research suggests that it *is* possible to improve one's intelligence—it just requires the belief that change is possible.

WORKING THE SCIENTIFIC LITERACY MODEL

Beliefs about Intelligence

Simulate
Survey: What Is Intelligence?

Although intelligence test scores are supposed to measure intelligence, as you've read in this module, scores on these tests can be influenced by a number of factors. Some of these are fairly obvious, like fatigue, illness, or stress; but some are very subtle, such as the beliefs we have about our own intelligence. Think about your own intelligence for a moment: Do you believe your level of intelligence is something innate to you, a basic quality of yours, like your height, which is relatively unchangeable? Or do you believe it is more changeable, something you could improve if you worked at it? Can you make yourself smarter?

Surprisingly to many people, intelligence is highly changeable. Yet many people hold implicit beliefs that their intelligence level is relatively fixed. Ironically, that belief itself will tend to limit people's potential to positively affect their own intelligence.

What do we know about the kinds of beliefs that may affect test scores?

Educators and parents have long been perplexed by students who consistently achieve below what their ability would predict. This is an especially important issue for students, as children's self-perceptions of their mental abilities have a very strong influence on their academic performance (Greven et al., 2009). For some students, it is simply a matter of apathy, but for others, it can be a very frustrating experience.

Thus it was truly a serious matter when psychologist Carol Dweck (2002) responded to a colleague's inquiry about "Why smart people can be so stupid." Her research has found some interesting conclusions in that there seem to be two influential beliefs about the nature of intelligence. First is **entity theory**: *the belief that intelligence is a fixed characteristic and relatively difficult (or impossible) to change*. Second is **incremental theory**: *the belief that intelligence can be shaped by experiences, practice, and effort*. According to Dweck and colleagues, beliefs based on entity theory and incremental theory have different effects on academic performance.

How can science test whether beliefs affect performance?

According to Dweck's research, the differences between the two theories are not nearly as important as the differences in behaviour that result. In experiments by Dweck and her colleagues, students were identified as holding either entity theories or incremental theories. The students had the chance to answer 476 general knowledge questions dealing with topics such as history, literature, math, and geography. They received immediate feedback on whether their answers were correct or incorrect. Those who held entity theories were more likely to give up in the face of highly challenging problems, and they were likely to withdraw from situations that resulted in failure. These individuals believe that successful people were born that way, so why keep punishing yourself if you simply do not have the ability to succeed? By comparison, people with incremental views of intelligence were more resilient (Mangels et al., 2006). If they are motivated to succeed at a task, then they will work through failures and challenges—if intelligence and ability can change, then it makes sense to keep pursuing goals.

Resilience is a desirable trait, so Dweck and her colleagues tested a group of junior high students to see whether incremental views could be taught (Blackwell et al., 2007). In a randomized, controlled experiment, they taught one group of Grade 7 students incremental theory—that they could control and change their ability. This group's grades increased over the school year, whereas the control group's grades actually declined (Figure 9.5). Thus, if you are skeptical about your own abilities, it might pay to look into Dweck's research more closely.

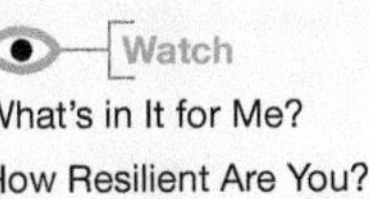

What's in It for Me? How Resilient Are You?

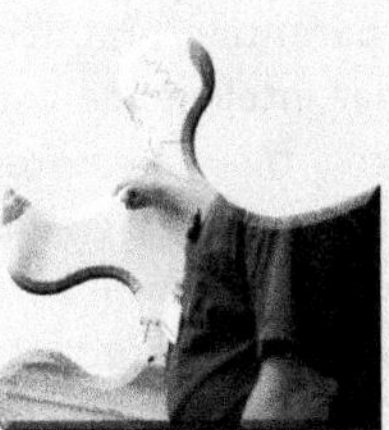

Can we critically evaluate this research?

These findings suggest that any time a belief about intelligence or ability can be changed to become more incremental, then that change should probably be made. One unanswered question raised by this research, however, is whether this is indeed always for the best. What if, in some situations, it is true that no matter how hard a person tries, he or she is unlikely to succeed? At what point do we encourage people to be more "realistic" and to accept their limitations? Is it truly always desirable to encourage people to "reach for the stars," or is it sometimes better to steer people away from the shattered dreams and heartache that would accompany striving only to fail?

An additional difficulty surrounding these studies is that it is not clear what mechanisms might be causing the improvements. Does the incremental view of intelligence lead to increased attention, effort, and time organizing study materials? Or is it actually just a positive mood manipulation?

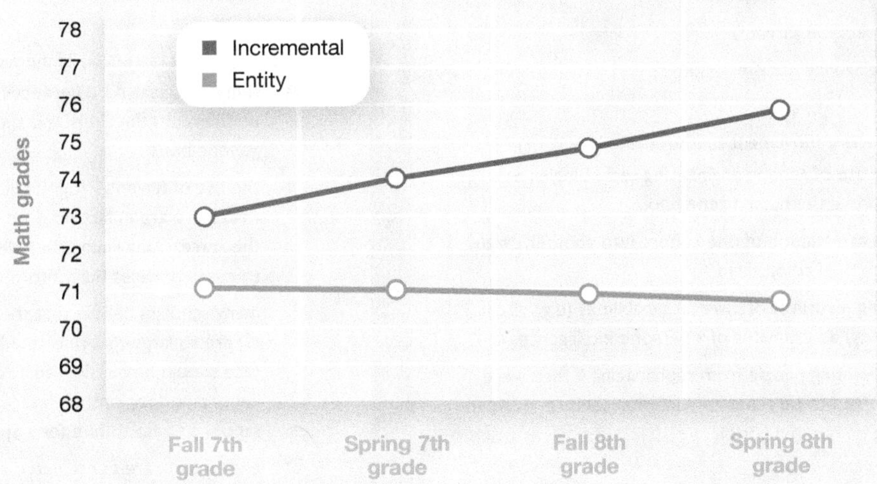

{FIG. 9.5} **Personal Beliefs Influence Grades** Students who hold incremental views of intelligence (i.e., the belief that intelligence can change with effort) show improved grades in math compared to children who believe that intelligence is an unchanging entity (Blackwell et al., 2007).

Positive moods have been shown to improve performance on tests of perception and creativity (Isenberg, 1987); perhaps the hope associated with the incremental view is influencing students' emotions, not their IQs.

However, regardless of the mechanism(s) involved, the fact that it is possible to help students by changing their view of intelligence could be a powerful force for educational change in the future.

Watch
The Big Picture: What Is Intelligence?

Why is this relevant?

This research has huge potential to be applied in schools and to become a part of standard parenting practice. Teaching people to adopt the view that intelligence and other abilities are trainable skills will give them a greater feeling of control over their lives; it may improve their grades in the process. Carol Dweck and Lisa Sorich Blackwell have designed a program called Brainology to teach students from elementary through high school that the brain can be trained and strengthened through practice. They hope that programs such as this could counteract the disempowering effects of stereotypes by helping members of stereotyped groups to have greater resilience and to avoid succumbing to negative beliefs about themselves. Not only is intelligence changeable, as this research shows, but perhaps society itself can be changed through the widespread application of this research, as it lurches toward a truly level playing field.

lisafx/iStockphoto

Quick Quiz 9.1b The Chequered Past of Intelligence Testing

KNOW ...

1 People who believe that intelligence is relatively fixed are said to advocate a(n) _______ theory of intelligence.

A incremental
B entity
C sexist
D hereditary

2 _______ is the situation in which, when people are aware of stereotypes about their social group, they may fear being reduced to that stereotype.

A Incremental intelligence
B Hereditary intelligence
C Stereotype threat
D Intelligence discrimination

3 Eugenics was a movement that promoted

A the use of genetic engineering technologies to improve the human gene pool.
B the assimilation of one culture into another, often as part of colonialism.
C using measures of physical capabilities (e.g., visual acuity) as estimates of a person's intelligence.
D preventing people from reproducing if they were deemed to be genetically inferior, so as to improve the human gene pool.

APPLY ...

4 As a major exam approaches, a teacher who is hoping to reduce stereotype threat and promote an incremental theory of intelligence would most likely

A remind test takers that males tend to do poorly on the problems.
B remind students that they inherited their IQ from their parents.
C cite research of a recent study showing that a particular gene is linked to IQ.
D let students know that hard work is the best way to prepare for the exam.

ANALYZE ...

5 According to the discussion of the race and IQ controversy

A there are clear IQ differences between people of different ethnicities, and these probably have a genetic basis.
B the use of Raven's Progressive Matrices has shown that there are in fact no differences in IQ between the "races"; any such group differences must be due to cultural biases built into the tests.
C many scholars believe that the ethnic differences in IQ are so large that one could argue that a person's race should be considered a relevant factor in important decisions, such as who to let into medical school or who to hire for a specific job.
D even if tests are constructed that are culturally unbiased, the testing process itself may still favour some cultures over others.

Answers can be found on page ANS-3.

Module Summary

Module 9.1

Now that you have read this module you should

KNOW ...

- ***The key terminology associated with intelligence and intelligence testing*:**

anthropometrics (p. 353)
entity theory (p. 361)
incremental theory (p. 361)
intelligence (p. 354)
intelligence quotient (IQ) (p. 354)
mental age (p. 354)
Raven's Progressive Matrices (p. 356)
Stanford-Binet test (p. 354)
stereotype threat (p. 359)
Wechsler Adult Intelligence Scale (WAIS) (p. 355)

UNDERSTAND ...

- ***The reasoning behind the eugenics movements and its use of intelligence tests.*** The eugenicists believed that abilities like intelligence were inborn, and thus, by encouraging reproduction between people with higher IQs, and reducing the birthrate of people with lower intelligence, the overall genetic pool of humankind could be improved.

APPLY ...

- ***The concepts of entity theory and incremental theory to help kids stay in school.*** One of the key reasons that people stop trying to succeed, and then eventually drop out of school, is that they internalize a belief that their basic abilities, such as their intelligence, are fixed and not something they can change. By not trying, they guarantee that they will perform poorly, which then reinforces their tendency to not try very hard. By training young people to think of themselves as changeable, to think of the brain like a muscle that can be strengthened through exercise, people can improve their scores on intelligence tests. At the same time, they may become much more resilient to negative circumstances, and much better able to cope when life offers them challenges or setbacks.

LesPalenik/Shutterstock.com

ANALYZE ...

- ***Why it is difficult to remove all cultural bias from intelligence testing.*** There are many reasons why the process of intelligence testing contains cultural bias, resulting in inaccuracies when testing people from certain cultural groups: Tests may contain content or knowledge that is more relevant to some cultures; the method of testing (e.g., paper and pencil multiple-choice questions) may be more familiar to people from some cultures; the environment of testing may make people from some cultures more comfortable; the presence of negative stereotypes about one's group may interfere with test-taking abilities; and the internalization of self-defeating beliefs, such as entity theory beliefs, may further interfere with the ability of members of disadvantaged cultures to have the optimism to believe that they can improve their performance.

Lane V. Erickson/Shutterstock

Module
9.2

Understanding Intelligence

Learning Objectives

After reading this module you should

KNOW ...	UNDERSTAND ...	APPLY ...	ANALYZE ...
The key terminology related to understanding intelligence	Why intelligence is divided into fluid and crystallized types Intelligence differences between males and females	Your knowledge to identify examples from the triarchic theory of intelligence	Whether teachers should spend time tailoring lessons to each individual student's learning style

Blind Tom was born into a Black slave family in 1849. When his mother was bought in a slave auction by General James Bethune, Tom was included in the sale for nothing because he was blind and believed to be useless. Indeed, Tom was not "smart" in the normal sense of the term. Even as an adult he could speak fewer than 100 words and would never be able to go to school. But he could play more than 7000 pieces on the piano, including a huge classical music repertoire and many of his own compositions. Tom could play, flawlessly, Beethoven, Mendelssohn, Bach, Chopin, Verdi, Rossini, and many others, even after hearing a piece only a single time. As an 11-year-old, he played at the White House, and by 16 went on a world tour. A panel of expert musicians performed a series of musical experiments on him, and universally agreed he was "among the most wonderful phenomena in musical history." Despite his dramatic linguistic limitations, he could reproduce, perfectly, up to a 15-minute conversation without losing a single syllable, and could do so in English, French, or German, without understanding any part of what he was saying. In the mid-1800s, he was considered to be the "eighth wonder of the world."

Today, Tom would be considered a **savant**, *an individual with low mental capacity in most domains but extraordinary abilities in other specific areas such as music, mathematics, or art.* The existence of savants complicates our discussion of intelligence considerably. Normally, the label "intelligent" or "unintelligent" is taken to indicate some sort of overall ability, the amount of raw brainpower available to the person, akin to an engine's horsepower. But this doesn't map onto savants at all—they have seemingly unlimited "horsepower" for certain skills and virtually none for many others. The existence of savants, and the more general phenomenon of people being good at some things (e.g., math, science) but not others (e.g., languages, art), challenges our understanding of intelligence and makes us ask more deeply, what *is* intelligence? Is it one ability? Or is it many?

Focus Questions

 Is intelligence one ability or many?

 How have psychologists attempted to explain intelligence as a collection of different abilities?

Bettmann/Corbis

In general, people believe that intelligence involves the ability to think, understand, reason, learn, and find solutions to problems. But how are these abilities related to each other? Does the content of a person's intelligence matter? To be intelligent, must a person be able to do these things well for math, history, poetry, music, and child rearing? Or does intelligence break down into sets of lower-level abilities? If so, does that mean that there isn't any such thing as "intelligence" per se, but rather a whole host of narrower "intelligences"? As you will learn in this module, a full picture of intelligence involves various perspectives on how many different abilities fall under the term "intelligence."

Intelligence as a Single, General Ability

When we say someone is intelligent, we usually are implying they have a high level of a generalized cognitive ability. We expect intelligent people to be "intelligent" in many different ways, about many different topics. Intelligent people are the kids who do well in almost every subject in high school, whereas the unintelligent seem to struggle in almost every class they take. We wouldn't normally call someone intelligent if she were good at, say, making up limericks, but nothing else. Intelligence should manifest itself in many different domains.

Scientific evidence for intelligence as a general ability dates back to early 20th-century work by Charles Spearman, who began by developing techniques to calculate correlations among multiple measures of mental abilities (Spearman, 1923). One of these techniques, known as **factor analysis**, *is a statistical technique that examines correlations between variables to find clusters of related variables, or "factors."* For example, imagine that scores on tests of vocabulary, reading comprehension, and verbal reasoning correlate highly together; these would form a "language ability" factor. Similarly, imagine that scores on algebra, geometry, and calculus questions correlate highly together; these would form a "math ability" factor. However, if the language variables don't correlate very well with the math variables, then you have some confidence that these are separate factors; in this case, it would imply that there are at least two types of independent abilities: math and language abilities. For there to be an overarching general ability called "intelligence," one would expect that tests of different types of abilities would all correlate with each other, forming only one factor.

SPEARMAN'S GENERAL INTELLIGENCE Spearman found that schoolchildren's grades in different school subjects were positively correlated, even though the content of the different topics (e.g., math vs. history) was very different. This led Spearman to hypothesize the existence of a **general intelligence factor** (abbreviated as "*g*"). Spearman believed that *g* represented a person's "mental energy," reflecting his belief that some people's brains are simply more "powerful" than others (Sternberg, 2003). This has greatly influenced psychologists up to the present day, cementing within the field the notion that *intelligence* is a basic cognitive trait comprising the ability to learn, reason, and solve problems, regardless of their nature. Spearman's concept of *g* is apparent today with a wide range of intelligence tests administered by psychologists (Johnson et al., 2008).

Watch Basics: Theories of Intelligence

Is *g* real? Does it predict anything meaningful? In fact, *g* does predict many important phenomena. For example, correlations between *g* and high school and university grades are about .5, which is a relatively strong association (Neisser et al., 1996). The general intelligence factor also predicts how many years a person will stay in school, as well as how much they will earn afterwards (Ceci & Williams, 1997).

General intelligence scores also predict many seemingly unrelated phenomena, such as how long you are likely to live (Gottfredson & Deary, 2004), how quickly you can make snap judgments on perceptual discrimination tasks (i.e., laboratory tasks that test how quickly people form perceptions; Deary & Stough, 1996), and how

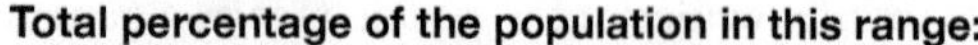

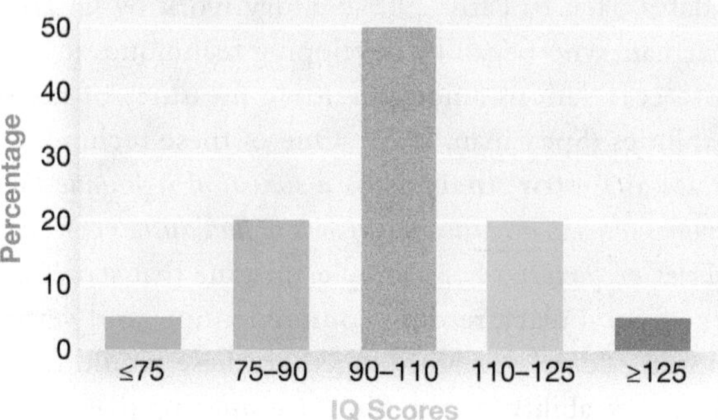

Watch Thinking Like a Psychologist: Intelligence Tests and Success

Individuals in this range who divorced within five years:

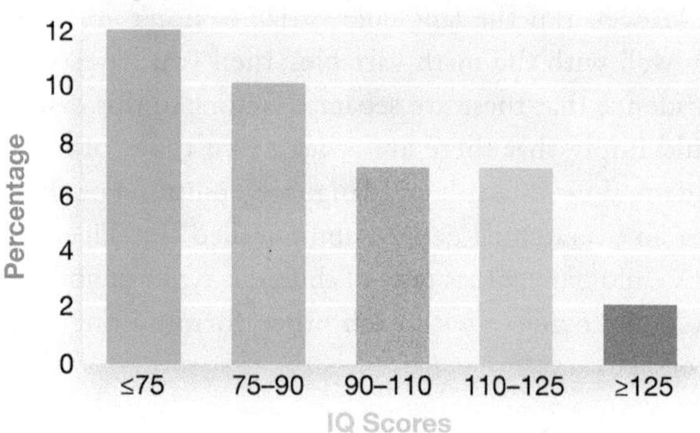

Individuals in this range who live in poverty:

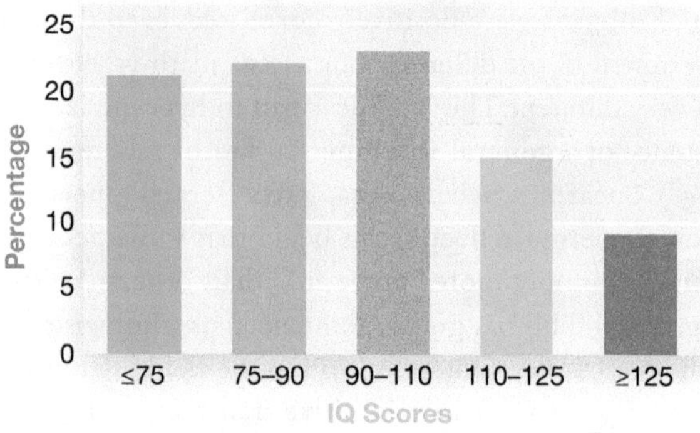

Individuals in this range who have been incarcerated:

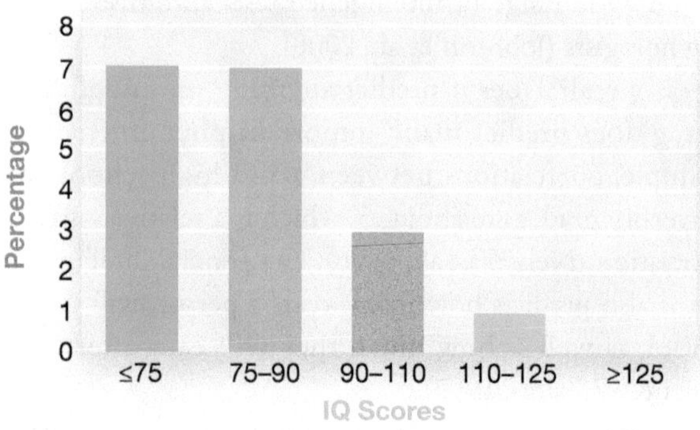

{FIG. 9.6} **General Intelligence Is Related to Many Different Life Outcomes** General intelligence (*g*) predicts not just intellectual ability, but also psychological well-being, income, and successful long-term relationships.

well you can exert self-control (Shamosh et al., 2008). Some other examples of *g*'s influences are depicted in Figure 9.6.

In the workplace, intelligence test scores not only predict who gets hired, but also how well people perform at a wide variety of jobs. In fact, the correlation is so strong that after almost a century of research (Schmidt & Hunter, 1998), general mental ability has emerged as the single best predictor of job performance (correlation = .53; Hunter & Hunter, 1984). Overall intelligence is a far better predictor than the applicant's level of education (correlation = .10) or how well the applicant does in the job interview itself (correlation = .14). It is amazing to think that in order to make a good hiring decision, a manager would be better off using a single number given by an IQ test than actually sitting down and interviewing applicants face to face!

The usefulness of *g* is also shown by modern neuroscience research findings that overall intelligence predicts how well our brains work. For example, Tony Vernon at Western University (formerly the University of Western Ontario) and his colleagues have found that general intelligence test scores predict how efficiently we conduct impulses along nerve fibres and across synapses (Johnson et al., 2005; Reed et al., 2004). This efficiency of nerve conduction allows for more efficient information processing overall. As a result, when working on a task, the brains of highly intelligent people don't have to work as hard as those of less intelligent people; high IQ brains show less overall brain activation than others for the same task (Grabner et al., 2003; Haier et al., 1992).

Thus, overall intelligence, as indicated by *g*, is related to many real-world phenomena, from how well we do at work to how well our brains function.

DOES *G* TELL US THE WHOLE STORY? Clearly, *g* reflects something real. However, we have to remember that correlation does not equal causation. It is possible that the effects of *g* are due to motivation—being motivated to succeed would lead to better grades, better IQ scores, and better job performance. Therefore, it is important to be cautious when interpreting these results.

We should also ask whether *g* can explain everything about a person's intelligence. A single number cannot possibly capture the kind of genius exhibited by the savants we discussed earlier. Or you can think closer to your own experience—surely you have known people who were very talented in art or music but terrible in math or science? Or did you ever know an incredibly smart person who was socially awkward, or a charismatic and charming person who you'd never want as your chemistry partner? There may be many ways of being intelligent, and reducing all of that diversity to a single number seems to overlook the different types of intelligence that people have.

The idea that it is important to appreciate the diversity of abilities different people possess is captured very well by a story told by Craig Kielburger, a famous young Canadian from Toronto who, at age 12, founded the charity Kids Can Free the Children (usually shortened to Free the Children). Craig quickly gained national and international acclaim as his organization inspired millions of kids to take action against child labour and poverty. He has now been nominated for the Nobel Peace Prize multiple times, won countless awards, and written several books. Craig and his brother, Mark, write,

> *Many of us have difficulty recognizing our skills and talents as the gifts they truly are. Craig learned this lesson a few years ago while he was doing a television interview on a show that was focusing on "accomplished youth." The other young interviewee was nineteen years old, had already completed his master's degree and PhD, and was working at an important job at a pharmaceutical company. Throughout the interview, he kept mentioning that he was "gifted," a fact that he had discovered when he passed a special IQ test. Thereafter, the boy's parents told him that he was "gifted," his teachers spent extra time with him because he was "gifted," and the media labelled him as "gifted." He must have said the word "gifted" at least five times during the interview. Finally, the host turned to Craig and asked, "Well, are you gifted, Craig?" Craig looked at her and shook his head.*
>
> *Later that day, Craig was still thinking about this interview when he went back to the Free The Children office. As he looked around at the remarkable people who work with us, he realized that he had given the host the wrong answer. Craig saw our webmaster, whom we all consider to be incredibly gifted when it comes to designing websites that are visited by millions of people around the world. He saw our young writing staff, gifted in translating their passion and energy into words to inspire others. He saw our amazing adult volunteers, who are gifted mentors, giving tirelessly of their time and expertise. The more he thought about it, the more Craig realized that he couldn't think of anyone he knew who wasn't gifted.*
>
> *In our society, we are often led to believe that only an extraordinary few people qualify as "gifted." In truth, everyone has a unique gift to share with the world, whether it's for creating beautiful works of art, healing the sick, being a compassionate listener, fixing things that are broken, raising money, being a good friend, or finding solutions to problems.* (Kielburger & Kielburger, 2006, pp. 258–259)

Moving beyond intelligence as a single ability may help us to better appreciate the different gifts we all have.

Quick Quiz 9.2a

Intelligence as a Single, General Ability

KNOW ...

1 Spearman believed that

- **A** people have multiple types of intelligence.
- **B** intelligence scores for math and history courses should not be correlated.
- **C** statistics cannot help researchers understand how different types of intelligence are related to each other.
- **D** some people's brains are more "powerful" than others, thus giving them more "mental energy."

UNDERSTAND ...

2 What is factor analysis?

- **A** A method of ranking individuals by their intelligence
- **B** A statistical procedure that is used to identify which sets of psychological measures are highly correlated with each other
- **C** The technique of choice for testing for a single, general intelligence
- **D** The technique for testing the difference between two means

3 Researchers who argue that *g* is a valid way of understanding intelligence would NOT point to research showing

- **A** people with high *g* make perceptual judgments more quickly.
- **B** people with high *g* are more likely to succeed at their jobs.
- **C** the brains of people with low *g* conduct impulses more slowly.
- **D** people with low *g* are better able to do some tasks than people with high *g*.

Answers can be found on page ANS-3.

Intelligence as Multiple, Specific Abilities

Spearman himself believed that *g* didn't fully capture intelligence. After all, although different items on an intelligence test were correlated with each other, their correlations were never 1.0, and usually far less than that. This is an important point, because correlations less than 1.0 mean that scores on one item do not perfectly predict scores on another item. Your performance when answering a given question is not determined by just one factor, global intelligence, but obviously reflects many other factors, such as idiosyncratic knowledge that helps you answer that particular question, or the amount of attention available to focus on the question in that moment (vs. being distracted, tired, stressed, or having other things on your mind).

To account for the idiosyncratic skill or knowledge factor, Spearman hypothesized a second kind of ability that was specific to each task (i.e., each item on a test). And in a flurry of creativity, he chose the inspired name "*s*" to represent this specific-level, skill-based intelligence. His two-factor theory of intelligence was therefore comprised of *g* and *s*, where *g* represents our general, overarching intelligence, and *s* represents our skill or ability level for a given task.

Nobody has seriously questioned the *s* part of Spearman's theory; obviously, each task in life, from opening a coconut, to using an ATM machine, to solving calculus problems, requires abilities that are specific to the task. However, the concept of *g* has come under heavy fire throughout the intervening decades, leading to several different theories of multiple intelligences.

The first influential theory of multiple intelligences was created by Louis Thurstone, who examined scores of general intelligence tests using factor analysis, and found seven different clusters of what he termed *primary mental abilities*. Thurstone's seven factors were word fluency (which is the person's ability to produce language fluently), verbal comprehension, numeric abilities, spatial visualization, memory, perceptual speed, and reasoning (Thurstone, 1938). He argued that there was no meaningful *g*, but that intelligence needed to be understood at the level of these primary mental abilities that functioned independently of each other. However, Spearman (1939) fired back, arguing that Thurstone's seven primary mental abilities were in fact correlated with each other, suggesting that there was after all an overarching general intelligence.

A highly technical and statistical debate raged for several more decades between proponents of *g* and proponents of multiple intelligences, until it was eventually decided, of course, that both of them were right.

THE HIERARCHICAL MODEL OF INTELLIGENCE

The controversy was largely settled by the widespread adoption of hierarchical models that describe how some types of intelligence are "nested" within others in a similar manner to how, for example, a person is nested within her community, which may be nested within a city, which is nested within a province. The general hierarchical model describes how our lowest-level abilities (those relevant to a particular task, like Spearman's *s*) are nested within a middle level that roughly corresponds to Thurstone's primary mental abilities (although not necessarily the specific ones that Thurstone hypothesized), and these are nested within a general intelligence (Spearman's *g*; Gustaffson, 1988). By the mid-1990s, analyses of prior research on intelligence concluded that almost all intelligence studies were best explained by a three-level hierarchy (Carroll, 1993).

What this means is that we have an overarching general intelligence, which is made up of a small number of sub-abilities, each of which is made up of a large number of specific abilities that apply to individual tasks. Figure 9.7 shows the evolution of these models.

However, even this didn't completely settle the debate about what intelligence really is, because it left open a great deal of room for different theories of the best way to describe the middle-level factors. And as you will see in the next section, even the debate about *g* has been updated in recent years.

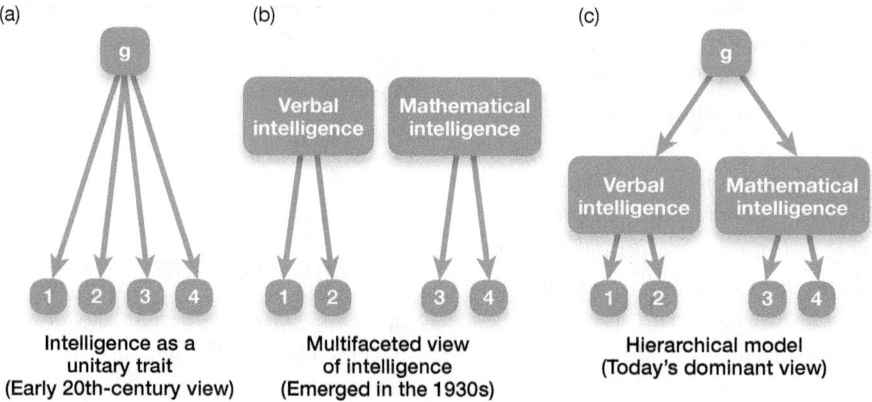

Notes:
- "*g*" stands for general, a single factor underlying all intelligent behaviour.
- Numbered boxes represent multiple tests of different intellectual abilities.

{FIG. 9.7} **Comparing Different Theories of Intelligence** Diagrams A and B summarize Spearman's and Thurstone's historical views. Diagram C represents the modern, general consensus that intelligence is a three-level hierarchy (although see the Working the Scientific Literacy Model section for a further wrinkle in this story . . .).

WORKING THE SCIENTIFIC LITERACY MODEL

Testing for Fluid and Crystallized Intelligence

The concept of g implies that performance on all aspects of an intelligence test is influenced by this central ability. But careful analyses of many data sets, and recent neurobiological evidence, have shown that there may be two types of g that have come to be called fluid intelligence (Gf) and crystallized intelligence (Gc).

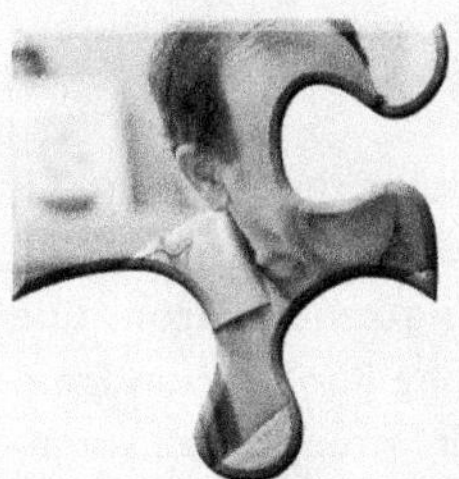

What do we know about fluid and crystallized intelligence?

The distinction between fluid and crystallized intelligence is basically the difference between "figuring things out" and "knowing what to do from past experience." **Fluid intelligence (Gf)** is *a type of intelligence used in learning new information and solving new problems not based on knowledge the person already possesses*. Tests of Gf involve problems such as pattern recognition and solving geometric puzzles, neither of which is heavily dependent on past experience. For example, Raven's Progressive Matrices, in which a person is asked to complete a series of geometric patterns of increasing complexity (see Module 9.1), is the most widely used measure of Gf. **Crystallized intelligence (Gc)**, is *a type of intelligence that draws upon past learning and experience*. Tests of Gc, such as tests of vocabulary and general knowledge, depend on individuals' prior knowledge to come up with the right answer (Figure 9.8; Cattell, 1971).

Gf and Gc are thought to be largely separate from each other, with two important exceptions. One is that having greater fluid intelligence means that the person is better able to process information and to learn; therefore, greater Gf may, over time, lead to greater Gc, as the person who processes more information and learns more things will gain more crystallized knowledge (Horn & Cattell, 1967). Note, however, that this compelling hypothesis has received little empirical support thus far (Nisbett et al., 2012). The second is that it is difficult, perhaps impossible, to measure Gf without tapping into people's pre-existing knowledge and experience, as we discuss below.

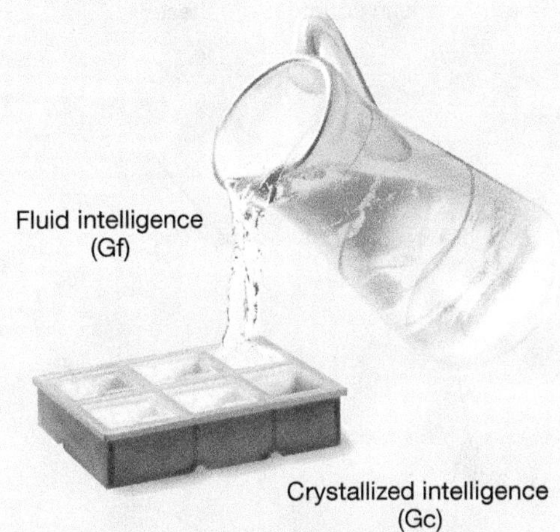

{FIG. 9.8} **Fluid and Crystallized Intelligence** Fluid intelligence is dynamic and changing, and may eventually become crystallized into a more permanent form.

The distinction between Gf and Gc certainly makes intuitive sense, but does scientific evidence support it?

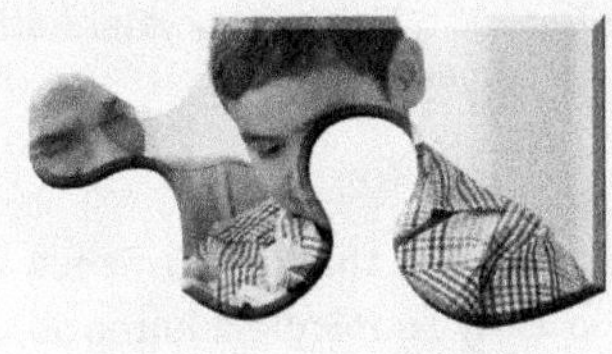

How can science help distinguish between fluid and crystallized intelligence?

One interesting line of research that supports the Gf/Gc distinction comes from examining how each type changes over the life span (Cattell, 1971; Horn & Cattell, 1967). In one study, people aged 20 to 89 years were given a wide array of tasks, including the Block Design task (see Figure 9.3), the Tower of London puzzle (see Figure 9.9), and tests

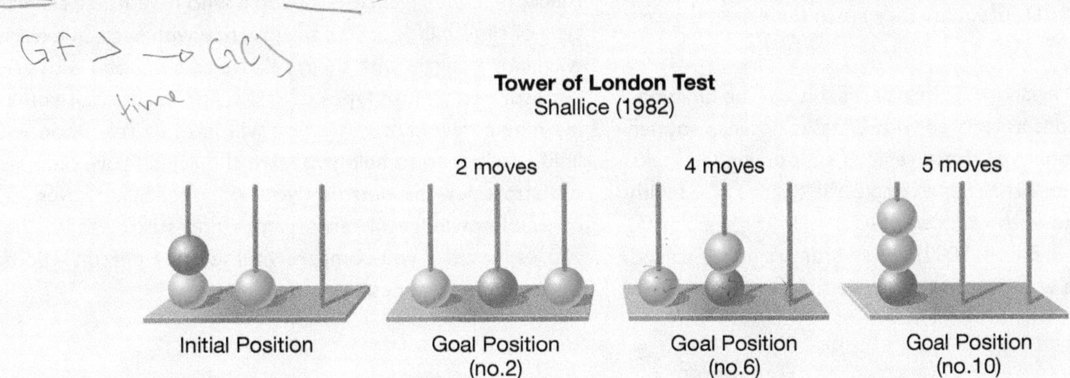

{FIG. 9.9} **Measuring Fluid Intelligence** The Tower of London problem has several versions, each of which requires the test taker to plan and keep track of rules. For example, the task might involve moving the coloured beads from the initial position so that they match any of the various end goal positions.

{FIG. 9.10} **Measuring Crystallized Intelligence** Crystallized intelligence refers to facts, such as names of countries.

of reaction time. Researchers have found that performance in tasks that require Gf peaks in early to middle adulthood and declines thereafter (Bugg et al., 2006). Other researchers have found a consistent decline after adolescence in tasks that require fluid intelligence (Avolio & Waldman, 1994; Baltes & Lindenberger, 1997). Gc, by comparison, shows greater stability than Gf as a person ages (Schaie, 1994). Examples of Gc are vocabulary and verbal ability (Figure 9.10). Healthy, older adults generally do not show much decline, if any, in these skills, at least until they reach their elderly years (Miller et al., 2009).

Neurobiological evidence further backs this up. The functioning of brain regions associated with Gf tasks declines sooner than the functioning of those regions supporting Gc tasks (Geake & Hansen, 2010). For example, the decline of Gf with age is associated with reduced efficiency in the prefrontal cortex (Braver & Barch, 2002), a key brain region involved in the cognitive abilities that underlie fluid intelligence. In contrast, this brain region does not play a central role in crystallized intelligence, which is more dependent on long-term memory systems that involve a number of different regions of the cortex.

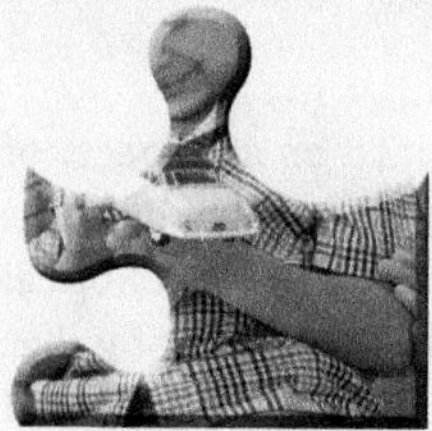

Can we critically evaluate crystallized and fluid intelligence?

There are certainly questions we can ask about crystallized and fluid intelligence. For one, is there really any such thing as fluid intelligence, or does it merely break down into specific sub-abilities? And, are fluid and crystallized intelligence *completely* different from each other, or are they related in some ways?

Cognitive psychologists generally accept that fluid intelligence is a blending of several different cognitive abilities. For example, the abilities to switch attention from one stimulus to another, inhibit distracting information from interfering with concentration, sustain attention on something at will, and keep multiple pieces of information in your working memory at the same time, are all part of fluid intelligence (Blair, 2006). If Gf is simply a statistical creation that reflects the integration of these different processes, perhaps researchers would be better off focusing their attention on these systems, rather than the more abstract construct Gf.

Another critique is that fluid and crystallized intelligence are not, after all, entirely separable. Consider the fact that crystallized intelligence involves not only possessing knowledge in your brain, but also being able to access that knowledge when it's needed. Fluid cognitive processes, and the brain areas that support them such as the prefrontal cortex, play important roles in both storing and retrieving crystallized knowledge from long-term memory (Ranganath et al., 2003).

Similarly, tests of fluid intelligence likely also draw upon crystallized knowledge. For example, complete-the-pattern tasks such as Raven's Progressive Matrices may predominantly reflect fluid intelligence, but people who have never seen any type of similar task or had any practice with such an exercise will likely struggle with them relative to someone with prior exposure to similar types of tasks. For example, if you are learning a new card game, you will have to rely upon your fluid intelligence to help you learn the rules, figure out effective strategies, and outsmart your opponents. However, your overall knowledge of cards, games, and strategies will help you, especially if you compare yourself to a person who has played no such games in his life.

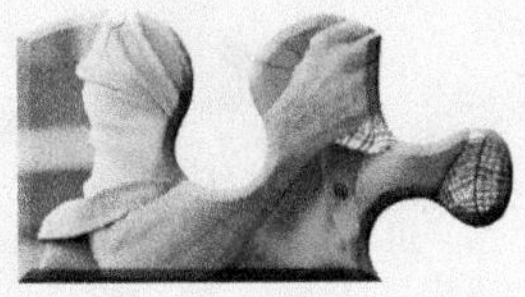

Why is this relevant?

Recognizing the distinctness of Gf and Gc can help to reduce stereotypes and expectations about intelligence in older persons, reminding people that although certain kinds of intelligence may decline with age, other types that rely on accumulated knowledge and wisdom may even increase as we get older (Kaufman, 2001). Also, research on fluid intelligence has helped psychologists to develop a much more detailed understanding of the full complement of cognitive processes that make up intelligence, and to devise tests that measure these components' processes more precisely.

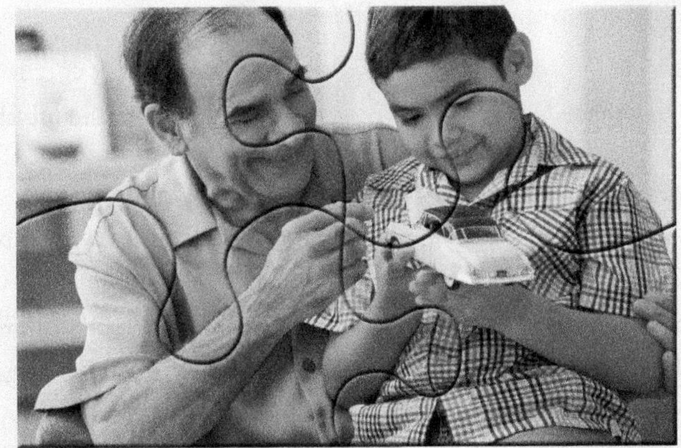

Jose Luis Pelaez/Glow Images

STERNBERG'S TRIARCHIC THEORY OF INTELLIGENCE Other influential models of intelligence have been proposed in attempts to move beyond *g*. For example, Robert Sternberg (1983, 1988) developed the **triarchic theory of intelligence**, *a theory that divides intelligence into three distinct types: analytical, practical, and creative* (see Figure 9.11). These components can be described in the following ways:

- *Analytical intelligence* is "book smarts." It's the ability to reason logically through a problem and to find solutions. It also reflects the kinds of abilities that are largely tested on standard intelligence tests that measure *g*. Most intelligence tests predominantly measure analytical intelligence, while generally ignoring the other types.
- *Practical intelligence* is "street smarts." It's the ability to find solutions to real-world problems that are encountered in daily life, especially those that involve other people. Practical intelligence is what helps people adjust to new environments, learn how to get things done, and accomplish their goals. Practical intelligence is believed to have a great deal to do with one's job performance and success.
- *Creative intelligence* is the ability to create new ideas and generate novel solutions to problems. Obviously, artists must have some level of creative intelligence, because they are, by definition, trying to create things that are new. It also takes creative intelligence to be a scientist because creative thinking is often required to conceive of good scientific hypotheses and develop ways of testing them (Sternberg et al., 2001).

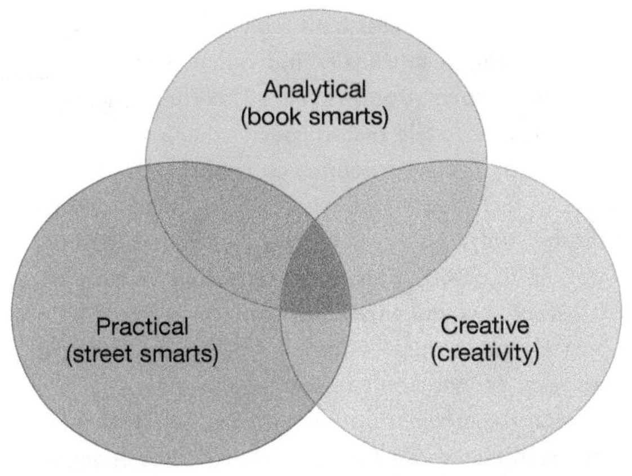

{FIG. 9.11} **The Triarchic Theory of Intelligence** According to psychologist Robert Sternberg, intelligence comprises three overlapping yet distinct components. **Click on this figure in your eText to see more details.**

Sternberg believed that both practical and creative intelligences predict real-world outcomes, such as job success, better than analytical intelligence (Sternberg et al., 1995). However, other psychologists have questioned whether Sternberg's theory adequately captures separate intelligences, or whether they are merely aspects of *g*. In particular, practical intelligence may be part of *g* (Gottfredson, 2003; Jensen, 1993), and creativity may not be an "intelligence" per se, but a tendency to think in ways that challenge norms and conventions. Furthermore, psychologists have criticized Sternberg's studies of job performance, arguing that the test items that were supposed to measure practical intelligence were merely measuring job-related knowledge (Schmidt & Hunter, 1993).

GARDNER'S THEORY OF MULTIPLE INTELLIGENCES Howard Gardner proposed an even more elaborate theory of multiple intelligences than Sternberg. Gardner was inspired by specific cases, such as people who were savants (discussed in the introduction to this module), who had extraordinary abilities in limited domains, very poor abilities in many others, and low *g*. Gardner also was informed by cases of people with brain damage, which showed that some specific abilities

Explore Sternberg's Triarchic Theory of Intelligence

Explore Creativity

Simulate Survey: What Is Creativity?

Watch Practical Intelligence: Robert Sternberg

Watch Intelligence: Robert Sternberg

Watch Successful Intelligence: Robert Sternberg

Simulate Gardner's Theory of Intelligence

Table 9.1 :: Gardner's Proposed Forms of Intelligence

Verbal/linguistic intelligence	The ability to read, write, and speak effectively
Logical/mathematical intelligence	The ability to think with numbers and use abstract thought; the ability to use logic or mathematical operations to solve problems
Visuospatial intelligence	The ability to create mental pictures, manipulate them in the imagination, and use them to solve problems
Bodily/kinesthetic intelligence	The ability to control body movements, to balance, and to sense how one's body is situated
Musical/rhythmical intelligence	The ability to produce and comprehend tonal and rhythmic patterns
Interpersonal intelligence	The ability to detect another person's emotional states, motives, and thoughts
Self/intrapersonal intelligence	Self-awareness; the ability to accurately judge one's own abilities, and identify one's own emotions and motives
Naturalist intelligence	The ability to recognize and identify processes in the natural world—plants, animals, and so on
Existential intelligence	The tendency and ability to ask questions about purpose in life and the meaning of human existence

would be dramatically affected but others would remain intact (Gardner, 1983, 1999). He also noted that "normal people" (presumably, those of us who are not savants and also don't have brain damage) differ widely in their abilities and talents, having a knack for some things but being hopeless at others. Gardner argued that if intelligence were a single ability, like *g*, then people would show greater consistency in their abilities.

Explore Gardner's Multiple Intelligences

Based on his observations, Gardner proposed a theory of **multiple intelligences**, *a model claiming that there are eight (now updated to at least nine) different forms of intelligence, each independent from the others* (see Table 9.1). As intuitively appealing as this is, critics have pointed out that few of Gardner's intelligences can be accurately and reliably measured, making his theory unfalsifiable and difficult to research. One of the key challenges to overcome in order to measure Gardner's different intelligences is that so many measurement techniques (e.g., self-report scales) may not be able to capture a person's intelligence in certain domains. As an analogy, you would not try to measure people's running speed by asking them questions on a paper and pencil test; you have to get them to run and see how fast they are. Similarly, you can't really measure an ability like "interpersonal intelligence" using paper and pencil scales, because then you are measuring people's verbal/linguistic intelligence, or perhaps their *beliefs* about their interpersonal abilities, but you are not getting a direct window into how well they can *actually* interact competently with other people. Developing proper measures to test Gardner's theory is therefore not a criticism against his theory as much as it is a challenge to researchers to develop better ways of measuring intelligence (Tirri & Nokelainen, 2008).

Thus far, these measurement challenges have not been adequately met, and there is therefore relatively little data supporting the existence and independence of Gardner's intelligences. Nevertheless, Gardner's model has been widely adopted in society, particularly in educational settings, where it has been quite influential. Educators often argue that if children have different intelligences, then you can teach children more effectively if you present information that appeals to the types of intelligence that are most dominant for them, or in other words, their *learning style*. Thus, teachers should be able to teach more effectively if they appeal to different intelligences, such as using visual displays for their "visual learners," the spoken word for their "auditory learners," and exercises that encourage kids to move around and use their hands for their "kinesthetic/tactile learners." But does this make a difference?

MYTHS IN MIND

Learning Styles

The proposal that humans have individual learning styles can be easily tested scientifically: Individuals should learn and retain more information presented to them through their preferred learning style than through other styles.

However, finding evidence to support this has proven difficult. In fact, dozens of studies have failed to show any benefit for studying according to an individual's learning style (Pasher et al., 2008). This result probably occurs because regardless of how you encounter something—reading, watching, listening, or moving—whether you retain it over the long term largely depends on whether you process and store the *meaning* of the information (Willingham, 2004). As a result, it makes much less sense for teachers to tailor their instructional styles to fit individual students than it does for teachers to teach in ways that help their students deeply process material rather than merely committing it to memory without much understanding.

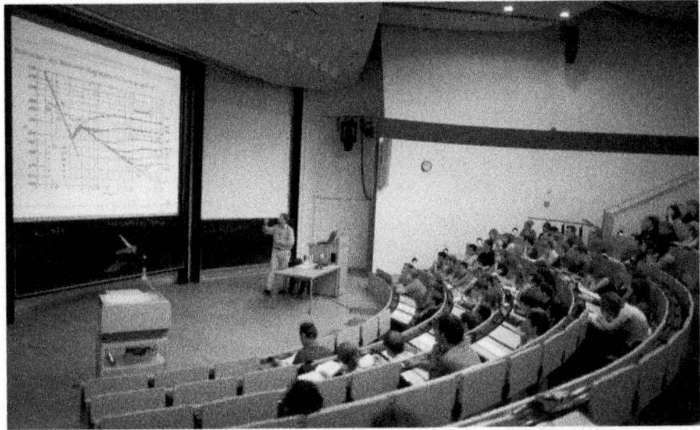

Photothek/Andia/Alamy

Are there actually "learning styles"? Educators have long argued that individual students learn better if instruction practices are adapted to suit their style of learning, but evidence supporting the existence of different learning styles is virtually nonexistent.

The concept of multiple intelligences can also be extended to domains that we don't typically associate with intelligence. Is an amazing actor showing a special form of intelligence? What about *hockey sense,* that skill to know where you should be on the ice in different situations? Clearly hockey sense (or soccer sense, etc.) involves intelligence in some way, as it requires a person to interpret rapidly changing patterns (player locations) and decide upon an optimal course of action. The challenge for sports teams—who would have to pay millions of dollars to draft picks in sports like hockey and football—is to find some test that could predict a player's ability to play a sport in an intelligent way. However, the attempts to link sports intelligence with more traditional measures of intelligence have proven quite elusive.

PSYCH @

The NFL Draft

Every spring, American football fans turn their attention to "the draft," during which professional teams in the National Football League (NFL) take turns selecting the best amateur football players to join their teams. Pride, potential championships, and a lot of money are at stake, so teams use all the information they can get to select the players whom they think will contribute the most to the team's success. As a part of the run-up to the draft, the candidates demonstrate their physical aptitude through tests focusing on speed, strength, coordination, and agility by running, lifting, jumping, and clearing obstacles.

But what about the cognitive aspects of the game? Football is a highly complex game, filled with strategy and counter-strategy. Players must memorize their responsibilities for each possible play, keeping in mind the rules for legal tackling and blocks in the midst of the action, and be able to update their play "on the fly" as optimal strategies change moment to moment depending on how the play unfolds. To assess their intelligence, for the past three decades, candidates participating in the NFL draft have completed the Wonderlic Personnel Test, a 50-question test that is completed in less than 12 minutes.

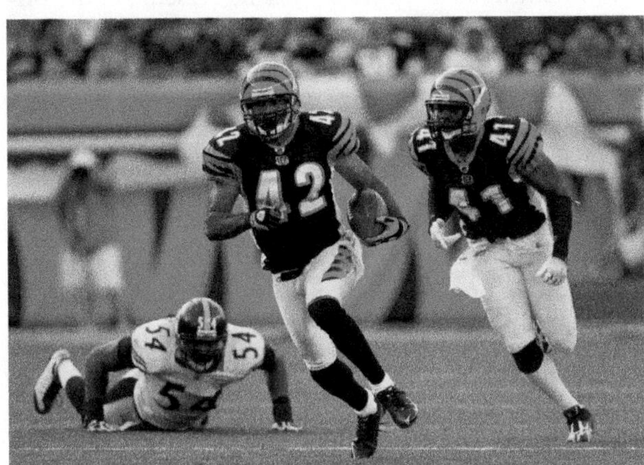

AP Photo/Ed Reinke

The Wonderlic is supposed to predict success in professional football, although it is not always very successful. This failure could be because of low validity.

Wonderlic scores have been shown to predict performance in a wide variety of jobs, regardless of the specific job, the tasks an employee has to perform, or the job's complexity (Schmidt & Hunter, 1998; Schmidt et al., 1981). But will they be a good predictor in the NFL, a setting that predominantly requires high levels of strength and athletic ability? The NFL certainly believes so, as the Wonderlic has been used to guide draft choice picks since the 1970s. This is an important question, considering the millions of dollars it costs teams to sign their players, particularly their first- and second-round draft picks. If the Wonderlic works, it should be the most helpful tool for picking players for the more complex and cognitively challenging positions, such as quarterback, relative to positions that rely more on athleticism, such as running back.

However, after studying 762 players from the 2002, 2003, and 2004 drafts and measuring their performance on the field in multiple ways, researchers concluded that there was no significant correlation between Wonderlic scores and performance. Contrary to the NFL's widely adopted practice, intelligence (as measured by Wonderlic scores) and football prowess seem to have nothing to do with each other. What's more, the performance of only two football positions, tight end and defensive back, showed any significant correlation with Wonderlic scores, and it was in a negative direction (Lyons et al., 2009). That means that *lower* intelligence scores predict greater football success for these positions.

It seems that NFL teams would be well advised to throw out the Wonderlic test entirely, or perhaps only use it to screen for defensive backs and tight ends, and choose the less intelligent players. No offence is intended whatsoever to football players, who may be extremely intelligent individuals, but in general, being highly intelligent does not seem to be an advantage in professional football. In the now immortalized words of former Washington Redskins quarterback Joe Thiesmann, "Nobody in the game of football should be called a genius. A genius is somebody like Norman Einstein."

Quick Quiz 9.2b

Intelligence as Multiple, Specific Abilities

KNOW ...

1 Which of the following is *not* part of the triarchic theory of intelligence?

- **A** Practical
- **B** Analytical
- **C** Kinesthetic
- **D** Creative

2 ________ proposed that there are eight different forms of intelligence, each independent from the others.

- **A** Robert Sternberg
- **B** Howard Gardner
- **C** L. L. Thurstone
- **D** Raymond Cattell

3 The ability to adapt to new situations and solve new problems reflects ________ intelligence(s), whereas the ability to draw on one's experiences and knowledge reflects ________ intelligence(s).

- **A** fluid; crystallized
- **B** crystallized; fluid
- **C** general; multiple
- **D** multiple; general

ANALYZE ...

4 The hierarchical model of intelligence describes that

- **A** some types of intelligence are more powerful and desirable than others.
- **B** intelligence is broken down into two factors, a higher-level factor called g, and a lower-level factor called s.
- **C** scores on intelligence tests are affected by different levels of factors, ranging from lower-level factors such as physical health, to higher-level factors such as a person's motivation for doing well on the test.
- **D** intelligence is comprised of three levels of factors, which are roughly similar to Spearman's g, Thurstone's primary mental abilities, and Spearman's s.

5 Which of the following statements is an argument for multiple intelligences?

- **A** Statistical analyses show that all varieties of intelligence tests are highly correlated with one another.
- **B** Most individuals who score high on verbal tests also score high on quantitative and performance tests.
- **C** Some individuals score high on verbal tests but very low on quantitative tests, and vice versa.
- **D** Some people would rather listen to a lecture than view a film because they are "auditory" learners.

Answers can be found on page ANS-3.

The Battle of the Sexes

The distinction between *g* and multiple intelligences plays an important role in the oft-asked question of whether males are smarter than females or vice versa. Although earlier studies showed some average intelligence differences between males and females, this has not been upheld by subsequent research and is likely the result of bias in the tests that favoured males over females. One of the most conclusive studies was conducted in 2007, using 42 different tests of mental abilities to compare males and females. They found almost no differences in intelligence between the sexes (Johnson & Bouchard, 2007).

Some research has found that although males and females have the same average IQ score, there is much greater variability in male scores, which suggests that there are more men with substantial intellectual challenges, as well as more men who are at the top of the brainpower heap (Deary et al., 2007; Dykiert et al., 2009). However, this may not be as simple as it appears. For example, one type of test that shows this male advantage at the upper levels of ability examines math skills on standardized tests. A few decades ago, about twelve times more males than females scored at the very top (Benbow & Stanley, 1983). This difference has decreased in recent years to 3–4 times as many males scoring at the top end of the spectrum. Not surprisingly, this change has occurred just as the number of math courses being taken by females—and the efforts made to increase female enrollment in such courses—has increased. So, the difference in results between the sexes is still there, but it's been vastly reduced by making math education more accessible and acceptable for females (Wai et al., 2010).

The apparent advantage enjoyed by males may be the result of an unintentional selection bias. More males than females drop out of secondary school; because these males would have lower IQs, on average, the result is that fewer low-IQ men attend university. Therefore, most of the samples of students used in psychology studies are skewed in that they under-represent men with low IQs. This biased sampling of males and females would make it seem like men have higher fluid intelligence, when in reality they may not (Flynn & Rossi-Casé, 2011).

So, who's smarter, males or females? Neither. The best data seems to show that they are basically equal in overall intelligence.

Top: Brand X Pictures/Thinkstock; bottom: Bob Daemmrich/PhotoEdit

Males and females are not equally distributed across all professions. Do these discrepancies arise because of inherent differences in cognitive abilities, or something else?

DO MALES AND FEMALES HAVE UNIQUE COGNITIVE SKILLS? Although the results discussed above suggest that males and females are equally intelligent, when multiple intelligences are considered, rather than overall IQ, a clear difference between the sexes does emerge. Females are, on average, better at verbal abilities, some memory tasks, and the ability to read people's basic emotions, whereas males have the advantage on visuospatial abilities, such as mentally rotating objects or aiming at objects (see Figure 9.12; Halpern & LaMay, 2000; Johnson & Bouchard, 2007; Tottenham et al., 2005; Weiss et al., 2003).

This finding is frequently offered as an explanation for why males are more represented in fields like engineering, science, and mathematics. However, there are many other factors that could explain the under-representation of women in these disciplines, such as prevalent stereotypes that discourage girls from entering the maths and sciences, parents from supporting them in doing so, and teachers from evaluating females' work without bias.

The under-representation of females in some disciplines may also be due to *stereotype threat,* when people become aware of stereotypes about their social group and become fearful of being reduced to that stereotype (see Module 9.1). So, if females are aware of the stereotype that "girls can't do math," the fear of living up to that stereotype may produce enough anxiety that it undermines their performance. As a result, they *do* underperform on that task compared to males, although not necessarily because of their mathematical abilities. Interestingly, a clever set of studies by Steve Spencer at the University of Waterloo showed that if subjects are told that a math test has shown gender differences in the past, females will do worse than males; however, if they are told the test has shown no gender differences in the past, females perform equally as well as males (Spencer et al., 1999). Thus, any evidence for group differences in abilities needs to be carefully examined to see whether negative beliefs about the groups could be causing the differences that are found.

Overlooking the many other factors that limit females' participation in the maths and sciences is a dangerous thing to do. This was dramatically shown in 2005 when the President of Harvard University, Lawrence Summers, was removed from his position shortly after making a speech in which he argued that innate differences between the sexes may be responsible for under-representation of women in science and engineering. The outrage many expressed at his comments reflected the fact that many people realize that highlighting innate differences while minimizing or ignoring systemic factors only serves to perpetuate problems, not solve them.

Watch Gender Differences: Robert Sternberg

Watch Gender and Spatial Ability: Nora Newcombe

Simulate Mental Rotation

Can you find the match?
One of the three figures below matches the one on top. Males often perform tasks like this mental rotation problem faster than females.

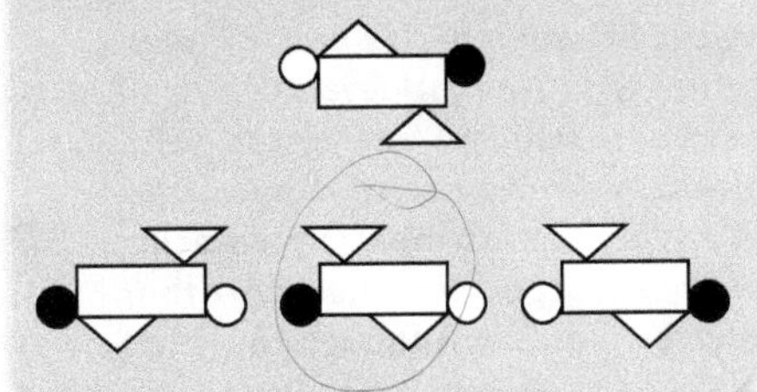

(a)

Conversely, women tend to outperform men on verbal fluency tasks like this one.

In 60 seconds, name as many words that start with the letter "G" that you can think of.

OR

In 60 seconds, name as many different kinds of animals you can think of.

(b)

{FIG. 9.12} **Mental Rotation and Verbal Fluency Tasks** Some research indicates that, on average, males outperform females on mental rotation tasks (a), while females outperform men on verbal fluency (b). **Click on this figure in your eText to see more details.**

Quick Quiz 9.2c The Battle of the Sexes

KNOW ...

1 Men tend to outperform women on tasks requiring ________, whereas women outperform men on tasks requiring ________.

A spatial abilities; the ability to read people's emotions

B practical intelligence; interpersonal intelligence

C memory; creativity

D logic; intuition

ANALYZE ...

2 Research on gender differences in intelligence leads to the general conclusion that

A males are more intelligent than females.

B females are more intelligent than males.

C males and females are equal in overall intelligence.

D it has been impossible to tell which gender is more intelligent thus far, because stereotype threat makes men underperform on some questions and women underperform on others.

Answers can be found on page ANS-3.

Module Summary

Module 9.2

Now that you have read this module you should

KNOW ...

- ***The key terminology related to understanding intelligence:***

crystallized intelligence (Gc) (p. 369)
factor analysis (p. 365)
fluid intelligence (Gf) (p. 369)
general intelligence factor (g) (p. 365)
multiple intelligences (p. 372)
savant (p. 364)
triarchic theory of intelligence (p. 371)

UNDERSTAND ...

- ***Why intelligence is divided into fluid and crystallized types.*** Mental abilities encompass both the amount of knowledge accumulated and the ability to solve new problems. This understanding is consistent not only with our common views of intelligence, but also with the results of decades of intelligence testing. Also, the observation that fluid intelligence can decline over the life span, even as crystallized intelligence remains constant, lends further support to the contention that they are different abilities.
- ***Intelligence differences between males and females.*** Males and females generally show equal levels of overall intelligence, as measured by standard intelligence tests. However, men do outperform women on some tasks, particularly spatial tasks such as mentally rotating objects, whereas women outperform men on other tasks, such as perceiving emotions. Although there are some male-female differences in specific abilities, such as math, it is not yet clear whether these reflect innate differences between the sexes, or whether other factors are responsible, such as reduced enrollment of women in math classes and the presence of stereotype threat in testing sessions.

Lane V. Erickson/Shutterstock

APPLY ...

- ***Your knowledge to identify examples from the triarchic theory of intelligence.*** Recall from page 371 that this theory proposes the existence of analytical, practical, and creative forms of intelligence. Classify whether the individual in the following scenario is low, medium, or high in regard to each of the three aspects of intelligence.

Katrina is an excellent chemist. She has always performed well in school, so it is no surprise that she earned her PhD from a prestigious institution. Despite her many contributions and discoveries related to chemistry, however, she seems to fall short in some domains. For example, Katrina does not know how to cook her own meals and if anything breaks at her house, she has to rely on someone else to fix it.

Check your answers on page ANS-3.

ANALYZE ...

- ***Whether teachers should spend time tailoring lessons to each individual student's learning style.*** Certainly, no one would want to discourage teachers from being attentive to the unique characteristics that each student brings to the classroom. However, large-scale reviews of research suggest that there is little basis for individualized teaching based on learning styles (e.g., auditory, visual, kinesthetic).

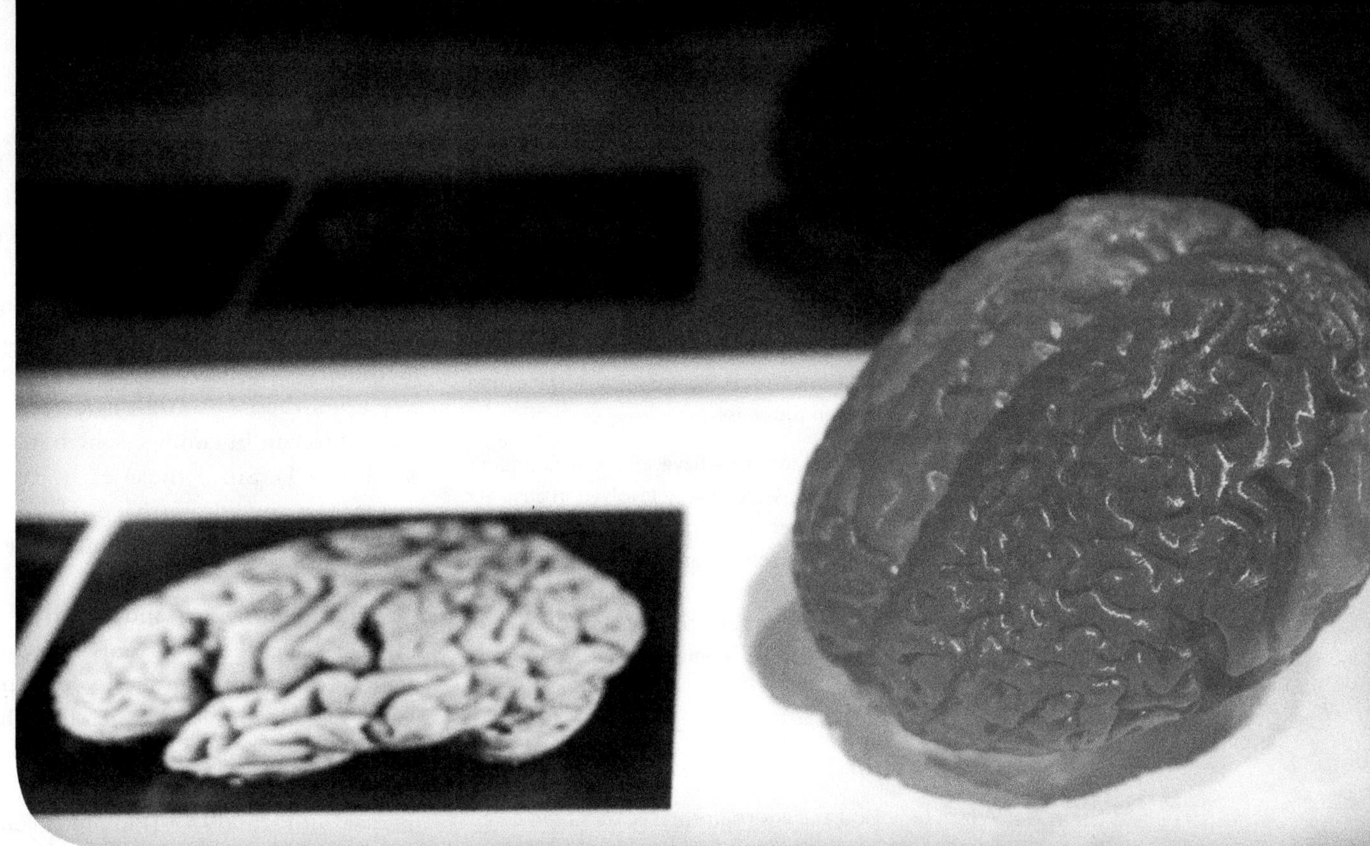

MIGUEL MEDINA/AFP/Getty Images/Newscom

Module 9.3

Biological, Environmental, and Behavioural Influences on Intelligence

Learning Objectives

After reading this module you should

KNOW ...	UNDERSTAND ...	APPLY ...	ANALYZE ...
The key terminology related to heredity, environment, and intelligence	Different approaches to studying the genetic basis of intelligence	Your knowledge of environmental and behavioural effects on intelligence to understand how to enhance your own cognitive abilities	Claims that infant intelligence is increased by viewing educational television programming

In 1955, the world lost one of the most brilliant scientists in history, Albert Einstein. Although you are probably familiar with his greatest scientific achievements, you may not know about what happened to him after he died—or more specifically, what happened to his brain.

Upon his death, a forward-thinking pathologist, Dr. Thomas Harvey, removed Einstein's brain (his body was later cremated) so that it could be studied in the hope that medical scientists would eventually unlock the secret to his genius. Dr. Harvey took photographs of Einstein's brain, and then it was sliced up into hundreds of tissue samples placed on microscope slides, and 240 larger blocks of brain matter, which were preserved in fluid. Surprisingly, Dr. Harvey concluded that the brain wasn't at all remarkable, except for being smaller than average (1230 grams, compared to the average of 1300–1400 grams).

You might expect that Einstein's brain was intensively studied by leading neurologists. But, instead, the brain mysteriously disappeared. Twenty-two years later, a journalist named Steven Levy tried to find Einstein's brain. The search was fruitless until Levy tracked down Dr. Harvey in Wichita, Kansas, and interviewed him in his office. Dr. Harvey was initially reluctant to tell Levy anything about the brain, but eventually admitted that he still had it. In fact, he kept it right there in his office! Sheepishly, Dr. Harvey opened a box labelled "Costa Cider" and there, inside two large jars, floated the chunks of Einstein's brain. Levy later wrote, "My eyes were fixed upon that jar as I tried to comprehend that these pieces of gunk bobbing up and down had caused a revolution in physics and quite possibly changed the course of civilization. Swirling in formaldehyde was the power of the smashed atom, the mystery of the universe's black holes, the utter miracle of human achievement."

Since that time, several research teams have discovered important abnormalities in Einstein's brain. Einstein had a higher than normal ratio of glial cells to neurons in the left parietal lobe (Diamond et al., 1985) and parts of the temporal lobes (Kigar et al., 1997), and a higher density of neurons in the right frontal lobe (Anderson & Harvey, 1996). Einstein's parietal lobe has been shown to be about 15% larger than average, and to contain an extra fold (Witelson et al., 1999). The frontal lobes contain extra convolutions (folds and creases) as well. These extra folds increase the surface area and neural connectivity in those areas.

Explore Factors Affecting Intelligence

Explore Correlations between IQ Scores of Persons of Varying Relationships

How might these unique features have affected Einstein's intelligence? The frontal lobes are heavily involved in abstract thought, and the parietal lobes are involved in spatial processing, which plays a substantial role in mathematics. Thus, these unique brain features may provide a key part of the neuroanatomical explanation for Einstein's remarkable abilities in math and physics. Einstein not only had a unique mind, but a unique brain.

Focus Questions

1. Which biological and environmental factors have been found to be important contributors to intelligence?
2. Is it possible for people to enhance their own intelligence?

Wouldn't it be wonderful to be as smart as Einstein? Or even just smarter than you already are? Imagine if you could boost your IQ, upgrading your brain like you might upgrade a hard drive. You could learn more easily, think more quickly, remember more. What benefits might you enjoy? Greater success? A cure for cancer? A Nobel Prize? Or at least you might not have to study as much to get good grades. As you will read in this module, there are in fact ways to improve your intelligence (although perhaps not to "Einsteinian" levels). However, to understand how these techniques can benefit us, we must also understand how our biology and our environment—"nature" and "nurture"—interact to influence intelligence.

Biological Influences on Intelligence

The story of Einstein's brain shows us, once again, that our behaviours and abilities are linked to our biology. However, although scientists have been interested in these topics for over 100 years, we are only beginning to understand the complex processes that influence measures like IQ scores. In this section, we discuss the genetic and neural factors that influence intelligence, and how they may interact with our environment.

THE GENETICS OF INTELLIGENCE: TWIN AND ADOPTION STUDIES The first step to understanding the genetic contributions to high intelligence is to determine the extent to which intelligence is, in fact, related to our genes. The belief that intelligence is a capacity that we are born with has been widely held since the early studies of intelligence. However, because early researchers lacked today's sophisticated methods for studying genetic influences, they had to rely upon their observations of whether intelligence seemed to run in families, which it seemed to do (see Module 9.1). Since those early days of intelligence research, many studies have been conducted to see just how large the genetic influence on intelligence may be.

Studies of twins and children who have been adopted have been key tools allowing researchers to begin estimating the genetic contribution to intelligence. Decades of such research have shown that genetic similarity does contribute to intelligence test scores. Several important findings from this line of work are summarized in Figure 9.13 (Plomin & Spinath, 2004). The most obvious trend in the figure shows that as the degree of genetic relatedness increases, similarity in IQ scores also increases. The last two bars on the right of Figure 9.13 present perhaps the strongest evidence for a genetic basis for intelligence. The intelligence scores of identical twins correlate with each other at about .85 when they are raised in the same home, which is much higher than the correlation for fraternal twins. Even when identical twins are adopted and raised apart, their intelligence scores are still correlated at approximately .80—a very strong relationship. In fact, this is about the same correlation that researchers find when individuals take the same intelligence test twice and are compared with themselves!

THE HERITABILITY OF INTELLIGENCE Overall, the heritability of intelligence is estimated to be between 40% and 80% (Nisbett et al., 2012). However, interpreting what this means is extremely tricky. People often think that this means that 40% or more of a person's intelligence is determined by genes. But this is a serious misunderstanding of heritability.

A heritability estimate describes how much of the differences *between people in a sample* can be accounted for by differences in their genes (see Module 3.1). This may not sound like an important distinction, but in fact it's extremely important! It means that a heritability estimate is not a single, fixed number; instead, it is a number that *depends on the sample of people being studied.* Heritability estimates for different samples can be very different. For example, the heritability of intelligence for

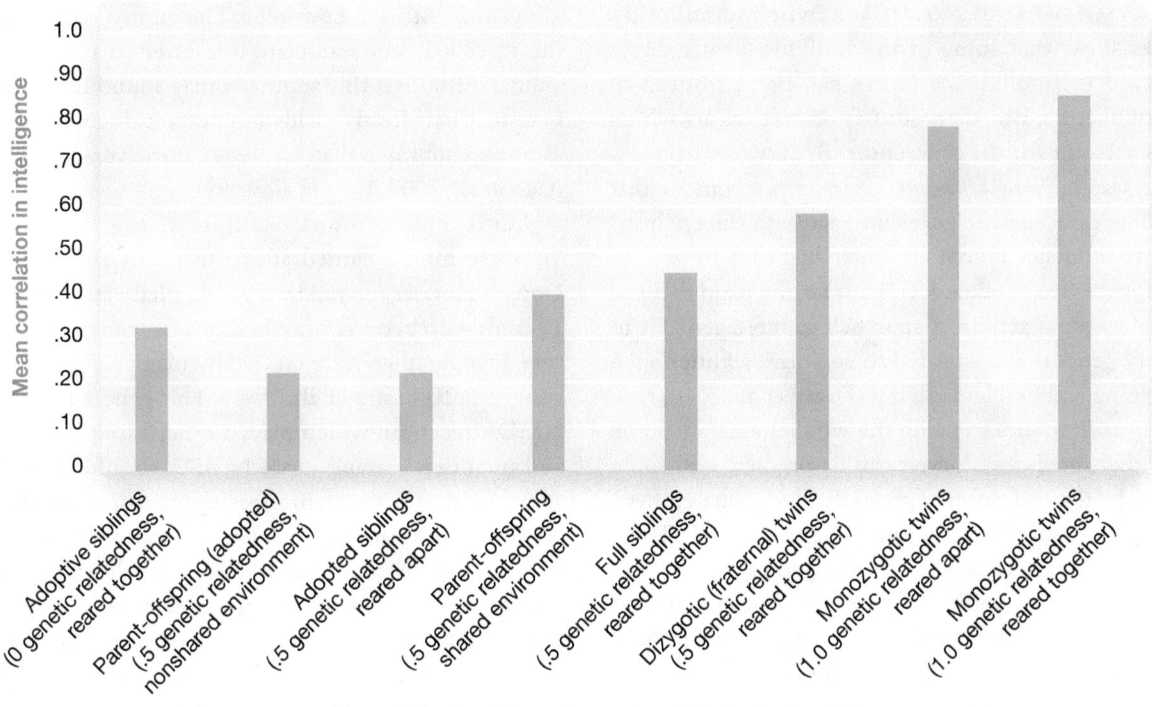

{FIG. 9.13} **Intelligence and Genetic Relatedness** Several types of comparisons reveal genetic contributions to intelligence (Plomin & Spinath, 2004). Generally, the closer the biological relationship between people, the more similar their intelligence scores. **Click on this figure in your eText to see more details.**

wealthy people has been estimated to be about 72%, but for people living in poverty, it's only 10% (Turkheimer et al., 2003).

Why might this be? Heritability estimates depend on other factors, such as how different or similar people's environments are. If people in a sample inhabit highly similar environments, the heritability estimate will be higher, whereas if they inhabit highly diverse environments, the heritability estimate will be lower. Because most wealthy people have access to good nutrition, good schools, plenty of enrichment opportunities, and strong parental support for education, these factors contribute fairly equally to the intelligence of wealthy people; thus, differences in their intelligence scores are largely genetic. But the environments inhabited by people living in poverty differ widely. Some may receive good schooling and others very little. Some may receive proper nutrition (e.g., poor farming families that grow their own food), whereas others may be chronically malnourished (e.g., children in poor inner-city neighbourhoods). For poorer families, these differences in the environment would have a huge impact on intelligence (as we discuss later in this module) leading to lower heritability estimates.

There are many other problems with interpreting heritability estimates as indications that genes *cause* differences in intelligence. Two of the most important both have to do with an under-appreciation for how genes interact with the environment. First, as discussed in Module 3.1, genes do not operate in isolation from the environment. The "nature vs. nurture" debate is no longer about whether it is nature OR nurture that contributes to development. Instead, we understand that "nurture shapes nature"; that is, environmental factors determine how genes express themselves and influence the organism.

Second, genes that influence intelligence may do so indirectly, operating through other factors. For example, imagine genes that promote novelty-seeking. People with these genes would be more likely to expose themselves to new ideas and new ways of doing things. This tendency to explore, rooted in their genes, may lead them to become more intelligent. However, in more dangerous environments, these novelty-seeking genes could expose the person to more danger, rather than to learning opportunities. In these contexts, genes that promote stability-seeking could be more adaptive, leading the stability-seeker to live longer and be better integrated into the community, thereby gaining knowledge and becoming more intelligent. In both cases, genes influence intelligence, but neither could be considered a "smart gene" because they have such different consequences in different environments.

BEHAVIOURAL GENOMICS Twin and adoption studies show that some of the individual differences observed in intelligence scores can be attributed to genetic factors. But these studies do not tell us which genes account for the differences. To answer that question, researchers use *behavioural genomics,* a technique that examines how specific genes interact with the environment to influence behaviours, including those related to intelligence (see Module 3.1). Thus far, the main focus of the behavioural genomics approach to intelligence is to identify genes that are related to cognitive abilities, such as learning and problem solving (Deary et al., 2010).

Overall, studies scanning the whole human genome show that intelligence levels can be predicted, to some degree, by the collection of genes that individuals inherit (Craig & Plomin, 2006; Plomin & Spinath, 2004). These collections of genes seem to pool together to influence general cognitive ability; although each contributes a small amount, these contributions add together to have a larger effect. However, although almost 300 individual genes have been found to have a large impact on various forms of mental retardation (Inlow & Restifo, 2004), very few genes have been found to explain normal variation in intelligence (Butcher et al., 2008). In one large study that scanned the entire genome of 7000 people, researchers found a mere six genetic markers that predicted cognitive ability. Taken together, these six markers only explained 1% of the variability in cognitive ability (Butcher et al., 2008).

One promising line of genetic research has been to conduct experiments by manipulating the genes of mice and seeing whether this affects their intelligence. **Gene knockout (KO) studies** *involve removing a specific gene and comparing the characteristics of animals with and without that gene.* In one of the first knockout studies of intelligence, researchers discovered that removing one particular gene disrupted the ability of mice to learn spatial layouts (Silva et al., 1992). Since this investigation was completed, numerous studies using gene knockout methods have shown that specific genes are related to performance on tasks that have been adapted to study learning and cognitive abilities in animals (Robinson et al., 2011).

Scientists can also take the opposite approach; instead of knocking genes out, they can insert genetic material into mouse chromosomes to study the changes associated with the new gene. The animal that receives this so-called gene transplant is referred to as a *transgenic* animal. Although this approach may sound like science fiction, it has already yielded important discoveries, such as transgenic mice that are better than average learners (Cao et al., 2007; Tang et al., 1999).

One now-famous example is the creation of "Doogie mice," named after the 1990s TV character Doogie Howser (played by a young Neil Patrick Harris), a genius who became a medical doctor while still a teenager. Doogie mice were created by manipulating a single gene, NR2B (Tang et al., 1999). This gene encodes the NMDA receptor, which plays a crucial role in learning and memory. Having more NMDA should, therefore, allow organisms to retain more information (and possibly to access it more quickly). Consistent with this view, Doogie mice with altered NR2B genes learned significantly faster and had better memories than did other mice. For example, when the Doogie mice and normal mice were put into a tank of water in which they had to find a hidden ramp in order to escape, the Doogie mice took half as many trials to remember how to get out of the tank.

The different types of studies reviewed in this section show us that genes do have some effect on intelligence. What they don't really show us is *how* these effects occur. What causes individual differences in intelligence? One theory suggests that these differences are due to differences in the size of the brain.

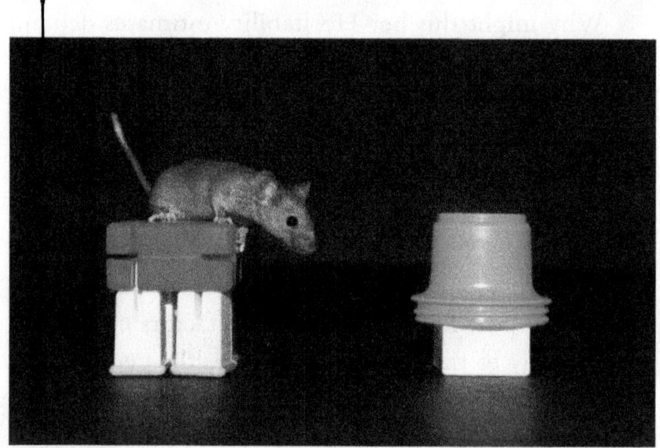

AP Photo/Princeton University

The Princeton University lab mouse, Doogie, is able to learn faster than other mice thanks to a bit of genetic engineering. Researchers inserted a gene known as NR2B that helps create new synapses and leads to quicker learning.

WORKING THE SCIENTIFIC LITERACY MODEL

Brain Size and Intelligence

Are bigger brains more intelligent? We often assume that to be the case—think of the cartoon characters that are super-geniuses; they almost always have gigantic heads. (Check out http://tvtropes.org/pmwiki/pmwiki.php/Main/MyBrainIsBig for an exhaustive list, in case you doubt this claim. . . .) Or think about what it means to call someone a "pea brain." Psychologists have not been immune to this belief either, and many studies have searched for a correlation between brain size and intelligence.

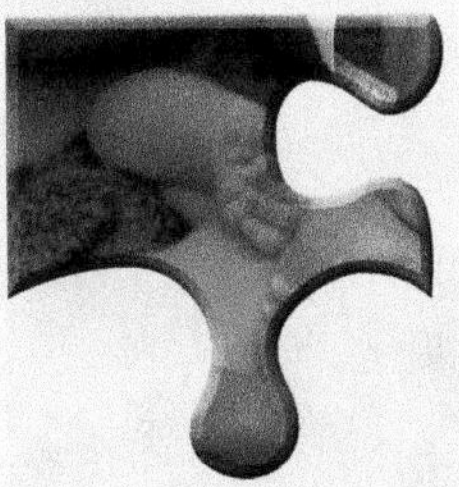

What do we know about brain size and intelligence?

Brain-based approaches to measuring intelligence rest on a common-sense assumption: Thinking occurs in the brain, so a larger brain should be related to greater intelligence. But does scientific evidence support this common-sense notion? In the days before modern brain imaging was possible, researchers typically obtained skulls from deceased subjects, filled them with fine-grained matter such metal pellets, and then transferred the pellets to a flask to measure the volume. These efforts taught us very little about intelligence and brain or skull size, but a lot about problems with measurement and racial prejudice. In some cases, the studies were highly flawed and inevitably led to conclusions that Caucasian males (including the Caucasian male scientists who conducted these experiments) had the largest brains and, therefore, were the smartest of the human race (Gould, 1981). Modern approaches to studying the brain and intelligence are far more sophisticated, thanks to newer techniques and a more enlightened knowledge of the brain's form and functions.

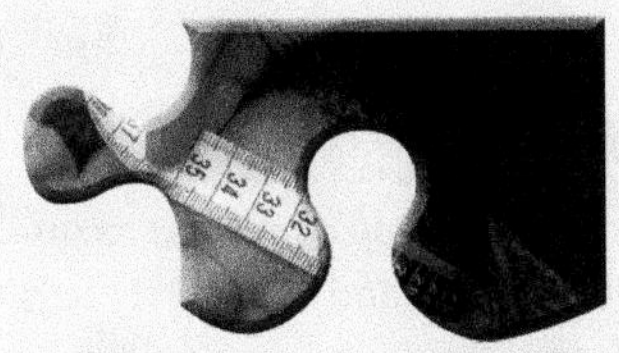

How can science explain the relationship between brain size and intelligence?

In relatively rare cases, researchers have two main sources of data available to them: a brain and an intelligence test score. In one modern and highly detailed study, Sandra Witelson at McMaster University and her colleagues (2006) collected 100 brains of deceased individuals who had previously completed the Wechsler Adult Intelligence Scale (WAIS). Detailed anatomical examinations and size measurements were made on the entire brains and certain regions that support cognitive skills. For women and right-handed men (but not left-handed men), 36% of the variation in verbal intelligence scores was accounted for by the size of the brain; however, brain size did not significantly account for the other component of intelligence that was measured, visuospatial abilities.

The size of the brain and its various regions is just one way of looking at intelligence. One of the most obvious features of the human brain is its convoluted surface. These convolutions (called gyri; pronounced "ji-rye") comprise the outer part of the cerebral cortex (see Figure 9.14). The number and size of these cerebral gyri is greater in species that have complex cognitive and social lives, such as elephants, dolphins, and primates (Marino, 2002; Rogers et al., 2010). But what about humans: Are individual differences in intelligence test scores related to convolutions of the cortex? Using brain imaging technology, researchers have scanned the brains of healthy adults who had completed the WAIS. The degree of convolution across the surface of the cortex was then correlated to the subjects' IQ score. It turns out that the higher the score on the WAIS, the more convolutions seen across several regions of the cortex; the degree of convolutions accounted for approximately 25% of the variability in WAIS scores (Luders et al., 2008).

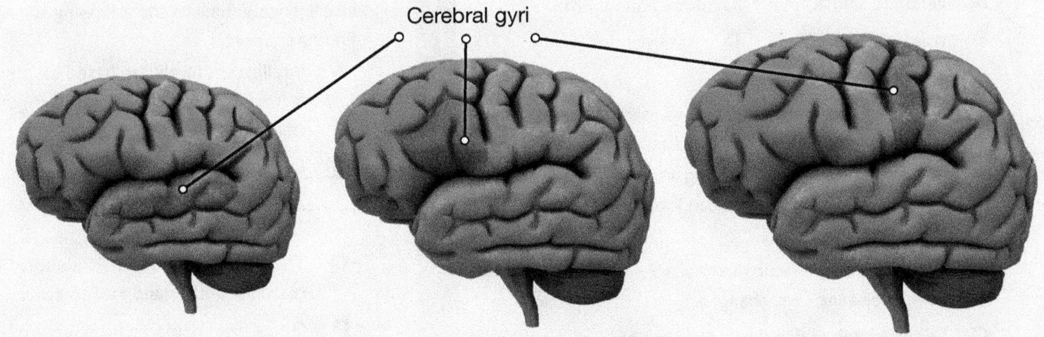

{FIG. 9.14} **Does Intelligence Increase with Brain Size?** While the size of the brain may have a modest relationship to intelligence, the convolutions or "gyri" along the surface of the cortex are another important factor: Increased convolutions are associated with higher intelligence test scores.

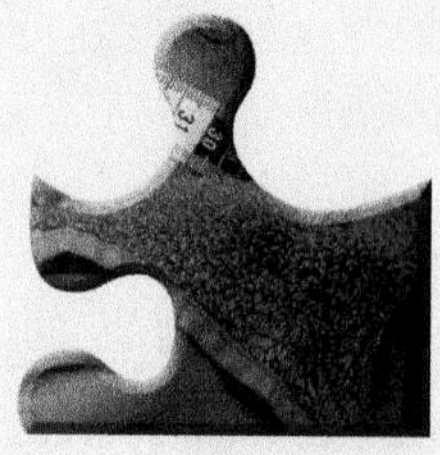

Can we critically evaluate this issue?

A common critique of studies examining brain size and IQ is that it is not always clear what processes or abilities are being tested. IQ scores could be measuring a number of things including working memory, processing speed, your ability to pay attention, or even your motivation to perform well on the test. Therefore, when studies show that brain size can account for 25% of the variability in IQ scores, it is not always clear what ability (or abilities) are underlying these results.

Similarly, there may be no causal connection whatsoever. It could be a *third-variable problem*; that is, brain size and performance on intelligence tests could both be related to other factors, such as the presence of toxins in a child's environment, stress, nutrition, physical health, or the amount of enriching stimulation experienced during childhood (Choi et al., 2008). These other factors might explain both brain size and intelligence. If so, then the brain-IQ relationship would be "spurious" (i.e., it would only be due to the common relationship both variables share with these other factors).

Furthermore, if brain size explains 25% of the variability in IQ scores, what about the other 75%? Clearly, there is more to intelligence than the mere biological fact of having a bigger or smaller brain. Size isn't everything . . .

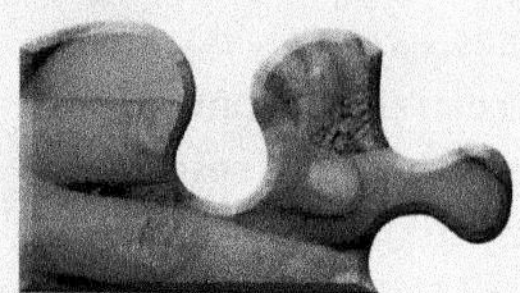

Why is this relevant?

This research furthers our understanding of the relationship between brain structure and function. This can help give us insight into many important phenomena, such as anorexia nervosa (a psychological disorder marked by self-starvation) or prolonged periods of alcohol abuse, both of which lead to the loss of brain volume along with cognitive abilities (e.g., McCormick et al., 2008; Schottenbauer et al., 2007). Measurements of brain volume have also played a key role in understanding the impaired neurological and cognitive development of children growing up in institutional settings (e.g., orphanages), as well as how these children benefit from adoption, foster care, or increased social contact (Sheridan et al., 2012). Better understanding of how experiences like anorexia, alcoholism, and child neglect affect brain development may provide ways of developing effective interventions that could help people who have suffered from such experiences.

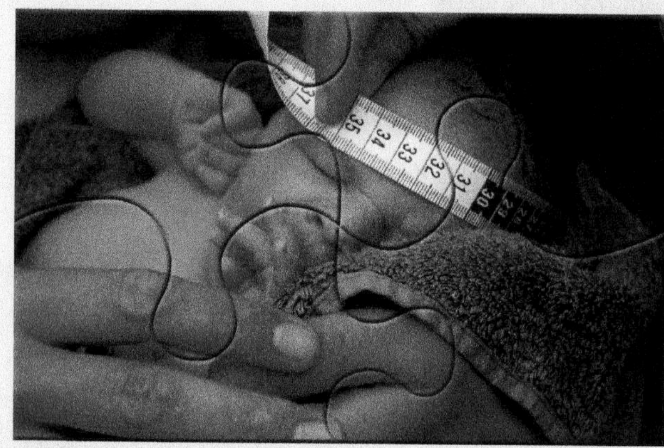

Janine Wiedel Photolibrary/Alamy

Quick Quiz 9.3a Biological Influences on Intelligence

KNOW . . .

1 When scientists insert genetic material into an animal's genome, the result is called a ________.

A genomic animal **C** knockout animal

B transgenic animal **D** fraternal twin

UNDERSTAND . . .

2 How do gene knockout studies help to identify the contribution of specific genes to intelligence?

A After removing or suppressing a portion of genetic material, scientists can look for changes in intelligence.

B After inserting genetic material, scientists can see how intelligence has changed.

C Scientists can rank animals in terms of intelligence, and then see how the most intelligent animals differ genetically from the least intelligent.

D They allow scientists to compare identical and fraternal twins.

ANALYZE . . .

3 Identical twins, whether reared together or apart, tend to score very similarly on standardized measures of intelligence. Which of the following statements does this finding support?

A Intelligence levels are based on environmental factors for both twins reared together and twins reared apart.

B Environmental factors are stronger influences on twins raised together compared to twins reared apart.

C The "intelligence gene" is identical in both twins reared together and reared apart.

D Genes are an important source of individual variations in intelligence test scores.

Answers can be found on page ANS-3.

Environmental Influences on Intelligence

As described earlier, research on the *biological* underpinnings of intelligence repeatedly emphasizes the importance of *environmental* factors. For example, environmental conditions determine which genes get expressed ("turned on") for a given individual; thus, without the right circumstances, genes can't appropriately affect the person's development. Also, brain areas involved in intelligence are responsive to a wide variety of environmental factors. The full story of how "nature" influences intelligence is intricately bound up with the story of how "nurture" influences intelligence.

Evidence describing the influence of environmental factors comes from many sources that include both animal and human studies. Controlled experiments with animals show that growing up in physically and socially stimulating environments results in faster learning and enhanced brain development compared to growing up in a dull environment (Hebb, 1947; Tashiro et al., 2007). For example, classic studies in the 1960s showed that rats who grew up in enriched environments (i.e., these rats enjoyed toys, ladders, and tunnels) ended up with bigger brains than rats who grew up in impoverished environments (i.e., simple wire cages). Not only were their cerebral cortices approximately 5% larger (Diamond et al., 1964; Rosenzweig et al., 1962), but their cortices contained 25% more synapses (Diamond et al., 1964). With more synapses, the brain can make more associations, potentially enhancing cognitive abilities such as learning and creativity. In this section, we review some of the major environmental factors that influence intelligence.

BIRTH ORDER One of the most hotly debated environmental factors affecting intelligence is simply whether you were the oldest child in your family, or whether you had older siblings. Debate about this issue has raged for many decades within psychology. However, a 2007 study of more than 240 000 people in Norway found that the IQs of first-born children are, on average, about three points higher than those of second-born children and four points higher than those of third-born children (Kristensen & Bjerkedal, 2007).

Carolyn A. McKeone/Photo Researchers, Inc.

Growing up in an enriched environment enhances brain development and functioning.

Why might this be? The most important factor, researchers believe, is that older siblings, like it or not, end up tutoring and mentoring younger siblings, imparting the wisdom they have gained through experience on to their younger siblings. Although this may help the younger sibling, the act of teaching their knowledge benefits the older sibling more (Zajonc, 1976). The act of teaching requires the older sibling to rehearse previously remembered information and to reorganize it in a way that their younger sibling will understand. Teaching therefore leads to a deeper processing of the information, which, in turn, increases the likelihood that it will be remembered later (see Module 7.2).

Before any first-born children reading this section start building monuments to their greatness, it is important to note that the differences between the IQs of first- and later-born siblings are quite small: three or four points. Indeed, many later-born kids have higher IQs than their first-born siblings. Nevertheless, this finding is one example of how environments can influence intelligence.

SOCIOECONOMIC STATUS Another key finding in the intelligence literature is that children growing up in wealthy homes have, on average, higher IQs than those growing up in poverty (Turkheimer et al., 2003). In general, wealthier people have access to greater resources and opportunities than the poor, leading to many environmental differences between the two populations. In fact, many of the environmental factors that affect intelligence and cognitive functioning are not evenly distributed between the rich and poor. For example, consider how much language kids are exposed to at home; one U.S. study estimated that by age three, children of professional parents will have heard 30 million words, children of working-class parents will have heard only 20 million words, and children of unemployed African-American mothers will have heard only 10 million words. Furthermore, the level of vocabulary is strikingly different for families in the different socioeconomic (SES) categories, with professional families using the most sophisticated language (Hart & Risley, 1995).

Other studies have shown that higher SES homes are much more enriching and supportive of children's intellectual development—high SES parents talk to their children more; have more books, magazines, and newspapers in the home; give them more access to computers; take

Left: Barry Lewis/Alamy; right: ONOKY-Photononstop/Alamy

Socioeconomic status is related to intelligence. People from low socioeconomic backgrounds typically have far fewer opportunities to access educational and other important resources that contribute to intellectual growth.

them to more learning experiences outside the home (e.g., visits to museums); and are less punitive toward the children (Bradley et al., 1993; Phillips et al., 1998).

Unfortunately, the effects of SES don't end here. Rather, SES interacts with a number of other factors that can influence intelligence including nutrition, stress, and education. The difference between rich and poor people's exposure to these factors almost certainly affects the IQ gap between the two groups.

NUTRITION It's a cliché we are all familiar with—"you are what you eat." Yet over the past century, the quality of the North American diet has plummeted as we have adopted diets that are highly processed, high in sugar and fat, low in fibre and nutrients, and laden with chemicals (e.g., preservatives, colour, flavour). There is some evidence suggesting that poor nutrition could have negative effects on intelligence. For example, research has shown that diets high in saturated fat quickly lead to sharp declines in cognitive functioning in both animal and human subjects. On the other hand, diets low in such fats and high in fruits, vegetables, fish, and whole grains are associated with higher cognitive functioning (Greenwood & Winocur, 2005; Parrott & Greenwood, 2007).

A massive longitudinal study on diet is currently underway in the United Kingdom. The Avon Longitudinal Study of Parents and Children is following the development of children born to 14 000 women in the early 1990s. This research has shown that a "poor" diet (high in fat, sugar, and processed foods) early in life leads to reliably lower IQ scores by age 8.5, whereas a "health-conscious" diet (emphasizing salads, rice, pastas, fish, and fruit) leads to higher IQs. Importantly, this was true even when researchers accounted for the effects of other variables, such as socioeconomic status (Northstone et al., 2012).

So what kinds of foods should we eat to maximize our brainpower? Although research on nutrition and intelligence is still relatively new, it would appear that eating foods low in saturated fats and rich in omega-3 fats, whole grains, and fruits and veggies are your smartest bets.

STRESS High levels of stress in economically poor populations is also a major factor helping to explain the rich-poor IQ gap. People living in poverty are exposed to high levels of stress through many converging factors, ranging from higher levels of environmental noise and toxins, to more family conflict and community violence, to less economic security and fewer employment opportunities. These and many other stresses increase the amounts of stress hormones such as cortisol in their bodies, which in turn is related to poorer cognitive functioning (Evans & Schamberg, 2009). High levels of stress also interfere with working memory (the ability to hold multiple pieces of information in memory at one time; Evans & Schamberg, 2009), and the self-control needed to persevere when faced with challenging tasks (Evans & Stecker, 2004), such as difficult questions on an IQ test. These self-control deficits interfere with learning in school (Blair & Razza, 2007; Ferrer & McArdle, 2004). The toxic effects of chronic stress show up in the brain as well, damaging the neural circuitry of the prefrontal cortex and hippocampus, which are critical for working memory and other cognitive abilities (e.g., controlling attention, cognitive flexibility) as well as for the consolidation and storage of long-term memories (McEwen, 2000). In short, too much stress makes us not only less healthy, but less intelligent.

EDUCATION One of the great hopes of modern society has been that universal education would level the playing field, allowing all children, rich and poor alike, access to the resources and skills necessary to achieve success. Certainly, attending school has been shown to have a large impact on IQ scores (Ceci, 1991). During

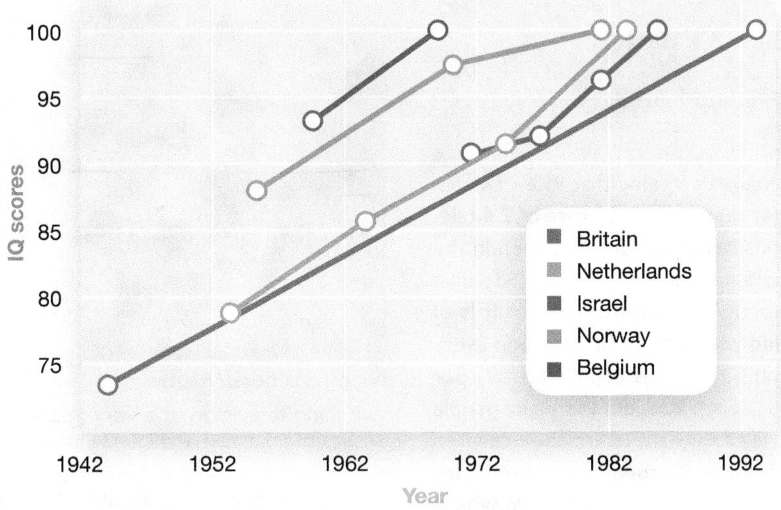

{FIG. 9.15} **The Flynn Effect** For decades, there has been a general trend toward increasing IQ scores. This trend, called the Flynn effect, has been occurring since standardized IQ tests have been administered.

school, children accumulate factual knowledge, learn basic language and math skills, and also learn skills related to scientific reasoning and problem solving. Children's IQ scores are significantly lower if they are not attending school (Ceci & Williams, 1997; Nisbett, 2009). In fact, for most children, IQ drops even over the months of summer holiday (Ceci, 1991; Jencks et al., 1972), although the wealthiest 20% actually show gains in IQ over the summer, presumably because they enjoy activities that are even more enriching than the kinds of experiences delivered in the classroom (Burkam et al., 2004; Cooper et al., 2000). However, although education has the potential to help erase the rich-poor gap in IQ, its effectiveness at doing so will depend on whether the rich and poor have equal access to the same quality of education and other support and resources that would allow them to make full use of educational opportunities.

Clearly, environmental factors such as nutrition, stress, and education all influence intelligence, which gives us some clues as to how society can contribute to improving the intelligence of the population. Interestingly, exactly such a trend has been widely observed across the last half-century or so; it appears that generation after generation, people are getting smarter!

THE FLYNN EFFECT: IS *EVERYONE* GETTING SMARTER? The **Flynn effect**, named after researcher James Flynn, *refers to the steady population level increases in intelligence test scores over time* (Figure 9.15). This effect has been found in numerous situations across a number of countries. For example, in the Dutch and French militaries, IQ scores of new recruits rose dramatically between the 1950s and 1980s—21 points for the Dutch and about 30 for the French (Flynn, 1987). From 1932 to 2007, Flynn estimates that, in general, IQ scores rise about one point every three years (Flynn, 2007).

The magnitude of the Flynn effect is striking. In the Dutch study noted above, today's group of 18-year-olds would score 35 points higher than 18-year-olds in 1950. The average person back then had an IQ of 100, but the average person today, taking the same test, would score 135, which is above the cutoff considered "gifted" in most gifted education programs! Or consider this the opposite way—if the average person today scored 100 on today's test, the average person in 1950 would score about 65, enough to qualify as mentally disabled.

How can we explain this increase? Nobody knows for sure, but one of the most likely explanations is that modern society requires certain types of intellectual skills, such as abstract thinking, scientific reasoning, classification, and logical analysis. These have been increasingly emphasized since the Industrial Revolution, and particularly since the information economy and advent of computers have restructured society over the past half-century or so. Each successive generation spends more time manipulating information with their minds, spending more time with visual media, in the form of television, video games, and now the Internet, as well as spending more time in school. It seems reasonable to propose that it is these shifts in information processing that have led to the increases in IQ scores (Nisbett et al., 2012).

This explanation of the Flynn effect suggests that spending time with various forms of media can be a kind of brain exercise, which can increase intelligence. This possibility has also been exploited by corporations seeking to market products to enhance brainpower, tapping into the almost universal wish of parents to have smart kids.

MYTHS IN MIND

Can the Media Make Babies Smarter?

A 2008 Statistics Canada Report revealed that 99% of Canadian households have a television, with an average of 2.4 televisions per home (Solutions Research Group, 2006). In the U.S., the average household has more TV sets (2.93) than people (2.5; Nielsen Research, 2010)! Almost two-thirds of children aged two years and younger watch television every day, and they average about 80 minutes of TV watching per day (Rideout & Hamel, 2006). Such statistics can make people feel self-conscious, wondering if they are letting their children down by planting them in front of the tube. Some parents try to reduce their guilt by insisting that most of the TV time is spent on educational programs. Surely that's better, right? It might even be beneficial! After all, aren't programs like *Sesame Street* and *Blue's Clues* specifically designed to facilitate learning? Indeed, research suggests that such programs produce cognitive benefits for children older than at least 24 months (Anderson et al., 2001; Wright et al., 2001).

Given that watching at least some educational programming has positive effects on pre-schoolers, parents widely believe that programming for infants must have similar benefits. Despite the American Academy of Pediatrics' recommendation that children younger than two years of age watch no television whatsoever (AAP, 1999), the majority of parents (68%) have ignored this (Certain & Kahn, 2002), feeling confident that videos targeting the very young can have a positive impact on their children's development (Rideout & Hamel, 2006; Robb et al., 2009). Companies, of course, rushed to create programs for infants that purported to be educational and beneficial. These became incredibly popular, particularly the Disney Corporation's *Baby Einstein* videos and related products; at its peak the *Baby Einstein* brand sold a staggering $200 million worth of products each year, a full 90% of the baby media market (Lewin, 2009).

So, do they work? The evidence is mixed. For example, highly publicized reports (Christakis et al., 2004; Zimmerman & Christakis, 2005; Zimmerman et al., 2007), concluded that infants and toddlers who view a great deal of television were more likely to have attention deficits, poorer language development, and lower achievement in school. On the other hand, other researchers have failed to replicate these findings, concluding that there is no relationship between the amount of television viewed in infancy and later attentional or cognitive outcomes (e.g., Foster & Watkins, 2010; Mistry et al., 2007; Schmidt et al., 2009). One major problem with the use of TV as a learning tool has been called the **video deficit**, which describes *how young children do not learn very much from information presented on screens* (Barr, 2010; Troseth, 2010), and certainly not as much as they learn from interacting directly with a person who teaches them (Barr & Hayne, 1999; Hayne et al., 2003). Furthermore, not only are very young kids not learning much from their TV time, they are being distracted from the activities that would be the most developmentally enriching—hands-on play; this is true even when the television is merely on in the background (Schmidt et al., 2008).

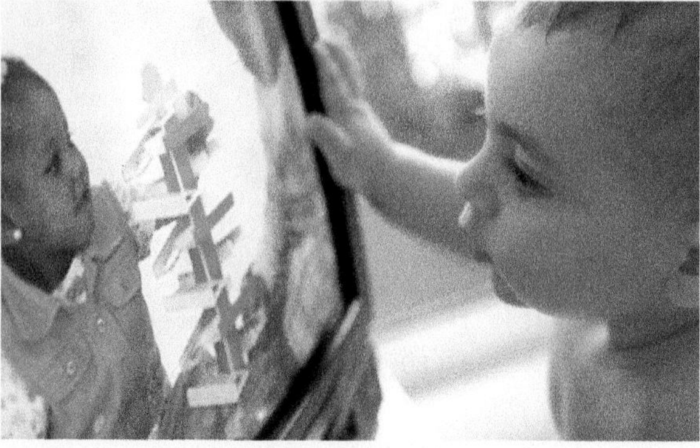

Niamh Baldock/Alamy

Watching television at a very young age may slow the processes of cognitive and intellectual development.

The bulk of evidence suggests that relying on the "electronic babysitter" for children is not a good idea, particularly if they are under three years of age. Interestingly, after a class action lawsuit was launched, the Walt Disney Company decided to refund the cost of *Baby Einstein* videos that people had bought, believing that they would boost their children's intelligence. Although the company claimed that this was merely part of their new "enhanced customer satisfaction guarantee," it does seem to imply that Disney did not have sufficient evidence of positive effects from those videos to justify their claims that the videos would improve children's intelligence.

Quick Quiz 9.3b

Environmental Influences on Intelligence

UNDERSTAND ...

1 What have controlled experiments with animals found in regard to the effects of the environment on intelligence?

- **A** Stimulating environments result in faster learning and enhanced brain development.
- **B** Deprived environments result in faster learning and enhanced brain development.
- **C** Stimulating environments result in slower learning and poorer brain development.
- **D** Deprived environments have no effect on learning and poorer brain development.

2 In which way have psychologists NOT studied the major environmental factors that, through their interaction with genes, influence intelligence?

- **A** By measuring stress hormones among poor and affluent children and correlating them with intelligence test scores
- **B** By depriving some children of education and comparing them to others who attended school
- **C** By measuring children's nutrition and then correlating it with intelligence scores
- **D** By correlating children's birth order in the family with intelligence scores

ANALYZE ...

3 Research on television viewing by children under the age of 2 shows that

A TV is especially detrimental to children aged 3 years or older.

B there is never any benefit from television, not even from educational programs.

C infants who watch educational shows are, on average, better learners when they reach school age.

D even educational programming shows no benefit, and can even slow some aspects of cognitive development.

Answers can be found on page ANS-3.

Behavioural Influences on Intelligence

If you want to make yourself more intelligent, we've covered a number of ways to do that—eat a brain-healthy diet, learn how to manage stress better, keep yourself educated (if not in formal schooling, then perhaps by continuing to be an active learner), and expose yourself to diverse and stimulating activities. But is there anything else you can do? For example, if you want bigger muscles, you can go to the gym and exercise. Can you do the same thing for the brain? Some fascinating recent research suggests that you can.

BRAIN TRAINING PROGRAMS The first technique is the use of "brain training" programs designed to improve working memory and other cognitive skills. Until recently, people generally believed this would not work, that although we can increase the amount of information we have in our heads, we can't change the actual functioning of the brain systems that make us intelligent.

However, in a ground-breaking line of research, a computer task (the "N-back" task) was used as an exercise program for working memory. In this task, people are presented with a stimulus, such as squares that light up on a grid, and are asked to press a key if the position on the grid is the same as the last trial. The task gets progressively more difficult, requiring participants to remember what happened two, three, or more trials ago (although it takes considerable practice for most people to be able to reliably remember what happened even three trials ago). Practising the N-back task was shown to not only improve performance at that task, but also to increase participants' IQ scores (specifically, their fluid intelligence; Jaeggi et al., 2008). This staggering finding showed that practising cognitive exercises could affect the cognitive abilities that underlie intelligence, and this seems to hold for a variety of populations, including children with attentional disorders (e.g., Klingberg et al., 2005) and people over 80 years of age (Buschkuehl et al., 2008). Furthermore, the benefits are not merely short term, but last for at least three months (Jaeggi et al., 2011).

NOOTROPIC DRUGS Another behaviour that many people believe improves their cognitive functioning is the use of certain drugs. **Nootropic substances** (meaning "affecting the mind") *are substances that are believed to beneficially affect intelligence*. Nootropics can work through many different mechanisms, from increasing overall arousal and alertness, to changing the availability of certain neurotransmitters, to stimulating nerve growth in the brain.

Certainly, these drugs can work for many people. For example, two drugs commonly used are methylphenidate (Ritalin) and modafinil (Provigil). Methylphenidate is a drug that inhibits the reuptake of norepinephrine and dopamine, thus leaving more of these neurotransmitters in the synapses between cells; although generally prescribed to help people with attentional disorders, Ritalin can also boost cognitive functioning in the general population (Elliott et al., 1997). Modafinil, originally developed to treat narcolepsy (a sleep disorder), is known to boost short-term memory and planning abilities by affecting the reuptake of dopamine (Turner et al., 2003).

Boosting the brain, however, does not come without risk. For example, the long-term effects of such drugs are poorly understood. There are also potential side effects, which may be severe; dependency issues, as people come to rely on such drugs and use them more regularly; and problems with providing unfair advantages to people willing to take such drugs, which puts pressure on others to take them as well in order to stay competitive (Sahakian & Morein-Zamir, 2007). Because of these risks, a September 2013 review in the *Canadian Medical Association Journal* recommended that doctors "should seriously consider refusing to prescribe medications for cognitive enhancement to healthy individuals" (Forlini et al., 2013, p. 1047).

These risks have to be weighed against the potential benefits of developing these drugs. For example, researchers in the United Kingdom have argued that if nootropic drugs could improve the cognitive functioning of Alzheimer's patients by even a small amount, such as a mere 1% change in the severity of the disease each year, this would be enough not only to dramatically improve the lives of people with Alzheimer's and their families, but to completely erase the predicted increases in long-term health care costs for the U.K.'s aging population (Sahakian & Morein-Zamir, 2007).

There are no easy answers when it comes to the nootropic drugs. But we would caution you—there are much safer ways to increase your performance than ingesting substances that will affect your brain in unknown ways.

MEDITATION Research on the cognitive benefits of meditation has exploded over the past decade or so. Numerous studies have linked mindfulness meditation with improvements in cognitive functioning. For example, going on a ten-day mindfulness retreat has been shown to improve working memory, which is very highly correlated with IQ (Chambers et al., 2008). Mindfulness practice also helps people to recover more quickly from negative emotions (Ortner et al., 2007); this may increase IQ test scores indirectly, by helping people keep stress or other negative feelings from interfering with their ability to concentrate on the test.

Meditation may not only help people in the short term, but may produce long-term benefits as well. For example, mindfulness meditation increases the thickness and density of the white-matter pathways connecting the anterior cingulate gyrus to a number of other brain regions. These networks play key roles in helping people to control their attention and emotional reactions, both of which could improve intelligence (Tang et al., 2010). Other forms of meditation have been shown to slow down the rate of cognitive decline and the loss of grey matter in the brain normally associated with aging (Pagnoni & Cekic, 2007). Meditation also increases the thickness of parts of the brain, especially the prefrontal cortex, that are in turn associated with performance on intelligence tests (Lazar et al., 2005).

With all of these cognitive and brain benefits, it should be no surprise that meditation can increase IQ. But what may surprise you is how little time it can take—one line of research showed that a mere five days of a mindfulness-based program improved the ability to pay attention and increased IQ scores on Raven's Progressive Matrices (Tang, Y., et al., 2007). Furthermore, the longer and more regularly one practises meditation, the greater the benefits seem to be, both for cognitive abilities and for beneficial effects to brain structure (Jha et al., 2010; Pagnoni & Cekic, 2007).

In sum, although few people are blessed with brains as abnormally intelligent as Einstein's, there are practical things anyone can do to maximize their potential brainpower. From eating better to providing our brains with challenging exercises, we can use the science of intelligence to make the most out of our genetic inheritance.

Quick Quiz 9.3c Behavioural Influences on Intelligence

KNOW ...

1 A commonly used nootropic drug is ________.

- **A** Tylenol®
- **B** Ecstasy
- **C** Ritalin®
- **D** Lamictal®

UNDERSTAND ...

2 Which of the following is NOT an effect of meditation?

- **A** Meditation can improve working memory.
- **B** Meditation reduces the number of unnecessary axons in the frontal lobes.
- **C** Meditation can increase the thickness of the prefrontal cortex.
- **D** Meditation can improve attentional abilities.

ANALYZE ...

3 Research on nootropic drugs shows that

- **A** they have a much larger effect on intelligence than do environmental factors such as socioeconomic status.
- **B** they show low addiction rates and are therefore quite safe.
- **C** they have a larger effect on long-term memory than on working memory.
- **D** these drugs can produce increases in intelligence.

Answers can be found on page ANS-3.

Module Summary

Module 9.3

Now that you have read this module you should

KNOW ...

- ***The key terminology related to heredity, environment, and intelligence*:**

Flynn effect (p. 385)
gene knockout (KO) studies (p. 380)
nootropic substances (p. 387)
video deficit (p. 386)

UNDERSTAND ...

- ***Different approaches to studying the genetic basis of intelligence.*** Behavioural genetics typically involves conducting twin or adoption studies. Behavioural genomics involves looking at gene–behaviour relationships at the molecular level. This approach often involves using animal models, including knockout and transgenic models.

APPLY ...

- ***Your knowledge of environmental and behavioural effects on intelligence to understand how to enhance your own cognitive abilities.*** Based on the research we reviewed, there are many different strategies that are good bets for enhancing the cognitive abilities that underlie your own intelligence. (Note: some of these strategies are known to be helpful for children, and the effects on adult intelligence are not well researched.)
    - Choose challenging activities and environments that are stimulating and enriching
    - Eat diets low in saturated fat and processed foods and high in omega-3 fatty acids, nuts, seeds, fruits, and antioxidant-rich vegetables
    - Reduce sources of stress and increase your ability to handle stress well
    - Remain an active learner by continually adding to your education or learning
    - Don't spend too much time watching TV and other media that are relatively poor at challenging your cognitive abilities
    - Practise playing brain-training programs, such as video games based on the N-back task
    - Practise meditation
    - The use of nootropic drugs remains a potential strategy for enhancing your cognitive faculties; however, given the potential side effects, addictive possibilities, and the uncertainty regarding the long-term consequences of using such drugs, this option may not be the best way to influence intelligence.

MIGUEL MEDINA/AFP/Getty Images/Newscom

ANALYZE ...

- ***Claims that infant intelligence is increased by viewing educational television programming.*** As you read in the Myths in Mind feature, television viewing appears to have no benefits for cognitive development for very young children (i.e., younger than two years old), and in some cases inhibits it. On the other hand, certain programs may have cognitive benefits for somewhat older children.

Work the Scientific Literacy Model :: Understanding Intelligence

1 What do we know about testing and evaluating intelligence?

To understand and evaluate intelligence tests—and indeed, any kind of research—you should know the difference between reliability and validity. *Reliability* means that the test provides consistent and stable scores across multiple observations. *Validity* means that the test measures what it claims to be measuring, in this case intelligence. If Helen took the same intelligence test twice and she received two very different results, then you would question the *reliability* of the test. If she found an online test that purports to measure IQ depending on how long she could hold her breath, then you would likely question its validity. Without reliability, a test will lack *validity*. Also, just because a test is reliable, that does not mean it is valid. Helen may be able to hold her breath for approximately 20 seconds each time she tries, but the amount of time she can hold her breath will never be a valid test of intelligence. While none of the IQ tests involve holding your breath for any length of time, many intelligence and aptitude tests do appear to measure a single, generalized intelligence.

There is still debate over the exact nature of intelligence. Consider Sternberg's triarchic theory of intelligence (**Figure 9.11 on page 371**) and Gardner's concept of multiple intelligences (**Table 9.1 on page 372**), and think about how each contrasts with Spearman's theory of a general, basic intelligence (*g*).

2 How can science help explain theories of intelligence?

As you can see in **Figure 9.6 on page 366**, research has shown a correlation between IQ, which is primarily an indicator of a single intelligence (*g*), and several other positive outcomes, such as higher income, better physical and psychological health, and successful relationships. Researchers have mixed opinions on the validity of aptitude tests such as the SAT (a standardized test taken by most American high school students), as there is only a slightly positive correlation between high test scores and later academic performance. By comparison, strong research evidence supports the idea that intelligence can be divided into the dual categories of fluid intelligence (the ability to adapt to new problems) and crystallized intelligence (the ability to solve problems based on past experience). Research involving the existence of savants—people with low mental capabilities in some areas and extraordinary abilities in others—also supports the idea that intelligence has multiple components. Gardner's speculation on the multiple dimensions of intelligence in particular has had a heavy influence on the emphasis on learning styles in educational practice.

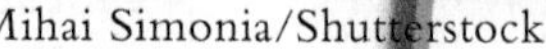

Mihai Simonia/Shutterstock

3 Can we critically evaluate claims about intelligence?

Does scientific research confirm that multiple kinds of intelligence exist, driving everything from your artistic ability to how you learn vocabulary terms? Are aptitude tests such as the SAT and the GRE (a test taken by university students applying to graduate school) a waste of your time? **Myths in Mind on page 372** highlights how researchers have failed to find evidence that people learn more efficiently when teaching is tailored to their particular learning style. Furthermore, critics of Gardner's theory of multiple intelligences question whether the ability to paint a beautiful picture is intelligence or whether it should just be considered a skill. Of course, despite the fact that the research is unclear on whether aptitude tests predict later academic success, the slight correlation between high scores and academic performance, and the relatively minor issues in reliability, have ensured that these scores are still used by many institutions.

4 Why is this relevant?

Watch the accompanying video excerpt on the theories of intelligence. You can access the video at MyPsychLab or by clicking the play button in the centre of your eText. If your instructor assigns this video as a homework activity, you will find additional content to help you in MyPsychLab. You can also view the video by using your smart phone and the QR code below, or you can go to the YouTube link provided.

After you have read this chapter and watched the video, provide real-world examples for the following types of intelligences as theorized by Gardner: verbal/linguistic, bodily-kinesthetic, and intrapersonal. Present some of the arguments critics have offered against Gardner's research.

MyPsychLab **Your turn to Work the Scientific Literacy Model:** Watch the accompanying video on YouTube, or on your phone (using the Layar app or QR code). If your instructor has assigned this as a homework activity, you can find the video clip and additional content at MyPsychLab. Answer the questions that accompany the video clip to test your understanding.

10

Lifespan Development

Dubova/Shutterstock

Paul Doyle/Alamy

Module 10.1

Physical Development from Conception through Infancy

Learning Objectives After reading this module you should	KNOW ...	UNDERSTAND ...	APPLY ...	ANALYZE ...
	The key terminology related to developmental research methods and prenatal and infant physical development	The pros and cons to different research designs in developmental psychology	Your understanding to identify the best ways expectant parents can ensure the health of their developing fetus	The effects of preterm birth

It is difficult to overstate the sheer miracle and profundity of birth. Consider the following story, told by a new father. "About two days after the birth of my first child, I was driving to the hospital and had one of 'those moments,' an awe moment, when reality seems clear and wondrous. What triggered it was that the person driving down the highway in the car next to mine yawned. Suddenly, I remembered my newborn baby yawning just the day before, and somehow, it hit me—we are all just giant babies. All of us, from the power broker in the business suit to the rebellious teenager in gangsta fashion, the tired soccer parent in the mini-van and the elderly couple holding hands on the sidewalk. Despite all of our cherished opinions, political beliefs, dreams and aspirations, the endless drama of our soap opera lives, and all the things we know and remember, we are, at our essence, giant babies. We have the same basic needs as babies—food, security, love, air, water, plus we've added a mountain of wants to those needs—the latest gadget, exciting ways to spend our weekends, feeling smarter than the people around us. But our bodies are basically the same, just a little bigger. Our brains are basically the same, just a little more developed. Our movements are even basically the same, just a little more coordinated. But fundamentally, we are just giant babies. I like to remember that now and then, when I feel intimidated by someone, or when I feel too self-important. It's humbling, and liberating."

The story of how we got from where we started "once upon a time" to where we are now, and what's going to happen to us as we continue to age, is a remarkable story that developmental psychologists have painstakingly pieced together over the past century or so of scientific research. And it starts with a single egg and a single sperm.

Focus Questions

 How does brain development occur, before and after birth?

 What are newborns able to sense?

Developmental psychology *is the study of human physical, cognitive, social, and behavioural characteristics across the lifespan*. Take just about anything you have encountered so far in this text, and you will probably find psychologists approaching it from a developmental perspective. From neuroscientists to cultural psychologists, examining how we function and change across different stages of life raises many central and fascinating questions.

Methods for Measuring Developmental Trends

Studying development requires some special methods for measuring and tracking change over time. A **cross-sectional design** *is used to measure and compare samples of people at different ages at a given point in time*. For example, to study cognition from infancy to adulthood, you could compare people of different age groups—say, groups of 1-, 5-, 10-, and 20-year-olds. In contrast, a **longitudinal design** *follows the development of the same set of individuals through time*. With this type of study, you would select a sample of infants and measure their cognitive development periodically over the course of 20 years (see Figure 10.1).

These different methods have different strengths and weaknesses. Cross-sectional designs are relatively cheap and easy to administer, and they allow a study to be done quickly (because you don't have to wait around while your participants age). On the other hand, they can suffer from **cohort effects**, which are *differences between people that result from being born in different time periods*. For example, if you find differences between people born last year with those born in the 1990s or 1970s, this may reflect any number of differences between people from those time periods—such as differences in nutrition, parenting norms, medical advances, cultural changes, environmental pollutants, or many other factors. This creates big problems in interpreting the findings of a study—do differences between the age groups reflect a normal developmental process or do they reflect more general differences between people born into these time periods?

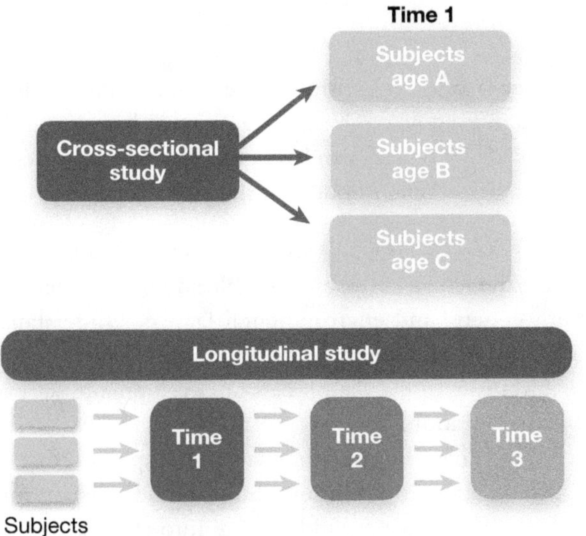

{FIG. 10.1} **Cross-Sectional and Longitudinal Methods** In cross-sectional studies, different groups of people—typically of different ages—are compared at a single point in time. In longitudinal studies, the same group of subjects is tracked over multiple points in time. **Click on this figure in your eText to see more details.**

A longitudinal study fixes the problem of cohort effects, but the demands of following a single group of people for a long period of time can be very costly and time-consuming. Longitudinal designs often suffer from the problem of *attrition*, which occurs when participants drop out of a study for some reason, such as losing interest or moving away. Despite these challenges, some very ambitious long-term studies have been done, sometimes following the same people for decades (e.g., the Seven Up series, the Minnesota Twins study).

PATTERNS OF DEVELOPMENT: STAGES AND CONTINUITY To parents, sometimes it may seem like children can't grow up quickly enough, and days crawl by with little apparent change. At other times, it seems like they grow up too fast and change so quickly you feel their childhood is slipping by; you leave on a weekend business trip and when you come back, you've missed their first steps or their vocabulary has advanced dramatically. To account for both periods of slow and rapid growth, development is seen as a progression of abrupt transitions in physical or mental skills, interspersed with slower, more gradual change. Psychologists often describe this pattern of change as a series of *stages*. The transition from stage to stage involves rapid shifts in thinking and behaving, and fundamental shifts in the *types* of abilities a child can perform.

Explore
Cross-Sectional and Longitudinal Research Designs

What accounts for the rapid physical and behavioural transitions that occur during early development? Complex interactions between genetics and the environment are constantly shaping developmental processes. Change occurs rapidly when individuals are "ready" for it; that is, there are certain times in development when individuals are particularly sensitive to the stimulation that facilitates physiological, neurological, behavioural, and cognitive development. The concept of a sensitive period helps explain how this transformation happens.

THE IMPORTANCE OF SENSITIVE PERIODS Timing is everything during key stages of development. A **sensitive period** *is a window of time during which exposure to a specific type of environmental stimulation is needed for normal development of a specific ability*. For example, to become fluent in their native language, infants need to be exposed to speech during their first few years of life. Long-term deficits can emerge if the needed stimulation, such as language, is missing during a sensitive period.

Watch
Chi Hae: Raising an Eleven-Month-Old, Part 1

Sensitive periods of development are a widespread phenomenon. They have been found in humans and other species for abilities such as depth perception, balance, and recognition of parents. A sensitive period for identifying with a culture may be uniquely human. Among immigrants of all ages, it is the younger individuals (0 to 20 years) who are quicker to identify more strongly with their new culture (Cheung et al., 2011).

Table 10.1 :: Phases of Prenatal Development

A summary of the stages of human prenatal development and some of the major events at each.

GERMINAL: 0 TO 2 WEEKS

Major Events

Migration of the blastocyst from the fallopian tubes and its implantation in the uterus. Cellular divisions take place that eventually lead to multiple organ, nervous system, and skin tissues.

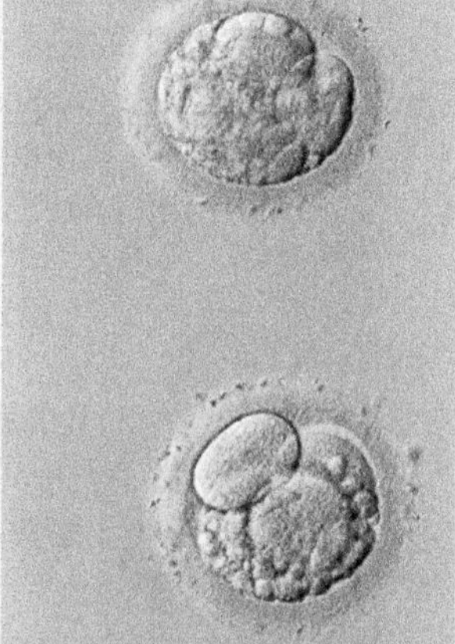

EMBRYONIC: 2 TO 8 WEEKS

Major Events

Stage in which basic cell layers become differentiated. Major structures such as the head, heart, limbs, hands, and feet emerge. The embryo attaches to the placenta, the structure that allows for the exchange of oxygen and nutrients and the removal of wastes.

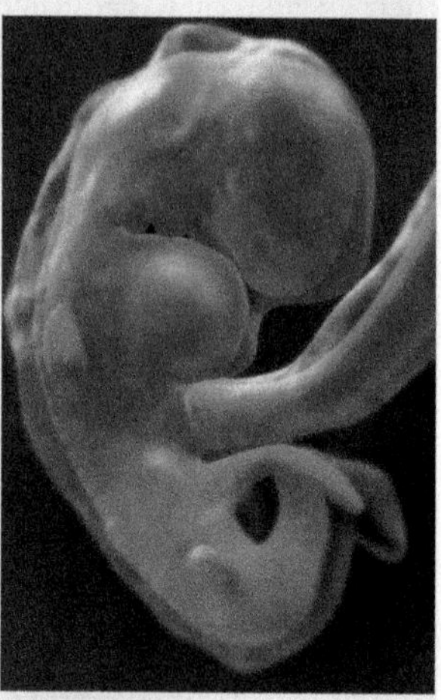

FETAL STAGE: 8 WEEKS TO BIRTH

Major Events

Brain development progresses as distinct regions take form. The circulatory, respiratory, digestive, and other bodily systems develop. Sex organs appear at around the third month of gestation.

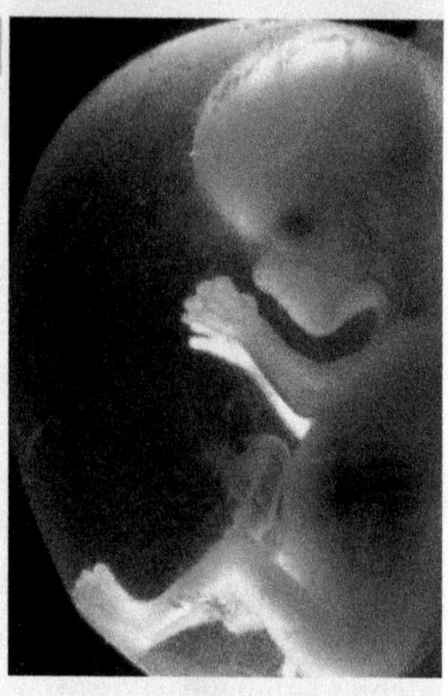

Top: Doug Steley A/Alamy; centre: MedicalRF.com/Alamy; bottom: Claude Edelmann/Science Source

Quick Quiz 10.1a

Methods for Measuring Developmental Trends

KNOW ...

1 The effects of language deprivation during infancy and childhood can be irreversible. This fact is best explained by which concept?

- **A** Cohort effects
- **B** Sensorimotor functioning
- **C** Sensitive period
- **D** Stage theories

APPLY ...

2 A researcher has only one year to complete a study on a topic that spans the entire range of childhood. To complete the study she should use a ________ design.

- **A** cohort
- **B** longitudinal
- **C** correlational
- **D** cross-sectional

ANALYZE ...

3 Which of the following is a factor that would be *least* likely to be a cohort effect for a study on cognitive development in healthy people?

- **A** Differences in genes between individuals
- **B** Differences in educational practices over time
- **C** Changes in the legal drinking age
- **D** Changes in prescription drug use

Answers can be found on page ANS-3.

Zygotes to Infants: From One Cell to Billions

We begin our exploration of developmental psychology from even before birth, because what happens in the prenatal environment can have consequences for psychological functioning throughout the rest of a person's life.

FERTILIZATION AND GESTATION During pregnancy, the fetus's development is already being shaped by both genetic and environmental factors. Understanding the complex interplay between nature and nurture requires examining the process of development, starting with fertilization.

Our lives begin when a single sperm (out of approximately 200 million who start the journey into the vagina) is able to find its way into the ovum (egg cell), at which point the ovum releases a chemical that bars any other sperm from entering. A **zygote**, *the initial cell formed when the nuclei of egg and sperm fuse*, mysteriously comes into being in this moment, and out of this single cell, the rest of our lives flow.

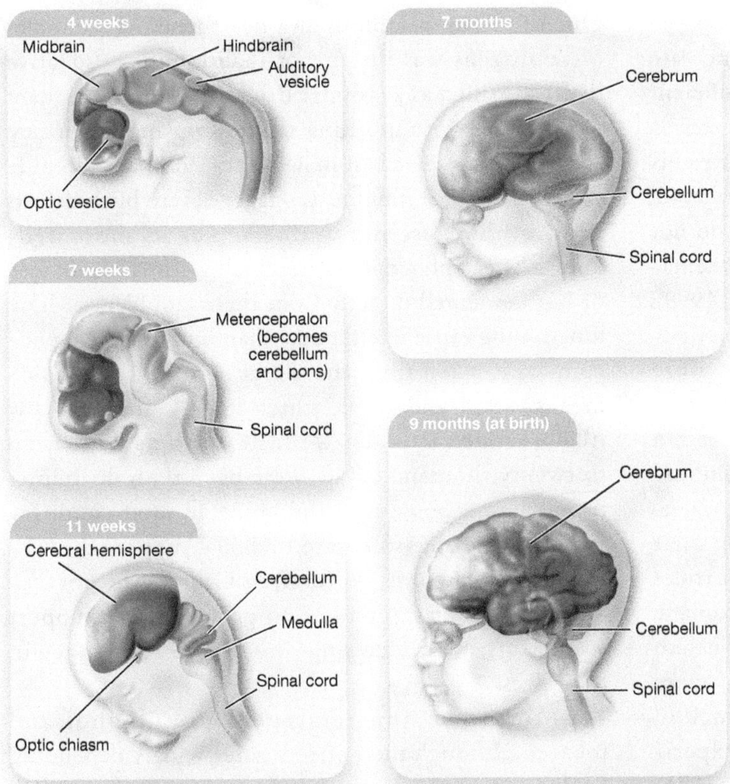

{FIG. 10.2} **Fetal Brain Development** The origins of the major regions of the brain are already detectable at four weeks' gestation. Their differentiation progresses rapidly, with the major forebrain, midbrain, and hindbrain regions becoming increasingly specialized. **Click on this figure in your eText to see more details.**

This is the beginning of the **germinal stage**, *the first phase of prenatal development, which spans from conception to two weeks.* Shortly after it forms, the zygote begins dividing, first into two cells, then four, then eight, and so on. It also begins travelling down the fallopian tubes toward the uterus, where it becomes implanted into the lining of the uterus (Table 10.1). The ball of cells, now called a blastocyst, splits into two groups. The inner group of cells develops into the fetus. The outer group of cells forms the placenta, which will pass oxygen and nutrients to, and expel waste from, the fetus.

The **embryonic stage** *spans weeks two through eight, during which time the embryo begins developing major physical structures such as the heart and nervous system, as well as the beginnings of arms, legs, hands, and feet.*

The **fetal stage** *spans week eight through birth, during which time the skeletal, organ, and nervous systems become more developed and specialized.* Muscles develop and the fetus begins to move. Sleeping and waking cycles start and the senses become fine-tuned—even to the point where the fetus is responsive to external cues (these events are summarized in Table 10.1).

FETAL BRAIN DEVELOPMENT Human brain development is an extremely lengthy process—continuing all the way to adulthood. The beginnings of the human brain can be seen during the embryonic stage, between the second and third weeks of gestation, when some cells migrate to the appropriate locations and begin to differentiate into nerve cells. The first signs of the major divisions of the brain—the forebrain, the midbrain, and the hindbrain—are apparent at only 4 weeks (see Figure 10.2). By 11 weeks, differentiations between the cerebral hemisphere, the cerebellum, and the brain stem are apparent. During the final months of pregnancy, a fatty tissue called myelin builds up around developing nerve cells, a process called *myelination*. Myelin insulates nerve cells, enabling them to conduct messages more rapidly and efficiently (see Module 3.2; Giedd, 2008).

Watch: Period of the Zygote

At birth, the newborn has an estimated 100 billion neurons and a brain that is approximately 25% the size and weight of an adult brain. Astonishingly, this means that at birth, the infant has created virtually all of the neurons that will comprise the adult brain, growing up to 4000 new neurons per *second* in the womb (Brown et al., 2001); what's missing from the newborn brain is most of the connections between these neurons (Kolb, 1989, 1995). This gives us a key insight into one of our core human capacities—our ability to adapt to highly diverse environments. In contrast with most other animal species, whose brains develop predominantly in the womb, human brains develop most of their neural organization through interaction with the outside environment. This means that the environment structures us to be the way we are, to a phenomenal degree.

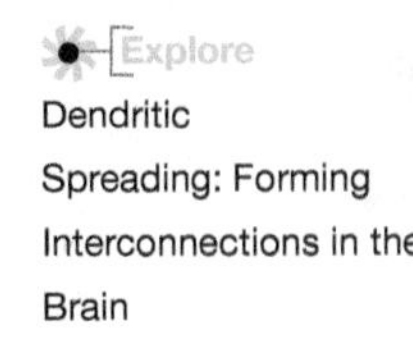

Explore: Dendritic Spreading: Forming Interconnections in the Brain

Explore: Virtual Brain: Development of the Brain

This reliance upon the outside world is why human babies are so, well, useless at birth! (No offence to babies, but seriously, they are pretty useless, just lying there in their own drool randomly waving their limbs about.) But it's also why human children and adults are able to adapt to the challenges of just about any environment on earth; we become the type of organism needed to live in the environment into which we're born.

Explore: The Embryonic Period: A Critical Period of Human Development

Watch: Fetal Development

Watch: Second Trimester

NUTRITION, TERATOGENS, AND FETAL DEVELOPMENT The rapidly developing fetal brain is highly vulnerable to environmental influences, such as the mother's nutrition and teratogens in the bloodstream.

Nutrition is critical for normal fetal development. In fact, aside from specific teratogens (as we discuss below), proper nutrition is the single most important non-genetic factor affecting fetal development

(Phillips, 2006). To provide this nourishment, pregnant women typically require an almost 20% increase in energy intake during pregnancy, including sufficient quantities of protein (which affects neurological development; Morgane et al., 2002) and essential nutrients (especially omega-3 fatty acids, folic acid, zinc, calcium, and magnesium). Given that most people's diets do not provide enough of these critical nutrients, supplementation is generally a good idea (Ramakrishnan et al., 1999).

Fetal malnutrition can have severe consequences, producing low-birth-weight babies who are more likely to suffer from a variety of diseases and illnesses, and are more likely to have cognitive deficits that can persist long after birth. Children who were malnourished in the womb are more likely to experience attention deficit disorders and difficulties controlling their emotions, due to underdeveloped prefrontal cortices and other brain areas involved in self-control (Morgane et al., 2002). Other surprising effects on mental health were illustrated after the citizens of Holland were severely malnourished during a famine that struck in World War II. Babies born during those years experienced a variety of physical problems (Stein et al., 1975) and, over time, had a much higher risk of developing psychological disorders, such as schizophrenia and antisocial personality disorder (Neugebauer et al., 1999; Susser et al., 1999).

Watch Brain Development and Nutrition

Simulate Teratogens and Their Effects

Watch Effects of Prenatal Smoking

Fetal development can also be disrupted through exposure to **teratogens**, *substances, such as drugs or environmental toxins, that impair the process of development.* One of the most famous and heartbreaking examples of teratogens was the use of thalidomide, a sedative that was hailed as a wonder drug for helping pregnant women deal with morning sickness during pregnancy. Available in Canada from 1959 to 1962, thalidomide was disastrous, causing miscarriages, severe birth defects such as blindness and deafness, plus its most well-known effect, phocomelia, in which victims' hands, feet, or both emerged directly from their shoulders or hips, functioning more like flippers than limbs; indeed, phocomelia is taken from the Greek words *phoke*, which means "seal," and *melos*, which means "limb" (www.thalidomide.ca/faq-en/#12). It is estimated that up to twenty thousand babies were born with disabilities from being exposed to thalidomide. In most countries, victims were able to secure financial support through class action lawsuits; however, in Canada, the government has steadfastly refused to provide much support to victims, who face ongoing severe challenges in their lives.

More common teratogens are alcohol and tobacco, although their effects differ widely depending on the volume consumed and when exposure occurs during pregnancy. First described in the 1970s (Jones & Smith, 1973), **fetal alcohol syndrome** *involves abnormalities in mental functioning, growth, and facial development in the offspring of women who use alcohol during pregnancy.* This condition occurs in approximately 1 per 1000 births worldwide, but is probably underreported (Morleo et al., 2011). Alcohol, like many

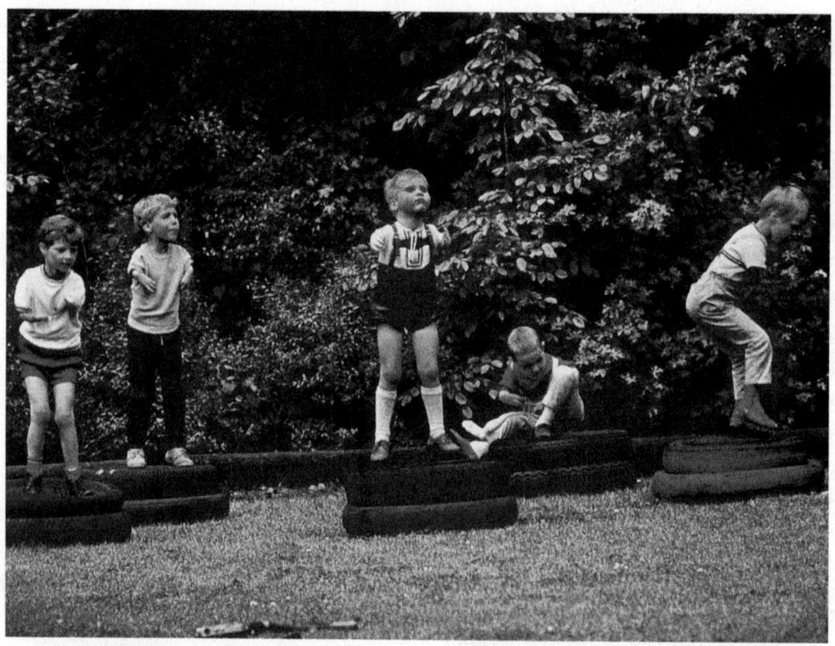

Dpa Picture Alliance/Alamy

Victims of Thalidomide; this sedative seemed like a miracle drug in the late 1950s, until its tragic effects on fetal development became apparent.

other substances, readily passes through the placental membranes, leaving the developing fetus vulnerable to its effects, which include reduced mental functioning (Olson, C., et al., 1997; Streissguth et al., 1999). The more alcohol the mother consumes, the more likely these birth defects will appear; nevertheless, there is no "safe limit"; even one drink per day can be enough to cause impaired fetal development (O'Leary et al., 2010; Streissguth & Connor, 2001).

Smoking can also expose the developing fetus to teratogens, decreasing blood oxygen and raising concentrations of nicotine and carbon monoxide, as well as increasing the risk of miscarriage or death during infancy. Babies born to mothers who smoke are twice as likely to have low birth weight and have a 30% chance of premature birth—both factors that increase the newborn's risk of illness or death. Smoking during pregnancy also increases the risk that the child will experience problems with emotional development and impulse control (Brion et al., 2010), as well as attentional problems and learning deficits (Makin et al., 1991). Babies exposed to smoke are also as much as three times more likely to die from SIDS (sudden infant death syndrome; Centers for Disease Control and Prevention [CDC], 2009; Rogers, 2009). Even exposure to second-hand smoke carries the same risk (Best, 2009).

Clearly, teratogens exact a major cost on society, causing deficits that range from very specific (e.g., blindness), to more general effects on development (e.g., premature birth).

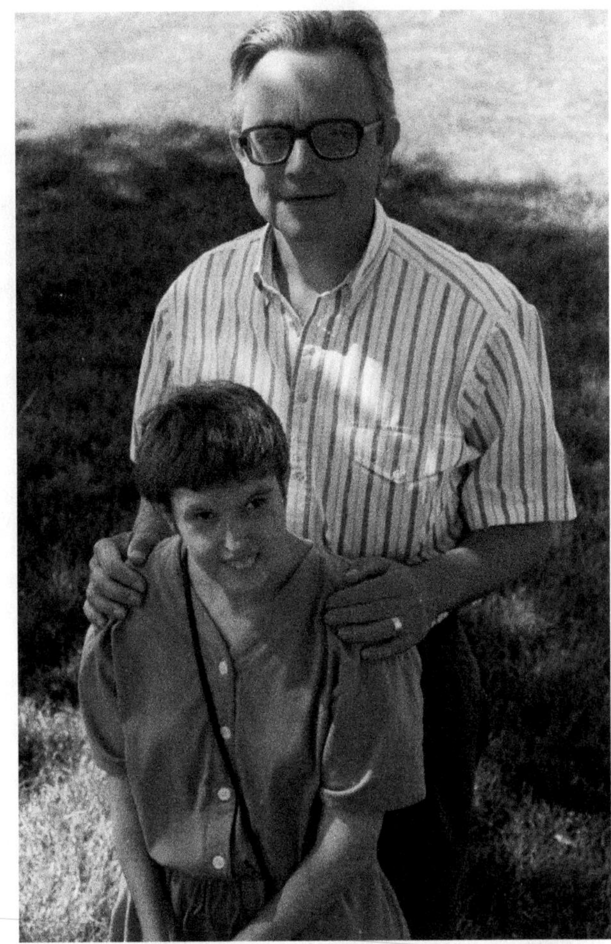
STUART WONG KRT/Newscom

Fetal alcohol syndrome is diagnosed based on facial abnormalities, growth problems, and behavioural and cognitive deficits.

WORKING THE SCIENTIFIC LITERACY MODEL

The Long-Term Effects of Premature Birth

Evolution has prepared the mother's womb to be a close-to-ideal environment for a fetus's delicate brain and body to prepare for life outside the womb. Premature birth thrusts the vulnerable baby into a much less congenial environment; what effects does this have on development?

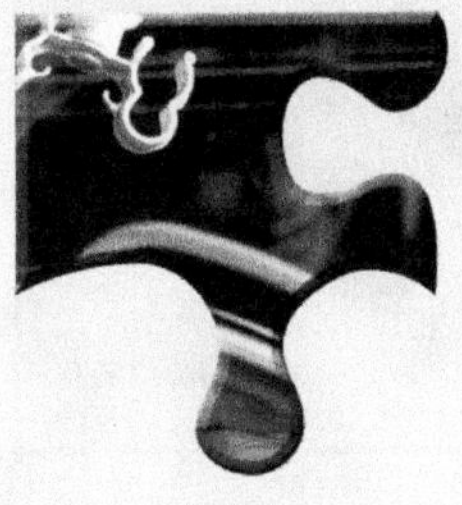

What do we know about premature birth?

Typically, humans are born at a gestational age of around 40 weeks. **Preterm infants** *are born earlier than 36 weeks.* Premature babies typically have underdeveloped brains and lungs, which presents a host of immediate challenges, such as breathing on their own and maintaining an appropriate body temperature. With modern medical care, babies born at 30 weeks have a very good chance of surviving (approximately 95%), although for those born at 25 weeks, survival rates drop to only slightly above 50% (Dani et al., 2009; Jones et al., 2005). Babies born at less than 25 weeks do often survive, but with very high chances of damage to the brain and other major organs. Because of these immense costs, medical science sorely needs better procedures for nurturing preterm infants.

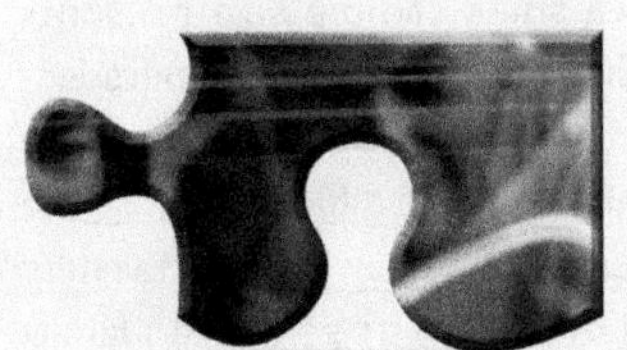

How can science be used to help preterm infants?

Researchers and doctors have compared different methods for improving survival and normal development in preterm infants. One program, called the Newborn Individualized Developmental Care and Assessment Program

Helen Mcardle/Science Photo Library/Corbis

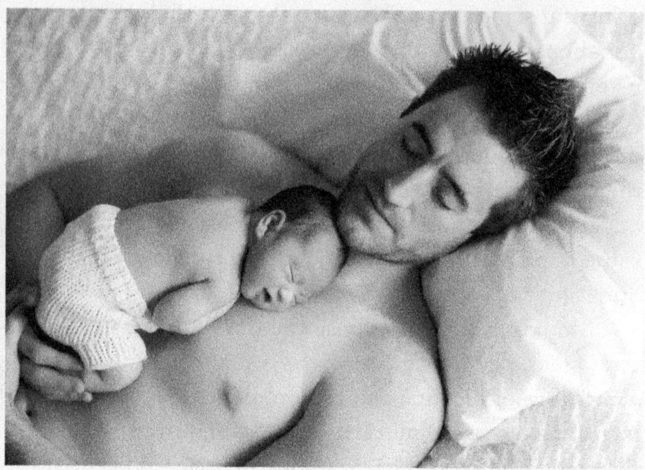

Victoria Boland Photography/Flickr/Getty Images

Kangaroo care—skin-to-skin contact between babies and caregivers—is now encouraged for promoting optimal infant development.

(NIDCAP), is a behaviourally based intervention in which preterm infants are closely observed and given intensive care during early development. To keep the delicate brain protected against potentially harmful experiences, NIDCAP calls for minimal lights, sound levels, and stress.

Controlled studies suggest that this program works. Researchers randomly assigned 117 infants born at 29 weeks or less gestational age to receive either NIDCAP or standard care in a prenatal intensive care unit. Within 9 months of birth, the infants who received the NIDCAP care showed significantly improved motor skills, attention, and other behavioural skills, as well as superior brain development (McAnulty et al., 2009).

Longitudinal studies show that these initial gains last for a long time. Even at eight years of age, those who were born preterm and given NIDCAP treatment scored higher on measures of thinking and problem solving, and also showed better frontal lobe functioning, than children who were born preterm but did not have NIDCAP treatment (McAnulty et al., 2010).

Can we critically evaluate this research?

The chief limitation of this study is its small sample size (only 22 children across the two conditions). Such a small sample size presents problems from a statistical perspective, increasing the likelihood that random chance plays a role in the results. Small samples also make it difficult to test the effects of interacting factors, such as whether the effectiveness of the program would depend on the child's gender, on family socioeconomic status, ethnicity, or other factors. This study also does not identify why the program works, what specific mechanisms it affects that in turn improves development. It is not known which brain systems are beneficially affected by the program, or which aspects of the treatment itself are responsible for the effects. These remain questions for future research.

Why is this relevant?

Worldwide, an estimated 9% of infants are born preterm (Villar et al., 2003). For these children, medical advances have increased the likelihood of survival, and behaviourally based interventions, such as NIDCAP, can reduce the chances of long-term negative effects of preterm birth. This fits with a growing literature on other behavioural interventions that have shown promise in improving outcomes for preterm infants. For example, massaging preterm infants for a mere 15 minutes per day can result in a 50% greater daily weight gain (Field et al., 2006) and reduce stress-related behaviours (Hernandez-Reif et al., 2007). Another method called *kangaroo care* focuses on promoting skin-to-skin contact between infants and caregivers, as well as encouraging breastfeeding; these practices have been shown to improve the physical and psychological health of preterm infants (Conde-Agudelo et al., 2011), and are becoming widely adopted into mainstream medical practice.

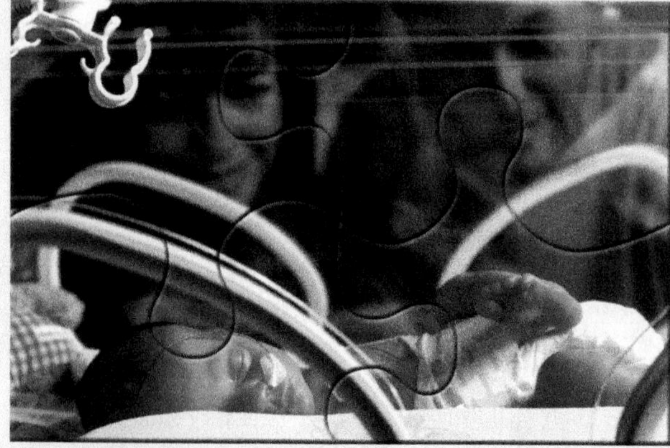

allOver photography/Alamy

Quick Quiz 10.1b

Zygotes to Infants: From One Cell to Billions

KNOW ...

1 A developing human is called a(n) ________ during the time between weeks 2 and 8.

A embryo
C fetus
B zygote
D germinal

2 In which stage do the skeletal, organ, and nervous systems become more developed and specialized?

A Embryonic stage
C Germinal stage
B Fetal stage
D Gestational stage

UNDERSTAND ...

3 Which of the following would not qualify as a teratogen?

A Cigarette smoke
B Alcohol
C Prescription drug
D All of the above are possible teratogens

ANALYZE ...

4 Which of the following statements best summarizes the effects of preterm birth?

A Preterm births are typically fatal.
B The worrisome effects of preterm birth are exaggerated. There is little to worry about.
C Preterm birth may cause physical and cognitive problems.
D Cohort effects make it impossible to answer this question.

Answers can be found on page ANS-3.

MYTHS IN MIND

Vaccinations and Autism

In the late 1990s, a team of researchers claimed that the combined vaccination for measles, mumps, and rubella (MMR) was linked to the development of autism (Wakefield et al., 1998). The MMR vaccination is given to millions of children at around their first birthday; a second dose is administered at approximately the time they start school. Of course, scientific evidence that such a widespread treatment could lead directly to autism alarmed many parents, many of whom refused to have the vaccine given to their young children.

The hypothesis that the MMR vaccine causes autism unravelled when other groups of scientists could not replicate the original findings. The knockout blow to the MMR–autism hypothesis came when it was discovered that Andrew Wakefield, the doctor who published the original study in 1998, was found to have financial interests in linking the disease with the vaccine. His research was funded by lawyers who sued makers of vaccines for damages. In 2010, the original 1998 paper was retracted by *The Lancet*, the medical journal that published it. Also, a thorough investigation revealed numerous counts of misconduct by Wakefield, and the UK revoked his medical licence.

There is no scientific evidence that the MMR vaccine causes autism.

Autistic Children

Sensory and Motor Development in Infancy

Compared to the offspring of other species, healthy newborn humans are relatively helpless. Horses, snakes, deer, and many other organisms come into the world with a few basic skills, such as walking (or slithering), that enable them to move about the world, get food, and have at least have a chance of evading predators. But human infants depend entirely on caregivers to keep them alive, as they slowly develop their senses, strength, and coordination. In this section, we shift our focus to newborns to find out how movement and sensation develop in the first year of life.

Watch Perception

It's weird to think about what the world of an infant must be like. As adults, we depend heavily on our top-down processes (see Module 4.1) to help us label, categorize, perceive, and make sense of the world, but infants have developed very few top-down patterns when they are born. Their brains are pretty close to being "blank slates," and life must be, as William James so aptly put it, a "blooming, buzzing confusion."

Suprisingly, however, babies have started to make sense of their world even while in the womb. By month four of prenatal development, the brain starts receiving signals from the eyes and ears. By seven to eight months, infants can not only hear, but they seem to be actively listening. This amazing finding comes from studies in which developing fetuses were exposed to certain stimuli, and then their preference for these stimuli was tested upon birth. In one study, mothers read stories, including *The Cat in the Hat,* twice daily during the final six weeks of pregnancy. At birth, their babies were given a pacifier that controlled a tape recording of their mother's voice reading different stories. Babies sucked the pacifier much more to hear their mothers read *The Cat in the Hat* compared to hearing stories the moms had not read to them in the womb (DeCasper & Spence, 1986). Newborn babies also show a preference for their mother's voice over other women's voices; for example, a study involving researchers at Queen's University showed that babies responded positively when they heard poems read in their moms' voice, but not when read by a stranger (Kisilevsky et al., 2003).

(But sorry, dads, babies up to at least 4 months old don't prefer your voice over other men's [DeCasper & Prescott, 1984; Ward & Cooper, 1999].)

The auditory patterning of babies' brains is so significant that they have already started to internalize the sounds of their own native tongue, even before they are born! Recently, researchers discovered that babies actually cry with an accent, by analyzing the crying sounds of 60 babies born to either French or German parents. The cries of French babies rose in intensity toward the end of their cry while German babies started at high intensity and then trailed off. This difference was apparent at only a few days of age and reflects the same sound patterns characteristic of their respective languages (Mampe et al., 2009). So, babies are actively learning about their cultural environment even while in the womb.

The visual system is not as well developed at birth, however. Enthusiastic family members who stand around making goofy faces at newborn babies are deluding themselves if they think they're interacting with the child; newborns have only about 1/40th of the visual acuity of adults (Sireteanu, 1999), and can only see about as far away as is necessary to see their mom's face while breastfeeding (about 30 cm or less). It takes 6 months or more before they reach 20/20 visual acuity. Colour vision, depth perception, and shape discrimination all get a slow start as well. Colour discrimination happens at about 2 months of age, depth perception at 4 months, and it takes a full 8 months before infants can perceive shapes and objects about as well as adults (Csibra et al., 2000; Fantz, 1961). Nevertheless, even newborns are highly responsive to visual cues if they're close enough to see them. They will track moving objects, and will stare intently at objects they haven't seen before, although after a while they habituate to an object and lose interest in looking at it (Slater et al., 1988).

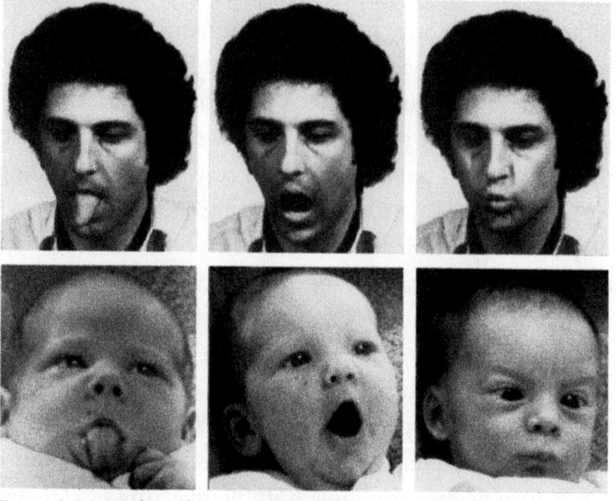

From A.N. Meltzoff & M.K. Moore, "Imitation of facial and manual gestures by human neonates." *Science,* 1977, 198, 75–78.

At just a few days of age, infants will imitate the facial expressions of others (Meltzoff & Moore, 1977).

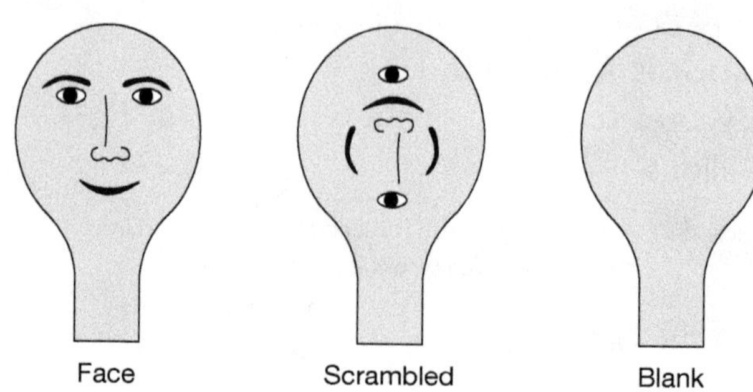

{FIG. 10.3} **Experimental Stimuli for Studying Visual Habituation in Infants** Infants were shown three types of stimuli, a face-like stimulus, a neutral stimulus, and a scrambled-face stimulus.

Babies' visual responses to the world illustrate a major theme within psychology, which is that humans are fundamentally social creatures. By a few days of age, newborns will imitate the facial expressions of others (Meltzoff & Moore, 1977). Newborns prefer to look at stimuli that look like faces, compared to stimuli that have all the same features but are scrambled so that they don't look like faces (see Figure 10.3). Infants also take longer to habituate to the face-like stimuli, suggesting that the human face holds particular importance even for newborns (Johnson et al., 1991). This social attunement is dramatically illustrated in one study, which showed that within *one hour* of birth, newborns begin to imitate facial expressions (Reissland, 1988) that they see!

Interestingly, the proper development of the visual system is not guaranteed to happen; it's not hardwired into our genes. Instead, the visual system develops in response to the infant experiencing a world of diverse visual input. Research at McMaster University has shown that even though babies possess the necessary "equipment" for proper vision, this equipment needs to be exposed to a diverse visual world in order to learn how to function effectively (Maurer et al., 1999); it is the patterns in the world which develop the appropriate neural pathways in the visual cortex (see Module 4.2).

Contrary to vision, the taste and olfactory systems are relatively well developed at birth. Similar to adults, newborns cringe when smelling something rotten or pungent, such as ammonia, and they show a strong preference for the taste of sweets. Odours are strong memory cues for infants as well. For example, infants can learn that a toy will work in the presence of one odour but not others, and they can retain this memory over several days (Schroers et al., 2007). Newborn infants can also smell the difference between their mother's breastmilk and that of a stranger. Infants even turn their heads toward the scent of breastmilk, which helps to initiate nursing (Porter & Winberg, 1999).

MOTOR DEVELOPMENT IN THE FIRST YEAR

Although the motor system takes many years to develop

Table 10.2 :: Infant Reflexes

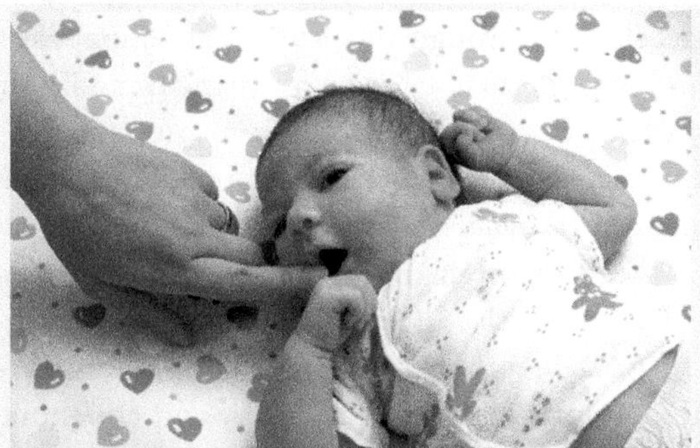	**THE ROOTING REFLEX** The *rooting reflex* is elicited by stimulation to the corners of the mouth, which causes infants to orient themselves toward the stimulation and make sucking motions. The rooting reflex helps the infant begin feeding immediately after birth.
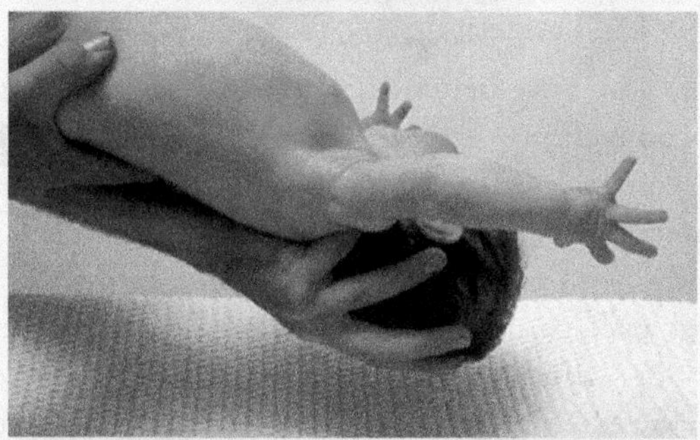	**THE MORO REFLEX** The *Moro reflex*, also known as the "startle" reflex, occurs when infants lose support of their head. Infants grimace and reach their arms outward and then inward in a hugging motion. This may be a protective reflex that allows the infant to hold on to the mother when support is suddenly lost.
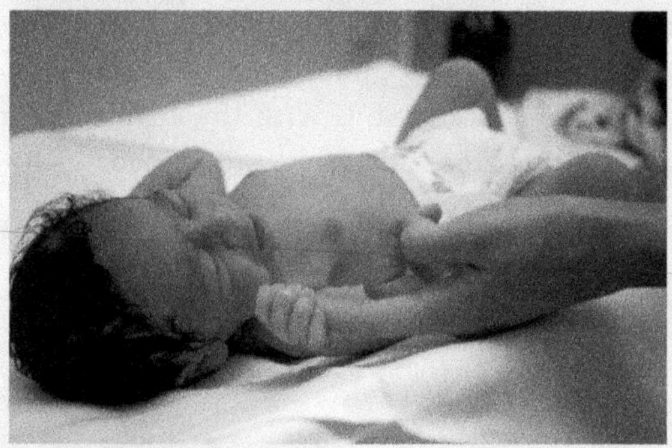	**THE GRASPING REFLEX** The *grasping reflex* is elicited by stimulating the infant's palm. The infant's grasp is remarkably strong and facilitates safely holding on to one's caregiver. Top: Cathy Melloan Resources/PhotoEdit; centre: Petit Format/Photo Researchers, Inc.; bottom: Denise Hager/Catchlight Visual Services/Alamy

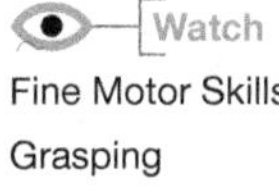
Watch
Fine Motor Skills: Grasping

Mark Richards/PhotoEdit

The visual cliff.

a high degree of coordination (e.g., good luck getting an infant to wield a steak knife), the beginnings of the motor system develop very early. A mere five months after conception, the fetus begins to have control of voluntary motor movements. In the last months of gestation, the muscles and nervous system are developed enough to demonstrate basic **reflexes**—*involuntary muscular reactions to specific types of stimulation*. These reflexes provide newborns and infants with a set of innate responses for feeding and interacting with their caregivers (see Table 10.2).

As the infant begins to navigate the world under her own power, her perceptual understanding sharpens as well. This was illustrated in research involving an ingenious device—*the visual cliff*. Originally, researchers in 1960 (Gibson & Walk, 1960) found that infants would be reluctant to crawl over the deep side, seeming to understand depth and danger right from birth. However, researchers eventually discovered that only babies who had some experience crawling showed fear of the deep end (Campos et al., 1992).

Watch
Gross Motor Skills

Over the first 12 to 18 months after birth, infants' motor abilities progress through reliable stages—from crawling, to standing, to walking (see Figure 10.4). The age at which infants can perform each of these movements differs from one individual to the next. In contrast to reflexes, the development of motor skills seems to rely more on practice and deliberate effort, which in turn is related to environmental influences, such as

Watch
Reflexes

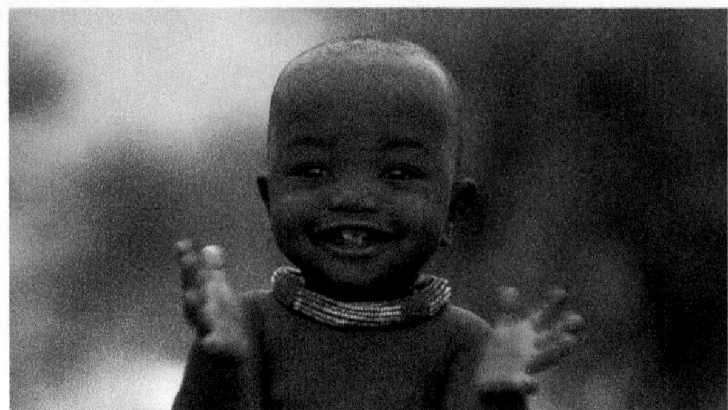

CANAL +/Album/CANAL +/Album/Newscom

Different childrearing practices and expectations result in cultural variations in the rate at which motor skills develop.

cultural practices. For example, Jamaican mothers typically expect their babies to walk earlier than British or Indian mothers, and sure enough, Jamaican babies do walk earlier, likely because they are given more encouragement and opportunities to learn (Hopkins & Westra, 1989; Zelazo et al., 1993).

One area of the body that undergoes astonishing development during infancy is the brain. Although the major brain structures are all present at birth, they continue developing right into adulthood. One key change is the myelination of axons, which begins prenatally, accelerates through infancy and childhood, and then continues gradually for many years. In addition, two key events occur at the level of synapses: synaptogenesis and synaptic pruning. **Synaptogenesis** describes *the forming of new synaptic connections*, which occurs at blinding speed through infancy and childhood, and continues through the lifespan. **Synaptic pruning**, *the loss of weak nerve cell connections*, accelerates during brain development through infancy and childhood (Figure 10.5), then tapers off until adolescence (see Module 10.3). Synaptogenesis and synaptic pruning serve to increase neural efficiency by strengthening needed connections between nerve cells and weeding out unnecessary ones.

In summary, the journey from zygote to you begins dramatically, with biological pathways being formed at a breakneck pace prenatally and into the first year of life, allowing for sensory and motor abilities to connect the infant to the external world. Most motor abilities require substantial time for the infant to learn to coordinate the many different muscles required, which depends heavily on the infant's interactions with the environment. Nature and nurture are inextricably intertwined.

Top, left: bendao/Shutterstock; top, right: Bubbles Photolibrary/Alamy; bottom, left: Glow Images; bottom, centre left: OLJ Studio/Shutterstock; bottom, centre right: Corbis Bridge/Alamy; bottom, right: Eric Gevaert/Shutterstock.com

{FIG. 10.4} **Motor Skills Develop in Stages** This series shows infants in different stages of development: (a) raising the head, (b) rolling over, (c) propping up, (d) sitting up, (e) crawling, and (f) walking.

Watch Motor Development in Infants and Toddlers: Karen Adolph

1. At birth, the infant's brain has a complete set of neurons but not very many synaptic connections.

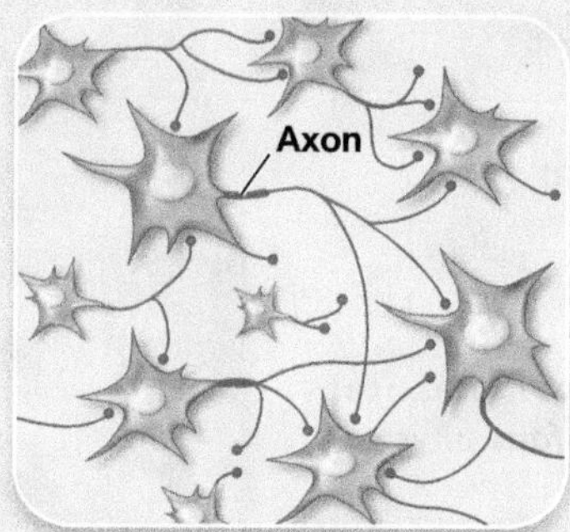

2. During the first year, the axons grow longer, the dendrites increase in number, and a surplus of new connections is formed.

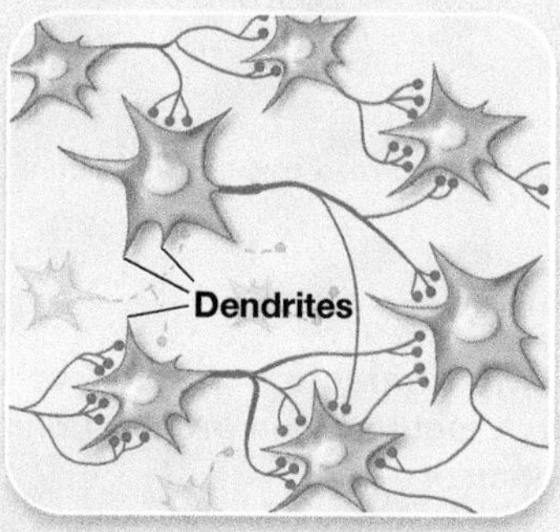

3. Over the next few years, active connections are strengthened, while unused connections disintegrate.

{FIG. 10.5} **The Processes of Synaptic Pruning**

Quick Quiz 10.1c Sensory and Motor Development in Infancy

KNOW ...

1 Three main types of processes account for the main ways in which the brain develops after birth. These three processes are

A myelination, synaptogenesis, synaptic pruning.

B myelination, synaptic reorganization, increased neurotransmitter production.

C synaptogenesis, synaptic pruning, increased neurotransmitter production.

D Actually, the brain is fully developed at birth; the only change afterwards is that new cells are formed while the child's brain grows (synaptogenesis).

UNDERSTAND ...

2 The development of infant motor skills is best described as

A a genetic process with no environmental influence.

B completely due to the effects of encouragement.

C a mixture of biological maturation and learning.

D progressing in continuous, rather than stage, fashion.

Answers can be found on page ANS-3.

Module Summary

Module **10.1**

Now that you have read this module you should

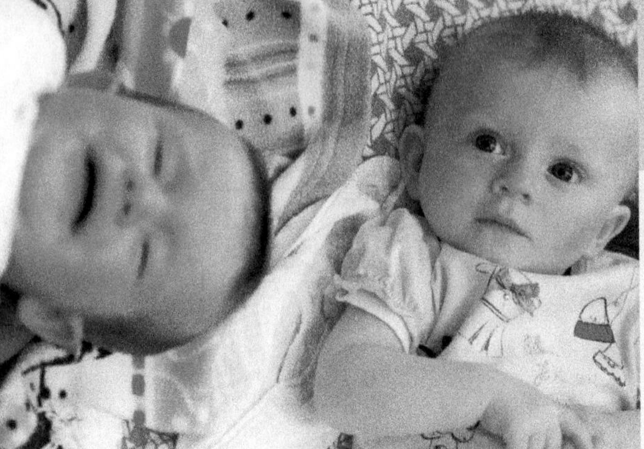
Paul Doyle/Alamy

KNOW ...

- ***The key terminology related to developmental research methods and prenatal and infant physical development*:**

cohort effect (p. 393)
cross-sectional design (p. 393)
developmental psychology (p. 393)
embryonic stage (p. 395)
fetal alcohol syndrome (p. 396)
fetal stage (p. 395)
germinal stage (p. 395)
longitudinal design (p. 393)
preterm infant (p. 397)
reflexes (p. 400)
sensitive period (p. 393)
synaptic pruning (p. 402)
synaptogenesis (p. 402)
teratogen (p. 396)
zygote (p. 394)

UNDERSTAND ...

- ***The pros and cons to different research designs in developmental psychology.*** Cross-sectional designs, in which a researcher studies a sample of people at one time, have the advantage of being faster, and generally cheaper, allowing research to be completed quickly; however, they may suffer from cohort effects because people of different ages in the sample are also from somewhat different historical time periods and, thus, any differences between them could reflect a historical process and not a developmental one. Longitudinal designs, in which a researcher follows a sample of people over a span of time, have the advantage of being able to track changes in the same people, thus giving more direct insight into developmental processes. However, such studies take longer to complete, thus slowing down the research process, and they can suffer from attrition, in which people drop out of the study over time.

APPLY ...

- ***Your understanding to identify the best ways that expectant parents can ensure the health of their developing fetus.*** The key to healthy fetal development is ensuring a chemically ideal environment. The most important factors are adequate nutrition and avoiding teratogens. Best nutritional practices include approximately a 20% increase in the mother's caloric intake, additional protein, and ensuring sufficient quantities of essential nutrients, which usually involves taking nutritional supplements. Avoiding teratogens involves giving up smoking and drinking alcohol, and getting good medical advice concerning any medications that the expectant mother may be taking.

ANALYZE ...

- ***The effects of preterm birth.*** Health risks increase considerably with very premature births (e.g., those occurring at just 25 weeks' gestation). Use of proper caregiving procedures, especially personalized care that emphasizes mother–infant contact, breastfeeding, and minimal sensory stimulation for the underdeveloped brain, increases the chances that preterm infants will remain healthy.

Inspirestock Inc/Alamy

Module 10.2

Infancy and Childhood: Cognitive and Emotional Development

Learning Objectives

After reading this module you should

KNOW ...	UNDERSTAND ...	APPLY ...	ANALYZE ...
The terminology associated with infancy and childhood	The cognitive changes that occur during infancy and childhood The importance of attachment and the different styles of attachment	The concept of scaffolding and the zone of proximal development to understand how to best promote learning	How to effectively discipline children in order to promote moral behaviour

Many parents have turned to Disney's "Baby Einstein" line of books, toys, and DVDs in hopes of entertaining and enriching their children. These materials certainly are entertaining enough that children watch them. But a major issue concerns whether they provide the advertised long-term benefits of increasing cognitive skills. These products are designed to help babies explore music, art, language, science, poetry, and nature through engaging images, characters, and music. The American Academy of Pediatrics, however, recommends that children younger than two years do not watch television at all. This recommendation is consistent with research showing that memory and language skills are slower to develop in infants who regularly watch television (Christakis, 2009). Furthermore, controlled studies show that the DVDs in question have no effect on vocabulary development (Richert et al., 2010; Robb et al., 2009). It turns out that the amount of time parents spend reading to their infants is related to greater vocabulary comprehension and production. As you can imagine, these results might give parents pause before they commit to using the DVDs.

Focus Questions

1. Which types of activities do infants and young children need for their psychological development?

2. Given that social interactions are so important, which specific abilities are nurtured by them?

Jerry Arcieri/Corbis

Baby Einstein: A very financially successful line of baby products; but do they really help develop infant brains?

Watch
Thinking Like a Psychologist: Smart Babies by Design

Watch
Basics: How Thinking Develops

Although human infants are relatively helpless for an extended period of time, the complexity of the human brain and behaviour begins to unfold immediately after birth. The physical, cognitive, and social transitions that occur between infancy and childhood are remarkably ordered, yet are also influenced by individual genetic and sociocultural factors. In this module, we integrate some important stage perspectives to explain psychological development through childhood.

Cognitive Changes: Piaget's Cognitive Development Theory

Explore
Piaget's Stages of Cognitive Development

One of the awesome things about getting a psychology degree is that you gain the knowledge required to run secret experiments on your friends and family whenever you want. Jean Piaget (1896–1980) did just that, observing and testing his children's abilities from infancy onwards. His extensive personal project and the theories that resulted laid much of the groundwork for the modern science of **cognitive development**—*the study of changes in memory, thought, and reasoning processes that occur throughout the lifespan.* In his own work, Piaget focused on cognitive development from infancy through early adolescence. In this section, we review his theory and offer insight into modern work that builds upon it. So, keep at it! Maybe you too will become a world-famous psychologist by performing studies on your loved ones . . . just don't tell anyone we told you to do it.

Piaget was interested in explaining how different ways of thinking and reasoning develop. According to Piaget, knowledge accumulates and is modified by two processes—assimilation and accommodation. **Assimilation** is *a conservative process, whereby people fit new information into the belief systems they already possess.* For example, young children may think that all girls have long hair and, as they encounter more examples of this pattern, they will assimilate it into their current understanding. Of course, eventually they're going to run into girls with short hair or boys with long hair, and their beliefs will be challenged by this information. They may, at first, misunderstand, assuming the short-haired girl is actually a boy and the long-haired boy is actually a girl. But over time they will learn that their rigid categories of long-haired girl and short-haired boy need to be altered. This process is **accommodation**, *a creative process whereby people modify their belief structures based on experience.* The processes of assimilation and accommodation continue throughout our lives, as our belief systems help us make sense of the world, and then get challenged by information that doesn't fit our beliefs; we have to either ignore or deny the information, or change our minds.

Piaget's observations revealed that cognitive development passes through four distinct *stages* from birth through early adolescence: sensorimotor, preoperational, concrete operational, and the formal operational stage. Passing out of one stage to the next occurs when the child achieves the important developmental milestone of that stage (see Table 10.3).

Table 10.3 :: Piaget's Stages of Cognitive Development

STAGE	DESCRIPTION
Sensorimotor (0–2 years)	Cognitive experience is based on direct, sensory experience with the world as well as motor movements that allow infants to interact with the world. Object permanence is the significant developmental milestone of this stage.
Preoperational (2–7 years)	Thinking moves beyond the immediate appearance of objects. The child understands physical conservation and that symbols, language, and drawings can be used to represent ideas.
Concrete operational (7–11 years)	The ability to perform mental transformations on objects that are physically present emerges. Thinking becomes logical and organized.
Formal operational (11 years–adulthood)	The capacity for abstract and hypothetical thinking develops. Scientific reasoning becomes possible.

THE SENSORIMOTOR STAGE: LIVING IN THE MATERIAL WORLD When we are adults, we understand that things continue to exist even if they are not physically present; the man committing adultery in Vegas knows, in reality, that his spouse exists, even if he is choosing not to think about her. But he *could* think about her, and she would exist in his mind as a kind of abstraction, a mental representation of his wife. Unlike adults, four-month-old infants do not appear to have the ability to form abstract mental representations. This explains why infants will often stare in awe at things that are mundane to adults, like snow. Imagine if you had no *idea* what snow was, had no previous experience that mapped onto snow and suddenly saw fluffy, white, sparkly . . . things . . . pouring out of the sky! You might stand in awe too.

Piaget named the earliest period of cognitive development the **sensorimotor stage**, *from birth to two years, during which infants' thinking about and exploration of the world are based on immediate sensory (e.g., seeing, feeling) and motor (e.g., grabbing, mouthing) experiences.* During this time, infants are completely immersed in the present moment, responding exclusively to direct, sensory input. In some ways this is a great way to live; little kids enjoy snow and mud puddles more than your average adult. But in other ways this is highly dysfunctional; you certainly wouldn't want to rely on an infant to pick you up at the airport. And if you were married to one, you'd be pretty worried when she went to Vegas . . .

According to Piaget's logic, as soon as an object is out of sight and out of reach, it will cease to exist (at least in the minds of young infants). Out of sight, out of mind. Thus, the first major milestone of cognitive development proposed by Piaget is **object permanence**, *the ability to understand that objects exist even when they cannot be directly perceived.* To test for object permanence, Piaget would allow a child to reach for a toy, and then place a screen or a barrier between the infant and the toy. If the infant stopped reaching for the toy or looking in its direction, then this infant would not yet have developed object permanence.

Notice that this is not a problem for a two-year-old child. He can be *very* aware that his favourite dinosaur toy awaits him in another room while he has to sit at the dinner table; in fact, he might not be able to get the toy out of his mind and take revenge on the evil beings who won't get it for him by screaming throughout the meal.

THE PREOPERATIONAL STAGE: QUANTITY AND NUMBERS According to Piaget, once children have mastered sensorimotor tasks, they have progressed to the **preoperational stage** (ages two to seven). This stage is devoted to *language development, using symbols, pretend play, and mastering the concept of conservation.* During this stage, children can think about physical objects, although they have not quite attained abstract thinking abilities. They may count objects (obsessively) and use numbers, yet they cannot mentally manipulate information or see things from other points of view.

Their inability to manipulate abstract information is shown by testing their understanding of **conservation**, *the knowledge that the quantity or amount of an object is not the same as the physical arrangement and appearance of that object.* For example, imagine that a child is presented with two identical rows of seven pennies each, as shown in the bottom of Figure 10.6. Next, the experimenter spreads out one of the rows so that it is longer, but has the same number of coins. If you ask a child, "Which row has more?" a three-year-old child would likely point to the row that was spread out. The child in the preoperational stage focuses on the simpler method of answering based on immediate perception, instead of the answer that would require more sophisticated mental operations.

Watch
Fine Motor Skills: Reaching

Watch
Sensorimotor Development

Watch
The Preoperational and Concrete Operational Stage

Watch
Conservation of Liquids

Watch
Piaget: Sensorimotor Stage

Explore
Infant's Perceptual and Cognitive Milestones

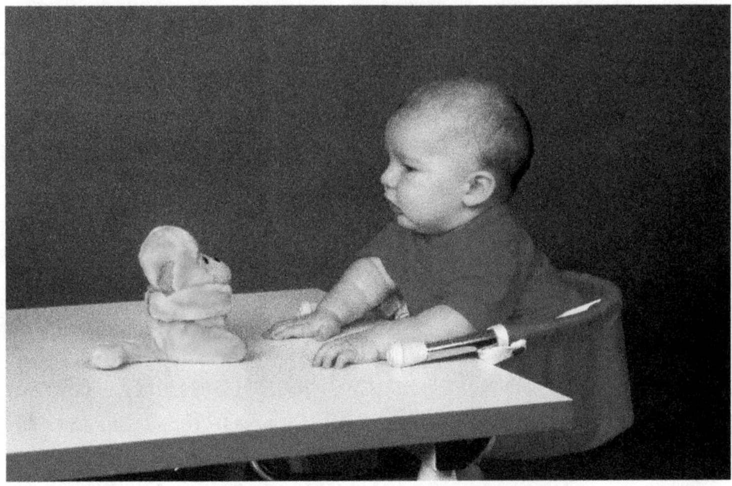

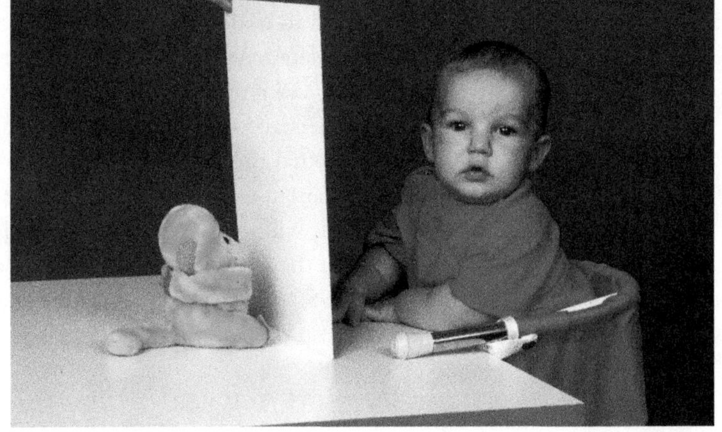

Doug Goodman/Photo Researchers/Getty Images

Object permanence is tested by examining reactions that infants have to objects when they cannot be seen. Children who have object permanence will attempt to reach around the barrier or will continue looking in the direction of the desired object.

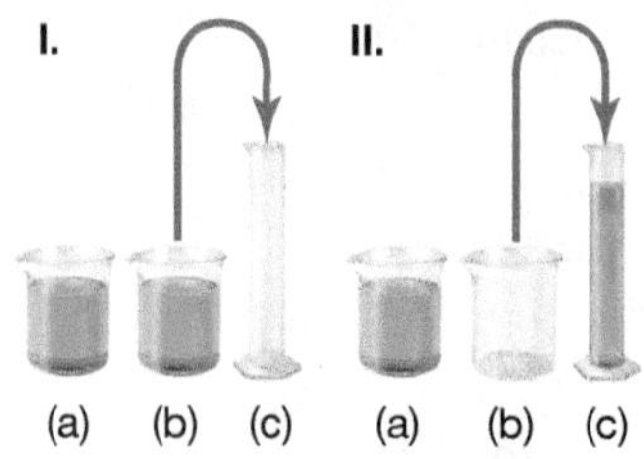

Which has more, row A or row B, or do they both have the same?

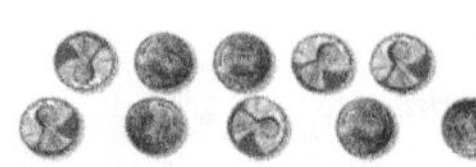

Now which has more, row A or row B, or do they both have the same?

{FIG. 10.6} **Testing Conservation** A child views two equal amounts of fluid, one of which is then poured into a taller container. Children who do not yet understand conservation believe that there is more fluid in the tall, narrow container compared to the shorter one. A similar version of this task can be tested using equal arrays of separate objects.

Watch Conservation Tasks

Other creative researchers have challenged Piaget's pessimism about the abilities of young children, arguing that their inability to perform certain tasks was a function of the child's interpretation of the task, not their underlying cognitive limitations (see Working the Scientific Literacy Model, next page). For example, when 3-year-old children are presented with a conservation test similar to the one described previously except with (1) M&Ms instead of pennies and (2) fewer M&Ms present in the row that is spread out, children will pick the tighter row, understanding that it contains more candy—especially if they get to eat the candy from the row they choose (Mehler & Bever, 1967). Attempting to trick kids out of candy is no joke! They will leap past entire milestones to obtain those tiny morsels of sugary goodness.

It is important to note that even before children start to use and understand numbers, they acquire a basic understanding of quantity. Very soon after they are born, infants appear to understand what it means to have less or more of something. This suggests that the infants who chose the longer row of pennies in the example above may simply have misunderstood the question, not the underlying rule of conservation. To them "more" could simply have meant "longer."

Although abstract thinking abilities are a work in progress for young children, they do begin to understand some basic principles. The children in Figure 10.7 are committing *scale errors* in the sense that they appear to interact with a doll-sized slide and a toy car as if they were the real thing, rather than miniatures (DeLoache et al., 2004).

However, by 2 to 2½ years of age, scale errors decline as children begin to understand properties of objects and how they are related. At around 3 years of age children begin to understand symbolic relationships. For example, 3-year-olds understand that a scale model of a room can symbolize an actual room (Figure 10.7). Children who view an experimenter placing a miniature toy within the scale model will quickly locate the actual toy when allowed to enter the room symbolized by the scale model (DeLoache, 1995). Abilities such as this are precursors to more advanced abilities of mental abstraction.

(a)

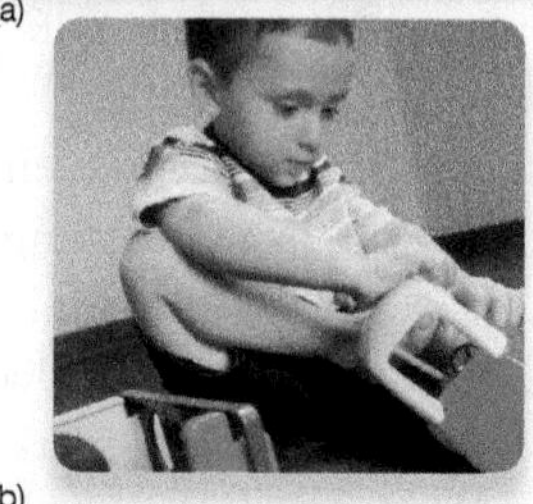
(b)

(c)

Courtesy of Judy DeLoache

{FIG. 10.7} **Scale Errors and Testing for Scale Model Comprehension** The children in photos (a) and (b) are making scale errors. One child is attempting to slide down a toy slide and another is attempting to enter a toy car. Three-year-olds understand that a scale model represents an actual room (c). The adult pictured is using a scale model to indicate the location of a hidden object in an actual room of this type. At around 3 years of age, children understand that the scale model symbolizes an actual room and will go directly to the hidden object after viewing the scale model.

THE CONCRETE OPERATIONAL STAGE: USING LOGICAL THOUGHT Conservation is one of the main skills marking the transition from the preoperational stage to the **concrete operational stage** *(ages 7 to 11 years), when children develop skills in logical thinking and manipulating numbers.* Children in the concrete operational stage are able to classify objects according to properties such as size, value, shape, or some other physical characteristic. Their thinking becomes increasingly logical and organized. For example, a child in the concrete operational stage recognizes that if X is more than Y, and Y is more than Z, then X is more than Z (a property called *transitivity*). This ability to think logically about physical objects sets the stage for them to think logically about abstractions in the fourth and final stage of cognitive development.

THE FORMAL OPERATIONAL STAGE: ABSTRACT AND HYPOTHETICAL THOUGHT The **formal operational stage** *(ages 11 to adulthood) involves the development of advanced cognitive processes such as abstract reasoning and hypothetical thinking.* Scientific thinking, such as gathering evidence and systematically testing possibilities, is characteristic of this stage.

WORKING THE SCIENTIFIC LITERACY MODEL

Evaluating Piaget

Piaget was immensely successful at opening our eyes to the cognitive development of infants and children. Nevertheless, advances in testing methods have showed that he may have underestimated some aspects of infant cognitive abilities. In fact, infants appear to understand some basic principles of the physical and social worlds very shortly after birth.

What do we know about cognitive abilities in infants?

The **core knowledge hypothesis** *proposes that infants have inborn abilities for understanding some key aspects of their environment* (Spelke & Kinzler, 2007). It is a bold claim to say that babies know something about the world before they have even experienced it, so we should closely examine the evidence for this hypothesis.

How can *we* know what infants know or what they perceive? One frequently used method for answering this question relies on the habituation–dishabituation response. **Habituation** *refers to a decrease in responding with repeated exposure to an event,* something infants are well known for doing. For example, if an infant views the same stimulus over and over, she will stop looking at it. Conversely, infants are quite responsive to novelty or changes in their environment. Thus, if the stimulus suddenly changes, the infant will display **dishabituation**, *an increase in responsiveness with the presentation of a new stimulus.* In other words, the infant will return her gaze to the location that she previously found boring. Knowing that infants respond to stimuli in these ways allows researchers to devise ways to test infants even younger than Piaget's tests were able to test.

How can science help explain infant cognitive abilities?

Habituation and dishabituation have been used to measure whether infants understand many different concepts, including abstract numbers—an ability that most people imagine appears much later in development. For example, Elizabeth Spelke and colleagues conducted a study in which 16 infants just *two days old* were shown sets of either 4 or 12 identical small shapes (e.g., yellow triangles, purple circles) on a video screen. The researchers also sounded a tone 4 or 12 times (e.g., tu-tu-tu-tu or ra-ra-ra-ra-ra-ra-ra-ra-ra-ra-ra-ra) at the same time they showed the shapes (see Figure 10.8). Researchers varied whether the number of shapes the infants saw matched the number of tones they heard (e.g., 4 yellow triangles and 4 ra-ra-ra-ra tones), or not (e.g., 12 ra tones and 4 purple circles). The infants were most attentive when what they saw and heard matched. In other words, they looked longer at the shapes when the tone that accompanied them matched in number, compared to when

Explore
Physical Knowledge in Infancy

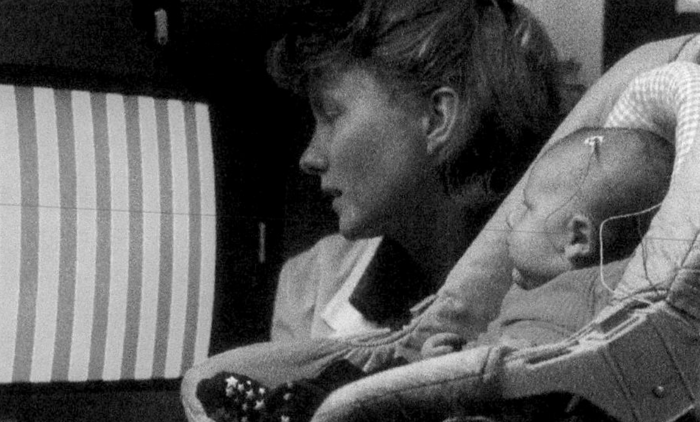
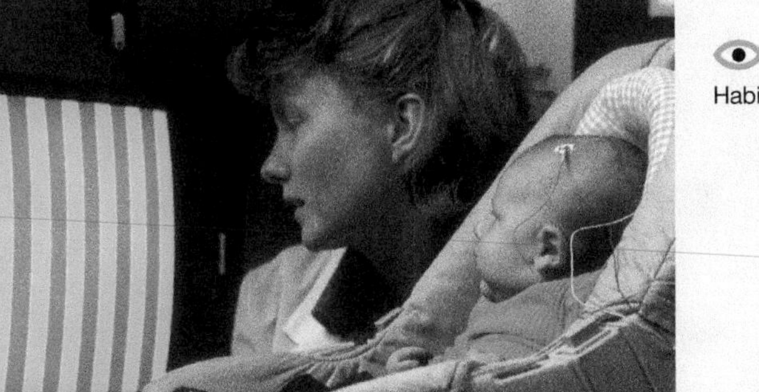

Lawrence Migdale/Photo Researchers, Inc.

A popular method for testing infant cognitive abilities is to measure the amount of time infants look at events. Researchers measure habituation and dishabituation to infer what infants understand.

Watch
Habituation

{FIG. 10.8} **Testing Infants' Understanding of Quantity** In this study, infants listened to tones that were repeated either 4 or 12 times while they looked at objects that had either 4 or 12 components. Infants spent more time looking at visual arrays when the number of items they saw matched the number of tones they heard.

they did not match. The researchers believe that this finding is evidence that even very young infants have a rudimentary appreciation for abstract numbers (Izard et al., 2009).

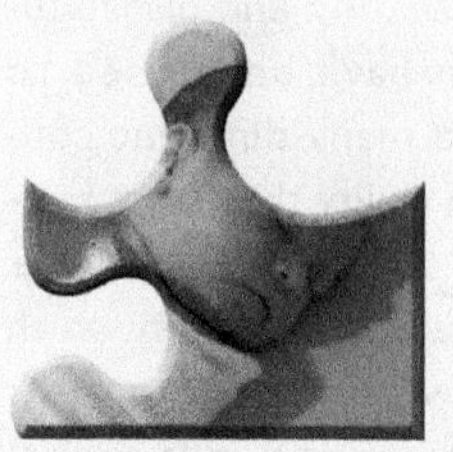

Can we critically evaluate alternative explanations?

Many of the studies of early cognitive development discussed in this module used the "looking time" procedure, although not all psychologists agree that it is an ideal way of determining what infants understand or perceive (Aslin, 2007; Rivera et al., 1999). We cannot know exactly what infants are thinking, and perhaps they look longer at events and stimuli simply because these are more interesting, rather than because they understand anything in particular about them. Inferring mental states when the participant cannot validate them certainly leaves room for alternative explanations. Also, the sample size was fairly small; in the study of shapes and tones just described, only 16 infants managed to complete the study. Forty-five others were too fussy or sleepy to successfully finish the task. (And can you blame them? Only in the world for two days and their parents already have them in a psychology lab!)

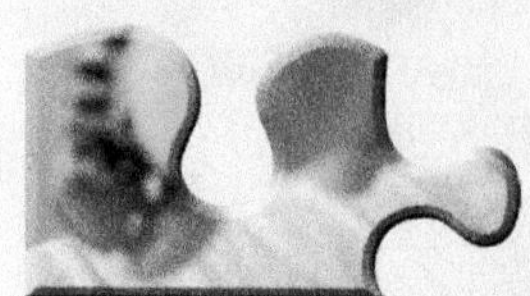

Why is this relevant?

The key insight provided by this research is that cognitive development in young infants is much more sophisticated than psychologists have assumed. With each study that examines the cognitive capacities of infants, we learn that infants are not just slobbery blobs that need to be fed and diapered—though it certainly can feel that way when you are a new parent. Instead, infants' brains are rapidly developing, and they are procedurally absorbing the logic of their world. In other words, infants can begin to understand more than we might realize, and their brains are actively being patterned by the world. Talking to them using diverse vocabulary, exploring rhythms, allowing them to feel different objects, and exposing them to different textures and sensations are all good ways to use their dominant modality (sensorimotor) to expand their emerging cognitive abilities.

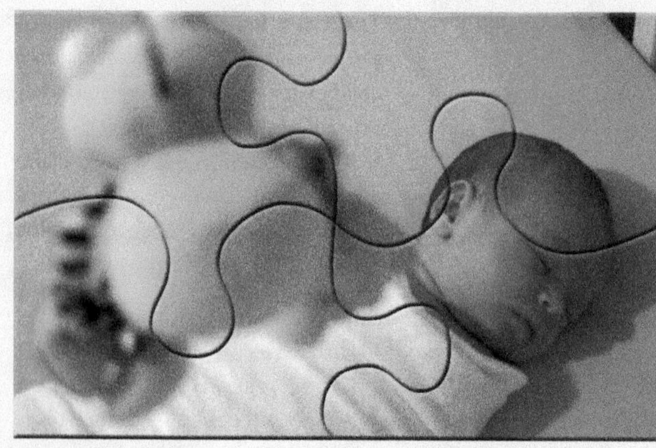

Jane Shauck Photography/Alamy

COMPLEMENTARY APPROACHES TO PIAGET

Piaget's theories have had a lasting impact on modern developmental psychology. Even so, some details of his theories have been refuted or challenged in the intervening decades. In particular, Piaget generally underestimated the abilities of infants and their rates of development, and his strong emphasis on cognitive tasks overlooked sociocultural and biological elements of cognitive growth.

Watch Zone of Proximal Development: Cognitive

Watch Zone of Proximal Development: Physical

The interactions that occur between children and other people form the sociocultural context in which cognitive development occurs; children's abilities are therefore responsive to their social environment. For example, children who try to master a skill by themselves may run into obstacles that would be much easier to overcome with a little assistance or guidance from another person. At the opposite extreme, imagine children who have everything done for them and who are not allowed to try things out and work through problems themselves; their development would be harmed, in this case by excessive involvement. Therefore, it seems logical that optimal development occurs somewhere in between these extremes. Russian psychologist Lev Vygotsky (1978) proposed that *development is ideal when children attempt skills and activities that are just beyond what they can do alone, but they have guidance from adults who are attentive to their progress;* this was called the **zone of proximal development** (Singer & Goldin-Meadow, 2005). Teaching in order to keep children in the zone of proximal development is

Gladskikh Tatiana/shutterstock.com

Caregivers who are attentive to the learning and abilities of a developing child provide scaffolding for cognitive development.

called **scaffolding**, *a highly attentive approach to teaching in which the teacher matches guidance to the learner's needs.*

Cross-cultural research on parent–infant interactions shows that scaffolding is exercised in different ways (Rogoff et al., 1993). For example, in one study, 12- to 24-month-old children were offered a toy that required pulling a string to make it move. Parents from Turkey, Guatemala, and the United States were observed interacting with their infants as they attempted to figure out how the toy worked. All parents used scaffolding when they spoke and gestured to their children to encourage them to pull the string, but mother–child pairs from Guatemala were much more communicative with each other, both verbally and through gestures such as touching and using the direction of their gaze to encourage the behaviour. Interestingly, this increased scaffolding results over time in children who are more seamlessly integrated into the daily life of the family and community, rather than merely relegated to "play" activities using specialized and highly unrealistic toys. In simple terms, this means that children who are appropriately scaffolded are able to be useful and self-sufficient at much earlier ages than is normal in contemporary North American society. This kind of scaffolding approach to everyday life tasks is one of the foundational practices in "alternative" education systems, such as the Montessori system.

Quick Quiz 10.2a

Cognitive Changes: Piaget's Cognitive Development Theory

KNOW ...

1 Recognizing that the quantity of an object does not change despite changes in physical arrangement or appearance is referred to as ________.

A object permanence **C** conservation

B scale comprehension **D** number sense

2 Parents who attend to their children's psychological abilities and guide them through the learning process are using ________.

A scaffolding

B tutoring

C core knowledge

D the zone of proximal development

3 What is the correct order of Piaget's stages of cognitive development?

A Preoperational, sensorimotor, concrete operational, formal operational

B Sensorimotor, preoperational, formal operational, concrete operational

C Sensorimotor, preoperational, concrete operational, formal operational

D Preoperational, concrete operational, sensorimotor, formal operational

APPLY ...

4 A child in the sensorimotor stage may quit looking or reaching for a toy if you move it out of sight. This behaviour reflects the fact that the child has not developed ________.

A core knowledge **C** conservation

B object permanence **D** to the preoperational stage

ANALYZE ...

5 Research on newborns indicates that they have a sense of number and quantity. What does this finding suggest about Piaget's theory of cognitive development?

A It confirms what Piaget claimed about infants in the sensorimotor phase.

B Some infants are born with superior intelligence.

C Piaget may have underestimated some cognitive abilities of infants and children.

D Culture determines what infants are capable of doing.

Answers can be found on page ANS-3.

Social Development: Attachment, Personality, and Reading Others

Think of how helpless infants and toddlers are upon being born. Subject to a chaotic world entirely different from the one they were in for nine months (wait . . . you mean I *don't* have a constant stream of food delivered straight into my stomach?!), they are utterly dependent on their caregivers in order to survive. This sense that they are being cared for forms the basis of an infant's feelings of security. We know from discussing Piaget that infants experience the world through sensation and movement; it makes sense, then, that a significant way in which this security is experienced is through touch, as well as other explicit physical cues that indicate a caregiver is close enough to respond to their needs, such as vocal reassurance and responsive facial expressions. If this physical responsiveness is missing, the attachment system can break down quickly, leaving the infant in a state of insecurity, feeling that they are vulnerable and that key figures in their life cannot be counted on to respond to their needs.

TYPES OF ATTACHMENT Intense social bonding between humans starts with **attachment**, *the enduring emotional bond formed between individuals,* initially between infant and caregiver. From an evolutionary perspective, safety and survival are the basic needs that give rise to the need for attachment (Bowlby, 1951). Thus, each human child forms a basic sense of security through the attachment bonds they form; attachment motivations are deeply rooted in our psychology, compelling us to seek out others for physical and psychological comfort,

Watch Attachment

particularly when we feel stressed or insecure. Infants use behaviours that are both cute and not-so-cute to seek attachment, such as crying, cooing, gurgling, smiling, and screaming, and adults are generally responsive to these communications.

Watch
Attachment in Infants

In the early decades of modern psychology, dominant theories of motivation emphasized biological drives, such as hunger and thirst, that motivated people to satisfy their basic needs. From this perspective, the reason why infants seem to love their moms was simple; mom fed them, reduced their hunger, and through simple conditioning (associating mom with food), they developed a behavioural interdependence with mom. Such a description of love is never going to fill many books of poetry, but it seemed "scientific" and "objective."

In the 1950s, psychologist Harry Harlow became passionately interested in the topic of bonding and attachment after noticing that infant rhesus monkeys who were being raised without mothers in his laboratory clung desperately to cloth pads that lined their cages and would panic when these pads were removed for cleaning. Obviously, the pads provided nothing of value in strict, practical terms; the monkeys didn't eat the pads, after all. This made Harlow start to wonder just how important primary drive reduction was after all; if the monkeys could be so attached to the cloth pads, maybe something similar was at work in normal infants' attachment to their moms. Maybe it's not about mom as a food provider; maybe babies just like physical comfort.

Watch
Classic Footage of Harlow's Monkeys: Contact Comfort

Harlow designed an ingenious set of studies, testing whether it was physical comfort or primary drive reduction that drove the formation of attachment. He raised rhesus monkeys from birth, and placed them in cages with two pseudo-parents: one was a cylinder of mesh wire wrapped with a piece of terry cloth that loosely resembled an adult monkey; the other was an identical cylinder but without the cloth covering. Some monkeys were raised in cages where the "wire mother" also had a bottle affixed to her and thus was the infant's food source, and other monkeys were raised in cages where the "cloth mother" was the food provider.

The question was, who would the monkeys bond with? Would they bond with whoever fed them? Or

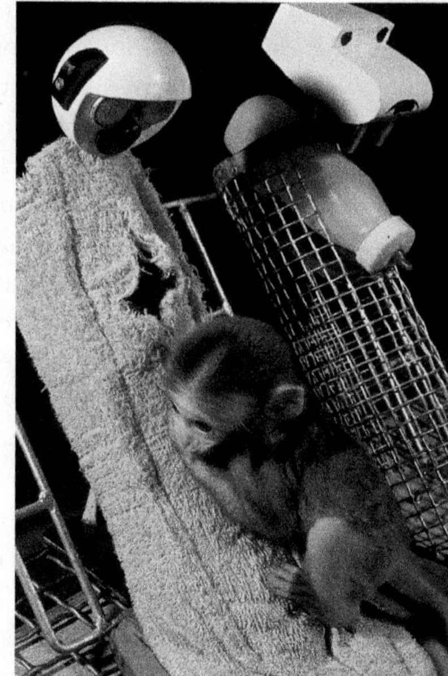
Nina Leen/Time & Life Pictures/Getty Images

A baby monkey clings to a cloth-covered object—Harlow called this object the *cloth mother*—even though in this case the wire "mother" provided food.

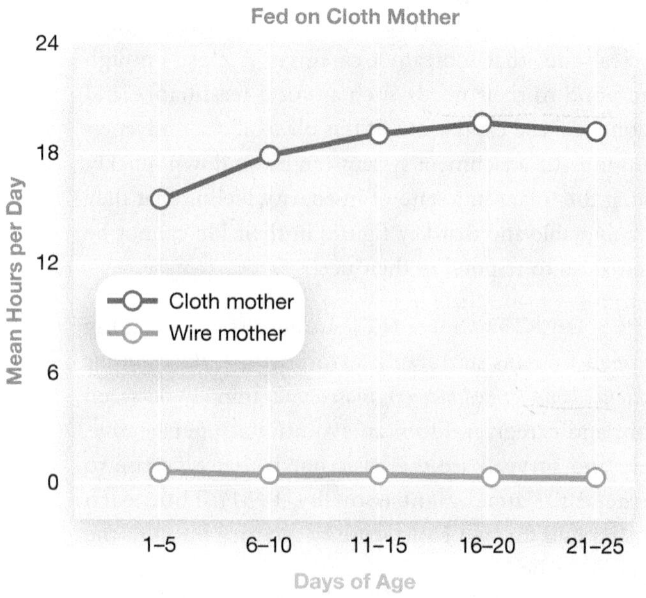

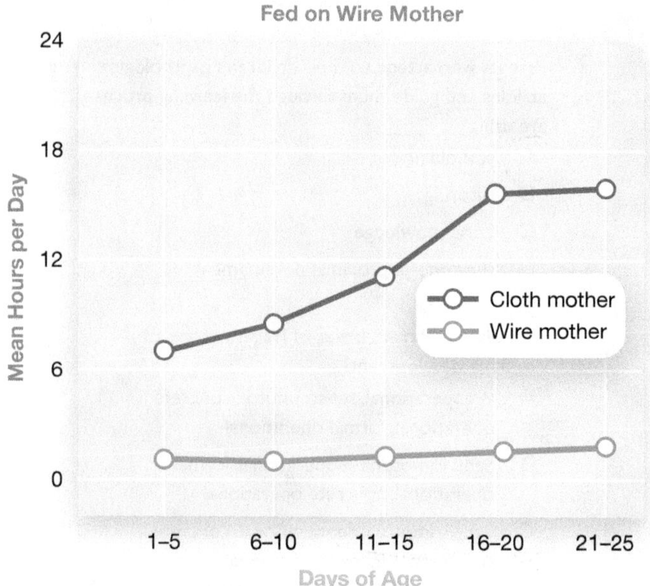

{FIG. 10.9} **Harlow's Monkeys: Time Spent on Wire and Cloth Mother Surrogates**

would they prefer the more comfortable cloth mother regardless of whether she fed them or not?

The contest between moms wasn't even close. No matter who had the bottle, the baby monkeys spent almost all their time with the cloth mom (see Figure 10.9). To test the degree of emotional dependence on the pseudo-mom, researchers arranged experiments in which the baby monkey would get scared (e.g., surprising them with a metallic contraption made to look, and sound, like a vicious monster), and they would watch which mother the infants would run to for comfort and security. Over and over again, they ran to the cloth mom. The implications were clear—attachment is not about reducing fundamental biological drives; attachment is based on feeling secure, which is based on physical comfort.

Unfortunately, Harlow's insights were not immediately adopted into mainstream parenting practice. In fact, the behaviourist approach to parenting remained dominant in North American society for decades, subjecting children to punishments in the form of time-outs (the modern replacement for spankings) and the removal of privileges ("No TV for the rest of the week!"), and the almost-continual use of rewards ("If you eat your broccoli, you can have ice cream for dessert") and praise ("Good job!"). Raising children as though they are animals learning to perform specific tasks makes a great deal of sense from a purely behaviourist perspective, although it ignores the emotional reality of the child.

In fact, parenting "wisdom" that stemmed from the behaviourist approach emphasized that children should be exposed to very limited bodily contact, in order to avoid spoiling them. John Watson, one of the pioneers of behaviourism, advised: "Never hug and kiss [your child], never let them sit on your lap. If you must, kiss them once on the forehead when they say goodnight. Shake hands with them in the morning. Give them a pat on the head if they have made an extraordinary good job of a difficult task." This quote probably made you laugh, but it's important to appreciate just how radical the research on attachment would have been on the heels of this sterile view of parenting—even though most of us now don't question the idea that physical affection is good for children. Sadly, gaining this knowledge has meant that many children nowadays are deprived of regular handshakes and pats on the head. Hugs and kisses will have to do.

In order to measure attachment bonds in human infants, obviously it is unethical to raise babies in cages with fake moms and then scare them half to death to see who they crawl to. Instead, psychologists have developed methods of studying infant attachment that are only mildly stressful and mimic natural situations. One method capitalizes on *stranger anxiety,* signs of distress that infants begin to show toward strangers, at about eight months of age.

{FIG. 10.10} **The Strange Situation** Studies of attachment by Mary Ainsworth involved a mother leaving her infant with a stranger. Ainsworth believed that the infants' attachment styles could be categorized according to their behavioural and emotional responses to the mother leaving and returning.

Simulate Attachment Classifications in the Strange Situation

Mary Ainsworth (1978) developed a procedure using the **strange situation** as *a way of measuring infant attachment by observing how infants behave when exposed to different experiences that involve anxiety and comfort.* The procedure involves a sequence of scripted experiences that expose children to some mild anxiety (e.g., the presence of a stranger, being left alone with the stranger), and the potential to receive some comfort from their caregiver (e.g., the return of the caregiver). For example, the child and caregiver spend a few minutes in a room with some toys; a stranger enters, the caregiver leaves, and then the caregiver returns. In each segment of the procedure, the child's behaviour is carefully observed. Ainsworth noted three broad patterns of behaviour that she believed reflected three different attachment styles (see Figure 10.10):

1. *Secure attachment.* The caregiver is a secure base that the child turns toward occasionally, "checking in" for reassurance as he or she explores the room. The child shows some distress when the caregiver leaves, and avoids the stranger. When the caregiver returns, the child seeks comfort and her distress is relieved.
2. *Insecure attachment.* Two subtypes were distinguished:
   - *Anxious/Resistant.* The caregiver is a base of security, but the child depends too strongly on the caregiver, exhibiting "clingy" behaviour rather than being comfortable exploring the room on his own. The child is very upset when the caregiver leaves, and is quite fearful toward the stranger. When the caregiver returns, the child seeks comfort, but then also resists it and pushes

Watch Stranger Anxiety

the caregiver away, not allowing his distress to be easily alleviated.

- *Avoidant*. The child behaves as though she does not need the caregiver at all, and plays in the room as though she is oblivious to the caregiver. The child is not upset when the caregiver leaves, and is unconcerned about the stranger. When the caregiver returns, the child does not seek contact.

3. Subsequent research identified a fourth attachment style, *disorganized* (Main & Solomon, 1990). What best characterizes disorganized attachment is instability; the child has learned (typically through inconsistent and often abusive experiences) that caregivers are both sources of fear and comfort, leaving the child oscillating between wanting to get away and wanting to be reassured. The child experiences a strong ambivalence, and reinforces this through his own inconsistent behaviour, seeking closeness and then pulling away, or often simply "freezing," paralyzed with indecision.

Watch
Self-Awareness Task

Attachment is important not only in infancy, but throughout one's life. For example, in adult romantic relationships, attachment styles (gained during infancy!) are still at work (Hofer, 2006). A longitudinal study spanning more than 20 years showed that people who were securely attached as infants were better able to recover from interpersonal conflict with their romantic partners (Salvatore et al., 2011). Our attachment styles hold evolutionary advantages in that they lead us to establish secure and long-lasting relationships, which, in humans, is an important component of childrearing (Bowlby, 1951; Fraley et al., 2005).

Watch
Egocentrism Task

Upon identifying the characteristic attachment styles, psychologists began to ask *how* infants developed their particular style. It may come as no surprise to you that the way parents/caregivers interact with infants influences their attachment style. Ainsworth's research (Ainsworth, 1978) showed that maternal sensitivity (i.e., being highly attuned to the infant's signals and communication, and responding appropriately) is key to developing a secure attachment style.

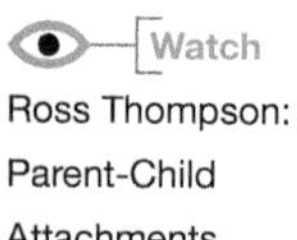
Watch
Ross Thompson: Parent-Child Attachments

While it was initially believed that ideal parenting called for parents to be highly sensitive to the child, leading to closely coordinated emotional interactions between them, recent studies have shown that highly sensitive caregivers actually demonstrate *moderate* coordination with their children (Hane et al., 2003). Both under-responsiveness and over-involvement/hypersensitivity to an infant's needs and emotions are correlated with the formation of insecure attachment styles (Beebe et al., 2010). The ideal parent does not reflexively respond to all the child's needs, but is sensitive to *how much* responsiveness the child needs. In the next section we will learn how this type of parental sensitivity is connected to the development of self-awareness, as well as the awareness of other minds.

SELF AWARENESS Between 18–24 months of age, toddlers begin to make a major shift in awareness, gaining **self-awareness**, *the ability to recognize one's individuality*. Becoming aware of one's self goes hand-in-hand with becoming aware of others as separate beings, and thus, self-awareness and the development of pro-social and moral motivations are intricately intertwined, as we discuss below.

The presence of self-awareness is typically tested by observing infants' reactions to their reflection in a mirror or on video (Bahrick & Watson, 1985; Bard et al., 2006). Self-awareness becomes increasingly sophisticated over the course of development, progressing from early recognition of oneself in a mirror or on video, to having the ability to reflect on one's own feelings, decisions, and appearance. By the time children reach their fifth birthday, they become self-reflective, show concern for others, and are intensely interested in the causes of other people's behaviour.

Young children are often described as **egocentric**, *meaning that they only consider their own perspective* (Piaget & Inhelder, 1956). This does not imply that children are selfish or inconsiderate, but that they merely lack the cognitive ability to understand the perspective of others. For example, a two-year-old may attempt to hide by simply covering her own eyes. From her perspective, she

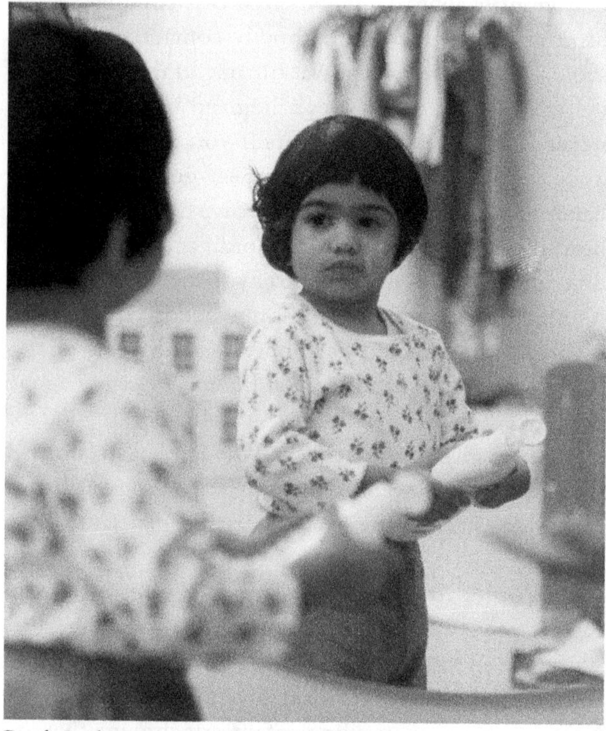

Ruth Jenkinson/Dorling Kindersley Ltd

By two years of age, toddlers can recognize themselves in mirrors.

is hidden. Piaget tested for egocentrism by sitting a child in front of an object, and then presenting pictures of that object from four angles. While sitting opposite the child, Piaget would ask him or her to identify which image represented the object from Piaget's perspective. Many children would select the image corresponding to their own perspective (Figure 10.11). Piaget concluded that children were egocentric through the preoperational phase (ending around age seven).

Modern research indicates that children take the perspective of others long before the preoperational phase is complete. Perspective taking in young children has been demonstrated in studies of **theory of mind**—*the ability to recognize the thoughts, beliefs, and expectations of others, and to understand that these can be different from one's own.* Adults may have difficulty putting themselves in another person's shoes from time to time, but young children find it next to impossible. Consider the following scenario:

> *An experimenter offers three-year-old Andrea a box of chocolates. Upon opening the box, Andrea discovers not candy, but rather pencils. Joseph enters the room and she watches as Joseph is offered the same box. The researcher asks Andrea, "What does Joseph expect to find in the box?"*

This is called the *false-belief task.* If Andrea answers "pencils," this indicates that she believes that Joseph knows the same thing she does. However, if Andrea tells the experimenter that Joseph expects to see chocolates, it demonstrates that she is taking Joseph's mental perspective, understanding that he does not possess her knowledge (Lillard, 1998; Wimmer & Perner, 1983). Children typically pass this test at ages four to five, although younger children may pass it if they are told that Joseph is about to be tricked. Of course, the shift away from egocentric thought does not occur overnight. Older children may still have difficulty taking the perspective of others; in fact, even adults aren't that great at it much of the time. As with many milestones of development, theory of mind is not a linear *outcome* of development, but rather a continual *process.*

Converging evidence now indicates that self-awareness and theory of mind are dynamic and in constant development right from birth. Our abilities to represent our own thoughts and another's thoughts are intimately tied together and may have similar origins within the brain (Keenan et al., 2000). Early in children's lives, emotions are often experienced as chaotic, overwhelming, and unintegrated combinations of physical sensations, non-verbal representations, and ideas. As caregivers respond to children's emotions, this provides a kind of "mirror," a "higher order representation" that assists children in organizing their emotion, helping them "know what they feel" (Fonagy & Target, 1997). As children gain the ability to understand their internal states with greater clarity, this scaffolds their ability to represent the mental states of others.

{FIG. 10.11} **Piaget's Test for Egocentric Perspective in Children** Piaget used the three-mountain task to test whether children can take someone else's perspective. The child would view the object from one perspective while another person viewed it from a different point of view. According to Piaget, children are no longer exclusively egocentric if they understand that the other person sees the object differently.

This helps to explain why it is important that caregivers not overidentify with a child's emotions. If their emotional exchange is completely synchronized (e.g., the child experiences fear and the adult also experiences fear) then the symbolic function of the caregiver's sensitive response is lost; the child simply gets fear reinforced, rather than gaining the ability to *understand* that she is feeling fear. There is a profound difference between being locked into an emotion, and being able to stand back from the emotion somewhat and understand it as an experience one is having. In a study of how mothers behave after their infants received an injection, Fonagey et al. (1995) observed that the mothers who most effectively soothed their child rapidly reflected their child's emotions, but also included displays of other affect in their mirroring, such as smiling or questioning. The mother's "complex" representation of the child's affect ensured that the child recognized it as related to, but not identical to his own emotion. This serves to modulate negative emotions by helping to implicitly build coping responses into the experience and understand experiences in a more organized, abstract fashion (Fonagy & Target, 1997).

Therefore, in the early stages of life, these face-to-face exchanges of emotional signals help the child's brain learn how to understand and "deal with" emotions (Beebe et al., 1997).

Watch
The Preschool Years: Egocentrism

PROSOCIAL BEHAVIOUR Being aware of one's own emotions, and then understanding the emotions of others, are extremely important parts of prosocial moral motivations and behaviours. However, the basic capacity for morality is built right into us and manifests long before we develop the cognitive sophistication to recognize "self" and "others." Children show a natural predisposition toward prosocial behaviour very early in their development (Hamlin et al., 2007; Warneken & Tomasello, in press). Even one-day-old infants experience distress when they hear other infants cry, exhibiting affective empathy, which is a spontaneous response to another person's affect.

However, at this point children have not sufficiently separated others' distress from their own, and are predominantly motivated to get rid of their experience of distress rather than act out of other-oriented concern (Eisenberg, 2005). For example, watching a parent cry is upsetting to a young child, and sometimes the child may seek to comfort the parent, such as by offering his teddy bear; other times, however, children might just close their eyes and plug their ears, thereby alleviating their own distress. In order for explicitly prosocial motives to develop, children must learn to attribute their negative feelings to the other person's distress, thereby becoming motivated to reduce the other person's suffering, not just their own reaction to it (Mascolo & Fischer, 2007; Zahn-Waxler & Radke-Yarrow, 1990). For this purpose, social and communicative support from adults is important scaffolding for children's understanding of both their own and others' intentional states (as explored in the previous section); basically, helping children be aware of themselves helps them be aware of others, which motivates and teaches them to be concerned for others' welfare (Carpendale & Lewis, 2004; Ruffman et al., 2006).

Recently, amazing work by researchers at the University of British Columbia and other universities has discovered that the roots of moral motivation go back much further than we once believed, all the way to very early infancy. This is truly groundbreaking work; the suggestion that children could be innately moral beings would have been greeted with ridicule for much of our cultural history. Western culture has been strongly influenced by the Christian notion of "original sin," leading to the general belief that people are fundamentally selfish, that religion and culture are necessary to curb human evil and keep life from becoming "nasty, brutish, and short" and that children are basically "bad" and need proper discipline in order to have their inherent evil beaten out of them; "spare the rod and spoil the child" was parenting wisdom for untold centuries.

However, even infants seem to recognize good from bad, and to prefer people (or teddy bears, as the research shows) who display good, moral behaviour, such as helping (Hamlin et al., 2007, 2010). Five-month-old infants indiscriminately prefer people who help others, showing that even before infants can crawl, they are processing kindness in others' behaviour. By eight months, infants are making complex moral discriminations; infants prefer others who are kind to someone who is prosocial, but they prefer others who are unkind to someone who is antisocial (Hamlin et al., 2011). This leads to a much more optimistic view of human nature. It doesn't seem that humans are inherently selfish; in fact, we seem to inherently prefer the good.

As children move from infancy to the toddler years, their prosocial behaviours increase in scope and complexity. Around their first birthday, children demonstrate *instrumental helping*, providing practical assistance such as helping to retrieve an object that is out of reach (Liszkowski et al., 2006; Warneken & Tomasello, 2007). By their second birthday, they begin to exhibit *empathic helping*, providing help in order to make someone feel better (Zahn-Waxler et al., 1992). In one study, children younger than two were observed to be happier when giving to others over receiving treats themselves, especially when the giving occurred at a cost to their own resources (Aknin et al., 2012).

In humans, the tension between helping others versus being concerned for oneself reflects a deep tension in our own biology. Humans possess two psychobiological systems, the **attachment behavioural system**, *which is focused on meeting our own needs for security*, and the **caregiving behavioural system**, *which is focused on meeting the needs of others*. Each system guides our behaviour when it is activated; however, the attachment system is primary, and if it is activated, it tends to shut down the caregiving system. What this means in everyday experience is that if a person feels insecure herself, it will be hard for her to reach out and take others' needs into consideration. However, if attachment needs are fulfilled and the person is in a state of basic security, then the caregiving system responds to signs of others' distress, motivating the person to care for others (Mikulincer & Shaver, 2005).

Understanding how these two behavioural systems function is critically important for understanding why secure attachment is related to prosocial behaviour. An insecurely attached person will often have his own needs (fear, insecurity, distress) activated, and the attachment system then effectively shuts down the caregiving system. Helping people feel securely attached, then, is important for building a truly compassionate society. Given that one of the central goals of parents is to raise kind, moral children, developmental psychology has helped us fully appreciate how this goal can only be met by helping parents understand how to raise securely attached children. One difficult set of conclusions drawn from this research is a deep critique of many aspects of common North American parenting practices; the hope is that the prevailing wisdom about parenting may change in the years to come.

Quick Quiz 10.2b

Social Development: Attachment, Personality, and Reading Others

KNOW ...

1 The emotional bond that forms between caregiver and child is referred to as ________.

A a love/hate relationship

B dependence

C attachment

D transference

UNDERSTAND ...

2 Marcus is very careful and consistent about how he raises his daughter, because he doesn't want to "spoil" her. When she misbehaves or cries, he gives her a "time out," whereas when she does what she is told to do, he gives her a big smile and enthusiastic "Good job!" Marcus's approach to parenting is heavily guided by ________.

A Piaget's theory of cognitive development

B behaviourism

C cognitive psychology

D humanistic psychology

APPLY ...

3 As you observe a child you know interacting with her parents, you watch the child behaving in a "clingy" and dependent manner, but later you notice that the child is behaving very independently from her parents and actively rejects their attention. It seems likely that the child has what sort of attachment style?

A Secure

B Anxious/resistant

C Avoidant

D Disorganized

Answers can be found on page ANS-3.

PARENTING Parenting is a topic of much debate and, all too often, intense judgment. Many parenting books lining the shelves of bookstores promise a simple, step-by-step method that will *get children to behave the way you want.* Certainly, this makes sense; parents constantly need their kids to get certain things done—get up, eat your breakfast, get dressed, brush your teeth, brush your hair, pack your things, get your lunch, go to school. . . .

The application of operant conditioning to parenting, in the form of providing children with rewards (e.g., Smarties, physical affection, loving words) and punishments (e.g., angry tone of voice, time-outs, criticism), has provided caregivers many tools for, basically, manipulating the behaviour of children. Although society has largely moved away from the use of harsh punishments (e.g., spankings), the use of both rewards and punishments is pervasive in modern parenting practices. In North American society particularly, the majority of people are unconcerned about trying to reinforce desired behaviour through the use of rewards, such as praise, verbal encouragement, or some form of advancement system (e.g., points, levels, ranks). Any amount of time spent actually interacting with children will make the benefits of such positive reinforcement unmistakably obvious.

However, children are not merely stimulus-response machines, and this pervasive use of *conditional approaches* sows the seeds for many problems that crop up over time. One of the almost invisible but highly damaging problems is that even though rewards do successfully produce the desired behaviours in children, these behaviours don't tend to persist; the children won't keep engaging in the behaviour unless they continue to receive rewards (Deci, Ryan, & Koestner, 1999). This encourages a whole generation of children to become addicted, in a sense, to praise and other rewards, finding it difficult to motivate themselves or even to explore their passions for the intrinsic interest and enjoyment of the activity.

Another downside to the conditional parenting approach (including positive reinforcement) is the impact it may have on children's self-esteem and emotional security. Because children learn to associate feeling good about themselves with the experience of receiving rewards, their self-esteem becomes more dependent upon external sources of validation, such as the attention or admiration of other people, or the tendency to compare oneself to others and seek to be "the best." In addition to the gradual erosion of children's motivation discussed above, an overuse of rewards builds a more conditional sense of self-worth, making people more dependent on external sources of validation or reward in order to feel good about themselves.

Despite their down sides, the immediate and obvious benefits of using rewards and punishments have led to their use in virtually every aspect of society, from families, to schools, to workplaces (think: grades, praise, candy, commission). Parents doling out praise, affection, TV, and treats for "good" behaviour, versus time-outs, anger, removal of privileges, and general withdrawal of affection for "bad" behaviour, is so normal that most of us don't even think twice about this approach.

Watch In the Real World: Parenting Styles and Socialization

Although this may seem fairly normal when it comes to raising children, think about it for a moment in a different context, such as your romantic relationship. Imagine if you and your partner decided to go to a couple's counsellor in order to work out some problems in your relationship. Now imagine that the counsellor

Top: Chamille White/Shutterstock.com; centre: Kali Nine LLC/E+/Getty Images; bottom: bonninturina/Fotolia

Rewards and punishments: The use of operant conditioning approaches in our daily lives

told you that every time your partner behaved in ways you didn't like, you should respond with immediate negativity, such as withdrawing affection and adopting a "cold" tone of voice, speaking sharply and angrily to him, physically forcing him into a corner for the amount of minutes equivalent to his age, or taking away one of his favourite possessions. You also should use rewards as a way of getting your partner to do things you want—promise him pie, or physical intimacy, or buy him something nice.

Our guess is that you would conclude it's time to get a different counsellor. Nobody would want to be in a relationship that operated through such manipulative, and even abusive, tactics. There are natural social rewards in relationships, but using them explicitly to manipulate behaviour just seems, well, manipulative! Nevertheless, this is often how we raise children.

A mountain of research has revealed the downside of taking this kind of conditional approach to parenting. One meta-analysis of 128 different studies revealed that *all forms of explicit reward undermined participants' interest in the activity for which they received the reward.* Even verbal rewards didn't work (Deci et al., 1999). For children, feeling controlled is associated with less creativity and motivation (Grolnick & Apoteleris, 2002). Furthermore, children who experience their parents' regard for them as conditional report more negativity and resentment toward their parents; they also feel greater internal pressure to do well, which is called **introjection**, *the internalization of the conditional regard of significant others* (Assor et al., 2004). The more that people motivate themselves through introjection, the more unstable their self-esteem (Kernis et al., 2000), and the worse they tend to cope with failure (Grolnick & Ryan, 1989).

So what works better? Research clearly shows that moral development is associated with more frequent use of **inductive discipline**, *which involves explaining the consequences of a child's actions on other people, activating empathy for others' feelings* (Hoffman & Saltzsein, 1967). Providing a rationale for a parent's decisions, showing empathy and understanding of the child's emotions, supporting her autonomy, and allowing her choice whenever possible all promote positive outcomes such as greater mastery of skills, increased emotional and behavioural self-control, better ability to persist at difficult tasks, and a deeper internalization of moral values (Deci et al., 1994; Frodi et al., 1985).

When it comes to raising moral children, the "golden rule" seems to apply just as well—do unto your children as you would have someone do unto you.

Module Summary

Module **10.2**

Now that you have read this module you should

KNOW …

- ***The key terminology associated with infancy and childhood:***

accommodation (p. 406)
assimilation (p. 406)
attachment (p. 411)
attachment behavioural system (p. 416)
caregiving behavioural system (p. 416)
cognitive development (p. 406)
concrete operational stage (p. 408)
conservation (p. 407)
core knowledge hypothesis (p. 409)
dishabituation (p. 409)
egocentric (p. 414)
formal operational stage (p. 408)
habituation (p. 409)
inductive discipline (p. 418)
introjection (p. 418)
object permanence (p. 407)
preoperational stage (p. 407)
scaffolding (p. 411)
self-awareness (p. 414)
sensorimotor stage (p. 407)
strange situation (p. 413)
theory of mind (p. 415)
zone of proximal development (p. 410)

UNDERSTAND …

- ***The cognitive changes that occur during infancy and childhood.*** According to Piaget's theory of cognitive development, infants mature through childhood via orderly transitions across the sensorimotor, preoperational, concrete operational, and formal operational stages. This progression reflects a general transition from engaging in the world through purely concrete, sensory experiences, to an increasing ability to hold and manipulate abstract representations of the world in one's mind.
- ***The concept of attachment and the different styles of attachment.*** In developmental psychology, attachment refers to the enduring social bond between child and caregiver. Based on the quality of this bond, which is dependent on appropriately responsive parenting, individuals develop an attachment style, which is their internalized feeling of security and self-worth. Children are either securely or insecurely attached, and insecure attachments can be further divided into disorganized, resistant, and avoidant styles.

Inspirestock Inc/Alamy

APPLY …

- ***The concept of scaffolding and the zone of proximal development to understand how to best promote learning.*** According to Vygotsky, cognitive development unfolds in a social context between caregivers/teachers and children. Adults who are attuned to the child's experience can help to scaffold children's learning, guiding them such that they focus on challenges that lie on the very edge of their capabilities. This keeps children engaged fully, in the zone of proximal development, maximizing their skill development and the intrinsic motivation that comes with a sense of emerging mastery.

ANALYZE …

- ***How to effectively discipline children in order to promote moral behaviour.*** Internalizing prosocial motives comes from children developing a secure attachment, and having empathy and inductive reasoning taught to them throughout their childhood. Children have an innate sense of morality, but this can be interfered with if their attachment needs are insufficiently met, and the attachment behavioural system takes precedence over the caregiving behavioural system. Therefore, responsive parenting that helps the child feel secure lays the foundation for the child to become less self-focused. As the child cognitively develops and can more explicitly take others' perspective, inductive reasoning that emphasizes perspective taking and having empathy for how the child's behaviour affects others builds the habit of "doing good" because the child genuinely cares, not because the child wants approval or to avoid punishment.

Picture Partners/Alamy

Module 10.3

Adolescence

Learning Objectives

After reading this module you should

KNOW ...	UNDERSTAND ...	APPLY ...	ANALYZE ...
The key terminology concerning adolescent development	The process of identity formation during adolescence The importance of relationships in adolescence The functions of moral emotions	Your understanding of the categories of moral reasoning	The relationship between brain development and adolescent judgment and risk taking

Do you spend too much time online? Does "screen time" remove you from "real life"? Or is the Internet a healthy part of your social life, and a necessary research tool for your schooling? Many people, including psychologists, are concerned that spending time on the Internet sets people up for social isolation. The image of lonely web surfers "unplugged" from the real world depicts a social reality that we would want to avoid. Research findings linking Internet use, loneliness, and depression (Amichai-Hamburger & Ben-Artzi, 2003; Ybarra et al., 2008) certainly haven't helped to alleviate these concerns. On the other hand, Brock University psychologist Dr. Teena Willoughby argues that as the Internet has become more of a platform for social networking, at least moderate use of the Internet is associated with greater social involvement (Gross, 2004) and stronger academic motivation (Willoughby, 2008).

Nevertheless, the Internet has its dangers. One is that use may become "pathological," as people turn to the Internet as a way of coping with life's difficulties, much the same as people turn to drugs, alcohol, sex, or their career. Even psychologically healthy adolescents can get "hooked" on the Internet, and such pathological use can lead to depression (Lam & Peng, 2010).

The Internet may also carry social dangers, such as Internet bullying and public humiliation, as one's indiscretions can now be posted online and haunt people for years to come. In 2012, 15-year-old Amanda Todd from British Columbia was cruelly ostracized and humiliated by her peers after revealing pictures of her were posted online. Although she switched schools and tried to leave the negativity behind her, she couldn't escape the online bullying, and tragically, committed suicide.

The Internet has revolutionized society in a single human generation. But we don't know how it will affect human development, particularly in the sensitive period of adolescence when people are forming their identities, and often committing some of their biggest mistakes. This will undoubtedly be a major focus for research, and will raise major questions for society in the years to come.

Focus Questions

 Does Internet use impair or enhance social relationships during adolescence?

 Which other psychological characteristics are major points of change during adolescence?

"It was the best of times; it was the worst of times." For many people, this pretty much sums up adolescence, a time of confusion, pimples, and existential angst, as well as hanging out with your friends and having greater interest in intimate relationships. This tumultuous time between childhood and adulthood involves many physical changes, increasing cognitive sophistication, and strong doses of emotional and social volatility.

Acne
Beard
Voice change
Underarm hair, chest hair, muscle development
Pubic hair
Enlargement of penis, scrotum, testes
Ejaculation
Acne
Underarm hair
Breast development
Rounded body contours
Pubic hair
Enlargement of uterus, clitoris, labia
Menstruation

{FIG. 10.12} **Physical Changes That Accompany Puberty in Male and Female Adolescents** Hormonal changes accelerate the development of physical traits in males and females. Changes involve maturation of the reproductive system (primary sex traits) as well as secondary sex traits such as enlargement of breasts in women and increased muscle mass in males. **Click on this figure in your eText to see more details.**

Physical Changes in Adolescence

The physical transition from childhood to adolescence starts with puberty, culminating in reproductive maturity. Puberty begins at approximately age 11 in girls and age 13 in boys, although there is a wide range. The changes that occur during puberty are primarily caused by hormonal activity. Physical growth is stimulated by the pituitary gland. The *hypothalamus* begins stimulating the release of hormones such as testosterone and estrogen, which contribute to the development of *primary and secondary sex traits* in boys and girls. **Primary sex traits** are *changes in the body that are part of reproduction* (e.g., enlargement of the genitals, ability to ejaculate, the onset of menstruation). **Secondary sex traits** are *changes in the body that are not part of reproduction*, such as the growth of pubic hair, increased breast size in females, and increased muscle mass in males (Figure 10.12).

MLADEN ANTONOV/AFP/Getty Images
Amanda Todd: A tragic case of cyber-bullying.

For girls, **menarche**—*the onset of menstruation*—typically occurs around age 12. The timing of menarche is influenced by physiological and environmental factors, such as nutrition, genetics, physical activity levels, and illness (Ellis & Garber, 2000). Even the absence of a father or the presence of a stepfather during development is associated with early onset of menarche (Bogaert, 2008). Boys are considered to reach sexual maturity at **spermarche**, *their first ejaculation of sperm*, at around age 14.

Interestingly, puberty happens much earlier now than 100 years ago. American teens in the 19th century started puberty at 16–17 on average; nowadays, about one-third of boys show the beginnings of physical maturation at age 9 (Reiter & Lee, 2001), as do almost 40% of European-American girls, and almost 80% of African-American girls (Herman-Giddens et al., 1997). This is probably because of behavioural changes that increase body fat (e.g., poor nutrition, insufficient exercise), and increased environmental stresses that increase stress hormones in the body. As the environment changes, our biology changes along with it.

Teens' changing bodies bring a host of developmental challenges, from feelings of self-consciousness and a heightened desire to be attractive and "fit in," to increasing sexual interest and experimentation, to the negative moods and adjustment problems that accompany hormonal fluctuations (Warren & Brooks-Gunn, 1989). Adolescents who begin to physically develop earlier than their peers can face extra challenges. Early-developing females often have to cope with being teased and having their bodies made into objects of others' attention. Early-developing boys tend to have it easier; their masculine traits are often regarded positively by both themselves and their peers. Nevertheless, early developers of either gender run a greater risk of drug and alcohol abuse and unwanted pregnancies.

Recent research has shown that adolescence is a time of major brain changes as well. In particular, the frontal lobes undergo a massive shift in myelination, speeding up neural firing by up to 100-fold in those areas (Barnea-Goraly et al., 2005; Sowell et al., 2003). The frontal lobes also undergo a wave of synaptic pruning, during which relatively unused synaptic connections are broken, leaving a more efficiently functioning brain. The net result of these changes is an increase in teens' abilities to exert self-control. However, during adolescence this process is merely under way, not completed, leaving teens often struggling with volatile emotional experiences.

Emotional Challenges in Adolescence

The physical and emotional changes associated with puberty are widely believed to be connected to each other. For example, mood swings and experimental high-risk behaviours are attributed to "raging hormones." But is this characterization of adolescence accurate? Are most teens hormonally supercharged animals, constantly desiring to hook up with the first attractive person to cross their path?

The belief that adolescence is tumultuous has held sway in popular culture as well as in psychology since at least the early 1900s (Hall, 1904); some theorists even believed that the absence of extreme volatility was an indication of arrested development (Freud, 1958). However, this belief came under fire from cultural anthropologists (Benedict, 1938; Mead, 1928), who discovered that in many non-Western cultures, the transition from childhood to adulthood happened remarkably smoothly; children simply began to take on more and more responsibilities, and then moved into their adult roles without a dramatic period of questioning "Who am I?" and "What do I want to be when I grow up?"

In the decades since, research has painted a somewhat mixed picture of adolescence. On the up side, the majority of teens keep their forays into debauchery fairly minimal and do not let their larger lives get unduly harmed by their experimentation; most also "grow out of" these patterns fairly readily and move into adulthood relatively unscathed by their teenage experiences (Bachman et al., 1997). Navigating adolescence successfully leaves teens feeling they know who they are, having constructed a healthy social identity, and having learned to identify at least some of their passions and intrinsically fulfilling goals.

However, the emotional road through adolescence contains its fair share of bumps. Adolescents are prone to experiencing particularly intense and volatile emotions (Dahl, 2001; Rosenblum & Lewis, 2003), including heightened feelings of anxiety and depression (Van Oort et al., 2009). Learning how to regulate their emotions effectively is of critical importance (McLaughlin et al., 2011). Research at Queen's University has shown that one key to adolescents effectively regulating their emotions is to be able to draw flexibly upon a diverse set of self-control strategies. Adolescents who rely upon a limited number of adaptive strategies (e.g., learning to suppress emotions, or conversely, learning to always reach out and talk to people about their feelings), and narrowly relying upon their chosen strategy, are at greater risk for developing symptoms of anxiety and depression (Lougheed & Hollenstein, 2012). One of the most flexible and powerful strategies for dealing with emotions is cognitive reframing, whereby we learn to look at our experience through a different "frame." For example, failure can be reframed as an opportunity to learn, and a threatening experience as a challenge to be overcome.

The ability to reframe is critical to one of the most important skills adolescents need to hone as they move into adulthood—the ability to **delay gratification**, *putting off immediate temptations in order to focus on longer-term goals*. For example, should you party with your friends, or study for the test next week? Adolescents who master this skill are far more likely to be successful in life.

An inability to delay gratification reflects a tendency to discount the future in order to "live in the moment," which lies at the heart of a wide range of dysfunctional behaviours, from addictions and unsafe sex, to racking up credit card debt and leaving everything to the last minute. Failing to appropriately delay gratification limits people's ability to live up to their potential, setting the stage for adulthoods in which they wonder "what might have been." Of course, people who discount the future don't care about what their eventual future selves might think. And therein lies the problem.

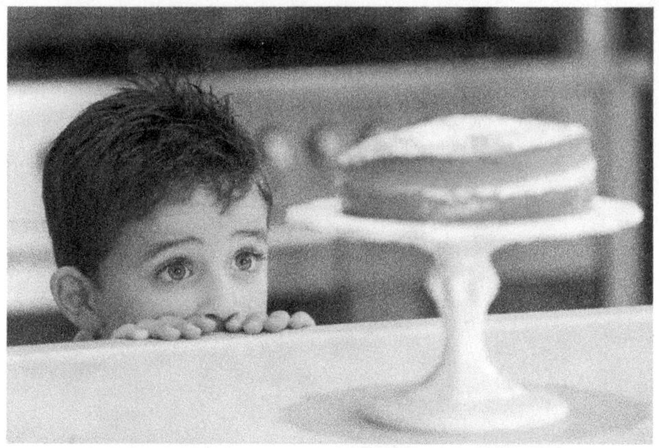
Monkey Business Images/Shutterstock

Unfortunately, the ability (or inability) to delay gratification tends to be quite stable throughout childhood and adolescence. A brilliant set of studies begun in the 1960s looked at what young children would do if given a difficult temptation—they could have a marshmallow immediately, or if they could wait for 15 minutes, they would be given two marshmallows. It's a pretty simple choice right? A mere 15 minutes, and the marshmallow feast doubles in size! However, preschool-aged children find it excruciating to resist this temptation. In one study (Mischel & Ebbesen, 1970), when the marshmallow was temptingly placed right in front of the children, they could only wait for, on average, one minute!

The finding that made these studies famous in psychology, though, was that the length of time kids could wait for the second marshmallow predicted how well adjusted they were many years later, in adolescence. The child who could wait longer for a marshmallow at age 4 was better adjusted both psychologically and socially at age 15, and by the end of high school, had higher SAT scores (Shoda et al., 1990)! (SATs are standardized tests written by American students at the end of high school, and are a major part of determining acceptance to college and university.) Clearly, being able to delay gratification is an important skill.

Importantly, this is also a skill that people can learn. In fact, the challenge of delaying gratification is basically the same as the challenge of controlling emotions, and the same strategies are useful, such as cognitive reframing. Even preschool-aged children can use them; in the simplest and most literal reframing study, children were instructed to simply imagine that the marshmallow was a picture, not a real object, and to do this by mentally drawing a picture frame around the object; incredibly, this simple imagination tactic increased the average wait time to a full 18 minutes (Moore et al., 1976).

The ability to effectively choose reframing strategies, especially when under the grip of strong emotions, relies on a sophisticated cognitive control network involving the frontal and parietal lobes (McClure et al., 2004). These are precisely the brain areas that are undergoing the most development during adolescence. Thus, helping adolescents learn self-control strategies is critically important, not only for developing good habits, but for helping them to develop the cognitive control systems in their brains. Failing to provide this guidance (which our culture regularly does, with its paucity of programs for cultivating self-control), is a lost opportunity for making a major difference in the lives of today's youth.

Quick Quiz 10.3a Physical Changes and Emotional Challenges in Adolescence

KNOW ...

1 One of the changes that occurs in puberty is the beginning of menstruation for females. This event is known as ________.

A estradiol
B menarche
C a primary sex trait
D spermarche

2 One of the major differences between primary and secondary sex characteristics is that

A primary sex characteristics are directly related to reproductive function.
B secondary sex characteristics are directly related to reproductive function.
C whether a person is male or female depends on the secondary sex characteristics.
D primary sex characteristics are unique to human reproductive anatomy.

UNDERSTAND ...

3 The length of time children can wait in the marshmallow task is an indicator of

A the age at which they begin to develop secondary sex characteristics.
B intelligence.
C self-control.
D emotional security.

Answers can be found on page ANS-3.

WORKING THE SCIENTIFIC LITERACY MODEL

Adolescent Risk and Decision Making

One of the nightmares of every parent is the smorgasbord of disasters waiting for adolescents as they explore their increasing independence—sexually transmitted diseases, drinking, drugs, and the whole panoply of alluring activities parents wish were never invented (despite their own fond memories of their younger years . . .). The adolescent says "Trust me!" and the parent thinks "No way; I know what you're going to do once you're out of my sight!"

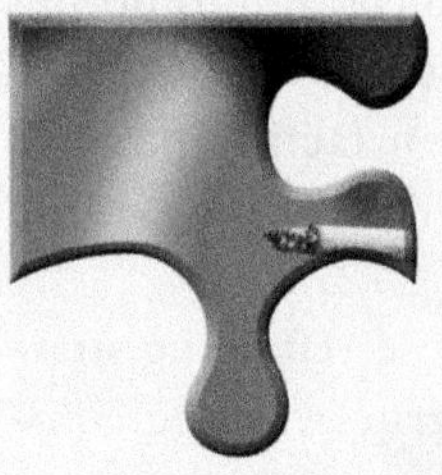

What do we know about adolescence and decision making?

Parents do have some reason to fear; adolescents are particularly prone to behaving impulsively and making risky decisions (Chambers et al., 2003; Steinberg, 2007). As a result, driving recklessly and having unsafe sex (Arnett, 1992), drug and alcohol abuse, accidents, and violence are more common during adolescence than during any other stage of life (Chambers & Potenza, 2003; Steinberg, 2008).

Watch
Special Topics: Risky Behaviour and Brain Development

Why do adolescents often make such bad judgment calls? This is due to a convergence of factors, such as a teenage culture that glorifies high-risk activities (e.g., binge drinking, fast driving), increased freedom from parents, and a growing intellectual ability to critically examine and question the values and traditions of society. These factors happen to converge at the same time as adolescent brains are still developing critical cognitive control systems, in particular the prefrontal areas, although they have well-developed reward systems, located in limbic areas (Galvan et al., 2006). This makes them especially responsive to rewards and incentives (Casey et al., 2008), setting up a tension within their own neurophysiology. The reward system acts like the devil on their shoulder, nudging them to "Do it! Do it!" while the underdeveloped prefrontal areas struggle along like the beleaguered angel, ineffectually pleading "Don't do it! It's not worth it!"

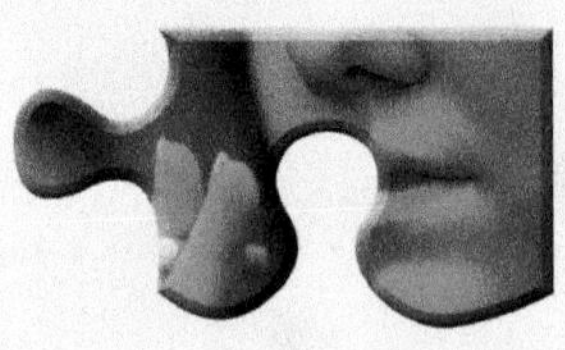

How can science test the link between brain function and decision making in adolescents?

Modern technology has enabled researchers to look at the actual brain activity of adolescents in the process of making risky decisions. In one study, adolescents had their brains scanned using functional magnetic resonance imaging while they played a betting game. In this experiment, participants had to make a decision between a high-risk, high-reward choice (placing a \$6 bet with a 25% chance of winning), and a low-risk, low-reward choice (placing a \$1 bet with a 50% chance of winning).

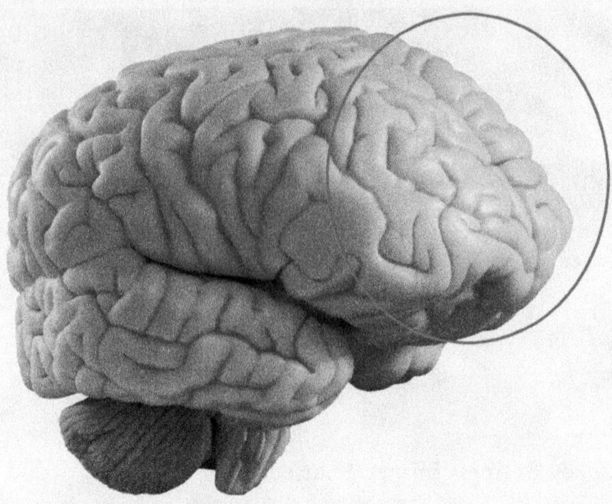

werbefoto-burger.ch/Fotolia

{FIG. 10.13} **Extended Brain Development** The prefrontal cortex (highlighted in blue) continues to develop through adolescence and even into young adulthood. **Click on this figure in your eText to see more details.**

Adolescents who selected the high-risk choice had less brain activity in their prefrontal cortex than those who selected the low-risk choice (Figure 10.13; Shad et al., 2011). It seems that choosing the high-risk gamble was, in a sense, easier; those teens simply focused on how much they wanted the bigger reward, and ignored the higher likelihood that they would lose. On the other hand, making the low-risk choice involved some neurological conflict; those teens wanted the bigger reward, but restrained themselves by taking into account the probabilities.

This study helps to shed light on adolescent decision making in general. Compared to adults, adolescents have less-developed frontal lobes, and are therefore more likely to default to their strong reward impulses, rather than restraining their desires as a result of more sober and complex calculations of what would be in their best interest overall. This study lends support to the hypothesis that risky decision making by adolescents has a basis in their still-developing frontal cortex.

Can we critically evaluate this explanation for risky decision making?

This brain-based explanation does not, in fact, fully *explain* adolescents' behaviour, in at least two important ways. First, in this particular study, it's not clear whether the prefrontal activation reflects teens thinking in more complex

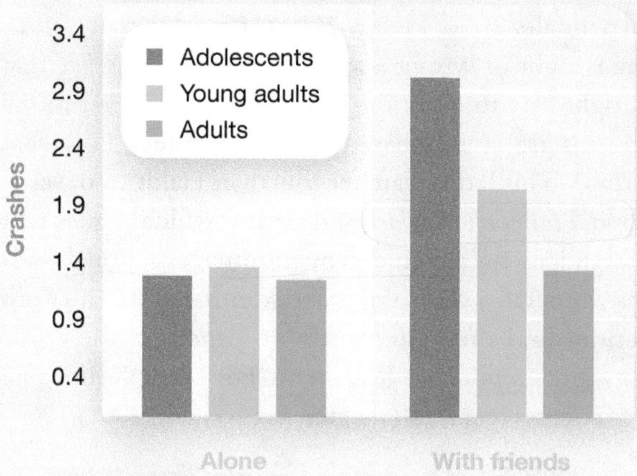

{FIG. 10.14} **What Drives Teenagers to Take Risks?** One key factor in risk taking is simply *other teenagers*. When teens play a driving video game with other teens, they crash more than when playing the same game when alone, and more than adults playing the game (from Steinberg, 2007).

ways, or whether it shows that they are effortfully restraining themselves from following their reward-focused desires. Is it about complex thought, or is it about self-control?

Second, in everyday decisions, other factors likely influence teens' preference for risk, such as size of rewards and costs, the importance of long-term goals, personality characteristics such as extraversion (which is related to reward-sensitivity), and the social context in which the decisions occur. For example, psychologists have found that in some situations, adolescents are no more likely to engage in risky behaviour than adults. But when other teens are around, this propensity changes (see Figure 10.14). Clearly, realistic strategies for reducing adolescent risk taking should also consider the important role that situational factors play in adolescents' decision making.

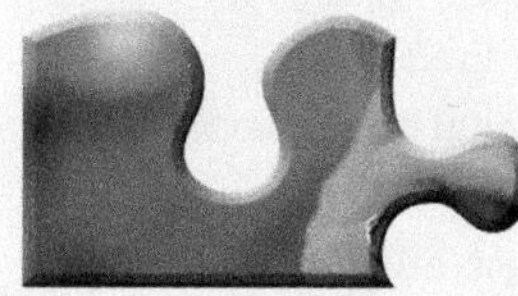

Why is this relevant?

Research on the developing adolescent brain helps explain problems with risk and impulse control, which could lead to the development of programs that could steer adolescents toward making better decisions. If we could figure out how to enhance prefrontal functioning in teens, or how to get more of them to engage in practices like meditation that would do the same thing, we could improve the emotional control and quality of life of a whole generation of young people.

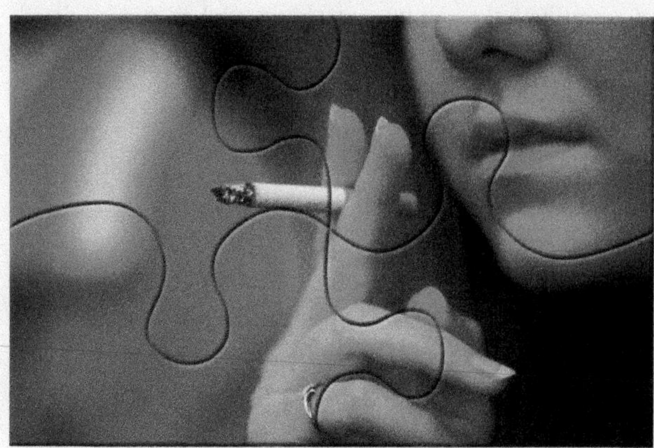

Rob Crandall/Stock Connection/Glow Images

Cognitive Development: Moral Reasoning vs. Emotions

As we have just seen, making wise decisions depends on the prefrontal cortex. This area is involved in higher cognitive abilities, such as abstract reasoning and logic (what Piaget referred to as *formal operational* thinking; see Module 10.2), which also begin to show substantial improvements starting at about age 12. This increase in complex cognitive ability allows people to view problems from multiple perspectives and to think more flexibly. Since Piaget, psychologists have generally believed that the shift to formal operational thinking laid the foundation for effective moral reasoning, allowing a person to consider abstract moral principles, and take into consideration multiple perspectives when reasoning through a problem.

KOHLBERG'S MORAL DEVELOPMENT: LEARNING RIGHT FROM WRONG The most influential theory of the development of moral reasoning was created by Lawrence Kohlberg, after studying how people reasoned through complex moral dilemmas. Imagine the following scenario, unlikely as it may be:

> *A trolley is hurtling down the tracks toward a group of five unsuspecting people. You are standing next to a lever that, if pulled, would direct the trolley onto another track, thereby saving the five individuals. However, on the second track stands a single, unsuspecting person, who would be struck by the diverted trolley.*

What would you choose to do? Would you pull the lever, directly causing one person to die, but saving five others? Or would you be unwilling to directly cause someone's death and therefore do nothing? Moral dilemmas provide interesting tests of reasoning because they place values in conflict with each other. Obviously, five lives are more than one, yet most people are also unwilling to take a direct action that would cause a person to be killed.

But even more important than *what* you would choose is *why* you would choose it. Kohlberg (1984) believed that people's reasons evolved as they grew up and became better able to think in complex ways. By analyzing people's reasons for their decisions in these sorts of dilemmas, he developed a stage theory of moral development, here organized into three general stages (see Table 10.4).

The shift to postconventional morality is a key development, for without this shift, it is unlikely that the individual will rebel against authority or work against unjust practices, if they are accepted by society at large. Indeed, social reformers always encounter resistance from members of society who hold to "traditional" values and think of change as a destabilizing influence to be resisted; reformers must adopt the language of values and rights, whereas those who seek to preserve the system invoke other values, such as tradition, social harmony, and authority.

Kohlberg regarded the three stages of moral reasoning as universal to all humans; however, because he developed his theory mostly through the study of how *males* reason about moral dilemmas, other researchers argued that he had failed to consider that females reason about moral issues differently. Carol Gilligan (1982) suggested that females base moral decisions on a standard of *caring for others*, rather than the "masculine" emphasis on standards of justice and fairness that Kohlberg emphasized. Some support has been found for this; women are more likely to emphasize the importance of maintaining harmony in their relationships with others (Lyons, 1983). On the other hand, men and women generally make highly similar judgments about moral dilemmas (Boldizar et al., 1989), and both genders make use of both caring and justice principles (Clopton & Sorell, 1993). This has led other researchers to question the importance of the gender distinction at all (Jaffee & Hyde, 2000).

Watch Moral Development: Preconventional

Watch Moral Development: Conventional

Watch Moral Development: Postconventional

However, an even more devastating critique has been made against the moral reasoning perspective in general, based on extensive research showing that moral reasoning doesn't actually predict behaviour very well (Carpendale, 2000; Haidt, 2001). *Knowing* that something is right or wrong is very different from *feeling* that it is right or wrong, and in our everyday lives our moral decisions are largely based on how we feel, not what we think. This led researcher Jonathan Haidt to develop the *social intuitionist model* of morality, which argues that moral judgments are guided by intuitive, emotional reactions. Generally, we make a decision based on our "gut reaction" and then afterwards we construct the arguments that support our judgments. For example, imagine the following scenario (adapted from Haidt, 2001):

> *Julie and Steven are brother and sister. They are travelling together in France on summer vacation from college. One night they are staying alone in a cabin near the beach. They decide that it would be interesting and fun if they shared a romantic kiss. At the very least it would be a new experience for each of them. They both enjoy the experience but they decide not to do it again. They keep that night as a special secret, which makes them feel even closer to each other.*

How do you react to this scenario? Was what took place between the two siblings morally acceptable? If you are like most people, you probably didn't think carefully through this scenario, consider different perspectives, and examine your reasoning before making a decision. Instead, you probably had a gut reaction, like "Brother and sister!?!? Gross! No way!" and made your decision almost instantly.

It is only after making a decision that most people then engage in more thoughtful and reflective reasoning, trying to justify their decision. For some scenarios, it is easy to come up with justifications, such as "Brothers and sisters should not engage in romantic acts, because it could lead to sexual intercourse, which could produce genetic problems for the offspring," or "They shouldn't do it because if the family found out, it would be devastating, and their responsibility to their family is more

Table 10.4 :: Kohlberg's Stages of Moral Reasoning

STAGE OF MORAL DEVELOPMENT	DESCRIPTION	APPLICATION TO TROLLEY DILEMMA
Preconventional morality	*Characterized by self-interest in seeking reward or avoiding punishment.* Preconventional morality is considered a very basic and egocentric form of moral reasoning.	"I would not flip the trolley track switch because I would get in trouble."
Conventional morality	*Regards social conventions and rules as guides for appropriate moral behaviour.* Directives from parents, teachers, and the law are used as guidelines for moral behaviour.	"I would not flip the switch. It is illegal to kill, and if I willfully intervened I would have probably violated the law."
Postconventional morality	*Considers rules and laws as relative.* Right and wrong are determined by more abstract principles of justice and rights.	"I would flip the switch. The value of five lives exceeds that of one, so saving them is the right thing to do even if it means I am killing one person who would otherwise not have died."

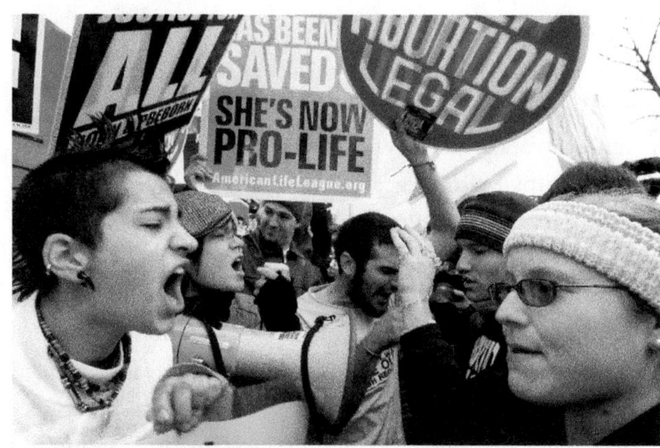

Alex Wong/Getty Images

Emotion is a major component of moral thinking and decision making.

important than their private desire to share an intimate experience together." However, it's not hard to construct a scenario that lies outside of such justifications, such as the brother and sister being infertile and having no other surviving family members. Faced with such a scenario, people might be hard pressed to find a justification; often, in such situations, people become flustered and confused, and resort to emphatically stating something like "I don't know—it just isn't right!" Their intuitive emotional reaction has told them it's wrong, but their more cognitive, effortful reasoning process has had a difficult time explaining *why* it's wrong; interestingly, in such situations, people generally do not change their judgments, instead trusting their intuitive reaction. The feeling of disgust is stronger than their inability to explain themselves, which is another piece of evidence that suggests that it's not moral *reasoning* that is important, but moral *feelings*.

BIOPSYCHOSOCIAL PERSPECTIVES

Emotion and Disgust

The social intuitionist perspective on morality describes moral judgments as being driven primarily by emotional reactions. Psychologists believe that these embodied processes draw upon evolutionarily ancient systems that evolved for highly functional reasons. For example, the disgust system evolved to keep us from ingesting substances that were harmful to us, such as feces and toxic plants. As we developed into more complex social beings, our judgments of "good" and "bad" involved neural circuits that were more cognitive and conceptual; however, these "higher-level" cognitive systems evolved after our more basic physiological responses. A major insight from psychology over the past decade has been that as the brain evolved, newer systems grew out of older systems, and therefore include the functioning of the older systems. In terms of our moral reasoning, what this means is that the cognitive systems that reason about right and wrong grew out of emotional systems that in turn grew out of systems representing very basic physiological responses of accepting or rejecting a substance from one's body. From this perspective, "good" and "bad" are not moral judgments, per se, but rather, are emotional judgments on top of which we have constructed a moral framework.

This surprising theory has been tested in several different ways. One creative set of studies first activated physiological symptoms of repulsion, for example by getting subjects to sit at a disgustingly dirty work station, or to smell fart spray (Schnall et al., 2008); these disgust-inducing experiences led people to make more severe judgments of moral violations. Also, neuroimaging studies show that certain moral dilemmas trigger emotional areas in the brain, and this emotional activation determines the decision that subjects make (Greene & Haidt, 2002; Greene et al., 2001).

At the other end of the spectrum, consider people who are clinically psychopathic; such people have an almost complete disregard for moral considerations, and feel no compunction to refrain from violating the rights of others or committing acts of violence (Hare, 1985). Physiologically, psychopaths tend to have chronically reduced emotional activity (Blair & Cipolotti, 2000; Lorber, 2004); with no emotional "signal," psychopaths simply do not *feel* that what they are doing is wrong.

It is interesting to consider that the development of key moral emotions, such as empathy, is intimately bound up with the extent to which one's social relationships have been healthy right from birth (see Module 10.2). People who are regularly socially included and treated well by others are the same people who develop trust and security, which results in well-developed areas of the prefrontal cortex necessary for good decision making, and well-developed moral emotional systems. In adolescence, the importance of social relationships is heightened even further, as adolescents seek to build an identity that helps them to "fit in" to their social world.

Social Development: Identity and Relationships

It doesn't take a rocket scientist, or even a psychologist, to understand the importance of friends during adolescence. To teenagers, friends are everything—the people who will support your story to your parents about why you came home late, who laugh hysterically with you at 3:00 in the morning, who help you feel that your choice of clothing is actually cool. Friends are central to two of the most important changes that occur during adolescence—the formation of a personal identity, and a shift away from family relationships and toward friendships and romantic relationships. These major changes in teens' lives are sources of growth and maturation, but are also often sources of distress and conflict.

WHO AM I? IDENTITY FORMATION DURING ADOLESCENCE A major issue faced by adolescents is forming an **identity**, which is *a clear sense of what kind of person you are, what types of people you belong with, and what roles you should play in society*. It involves coming to appreciate and express one's attitudes and values (Arnett, 2000; Lefkowitz, 2005), which are to some degree realized through identifying more closely with peers and being included into valued social groups.

Watch
Peer Pressure

Adolescents may actually experience numerous *identity crises* before they reach young adulthood. An identity crisis involves curiosity, questioning, and exploration of different identities. One month a teenage boy might be interested in playing varsity football and lifting weights, and the next month he might ponder abandoning sports to pursue music. All the while, he may be wondering where he would best fit in, be most successful, or make more friends.

The process of exploring different identities, and enjoying more independence from the family, sets the stage for potential conflict, particularly with parents. Even well-meaning parents may feel somewhat threatened as their teenage son or daughter starts to establish more distance or starts to experiment with identities they feel are unwise. They may feel hurt and want to hold onto their closeness with their child. They may also feel concerned and want to protect their child from making mistakes they will later regret. So, parents may simply be trying to help, but their advice, rules (like curfew), or insistence that the teen abandon certain goals ("There's no way you're giving up math and science to take drama and music!") may get interpreted as being restrictive or controlling. Net results? Conflict.

PEER GROUPS Friendships are a priority to most adolescents, and teenagers typically spend more time with peers while gaining independence from their parents. Friendships take place within a broader social context of small groups or *cliques,* and the membership and intensity of friendships within a clique are constantly changing (Cairns & Cairns, 1994). Adolescent *crowds*—often referred to with labels such as "jocks," "geeks," "Goths," and "druggies"—are larger than cliques and are characterized by common social and behavioural conventions.

Adolescents who can't find their place in social networks have a difficult time; social exclusion is generally a devastating experience. When rejected by peers, some adolescents turn to virtual social networks for online friendships, or join distinctive sub-groups in order to gain acceptance within the group and to devalue the "mainstream" from which they feel rejected. Both psychologists and the media have given these low-status adolescents a great deal of attention because of the widespread belief that they are at high risk for committing violence and engaging in other antisocial behaviours.

One of the most troubling outcomes of social rejection is the experience of shame, which is a feeling that there is something wrong with oneself: one is worthless, inferior, defective. Shame-prone individuals have often experienced substantial social rejection, and feeling powerless and in pain, are at increased risk for blaming others for their problems. Many psychologists believe that shame and other negative emotions that are connected to social rejection, bullying, teasing, and being publicly humiliated can lead to tragic outbursts of violence, such as the school shootings that have become disturbingly frequent recently. In almost all cases of school shootings, social rejection is a key factor that precedes the violent outburst (Leary et al., 2003; Tangney & Dearing, 2002). Just as the *security* from having one's belongingness needs satisfied leads to

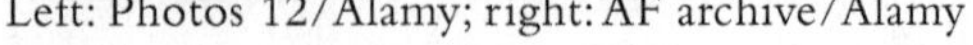

Left: Photos 12/Alamy; right: AF archive/Alamy

For decades, television shows and movies have offered glimpses into life within adolescent cliques and crowds. The portrayals may be exaggerated, but they are often successful because viewers can closely identify with the characters' experiences.

the development of empathy and moral behaviours (see Module 10.2), the *insecurity* from having one's belongingness needs brutally unmet can lead to terrible violence, sometimes against others, sometimes against oneself.

ROMANTIC RELATIONSHIPS In addition to friendships taking prominence over family, teens' social lives also begin to revolve around seeking, or being involved in, romantic relationships. This opens up new worlds of exploring both emotional and physical intimacy.

Many people in North American culture may feel uncomfortable with adolescents exploring and engaging in sexual behaviour—but teens themselves don't seem to agree. Between 40–50% of Canadian teens aged 15–19 report having had sexual intercourse (Boyce et al., 2006; Rotermann, 2008), although the proportion who have engaged in other forms of sexual acts such as oral sex or mutual masturbation is higher; for example, more than 80% of American adolescents report engaging in non-intercourse sex acts before the age of 16 (Bauserman & Davis, 1996); more than half of Canadian teens in Grade 11 report having experienced oral sex (Boyce et al., 2006). Some teens turn to oral sex because they see it as less risky than intercourse, both for one's health and social reputation (Halpern-Fisher et al., 2005).

Same-sex sexual encounters are also very common and typically occur by early adolescence (Savin-Williams & Cohen, 2004), although contrary to stereotypes, such an experience is not an indication of homosexuality; approximately 60% of people who identify as heterosexual have had at least one same-sex encounter (Remafedi et al., 1992). For many, this is part of the experimentation that comes with figuring out who you are and establishing an identity.

The process by which adolescents come to recognize their sexual orientation depends on many factors, including how they are perceived by their family and peers. Because of some people's still-existing prejudices against non-heterosexual orientations, it is not uncommon for many people who don't identify as heterosexual to experience some difficulty accepting their sexuality, and thus, to struggle with feelings of rejection toward themselves. However, this process is not always difficult or traumatic; it largely depends on how supportive their family and peer relationships are. Nevertheless, despite these extra identity challenges, homosexuals have about the same level of psychological well-being as heterosexuals (Rieger & Savin-Williams, 2011).

Although sexual exploration is a normal part of adolescence, it can unfortunately be dangerous for many people. Research at the University of New Brunswick has shown that among Canadian teens in Grade 11, approximately 60% of both males and females reported having experienced psychological aggression against them by their romantic relationship partner. About 40% experienced sexual aggression, generally in the form of being coerced or pressured into having sex (Sears & Byers, 2010). In addition, each year in North America, millions of teens face the life upheaval of an unplanned pregnancy, sexually transmitted diseases, or simply having sex they will later regret.

Overall, the emotional upheaval of relationships, from the ecstasy of attraction, to the heartbreak of being rejected or cheated on, to the loneliness one may feel in the absence of relationships, consumes a great deal of many teenagers' attention and resources and is a primary part of the experience of adolescence.

Quick Quiz 10.3b

Decision Making, Moral Reasoning, and Social Development

KNOW ...

1 Rachel believes that it is wrong to steal only because doing so could land her in jail. Which level of Kohlberg's moral development scheme is Rachel applying in this scenario?

- **A** Postconventional
- **B** Preconventional
- **C** Preoperational
- **D** Conventional

UNDERSTAND ...

2 Adolescent decision making is often problematic or dangerous because teens have

- **A** underdeveloped limbic areas responsible for reward, and well-developed prefrontal areas.
- **B** well-developed limbic areas responsible for reward, and underdeveloped prefrontal areas.
- **C** only partly moved out of the concrete operations stage of cognitive development.
- **D** poorly formed sets of goals.

3 The length of time children can wait in the marshmallow task is an indicator of

- **A** the age at which they begin to develop secondary sex characteristics.
- **B** intelligence.
- **C** self-control.
- **D** emotional security.

4 For most teens, the most devastating experience would be one of

- **A** failing at an important competition.
- **B** being rejected by their friends.
- **C** being rejected on a first date.
- **D** having a physical injury.

Answers can be found on page ANS-3.

Module Summary

Module 10.3

Now that you have read this module you should

KNOW ...

- ***The key terminology concerning adolescent development:***

conventional morality (p. 426)
delay gratification (p. 422)
identity (p. 428)
menarche (p. 421)
postconventional morality (p. 426)
preconventional morality (p. 426)
primary sex traits (p. 421)
secondary sex traits (p. 421)
spermarche (p. 421)

UNDERSTAND ...

- ***The process of identity formation in adolescence.*** A major challenge of adolescence is the formation of a personal identity, which involves exploring different values and behaviours, and seeking inclusion in different social groups. The eventual outcome, if navigated successfully, is a relatively stable and personally satisfying sense of self.
- ***The importance of relationships in adolescence.*** Teenagers undergo a general shift in their social attachments as family becomes less central and friends and intimate relationships take on increased significance. The failure to establish a sense of belonging is an important precursor to dysfunctional behaviours and violence.
- ***The functions of moral emotions.*** Contrary to theories of moral reasoning, recent research on moral emotions, such as disgust, suggests that these feelings are what leads to moral behaviour, and reasoning generally follows as a way of justifying the behaviour to oneself.

APPLY ...

- ***Your understanding of the categories of moral reasoning.*** Read the following scenarios and identify which term applies to each. Check your answers on page ANS-3.
    1. Jeff discovers that the security camera at his job is disabled. He decides it is okay to steal because there's no way he's going to get caught. Applying Kohlberg's theory, which type of moral reasoning is Jeff using?

Picture Partners/Alamy

    2. Margaret is aware that a classmate has been sending hostile text messages to various people at her school. Although she does not receive these messages, and she does not personally know any of the victims, Margaret reports the offending individual to school officials. Applying Kohlberg's theory, which type of moral reasoning is Margaret displaying?

ANALYZE ...

- ***The relationship between brain development and adolescent judgment and risk taking.*** Many problems with judgment and decision making involve a kind of "tug of war" between emotional reward systems involving limbic areas of the brain and the prefrontal cortex, which is involved in planning, reasoning, emotion, and impulse control. Because the prefrontal cortex is still developing during adolescence, particularly through myelination and synaptic pruning, it is often not sufficient to override the allure of immediate temptations, leading to failures to delay gratification.

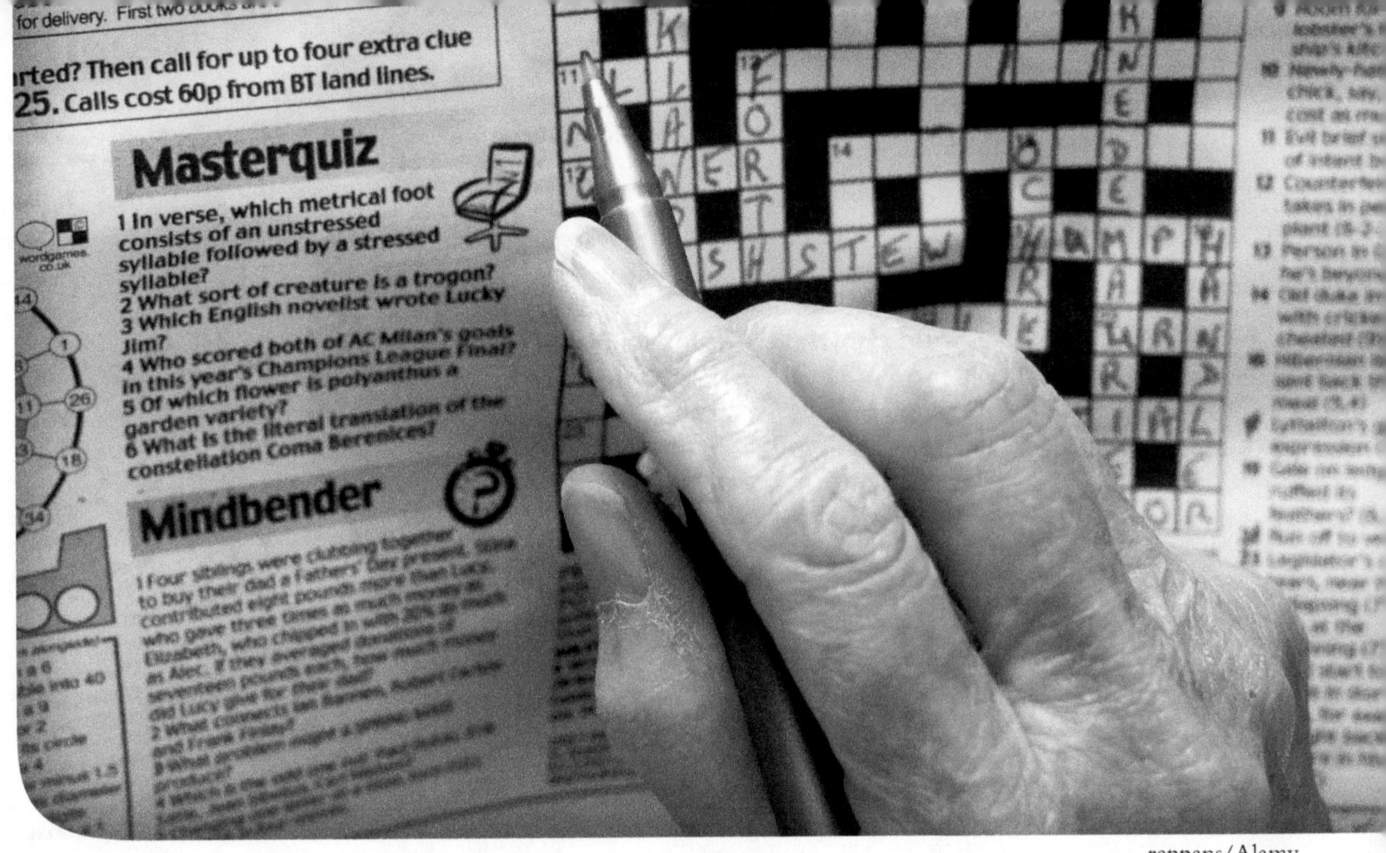

reppans/Alamy

Module **10.4**

Adulthood and Aging

Learning Objectives

After reading this module you should

KNOW ...	UNDERSTAND ...	APPLY ...	ANALYZE ...
The key areas of growth experienced by emerging adults	Age-related disorders such as Alzheimer's disease How cognitive abilities change with age	Effective communication principles to the challenge of improving your own relationships	The stereotype that old age is a time of unhappiness

"Use it or lose it." This is one of those sayings that you grow up hearing, and you think, "Yeah, whatever, I'm young and awesome; I'm never going to lose it." But time goes by, and like it or not, the day is not far away when may find yourself puffing at the top of a flight of stairs, or standing in the kitchen wondering why you're there. You may wonder, what's happened to me? Why do I feel so old?

We all know that if you stay physically active, your body will stay stronger and healthier as you age, maintaining better cardiovascular fitness, muscle tone, balance, and bone density. Thankfully, recent advances in neuroscience confirm that the same thing is true for the brain. If you use it, you're less likely to lose it. And unfortunately, brain connections are exactly what people lose as they age, particularly from their 60s onward, resulting in less neural connectivity and grey and white matter volume. These neurological losses are accompanied by gradual declines in some types of cognitive functioning. But not all aging people are doomed to the same rate of cognitive decline, because if they "exercise" their brains, they can dramatically reduce these neurological and cognitive losses. Furthermore, more mentally active adults are less likely to develop age-related disorders such as Alzheimer's disease.

So this is good news. And even better news is that exercising your brain is actually fun! It's not like spending countless hours on the brain equivalent of a treadmill. Instead, neurological exercisers are those who regularly solve puzzles and brain teasers, play games, stay socially active, pursue hobbies, and remain lifelong active learners. The take-home message for all of us, young and old, is not a grim "go to the brain gym or get stupider"; instead it's a joyful message, more like "Play! Learn! Do what you love!" This kind of advice makes getting old sound not so bad after all . . . .

Focus Questions

1. What are the key developmental challenges adults face as they age?
2. How does aging affect cognitive functioning?

Becoming an adult does not entail crossing any specific line. It's not as clear-cut as adolescence; after all, puberty is kind of hard to miss. In Canada, you are considered to be an adult from a legal perspective at 18. Still, it's questionable whether 18-year-olds are fully-fledged adults; they have essentially the same lifestyle as 17-year-olds, often at home or in student housing, with relatively few responsibilities beyond brushing their teeth and dragging themselves to work or school. As time goes by, people get increasingly integrated into working society, begin careers, usually establish long-term relationships, pay bills (or fend off bill collectors . . .), possibly have children, and in a variety of ways conform to the expectations and responsibilities of adulthood. As they move slowly from adolescence toward retirement and beyond, adults go through a series of roughly defined stages based loosely on age: Young adulthood spans 18 to 40 years, middle adulthood from 40 to 65 years, and older adulthood from 65 years onward. As they mature through these stages, people experience many different changes physically, socially, emotionally, cognitively, and neurologically.

Watch
What's in It for Me? Identity

Watch
Physical Development after 40

Explore
Major Changes in Important Domains of Adult Functioning

Simulate
Aging and Changes in Physical Appearance

EMERGING ADULTS: MOVING FROM ADOLESCENCE TO ADULTHOOD The undefinable no-man's-land between adolescence and adulthood is a time of great personal challenge and growth. "Emerging adults" confront many adaptive challenges; they may leave home for the first time, start college or university or full-time work, become more financially responsible for themselves, commit to and cohabit with romantic partners, and of course, deal with the endless crises of their friends. Navigating this challenging time can strongly affect people's feelings of self-worth, competence, and their ability to handle the complex challenges of adulthood.

Watch
Cognitive Changes Secondary to Menopause in Middle Adulthood

Watch
Stress about the Future: Amanda, 22 Years Old

Explore
Physical Changes in Late Adulthood

Researchers at the University of Guelph conducted an in-depth study (Gottlieb & Newby-Clark, 2007) of the experiences of these emerging adults, identifying three main areas of personal growth: relationships, new possibilities, and personal strengths. Interestingly, these map on perfectly to the domains of relatedness, autonomy, and competence that are widely viewed as key pillars of healthy development throughout the lifespan.

In the relationships domain, the majority of people felt that they had matured in their ability to put effort into building lasting relationships, to trust others and rely on others for support, and to be able to establish strong and intimate connections. This increased intimacy is an outgrowth of people learning to "be themselves" with others and invest in relationships in which their authenticity is accepted and encouraged. The domain of new possibilities reflects the greater freedom that emerging adults enjoy to choose activities that better fit their goals and interests, to broaden their horizons, and actively search for what they want to do with their lives. The domain of personal strength reflects the confidence young adults gain as they confront more serious life challenges and discover that "they can handle it." Taken together, this growth in three important domains of life suggests that emerging adulthood is a time of great opportunity.

Watch
Speaking Out: Alvin: Living with Dementia

Physical Changes in Adulthood

Physical changes happen fairly slowly in adulthood, which is good news for 20-somethings who still feel and look young, and 30- and 40-somethings who want to feel and look like they're still in their 20s. The most obvious signs of age-related physical changes in adulthood typically appear at middle adulthood. These include an increased likelihood of weight gain, thinning and greying of the hair, and a gradual decline in sensory abilities such as hearing and sight. For healthy adults, these changes progress slowly and are typically easy to manage.

One major physical change affecting women at approximately age 50 is **menopause**, *the termination of the menstrual cycle and reproductive ability*. The physical changes associated with menopause, particularly the reduction in estrogen, can result in symptoms such as hot flashes, a reduced sex drive, and mood swings. The severity of these symptoms varies widely among individuals. Men, on the other hand, don't experience a physical change as substantial as menopause during middle adulthood, although testosterone production and sexual motivation typically decline.

The brain, just like other physical systems, shows structural changes and some functional decline with age. These changes include reduced volume of white and grey matter of the cerebral cortex, as well as the memory-processing hippocampus (Allen et al., 2005). The prefrontal cortex and its connections to subcortical regions are also hit hard by aging (Raz, 2000), which helps to explain much of the cognitive decline typically experienced by older adults.

Some of the most severe consequences of aging are the *neurodegenerative* conditions, characterized by loss of nerve cells and nervous system functioning. **Dementia** *refers to mild to severe disruption of mental functioning, memory loss, disorientation, poor judgment, and decision making*. Approximately 14% of people older than 71 years of age have dementia. Nearly 10% of these cases involve a

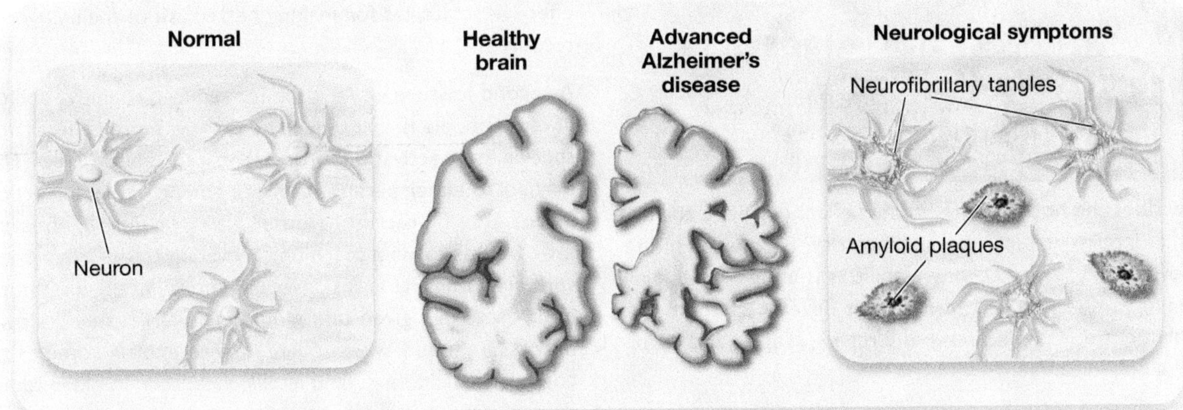

{FIG. 10.15} **How Alzheimer's Disease Affects the Brain** Advanced Alzheimer's disease is marked by significant loss of both grey and white matter throughout the brain. The brain of a person with Alzheimer's disease typically has a large buildup of a protein called beta-amyloid, which kills nerve cells. Also, tau proteins, which maintain the structure of nerve cells, are often found to be defective in the Alzheimer's brain, resulting in neurofibrillary tangles.

type of dementia called **Alzheimer's disease**—*a degenerative and terminal condition resulting in severe damage of the entire brain.* Alzheimer's disease rarely appears before age 60, and it usually lasts 7 to 10 years from onset to death (although some people with Alzheimer's live much longer). Early symptoms include forgetfulness for recent events, poor judgment, and some mood and personality changes. As the disease progresses, people experience severe confusion and memory loss, eventually struggling to recognize even their closest family members. In the most advanced stages of Alzheimer's disease, affected individuals may fail to recognize themselves and lose control of basic bodily processes such as bowel and bladder control.

What accounts for such extensive deterioration of cognitive abilities? Alzheimer's disease involves a buildup of proteins that clump together in the spaces between neurons, interrupting their normal activity. In addition, another type of protein forms tangles within nerve cells, which severely disrupts their structural integrity and functioning (Figure 10.15). Many different research groups are currently searching for specific genes that are associated with Alzheimer's disease. The genetic risk (i.e., the heritability of the disease) is very high for people who develop an early-onset form (age 30–60) of Alzheimer's disease (Bertram et al., 2010). In those individuals with later-onset (age 60+) disease, the genetic link is not as consistent.

Alzheimer's disease illustrates a worst-case scenario of the aging brain; however, in normal brains, structural changes occur which also cause a variety of cognitive challenges that increase as the person gets older.

Quick Quiz 10.4a Physical Changes in Adulthood

KNOW ...

1 Which of the following is not a symptom of Alzheimer's disease?

- **A** Memory problems
- **B** Disorientation
- **C** Obsessive behaviours
- **D** Personality changes

UNDERSTAND ...

2 Deterioration of cognitive abilities and memory in Alzheimer's patients may be attributable to

- **A** nonprescription drug usage earlier in life.
- **B** a buildup of proteins that clump together in the spaces between neurons, interrupting their normal activity.
- **C** normal aging processes that are unavoidable.
- **D** one gene that definitively determines whether the disease will appear.

Answers can be found on page ANS-3.

WORKING THE SCIENTIFIC LITERACY MODEL

Aging and Cognitive Change

How does the normal aging process affect cognitive abilities such as intelligence, learning, and memory? People commonly believe that a loss of cognitive abilities is an inevitable part of aging, even for those who do not develop dementia or Alzheimer's disease. However, the reality of aging and cognition is not so simple.

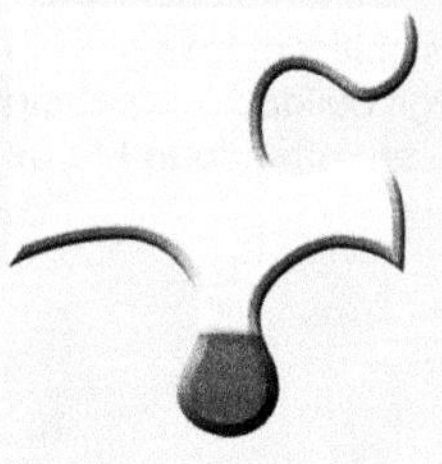

What do we know about different cognitive abilities?

There are many different cognitive abilities, including different memory and attentional abilities. One useful distinction is made between cognitive tasks that involve processes such as problem solving, reasoning, processing speed, and mental flexibility; these tasks are said to involve *fluid intelligence*. Other tasks tap into *crystallized intelligence*, which is based on accumulated knowledge and skills (Module 9.2), such as recognizing famous people like David Suzuki or Justin Bieber. Although fluid intelligence reaches a peak during young adulthood and then slowly declines, crystallized intelligence remains largely intact into old age.

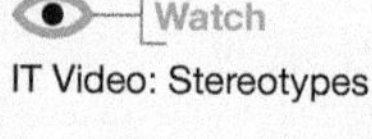

Watch
IT Video: Stereotypes

Watch
A 92-Year-Old Volunteer

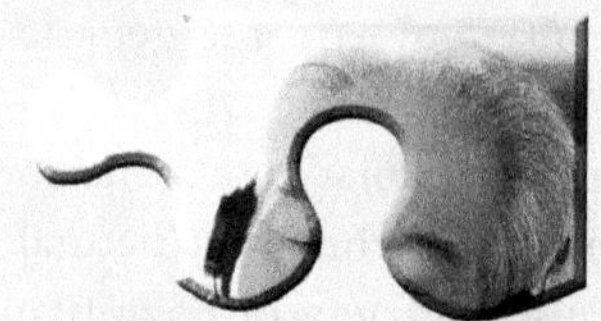

How can science explain age-related differences in cognitive abilities?

Researchers have not yet fully solved the riddle of why some cognitive abilities decline with age. There are many different potential explanations. Neurological studies of brain function suggest two leading possibilities.

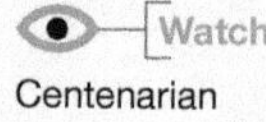

Watch
Centenarian

The first is that older adults under-utilize neural resources, leading to lower levels of activation of relevant brain areas, which has been repeatedly found (Logan et al., 2002; Madden et al., 1996). Interestingly, it may be possible to enhance neural function in older people simply by reminding them to use effective strategies. For example, Logan and her colleagues (2002) found that, compared to subjects in their 20s, older subjects (in their 70s and 80s) performed worse on a memory task, and showed less activation of key frontal lobe areas. However, by giving older adults strategies that would help them more deeply encode the information, older adults were able to activate these brain areas to a greater extent, thus improving their memories for the information. This work suggests that a key to helping older adults resist the decline of their cognitive abilities is to help them learn effective strategies for making better use of their cognitive resources.

Watch
Successful Aging, Independent Lifestyle: Thelma, 81 Years Old

A second possible explanation for reduced cognitive abilities in older people is that older brains show more general, nonspecific brain activation for a given task (Cabeza, 2002). They may do so either because they are compensating for deficits in one area by recruiting other areas, or possibly because they are less capable of limiting activation to the appropriate, specialized neural areas. Involving more widely distributed brain areas in a given task would generally result in slower processing speed, which could help to explain some of the cognitive deficits (e.g., fluid intelligence) seen in older adults.

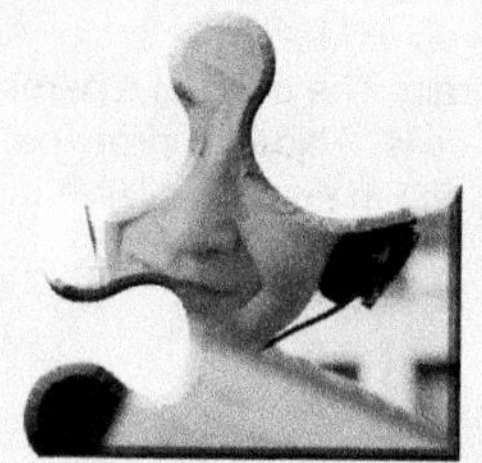

Can we critically evaluate our assumptions about age-related cognitive changes?

Although older people show declines on laboratory tests of some cognitive functions, we should guard against the stereotypic assumption that the elderly are somehow less intellectually capable than the rest of us. In most cultures and for most of history, older people have been widely respected and honoured as wisdom keepers for their communities; respect for one's elders is, in fact, the historical norm, whereas modern Western society's tendency to disregard the perspectives of the elderly, assuming that they are out of touch and their opinions are no longer relevant, is the aberration.

The wisdom of elderly people is evident in their approach not only to emotional well-being, as we discuss later in this module, but also in how they deal with their own cognitive abilities. In everyday life, as opposed to most laboratory tests, the decline in cognitive abilities does not necessarily translate into decline in practical skills, for at least two important reasons. The first is that while the episodic memory and working memory systems work more poorly, the procedural and semantic memory systems show a much reduced rate of decline with age; thus, older people's retention of practical skills and general knowledge about the world remains largely intact for most of their lives.

The second reason the elderly fare better than might be expected from laboratory tests is that they learn to compensate for their poorer raw cognitive power by using their abilities more skillfully. For example, in a chess game, older players play as well as young players, despite the fact that they cannot remember chess positions as well as their young opponents; they compensate for this reduction in working memory during a game by more efficiently searching the chessboard for patterns (Charness, 1981). Having more experience to draw upon in many domains of life gives older people an advantage because they will be better able to develop strategies that allow them to process information more efficiently (Salthouse, 1987).

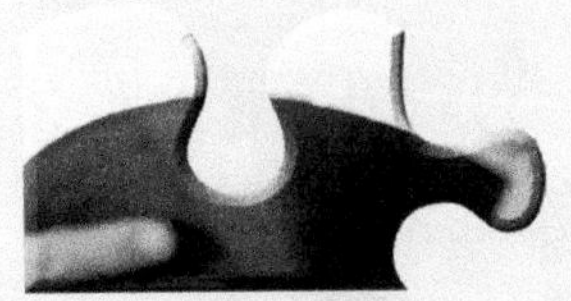

Why is this relevant?

In a society that increasingly relegates its elderly to seniors' residences, largely removing them from their families and the larger community, it is important to remember that older people actually retain their faculties much better than might be expected. This is especially true for older adults who practise specific cognition-enhancing behaviours. What keeps the aging brain sharp? It's pretty simple really, as researchers at the University of Alberta and others have shown—staying physically active, practising cognitively challenging activities (and they don't have to be crosswords and brain teaser puzzles; intrinsically enjoyable hobbies work just fine), and remaining socially connected and active (Small et al., 2012; Stine-Morrow, 2007). In addition, diets low in saturated fats and rich in antioxidants, omega-3 fatty acids, and B vitamins help to maintain cognitive functioning and neural plasticity (Mattson, 2000; Molteni et al., 2002). As a society, providing opportunities and resources for seniors to remain active, socially engaged, and well nourished will allow them to enjoy high-quality lives well into old age.

Watch
Physical Fitness: Joan and Bill, Early 70s

Imagesource/Glow Images

PSYCH @

The Driver's Seat

Thanks to technology, the current generation of elderly adults faces issues that previous generations never did. Take driving, for example. Many older adults depend on their cars to shop, maintain a social life, and keep appointments. Research, however, has shown that the cognitive and physical changes in old age may take a toll on driving skill. This decline presents a dilemma for many seniors and their families: How can individuals maintain the independence afforded by driving without endangering themselves and other drivers?

To address this problem, psychologist Karlene Ball developed an intervention called Useful Field of View (UFOV) Speed of Processing training. UFOV uses computer-based training exercises to increase the portion of the visual field that adults can quickly process and respond to. Laboratory studies show that UFOV actually increases the speed of cognitive processing for older adults. Records from several states that have studied the UFOV show that drivers who completed the training were half as likely to have had an accident during the study period.

{FIG. 10.16} **Memory and Aging** Several types of memory systems exist, not all of which are equally affected by age. An older person's ability to remember events, such as words that appeared on a list (episodic memory), is more likely to decline than his or her memory for facts and concepts (semantic memory).

Psychosocial Development across the Lifespan

Psychologists seeking to understand the general experience of aging across the lifespan have been heavily influenced by Erik Erikson's (1963) theory of psychosocial development. Erikson, who was trained as a psychologist by Sigmund Freud's daughter, Anna, divided the lifespan into eight psychosocial stages (see Table 10.5; also note that earlier stages have been discussed in Modules 10.2 and 10.3 as well). In each stage, the individual's development hinges on whether she successfully resolves a specific developmental challenge, or "crisis of development." If successfully resolved, the individual becomes better able to rise to the challenges of subsequent stages. If not resolved, specific problems result that can interfere with her subsequent development.

Watch
Classic Footage of Erik Erikson

Table 10.5 :: Erikson's Stages of Psychosocial Development

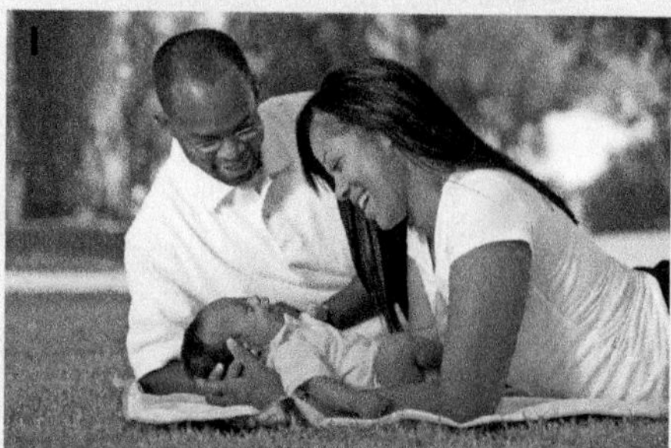

Infancy: trust versus mistrust: Developing a sense of trust and security toward caregivers.

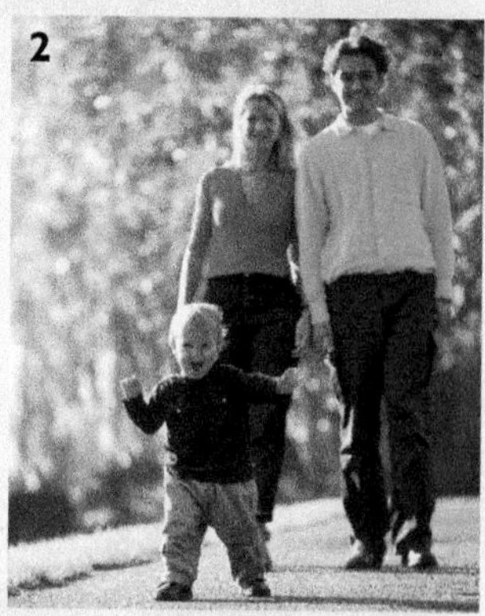

Toddlerhood: autonomy versus shame and doubt: Seeking independence and gaining self-sufficiency.

Preschool/early childhood: initiative versus guilt: Active exploration of the environment and taking personal initiative.

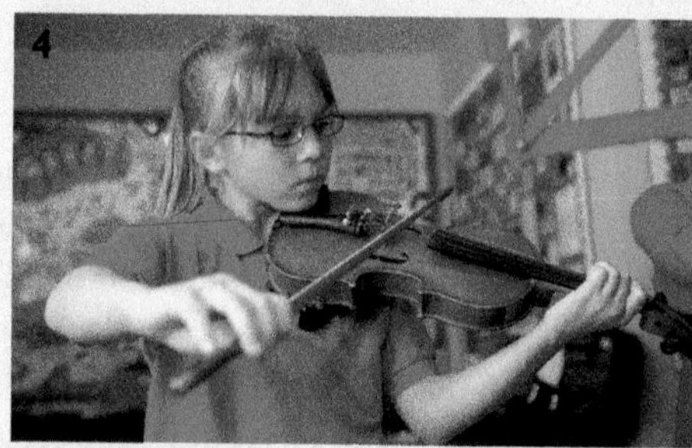

Childhood: industry versus inferiority: Striving to master tasks and challenges of childhood, particularly those faced in school. Child begins pursuing unique interests.

Adolescence: identity versus role confusion: Achieving a sense of self and future direction.

Young adulthood: intimacy versus isolation: Developing the ability to initiate and maintain intimate relationships.

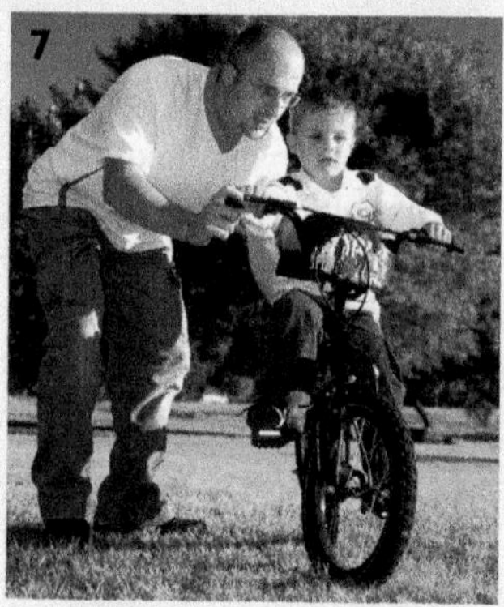

Adulthood: generativity versus stagnation: The focus is on satisfying personal and family needs, as well as contributing to society.

Aging: ego integrity versus despair: Coping with the prospect of death while looking back on life with a sense of contentment and integrity for accomplishments.

1. ClickPop/Shutterstock; 2. Picture Partners/Alamy; 3. Monkey Business Images/Shutterstock; 4. keith morris/Alamy; 5. Tracy Whiteside/Shutterstock.com; 6. OLJ Studio/Shutterstock; 7. Belinda Pretorius/Shutterstock.com; 8. Digital Vision/Thinkstock

Explore
Erikson's First Four Stages of Psychosocial Development

Explore
Erikson's Last Four Stages of Psychosocial Development

According to this model, by the time of adulthood people have already navigated (successfully or not) many challenges, ideally developing a sense of security, feelings of agency and self-worth, self-confidence in their abilities in social and general life domains (see Module 10.2), and a coherent identity (see Module 10.3). It is important to recognize that at each stage, the impact of the social world is profound; the person's key relationships largely determine both the challenges inherent in each stage, and the person's ability to resolve them successfully. The other primary factor is the person's feeling of being competent and capable, although this is also related to feedback received from the social world.

Intimate relationships take on a central focus as people enter into adulthood; the challenge is to establish a genuinely intimate, committed relationship with another person. Because true intimacy involves some degree of compromise, it requires openness, a lack of selfishness, empathy, and even courage in order to risk rejection and bring one's real self into the relationship. As any dismissively attached person well knows, holding back your "true self" is an effective defensive strategy that will protect your feelings if you are rejected by someone you love. However, in order to create truly intimate relationships, one must have the courage to, as poker players say, "go all in." If this challenge is not met, people may enter relationships that lack true intimacy and openness, leaving their intimacy needs never fully met; over time this can cause people to push away and deny their need for intimacy and emphasize their independence.

As individuals enter middle adulthood, the challenge shifts to *generativity versus stagnation*. People become more focused on giving back to society and producing something of value for future generations. Typically, the focus is on raising children and being productive through work, ideally in a way that the individual feels makes a meaningful contribution to society.

Erikson's final major stage of psychosocial development, spanning 65 years onward, is *ego integrity versus despair*. During this time the older adult contemplates whether he or she lived a full life and fulfilled major accomplishments, or looks back and dwells upon disappointments and failures.

Despite the huge impact that Erikson has had on theories of development, James Marcia (2002) from Simon Fraser University notes that there is sparse research support for some aspects of his theory, such as whether there are clearly defined stages that individuals proceed through in sequence, exactly how issues at one stage affect the person later on in life, and whether individuals may be able to compensate fully for not meeting the challenges of a stage.

Nevertheless, Erikson's model is often regarded as a useful guide to the key challenges individuals experience as they go through life, and helps frame our discussion of some of the major aspects of adulthood, including marriage, parenting, careers, and the experiences of older adulthood.

Explore
Theories of Social and Personality Development

Social Development: Intimacy and Generativity

As adolescents transition into adulthood, the nature of their social relationships begins to change. Intimate relationships take central stage, and typically, people begin to pair off into long-term committed relationships (although this is not true for many people, who stay single for a variety of reasons).

LOVE AND MARRIAGE Although not all long-term committed relationships proceed to marriage, it remains the norm, with 67% of Canadian families involving a married couple (with or without children). In recent years the proportion of married-couple families has been dropping, however, from 70.5% in 2001, with a simultaneous increase in common-law and lone-parent families, each of which accounts for about 16% of families (Statistics Canada, 2012).

Watch
Love Marriage: Scherazade and Roderick—Late 30s

Consistent with Erikson's theorizing, being able to establish a committed, long-term relationship seems to be good for people, although of course not in all cases, such as abusive relationships. On average, however, being in such a relationship associated with greater health, longer life (Coombs, 1991; Koball et al., 2010), and increased happiness (Wayment & Peplau, 1995). There are various reasons why, for example, married couples encourage each other to stay active and eat healthier diets, are more satisfied with their sex lives (and have sex more frequently than those who stay single, "swinging single" myths notwithstanding), and enjoy greater financial security (Waite & Gallagher, 2000).

But is it really marriage, per se, that makes people happier? Or is it due to living together in a committed relationship? Until recently, researchers believed that marriage itself got the credit (e.g., Stack & Eshleman, 1998). However, a large international study of relationships across 27 different countries (Lee & Ono, 2012) has shown that the reason people in common-law relationships seem less happy, on average, is because of cultural intolerance of these types of relationships. In cultures with more traditional gender roles, cohabiting outside of marriage is frowned upon, and couples who do so suffer a social cost. This negatively affects women in particular, whose happiness depends more heavily on family relationships and interpersonal ties (Aldous & Ganey, 1999). In more

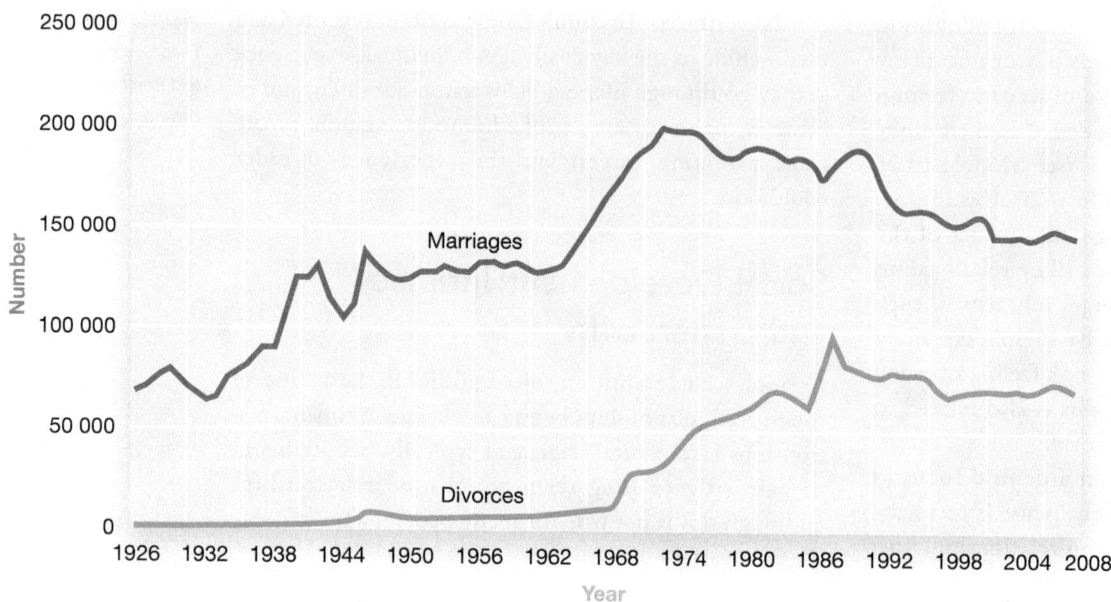

{FIG. 10.17} **Marriage and Divorce Trends in Canada** Starting in the 1960s, Canadian divorce rates began rising quickly. They have been fairly steady for the past 20 years.

egalitarian societies, common-law relationships are not judged as negatively, and consequently, marriage no longer makes people happier than simply living together.

Despite "until death do us part," about 40% of Canadian marriages end in divorce (Statistics Canada, 2004). Many different factors can lead to divorce, but decades of behavioural studies of relationships have shown that a critical factor is how well couples are able to communicate, particularly during conflict. Dr. John Gottman has identified what he calls the "Four Horsemen of the Apocalypse," four communication patterns that are toxic to relationships (Gottman & Levenson, 1992, 2002). Learning to fight fair requires practising a few simple strategies during conflict, and it can make all the difference between maintaining a happy relationship or having to start the dating game all over again.

If you find yourself having conflicts in your relationship, watch out for the following patterns, and if they start happening, fix them!

The First Horseman—Criticism: Complaining about what's wrong in a relationship is okay, but stay focused on what you want to see change. Once the complaint shifts from the problem itself to how it's all your partner's fault, criticism is rearing its ugly head. Watch out for words like "always" and "never." This first horseman is often followed by . . .

The Second Horseman—Defensiveness: "It's not my fault! You do x, y, and z too!" When you feel attacked, it's natural to want to defend yourself, but it undermines communication and turns a problem-solving dialogue into a war. Instead of defending, take responsibility for your part of the problem, let your partner know you're listening and you're open to what your partner is saying, and try to find solutions together rather than just "proving" it's not all your fault.

The Third Horseman—Contempt: "If you were my husband, I'd poison your coffee!" "Yeah, well if you were my wife, I'd drink it!" Although this is a joke, contempt is basically relationship poison. Contempt creeps in when one partner feels superior to the other, feels that what upsets the other is not that big of a deal and engages in name-calling, sarcastic retorts, and eye-rolling during a conflict. To avoid contempt, make the choice to focus on all those things you love and appreciate about your partner, and try to understand the concerns from your partner's perspective, not yours. Just because something seems like "no big deal" to you, it is to them, and they have good reasons for their reactions, perhaps reaching into painful experiences they've had in the past. Instead of judging them, practise empathizing, and instead of focusing on how much they have failed, focus on how hard they are trying.

The Fourth Horseman—Stonewalling: This one seems straightforward—the stony silence, one-word answers, going cold and acting like you don't care. What's not straightforward is realizing that what causes stonewalling is often that the person feels so emotionally overwhelmed that she or he doesn't know what to say or how to respond. But instead of disengaging, it's better to be honest, tell your partner that you don't know what to say, you're confused or upset or just feeling a lot of

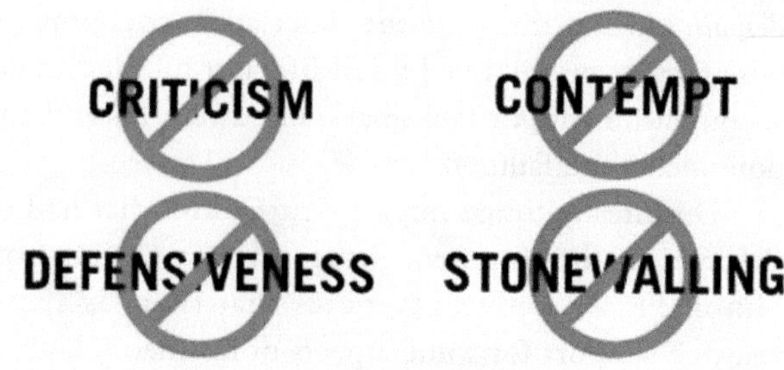

The Gottman Institute

Recognizing the Four Horsemen of the (Relationship) Apocalypse—Learning to recognize and change these negative communication patterns can make many relationships better.

emotions, and you need to take a break. It's a lot easier to try again once the emotions have settled down, and it's a lot easier for your partner to know that you aren't shutting her or him out.

The up side of this research is that, by changing communication patterns, people can dramatically improve their relationships. What was once a climate of contempt and escalating conflict can again become one of love and intimacy.

PARENTING Parenting is another major experience that shapes the young and middle adult years. Parenting basically takes over your life, especially in the beginning when children are young and have virtually no independence. As people become parents, they often experience a major shift in identity; not only can they kiss goodbye to sleeping in on Saturday mornings, but they change their whole way of looking at life. Becoming 100% responsible for a little bundle of joy, and feeling loved in a way you've never known before, makes many people realize that their life is about much more than their own personal wants and needs.

Of course, making this transition, with the exhaustion, stress, and massive changes that accompany it, is not easy. As a result, although parenting young children brings unfathomable love and rewards, and marriages can be stabilized as parents pull together "for the sake of the kids," it also exacts a cost; within the first two years of having children, parents typically report that marital satisfaction declines (Belsky & Rovine, 1990). Marital satisfaction is usually highest before the birth of the first child, then is reduced until the children enter school (Cowan & Cowan, 1995; Shapiro et al., 2000), and not uncommonly, remains low until the children actually leave home as young adults themselves (Glenn, 1990).

In fact, the notion of parents suffering in their "empty nest" once their children leave home is largely a myth. Although some parents may take a fresh look at their relationship once it's just the two of them again and discover they really don't have anything in common anymore, the general trend is the opposite; married older adults are just as likely to report being "very satisfied" with marriage as are newlyweds (Rollins, 1989). However, empty nest feelings do occur in some cases, particularly for women if they stayed at home to raise the children, if they are not well connected to the extended family (which is generally rare in all except White, Euro-American cultures), and if they tended to define themselves largely through their role as "mom" (Borland, 1982). In most other cases though, having children (finally) leave home leads to an increase in both marital and life satisfaction (Black & Hill, 1984).

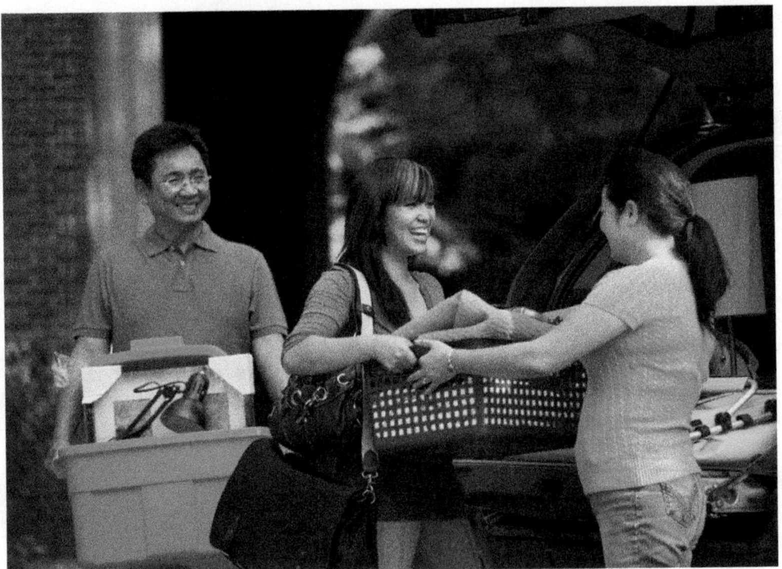

Ariel Skelley/lend Images/Alamy

Although parents may experience sadness or even divorce when their children move out, the general trend is toward an increase in marital satisfaction.

CAREER In addition to parenting, having a satisfying career is a component of **generativity** in adulthood. Erikson believed that generativity involves *being engaged in meaningful and productive work, as well as making contributions to future generations*. Failure to fulfill these goals leads to being self-absorbed (see Table 10.5 on page 436).

Watch: In the Real World: Parenting Styles and Socialization

Career choice is a major decision that affects the lifestyle of the majority of adults. Although career changes are very common, most choices that adults make about their career reflect their own self-concept (Super et al., 1996)—that is, what people believe about what they can do well and what they are happy doing influence the jobs they choose. Several variables influence career happiness. For example, salary or wage earnings contribute to career satisfaction, but other factors such as job interest and relationships with managers and supervisors are important as well (Sousa-Poza & Sousa-Poza, 2000).

Most adults who are financially able to do so retire during late adulthood. Primary concerns at this life stage may switch to grandparenting roles, staying healthy, travelling, and leisure activities. Of course, not all adults are able to enjoy the luxuries associated with retirement, depending on their health and economic resources.

Watch: Transitioning to Retirement: Mary and George

EMOTIONAL CHANGES One of the biggest benefits to growing older is that the emotional turmoil of youth often (of course not always) gives way to an emotional stability and positivity that makes late adulthood particularly enjoyable. The famous Buddhist monk Thich Nnat Hanh has described youth as being like the chaotic mountain stream tumbling down the mountainside, whereas old age is when the stream has broadened into a serene river calmly making the final leg of its journey to the ocean.

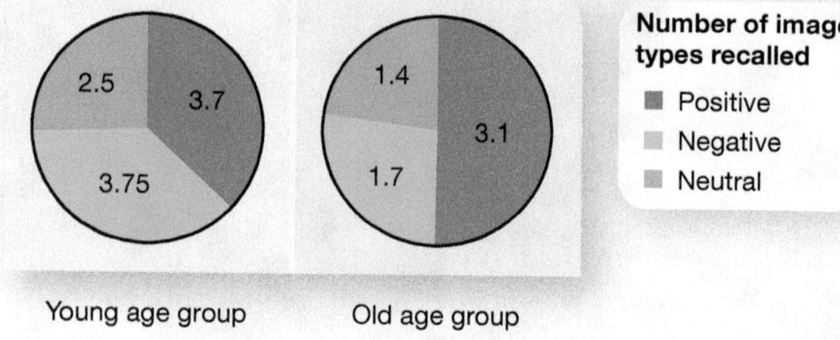

{FIG. 10.18} **Emotion, Memory, and Aging** Younger people have superior memory for whether they have seen positive, negative, or neutral pictures compared with older people. However, notice that younger people remember positive and negative pictures equally, whereas older people are more likely to remember positive pictures (Charles et al., 2003).

Then again, the older years certainly bring their share of challenges: Older people may experience the death of their spouse, the loss of close friends and acquaintances, the fading of their physical capabilities which then brings the loss of personal freedoms such as driving or living without assistance, and the almost inevitable health challenges. Older adults also must, sooner or later, face the growing awareness that their time on this earth is drawing to a close. It doesn't take a lot of imagination to understand why younger people often assume that the elderly are unhappy and depressed as they face the imminent "dying of the light." Certainly, depression and even suicide are not unknown to the elderly, although contrary to the stereotype of the unhappy, lonely old person, healthy older adults are no more likely to become depressed than are younger people. The reality is that as long as basic emotional and social needs are met, old age is often a very joyous time (Charles & Carstensen, 2009).

In fact, many of the challenges of growing old that we noted above bring their own rewards. It is often through loss, trauma, and difficulty that people experience personal growth, a shift in their priorities, a deepened awareness of their values, a heightened appreciation for other people, and a fresh sense of gratitude for the simple joys and pleasures of being alive (Tedeschi & Calhoun, 2004). Even the contemplation of death can help people to become more grateful for life (Frias et al., 2011).

Older adults have had enough experience dealing with the slings and arrows of life that they've learned how to emotionally cope, how to see the glass as half-full rather than half-empty, how to focus on the positives even as they face the negatives. The active cultivation of positive emotions has been shown to be a key resource that helps people cope with life's challenges (Cohn et al., 2009; Garland et al., 2010). For example, groundbreaking research at Kwantlen University has shown that many older people respond even to the loss of their beloved spouse by focusing on positive emotions (Tweed & Tweed, 2011); this enhanced positive focus leads to better coping overall, such as less depressed mood, the experience of greater social support, and even the ability to provide more support to others in the community. This flies in the face of earlier theorists who argued that grief needed to be "fully processed" in order for people to recover (Bonanno, 2004), and experiencing frequent positive emotions while grieving was actually a sign of pathology (Bowlby, 1980)!

Socioemotional selectivity theory describes how older people have learned to pay more attention to positive experiences, and set goals that emphasize positive emotions and meaningful connection (Carstensen et al., 1999). The net result of this wiser approach to life is that negative emotions tend to decline with age, while positive emotions actually increase in frequency (Figure 10.18), resulting in greater emotional well-being as people get older (Charles & Carstensen, 2009).

Quick Quiz 10.4b Cognitive and Psychosocial Changes in Adulthood

KNOW ...

1 In Erikson's theory of psychosocial development, what does generativity refer to?

A The desire to generate an income

B The desire to generate knowledge and learning for oneself

C The desire to have offspring

D The desire to have a positive impact on the world

UNDERSTAND ...

2 Which of the following best describes the effects of aging on intelligence?

A Fluid intelligence tends to decrease, but working memory tends to increase.

B Fluid intelligence tends to decrease, but crystallized intelligence tends to increase.

C Crystallized intelligence tends to increase, but the ability to skillfully use one's abilities decreases.

D Aging is unrelated to intelligence, except in the case of brain disorders and diseases such as dementia or Alzheimer's.

Answers can be found on page ANS-3.

Module Summary

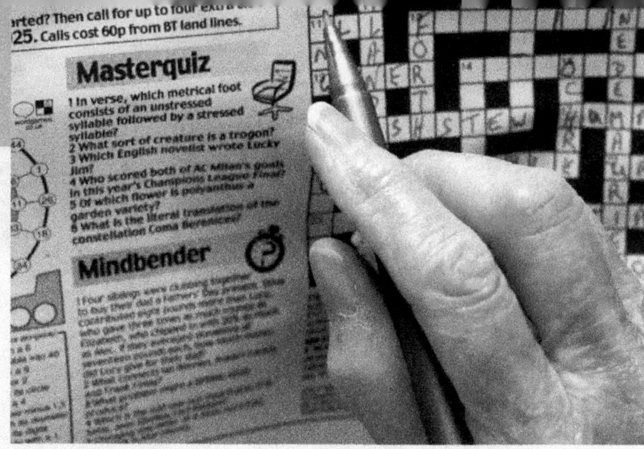

reppans/Alamy

Now that you have read this module you should

KNOW ...

- ***The key terminology concerning adulthood and aging:***

Alzheimer's disease (p. 433)	generativity (p. 439)
dementia (p. 432)	menopause (p. 432)

- ***The key areas of growth experienced by emerging adults.*** People making the transition from adolescence to adulthood face substantial life challenges that contribute to personal growth in three main areas: relationships (i.e., cultivating true intimacy and trust); new possibilities (i.e., exploring what they really want to do with their lives and choosing a compatible path that reflects their interests); and personal strengths (i.e., the skills and competencies that come from successfully facing challenges and learning that "you can do it").

UNDERSTAND ...

- ***Age-related disorders such as Alzheimer's disease.*** Alzheimer's disease is a form of dementia that is characterized by significant decline in memory, cognition, and, eventually, basic bodily functioning. It seems to be caused by two different brain abnormalities—the buildup of proteins that clump together in the spaces between neurons, plus degeneration of a structural protein that forms tangles within nerve cells.
- ***How cognitive abilities change with age.*** Aging adults typically experience a general decline in cognitive abilities, especially those related to fluid intelligence, such as working memory. However, older adults also develop compensatory strategies that enable them to remain highly functional in their daily lives, despite their slow decline in processing capability.

APPLY ...

- ***Effective communication principles to the challenge of improving your own relationships.*** Improving communication in relationships requires being wary of the "Four Horsemen of the Apocalypse" and learning to fix those destructive communication patterns.

  1. Criticism—When complaints focus on the person, not the issue, and global statements like "always" and "never" become common, partners should work on remaining focused on specific issues and how to work together to change them, rather than making it one person's fault.
  2. Defensiveness—Often the response to perceived criticism, defensiveness is about making oneself blameless; to fix it, focus on taking responsibility for your part of the problem and work together to find solutions.
  3. Contempt—This involves seeing the other person as weaker and inferior to oneself, which leads to not taking the other seriously anymore or really listening to that perspective; to fix it, focus on empathizing with your partner and appreciating his or her efforts to change things, rather than any failure to do so in the past.
  4. Stonewalling—This involves shutting down during conflict and ceasing to respond, or even walking out and leaving the situation; to fix this pattern, focus on being honest and telling your partner that you are feeling too emotional right now to keep talking, but you'll try again after the two of you take a bit of a break.

ANALYZE ...

- ***The stereotype that old age is a time of unhappiness.*** Research shows that older adults do face issues that might lead to unhappiness—health problems, loss of loved ones, reductions in personal freedom. However, such challenges often lead to growth and a deepened appreciation for life and other people; the result is that many older people become skilled at focusing on the positives of life and paying less attention to the negatives, leading to an *increase* in life satisfaction, not a decrease.

Work the Scientific Literacy Model :: Understanding Cognitive Development

1 What do we know about Piaget's theory of cognitive development?

Table 10.3 on **page 406** reviews Piaget's stage approach to cognitive development in children. The discussion on **pages 407–408** describes some important milestones achieved in each phase. Piaget's theory is based on the idea of developmental milestones—that children transition from one stage to the next upon developing a new cognitive skill. Also, two processes supporting cognitive development are the twin concepts of assimilation and accommodation.

If you are having trouble telling the difference between the two, it might help to think about learning motor skills in the sensorimotor stage. Once an infant learns to grasp an object in one hand, he will soon learn to grasp all sorts of things—your finger, a pacifier, or a toy. If you give him a new toy, the child can quickly assimilate the new object and learn to grasp it with one hand—unless, of course, that toy happens to be a great big ball that does not fit in one hand. In that case, the infant must accommodate the new object by modifying what he knows about grasping objects. In this case, the task involves devising a technique that uses both hands.

2 How can science help explain cognitive development?

Research, such as the study on errors of scale illustrated in **Figure 10.7 on page 408** and the conservation study described in **Figure 10.6 on page 408**, has provided extensive support for Piaget's ideas. More recently, researchers like Elizabeth Spelke have shown that even infants may actually have some appreciation for abstract numbers. Other studies suggest that children may be able to take on the perspective of others as early as 4 or 5 years of age. The dynamics between caregivers and children's cognitive development have been explored via the idea of scaffolding, and the text on **page 411** highlights cross-cultural research on caregiver/child interaction suggesting that cultural issues might also have a noticeable effect on cognitive development.

Dubova/Shutterstock

3 Can we critically evaluate theories of cognitive development?

Piaget's early work on cognitive development from infancy through adolescence has exerted an enormous influence on developmental psychology, but modern research has raised some questions about when and how children move through each stage. The possibility that children are born with some innate cognitive abilities and the recent studies on egocentrism have added to an already rich discussion. Similarly, evidence of the link between social influences and cognitive development suggests that the interplay between cognitive development and sociocultural factors may be stronger than Piaget originally thought.

4 Why is this relevant?

Watch the accompanying video excerpt on how thinking develops. You can access the video at MyPsychLab or by clicking the play button in the centre of your eText. If your instructor assigns this video as a homework activity, you will find additional content to help you in MyPsychLab. You can also view the video by using your smart phone and the QR code below, or you can go to the YouTube link provided.

Once you have read this chapter and watched the video, using specific examples, differentiate between the thinking patterns of a 3-year-old preschooler and a 9-year-old student, according to Piaget's theory of cognitive development.

MyPsychLab **Your turn to Work the Scientific Literacy Model:** Watch the accompanying video on YouTube, or on your phone (using the Layar app or QR code). If your instructor has assigned this as a homework activity, you can find the video clip and additional content at MyPsychLab. Answer the questions that accompany the video clip to test your understanding.

youtube.com/workthemodel

SCAN WITH LAYAR

11

Motivation and Emotion

Dudarev Mikhail/Shutterstock

Satchan/Corbis/Bridge/Glow Images

Module 11.1

Hunger and Eating

Learning Objectives

After reading this module you should

KNOW ...	UNDERSTAND ...	APPLY ...	ANALYZE ...
The key terminology of motivation and hunger	The biological, cognitive, and social processes that shape eating patterns The major eating and weight-control problems people face	Your knowledge of hunger regulation to better understand and evaluate your own eating patterns	The role of the media on people's body image

It was Janice's first year of university. She'd made it through the first three months of the semester with impressive grades, but was now dealing with her first ever "Finals Week." After a long afternoon of studying History, Janice felt like she was starving. She walked over to the cafeteria and was overwhelmed by the number of options. She saw a friend eating a greasy pizza, and immediately ordered one for herself (but with a salad, which of course made the meal healthy). She finished the enormous plate of food and felt like she couldn't eat another bite. She crawled back to the library and began studying for her Chemistry exam that was scheduled for the next morning. But, despite having just eaten a large meal, Janice found herself munching on candy that she'd snuck into the library (a guilty habit that was now as much a part of studying as her textbooks). The more anxious she got about this exam, the more she mindlessly moved the sugary snacks from their bag into her mouth. Janice's experience shows us that eating isn't just a simple behaviour we use for survival. Hunger is a biological drive that influences what we pay attention to and interacts with our past experiences and current mental states such as excitement and anxiety. Hunger is a psychological behaviour.

Focus Questions

 What are some ways that our physical and social environments affect eating?

 What makes us feel hungry or full?

The study of **motivation** *concerns the physiological and psychological processes underlying the initiation of behaviours that direct organisms toward specific goals.* These initiating factors, or *motives*, include the thoughts, feelings, sensations, and bodily processes that lead to goal-directed behaviour. For example, when the body's water levels fall below normal, cells release chemical compounds that maintain the structure and fluid levels of cells. Receptors in the body respond to the increased concentrations of these compounds, as well as to the

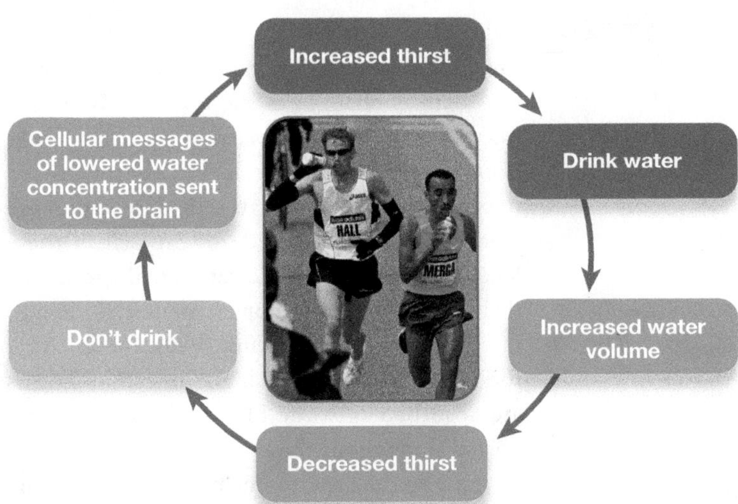

Boston Globe/Getty Images

{FIG. 11.1} **Drives and Incentives** Our motivation to reduce a drive, or in response to an incentive, can lead to the same behaviour.

lower water volume, and send messages to the brain. The result is the sudden awareness that you are thirsty, which motivates you to drink water. This process is known as a **drive**, *a biological trigger that tells us we may be deprived of something and causes us to seek out what is needed, such as food or water* (Figure 11.1). When a drive is satisfied, reward centres in our brains become activated. This reinforces our behaviour, making it more likely that we'll respond to these drives—such as Janice's decision to eat pizza—again in the future.

As you can see from this example, motivation is essential to an individual's survival because at its most basic level it contributes to **homeostasis**, *the body's physiological processes that allow it to maintain consistent internal states in response to the outer environment* (see Figure 11.2). However, sometimes humans and animals are motivated to engage in behaviours that cannot be explained by homeostasis. Think back to Janice eating candy while stressing out about her exams. The experience of anxiety uses a lot of energy, as does the effort required to control your emotions. It is also never clear exactly how long these feelings will be experienced (it's tough to schedule "stress" in your dayplanner). If Janice didn't increase her food consumption to meet these new energy demands, her energy level would quickly dip below the level that homeostasis was trying to maintain. Her physical and mental well-being would then suffer. Luckily, there are mechanisms in our brain that take note of these changes in energy consumption—particularly those caused by mental states—and predict how much food should be consumed to account for this increased need for energy. In other words, *motivation is not only influenced by current needs, but also by the anticipation of future needs* (Sterling, 2011). This process is known as **allostasis**.

Of course, our ability to predict our future needs is not perfect, which explains why psychological variables (e.g., stress, desire to appear attractive, the need to feel "in control") can have such a strong influence on behaviours like eating and drinking, which don't seem "psychological" at all.

In this module, we will examine how these physical and psychological factors influence our motivation to eat. We will also examine how social factors can alter our eating habits in negative and self-destructive ways.

Explore
Evolutionary Drive, Arousal, Cognitive, and Humanistic Theories of Motivation

Physiological Aspects of Hunger

Hunger is not simply a homeostatic mechanism. The need to consume enough nutrients so that you have enough energy to function involves physiological responses *as well as* more complex cognitive and emotional factors (Dagher, 2012). The brain areas involved with these factors interact with the brain areas that control our appetites.

Watch
How Food Impacts the Brain

The "on" and "off" switches involved in hunger can be found in a few regions of the hypothalamus, a set of nuclei found on the bottom surface of the brain. Researchers have found that electrically stimulating the lateral hypothalamus causes rats to begin to eat; thus, this structure may serve as an "on" switch (Delgado & Anand, 1952). In contrast, stimulating the ventromedial region of the hypothalamus causes rats to stop eating. Damaging the ventromedial region removes the "off switch" in the brain; in lab animals, this damage leads to obesity because the animals don't stop eating (Figure 11.3).

Explore
Virtual Brain: Hunger and Eating

The activity of the hypothalamus is influenced by hormones that are released in response to the energy needs of your body. So, your brain influences your body *and* your body influences your brain! A key function of the hypothalamus is to monitor blood chemistry for

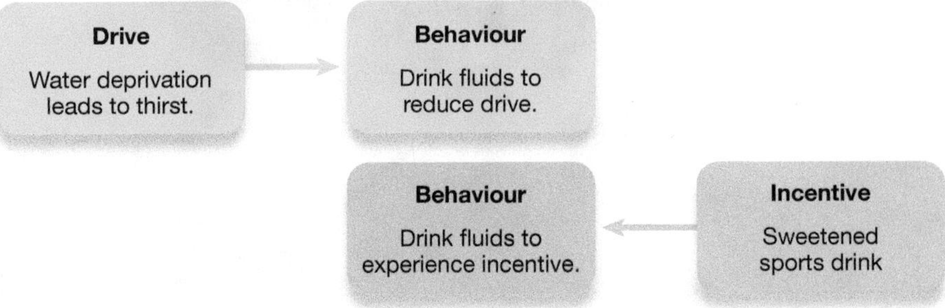

{FIG. 11.2} **Maintaining Balance** Homeostasis is the process of maintaining relatively stable internal states. For example, this diagram illustrates how homeostasis regulates thirst and the body's fluid levels.

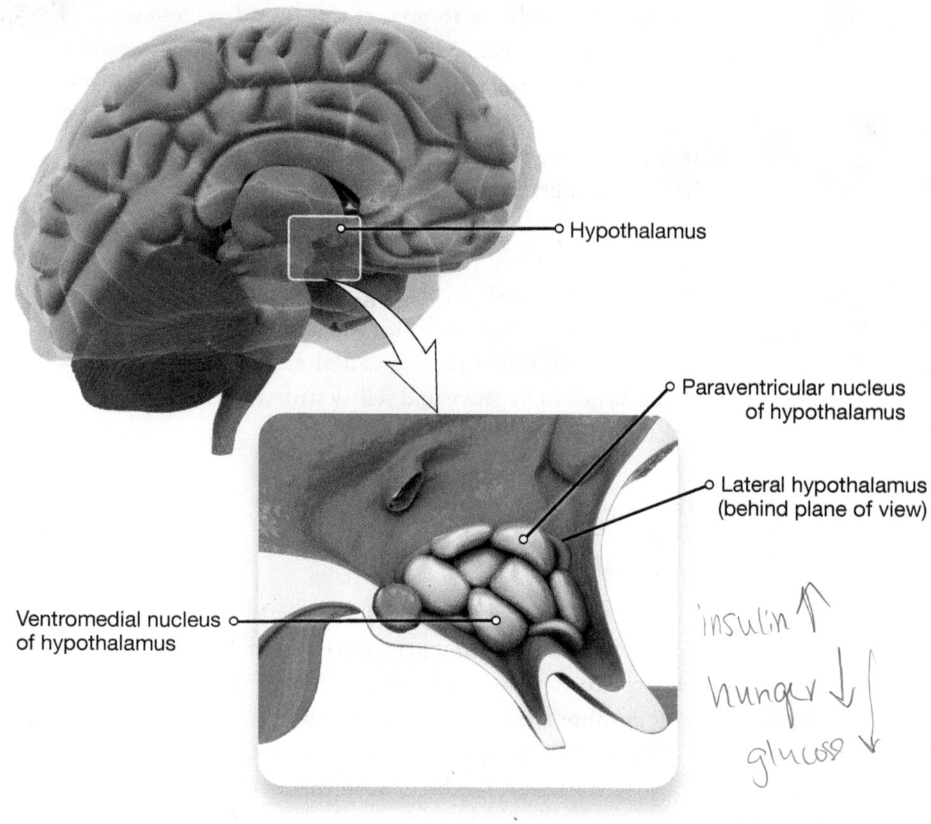

{FIG. 11.3} **The Hypothalamus and Hunger** The hypothalamus acts as an on/off switch for hunger. The lateral region of the hypothalamus signals when it is time to eat, while the ventromedial and paraventricular regions signal when it is time to stop eating.

Explore

The Effects of the Hypothalamus on Eating Behaviour

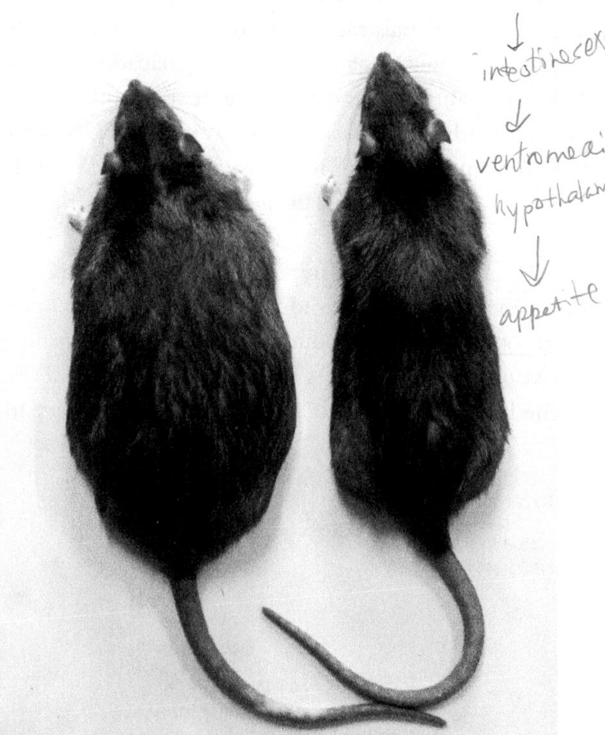

Olivier Voisin/Photo Researchers, Inc.

The rat on the left has swollen to enormous proportions after researchers created lesions to its ventromedial hypothalamus. Compare it to the more typical rat on the right.

indicators of the levels of sugars and hormones involved in energy. For example, the hypothalamus detects changes in the level of **glucose**, *a sugar that serves as a primary energy source for the brain and the rest of the body.* Highly specialized neurons called glucostats can detect glucose levels in the fluid outside of the cell. If these levels are too low, glucostats signal the hypothalamus that energy supplies are low, leading to increased hunger (Langhans, 1996a, 1996b). After food reaches the stomach and intestines, sugars are absorbed into the bloodstream and transported throughout the body. Insulin, a hormone secreted by the pancreas, helps cells store this circulating glucose for future use. As insulin levels rise in response to consumption of a meal, hunger decreases—but so do glucose levels, which, after a few hours, leads to hunger again.

We have all experienced the feeling of being "full." A full stomach is one cue for **satiation**—*the point in a meal when we are no longer motivated to eat.* That feeling is caused, in part, by cholecystokinin (mercifully abbreviated to CCK) (Badman & Flier, 2005). Neurons release CCK when the intestines expand. The ventromedial hypothalamus receives this information and decreases appetite.

The feeling of satiation can also influence how rewarding we find a food. For example, have you ever eaten a food so many times that you started to feel "sick of" it? Scientists at the Montreal Neurological Institute used neuroimaging to investigate the areas of the brain related to this feeling. In one experiment, these researchers scanned people's brains while feeding them pieces of chocolate. At first, the participants rated the chocolate as being quite tasty and pleasurable; this led to activity in the orbitofrontal cortex (the part of the frontal lobes just above your eyes), a brain area that judges the reward value of foods (Small et al., 2001). Activity was also found in the insula, which receives information about taste, and the basal ganglia, which respond to physical rewards. But, after participants had consumed several pieces of chocolate, this formerly pleasurable food became somewhat aversive. Interestingly, as participants' ratings of the chocolate became more negative, the activity in reward centres decreased and was replaced by activity in other areas of the frontal lobes. This study shows that a number of different brain areas are involved when we are motivated to eat—it is not simply a case of the hypothalamus controlling this complex behaviour. It also shows us that our physiological and psychological motivations to eat influence each other.

Quick Quiz 11.1a
Physiological Aspects of Hunger

KNOW ...

1 The __________ region of the hypothalamus is associated with the onset of eating, while the __________ region is associated with the offset.

- **A** lateral; ventromedial
- **B** ventromedial; lateral
- **C** anterior; posterior
- **D** anterior; ventromedial

2 __________ is a sugar that serves as a vital energy source for the human body; its levels are monitored by the nervous system.

- **A** Ghrelin
- **B** CCK
- **C** Glucose
- **D** Insulin

UNDERSTAND ...

3 Why do psychologists believe the lateral hypothalamus generates hunger signals that contribute to people's motivation to eat?

- **A** This brain structure responds to glucose levels.
- **B** When the lateral hypothalamus is stimulated, laboratory animals eat more.
- **C** Skinny people have smaller nuclei in this area.
- **D** The lateral hypothalamus releases CCK, which reduces hunger.

Answers can be found on page ANS-3.

Psychological Aspects of Hunger

In the example that started this module, poor stressed-out Janice ate pizza, salad, and candy. But, humans evolved in environments in which food was not this plentiful or rich in variety. Sometimes, after a successful hunting expedition, food was abundant; however, at other times, food was quite scarce. Humans quickly learned that the best strategy was to "eat while you can" because there was no guarantee that another meal would be forthcoming any time soon. And, given that we need a great deal of energy to keep our bodies functioning properly, it would make sense to consume fatty foods, a very rich source of energy. Over the course of evolution, our bodies responded to this need with a number of systems that made the consumption of high-energy foods pleasurable. In other words, we developed bodies that were hard-wired to *like* some foods more than others.

Imagine eating poutine, Quebec's cardiovascular equivalent of Russian roulette. It's clearly bad for you (there is no diet poutine), yet people still enthusiastically eat it. Indeed, some of the most popular foods in Canada are loaded with fats, including red meat, cheese, ice cream, and anything deep-fried. Psychologists and neuroscientists are discovering why people can be so driven to consume these and other fattening foods. Scientists suggest that we crave fats because we have specialized receptors on the tongue that are sensitive to the fat content of food (Figure 11.4). Research with animals shows that these receptors send messages to the brain that stimulate the release of endorphins and dopamine, both of which are responsible for the subjective sense of pleasure and reward (Mizushige et al., 2007). Similar results were found in brain imaging studies with human participants (Rolls, 2010). In one study, participants had their brains scanned while they tasted various substances. At different times, the participants tasted either a fatty solution (vegetable oil), sucrose (a sweet taste), or a tasteless control substance. Brain activity was recorded while these different taste stimuli were delivered in liquefied form into the mouths of the participants through a small plastic tube. The participants were also asked to rate the pleasantness of each stimulus. Overall, the participants rated the fatty substance favourably, and the brain scans showed activity in regions of the brain associated with pleasure sensations when they tasted fat (de Araujo & Rolls, 2004).

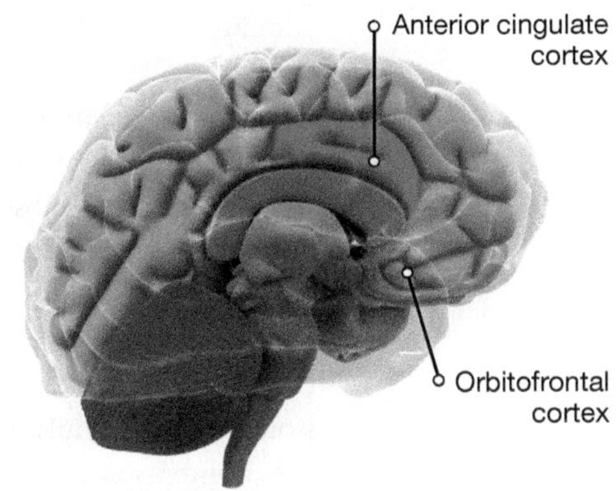

{FIG. 11.4} **The Pleasure of Taste** When fat receptors of the tongue are stimulated, the cingulate cortex—a region of the brain involved in emotional processing—is activated. The orbitofrontal cortex is involved in linking food taste and texture with reward.

In some situations, high-energy food can be a more powerful reinforcer than highly addictive drugs (Christensen et al., 2008). Some people even report cravings for a "sugar fix"—a term that seems to imply that addiction to candy and chocolate bars is comparable to an addiction to a drug like heroin. The phrase "sugar fix" may seem an exaggeration, but is it possible that sugar actually does act like a drug? Sugar and some

studiovitra/Shutterstock

Cells in the orbitofrontal cortex respond to perceptual qualities of food texture, such as the difference between a runny spaghetti sauce and a thick one.

addictive drugs share an interesting similarity. Ordinary sucrose—plain white granulated sugar—can stimulate release of the neurotransmitter dopamine in the nucleus accumbens, a brain region associated with the reinforcing effects of substances such as amphetamines and cocaine (Rada et al., 2005; see Module 5.3).

So why did Janice have greater cravings for fatty and sugary foods while stressed out? One possibility is that stress modulates *ghrelin*, a hormone secreted in the stomach that stimulates stomach contractions and appetite (Kristensson et al., 2006). Additionally, feeling stressed means that you are viewing a particular situation as being threatening in some way, even if you are not in physical danger. Based on the principle of allostasis discussed above, if you predict that an upcoming event will be threatening, you will react by stocking up on energy reserves so that you are better able to deal with this threat. So, even though homeostasis would indicate that Janice should stop eating, her psychological interpretation of her situation will lead her to continue munching away. While such a strategy is not good for your health, at the species level, it did help us survive some very threatening times, when exam results were the least of our worries.

ATTENTION AND EATING The quantity of food that we eat is not entirely controlled by the brain or by evolutionary mechanisms. Instead, something as simple as attention can have a huge effect on how much we consume. Imagine sitting down to your favourite meal. Many of us would eat a lot, but then watching each helping disappear would probably serve as a reminder that it is approaching time to stop. But what if someone (or some drug) interfered with your ability to keep track of how much you had eaten? This scenario is not what we would expect in normal situations, but it would allow for an ideal test of how food availability affects how much you will eat.

Psychologists have created such a situation in the laboratory through a technique known as the bottomless bowl of soup. Volunteers were asked to eat soup until they had had enough. In the experimental condition, a tube continued to fill the soup bowl from the bottom so that it could not be detected by the volunteers. These individuals stopped eating after consuming, on average, over 70% more than those participants who knowingly refilled their bowls. Even more interesting is what happened—or did not happen—in terms of feelings and thoughts: The individuals eating from bottomless bowls did not feel any more satiated, nor did they believe they had eaten any more than the individuals in the control group. It turns out we are not so good at putting on the brakes when we cannot keep track of how much we have consumed (Wansink et al., 2005).

The results of the bottomless soup bowl study can be explained by **unit bias**, *the tendency to assume that the unit of sale or portioning is an appropriate amount to consume.* In some cases, this assumption works well. A single banana comes individually wrapped and makes for a healthy portion; it is an ideal unit (Geier et al., 2006). In contrast, packaged foods often come in sizes that are too large to be healthy. A bottle of pop today is likely to be 600 mL, but a few decades ago the same brand of soda came in a 177 mL bottle. Despite the huge difference in volume, each is seen as constituting one unit of pop. As a consequence, you are now likely to consume more than three times as much pop in one sitting as your grandparents would have. Surprisingly, the unit bias affects our consumption almost as much as the taste of the food! In one study, participants were given fresh or stale (14-day-old) popcorn in either a small (120 g) or large (240 g) container. When the container was large, participants ate more popcorn . . . even if it was incredibly stale and tasted like Styrofoam (Wansink & Kim, 2005). A similar effect was found for people at a Super Bowl party. The larger bowls implied that it was "normal" for people to eat more (Wansink & Cheney, 2005). Researchers have concluded that increasing the size of the dishes increases consumption by 18–25% for meals and 30–45% for snack foods (Wansink, 1996).

This expansion of portion sizes—and waistlines—is being felt worldwide. As North American style fast-food chains expand into Asia, the prevalence of diabetes has increased (Pan et al., 2012). This is likely why some countries limit portion sizes and others, such as France, require all fast-food chains and snack products to have warning labels. But, before we beat ourselves up about how greedy our culture is, we should get some perspective: This upward trend in the size of our meals has been going on for a long time. This was demonstrated in a clever study examining the portion sizes of food in paintings depicting the same scene from the Bible (the last supper of Jesus). The study examined portion sizes in paintings over the last millennium (1000–2000 C.E.). Sure enough, the plate sizes and portion sizes increased over the years (Wansink & Wansink, 2010).

Given this information about the role of attention, container sizes, and culture, what changes do you think should be made in the food industry to make Canada a healthier place?

EATING AND THE SOCIAL CONTEXT In addition to physical and attentional influences, food intake is affected by social motives as well. Have you ever gone to a party feeling not a hint of hunger, yet spent the first hour sampling each of the snacks laid out on the dining room table because you were nervous and didn't know what else to do with yourself? Whether the presence of other people increases or decreases our motivation to eat is influenced by the social situation (Herman et al., 2003). Here are a few examples:

- *Social facilitation: Eating more.* Dinner hosts (and grandmothers) may encourage guests to take second and even third helpings, and individuals with a reputation for big appetites will be prodded to eat the most. Perhaps the strongest element of social facilitation is just the time spent at the table: The longer a person sits socializing, the more likely he or she is to continue nibbling (Berry et al., 1985).
- *Impression management: Eating less.* Sometimes people self-consciously control their behaviour so that others will see them in a certain way—a phenomenon known as *impression management*. For example, you probably know that it is polite to chew with your mouth closed. Similarly, the *minimal eating norm* suggests that another aspect of good manners—at least in some social and cultural settings—is to eat small amounts to avoid seeming rude (Herman et al., 2003).
- *Modelling: Eating whatever they eat.* At first exposure to a situation, such as a business dinner, a new employee may notice that no one eats much and everyone takes their time. The newcomer will see the others as models, and so he too will restrain his eating. Later, he may drop by his friend's family reunion where everyone is having a second or third helping and undoing their belts so their stomachs can expand more. In this case, he will be likely to eat more, even if he is already feeling full (Herman et al., 2003).

Clearly, eating is not just a matter of maintaining homeostasis. It is best described as a behaviour motivated by biological, social, and individual psychological factors.

Top: Image Source/Corbis; bottom: Akg-images/Newscom

Compare a modern soft drink serving (top) to the historical serving size (bottom). Despite the massive increase in volume, modern consumers still consider the unit of packaging as a normal-sized serving.

Quick Quiz 11.1b

Psychological Aspects of Hunger

KNOW ...

1 The minimal eating social norm is the observation that people tend to

A eat as little as possible in just about every social situation imaginable.

B view eating reasonably sized portions as the polite thing to do.

C encourage one another to eat too much.

D eat as much as possible to flatter the cook.

UNDERSTAND ...

2 Sometimes being around others can

A lead you to eat more than you normally would.

B lead you to eat less than you normally would.

C both a or b, depending on what others were doing.

D neither a nor b; others do not influence our eating.

APPLY ...

3 In Europe, the typical container of fruit and yogurt is roughly 177 mL. In North America, the same food item is usually packaged in 237 mL containers. The unit bias suggests that

A a German person visiting Canada would be likely to eat the entire container, even though it contains 25% more than the typical German serving.

B a Canadian visiting Germany would almost certainly miss the extra 50 mL of yogurt.

C a German person visiting Canada would carefully evaluate the differences in packaging to ensure that he or she does not consume more than usual.

D all people would be unsatisfied with the 177 mL serving in Germany.

ANALYZE ...

4 How do evolutionary psychologists explain our desire to eat particular foods?

A We eat fatty foods because they are most accessible.

B The foods we now find pleasurable are often high-energy foods that would have enhanced our chances for survival in the past.

C People who consume sugar-free food have less energy and are less likely to reproduce, thus making them less evolutionarily fit.

D People have adapted our food intake to match our current North American lifestyle.

Answers can be found on page ANS-3.

Watch In the Real World: Eating Disorders

Disorders of Eating

Our dietary habits are influenced by biological dispositions, our beliefs and perceptions about eating and our bodies, and sociocultural factors. Unfortunately, these motivational systems do not always lead us to good health.

OBESITY **Obesity** *is a disorder of positive energy balance, in which energy intake exceeds energy expenditure.* Some refer to this phenomenon as an epidemic which has spread across the world. Over the last 15 years, surveys have consistently shown that approximately 20% of Canadians had a height and weight ratio that would classify them as obese; over 60% of Canadian adults could be classified as overweight (Figure 11.5; Statistics Canada, 2010). Obesity rates were lowest in Quebec, and highest in Atlantic Canada, the Territories, and Saskatchewan (Dutton & McLaren, 2011). So, why are obesity rates so high? There is no simple answer to this question. One issue is the huge variety of foods available. As you read above, if we eat the same foods a lot, we desire them less. So, if there are a large number of different foods to choose from, we are less likely to grow tired of any of them. (Think about this the next time you walk into a food court at a mall.) A second issue relates to our discussion of the evolutionary need to crave fatty foods, and to store the excess energy in our bodies in case no food is available later. We still crave fatty and energy-rich foods—however, for most people, there are few periods of time in which we are going hungry. The result is that the excess food is stored as fat. Another factor is economics. In developed countries like Canada, obesity tends to affect the poor more than the rich (Evans et al., 2000) because unhealthy, energy-dense foods are less expensive than healthy ones (Darmon et al., 2004). Fast-food outlets are also more numerous in low-income neighbourhoods than in richer areas (Hemphill et al., 2008). As the number of people who are struggling economically increases, so will the obesity rates. Sadly, obesity is linked to health problems, which will make it more difficult (but not impossible!) for these individuals to earn enough money to afford healthy food (see Module 14.1).

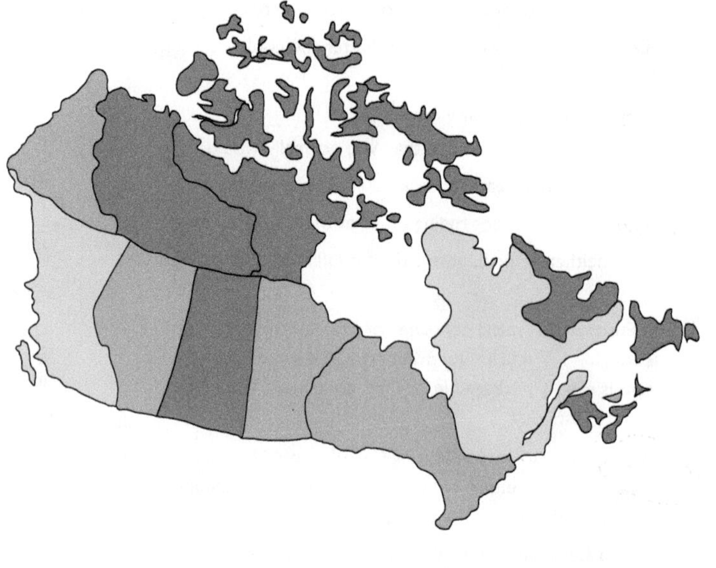

{FIG. 11.5} **Obesity Rates in Canada** The rates of obesity differ from province to province. For more information about Canadian obesity rates, go to the Canadian Community Health Survey www.statcan.gc.ca/daily-quotidien/110621/dq110621b-eng.htm.

All of these factors combine to explain our different motivations to over-eat. However, in some individuals, hunger-related motivations move in the opposite direction—leading them to under-eat. While skipping dessert at Dairy Queen might not be a bad idea, avoiding or restricting the consumption of healthy food is obviously problematic. In the next section, we discuss some of the motivations underlying these behaviours.

ANOREXIA AND BULIMIA The two most common forms of eating disorders are anorexia nervosa and bulimia (see Table 11.1). **Anorexia nervosa** *is an eating disorder that involves (1) self-starvation, (2) intense fear of weight gain and dissatisfaction with one's body, and (3) a denial of the serious consequences of severely low weight.* In contrast, **bulimia nervosa** *is an eating disorder that is characterized by periods of food deprivation,*

Table 11.1 :: Statistical Characteristics of Eating Disorders

Lifetime prevalence of anorexia	Women: 0.9%	Men: 0.3%
Lifetime prevalence of bulimia	Women: 1.5%	Men: 0.5%
	Women and Men combined	
Percentage of people with anorexia who are receiving treatment	34%	
Percentage of people with bulimia who are receiving treatment	43%	
Average duration of anorexia	1.7 years	
Average duration of bulimia	8 years	

Source: Hudson et al., 2007.

binge-eating, and purging. The periods of binging involve short bursts of intense calorie consumption. These are followed by purging (generally self-induced vomiting), fasting, laxative or diuretic use, and/or intense exercise. Both disorders usually occur during mid- to late adolescence and have been on the rise during the 20th century (Hudson et al., 2007).

Studies of these disorders have found that bulimia is marked by a tendency to be impulsive, whereas anorexia is not (Matsunaga et al., 2000). Bulimics are also much more likely to enter treatment programs because they find the binge-purge cycle disturbing. Anorexics, on the other hand, often appear indifferent to the negative effects the food deprivation is having on their health (Polivy & Herman, 2002). Although there are clear differences between anorexia and bulimia, both involve changes in the motivation to eat and both are dangerous. A critical question, then, is why eating disorders develop in some people but not others.

One factor is stress. Patients with eating disorders report greater levels of premorbid (before the disorder began) life stress than do age- and gender-matched individuals without eating disorders (Schmidt et al., 1997). These life stresses tend to make people feel as though they have no control over their lives. However, stress alone isn't enough to create an eating disorder. Instead, the perceived loss of control interacts with psychological variables such as depression, guilt, anxiety, and perfectionism (Vohs et al., 1999); low self-esteem (Button et al., 1996); and/or suppressed anger (Geller et al., 2000). This *combination* of stress and psychological vulnerability dramatically increases the chances of developing an eating disorder (Ball & Lee, 2002; Raffi et al., 2000).

There are also a number of social factors that can lead to eating disorders. Peer influence is often viewed as the number one cause of these conditions (Stice, 1998). Adolescents, particularly females, learn attitudes and behaviours from their friends. This learning comes in the form of examples and encouragement as well as from teasing and nasty remarks when an individual doesn't live up to the idealized (thin) standards depicted in the media (Levine et al., 1994). In fact, numerous pro-anorexia websites have emerged over the past decade offering "thinspiration" for people engaging in extreme dieting; similar messages are now appearing on social media sites such as Pinterest. By posting photographs and messages on these sites, individuals with eating disorders create a much larger peer group than before, making dangerous eating disorders seem normal. This is a worrisome trend. Families are also a major influence on individuals with eating disorders. They often compliment anorexic girls for being slim and praise their self-control. This serves as a source of reinforcement for the eating disorder (Branch & Eurman, 1980). Bulimic patients reported that their families were competitive, prone to jealousy, and tended to intrude in each other's lives (Rorty et al., 2000). Importantly, adolescent girls whose families allow them to have some autonomy (i.e., control over their own lives) tend to have lower rates of eating disorders, suggesting that control is a major factor in these conditions (Polivy & Herman, 2002).

Watch
Eating Disorders

So, how do stress, peer pressure, and family issues lead to eating disorders? Researchers suggest that some people use eating disorders as a coping mechanism to deal with their difficult-to-control lives (Troop, 1998). By making weight and eating the primary focus of one's life, individuals gain some feelings of security (both physical and emotional) as well as a feeling of being in control of some aspect of their life. Indeed, after binging in the laboratory, individuals with bulimia reported feeling less anxiety, tension, and guilt, although feelings of depression remained the same (Kaye et al., 1986). In contrast, when these feelings of control are reduced, studies have shown that individuals with eating disorders become more pessimistic and report feeling fatter than before (Waller & Hodgson, 1996). Evolutionary psychologists have suggested that this need for control

Watch
College Students and Eating Disorders: Sue Mineka

extends to the woman's reproductive system as well. The *reproduction suppression hypothesis* states that females who believe they have low levels of social support from romantic partners and family members are more likely to engage in dieting behaviour (Juda et al., 2004). This change in food intake can influence ovulation (Frisch & Barbieri, 2002) and lead to a loss of menstrual periods (amenorrhea), making it less likely that the woman will become pregnant. Such data again suggest that eating disorders are an attempt to gain control over complex and stressful lives (Wasser & Barash, 1983).

Males, although less prone to these problems than females, also develop eating disorders. Adolescents and young men may starve themselves during periods of high exercise to lose weight and achieve muscle mass (Ricciardelli & McCabe, 2004). Ironically, although they have positive views of their own bodies, these men with "reverse anorexia" are just as obsessive and perfectionistic about their bodies as people with anorexia (Davis & Scott-Robertson, 2000). And, both groups are particularly sensitive to media depictions of "perfect bodies" that, for almost everybody, are unattainable.

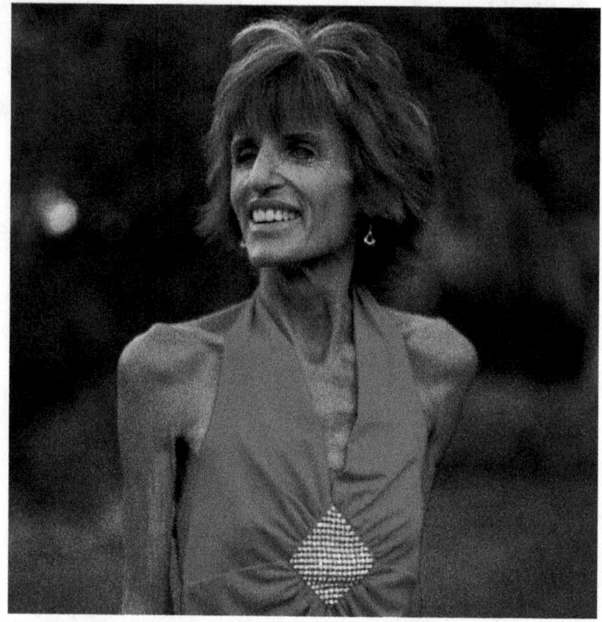

TIFFANY BROWN/WPN/Photoshot

People with anorexia experience severely distorted views of their body. Although dangerously underweight, they continue to both fear and *feel* being fat. Both males and females may become anorexic.

Watch
Body Image and Eating Disorders

WORKING THE SCIENTIFIC LITERACY MODEL

The Effect of Media Depictions of Beauty on Body Image

One concern regarding eating disorders is the role that culture plays in their onset. Specifically, people with regular exposure to Western culture are more likely to develop bulimia than members of cultures without such exposure (Keel & Klump, 2003).

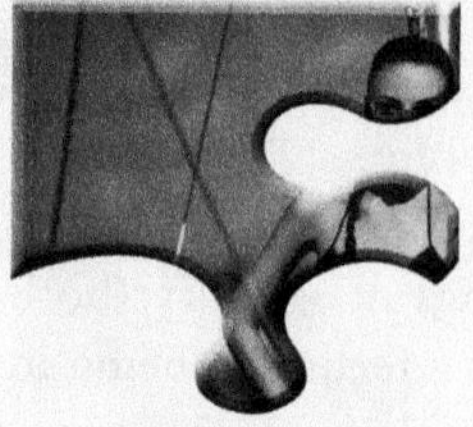

What do we know about the effect of media depictions of beauty on body image?

We often don't critically analyze the effects that media depictions of beauty can have on people, particularly on sensitive teenagers. In the 1950s, Marilyn Monroe—who was busty and had big hips—was considered gorgeous. Today, A-list actresses are pressured to have body shapes that are virtually impossible: a very thin body and large breasts. Failure to meet this standard will lead to mockery in magazines and on gossip websites. For example, in *People* magazine's "Worst Dressed" section, the writers freely use weight-related words when discussing why an article of clothing is a fashion "fail" (Crumpton, 1997). The result is that people who are not unnaturally thin may view their bodies as being ugly. But, do these media depictions of "perfection" influence how girls and women view themselves?

How can science explain the effect of the media on people's body image?

The average North American woman is 163 cm (5'4") and weighs 64 kg (140 lb); the average model is 180 cm (5'11") and weighs 53 kg (117 lb) (National [U.S.] Eating Disorders Association, 2002). Studies have shown that increased exposure to media (TV, magazines, Internet) is related to decreased satisfaction with one's body (Hofschire & Greenberg, 2002); it is also related to a greater internalization of the slender ideal for female body shape (Stice et al., 1994). Researchers at Wilfrid Laurier University found that females were more likely to compare themselves to unrealistic popular culture figures than were men when they were describing their own bodies; they did not do so when describing their social skills (Strahan et al., 2006). When the prominence of cultural norms was increased, all participants (female and male) were more likely to compare themselves with a model and felt worse after doing so. These results suggest that women are more consistently exposed to media depictions of "perfect bodies," but that men are also sensitive to these pressures. In a follow-up study, female participants were either exposed to commercials containing attractive and thin women or to neutral stimuli. The results indicated that viewing media depictions of beauty decreased women's satisfaction with their own bodies and made them more concerned with what other people thought of them (Strahan et al., 2008).

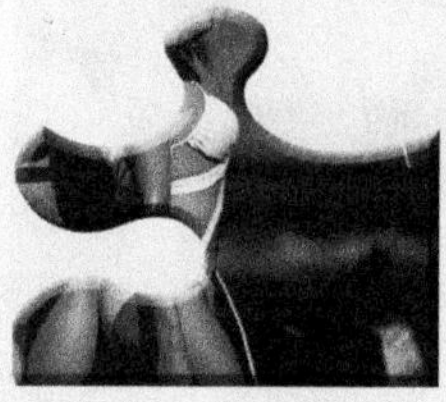

Can we critically evaluate this research?

It is easy to say that participants in psychology studies are simply answering the way they think the experimenter wants them to. However, the studies described above are consistent with recent brain-imaging data as well. Individuals with anorexia showed increased activity in the amygdala, a brain area related to fear and emotional arousal, when they were shown negative words related to body image; neutral words did not have this effect (Miyake et al., 2010). Women with bulimia had greater levels of activity in medial frontal lobe regions related to emotional processing during the viewing of overweight as opposed to thin bodies; non-bulimic women did not show this activity. Finally, when women with eating disorders were shown images comparing themselves to idealized (model) bodies, the insula—a brain region related to disgust—fired (Friederich et al., 2010). Together, these studies corroborate the questionnaire-based results that idealized media depictions of beauty have negative emotional consequences on vulnerable individuals.

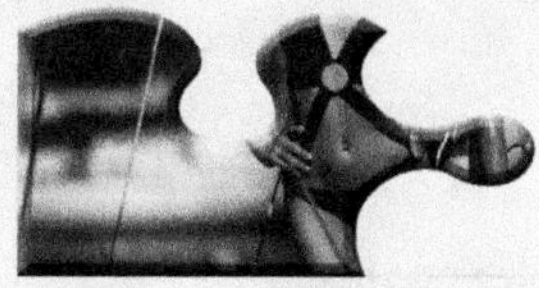

Why is this relevant?

Understanding the relationship between the media and disorders of body image allows teachers, parents, and health-care practitioners to design programs to help image-conscious individuals. Several programs are now being instituted in Canada, with the goal of teaching people to deal with social pressures and to have a realistic body image (McVey et al., 2009; Yuile & McVey, 2009). Importantly, knowledge about media influences can reduce its effects. When public school students completed activities that contested the idea that women needed to be thin and beautiful and men needed to be tall and muscular in order to succeed, the influence of media depictions decreased substantially (Strahan et al., 2008). Not everyone needs to keep up with the Kardashians.

OLGA ILYINA/Shutterstock

Quick Quiz 11.1c Disorders of Eating

KNOW ...

1 What is one difference between anorexia and bulimia?

- **A** Anorexia involves periods of self-starvation, whereas bulimia does not.
- **B** Bulimia involves purging (such as self-induced vomiting), whereas this is less characteristic in anorexia.
- **C** Anorexia occurs in females only, whereas bulimia occurs in both females and males.
- **D** Anorexia and bulimia are actually two terms for the same disorder.

UNDERSTAND ...

2 Why do psychologists believe that obese people respond differently to food reinforcement than do people of normal weight?

- **A** Obese people typically have less exposure to diverse food groups.
- **B** Brain-imaging studies show less activity in obese individuals' brains in response to food compared to the brains of people of normal weight.
- **C** Brain-imaging studies show greater activity in obese individuals' brains in response to food compared to the brains people of normal weight.
- **D** Obese people do not respond differently to food reinforcement than people of normal weight.

APPLY ...

3 Which of the following is the most likely predictor of someone's chances of developing an eating disorder or obesity?

- **A** Activity of the parietal somatosensory cortex
- **B** Decreased sensitivity to the reward value of food
- **C** Exposure to idealized versions of body type and thinness
- **D** Fat receptors on the tongue

Answers can be found on page ANS-3.

Module Summary

Now that you have read this module you should

KNOW . . .

- ***The key terminology of motivation and hunger:***

allostasis (p. 445)
anorexia nervosa (p. 450)
bulimia nervosa (p. 450)
drive (p. 445)
glucose (p. 446)
homeostasis (p. 445)
motivation (p. 444)
obesity (p. 450)
satiation (p. 446)
unit bias (p. 448)

UNDERSTAND . . .

- ***The biological, cognitive, and social processes that shape eating patterns.*** Energy is delivered through the bloodstream in the form of glucose found in food; the hormone insulin helps the cells throughout the body store this fuel. CCK signals fullness (satiety). These substances are monitored by the hypothalamus, which signals hunger when not enough glucose is available to the cells. You should also have an understanding of the effects of psychological cues, such as the unit bias and the variety of available foods, as well as social cues, such as the minimal eating norm.
- ***The major eating and weight-control problems people face.*** This module discussed issues related to obesity and the difficulties that individuals face when trying to slim down. For example, restricting food intake may actually increase the reward value of food. Other problems include anorexia and bulimia, both of which involve periods of self-starvation and a fear of gaining weight. Bulimia also includes purging, such as through vomiting or the use of laxatives.

APPLY . . .

- ***Your knowledge of hunger regulation to better understand and evaluate your own eating patterns.*** Do you finish an entire package of a food item, as the minimal eating norm would suggest? Or do you check to ensure you are getting an appropriate serving size? Try this activity to find out exactly how you eat. Starting first thing tomorrow, keep a food diary for the next three days. In other words, keep a record of everything you eat over this period, recording when you ate, what you ate, and what made you feel like eating. It is important to be honest with yourself and to be reflective: Did you eat because your stomach rumbled, because you were craving something, or perhaps because the food was just there? It is okay to list more than one reason for each entry in your food diary. At the end of the three-day period, tally how often each reason for eating appeared in your diary. Make note of what proportion of the time you ate for each reason. Ask yourself: Are the results surprising? Do they make you want to think more about the reasons you eat? (Note: You can also try to work from memory and recreate a food diary from the past three or four days, but the results might not be as accurate).

Satchan/Corbis/Bridge/Glow Images

ANALYZE . . .

- ***The role of the media on people's body image.*** A number of studies using different methodologies—questionnaires and brain scanning—have shown that the media's idealized depictions of beauty have a negative influence on people's body image (and happiness). With this knowledge, you should be able to identify these misrepresentations of what a normal body should look like, to recognize that the motivation to eat is important, and to see that beauty is not necessarily Size 2.

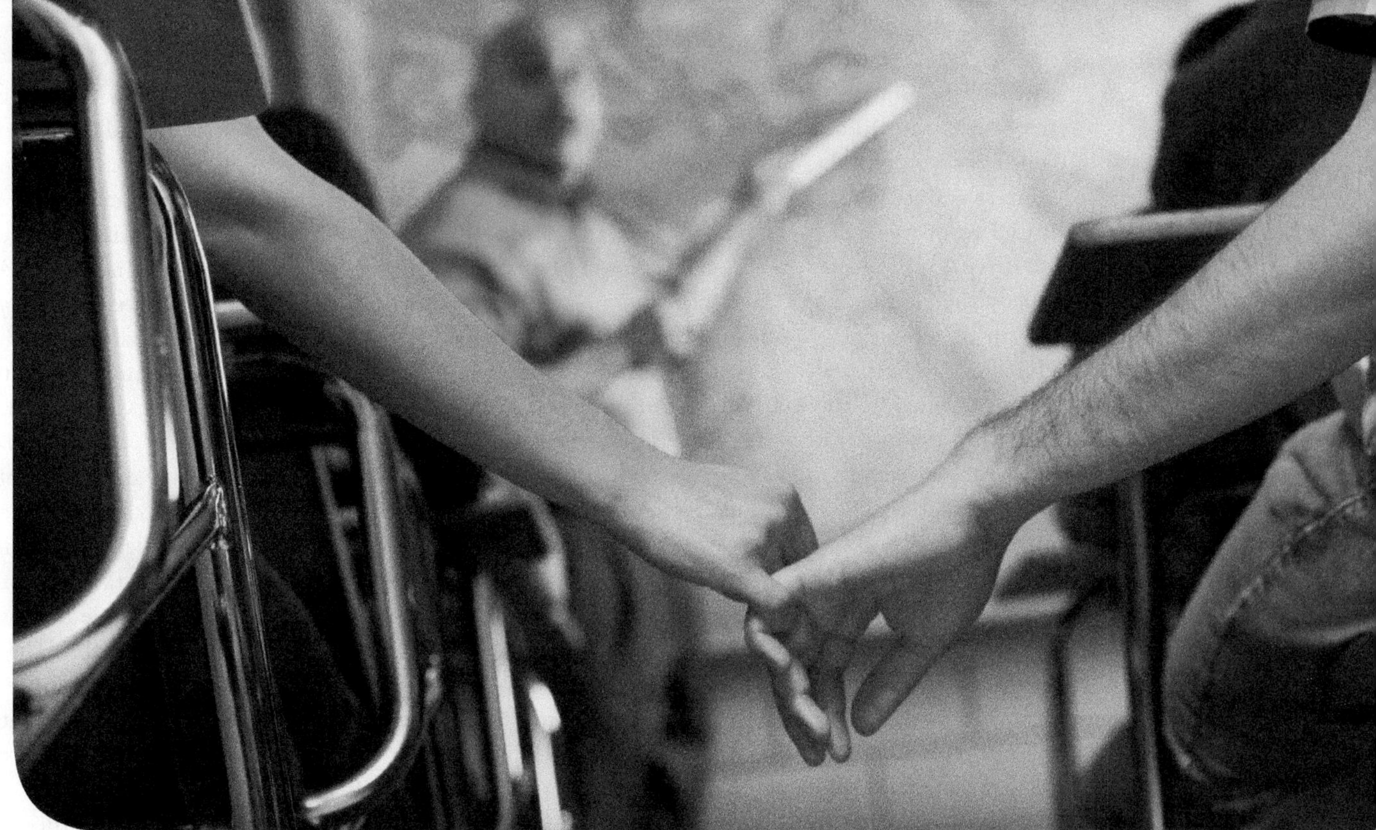

Somos Images/Alamy

Module 11.2

Sex

Learning Objectives

After reading this module you should

KNOW ...	UNDERSTAND ...	APPLY ...	ANALYZE ...
The key terminology associated with sexual motivation	Similarities and differences in sexual responses in men and women	Information from surveys to understand your own views of sexuality	Whether sexual imagery influences consumer behaviour

Why do humans have sex? Psychologists Cindy Meston and David Buss have asked just this question in their research on human sexual motivation. Specifically, they asked American college students why they have sex and tabulated the many different responses offered by both males and females (Meston & Buss, 2007). There are so many possible answers to this very open-ended question—how many do you think they came up with? Certainly more than if we asked the same about why birds, bees, or meerkats have sex. Here are some of the reasons the students came up with:

- "I wanted to get back at my partner for cheating on me."
- "Because of a bet."
- "I wanted to end the relationship."
- "It feels good."
- "I wanted to show my affection toward the other person."
- "I wanted to feel closer to God."

Although we will never know for sure, birds, bees, and meerkats likely have sex to reproduce (a reason that was far down the list for college students). The motivation to have sex naturally has its complex, underlying physiology. As we will see in this module, however, human sexual motivation is expressed and experienced in diverse ways—at least 237 different ways, according to Meston and Buss's research.

Focus Questions

 How do psychologists explain the diverse sexual motivations of humans?

 How do psychologists explain variations in sexual orientation?

Imagine seeing an attractive person walking along the beach, a toned body glistening in the hot summer sun. Then you and the object of your desire make eye contact and it is clear that the interest is mutual. Your initial response will seem like a white-hot biological drive. This is your **libido**—*the motivation for sexual activity and pleasure*. But, whether you act on this motivation is dependent upon a number of factors, not just "hotness." As researchers delve into the complex topic of sexual behaviour, it is becoming increasingly clear that our motivations are shaped by physiological, psychological, and social factors, and that these factors interact with each other differently in different people.

Human Sexual Behaviour: Psychological Influences

Humans have many motives for pursuing and having sex, and one notable observation is that sex frequently occurs *without* an end goal of reproduction. In other words, sex serves many purposes other than what seems to be its primary biological purpose. But sex is not unique in this regard; people eat when they are not hungry and drink when they are not thirsty, without considering the nutritional purpose of their behaviour. However, sex for purposes other than reproduction appears to be rare in nonhuman species. Interestingly, masturbation occurs in some primate species, and the bonobo chimpanzee engages in frequent genital contact, touching, and other sexual behaviours without actually copulating (de Waal & Lanting, 1997; Starin, 2004).

By comparison, among humans, expressions of sexual motivation are vast and diverse. Sexual themes are common in television, movies, humour, advertising, and other media, and discussions of sex and sexuality influence social life, the workplace, and politics. Obviously, sex is a very important and relevant topic for psychology, but it is also one of the most challenging to study. Sex generally happens in private, and many people prefer to keep it that way. Nonetheless, psychologists use a variety of methods to understand the complexities of human sexual behaviour, including interviews, questionnaires, physiological measures, and even direct observations of behaviour. Interviews and questionnaires are (obviously) the least intrusive techniques and, therefore, are the most commonly used.

PSYCHOLOGICAL MEASURES OF SEXUAL MOTIVATION One of the first scientists to tackle the topic of human sexual behaviour was zoology professor Alfred Kinsey. Kinsey began his research on human sexuality by interviewing his students about their sexual histories. Between 1938 and 1952, Kinsey and his colleagues at Indiana University interviewed thousands of people and published their results in a pair of books known informally as the Kinsey Reports (1948, 1953). By modern standards, Kinsey's methods were quite flawed and rather controversial. Kinsey tended to make sweeping generalizations about his findings that were based on very limited samples. Despite these practices, Kinsey's work on sexuality continues to influence discussion on sexual behaviour and motivation.

The fact that Kinsey dared to apply science to sexuality was offensive to many people at the time. During an era when the phrase "sexual orientation" did not even exist, Kinsey reported that 37% of the males whom he interviewed had at least one homosexual experience resulting in orgasm; this was absolutely shocking at the time. (The corresponding figure for females in his studies was 13%.) Contrary to the conventional thinking of his time, Kinsey believed that heterosexuality and homosexuality fell on a continuous scale.

His studies opened up further opportunities for current researchers to find out what motivates human sexual behaviour. Since Kinsey conducted his investigations, however, the methods used for such research have changed—to include more representative samples, for example—and the extensive interviews have been largely replaced with anonymously completed questionnaires that encourage participants to provide more candid responses.

The questionnaire method of studying human sexual motivation has continued since Kinsey's time. At the beginning of this module, we introduced a study conducted by psychologists Cindy Meston and David Buss, who asked more than 1500 U.S. college students to identify their reasons for having sex. We listed a few reasons provided by the students—some conventional (to express affection) and others perhaps more surprising (to feel closer to God). We return to this study to discuss some general themes that emerged—notably, the four shown in Figure 11.6.

As you can see in Figure 11.6, physical, personal, and social factors underlie sexual motivation. For the respondents in Meston and Buss's study, physical reasons were related to pleasure of the sex itself as well as to orgasm. Many respondents used sex for what might be described as instrumental reasons—sex was a means of accomplishing a goal such as financial or personal gain, or revenge. Students were also motivated by emotional reasons and because of feelings of insecurity (although there is little evidence to suggest that sex leads to any long-term improvements in this regard). Reproduction ranked very far down the list. But, can you think of a

1. For physical reasons.

"The person's physical appearance turned me on."

"I want to achieve an orgasm."

2. To help attain a goal.

"I wanted to get a raise."

"I wanted to hurt an enemy."

3. For emotional reasons.

"I realized I was in love."

"I wanted to intensify my relationship."

4. Because of insecurity.

"I felt obligated to."

"I wanted to be nice."

Michaelpuche/Shutterstock

{FIG. 11.6} **Why Have Sex?** Self-reported reasons for having sex by undergraduate students (Meston & Buss, 2007).

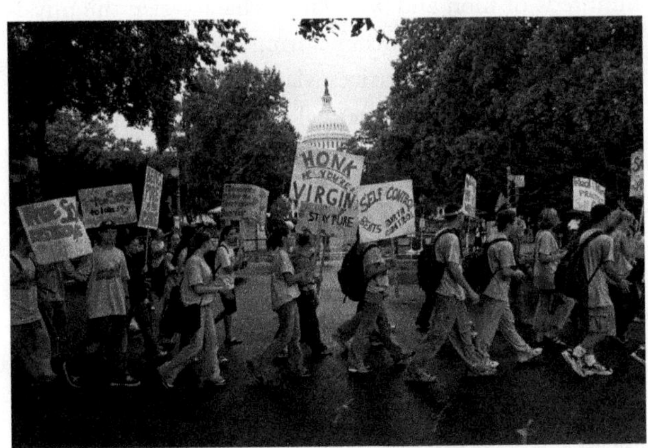

The Washington Times/ZUMAPRESS/Newscom

There are also reasons for avoiding sex. Each year thousands of teenagers experience unplanned or unwanted effects of sexual behaviour, such as pregnancy, sexually transmitted diseases, or being in a relationship that may be abusive or simply too complex for a younger person to handle. Sexual abstinence clubs have been cropping up across high school and college campuses across the U.S.; fewer such clubs are found in Canada. Can you think of a reason why?

limitation of this study? The fact that the study surveyed students, most of whom are the same age and at the same level of education, means that the data don't necessarily apply to the entire population. To do so, it would be necessary to interview people from a number of different ethnicities, economic backgrounds, education levels, and, most importantly, age groups.

MYTHS IN MIND

Sex after Sixty?

Living in a culture that emphasizes youth can make it difficult to talk about—or even think about—the sexual lives of older people. Sex often seems like something that only younger people care about, starting with the surge of hormones in adolescence and lasting until parenthood. However, surveys indicate that the motives of middle-aged women are the same as women aged 18 to 22 years: pleasure, love, and commitment

Fancy/Alamy

Research confirms that many senior adults remain sexually active.

(Meston, Hamilton, & Harte, 2009). A recent wave of advertisements showing older couples discussing sexual intimacy suggest that sex is a common motivation in older populations as well. Since sexuality is such an important part of life, it is worth asking what happens to sex and sexuality as people age.

In one survey (Lindau et al., 2007), almost three-fourths of the 57- to 64-year-old respondents reported sexual contact with a partner in the past year, as did half of the 64- to 75-year-olds and one-fourth of the respondents between ages 75 and 85 (a fact that might make your next family reunion awkward for you). Sexuality does not always require a partner: Almost half of the men and one-fourth of the women in the survey reported masturbating within the past year.

Does sexuality decline in the senior years? It seems that for many people, it does. Nevertheless, these data clearly show that many seniors remain sexually active into their 80s. This sexuality is not without problems; approximately 40% of women in the survey cited lack of desire as a problem, and almost the same percentage of men reported erectile problems.

The survey and interview methods discussed to this point have provided a rich set of data about human sexuality. Other researchers have approached this topic from a biological standpoint by looking at the physiological and brain basis of sexual motivation (Pfaus et al., 2012), a topic we will consider in the next section of this module.

Quick Quiz 11.2a

Human Sexual Behaviour: Psychological Influences

KNOW ...

1 __________ refers to one's motivation for sexual behaviour and pleasure.

A Libido

B Excitement

C Orgasm

D Cybersex

2 According to research on sexual motivation in college students, which of the following is not a primary reason students offer for having sex?

A Emotional reasons

B Physical reasons

C Social reasons

D Reproduction

Answers can be found on page ANS-3.

Human Sexual Behaviour: Physiological Influences

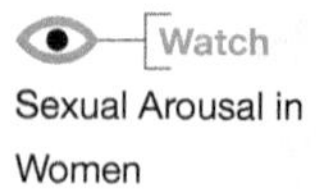

Sexual Arousal in Women

PHYSIOLOGICAL MEASURES OF SEX Our physiological and psychological motives for having sex are not separate. Sexual arousal (a biological state) can influence what we pay attention to and how we respond to it; in other words, it can influence our feelings of desire (Pfaus & Scepkowski, 2005). Although several decades of research have helped identify many of the biological processes associated with sexual motivation, it is important to remember that all of these biological processes are influenced by a person's psychological state.

William Masters and Virginia Johnson performed some of the earliest studies of sexual behaviour in the 1950s. These researchers described the human sexual response cycle based on their observations of 27 male and 118 female prostitutes who agreed to masturbate or to have intercourse while under observation (Masters & Johnson, 1966). Participants were monitored with heart rate and blood pressure equipment, as well as with more peculiar devices such as the penile plethysmograph or vaginal photoplethysmograph, which are designed to measure blood flow to the genitalia in men and women, respectively. Masters and Johnson's initial study allowed them to develop their methods and work with participants who, according to the researchers, were less likely to be sexually inhibited than non-prostitutes. Masters and Johnson followed up this study with observations of hundreds of men and women to characterize the physiological changes that occur during sex.

Figure 11.7 summarizes Masters and Johnson's (1966) observations of human sexual responding in males and females. The **sexual response cycle** *describes the phases of physiological change during sexual activity, which comprises four primary stages: excitement, plateau, orgasm, and resolution.* Dividing the sexual response cycle into phases allowed the researchers to describe the cascade of physiological changes that occur during sexual behaviour. The cycle applies to both male and female sexual responses, although there are differences between sexes in how these stages are experienced and their duration. The work of Masters and Johnson and those who have followed in their footsteps reveals a complex picture of male and female sexual responses.

One topic of particular interest is how males and females differ in their patterns of orgasm. In one study, 21% to 32% of women reported that they did not experience orgasm during masturbation or sexual intercourse (Dunn et al., 2005), whereas only 2% of men did not experience orgasm. Men usually experience a single orgasm followed by a **refractory period**, *a time period during which erection and orgasm are not physically possible.* In contrast, some women experience multiple orgasms without a refractory period.

What about the subjective experience of orgasm? Do women and men feel differently during orgasm? This challenging question was taken up by a group of researchers who asked American college students to write detailed descriptions of their orgasm experiences.

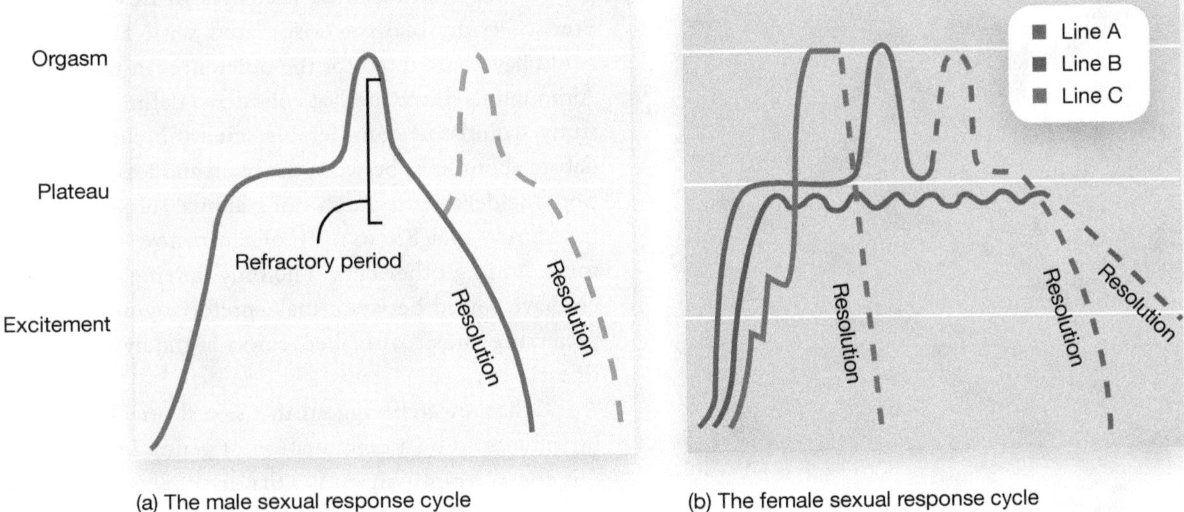

{FIG. 11.7} **Sexual Response Cycles** (a) Masters and Johnson's studies showed that males typically experience a single orgasm followed by a refractory period—a time during which orgasm cannot be physically achieved again. Then they experience resolution, unless they continue sexual activity. (b) Women typically have a more varied sexual response profile than men. Here are a few examples. Line A indicates a woman who has multiple orgasms, Line B a woman who does not experience orgasm, and Line C a woman who has a single orgasm. **Click on this figure in your eText to see more details.**

Researchers removed clues to the sex of each writer by changing terms such as "penis" or "vagina" to "genitals." Then, male and female physicians, psychologists, and medical students judged whether each description came from a male or female. The judges were no better than chance at guessing the gender of the authors, and neither female nor male judges were any better than the other at guessing (Vance & Wagner, 1976). This outcome suggests that, to some degree, males and females have similar subjective experiences during orgasm.

Although sexual activity involves the whole body, researchers have recently focused on brain activity in women who experienced orgasm while being monitored by functional MRIs (Komisaruk et al., 2005). Stimulation of the breasts, nipples, and vaginal areas causes sensory nerves to send signals to the hypothalamus. The hypothalamus, in turn, stimulates the pituitary gland to release a hormone called oxytocin, which plays a role in orgasm and post-orgasm physiology as well as in the feeling of trust (Zak, 2008). Blood levels of oxytocin surge just after orgasm and may remain elevated for at least five minutes (Carmichael et al., 1994). Oxytocin is released during orgasm in males as well (Murphy et al., 1990). In addition, the dopamine-rich reward centres of the brain become highly active during orgasm (Holstege et al., 2003). However, once ejaculation has taken place, dopamine levels in the brain's reward centres decrease and serotonin levels in parts of the hypothalamus increase (Lorrain et al., 1997). This suggests that, as with hunger, the brain's activity changes dramatically once that motivation has been satisfied.

SEXUAL ORIENTATION: BIOLOGY AND ENVIRONMENT Although the research discussed thus far has shed light on many aspects of sexual behaviour, there are still questions that have not been answered. A topic that has garnered considerable interest is **sexual orientation**, *the consistent preference for sexual relations with members of the opposite sex (heterosexuality), same sex (homosexuality), or either sex (bisexuality).* Current definitions of sexual orientation focus on the psychological aspects of sexuality (e.g., desire, emotion, identification) rather than strictly behavioural criteria (Bailey et al., 2000). For example, a person can have a sexual orientation but never have sexual contact throughout his or her life. Psychologists have long struggled to find a satisfactory explanation for variations in sexual orientation. Sigmund Freud (1905) advanced the theory that male homosexuality could be traced to the presence of a domineering mother and a weak father figure. As recently as 1987, Ellis and Ames argued that homosexuality could be caused by experiencing seduction from an older sibling or playmate. Both theories lack scientific evidence to confirm their validity. An ongoing debate is now considering why a significant number of humans prefer emotional and sexual relationships with members of the same sex. Researchers question whether sexual orientation is based on choices people make or on biologically related factors such as genetics or differences in brain anatomy. Thus, modern scientific explanations of homosexuality focus on interactions between biological and sociocultural factors.

BananaStock/Thinkstock

Sexual orientation is not exclusively determined by patterns of sexual behaviour. It also includes aspects of identity and emotional connection. Scientists are discovering that sexual orientation is an outcome of complex gene and environmental interactions.

In the early 1990s, neuroscientist Simon LeVay compared the brains of deceased gay and heterosexual males. In his work, he found that an area of the hypothalamus was, on average, smaller in gay men compared to heterosexual men (Figure 11.8; LeVay, 1991). LeVay's results created a storm of controversy among both scientists and the public. Many people incorrectly interpreted his findings as proof that homosexuality was biologically, and therefore genetically, determined. In fact, the differences in the hypothalamus could have been due to environmental factors—LeVay's study was not designed to test either conclusion. As with many other topics you have encountered in this text, disentangling the "nature versus nurture" issues in relation to sexual orientation is a challenge that many researchers are now addressing. Modern research on the brain has shown how environmental factors, even those occurring in the prenatal environment, contribute to anatomical and functional differences in the brain (Roselli & Stormshak, 2009).

Scientists have been skeptical of LeVay's results, in part because they have proved difficult to replicate (Lasco et al., 2002). The region of the hypothalamus he identified was only smaller on average in gay men versus heterosexual men, and the ranges in size were overlapping, with some gay men having a larger hypothalamic region than some heterosexual men. In addition, the purportedly homosexual men whom LeVay studied died of complications associated with HIV, which could have accounted for the differences in their brains. Although its results are not considered definitive, LeVay's study stimulated considerable scientific curiosity and debate about links between the brain and sexual orientation. Incidentally, research using animal subjects (sheep) has shown that 8% to 10% of rams show preferences for mounting other rams. The only difference researchers have found between male-preferring and female-preferring rams is a smaller region of the hypothalamus (Roselli et al., 2004).

Other research suggests that sexual orientation may be influenced by a combination of genes. Evidence for this comes from twin studies that have identified higher genetic correlations between identical twins compared with fraternal twin pairs. Several twin studies examining the genetic basis of sexual orientation have been conducted. Genetic correlations between .30 and .60 for homosexuality have been reported for both men and women, suggesting that approximately half of the individual differences found in sexual orientation are due

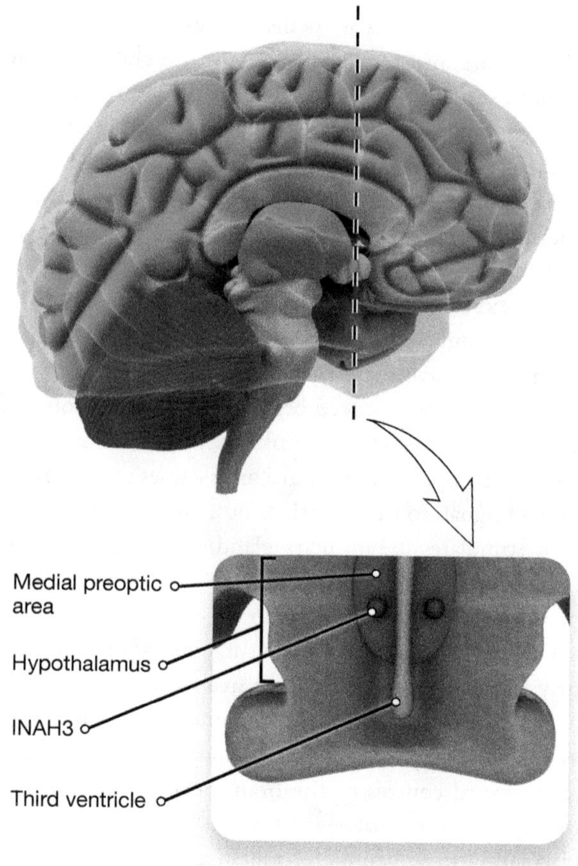

{FIG. 11.8} **Sexual Orientation and the Brain** An early study of the brain basis of sexual orientation found that homosexual males had a smaller subregion (INAH3) of the hypothalamus within the medial pre-optic area (LeVay, 1991).

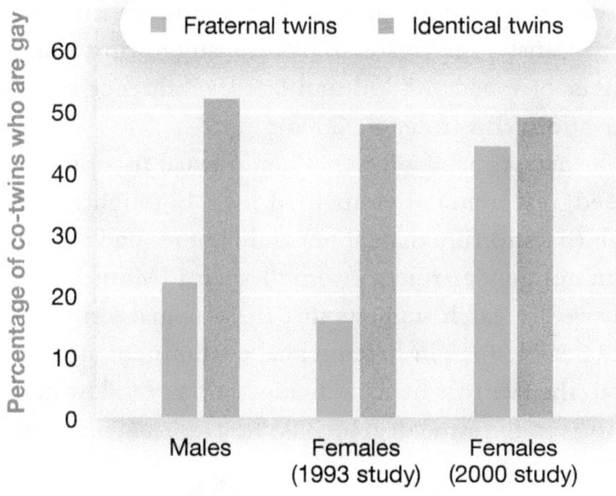

{FIG. 11.9} **Genetics and Sexual Orientation** Twin studies tend to show consistently higher genetic correlations for sexual orientation between male identical twins compared to fraternal twins. This finding indicates that male homosexuality has a genetic basis. Results of studies comparing female identical and fraternal twins are not as consistent.

to genetic factors (Figure 11.9; Bailey & Pillard, 1995; Bailey et al., 1993; Kirk et al., 2000). This result tends to hold true for gay men across multiple studies. In contrast, studies have failed to confirm a genetic relationship between genes and homosexuality in women (Bailey et al., 2000; Långström et al., 2010). Thus, genes appear to play at least some role in sexual orientation, particularly for men. However, this statement does not mean that sexual orientation is *determined* by genetics. The brain and endocrine system are remarkably sensitive to the environment, and they interact with a variety of sociocultural factors (Meston & Ahrold, 2010). More research investigating these interactions is clearly necessary.

Quick Quiz 11.2b

Human Sexual Behaviour: Physiological Influences

KNOW ...

1 In what order do the phases of the sexual response cycle occur?

- **A** Plateau, orgasm, resolution, excitement
- **B** Excitement, plateau, orgasm, resolution
- **C** Orgasm, resolution, excitement, plateau
- **D** Excitement, orgasm, resolution, plateau

UNDERSTAND ...

2 The male sexual response cycle includes a(n) _______ during which erection and orgasm are not physically possible, whereas the female sexual response cycle most often does not.

- **A** plateau
- **B** refractory period
- **C** oxytocin release
- **D** sensitive period

ANALYZE ...

3 Brain differences between homosexual and heterosexual adults should be interpreted as

- **A** a result of both genetic and environmental factors.
- **B** due solely to inherited, genetic differences.
- **C** proof that the brain structure between homosexual men and heterosexual women is identical.
- **D** due solely to environmental factors.

Answers can be found on page ANS-3.

Human Sexual Behaviour: Cultural Influences

Simulate Perceptions of Attractiveness

How is an 18-year-old woman "supposed to" act when she is interesting in having sex? How about an 18-year-old guy? Although we'd all love to say that people should act any way they want, **gender roles**, *the accepted attitudes and behaviours of males and females in a given society*, exist. These gender roles are flexible over time, however. Your great-grandmothers were unlikely to wear revealing clothing or have "hook ups" or "friends with benefits"; this norm changed across generations. Indeed, across generations, there have been significant changes in male and female **sexual scripts**, *the set of rules and assumptions about the sexual behaviours of males and females*. As you read in Module 3.1, for most of human history, male sexual behaviour was based on competition. Men would value sexual conquests and the physical attractiveness of females. Females, on the other hand, would be taught to be less promiscuous and to focus on developing a stable relationship before engaging in sexual intercourse. There are a number of reasons for this difference. First, females have a limited supply of eggs that can be fertilized. They therefore have to be careful about which male does the fertilizing (Trivers, 1972; see Module 3.1). Because children require resources (food, clothing, shelter, money, etc.), and females were not traditionally in the workforce, it was important to be certain that a potential mate would be a good provider. Males, on the other hand, have a seemingly unlimited supply of sperm that can be replenished quickly. If their evolutionary goal is to pass on their genetic information to as many people as possible, males are able to do this by impregnating as many women as possible (whereas women would have to give birth a large number of times, which is much more difficult). Although this might not be the stated goal of most men, the sexual motivation to have sex with large numbers of women still exists. Additionally, males have higher levels of **testosterone**, *a hormone that* *is involved in the development of sex characteristics and the motivation of sexual behaviour.* Thus, there are social, evolutionary, and hormonal reasons for the sexual scripts in our culture.

But, this evolutionary explanation is only part of the explanation for gender roles and sexual scripts. For a large part of human history, societies were set up in a way that gave men greater power than women. Indeed, in many cultures, women were viewed as possessions—first of their fathers and then of their husbands. Limiting the sexual expressiveness of women limited their ability to feel empowered, and allowed the "status quo" of the patriarchy (male-dominated society) to continue.

But, as we noted, these scripts are changing. Why do you think that is? Although there are dozens of potential explanations, there are three that are particularly important. The first is the emergence of the Women's Rights Movement over the last 130 years. This movement challenged the core values of the patriarchal society and put pressure on lawmakers to allow women to have equal economic and political rights such as voting. The result was that women were perceived as people rather than possessions. A second, related, cause was the increasing presence of women in the workforce. This economic independence meant that females could take care of themselves if they became pregnant. Therefore, they didn't need to be as careful about who they had sex with. The third reason for changing sexual scripts was "the pill." The U.S. Federal Drug Administration approved the drug *Enovid* for use as a contraceptive on June 23, 1960 (Marks, 2001); the pill was legalized in Canada in 1969. This allowed women to have control over when they were going to become pregnant, thus giving them much more control over their sexual behaviours. The importance of birth-control pills cannot be overstated. Imagine how people's lives would be changed if pregnancy was a strong possibility every time someone had sex.

Watch Online Dating Advice

Of course, it is important to note that not all females or males follow the same sexual scripts. Different ethnicities or religious backgrounds have their own scripts as well. For instance, researchers at the University of British Columbia found that Chinese women (born in China or Taiwan, but living in Canada) reported more conservative sexual attitudes (Woo et al., 2010) and lower levels of sexual desire than Euro-Canadian women (Woo et al., 2012). Why would this occur? Researchers have found that **sex guilt**, *negative emotional feelings for having violated culturally accepted standards of appropriate sexual behaviour*, is a major factor in these differences. Interestingly, these differences decrease for individuals who become more involved with mainstream Western culture, suggesting that a number of social and cultural factors influence sexual motivations (Brotto et al., 2005).

Sexual scripts also exist in homosexual relationships. Indeed, researchers in this field have highlighted the butch (traditionally masculine) and femme (traditionally feminine) gender roles of some lesbians (Munt, 1998). However, research suggests that these sexual scripts are more flexible than in heterosexual relationships, possibly due to the fact that many individuals do not follow gender roles to the same degree as do heterosexual individuals (Kurdek, 2005).

SEX AND TECHNOLOGY What type of sexual scripts would develop if people could engage in sexual behaviour anonymously without having to physically interact with another person? Although your grandparents would have considered that question to be science fiction pornography, in the past two decades, electronic media such as the Internet, text messaging, instant messaging, and social networking sites have become common outlets for sexual expression. Electronic media are often used for viewing pornography, having online sexual encounters, and meeting others for sex offline (i.e., in the real world). Adolescents, as well as both single and married adults, may engage in cybersex—that is, the use of the Internet and computer equipment for sending sexually explicit images and messages to a partner. An estimated one in three adults today has engaged in cybersex (Daneback et al., 2005).

Unplanned pregnancy and STDs are obviously not an immediate risk of cybersex. However, people tend to communicate with less inhibition via digital media compared to face-to-face encounters. This opens up the possibility for impulsive behaviour such as sending sexually explicit pictures and messages ("sexting"). Many teens have suffered rather harsh legal consequences for sexting. Some U.S. states consider sexting to be a form of underage pornography and those convicted could be required to register as sex offenders. The Supreme Court of Canada has indicated that under-aged teens can possess sexual images of each other assuming it is consensual; however, the distribution of such images is illegal (*R. v. Sharpe*, 2001 SCC 2; [2001] 1 S.C.R. 45 (January 26, 2001)).

Regardless of your opinions of, or experience with, cybersex, it is impossible to ignore the fact that sexual imagery is becoming increasingly common in our society. What is less clear is how this sexuality will affect our day-to-day behaviours.

WORKING THE SCIENTIFIC LITERACY MODEL

Does Sex Sell?

The American Apparel® advertisement showed a topless model with her back to the camera, her nylon-clad buttocks thrust provocatively toward the viewer. Needless to say, this ad got noticed, as did several other (equally subtle) ads by the same company. But American Apparel isn't alone in using sex to sell its products. H&M® features giant billboards displaying David Beckham in his underwear. Soft drink companies have young and attractive people drink their products in commercials. And, in a sure sign of the Apocalypse, Paris Hilton wore a skimpy swimsuit, soaped herself up, and writhed on a car in order to sell Carl's Jr.® hamburgers. The ad's caption was, "She tells you size doesn't matter. She's lying." Although there is no doubt that such ads attract attention, are they effective in changing consumers' brand preferences? Does sex really sell?

Gregory Holmgren / Alamy

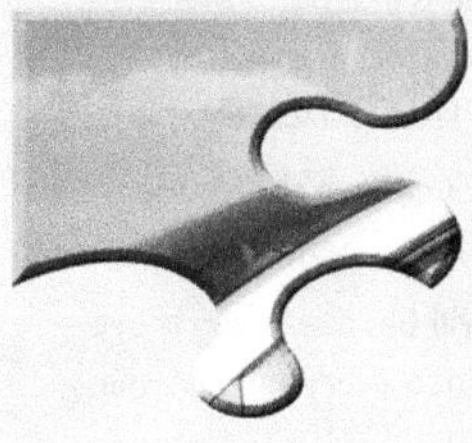

What do we know about sex and advertising?

There are a number of examples of companies being saved by sexual advertising. Woodbury's Facial Soap was near bankruptcy in 1910; however, when a new ad campaign depicted romantic couples and promised that using the product would lead to greater intimacy, sales skyrocketed (Reichert, 2003, 2012). Jovan Musk Oil, a fragrance for men, had advertisements that suggested that it would increase a user's sexual attractiveness; revenue from Jovan's Musk increased from $1.5 million in 1971 to $77 million in 1978. Based on these, and many more, success stories, the frequency of sexual imagery in ads has increased substantially in the past three decades. A study of 3343 full-page ads that were published in 1983, 1993, and 2003 in popular magazines such as *Esquire, Playboy, Newsweek, Time, Cosmopolitan,* and *Redbook* found that the proportion of sexual ads increased from 15% in 1983 to 27% in 2003 (Reichert et al., 2012). Sexual imagery was most often used to sell health and hygiene products (38%), beauty products (36%), medicine (29%), and clothing (27%). This trend leads to the obvious question: How is sex being used to influence our buying behaviour?

How can scientists explain the effect of sexual imagery on advertising success?

Some advertisements use sexual imagery to attract attention to a product. For example, an attractive model standing next to a car or eating a bowl of cereal will make us pay more attention to that image than we otherwise would. Such image-product pairings are not always effective. Although the consumer might remember the *ad*, they are less likely to remember the *brand* that is being advertised (Reichert & Alvaro, 2001); after Paris Hilton's hamburger ad, Carl's Jr. experienced a 1.7% increase in sales . . . *but archrival Hardees had a similar increase!* However, if sexuality is an integral part of the brand's identity or if the sexuality in the ad is related to the product's function (e.g., condoms), then sexual imagery will enhance our memory for that product (Richmond & Hartman, 1982). This effect is likely due to the sexual imagery being a memory retrieval cue for that product.

Sex has another interesting effect on how we perceive advertisements: It interferes with our ability to think rationally about persuasive material (Riechert et al., 2001). A recent brain-imaging study compared neural responses to advertisements containing sexual or emotional images with responses to advertisements in which an image of the product was presented alongside factual information about the product. The researchers found that sexual ads generated smaller neural responses in several areas of the frontal lobes (Cook et al., 2011). These results suggest that sexual images may lead to less analysis of an ad's contents than a purely fact-based appeal, making us more vulnerable to persuasive material. (This research would certainly make election ads more interesting. . . .)

Can we critically evaluate this evidence?

Although the psychology research investigating whether sex sells is interesting, we do have to be cautious in interpreting it. That's because the stimuli are being used in a way that differs from how they will be used in the real world. Most television or radio ads are seen or heard numerous times; in an experiment, they are often presented only once. Additionally, most ads are targeted at specific demographic groups (e.g., females aged 18–25). Therefore, we, as consumers of research, need to be sure that the experimenters paid attention to the same variables as the marketers. Otherwise, their data don't buy us much.

We also have to remember that not all participants in a study are alike in their sexual views, a fact that was overlooked in many early studies on this topic. Overall, women are less accepting of sexual ads than men, likely due to the fact that most sexual ads are targeted toward heterosexual males (Monk-Turner et al., 2008). Women with more liberal views toward sexuality respond similarly to men—they are much more likely to accept unnecessary sexual imagery than more conservative women (Sengupta et al., 2008). Additionally, women are more likely to accept a sexual advertisement if sex is depicted in a way that is respectful, focusing on devotion rather than on primitive biological urges (Dahl et al., 2009).

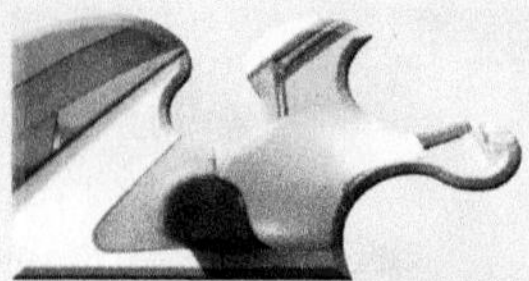

Why is this relevant?

The results of numerous studies show that sex *can* sell, *in certain situations*. But, if psychologists and marketers wish to use sex to sell a product, they have to be extremely careful about when and where these ads are going to be displayed, and how sex is depicted. If they fail to do so, then their sexy ad campaign might end up being a bust.

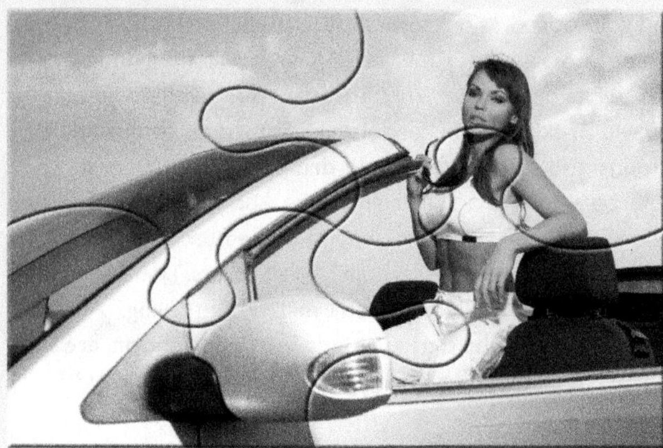

Daniel_Dash/Shutterstock.com

Quick Quiz 11.2c Human Sexual Behaviour: Cultural Influences

KNOW ...

1 The accepted attitudes and behaviours of males and females in a given society are known as

- **A** sexual orientation.
- **B** sex guilt.
- **C** gender roles.
- **D** sexual scripts.

UNDERSTAND ...

2 Sexual content in advertisements can be effective in all of the following cases EXCEPT

- **A** when the viewers are liberal-minded males.
- **B** when the sexual content is related to the purpose or function of the product being advertised.
- **C** when paired with a logical argument for buying the product.
- **D** when the viewers are conservative-minded females.

ANALYZE ...

3 Future computers will likely include face-recognition software that keeps the computer screen lit up when you're looking at it (this technology is already found in some smart phones). This technology may also make it more difficult for users to remain anonymous in social networking sites or chat rooms. Based on what you've read in this module, what effect will this have?

- **A** The loss of anonymity will make people more inhibited because the sexual scripts will become similar to those found in face-to-face encounters.
- **B** The loss of anonymity will change the gender roles for males and females, making them more similar.
- **C** Social networking sites will become even more popular and sexualized once everyone can see everyone else.
- **D** From an evolutionary perspective, the loss of anonymity will influence male sexual behaviour, as it will be possible for them to identify a larger number of potential mates.

Module Summary

Module 11.2

Now that you have read this module you should

KNOW ...

- ***The key terminology associated with sexual motivation:***

gender roles (p. 461)
libido (p. 456)
refractory period (p. 458)
sex guilt (p. 462)
sexual orientation (p. 459)
sexual response cycle (p. 458)
sexual scripts (p. 461)
testosterone (p. 461)

UNDERSTAND ...

- ***Similarities and differences in sexual responses in men and women.*** The similarities in sexual response cycles found in men and women can be explained by a common reproductive physiology in both sexes. However, males experience a distinct phase called the refractory period, during which erection or orgasm is not physiologically possible. Both males' and females' sexual behaviours are also influenced by gender scripts and sexual roles, factors that are affected by the culture in which the sexual behaviours are taking place.

APPLY ...

- ***Information from surveys to understand your own views of sexuality.*** People express sexuality for many different reasons, in different ways, and with varying frequency. How do you feel about sexuality? You can apply what we have learned from research to understand if you take a generally permissive attitude (people have the right to do what they want) or a more conservative one. Respond to each of the items below by assigning a score on a scale from 1 (strongly agree) to 5 (strongly disagree). Note that it is not necessary to be sexually active to complete this scale—simply respond to the general principle of each item.

1. I do not need to be committed to a person to have sex with him or her.
2. Casual sex is acceptable.
3. I would like to have sex with many partners.
4. One-night stands are sometimes enjoyable.

Somos Images/Alamy

5. It is okay to have ongoing sexual relationships with more than one person at a time.
6. Sex as a simple exchange of favours is okay if both people agree to it.
7. The best sex is with no strings attached.
8. Life would have fewer problems if people could have sex more freely.
9. It is possible to enjoy sex with a person and not like that person very much.
10. It is okay for sex to be just a good physical release.

Once you have assigned a number to each item, average your responses to get your overall score. In one study of slightly more than 200 university students, men averaged a score of 3.63 and women averaged a score of 4.47 on this scale (Hendrick et al., 2006). How do you compare? Given what you have learned about the biological and cultural factors that influence sexuality, are you surprised by the gender difference? Which other factors might influence the norms?

ANALYZE ...

- ***Whether sexual imagery influences consumer behaviour.*** Depictions of sex and sexuality have occurred throughout the history of advertising. However, the frequency of this type of content has increased dramatically in the last two decades. Although most people believe that "sex sells," research indicates that specific limitations do exist. The sexuality must be linked with a product's identity (e.g., a perfume) or function (e.g., condoms), and the sexual acts depicted must be respectful. If these conditions are not met, consumers may remember the advertisement but forget the brand being advertised, a result that marketers would not find sexy at all.

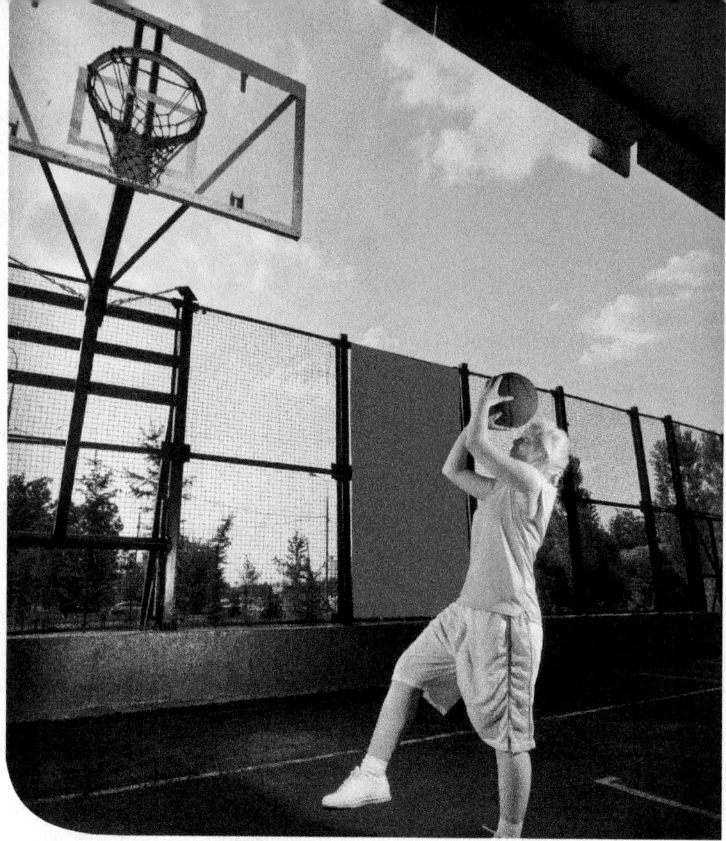

Nikita Buida/Fotolia

Module 11.3

Social and Achievement Motivation

Learning Objectives

After reading this module you should

KNOW ...	UNDERSTAND ...	APPLY ...	ANALYZE ...
The key terminology of social and achievement motivation	How people experience a need to belong How we can harness the power of intrinsic motivation	Theories of motivation to understand your personal motivation to achieve in school or your career	Claims that a sense of belonging is something people need versus something they want

Michelle sat at the end of the gymnasium, watching the varsity girls' basketball team warming up for their game. She was younger than most of the women on the team, but still desperately wanted to be a part of it. She loved playing basketball with her friends, a couple of whom made the team, and decided that if she was going to be a part of it next year, she would have to practise every day. She would also have to work on the skills that were currently weaknesses, so that she could become a better player.

This story is very familiar—all of us know someone who vowed to work hard in order to make a team or to improve their position in an organization. The over-arching question of this module is "Why do we try to achieve these goals?" What is motivating Michelle to work hard to be on the high-profile basketball team with her friends? And, what factors will make it more or less likely for Michelle to succeed?

Focus Questions

 How critical are external rewards in motivating us to achieve?

 How is achievement motivation influenced by the amount of control we have over our actions?

In addition to satisfying basic biological drives, motivation entails meeting our complex social and personal needs. In this module, we explore our motivation to feel as though we belong as well as our motivation to achieve.

Belongingness and Love Needs

Everyone acknowledges that humans need to satisfy needs for food, water, clothing, and shelter in order to survive. Each of these needs is associated with a motivation, some sort of psychological process that will cause us to perform a particular behaviour. The need for food would lead to the behaviour of eating; the need for water would lead to the behaviour of drinking. But, humans have many different types of needs, some of which are less straightforward than the need to eat. These involve social processes, as well as our need for meaning and a purpose in life. In this module, we discuss some of these social and achievement needs, and try to understand the psychological processes that accompany them.

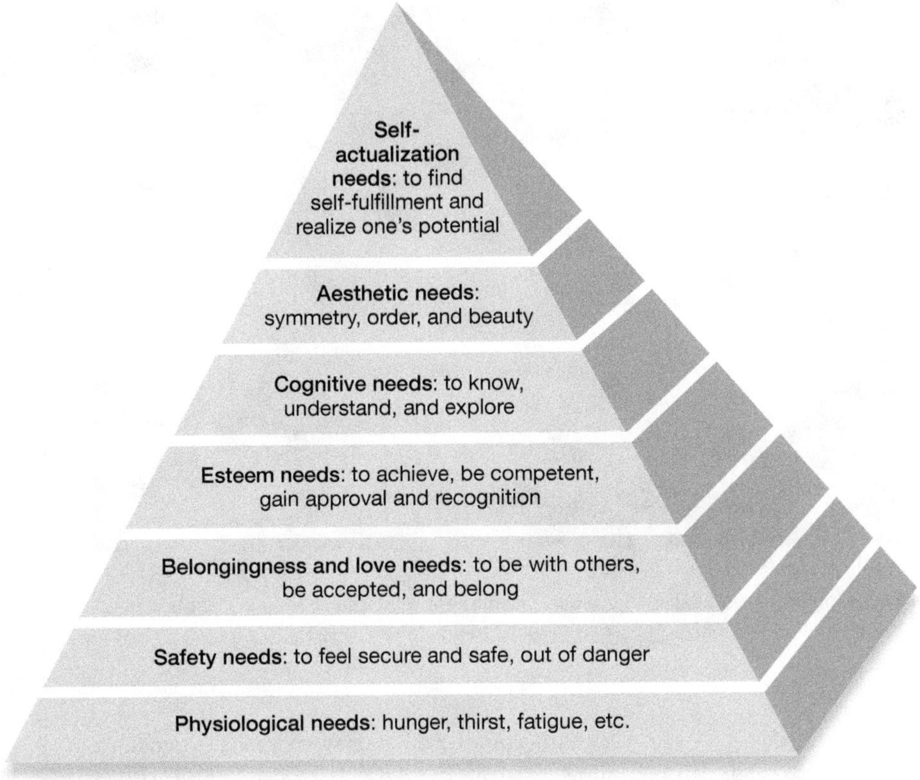

Self-actualization needs: to find self-fulfillment and realize one's potential

Aesthetic needs: symmetry, order, and beauty

Cognitive needs: to know, understand, and explore

Esteem needs: to achieve, be competent, gain approval and recognition

Belongingness and love needs: to be with others, be accepted, and belong

Safety needs: to feel secure and safe, out of danger

Physiological needs: hunger, thirst, fatigue, etc.

{FIG. 11.10} **Maslow's Hierarchy of Needs** According to Abraham Maslow, human needs are organized as a hierarchy, with basic needs at the bottom, and personal fulfillment and other uniquely human characteristics at the top. **Click on this figure in your eText to see more details.**

HIERARCHY OF NEEDS When we think about our different needs, it seems like common sense that some things are more important than others. Eating would obviously be more important than having high self-esteem, for example. In an early attempt to understand the different motivations that drive human behaviour, Abraham Maslow (1943, 1954) described a "hierarchy of needs," with needs associated with our basic physiological survival being more important than social or achievement needs (see Figure 11.10). According to Maslow, once survival needs are met, then we can move to higher-level needs such as belonging or the need for self-esteem. At the highest point of this model lies *self-actualization*, the point at which a person reaches his or her full potential as a creative, deep-thinking, and accepting human being.

Although Maslow's depiction of human needs and motivations seems logical, numerous researchers have criticized this model. First, the idea that we must fulfill one need before moving on to the next (a way that is similar to levels of a video game) is simplistic (Wahba & Bridwell, 1974). You know from your own life that it is possible to have multiple motivations simultaneously—you can be striving to self-actualize while also experiencing the need to achieve at school. A second criticism was that the hierarchy appeared to be biased toward an individualistic (Western) culture (Hofstede, 1984). Self-actualization, the peak state of Maslow's model, consists of a number of characteristics that put the individual's needs or goals first, sometimes at the expense of humanity as a whole. In collectivistic (primarily Eastern) cultures, such needs would be much less important than acting to ensure that everyone was getting along and that the community, not just the individual, was successful.

However, although the *hierarchy* element of Maslow's model may be inaccurate, his work has highlighted the fact that human motivation extends to a number of different areas rather than being simply a matter of eating, sleeping, and reproducing. Later researchers have noted that we have a number of needs that can, at times, feel as pressing as a grumbling stomach. For example, research suggests that humans have a fundamental need to belong (Baumeister & Leary, 1995), which motivates us to affiliate with other people and to seek meaningful, long-term bonds.

Explore
Maslow's Hierarchy of Needs

BELONGING IS A NEED, NOT A WANT The **need to belong** (sometimes known as affiliation motivation) *is the motivation to maintain relationships that involve pleasant feelings such as warmth, affection, appreciation, and mutual concern for each person's well-being.* In addition, an individual must have the sense that these feelings are part of a permanent relationship, such as a friendship, kinship, or shared group membership (Baumeister & Leary, 1995). A strong sense of belonging brings more than warmth and happiness; it appears to be fundamental in the same way that food and shelter are needs—these are all things that humans cannot survive without.

Watch
What's in It for Me?: Meeting Our Needs

Blend Images/Shutterstock.com

Psychologists hypothesize that close, permanent relationships are as important as food and water are for normal psychological functioning.

AF archive/Alamy

George Clooney's character in *Up in the Air* shunned all permanent relationships, opting instead for brief, passing encounters. He was soon confronted with his own need to belong.

Although we all probably want to have pleasant interactions, it is the second part of the definition—a sense of permanence—that is most important for our well-being. Specifically, an individual who has many positive social interactions with a series of different individuals does not enjoy the same satisfaction and other benefits as an individual who interacts with only a few people, but regularly and for a long period of time. For example, an executive who flies all over the continent may have fascinating conversations with fellow passengers every week, yet feel extremely lonely. Meanwhile, imagine a couple living on a rural farm who see only a few neighbours during the week, but see the same people frequently and know them very well. The permanence of their family and community is significant, and they will probably be much more satisfied with their sense of belongingness over the long run than will the high-flying executive. Indeed, a substantial number of studies have shown that lonely people like the executive are more likely to feel depressed than are socially connected individuals like the rural farmers (Cacioppo et al., 2006); this leads to substantially lower ratings of happiness and life satisfaction (Cacioppo et al., 2011).

Watch Relationships and Love

In addition to its effects on mental health, psychologists have found that social connectedness has a dramatic effect on physical health as well. Research has demonstrated that loneliness is a risk factor for illnesses such as heart disease and cancer (Cacioppo et al., 2003). It also elevates a person's risk for having hypertension, a weaker immune system, and high levels of stress hormones. This relationship holds true even when lonely and non-lonely individuals have the same amount of social interaction—it is the *sense of belonging* that counts (Hawkley et al., 2003). Even very simple indicators such as living alone or an individual's rating of the statement "I feel lonely" predict chances of survival after heart attacks and bypass surgeries (Herlitz et al., 1998; Rozanski et al., 1999). Given that belonging is important for our health and happiness, it makes sense that so much of our life is focused on friends, family, and romantic partners.

LOVE In some cases, the feeling of belonging that accompanies your friendship and family bonds becomes a form of love. You'd be willing to make great sacrifices for these lucky people and you know they would do the same for you. You trust them, look forward to spending time with them, and genuinely cheer for them as they go through life. Of course, this isn't the only type of love that we experience. As you stumble through your teenage years and enter early adulthood, many of you will desire and experience romantic relationships. Some of these will produce an intense feeling that we think of as romantic love.

What *is* romantic love? This is a question that has permeated our culture for thousands of years. Armies of anemic English poets have worked furiously, desperately trying to find the perfect words to describe this wonderful feeling. For most of our history, love has not been seriously discussed in scientific circles. However, this has changed in the last 40 years. In 1974, Berscheid and Walter proposed the first scientific model of love, one that is still widely accepted today (Fehr, 2003). These psychologists suggested that love is composed of two main components: passionate love and companionate love. **Passionate love** *is associated with a physical and emotional longing for the other person.* We feel passionate love at the beginning of a relationship, when we are just getting

berc/Fotolia

Darren Baker/Fotolia

to know the other person and everything is new. Recent brain-imaging research has shown that feelings of passionate love are associated with activity in areas of the brain related to physical rewards as well as the insula, a region that is sensitive to internal bodily feelings such as having "butterflies in the stomach" (Bartels & Zeki, 2004; Beauregard et al., 2009).

Companionate love, on the other hand, *is related to tenderness, and to the affection we feel when our lives are intertwined with another person* (Hatfield & Rapson, 1993). Although passionate love is certainly more exciting, companionate love appears to have a greater influence on the long-term stability of a relationship. Undergraduate research participants viewed increases in companionate features of love to be more indicative of a loving relationship than passionate features of love. Decreases in companionate love suggested that the relationship was in trouble (Fehr, 1988), and may suggest that the people do not feel as committed to each other as they once did.

Love, therefore, seems to be a very pleasant state. But, what *motivates* people to seek it out? Art Aron and his colleagues (2005) have suggested that "love is a mammalian drive to pursue preferred mates" (p. 327). In other words, love may be a goal-oriented state in a way that is similar (but obviously not identical) to hunger and sex drives. To test this hypothesis, these researchers performed fMRI scans on 17 people who were in love. While in the scanner, these participants viewed images of their special someone, as well as photographs of a familiar person. The brain responses to images of the loved one were stronger in dopamine-rich areas that are part of the reward system. Even better, activity in some parts of this system correlated with the participants' responses on a passionate love questionnaire (see Figure 11.11). Activity in other parts of the reward system correlated with the intensity of their reported love and with ratings of facial attractiveness. Importantly, many of these brain areas contain many receptors for *oxytocin*, a hormone related to feelings of trust and the desire to be close to someone (Aron et al., 2005).

Watch
IT Video: Finding a Mate

Watch
Dating and Finding a Mate: Ralf, 33 Years Old

Watch
Dating and Finding a Mate: Stephanie, 31 Years Old

It's important to note that this motivational view of love is still consistent with the passionate-companionate theory of love. In fact, it adds a mechanism that can explain why we seek out passionate love in the first place: a reward state similar to many other types of motivations.

LOVE AND COMMITMENT There are obviously numerous reasons to seek out love; however, as many of you are painfully aware, love does not always last forever. In fact, in many cases, loving relationships become stale and people feel the desire to leave. Why do you think this happens?

Watch
Triangular Theory of Love: Robert Sternberg

According to researchers, there are a number of factors influencing commitment. One is the initial strength of the attraction; this could include the happiness associated with companionship and finding someone similar to yourself, the enjoyment of sex, and the economic benefits of being in a stable relationship (Levinger, 1965). A second factor is the number of barriers to leaving the relationship; these include children, religious convictions, and social and economic pressures. These positive

Explore
Passionate Love Scale

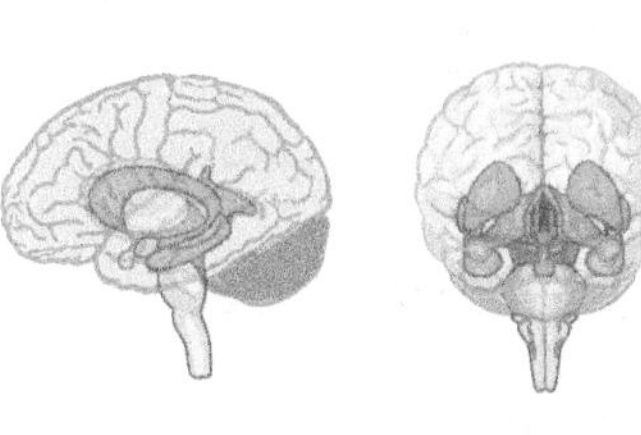

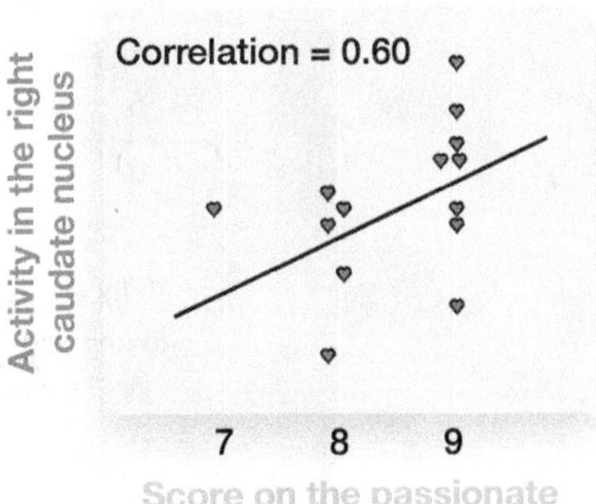

{FIG. 11.11} **Love as a Motivational System** (*Left*) Neuroimaging data show that viewing images of your beloved (as opposed to someone else) activates the caudate nucleus (the green structures in the above image), an area in the brain related to experiencing rewards. (*Right*) People who felt greater levels of passionate love showed larger reward responses.

and negative factors must be weighed by people who are considering leaving a relationship. The decision to stay or leave a relationship will be, to a large degree, dependent upon how much weight an individual gives to each of these variables. However, there is a third factor that comes into play: the availability of alternatives (Thibault & Kelley, 1959). If people think that there are few alternatives, then they are more likely to remain committed. Of course, there aren't many pop songs about *that*.

Incidentally, researchers have examined brain activity in people whose partners had left the relationship (i.e., people who had been dumped). These participants viewed images of their ex-boyfriend or ex-girlfriend along with images of a familiar person. The results confirmed a motivational view of love. Responses to images of a former partner activated brain areas in reward centres—this activity was very similar to that shown by drug addicts who were craving a drug (Fisher et al., 2010). However, the researchers noted that as the number of days after the break-up increased, the activity in brain areas related to craving decreased. In other words, the attachment decreased over time. So, if you've recently experienced a break-up and are upset, listen to your friends when they say that you'll feel better after some time passes. Your brain will one day agree.

Quick Quiz 11.3a

Belongingness and Love Needs

KNOW ...

1 Affiliation motivation is

- **A** the drive to have as many friends as possible.
- **B** the desire to be around other people as often as possible.
- **C** the need to have at least a few permanent meaningful relationships.
- **D** the desire to be isolated from others.

2 Which of the following factors increases an individual's risk for illness, heart disease, and even cancer?

- **A** Self-actualization
- **B** Loneliness
- **C** Happiness
- **D** Low self-esteem

UNDERSTAND ...

3 Why do people leave relationships that were once loving and supportive?

- **A** There are too many alternative relationship partners to cope with.
- **B** The level of companionate love is not sufficient to maintain the relationship.
- **C** There are too few barriers for leaving the relationship.
- **D** The levels of passionate love are not increasing at a fast enough rate to be satisfying.

ANALYZE ...

4 What point did Maslow intend to communicate when he placed belonging in the middle of his hierarchy of needs?

- **A** Individuals generally must take care of physiological needs first, but must satisfy belonging needs before developing healthy self-esteem.
- **B** Belonging is not an essential human need.
- **C** Individuals generally must first have a healthy self-esteem before one can satisfy the need to belong.
- **D** Belonging is more important than physiological needs.

Answers can be found on page ANS-3.

Achievement Motivation

At the beginning of this module, you read about Michelle, a student who desperately wanted to be on the varsity basketball team. Part of that desire was likely related to the need to belong, to be part of a team with her friends. But, that can't explain why she vowed to practise every day so that she would make the team next year. It would be much easier to join a team in a lower-level basketball league, or to have her friends put together a team in a different sport. But, these solutions weren't part of Michelle's story. Instead, she wanted to improve her basketball skills so that she could be part of the competitive and prestigious league. In other words, she wanted to achieve a specific goal.

Achievement motivation is a very strong force in human behaviour, and refers to *the drive to perform at high levels and to accomplish significant goals*. But, this motivation isn't as simple as it sounds. There are a number of reasons *why* Michelle could be motivated to achieve. For example, Michelle might want to make the team in order to receive more respect and attention from her fellow students; she might also really enjoy the game and could have a desire to play it as much as possible. In both cases, Michelle would be attempting to achieve an **approach goal**, *an enjoyable and pleasant incentive that a person is drawn toward, such as praise, financial reward, or a feeling of satisfaction*. But, what if Michelle were motivated to make the team in order to avoid the embarrassment of being "cut" from the team this year? That's a very different mindset than an approach goal. Instead, her behaviour would be motivated by an **avoidance goal**, *an attempt to avoid an unpleasant outcome such as shame, embarrassment, losing money, or feeling emotional pain*.

If achievement motivation were this simple, we could explain most of our behaviour in terms of seeking a reward and/or avoiding suffering. Although both are elements of our behaviour, our motivation to achieve is also influenced by numerous other factors, including (but not limited to) personal preferences, values, the setting we are in, and whether we feel that we actually have the ability to achieve our goal. In the rest of this module, we will discuss how these different factors can influence our motivation to achieve our goals, and will provide examples that will allow you to apply what you learn in this module to the real world (if you feel motivated to do so).

SELF-DETERMINATION THEORY When we think about achieving our goals, we can't help but think about making up to-do lists or pro-and-con lists that will help us organize our lives. But, while these techniques provide us with a practical way of examining the choices we face, they don't really tap into the deeper motivation for why we are, or are not, performing a behaviour. Recent psychological research has attempted to fill this void by examining what researchers refer to as universal needs, needs that (almost) all humans experience. Our attempts to satisfy these needs likely influence our motivation to perform one behaviour or another, and can therefore have a huge effect on how we act. One universal need is *relatedness,* feeling connected with others. This need is satisfied by forming meaningful bonds with other people, such as family members, teammates, or colleagues at school or work. A second need is that of *autonomy,* the need to feel in control of your own life (Deci & Vansteenkiste, 2004). If you have no control over elements of your life, you will feel less motivated to succeed in them. For example, if your boss "micro-managed" every single thing you did while you were putting together a presentation, would you feel more motivated to do a great job than if you controlled how it was put together? Probably not. But, if your boss were kindly teaching you the presentation software so that you would know how to do the work on your own next time, you might feel differently. This leads to the third universal need, *competence,* or the ability to perform a task at a skill level that is satisfying to the individual. Most of you are quite computer savvy, but likely have elderly relatives who think that "phishing" is a spelling error. You would therefore have a greater feeling of competence than these relatives when it comes to computers.

But, our motivation isn't necessarily influenced by how competent we *are.* Instead, it is influenced by how competent we *think* we are. If a very skilled basketball player didn't think she was good enough, she wouldn't practise as hard as she would if she believed in her abilities. (In contrast, watch some of the awful singers making the judges' ears bleed on *American Idol*-type shows; they believe they are good, so they continue to sing . . . sometimes even while security drags them away.) The effect that your perception of your own ability has on motivation is known as **self-efficacy**, *an individual's confidence that he or she can plan and execute a course of action in order to solve a problem* (Bandura, 1997). When people experience high levels of self-efficacy, their performance improves and they are motivated to choose more challenging tasks to perform (Eccles & Wigfield, 2002). So, if you believe that you can competently do something, you will be more motivated to attempt to do so.

A theme running through all three of our universal human needs—relatedness, autonomy, and competence—is the need to feel in control of your life and your decisions. We want to be able to choose who we associate with and the form those relationships are going to take (relatedness), control the decisions that affect our lives (autonomy), and be in control of the actions necessary to carry out those decisions (competence). These themes are part of **self-determination theory**, a theory that states that *an individual's ability to achieve their goals and attain psychological well-being is influenced by the degree to which he or she is in control of the behaviours necessary to achieve those goals* (Ryan & Deci, 2000). So, if we are able to achieve this control, or at least feel like we have control, then we will be more motivated to perform the actions necessary to achieve that goal. We will also be happier. Self-determination theory has been used to explain a number of behaviours ranging from the likelihood of successfully learning a second language (Noels et al., 2000), the motivation to exercise (Wilson et al., 2008), the establishment of healthy identities (La Guardia, 2009), and the ability to adapt to life as an international student studying in Canada (Chirkov et al., 2007, 2008). In each case, increasing feelings of competence, autonomy, and relatedness increased motivation.

But, at this point in our discussion, our explanation for why we are motivated to achieve goals only explains very general, deep-seated needs. To more thoroughly explain our behaviours, we need to look more closely at specific factors that could influence motivation.

EXTRINSIC AND INTRINSIC MOTIVATION One way to examine the question of "Why do we try to achieve a goal?" is to determine whether our motivation is externally or internally generated. If you wanted to be on a basketball team in order to be popular, you would be experiencing **extrinsic motivation** (or a **performance motive**), *motivation geared toward gaining rewards or public recognition, or avoiding embarrassment* (Deci, 1971; Vansteenkiste et al., 2006). This form of motivation is not always the most effective, as it requires a person to give up some autonomy. If you play basketball to seem cool, then you must rely on other people's reactions to determine if you succeeded in your goal (i.e., other people control if you are viewed as "cool"). Taken to its most extreme, people can become **amotivational**, *a feeling of having little or no motivation to perform a behaviour.* If your parents forced you to play basketball against your will, you might stop trying putting forth any effort. In this case, neither the feelings of autonomy nor competence would be met.

Luckily, not all of our motivation is controlled by outside forces; sometimes we do things simply because we enjoy doing them. For example, what if you wanted to become a better basketball player simply for the joy of playing and improving yourself? In this case, the motivation to improve came from within yourself rather than from some external source. This would be an example of **intrinsic motivation** (or **mastery motive**), *the process of being internally motivated to perform behaviours and overcoming challenges (e.g., a genuine desire to master a task rather than being motivated by a reward).*

Simulate Survey: What Motivates You?

A study of Grade 5 students shows the profound effect that intrinsic and extrinsic motivation can have on how we respond to challenges and to failures. Children were given sets of puzzle problems and were asked to complete them independently. After successfully solving the first set of puzzles, some of the students were praised for their intelligence (e.g., "You must be smart to do these problems") while others were praised for their work ethic (e.g., "You must have worked hard at these problems"). The psychologists then gave the children another, more difficult, set of problems to complete. This time, the researchers told the children that they had scored lower on these questions. Finally, the children were asked to select the goals that they tended to work toward. This list included performance/extrinsic goals such as choosing easy questions to avoid getting many wrong, as well as mastery/intrinsic goals such as selecting problems that one could learn from.

The results of the experiment were remarkable. The children praised for being smart tended to feel less pleasure during learning and instead tended to worry about how well they were doing. They gave up more easily and performed more poorly. Just under 70% of these students selected performance/extrinsic goals when given a list of options. In contrast, only 10% of the students who were praised for their effort chose performance/extrinsic goals when asked what motivated them. Instead, they focused on working hard, overcoming challenges, and learning from their mistakes. Even more stunning was the fact that the students praised for being smart were three times more likely to lie about their results to other people. Almost 40% of the "smart" students lied about their results, compared with only 13% of the "effort" students. In summary, the students praised for intelligence felt incredible pressure to live up to that label and went to great extents to preserve that image, including selecting easier questions and lying about their results. Based on this study, what parenting techniques do you think would help kids become well-adjusted?

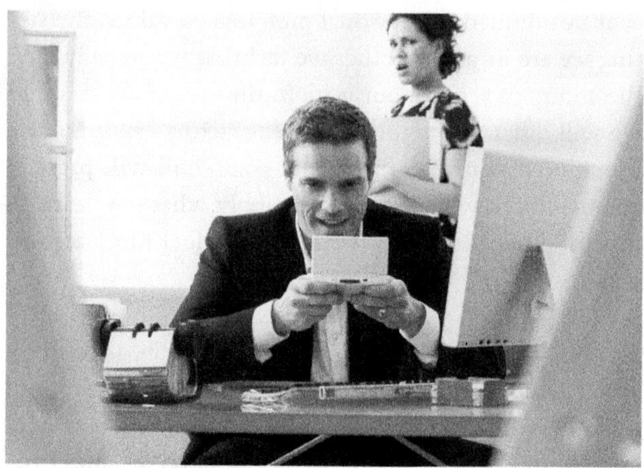

Radius Images/Alamy

This person is clearly procrastinating—there is a good chance that his work is a performance-avoidance goal.

A CONTINUUM OF MOTIVATION It is important to note that intrinsic and extrinsic motivation are not completely separate. Rather, intrinsic motivation, extrinsic motivation, and amotivation can be placed on a continuum that depicts how much self-determination an individual might feel for those behaviours (see Figure 11.12). Critically, where a given behaviour lies on this continuum can change over time or across situations. For instance, if you give someone a reward (other than verbal praise) for an intrinsically motivated behaviour, the intrinsic motivation decreases, as does the frequency of the behaviour. This change in motivation is known as *the over-justification effect* (Lepper et al., 1973). This decrease in motivation is likely due to the change from being internally motivated (high autonomy) to being dependent

Amotivation	Extrinsic Motivation	Intrinsic Motivation

Nonself-determined ⟷ Self-determined

{FIG. 11.12} **The Continuum of Self-Determination Theory** On this continuum, amotivation would reflect very low levels of self-determination. Intrinsic motivation, on the other hand, would reflect a high degree of self-determination.

upon a reward (low autonomy). So, if you loved basketball, but then started receiving money from your parents for each basket, you would actually feel less motivated to play than you did before! This effect has profound implications for parenting, education, and the business world. For example, if a good student were given rewards for getting good grades, it might reduce how much she identified herself with learning. Businesspeople who work in the hopes of getting a bonus monetary reward will be less likely to identify with the projects or products they are working on. In both cases, the rewards have moved their motivation along the continuum from intrinsic toward extrinsic. This isn't to say that rewards should never be given; sometimes this is the only option to motivate someone. However, as we learn more about the over-justification effect, it is becoming increasingly clear that we need to more carefully consider the effects of rewards on behaviours that were already intrinsically motivated.

A different, but potentially more powerful, change along the continuum can occur for behaviours that were initially extrinsically (externally) motivated. Generally, these behaviours are not associated with much passion, as some outside motivation (e.g., money or another person) is stimulating this behaviour. But, over time, it is possible that some of these behaviours will become *internalized* so that they are part of a person's identity. A basketball player might begin working out because it will increase the odds that she will be recruited to play for a team and will become popular. Over time, however, she might become enthusiastic about exercising for its own sake, and could make that part of her identity long after her basketball career ended. By making exercising part of her identity, the basketball player gains autonomy over this behaviour, because *she* is the one motivating it, not some external source like a coach. Internalized behaviours are more likely to be performed—and performed well—than extrinsically motivated behaviours that are not internalized. The challenge, therefore, is to find a way to increase the likelihood that behaviours will undergo this transition. In other words, how do you harness the power of intrinsic motivation?

To answer this question, we have to remember that intrinsic motivation is, in many ways, about a behaviour having some sort of meaning to an individual. Intrinsically motivated behaviours are generally consistent with your values, are enjoyable, and are part of your image of your future self (Sheldon et al., 2003). When you encounter a new situation, your motivational response will therefore change depending upon whether it has meaning to you. For instance, most of us like to be frugal with our money. So, if you were asked to drive less and use public transportation more, you would be more likely to internalize the idea of being a public transportation user if you thought about it in terms of saving yourself money. In contrast, abstract ideas such as reducing greenhouse gas emissions are less likely to grab your attention because they are more difficult to attach a concrete meaning to (Schultz & Zelezny, 2003).

But if personal meaning has a powerful effect on intrinsic motivation, could we alter motivation if we made a behaviour more or less meaningful? If we wanted to influence *other people's* motivation, could we tailor messages in such a way that we could increase their intrinsic motivation? And, could these changes allow us to convince people to behave in a way that would benefit not just themselves, but society as a whole?

WORKING THE SCIENTIFIC LITERACY MODEL

Framing, Values, and Pro-Environmental Messages

Although not all of you are avid campers who love to be covered in mud, it's safe to assume that most of you want the environment to be preserved and protected. Polls indicate that a large proportion of Canadians are concerned about air and water pollution, climate change, and the use of toxic chemicals (Environics, 2005a, 2005b). These people also agree that we have a responsibility to do everything we can to address environmental issues (Ekos, 2003). That said, in July 2012, Canada was ranked 11 out of 12 wealthy nations in terms of energy conservation (Hayes, Young, & Sciortino, 2012). How can psychology be used to motivate people to act in the environmentally friendly ways that Canadians claim they value?

What do we know about framing pro-environmental messages?

Although most Canadians are sympathetic to environmental messages, there is little evidence that concern for the environment is linked to any consistent behaviour change (Oskamp et al., 1991). Some experiments using extrinsic rewards have shown short-term changes in behaviours (Geller et al., 1982); however, as you would have guessed based on what you've read in this module, these changes tend to disappear as soon as the reward does (Aronson & Gonzales, 1990; Lehman & Gellar, 2004). In order to maintain pro-environmental behavioural changes, psychologists have focused on framing messages in ways that promote intrinsic motivation.

The **framing effect** states that *when the correct course of action is not obvious, the different phrasing of the question or problem can produce different results* (Tversky & Kahneman, 1981; see Module 8.2). Generally, if a situation is framed in a positive way (e.g., "Reducing pollution will make our rivers clean"), people choose the less uncertain option. This is likely because positive emotions make the situation seem less threatening; therefore, there is less motivation to change things. In contrast, if a situation is framed negatively (e.g., "If we don't reduce pollution, then our streets will be filled with streams of deadly toxic waste"), then people choose the most uncertain option because it appears that larger changes are needed (Piñon & Gambara, 2005). This tendency is magnified when there is a particularly pressing need or threat (Mishra et al., 2012). Note that both examples of messages dealt with the same behaviour: reducing pollution. But, how the messages were conveyed differed dramatically and could produce different results. Therefore, if people want to create *rapid* behavioural change, this research would suggest that focusing on how environmental problems could have frightening effects on humanity would influence how people thought about these issues.

How can science explain the framing of pro-environmental messages?

Rothman and Salovey (1997) found that framing the message in a threatening manner (e.g., driving your cars will create harmful greenhouse gas emissions) attracts more attention than framing messages in terms of benefits to society (e.g., using public transportation reduces greenhouse gas emissions). *But,* framing messages in a fear-inducing manner appears to lose its effect quickly; people tend to build up defensive reactions (e.g., ignoring the message) after a while (Leventhal, 1970). So, given that so many Canadians are already aware of environmental dangers, this type of message framing will be unlikely to lead to increased motivation to perform pro-environmental behaviours.

Instead, researchers have focused on using self-determination theory to promote environmentally friendly behaviours (Pelletier et al., 1998). If people are already aware of a danger, then approach-related messages that focus on a positive outcome appear to be more effective, especially when the message also explains the benefits of changing a behaviour (Pelletier & Sharp, 2008). This information about *how* to act in an eco-friendly way increases people's feelings of competence and autonomy, which makes them more likely to act.

Researchers have also found that framing a message in a way that is congruent with a person's values can influence the likelihood that people will become intrinsically motivated. In one study, U.S. researchers asked 898 people from different political affiliations (Republican, Democrat, or independent voters who were not linked to either party) whether they would support paying a surcharge for the carbon dioxide emissions. However, they framed this question in two ways: as a "tax" or as an "offset." The framing did not affect the Democrats. Republicans and independents, on the other hand, strongly opposed the same behaviour when it was labelled a "tax" but were in favour of it when it was labelled an "offset." The reason was that taxes are a value-laden term, with Republicans in particular opposing, on principle, any tax (Hardistry et al., 2010).

Can we critically evaluate this evidence?

The idea of framing messages is quite intuitive—advertisers, politicians, and kids in trouble with their parents frame messages all the time. But, to critically evaluate the effects of framing, we have to examine what the researchers are actually manipulating. In the tax vs. offset study, a few words in a persuasive sentence were changed. This change then tapped into the participants' values and past experiences, which then triggered some sort of emotional response (at least in Republicans and independents). The result of this emotional response was a motivation to support or oppose the proposed charge for carbon use. Given the role that emotion appears to have on the subsequent behaviour, a critical evaluation of these effects has to examine whether the framing of an idea really does elicit different emotions. Brain-imaging research suggests that this is the case. Framing a gambling decision in terms of how likely you are to lose money activates fear centres in your brain (De Martino et al., 2008). Emily Falk and colleagues (2010) have also shown that neural activity in the medial (close to the middle) region of your prefrontal cortex occurring in response to a persuasive message is linked with whether you will actually act on that message over the next week; this same region is involved with a number of emotional functions. Although more research needs to be performed on this topic, the existing evidence does suggest that framing, emotion, and the motivation to act are related processes.

Why is this relevant?

Psychologists have noted that people who are intrinsically motivated to engage in pro-environmental behaviours will continue to act this way even if it is difficult to do so (e.g., having to drive recycling to a depot rather than having curbside pick up; Green-Demers et al., 1997). The challenge for environmentalists, then, is to increase the number of people who are intrinsically motivated. Given that such a large proportion of Canadians are concerned about the environment, the use of framing techniques could motivate people to act on their emotions and to internalize that motivation. But, as you read earlier in this module, the message must include some information about *how* a person can solve the problem (Gollwitzer, 1999). By providing a person with possible actions that he or she can perform to help solve an environmental problem, it increases that person's autonomy and feelings of competence because they are able to *do something*; but, they aren't being forced into doing it (De Young, 2000).

Goodluz/Fotolia

Quick Quiz 11.3b Achievement Motivation

KNOW ...

1 If a student is a pre-med major because he is curious about how the body works and how it recovers from disease, psychologists would say that he has ________ motives. If the student is studying pre-med only because he thinks this major will impress people, then psychologists would say that he has ________ motives.

A mastery; performance
B performance; mastery
C performance; avoidance
D avoidance; mastery

2 An individual's belief that he or she will be able to complete a task is known as

A implicit motivation.
B self-efficacy.
C approach motivation.
D avoidance motivation.

APPLY ...

3 What method would be most effective in helping someone stop smoking?

A Explain the dangers of smoking and provide photographs of its effects on a person's body.
B Increase the extrinsic motivation she would feel about stopping smoking.
C Give her encouraging messages as well as a list of specific ways to stop smoking.
D Have her run up and down hills until she coughs and feels shame.

Answers can be found on page ANS-3.

Module Summary

Now that you have read this module you should

Nikita Buida/Fotolia

KNOW ...

- ***The key terminology of social and achievement motivation:***

achievement motivation (p. 470)
amotivation (p. 472)
approach goal (p. 470)
avoidance goal (p. 470)
companionate love (p. 469)
extrinsic motivation (p. 471)
framing effect (p. 474)
intrinsic motivation (p. 472)
mastery motive (p. 472)
need to belong (p. 467)
passionate love (p. 468)
performance motive (p. 471)
self-determination theory (p. 471)
self-efficacy (p. 471)

UNDERSTAND ...

- ***How people experience a need to belong.*** Psychologists have discovered a number of ways in which people are motivated to enter into personal relationships. People seek out friendships, romantic relationships, and group membership to satisfy this need.
- ***How we can harness the power of intrinsic motivation.*** Intrinsic motivation can be a powerful tool in our attempts to achieve our goal. If we can make behaviours that used to be extrinsically motivated part of our identity, a process known as internalization, then we are more likely to continue to perform those behaviours. A number of factors can influence this process including whether the behaviour fits with a person's values, is fun, is consistent with a person's view of him- or herself, and has a clear behaviour associated with it (which will tap into a person's need to feel competent).

APPLY ...

- ***Theories of motivation to understand your personal motivation to achieve in school or your career.*** How would you describe your motivation for school? Are you just trying to earn good grades, or do you find yourself motivated because you are interested in learning? Complete the four brief questionnaires included in **Table 11.2** to see how your motives stack up relative to other students.

ANALYZE ...

- ***Claims that a sense of belonging is something people need versus something they want.*** Although belonging may not be the most basic type of need on the hierarchy of needs—those positions are usually assigned to food, water, and shelter—it is a significant need nonetheless. Research has shown that living without a feeling of belonging has some drastic consequences. Not only is loneliness related to depression, but it is also associated with a reduced life span. The fact that belonging is essential to good health and longevity provides strong support for classifying it as a need, not just something people want.

Table 11.2 :: Application Activity

Thinking about your Psychology course, respond to each statement by assigning a score on a scale of 1 ("Not at all true of me") to 7 ("Very true of me"). Then find your average response for each set of three questions. Compare your scores to the averages for each score.

	MASTERY	PERFORMANCE
APPROACH	1. I want to learn as much as possible from this class. 2. It is important for me to understand the content of this course as thoroughly as possible. 3. I desire to completely master the material presented in this class. Average score: 5.52	1. It is important for me to do better than other students. 2. It is important for me to do well compared to others in this class. 3. My goal in this class is to get a better grade than most of the other students. Average score: 4.82
AVOIDANCE	1. I worry that I may not learn all that I possibly could in this class. 2. Sometimes I'm afraid that I may not understand the content of this class as thoroughly as possible. 3. I am often concerned that I may not learn all that there is to learn in this class. Average score: 3.89	1. I just want to avoid doing poorly in this class. 2. My goal in this class is to avoid performing poorly. 3. My fear of performing poorly in this class is often what motivates me. Average score: 4.49

Source: These items and the averages are provided in Elliot & McGregor, 2001.

Matteo photos/Shutterstock

Module 11.4

Emotion

Learning Objectives

After reading this module you should

KNOW ...	UNDERSTAND ...	APPLY ...	ANALYZE ...
The key terminology associated with emotion	How the nervous system responds to emotions Cultural similarities and differences in emotional expressions	Your knowledge of theories of emotion to new examples	What purpose(s) do facial expressions serve

Imagine the following scenario: You are sitting in your bedroom watching television. Suddenly, you notice something moving beside one of your textbooks. Your heart rate increases slightly and your palms begin to sweat as you move closer to the moving object.

At this point—before we know how this story resolves itself—it is important to examine some details about your emotional response. First, the "you" in this story was very quick to locate and pay attention to a potentially threatening stimulus; nothing else in your environment seemed to matter for that instant. The moving object could have been a leaf or clump of dust that was being moved by the air conditioning in your house. Or, it could have been a spider or, worse yet, a spider with a knife. What is important to note is that before you were even able to consciously identify what the object was, your body was preparing itself to act. You were afraid, and your body responded with an increase in heart rate, sweating, and muscle tension. Once you've determined whether the moving object was dangerous or not, you can either increase or decrease your emotional reaction. If it is just a "dust bunny," you don't need to feel fear. However, if it is a well-armed spider, then your initial emotional response may be appropriate.

This example illustrates the key parts of an emotional experience: We detect an emotional item, we have an initial emotional reaction preparing us to respond, and then, after we analyze the situation, we increase or decrease that response. In this module, we will take a closer look at these different parts of our emotional responses in an effort to better understand the emotions that we experience every day.

Focus Questions

 1. What role does the brain play in our emotional experiences?

 2. How do the labels we give our emotions, such as fear, happiness, and sadness, relate to their corresponding physical sensations?

Watch
The Big Picture: Motivation and Emotion

Darren Greenwood/Vibe Images/Alamy

Children who are born both deaf and blind show the same facial expressions and emotions as people who see and hear. This is one of many pieces of evidence that our emotions have a strong biological basis.

Simulate
Transfer of Emotions

Like most concepts in psychology, the term "emotion" can mean a number of different things. Common convention in psychology is to define an **emotion** as being *a behaviour with the following three components: (a) a subjective thought and/or experience with (b) accompanying patterns of neural activity and physical arousal and (c) an observable behavioural expression (e.g., an emotional facial expression or changes in muscle tension)*. Although this definition still includes thoughts and *feelings,* it also shows that our current understanding of emotion encompasses other elements as well. In particular, it shows us that the emotions we experience include a biological response.

Physiology of Emotion

In the example at the beginning of this module, we noted that emotional behaviours are actually quite complex and involve a number of different components or stages. Each of these stages uses a distinct set of brain regions. The brain regions are connected to each other in such a way that the firing associated with one stage of an emotional response will influence the patterns of firing associated with subsequent stages of that response. Importantly, your emotional system also allows for later stages to provide feedback to earlier stages. This allows you to modify your emotional responses as you learn more about your situation. In this section, we will discuss the different areas of the nervous system that are involved in emotions and will show how different areas work together to produce the emotional behaviours that have allowed our species to survive in a dangerous world.

THE INITIAL RESPONSE The human brain shows emotion-dependent responses within approximately 150 ms of seeing or hearing a potential threat (Pizzagalli et al., 2002). The goal of this early activity isn't to consciously identify an emotional stimulus. Instead, the purpose of this initial brain activity is to tag or highlight that stimulus so that it receives extra processing by brain structures at later stages of perception. For an example of this phenomenon, look at Figure 11.13. There are many different objects in this scene, yet you likely paid more attention to the snake than to anything else. Why does this happen? How does your brain make some stimuli more important than others, and what consequences follow from that?

A critical brain area involved in this process is the **amygdala**, a group of nuclei in the medial portion (near the middle) of the temporal lobes in each hemisphere of the brain. The amygdala fires when we perceive stimuli that are emotionally arousing, and is especially sensitive to fear-relevant images and sounds. However, the firing of the amygdala on its own does very little—it is the amygdala's projections to other brain structures that lead to the observable behaviours that we think of as being emotional responses. When the amygdala receives input about a stimulus that might be emotionally meaningful or threatening, it stimulates activity in sensory areas so that they fire more than they would for a non-emotional stimulus. So, when you see a spider or hear a dog growling, your amygdala will help to increase the activity in your visual and auditory cortices, respectively. The result is that we end up paying more attention to these potentially emotional stimuli.

THE AUTONOMIC RESPONSE: FIGHT OR FLIGHT? An emotional response obviously involves more than simply perceiving a threat—we need to

Roy Toft/National Geographic/Getty Images

{FIG. 11.13} **An Example of How Emotional Elements of a Scene Attract Our Attention**

prepare our body to physically respond to the emotional stimulus, if necessary. Importantly, this preparation needs to occur instinctively and as rapidly as possible. The *autonomic nervous system* (ANS) specializes in such responses. As you read in Module 3.3, the ANS consists of two systems: (1) the *sympathetic nervous system*, which helps recruit energy to prepare you for a response, and (2) the *parasympathetic nervous system,* which helps preserve energy and calms you down if no response is necessary (Figure 11.14). Think back to the example at the beginning of this module. If the moving object were a large and angry spider, the sympathetic nervous system would mobilize resources so that you had enough energy to either do battle with this threatening creature or to run away from it. If you discovered that you weren't in immediate danger (e.g., a moving object is a leaf, not a spider), the parasympathetic nervous system would become active in an attempt to return you to a normal level of emotional arousal.

Parasympathetic		Sympathetic
Pupils constricted	**Eyes**	Pupils dilated
Salivating	**Mouth**	Dry
No goose bumps	**Skin**	Goose bumps
Dry	**Palms**	Sweaty
Constricted passages	**Lungs**	Dilated passages
Decreased rate	**Heart**	Increased rate
Directed toward internal organs and muscles	**Blood**	Directed to muscles
Decreased activity	**Adrenal glands**	Increased activity
Stimulated	**Digestion**	Inhibited

{FIG. 11.14} **The Autonomic Nervous System and Emotional Responding** The ANS is involved in emotional responding. The sympathetic division prepares the body to respond to stress, and the parasympathetic division restores the body to normal conditions.

THE EMOTIONAL RESPONSE: MOVEMENT If your body is going to mobilize its energy resources during an emotional response, it also needs to plan for what it is going to do with them. In other words, the nervous system needs to prepare your body to make a movement in response to the emotion you are experiencing (e.g., squishing the spider). The problem for us is that even the simplest of movements requires the coordination of a number of different parts of your nervous system so that the muscles move in the appropriate order. Research in the last couple of years has found that emotional stimuli—particularly *threatening* emotional stimuli—trigger an increase in activity in brain areas related to planning movements (Pereira et al., 2010) and in several regions of the spinal cord (Smith & Kornelsen, 2011). This activity suggests that our nervous system is becoming prepared to make a movement if one is necessary—this preparation likely increases the speed and efficiency of our emotional responses.

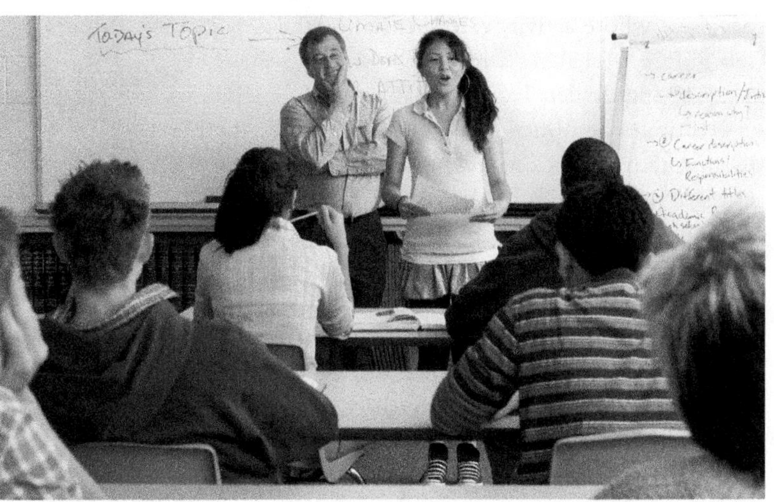

Left: Art_man/Fotolia; right: Radius Images/Alamy

Would a snarling dog startle you? How about the prospect of speaking in front of your Psychology class? Autonomic arousal prepares the body to respond to real or perceived threats.

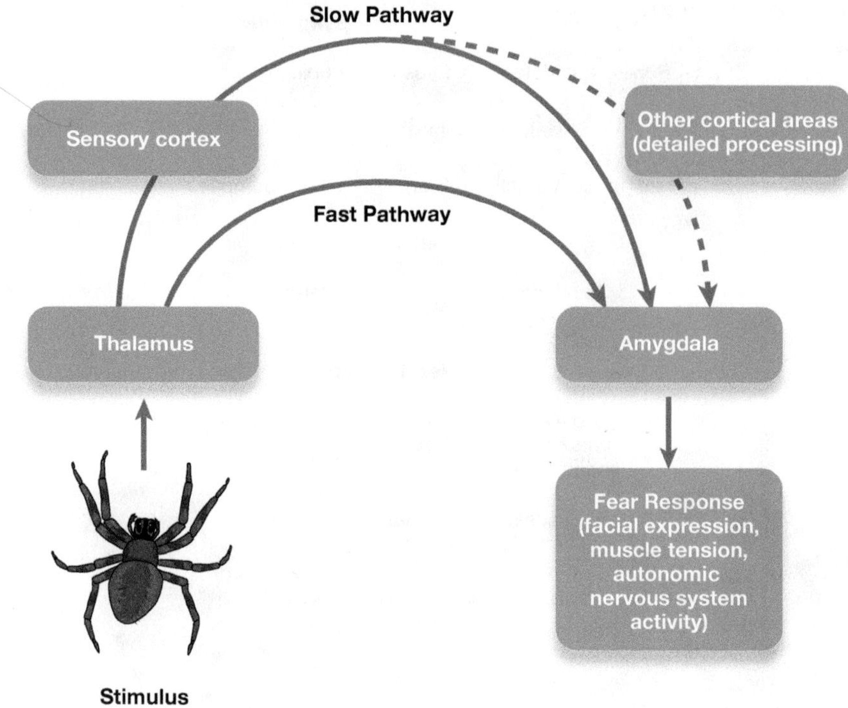

{FIG. 11.15} **Emotion and the Amygdala** The amygdala is a key brain structure in the processing of emotion. Neuroscientist Joseph LeDoux has described this processing as functioning through both "slow" and "fast" pathways. Fast pathways are routed from sensory areas of the brain through the amygdala and directly to the autonomic nervous system for quick action. The slow pathway is routed through the cortex where the situation is processed at a higher level of awareness.

Watch Emotion Processes and Aging: Susan Charles

Simulate Emotion and Motivation

EMOTIONAL REGULATION As we saw in the example at the beginning of this module, it makes sense from a survival standpoint to have rapid emotional responses and *then* to decide if the responses are correct or not. However, this final, evaluative stage of emotional responses is the most complex and involves a number of areas within our frontal lobes. The frontal lobes receive information directly from the amygdala and from sensory areas whose activity is influenced by the amygdala (see Figure 11.15). As a result, the frontal lobes have access to highly detailed information about a stimulus or situation. The frontal lobes must determine whether the instinctive emotional response produced by earlier stages of processing is the best one for that given situation. In some cases, the frontal lobes will analyze the situation and agree that an emotional response is necessary. It will then generate a behaviour that is appropriate for that situation (e.g., you should continue to run away from the spider). In other cases, the frontal lobes will analyze the situation and decide that a stimulus is not emotional (e.g., the moving object was just dust or a leaf, not a spider). In this case, it is necessary to decrease the emotional responses so that the ANS is not depleting the body's resources. So, in the first situation (running away from the spider), the amygdala and ANS influence the frontal lobes; in the second situation, the frontal lobes send feedback that reduces the intensity of the initial emotional response. This constant communication between brain regions is an important characteristic of our emotional system (Mayberg et al., 1999), and explains why we can sometimes feel emotionally out of control and at other times feel "cool, calm, and collected."

Quick Quiz 11.4a
Physiology of Emotion

KNOW ...

1 The ________ influences the firing of your visual and auditory cortex.
- A hippocampus
- B hindbrain
- C amygdala
- D hypothalamus

UNDERSTAND ...

2 After narrowly avoiding a car accident, your arousal returns to a baseline state because of activity in the ________.
- A sympathetic nervous system
- B parasympathetic nervous system
- C hypothalamus
- D amygdala

APPLY ...

3 Elizabeth has a form of epilepsy that cannot be controlled by medications. In an effort to stop her seizures, doctors removed the amygdala from both sides of her brain. How should that affect her experience of fear?
- A She should have difficulties with emotional regulation.
- B Her parasympathetic nervous system should no longer function properly.
- C She should have a smaller initial reaction to emotional images.
- D She should be unaffected by this surgical procedure.

Answers can be found on page ANS-3.

Experiencing Emotions

Try this: hold a pencil or straw in your mouth sideways without letting your lips touch it—just your teeth. Wait for a few seconds. How do you feel? Happy? Sad? Afraid? Why do you think you feel this way?

When we think of the term *emotion,* we rarely think about complex interconnected responses in our brains. Instead, we think of the subjective, personalized *feelings* that we experience such as happiness or fear. For example, we've already discussed how seeing an unidentified moving object in your bedroom can trigger activity in a number of physiological systems leading to the firing of millions of neurons in your brain and in the autonomic nervous system throughout your body. But, you would think of that experience as a *feeling of fear*. How are the physiological response and the psychological feeling related? Which comes first and, importantly, how would one test this question?

The earliest scientific theory of emotions was independently developed by William James, one of the founders of psychology in North America, and a Danish researcher named Carl Lange. Now known as the **James-Lange theory of emotion**, *this view suggested that our physiological reactions to stimuli (e.g., a racing heart) precede the emotional experience (e.g., the fear)*. In other words, your subjective feelings such as happiness or fear follow your physiological responses. But, the James-Lange theory goes one step further, claiming that your feeling of fear is *determined* by how your body responds. According to this theory, emotion would be experienced in the following way: (1) based on your initial perception of a stimulus, your heart starts to race, (2) your brain receives feedback about that response, and then (3) the brain decides that based on the feedback it has received, you should feel fear. This sequence of events may contradict your own common sense experience of emotion. If so, you are not alone. Some prominent researchers from the same era disagreed with James and Lange.

Walter Cannon and Philip Bard developed an alternative to the James-Lange theory (see Figure 11.16). They noted that some of the internal organs involved in emotional feelings could not respond quickly enough to be the first step in an emotional response. They also suggested that the feedback from the body was not specific enough to create the different emotions that we experience. Instead, the **Cannon-Bard theory of emotion** *suggested that the brain interprets a situation and generates subjective emotional feelings, and that these representations in the brain trigger responses in the body*. This theory suggests that these emotional processes occur very quickly, so that the steps occur almost simultaneously.

Watch Basics: Theories of Emotion and Motivation

Explore Physiological, Evolutionary, and Cognitive Theories of Emotion

For several decades, the Cannon-Bard theory was the most widely accepted view of our emotional behaviours. However, as clever researchers examined emotions in more detail, this "common-sense" theory began to show its limitations (another example of scientific knowledge evolving). In fact, there is more empirical support for the James-Lange theory than for the Cannon-Bard theory. This is likely due to the fact that some of the bodily feedback involved in emotional responses is caused by facial responses that have direct connections to the brain rather than by slow responses from internal organs. Indeed, the **facial feedback hypothesis** is a key feature in modern interpretations of the James-Lange theory (see Figure 11.17). This hypothesis *suggests that our emotional expressions can influence our subjective emotional states*. So, if your lips are smiling, you will feel happier. Did you feel happier when you held your pencil or straw in your teeth a few minutes ago? Research participants who performed this action were essentially smiling whether they meant

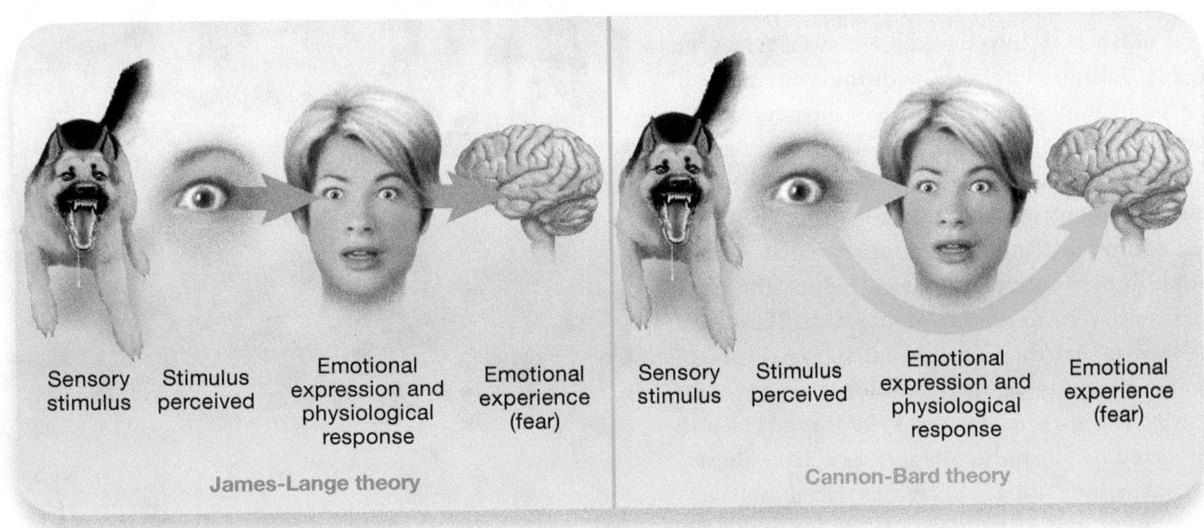

{FIG. 11.16} **Competing Theories of Emotion** What is the correct order of events when it comes to emotional experiences? The James-Lange and Cannon-Bard theories differ in their predictions. **Click on this figure in your eText to see more details.**

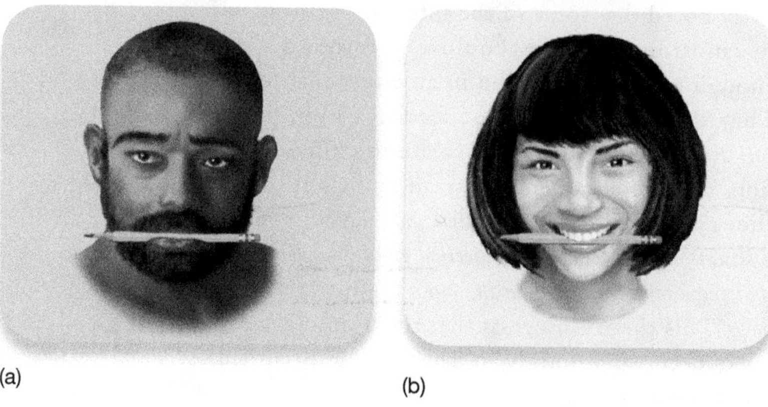

{FIG. 11.17} **The Facial Feedback Hypothesis** Psychologists have found that inducing a facial expression, such as a frown or a smile, can have mild effects on how people feel. This lends support to the facial feedback hypothesis.

to or not. As the facial feedback hypothesis predicted, the participants reported elevated levels of happiness (Strack et al., 1988).

What is a potential alternative explanation for this result? If you tried this example in front of other people, the answer would become readily apparent: You look and feel silly. In order to rule out the possibility that making *any* artificial face would improve your mood, researchers had participants make a different facial expression. Hold the pencil sideways in your mouth using only your lips—don't let your teeth come into contact with the pencil. The result is a slight pout. This is an experimental method of producing a sad face and, sure enough, it leads to a less positive mood (Larsen et al., 1992).

Research support for the facial feedback hypothesis has been mixed. In support of this hypothesis is a study by researchers who tested the effect of Botox™ injections on emotions (Havas et al., 2010). Botox interferes with the movement of muscles by inhibiting the release of the neurotransmitter acetylcholine, which is found at the junctions between muscles and nerves (see Module 3.2). Less movement of the skin leads to fewer wrinkles. Although Botox injections can make some people look younger, they also reduce the person's ability to move his or her face. Research has shown that this impairment in facial movement can slightly dampen emotional experiences. However, the facial feedback hypothesis is not supported by all studies. Researchers have shown that surprise is not as affected by facial feedback as other emotions (Reisenzen & Studtman, 2007). Therefore, we need to be cautious about overgeneralizing this hypothesis to all emotions and all situations.

Additional studies in support of the James-Lange theory note that physical touch can influence our emotional experiences (Hertenstein et al., 2006). In one such study, researchers had participants hold a warm cup of coffee or a cup of iced coffee while describing another person. Participants in the warmth condition used "warmer" terms to describe the target individual (e.g., generous and caring) than did participants in the iced coffee condition (Williams & Bargh, 2008). In another study examining bodily sensations and emotions, researchers watched National Basketball Association (NBA) games involving 294 players from a number of different teams. It turns out that the teams and players who do the most interpersonal touching—fist-pumping, high fives, chest-bumping, etc.—are more cooperative, score more points, and are more likely to win (Kraus et al., 2010). These results, among many others, suggest that how our body feels influences how our brain responds.

Peter Jones/Reuters/Corbis

Players who engage in more interpersonal contact such as chest-bumping and flying shoulder bumps play more cooperatively. Their teams are also more likely to win. Can psychology improve the Raptors?

WORKING THE SCIENTIFIC LITERACY MODEL

The Two-Factor Theory of Emotion

To this point, our discussion of emotions has focused on physical reactions. However, our emotional feelings also involve thoughts, memories, beliefs, and interpretations of different stimuli and situations. How do these different factors interact to produce our emotional experiences? In the 1960s, two researchers developed a theory of emotion that addressed this question.

What do we know about the two-factor theory of emotions?

Researchers Stanley Schachter and Jerome Singer (1962) agreed with James and Lange that our physical reactions give rise to our emotional experiences. However, they also pointed out that many different emotions can elicit physiological arousal. How do we choose which emotion goes with this arousal? Schachter and Singer suggested that it is our interpretation of *why* we are aroused that creates the emotional experience. Their theory, the **two-factor theory**, *holds that patterns of physical arousal and the cognitive labels we attach to them form the basis of our emotional experiences*. Physical arousal is the first factor to come into play (as James and Lange predict) and along with this comes a cognitive label for the experience, such as "I am sad." Combining the two factors, the physical and cognitive, gives rise to the emotional experience of sadness (see Figure 11.18).

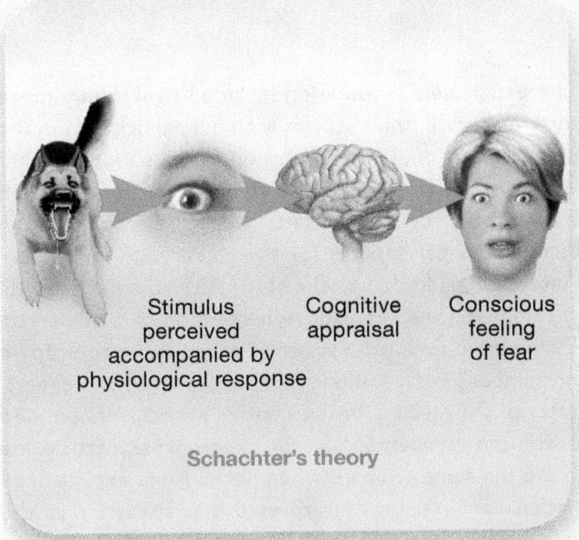

{FIG. 11.18} **Two-Factor Theory of Emotion** According to Schachter and Singer, emotions are experiences composed of physiological responses and the cognitive labels we give them.

How can science explain the two-factor theory?

To test this theory, Schachter and Singer performed a study in which participants were given different cognitive labels for the same physical feeling. These researchers injected three groups of volunteers with adrenaline (epinephrine), a stimulant that increases a person's heart rate, causes sweating, and makes a person's face feel warm and flushed. So, all participants experienced the same physical symptoms. However, the cognitive explanation for those symptoms was manipulated by the experimenters. One group of participants was correctly informed about the symptoms (the Informed Group). Another group was provided no information at all; they were (politely) called the Ignorant Group. The third group of participants was given incorrect information about the injection; these people were told that adrenaline leads to numbing, itchiness, and a slight headache (the Misinformed Group). Thus, only the Informed Group had a correct cognitive explanation for their physical feelings. A final group of participants was injected with a saline solution; this was the control condition. The experimenters then had each participant sit in a room with another participant who, in reality, was an actor paid to create an emotional scene. In one version of the study, the experimenters told the participants that they would have to wait for 20 minutes before receiving a vision test, and that they could doodle on the papers left in the room. After the experimenter left the room, the actor began to behave in an excited fashion, playing basketball with crumpled up paper and playing with props that had been left in the room (e.g., hula-hoops). In other words, the actor was behaving euphorically (extremely happily). In other version of the study, the participants were asked to fill out questionnaires during the 20-minute delay period. The questions were quite personal in nature, and oftentimes mildly offensive (e.g., "With how many men (other than your father) has your mother had extramarital relationships? 4 and under ______, 5–9 ______, 10 and over ______"). After reading these questions, the actor became quite angry and tore up the sheet of paper while swearing.

The question the experimenters wanted to answer was whether the participant's response to the actor was affected by the cognitive explanation they had been given for the effects of adrenaline. Presumably, if you knew that you were going to have your heart rate increase due to a drug, then you would attribute any changes in your heart rate to the drug, not to the actor. In contrast, if you didn't know about the effects of adrenaline, then you would assume that your heart was racing because you were having an emotional response to the actor. As predicted, in both the euphoria and the anger conditions, the participants' emotional responses were influenced by their ability to explain their physical symptoms. When people understood the adrenaline was going to make their heart race, they reported smaller

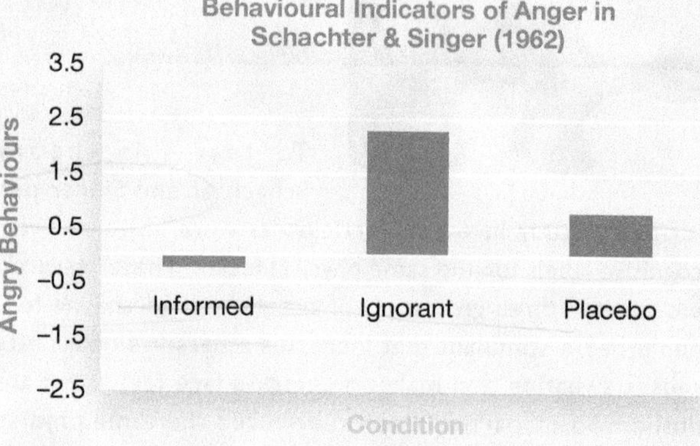

{FIG. 11.19} **Results from Schachter and Singer's Study** If participants knew that their racing heart was due to a drug injected by the experimenter, their emotional responses to the actor in the study were smaller. This graph depicts the number of angry statements and acts performed by participants in the angry condition of the experiment.

emotional reactions to the actor than when they were ignorant of the drug's effects (see Figure 11.19). This classic study provided the first evidence that our cognitive interpretation of an emotional event can have a dramatic effect on how we experience that situation.

Can we critically evaluate these findings?

One criticism of Schachter and Sutton's experiment is that it might not apply to the real world. Very few of us are given injections of adrenaline and made to watch someone acting in an emotionally extreme manner. In order to test the generalizability of these results, Donald Dutton and Arthur Aron (1974) from the University of British Columbia performed an innovative study that provided strong support for the two-factor theory. In this study, a female experimenter told male participants that she was investigating the effects of scenic attractions on creative expression. Participants were asked to cross a bridge before completing the Thematic Apperception Test, an open-ended test in which participants create stories to go along with a set of pictures. The independent variable of this study was the bridge the participants crossed. In the control condition, individuals crossed a solid wooden bridge that was approximately 3 metres above a small, shallow stream. In the experimental condition, individuals crossed the Capilano Canyon Suspension Bridge, which, as the name would suggest, crosses the Capilano Canyon near Vancouver. This bridge was 120 metres long and had a tendency to sway, which created the impression that one was about to fall over the edge. The bridge was 75 metres above rocks and rapids. Needless to say, the experimental condition would produce greater levels of emotional arousal. Interestingly, participants who were in the experimental condition included significantly more sexual imagery in their stories than did participants in the control condition. The explanation for this result is that the participants experienced stronger emotions when crossing the bridge, but misattributed the arousal to the pictures. Stronger support for this explanation came from an interesting addition to the study. After the participants had completed the Thematic Apperception Test, the female experimenter tore off a sheet of paper and wrote down "her number" (a fake phone number set up by the experimenters). Only 12.5% of the control participants phoned the woman's number; 50% of the experimental participants phoned the same woman. When participants experienced emotional arousal, they interpreted it as attraction to the experimenter. Keep this result in mind the next time someone wants to take you to a scary movie for a first date.

Bill Aron/PhotoEdit

An example of the Thematic Apperception Test stimuli used in the Capilano bridge experiment. Males in the high-arousal condition produced stories that included more sexual imagery than did participants in the control condition.

Why is this relevant?

Studies of the two-factor theory of emotions show us that although we do have rapid physiological responses to emotional situations, it is our *interpretation* of those events that leads to our emotional experiences. This obviously doesn't mean that you will never be upset. But, knowing that you *can* control how you interpret the emotional (or even the aggravating day-to-day) events of your life means that you can try to reduce the negative effects that emotional situations can have on you. So, ironically, a study involving an injection of adrenaline and the induction of angry emotions may help you become happier. It's up to you.

Alison Wright/Alamy

Quick Quiz 11.4b
Experiencing Emotions

UNDERSTAND ...

1 Which of the following is a weakness of the James-Lange theory of emotion?

- **A** Cognitive appraisal is not a component.
- **B** The theory does not address the subjective feeling of emotion.
- **C** The theory ignores the role of physiological reactions.
- **D** Awareness always precedes physiological reactions during emotions.

APPLY ...

2 Raj's mother tells him to smile more if he wants to feel better. She is applying the ________ theory of emotion.

- **A** Cannon-Bard
- **B** two-factor
- **C** James-Lange
- **D** slow/fast path

3 Nguyen is paralyzed from the neck down and does not experience the autonomic responses that usually accompany fear. Despite this injury, he continues to experience fear. Which theory of emotion is contradicted by this observation?

- **A** Cannon-Bard
- **B** Two-factor theory
- **C** James-Lange theory
- **D** Physiological theory

Answers can be found on page ANS-3.

Expressing Emotions

Are you a good liar? Can you tell when someone else is lying to you? How confident are you in your lie detection abilities? Although most of us believe we are quite good at spotting someone else's deception, the truth is that our accuracy is quite poor. In order to fix this problem, researchers attempted to create a lie detector test that measured the responses of our autonomic nervous system. This machine, a *polygraph,* measures whether heart rate and sweating increase when a person responds to different events or questions. Sudden changes in these levels suggest that the person is experiencing stress, and may be hiding something. However, after extensive testing, the polygraph was shown to be an inaccurate measure of lie detection; evidence gathered using this technique is not admissible in Canadian courts.

Watch Special Topics: Detecting Lies

Fortunately, psychologist Paul Ekman and his colleagues (Ekman et al., 1999) have developed a new technique for lie detection. Using videotapes of several research participants, Ekman and colleagues found that our faces give us away when we try to lie. Although we can fake an emotional expression within a fraction of a second, our real emotional response can be seen on our faces before this mask is in place. Ekman called these brief expressions of our true feelings *microexpressions,* and is training police officers to detect them in order to catch criminals. But, use your critical thinking skills for a moment: What do microexpressions really tell you? Yes, the face is expressing someone's inner state, and yes, it appears that a person is concealing how they are feeling. But, microexpressions cannot tell you *why* they are doing so. Instead, police officers have to make assumptions about the person's motives based on the microexpressions on his or her face.

This all sounds very dramatic, but we make assumptions about other people's feelings and motives all the time. It is quite rare for someone to tell you exactly how he or she feels. Instead, you observe other people's faces and body movements in order to make an educated guess about what thoughts and feelings are going on inside their heads. And, they do the same with you. In this section of the module, we will examine these processes, as well as how culture can influence how emotions are expressed and interpreted.

EMOTIONAL FACES AND BODIES Our primary method of communicating our emotional feelings is through our facial expressions. Each of these expressions has its own unique combination of muscle movements, such as the crinkling of muscles near the eye (*orbicularis oculi*) and the movement of the mouth (*zygomatic major*)

Watch IT Video: Basic Emotions

Paul Ekman, Ph.D./Paul Ekman Group, LLC

The meaning behind facial expressions changes with subtle modifications. For example, one version of smiling is genuine, while another is reserved for social graces. Genuine smiles, known as *Duchenne's smiles,* involve a crinkling of muscles at the corner of the eye. Fake smiles tend not to have this crinkling (unless you practise, which is mildly creepy). However, even if you learn to fake your emotions, your face can give you away. Psychologist Paul Ekman (pictured above) has shown that our real emotional responses appear on our faces for a fraction of a second before being covered up with our social mask.

Explore
Recognizing Facial Expressions of Emotions

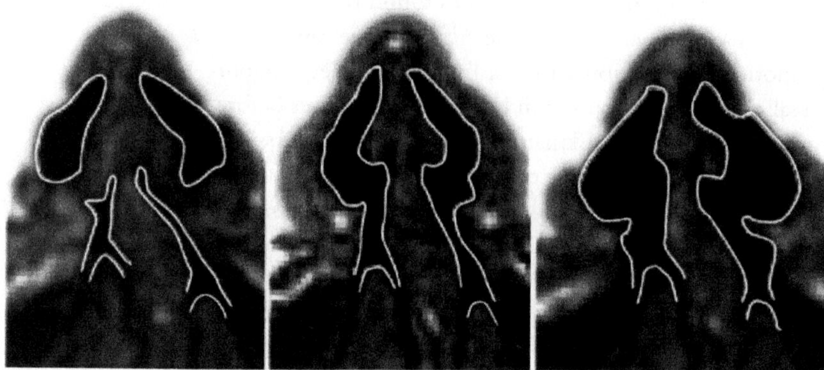

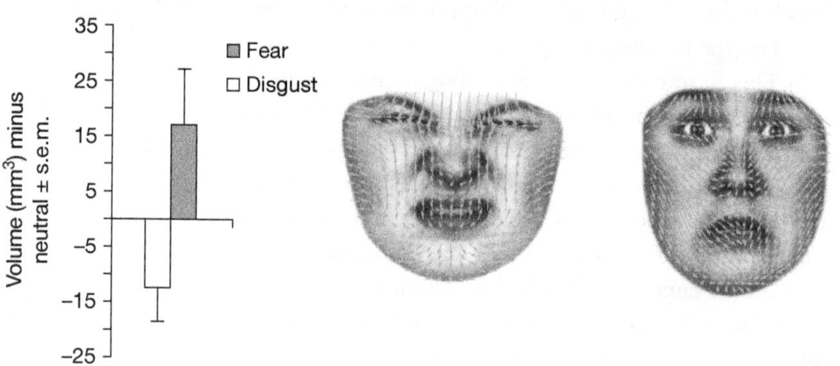

{FIG. 11.20} **Nostril Airflow Associated with Disgust and Fear** The images depict the opening of nasal passageways during the experience of disgust (left), a neutral emotion (centre), and fear (right). Note that the passageways are constricted during disgust, but opened wider during fear. This difference is reflected in the volume of airflow breathed in during each facial expression.

Source: Image from Susskind et al. (2008). *Nature Neuroscience, 11*, p. 846.

during smiling. But why are certain combinations of muscle movements associated with particular feelings? Although researchers are still trying to solve parts of this puzzle, researchers at the University of Toronto have highlighted some important characteristics of expressions of fear and disgust. Imagine changing a really stinky diaper—something even dung beetles would walk away from. The powerful odour feels like it's crawling up your nostrils. Your natural reaction is to make a disgusted face, which involves scrunching up your nose. This expression isn't just for show, however. It also reduces airflow into your nostrils, thus limiting the amount of the disgusting substance(s) that can enter your body (Chapman et al., 2009; Susskind & Anderson, 2008). This makes evolutionary sense, as some disgusting substances could threaten a person's health. In contrast, when we experience fear, our eyes open wide and we tend to inhale deeply (Susskind et al., 2008). This is likely due to the fact that when we're afraid, we are being threatened and therefore need to be able to take in as much information as possible in order to develop the best plan of action to keep ourselves safe. These results show that the strange facial geometry that makes up our emotional expressions is not random—our expressions have a purpose that will enhance our ability to survive (see Figure 11.20).

Importantly, these expressions appear all over the world, suggesting that they are an innate part of being human. Charles Darwin (1872) was the first person to recognize that facial expressions of emotion were universal. During his extensive travels, he noted that people from different cultures formed similar facial expressions and were able to understand the emotions of others. In the late 1960s, Paul Ekman performed cross-cultural studies that supported Darwin's hypothesis. Ekman and his colleagues photographed North Americans expressing six basic emotions—fear, happiness, disgust, anger, surprise, and sadness. They then travelled to an isolated region of Papua New Guinea (an island country north of Australia) to see if individuals who were unfamiliar with Caucasian faces could still recognize the emotions they displayed. Sure enough, tribesmen from the Fore ethnic group were able to accurately identify the emotions of the actors (Ekman & Friesen, 1969). The researchers then asked the tribesmen to make their own facial expressions for each emotion. As would be expected, research participants in the U.S. were able to recognize these emotions as well.

But, facial expressions aren't our only way of communicating our emotional states. Imagine that you are sitting across a table from someone that you find attractive. Or, what if you found the person annoying and really wished your friend would return from the washroom so that you could leave? Even if you didn't express any emotion with your face, your body would likely give away what you were feeling in both situations. *Body language* provides

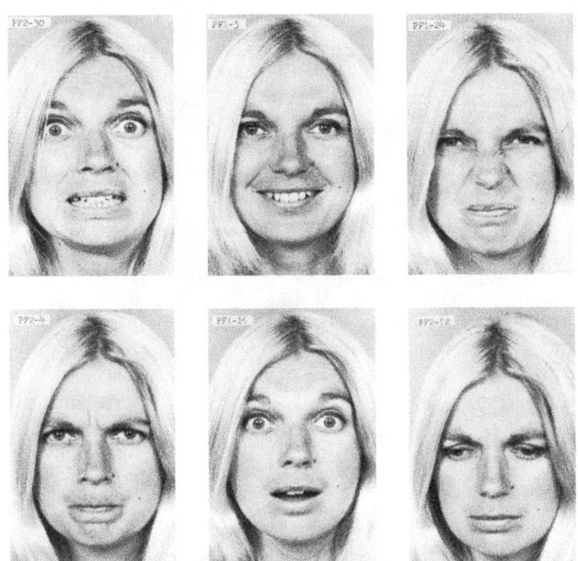

Paul Ekman Group, LLC

Individuals in isolated areas of the world were able to identify the emotions expressed by these faces, suggesting that these expressions are universal.

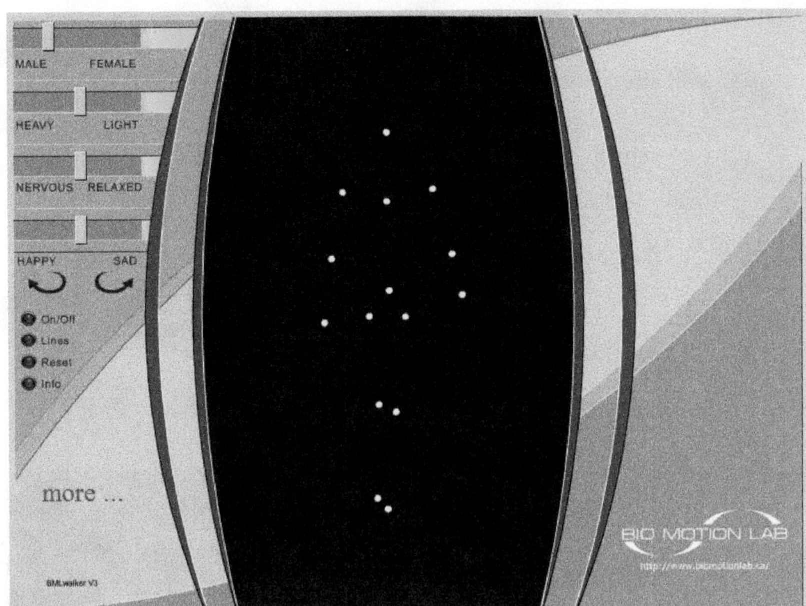

Biomotion Lab, Queen's University. Published in: Troje NF (2002) *Journal of Vision* 2:371–387. http://www.biomotionlab.ca/Demos/BMLwalker.html

Point-of-light technology can be used to infer a number of characteristics from a person's biological motion, including his or her emotional state. See http://www.biomotionlab.ca/Demos/BMLwalker.html.

almost as much emotional information as facial expressions; it also activated a number of similar brain areas (de Gelder & Hadjikhani, 2006). Researchers at Queen's University have created a novel method of examining body language and biological motion. Experimental stimuli are created by attaching motion capture sensors to different parts of people's bodies and having them make different movements such as walking. By averaging the types of movements across a number of individuals, it is possible to see the different body movement patterns of men and women, happy and sad people, and nervous or relaxed people (Troje 2002a, 2002b, 2008). Importantly, like the recognition of faces, detecting characteristics of body language and body motion appears to be universal, as many of the effects were observed in Mundurucu indigenous people in Amazonian regions of Brazil (Pica et al., 2011).

CULTURE, EMOTION, AND DISPLAY RULES Despite the universality of many aspects of emotion, people raised within a specific culture show characteristics that are specific to their region (Elfenbein & Ambady, 2003). Put simply, cultural groups have unique **emotional dialects**, or *variations across cultures in how common emotions are expressed*. For example, people from North America and from Gabon (a country in West Africa) both experience contempt. However, North Americans are more likely to lower their brow, and Gabonese people are more likely to raise their upper lip when expressing this emotion.

The situation or context is a major factor in determining when members of different cultures express specific emotions. **Display rules** *refer to the unwritten expectations we have regarding when it is appropriate to show a certain emotion*. Think about embarrassing situations. In North America, we tend to blush and look away when embarrassed. In Japan, on the other hand, people tend to smile. They aren't happy, but do their best not to show embarrassment. As another example, think about funerals. The British norm is to "keep a stiff upper lip" and to limit the emotions one shows. At Irish funerals, people are singing and very few beer mugs are empty. The people at both types of funerals are equally upset, but express their grief in different ways. Culture-specific display rules such as these can be found the world over and show us that we need to be cautious about overgeneralizing the meaning of different displays of emotions (Elfenbein et al., 2007).

In addition to trying to understand *which* emotion is being displayed, people also must attempt to figure out *why* a person is expressing that emotion. How this interpretation is performed seems to differ across cultures. Some cultures (e.g., Western countries) focus on the person expressing the emotion; people in other cultures (e.g., Asian countries) tend to also pay attention to those *around* the person expressing that emotion. So, do these different ways of looking at a situation translate into differences in how people of various cultures interpret emotions? To answer this question, psychologists asked students from both Western and Asian universities to judge the emotion of the central figure in the scenes depicted in Figure 11.21. Western students tended to focus on the facial expression of the central figure. Thus, if the individual was smiling, they would report he was happy, and they did not interpret his happiness with respect to how the surrounding

Watch Interview: Shinobu Kitayama

{FIG. 11.21} **How is the man in the middle of these pictures feeling?**

DDAA/ZOB WENN Photos/Newscom

Even in the most formal occasions, and even among royalty, it can be impossible to stifle emotions. Web surfers were thrilled to catch England's Prince Harry succumbing to a fit of laughter during this formal state ceremony. What could have been so funny?

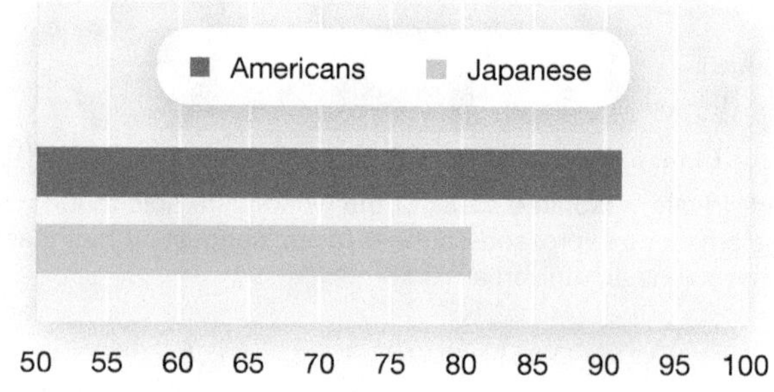

{FIG. 11.22} **East–West Differences in Interpreting Emotion** In comparison to Asian people, Westerners spend more time looking at the focal individual in a scene and interpret his or her emotions without reference to surrounding individuals (Masuda et al., 2008).

people appeared to feel. In contrast, Asian students interpreted the central figure's emotion in reference to what people in the background might be feeling (Masuda et al., 2008). So, in the right panel of Figure 11.21, a Westerner might report that the central figure was happy, while an Asian person might assume that the central figure was happy at the expense of the other people.

The tendency for Asian students to focus on people in the background was further confirmed in two different ways. First, Asian students were more accurate than Western students in remembering whether they saw specific individuals in the background. Also, using a device that tracks the eye movements of the participants, the researchers discovered that Asian students spent more time actually looking at the entire picture, rather than just the central character (Figure 11.22; Masuda et al., 2008). These results indicate that although the perception of emotional expressions is universal, the interpretation of why those expressions are being displayed is very culture-dependent.

Quick Quiz 11.4c

Expressing Emotions

KNOW ...

1. A(n) _______ refers to when it is appropriate to show a specific emotion.
   - **A** emotional dialect
   - **B** display rule
   - **C** context rule
   - **D** display dialect

UNDERSTAND ...

2. Which of the following is an example of an emotional dialect?
   - **A** Experiencing anger
   - **B** Avoiding laughter in church
   - **C** Raising one's chin in contempt
   - **D** Smiling as a sign of happiness

3. Which of the following is an example of a display rule?
   - **A** Biting one's lip in embarrassment
   - **B** Dropping one's jaw in surprise
   - **C** Suppressing anger during a debate
   - **D** Expressing happiness to a loved one

Answers can be found on page ANS-3.

Module Summary

Module 11.4

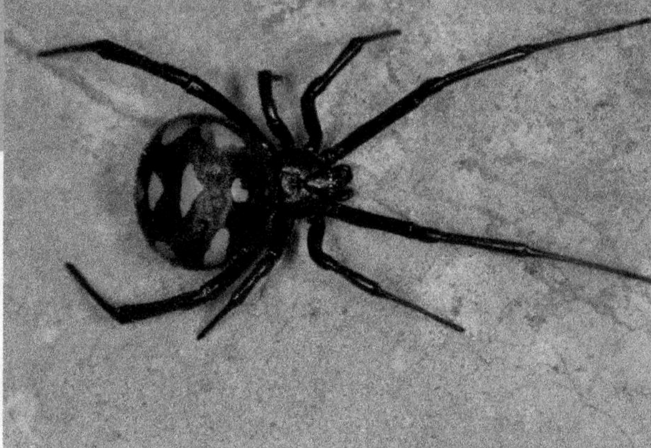
Matteo photos/Shutterstock

Now that you have read this module you should

KNOW ...

- ***The key terminology associated with emotion:***

amygdala (p. 478)
Cannon-Bard theory of emotion (p. 481)
display rules (p. 487)
emotion (p. 478)
emotional dialects (p. 487)
facial feedback hypothesis (p. 481)
James-Lange theory of emotion (p. 481)
two-factor theory (p. 483)

UNDERSTAND ...

- ***How the nervous system responds to emotions.*** Our biological responses to emotions occur in many different parts of our nervous system. Our brain has a rapid-response system involving the amygdala, which can fire within a few hundred milliseconds. This system triggers activity in other brain areas and influences how much attention a stimulus will receive. Our sympathetic nervous system also responds quickly. Soon after, brain and spinal cord areas related to movement become active in order to prepare us for a response. Finally, frontal lobe regions examine the situation to determine whether we should continue the emotional response or change our behaviour to conserve energy.

- ***Cultural similarities and differences in emotional expressions.*** Emotions such as fear, anger, happiness, sadness, surprise, and disgust appear to be human universals—all people experience them regardless of culture. At the same time, we cannot completely explain human emotions without references to cultural variation in the form of dialects and display rules.

APPLY ...

- ***Your knowledge of theories of emotion to new examples.*** Try this exercise. Spend 10 seconds looking at the Sanskrit figure on the left in **Figure 11.23** while slowly nodding your head. Now, spend about 10 seconds looking at the figure on the right while slowly moving your head from side to side.

  Now, imagine that you had to choose one image to display on the wall of your home. Which one would you choose—the one on the left or the one on the right?

{FIG. 11.23} **Application Activity**

What is important about this exercise is not which figure you chose; rather, it is the application of emotion theories to the problem. Consider the facial feedback study, and try to explain how the head movements could potentially influence one's preference for a symbol. This module provided examples of what researchers have found using similar techniques.

ANALYZE ...

- ***What purpose(s) do facial expressions serve?*** Facial expressions allow us to show the outside world what we are feeling. But, they serve other functions as well. For instance, facial expressions of disgust actually restrict the amount of air entering the body, possibly to protect us from contaminants. Expressions of fear serve to increase the amount of sensory information available to us, thus helping us to select the more appropriate response to that stimulus or situation.

Work the Scientific Literacy Model :: Understanding Emotion

1 What do we know about theories of emotion?

Figures 11.16 (p. 481) and **11.18** (p. 483) review the three major theories of emotion covered in this chapter. If you are trying to differentiate between them, it may help to remember that they vary in the order of the various responses. According to the James-Lange theory, if you saw an aggressive dog (stimulus), your heart would race (physiological response) and you would feel fear (emotional response). But according to the Cannon-Bard theory, you would see the aggressive dog (stimulus), and then experience a racing heart and a feeling of fear simultaneously (physiological and emotional response). In the cognitive category, Schachter-Singer's two-factor theory holds that the dog (stimulus) would cause your heart to race (physiological response); you would label that response "I am afraid" (cognitive response) and then feel fear (emotional response).

A common thread running through these theories is the agreement on the biological basis for emotional responding. The amygdala is a key player in the body's initial response to a stimulus, and specialized structures in the brain stimulate the body by sending messages to the autonomic nervous system **(Figure 11.14 on page 479)**

2 How can science help explain emotional responses?

As discussed on **page 481**, research on the facial feedback hypothesis supports the idea that our emotional responses are influenced by the bodily processes that precede them. When we smile, mood can be elevated and when we frown, mood can be dampened. Brain-imaging studies suggest that all of the emotions we feel regularly involve components of the nervous system, and that certain areas of the brain are more active depending on the emotion being experienced. There is also evidence that cells in our spinal cords show increased activity in response to emotions, suggesting that our bodies are preparing to respond.

Emotional experience is also influenced by cultural factors. Scientists have observed some emotions across all cultures, although emotional dialects and display rules alter how and when they are expressed.

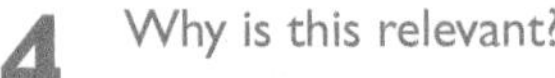

Dudarev Mikhail/Shutterstock

3 Can we critically evaluate claims about emotional responses?

While the facial feedback hypothesis provides some support for the James-Lange theory of emotion, the fact that some emotions can be experienced in the absence of facial expression seems inconsistent with the theory. Also, research investigating the usefulness of a polygraph, a "lie detector test" that relies on responses from the autonomic nervous system, suggests that physiological responses do not always predict emotional responses. Finally, the fact that patients with damage to the spinal cord can still experience some emotions despite not having much feedback from the body suggests that this feedback might not be *necessary* for emotional experiences (although it may still play a supporting role in these experiences). These results imply that the James-Lange theory might only be a part of the full explanation for how we feel emotions.

4 Why is this relevant?

Watch the accompanying video excerpt on the theories of motivation and emotion. You can access the video at MyPsychLab or by clicking the play button in the centre of your eText. If your instructor assigns this video as a homework activity, you will find additional content to help you in MyPsychLab. You can also view the video by using your smart phone and the QR code below, or you can go to the YouTube link provided.

After you have read this chapter and watched the video, imagine you are walking alone late at night and hear footsteps behind you. Think about your emotional reaction to this situation. Consider the major theories of emotion: James-Lange theory, Cannon-Bard theory, and Schachter-Singer theory. From the perspective of these major theories of emotion, describe how each would predict the sequence of events that would occur as you experience a reaction to this situation.

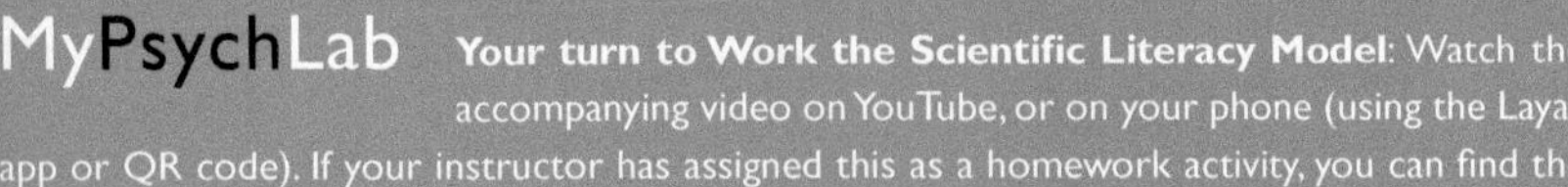

MyPsychLab **Your turn to Work the Scientific Literacy Model**: Watch the accompanying video on YouTube, or on your phone (using the Layar app or QR code). If your instructor has assigned this as a homework activity, you can find the video clip and additional content at MyPsychLab. Answer the questions that accompany the video clip to test your understanding.

youtube.com/workthemodel

SCAN WITH LAYAR

12

Personality

ollyy/Shutterstock

Patrick Sheandell O' Carroll/Glow Images

Module **12.1**

Contemporary Approaches to Personality

Learning Objectives

After reading this module you should

KNOW . . .	UNDERSTAND . . .	APPLY . . .	ANALYZE . . .
The key terminology associated with contemporary approaches to personality	The behaviourist and social-cognitive views of personality	The Big Five personality traits to understand your own personality	The personality roots of violence and prejudice The relative roles of personality traits and psychological and physical states in determining behaviour

What does your living space say about you? That alphabetized bookshelf and bathroom full of grooming products suggest conscientiousness. The photos of Mount Everest and major European cities reveal an openness to experiencing new and exciting things. The three pet cats and extensive DVD collection? Possibly signs of an introverted homebody.

It might sound like we are just making assumptions here, but scientific research backs up the notion that personality can be measured by examining the details of our dwellings. Psychologist Sam Gosling and his students have, with permission, closely scrutinized people's offices and bedrooms for clues about their personality (Gosling, 2008; Gosling et al., 2002). Teams of seven or eight observers entered people's bedrooms and offices and rated the personality types of the occupants with a standardized personality test. Not only did the observers reach close consensus on many measures of personality, but their ratings also matched up with how the occupants rated their *own* personality.

If you look around your own room, some parts of it may symbolize the "core" of who you are, whereas others reflect less "deep," more superficial details about yourself. For example, your book collection and most treasured belongings may be very revealing, but what about the clothing strewn all over the floor? Does it mean that you are a lazy slob? Or that you are ambitious and live a busy life? Or simply that you are enjoying the freedom of not living with your parents? Which is more appropriate as an explanation: the dispositional (i.e., rooted in the kind of person you are) or the situational (i.e., external, circumstantial factors)? A key challenge for personality psychologists is figuring out how our personalities and circumstances work together in shaping our behaviour. This raises many important questions, to be addressed later in this module.

Focus Questions

 What are the basic traits that make up human personality?

 To what extent are our preferences, thoughts, and behaviours determined by situational factors versus more stable personality traits?

What is personality? Psychologists describe **personality** as *a characteristic pattern of thinking, feeling, and behaving that is unique to each individual, and remains relatively consistent over time and situations.* Psychologists have long searched for a theory of personality that would describe and explain how people develop these patterns. One major challenge for the field has been to develop measures of people's personalities, which has resulted in two broad approaches to personality measurement: the *idiographic approach* and the *nomothetic approach.*

When you try to figure out the people you know very well, you probably intuitively adopt an **idiographic approach**, focusing on *creating detailed descriptions of a specific person's unique personality characteristics.* So, when you are "trying to figure yourself out," trying to understand why your cousin Bobby is so weird, or why your friend Alexis keeps making such terrible relationship choices, you are taking an idiographic approach.

Idiographic approaches are helpful not only for understanding yourself and your social world, but also can be applied to the full range of human experience, from the most disturbed to the healthiest and most highly functioning individuals. For example, criminal profilers may focus on a detailed study of a serial killer in order to help police in their investigation. At the other extreme, Abraham Maslow wanted to understand the people who had lived up to their fullest potential, who were in Maslow's terms, "self-actualized." Accordingly, Maslow performed detailed analyses of the biographies of famous people who were widely regarded as being wise and fully functioning (Maslow, 1970). Maslow's findings launched decades of work trying to uncover what makes human beings thrive and develop to their maximum potential.

In contrast, psychologists who take a **nomothetic approach** *examine personality in large groups of people, with the aim of making generalizations about personality structure.* Rather than trying to understand a specific person, psychologists taking a nomothetic approach may want to understand the factors that predict certain behaviours across people in general.

There are many examples of nomothetic research in Canadian universities. Dr. Gordon Flett at York University has examined personality predictors of alcohol, drug use, and depression in university students (e.g., Flett et al., 2009; Goldstein et al., 2009; Goldstein & Flett, 2009). Dr. Lawrence Walker at the University of British Columbia has sought to identify the "moral personality," seeking the personality factors that predict courage and heroism (Walker & Frimer, 2007; Walker et al., 2010). Dr. Jacob Hirsh at the Rotman School of Management in Toronto has examined the personality predictors of pro-environmental motivations (Hirsh, 2010; Hirsh & Dolderman, 2007). Taking a nomothetic approach allows psychologists to examine what types of people are more or less likely to engage in certain behaviours, which is an important step toward being able to change behaviours of societal importance, such as substance abuse or energy conservation.

The key to nomothetic research is to identify the important personality traits that are related to whatever it is that you are interested in understanding.

Explore
Approaches to Personality

The Trait Perspective

So, who are you anyway? What kind of person are you?

Try to answer these questions. Seriously—stop reading right now, take out a piece of paper, and try to describe the kind of person you are. Write down "I am . . ." and complete the sentence 10 times.

Okay, now take a look at your list. If you're like most people, your list probably has quite a few personality traits—words like extraverted or introverted, funny, ambitious, lazy, anxious, and easy-going. A **personality trait** describes *a person's habitual patterns of thinking, feeling, and behaving*; how that person is "most of the time." Trait descriptors are useful as short-cuts to understanding people. Traits summarize a great deal of information about a person, and help to predict how that person will behave across a range of different situations. For example, an "extraverted" person is more likely to be comfortable in social situations, go to parties, and have a large number of friends than someone who is "introverted."

As you can imagine, many different traits could be used to describe people, such as "shy," "cheerful," "outgoing," and "adventurous." The first systematic attempt to identify all possible traits (in the English language) was made in the 1930s by Gordon Allport, who tallied nearly 18 000 English words that could be used to describe an individual's physical and psychological attributes (Allport & Odbert, 1936). (Perhaps Allport himself would be described as "patient," "methodical," and "weird to talk to at a party.") Allport then developed a theory of personality structure by organizing these words into traits, launching a strong trend in personality psychology that continues to this day—attempting to identify and measure the key personality traits.

Watch
Classic Footage of Gordon Allport on Personality Traits

Watch
Thinking Like a Psychologist: Measuring Personality

To accomplish this, trait researchers have devised a variety of personality tests. Some tests present a list of trait labels and ask an individual to rate how well the trait describes him or her. Other measures present specific behaviours that represent traits. Items on these kinds of personality tests might, for example, ask you to rate your agreement with statements such as "I like to meet new people" to assess how outgoing you are. These approaches have spawned countless "personality scales." Some, like the ones used in psychology research and described later in this chapter, are rigorously evaluated. Others, like the ones you find in popular magazines, are

((Listen
Psychology in the News: Theories of Personality—Personality Tests

Watch
In the Real World: Popular Personality Assessments

Explore
The Five Factor Model

of questionable value. For example, *Cosmopolitan* regularly includes "personality scales" in which you can discover all sorts of things about yourself; while it is possible that *Cosmo* has a team of highly qualified psychologists rigorously designing these scales, we do recommend that you not base your life decisions on your results to the "Are You Enough of a Bad Girl?" quiz.

It is clear that people love to know "what kind of person they are." However, it is often easier to make people believe that you are measuring their personality than it is to actually measure it. In fact, it is remarkably easy for people to be convinced that a personality profile describes them well. Surprisingly, this can occur even when the profile is patently false and was not generated to describe them at all. This is popularly known as "the Barnum effect," after the circus showman P. T. Barnum, due to his apparent statement "there's a sucker born every minute." (Ironically, P. T. Barnum never actually said this quote, which is widely attributed to him [Saxon, 1989].) The Barnum effect harkens back to the late 1940s, when psychologist Bertram Forer gave research participants a personality test and then generated a description of subjects' personalities, which they believed was based on their test responses. Participants found the profiles very convincing; when asked to rate how well the profile described them, on a scale ranging from 0 (very poor) to 5 (excellent), the average rating was an impressive 4.26. Astonishingly, however, every participant was given the exact same personality description (Forer, 1949)!

As you can see from the profile Forer used below, the statements were fairly general and most could apply to most people, at least some of the time. It is easy for people to see themselves in statements such as "While you have some personality weaknesses, you are generally able to compensate for them," and of course, just about everybody tends to be extraverted *sometimes* and introverted other times, or to have unrealistic goals. The Barnum effect may be a key reason why personality tests of questionable validity are so widely believed, as well as horoscopes, astrologers, psychics, and the like.

You have a great need for other people to like and admire you. You have a tendency to be critical of yourself. You have a great deal of unused capacity that you have not turned to your advantage. While you have some personality weaknesses, you are generally able to compensate for them. Your sexual adjustment has presented problems for you. Disciplined and self-controlled outside, you tend to be worried and insecure inside. At times you have serious doubts as to whether you have made the right decision or done the right thing. You prefer a certain amount of change and variety and become dissatisfied when hemmed in by restrictions and limitations. You pride yourself as an independent thinker and do not accept others' statements without satisfactory proof. You have found it unwise to be too frank in revealing yourself to others. At times you are extroverted, affable, sociable, while at other times you are introverted, wary, and reserved. Some of your aspirations tend to be pretty unrealistic. Security is one of your major goals in life.

In contrast, rigorous empirical research over the past several decades has narrowed the many potential personality traits into a small number of factors. The statistical technique called **factor analysis** is *used to group items that people respond to similarly*; for instance, the terms *friendly*, *warm*, and *kind* have similar meanings, and can be grouped in a cluster, referred to as a *factor*.

THE FIVE FACTOR MODEL Using factor analysis, psychologist Raymond Cattell (1946) narrowed the list of key personality traits to 16, thereby simplifying and standardizing the number of dimensions psychologists needed to describe the composition of personality. Forty years later, McCrae and Costa (1987) created the **Five Factor Model**, *a trait-based theory of personality based on the finding that personality can be described using five major dimensions*; this model has become the most popular trait-based approach for academic personality researchers, and has been cited in hundreds of research articles.

To understand the Big Five traits, consider what characteristics are associated with people high and low on that trait. These are the "kinds of people" described by each trait (see Figure 12.1):

Openness: Individuals high in openness (high Os) are the dreamers and creatives; they tend to be more "open" to new things (no big surprise there . . .)—ideas, opinions, and perspectives that differ from theirs, and new ways of seeing a problem that they had not considered. They are more open to new experiences, tending to be curious and appreciative of art and unusual ideas. As a result, they often hold beliefs that would be considered "unconventional." High Os are also likely to think more abstractly and to be more sensitively aware of their emotions.

Individuals low in openness (low Os) are the defenders of the system, preferring the conventional, the tried and true. They avoid the unknown and find security in the known. They prefer things that are tangible rather than symbolic, priding themselves on being "practical." Low Os prefer things to be straightforward and generally dislike subtlety and complexity. They approach new information somewhat defensively—preferring to learn about things they already believe in, and paying less attention to information that challenges their perspective. Low Os tend to be resistant to change and suspicious of their emotions, placing more emphasis on the attempt to be rational and logical.

Conscientiousness: Highly conscientious people (high Cs) are the organizers—efficient, self-disciplined, and dependable. They are the ones who meet deadlines, plan ahead to achieve their goals, and are comfortable with schedules and lists, although at the expense of being flexible and spontaneous at times. High Cs are great

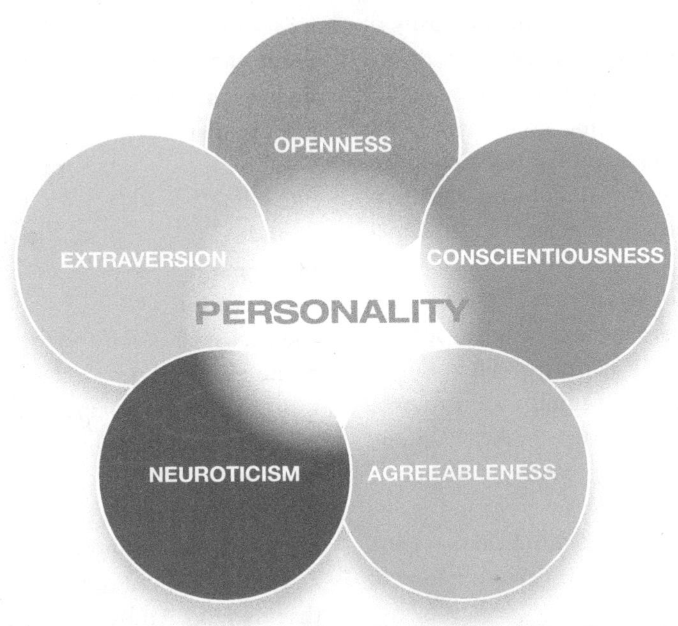

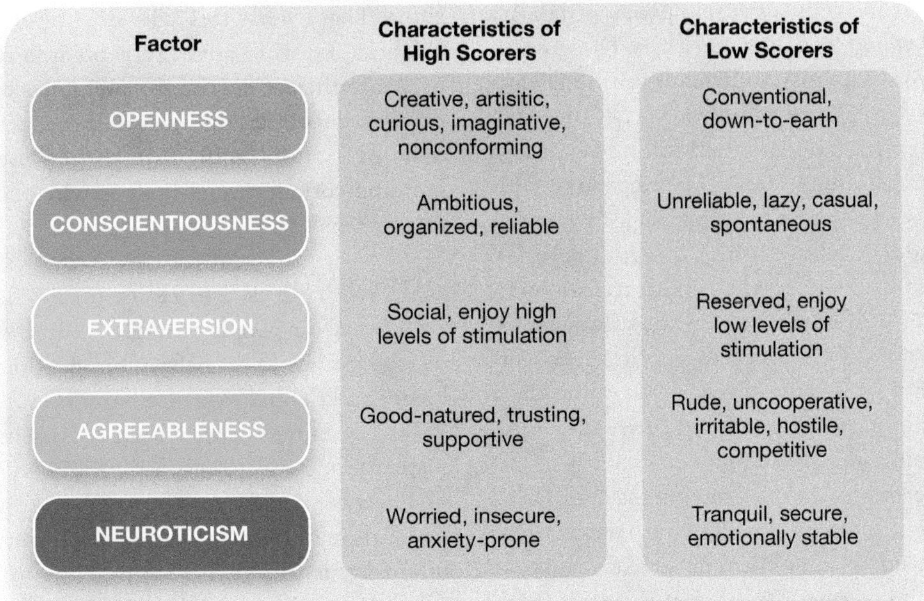

Factor	Characteristics of High Scorers	Characteristics of Low Scorers
OPENNESS	Creative, artisitic, curious, imaginative, nonconforming	Conventional, down-to-earth
CONSCIENTIOUSNESS	Ambitious, organized, reliable	Unreliable, lazy, casual, spontaneous
EXTRAVERSION	Social, enjoy high levels of stimulation	Reserved, enjoy low levels of stimulation
AGREEABLENESS	Good-natured, trusting, supportive	Rude, uncooperative, irritable, hostile, competitive
NEUROTICISM	Worried, insecure, anxiety-prone	Tranquil, secure, emotionally stable

{FIG. 12.1} **The Big Five Personality Dimensions** A widely used measure of personality is the NEO-PI-R. Individuals rate themselves on multiple questions that reflect the traits of openness, conscientiousness, extraversion, agreeableness, and neuroticism. (To help you remember the Big Five, note that the first letters of the traits spell out OCEAN.)

employees and students, tending to achieve more in their careers due to their achievement orientation and tendency to get things done on time. They also live longer, perhaps because they are more likely to engage in the positive health behaviours (e.g., eating well and exercising regularly) that the less conscientious among us never quite get around to doing. . . .

Low Cs are the easy-going ones, fun to hang out with, but not so great as collaborators on a project. Low Cs tend to be disorganized, careless with details, and have difficulty meeting deadlines. Although they may want to perform well at a task, they have difficulty disciplining themselves enough to actually get things done. Low Cs feel uncomfortable with schedules and detailed plans, preferring to "be in the moment." Although low Cs suffer somewhat in life due to their lack of self-discipline, they benefit by not being as stressed about details and able to still enjoy themselves when things don't go according to plan.

Extraversion: Extraverts (high Es) are the socializers and sensation seekers. They are comfortable in more stimulating environments, and thus love the company of others, being seen as outgoing and energetic. Extraverts tend to be more assertive, talkative, and enthusiastic, preferring high levels of stimulation and excitement much of the time. They are fun to be around, but sometimes take things too far, as their love of stimulation puts them at higher risk for dangerous activities such as substance abuse.

Introverts (low Es) are the quiet ones. Although they like social contact, introverts also need time for solitary activities and "recharging their batteries." They can be overwhelmed by the high levels of stimulation preferred by extraverts, so while the extraverts party it up and compete for all the attention, the introverts sit on the couch in the corner having great conversations with a friend or two. Introverts tend to be more cautious and reserved, and they are great when you need someone to really talk to.

Agreeableness: If highly agreeable people (high As) were dogs, they would be golden retrievers. These warm and friendly people are easy to like, easy to be friends with, easy to have as part of your group. They are kind, compassionate, empathetic, and tend to be helpful and altruistic. They place strong value on getting along with people and are generally willing to put their own interests aside in order to please others or avoid conflict. Agreeable people are the ones who make it really hard to choose what movie to watch, because they always want to know what movie YOU want to watch. . . . As you might expect, they make great team members, but their leadership skills often suffer because they are unwilling to assert their opinion.

Low As are the type who "put themselves first." They value being authentic more than pandering to other people's needs, making them more likely to assert their opinions and engage in conflict if necessary. Low As suffer socially somewhat, as they tend to be seen as cold, unfriendly, uncooperative, and unkind. They are often skeptical of other people's motives, and tend to be less trusting of human nature in general. As you might expect, low As don't experience much empathy, and tend to be self-interested rather than altruistic.

Neuroticism: To be called "neurotic" is not generally considered a compliment. Indeed, people high in neuroticism (high Ns) are often difficult to deal with, as their emotional volatility and general tendency to experience negative emotions makes them not much fun to be around. High Ns tend to be quite sensitive and experience strong reactions to stressful situations; as a result, they often interpret situations as overly threatening and magnify small frustrations into major problems. When they experience negative emotions, they have difficulty relaxing and "letting go" of their negative feelings, which makes these feelings persist, and persist, and persist. As a result of their difficulties regulating negative emotions, high Ns are the most vulnerable to anxiety and depressive disorders.

Low Ns, on the other hand, are the prototypical mentally healthy people. They tend to be secure and confident, let go of negative emotions easily, and are highly resilient to stress. Rather than "blowing things out of proportion," the low Ns take the good with the bad, and deal with problems as they arise, but feel no need to create problems where there aren't any, or to obsessively look for problems until they find them. Low Ns are excellent at managing their emotions, and are regarded by others as "stable."

Taken together, the Big Five factors are extremely useful for understanding people's behaviours, thoughts, and emotions, and predicting why people do the things that they do. And that's what we really want to know, right? That's what this whole psychology business is all about, figuring out why people do the things they do. Nevertheless, despite the usefulness of the Big Five, psychologists often find that there are other personality traits, outside of the Big Five, that are useful for understanding certain things, such as why people do things that are "evil."

BEYOND THE BIG FIVE: THE PERSONALITY OF EVIL? Most people struggle when they think about truly negative human behaviours: prejudice, hatred, violence, child abuse, wartime atrocities, the Holocaust, 9/11. The more horror we allow ourselves to contemplate, the more we must ask *why?* Why do people do such terrible things?

Following World War II, such questions were a major focus in personality psychology, as the world wanted to understand the rise of fascism and Hitler's ability to mobilize millions of people to carry out his plans of destruction. Early research by Theodore Adorno suggested that a key personality type, the *authoritarian personality*, was a big piece of the puzzle. Authoritarians were theorized to be rigid and dogmatic in their thinking, to separate their social world into strict categories of *Us* and *Them*, and then to believe strongly in the superiority of *Us* and the inferiority of *Them*. As a result, authoritarians were more likely to endorse and engage in prejudice and violence, particularly toward people in the "them" category (Adorno et al., 1950). At first glance, this sounds like people low in openness, but over the past several decades, personality researchers have discovered important personality traits that extend the Five Factor Model and help to shed light on the problem of human "evil." Three lines of research (all by Canadian researchers, incidentally) are particularly important.

Honesty–Humility First, Michael Ashton at Brock University and his colleagues have developed the **HEXACO model of personality**, *a six-factor theory that generally replicates the five factors of the FFM and adds one additional factor: Honesty–Humility*. Individuals scoring highly on this factor (high HHs) tend to be sincere, honest, faithful, and modest, whereas those with low scores (low HHs) are deceitful, greedy, and pompous (Ashton & Lee, 2007). Whereas high HHs are more likely to perform altruistic, pro-social behaviours, low HHs harbour more selfish, anti-social, and violent tendencies (Ashton & Lee, 2008; deVries & van Kampen, 2010). Low HHs are also more likely to be materialistic and to "do whatever it takes" to get what they want, using flattery to manipulate others, being more willing to break the rules, even being unfaithful to relationship partners (Bourdage et al., 2007). Interestingly, low HHs feel a strong sense of self-importance and a feeling of entitlement, like they deserve to have their desires fulfilled.

The Dark Triad One important set of personality factors that are related to Honesty–Humility has been labelled the Dark Triad by researchers at the University of British Columbia. The **Dark Triad** *refers to three traits—Machiavellianism, psychopathy, and narcissism—that describe a person who is socially destructive, aggressive, dishonest, and likely to commit harm in general* (Paulhus & Williams, 2002).

Machiavellianism is a tendency to use people and to be manipulative and deceitful. Individuals scoring high in Machiavallianism tend to lack respect for others and focus predominantly on their own self-interest. As a result, they treat others as means to their own desired ends and approach relationships strategically, in terms of "what's in it for me?"

Psychopathy, on the other hand, is a general tendency toward having shallow emotional responses. Thus, individuals scoring high in psychopathy veer toward highly stimulating activities and tend to feel little empathy for others. They often get a thrill out of conflict, exerting control, or even harming others, and feel little remorse for their actions.

Narcissism reflects an egotistical preoccupation with self-image and an excessive focus on self-importance. The extreme narcissist is "full of himself" (or herself). In Greek legend, the hunter Narcissus was filled with excessive pride and adoration toward himself. This was his fatal flaw, however, as he was so transfixed by his own gaze reflecting in a pool of water that he died by the poolside, still staring at his reflection. Narcissists can often be charming, but are difficult to have as relationship partners because they tend to always put themselves first rather than considering their partner's needs.

Considering these traits separately yields some important insights; for example, people high on different traits may become aggressive for different reasons. One study showed that high Ps became aggressive when they felt physically threatened, but high Ns responded aggressively when their self-esteem was threatened. High Ms responded to neither type of threat; it seems the Machiavellian individuals only become aggressive when it serves their goals (Jones & Paulhus, 2010).

Considering all three traits together is important because they strongly predict anti-social tendencies; people characterized by all three of the Dark Triad traits are substantially more likely to commit harm to others, having little empathy or other constraints to prevent them from doing so.

Right-Wing Authoritarianism In a third line of research, Bob Altemeyer at the University of Manitoba has identified **Right-Wing Authoritarianism (RWA)** *as a highly problematic set of personality characteristics that involve three key tendencies:*

1. *obeying orders and deferring to the established authorities in a society;*
2. *supporting aggression against those who dissent or differ from the established social order; and*
3. *believing strongly in maintaining the existing social order* (Altemeyer, 1996).

At the centre of the RWA personality is a strong tendency to think in dogmatic terms, where, metaphorically speaking, everything is either black or white, with no shades of grey. RWAs tend to hold strong beliefs and are highly resistant to changing them. In order to maintain their rigid beliefs, RWAs process information in highly biased ways, ignoring or rejecting evidence that contradicts their views and uncritically accepting evidence that is consistent with their beliefs. As a result, RWAs rarely encounter information that challenges their views, leading them to hold their opinions with complete certainty (Altemeyer, 1996).

A person high in RWA is likely to be seething with prejudice. Because RWAs see "their way" as right, they tend to judge people harshly who have different perspectives. Drawing strict boundaries between social groups, they see a world of *Us* vs. *Them*. This supports strong prejudices against people in the "them" category—people who are members of cultural "outgroups" (see Module 13.2). As a result, RWAs are likely to advocate a harsh stance—social rejection, aggression, even arrest and detention—toward people who deviate from the established social order, such as political activists, feminists, atheists, and members of ethnic minorities (Goodman & Moradi, 2008; Haddock et al., 1993; Narby et al., 1993). High RWAs also play problematic roles as citizens of a society. Given their unquestioning acceptance of authority figures, they are more likely to agree with unethical decisions made by leaders (Son Hing et al., 2007). They also are more likely to have positive attitudes toward corrupt governments and the violation of civil liberties by the state, such as the use of illegal wiretaps (Altemeyer, 1996).

As a result of these tendencies, high RWA individuals were likely instrumental in the rise of fascism that led to World War II, and will likely play important roles in the future helping to maintain repressive dictatorships, problematic business practices, and unhealthy family structures. According to Altemeyer, the various "shortfalls of authoritarian thinking eminently qualify them to follow a would-be dictator. As Hitler is reported to have said, 'What good fortune for those in power that people do not think'" (Altemeyer, 2006, p. 75).

WORKING THE SCIENTIFIC LITERACY MODEL

Right-Wing Authoritarianism at the Group Level

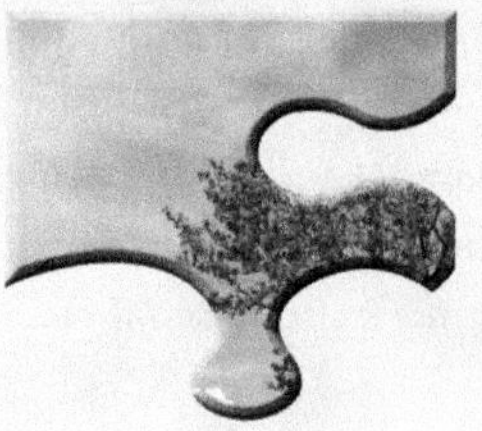

What do we know about RWA?

As we discussed above, personality researchers have identified RWA as a cluster of characteristics that make society a less warm and friendly place, being related to generally harmful tendencies such as holding prejudiced views against other groups and an excessive and closed-minded allegiance to societal conventions plus a tendency to obey orders unquestioningly.

One would expect that the more RWAs in a society, the more intolerance and inter-group aggression will plague that society. However, most of this research has focused on *individuals*. But what happens when RWAs get into groups?

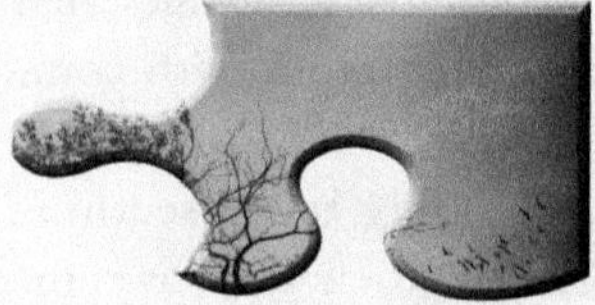

How can science determine how RWA affects groups?

In one fascinating and highly disturbing study, Altemeyer selected high and low RWAs to play a complex role-playing simulation of the Earth's future, called the Global Change Game. This game is generally played by 50–70 people who are organized into groups that represent different regions of the world; these groups then make decisions about how their region behaves on the international stage. For example, participants decide how their region will deal with problems such as environmental degradation, poverty, overpopulation, and military threats. The simulated conditions of the Earth change depending on the actions of the players, thus providing a realistic simulation of the challenges of governance in the international community.

In order to test how RWAs play the game, Altemeyer ran through the game two times, once with 67 individuals who scored very low on the RWA scale, and once with 68 people who scored very high. Each simulation covered 40 years of time into Earth's future. The results were astonishing.

In the low RWA group, there were no wars or military build-up over the 40-year time period. Instead, regions steadily downsized their militaries and diverted the money into humanitarian and environmental projects. They also collectively resolved challenges through international meetings and cooperation. At one point, a global crisis occurred due to a threat to the Earth's ozone layer; players responded by holding a group meeting, and agreeing to make large investments in technology development so that they could collectively solve the problem. By the end of the game, food, health services, and jobs were provided for almost all people on Earth, resulting in a peaceful, stable world.

In the high RWA group, players tended to interpret the actions of others as aggressive, and responded in kind. Militaries quickly grew and war ensued, leading to a global nuclear war that killed every person on the planet. At this point, the players were given a second chance to play, starting at a point prior to the nuclear war. Despite having the chance to learn from their earlier mistakes, the players nevertheless were incapable of getting along with each other. When the ozone crisis occurred, no international summit was called and no region except Europe took action to avert the crisis. Instead of cooperation, players remained suspicious of each other and rapidly developed their militaries. One major military conflict killed 400 million people, and players poured so much money into military expenses that devastating social and environmental problems were never dealt with. At the end of the 40-year period, the world was again divided into armed camps on the brink of all-out war.

Obviously, this simulation suggests that high vs. low RWAs may have a huge impact on the way that our society behaves as a whole.

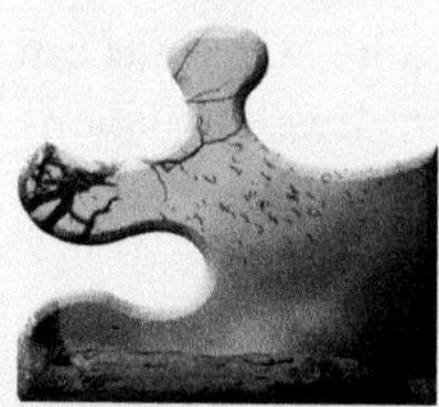

Can we critically evaluate this research?

There are several methodological limitations to this study that should be taken into consideration when evaluating the findings. First, there are external validity concerns; for example, playing a game with no real consequences does not necessarily indicate how people would respond in a real-life situation. It is possible that in a real situation, people would be more sensitive to the consequences of their actions, and would not be so willing to risk human lives. Furthermore, the simulations were only performed on one night with each group; therefore, results could have been due to chance factors, such as particular individuals having a strong impact on the outcomes. Also, because only university students participated in the study, the results may not generalize to the rest of the population.

Why is this relevant?

This research illustrates the highly destructive impact that authoritarian personalities can have in group settings, and sounds a clear bell of warning in the 21st century. We are living in a time in which our world faces unprecedented challenges requiring international cooperation, yet this is also a time when intolerance and intergroup hostilities are rampant and when ideological fundamentalism and fanaticism are having a major impact on politics in many countries. Understanding the potential roots of intergroup hostility in individuals' personalities is urgently needed at this time, as it may help us to understand how best to counteract such tendencies and to recognize the role they may play on the political stage.

LilKar/Shutterstock

PSYCH @

Test Yourself!

Personality researchers have developed online tests of the personality attributes discussed in this module so that you can learn more about your own personality tendencies. Go to MyLab to find links for personality tests online!

PERSONALITY TRAITS OVER THE LIFE SPAN Have you ever looked back on something you wrote several years ago, perhaps in your diary, and wondered, "Who was that person who wrote these things?" Or have you ever considered someone you once dated and wondered, "Who was I when I chose to date that person? It certainly wasn't 'me'!" One of the most fascinating issues in personality psychology is whether we are the same people as we get older, or whether our fundamental personalities tend to change.

A mountain of research from different areas within psychology has revealed considerable stability in our personalities. In fact, given the large genetic contribution to personality factors, our personalities start even before we are born (Plomin & Caspi, 1999). Research on monozygotic and dizygotic twins in Canada, Germany, and Japan found clear genetic contributions to personality structure that were similar across these different cultures (Yamagata et al., 2006). Thus, our genes predispose us to forming a certain lifelong personality.

In child development studies, researchers have found that infants possess different *temperaments* right from birth, suggesting that the seeds of our personalities are present right from the start. Temperaments are relatively rudimentary; infants do not have the same complexity of personalities as adults, but they do vary on characteristics such as activity level, mood, attention span, and distractibility (Rothbart & Bates, 2006; Thomas & Chess, 1977). As most parents of more than one child can attest, kids come "hard-wired" to be a certain way. Some infants are generally active and happy, whereas others are more tranquil, and still others are easily upset. So, if you happen to be a parent of an easy-going child and you think, "This parenting thing isn't so hard," don't pat yourself on the back too much and walk around judging those exhausted-looking parents who "must be doing something wrong." Your next kid might just show you that you had it easy the first time. And if you're a parent pulling your hair out with your chronically distressed child who seems impossible to deal with, don't judge yourself too harshly (or listen to the grandparents who tell you that they never had such problems with their babies!). Remind yourself that infants have different temperaments and your power as a parent is small compared to the power of their genes.

Thus, temperament seems to represent an innate, biological foundation upon which personality is built. This, combined with the genetic research, suggests that personality traits should be stable over time. To some extent, research confirms that this is the case: Infant temperament predicts the adult personality traits of neuroticism, extraversion, and conscientiousness (Evans & Rothbart, 2007).

One amazing study that followed the same children from age 3 until adulthood showed that temperament at 3 years of age was strongly predictive of behavioural tendencies, personality, and life outcomes many years later (Caspi, 2000). Three main temperaments were identified: *well-adjusted* (capable of self-control, confident, not overly upset by new people or situations); *under-controlled* (impulsive, restless, distractible, emotionally volatile); and *inhibited* (socially uncomfortable, fearful, easily upset by strangers). Just over 10 years later, children of different temperaments had developed quite different behaviour patterns. The *under-controlled* children (relative to the other groups) had become much more likely to engage in *externalizing behaviours* (fighting, bullying, lying, disobeying) and somewhat more *internalizing behaviours* (worrying, being fussy, crying easily). The *inhibited* children had also developed strong *internalizing* behaviour patterns. By age 18, their emerging adult personalities were reflections of their temperaments at age 3. By age 21, the formerly *under-controlled* children were showing serious relationship difficulties. Both their relationships with roommates and romantic partners were filled with conflict and tension, and their romantic relationships especially suffered low levels of intimacy and trust.

In general, a person's personality tends to reinforce itself and exhibit remarkable stability over time (Heatherton & Weinberger, 1994). Your personality conditions how you tend to feel, perceive, interpret, and behave; this sets in motion processes that feed back to reinforce the original personality structure. Take the personality factor of conscientiousness as an example. As we discussed earlier, highly conscientious people will tend to be organized, punctual, and dependable; they are therefore more likely to succeed, be respected by others, and create professional opportunities for themselves. As they experience success, this feeds back to reinforce those qualities. On the other hand, people low in conscientiousness are likely to be disorganized, unreliable, and have difficulty meeting deadlines. As a result, their professional accomplishments will tend to suffer, their lives will increasingly spiral out of their control, and they will feel constantly overwhelmed by the looming crises that are bearing down on them. As you can see from this example, our personality tendencies are likely to reinforce themselves in the myriad ways they play out in our lives.

A simpler way of understanding how "personality is destiny" is to consider the basic insight of neuroscience: that neurons that fire together wire together. One consequence of this is that the more that people practise a certain skill, the more they train their brains to be good at that skill. Similarly, the more that people practise being extraverted, or open-minded, or conscientious, or neurotic, etc., the more they train their brains to function in that manner. This can also be seen as a positive feedback system; personality structures influence patterns in the person's life and build networks in the person's brain in ways that reinforce themselves, leading personality to be quite stable over time.

This seems to have been understood by William James, who asserted over 100 years ago that ". . . in most of us, by the age of thirty, the character has set like plaster, and will never soften again" (James, 1890, p. 121). Indeed, people's personalities are much more labile when they are young and tend to become more "fixed" as we age; researchers analyzing the results of over 150 studies involving almost 50 000 participants showed that personality stability is lowest for young children and highest for people over 50 (Roberts & DelVecchio, 2000).

However, research has shown that James may have been a little too pessimistic. For example, young adults tend to experience fewer negative emotions than do adolescents, reflecting decreases in neuroticism. Also, conscientiousness, agreeableness, and social dominance (an aspect of extraversion) all increase in early adulthood (Roberts et al., 2006; see Figure 12.2).

Nevertheless, even these data describe a kind of personality stability, in that although people's personality traits may fluctuate over time, their rank ordering in the population remains very stable. That is, people who are more extraverted than others at time one also tend to be more extraverted than others at time two, even though the overall level of extraversion may change over that time period (McCrae & Costa, 1990). Thus, although individuals may change over time, their personal characteristics relative to other people remain remarkably stable.

Take a moment and consider why personalities change in these systematic ways over time. What could be causing these changes? One likely explanation is that, over time, our environments change as well as the roles we play in those environments. For example, adults have to be more conscientious than children, because they have so many more responsibilities—like taking care of their unconscientious children! Or, in the case of emotional stability, which increases from childhood to young adulthood, there may be psychological changes that occur, such as increased sense of identity—knowing who you are—which could help young adults feel less insecurity and therefore experience fewer negative emotions. Or, perhaps young adults have greater choice over their activities than teenagers and children; as a result, they rarely find themselves in situations in which they are unsure of themselves, whereas children regularly end up having to perform in a domain in which they feel incompetent (one of your authors is remembering art class

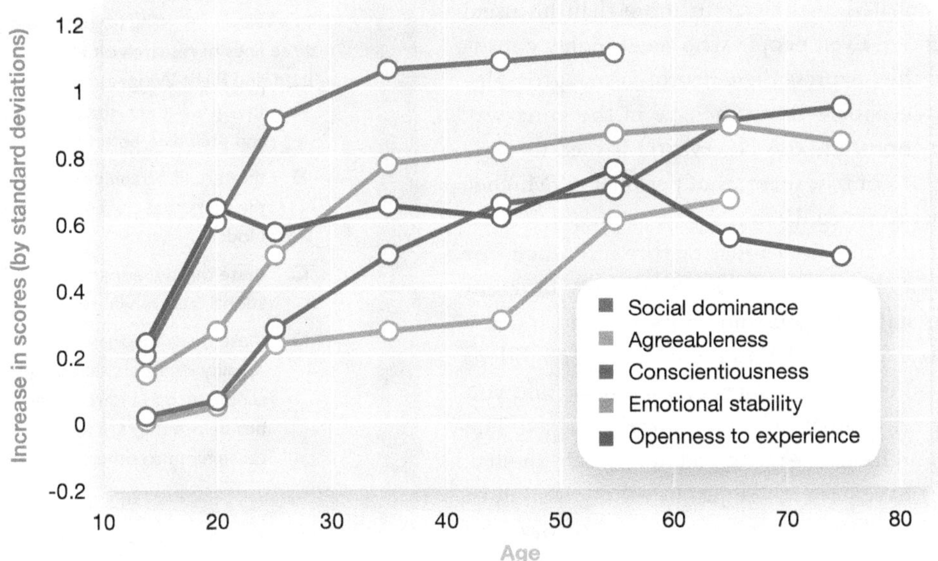

{FIG. 12.2} **Personality Stability and Change over the Lifespan** Average scores of Big Five traits change over the life span. Generally, most traits become more positive through adulthood, although there are anomalies. Social dominance (an aspect of extraversion) remains stable after age 40. Conscientiousness does not begin rising until after the college years. Openness to experience only rises up to the college years, then remains largely stable until old age, when it declines (Roberts et al., 2006).

in elementary school, and shuddering . . .). The point is, over time there are many changes—in our environments, our roles, the amount of choice and power we have, the sophistication of our thinking processes, our bodies and brains themselves, and many other things—so there may be many reasons why personalities change over time, which is a current focus of personality research.

PERSONALITY TRAITS AND STATES Trait labels may go a long way toward describing what people are like. However, many psychologists are quick to point out that no matter how useful traits may seem, people's behaviour is also determined by situational factors and context. You may know someone whom you would describe as very calm and tranquil, yet when the restaurant waiter brings him the wrong dish he loudly protests. Definitions of personality typically include an element of consistency, but this does not mean that people are always consistent in the ways they behave. In contrast to a personality trait, a **state** *is a temporary physical or psychological engagement that influences behaviour.* Perhaps your normally calm friend lashed out at the waiter because he was hungry to the point of irritability. In this case, the

RimDream/Shutterstock

Children are regularly placed in activities at which they are not yet very competent.

Monkey Business/Fotolia

Adults have the ability to choose activities that play to their strengths and skills.

situation motivated his behaviour more than his usual calm demeanour. Even people who seem highly consistent in how they express their neuroticism, agreeableness, or extraversion will not behave in the same way across all situations, and this observation has led to some strong criticisms of trait theories of personality (Mischel, 1968; Mischel & Shoda, 1998).

How states and situational factors influence our behaviour is a challenging topic. How many different situations or states do you find yourself in during any particular day? You can be awake or asleep; confident or unsure; you may have money or no money; and you may be in a crisis situation or completely relaxed. The list could go on forever—and as you might have guessed, psychologists have tried to see just how long it goes. In one study, 77 college students were asked to describe as many situations as they might encounter. Their total reached more than 7000. Perhaps you can now see why many psychologists would rather focus on five personality dimensions. Fortunately, Saucier and colleagues (2007) took these 7000 situations and reduced them to four general aspects of situations that are most likely to influence our behaviour:

1. Locations (e.g., being at work, school, or home)
2. Associations (e.g., being with friends, alone, or with family)
3. Activities (e.g., awake, rushed, studying)
4. Subjective states (e.g., mad, sick, drunk, happy)

These situations influence how and when our personality traits are expressed. Identifying these situations is important because they contribute to our psychological states, and they interact with personality traits to determine our behaviour.

Quick Quiz 12.1a

The Trait Perspective

KNOW ...

1 Which of the following statements best describes the difference between the nomothetic and idiographic approaches to personality?

A The nomothetic approach focuses on traits found across large groups, whereas the idiographic approach focuses on individuals.

B The idiographic approach focuses on traits found across large groups, whereas the nomothetic approach focuses on individuals.

C The idiographic approach relies on measures such as the Big Five, whereas the Big Five is of no use to a nomothetic approach.

D The idiographic approach allows psychologists to ask questions about the genetic and cultural basis of personality traits.

UNDERSTAND ...

2 One reason for going beyond the Big Five, such as the three lines of research on Honesty–Humility, the Dark Triad, and Right-Wing Authoritarianism, is

A they predict anti-social tendencies, such as violence and prejudice, better than the Big Five traits.

B they are idiographic approaches, which supplement the nomothetic approach taken in the Five Factor Model.

C these three theories account for states and situational factors, whereas the Big Five does not.

D these three theories can be used to diagnose personality disorders that could justify preventative action, such as incarcerating "dangerous" personalities before they are able to commit any crimes and cause harm to others.

APPLY ...

3 You are the type of person who tends to go to the same restaurant and order the same thing, sticking to your daily routine. You have even turned down opportunities to travel to new destinations. Which of the Big Five factors would account for this description of your personality?

A Agreeableness
B Conscientiousness
C Openness
D Neuroticism

ANALYZE ...

4 Your friend, who is normally introverted, is outraged at the taxi driver who is trying to overcharge you. He is cursing at the driver in a verbal altercation. This event is most likely due to his ________.

A temperament
B subjective state
C idealized self
D Big Five personality traits

5 The theory that our personalities consist of a stable set of traits is very useful to psychologists, but there are some notable problems with trait theories. Which of the following is *not* a problem?

A Trait theories typically rely on self-reported behaviours, rather than actual observed behaviours.

B Situational factors, in addition to personality traits, also determine our behaviour.

C Factor analysis is not considered a valid technique in the study of personality.

D Historically, psychologists have not agreed on the traits that make up someone's personality.

Answers can be found on page ANS-3.

Behaviourist and Social-Cognitive Perspectives

You probably didn't have much trouble understanding the trait perspective to personality; indeed, using traits to describe ourselves and others is something we do regularly, particularly in Western cultures. However, the trait approach does tend to reinforce certain assumptions that other psychologists have called into question. Most importantly, the trait approach reinforces the assumption that we carry our personality characteristics around inside us; traits are these "things" that we "have," which then influence our thoughts, feelings, and behaviours.

Psychologists with a behaviourist perspective would not adopt the same assumptions. To a behaviourist, it is unnecessary to posit the existence of some sort of internalized trait; instead, the behaviourist would seek to understand the relationship between specific environmental stimuli and an observed pattern of behaviour. Notable psychologist B. F. Skinner, for example, believed that "personality" is simply a description of the response tendencies that occur in different situations. For example, if you find yourself hanging out with a group of people, your behavioural responses to that situation might include dominating the conversation, asking a lot of questions, laughing along at other people's jokes, or generally remaining silent. Presumably, the behaviours you engage in are based on your past experiences; if you tend to dominate the conversation and laugh at people's jokes, then you were likely reinforced for those behaviours in the past. A behaviourist might note that using the personality dimension of "extraversion" is an unnecessary addition—it is just a label that does not help us understand the simple relationship between stimulus and response. Thus the behaviourist perspective emphasizes the importance of the stimulus-response associations that are learned through exposure to specific situations, rather than emphasizing internalized, relatively stable personality traits (Figure 12.3).

One major point of agreement between the behaviourists and other psychologists was the emphasis on how learning contributes to personality. However, most modern theorists have gone beyond the behaviourist account to develop more holistic and integrated models of how personality functions and develops. One prominent psychologist, Albert Bandura, advanced a social cognitive theory of personality in order to emphasize the role of beliefs and the reciprocal relationships between people and their environments. According to Bandura, environmental stimuli do not automatically (in most cases) trigger specific behaviours; instead, environmental stimuli, such as rewards or punishments, inform individuals' beliefs about the world, and in particular, their beliefs about what consequences are likely to follow from certain behaviours.

Furthermore, people are not affected by their environments in a strictly one-way causal process; instead, people exist in a relationship with their environments, both affecting and being affected by environmental circumstances. One of Bandura's central ideas was the theory of **reciprocal determinism**, which posits that *behaviour, internal (personal) factors, and external (situational) factors interact to determine one another, and that our personalities are based on interactions among these three aspects* (see Figure 12.3). From this perspective, personality is not something "inside" the person, but rather exists "between" the person (their thoughts, feelings, and behaviours) and the environment.

For example, the classic trait perspective would predict that people who are high on neuroticism are likely to view the world as threatening, and therefore are likely to notice negative information and to accentuate the potentially threatening aspects of situations they are in. The behaviourist would emphasize the environment that led to these neurotic behaviours—perhaps the person experienced a great deal of negativity in their lives, and learned that when they let their guard down, they end up getting hurt. But adding a social-cognitive perspective to this situation reveals a huge amount of complexity and richness that is otherwise missed.

Explore
Behavioural versus Social Learning Theories of Personality

In this example, a social-cognitive theorist like Bandura would emphasize the neurotic individual's beliefs and behaviour, and how these then influence what they experience back from the world. For example, one way

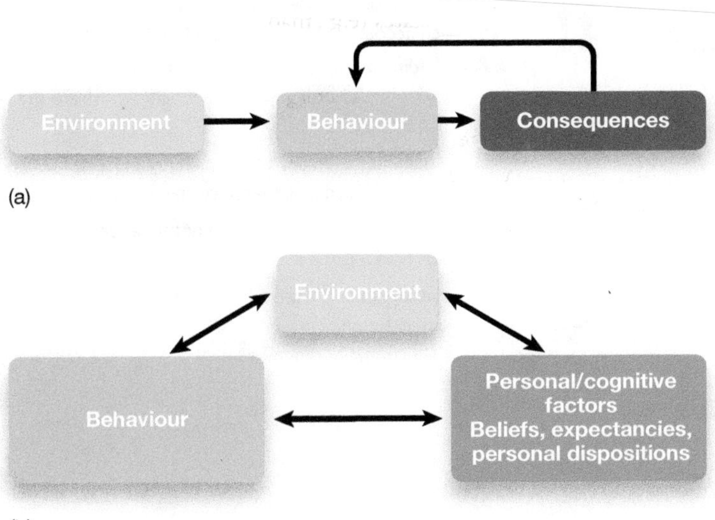

{FIG. 12.3} **(a) Behaviourist Account of Personality.** Behaviourists thought that what psychologists call personality was an expression of relationships between behaviour, rewards, and punishment. Behaviourists avoided referring to personality traits and dispositions, but rather focused on how past experiences predict future behaviours. For example, whether someone tends to be pessimistic might be based on past experiences of feeling a lost sense of control. **(b) Reciprocal Determinism and the Social-Cognitive Approach.** According to Albert Bandura and colleagues, personality is a product of dynamic interactions between behaviour and reinforcement, and, importantly, the beliefs, expectancies, and dispositions of the individual. **Click on this figure in your eText to see more details.**

that a neurotic person could deal with anxiety could be to attempt to control people and events. When they successfully exert control, things go according to plan and they are reinforced for exerting control. But as a result of their regular exercise of control, they also develop higher expectations that people will meet their standards of approval, and that events will turn out as they want them to. Unfortunately for them, life is full of surprises, and other people generally do not like being controlled and will act in ways that assert their own independence (which is not what the neurotic person wants them to do). Thus, the neurotic person continually experiences things *not* going according to plan, which then reinforces their anxiety and leads them to try to control things even more. As this pattern develops in their lives, they may suffer social costs as a result of excessively trying to manage other people and continually finding fault in the behaviours of those around them; these social costs and experiences of rejection then further reinforce the anxiety that underlies neuroticism.

According to Bandura, people's personalities and their environment are interdependent in many different ways, linked together in feedback loops that connect their perceptions, cognitions, emotions, behaviours, the ways they structure their environments, and the ways that their environments, in turn, structure them.

Quick Quiz 12.1b :: Behaviourist and Social-Cognitive Perspectives

KNOW ...

1 Which of the following concepts developed by Bandura refers to interactions that occur among behaviour, internal factors, and external factors as an explanation for personality?

A Reciprocal determinism **C** Intersubjectivity

B Positive psychology **D** Egocentrism

UNDERSTAND ...

2 Kaitlin describes herself as unmotivated. She has not felt rewarded by her attempts to succeed at school or work and, therefore, has given up trying. How might a psychologist who adopts a strict behaviourist approach account for Kaitlin's behaviour?

A Kaitlin believes that she cannot succeed and, therefore, avoids putting herself in situations where she might fail.

B Kaitlin has a history of not being reinforced for trying to succeed and, therefore, has stopped trying.

C Kaitlin focuses too much on negatives and does not have a positive outlook on life.

D Kaitlin has low levels of the trait known as extraversion.

ANALYZE ...

3 Alternative approaches to personality such as the behaviourist and cognitive approaches complement trait theories of personality because .

A these alternative approaches help to account for how traits interact with behaviour and personal experience.

B trait theories focus on the negatives of personality.

C it is easier to observe behaviour than to ask someone to fill out a personality inventory.

D trait theories focus only on the positive aspects of personality.

Answers can be found on page ANS-3.

Module Summary

Module 12.1

Now that you have read this module you should

KNOW ...

- ***The key terminology associated with contemporary approaches to personality:***

the Dark Triad (p. 497)	personality (p. 493)
factor analysis (p. 494)	personality trait (p. 493)
Five Factor Model (p. 494)	reciprocal determinism (p. 503)
HEXACO model of personality (p. 497)	Right-Wing Authoritarianism (RWA) (p. 497)
idiographic approach (p. 493)	state (p. 501)
nomothetic approach (p. 493)	

UNDERSTAND ...

- ***The behaviourist and social-cognitive views of personality.*** A strict behavioural account of personality identifies the stimuli that control a person's responses. From a behaviourist perspective, there is little need for trait terminology, such as neuroticism or conscientiousness, and no reference to cognitive factors such as beliefs or thoughts. The social-cognitive approach to personality also accounts for situational factors and behaviour, but adds a cognitive element that interacts with the environment in such a way that situations, behaviour, and thoughts are determined in reciprocal fashion.

APPLY ...

- ***The Big Five personality traits to understand your own personality.*** Psychologists usually describe individuals based on their scores on personality tests involving the Big Five traits, such that someone might rate high, medium, or low on each trait. Use **Table 12.1** to describe your own personality in terms of the Big Five, and cite examples of specific behaviours and habits that correspond to each trait. Before you begin this exercise, review **Figure 12.1** (p. 495), which outlines some of the major characteristics of high and low scores on each of the five factors.

Patrick Sheandell O' Carroll/Glow Images

ANALYZE ...

- ***The personality roots of violence and prejudice.*** Canadian researchers have identified three sets of factors that predict violence and prejudice that are not fully captured by the Five Factor Model. The first is the Honesty–Humility dimension of the HEXACO model of personality. The second is the Dark Triad of Psychopathy, Machiavellianism, and Narcissism. The third is Right-Wing Authoritarianism. Research has found that these traits predict many dysfunctional patterns of thoughts, emotions, and behaviours. Understanding the causal underpinnings of these traits and developing strategies to help individuals with such personality traits would be a key advance in promoting a healthier and more peaceful society.
- ***The relative roles of personality traits and psychological and physical states in determining behaviour.*** The debate over whether personality traits influence behaviour or whether situational factors play a bigger role in behaviour has been ongoing in the field of personality psychology. In reality, both sets of factors are important. Personality traits can be remarkably consistent, yet the situations we find ourselves in can lead to unexpected behaviour.

Table 12.1 Applying the Five Factor Model

For each trait, try to determine if you would score low, medium, or high if you were to complete a test based on the Five Factor Model. Cite specific examples of behaviours and preferences that support your ranking.

FACTOR	LOW, MEDIUM, OR HIGH?	SPECIFIC EXAMPLES
Openness		
Conscientiousness		
Extraversion		
Agreeableness		
Neuroticism		

Randy Faris/Glow Images

Module 12.2

Cultural and Biological Approaches to Personality

Learning Objectives

After reading this module you should

KNOW ...	UNDERSTAND ...	APPLY ...	ANALYZE ...
The key terminology associated with cultural and biological approaches to personality	How evolutionary theories explain personality	Your knowledge to understand personality differences between cultures	Claims that males and females have fundamentally different personalities The genetic basis of personality

Apparently, if you're backpacking in Europe, it's a good idea to highlight your Canadian heritage. Or even pretend to be Canadian if you're not. Sewing the Canadian flag onto one's backpack is so well known that it has become a cliché. But why has this become so popular?

Well, because Canadians are nice, eh? Polite! Friendly. A little backwards maybe, eh? But good people. So when you're travelling, show off the maple leaf and people will like you.

Are these beliefs about Canadians true? More generally, are there personality differences between different countries? Is there a "national character"? There certainly *seem* to be certain types of people from certain countries. Just try this—imagine the prototypical Swedish person. Now notice what came to your mind. The manic Swedish chef? Icy blond supermodels drinking vodka in a snowbank and looking at you with cool disdain? What are you basing your assumptions on? Now think about a Japanese person? American? Australian? Iraqi? Jamaican? Greek? In each case, probably some images and basic character traits pop into your head. We often reason this way about our social world, feeling like we gain insight into other people simply by knowing what country they call home.

We see personality differences at smaller levels of scale as well. We believe there are differences between people of different regions within a country (e.g., the urban Torontonian and the rural Manitoban), and even differences between the personalities of cities (e.g., think of "what type of people" tend to live in Calgary or Montreal, Vancouver or St. John's). Residents of one neighbourhood or small town feel that they are different from "those people," who live in a different place. In the TV show *The Simpson's*, the people of Springfield assumed that the townspeople of neighbouring Shelbyville were particularly disagreeable and untrustworthy types.

Although some of these examples may seem harmless, even humorous, many examples of group-based stereotypic thinking obviously are neither. All too readily, we split the world into *Us* vs. *Them*, overemphasizing any possible differences between groups of people, and underemphasizing the ways in which we are similar and interdependent. Nevertheless, in some cases there are real differences between people in different groups, and it is important to understand both these differences as well as the similarities.

Personality psychology researchers have looked extensively at cultural differences and similarities in personality, helping us to understand how culture, the environment, and people shape each other across time. In this module, we will explore personality from cross-cultural, evolutionary, and biological perspectives.

Focus Questions

 Does culture influence the types of personality traits we find across human societies?

 How do evolutionary and biological approaches add to our understanding of personality?

Culture and Personality

Would you say Americans are WEIRD? Of course you would! They're very WEIRD! But we're not pointing fingers—Canadians, Western Europeans, Australians, and others are WEIRD too. In this context, WEIRD stands for "Western, Educated, Industrialized, Rich, and Democratic," outlining key characteristics of certain cultures (Henrich et al., 2010). Do you think it is likely that people from WEIRD cultures differ in important ways from people in the rest of the world's cultures? Would it matter if they do?

One troubling fact that was uncovered recently puts this in perspective; researchers at the University of British Columbia calculated that 96% of psychology studies have been conducted on people from WEIRD cultures. Now consider that the entire population of WEIRD cultures accounts for a mere 12% of the earth's population (Henrich et al., 2010). So, 96% of our knowledge in psychology is based on studying samples that represent only 12% of humanity. What does this mean? At the very least, it means we should be cautious in making inferences about "human nature" when extrapolating from the findings of psychology studies to the human species at large. And it means that we need to better understand the similarities and differences between people in different cultures. For example, in terms of personality, there may be important differences, on average, between the WEIRD and the non-WEIRD.

UNIVERSALS AND DIFFERENCES ACROSS CULTURES: THE BIG FIVE The Five Factor Model of personality centres around five personality dimensions: neuroticism, extraversion, openness to experience, agreeableness, and conscientiousness. However, because these factors were discovered by researchers working in WEIRD places—the United States, Canada, and Europe—it is possible that the Five Factor Model only accounts for personality in WEIRD populations, and may not extend to the rest of the world.

To find out whether the Big Five traits are truly universal, an enormous team of psychologists (there were 127 authors on this single article) measured the Big Five dimensions in more than 17 000 people speaking 28 different languages and inhabiting 56 countries on 6 continents (they did not visit Antarctica). In all cultures that were studied, the Big Five factors were reliably found. Despite the many differences that may exist between cultures, the people in those cultures share the same basic personality structures (McCrae et al., 2005; Schmitt et al., 2007). This is an incredible finding, suggesting that the basic systems in the human personality are, in a sense, deeper than culture; although individual personalities differ enormously, the basic machinery of the human personality system is universal.

PERSONALITY STRUCTURES IN DIFFERENT CULTURES The study described above is groundbreaking in its global scope, but a key methodological challenge remains. Because the Five Factor Model was originally created by factor-analyzing personality adjectives in the English language, the kinds of questions that are asked on Big Five questionnaires are designed to measure the Big Five factors, and no others. Thus, when the scale is given to people from other cultures, the scale itself brings the biases of Western culture and the English language right along with it. What if other languages used different types of adjectives to describe personality? What if other cultures had different personality traits than the ones that emerge in the West? Re-analyzing personality from different linguistic starting points might reveal new personality factors that lie outside of the Big Five.

Researchers have begun to address this limitation, analyzing personality structure using personality descriptors in other languages; this work has already revealed unique personality factors not captured in the Big Five (Heine & Buchtel, 2009). For example, Cheung et al. (1996) factor-analyzed indigenous Chinese personality traits, looking for patterns among the personality descriptors used in Chinese, rather than English. They found 26 new personality traits in total, and when they factor-analyzed all the traits including these 26 new ones, they found a quite different structure from the Big Five.

Instead of five traits, these researchers found four: dependability, social potency, individualism, and interpersonal relatedness. The first three traits were very similar to three of the Big Five traits (neuroticism, extraversion, and agreeableness, respectively), but the fourth, Interpersonal Relatedness, was unique. Interpersonal Relatedness is a combination of characteristics concerning social harmony, tradition, and an emphasis on one's social relationships. This may reflect a distinct personality dimension in the Chinese psyche, emphasizing the more socially interdependent nature of the self in this culture.

Other researchers have added to our multicultural understanding of personality, factor-analyzing the personality traits found in Filipino, Spanish, and Greek languages, and seeking a more integrated cross-cultural theory of personality (Benet-Martinez & John, 1998; Church, 2001; Saucier et al., 2005). Each analysis has revealed new factors that seem to be independent of the Big Five.

Cross-cultural work on personality is still in its infancy, and clearly, many questions remain. At this point, most psychologists would agree that the Five Factor Model captures important and perhaps universal dimensions of personality, but also might miss important cultural-specific qualities that can only be understood by analyzing personality from that culture's own perspective.

COMPARING PERSONALITY TRAITS BETWEEN NATIONS Despite the difficulties noted above, one important advantage of personality scales that have been translated into different languages is that psychologists can test for personality differences across cultures. Many such differences have been found. For example, consider the countries with the highest and lowest averages on each of the Big Five traits in Table 12.2 (Schmitt et al., 2007). (Interestingly, Canada falls roughly in the middle in each case.)

What do these differences really mean? Do they reflect actual personality differences between the people in those countries? Or could other things account for the findings? Many of the personality differences do seem puzzling. For example, why are Argentinians so neurotic, compared to people from the Democratic Republic of the Congo? Why are the Japanese so much less conscientious than Ethiopians? In fact, many of the findings in these large-scale cross-cultural studies defy cultural stereotypes (Terracciano et al., 2005), and it is a huge challenge for researchers to understand whether or not these differences are real.

One striking cultural difference that researchers struggled to understand is also illustrated in the results below. Isn't it interesting that a single country, Japan, ranked lowest of all countries on three out of the five traits (openness, agreeableness, and conscientiousness)? Given the general desirability of these traits, that is a fairly critical evaluation of the Japanese personality! In fact, people from the entire South Asian part of the world rated their own personalities relatively negatively. Are these differences real? Is such a vast swath of humanity really so different from the rest of the world?

CHALLENGES IN CROSS-CULTURAL RESEARCH
Researchers attempting to answer these questions face two central challenges: how to translate measures of personality such that they will mean exactly the same thing in different languages, and how to ensure that people are using the exact same reasoning process when answering them. The translation challenge is somewhat easier to overcome, although researchers have to be constantly on guard that unintended nuances of meaning do not sneak into a scale item when it is translated into another language.

The second challenge, ensuring that people use the same kind of reasoning process when answering the questions, is much more difficult to overcome and occupies a great deal of attention in cross-cultural studies of personality. For example, it is possible that people from different cultures have different *response styles*—characteristic ways of responding to questions; these response styles can be strongly influenced by cultural norms. For example, in one culture it may be more socially acceptable to say highly positive things about yourself, whereas in another culture the same behaviour may be considered rude or boastful. Indeed, researchers at the University of British Columbia have shown that there are such norms in South Asian cultures, discouraging people from emphasizing their strengths and successes, and instead encouraging people to be modest, humble, even self-critical (Heine, 2003; Markus & Kitayama, 1991; Mezulis et al., 2004).

As a result, people from South Asian cultures would tend to answer personality questions more modestly,

Table 12.2 :: Cultural Differences in the Big Five Personality Traits

	HIGHEST	LOWEST
Extraversion	Serbia, Croatia	Bangladesh, France
Openness	Chile, Belgium	Hong Kong, Japan
Agreeableness	Jordan, Democratic Republic of the Congo	Japan, Lithuania
Conscientiousness	Ethiopia, Democratic Republic of the Congo	Japan, South Korea
Neuroticism	Japan, Argentina	Democratic Republic of the Congo, Slovenia

especially when compared to North Americans, who self-enhance practically every chance they get. Ironically then, South Asian people could be the most well-adjusted population in the world, but their self-effacing culture would tend to hide that fact and even make them appear maladjusted! Clearly, it is important to understand the possible impact of cultural norms and response styles when interpreting the findings of this research.

A further critique concerns the problem of *essentializing* cultural differences. To essentialize a cultural difference is to attribute that difference to something fundamental to the cultures, some sort of basic difference between the "essences" of each culture. Essentializing in general is a challenge for our sciences and culture to overcome, because we create and accentuate differences between what are simply human beings living on this planet. As soon as we start essentializing groups and attributing specific qualities to the essences of those groups, we start seeing the world in terms of *Us* and *Them*, and we are one step away from justifying inequalities favouring *Us* over *Them*. The tendency to essentialize cultural differences lies at the heart of prejudice, inequality, and social injustice (Allport, 1954; Levy et al., 2006). Furthermore, focusing on average differences between cultures tends to overlook the fact that there are vast individual differences within each culture, generally much bigger than the average difference between cultures. Therefore, it is important not to over-emphasize small average differences between groups and unduly reinforce group-based stereotypes.

Interestingly, despite all of the emphasis placed on cultural differences in personality, the authors of the huge study discussed earlier finally concluded that the differences found in average trait ratings in different cultures are not sufficiently strong to justify beliefs in national character. "No convincing evidence has demonstrated that beliefs about national character" have any basis in fact, "despite their wide adoption and resistance to change" (Schmitt et al., 2007).

Corbis/PhotoLibrary

Psychologists find many commonalities in personality dimensions from people of diverse cultures. However, there may be some culturally unique personality dimensions.

While acknowledging the methodological limitations discussed above, the overall cross-cultural research on the Big Five suggests that there is a great deal of cross-cultural consistency in the basic structure of personality (McCrae, 2001). Personality theorists argue that the Big Five traits are built into the human organism in a fundamental way, which is reflected in our biology, such as our genes and neural systems (e.g., DeYoung et al., 2010). Examining the biological processes underpinning personality has become a major focus of researchers in the 21st century.

BIOPSYCHOSOCIAL PERSPECTIVES

How Culture Shapes Our Development: Cultural Differences in the Self

During the 2000 Olympics in Sydney, Australia, two gold-medal–winning athletes were being interviewed about their success. In explaining her success during the race, Misty Hyman, who won the 200-metre butterfly for the United States, said, "I think I just stayed focused. It was time to show the world what I could do. I am just glad I was able to do it. I knew I could beat Suzy O'Neil, deep down in my heart I believed it, and I know this whole week the doubts kept creeping in, they were with me on the blocks, but I just said, 'No, this is my night.'"

In contrast, Naoko Takahashi, after winning the marathon for Japan, said, "Here is the best coach in the world, the best manager in the world, and all of the people who support

JEFF HAYNES/AFP/Newscom

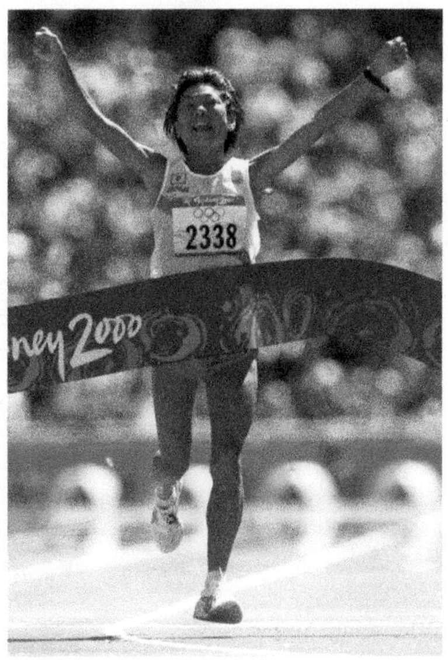

Reuters/Corbis

me—all of these things were getting together and became a gold medal. So I think I didn't get it alone, not only by myself" (Markus et al., 2006).

This striking example illustrates how people's behaviour can be shaped by broad cultural factors. Misty Hyman, from the individualistic United States, seems to be more self-promoting, explaining her success as being due to her own characteristics, her willpower, and belief in herself. Naoko Takahashi, from collectivistic Japan, takes her moment of Olympic glory as an opportunity to highlight the ways in which she was assisted by so many people in her life, de-emphasizing her own contribution in favour of honouring others.

Whether a culture predominantly emphasizes individualism or collectivism has many effects on personality, affecting how people see themselves and how they behave in many situations. Researchers have found that when describing themselves, predominantly individualistic people use more personal adjectives (e.g., "I am extraverted"; "I have a good sense of humour"). Predominantly collectivistic people tend to describe themselves more relationally, in terms of their connections to other people ("I am a son"; "I am a sister"), and their affiliations with specific social groups ("I am Canadian"; "I am a Trekkie").

This difference in self-definition results in differences in the stability of personality across different situations. The individualistic person is the same across most situations, whereas the more collectivistic person feels that who you are depends on who you're with; the self that you are emerges within a social context and is attuned to that context.

Perhaps because they define their self-concepts more rigidly, individualistic people are more likely to be defensive in specific ways. To the collectivistic person, the self is fluid and changeable from situation to situation; thus there is not the same need to defend a single specific self-concept. But to the individualist, the self is supposed to exist as a separate "thing," one that persists from situation to situation, and as a result, individualists have a stronger need to maintain a positive view of their self-concepts. Individualists are likely to emphasize their positive qualities ("I love to really challenge myself, like doing triathlons and extreme mountaineering. Yes, and I'm going on tour next month to promote my new book. . . ."). And as with Misty Hyman, when things turn out well for them, they take most of the credit themselves. On the other hand, if the individualist fails, they are pretty good at finding other circumstantial factors to blame (Heine, 2003; Markus & Kitayama, 1991).

The influence of culture can even be seen in the brain. In one study (Chiao et al., 2009), participants were put into fMRI scanners to monitor their brain activity while they made judgments about different sentences. In order to manipulate whether subjects were thinking of themselves in a more individualistic or collectivistic manner, researchers asked subjects to make different types of judgments about the sentences. For some sentences, they judged the degree to which it described them in general (individualistic self task), whereas for others they judged how well it described them when they were with their mothers (collectivistic self task). Amazingly, their brain scans were able to tell the difference between individualists and collectivists. In the brain, part of the medial prefrontal cortex is involved when processing information related to the self. This area was most active for individualistic participants when they were making judgments about themselves in general, whereas collectivists showed the greatest amount of activation in this area when making judgments about their selves in relation to their mothers. Thus, to individualists, the individualistic task was processed by their brains as most self-relevant, whereas for collectivists, it was the collectivistic task that was most self-relevant.

This study provides direct evidence that different cognitive processes are considered self-relevant for individualists and collectivists. This is like having a neurological fingerprint that can predict which culture a person is from. In other words, culture is built right into our brain matter. Much current research in personality, such as this study, addresses questions at multiple levels of analysis, seeking to understand the connections between biological functioning, personalities, and culture.

Quick Quiz 12.2a Culture and Personality

KNOW ...

1 What does the WEIRD acronym refer to?

A Psychologists' preoccupation with abnormal personalities

B A single, specific group on which major perspectives and theories of personality are based

C A database that compiles personality profiles from people of all walks of life

D The application of personality to the various cultures from East Asia

2 Psychologists have primarily relied on ________ to measure personality traits in other cultures.

A behavioural observations

B interviews

C the Cannon-Bard theory

D the Big Five trait theory

ANALYZE ...

3 Results from applying the Big Five personality traits in other countries reveal that

A people all over the world are identical in the patterns of their personality traits.

B people all over the world are radically different in the patterns of their personality traits.

C there are some cross-cultural differences as well as many similarities in the patterns of people's personality traits.

D the Big Five was not understood in other parts of the world because of language translation problems.

Answers can be found on page ANS-3.

How Genes Affect Personality

Do you have your mother's eyes? Your father's nose? You may have at some point heard friends and relatives commenting on the physical resemblance you share with your parents or siblings. But what about personality? Can you be born with your grandpa's sense of humour, or your grandma's tendency to lose her temper? If you catch yourself behaving like your mom or dad, should you conclude that "it must be genetic"?

Or do you believe more in the role of the environment in shaping your personality? Like many psychologists, you may assume that if you have certain traits, like a propensity for alcoholism, or for being friendly and outgoing, then you must have picked these up from other people (e.g., Mischel, 1981). Indeed, if you had been raised in an Amish village, a Toronto highrise, a working-class neighbourhood in the north end of Halifax, or as a member of the royal family, then obviously, you would turn out quite differently in each case.

We know that nurture matters. And to be honest, most of us love that! It gives us comfort, because if the environment shapes us, then we can shape our own destinies. We can decide for ourselves the kind of people we are going to be. And we can help other people shape their own future selves. But we know that nature matters too; mountains of research findings over the past few decades lead to the overwhelming conclusion that genetic factors contribute substantially to personality (Plomin & Caspi, 1999). Exactly how much of who we are is determined by nature, and how much remains under the control of nurture, has profound implications. For example, how would you make sense of yourself if you found out that the home you grew up in is much less important than the genes you inherited at the moment of conception?

TWIN STUDIES Researchers attempting to tease apart the contributions made by our genes and our environments faced a key challenge, which was that families share not only genes, but also many environmental factors. For example, if you were to observe a behaviour pattern that runs in families, such as alcoholism or anxiety, you might be tempted to conclude that because of the strong family inclination toward this pattern, there must be genetic roots. But family members also often live in the same home, spend much of their time together, share many common experiences, and share other similarities. How then do you know if the pattern you observe is due to the shared genes or the shared environments?

The use of twins as research subjects was a brilliant way of overcoming this challenge. Comparing twins who were identical (monozygotic) to twins who were fraternal (dizygotic) allowed researchers to estimate the influence of genetic factors on personality. Research on the Big Five personality traits of twins has shown that identical twins show a stronger correlation for each personality trait than do fraternal twins. The correlations for identical twin pairs are approximately .50 for all five factors, significantly higher than the correlations for fraternal twin pairs (who average approximately .20). This implies that the increased similarity in the personalities of identical twins is due to their shared genes.

Special Topics: Twins and Personality

AP Photo

Gerald Levey and Mark Newman are identical twins who were reared apart. When they eventually met it turns out they had many similarities—for example, both chose the same profession, loved John Wayne movies and The Three Stooges, and had a fondness for professional wrestling.

ZAK BRIAN/SIPA/ZAK BRIAN/SIPA/Newscom

Paula Bernstein and Elyse Schein are identical twins who were separated at birth, and upon uniting at age 35 discovered they shared some uncanny similarities. They were editors for their high-school newspapers, chose to study film in university, sucked their fingers but not their thumbs as toddlers, have an odd habit of typing into the air, and share very similar tastes in books, among other similarities.

But you might ask, how do researchers know that it's the increased genetic similarity of identical twins that is responsible for their similar personalities? Maybe identical twins also tend to share more similar environments than fraternal twins, and this is the reason for their personality similarity. Identical twins are often treated in very similar ways, especially during their younger and formative years. If this is true, then the strong correlations between identical twin pairs might be environmentally based.

An impressive line of research directly examines this question. The Minnesota Study of Twins Reared Apart located over 100 sets of twins and triplets who were raised in separate households, and compared them to those raised in the same household. Amazingly, identical twins raised *in different households* nevertheless were quite similar in many ways, more similar than fraternal twins raised in the same household; this is amazing when you consider how important a person's family is in general, and yet, family does not have a stronger impact than genes when shaping personality. Identical twins raised in different households are about as similar to each other as identical twins raised in the same household! Studies such as these argue strongly that in terms of basic personality characteristics, your genes are indeed more important than your home (Bouchard et al., 1990; Tellegen et al., 1998).

Watch
Twins Separated at Birth, Reunited

Other studies of adopted children support these findings. On average, the personalities of adoptive parents have no influence on the personality characteristics of their adopted children. Although it may be hard to believe, siblings who are adopted (i.e., not genetically related) and raised in the same household are *no more similar in personality than two people picked randomly off the street* (Plomin & Caspi, 1999). The genetic influences on personality are strong indeed.

It is important to note that this does not mean that parents are incapable of influencing their children's personality development. Obviously, parents who abuse their children, or on the positive side, parents who put extraordinary efforts into cultivating positive personality traits in their children, are likely to have an impact on their children's personalities. The genetic evidence just discussed simply implies that most parents do not do these things; most parents do not expose their children to experiences so far outside the norm that they are likely to shape their children's personalities in a strong way. The conclusion, then, is that most of the time, the influence of parenting on personality is overshadowed by the contributions made by our genes.

One further challenge of this research is to move beyond estimating the overall heritability of traits, and begin to uncover which specific genes are linked to personality outcomes. New advances in gene sequencing techniques and molecular genetics methods are allowing scientists to do just that.

WORKING THE SCIENTIFIC LITERACY MODEL

From Molecules to Personality

It's pretty mind-blowing to know that who you are was determined to a fair degree before you were even born, by whatever genes you happened to inherit from your parents. Researchers are just beginning to piece together which specific genes influence which traits.

What do we know about specific genes and personality?

Although scientists have not identified a specific gene or genes involved in the expression of specific personality factors, such as neuroticism or agreeableness, they have discovered genes that code for specific brain chemicals that, in turn, are related to personality. For example, one of the genes that codes for serotonin activity has been found on human chromosome 17. Specifically, this gene codes for proteins that transport serotonin molecules within the tiny spaces (synapses) between nerve cells. Many of our genes are polymorphic (*poly* = "multiple"; *morph* = "form"), meaning that there are different versions of the same gene that lead to different physical or behavioural characteristics. Two possible variations of the "serotonin transporter gene" have been identified: a short copy and a long copy.

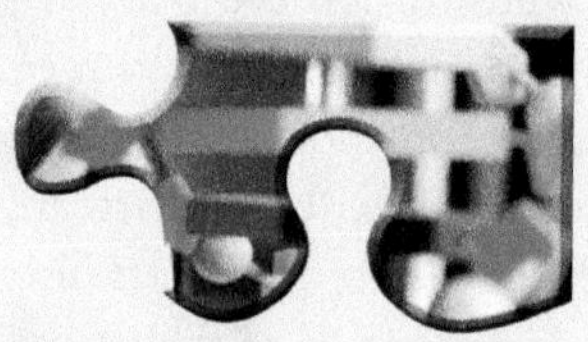

How do scientists study genes and personality?

To study genes and personality, one method is to compare responses on self-report questionnaires of people who have inherited different copies of a specific gene. People who inherit short copies of the serotonin transporter gene from one or both parents seem predisposed to anxiety, shyness, and experiencing negative emotional reactions in interpersonal situations (Battaglia et al., 2005; Lesch et al., 1996). However, other researchers have suggested that these differences may depend on which of the many different varieties of self-report questionnaires are used (Schinka et al., 2004).

Another method for studying genes and personality is to conduct experiments and compare the responses of people with different copies of a gene. In one study, participants provided a hair sample so researchers could extract DNA to determine which combination of serotonin transporter genes they had inherited. The participants completed a task that monitored their attentional focus to pictures of positive (e.g., a smiling infant), negative (a black widow spider), or neutral (a kitchen table) stimuli. Previous research has shown that people who have problems with anxiety focus their attention on threatening stimuli more than nonanxious people (Bar-Haim et al., 2007). Researchers found that participants who had inherited two long copies of the gene were biased toward looking at positive images more frequently and for longer periods of time. On the other hand, people who inherited one or two short versions of the gene spent more time looking at negative images (Figure 12.4; Fox et al., 2009). It seems that inheriting short copies of this gene increases anxiety levels in general, and seems to steer people toward giving excessive attention to negative and threatening information.

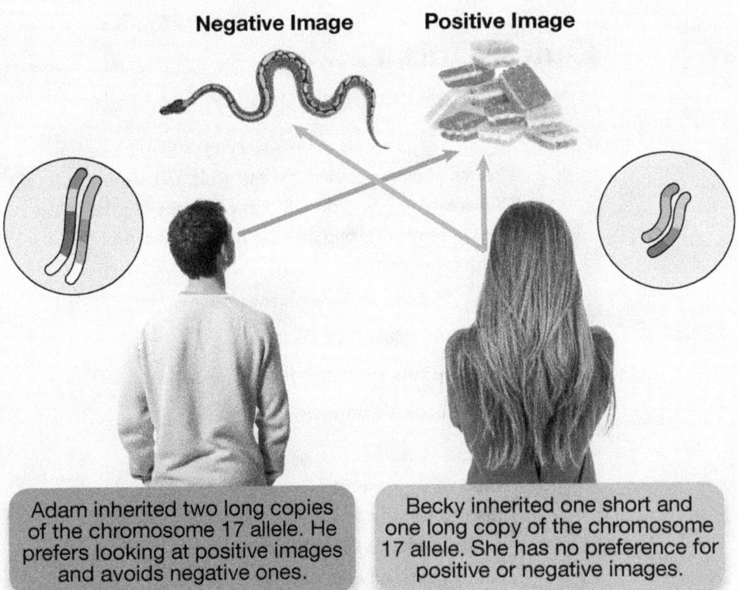

{FIG. 12.4} **Genes, Serotonin, and Personality** People who inherit two copies of the long version of the serotonin transporter gene fixate on positive images and avoid looking at negative images. People who inherit the short version of this gene are not biased toward attending to positive imagery.

Can we critically evaluate this evidence?

It is important to keep in mind that, in most cases, there is no single gene causing a single outcome in a person. Most phenomena are understood to be caused by multiple genes interacting with the environment. At this point the general consensus is that a vast number of genes, each of which has only a very small effect, account for individual differences in personality (Terracciano et al., 2010). It is also important to note that these are correlational studies, and inferring causality from such data is highly problematic.

Why is this relevant?

Knowledge about how genes and personality are related can help psychologists identify risk factors for developing mental disorders. As we will see in other parts of this text, genetic studies of personality help us better understand the biological basis of psychological disorders such as anxiety and depression. This work raises some interesting possibilities, such as the potential to screen individuals to assess their risk of developing a disorder. In turn, at-risk individuals might be better helped with early detection and treatment. Also, knowing about the genetic underpinnings of personality is highly informative to theorists seeking to understand how our personality traits, and the variability of traits across cultures, evolved in the first place.

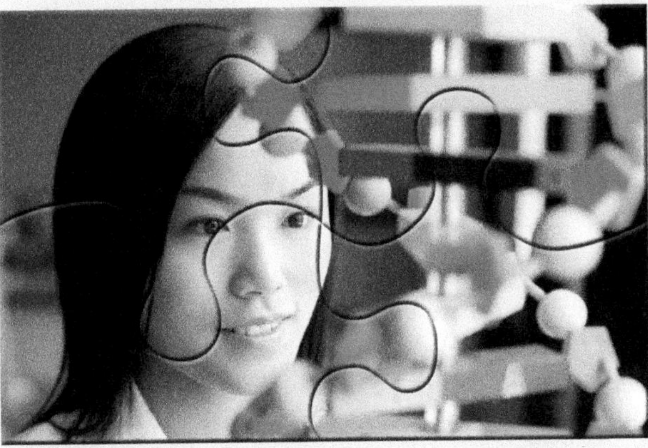

GoGo Images Corporation/Alamy

Quick Quiz 12.2b

How Genes Affect Personality

KNOW ...

1 ________ refers to the tendency to define the self in terms of one's personal identity, goals, and attributes, whereas ________ describes the tendency to define the self in terms of group memberships and relationships with other people.

A Motivation; agreeableness

B Individualism; collectivism

C Autonomy; dependence

D Collectivism; individualism

UNDERSTAND ...

2 Even when identical twins are reared apart, they still tend to be very similar in personality. How is this strong evidence that genes contribute to personality?

A Identical twins who were reared apart were most likely treated in very similar ways.

B The similarities remain, even though there were probably significant differences in how the siblings were raised.

C There are fewer similarities when twins are reared together.

D Actually, identical twins who are raised apart show very little similarity.

3 Which of the following statements best describes what psychologists now know about the genetic basis of personality?

A Hundreds of genes have been identified that are directly linked to specific personality traits.

B Technology is not sophisticated enough to link genes and personality characteristics.

C Some genes have been identified that are related to certain aspects of personality function.

D Genes do not contribute to personality characteristics.

Answers can be found on page ANS-3.

The Role of Evolution in Personality

Evolutionary psychologists emphasize that our personality structures are built right into our species because they conferred selective advantages to humans possessing certain traits. But the human species is related to other species as well, and so one would expect that we may share at least some aspects of our personalities with other species.

ANIMAL BEHAVIOUR: THE EVOLUTIONARY ROOTS OF PERSONALITY One compelling argument for the usefulness of the evolutionary perspective on personality is the presence of personality traits in numerous nonhuman species. For example, scientists have studied one particular species of bird (*Parus major*) that lives in Europe and Asia. These birds display two different patterns of behaviour when they encounter new environments, corresponding to a "fast-exploring" or "slow-exploring" personality type. The fast-exploring types are aggressive, bold in their exploration of new environments, and tend to rely more on routine ways of responding to the environment rather than being responsive to external cues. The slow-exploring types are passive, shy when confronted with new environments, and are more responsive to the external environment, changing their behaviour more readily to suit changes in the environment. These two personality types are known to have a strong genetic basis. Which of the two personality types is adaptive depends on what kind of year the birds are having. If there are limited resources, aggressive, fast-exploring females, and timid, slow-exploring males have greater reproductive success. In years where resources are plentiful, it is the opposite—slow-exploring females and fast-exploring males have greater success. There are complex reasons why males and females have personality factors that are oppositely adaptive to the environment, but the important point is that the basic personality dimension of aggressiveness vs. passivity is represented in these birds and has been clearly tied to the birds' adaptive advantage in different environments (Dingemanse et al., 2004).

The suggestion that animals have personalities may not strike you as all that surprising. Many people who have had close and extended experience with animals, from farmers to pet owners, would say that animals have personalities. For example, dog lovers don't feel that their pet is a totally incomprehensible beast; instead, they attribute qualities, emotions, and personality quirks that are very "human" to the beloved animal. This may merely illustrate our tendency to anthropomorphize the living world, seeing other species through our own egocentric lens, but it may also reflect our shared genetic heritage with other species.

Researchers who wish to study animal personalities face a daunting task, particularly considering that nonhuman animals are usually not very adept at filling out personality scales. To overcome this problem, individuals who are familiar with the animals rate their behaviours according to the five factors. Typically, observers strongly agree on their ratings of extraversion and neuroticism in the animals studied (Gosling, 2001). In fact, several of the Big Five personality traits have been found in a rich diversity of species—such as rhinos, primates, hedgehogs, and even ants (Gosling, 2001)! In one study of chimpanzees, our closest primate relatives, a list of adjectives was taken from the Big Five test and people who

Left: poeticpenguin/Shutterstock.com; centre: Rena Schild/Shutterstock.Com; right: dmvphotos/Shutterstock.com

Psychologists are finding that measures of human personality are applicable to diverse species such as hyenas, octopuses, and chimpanzees, among many others.

were familiar with the chimpanzee subjects rated how well the adjectives applied to each chimp on a 1 to 7 scale. Of the Big Five traits, extraversion, conscientiousness, and agreeableness were reliably found in the chimps (Weiss et al., 2007).

The presence of basic personality dimensions may be extremely widespread in the living world; some researchers even argue you do not need a backbone to have a personality! Researchers at the University of Lethbridge, Alberta, have shown that octopuses show stable individual differences in measures of activity, reactivity, and avoidance (Mather & Anderson, 1993).

WHY THERE ARE SO MANY DIFFERENT PERSONALITIES: THE EVOLUTIONARY EXPLANATION

David Zuroff of McGill University argues that evolutionary perspectives can make a major contribution to our understanding of personality, helping us to go beyond the Five Factor Model. According to Zuroff, the FFM has answered the "content" question of personality quite well, outlining the key factors that comprise personality. However, it leaves largely unaddressed the "process" questions, such as why we acquired the specific traits that we did (Zuroff et al., 2010).

Evolutionary perspectives can help us to understand why humans have evolved the particular personality traits that we have. To the extent that the Big Five traits are built right into our biology, these traits must have been selected for by being adaptive in past evolutionary epochs, helping to promote our survival and reproductive success.

For example, individuals high in extraversion would be more likely to rise in social hierarchies, playing leadership and social networking roles in a community; on the other hand, extraverts tend to be risk takers and sensation seekers, and it would therefore be desirable to offset these qualities with a healthy proportion of introverts in a group.

People high in conscientiousness would be reliable and dependable, and others would learn to count on them to get things done, clearly desirable qualities in a mate. However, the person low in conscientiousness may be an attractive partner to mate with for other reasons, such as their spontaneity and willingness to not always take life too seriously.

People low in neuroticism would be the emotional stalwarts of the community, the people who didn't crack under pressure but kept a level head and could be counted on in crises. However, being high in neuroticism could pay off at times; for example, groups may benefit from having some highly neurotic people around, because they would be more attuned to danger and act as the voice of caution that keeps others from making dangerous decisions.

People high in agreeableness would be the friends who are there for you when you need them, and they would generally help to promote harmony and solidarity as groups work together on larger projects; whereas those low in agreeableness may be useful for providing a critical perspective and ensuring that the group doesn't make rash decisions.

People high in openness would be imaginative and creative, helping to build bridges between members of different subgroups in the community, and challenging ideas so that the community doesn't rigidify into dogma and closed-mindedness. On the other hand, those low in openness may be useful for preserving traditions, and helping to identify a coherent sense of identity within the community.

MYTHS IN MIND

Men Are from Mars, Women Are from Venus

Much is often made about apparent differences in how men and women think and behave. This comparison can sometimes get stretched pretty far, such as the implication inherent in the title of the 1992 self-help book *Men Are from Mars, Women Are from Venus* (Gray, 1992). The notion that men and women may as well be from different planets is strongly reinforced by the popular media.

To what extent does science back up this hypothesis when it comes to personality? On the one hand, there is strong evidence that men and women differ on their Big Five personality ratings. Women generally report higher levels of extraversion, conscientiousness, agreeableness, and neuroticism than men. This finding has been noted in comparisons made across dozens of cultures (Schmitt et al., 2008). On the other hand, these gender differences are quite small, and are vastly overwhelmed by the variability *within* each gender. In other words, there are a lot of men who seem like they're from Venus, and a lot of women who seem like they're from Mars. So, even though there is a gender difference in personality, it is so small as to hardly allow the characterization that men and women are fundamentally different from each other.

In an interesting twist, however, this research also found that the gender differences are related to economic factors. Specifically, the countries showing the *largest* gender differences in personality also have greater access to resources such as health care, education, and wealth. Men and women in countries with fewer social and economic resources tend to be more similar in their self-reported personality scores. This phenomenon may occur because a lack of resources tends to constrain the behaviours and social roles of individuals, thus making people more similar to each other at the expense of their personal individuation. On the other hand, abundant prosperity opens up more opportunities for personal expression and allows individual differences to flourish (Schmitt et al., 2008). The authors argue that economic development allows people to express the "true" gender differences that exist whereas a lack of development imprisons people in their social roles, artificially narrowing what is considered to be acceptable behaviour for men and women.

The conclusion seems to be that men and women actually are from Mars and Venus, so to speak; they do have different personalities on average. Nevertheless, the differences are so small that Mars and Venus must be pretty similar places. A good title will sell a lot of self-help books, but does little to inform the general public about what scientific studies truly reveal about human behaviour.

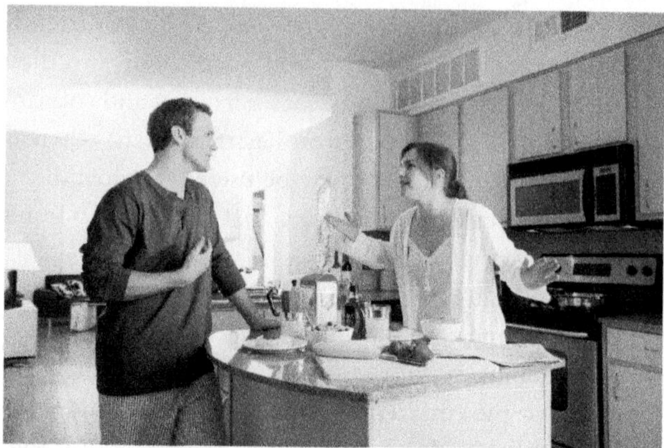

Jupiterimages/Brand X Pictures/Thinkstock

Men and women tend to differ in some personality dimensions. However, these differences are often greatly exaggerated—especially in the pop psychology industry.

Quick Quiz 12.2c
The Role of Evolution in Personality

APPLY ...

1 What is an important piece of evidence supporting an evolutionary basis of personality?

- **A** Changes in personality can be seen over generations.
- **B** Personality traits are stable in the sense that they are common among humans and can be found in nonhuman species.
- **C** Personality traits are not stable and cannot be found in nonhuman species.
- **D** No valid evidence supports an evolutionary approach to personality.

ANALYZE ...

2 According to evolutionary psychologists, there is great diversity in human personality because

- **A** certain personality traits (e.g., extraversion) were most adaptive and were therefore selected for over our evolutionary history.
- **B** different traits are most adaptive in different situations.
- **C** a person with a diverse personality is best able to adapt to different situations.
- **D** some personality traits are most adaptive for mating, whereas others are more adaptive for survival.

3 Which of the following statements best summarizes personality differences between men and women?

- **A** Averages of some traits such as extraversion and neuroticism tend to differ between men and women, but these differences are very small.
- **B** Males and females inherit separate sets of genes that cause their differences in personality.
- **C** Research shows that men and women really do not differ in personality.
- **D** Males are generally agreeable, whereas women are generally conscientious.

Answers can be found on page ANS-3.

As you can see, being either high or low in each Big Five trait could be desirable, depending on the situation. Thus, the complex blends of personality types across society evolved because different traits were desirable in different circumstances. Just as there are different niches to which animal species adapt in an ecosystem, there are different social niches to which people can adapt in society. The extravert and the introvert, the neurotic and the secure, the conscientious and the careless gravitate toward the respective niches they best fill.

The Brain and Personality

Modern biological approaches for investigating the brain and behaviour build on many ancient traditions of medicine that connected the mind to the body and sought to understand the person in terms of bodily processes. For example, for much of the past 2000 years, Western medicine was guided by the theory of **humourism**, *which explained both physical illnesses and disorders of personality as resulting from imbalances in key fluids in the body*—the four "humours," including blood, phlegm, black bile, and yellow bile. For example, too much black bile resulted in melancholy and irritability; too much yellow bile resulted in becoming hot-tempered and prone to anger.

By the late 1700s, physicians began looking more specifically at the brain for clues to people's personalities. The initial attempts weren't exactly high-level personality neuroscience, because scientists of the day did not have access to the biological research technologies necessary for studying the brain. One influential German doctor, Franz Gall, attempted to overcome this deficit by carefully measuring the shape and contours of the outer skull, and inferring the size of the brain areas inside. Gall developed **phrenology**—*the theory that personality characteristics could be assessed by carefully measuring the outer skull*; the specific dimensions of the skull indicated the size of the brain areas inside, which in turn corresponded to specific personality characteristics. Phrenology held sway well into the 1800s. Ironically, phrenologists were on the right track in postulating that different psychological functions were localized in specific regions of the brain; however, it turns out that measurements of the skull do not correspond meaningfully to the size and power of different brain areas, nor does the shape of the skull have anything to do with personality.

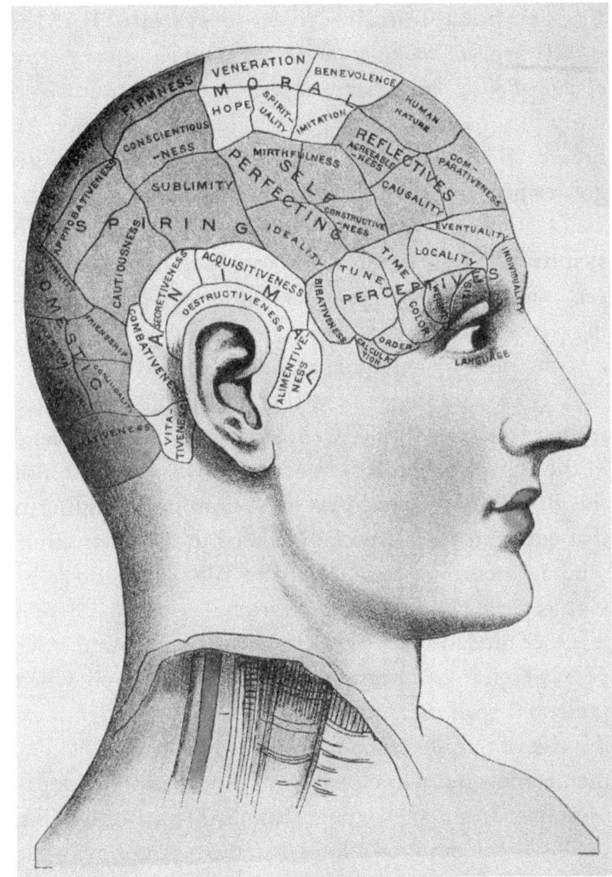

Classic Image/Alamy

Phrenologists believed that different personality traits were housed in different regions of the brain.

EXTRAVERSION AND AROUSAL By the mid-20th century, researchers working at the nexus of the biological and psychological sciences began convincingly linking personality characteristics with specific brain systems. One of the most influential pioneers in this field, Hans Eysenck (1967), proposed an **arousal theory of extraversion**, *arguing that extraversion is determined by people's threshold for arousal*; according to this theory, people high in extraversion (i.e., extraverts) have a higher threshold for arousal than people low in extraversion (i.e., introverts). As a result, extraverts generally seek greater amounts of stimulation, whereas introverts seek to limit the amount of stimulation they experience so as to not become overwhelmed with excessive arousal. One brain system, the **ascending reticular activating system (ARAS)**, *plays a central role in controlling this arousal response.* Eysenck initially proposed that extraverts have a lower resting baseline of activation of the ARAS than introverts; that is, extraverts are in a chronically lower state of arousal than introverts and therefore can handle a greater "kick" before becoming over-aroused. It turns out that it's not the average level of arousal of the ARAS, but its reactivity that differentiates extraverts from introverts. Put simply, for a given "kick," introverts have a stronger response.

Another influential model of the brain-personality relationship was proposed by Jeffrey Gray, whose approach/inhibition model of motivation (Gray, 1991) describes two major brain systems for processing rewards and punishments: the behavioural activation system and the behavioural inhibition system.

The **behavioural activation system (BAS)** *is a "GO" system, arousing the person to action in the pursuit of desired goals.* This system is responsive to rewards and fairly unresponsive to possible negative consequences; greater BAS activation therefore is associated with greater positive emotional responses and approach motivation. The other system, the **behavioural inhibition system (BIS)**, *is more of a "danger" system, motivating the person to action in order to avoid punishments or other negative outcomes.* The BIS is therefore associated with greater negative emotional responses and avoidance motivation.

As you might expect, the BIS/BAS systems are related to personality as well. Studies show that several of the Big Five factors are correlated with activation of the BIS/BAS systems. The most consistent finding is that extraversion is especially related to BAS activation, whereas neuroticism is related to BIS activation (e.g., Gomez et al., 2000). Research studies at many different levels of analysis back this up. At the behavioural level, people high in extraversion tend to act impulsively when presented with the possibility of rewards, even ignoring the risk of punishment (Patterson & Newman, 1993). At the neurochemical level, extraverts show a stronger dopamine response to rewarding stimuli (Depue & Collins, 1999). At the emotional level, extraverts tend to experience more positive affect in a range of situations (Ashby et al., 1999; Lucas et al., 2000). Thus, a trait measure of extraversion reflects the functioning of many different systems, providing a great example of the integration of science across many different areas of study.

CONTEMPORARY RESEARCH: IMAGES OF PERSONALITY IN THE BRAIN Modern-day researchers use brain-imaging technology to test for relationships between personality and the brain. Neuroscientists have tested whether each of the Big Five personality traits is associated with a different brain region, and whether these regions correspond to the behaviours associated with these traits. The general conclusion has been that indeed, there are many relationships between personality traits and the size of specific brain areas.

Extraversion: Extraverts have a larger medial orbitofrontal cortex (part of the PFC; DeYoung et al., 2010), and generally have less activation in the amygdala (Canli et al., 2002). The medial orbitofrontal cortex is involved in processing reward, which is consistent with extraverts' greater reward sensitivity. The amygdala, on the other hand, is involved in processing novelty, danger, and fear, which extraverts tend to pay less attention to, hence their *under*-active amygdalae (see Figure 12.5).

Neuroticism: Neuroticism is associated with the size of various brain areas, such as a smaller dorsomedial prefrontal cortex, a smaller hippocampus, and a larger mid-cingulate gyrus (an area right above the corpus callosum; DeYoung et al., 2010). Each of these areas is involved in abilities that are central to neuroticism.

The dorsomedial prefrontal cortex is involved in controlling emotions (Ochsner & Gross, 2005), the hippocampus in controlling obsessive negative thinking (Gray & McNaughton, 2000), and the mid-cingulate gyrus in detecting errors and perceiving pain—whether physical or emotional pain (Carter et al., 1998; Eisenberger & Lieberman, 2004). These are the kinds of processes that define highly neurotic people. They have difficulty controlling their emotions, often fall prey to obsessive negative thinking, and are highly sensitive when they make mistakes, or when they feel pain.

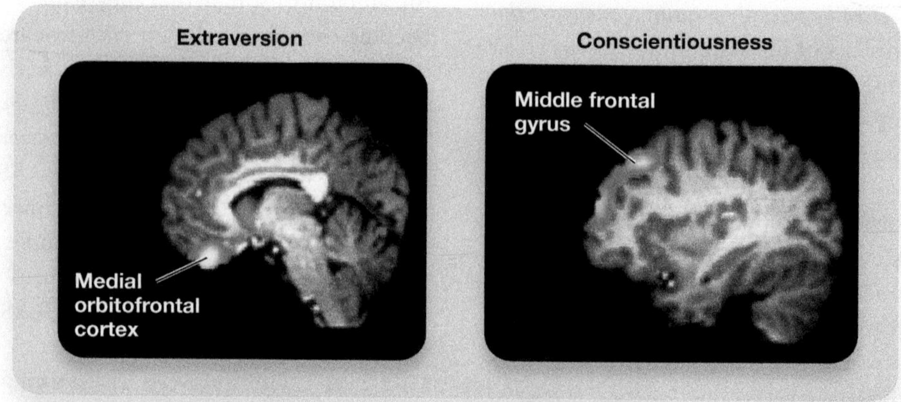

DeYoung, C. G., Hirsh, J. B., Shane, M. S., Papademetris, X., Rajeevan, N., & Gray, J. R. (2010). Testing predictions from personality neuroscience, Brain structure and the big five. *Psychological Science, 21*(6), 820–828. Reprinted by Permission of SAGE Publications

{FIG. 12.5} **Measuring Personality and Brain Anatomy** People's self-ratings of the Big Five traits correspond to their brain volume in specific regions. Here we see two (among several) regions of the brain where size is positively correlated with ratings of extraversion and conscientiousness (DeYoung et al., 2010).

Agreeableness: People high in agreeableness show less brain volume in an area called the left superior temporal sulcus (DeYoung et al., 2010), which is activated when one is interpreting another person's actions or intentions (Pelphrey & Morris, 2006). They also show greater volume in an area called the posterior cingulate cortex, which is involved in empathy and perspective-taking (DeYoung et al., 2010). These brain areas match the tendency for people high in agreeableness to be more socially attuned and to have more empathy for others.

Conscientiousness: People high in this trait have larger brain volume in the middle frontal gyrus in the left prefrontal cortex (DeYoung et al., 2010), which is involved in working memory processes and in carrying out actions that you have planned. These functions are implicated in effective self-control, which is a key strength of the highly conscientious person.

Openness to Experience: Individuals high in openness to experience have been shown to have greater activation in the dorsolateral prefrontal cortex, which is involved in creativity and intelligence, as well as other brain systems involved in the integration of the self and the environment (Adelstein et al., 2011). These systems reflect the tendencies for people high in openness to be creative, integrative thinkers.

Although the ability to link brain regions to personality processes at such a fine-grained level has only become possible recently, neuroscientists are beginning to find brain regions that differ reliably between people with different personality traits. This does not mean that these differences *cause* the personality differences, but it does suggest that these brain regions are involved in serving neurological functions that are related to personality processes at some level. The causal connections might be indirect and highly varied, challenging us with incredible complexity, both of personality itself but also complexity of the neurological architecture of the brain. This complexity reminds us that in most cases, there will be no specific brain area involved uniquely in a personality trait; for example, there is no "centre of extraversion" in the brain. Any trait plays itself out through many different thoughts, feelings, and behaviours, each of which involves many different brain systems. What ends up manifesting as a stable pattern that we identify as a personality trait therefore represents patterns of activation across many different brain systems.

So we may never be able to point at a single region (or even a few regions) and declare it to be the centre of any single personality trait. That said, we have come a long way from the days when personality was described in terms of the four humours of blood, phlegm, and black and yellow bile.

Quick Quiz 12.2d The Brain and Personality

KNOW ...

1 An outdated approach claiming that behaviour and personality were based on the sizes of various regions of the skull surface was called

A magnetic resonance imaging.

B alchemy.

C phrenology.

D humourism.

2 Hans Eysenck believed that extraversion was tied most closely to the functioning of the

A kimbic system.

B parasympathetic nervous system.

C ascending reticular activating system.

D amygdala.

APPLY ...

3 You are looking at an fMRI brain scan of a subject in a research study. The scan shows that the person generally has greater activation in the dorsolateral prefrontal cortex, and less activation in the amygdala. Based on this information, what guess would you make about the person's personality profile?

A Low on extraversion, high on conscientiousness

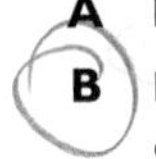

B High on extraversion, high on openness to experience

C Low in neuroticism, high on extraversion

D Low in neuroticism, high on conscientiousness

Answers can be found on page ANS-3.

Module Summary

Module 12.2

Now that you have read this module you should

Randy Faris/Glow Images

KNOW ...

- ***The key terminology associated with cultural and biological approaches to personality:***

arousal theory of extraversion (p. 517)
ascending reticular activating system (ARAS) (p. 517)
behavioural activation system (BAS) (p. 518)
behavioural inhibition system (BIS) (p. 518)
humourism (p. 517)
phrenology (p. 517)

UNDERSTAND ...

- ***How evolutionary theories explain personality.*** Evolutionary psychologists theorize that personality traits evolved because they solved environmental and social problems encountered by our distant ancestors. Although this hypothesis is difficult to test directly, different sources of evidence lend support to it. The widespread occurrence of these personality traits among different species indicates that they are adaptive.

APPLY ...

- ***Your knowledge to understand how arousal is related to extraversion.*** Although extraversion is commonly interpreted to indicate how sociable and friendly people are, it is more fundamentally related to how reactive people are to stimulation. Highly extraverted people have less reactive ascending reticular activating systems (ARAS), which means that they don't get as big of a "kick" out of a given level of stimulation; this causes them to prefer more stimulating environments, relative to introverts, who have more reactive ARASs, and therefore prefer lower levels of stimulation so that they do not feel overwhelmed.

ANALYZE ...

- ***Claims that males and females have fundamentally different personalities.*** Claims of major gender differences in personality are sometimes made to support popular-book sales. In reality, the general consensus in psychological science is that males and females are more alike than different when it comes to personality. Both, of course, share common personality dimensions. Although females tend to be, on average, more conscientious, agreeable, extraverted, and neurotic than males, these differences are very small, and there is no evidence to support claims that men and women are fundamentally different in personality.
- ***The genetic basis of personality.*** Heritability studies show that personality traits are substantially predicted by genetic variation. Studies of twins and adopted children also back this up, showing that identical twins are far more similar in personality than fraternal twins, and that the home in which people grow up has much less influence over their personalities than the genes they inherited from their biological parents. However, despite this evidence for genetic influences on personality, one cannot conclude that personality is "hard wired" and therefore unchangeable. Personality emerges through the interaction of genes and the environment; thus, a given genetic make-up can express itself differently in different environments.

blas/Fotolia

Module 12.3

Psychodynamic and Humanistic Approaches to Personality

Learning Objectives

After reading this module you should

KNOW ...	UNDERSTAND ...	APPLY ...	ANALYZE ...
The key terminology related to the psychodynamic and humanistic approaches to personality	How people use defence mechanisms to cope with conflicting thoughts and feelings The developmental stages Freud used to explain the origins of personality	Both psychodynamic and humanistic perspectives to explain personality	Whether projective tests are valid measures of personality The strengths and weaknesses of psychodynamic perspectives

Have you ever wondered, are you living your life as well as you possibly could? Are you the most empowered, vibrant self you could possibly be? Have you reached the pinnacle of what is possible for a human to become? To paraphrase the old U.S. army recruiting slogan, are you being all that you could be?

If you are being honest, your answer is probably no. And that's okay. Seriously, who has "reached the pinnacle of human development"? Almost all of us haven't developed our personalities to their utmost potential. We have shortcomings and flaws, and live decidedly less-than-ideal lives. Why is this? What is holding us back? What would we be like if we did "reach the pinnacle"?

Abraham Maslow was fascinated by questions like these. He was inspired by the potential he believed that human beings possess to become fully developed, or "self-actualized." In striking contrast to much of the cynicism of the 20th century, Maslow believed that although we have the capacity for great evil, at the very foundation of our being we are inherently good. He argued that the more we open ourselves to our inherent goodness, the more we will see reality clearly, rather than through our biases; the more we will be empowered and able to confront life courageously, rather than shrinking from challenges because of our insecurities; and the more we can focus on helping others rather than tending to our own needs and wants. The end result of pursuing personal growth is to become fully, vibrantly alive.

"Laboring under the effects of deficiency motivation is like looking at the world through a clouded lens, and removing those effects is like replacing the clouded lens with a clear one. Self-actualizing persons' contact with reality is simply more *direct*. And along with this unfiltered, unmediated directness of their contact with reality comes also a vastly heightened ability to appreciate again and again, freshly and naively, the basic goods of life, with awe, pleasure, wonder, and even ecstasy, however stale those experiences may have become for others." (Maslow, 1968)

Is it possible to live such a life? Maslow thought so, and studied the biographies of people who he deemed to be "self-actualized," people like Abraham Lincoln, Albert Einstein, Eleanor Roosevelt, and Aldous Huxley. Despite this rather unscientific approach, his study revealed a host of characteristics that seemed universal among the self-actualized, including the following:

They are attuned to reality as it is, rather than engaging in wishful thinking or filtering their experiences through their wants and needs.

Rather than bowing to social pressures or fearing the judgment of others, they strive to be "authentic," to present their true selves to the world.

They tend to be spontaneous and creative, responding freely and naturally to their circumstances.

They ground their awareness firmly in the present moment, not dwelling on the past or dreaming of a brighter future for themselves.

They possess a profound capacity for gratitude, appreciation, and wonder, taking great delight in the world around them.

They experience a strong, universal sense of connection and empathy for all of humanity.

They frequently seem to have "peak experiences"—moments of ecstasy, wonder, awe, and feeling "one with the universe."

Maslow hoped that his work would help people learn how to cultivate these qualities within themselves. His optimistic vision of human nature was a major break with the psychology of that time, which was dominated by behaviourism and Freudian psychoanalysis. To the behaviourists, "personality" was an unnecessary concept, because behaviour was merely the result of a complex accumulation of rewards and punishments that had been conditioned into the person over the course of her lifetime. And as we discuss below, to the Freudians, personality was a battleground between opposing forces in the psyche, as people struggled to defend themselves against the negativity that loomed in their unconscious.

Simulate What Has Shaped Your Personality?

Although neither Freudian psychoanalysis nor Maslow's humanistic theories have retained their once-prominent positions in psychology, they remain highly influential approaches in society at large, and have inspired and guided generations of people to more fully live their lives. In this module, we explore these exciting approaches that tried to get right to the heart of what it means to be human.

Focus Questions

 How do the psychodynamic and humanistic approaches give you insight into your own personality?

 How do people use psychological defences to protect themselves from emotionally troubling events?

Sigmund Freud does not get much respect in our society today. Many of his theories have not stood the test of time and are now largely ignored. Some of his theories are even regarded as ridiculous by most people (e.g., the Oedipus complex, which we discuss later in this module). He was a passionate user and advocate of cocaine before its addictive and destructive properties were known. He is said to have been a tyrant in some ways, allowing his followers little freedom to dissent from his views. He has been critiqued as having an obsession with sex, to have created unfalsifiable and therefore unscientific theories, and to have created grand theories of the psyche based on studying an extremely narrow cross-section of humanity (mostly women seeking counselling in Victorian-era Europe).

However, despite the criticisms, Sigmund Freud is one of the most influential psychologists in history. Freud was a pioneer in the study of personality and the treatment of psychological disorders, and many of his ideas about human consciousness continue to resonate with many psychologists, and are widely accepted and used in contemporary society. When a drug addict admits to being "in denial" of his addiction, an abuse survivor talks about how she "repressed" her memories and feelings for many years, or someone accuses you of "projecting" your anger onto other people, they are hearkening back to Freud.

Interestingly, Freud was not trained in psychology, but was instead a neurologist. The launch of his scientific career was anything but glamorous; he spent many hours peering through microscopes at tissue samples, searching for the elusive testicles of the male eel. Scientists of the day had not yet been able to locate the eel's testicles, but Freud's extraordinary attention to detail allowed him to eventually make the discovery, after dissecting many hundreds of eels. Which might make you ask, what kind of person exhaustively searches for eel testicles? Freudian theorists would have an interesting answer to that question.

After leaving his scientific career to be trained as a physician, Freud began to accept clients who sought his help for psychological difficulties. Initially, Freud believed that their issues could be resolved through investigating their physiology and isolating the biological factors that contributed to their problems. However, after thoroughly examining some of his patients, he realized that their emotional struggles often could not be understood at the physiological level; instead, he had to delve into the mysterious depths of the mind. This led him to begin trying to understand the personalities of his patients, and the psychological dynamics that led to the problems they were experiencing.

Over time, his observations and ideas coalesced into his *psychodynamic theory*, which isn't really a "theory" at all, but rather an evolving family of different theories and ideas that share many key features, which we discuss in this module (also, see Westen, 1998).

The Psychodynamic Perspective

A universal assumption of psychodynamic theories is that personality and behaviour are shaped by powerful forces in consciousness, a great deal of which is hidden from our awareness in the mysterious unconscious. By emphasizing the unconscious, Freud threw into doubt many of our common feelings and beliefs. For example, we like to feel like we are in control of ourselves and our behaviour reflects conscious choices that we make. We believe that we know why we do the things we do, that our behaviour makes sense to us. We also like to believe that when we do something embarrassing, immoral, or just plain stupid, that we were somehow "out of control" or that it was a mistake.

From a psychodynamic perspective, however, there are no mistakes, and we have very little control over ourselves, and remarkably little insight into the reasons for our own behaviours. Everything we think, feel, and do results from psychological dynamics that are so deeply buried in our unconscious that we have no direct access to them; our mind is a "black box," even to ourselves.

To understand the implications of Freud's psychodynamic theory, we will explore its key concepts and how they apply to personality psychology.

UNCONSCIOUS PROCESSES AND PSYCHODYNAMICS Freud grounded his theories on a model of consciousness that distinguished between different levels of mental life, most importantly between the conscious mind and the unconscious. The **conscious mind** *is your current awareness, containing everything you are aware of right now.* The **unconscious mind** *is a much more vast and powerful but inaccessible part of your consciousness, operating without your conscious endorsement or will to influence and guide your behaviours.* The unconscious mind houses your full lifetime of memories and experiences, including those that you can no longer bring into conscious awareness, such as emotional patterns that were created in early childhood or even infancy. It also contains your preferences and desires, thus powerfully influencing your motivations, but usually so subtly that you are not even aware of it. The relationship between these two levels of consciousness is often described using an iceberg metaphor of consciousness (Figure 12.6). With icebergs, the part you can see above the surface is a small fraction of the entire iceberg, while most of its bulk lurks beneath the surface; similarly, the conscious mind is a small fraction of the entire psyche, while most of the psyche lurks beneath the surface of our awareness in the depths of the unconscious.

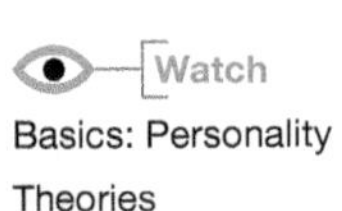

Because the unconscious is fairly inaccessible to consciousness and is much more powerful than the conscious mind, it is the primary driver of our behaviours. Even seemingly trivial behaviours, such as slips of the tongue, reflect the workings of the unconscious. In fact, these slips, famously called "Freudian slips," are very useful to the observant person, because they offer a glimpse into the otherwise inaccessible workings of the unconscious. When people make a Freudian slip, their conscious mind intends to say something appropriate to the circumstances, but their unconscious mind leads them to say what they were "really thinking." One of the most famous in recent cultural history occurred during a TV wedding on *Friends* between Ross and Emily. You may remember the fateful, "I, Ross, take thee, Rachel. . . . "

Freud believed fervently in the value of these "psychopathologies of everyday life" and developed several techniques that psychoanalysts could employ to use these small hints to gain access into the netherworld of the unconscious. (We revisit this later in this module.) These techniques were necessary because understanding the relationship between the conscious and unconscious minds was thought to give important

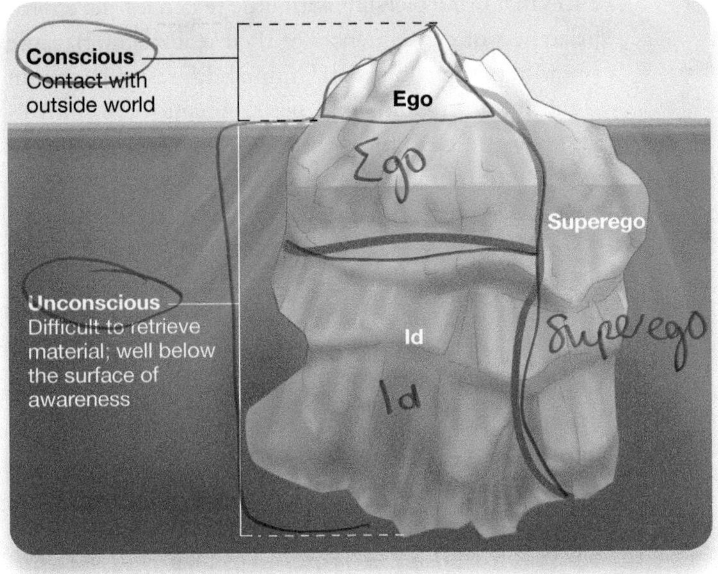

{FIG. 12.6} **The Freudian Structure of Personality** A popular depiction of how Freud viewed personality features an iceberg, with the unconscious mind residing below the surface and conscious awareness at only the tip of the iceberg. The id is completely submerged, whereas the ego and the superego operate at both unconscious and conscious levels. **Click on this figure in your eText to see more details.**

insights into human personality. Freud and other psychoanalysts argued that much of what manifests as personality reflects patterns that emerge from individuals' attempts to resolve conflicts within themselves, conflicts that are played out through the interactions between the conscious and unconscious minds. How does this occur? How do the conscious and unconscious minds interact with each other?

THE STRUCTURE OF PERSONALITY Have you ever done something you knew at the time was wrong? Like eating that brownie when you were trying to improve your diet? Losing your temper? Hooking up with that attractive person even though they have a boyfriend or girlfriend (or you do)? It's a cliché that desire and our conscience often are at odds with each other; think of the cartoon images of the devil sitting on one shoulder urging you to "do it!" and the angel on the other pleading with you not to.

To explain this all-too-common conflict, Freud hypothesized that the human psyche consists of three basic structures, which are often in conflict with each other: the *id*, the *ego*, and the *superego* (Figure 12.6).

Explore The Id, Ego, and Superego

The **id** *represents a collection of basic biological drives, including those directed toward sex and aggression*. Freud believed the id was fuelled by an energy called *libido*. Although this term is more commonly used in reference to sexual energy, the libido also controls other biological urges such as hunger. The id operates according to the *pleasure principle*, motivating people to seek out experiences that bring pleasure, with little regard for the appropriateness or consequences of their realization. Because the id represents our basic animal desires, it is present right from birth and is the predominant force controlling our actions in the earliest stages of our lives. The id gets us into trouble though, and increasingly so as we get older and society frowns on us hitting people in a rage or touching ourselves "down there" while we're in the living room with our family (a not uncommon activity for very young children to engage in, until they realize it is considered "bad"). Because society imposes constraints on our behaviour, the id must be restrained from its animal nature; and that is where the ego and superego come into play.

The **superego** *is comprised of our values and moral standards*. Our superego tells us what we *ought* to do, whereas the id tells us what our animal body *wants* to do. Freud believed that the superego forms over time as we become socialized into our family and larger community, and we are taught the values and norms of our society. The superego represents a process of internalization, through which we initially learn what is "right" and "proper" through being praised or punished by our caregivers, and we eventually internalize this praise and punishment until we apply it to ourselves. Thus, when we behave immorally, the superego chastises us, similarly to how our parents may have done, thereby encouraging us to "do the right thing."

In between the devilish id and the angelic superego sits the beleaguered **ego**, *the decision maker, frequently under tension, trying to reconcile the opposing urges of the id and superego*. So, instead of hitting someone when we are angry, we find more socially acceptable ways of expressing it, like being sarcastic and telling them off, or waiting until we get home so we can yell at our pillow or phone up a friend and vent our frustrations. The ego has to be plugged into reality; if it listened to the id all the time, we would be hedonic deviants, instantly gratifying ourselves at every turn, but if it listened to the superego all the time, we would cut ourselves off from much of our raw passion and zest for life. The ego seeks to balance the two forces, pulled by the tension between the id's need for instant gratification, and the superego's urging to do what is appropriate or moral. Thus, the ego operates according to the *reality principle*, still interested in gratifying its desires, but striving to postpone it until the appropriate situation.

According to Freud, personality arises out of the interactions among these three different systems in the mind. The id, ego, and superego are in constant tension, the id urging "Yes! Do it now!," the superego admonishing "No, that is inappropriate," and the ego mediating this dispute between the two, seeking an acceptable resolution. The tension between these three systems gives rise to personality in two key ways.

One is that different people will have deep personality differences because of the relative strengths of their id, ego, and superego. You can imagine the difference between a person guided by an extremely strong superego, and a person guided by an extremely strong id. The purist and the carnal are a far distance apart indeed. In this deep, structural sense, individuals' personalities are patterned by their own particular ego, as it figures out a way through the unfriendly tension between the id and superego; each system helps shape the other two, giving rise to each individual's particular personality.

The second key dynamic that generates much of our personality is how we react to anxiety. Anxiety plays a huge role in psychodynamic thought, because anxiety is the experiential—what we feel—result of the tension between the id, ego, and superego. When these systems are out of balance, we experience the deprivation of one system as a kind of basic anxiety. This drives negative thoughts and feelings, which ideally would serve as a messenge to us, a signal that "something is wrong; this system is not in harmony."

We experience anxiety about the profound as well as the mundane and everyday; it is important to realize that anxiety can be huge and overwhelming in the moment, or it can be a kind of small threat that one has to pay attention to and deal with. For example, you can feel anxiety over ways that you were mean to someone in the past; perhaps you were a bully, or cheated on your partner, or even killed people during a war. You feel guilty over your past, fearing that maybe you are not the good person you once believed you were. Dealing with those negative feelings is a challenge for the ego.

But the ego is also engaging in more minor anxiety-defence throughout our days. When we are afraid we failed, we experience anxiety. When we don't answer the phone call from our mom because we are too busy listening to our id's urgings to pay attention to the attractive person in our apartment, we experience anxiety. Similarly, if we do decide to answer the phone (because our superego tells us to), our id screaming at us, "No, you dummy, don't do it!" also creates anxiety. And when we're caught in the middle, unable to choose what to do, the result is, not surprisingly, more anxiety. From Freud's perspective, the psyche is a constant battleground, with the ego trying to keep both the id and superego happy, while protecting itself from anxiety.

DEFENCE MECHANISMS Oftentimes, the ego is unable to resolve the anxieties that plague it. Instead, it falls back to a defensive position and focuses merely on protecting itself from excessive anxiety, seeking some way of minimizing or avoiding the negativity it is experiencing. Imagine a young child caught between Mom and Dad screaming at each other, but having no way to resolve their conflict, he plugs his ears and hides in the closet. The child can't resolve the negativity, so he directly tries to escape it. This is what the ego does when it employs its **defence mechanisms**, *unconscious strategies the ego uses to reduce or avoid anxiety* (Freud, 1936; see Table 12.3). In fact, the literal acts of plugging one's ears and running into the closet are examples of *denial*, which is a very common defence mechanism.

Explore Defence Mechanisms

Defence mechanisms play key roles in many important social phenomena, such as prejudice and discrimination. For example, imagine a CEO of a company choosing not to hire a member of an ethnic minority; the CEO may protect himself or herself from admitting the possibility that the choice was racially motivated by engaging in *rationalization*, reasoning that the applicant didn't seem as impressive, professional, or "like she will fit into our team." You can imagine the thought, "It had nothing to do with race, of course! I just want to hire the best person for the job, and I felt that she wasn't the right fit. After all, I have a lot of experience in this company, and I trust my sense of who is going to work out and who isn't." You can see how easily a person's own reasoning process can be hijacked by the ego in order to

Table 12.3 :: Examples of Some Major Defence Mechanisms

DEFENCE MECHANISM	DEFINITION	EXAMPLE
Repression	Keeping distressing information out of conscious awareness by burying it in the unconscious.	Many people believe that victims of abuse or violence are sometimes able to *repress* memories, essentially "forgetting" that the violence occurred. Of course, the impact of what they experienced nevertheless conditions them in many different ways, driving their characteristic thoughts, emotions, and behaviour patterns. In some cases, these memories seem to resurface, coming back into the person's conscious awareness.
Denial	Refusing to acknowledge unpleasant information, particularly about oneself.	People in relationships often deny to themselves the many ways in which they themselves contribute to the problems in their relationship. It's not just their partner's fault! They themselves may be excessively critical, judgmental, or sarcastic. They may subtly control their partner through their own negative emotions such as anger or anxiety. They may be defensive or jealous or become angry when disagreed with. But they may simply refuse to consider these negative aspects of themselves, and find other explanations for the problems in their relationship.
Rationalization	Attempting to hide one's true motives (even from oneself!) by providing what seems like a reasonable explanation for unacceptable feelings or behaviours.	People who are prejudiced against certain types or groups of other people may not see themselves as racist, but may instead believe that the group they are prejudiced against actually does possess certain negative qualities. By believing that people from the disliked group are hostile, or lazy, or unintelligent, the person never has to confront their prejudice. It is important to note with an example such as this that of course the rationalization does not need to be true or even reasonable; it simply must feel like a reasonable explanation to the person using it.

protect itself, and the line between what is true and what merely appears to be true can so easily be blurred.

- Displacement—transforming an unacceptable impulse into a less unacceptable or neutral behaviour. For example, if you have ever stomped to your bedroom and slammed the door instead of telling your parents off, you have engaged in displacement. Ditto for throwing a plate at the wall or swearing at your cat.
- Identification—unconsciously assuming the characteristics of a more powerful person in order to reduce feelings of anxiety or negative feelings about the self. By expressing those qualities oneself, the insecure or anxious person makes himself feel like a stronger, more competent, more worthy person. For example, someone who was bullied when she was young may begin to adopt the characteristics of the bully, especially when she is with a less powerful person. In this way, the child bullied by an abusive parent often becomes a bully in other contexts, or with his or her own children eventually.
- Projection—keeping yourself unaware of undesirable qualities that you possess by instead attributing those qualities to other groups or people. For example, the particularly selfish person may tend to see other people as selfish and aggressive, believing that we live in a "dog-eat-dog" kind of world, where everybody is looking out for themselves.
- Reaction formation—altering an impulse that one finds personally unacceptable into its opposite. For example, men who are homophobic show greater penile arousal (compared to non-homophobic men) when looking at pornography of males engaging in sexual acts with other men (Adams, Wright, & Lohr, 1996).
- Sublimation—transforming unacceptable impulses into socially acceptable or even pro-social alternatives. For example, someone with a great deal of hostility and aggressive tendencies may become a football player, whereas someone with intense sexual desire may become an artist. (Which puts an interesting twist on the dilemma of whether to date jocks or artsy types . . .) Freud believed that sublimation was one of the cornerstones of civilization, the mechanism by which base human desires were harnessed to give rise to great works of art, invention, and scientific advance.

Explore
Freud's Five Psychosexual Stages of Personality Development

Unfortunately, although defence mechanisms may keep us from feeling anxiety in the moment, they are ultimately dysfunctional, for a variety of reasons. One is simply that undesirable tendencies are not confronted and problems are not dealt with; instead, immense energy is devoted to maintaining the defence mechanisms and trying to feel okay. For example, alcoholics (and often their families) sometimes go to great lengths to avoid having to admit that they have a problem, which only worsens the impact of alcohol on their lives. Freud's (and others') work on defence mechanisms remains influential to this day, particularly in the mental health field, where defence mechanisms often play important roles in therapy for psychological disorders.

PERSONALITY DEVELOPMENT: THE PSYCHOSEXUAL STAGES Freud also proposed a theory of personality development based on psychodynamic principles. To Freud, the infant is a bundle of impulses, ruled by the id; it is only through experience that the ego and superego can emerge. He believed that childhood could be divided into a series of important stages, which occur mostly in the first five years of life (as summarized in Table 12.4). At each stage, the libido manifests

Table 12.4 :: Freud's Stages of Psychosexual Development

STAGE	PLEASURE FOCUS	KEY DYNAMICS
Oral (0–18 months)	Actions of the mouth—sucking, chewing, swallowing	This stage is about the very foundation of the ego. Fixation at this stage represents a basic lack of self-confidence and "ego-strength," leaving the person more vulnerable, and more dependent on outside supports, such as relationships or even addictions.
Anal (18–36 months)	Bowel elimination, control	This stage is about the development of a sense of control, and competence. Fixation at this stage leads to "anal retentive" personality or "anal expulsive" personality, manifesting either as an obsession with cleanliness, order, and control, or as a disorganized slacker with utter disregard for order.
Phallic (3–6 years)	Genitals	The key personality challenge is the Oedipus complex, through which a person further develops the superego, due to the internalization of values from the parents. Fixation at this stage leads to problems with jealousy, and obsessions with power and sex.
Latency (6 years until puberty)	External activities	Ideally, this stage is fairly conflict-free. People focus on developing themselves, discovering their interests through sports, arts, school, and general activities. Fixation at this stage was not considered to be a big concern.
Genital (puberty to adulthood)	Sexual activities with others	Ideally, this stage is also fairly conflict-free. People focus on fully entering the world as themselves, further developing and expressing their mature, adult personality, provided they are not fixated at earlier stages.

Stockbyte/Getty Images

Psychodynamic theories of personality emphasize early childhood development, especially in terms of emotion. In particular, the dynamic between parent and child is thought to determine how personality develops.

in particular areas of the body, depending on what areas are most important for providing the person with pleasure; the id therefore focuses on these areas, attempting to derive as much pleasure as possible from them. Thus, each of these important regions becomes a battleground pitting the child's id against the restrictions of the adult world.

In order for proper development to occur, the individual must learn to transition from one stage to the next, which can be helped or harmed by the behaviours of one's caregivers. Children who fail to make this transition effectively are said to experience **fixation**, *becoming preoccupied with obtaining the pleasure associated with a particular stage.* Fixation can occur either because of conflict and excessive parental interference (e.g., criticizing the child for making mistakes during toilet training), or because the child is allowed to overindulge in that form of pleasure-seeking behaviour (e.g., the *Simpsons* character, Maggie, is in serious danger of developing an oral fixation).

The oral stage: An oral fixation can occur if the infant fails to transition out of the *oral stage* (0–18 months). For babies, life is all about sensations of the mouth. Imagine being an infant—in the beginning, life is sweet; you don't have to do anything, get fed whenever you are hungry, and you get to suck on whatever you can reach, including things that feed you. But as time goes on and infancy fades into toddlerhood, more restrictions start getting placed on you. With your increased mobility and ability to get more objects into your mouth, you start getting scolded more and more often for putting things in your mouth. This is a major adjustment!

Because infancy lays the basic foundation of experience upon which consciousness is built, what happens in infancy has a profound effect on the rest of one's life. Infants who are fixated at this stage fail to fully develop their ego. As a result, the orally fixated adult is somewhat more vulnerable, less capable at adjusting to social reality (i.e., impaired in following the reality principle), and less able to deal with anxiety through the use of defence mechanisms. Freud might explain that habits such as biting your fingernails or excessive gum chewing stem from unresolved conflict during the oral stage. But these are just behavioural clues as to what might be happening in the personality. The orally fixated nail biter is likely, in Freud's view, to be the kind of person who struggles with over-indulgence of many forms (e.g., overeating, addiction) and being orally aggressive (i.e., "mouthing off" to others), envious, and generally demanding, among other things.

The anal stage: This stage occurs during the toddler years (2–3), during which toilet training and the control of bowel movements takes up a lot of the toddler's awareness. Freud believed that if these bathroom skills were learned successfully and positively with support and encouragement from caregivers, the result was a sense of competence and confidence that would lead the toddler to develop into a well-adjusted and productive adult. But if parents were too strict and critical of toddlers, making them feel bad about "having an accident"

Left: Jupiterimages/Thinkstock; right: Exactostock/SuperStock

According to Freud, during the oral stage of psychosexual development pleasure is derived from actions of the mouth—particularly breastfeeding. Later, during the anal stage, attention turns toward potty training.

and putting too much pressure on them, they could be fixated at this stage. Eventually, they would become "anal retentive" adults, a rather rigid personality excessively concerned with cleanliness and order, with a high need for control and not a great deal of emotional openness. Or the parents might be too lenient and provide too little support for toilet training. This would produce an "anal expulsive" adult who exhibits opposite qualities of slovenliness, disorganization, and general irresponsibility.

The phallic stage: Ages 3–6 are a monumentally important time in the child's development. Bodily attention shifts to the genitals as children become aware of the differences between boys and girls and start to heavily identify with one gender. Boys go through the now-infamous *Oedipus complex*, during which they become sexually attracted to their mothers. However, they also realize that they are in competition with their fathers for their mothers' affections; this creates resentment toward their fathers, and in the wonderful logic of young children, they want to kill the fathers. During this time, boys struggle with highly conflicted feelings toward their fathers, feeling both attached to and hostile toward them. This is an excruciating time emotionally, as boys are torn between such strong feelings and longings. Freud represents this anguish with the Greek tragedy of *Oedipus Rex* (by Sophocles); in this story, the main character, Oedipus, kills his father without knowing he has done so, and ends up marrying his mother. When he eventually learns what he has done, he is so overcome with horror that he stabs his own eyes, blinding himself. (The ancient Greeks were fairly intense.)

Freud used highly sexual language to describe the phallic stage, although it is important to remember that the literal descriptions can also be understood to provide metaphoric insights into personality. According to Freud, little boys are quite distressed to learn that their mothers do not have penises; they reason that something must have happened to cut them off. And if that happened to their mothers, it might happen to them! Furthermore, it stands to reason that it was the powerful father figure who did the nasty deed, thus causing a great deal of *castration anxiety*, the fear of castration by one's father. (Metaphorically, castration anxiety is the fear of emasculation.) Boys resolve this fear, and thus the Oedipus complex, by learning to identify with the father, developing a close bond with him, while repressing sexual feelings for the mother.

For girls, the logic was considerably more complicated and Freud revised his theories somewhat over time. Basically, Freud believed that girls also want to sexually possess their mothers, and are in competition with their fathers. However, discovering that they themselves are lacking a penis, girls experience *penis envy*, which is, well, pretty much exactly what it sounds like. As a result, girls redirect their sexual interest to their fathers, and subsequently men in general, because having a child with a man (a boy, that is) provides the girl with a penis (sort of), which she never completely stops envying. (It's safe to assume the critiques of Freud's ideas about women are painfully obvious at this point; indeed, these critiques of the phallic stage, as well as its general inaccuracy as a description of the psychological experiences of most people, have been devastating to this part of Freud's theories.)

The importance of the phallic stage is that, at its resolution, the child has formed a healthy relationship with the parents, resulting in the internalization of parental values, which completes the formation of the superego. Successfully transitioning out of this stage leaves the child well prepared as a moral being. On the other hand, becoming fixated at this stage has striking negative consequences. People become plagued with jealousy and preoccupied with sex, seduction, competitiveness, and power.

Freud believed that girls never entirely resolve their Oedipus complexes (the term *Electra complex* was coined by Carl Jung, and rejected by Freud), leaving women with somewhat less well-developed superegos and thus, a less reliable morality. To the extent that Oedipal issues remain, the woman will seek to control and dominate men, because of course, men have the penises that women envy, and one way of possessing them is to dominate men. According to Freud, women dominate men through their sexuality or through manipulative submissiveness.

The latency stage: After the lurid sexuality and emotional drama of the phallic stage, the *latency stage* is downright boring. Between ages 5 and 13, the ego and superego have achieved a degree of general calm. The sexual nature of the libido is deemphasized, and it is instead directed into more productive activities than trying to mate with and murder one's parents, such as education, hobbies, and hanging out with friends. This is a period of rich personal development for children, during which they gain many of their intellectual, social, artistic, and physical skills. Interestingly, people don't get fixated at this stage, because personality is largely formed by the end of the phallic stage. If the previous three stages are successfully navigated and people are not fixated at an earlier stage, they become relatively free to pursue their interests.

The genital stage: The onset of puberty marks the beginning of this stage, which continues throughout adulthood. This is the time during which the person emerges into a mature adult personality, with a fully developed capacity for productive work and satisfying and loving relationships. However, those who remain fixated at previous stages will suffer from underdeveloped adult personalities, which cause any number of problems in their subsequent adulthoods.

Modern psychodynamic psychologists generally agree that Freud's stages of psychosexual development are not an accurate view of personality development. However, even this is not entirely clear; clinical psychologists often report observing patterns that are consistent with Freud's observations of each stage of psychosexual development (Westen, 1998). For example, one study reported that young children are more likely to show affection to the same-sexed parent and aggression toward the opposite-sexed parent (Watson & Getz, 1990). This is reminiscent of the Oedipus complex, although the underlying mechanisms are not necessarily the same (i.e., notice there is no reference to sexual attraction or murderous intent toward the parents).

A huge challenge faced (and never fully surmounted) by Freudian thinkers was how to empirically measure many of the concepts and processes described in Freud's theories. For example, how exactly does one measure the contents of the unconscious? How can we measure something that, by definition, people are unaware of?

EXPLORING THE UNCONSCIOUS WITH PROJECTIVE TESTS As discussed earlier in this module, Freud devised a number of techniques for peering into the inner workings of the unconscious, such as analyzing the "psychopathologies of everyday life" for evidence of defence mechanisms and hidden motivations. Freud also refined methods, such as dream analysis and free association, which were believed to reveal unconscious material by side-stepping the conscious mind. For example, dream analysis was based on the belief that the material in the unconscious, although not accessible to the conscious mind, nevertheless was depicted in our dreams. However, because much of the unconscious operates without language, dreams would not be literal, but symbolic representations of the contents of the unconscious. Thus, the dream analyst had to learn to properly interpret the symbolic meaning of dreams in order to understand what could be learned from the unconscious.

Explore Personality Assessment

Since Freud's time, psychodynamic psychologists have attempted to develop more standardized techniques for probing the unconscious. One popular approach is to use **projective tests**, *personality tests in which ambiguous images are presented to an individual to elicit responses that reflect unconscious desires or conflicts.* They are called "projective" because the image can be interpreted in different ways, and the particular interpretation a person chooses is thought to be a projection of her unconscious.

One of the most familiar projective tests (see Figure 12.7) is the **Rorschach inkblot test**, *in which people are asked to describe what they see on the inkblot, and psychologists interpret this description using a standardized scoring and interpretation method* (Exner, 1991). Another projective test is the **Thematic Apperception Test (TAT)**, *which asks respondents to tell stories about ambiguous pictures involving various interpersonal situations* (Figure 12.8). For example, a picture might show a man and woman looking at each other with blank expressions. Subjects are asked to tell a story

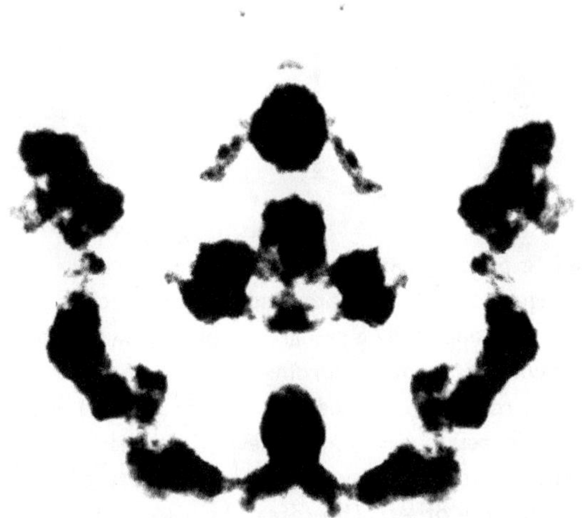

Equinox Imagery/Alamy

{FIG. 12.7} **The Rorschach Inkblot Test** Some psychologists attempt to measure personality characteristics by analyzing the verbal responses clients use to describe what they see in an inkblot such as this. **Click on this figure in your eText to see more details.**

Ken Karp/Pearson Education

{FIG. 12.8} **The Thematic Apperception Test** In this projective test, the individual is asked to tell a story about what is happening in the image. The responses to this task are believed by some to give important insights into an individual's personality.

about the picture. Who are these people? What emotions are they feeling? Why are they looking at each other that way? The details in the story that a person makes up are thought to be a projection of their personality functioning, and thus, a way of illuminating their unconscious.

Unfortunately for proponents of projective tests, they have not fared well in empirical research, receiving criticism for low reliability and validity. Low reliability indicates that the test will not give the same measurement on subsequent assessments of the same person. Low validity indicates that the test does not actually measure what it purports to measure. For example, although projective tests are supposed to measure personality functioning, in some cases, such as the figure-drawing test shown in Figure 12.9, they actually measure a combination of artistic ability and intelligence (see Lilienfeld et al., 2000). Time and again, research has indicated serious limitations regarding the reliability and validity of projective tests (Garb et al., 2005; Lilienfeld et al., 2000).

{FIG. 12.9} **Figure Drawing as a Projective Test** Figure drawing is another projective technique used by many psychologists. The content of the drawings is analyzed and interpreted by the therapist. It turns out that these drawings are somewhat related to artistic ability and intelligence, but not personality (Lilienfeld et al., 2000). **Click on this figure in your eText to see more details.**

Despite criticisms from some researchers, many clients and therapists claim that they have experienced significant breakthroughs toward understanding personality by using projective tests. A survey in the mid-1990s estimated that 43% of clinical psychologists and psychiatrists made frequent use of projective tests (Watkins et al., 1995). More recently, a survey of school psychologists showed that the TAT and Rorschach were used by 30% and 14% of these professionals, respectively, but their popularity appears to be declining (Hojnoski et al., 2006). However, researchers continue to look for projection in other areas.

WORKING THE SCIENTIFIC LITERACY MODEL

Perceiving Others as a Projective Test

There are clearly problems with the reliability and validity of some projective tests, but the basic idea of projection remains compelling to many psychologists. Could there be some way to measure projection with greater accuracy? One promising direction is to look at how people make judgments about what other people are like.

What do we know about the way people perceive others?

People have a seemingly natural inclination to make assumptions about what others are like, even if only very limited information is available. We may judge people we hardly know as friendly, aggressive, selfish, or trustworthy, for example. But with virtually no information to guide us, how do we make these judgments? One possibility is that we make guesses as to what other people are like by using our own self-concepts as a guide. With no other information to go on, we tend to assume that most people are kind of like us. The trait of Machiavellianism provides a great example. People who exhibit this trait are generally willing and able to manipulate and deceive others to get what they want. Interestingly, they are more likely than the general population to see others as being cynical and selfish (Christie & Geis, 1970). Thus, psychologists suggest that the degree to which an individual sees people as selfish and cynical is, to an extent, a projection of his own Machiavellianism (Wood et al., 2010).

How can scientists study how projection relates to personality?

Although projection was initially a psychodynamic idea, contemporary researchers have begun to apply it to other approaches, such as the trait approach. In one study, a research team had participants rate their own personality according to the Big Five personality factors, narcissism (i.e., excessive self-importance), and symptoms of depression. They found several correlations showing that the way people view themselves is, in fact, related to how they view others. The researchers identified a general trend in which people who view themselves positively (as agreeable, intelligent, and satisfied with life) are likely to view others the same way (Wood et al., 2010). In other words, how people perceive others appears to be a projection of how they perceive themselves.

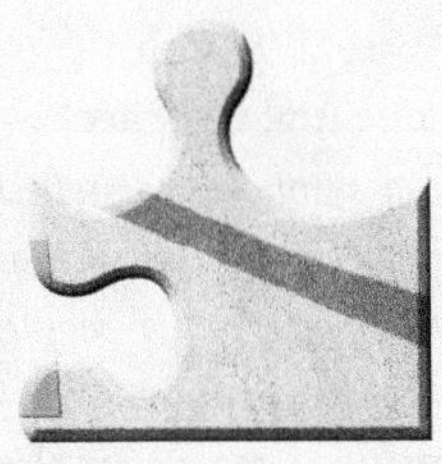

Can we critically evaluate this research?

The results of this study indicate that self-ratings and ratings of others are correlated. However, the correlations themselves are not very large, meaning that psychologists cannot make *precise* predictions about a rater's personality based on that individual's ratings of others, but rather can make only *general* statements. Furthermore, this study does not provide evidence that projection is actually occurring in which people actually use their own self-concepts to guide their impressions of others. It could be the case that people are simply positive or negative in general, such as being optimistic or pessimistic. The positive, optimistic person would tend to see herself and others positively, and the negative, pessimistic person would do the opposite. Thus, the correlation between ratings of self and other simply reflects a general disposition, not a specific process of projection.

Why is this relevant?

Standard projective tests such as the Rorschach inkblot test and the Thematic Apperception Test are fraught with problems and controversy. It would be unheard of for modern medical doctors to diagnose disorders using procedures that are as unreliable and of as questionable validity as these tests. Thus it is important to search for new and better methods that might reveal meaningful information about the individuals taking them. Psychology need not necessarily abandon projective tests altogether, as the benefits of adding rigour and scrutiny to them has shown that they can be of value (e.g., Schultheiss & Brunstein, 2001).

Martin Barraud/Alamy

Quick Quiz 12.3a The Psychodynamic Perspective

KNOW ...

1 According to Freud, the ______ is the personality component that is responsible for seeking to immediately satisfy basic biological needs.

A id
B ego
C superego
D libido

2 Which of the following is *not* a point of emphasis for psychodynamic theories of personality?

A The role of unconscious motives
B The importance of early social relationships
C Learning how to cope with and regulate emotion
D Using trait descriptions to describe personality

3 According to Freud, in which order do the stages of psychosexual development occur?

A Oral, anal, phallic, latency, genital
B Oral, anal, genital, phallic, latency
C Anal, oral, phallic, latency, genital
D Latency, oral, anal, genital, phallic

UNDERSTAND ...

4 A defence mechanism would be employed

A by the id to create anxiety.
B by the superego to reduce or avoid anxiety.
C by the ego to reduce or avoid anxiety.
D by the superego to create anxiety.

APPLY ...

5 Steven lied about his brother to avoid getting in trouble with his parents, but now he is experiencing anxiety caused by extreme guilt. According to Freud, these negative feelings would arise due to the activity of the ______.

A Oedipus complex
B ego
C superego
D libido

ANALYZE ...

6 Why have some psychologists questioned the reliability of projective tests?

A Judges very often agree on how to interpret an individual test.
B Individuals often score quite differently if tested at two different times.
C The tests may not measure what they claim to measure.
D These tests often provide disturbing details about a person's unconscious.

Answers can be found on page ANS-3.

Warner Bros./Everett Collection

According to Carl Jung, the "Hero" archetype is a universal notion of the individual who embodies good and strength.

Alternatives to the Psychodynamic Approach

Freud attracted many followers, but some of his contemporaries took psychodynamic psychology in different directions. They recognized that sex and aggression are not the only motives driving personality development; indeed, other motivational forces, such as the need for belonging, the need for achievement, and the need for integrity or wholeness are important aspects of personality.

Watch
Classic Footage of Carl Jung on Unconscious

Carl Jung (1875–1961) made a dramatic break from Freud over disagreements about a number of issues, founding the analytical psychology movement. **Analytical psychology** *focuses on the role of unconscious archetypes in personality development.* The archetypes were believed to be housed in a region of the unconscious unique to Jung's theories. In contrast to the Freudian unconscious, Jung believed that there were two main types of the unconscious, a **personal unconscious**, which was basically the same as the Freudian unconscious, *a vast repository of experiences and patterns that were absorbed during the entire experiential unfolding of the person's life*, and a collective unconscious, which is not held within the individual person. The **collective unconscious** is *a separate, non-personal realm of the unconscious that holds the collective memories and mythologies of humankind, stretching deep into our ancestral past.* Thus, the personal and collective unconscious are different levels of consciousness, one being held within the person and representing the person's own life experience, and the other being held within the collectivity of humankind and representing humanity's collective experience.

Within analytical psychology, archetypes played a central role; **archetypes** *are images and symbols that reflect common "truths" held across cultures, such as universal life experiences or types of people.* The archetypes were thought to represent major narrative patterns in the unconscious, and thus, the appearance of archetypal symbols in the unconscious (which could be found in a person's dreams, for example) could give the person great insight into herself and her personality dynamics. For example, there are archetypes of Mother and Father, the Hero, and the Shadow, among others. The Hero archetype represents the special force or being that wins mighty battles against dangerous or evil foes. The Shadow archetype represents unwanted aspects of the self that the person is unwilling to acknowledge; the Shadow archetype has been particularly influential, particularly among people who emphasize personal growth, individual empowerment, and healing from trauma (e.g., Ford, 2002).

Alfred Adler (1870–1937) initially differentiated himself from Freud by arguing for the importance of social dynamics and conscious thoughts (as opposed to sexual and aggressive drives in the unconscious) as determinants of behaviour. He rejected the centrality of the pleasure principle, instead emphasizing the **inferiority complex**, *the struggle many people have with feelings of inferiority, which stem from experiences of helplessness and powerlessness during childhood.* The term *inferiority complex* stems from Adler's work; he described how people strive to compensate for their feelings of inferiority by trying to appear competent and, in many cases, overcompensate for inferior feelings by trying to be or appear superior to others. Adler's theories of the importance of the need for power have had a profound influence on the field of psychology and continue to inspire contemporary research (e.g., Watts, 2000).

Karen Horney (1885–1952) also disagreed with Freud's heavy emphasis on sex, and especially infantile sexuality. Instead, Horney (disappointingly pronounced "HORN-eye") focused on the importance of social and cultural factors, arguing that to understand personality one should focus on the functioning of a person's present self, rather than overwhelmingly focusing on the unconscious, which was largely formed in early childhood. Horney highlighted the role of interpersonal conflict between children and their parents as important to personality development. She also strongly advocated against Freud's "phallocentrism" (i.e., emphasis on the penis). To counter his theory of the Oedipus complex, Horney argued instead that men suffer from "womb envy," because men could never experience the miracle of birth and of carrying another human life as part of oneself, as well as the experiences of breastfeeding and other biological acts of motherhood. She said that men attempted to compensate for their perceived deficiencies by focusing on work and by devaluing and subjugating women. While Freud believed that women suffered from penis envy, Horney argued that any "envy" Freud observed in the female psyche was envy of the patriarchal power enjoyed by men, not of men's sexual equipment (Paris, 1994).

As you can see, psychodynamic theorists have separated themselves in a number of important ways. Contemporary psychodynamic psychologists work mostly in the field of clinical psychology and counselling. And, despite some differences, modern psychodynamic psychologists do share many of the core attributes of psychoanalytic thought: an emphasis on the unconscious, internal conflicts between opposing forces within personality, and the influence of early experiences on adult personality (Westen, 1998).

Quick Quiz 12.3b

Alternatives to the Psychodynamic Approach

KNOW ...

1 The aspect of consciousness proposed by Carl Jung that is a store of archetypes representing symbols and experiences common to all cultures is called the ______ .

- **A** preconscious
- **B** subconscious
- **C** analytical conscious
- **D** collective unconscious

APPLY ...

2 Alexandra's older sister is praised for being good at math, but Alexandra struggles with the subject. What would the resulting feelings of being "not good enough" be called?

- **A** Negative reinforcement
- **B** Negative archetype
- **C** Inferiority complex
- **D** Oedipus complex

ANALYZE ...

3 Which of the following is not a critique of Freud's psychodynamic approach to personality?

- **A** It focuses on situations we cannot control.
- **B** It does not yield many scientifically testable hypotheses.
- **C** It was based on a very limited sample of subjects.
- **D** It has not been found useful or applicable to clinical psychology.

Answers can be found on page ANS-3.

Humanistic Perspectives

Reacting against the pessimism and disempowerment inherent in Freudian approaches, the humanistic psychologists wanted to explore the potential for humans to become truly free and deeply fulfilled. Thinking outside the boxes of behaviourism and psychodynamic theories, the humanistic psychologists emphasized the individual's free will to make choices, highlighted positive motivations for personal growth and development, and explored the upper ranges of human experience, such as feelings of transcendence, love, and fulfillment. Proponents of the humanistic approach believed it would become the "third force" in psychology, after psychoanalysis and behaviourism.

Among the many influential humanistic psychologists, Carl Rogers was perhaps uniquely responsible for helping to launch the movement and for cementing certain ideas in the field that remain to this day. Rather than the Freudian depiction of people plagued by complexes and defences, Rogers championed a **person-centred perspective**, founded on the assumption *that people are basically good, and given the right environment their personality will develop fully and normally.* Rogers believed that people possess immense inner resources for growth and resilience, and an inner drive toward **self-actualization**, *which is the drive to grow and fulfill one's potential.*

Watch What's in It for Me? Psychological Resilience

According to Rogers, fully functioning, self-actualized people deeply accept themselves and are highly self-aware; having moved beyond the need to erect defences to ward off negative feelings, they become aware of their inherent goodness. Rogers believed that the more self-actualized a person becomes, the more his inherently good nature will dominate his personality.

These themes predominate throughout humanistic psychology, influencing many great theorists, including Abraham Maslow. Maslow not only created his influential theories of motivation and self-actualization, but also explored the outer ranges of human experience. His investigations into self-transcendence, peak experiences, and mysticism were regarded as ground-breaking and inspiring by many, but also garnered critique from research psychologists who felt that humanistic theories were not well grounded in empirical research, and explored topics that were outside of the realm of scientific investigation. As the cognitive revolution within psychology became increasingly dominant in the 1960s and 1970s, the humanistic movement became increasingly marginalized and largely disappeared from mainstream discussion.

Almost 40 years later, in 1998, a well-respected psychologist, Martin Seligman, became president of the

American Psychological Association, and used his term as president to resurrect the humanistic approach. Seligman had built a successful career studying depression and the self-defeating cognitions that accompany depression, but became dissatisfied with what the traditional approaches to personality and clinical psychology had been able to accomplish. He became convinced that an absence of pathology was not the same as fulfillment and optimal living, and launched the *positive psychology* movement.

In his seminal publication introducing the field of positive psychology, Seligman and Csikzentmihalyi (2000) explain how the focus on people's problems and personality dysfunctions turned psychology into a "victimology. Psychologists saw human beings as passive foci: Stimuli came on and elicited responses (what an extraordinarily passive word!). External reinforcements weakened or strengthened responses. Drives, tissue needs, instincts, and conflicts from childhood pushed each of us around" (Seligman & Csikzentmihalyi, 2000, p. 6). In contrast, their "message is to remind the field that psychology is not just the study of pathology, weakness, and damage; it is also the study of strength and virtue" (Seligman & Csikzentmihalyi, 2000, p. 7).

The positive psychologists quickly gained attention in the field, focusing on the same deep questions of human growth and fulfillment as the humanists, but attempting to approach these questions using more rigorous, empirical methods. In the decade to follow the official launch of this movement, almost 1000 articles were published on positive psychology topics, new journals were launched (e.g., the *Journal of Positive Psychology*, the *Journal of Happiness Research*), and research on such long-neglected topics as fulfillment, compassion, kindness, joy, and gratitude have attained positions of respect in mainstream psychology. Positive psychology research is being applied in business, education, and even the military. In fact, the foundation of the U.S. Army's Comprehensive Soldier Fitness Program is based on positive psychology principles, and they are systematically evaluating how to best cultivate positive personality traits in military personnel, so as to help them become more resilient to the stresses that come with military service and combat experience (Azar, 2011).

In conclusion, the humanistic and positive psychology movements have contributed a great deal to our understanding of personality, helping us to understand and appreciate the incredible potential people have to cultivate the kinds of personality strengths that will allow them to be truly happy.

Quick Quiz 12.3c Humanistic Perspectives

KNOW ...

1 According to Maslow, what is the most advanced stage of personality development?

- **A** Collective unconscious
- **B** Self-actualization
- **C** Hierarchy of needs
- **D** Action potential

2 In contrast to psychodynamic theories, humanistic theories emphasize

- **A** free will.
- **B** how personalities are determined by biology.
- **C** how personality is determined by the environment.
- **D** how defence mechanisms affect behaviour.

APPLY ...

3 If faced with trying to help a troubled youth, how would a positive psychologist's approach differ from a psychoanalytic approach?

- **A** The positive psychologist would place greater emphasis on building the person's psychological resilience and helping him recover his sense of what is truly important in life.
- **B** The psychoanalyst would place more emphasis on understanding the personal strengths and deep values of the individual in order to know best how to help him.
- **C** The positive psychologist would focus on uncovering the defence mechanisms the young person uses in order to avoid anxiety, and would then work with the youth to develop more positive strategies for dealing with anxiety.
- **D** The positive psychologist would focus more on understanding childhood traumas and early experiences with one's parents.

Answers can be found on page ANS-3.

Module Summary

Module 12.3

blas/Fotolia

Now that you have read this module you should

KNOW …

- ***The key terminology related to the psychodynamic and humanistic approaches to personality:***

analytical psychology (p. 532)
archetypes (p. 532)
collective unconscious (p. 532)
conscious mind (p. 523)
defence mechanisms (p. 525)
ego (p. 524)
fixation (p. 527)
id (p. 524)
inferiority complex (p. 532)
person-centred perspective (p. 533)
personal unconscious (p. 532)
projective tests (p. 529)
Rorschach inkblot test (p. 529)
self-actualization (p. 533)
superego (p. 524)
Thematic Apperception Test (TAT) (p. 529)
unconscious mind (p. 523)

UNDERSTAND …

- ***How people use defence mechanisms to cope with conflicting thoughts and feelings.*** According to the psychodynamic perspective, defence mechanisms activate whenever we are threatened by feelings of anxiety due to conflicts between different systems within consciousness. These mechanisms include denying and repressing urges, displacing them, or finding more acceptable ways of expressing them.
- ***The developmental stages Freud used to explain the origins of personality.*** To explain personality development, Freud began with the concept of libido—the id's energy source for the drives that originate at different focal points of the body from infancy to adolescence. Each of the stages of psychosexual development—oral, anal, phallic, latent, and genital—is associated with a unique form of conflict as the ego and superego develop. Failure to resolve the corresponding conflict can result in a fixation by which the person is stuck at a certain phase of development, and this can cause many problems later in life.

APPLY …

- ***Both psychodynamic and humanistic perspectives to understand personality.*** If you are applying the psychodynamic approach to understand someone's personality, you would consider the role that unconscious processes play in determining behaviour, as well as the conflicts that exist between a person's impulses and his need to regulate them. Review Freud's structure of the mind in **Figure 12.6** (p. 523) and the psychosexual stages of development (pp. 526–529). What might each of the following situations mean from Freud's perspective?

1. A student cannot concentrate on her homework until every little item on her desk is in its appropriate place.
2. An individual commits violent acts against others without feeling any remorse.

If you are applying the humanistic perspective to understand personality, you would look at the person's motivations for personal growth and fulfillment, and consider whether they embody the set of traits described by Maslow as characterizing self-actualized people. In each of the following scenarios, which personality characteristic could the person work on changing, in order to move toward becoming self-actualized?

3. Dave is a pragmatic guy, preferring the hard, cold facts of reality to fantasies about how life could be different. He is not afraid to express what he really thinks, and is not very concerned about whether other people accept or reject him. Because he is so comfortable with himself, he has little anxiety and can behave spontaneously and freely in most situations. He feels strongly patriotic toward his country, and thinks that government should focus on issues like taxes and the economy, rather than trying to help people who are disadvantaged due to poverty.
4. Zoe is enthusiastic about life and has a strong spiritual practice, using meditation and prayer to feel closer to the divine. She feels profound empathy for people in all parts of the world and is described by her family as a "bleeding heart," someone who cares strongly for people who are worse off than her. She is regretful about some of the choices she made earlier in life, and although she tries to learn from them, finds herself often nostalgically thinking about the past. She has many friends and is very socially active, in part because she is such a people-pleaser that she is good at presenting herself in such a way that she makes other people comfortable.

ANALYZE …

- ***Whether projective tests are valid measures of personality.*** In this module you learned about projective tests such as the Rorschach inkblot test and the Thematic Apperception Test, which some psychologists believe are useful tools that give them insight into unconscious processes. However, projective tests do not appear to be valid ways of accessing what is being processed.
- ***The strengths and weaknesses of psychodynamic perspectives.*** Psychodynamic theories can provide some compelling explanations for human motivation. For example, it is easy to understand how social and moral conflicts arise when couched in terms of a struggle between the id and the ego. At the same time, this approach does not have a lot of scientific support. Its key concepts, such as the id, ego, and superego, are theoretical constructs that cannot be empirically measured. Also, the psychosexual stages of development are no longer believed to be accurate descriptions of stages that children go through while growing up.

Work the Scientific Literacy Model :: Understanding Personality

1 What do we know about personality?

Review what it means to approach the study of personality from an idiographic or nomothetic perspective on **page 493**. The nomothetic approach is what allows researchers to arrive at global characterizations of personality, such as the Five Factor Model (review **Figure 12.1, p. 495**). Research using the Big Five indicates that individuals tend to have relatively stable traits from day to day—an observation that, as demonstrated in twin studies, indicates a strong genetic component to personality. But as we mention, personality is also affected by factors like culture, environment, and the situation. On **pages 501–502** we discussed the dynamic relationship between states and traits. This is a complicated but important idea. Remember that traits are stable characteristics, while states are temporary but highly influential determinants of behaviour that are influenced by context. States influence how and when personality traits are expressed. For example, you may normally be highly agreeable, but if you start your morning by losing your bus pass, and then wait in a long line at the coffee shop, you may be in a state of anger by the time the barista hands you a cappuccino instead of the iced coffee you ordered.

2 How can science help explain personality?

Researchers use a variety of tests to understand personality. The Five Factor Model and other trait approaches rely on statistical analyses, such as factor analysis, to determine the structure of personality. However, some question the validity of self-reports: Can people be trusted to evaluate their own characteristics, and do they report their behaviour accurately? As we described on **page 495,** research shows that people's self-reporting on trait inventories matches with the reports of people who know them well, and studies on self-presentation on Facebook also suggest that people accurately report their personality characteristics. Projective personality tests like the Rorschach inkblot test are commonly used by psychodynamic psychologists. Research has shown that we do process information without being aware of it, although psychologists have generally struggled to demonstrate that projective tests are reliable or valid. Psychologists argue that our personality dimensions evolved to solve adaptive problems in our physical and social environments. So, for example, each of the Big Five traits is thought to have an adaptive function. Evidence for this argument comes from several sources, namely that of studies showing that numerous nonhuman species also share some of the basic personality dimensions that people have.

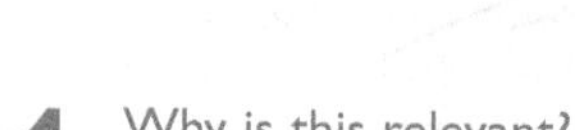

ollyy/Shutterstock

3 Can we critically evaluate claims about personality?

Some popular psychology authors have argued that men and women are so different that they might as well be from different planets—but is this supported by research? The answer is no, at least not when it comes to personality characteristics. The **Myths in Mind on page 516** raised the point that although women and men differ on their Big Five personality ratings, the differences are actually quite small and are often based on states or situational factors. Similar claims have been made about culturally based personalities. The research shows that there is remarkable consistency across cultures on core personality traits; however, it would be wrong to assume that culture has no effect on personality. For example, average levels of Big Five traits differ significantly between different cultures, and personality tests that are constructed from the perspective of other cultures and using other languages often show personality characteristics that are unique to that culture or language. Finally, when it comes to projective tests and probing the unconscious mind, it seems as though some projective tests are not measuring personality, but artistic ability, intelligence, or something altogether different, so it is wise to be skeptical of their results.

4 Why is this relevant?

Watch the accompanying video excerpt on testing personality. You can access the video at MyPsychLab or by clicking the play button in the centre of your eText. If your instructor assigns this video as a homework activity, you will find additional content to help you in MyPsychLab. You can also view the video by using your smart phone and the QR code below, or you can go to the YouTube link provided.

After you have read this chapter and watched the video, identify and explain the four major approaches to personality assessment, including the advantages and disadvantages of each type.

MyPsychLab **Your turn to Work the Scientific Literacy Model:** Watch the accompanying video on YouTube, or on your phone (using the Layar app or QR code). If your instructor has assigned this as a homework activity, you can find the video clip and additional content at MyPsychLab. Answer the questions that accompany the video clip to test your understanding.

13

Social Psychology

wong yu liang/Shutterstock

Ted Pink/Alamy

Module 13.1

The Power of the Situation: Social Influences on Behaviour

Learning Objectives

After reading this module you should

KNOW ...	UNDERSTAND ...	APPLY ...	ANALYZE ...
The key terminology associated with social influence	Why individuals conform to others' behaviours How individuals and groups can influence behaviours	Your knowledge of the bystander effect to ensure that you will be helped if you are in an emergency	Whether guards who participate in abuse are inherently bad people, or whether their behaviour is the product of social influences

In an interview for the BBC, Darby described what it felt like when he started looking at the pictures. In early 2004, military policeman Joe Darby's life changed forever, when one of his colleagues, Charles Graner, gave him a CD of pictures. Most were of soldiers and scenes around Baghdad. But then he saw some photos that he would never forget, photos that, three weeks later, he decided to turn over to the Army's criminal investigation unit. You have probably seen some of these photos yourself, as they were splashed across newspapers and websites around the world, bringing to light the horrible abuse of Iraqi detainees in the Abu Ghraib prison. This prison was, ironically, once used by Saddam Hussein, as a brutal prison renowned for its use of torture and cruelty. And now Abu Ghraib was being used by the U.S. military in basically the same way, at least in some cases.

In an interview for the BBC, Darby described what it felt like when he started looking at the pictures. When Darby first looked at the pictures, he didn't initially realize that the subjects of the images were Iraqi prisoners. The first picture he saw was one of a pyramid of naked people, which made him laugh, as he thought that it was a photo of a group of soldiers fooling around. However, as he saw more of the images, he realized it was a very different scenario. He saw images of Charles Graner physically assaulting a group of handcuffed prisoners. He saw a photo of naked male prisoners with bags over their heads positioned in sexually suggestive poses. And he saw many images of Lynndie England—leading prisoners around on a leash, standing behind a pile of naked prisoners while giving a thumbs-up sign, and posing with an Iraqi prisoner who had died.

When he decided to hand over the pictures, Darby feared that he would be putting himself at serious risk for retaliation from his fellow soldiers. Sleeping at night, he feared that someone would take the opportunity to quietly remove him from the picture. However, none of the other soldiers knew that he had been the one to turn in the photos. His anonymity was protected until, astonishingly, then-Secretary of Defense, Donald Rumsfeld, appeared on TV and personally thanked Joe

Darby, by name, for turning in the photos; this astonishing act destroyed Darby's cover, leaving him vulnerable to any who would seek revenge.

When his fellow soldiers found out, he was widely congratulated, putting most of his fears to rest. But back in his home town, Darby was regarded as a traitor. In his words, "You have some people who don't view it as right and wrong. They view it as: I put American soldiers in prison over Iraqis." For their own security, Darby, his wife, and children were placed in protective custody. Today, they remain in an undisclosed location, accompanied by a military escort whenever they go out—even for something as simple as a trip to the grocery store.

When we learn about atrocities like Abu Ghraib, we want to understand how people could ever do such things. The hope is that by understanding the social and psychological dynamics that lead to these tragedies, we may be able to prevent them in the future, or at least make it easier for heroes such as Joe Darby to come forward and expose the perpetrators. One thing is certain, people *can* resist social pressures in any circumstance. And when they "do the right thing," it pays off in a deep sense of inner conviction, a clear conscience. Joe Darby says that after all he and his family have been through, "I've never regretted for one second what I did when I was in Iraq, to turn those pictures in."

BRIAN SNYDER/Landov

Courtesy Wikepedia/ZUMA Press/Newscom

Focus Questions

 What leads people to engage in horrific acts against other human beings?

 How powerfully are people affected by the behaviour of others?

The Person and the Situation

Most of us grow up with a clear distinction between right and wrong and the belief that the world is comprised of "good guys" and "bad guys." This is reassuring because, of course, we feel that we are good; after all, we don't go around murdering and torturing people. When we turn on the news and hear about terrible things, we assume that it's "other" people who do these things. It's the bad guys, and they are fundamentally different from us. One consequence of this way of seeing the world is that when terrible things occur, we generally don't question the larger system; instead we assume it's the few bad apples who spoil things for everyone else.

Philip Zimbardo, a prominent social psychologist, has a very different view. He says it's not the bad apples, but the bad barrels. He believes that the tragedy of Abu Ghraib was a failure of the whole system, involving not just a few sadistic individuals but many social psychological forces that, together, set up a situation that was hard to resist. For example, there was a general lack of supervision over guards' treatment of detainees, a sense of constant threat from terrorists, the presence of many non-military personnel hired from private security companies who didn't have the same public accountability as military officers, the danger and stress and exhaustion experienced by soldiers working in that region, language and cultural barriers that would make it easier to fall into *Us* vs. *Them* ways of thinking (see Module 13.2), frequent changes made to the official rules on what were considered acceptable methods for interrogation, and finally, strong pressure coming from higher up the chain of command to "get results" when interrogating detainees. Not that the situation strictly caused a specific act of torture or violence to occur, but these situational factors

Watch
The Big Picture: The Social World

would have made it far more likely that soldiers working in those conditions would commit violent or sadistic acts. It is too simplistic to solely blame the individual perpetrators; you have to also look at the situational forces (Zimbardo, 2004, 2007).

It's disturbing to fully consider the situational explanation for "evil." Most of us would rather believe in the dispositional, bad apples explanation. Otherwise we have to face the possibility that we also have the capacity to do terrible things; if we fall into the wrong circumstances, then who knows what might happen? On the other hand, if we fail to appreciate the power of the situation, how can we prevent history from repeating itself? How can we learn the lessons taught by Abu Ghraib, or by the Holocaust, if we assume that these things occurred as a mistake, a faulty pattern of human behaviour? Clearly, we need to have a full understanding of the situational forces that influence the occurrence of these types of events.

We must also remember that the situational analysis is never enough to fully explain a behaviour pattern. Individuals retain free will (or so we assume). People are still, in the final analysis, responsible for their behaviour. In Abu Ghraib, most of the soldiers did not behave abusively; they seemed to be able to resist the power of the situation. Joe Darby even had the courage to step forward and report the abuses so that the rest of the world found out what was going on.

To try to fully understand social reality, social psychologists study the *interaction between the person and the situation.* Kurt Lewin (1936), a key founder (often regarded as the grandfather) of social psychology, expressed this insight as $B = f(P,E)$: *Behaviour* is a function of the *Person* and the *Environment*. This insight challenged the Freudian theories of the early 20th century, which painted a picture of a person's behaviour being guided by psychological dynamics that were rooted in that person's distant personal past. It also challenged behaviourism, with its emphasis on the person's past history of conditioning. In contrast, social psychologists focused on the present moment, arguing that the situation a person happens to be in at a particular time is a key influence on behaviour. Lewin brought a metaphor from physics into psychology, arguing that a person's behaviour was the consequence of sets of forces operating on the person, and once an analyst sufficiently understood the forces, then the person's behaviour could be predicted, just as one could analyze the trajectory of an object by understanding the physical forces (gravity, friction, etc.) operating on the object. This general approach was extremely influential in social psychology and has been widely applied in the business world. Theories of how to create change in organizations often incorporate Lewin's force-field logic, analyzing the forces operating in the situation and determining which forces to change.

Watch
Introduction to Social Psychology

INTERFOTO/Alamy

The past 80 years or so of research in social psychology that has flowed from this insight has pieced together a deep understanding of the situational forces and individual characteristics that determine human behaviour.

MIMICRY Our analysis begins by considering the powerful, and often overlooked, ways in which we are influenced by the people who are around us. For example, in many subtle ways of which we are typically not even aware, we engage in **mimicry**, *taking on for ourselves the behaviours, emotional displays, and facial expressions of others.* Although we aren't merely "sheeple," much of the time we do simply follow the herd.

It's important to point out that there are very good reasons for doing so! Humans are a social species, and coordinating our behaviour with others is a key part of learning to get along with each other. It is often highly desirable to see what other people are doing and "go with the flow." It sets the foundation for observational learning, which is how chimpanzees learn techniques for cracking open hard nuts by banging them with rocks in specific ways, how you may have learned to eat with chopsticks, which fork to use when you sit down at a fancy dinner, and how to walk down the street without bumping into people. The whole complex navigation of the modern world is facilitated by coordinating our behaviour with other people, from learning specific skills to developing relationships and coordinating projects. Everything depends on communication and behavioural coordination.

Although some of this communication and behavioural coordination occurs through explicit levels of consciousness, such as the decisions and intentional actions we take, the vast bulk of our consciousness is determined through implicit, "unconscious" processes. (In this way, Freud's iceberg metaphor of consciousness was genuinely getting at something real.) This nonconscious realm of experience is built out of many different aspects, from the implicit processes of attention, perception, emotions, and behaviour in social psychology, to the neural systems such as mirror neurons that enable people's brains to harmonize with each other, to the physiological synchronization that people experience when in close proximity with each other over long enough periods of time that their own bodily processes become synchronized with each other.

Our motor systems involve the cerebellum and its procedural learning functions. This form of learning, which ties together subtle physical coordination with emotional functioning, depends on patterns formed through active, embodied learning (learning involving the body) that forms the procedural knowledge networks in the cerebellum and other areas.

We took this digression in our discussion to point out just how fundamental the involvement of the body and nonverbal, movement-based activities are to human consciousness. It is important to appreciate the full extent of this, because this lays a foundation for understanding that this whole implicit, unconscious level of our awareness, of *who we are, is constantly shaped and patterned by other people.*

For example, the **chameleon effect** (Chartrand & Bargh, 1999) describes how *people mimic others non-consciously, automatically copying others' behaviours even without realizing it.* You tend to laugh when others are laughing. You make the same emotional expressions on your face as those you see on the faces around you (and then pick up their moods as well). And if someone else is whispering, you will likely whisper as well, even if it is to ask, "Why are we whispering?" The examples are literally endless; practically every moment of social interaction between people involves mimicry, the moment-by-moment behavioural synchronization between people.

This kind of subtly attuned mimicry is highly functional (Lakin et al., 2003), much of the time serving as a "social glue," helping to coordinate behaviours in social settings, helping people to feel reassured and validated by each other, sending the unconsciously processed message to others that you are similar to them and, thus, they should like and trust you. In this sense, mimicry represents another set of interdependencies between ourselves and other people; our social nature as a species is programmed right into our automatic behaviour patterns.

In some situations, of course, people try to use the powers of mimicry to their advantage. For example, when people are trying to make a good impression, wanting to be liked or to be part of a group, they mimic others' behaviours even more (Lakin & Chartrand, 2003). This tactic seems to work; people who are mimicked have more favourable views of the person who is mimicking them. Even something as subtle as mimicking the gestures and bodily movements a person makes will tend to make that person like you more (Chartrand & Bargh, 1999). However, don't do it too obviously, or the person might notice, which will make that person like you less (Maddux, Mullen, & Galinsky, 2008). This discrepancy reflects the functional value of the mimicry system. After all, mimicry didn't evolve at the conscious level as a tool for manipulation. Mimicry occurs at the unconscious level, reflecting genuine behavioural similarity, understanding, and, presumably, trustworthiness. The point, therefore, of knowing about the social value of mimicry is not to learn how to use it manipulatively, but instead to learn the value of getting oneself fully attuned to the people one interacts with; what can emerge from this is the most healthy and genuine flourishing of trusting relationships. After all, as the saying goes, imitation is the sincerest form of flattery. And we might add, mimicry is the sincerest form of imitation.

kiuikson/Shutterstock

Given that mimicry and imitation are deeply ingrained, it makes sense that people find it difficult to resist the influence of others, which can become a big problem in some situations. Although it usually makes sense to follow the crowd, what happens when the crowd is going in the wrong direction? Will we go along anyway, even if we know it to be wrong? Many people, as children, have had the uncomfortable experience of standing in front of a parent after being caught for doing something the parent considers "wrong." "But Mom/Dad!" the child protests, "All of my friends were doing it!" The parent responds sharply, "If all of your friends jumped off a bridge, would you?" At this point, this child usually scuffs his/her feet, looks down, and mumbles a reluctant, "No . . ."

But the question gets at a very important social phenomenon, conformity pressure, more commonly called "peer pressure." The fact is, if ALL your friends really were jumping off a bridge, there would be a lot of pressure for you to do it as well. After all, who wants to be the "chicken" who was too afraid to do what EVERYONE else was doing? Looking into the social influences that push us around has been an important focus for social psychologists.

For example, similar to mimicry, we often conform to the **social norms** that are evident in a situation. Social norms are *the (usually unwritten) guidelines for how to behave in social contexts*. Norms influence everything from the manners we use (e.g., compare the jokes you tell to your friends or to your grandparents), to the amount of alcohol we drink, food we eat, clothes we wear, and even our beliefs and attitudes. Norms govern much of our behaviour even when we don't realize it. People's behaviour is often strongly affected by social norms, yet they generally fail to realize this, instead believing that their behaviour reflects their belief that "it's the right thing to do," or some logical, carefully thought out rational argument for doing so (Nolan et al., 2008). This reflects a more general lack of understanding that people tend to have about their own implicit decision-making processes (Nisbett & Wilson, 1977).

Juergen Hasenkopf/Alamy

As a result of social pressures being so powerful, and so unnoticed by individuals in groups, a variety of fascinating group dynamics emerge that are unique to groups. Understanding how to work with these dynamics can dramatically improve the future group environments in which you will find yourself. Having a full understanding of how one person's behaviour patterns emerge from and reflect back to affect the behaviour patterns of the other members of the group, understanding how clusters of social influence can develop as people interact with each other in groups, and understanding how to watch out for some of the key pitfalls that develop as a result can only help as one goes forward in life.

GROUP DYNAMICS: SOCIAL LOAFING AND SOCIAL FACILITATION How do you feel about group assignments? Do you like them because they're an opportunity to get to know people and because the group together can do a more impressive project than individuals typically can do alone? Or do you hate them because people often have ideas you don't like, and because some people are slackers whose work doesn't meet your standards (or doesn't happen at all!), so that you end up having to do everything? Whether you like them or not, the fact is you are very likely going to be working in groups throughout your life, whether it's the fundraising team at your children's school, the work team you are part of, or the group project your evil professor assigns to your class.

Do groups produce better work, making the most out of individuals' ideas and encouraging their best effort? Or do they produce poorer outcomes, limiting people's creativity and encouraging them to slack off? Oddly enough, the answer to both questions is "yes, sometimes."

Groups can produce poorer outcomes due to **social loafing**, *which occurs when an individual puts less effort into working on a task with others.* There are various phrases for describing this—coasting, slacking, free-riding. Social loafing can occur in all sorts of tasks, including physical activities (e.g., swimming, rope-pulling), cognitive activities (e.g., problem solving, perceptual tests), and creativity (e.g., songwriting), and across all types of groups, regardless of age, gender, or nationality (Karau & Williams, 2001; Latané et al., 2006). One reason why people loaf is because they think others in the group are also not doing their best, setting up an apparent social norm that "people in this group don't work very hard." The likely result? A group that crashes and burns, or a small number of people who end up saving the group by doing everything themselves.

Given the importance and inescapability of group work, it is important to understand what factors encourage loafing, so we can avoid them.

- **Low efficacy beliefs.** This occurs if tasks are too difficult or complex, so people don't know where to start. It can be overcome by structuring tasks so people know exactly what to do, providing clear deadlines, and giving people feedback so they know how well they are doing and how they can improve.
- **Believing that one's contributions are not important to the group.** This occurs if people can't see how their own input matters to the group. Ways of overcoming this include giving people a larger understanding of how the different group members rely on and affect each other, and assigning tasks to people that they feel are significant, as much as possible.
- **Not caring about the group's outcome.** This occurs when a person is not personally identified with the group; this can be the result of feeling rejected from the group or perceiving that the group is unsuccessful or unimportant. This can be overcome by making the group's goals clear and explicit, so that people know what the group stands for. Identification with the group will also follow from identifying with the people in the group, so encouraging personal relationships, making time for socializing, and making the group more fun and socially rewarding will help people care more about the group.
- **Feeling like others are not trying very hard**. As discussed earlier, people loaf if they feel others are loafing (Karau & Williams, 2001). This can be overcome by providing feedback about the progress of group members on their individual tasks; strong groups often have regular meetings where people's progress is discussed and, ideally, celebrated!

In contrast to social loafing, **social facilitation** *occurs when one's performance is affected by the presence of others*. For example, in probably the first social psychology experiment ever published, Norman Triplett (1898) found that cyclists ride faster when racing against each other than when trying to beat the clock. Many other researchers have found similar effects, even in animals. For example, ants are able to dig more when other ants are working alongside them (Chen, 1937) and even cockroaches run down a runway more quickly when other cockroaches are around (Zajonc et al., 1969).

JOHN MACDOUGALL/AFP/GETTY IMAGES/Newscom

Cockroaches run faster down a simple runway when in the presence of other cockroaches than they do by themselves. We don't think it's because they're trying to win a race though. . . .

The presence of others doesn't always improve performance, however. We're all familiar with the athlete who "choked" at the big moment. The presence of others is likely to interfere with our performance when our skills are poor or the task is difficult. Even the cockroaches mentioned earlier did more poorly when other cockroaches watched them try to navigate a more complex maze (Zajonc et al., 1969).

There are many different mechanisms that explain parts of the social facilitation effect (Uziel, 2007). One of the most important is that the presence of others is arousing, and arousal tends to strengthen our dominant responses. When the task is simple (e.g., run in a straight line), our dominant responses are the right ones, but when the task is very complex (e.g., juggle three axes), we need to be able to control our responses more carefully, and then arousal decreases performance. Thus, the effects of arousal due to social facilitation depend on one's skills and the difficulty of the task; the greater the skills and the simpler the tasks, the more likely the presence of others will enhance performance. For true masters of a skill, audiences and competitors generally

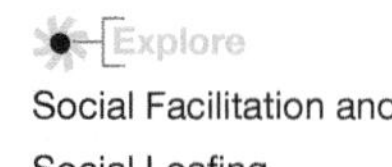

Social Facilitation and Social Loafing

enhance performance, but novices tend to perform best in practice sessions when nobody's watching (Bell & Yee, 1989; MacCracken & Stadulis, 1985). In fact, the audience doesn't have to actually exist; they can just be present in one's mind. This often happens when people feel they are being evaluated; it is as though they construct a "private audience" in their minds that then creates anxiety and arousal and disrupts performance in the same way.

GROUPTHINK In the same way that feeling evaluated tends to limit one's full abilities, the pressures that build within groups also limit creativity, and shut down the ability for different perspectives to be heard or considered. As a result, group brainstorming sessions are often less effective than they could be, particularly to the extent that group members feel evaluative or competitive pressures in the group. Of course, it is possible for brainstorming to work, particularly if group members trust each other and maintain a spirit of light-hearted acceptance of whatever ideas people come up with, much in the same way that comedians learn to perform together, creating a kind of bubble of utter safety and acceptance. Obviously, and unfortunately, this is not what groups tend to accomplish. Numerous kinds of social pressures arise in groups that lead people to "hold back" their ideas, and focus more on maintaining harmony and agreement in the group, than on considering different perspectives. **Groupthink** *refers to this stifling of diversity that occurs when individuals are not able to express their true perspectives, instead having to focus on agreeing with others and maintaining harmony in the group.*

Watch
IT Video: Group Thinking

When everyone is overly concerned with avoiding disagreements, three main problems occur in terms of the group's effectiveness. First, group members may minimize or ignore potential problems and risks in the ideas they are considering. Second, they may apply social pressure to influence people who are not fully in support of an idea in an effort to get them to conform, leading to decisions that are sub-optimal. Third, the group often becomes overconfident and fails to think carefully or critically about its conclusions and decisions, leading it to be incapable of learning from its mistakes (Ahlfinger & Esser, 2001; Janis, 1972).

But in order to fully understand the effects of groupthink on individuals, you have to go beyond these group-level consequences and think of the many specific instances in which specific people are affected by groupthink. For example, think of the groupthink that may occur in families with a parent who is abusive, emotionally unstable, manipulative, neglectful, or simply emotionally immature or unskilled. Many people, in many families, have experienced that climate of fear and the constant need to keep "person X" happy, a family control tactic that keeps each person locked in a certain role, but all in deference to the emotional manipulator. When difficult decisions arise in such families, such as where to live, what kinds of activities a child should be encouraged to pursue, or how money should be spent, the person with the most emotional power over the rest of the family will exert groupthink pressures on everybody in the family. The results are written in the lives of all of us, given that everybody has experienced this in different ways in different relationships and social situations.

At the broader, cultural level, groupthink has been identified in some famously disastrous political decisions, including the 1986 space shuttle *Challenger* explosion; the escalation of the Vietnam War; and the 1961 Bay of Pigs invasion, when U.S. forces attempted to orchestrate an overthrow of Fidel Castro and were soundly defeated. In each case, leaders committed themselves to a course of action without taking into consideration all the different perspectives and opinions that were available. In recent years, the U.S. war in Iraq has been criticized as being due to groupthink; the original official justification for the invasion was that Saddam Hussein had a vigorous program manufacturing weapons of massive destruction (WMDs). However, the Bush administration was widely criticized for making its decisions after not giving equal consideration to different types of information. Specifically, information that supported the assertion that Saddam Hussein was manufacturing WMDs was considered valid and given serious weight, whereas information that countered this assertion tended to be rejected as invalid or based on uninformed testimony. In the end, the military action that resulted from this decision involved the deaths of hundreds of thousands of Iraqi citizens and thousands of U.S. soldiers. In the end, no WMDs were found, and that region remains in turmoil.

Obviously, it lies far beyond our analysis here to consider what other ways the United States and Iraq may have negotiated their relationship, and what other decisions the Bush administration may have made. The point of this psychological analysis is to show that when groupthink is involved, the search for alternative solutions and creative ideas does not happen in the first place. Few options are considered, action is taken, and let the chips fall where they may. If only that strategy always turned out well. . . .

Some groups are more susceptible to groupthink than others, as Table 13.1 shows. Laboratory research revealed that when groupthink occurs, there is often a strong or "directive" leader—specifically, an individual who suppresses dissenters and encourages the group to consider fewer alternative ideas (Ahlfinger & Esser, 2001). Also, groups in which members are more similar to each other, especially in terms of shared sociopolitical perspectives, are more likely to fall into groupthink (e.g., Schulz-Hardt et al., 2000).

The Asch Experiments: Conformity

Groupthink can occur easily without a strong leader simply because of conformity pressures that arise spontaneously in groups. The classic experiments on conformity were performed in the 1950s by Solomon Asch. In his now-famous studies, participants were seated at a table along with several other people who seemed like other participants but who were, in fact, "confederates," people who were secretly working with the experimenter. Participants and confederates were asked to look at an image of three lines, and choose which was the same length as a "standard line." The task was designed to be very easy (see Figure 13.1); Asch showed that when people were allowed to give their answers privately, they were correct almost 100% of the time. However, things changed when answers were spoken aloud in front of a group. For the first couple of trials, everybody gave the right answer, making the participant's job easy. But then, something weird happened; each of the confederates started giving the same wrong answer, one after another. Then it was the participant's turn. What would he do? Would he go along with the rest of the group and give the clearly wrong answer? Or would he say what he knew to be the right answer?

This is a situation in which unconscious mimicking doesn't apply, because the behaviour is very consciously chosen. And it is not an ambiguous situation at all. And yet, conformity pressures were strong enough that 75% of people gave the wrong answer on at least one of the 12 trials in which the confederates gave the wrong answer. Each time confederates gave the wrong answer, about ⅓ of participants conformed (Asch, 1951, 1955, 1956).

{FIG. 13.1} **Perceptual Judgment Task in Asch's Conformity Studies** Which of the comparison lines is the same length as the standard line? In Asch's experiments, many people conformed to the confederates and gave the wrong answer. **Click on this figure in your eText to see more details.**

Why would people choose an answer they knew to be wrong? After the experiments, some of the conforming participants said that they might have misunderstood the test, or thought that there was a "trick" or an optical illusion involved. Others simply wanted to avoid making a scene or being the odd one out. This experiment showed that conformity can happen through either **normative influence**, *a social pressure to adopt a group's perspective in order to be accepted, rather than rejected, by a group*, or **informational influence,** *which occurs when people internalize the values and beliefs of the group, coming to believe the same things and feel the same ways themselves.* There is a big difference between these two types of social influence. Normative influence leads to public acceptance, but not necessarily private acceptance, whereas informational influence leads more directly to the person privately accepting the group norm.

Watch
Conformity and Influence in Groups

In conformity situations more generally, there are numerous factors that influence whether someone conforms or goes against the grain (see Table 13.1).

Table 13.1 :: Personal and Situational Factors Contribute to Conformity

PEOPLE TEND TO BE LESS LIKELY TO CONFORM WHEN . . .	PEOPLE TEND TO BE MORE LIKELY TO CONFORM WHEN . . .
Only one other person is in the vicinity	There is a larger group in the vicinity
There are only male group members	There is a high proportion of female group members
There are only strangers in the room	There are friends, family, or acquaintances in the vicinity
There are extremely clear and simple tasks	The task is unclear or ambiguous
There is one other nonconformist in the room	Others conform first
Responses are made anonymously	Responses are made publicly

WORKING THE SCIENTIFIC LITERACY MODEL

Examining Why People Conform: Seeing Is Believing

For more than half a century, social psychologists have wondered why subjects in the Asch experiment conformed to the group. Did they consciously choose to conform solely because they didn't want to incur a social cost by seeming different from everyone else (although they still knew the right answer), or did the group's collective opinion actually change the subjects' own perceptions of the lines? Is it possible that if enough people insist that reality is different from how it appears, then you will actually perceive a different reality?

What do we know about measuring choosing vs. perceiving?

Recent advances in neuroscience have given researchers the ability to see which areas of the brain are associated with consciously making a choice and with straight perceptual processes, such as seeing. Consciously making a choice that one knows to be wrong should activate parts of the prefrontal cortex that involve executive function abilities, such as choosing between alternatives, whereas the act of perceiving visual stimuli activates certain parts of the frontal, occipital, and parietal cortices. If it turns out that the group's perception actually changes the way that people perceive a stimulus, then when people are conforming to the group, the perceptual networks of their brains should be activated. On the other hand, if people are conforming to the group merely in order to "fit in," they shouldn't show this same pattern of activation.

How can science study people's reasons for conforming, if the people themselves don't necessarily know why they do so?

The simplest way of assessing why people conform is, of course, to ask them, which Asch did in some of his original studies. However, other research has shown that people often don't have accurate insight into their own reasons for doing things (Nisbett & Wilson, 1977). Relying on self-reports only gives you insight into the theories people have about their own behaviour, not necessarily the actual reasons why they did what they did. By having subjects go through an Asch-like procedure while their brains are being scanned in an fMRI machine, researchers can look for whether the brain shows evidence of actual perceptual changes, or whether people seem to be consciously choosing to conform for other, presumably more social, reasons.

One ingenious study did exactly this (Berns et al., 2005). Subjects were put into a situation similar to Asch's original studies, in which they were asked to make perceptual judgments but were also given information about the perceptions of other people in the experiment, many of which were wrong. One key difference was that instead of line judgments, these subjects were asked to mentally rotate figures in order to determine whether a shape was the same or different from a comparison shape. The reason for choosing these stimuli rather than the lines that Asch used was that other research has mapped out the brain areas that are involved in this type of mental rotation task.

This study showed that when subjects conformed to the incorrect judgments of the group, they activated regions of the brain involved in visual perception (i.e., parts of the visual cortex and parietal lobes). This indicates that they were, in fact, perceiving these stimuli in a different way—that the difference was in their *perceptions*. On the other hand, when subjects refused to conform to the group's incorrect judgments, they activated areas of the amygdala that are associated with negative emotion (LeDoux, 2000) and with processing social information (Amaral et al., 2003; Singer et al., 2004). This suggests that going against a group's judgments is a difficult thing for people to do, involving negative emotion and a heightened social awareness. This may be the brain indicator of the heavy emotional load of standing up for what you believe in.

Can we critically evaluate this evidence?

This fascinating study may give us insight into what can happen when people conform to groups, but it leaves wide open the question of what happens in different situations, including the Asch study. In this study, people were mentally rotating shapes, which is a more challenging task than the line judgments in Asch's study. Although people's perceptions on the mental rotation task could be swayed by the group's judgment, this does not necessarily imply that people's perceptions on Asch's much simpler task could also be swayed in the same way. It is important to keep in mind that the different operational details of the experiments, indeed of any experiment, have important implications for how the results should be interpreted.

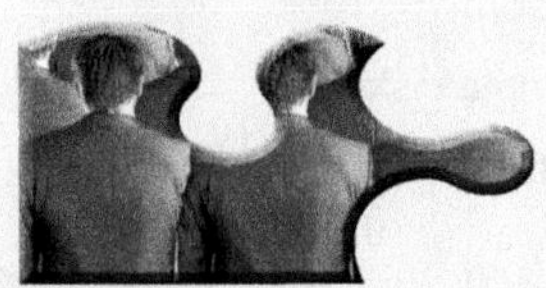

Why is this relevant?

This study shows that when people conform to a group, it can potentially change their basic perceptions about the world at a deep level. This suggests that if enough people say something is true, not only may we go along with the group, we may start to experience the world in the same way. This study also shows that going against the group, standing up for what you believe, is a threatening experience, making us feel negative emotions such as fear or self-doubt.

Empowering people to resist the influence and pressures of destructive groups or authority figures is a huge puzzle science is still trying to solve. Certainly it's true that overcoming the power of the group, and all the negative emotions that go along with it, requires some form of strong opposing force. For example, people are more likely to resist a group's influence if they have deep moral conviction that their own perspective is right and the group is evil or otherwise in the wrong. But many forces operating together, some seemingly positive and others seemingly negative, all influence how empowered a person feels to go against a group: self-esteem, nationalistic pride, courage, compassion, empathy, prejudice, a feeling of certainty or expertise in the relevant area (e.g., a heart specialist disagreeing with a group's diagnosis), having authority or status in society, religious or ideological certainty, and undoubtedly many others.

The question of why people conform therefore relates to deep questions about when people will or will not stand up for the good, how destructive institutions and social movements arise, why situations occurred like Abu Ghraib and the Stanford Prison study, and in short, questions about how to make the world a better place and avoid making it a worse one. In recent years, many psychologists, including the field of positive psychology, have put these questions at the forefront of their agendas.

Nomad_Soul/Fotolia

Follow-up experiments to the Asch study illuminated two additional, very important aspects of conformity situations. First, there is a fascinating relationship between conformity rates and the size of the group. Asch found very low conformity if only one or two people gave a wrong answer. But once there are 3 or more people, conformity rates instantly reach their maximum level (Asch, 1951).

This means that it doesn't take many people to build group pressure; in fact, group norms would arise in countless small groups with which people are involved in their daily lives. Group norms are not some sort of overarching set of abstract cultural forces that influence our behaviour; norms are also created at the micro-level of our everyday situations and circumstances—people laughing with their friends to a demeaning joke, co-workers passing along malicious gossip, homeowners pressuring their neighbours to maintain certain front lawn standards, the decision to have a coffee and a bagel in the morning, or the decision of a few friends to take away someone's car keys because he has had too much to drink. As you go through your day, social norms are operating continuously, shaping your behaviour in countless ways.

The second finding was that, even though groups are powerful, individuals can also be very powerful. In some variations of Asch's studies, one of the confederates would also give the right answer, going against the rest of the group. This single dissenting voice was enough to shatter the group's power, reducing the rate

Arthur Tsang/Files/Reuters/Landov

"Tank man"—this image shows a lone Chinese man who was able to temporarily stop a line of tanks by refusing to get out of the way. This brave act occurred one day after the Tiananmen Square massacre of 1989.

Todd Bannor/Alamy

Being willing to stand out from the crowd is not all about grim and serious things. It can also just be about good times! Imagine if people could be like this guy more often.

of conformity to ¼ of its original level (Asch, 1955). This shows that groups are most powerful when they are unanimous, but a single person's courage can burst that bubble of unanimity and liberate the voices of others who may privately disagree with the group. This is a key reason why it is so important to speak out about what you believe in.

Interestingly, this may be one of the situational factors that led to the Abu Ghraib abuses. Because of the general need for soldiers to not question orders and to maintain solidarity in the ranks, soldiers were unwilling to voice their disapproval of what they saw others doing; however, once it was revealed that Joe Darby had reported the pictures, most of the others congratulated him and appreciated his courage. However, because of the general tendency to not want to be the first one who appears different from the group, it is all too common for kindness, caring, and courage to be suppressed. In a strange irony, the seemingly good desire to maintain harmony leads all too often to ignoring those who are truly in distress and need help.

Quick Quiz 13.1a

Norms, Roles, and Conformity

KNOW ...

1 According to Kurt Lewin, human behaviour is governed by the formula $B = f(P,E)$. In this formula E refers to

A environment.

B education.

C ego.

D extraversion.

UNDERSTAND ...

2 The chameleon effect occurs when

A individuals withdraw from social interactions.

B individuals try to use subtle means of persuasion.

C individuals turn their backs on a group member.

D individuals unintentionally mimic another's behaviour.

3 Groupthink is least likely to occur when

A group members have very different sociopolitical values.

B group members become excited about their progress.

C a leader emerges who suppresses dissent.

D the group refuses to consider alternatives.

APPLY ...

4 Which of the following is a reasonable conclusion to draw from the Asch studies?

A Conformity pressures are so powerful that it is almost impossible to help people stand up against a group's majority opinion.

B Conformity always happens because people simply choose to agree with the group just to fit in; conformity can never, however, lead people to privately accept a group's perspective.

C People will conform in most situations where there is a great deal of uncertainty; but when people are certain of what is "right," most will disagree with the group if the group holds a different opinion from them.

D Even a single individual has a great deal of power in group settings, because by being willing to publicly disagree with the group, conformity pressures are significantly reduced for others.

ANALYZE ...

5 Which of the following does not explain why social loafing may occur?

A The individual believes that even if the group succeeds, there will be very little reward in it for each individual group member.

B The individual believes that the group will fail no matter what his or her contribution is.

C The individual believes that he or she has little to contribute to a group.

D The group is engaged in a particularly complicated project.

The Bystander Effect: Situational Influences on Helping Behaviour

In the middle of the night on March 13, 1964, a young woman, Kitty Genovese, was attacked outside an apartment complex in New York City. She screamed and made enough noise that many people (38, it was later revealed) came to their windows to try to see what was

NY Daily News Archive/Getty Images

Kitty Genovese: Her tragic murder in 1964 led to groundbreaking studies on the bystander effect.

going on. One person shouted through his window, which scared the attacker off, and Kitty stumbled around the corner of the building, out of sight of most of the residents. Kitty's attacker came back and attacked her again, stabbing and sexually assaulting her. In total, her ordeal lasted more than half an hour. When the police were finally called, it was too late to save Kitty's life.

A couple of weeks later, *The New York Times* published a front-page article, with the headline, "37 Who Saw Murder Didn't Call the Police. Apathy at Stabbing of Queens Woman Shocks Inspector." People were shocked and outraged that so many people could have watched a young woman get assaulted and not lift a finger to help her. How is it possible that not a single person could have intervened? Have we become so selfish and disconnected from our neighbours that we don't want to get involved even when a life is on the line?

Note: Before continuing, we should mention that several decades later, it has been revealed that the murder did not really occur the way it was reported, which is the way that most psychology textbooks have repeated ever since. Only a few people seem to have been able to see anything in the parking lot, and only for a few moments; it was not clear to them exactly what was going on. Some people also reported that they did, in fact, phone the police (Manning et al., 2007).

Nevertheless, the horrifying (if mistaken) belief that 38 people could have watched a woman get murdered and do nothing to help her launched an important line of research. The **bystander effect** describes the counterintuitive finding that *the presence of other people actually reduces the likelihood of helping behaviour.* You might assume, for a given situation, that if one person had a certain chance of helping, then each additional person would make it even more likely that someone would help. However, research says exactly the opposite; as you add people to a situation, helping rates actually decrease!

Watch Basics: Under the Influence of Others

There are different reasons for the bystander effect in different situations. The first was offered by social psychologists Bibb Latané and John Darley after the Genovese murder. They reasoned that, instead of thinking that it was surprising that nobody intervened, out of such a large number of people, what if they considered that it was *because there were so many people* that nobody intervened.

This brilliant flip of the logic reveals a very common pattern of behaviour, one that occurs for many reasons. Just think of the embarrassment you might feel in a situation if something were wrong but you weren't entirely sure what to do, or you were in a circumstance in which you had no familiarity or power. Unsure of yourself, it would be very easy to step back and let others deal with the situation, convincing yourself that it's probably for the best anyway, and you'll keep an eye on everybody else to see what they're doing . . .

Consider the perspective of each person, standing by their window that night in New York in 1964, looking out at a dark parking lot where they heard a bit of shouting. They wonder, is it serious? Is it just a drunken argument or even people having fun? Is it an argument between two people in a relationship? Or is it something worse? Maybe somebody needs help! What should I do? Call the police? . . . And then they notice all the other people looking out of their own windows, and they conclude, "Somebody else probably has a better idea of what is going on and has called the police."

The problem is, of course, that if everybody thinks that way, nobody ends up doing anything. Latané and Darley called this **diffusion of responsibility**, *which occurs when the responsibility for taking action is spread across more than one person, thus making no single individual feel personally responsible.*

Other studies have explored this effect by simulating emergencies. For example, in one study, subjects believed they were interacting with other people who were in different rooms in the experiment, talking over an intercom system with each other. One of the other voices on the intercom started to clearly have a seizure and require some help. Latané & Darley varied the number of other people (including the subjects themselves and the person having the seizure) that subjects assumed were part of the intercom conversation: 0, 2, and 5. The more people there were, the longer it took participants to react to the calls for help (Latané & Darley, 1968). The take-home message is that the more people there are in a situation, the more likely it is that any one person will assume "someone else will do it."

Explore
Helping a Stranger

The second explanation is that you may not be sure what to do, or how to interpret the situation, and so you look around to see what other people are doing. This is a search for informational influence, which seems sensible enough, right? And indeed it often is, as we have discussed. But being guided by the group can in some circumstances backfire terribly, leading to a phenomenon called **pluralistic ignorance.** *This occurs when there is a disjunction between the private beliefs of individuals and the public behaviour they display to others.* Although that might seem abstract for a moment, pluralistic ignorance is one of the most important and powerful ideas in theories of social change. Think about the implications of one of its conclusions: It is possible for a social norm, which is not privately held by a single person in the group, to develop in a group and exert pressure on each person in the group. This means that groups can pressure people to do things that not only do they themselves not agree with, neither does a single person in the group.

The bystander effect, diffusion of responsibility, and pluralistic ignorance can often work together to ensure that people who need help don't get it.

Let's see how this works: Imagine that you are sitting in a room filling out questionnaires, when you notice smoke wafting into the room from a vent. What do you do? If you are by yourself, you probably will quickly get up to investigate, look for the experimenter, or even leave the building. But what if you are sitting in the room with other people? In this case, you might not want to embarrass yourself by jumping up right away; after all, maybe the "smoke" is just mist from a broken air conditioner or something equally benign.

So, in this situation, you pause, considering what to do, looking out of the corner of your eyes at the others in the room. But everyone else isn't doing much either, just filling out their questionnaires, perhaps occasionally looking around as well. Nobody gives any indication that they are worried, so you conclude there's nothing to be worried about. It's possible that every single person is privately thinking, "There might be a fire!" but publicly, each person is displaying no evidence of their private concerns. So, nobody takes action because nobody takes action.

Exactly this pattern of behaviour was observed in the "smoke-filled room study" (Latané & Darley, 1968), which had subjects go through that experience. Most subjects (75%) who sat in the smoky room by themselves got up to investigate within six minutes, but if the subjects were in a room with two other people who gave no indication of being concerned about the smoke, only 10% of the subjects took action to investigate.

Political scientist Timur Kuran (1995) has even argued that pluralistic ignorance lies at the heart of why social and political revolutions happen so suddenly, and often unpredictably. Revolutions usually occur when there is a widespread dissatisfaction with the current system, but widespread dissatisfaction is not a good predictor of when a revolution might occur. Pluralistic ignorance helps us to understand why this is. If there is an unpopular government in place, such as a dictator, there are often serious costs that the individual would be risking by speaking out against the government. As a result, most people keep their beliefs privately to themselves. If the government also controls most of the media, then it might easily occur that the majority of the population privately disagrees with the government, but so little of this gets expressed publicly that what people see is very little support for taking action against the government. As a result, people don't take action, the illusion is maintained, and the oppressive system remains in power. This example helps illustrate the more general insight that individual-level processes, such as pluralistic ignorance, can operate at larger scales and become forces that shape the nature of a society.

Understanding pluralistic ignorance is important also because it indicates that a social system is ready for change. If most people in a nation, for example, disagree strongly with an oppressive government but are afraid to speak up, they may all fail to realize how much support exists for a revolution. As people speak up, it is possible for such a social system to change very quickly, as people suddenly become aware of how many other people think the same way they do. Remember the power of the dissenter in the Asch study? As enough dissenters speak up, support builds for others to do the same. Because pluralistic ignorance can be so rapidly dispelled, social changes such as revolutions often happen suddenly and seemingly by surprise.

It should be obvious how much potential power exists in understanding these social forces within a society. Understanding the values, beliefs, and norms that are held within a population provides leverage for how to communicate with and connect with different groups in that population. Understanding any important areas of pluralistic ignorance provides great power, because these are areas that are ripe for change, areas in which small numbers of people could potentially have a great impact, if only they can raise enough awareness to dispel the pluralistic ignorance they believe is held by society.

In a specific crisis situation in which people would normally help or take action, the mere presence of other people sets up social forces that can prevent people from doing so. This can occur for many possible reasons, including embarrassment (Karakashian et al., 2006), uncertainty and pluralistic ignorance (Prentice & Miller, 1993), and diffusion of responsibility (see Figure 13.2; Darley & Latané, 1968).

As something to remember for your own life, if you are ever in an emergency situation and need someone's help, it is important to cut through any confusion or diffusion of responsibility. If possible, clearly ask for help, from a specific person, with a specific command: "Hey you! In the red shirt! This is an emergency! Call 911! Get an ambulance!" (Schroeder et al., 1995).

In contrast to social norms, which are general rules that apply to members of a group, **social roles** *are more specific sets of expectations for how someone in a specific position should behave.* The key word here is "specific." Roles emerge within a specific position in society—such as professor, student, parent, and prison guard—because the rest of society expects the person to behave in accordance with the role. In a sense, the person's individuality gets subsumed by the role, and what they might freely choose to do takes a back seat to what society expects of someone in that role. Roles can be incredibly powerful, leading people to do things they would never believe themselves capable of. Perhaps the best illustration of this is the now famous Stanford Prison study.

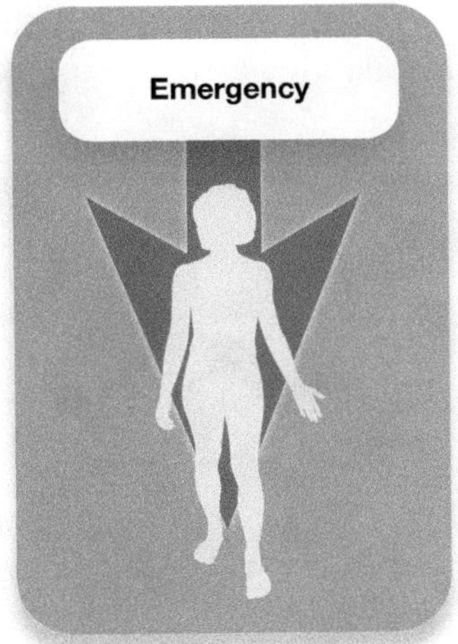

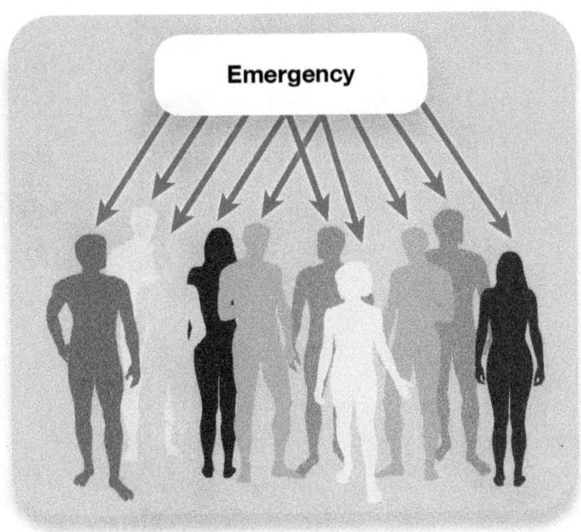

{FIG. 13.2} **Diffusion of Responsibility** If one person witnesses an emergency, it is as if 100% of the responsibility for helping falls on that person. If 10 people witness an emergency, that responsibility is diffused, so it is as if each person feels only 10% of the responsibility—which may not be enough to motivate a person to act. **Click on this figure in your eText to see more details.**

Explore
Bystander Intervention

Social Roles: The Stanford Prison Study

In 1971, Philip Zimbardo, a social psychologist at Stanford University, wanted to study the impact that situations could have on people. Would otherwise "good" people do "bad" things if placed in a bad situation? He placed an ad in the paper asking for volunteers for a prison simulation experiment. After giving the respondents a battery of psychological tests, Zimbardo selected the most psychologically stable people to be participants. He then randomly assigned nine to take on the role of prison guards, and nine to become prisoners.

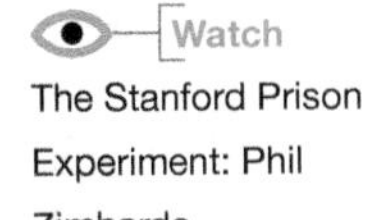
Watch
The Stanford Prison Experiment: Phil Zimbardo

The study began dramatically, as the police arrested the new "prisoners" outside of their homes, in full view of their neighbours. (Zimbardo had enlisted the help of the local police department to help maximize the realism of this part of his study.) These newly arrested men were taken to the police station, where they were fingerprinted and held in a cell, then blindfolded and transferred to the basement of Stanford University's Psychology Department. Zimbardo had transformed the basement into a simulated prison, complete with cells with barred doors and cots for sleeping. The prisoners were strip-searched and sprayed with de-lousing spray, then given a smock to wear (with no underwear), a nylon stocking for their heads, a chain around their ankles, and an ID number, which was to be their only personal identification while in the study (i.e., they couldn't use their names anymore). The guards were given uniforms, and were given authority to oversee the daily lives of the prisoners. And thus the study began.

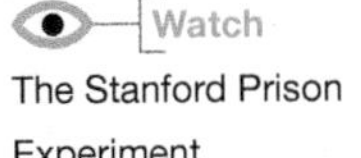
Watch
The Stanford Prison Experiment

What happened next was truly surprising, and horrifying. By the morning of the second day, the prisoners

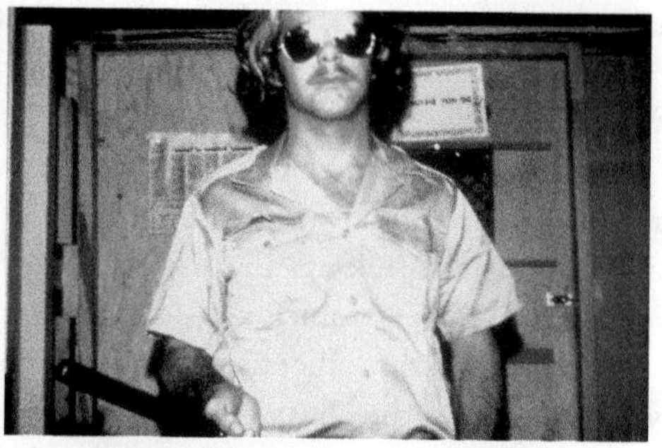

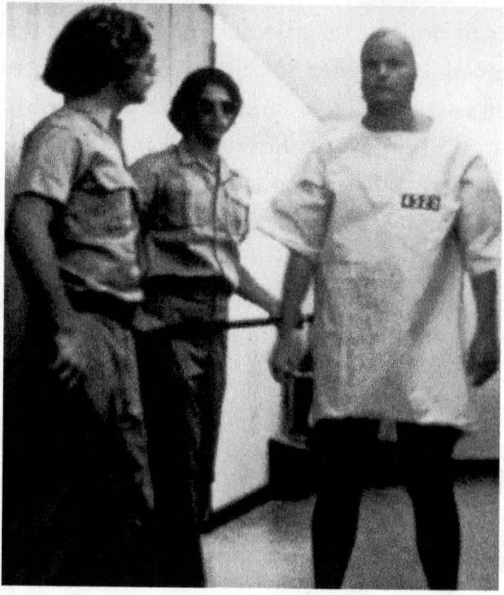

Philip G. Zimbardo

Volunteers were randomly assigned to play guards or prisoners in the Stanford Prison Study in 1971. Each group took their roles so seriously, and their behaviours degraded so quickly, that the researchers called off the experiment before it was even halfway completed.

staged a rebellion and refused to cooperate with the guards. The guards decided to physically subdue the prisoners, so using the chilling spray from a fire extinguisher, they forced the prisoners to back away from their cell doors, whereupon the guards went in and subdued them. The stress was so intense that less than 36 hours into the experiment, one of the prisoners completely broke down, exhibiting such severe signs of emotional distress that he was taken out of the study.

Afterwards, the prisoners quickly became absorbed into their roles, followed the guards' orders, and generally tried to be "good prisoners"; no individual wanting to risk being singled out by the guards for some sort of punishment or harsh treatment. They left their names behind and only referred to themselves by number. The guards also fell into their roles, quickly learning to treat the prisoners with disrespect, engaging in ever-escalating tactics of control and humiliation. Prisoners were made to do push-ups and their sleep was interrupted for "counts" during which they had to line up and say their ID numbers, which lasted for a very long time, in some cases, up to a few hours. Some guards became particularly creative and committed to being abusive toward the prisoners. Guards mocked and verbally harassed the prisoners, forced them to clean toilets with their bare hands, controlled when the prisoners were allowed to use the toilet, even played humiliating games in which they forced prisoners' bodies together in various postures and simulations that were degrading. For prisoners who were rebellious or difficult, the guards set up a solitary confinement cell in what had previously been a broom closet.

Zimbardo himself, who had assumed the title of Prison Superintendent, even fell into his role. As he freely admits, he quickly lost his more objective perspective as a psychologist running a study, and instead started to view it as "his prison" containing "prisoners and guards," not young men from the community who were research participants.

The situation took a serious toll on the prisoners; many exhibited stress-related symptoms including screaming, crying, even becoming ill. Amazingly, although at least 50 outside observers were allowed to see what was going on, nobody questioned the ethics or expressed significant concern for the prisoners, until one graduate student, upon seeing the prisoners being marched down the hall on a "toilet run" with sacks over their heads, confronted Zimbardo with the unethical nature of the study. At that point, Zimbardo realized things had gotten out of hand and called off the study, a mere six days into the planned two-week simulation of prison life.

The Stanford Prison Study could not be repeated today due to the ethical standards that have since come into force. Nevertheless, it taught us a great deal about human behaviour and, in particular, the power of social roles. It seems that a role, even a randomly assigned role, can make otherwise bright, well-adjusted people do things that they would never dream possible for themselves. You can likely see the connection between the Stanford experiment and the tragedies of Abu Ghraib. In both cases, a host of situational factors encouraged brutal behaviour. This is the power of the situation. However, as we discussed earlier, situational forces don't deserve all the blame; in both Abu Ghraib and Zimbardo's prison study, not all people were affected equally. In Abu Ghraib, only a relatively few soldiers seemed to have committed the majority of the documented abuses. In Zimbardo's study, some people took on their role as guards with far more sadism than others, whereas other guards treated the prisoners much more kindly. Understanding precisely what personal factors lead people to be better able to resist destructive situations is a key focus in the field today.

Obedience to Authority: The Milgram Experiment

One additional factor in Abu Ghraib was the military command structure. Prison guards were often given orders to "soften up" the detainees for questioning; softening up implied a variety of tactics, including general harassment and rough treatment, humiliating prisoners through forcing them to be naked or perhaps to wear women's underwear on their heads, terrorizing prisoners with attack dogs and electrical cables, and committing outright physical torture, such as hanging prisoners by their arms for many hours at a time. It is important to appreciate that once the power of authority is added to the mix of social influence factors, the power of the situation becomes truly profound.

Nevertheless, you probably believe that if you were ever in a situation where you were ordered to do something that went completely against your values, such as torturing or killing an innocent person, you would refuse. Especially if the person giving the orders had no real power over you, then you would just say no. Right? Although we would all like to believe this of ourselves, the results of the Milgram obedience experiments have thoroughly shattered this belief. Consider what happened in Milgram's study:

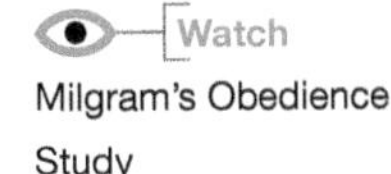

Milgram's Obedience Study

- Participants are told the study is about the effects of punishment on memory. They, and the other participant (who is actually a confederate, although the real participants don't know that), a friendly middle-aged man, draw slips of paper in order to determine who will play the role of "teacher" and who will be the "learner." The draw is rigged so that the real subjects are always the teacher (but again, they don't know that).
- The teacher's job is to read a series of word pairs to the learner, and then to test him on his memory of the word pairs. The learner will be in a separate room hooked up to an electric shock machine. Each time the learner gets an answer wrong, the teacher is to administer a shock, by flipping a switch on a panel in front of him, and increasing the voltage after each wrong answer. The switches go up by 15 volts until reaching a maximum of 450 volts, which is labelled "xxx." This process is watched by an "experimenter" wearing a lab coat.

From the film *Obedience* © 1968 by Stanley Milgram, © renewed 1993 by Alexandra Milgram, and distributed by Penn State Media Sales.

The "shock generator" that the teacher operated, purportedly to punish the learner.

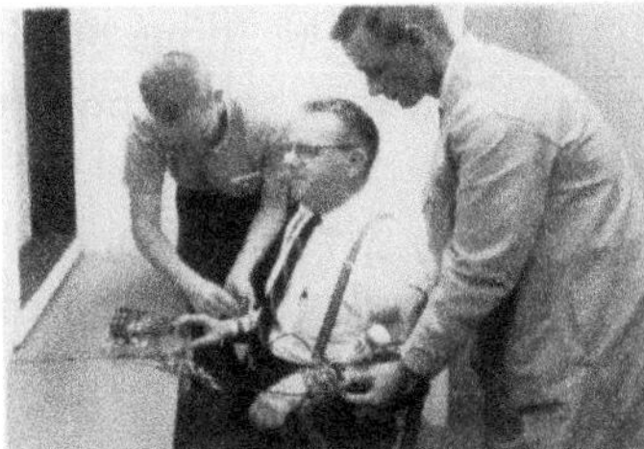
From the film *Obedience* © 1968 by Stanley Milgram, © renewed 1993 by Alexandra Milgram, and distributed by Penn State Media Sales.

The "learner" gets set up to participate in the experiment. He is being hooked up to the device that the teacher believes will deliver a shock.

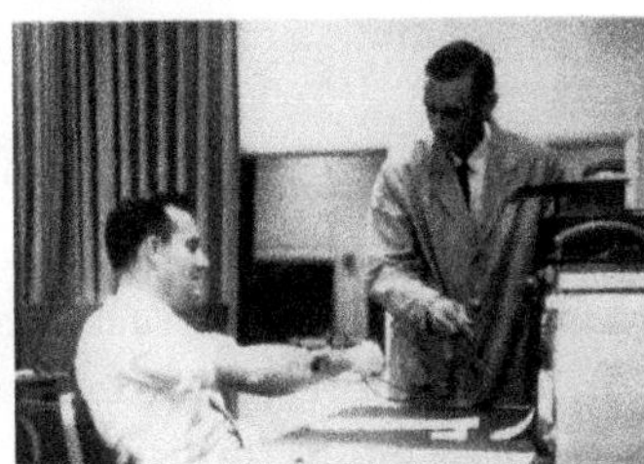
From the film *Obedience* © 1968 by Stanley Milgram. © renewed 1993 by Alexandra Milgram, distributed by Penn State Media Sales.

The experimenter explains to the "teacher" what the experimental procedure entails and how to use the shock generator.

1965 Stanley Milgram. From the film "Obedience," distributed by Pennsylvania State University, Media Sales.

Although most subjects were highly obedient, some, such as this person, refused to continue complying with the experimenter's orders.

- As the experiment progresses, the learner starts to make sounds of discomfort in the other room, grunting audibly as he is shocked. By 150 volts he is protesting loudly and saying that he no longer wants to continue in the study. If the subjects continue reading the word pairs and increasing the shock level, the learner gets to the point of screaming in pain, demanding and pleading, over and over again, to be let out, pleading that he can't take it any more, even that his heart condition is bothering him and his heart is acting up. And then, at 330 volts, the learner falls silent and gives no further responses. At this point, subjects are informed by the experimenter that a non-response is to be considered "wrong," and the punishing shock is to be administered.
- If, at any point, subjects express concern for the learner, or say that they don't want to continue, the experimenter simply says a few stock responses, such as "Please continue" or, "The experiment requires that you continue."

Now, let's step back for a moment and put the situation in perspective. As part of a psychology experiment, people are asked to shock a person in another room and ignore this person as he expresses increasing discomfort, screams repeatedly, begs and pleads to be let out of the experiment, angrily refuses to continue, indicates that he might be having a heart attack, and eventually falls completely silent. And there is no compelling reason for people to continue, except a guy in a lab coat telling them to do so. That seems absurd, when you stop and think about it. Surely almost nobody would actually do such a thing!

Think about yourself in the teacher's chair. What would you do? You probably feel that, at the very least, you would stop shocking the poor man once he said that he didn't want to continue in the experiment, right? What kind of person would force someone to receive electric shocks once the recipient stated he no longer consented to it?

A recent analysis of obedience rates across multiple replications of the Milgram study concluded that this moment of decision making is, in fact, the critical point (Packer, 2008). In most studies, more subjects disobey the experimenter and terminate the experiment at this point than at any other. This is the point at which the true moral conflict becomes clear, between the rights and safety of the learner versus the authority of the experimenter and the power of the situational forces acting on the subjects. It is heartening that this is a choice point at which many people choose to follow their morals and disobey the experimenter; but it's hard not to be disheartened overall, because far more people waver at this point, unprepared and therefore ineffective at resisting the influence of the authority figure.

It is worth repeating this, because this finding is truly astonishing—most of the people, across all the replications of these experiments, made the decision to bow to authority pressure, choosing to deliver electric shocks to another person, even though the other person was obviously in pain and expressed very clearly and eventually, desperately, that they did not consent to being involved any further. It's frightening to think of how easily people can be pressured to commit such harm, because surely few of us believe that we would do this ourselves. After all, how difficult can it really be to simply say no to the experimenter?

It wasn't, in fact, difficult to say no to the experimenter; almost everybody protested and argued with the experimenter, even repeatedly saying that they wouldn't continue. But the experimenter was implacable, refusing to take no for an answer and just stating his prompts of how necessary it was that the experiment continue, and how subjects had no choice but must simply continue. The experimenter forced subjects into a situation where "just saying no" wasn't enough; they had to *insist*, even beyond the point of being polite. It is quite telling that many of the participants in Milgram's study found it difficult to resist the experimenter because they didn't want to seem rude, and were simply uncomfortable disagreeing with someone so emphatically and taking action; this embarrassment held people back, astonishingly having more power than the man in the other room, screaming and begging to be let out of the experiment.

But, surely, if you were in this situation yourself, you would stop at some point! Surely *you* wouldn't go all the way to the end, shocking that other person even after they fell silent, gave no responses, or made noises of any kind. Surely you wouldn't shock that man to death, would you?

This is one of the most unbelievable findings in the history of psychology. Milgram found that two out of every three people (65% to be exact), would do just that, slowly electrocute an innocent, desperately protesting man into oblivion, simply because a psychology experimenter insisted that they do so.

Incidentally, a group of psychiatrists at Yale University were asked to predict ahead of time how many people would go to the end, and they thought it would only be about 1 in 1000—the base rate of sadistic or psychopathic individuals in the population (Milgram, 1974). Similarly, the experimental sessions were observed by people through one-way mirrors, who were unequivocably surprised and appalled at what the teachers were doing, expecting that they would definitely have stopped long before they did.

Clearly, the commands of an authority figure carry great power, able to override even the strong moral conviction not to harm another innocent person. It's important to emphasize that it wasn't easy for the subjects in this experiment; they were clearly very distressed by what they were doing to the learner. They became very tense and frequently turned to the experimenter, saying that they didn't want to continue, expressing concern for the learner, even worrying that they might be killing him. But time and time again, when commanded to by the experimenter, they would turn back to the shock machine and keep increasing the voltage.

Milgram (1963) wrote,

> *In a large number of cases, the degree of tension reached extremes that are rarely seen in sociopsychological laboratory studies. Subjects were observed to sweat, tremble, stutter, bite their lips, groan, and dig their fingernails into their flesh. These were characteristic rather than exceptional responses. . . . At one point he (one of the participants) pushed his fist into his forehead and muttered, 'Oh God, let's stop it.' And yet he continued to respond to every word of the experimenter, and obeyed to the end . . . I observed a mature and initially poised businessman enter the laboratory smiling and confident. Within 20 minutes he was reduced to a twitching, shuddering wreck, who was rapidly approaching nervous collapse. . . .* (pp. 375–377)

Clearly, it was not easy for the subjects to commit harm to another person, but it was even more difficult to break out of the power of the situation and refuse to obey.

Interestingly, Milgram ran other variants of this experiment, trying to see what would increase or decrease obedience rates and to understand what gives the situation such power. Milgram tried to reduce the situational pressure in several ways, such as having the experimenter deliver his orders from a different location using the telephone, or reducing the stature and reputation of the organization, holding the experiment in a downtown commercial space as research being conducted by a private firm working for industry rather than at prestigious Yale University.

Milgram also tried to increase the personal directness with which subjects would experience the learner's distress, such as by having subjects and learners in the same room so that subjects had to watch the learner shout and writhe in pain; in one condition, the learner had to press a shock plate in order to receive their shock, and when they resisted, the subjects would have to physically force their hand onto the shock plate while the learner struggled against the subject. Astonishingly, although the rates of obedience are slightly lower, they remain disturbingly high. At least in this context, being directly physically exposed to another person's suffering does not seem to be sufficient to overwhelm the power of authority. The fact that 30% of us would physically force a struggling person to receive pain against his will is disturbing, to say the least.

There were two especially interesting and powerful variations. One experiment looks at whether it is easier for a group to resist the experimenter, pitting the power of the group against the power of authority. In this experiment, there were three teachers making decisions collectively; two of the teachers were confederates, pretending to be real subjects; the other teacher was the actual subject. When the two confederate teachers would make the decision to not continue with the experiment, 90% of subjects also refused. (We would note that it seems surprising that a full 10% of people would still go to the maximum shock value; in this study, the power of authority was strong enough to resist even an open revolt against the authority figure!)

This particular variation is important because it illustrates again the power of dissent. As in the Asch study, if even a couple of people are courageous enough to fight for what is "right," they make it much easier for others to do the same; on the other hand, if those people fail to take action or support the "wrong," they can turn many of us into monsters.

Then there is one final condition, examining a crucial piece of the puzzle of World War II and the Holocaust, known as the Eichmann factor. Milgram ran one experiment in which subjects only had to read the word pairs to the learner; it was another person who actually threw the switches to deliver the electric shocks. This allowed subjects to feel even less responsible; by splitting the process of what was essentially torture into multiple components, with multiple people involved in different ways, it was easy for each individual to feel not responsible, and not powerful enough to do anything about it. The result was that 92.5% (37/40) of subjects obeyed the experimenter right to the end.

Milgram himself believed that these studies provided insight into the horrors of the Holocaust in World War II. Clearly, the Holocaust is the result of many different factors converging, but the Milgram study helps to shed light on one key aspect of it, which is often overlooked: how the behaviours of so many millions of people working for the Nazi death camps and all of the infrastructure that went along to support it created incredibly powerful situations, which swept most people up. Without understanding how these social forces can create such intense pressures, it is hard to understand. Specifically, it is hard to understand how so many millions of people could willingly participate in the immense Nazi operation that enabled the Holocaust, and how so many more millions of people could stand passively by, while one of the most brutal genocides of all time took place. How could so many people be so "evil"?

The disarmingly simple insight from the Milgram study is that it's not a question of people being good or evil; it's a question of the power of social situations.In some cases, they can be powerful enough to overwhelm even the deep moral beliefs of most people that committing harm to an innocent person is wrong. As Milgram (1974) noted, "This is, perhaps, the most fundamental lesson of our study: Ordinary people, simply doing their jobs, and without any particular hostility on their part, can become agents in a terrible destructive process. Moreover, even when the destructive effects of their work become patently clear, and they are asked to carry out actions incompatible with fundamental standards of morality, relatively few people have the resources needed to resist authority" (p. 6).

Simulate Could You Be a Hero?

In sum, situational forces can exert immense pressure on individuals, making an analysis of personal responsibility very tricky. However, social psychologists would generally agree that, in the final analysis, people are responsible for their behaviours; no matter how powerful the situational forces may be, individuals can always resist them and make a free choice, and history is replete with examples of such courageous behaviour. In fact, one of Dr. Zimbardo's current projects, the Heroic Imagination Project, is focused on understanding the factors that lead people to behave heroically. It is hoped that, by unlocking the secrets of heroism, courage, bravery, and compassion, we can help society evolve in a healthier direction, and potentially avoid future atrocities.

Quick Quiz 13.1b Group Influence and Authority

KNOW ...

1 ______ is complying with instructions from an individual who has authority.

A Obedience
B Groupthink
C Conformity
D Mimicry

UNDERSTAND ...

2 How did the Stanford Prison Study researchers come to the conclusion that roles, and not individual personalities, were the main influence on the volunteers' behaviour?

A The volunteer "prison guards" were specifically instructed to respond brutally.
B The "prisoners" were actually actors hired by the researchers.
C The prisoners and prison guards were psychologically similar prior to the start of the experience.
D The researchers actually believed that personality is more important than social roles.

APPLY ...

3 According to variations of the Milgram experiment

A women are much more obedient to authority figures than men are.
B most of the power of the situation was the general reputation of Yale as an institution; people assumed that the consequences of the shocks couldn't be too terrible, because it was, after all, happening at Yale.
C people are much less obedient now than they were shortly after World War II; so, Milgram's findings are historically important, but are not relevant to modern generations.
D one of the most effective ways to get people to disobey an authority figure is to make sure they have some companions who will do it too.

Answers can be found on page ANS-3.

Module Summary

Ted Pink/Alamy

Module 13.1

Now that you have read this module you should

KNOW ...

- ***The key terminology associated with social influence*:**

bystander effect (p. 549)
chameleon effect (p. 541)
diffusion of responsibility (p. 549)
groupthink (p. 544)
informational influence (p. 545)
mimicry (p. 540)
normative influence (p. 545)
pluralistic ignorance (p. 550)
social facilitation (p. 543)
social loafing (p. 542)
social norms (p. 542)
social roles (p. 551)

UNDERSTAND ...

- ***Why individuals conform to others' behaviours*.** At its most basic level, conforming begins with mimicry, in which people simply imitate others' behaviours. Mimicry seems to help form social bonds and encourages prosocial behaviour. Conformity usually describes the way an individual's more complex behaviours evolve to become like the behaviours of the group. People may conform because they want to be accepted by the group, or they may conform because the group's way of perceiving reality actually influences the person's own perceptions.
- ***How individuals and groups can influence behaviours*.** In many different situations, other people can change how we behave. In helping situations, the presence of others tends to decrease the likelihood that someone will help another in distress. In other situations, the presence of even a few more people can set up conformity pressures that influence us to behave like the others in the group. Interestingly, these conformity pressures can be largely eliminated in at least some situations if even a single individual is willing to go against the group and break its unanimity. In many situations we are placed into social roles and feel like we have to live up to the responsibilities of that role, even if we would normally behave differently. When authority figures are involved, these social pressures can become even more powerful, so powerful that many people cannot resist complying.

APPLY ...

- ***Your knowledge of the bystander effect to ensure that you will be helped if you are in an emergency*.** People are least likely to help if they don't feel personally responsible for taking action, if they are unsure what to do to help, or if they are unsure whether the situation is a genuine emergency. Thus, you can best ensure that others will help you if you make very clear that it's an emergency and you need help, if you make a specific person responsible for helping, and if you tell that person exactly what he or she needs to do.

ANALYZE ...

- ***Whether guards who participate in abuse are inherently bad people, or if their behaviour is the product of social influences*.** Behaviour is a function of the person and the situation. Therefore it is impossible to say in general the extent to which guards who participate in abuse were driven by their own character traits or by situational forces. A full analysis must take both sets of factors into consideration. Clearly though, in situations in which people are pressured to abuse prisoners, peer pressure is exerted through the expectations and behaviours of others, the authorities in charge condone the abuse, and other factors align with abusive behaviour, it becomes far more likely that some guards will become abusive. Nevertheless, even the most strict social psychological analysis would never remove the final responsibility from the person; no matter the situation, we can always choose how to respond.

w85/ZUMA Press/Newscom

Module 13.2

Social Cognition

Learning Objectives

After reading this module you should

KNOW ...	UNDERSTAND ...	APPLY ...	ANALYZE ...
The key terminology associated with social cognition	How we form first impressions and how these impressions influence us	Your understanding of social cognition to the problem of overcoming prejudice and discrimination	Whether people who commit discriminatory acts are necessarily prejudiced

One February night in 1999, four New York City plainclothes police officers were patrolling a Bronx neighbourhood when they saw a lone man on the street. The officers thought he was behaving suspiciously, so they decided to question him. Upon orders from the police to stop, the man ducked into the vestibule of an apartment building, reaching for the door with one hand and putting the other into his pocket. Officers feared he was reaching for a gun. One officer opened fire on the man, and the other three followed, firing a total of 41 shots, 19 of which hit the man and killed him on the spot.

Tragically, the victim of the shooting was a peaceful and unarmed 24-year-old man named Amadou Diallo. By all accounts, Diallo was a friendly, industrious, and law-abiding man from Guinea, West Africa, who had come to New York in hopes of attaining a college education. He had run from the police presumably because he didn't know they were police (they were not in uniform and were driving an unmarked car); besides, whenever four guys jump out of a car in the middle of the night in the Bronx and start yelling and running toward you, running into the safety of your home is a sensible thing to do. His hand went into his pocket because he was reaching for his wallet.

Much of New York was in an uproar over the shooting, and the turmoil was only heightened after the four police officers were found not guilty of any criminal wrongdoing in court. Half of all New Yorkers disagreed with the verdict, and that figure reached almost 80% among Africans and African Americans (Connelly, 2000). People of all backgrounds attributed the shooting to hostile prejudice. On the other hand, many other people and most police officers defended the actions of the four officers, blaming the stressful environment in which they work and the need for them to make a snap decision in a potentially life-threatening situation.

Was prejudice an issue in Diallo's death? If he had been a White man, would the police have reacted the same way? These questions go right to the heart of how stereotypes and prejudice colour our perceptions and can influence our behaviours, topics we turn to in this module.

Focus Questions

1. How do we make judgments and form impressions about other people?
2. Can stereotypes affect our behaviour in ways that we are unaware of? Could such processes have played a role in the killing of Amadou Diallo?

The field of social-cognitive psychology is a fusion of social psychology's emphasis on social situations, with cognitive psychology's emphasis on cognitions (perceptions, thoughts, and beliefs). Social-cognitive researchers study the cognitions that people have about social situations, and how situations influence cognitive processes. It is an exciting area to study, because it deals directly with the everyday social experiences we encounter in our lives.

One of the central ideas in social-cognitive psychology is the idea that there are two major types of processes in our consciousness: explicit processes and implicit processes. **Explicit processes**, *which correspond roughly to "conscious" thought, are deliberative, effortful, relatively slow, and generally under our intentional control.* This explicit level of consciousness is our subjective inner awareness, our "mind" as we know it. **Implicit processes** *comprise our "unconscious" thought; they are intuitive, automatic, effortless, very fast, and operate largely outside of our intentional control.* The implicit level of consciousness is the larger set of patterns that govern how our mind generally functions, all the "lower-level" processes that comprise the vast bulk of what our brains actually do (Chaiken & Trope, 1999; Kahneman, 2003; Todorov et al., 2005).

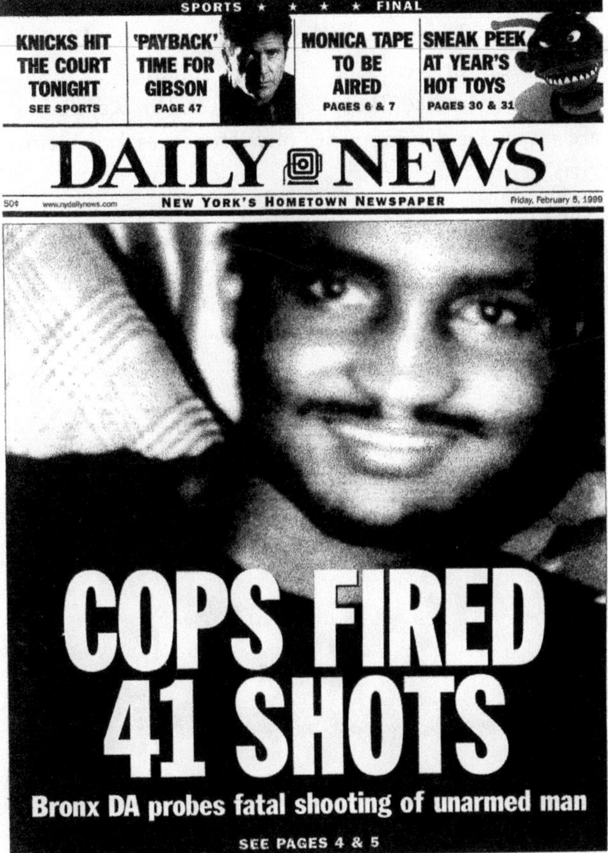

SPORTS ★ ★ ★ ★ FINAL

KNICKS HIT THE COURT TONIGHT
SEE SPORTS

'PAYBACK' TIME FOR GIBSON
PAGE 47

MONICA TAPE TO BE AIRED
PAGES 6 & 7

SNEAK PEEK AT YEAR'S HOT TOYS
PAGES 30 & 31

DAILY NEWS

50¢ www.nydailynews.com NEW YORK'S HOMETOWN NEWSPAPER Friday, February 5, 1999

COPS FIRED 41 SHOTS

Bronx DA probes fatal shooting of unarmed man

SEE PAGES 4 & 5

NY Daily News Archive/Getty Images

Amadou Diallo—Was his tragic death the result of racial prejudice?

These two sets of processes work together to regulate our bodies, continually update our perceptions, infuse emotional evaluations and layers of personal meaning to our experiences, and affect how we think, make decisions, and self-reflect. But not only do these two sets of processes carry out their independent functions, they also can influence each other. For example, explicit processes influence implicit processes when our beliefs (e.g., my friend Bob is a kind person!) influence how we process information (e.g., how much attention we pay to Bob's positive and negative behaviours). On the other hand, implicit processes can influence explicit processes, such as when our automatic tendency to categorize a person into a stereotyped group influences the judgments we make about that person or our decisions about how to behave toward him. You can see how explicit and implicit processes are intertwined, each influencing the other as we navigate the social world. *Models of behaviour that account for both implicit and explicit processes are called* **dual-process models** in social-cognitive psychology (Chaiken & Trope, 1999).

Because implicit processes happen so quickly, they occur even before we consciously can think and deliberate about something. Thus, as we consciously think about things and make decisions, we are already being influenced and guided by our implicit processes, without being aware of this at all. For example, consider the police officers in the Diallo case. As soon as they saw a Black man on the street late at night in the Bronx, the Black male stereotype may have become implicitly activated (Bargh, 1999); this stereotype then would have guided their explicit thinking, which then had disastrous consequences. For example, they would have been primed for information related to the Black stereotype, which may have made them more likely to interpret Diallo initially as somebody "acting suspiciously," and more likely to interpret later that he was reaching for a gun.

That's the double-edged sword nature of implicit processes; they bias us in ways that often help us process information efficiently and function effectively; but because they operate outside of conscious awareness, when they are faulty it is very difficult to protect yourself from their influence.

Person Perception

The effects of implicit processes are dramatically illustrated by research on **person perception**, *the processes by which individuals categorize and form judgments about other people* (Kenny, 2004). Person perception begins the instant we encounter another person, guided by our past experiences with people and the interpersonal knowledge we have absorbed from our culture. When we make a first impression of someone, we rely heavily on implicit processes. Because we have very little personal knowledge of someone we have just met, we rely on schemas to guide our impressions. Schemas are organized clusters of knowledge, beliefs, and expectations about individuals and groups, which influence our attention and perceptual processes in many ways (see Module 7.3). For example, a person's visible characteristics (e.g., gender, race, age, style of dress) all activate schemas, and these schemas can bring certain traits to mind automatically.

Attitudes and Attitude Change

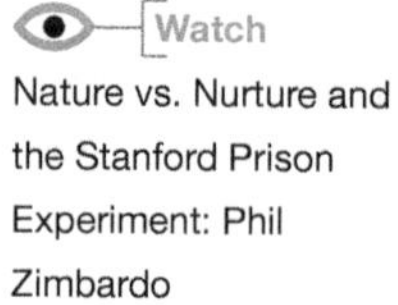

Nature vs. Nurture and the Stanford Prison Experiment: Phil Zimbardo

THIN SLICES OF BEHAVIOUR One amazing aspect of these implicit processes is just how accurate and instantaneous they can be. For example, within the first minute of seeing your professor at the front of the room, you have already evaluated her and made some basic judgments; if you were to fill out your course evaluations after a mere 30 seconds of the first class (which would seem highly unfair), your ratings would likely be very similar to your course evaluations after an entire semester's worth of exposure to that person (Ambady & Rosenthal, 1993; Tom et al., 2010). What happens in these situations is that we make very rapid, implicit judgments of people based on **thin slices of behaviour,** very small samples of a person's behaviour. Our implicit processes, guiding our perceptions holistically and using well-practised heuristics, are able to perceive very small cues and subtle patterns shaping our judgments so fast, and sometimes so accurately, that our "thin slice" judgments are often helpful guides to navigating our social world.

Surprisingly, many of our social judgments are made in this way—instantaneously, based on very little information. Whether it's judging people based on tiny snippets of conversations we happen to overhear (Holleran et al., 2009; Mehl et al., 2006), or based on a mere glimpse of their face (e.g., we judge trustworthiness, competence, likability, and aggressiveness after seeing a photograph for a mere half a second; Willis & Todorov, 2006), the fact is, our implicit judging and evaluating processes are sizing people up all the time. Research by Nicholas Rule from the University of Toronto has shown that we can tell surprising things about people given incredibly little information; for example, people can guess a male's sexual orientation (i.e., gay vs. straight) at rates greater than chance after viewing his photograph for a mere 1/20th of a second (Rule & Ambady, 2008), and Americans can accurately guess whether other people tend to vote Republican or Democrat merely by looking at a photograph of their face (Rule & Ambady, 2010). Republicans are viewed as having more powerful faces, but Democrats' are seen as warmer.

Left: Monkey Business Images, 2009/Used under license from Shutterstock.com; right: Glow Asia RF/Alamy

Thin slices of behaviour research shows that, in mere seconds, people form impressions that are surprisingly accurate. For example, you could get students to fill out course evaluations in university, evaluating the teaching capability of their professor, in the first minute of the first class, and they would be about the same as ratings taken after an entire semester of being taught by that professor.

Mark Burnett/Alamy

According to research on thin slices, our perceptions of others are formed immediately and with only physical appearance as a source of information. It turns out that our initial perceptions can be quite accurate. We have a strong tendency to judge personality characteristics based on physical appearances.

Thin-slice research demonstrates just how quickly impressions are formed, and how surprisingly accurate they often can be. Of course, they are not perfectly accurate, but they can have a large impact on how our social reality unfolds, sometimes for better, sometimes for worse.

SELF-FULFILLING PROPHECIES AND OTHER CONSEQUENCES OF FIRST IMPRESSIONS First impressions have a big impact on many of our social behaviours. Even very simple cues, such as facial appearance, guide a wide range of behaviours, from how a jury treats a defendant to how people vote. For example, one study asked participants to act as jurors and evaluate evidence against a defendant. If shown a photograph of a defendant who simply "looked more trustworthy," participants were less likely to come to a guilty verdict (Porter et al., 2010). In another study, the outcome of U.S. elections of congressional candidates could be predicted 70% of the time simply using participants' judgments of how competent the candidates appeared in photographs (Todorov et al., 2005).

The fact that our implicit judgments can influence our perceptions and behaviours has countless implications for our social lives, particularly in terms of **self-fulfilling prophecies**, *which occur when a first impression (or an expectation) affects one's behaviour, and then that affects other people's behaviour, leading one to "confirm" the initial impression or expectation.* In other words, your beliefs affect your actions, which affect other people's actions, which then reinforce your beliefs. For example, if you expect someone you meet to be warm and friendly, you will probably be more at ease with them and will treat them in a warm and friendly manner yourself. This friendly behaviour will make them comfortable and will lead them to behave warm and friendly in return, leaving you with the conclusion that they are—surprise!—warm and friendly. You can easily imagine the opposite process, if your initial expectation is that the person will be cold and unfriendly.

Self-fulfilling prophecies have been found in many important contexts, such as school and work. Back in the 1960s, Rosenthal and Jacobson (1968) told teachers of an elementary school class that certain students in the class had shown through IQ testing that they were exceptionally bright (see Module 2.1 for more information). By the end of the year, these same children experienced a whopping increase in their scores on IQ tests! This increase was surprising though, given that the children were randomly chosen and, therefore, were no more intelligent on average than the other students.

Why did these randomly chosen students do so much better by the end of the year? According to Rosenthal (1974), teachers were more friendly toward them, gave them more challenging work to do, gave more specific and immediate feedback (both positive and negative) on their work, and were more likely to select those students to participate in class. Receiving all of this positive feedback over the year would reinforce these students' motivation to do well in school, as well as their self-confidence and beliefs in their own intelligence. Through a variety of processes, students would end up performing more highly on an IQ test at the end of the year; the teacher's expectations became the students' reality. This is one example of how implicit processes can create their own social realities through self-fulfilling prophecies.

The Self in the Social World

How do we decide what information to use when we're trying to understand other people or form impressions of them? What schemas do we activate to guide our judgments? As discussed above, we may use subtle cues in people's faces or non-verbal behaviours, but what else guides our judgments? Certainly, if the person falls into a group about which there are specific stereotypes, such as categories based on race, class, and gender, then these stereotypes often are automatically activated and can colour our judgments (Bargh, 1999). But one additional schema that is highly accessible, contains a vast amount of information, and is therefore often used in guiding our social judgments—is ourselves! Much of the time, we look out at the social world through the lens of our own self-concepts.

This has two very important consequences. The first is that we tend to think that the way we are is the way people should be, and therefore, people who are substantially different from us have something wrong with them. The second is that we have a strong tendency to split the world into *Us* and *Them*, and we are motivated to see *Us* more positively than how we see *Them*. Understanding these dynamics gets right to the heart of why there is so much intergroup hostility in the world. It also reveals a tragic irony, which is that in the quest to feel good about ourselves and be happy, we sow the seeds that will grow into distrust, prejudice, and discrimination, thereby causing much suffering and unhappiness. Let's examine these arguments carefully, for they have major implications for understanding why the world is the way it is.

Watch
Cultural Psychology: Kaiping Peng

PROJECTING THE SELF ONTO OTHERS: FALSE CONSENSUS AND NAIVE REALISM One way in which our self-concept affects our social perceptions is that we tend to *project* our self-concepts onto the social world; this means that the qualities we see in ourselves and the attitudes and opinions that we hold, we tend to assume are similar for society at large. If we are sports fans, we assume that sports is generally important for other people as well. Even qualities we have that we know for certain are not popular enough to be mainstream are still projected onto society; so, for example, if we are believers in Scientology, we will tend to assume that a larger proportion of the population believes in Scientology than is likely the case, and we will certainly assume there are more Scientology believers out there than a non-believer would assume. *This tendency to project the self-concept onto the social world is known as the* **false consensus effect** (Marks & Miller, 1987). It's important to understand that this is a pretty sensible way to be, much of the time; after all, if we have to make guesses about people, why not base these guesses on ourselves?

We also tend to assume that the way we see things is the way that they are, that our perceptions of reality are accurate. Of course we want to believe that we make sense. By extension, this means that people who differ from us are not only a little weird, they are wrong as well. This tendency, called **naive realism** (Ross & Ward, 1996), also makes sense to some degree. After all, imagine the opposite: if you had no trust in your own perceptions of reality, you would be so beset by doubts and uncertainty that life would be difficult and stressful. So, it makes sense to assume, most of the time, that the way you see things is the way they are.

SELF-SERVING BIASES AND ATTRIBUTIONS This tendency toward naive realism reflects a larger, more general need to want to feel positively about ourselves, to have a positive sense of self-evaluation or self-esteem (Allport, 1955; Maslow, 1968; Sedikides & Strube, 1995). Undergraduate students clearly enjoy boosts to their self-esteem, reporting preferring to receive such a boost even over eating a favourite food, getting paid, having sex, or seeing a best friend (Bushman et al., 2011). We strive to maintain our positive self-feelings through a host of **self-serving biases**, *which are biased ways of processing self-relevant information to enhance our positive self-evaluation* (Miller & Ross, 1975). For example, we tend to take credit for our successes, but blame our failures on other people, circumstances, or bad luck.

Also, on many different dimensions, we tend to assume that we are better than average; this *better than average effect* is just another way we keep our self-esteem intact, and has been shown in many different domains. We tend to prefer the letters in our name, especially our initials, over the other letters of the alphabet (Nuttin, 1985; Pelham et al., 2005). An extreme example was shown in one study of almost one million American students; a whopping 85% viewed themselves as above average in their ability to get along with other people, and 25% believed they were in the top 1% of this ability (Alicke & Olesya, 2005).

These self-serving processes also influence the types of attributions, or explanations, that we make for our own and others' behaviours. Much in the same way that our first impressions are formed implicitly, attributions tend to start out as automatic, intuitive explanations. Imagine that you're driving down the highway, and all of a sudden some other driver swerves in front of you, honking; you slam on the brakes and turn the wheel sharply, narrowly avoiding a collision. Quick—what is the first thing that comes to mind about the other driver? Probably, your first thought is not the kindest or gentlest; you assume the other driver is an aggressive jerk! This is an **internal attribution** (also known as a *dispositional* attribution), *whereby the observer (yourself, in the above example) explains the behaviour of the actor (the driver who cut in front of you) in terms of some innate quality of that person (being an aggressive jerk)* (see Figure 13.3).

But of course, there may be other reasons for the driver's behaviour. Perhaps he is swerving out of the way of a piece of debris on the road, or he just blew a tire, or he just received a phone call that his wife is in the hospital and so he is panicked and distracted, or he's a surgeon driving home after a 36-hour shift at the hospital and he is completely exhausted and falling asleep. These are **external attributions** (also known as *situational* attributions), *whereby the observer explains the actor's behaviour as the result of the situation* (Heider, 1958). Generally, these external attributions are not what first come to mind, but rather, they take a bit of time as we

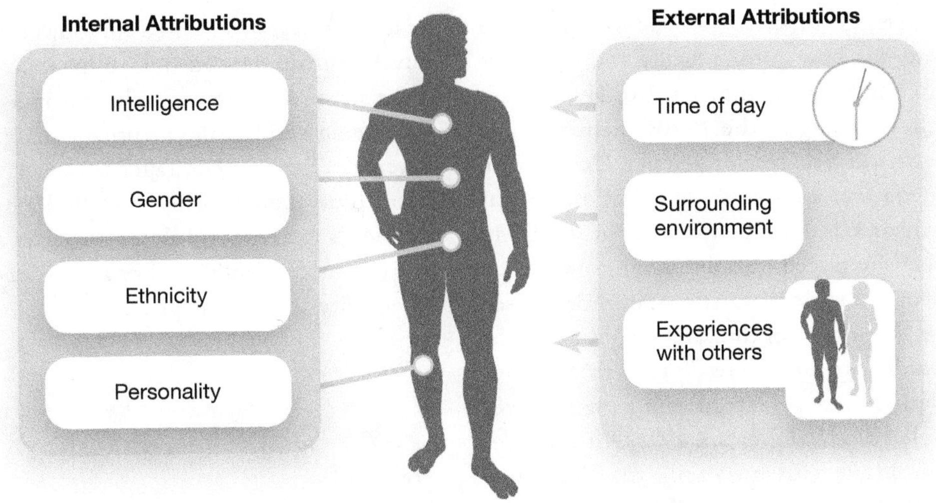

{FIG. 13.3} **Internal and External Attributions** Internal attributions are based on qualities or actions of the individual, whereas external attributions focus on the context in which the individual is situated. **Click on this figure in your eText to see more details.**

Explore
Internal and External Attributions

continue thinking about the situation and then realize that perhaps our snap judgment of the person's character may not have been warranted because there are other possible explanations we did not initially consider. *This tendency to over-emphasize internal (dispositional) attributions, and under-emphasize external (situational) factors, is known as the* **fundamental attribution error (FAE)** (Ross, 1977).

On the other hand, when we explain our own behaviours, we tend to emphasize whichever kind of explanation paints us in the best light. For our negative behaviours, our attributions are much more generous; we emphasize the situational factors that cause us to do undesirable things (e.g., we had a headache, our dog died last week, we were under a lot of stress, we had bad luck, etc.), rather than assuming that we are incompetent. And of course, when the behaviour is desirable, the self-serving bias works in the opposite direction; we take as much credit as we can for our successes (e.g., we worked really hard to deserve that promotion, we faced a lot of setbacks but we persevered and just didn't give up), but blame away our failures on people and circumstances beyond our control.

We should point out that the fundamental attribution error (FAE) is influenced by culture. People make the FAE the most in predominantly individualistic cultures such as Canada or the United States, and the least in more collectivistic cultures such as China or Japan. This different approach to explaining others' behaviour can be seen in how people interpret social events such as news stories. For example, after reading about recent mass murderers in the newspaper, subjects from China are more likely to emphasize situational explanations for the murders (such as recent stressful events in the person's life), whereas North American subjects are much more likely to emphasize dispositional explanations (such as the murderer being an evil person; Morris & Peng, 1994). This greater emphasis on situational factors in collectivistic societies reflects stronger values toward maintaining harmony in interpersonal relationships and fulfilling one's social roles in the larger community; this orientation leads people to become more sensitively attuned to and aware of situational information (Choi et al., 1999; Nisbett, 2003).

INGROUPS AND OUTGROUPS Although this desire to feel good about ourselves seems functional and healthy, it often has negative side effects, because these self-serving processes reinforce a tendency to be biased against others. We are motivated to be biased against others because one of the key ways we maintain positive feelings about ourselves is through our identification with larger social groups (Fein & Spencer, 1997). *Groups we feel positively toward and identify with* are our **ingroups**, including our family, home team, group of best friends, etc. In contrast, **outgroups** *are those "other" groups that we don't identify with.* In fact, we actively *dis*-identify with outgroups, which is one way we maintain high levels of self-esteem—we carve our social world into categories of *Us* and *Them* and then we automatically show a preference for *Us* over *Them.*

This where our self-serving biases begin to be so destructive. *As positive biases toward the self get extended to include one's ingroups, people become motivated to see their ingroups as superior to their outgroups—engaging in* **ingroup bias**. (Obviously, from the "outgroup's" perspective, it's the other way around, therein sowing the seeds for much social conflict.)

The final, crucial piece of this self–other puzzle is to appreciate just how automatically and easily we categorize our social world into *Us* and *Them*. A set of clever studies starting in the 1970s examined just *how easily people will form social categories, Us vs. Them, even using criteria that are meaningless*. The **minimal group paradigm** was described in a set of studies in which subjects were placed into different groups based on essentially meaningless distinctions, in order to see whether *Us* vs. *Them* ways of thinking would take root. In different studies, people were divided into groups based on whether they preferred one painting over another (Tajfel, 1970; Tajfel et al., 1971), or whether they flipped heads or tails on a coin toss (Locksley et al., 1980). Perhaps the most strikingly meaningless exercise was conducted by Richard Sorrentino at Western University and Gordon Hodson at Brock University, who simply randomly assigned people to "Group X" or "Group Y." Amazingly, even these completely meaningless ways of categorizing people into ingroups and outgroups are enough to drive prejudice and discrimination; for example, if people are asked to distribute money between the two groups, they consistently give more to their new ingroup members.

Imagine, if ingroup favouritism is so easily triggered based on essentially meaningless criteria, how much more powerful must such processes be when they are based on real-world distinctions, such as race, class, gender, or national identity? If the people in meaningless Group X prefer their fellow Xs over those nasty Ys, even though they have no history of animosity, no competition over resources, or any other grounds whatsoever on which to base their preferences, imagine how much more powerful people's biases will be when faced with real-world distinctions and long histories of conflict and violence. Appreciating the deeply biasing influences of making ingroup-outgroup distinctions in the first place adds an important layer to our understanding of these larger conflicts.

Finally, it is important to highlight that we cannot simply dispense with these psychological processes, despite all the trouble they cause us. All of these processes serve important functions for us. Without the false consensus effect and our tendency to project our self-concept onto others, we would be in a great deal of uncertainty about what other people are like; it would be like living on a planet of aliens about whom one can't make any assumptions except that they're mysterious and unpredictable. Without naive realism, we would be plagued by doubts as we constantly second-guessed our perceptions of the world. Without a positive sense of self-evaluation, it would be easy to feel useless, helpless, and generally miserable. Without the ability to attach ourselves to desired ingroups and distance ourselves from undesired outgroups it would be hard to feel a sense of belonging, which is indispensable to our well-being and healthy identity (Cacioppo et al., 2003; Myers & Diener, 1995; Tajfel & Turner, 1986). What we need to do then, is to learn to find a balance between our needs to feel good about ourselves and our groups, and our more enlightened awareness of our fundamental equality with all people.

Quick Quiz 13.2a

Person Perception

KNOW ...

1 ________ are very quick, effortless, and automatic, whereas ________ are slower, more careful, and effortful.

- **A** Explicit processes; implicit processes
- **B** Implicit processes; explicit processes
- **C** Internal attributions; external attributions
- **D** External attributions; internal attributions

UNDERSTAND ...

2 Which of the following statements about thin slices of behaviour is most accurate?

- **A** Thin slices of behaviour lead to inaccurate impressions of others.
- **B** In many instances, lasting and often accurate impressions of others form in just a few moments.
- **C** Thin-slice impressions are 100% accurate.
- **D** Thin slices work only when rating the attractiveness of others.

APPLY ...

3 Shania feels sure that her boss doesn't like her. As a result, every time her boss is around, Shania acts more restrained and less warm and friendly. This causes her boss to, in fact, find her unfriendly and start to not like her. This is an illustration of

- **A** thin slices of behaviour.
- **B** a self-fulfilling prophecy.
- **C** implicit processes being stronger than explicit processes.
- **D** explicit processes being stronger than implicit processes.

4 Donald, once poor, inherited $5 million and decided to donate $1000 to a local charity. Donald believes he took this step because he is a kind and generous man. Donald might be demonstrating ________.

- **A** the fundamental attribution error
- **B** hindsight bias
- **C** self-serving bias
- **D** concepts of cognitive dissonance

Answers can be found on page ANS-3.

Stereotypes, Prejudice, and Discrimination

Obviously, the roots of prejudice are planted very deeply in our psyches, stemming ultimately from our deep-rooted attachment to our own selves. Thus, while at the explicit level we may strive to be egalitarian, seeing all people as equal and not discriminating based on dimensions such as race, class, and gender, our normally functioning implicit processes continually split the world into *Us* and *Them*. In fact, using ERP technology to measure brain activation, research has shown that the perceptual system starts to react differently to people based on race and gender within a mere 200 milliseconds (Ito & Urland, 2003).

When we try to change these implicit tendencies, we are battling our vast and speedy implicit system with our weak and ponderously slow explicit system. Much of the time, our explicit, consciously controlled self is going to lose, and we will fall prey to our implicit biases. This can have highly destructive effects on society, because these implicit biases lay the foundation in our social-cognitive systems for stereotyping, prejudice, and intergroup discrimination.

It is important to understand that these three terms mean quite different things, although they are highly related to each other.

A **stereotype** *is a cognitive structure, a set of beliefs about the characteristics that are held by members of a specific social group; these beliefs function as schemas, serving to guide how we process information about our social world.*

Prejudice *is an affective, emotionally driven process, including negative attitudes toward and critical judgments of other groups.* Prejudice itself is an emotional process, but it in turn is reinforced by negative stereotypes.

Discrimination *is behaviour that disfavours or disadvantages members of a certain social group in some way.*

Taken together, stereotyping, prejudice, and discrimination underlie many of the destructive "isms" in society—racism, sexism, classism, etc. One of the central goals of social-cognitive psychology has been to understand how these processes work.

MYTHS IN MIND

Are Only Negative Aspects of Stereotypes Problematic?

The first examples that come to mind when stereotyping a group are usually based on negative characteristics. However, it is certainly not the case that all stereotypic associations are negative; men and women are stereotypically associated with different strengths, for example.

What might be counterintuitive to many people is that even the positive aspects of a stereotype carry a kind of hidden danger, leading to a tendency for people to believe it is okay to emphasize the positive aspects of a stereotype in a "benevolent or well-intentioned way." This has been examined a great deal with regard to sexism. For example, researchers have distinguished between hostile sexism, or stereotypes that have negative views of one or both sexes, and benevolent sexism, which includes positive views of one or both sexes (Glick & Fiske, 1996, 2001). For example, consider the somewhat dated saying that women are "the fairer sex." A person using this phrase may mean it as a compliment, implying that women are virtuous, nurturing, and empathetic. However, even stereotypes that a person may defend as being "well-intentioned" can place restrictions on an individual's behaviour. If we consider women to be "virtuous," they may be held to different sexual standards than men and, as a result, may be judged more harshly when they violate those standards. Similarly, considering women to be nurturing and empathetic reinforces the notion that women are the primary hubs of family life, and therefore less inclined toward career advancement in our competitive world; the belief in women's nurturance may feed the belief that their career is never the "primary" one in a two-gender household, and that when it comes time to raise a family, they will step back from their careers while the man will be the primary breadwinner, thus setting discriminatory practices in motion in the workplace and contributing to making women more dependent on men for financial security. Even when women try to go toe-to-toe in the workplace, they may be hindered in careers that call for assertive or aggressive behaviours (such as being successful in the business world) because the "fairer sex" stereotype is pervasive in the organization (Glick & Fiske, 1996, 2001). Thus, even seemingly positive aspects of a stereotype, from one perspective, can be perceived negatively from another perspective, and can result in negative consequences that were unforeseen.

PREJUDICE IN A POLITICALLY CORRECT WORLD? In recent decades, norms have changed greatly in terms of what is appropriate to say about other people. This increased sensitivity to social diversity and equality, such as society's greater acceptance of LGBTQ expressions of sexuality, or belief in gender and ethnic equality, is sometimes disparagingly referred to as "political correctness." The label carries the suggestion that the battles for equality are basically over, and now if people in disadvantaged groups raise concerns about how they are treated in our society, they are just looking for excuses, such as when people say someone is "playing the race card" as though they are using their ethnicity merely as a tool with which to try to take advantage of society. The truth is quite different. Outgroup stereotypes and prejudices are by no means a thing of the past, and neither are the discriminatory practices that go along with them. Just ask Muslims in the post-9/11 world how stigmatized they feel every time there is a "terrorist" attack somewhere in

Watch
In the Real World: Are Stereotypes and Prejudice Inevitable?

the world. Or ask a young Black person whether they feel they are treated exactly the same as Whites by their teachers, or the police, or potential employers. Or look at the outcry after a young girl in Steubenville, Ohio, was sexually assaulted while unconscious at a party, and two prominent high school football players in the community were found criminally responsible; many people felt that *she* had ruined *their* lives, and not the other way around. Or look at the disturbingly common and unabashed expression of negative views against Canada's Native people in the wake of the Idle No More protests of recent years. Clearly, the full story of stereotypes and prejudice plays out in the lives of millions of people who are placed into the category of "other" by one group or another.

For example, in the United States, despite the victories of the civil rights movement in shifting the racial attitudes of the general North American population, there is still prejudice toward non-White cultural groups. For example, it still seems as though Black men in particular experience the legal system differently from others. Black men in the U.S. are incarcerated far more often than any other groups, and experience substantially more physical and aggressive treatment from police (Smith, 2004). Records of police encounters over the past 30 years confirm what many minority groups have long claimed, that the police use more aggressive techniques on minority suspects than White suspects (Inn, Wheeler, & Sparling, 1977; Smith, 2004; Weitzer & Tuch, 2004). Historically, Black suspects have also been five times more likely to die in police confrontations than White suspects (U.S. Department of Justice, 2001).

This prejudice has seeped into the basic social-psychological functioning of many people, probably most people. For example, even though the general public denounces prejudice and discrimination and holds values of universal equality, studies of implicit processes tell a different story; when people (generally, White people) first are exposed to Black faces, this automatically influences a variety of physiological responses, including the activation of facial muscles, cardiovascular responses, and brain activity related to fear and negative emotions (Cunningham et al., 2004; Eberhardt, 2005).

In fact, measures of brain activity reveal the battle between implicit and explicit processes. Over very short amounts of time, exposure to White or Black faces activates implicit processes such as described above, indicating a racially biased pattern of processing. However, over longer periods of time, such as 30 seconds, brain activity shifts, showing heightened activity in the prefrontal cortex. This area relates to the control of emotions and abstract thinking, consistent with a neurological effort to bring values into one's mind in order to control emotional reactions.

This teaches us a powerful lesson: Even if people abhor prejudice at the explicit level of their awareness, they may implicitly hold negative stereotypes and experience prejudiced emotional reactions.

Clearly, there can be important discrepancies between stereotyping, prejudice, and discrimination at the explicit and implicit levels. This has created huge challenges for researchers attempting to study these processes, because of course simply asking subjects how they feel is only going to reveal their explicit processes, which may appear very egalitarian. Trying to overcome these challenges has led to the invention of measurement techniques to try to reveal implicit processes.

WORKING THE SCIENTIFIC LITERACY MODEL

Explicit versus Implicit Measures of Prejudice

If a great deal of modern prejudice has "gone underground" in the sense that people hide it and give politically correct responses at the explicit level, how can researchers accurately measure prejudice in today's society?

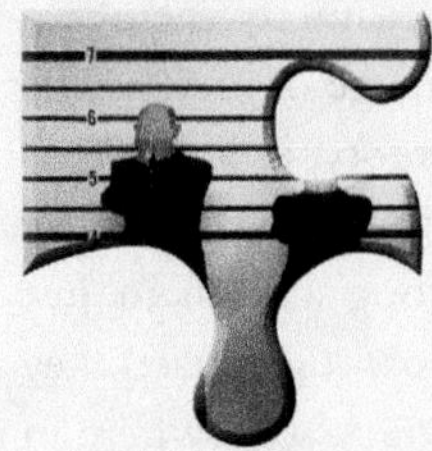

What do we know about measuring prejudice?

Psychologists have developed clever ways of measuring the forms of stereotyping and prejudice that are kept silent, either intentionally or because individuals are unaware of their own prejudices (Greenwald & Banaji, 1995; Nosek, 2007). In order to do so, researchers needed to come up with measurement devices that would reveal people's implicit processes. This is no easy challenge, because implicit processes can operate so quickly (in less than a second), and so subtly that we are typically not consciously aware of them.

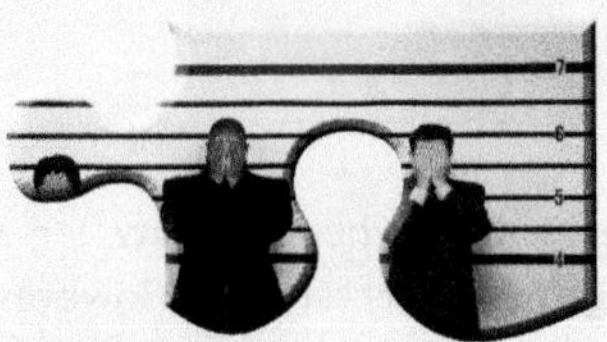

How can science study implicit prejudice?

A major research breakthrough occurred in the 1990s with the invention of the **Implicit Associations Test** (**IAT**; Greenwald et al., 1998). The IAT *measures how fast people can respond to images or words flashed on a computer screen.* To complete the test, a person uses two fingers and

(a)

(b)

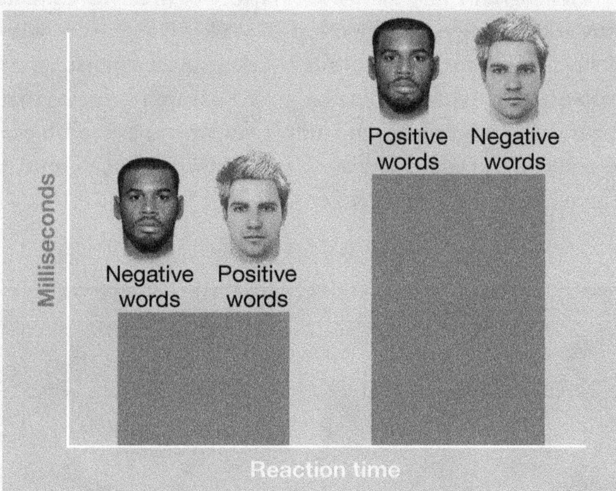

(c)

{FIG. 13.4} **The IAT Procedure** To complete one condition in the IAT (a), participants must use one button to identify Black faces and negative words and another button to identify White faces and positive words. In the other condition (b), the positive and negative words are switched to be paired with the other race (Black/positive and White/negative). Average response times are faster when Black is paired with negative words and White is paired with positive words (c). Is this a sign of hidden prejudice?

two computer buttons, and responds to stimuli on a computer screen (see Figure 13.4). In round 1, subjects are supposed to press one button if they see a Caucasian face or a positive word (such as "peace"), and a different button if they see a Black face or a negative word (such as "war"). Thus, in this round, the buttons are associating stereotype-consistent stimuli. With these particular pairings, it takes people around 800 milliseconds (four-fifths of a second) to press the correct button.

Watch
Implicit Attitudes

Round 2 rearranges the associations. This time subjects press one button if they see a Caucasian face or a negative word, and a different button if they see a Black face or a positive word. Thus, in this round, the buttons are associating the stimuli in stereotype-inconsistent ways. In this situation, people take an average of 1015 milliseconds to press the correct button, more than one-fifth of a second longer than in round 1. (To control for any possible effects of going first vs. going second, the order in which a person goes through these tasks is usually counterbalanced across subjects, with some going in the order presented here, and others in the reverse order.)

Why does it take longer to respond when there is a Black/positive button than when there is a Black/negative button? The researchers reasoned that our racial schemas associate more negativity with Blacks than with Whites. Because schemas guide our information processing, they facilitate the processing of information that is schema-consistent; thus, it is easier for a person to make snap judgments to always press one button for either Black or negative stimuli. But schema-inconsistent information is more difficult to process; thus, having two different buttons for Black and for negative means that a person has to override their automatic, implicit association between Black and negative, in order to choose the correct response. Thus, by measuring participants' abilities to process information extremely quickly, the IAT starts to reveal a person's schematic, implicit "programming." The size of the reaction time discrepancy between these two rounds is believed to be a direct measure of the strength of people's implicit prejudice toward Blacks.

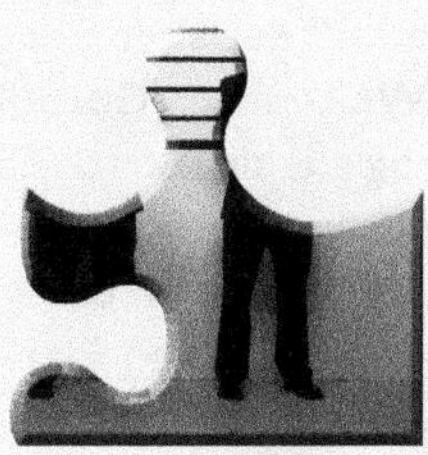

Can we critically evaluate this evidence?

Although the data gathered with this instrument show reliable results, some psychologists have questioned the test's validity: Is the IAT really a measure of prejudice? Or is it possible that the IAT is merely measuring the extent to which people have been exposed to negative stereotypes, but have not necessarily developed prejudices? After all, simply knowing about a stereotype does not mean an individual believes it, uses it to judge people, or engages in discriminatory behaviour.

Studies by Elizabeth Phelps and her colleagues (2000) suggest that the IAT reflects a person's emotional reactions to outgroup members. In her studies, White participants were shown pictures of Black and White faces, while having their brains scanned for activity in the amygdala. The amount of amygdala activation measured when looking at Black faces was positively correlated with participants' IAT measures of implicit prejudice. This suggests that the IAT is measuring something real enough to be reflected in neurological activity in areas related to fear and emotional processing.

Why is this relevant?

The development of the IAT has fostered a great deal of research and has been applied to at least a dozen forms of stereotyping, including stereotypes of social classes (Rudman et al., 2002), sexual orientation (Banse et al., 2001), and even fraternity and sorority members (Wells & Corts, 2008). The results of all these tests illustrate that implicit prejudice seems to be more prevalent than what people are willing to express in explicit tests (Nosek et al., 2002). The IAT is also being applied to clinical settings. For example, one research group developed an IAT that measures attitudes about alcohol use. This instrument can successfully predict how much alcohol someone is likely to consume, even when explicit measures fail to do so (Ostafin et al., 2008). To the extent that this methodology is valid, it is extremely valuable, giving us a window into people's private minds.

Blend Images/Alamy

PSYCH @

The Law Enforcement Academy

Imagine that instead of linking positive or negative terms with Black faces in the IAT, you were asked to make a snap decision whether or not to shoot a potential criminal. A number of researchers have used video-game-like tasks to put participants in these situations. In these video simulations, a figure will suddenly appear, either holding a weapon or a non-weapon (e.g., a wallet or a cell phone). It turns out that when making these split-second decisions, people are a little bit slower to decide whether or not to shoot a Black man holding a non-weapon, and they make the wrong decision more often. When a Black man is holding a gun, however, they make the "shoot" decision more quickly than if the gun is held by a White man (Correll et al., 2007; Correll et al., 2006). The logic is similar to the IAT discussed above. Because Black and "gun" are stereotypically consistent with each other, people have an easier time processing these stimuli together than when Black and "wallet" are paired with each other. Just like the situation in the Amadou Diallo case then, people are more likely to mistakenly shoot a Black man holding a wallet, believing that he might be holding a gun; at least, they're more likely to do this in a video game.

Certainly a video game pales in comparison to the adrenaline-fuelled confrontation that occurred that fateful night in the Bronx. It is easy to imagine that the stress of a real confrontation, combined with the complexity of a real-world situation, would lead to an even higher chance of a mistaken shooting occurring (Saus et al., 2006). To combat any implicit influence of race on an officer's decision to shoot, most law enforcement agencies in North America have developed extensive training programs, part of which focuses on making shoot–don't-shoot decisions (Cordner & Shain, 2011). Programs may simulate a variety of firearms combat situations, using a combination of walk-through sets with cardboard figures, and realistic mock-combat against other people armed with foam pellet guns. Research suggests that this training is helpful; even student volunteers in the lab can be trained to reduce shooting errors through such means (Correl et al., 2007; Plant & Peruche, 2005).

83/ZUMA Press/Newscom

The split-second differences in the IAT may be related to officers' increased use of deadly force with Black suspects, including cases where the suspect is unarmed. Here, a police officer undergoes virtual reality training designed to reduce shooting errors.

Quick Quiz 13.2b
Stereotypes, Prejudice, and Discrimination

KNOW ...

1. The concept of self-serving bias is similar to _________, in which we attribute positive qualities to the social group we belong to.
   - **A** ingroup bias
   - **B** outgroup bias
   - **C** discrimination
   - **D** implicit bias

2. _________ prejudice refers to situations in which a person stereotypes a group of people based on hidden, unacknowledged feelings.
   - **A** Explicit
   - **B** Discriminative
   - **C** Associative
   - **D** Implicit

UNDERSTAND ...

3. Unconscious forms of prejudice are believed to be measured with the implicit associations test. This test is based on
   - **A** the types of words people typically make up when they see a person of a specific race.
   - **B** how long it takes people to respond to positive or negative words along with Black or White faces.
   - **C** changes in heart rate that accompany photos of people from different racial backgrounds.
   - **D** increased activity in the emotional centres of the brain that are associated with specific races.

ANALYZE ...

4. Which of the following statements about stereotypes and prejudice is false?
   - **A** Stereotypes can be expressed outwardly and very explicitly.
   - **B** All stereotypes are of negative characteristics.
   - **C** Stereotypes are often experienced implicitly.
   - **D** Prejudice has become increasingly unpopular in the United States.

Answers can be found on page ANS-3.

Improving Intergroup Relations

We are left with an immense practical challenge: How can we overcome the implicit processes we have examined in this module, and work toward eliminating harmful stereotypes, prejudices, and discrimination from our society? Unfortunately, there are no easy answers. But there are some promising possibilities.

Keri Kawakami at York University has spent more than a decade researching how to overcoming implicit stereotyping and prejudice. Research in her lab has shown that people's implicit networks can be "reprogrammed" through practice. For example, people can be trained to make situational attributions for negative behaviours by stereotyped group members, thereby overcoming the fundamental attribution error; this helps to prevent people from thinking of others in stereotypic ways (Stewart et al., 2010). In another study, Kawakami and her colleagues used a computer task to directly teach people to make different associations to a stereotyped group. Subjects were presented with photographs of Blacks and Whites, coupled with either stereotypic or non-stereotypic traits, and were instructed to respond "NO" to stereotypic pairings, and "YES" to non-stereotypic pairings. After extensive training involving many such trials, subjects no longer activated negative racial stereotypes, even at the implicit level (Kawakami et al., 2000). This suggests that, over time, as our society continues to evolve in an increasingly egalitarian, non-prejudiced direction, it may be possible for people to un-learn the stereotypes that history has provided us with. However, there is a huge gap between the kind of intensive training that Kawakami's participants experienced in the lab and the real-world experience of individuals who are bombarded with both stereotypic and non-stereotypic messages on a daily basis. Nevertheless, these results suggest that it is at least possible for people to "reprogram" themselves.

One of the most well-supported ideas in all of social psychology is the **contact hypothesis**, *which predicts that social contact between members of different groups is extremely important to overcoming prejudice* (Allport, 1954; Pettigrew & Tropp, 2006), especially if that contact occurs in settings in which the groups have equal status and power, and ideally, in which group members are cooperating on tasks or pursuing common goals (Sherif, 1961). Negative stereotypes and the attendant prejudices thrive under conditions of ignorance, whereas allowing people to get to know members of outgroups, to work together to pursue common goals, to come to appreciate their membership in common groups or as part of the same ingroup (e.g., we're both Leafs fans, Canadians, or members of the human species; Gaertner & Dovidio, 2000), and to develop friendships with members of outgroups (Pettigrew, 1997, 1998) are all different ways in which contact helps to overcome prejudice. In fact, contact between members of different groups not only helps to combat their own prejudices, but that of their friends as well; simply knowing that someone is friends with an outgroup member serves to decrease the prejudice of that person's friends (Wright et al., 1997).

Coming to see our fellow human beings as all part of the same human family is an opportunity that recent advances in technology (the Internet, space exploration), economics (globalization), and ironically, global problems (climate change, nuclear proliferation) have made available to all of us. This global perspective shift may, one hopes, help us to overcome our age-old group prejudices. Astronauts who travel into space and look back on this one little planet that we inhabit often report that the experience profoundly affects them.

"The first day or so we all pointed to our countries. The third or fourth day we were pointing to our continents. By the fifth day, we were aware of only one Earth."
—Sultan bin Salman Al-Saud

Module Summary

Module 13.2

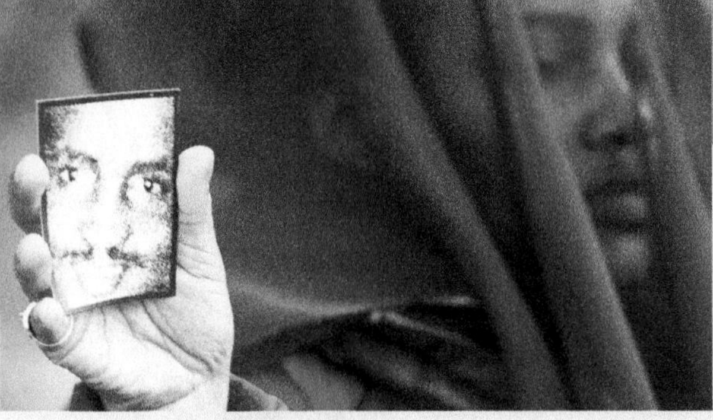
w85/ZUMA Press/Newscom

Now that you have read this module you should

KNOW ...

- ***The key terminology associated with social cognition*:**

contact hypothesis (p. 569)
discrimination (p. 565)
dual-process models (p. 559)
explicit processes (p. 559)
external (situational) attribution (p. 562)
false consensus effect (p. 562)
fundamental attribution error (FAE) (p. 563)
Implicit Associations Test (IAT) (p. 566)
implicit processes (p. 559)
ingroup bias (p. 563)
ingroups (p. 563)
internal (dispositional) attribution (p. 562)
minimal group paradigm (p. 564)
naive realism (p. 562)
outgroups (p. 563)
person perception (p. 560)
prejudice (p. 565)
self-fulfilling prophecy (p. 561)
self-serving bias (p. 562)
stereotype (p. 565)
thin slices of behaviour (p. 560)

UNDERSTAND ...

- ***How we form first impressions and how these impressions influence us.*** We quickly form impressions, even when only thin slices of behaviour are available to us. These impressions can be surprisingly accurate, but they can also affect our behaviour in ways that often tends to confirm our initial impressions; this is the phenomenon of self-fulfilling prophecies.

APPLY ...

- ***Your understanding of social cognition to the problem of overcoming prejudice and discrimination.*** The key to overcoming prejudice and discrimination seems to be to help people create different schemas in their mind for members of outgroups. This can be done through retraining the person to make different automatic associations with outgroup members, such as training them to consciously reject any pairing of the outgroup with any negative or stereotyped traits. Different schemas can also be created through realizing a common identity between oneself and the other person, which can occur from extended contact, cooperation on mutual goals, or adopting more inclusive and abstract categories (e.g., human family) by which to think about people.

ANALYZE ...

- ***Whether people who commit discriminatory acts are necessarily prejudiced.*** It is certainly possible for people to commit discriminatory acts without being prejudiced. Regardless of prejudice, stereotypes are absorbed from the larger culture, and these can function as interpersonal schemas that can guide how we see things, and how we process information implicitly. This can cause us to behave in a discriminatory fashion without us intending to, such as being more likely to assume an ambiguous object is a gun if held by a Black man, compared to when it is held by a White man.

Anton Balazh/Shutterstock

Module 13.3

Attitudes, Behaviour, and Effective Communication

Learning Objectives

After reading this module you should

KNOW ...	UNDERSTAND ...	APPLY ...	ANALYZE ...
The key terminology in research on attitudes, behaviour, and effective communication	How behaviours influence attitudes in terms of cognitive dissonance theory	Your understanding of the central route to describe how a message should be designed	The difficulties communicators face in trying to convince the public to take action on climate change

Bill McKibben is a man on a mission. He wants to save the planet; actually, to be more accurate, he wants to save the kind of planet that humans can live on. But unlike many people with such ambitious dreams, Bill has a few very important factors on his side.

First, he knows what he is talking about when it comes to saving the planet, having published many books and articles on the topic over the past few decades. Second, he has the full weight of the scientific community behind his cause, which agrees that the human species is heading rapidly for catastrophe as we push global warming higher and higher. And third, he has a global organization, 350.org, spanning almost every country on Earth, with hundreds of thousands of members. He also has some significant victories under his belt, from organizing the most widespread days of political activism in history to raising unprecedented opposition to key government decisions, such as whether or not to pass the Keystone XL pipeline that would take oil from Alberta's oilsands and transport it across the United States.

For Bill McKibben, and for the human species more generally, to succeed in the fight against climate change, there are some big barriers to overcome. Psychology provides a great deal of insight into how to rise to such a societal challenge. Any social problem is, at some level, a problem of human behaviour, and finding solutions therefore inevitably involves changing human behaviour. Social psychology provides many insights for how to do exactly this, which is what this module is about.

Focus Questions

 What is the relationship between attitudes and behaviour?

 How should communications be structured so as to be as persuasive as possible?

ZUMA Press, Inc./Alamy

Bill McKibben, author, activist and founder of 350.org

According to the American Psychological Association's official task force on climate change, "Addressing climate change is arguably one of the most pressing tasks facing this planet and its inhabitants" (American Psychological Association, 2010, p. 6). The task force was comprised of a carefully chosen group of highly regarded senior scientists, including the University of Victoria's Robert Gifford. Their overall assessment agrees with the perspective of the United Nations, whose Secretary General Ban Ki-Moon said in 2009 that climate change was the greatest issue of the 21st century. Using the insights of psychology to find solutions to climate change is increasingly becoming a focus for applied psychologists who specialize in communication and behaviour change.

Changing People's Behaviour

Four of the most common approaches taken to attempt to change the public's behaviour on a large scale are technological, legal, economic, and raising awareness. The technological approach focuses on making the desired behaviour as easy as possible through changing the technologies and structures that influence the person. For example, people will have a smaller carbon footprint if there are alternative energy technologies widely available; similarly, people will be less likely to throw their litter on the ground if there are easily accessible garbage cans nearby. The idea is to get the technology right, and people will behave in the desired way. The legal approach focuses on policy change—get the laws right and people will behave in the desired way. The economic approach focuses on financial incentives and penalties, generally through taxes and pricing—make the "right" thing to do cheaper, and the "wrong" thing to do more expensive, and people will behave in the desired way. The raising awareness approach focuses on information—get the information right, educate everybody, and people will behave in the desired way.

Watch

What's in It for Me?: Persuasion

Although each of these approaches obviously can have an impact on public behaviour, each one by itself is insufficient for solving the climate change crisis. The biggest problem with the technological, legal, and economic perspectives (aside from the problem that you can't, realistically, apply them to every behaviour that is relevant to climate change) is that developing and implementing the technological solutions, or passing the laws and setting the price incentives that would be required to sufficiently change behaviour, can only happen if the public at large will support such changes. Any politician who tries to, for example, increase gas taxes in order to encourage the shift to a sustainable energy economy is going to have to overcome some stiff public resistance. Clearly, finding solutions to our environmental challenges requires that the public supports those solutions.

Inevitably, as you consider how to achieve the technological, legal, or economic changes that might change public behaviour, you often end up at the problem of how to get the support of the general public. This takes us to the fourth approach: raising awareness. The assumption behind the raising awareness approach is that people will generally do the right thing, provided they have the right information. In turn, this is based on the assumption that information drives attitudes, and attitudes drive behaviour. So to change behaviour, you have to change the beliefs upon which attitudes are based, which means you have to give people information. Therein lies the logic behind public service announcements, pamphlets, billboards, education campaigns, and the vast majority of the behaviour change attempts occurring in society (McKenzie-Mohr, 2000). Learning how to communicate effectively in order to influence attitudes and behaviour has been a major focus of psychology for most of its history, and we have learned a great deal about how to do so.

PERSUASION: CHANGING ATTITUDES THROUGH COMMUNICATION Social psychologists have discovered many important principles underlying effective communication, giving us a set of tools for influencing all sorts of behaviours, from wearing condoms to eating chocolate bars. These tools are regularly employed in the marketing world to get us to, basically, buy more stuff. But they are also being employed in the social marketing world, which uses principles of marketing psychology to promote positive, pro-social behaviour changes, changes that benefit other people and society in general, such as donating blood or giving your time or money for a charitable cause.

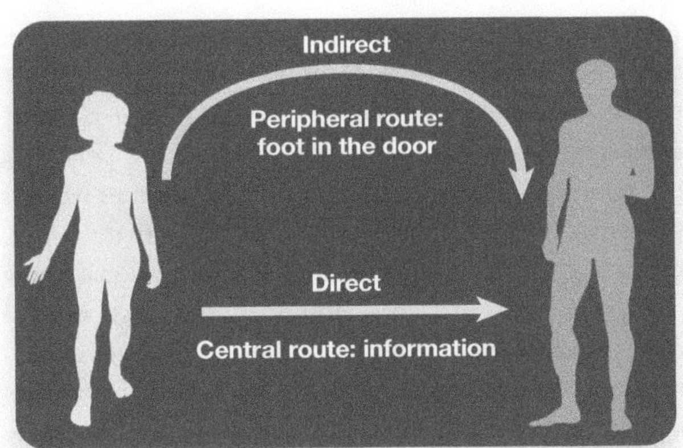

{FIG. 13.5} **Central and Peripheral Routes to Persuasion** There are two ways that communications can persuade people. In the "central route" people are persuaded by the content of a message, while in the "peripheral route" they are influenced by the way the content is presented, the "style" over the "substance." **Click on this figure in your eText to see more details.**

If you are preparing a persuasive message, understanding what is likely to be convincing to your audience is extremely important. One of the key theories that provide guidance for how to approach convincing your audience is the **elaboration likelihood model**. This model predicts that *when audiences are sufficiently motivated to pay attention to a message (i.e., they care about the issue) and they have the opportunity for careful processing (i.e., they have the cognitive resources available to understand the message), they will be persuaded by the facts of the argument, the substance; when either of these two factors, motivation and opportunity, are missing, people will tend to be persuaded by other factors*. According to this model of persuasion, information can appeal to people through two general "routes": *the central route* and *the peripheral route* (Cacioppo et al., 1986).

The **central route to persuasion** is all about substance. It *occurs when people pay close attention to the content of a message, evaluate the evidence presented, and examine the logic of the arguments*; if the message is sufficiently compelling, they will be convinced, internalizing the message as something they believe in (see Figure 13.5). As a result, attitude or belief change that occurs through the central route tends to be strong and long-lasting.

However, much of the time, people are not going to pay sufficient attention to the content of a message, and instead, *persuasion will depend upon other features that are not directly related to the message itself, such as the attractiveness of the person delivering the information*, or the sheer amount of information, such as the number of arguments made. When taking the **peripheral route to persuasion** it's all about style, not substance. Although persuasion is typically not as powerful through the peripheral route, it is nevertheless often a superior route through which to reach people, in part because it's so much easier. Even though people may not be paying much attention or may not really care about your issue, they can be convinced through the peripheral route. Also, even if you have a relatively weak set of arguments, people can often be persuaded through the peripheral route. We will explore the use of the peripheral route later in this module.

Watch: Becoming a Detective of Social Influence: Robert Cialdini

Using the Central Route Effectively

First, you need to be confident that you have the facts on your side. If you feel your perspective makes logical, rational sense, then it makes sense to appeal to the central route. This means getting your audience to pay close attention to your arguments; in order to do that, you have two key factors to work with: motivation and opportunity. People will be more likely to process information through the central route when they are highly motivated and when they have the knowledge or expertise to understand the information. Thus, the central route is most reliable when people are highly motivated about the topic, when they have sufficient time and freedom from distraction, and when the information is not overwhelmingly complex relative to their knowledge (i.e., if the audience is not very knowledgeable, the information has to be simple, but if the audience has more expertise, then obviously the information can be more nuanced and complex).

Watch: What's in It for Me? Persuasion

Keeping these factors in mind suggests some key strategies for maximizing the central route:

MAKE IT PERSONAL Imagine for a moment that your friend has some juicy, scandalous gossip to tell you. There would be a big difference in your desire to hear it if it were about (1) one of her friends who you do not know; (2) one of your friends; (3) you! Clearly, your desire to get this information is directly related to how personally relevant it is. Making a message self-relevant is crucially important to motivating people to care and pay attention.

Interestingly, it can be very easy to make information self-relevant, as simple as shifting from describing something to a person to getting them to imagine themselves in the situation. In the previous paragraph, our opening sentence could have been, "Making a message self-relevant is very important. . . ." Instead, we said "Imagine for a moment that your friend has some juicy, scandalous gossip. . . ." Crafting effective communications involves a subtle consideration of nuances such as this rewording that can make a message more personally engaging.

Consider one striking study from the early 1980s (Gregory et al., 1982), a time when cable television (CATV) was still making its way into the North American viewing market. Researchers compared two highly similar persuasive appeals, which were presented to two samples of homeowners to try to convince them to subscribe to CATV.

> In the information-only condition, homeowners were presented with this appeal: *CATV will provide a broader entertainment and information service to its subscribers. Used properly, a person can plan in advance to enjoy events offered. Instead of spending money on the babysitter and gas, and putting up with the hassles of going out, more time can be spent at home with family, alone, or with friends.*
>
> In the imagination condition, homeowners received this appeal: *Take a moment and imagine how CATV will provide you with a broader entertainment and information service. When you use it properly, you will be able to plan in advance which of the events offered you wish to enjoy. Take a moment and think of how, instead of spending money on the babysitter and gas, and then having to put up with the hassles of going out, you will be able to spend your time at home, with your family, alone, or with your friends.*

As you can see, the two appeals are almost identical, providing the exact same arguments; from a purely logical perspective, they should have exactly the same impact. However, their impact differed dramatically: Only 19.5% of the people who received the information-only appeal signed up for CATV, whereas a whopping 47% subscribed when they were simply told to imagine themselves in the scenario! Imagine the profit difference between selling your product to 1 in 5 people or 1 in 2 people. This is the power of making things personal.

This power has been explained by **construal-level theory** (Trope & Liberman, 2010), *which describes how information affects us differently depending on our psychological distance from the information.* Information that is specific, personal, and described in terms of concrete details feels more personal, or closer to us; whereas information that is more general, impersonal, and described in more abstract terms feels less personal, or more distant. Importantly, psychological distance depends not only on geography (people or places that are farther away are less personal), but temporal factors (distant future or past times feel less personal), social factors (people or groups that are further removed from one's identity are less personal), how abstract the information is (abstractions are less personal than things that are specific), and even the level of certainty one feels about an outcome (outcomes that are less certain are less personal). Communicators should be able to make their messages feel more personally relevant to the audience by working with these factors, bringing the message close to home in time and space, showing how it affects the audience themselves or their social groups, and making consequences or outcomes as certain as possible.

Unfortunately for climate change communicators, they have struggled in making climate change personal. Climate change communications have traditionally fared poorly on all the factors of psychological distance mentioned above. The term "climate change" itself implies something global and abstract, and when people do think of specific others who may suffer due to climate change, they tend to think of others in the distant future or in distant parts of the world (Leiserowitz et al., 2010; Lorenzoni & Pidgeon, 2006), and scientists have been honest about communicating the inherent uncertainty of scientific predictions. As a result, people often experience climate change as "psychologically distant," rather than personally relevant (Liberman & Trope, 2008; Milfont, 2010). Clearly, bringing the consequences of climate change home for a given audience, bringing them close in time and space, and changing the focus of the discussion to the certainty of what scientists do know rather than the uncertainty of what they don't, should make the message much more powerful (Spence et al., 2012).

WORKING THE SCIENTIFIC LITERACY MODEL

The Identifiable Victim Effect

It is practically a daily event on the news to focus on some human tragedy and cover it in excruciating detail, from children who have fallen down wells to individuals who have been tragically murdered. We focus an incredible amount of media attention to certain tragedies in particular, such as the horrendous shooting death of 20 children and six adults at Sandy Hook Elementary School in 2012. It makes sense that we do these things, to convey these tragedies to the public, to keep people informed about what's going on in the world, and to honour the dead by telling their stories. However, we also regularly ignore much larger tragedies. One astonishing example occurred in Rwanda, when 800 000 people were killed by machete attacks over a matter of weeks; almost as astonishing as the genocide itself was the world media's response, which was to largely ignore it, with most of the major news agencies devoting only a few minutes of a newscast to the genocide (Slovic, 2007). As a result, it was difficult to marshall public support for action.

A similar puzzle has held back the public from taking climate change action. The problem itself couldn't be much more threatening; for example, in March 2013, a major publication in the prestigious *Proceedings of the Royal Society*, by renowned scientists Paul and Anne Ehrlich at Stanford University, concluded that human civilization is headed rapidly toward global collapse due to an escalating mix of environmental problems such as climate change and the acidification of the oceans (Ehrlich & Ehrlich, 2013). Already, approximately 400 000 people die every year due to climate change–related disasters (DARA, 2012). Yet we largely ignore these news stories.

The mystery is not why we pay so much attention to a tragedy like the Sandy Hook shootings; they certainly deserve our shock, horror, and collective mourning. The mystery is why we give so much less attention to tragedies at much larger scales. Why is it so difficult, for instance, to persuade the public to force governments to take action on climate change?

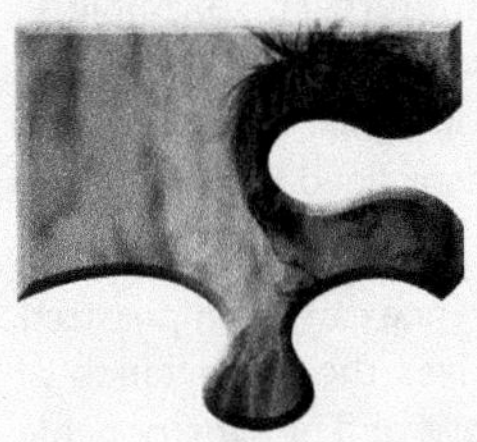

What do we know about communicating about tragedy?

Many experiments have shown that information about tragedies has much more impact if it focuses on specific, concrete events and specific people's experiences than if it relies upon more abstract, statistical information to try to convey the sheer scope and overall impact of the tragedy. For example, the **identifiable victim effect** *describes how people are more powerfully moved to action by the story of a single suffering person, than by information about a whole group of people.*

In one study (Small et al., 2007), researchers gave subjects a chance to donate up to $5 of their earnings from participating in the study to an organization, Save the Children, based on information provided in one of three different conditions. In the identifiable victim condition, participants read about Rokia, a 7-year-old girl from Mali, Africa, who was desperately poor and facing severe hunger and possibly starvation. In the statistical victims condition, participants read about food shortages and rainfall deficits affecting more than 20 million people and children in four countries in Africa. In the third condition, the information was combined; participants read about Rokia and then were also given statistical information about mass suffering in African countries.

Perhaps not surprisingly, people who read specifically about Rokia gave significantly more ($2.38) than people who read general statistical information ($1.14). Clearly, Rokia tugs on the heart-strings more than abstract numbers do. But amazingly, when given information about Rokia combined with the statistics, people still gave less than they did when reading solely about Rokia ($1.43) and no more (statistically speaking) than they gave when presented with the statistics alone. It seems that appealing to the head and heart simultaneously doesn't work.

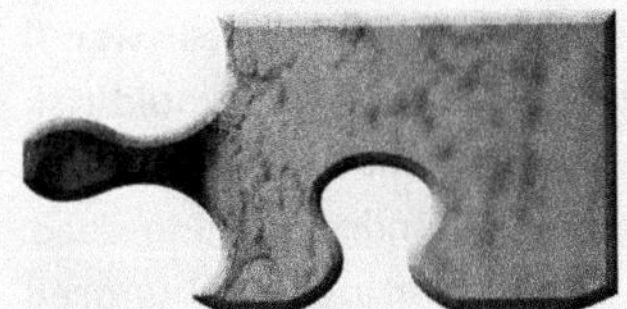

How can science explain the identifiable victim effect?

Earlier in the module, we mentioned that abstract information is experienced as more "psychologically distant" than concrete, specific information. But this doesn't go far enough to help us understand the findings in this Rokia study. There are two key findings to explain. First, why is Rokia's individual story more impactful than millions of Rokia stories presented in the form of statistical information? Second, why does combining Rokia's story with statistics actually make it *less* likely for people to act?

To understand these findings, psychologists rely upon dual-process models (see Module 13.2) of information processing, involving two systems in the brain that process information differently. System One (Stanovich & West, 2000), the **experiential system** (Epstein, 1994), *operates more implicitly, quickly, and intuitively and is predominantly emotional*; the experiential system responds to personal experiences, images, stories, and other people's emotions, making snap judgments based on intuitive, affective reactions to images, stories, and other people's emotions. System Two, the **analytic system**, *operates more at the explicit level of consciousness, is slower and more methodical, and uses logic and discursive thinking (i.e., reasoning using language)* to try to understand reality. The experiential system is more about *feeling with* something; the analytic system is more about *understanding* that "other" thing.

With these systems in mind, you can begin to see why Rokia's story would be so powerful; Rokia's story speaks to the experiential system, thereby triggering the affective responses, such as empathy, that would motivate people to give money to charity. The abstract statistics, however, speak to the analytic system, the head rather than the heart. With less emotional impact, they have less motivational strength (Barrett & Salovey, 2002; Forgas, 2000). Without emotions, information about the suffering of millions of people becomes "just a number," an abstraction, something that is difficult to *feel with*.

In some situations, appealing to the analytic system can backfire, because the analytic system effectively shuts down the experiential system, putting people in more of a cold, analytic frame of mind rather than a hot, emotional state. This may be why the condition that included both Rokia and the statistics was no more motivating than the statistics alone. The cold, analytic way of thinking that was activated by the statistics made Rokia's emotional story have less impact. When information is "just information," it is stripped of its meaning and therefore less likely to guide behaviour (Loewenstein et al., 2001; Slovic et al., 2002).

The system that FEELS, feels for the small, not the large. Nobel prize–winning biochemist Albert Szent Gyorgi sums this up well when he talks about the difficulties trying to wrap your head around the consequences of nuclear war. "I am deeply moved if I see one man suffering and would risk my life for him. Then I talk impersonally about the possible pulverization of our big cities, with a hundred million dead. I am unable to multiply one man's suffering by a hundred million" (Slovic, 2007).

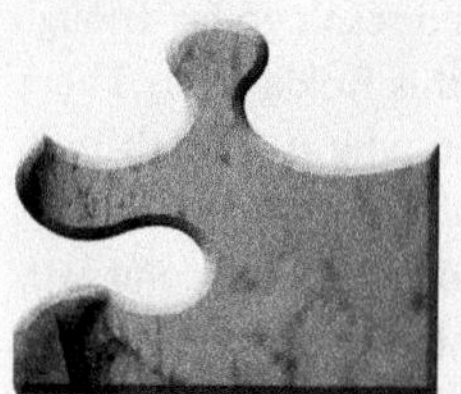

Can we critically evaluate this evidence?

Taken by itself, this single study cannot tell us whether individual stories are more motivating than statistics; it merely tells us that this particular story is more motivating than these particular statistics. But it obviously cannot be the case that all information that appeals to the logical mind is therefore undesirable or that it will interfere with the motivation to act. There are two main arguments against this.

First, specific stories and specific statistics will have different impacts in specific situations with specific people. Obviously, every particular convergence of circumstances is different. Sometimes, a certain story will be particularly powerful; other times a certain statistic will be. Sometimes, a particular combination of story and statistics will work the best, and other times one may disempower the other, as with Rokia.

Second, we don't know what the long-term impacts may be of statistical information and emotional stories. For example, a given statistic may have little impact in the first moment when a person hears it, but it may become part of a larger understanding of what is happening in the world that operates over a longer period of time. It seems highly possible that information that appeals to the analytic system may have more impact over longer periods of time; after all, this system, by its very nature, operates more slowly. We also don't know how the impacts of specific stories or statistics may change over time, or with repeated exposure. Do we get used to hearing about each of them and habituate to them so that they have less impact over time? Or do repeated exposures accumulate over time into a larger understanding that motivates us to act?

Obviously, we cannot dispense with talking about statistical, abstract information if we are to communicate with each other about what is happening in the world. It therefore becomes extremely important to understand how the experiential and analytic systems can work together, and how to make the best use of them in crafting effective communication strategies.

Why is this relevant?

This research is highly relevant to the challenge of motivating people to take action on major societal issues such as climate change (e.g., Slovic, 2007). The basic principle for communicating in a way that motivates behaviour change is to personally engage the person, to reduce the psychological distance of the information. There are many ways to do this, as illustrated by a recent TED talk on climate change.

- Information can be framed in a personal way. For example, the talk is titled, "Everything You Love," immediately framing the climate change message not in terms of "the environment" or something external to the person, but instead highlighting for people that this is, in fact, highly personal.
- Abstract information can be described in terms of personal experiences. For example, the fact that climate change is affecting the oceans is described not as a summary of environmental facts, but rather as a story about a little boy who loves the ocean so much, but is going to grow up to find that it has become a graveyard of his beloved species.
- The timeframe can be shortened, emphasizing the present and near future, rather than distant future. For example, in the talk, major consequences and opportunities for action are described in terms of the next few years, including the melting of the Arctic and the imminent need to change our energy systems.
- Specific actions that will make a difference can be emphasized. For example, the TED talk emphasizes the importance of joining organizations (such as 350.org or The Unstoppable Snowball) that are lobbying politicians to take action on climate change.
- Information can be more personally engaging if it is told to a person by their friends, rather than a more impersonal news source. For example, the TED talk advocates that people make use of social media strategies for sharing information about opportunities to take action.

How to make the best use of our understanding of the psychology of communication, in order to have a positive impact on the world, remains a major puzzle for humanity to solve.

SHAH MARAI/AFP/Getty Images

VALUE APPEALS As any good marketer knows, audiences are much more likely to listen to a message that is framed in such a way that it seems relevant to their values (see also Module 11.3). Most pro-environmental behaviours have been framed in ways that go *against* people's self-interest, involving trade-offs between the economy *or* the environment, jobs *or* trees, comfort and convenience *or* personal sacrifice (Schultz & Zelezny, 2003). And as noble as it might be to sit in the dark, shivering through the winter and eating only locally grown root vegetables while having two-minute showers once a week, these are unlikely to be the next hot behaviour trends.

The value frames that are adopted by most environmental messages are *biospheric* (e.g., save the rain forests; save the polar bears!) or *social-altruistic* (e.g., the poor will be more severely affected by climate change; climate change should be stopped to protect our children, grandchildren, and future generations) (Stern & Dietz, 1994). However, these value frames are not compatible with the dominant North American value system, which is *egoistic*, focused on self-enhancement, personal success, material wealth, and independence (Schultz & Zelezny, 2003; Schwartz, 1994).

Environmental messages might be more motivating if they are framed in more egoistic terms. For example, messages could emphasize financial savings (saving energy = saving money), personal empowerment (you can make a difference), the importance of community (community gardening will make your neighbourhood safer), economic opportunities (renewable energy is the fastest-growing sector of the energy economy), and even fun and friendship (going to protests is exciting and you meet interesting people). The increasingly popular youth movement, Power Shift (www.wearepowershift.org) emphasizes what people can do in their own communities to encourage the transition to a sustainable society; it's about inspiration through action, and has rapidly gained thousands of members in Canada and several other countries. Bill McKibben's organization, 350.org, has placed its members' creativity and inspiration front and centre for its whole existence; for example, in one of its first years of existence, 350.org's major campaign for the year was not explicitly environmental at all; it was simply a challenge for groups all over the world to take pictures of themselves making the 350 symbol in some creative way. Although this doesn't accomplish a thing in terms of reducing carbon emissions or helping the climate, it does show people that this organization is fun, inspiring, and has inspired many people from almost every country on the planet to get involved, helping to take the whole notion of environmental activism out of the fringe and into the mainstream.

From a strategic point of view, these strategies make sense. Appealing to your audience's values generally enhances the impact of messages; however, as we'll discuss at the end of this module, appealing to your audience's existing values may, in some cases, be detrimental to your cause . . .

PREACHING OR FLIP-FLOPPING? ONE-SIDED VS. TWO-SIDED MESSAGES One final consideration about message content is whether you should "preach," that is, give a one-sided appeal whereby you only argue for your own perspective, or whether you should risk being seen as a "flip-flopper," giving a two-sided appeal that acknowledges different perspectives. You might think that the one-sided message is strongest, because it's least likely to raise doubts in the audience's mind, but research suggests otherwise (O'Keefe, 1999). It is actually more persuasive if you acknowledge opposing arguments than if you just preach from your own soap-box, unless your audience is unlikely to ever hear information that counters your message. So, if you're trying to convince people the Earth is round, then it's okay to go with a one-sided message. But if you're wading into a real debate, it's best to show your audience the opposing side's arguments (and then, of course, show them why those arguments are wrong).

By giving a two-sided message, you make it more likely that your audience will see you as trustworthy and honest. But you gain in another, sneakier way as well. By bringing up, and shooting down, opposing arguments, you are helping your audience resist those arguments in the future. This is a strategy of **attitude inoculation,** which is *a strategy for strengthening attitudes and making them more resistant to change by first exposing people to a weak counter-argument and then refuting that argument* (Compton & Pfau, 2005; McGuire, 1961). This strategy operates in an analogous way to how the flu shot protects you from the flu. When you get injected with a weakened version of the flu virus, your immune system has a chance to respond, building up the antibodies it will need when the real flu comes along. Analogously, by exposing your audience to counter-arguments, and then showing why those counter-arguments are not correct, you are giving your audience the necessary information they will need to resist those counterarguments when they hear them later. The result is that the audience's attitudes are likely to be more resistant to change, even when presented with opposing viewpoints.

EMOTIONS IN THE CENTRAL ROUTE Taking the central route has been the chief strategy of climate change communicators, and unfortunately, they've had a pretty tough go of it. The well-funded "climate change denial" movement has been able to spread enough misinformation through the media that many people have been left confused about what is the truth and who to believe. Negative emotions such as confusion are much more damaging than you might expect, influencing people to process information in a different way. Even very subtle manipulations of confusion can have this effect.

For example, research by Norbert Schwarz and his colleagues has shown that even the font or the colour of the text used in a message can change how skeptical people are of the information. If the font is a little bit more difficult to read (e.g., **font like this**, compared to *font like this*), or if the text doesn't contrast as starkly from the background and thus is also more difficult to read, people tend to be more skeptical of the message (Winkielman et al., 2002).

What seems to happen is that the person experiences a subtle amount of negative emotion, which biases their information processing in a negative manner. As a result, they pay more attention to weaknesses in the information and claims that they disagree with, the net result being that they are less easily persuaded. Schwarz explains that **processing fluency**, *which is the ease with which information is processed,* biases the person's processing of the information; thus, even insignificant aspects of a communication can, through triggering negative affect, influence the communication's persuasive impact. Political strategists attempt to influence the public's emotions for similar reasons through the use of negative political advertising (attack ads; see Module 6.1).

Another key factor that can easily derail communication is the message's complexity. If your arguments are overly technical, complex, convoluted, or use specialized language, this can also activate negative emotion for people, biasing them against your message. Also, people will simply lose interest in a message they don't understand, and stop paying attention. This is a big challenge for communicating about technical topics like climate change. Strangely, experts are often terrible at communicating their knowledge. They don't realize that even though they understand the language they use and the subtleties of what they are saying, their audience may not. Chip and Dan Heath (2007) call this the "curse of knowledge." Anybody who has ever attended an academic conference or listened to an expert being interviewed on the news has likely experienced this phenomenon. Even though to the expert the conversation is fascinating and rife with meaning, to the audience it sounds like a monotonous drone.

The curse of knowledge was shown in an innovative experiment (Newton, 1991) in which subjects were assigned to be "tappers" or "listeners." The tappers were asked to tap the rhythm to a selection of extremely well-known songs, like "Happy Birthday," while the listeners tried to guess the songs. To the tappers, the songs were totally obvious; when they tapped out "Happy Birthday," they would hear the words and the tune in their heads and it seemed pretty likely that the listeners would be able to guess the song; in fact, they estimated that listeners would guess about 50% of the songs. To the listeners, however, the vague "tap-tap-TAP-tap TAP TAP" didn't amount to much; they guessed the correct songs a mere 2.5% of the time!

When you are communicating, you are the tapper; fight the urge to use impressively long words, acronyms, and technical lingo. Saying less, and in less complex ways, is often saying more.

Using the Peripheral Route Effectively

To be an effective communicator, you can't ignore the peripheral route. Half a century of social psychology research has identified several powerful factors of influence. There are more than can be represented here, but we will discuss several of the most important ones. You may recognize many of these, because they have undoubtedly been used against you many times, from corporations trying to sell you products to people trying to get you to do them a favour.

AUTHORITY The use of experts and authority figures to deliver a message can often enhance the impact of the message (Cialdini, 2001). Even people who look like experts but have no real authority on a subject can be used effectively. For example, an extremely successful ad campaign in the 1970s for decaffeinated coffee used a man who had absolutely no expert knowledge of coffee or its health effects; however, as an actor, he played Marcus Whelby, M.D., who was a very popular TV doctor at the time. Dressing the part is important as well; a man wearing a suit who jaywalks across a red light will be followed by 3.5 times as many people as the same man wearing casual clothes.

Basically, we believe people we like. Communicators who "connect" with their audience are going to get their message across more effectively (Cialdini, 2001). Liking can be influenced by numerous factors, including attractiveness. For example, in a study performed for the American Heart Association, "good-looking" fundraisers generated almost twice as many donations (42% versus 23%) as their less-attractive counterparts (Reingen & Kernan, 1993). In the 1972 Canadian federal election, candidates who were rated as physically attractive got three times as many votes as unattractive ones (Efrain & Patterson, 1974); in fact, politically unpopular parties had substantially less attractive candidates, which may have been the result of their party's lack of success at the polls! It is interesting to note that voters themselves insisted that their choices were not influenced by something as superficial as appearance.

Thus, there are good reasons to be pleasant and appealing, and to look your best, at least from a persuasion perspective. Highlighting any similarities you may share with your audience, loosening up a little and speaking informally, the appropriate use of humour, even complimenting the audience, can all enhance your likability and increase the effectiveness of your communication.

SOCIAL VALIDATION Because humans are such a social species, we use the behaviour of others as a guide to inform us what we should do. Elsewhere (Module 13.2) we discussed the importance of social norms and the effects of conformity pressures, and indeed, as an influence tactic, social validation can be incredibly powerful. Social validation is at work whenever you hear that a novel is a best-seller, or a piece of music has hit the charts, or "polls indicate" that a political party is supported by a certain percentage of the population.

One such example of social validation used in climate change communication occurred in the spring of 2013 when Bill McKibben's organization, 350.org, and several other organizations submitted a petition with one million signatures, urging President Obama to not allow the Keystone XL pipeline to transport oil from Canada's oilsands to the United States. Afterward, the fact that a million signatures were gathered became a major part of their organization's marketing messages. You can see how social validation becomes a major tool for communicators; obviously, proponents of the pipeline would want to downplay these facts, whereas opponents of the pipeline would want to highlight them.

Social validation is also often misused by communicators, somewhat ironically. For example, people may try to highlight the urgency of a behaviour change or the seriousness of an issue by pointing out how few people are currently doing something desirable (such as wearing condoms every time they have casual sex, or reducing their carbon footprint), or how many people are currently doing something undesirable (eating a high sugar diet, or leaving the lights on all the time). Although the information may be true, and the intentions are good, these communications can easily backfire. In one study, a suicide intervention program in New Jersey told people about the high rates of teenage suicides; as a result, people who went through the program became MORE likely to think of suicide as a way out of their problems (Cialdini, 2001).

RECIPROCITY You scratch my back, I'll scratch yours. All cultures have a strong social norm that obligates people to repay to others what they have received. If someone does you a favour, you "owe them one." This strong social norm is used by influence specialists all the time, and it can be so sneaky we often don't realize it. Just think of the "free samples" offered by vendors, the "free trial workout" offered by health clubs, even the "free personality assessments" offered by the Church of Scientology. The principle of reciprocity is one reason why corporations donate to politicians' campaigns, and why pharmaceutical companies spend millions of dollars funding research, organizing conferences, providing gifts, stationery, calendars, and even pens to doctors and family health clinics (Cialdini, 2001).

Reciprocity is often used in a two-step manner called the **door-in-the-face technique**, *which involves asking for something relatively big, then following with a request for something relatively small.* The logic is that once someone has scaled back their request, you are obligated to meet them part way. Professional negotiators will always start with a proposal they don't really expect to get; but they know that once they "give up" some of the things they want, the opposing side is obligated to do the same. The door-in-the-face technique can be used to surprising effectiveness.

In one well-known study by Bob Cialdini (Cialdini et al., 1975), people were approached on the street and asked whether they would be willing to volunteer to chaperone inmates from a juvenile detention centre for a day trip to the zoo. When simply asked, 17% said yes. A second set of people were approached and submitted to a door-in-the-face manipulation; they were first asked if they would be willing to volunteer for two hours per week as a counsellor at the juvenile detention centre, and make a commitment for two years. Everybody said no. But when they were subsequently asked whether they would merely agree to volunteer to chaperone inmates from the detention centre on a trip to the zoo for the day, an astonishing 50% said yes. This one-two punch is very effective, both because it makes the person feel obligated to say yes after you have "backed down," and because the second request doesn't *seem* as onerous, after being presented with the first, bigger request.

CONSISTENCY One of the most powerful influence techniques, especially for long-term behaviour change, is an old salesperson's trick called the **foot-in-the-door technique**, *which involves making a simple request followed by a more substantial request.* To the travelling salesmen of days gone by, literally getting one's foot in the door meant that a homeowner could not shut you out. In social psychology, the idea is that once you get the person to agree to even a small request, it's harder for them to say no to a subsequent request (Burger, 1999; Cialdini, 2000).

Explore
Cognitive Dissonance and Attitude Change

{FIG. 13.6} **Two-Step Persuasion Techniques to Encourage Community Service** The foot-in-the-door technique (top) starts with a small request and then moves on to a larger request. The door-in-the-face technique (bottom) does the reverse. It begins with a highly demanding request and then appears to settle for a much smaller one.

The foot-in-the-door technique is a very sneaky strategy, because the initial request can be so small that virtually everyone would say yes to it; nevertheless, it's powerful, because it makes use of a very strong motivation held by many people—the need for psychological consistency. We'll describe this in more detail, but just think of how people usually react to being called a "hypocrite" and you'll get a sense of the power of the need for consistency. So the foot-in-the-door technique packs another powerful one-two punch—an initial request that's hard to refuse locks you in, and then you get cornered into agreeing to a much larger request (see Figure 13.6).

Watch Thinking Like a Psychologist: Changing Attitudes and Behaviours

Explore Cognitive Dissonance

For example, if you are at the beach and you want to go swimming, how can you be sure nobody is going to steal your stuff? Just ask someone to watch your things for you. This is amazingly powerful. In one experiment, the experimenter posed as a person sunbathing on the beach; he then got up and asked whoever was close them to watch his things; everybody said yes. In a control condition, he simply got up and walked away from his things without asking anybody. After he left, as you might expect, a mock-thief came along and attempted to steal the experimenter's radio. An astonishing 95% of the people who agreed to watch his things attempted to interfere with the would-be thief, even to the point of chasing the thief down the beach! But if no one was asked and the experimenter just abandoned his things, only 20% of people tried to stop the thief (Cialdini, 2001). Imagine that—an additional 75% of us will become heroic vigilantes just because some stranger casually asks us on a beach to watch his stuff.

Commitments can be extremely subtle, another reason they are very sneaky. For example, one restaurant owner was able to reduce the rate of no-shows (people who reserve a table, but then don't show up) from 30% all the way down to 10% by changing two words in the script that his employees used when scheduling reservations over the phone. In the old script, the receptionist would say, "Please call if you have to change your plans." Now, she would say, "Would you please call if you have to change your plans?" And then, she would wait for a couple of seconds, until the person responded and said yes (Cialdini, 2001). Saying "yes" is an active commitment, and that tiny act was enough to get two-thirds of his no-shows to call first and cancel. Other studies have shown that written commitments ("sign here . . .") are even more effective than verbal commitments, and commitments that can be made public are the most effective of all.

The Attitude-Behaviour Feedback Loop

As we mentioned earlier, the reason the foot-in-the-door approach works so well is because people have a general need to be psychologically consistent—for their attitudes, beliefs, and behaviours to match up with each other. Much of the time, we maintain a feeling of consistency by letting our beliefs and attitudes guide our behaviours; we act in the way we think and feel is right. But groundbreaking work by Leon Festinger (1957) showed that we can also maintain a feeling of consistency by simply changing our beliefs to be consistent with our behaviour. Festinger (1957) proposed **cognitive dissonance theory**, describing that *when we hold inconsistent beliefs, this creates a kind of aversive inner tension, or "dissonance"; we are then motivated to reduce this tension in whatever way we can*, often by simply changing the beliefs that created the dissonance in the first place.

This sort of belief change was observed in a dramatic way by Festinger and two of his colleagues when they infiltrated a doomsday cult in the 1950s. December 21, 1954, was the date the world was supposed to end, according to the cult's leader, Marian Keech (not her real name). Keech told her followers that she was receiving messages from aliens who lived on the planet Clarion. The aliens had warned of an impending flood that would destroy life on Earth, but they promised to come in a spaceship and rescue Keech and her followers before the final cataclysm. If the members kept their faith, the aliens were supposed to contact them at midnight. The cult members were so convinced of impending doom that they gave away their possessions, quit their jobs, and prepared for the end.

Festinger and his colleagues, not being big believers in alien messages about the end of the world, wondered what would happen when the prophecy failed to come true. So, on December 20th, the cult members, including Festinger and his colleagues, gathered together and waited for the spaceship to arrive.

Midnight came . . . and went. A few minutes after midnight the group decided the clocks were fast and any minute now, the aliens would be contacting them. Then an hour passed. And another. The group waited all night, increasingly confused, wondering what was going on.

Finally, at 4:45 a.m., it was apparent the Clarions weren't coming to whisk them away. Keech had been wrong. The cult members had made fools out of themselves and ruined their lives. You might think that they would slink back to their normal lives, beg for their jobs back, and try to recover from the embarrassment. But no, the opposite happened. Keech suddenly got another message from the Clarions! They told her that because her little group had been so faithful, waiting all night for them to come, God had decided not to destroy the Earth after all. They weren't fools; they were heroes! Convinced that they had saved the world, Keech and most of her followers (some decided this was ridiculous and ditched them at this point) became even more evangelical, contacting newspapers and media outlets, spreading the good word that the world had been saved (Festinger, 1956).

Festinger and Carlsmith (1959) tested cognitive dissonance theory by having subjects come to their lab and spend an hour engaged in a mind-numbing study that required them to perform menial, repetitive tasks. Afterward, the subjects were told that in a different condition of the study, a research assistant meets subjects beforehand and gives them positive expectations of the study, telling them that it's a fun and interesting study. Unfortunately, the person called in sick that day, and so the subjects were asked if they would play the part of the research assistant for the next, incoming subject. All they had to do was sit in the waiting room, and when the next subject came in, chat with them and tell them the study was fun and interesting. Little did the unsuspecting participants know that this was what the real study was about, getting them to tell a "little white lie" and then seeing how it affected their attitudes.

The subjects were also offered one of two amounts of payment if they agreed to go along with the deception. Some subjects were paid $1 (the equivalent of $8 today), and others were paid $20 (the equivalent of $167 today). After agreeing to play along and deceiving the person in the waiting room, subjects then filled out a few measures of their perceptions of the study. Lo and behold, after lying about the study, the subjects actually felt more positively toward it! But not all the subjects felt this way, only those who were paid $1. Why might this be?

The subjects who were paid $20 had more than enough justification for telling a little white lie—"I did it for the money." But getting paid $1 seems hardly worth it; these subjects were left in a state of uncomfortable dissonance, caught between the beliefs "deceiving people is wrong" and "I just lied to somebody for a measly $1." However, by changing their attitudes—"This study actually wasn't mind-numbingly dull; it was pretty interesting! I didn't lie after all!"—subjects were able to resolve their dissonance and feel good again.

Cognitive dissonance theory can help to explain many puzzling phenomena of everyday life. For example, why would perfectly sane young people crawl through ice water in their underwear while others stood around shouting at them, throwing snowballs, and even spanking them? In the winter of 2013, exactly such an event happened at Ryerson University, when aspiring frosh leaders went through a "hazing ritual." When it came to light, university administrators and even Ontario's premier were shocked and appalled, although no official action was taken except to express disapproval.

Students at Dalhousie University, in the same year, were not so lucky; Dalhousie suspended its entire women's hockey team in January, except for the rookies, who also lost their season as a result of not having a team to play with. The previous September, the team had held a party at which the rookies were subjected to hazing, and when it came to light, the university administration reacted based on a "zero tolerance" policy.

But why does hazing occur? Why do groups so often require people who want to join them to submit to embarrassing, humiliating, even painful and dangerous initiation rituals? People have traditionally believed that such rituals help to bond members of the organization together; cognitive dissonance theory helps to explain why this seems to happen. Engaging in such rituals would be generally dissonant with the belief "I am a reasonable person who would not harm myself or do ridiculous things for no good reason." How can you reduce this dissonance after harming yourself or doing ridiculous things? One handy strategy is to assume that you did indeed have a good reason, that the group you suffered in order to join was worth it! By enhancing your positive attitude toward the group, you create a justification for your behaviour.

Cognitive dissonance is created when we make difficult choices between attractive alternatives. For example, imagine that you have to choose to date only one of two people who like you. You are attracted to both of them; one is funny and spontaneous and appeals to your fun-loving side, while the other is deep and intense and appeals to your existential, serious side. You're unsure who would be the better match, but then, after some soul-searching (or maybe on a mysterious whim), you make your choice.

After making such a difficult choice, we often feel some dissonance, as we consider what might have been had we chosen differently. To reduce this dissonance, we may bias our perceptions, highlighting for ourselves all the good things about our chosen option, and all the bad things about the rejected option, making the options seem farther apart afterwards than they were initially.

Interestingly, because cognitive dissonance is based on the need for self-consistency, it does not appear to work in quite the same way across cultures. In more collectivistic societies, for example, the need for self-consistency is not as strong, because it is more widely recognized that one's "self" is more fluid, manifesting differently in different social situations. This is reflected in collectivists experiencing less dissonance after making choices. However, research conducted at the University of Waterloo has shown that people from collectivist cultures do experience dissonance after making difficult choices for their friends (Hoshino-Browne et al., 2005). It appears that the need for self-consistency still exists; it's just that the "self" is more interpersonal than personal.

If attitudes influence behaviours, and behaviours influence attitudes, then you can see that the two are connected to each other in a circular fashion, with each affecting the other in a self-reinforcing cycle. Because each process affects the other, what happens in these causal loops is that initially small changes can grow into very large changes over time. For example, an initially small behaviour change can feed back to strengthen the person's attitude toward that behaviour, which leads in turn to greater behaviour changes in the future (see Figure 13.7).

Clearly, sometimes this works, as we saw earlier with the cognitive dissonance examples, the power of commitments, and the foot-in-the-door technique. With regard to climate change and the environmental movement, the hope for many decades has been that this "foot-in-the-door" approach would build increasingly pro-environmental attitudes in the general public in order to move society toward sustainability. By getting the public to adopt relatively easy behaviours, like recycling or using compact fluorescent light bulbs, the hope has been that this would strengthen pro-environmental attitudes and spill over, or generalize, to other behaviours and greater support for environmental laws and policies. This "spillover" effect has been the basic rationale for the general marketing approach to environmental behaviour change: appeal to whatever values people hold (e.g., the money they'll save), and encourage the adoption of whatever behaviours seem most likely. For example, you may recall a TV commercial of recent years by the David Suzuki Foundation, in which a man was informed of how much beer money he would save if he got rid of his extra fridge in the basement. Unplugging your fridge today, protesting in the streets tomorrow!

Unfortunately for anybody hoping to use the foot-in-the-door technique to change society in major ways, the strategy seems most effective for encouraging the adoption of similar behaviours (e.g., signing a petition for a cause today will make it more likely that you'll volunteer for that cause in the future), but it does not reliably spill over to a wider range of behaviours. Spillover is even less likely if there are clear, extrinsically motivating reasons for engaging in the behaviour, such as saving beer money (see Module 11.3). Just like Festinger's subjects didn't need

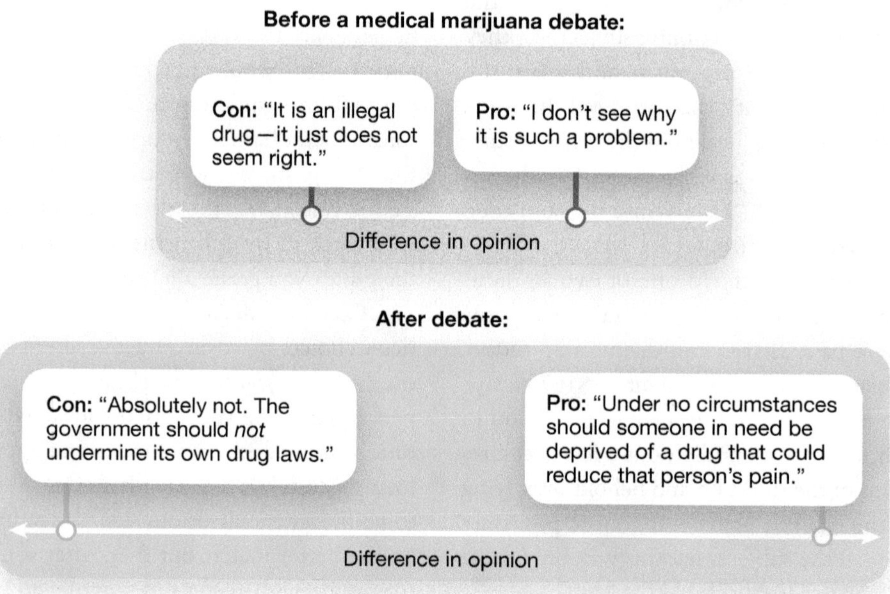

{FIG. 13.7} **The Circle of Attitudes and Actions**

to change their attitudes when they were paid $20 for lying, people whose primary reason for conserving energy is to save money are not likely to strengthen their pro-environmental attitudes more generally. After all, they just did it for the money.

Nevertheless, as we have reviewed, psychologists have provided many insights and tools for more effectively communicating and helping to change people's behaviour. Obviously, these same insights could be used to either benefit society or to harm it, just as they could be used to sell people cigarettes and alcohol or to help people kick their addictions. There is no inherent morality in the tools themselves, but with them, we can certainly help to shape our society.

Module Summary

Module 13.3

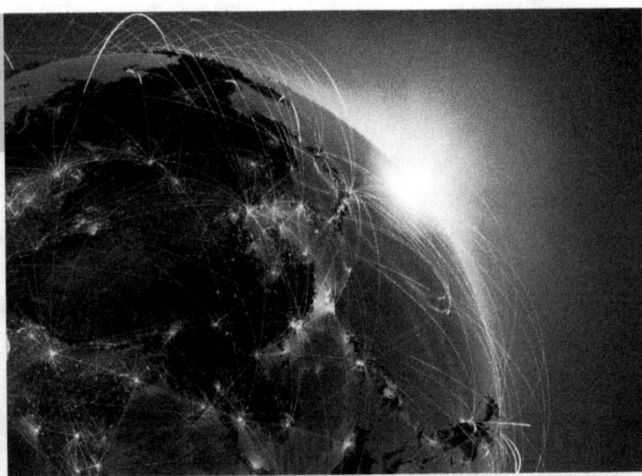
Anton Balazh/Shutterstock

Now that you have read this module you should

KNOW ...

- ***The key terminology in research on attitudes, behaviour, and effective communication:***

analytic system (p. 575)
attitude inoculation (p. 577)
central route to persuasion (p. 573)
cognitive dissonance theory (p. 580)
construal-level theory (p. 574)
door-in-the-face technique (p. 579)
elaboration likelihood model (p. 573)
experiential system (p. 575)
foot-in-the-door technique (p. 579)
identifiable victim effect (p. 575)
peripheral route to persuasion (p. 573)
processing fluency (p. 578)

UNDERSTAND ...

- ***How behaviours influence attitudes in terms of cognitive dissonance theory.*** When people hold cognitions that conflict with each other, such as when they are aware that they have behaved in a way that runs counter to their beliefs or attitudes, they experience an uncomfortable state of arousal known as cognitive dissonance. In order to reduce this dissonance, they need to change one of their conflicting cognitions, which often results in changing their attitudes in order to reflect the behaviour they just performed. In this way, behaviours and attitudes influence each other.

APPLY ...

- ***Your understanding of the central route to describe how a message should be designed.*** In order to design an effective message using the central route to persuasion, you must start with solid, convincing facts. Then personalize the message, making it self-relevant for your audience, such as by directly engaging them in a scenario you describe, or by describing how the message is relevant to them personally, or by framing the message in terms of values that your audience members hold. Also, keep your message from being unnecessarily complex, so as to maintain the interest of your audience. But if your audience is likely to hear opposing viewpoints, be sure to construct a two-sided message that includes those opposing arguments, and then provide solid reasons for why the opposing arguments are not valid. It also makes sense to use peripheral cues to further strengthen your message, such as appealing to authority, mentioning similarities between yourself and the audience, using humour appropriately, and relying predominantly on specific stories rather than on abstract data and statistics.

ANALYZE ...

- ***The difficulties communicators face in trying to convince the public to take action on climate change.*** Climate change communicators face some key challenges. Traditionally, the environmental movement has framed its messages in ways that run counter to predominant North American values, making many people wary of environmental messages or at least likely to see them as not relevant to themselves. Furthermore, climate change is experienced as psychologically distant from the public, with consequences that people feel are generally going to be experienced by people in other parts of the world and future generations. Climate change information is also highly technical and complex, and is abstract and statistical in nature, given that climate change is a global phenomenon that doesn't easily boil down to specific stories about specific people. There is also inherent uncertainty in scientific research, which has made it difficult to express climate change information in a way that would seem "certain" to the public.

Work the Scientific Literacy Model :: Understanding Social Cognition

1 What do we know about social cognition?

Review **Figure 13.3** on **page 563** for a recap of internal and external attributions, and take a moment to think about how you attribute behaviour in your daily life. Consider the fundamental attribution bias by thinking about this scenario: Imagine you are at the movies and another person in the theatre snaps at you and your friends for talking too loudly. You might assume that she is simply unpleasant and uptight (internal attribution) rather than assuming that she was having a bad day (external attribution). In contrast, an example of the self-serving bias would be snapping at your roommate for talking on the phone too loudly, but rationalizing your behaviour because you were feeling cranky after a long shift at work—not to mention your roommate was being rude first.

You may be surprised to learn that the terms "stereotype," "prejudice," and "discrimination" are not interchangeable. Remember that a stereotype is a generalized set of beliefs about a group of people (a type of schema), prejudice is a prejudgment of members of a group based solely on their membership in that group (an attitude), and discrimination is actual positive or negative behaviour that is based on that prejudice (actions).

2 How can science help explain stereotypes and prejudice?

Recent research has shown that people are increasingly concerned about appearing prejudiced, yet there is still evidence of pervasive stereotypes. For instance, examination of police records reveals that Black suspects are over five times more likely to die in a police encounter than White suspects. Psychologists interpret this type of evidence to suggest that many of us unknowingly or implicitly harbour prejudice. The discussion on **page 566** supports this claim with a study in which researchers found subtle but remarkable differences in facial expressions and brain activity when subjects looked at Black and White faces, even when the participants claimed that they were not prejudiced. Similarly, on **page 566** we described the Implicit Associations Test, which researchers say can reveal implicit prejudice through a series of responses to images or words flashed on a computer screen (see **Figure 13.4, p. 567**). For example, a person who believes he is free from prejudice might exhibit an implicit (unconscious) association between positive words and images of White faces, and negative words with images of Black faces.

wong yu liang/Shutterstock

3 Can we critically evaluate claims about stereotypes, prejudice, and discrimination?

Even "positive" stereotypes can be harmful. In the **Myths in Mind** feature on **page 565**, you were asked to think about how seemingly harmless stereotyping, such as labelling women as nurturers, can affect the group being stereotyped. If all women are nurturing and gentle, then certainly women would be out of place in a field like finance or politics, where leaders often have to make unpopular and assertive decisions. This kind of categorization can have other negative effects as well, such as the exclusion of women from executive or other high-level positions.

Are stereotypes just too powerful to fight? Keep in mind that training can undermine stereotypes. The **Psych @** feature on **page 568** described the success that law enforcement retraining has had in changing shoot/do not shoot procedures, and the encouraging data that suggest this kind of training can work even with people who are not making life-and-death decisions. Also, keep in mind that the research on implicit prejudice, while interesting, raises some questions about validity and whether the IAT is testing prejudice or simply the knowledge of pervasive stereotypes.

4 Why is this relevant?

Watch the accompanying video excerpt on stereotypes and prejudice. You can access the video at MyPsychLab or by clicking the play button in the centre of your eText. If your instructor assigns this video as a homework activity, you will find additional content to help you in MyPsychLab. You can also view the video by using your smart phone and the QR code below, or you can go to the YouTube link provided.

After you have read this chapter and watched the video, discuss the factors that contribute to prejudice and discrimination and identify some techniques for reducing the development of prejudice and discrimination.

MyPsychLab **Your turn to Work the Scientific Literacy Model:** Watch the accompanying video on YouTube, or on your phone (using the Layar app or QR code). If your instructor has assigned this as a homework activity, you can find the video clip and additional content at MyPsychLab. Answer the questions that accompany the video clip to test your understanding.

YouTube

youtube.com/workthemodel

SCAN WITH LAYAR

14

Health, Stress, and Coping

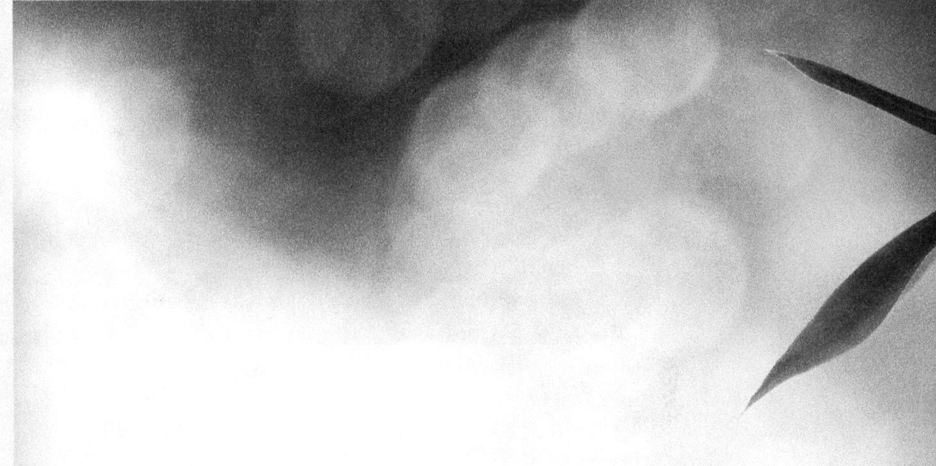

Ase/Shutterstock

stock_wales/Alamy

Module 14.1

Behaviour and Health

Learning Objectives

After reading this module you should

KNOW ...	UNDERSTAND ...	APPLY ...	ANALYZE ...
The key terminology related to health psychology	How genetic and environmental factors influence obesity	Your knowledge of persuasion and health to examine the effectiveness of different types of cigarette warnings	Whether associations with people who smoke affect smoking in adolescents

Should a person's body weight be a basis for how much tax the person pays? Some politicians, hospital administrators, and other members of society advocate a "fat tax"—taxing individuals for their excess weight, or for the nonessential food items that contribute to being overweight. Sugary soft drinks contribute hundreds of calories to our daily diet without providing any nutrition, and do little to leave a person feeling full and satisfied. So, like cigarettes, should additional taxes be attached to these products for the same reasons that cigarettes are so heavily taxed? Some health-care providers are pursuing such a plan. In 2009, for example, public employees in the U.S. state of Alabama who were obese discovered that they had to lose weight by year's end or face increased monthly health insurance costs. On one hand, this may sound like blatant discrimination. On the other hand, there is a parallel precedent for fat tax plans—namely, the massive taxes on cigarettes that serve to discourage smoking and help cover the costs of treating smoking-related illnesses. Plans such as fat taxes—or Samoa Airlines' pay-what-you-weigh ticket prices—tell us that issues related to health and behaviour are becoming common topics of conversation in many areas of society.

Focus Questions

 Which factors contribute to weight problems, and how much control over them can people expect to have?

 To what extent is physical health based on psychological processes such as choice and decision?

To what degree do you believe your behaviour affects your health? Each day we make choices that shape our physical and mental health. We decide what to eat and what to avoid eating, whether to exercise or relax on the couch. Some people choose to

Table 14.1 :: Health Costs of Tobacco Use

- Tobacco use causes an estimated 5 million deaths worldwide each year.
- Cigarette smoking is the leading preventable cause of death in North America.
- One in five Canadian deaths is due to cigarette smoking.
- Close to 1000 Canadians die each year as a result of second-hand smoke.

Sources: CDC, 2009b; Rehm et al., 2006; Statistics Canada, 2012b.

light up a cigarette whenever the chance arises. Others make a point of avoiding places where people are likely to smoke. The choices people make about their career paths similarly influence their health. Workplace stress levels for air traffic controllers are quite different from those experienced by small-town librarians. The numerous and complex connections between behaviour and health certainly have created an important niche for *health psychologists*. These researchers study both the positive and negative effects that humans' behaviour and decisions have on their health, survival, and well-being.

The need for health psychologists has increased considerably over the last century, as most premature deaths today are attributable to lifestyle factors. In the early 1900s, people in Canada were likely to die from influenza, pneumonia, tuberculosis, measles, and other contagious diseases. Advances in medicine have served to keep these conditions under much better control. Instead, people are now much more likely to die from tobacco use, alcohol use, obesity, and inactivity. In fact, more than half of all deaths in Canada in 2009 were caused by heart disease, cancer, stroke, and diabetes; although genetics plays a role in these diseases, they have also been linked to unhealthy behaviours such as a poor diet and smoking (Statistics Canada, 2012a). Clearly, then, our physical and mental well-being are connected to the health decisions that we make.

Smoking

One of the most widely studied health behaviours is tobacco use. Smoking cigarettes causes life-shortening health problems including lung, mouth, and throat cancer; heart disease; and pulmonary diseases such as emphysema. Recent reports indicate that 21% of all deaths in Canada over the past decade were due to smoking-related illnesses (Jones et al., 2010). The life expectancy of the average smoker is between 7 and 14 years shorter than that of a nonsmoker (U.S. Centers for Disease Control [CDC], 2002; Streppel et al., 2007). This number depends upon how much, and for how long, a person smoked. Quitting by the age of 30 greatly reduces the likelihood that a person will die of smoking-related cancers, a statistic that is quite relevant to university students (Statistics Canada, 2012b)! The costs in lives and money attributable to smoking are massive, as shown in Table 14.1. Despite these starkly ominous figures, 19.9% of Canadian adults—22.3% of males and 17.5% of females—smoke cigarettes (Statistics Canada, 2012b). In other words, 5.8 million Canadians perform a behaviour that is quite likely to harm or even kill them. It should come as no surprise that such a statistic would interest psychologists.

Watch
The Big Picture: Health Psychology

A. Ramey/PhotoEdit

The tobacco industry attempts to make everyone think of cigarettes as a familiar part of life; it spends more than $36 million each day on cigarette advertisements (U.S. Federal Trade Commission, 2011). This is approximately three times the amount of money spent on lung cancer research world wide.

WORKING THE SCIENTIFIC LITERACY MODEL

Media Exposure and Smoking

If smoking is so dangerous, why do people do it? Why don't they do something safer, like juggle scorpions? This is a perplexing question not only for psychologists, but also for many smokers. One reason may be the exposure young people have to other people who smoke: parents, friends, and even characters on television and in the movies.

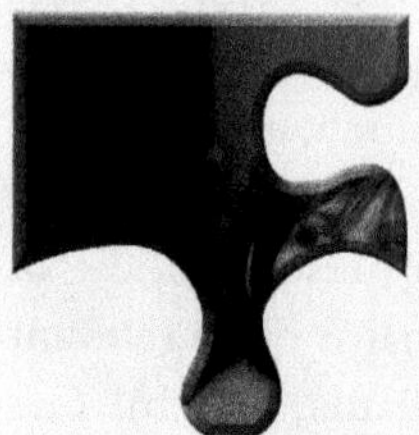

What do we know about media influences on smoking?

Each day approximately 250 adolescents in Canada try their first cigarette, and many will go on to become full-time smokers (Health Canada, 2008). An important question that health psychologists grapple with concerns the societal factors that lead young people to smoke. Many such factors come into play, including whether family members smoke, whether smoking is common in their culture, personality characteristics, and socioeconomic status. Adolescents may also begin smoking because they associate it with particular traits such as attractiveness, rebelliousness, and individualism. One factor that has received an increasing amount of attention from psychologists and health-care providers is the role of the media. Specifically, does exposure to smoking in movies and entertainment lead teens to begin smoking? Actors in many popular television shows and movies smoke. Additionally, photographs in fashion and entertainment magazines show stars such as Johnny Depp and Kristen Stewart looking cool and smoking cigarettes. Indeed, many smokers are portrayed as sophisticated and self-assured, traits that many adolescents hope to possess. In contrast, very few movies and magazines show someone with emphysema or lung cancer.

How can science help us analyze the effects of smoking in the movies?

To what extent do positive images of smoking in movies (and TV and magazines) contribute to adolescent smoking? This question has been addressed using a variety of methods. In one study, researchers conducted a random-digit-dialing survey of 6522 U.S. adolescents from all major geographic regions and socioeconomic groups (Sargent et al., 2005). The adolescents reported their age and indicated whether they smoked, and were asked to identify whether they had seen specific popular movies that featured smoking. The more exposure the adolescents had to movies that featured smoking, the more likely they were to have tried smoking. This relationship persisted even after the researchers controlled for important variables such as socioeconomic status, personality, and parental and peer influences on smoking (Heatherton & Sargent, 2009). Although this study showed a clear correlation linking smoking in movies and adolescent smoking, it did not explain why this correlation exists.

It appears that how people identify with smokers may influence their decision to smoke. An experimental study showed that adolescents who had positive responses to a protagonist in a movie clip who smoked were much more likely to associate smoking with their own identities. This correlation was observed in both adolescents who already smoked and even those who did not smoke (Dal Cin et al., 2007).

Can we critically evaluate this evidence?

It is very difficult to establish that watching movie stars smoke cigarettes causes adolescents to take up smoking, even though the correlations might suggest that it does. When researchers tracked the amount of smoking featured in popular movies from 1990 to 2007, they found that as the incidence of smoking in movies rose, smoking among adolescents increased after a short period of time. Likewise, when smoking in movies decreased, a decline in adolescent smoking followed (Heatherton & Sargent, 2009). However, the problem with these correlations is that multiple explanations could be put forth for why they exist. Although the researchers would like to demonstrate that smoking in movies influences audience members, perhaps the truth is the other way around: People who are already willing to smoke might be more attracted to movies that feature smoking.

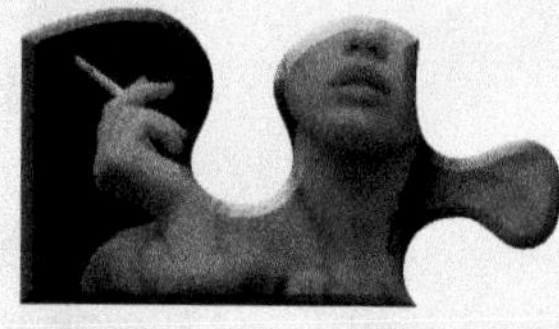

Why is this relevant?

Smoking by young people raises serious concerns about the health and well-being of those individuals who start smoking at such an early age. In addition, cigarette-related illness imposes a major societal burden in terms of lost work productivity and rising health-care costs. As the research shows, cigarette smoking in movies is just one of many influences on smoking behaviour. Of course, it may be one influence that could be easier to control than,

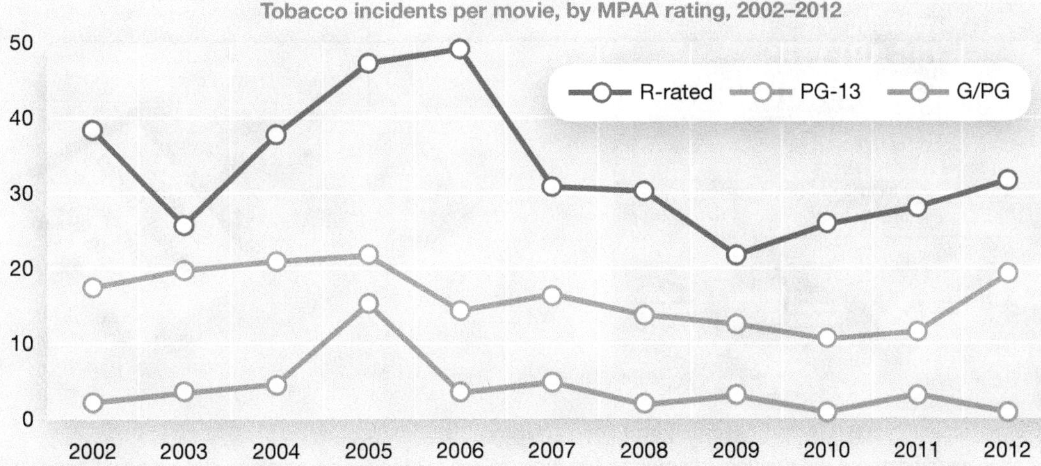

{FIG. 14.1} **Number of Smoking Images in Popular Movies from 2002–2012** This graph depicts the number times tobacco appears in movies from 2002–2012; note the recent increase in these incidents (from Polansky et al., 2013).

say, peer pressure. With scientific research in hand, advocacy groups such as Smoke Free Movies, the (U.S.) National Association of Attorneys General, and Physicians for a Smoke-Free Canada have a sound basis for arguing against smoking in movies—especially those that adolescents are likely to watch.

Unfortunately, the rate of smoking in films appears to be *increasing* (see Figure 14.1). After peaking in 2004, the number of scenes involving cigarettes decreased steadily until 2010; but, the numbers rose again in 2011 and then again in 2012. Importantly, the number of "tobacco incidents" in PG-13 movies specifically targeted to teens increased from 565 in 2010 to 1155 in 2012; therefore, the curtain hasn't fallen on this issue.

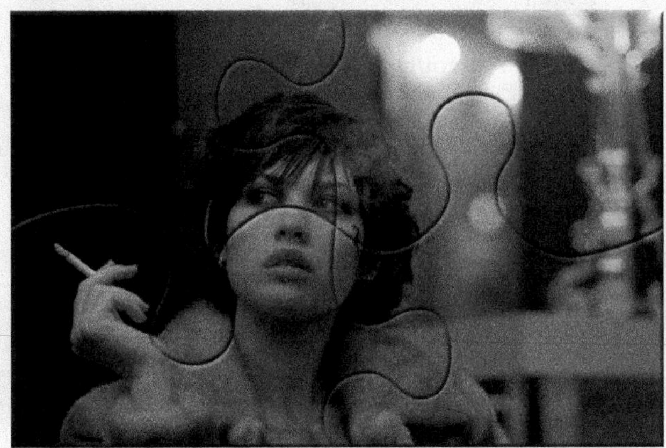

Splash News/Newscom

EFFORTS TO PREVENT SMOKING Given the health problems (to the smokers *and* to the people who are around them) and enormous health-care costs associated with smoking, both health-care workers and government officials recognize that more work has to be done to reduce smoking levels. Provincial and municipal laws are reducing the risks posed by secondhand smoke exposure by banning smoking in many public places—especially restaurants and public buildings. As mentioned at the beginning of the module, steep taxes applied to unhealthy products such as tobacco also act as a deterrent against their use. Not only does such a policy tend to reduce the number of smokers, but it also raises funds for health care and anti-smoking campaigns.

In the 1990s, several countries added written warnings to cigarette packages (e.g., "Smoking seriously harms you and others around you") in an attempt to reduce smoking rates. Unfortunately, these labels have had relatively little effect. However, in 2001, Canada became the first country to require companies to include graphic pictorial warnings on cigarette packages. These images included rotting teeth, black lungs, diseased hearts, and sick children; they were also paired with a verbal message. Researchers found that the image-based warnings were much more likely to be noticed by both smokers and non-smokers than were text-only messages (Fong et al., 2009; Hammond et al., 2003). They were also more useful than text-only messages in educating people about the risks associated with smoking (Environics Research Group, 2007; Li & Yong, 2009).

Image-based warnings on cigarette packages are now used in over 30 countries (Hammond, 2011). Numerous studies have shown that these warnings are quite memorable and are having the desired effect. Over 40% of Canadian smokers indicated that the graphic warnings motivated them to quit (Hammond et al., 2007).

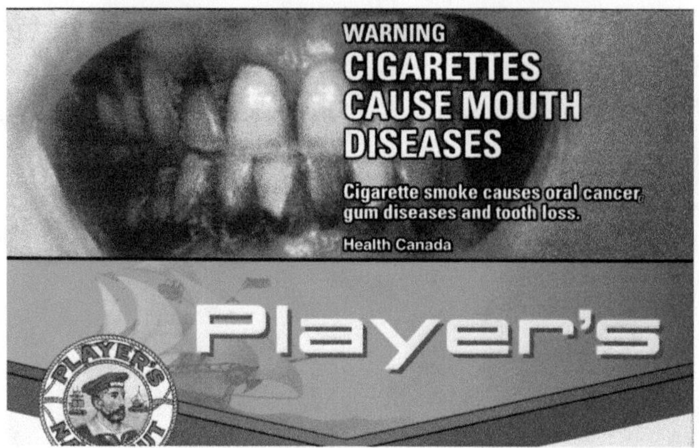

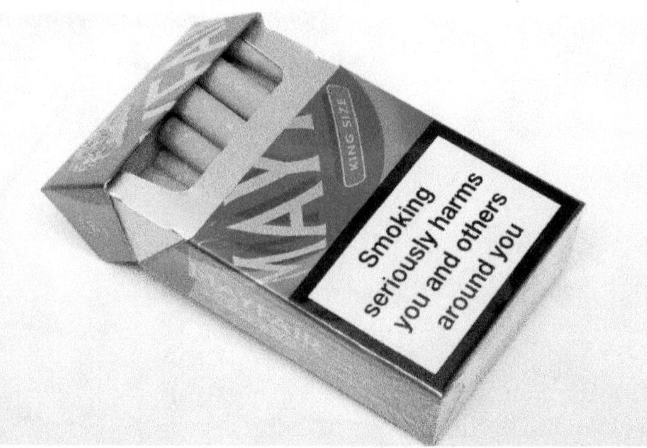

Left: Pierre Roussel/Getty Images News/Getty Images; right: David J. Green – studio/Alamy

Research shows that images warning about the dangers of smoking are more effective at reducing smoking rates than written warnings.

And, although it is impossible to accurately state how many people avoided smoking because of the ads, surveys of Canadian adolescents suggest that these warning labels do discourage teens from taking up smoking (Environics Research Group, 2007). These smoking-prevention programs are therefore a wonderful example of psychologists and government officials working together to improve people's health.

Indeed, there is some good news related to smoking rates. The prevalence of smoking in Canada declined steadily over the 1990s and early 2000s (Statistics Canada, 2012b); in 2001, 28.1% of men and 23.8% of women smoked, 5.8% and 6.3% higher than the current rates. But, there is still work to be done.

Quick Quiz 14.1a

Smoking

KNOW ...

1 What does a health psychologist study?

A The positive impacts that our behaviour has on our health

B The negative impacts that our behaviour has on our heath

C The chance that we will survive based on our decisions

D Both the positive and the negative impacts that our behaviour and decisions have on our health and survival

2 In modern times, the leading causes of death in industrialized nations such as Canada are ________ .

A viral infections

B bacterial infections

C lifestyle factors

D each of these are equal contributors

ANALYZE ...

3 Which of the following statements is the best evidence that viewing smoking in movies plays a causal (rather than correlational) role in influencing people's perception of smoking and willingness to try smoking?

A Long-term trends show that increased or decreased incidence of smoking by adolescents follows increases or decreases in rates of smoking in movies.

B The more adolescents smoke, the more smoking occurs in movies.

C Advertisements for smoking occur more frequently when smoking rates decrease.

D Adolescent smoking occurs at roughly the same rate regardless of how smoking is depicted in films.

Answers can be found on page ANS-3.

Obesity

You have likely heard the term "freshman 15"—the supposed number of pounds university students can expect to gain during their first year of school (15 pounds equals 6.8 kg). This term has stuck because weight gain during the first year of university (at least in North America) has seemingly become so common, if not expected. It is unclear exactly how the term originated, and research has shown that the 15-pound estimate is actually inflated. In reality, those male and female students who gain weight during their early university career put on an average of 6 pounds, or 2.7 kg (Gropper et al., 2009).

What accounts for this phenomenon? Several factors that are probably all too familiar to many readers: increased food intake, decreased physical activity, and, for many students, increased levels of alcohol consumption. The lifestyle changes that students face during university affect physical health. In addition, university in general, and the first year in particular, presents new challenges that bring on a great deal of both positive and negative stress. The freshman 15 (or 6) and other health-related issues are based on lifestyle decisions we make. Six pounds (2.7 kg) is not a lot of weight—but habits formed during any period of time, first year or otherwise, can be difficult to break. In this section, we will examine factors that lead us to put on weight as well as ways to use our knowledge of psychology to help us lose it.

DEFINING HEALTHY WEIGHTS AND OBESITY As you've read in different modules of this text, it is important to define your terms when discussing a concept. Doing so ensures that all researchers are talking about the same thing when they use terms like *overweight* or *obese.* When discussing weight, psychologists and health-care workers must also factor in a person's height; being 200 pounds (91 kg) is healthy for someone who is 6'4" (193 cm), but would be quite unhealthy for someone who is 5'2" (157 cm). To account for height differences, people use the **body mass index (BMI)**, *a statistic commonly used for estimating a healthy body weight given an individual's height.* The BMI is calculated by dividing the person's weight (kg) by the square of the person's height (in metres). So, if a person were 180 cm tall and weighed 100 kg, the BMI would be $100 / 1.8^2$; the outcome of this equation, 30.9, would be found on a table of BMI scores. In everyday usage, the BMI is used to screen people for weight categories that indicate whether they are considered normal weight, underweight, overweight, or obese. Someone in the healthy weight range would have a BMI between 18.5 and 24.9. People with a BMI that is less than 18.5 are considered to be underweight and may be at risk of having an eating disorder (see Module 11.1). A BMI of 25–29.9 is considered overweight, and a BMI over 30 is considered obese. Obesity is becoming a growing concern across Canada. It is associated with numerous detrimental health consequences, such as cardiovascular disease, diabetes, osteoarthritis (degeneration of bone and cartilage material), and some forms of cancer. According to Statistics Canada (2011), 24% of Canadian adults are obese, with almost identical percentages for males and females. Although this number is significantly lower than the 34.4% obesity rate in the U.S. (Shields et al., 2011), we cannot afford to become arrogant. With a quarter of our population being obese and another quarter reporting a body-mass index that is overweight (Statistics Canada, 2008), it is clear that body weight is a major health issue in our society. Even more alarming is that obesity rates are on the rise. When examining obesity rates from the mid-1970s until 2004, researchers found that these rates remained constant until the mid-1990s, at which point they spiked upward to the current levels (Shields & Tjepkema, 2005). This report also noted that Canadians—particularly males—are becoming obese earlier in life, which means that weight-related health problems could occur at an earlier age than they have for previous generations. In fact, some researchers are concerned that these health problems could lead to shorter life expectancies than were enjoyed by previous generations (Olshansky et al., 2005).

It should be pointed out that Canada is not alone in facing these problems. Obesity is also a significant problem in the United States as well as in other regions of the world—particularly in urban areas—in which the culture of fast food and processed, prepackaged meals has spread. The World Health Organization (WHO, 2009) estimates that 1 billion people across the world are overweight and 300 million are obese.

Given that obesity is common *and* has a number of negative health consequences, researchers are actively trying to understand its causes. As discussed in Module 11.1, weight is gained because of a positive energy balance, meaning that too many calories come in and not enough are expended. Obviously overeating can lead to obesity. But why might a 6-foot-tall (183 cm) male weigh 170 pounds (77 kg) while enjoying massive amounts of food and a relatively inactive lifestyle, while another person of similar height and lifestyle weighs in at 200 pounds (91 kg)? Several factors explain this difference, including genetic, lifestyle, and social variables.

GENETICS AND BODY WEIGHT Twin, family, and adoption studies all suggest that genes account for between 50% and 90% of the variation in body weight (Maes et al., 1997). Genetic factors influence body type, metabolism, and other physiological processes that contribute to body weight and size.

Some researchers have suggested that genes contribute to the development of a **set point**, *a hypothesized mechanism that serves to maintain body weight around a physiologically programmed level.* The set point is not an exact number of pounds or kilograms, but rather a relatively small range encompassing 10% to 20% of one's weight (Garrow & Stalley, 1975; Harris, 1990). Your initial set point is controlled by genetic mechanisms, but your actual weight can be modified by environmental factors—namely, what and how much you eat. According to set point theory, if an individual gains 10% of his body weight (e.g., increasing from 150 to 165 pounds, or 68 to 75 kg) his set point would make a corresponding shift upward—the body acts as though its normal weight is now the larger 165 pounds. Metabolism slows correspondingly, such that this person now requires additional energy expenditure to take the weight off. This process explains why people who gain extra weight may shed a few pounds with relative ease, but find it overwhelmingly difficult to continue losing or even maintaining their weight once they reach an initial goal. Their bodies naturally pull their weight back to the set point.

Set point theory has a long tradition in the field of nutrition, but its validity is challenged by research suggesting that weight gain and difficulty with weight loss are unrelated to a physiological set point. Rather, individual differences in physical activity may be a stronger determinant of who succeeds at losing weight and keeping it off. Specifically, people who gain weight expend less energy in their normal day-to-day activities (Weinsier et al., 2002). Thus, the difficulty with losing the weight may be related to lower activity levels, rather than to any elevation of a set point.

Listen
Psychology in the News: Sleep Obesity

Watch
What's in It for Me?: The Challenge Of Quitting Bad Health Habits

THE SEDENTARY LIFESTYLE How do you spend your time when you're not at school or at work? Do you watch television? Or do you work out, or curl up with a good book? Research shows us that how you spend your time can have a large effect on your waistline.

Although there are number of activities that could increase the likelihood of someone being obese, data from the 2007 Canadian Community Health Survey (CCHS) suggest that television is the biggest culprit (see Figure 14.2). This survey showed that as the number of hours of television viewing increased, so did obesity rates. Only 13.7% of men who watch five or fewer hours of television per week were obese; compare this to the 25.0% obesity rate for men who watched 21 or more hours of television. Similar patterns were observed for females.

In contrast, the number of hours spent in front of a computer did not affect obesity rates, at least in males; females who spent more than 11 hours/week in front of a computer had a *slightly* higher rate of obesity than those who spent little time using a computer (18.2% vs. 15.3%, respectively). Why was there a strong relationship between television viewing and obesity and a weak relationship between computer use and obesity? Both involve sitting in front of glowing rectangles. One possibility is that computer use—be it video games, using social media like Facebook or Twitter, or even typing up an essay for history class—involves a greater degree of engagement than sitting on the couch and passively watching television. It is therefore more likely that people will snack while watching television.

Studies of children's obesity rates are less ambiguous. In addition to the strong relationship between television viewing and weight, researchers also have found that the amount of time that children spend playing video games is positively correlated with levels of obesity (Stettler et al., 2004). Although some video games such as the Wii involve physical activity, these options claim only a small portion of the overall market. Instead, many games involve sitting in front of a computer or television screen rather than engaging in exercise; this sedentary lifestyle can lead to poor dietary and exercise habits (which may

{FIG. 14.2} **Obesity Rates and Television Viewing in Canadian Adults Aged 20–64** For both males and females, obesity rates were positively correlated with the number of hours spent watching television each week.

foto-begsteiger/vario images GmbH & Co.KG/Alamy

The number of hours children spend playing video games is directly related to increased body weight.

continue into adulthood), and helps to explain the high childhood obesity rates found in many industrialized countries, including Canada.

SOCIAL FACTORS In addition to genetics and activity levels, obesity rates are also affected by social factors, including influences from one's family. Similarities in body weight among family members are naturally influenced by what and how much they are eating. What children eat is largely based on what their parents provide and allow them to eat, and eating patterns developed in childhood are generally carried into adulthood.

Sociocultural influences on eating certainly extend beyond the family. Food advertisements trigger eating—after watching a commercial for buttery microwave popcorn, you have probably found yourself rummaging around in the kitchen in search of that last bag you hope is still there. If your popcorn supply is depleted, you are still far more likely to snack after watching commercials about food (Harris et al., 2009). Researchers have found that children who see food commercials while watching a 30-minute cartoon program consume 45% more snack food than do children who view nonfood commercials. The researchers estimated that this difference could lead to an additional 10 pounds (4.5 kg) of extra weight gained each year (Harris et al., 2009). Of course, corporations selling unhealthy food are aware of the power of advertising and use clever marketing techniques to promote unhealthy foods, often targeting children by linking their food with positive emotions (and toys). Luckily, in some regions of North America, lawmakers are attempting to prevent the corporations from directly targeting children by limiting when commercials can air (e.g., not during Saturday morning cartoons) and preventing them from including toys in kids' meals. The hope is that these restrictions will reduce unhealthy eating behaviours in children, thus helping them avoid the dangers of obesity.

PSYCHOLOGY AND WEIGHT LOSS Given that obesity is quite common and needs to be dealt with, how can people use psychological research to help them lose weight? The first step is to think critically about the weight-loss options that are out there. Some advertisements tell people that they can lose weight without exercising, just by taking a pill. Such options are often gimmicks. Instead, we need to find a way to effectively motivate people to change their behaviours (i.e., to eat healthy foods and exercise). A recent study from the University of Waterloo suggests that thinking positively about oneself can promote healthy weight loss. In the first part of the study, participants wrote about either self-defining values that made them feel positively about themselves (e.g., friendships, religious beliefs, relationships) or about other values. At a follow-up session two-and-a-half months later, the self-defined value group weighed less, had lower body-mass indices, and had smaller waistlines (Logel & Cohen, 2012). It is likely that the positive emotion manipulation reduced the participants' stress regarding dieting. Given that stress leads to an increase in the number of calories consumed (see Module 11.1), reducing stress would likely lead to a reduction in the amount of food consumed.

Of course, losing weight is only half the battle; we also have to maintain that weight loss. There are a number of challenges involved with this. First, obese individuals pay more attention to food cues (Polivy et al., 2008) and find them more rewarding than non-obese people (Stice et al., 2008). Additionally, the drive to eat and the perceived value of food increase as more time passes since the last meal (Raynor & Epstein, 2003); this makes it difficult to remove snacks from one's routine. Several studies have shown that girls and adolescents who attempt to diet are heavier later in life (Field et al., 2003; Stice et al., 2005). The restraint involved in dieting—especially avoiding certain highly reinforcing foods—may actually make the foods even more reinforcing in the long run. All of these factors help explain why obesity is such a difficult condition to overcome—it's not simply a matter of losing a few pounds.

BIOPSYCHOSOCIAL PERSPECTIVES

Obesity

Genetics, social influences, and lifestyle factors all play roles in obesity. But what about broader influences, such as socioeconomic status and ethnicity? To address this question, start by classifying the following statements about obesity as either true or false:

1. In Canada, obesity rates are unrelated to ethnicity.
2. Obesity has no effect on a person's wages.
3. Obesity is related to socioeconomic factors in Canadian adults.
4. Obesity can have a negative, long-term impact on the brain.

Nutritious, nonprocessed foods tend to be more expensive, which might have led you to predict that obesity would be more prevalent in people in lower socioeconomic brackets (e.g., low income or poverty). Also, diet seems to be influenced by sociocultural factors, including the types of foods people grow up eating. What do the data say about these issues?

1. False. Statistics Canada reports that First Nations people who did not live on reserves, Métis, and Inuit people have, on average, a greater prevalence of obesity than other Canadians (Statistics Canada, 2013).
2. False. Research on employment statistics indicates that workers who are overweight or obese are paid less than thin colleagues with similar qualifications—a finding that has led economists to suggest that the disparity in wage earnings is about equal to the size of the difference in medical costs incurred by thin versus overweight and obese people (Bhattacharya & Bundorf, 2005).
3. False. Recent Statistics Canada reports show that although obesity used to be more common in people with lower income levels, this difference is disappearing. There are even some patterns based on gender. Men at high income levels are more likely to be obese than men at lower levels. Conversely, among women, obesity increases at lower income levels. One difference that still exists, however, is the availability of healthy food options. Fast-food outlets are still more numerous in low-income neighbourhoods than in richer areas (Hemphill et al., 2008).
4. True. Obesity can have a negative, long-term impact on the brain. Researchers have found that people who are obese have, on average, 8% less brain tissue than people who are lean. The average brain of an individual with obesity in his 70s looks approximately 16 years older than a lean person of the same age (Raji et al., 2010).

Quick Quiz 14.1b
Obesity

KNOW ...

1 ________ is a hypothesized mechanism that serves to maintain body weight around a physiologically programmed level.

A BMI
B Set point
C Obesity
D A sedentary lifestyle

2 In Canada, researchers have found that obesity rates are related to ethnicity in what way?

A Obesity rates are not related to ethnicity.
B Caucasian adults have a greater prevalence of obesity.
C First Nations adults have a greater prevalence of obesity.
D Asian adults have a greater prevalence of obesity.

UNDERSTAND ...

3 Which of the following factors is not related to a person's weight?

A Exposure to food advertisements
B Sedentary lifestyle
C Ethnicity
D All of these are related to weight.

APPLY ...

4 To avoid gaining weight during the first year of university, a person should do all of the following except

A increase physical activity.
B decrease caloric intake.
C be aware of the new stressors the individual will face.
D increase alcohol intake.

Answers can be found on page ANS-4.

Psychosocial Influences on Health

The environments where we work, live, and play and the people with whom we interact influence both our physical and mental health. University dormitories are a prime example, especially in the fall of each academic year. Frequently, dormitory space is overbooked, leaving some students without an established living space, and forcing people to live in cramped conditions. Perhaps not surprisingly, these conditions lend themselves to the increased spread of influenza and other viruses amid a fairly stressed group of individuals. In addition, these conditions affect the way that individuals interact with one another.

Years ago psychologists compared students who lived in well-designed dormitory arrangements versus those living in improvised and poorly designed conditions. The crowded, poorly designed accommodations caused students to lose their sense of control over whom they could interact with or avoid. The researchers found that students living in the stressful environment were less

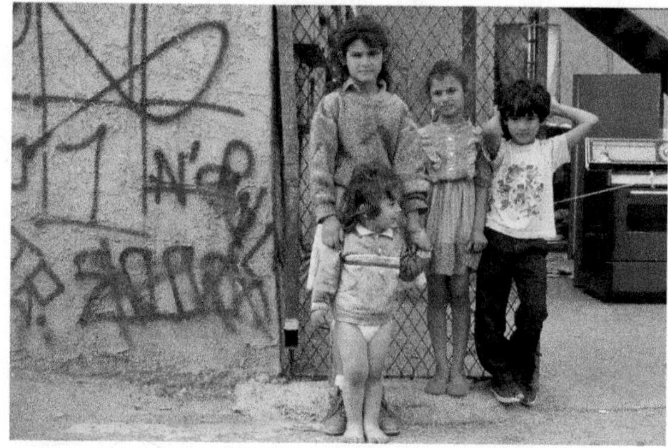

Visions of America, LLC/Alamy

People who are of low socioeconomic status are at increased risk for poor health. Numerous factors, including limited access to health care, stress, poor nutrition, and discrimination, collectively place children growing up in these communities at greater risk for developing health problems.

socially interactive with strangers, had difficulty with working in small groups, and gave up more easily in a competitive game (Baum & Valins, 1977). These students also seemed to feel helpless, which in turn affected how they interacted with others. For most students, better accommodations await them at home, and larger spaces open up at the end of the semester. However, for many living with very low incomes, the stresses of poor housing may be permanent.

POVERTY AND DISCRIMINATION Health and wealth increase together, and it appears that socioeconomic factors have numerous positive and negative effects. People who live in affluent communities not only enjoy better access to health care, but also have a greater sense of control over their environments and have the resources needed to maintain a lifestyle of their choosing. Individuals who lack this sense of control live in circumstances that can compromise their health. People who experience poverty, discrimination, and other social stressors have higher incidences of depression, anxiety, and other mental health problems (Tracy et al., 2008).

Furthermore, health problems are magnified by stress. Heart disease is prevalent in socioeconomically disadvantaged populations, and children who experience adverse socioeconomic circumstances (e.g., less than 12 years of education or living in a low-income household) are at greater risk for developing heart disease in adulthood (Fiscella et al., 2009; Galobardes et al., 2006). This relationship likely reflects the compound effects of stress, as well as the poorer diet that is often found among individuals residing in communities of low socioeconomic status.

Discrimination is another stressor that can compromise both physical and mental health. This kind of stressor is particularly problematic because it is often uncontrollable and unpredictable. Being a target of prejudice and discrimination is linked to increased blood pressure, heart rate, and secretions of stress hormones, which when experienced over long periods of time compromise physical health. For example, when people perceive that they are the targets of racism, their blood pressure remains elevated throughout the day, and it recovers poorly during sleep (Brondolo et al., 2008a, 2008b; Steffen et al., 2003). Discrimination also puts people at greater risk for engaging in unhealthy behaviours such as smoking and substance abuse (Bennett et al., 2005; Landrine & Klonoff, 1996). Finally, discrimination, or even the perception of discrimination, can put the body on sustained alert against threats. The stress response that this state elicits can have negative, long-term effects on physical health, as you will read in Module 14.2.

leungchopan/Shutterstock.com

People living in economically disadvantaged neighbourhoods feel as though they have less control over their environments. This leads to greater stress levels and poorer health.

FAMILY AND SOCIAL ENVIRONMENT Our close, interpersonal relationships have a major impact on health. In fact, chronic social isolation is as great a mortality risk as smoking, obesity, and high blood pressure (House et al., 1988). Marriage is typically the primary social relationship that people establish and has been shown to have long-term health benefits. Married people tend to live longer and have better mental and physical health than do nonmarried adults. Married couples enjoy the benefits of social support and combined resources, and they tend to have better health habits (Kiecolt-Glaser & Newton, 2001).

This is good news for married couples, but are both members of a heterosexual marriage benefiting equally from their union? It turns out that men enjoy greater health benefits from marriage. Unmarried women are 50% more likely to die from heart disease, several forms of cancer, cirrhosis of the liver, and other preventable diseases than are married women; this effect of marriage is even higher in men, with unmarried men being 250% more likely to die from these causes (Berkman & Breslow, 1983; Ross et al., 1990). Several possible reasons for this disparity in the health benefits gained from marriage have been suggested. One likely contributor is the greater role that women take in recognizing and supporting healthy behaviours in others. It should be noted that heterosexual marriages are not the only form of relationship. Currently, there are relatively little data about the health benefits of homosexual marriages; as more countries and U.S. states legalize these marriages, it will be possible to investigate whether both partners benefit equally or if, like heterosexual marriages, one partner appears to gain more health benefits than the other.

Of course, marriage can also be a considerable source of stress. Marital problems are among the most stressful experiences that people can have. Married couples who are experiencing ongoing problems with their relationship tend to experience more depression and greater incidences of physical illness than happily married couples (Kiecolt-Glaser & Newton, 2001). Marital problems and divorce also affect the emotional and physical health of children, particularly if they are younger during problematic periods of a marriage or during the parents' actual divorce. Adolescents of divorced parents are at a slightly higher risk of engaging in delinquent behaviours (Amato, 2001). While divorce can negatively affect the health of children, parents who continue engaging in high-quality parenting during marital discord protect children from many of the negative effects on health attributable to divorce (Hetherington et al., 1998).

SOCIAL CONTAGION Families are not the only interpersonal influence on how we think and act. The social group(s) that we belong to can also have a large effect on our health-related behaviours. Social scientists have found unhealthy behaviours such as smoking or having a poor diet spread throughout one's social group. You have likely observed this phenomenon in action—if one or two people in a group of friends start to eat a lot of junk food, it is easy for the others in the group to pick up this habit as well. These changes can work in either direction, positive or negative. Just as social groups can lead to smoking, they can also lead to training for a half-marathon.

These phenomena are examples of **social contagion**, *the often subtle, unintentional spreading of a behaviour as a result of social interactions*. Social contagion of body weight, smoking, and other health-related behaviours has been documented in the Framingham Heart Study. The U.S. National Heart Institute began this ongoing study in 1948 to track 15 000 residents of Framingham, Massachusetts. Participants made regular visits to their doctors, who recorded important health statistics such as heart rate, body weight, and other standard physical measures. Scientists working with the Framingham data noticed that over time, clusters of people from this study group became increasingly similar in certain characteristics—such as body weight increases or decreases, starting or quitting smoking, and even levels of happiness (Christakis & Fowler, 2007, 2008; Fowler & Christakis, 2008). It turns out that the groups who showed similar patterns in their health statistics were also friends with one another. This work demonstrates just how powerful social factors can be. Of course, this research doesn't only mean that you should be wary of your friends and their unhealthy behaviours. It also shows that through social contagion, you can be a positive force in the lives of the people around you.

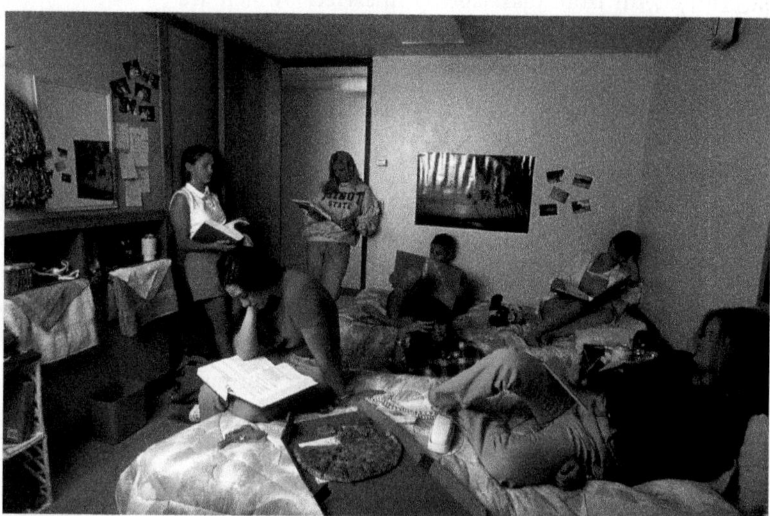

Barbara Stitzer/PhotoEdit

Social contagion in the dorms. Your roommate may influence your GPA more than you know—for better or for worse. At Dartmouth College in the U.S., students are randomly assigned to their dorm rooms rather than matched on various characteristics, as is customary at many schools. This practice makes Dartmouth's roommate pairs a diverse mixture. Professor Bruce Sacerdote (2001) found that GPA levels are influenced by one's roommate. Students with high GPAs elevate the GPAs of their lower-scoring roommates, and vice versa.

Quick Quiz 14.1c

Psychosocial Influences on Health

KNOW ...

1. Which psychological term refers to the often subtle, unintentional spreading of a behaviour as a result of social interactions?
   - **A** Health psychology
   - **B** Social contagion
   - **C** Discrimination
   - **D** Observational learning

2. Based on the research discussed in this module, which of the following is the lowest risk factor for health problems?
   - **A** Being an unmarried adult
   - **B** Experiencing discrimination
   - **C** Having an identical twin who is overweight
   - **D** Being a married adult

UNDERSTAND ...

3. Which of the following statements about how discrimination influences health is most accurate?
   - **A** Discrimination is unrelated to poor health.
   - **B** People who experience discrimination are likely to compensate for it by making positive health-related choices.
   - **C** An immediate increase in heart rate is the biggest problem associated with experiencing discrimination.
   - **D** Experiencing discrimination stimulates the stress response, which can bring about long-term health problems.

Answers can be found on page ANS-4.

Module Summary

Module
14.1

Now that you have read this module you should

KNOW ...

- ***The key terminology related to health psychology:***

body mass index (BMI) (p. 591)
set point (p. 591)
social contagion (p. 596)

UNDERSTAND ...

- ***How genetic and environmental factors influence obesity.*** Some research suggests that genetics influences our set point, a weight (or range of weights) that our body tends to maintain; however, weight is influenced by several other factors as well. Environmental influences on weight gain are abundant. Cultural, family, and socioeconomic factors influence activity levels and diet, even in very subtle ways, such as through social contagion.

APPLY ...

- ***Your knowledge of persuasion and health to examine the effectiveness of different types of cigarette warnings.*** In this module, you read about efforts by different countries to reduce smoking rates. In Canada, cigarette packages contain different types of emotional images depicting the dangers of smoking. But, the audience for these packages is diverse—some people viewing the images are life-long smokers who *should* quit whereas others are teenagers who are considering smoking. When looking at the images on the right, which images are targeting young people and which images are targeting longtime smokers? What differences do you see between the two types of images? What types of imagery do you think would be most effective in influencing the behaviour of the two groups?

  Now try using a search engine like Google Image to look at cigarette packages from different countries. How does the packaging differ from Canadian cigarette packages? Why do you think these cultural differences exist?

stock_wales/Alamy

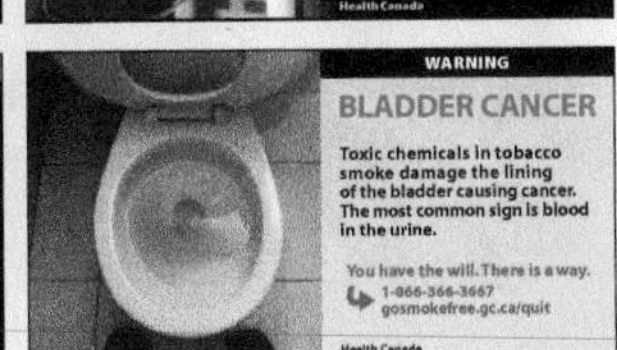

Health Canada

ANALYZE ...

- ***Whether associations with people who smoke affect smoking in adolescents.*** Correlational trends certainly show that smoking in popular movies is positively related to smoking among adolescents (e.g., increased exposure is related to increased incidence of smoking). Controlled laboratory studies suggest a cause-and-effect relationship exists between identification with story protagonists who smoke and smoking behaviour by young viewers.

Imagesource/Glow Images

Module 14.2

Stress and Illness

Learning Objectives

After reading this module you should

KNOW ...	UNDERSTAND ...	APPLY ...	ANALYZE ...
The key terminology associated with stress and illness	The physiological reactions that occur under stress How the immune system is connected to stress responses	A measure of stressful events to your own experiences	The claim that ulcers are caused by stress

The frustration and embarrassment of choking under pressure is undeniable. Whether the stakes are a championship title or admission to an elite university, a sudden, inexplicable shift to subpar performance can be devastating. According to psychologist Sian Beilock, the culprit in such a case may be the negative effects that stress has on working memory—the short-term capacity to hold and manipulate information. Calculating a 15% tip for a bill of $43.84 at a restaurant, or while the pizza delivery person waits, requires working memory processes. The pressure of your date watching you or the pizza delivery person looking on impatiently may result in your appearing either foolishly generous or just plain cheap.

Beilock has conducted experiments on how stress affects the cognitive resources needed for problem solving. For example, in one study, research volunteers were asked to solve math problems. Some were told that if they solved the problems correctly, they would earn money for themselves as well as for a partner they were paired with; if they did not perform well, both the volunteer and the partner would lose money. Beilock and her colleagues have found that this type of pressure draws resources away from the working memory processes needed for success (Beilock, 2008, 2010). Stressful thoughts readily occupy working memory space and cause the unfortunate experience of choking under pressure. The fact that the physiological response of stress can be caused by a social situation and can then affect a cognitive ability like working memory demonstrates, once again, the importance of the biopsychosocial model in understanding human behaviour.

Focus Questions

1. How does stress affect the brain and body?

2. How do individuals differ in how they handle stress?

Imagine a student near the end of the semester with several papers due and final exams looming. Now imagine someone who has worked at the same job for 25 years being told that he needs to learn a new computer system or he will be laid off. Or, think about a soccer player in a championship game that will be decided by penalty kicks; she walks up to place the ball on the penalty spot, knowing that if she misses her team will lose. If you were asked to find one work that connected all of these scenarios, what word would that be? For most people, that word would be stress. **Stress** *is a psychological and physiological reaction that occurs when perceived demands exceed existing resources to meet those demands.* Stress refers to both events (stressors) and experiences in response to these events (the stress response). Stressors can take a wide variety of forms, such as acute events (giving a speech, experiencing an assault, getting in a car accident) and chronic events (illness, marital problems, job-related challenges); the effects these stressors have on performance can be positive or negative.

WHAT CAUSES STRESS? Have you noticed how some people seem overwhelmed by stressful events while others seem calm and focused? These differences are not a figment of your imagination—people do differ in their responses to stress. To attempt to explain why and how people differ, psychologists Richard Lazarus and Susan Folkman developed a cognitive appraisal theory of stress (Lazarus & Folkman, 1984). Here, the term *appraisal* refers to the cognitive act of assessing and evaluating the potential threat and demands of an event. These appraisals occur in two steps. First, the individual perceives a potential threat and begins the *primary appraisal* by asking herself, "Is this a threat?" Threats can be physical (e.g., someone trying to harm you) or psychosocial (e.g., trying to study for two exams on the same day or trying to deal with interpersonal conflicts). If the answer is no, then she will not experience any stress. But, if the answer is yes, she will experience a physiological stress reaction (perhaps a racing heart beat and sweaty palms) as well as an emotional reaction (perhaps anxiety and fear). As these events unfold, the *secondary appraisal* begins—she must determine how to cope with the threat. During the secondary appraisal, she may determine that she knows how to cope with the stressor (e.g., studying for the exams over the course of several days); in this case, she will not feel much stress. However, if she believes that the stressor goes beyond her ability to cope, the physiological and emotional reactions to the stress will continue.

Imagine that a teenager experiences his first traffic accident. During his primary appraisal of the event, he will probably assess the situation as stressful even though it was a minor collision; his stomach may feel like it is in a knot and he may begin to worry about the consequences. As the stress sets in, his secondary appraisal may help him cope if he remembers that he has insurance to cover the damage, he considers that nobody was injured, and remembers how his parents have always been supportive and understanding. If, instead, he were illegally driving his older sister's car with no insurance, then his secondary appraisal would lead to a continuation (or an increase) of the initial stress response.

Although the causes of stress can vary from person to person, there are some patterns that tend to emerge. In the workplace, Canadians experience stress due to long hours, high work demands, safety concerns, and interpersonal relationships (Statistics Canada, 2003). Life changes such as marital difficulties, the birth of a child, or the death of a family member are also a major source of stress. Of course, not everyone finds all of these events or situations are equally stress-inducing. Psychologists have actually ranked stressful events according to their magnitude, as can be seen in the Social Readjustment Rating Scale (SRRS) in Table 14.2 (Holmes & Rahe, 1968). The highest-stress events include death of a spouse and divorce, while holidays and traffic tickets occupy the lower end of the spectrum. According to the psychologists who developed this scale, as the points in the left column of Table 14.2 accumulate, a person's risk for becoming ill increases. For example, 300 or more points put people at significant risk for developing heart problems, illnesses, and infections.

Importantly, life-stress experiences for adults will not necessarily be the same across all age groups. Students can have all of the stressors discussed above along with the obvious additions of school work, a lack of money, and all of the social excitement associated with one's late teens and early 20s. In addition to these stressors, students from immigrant minority groups must overcome additional challenges such as harassing comments from people who are not part of the person's minority group (Lay & Safdar, 2003). They also must deal with family conflicts associated with balancing the family's traditions with the desire to embrace Canadian culture (Safdar & Lay, 2003). Clearly, stress can be caused by a number of different forces.

At this point in the module, it would appear as though stress were always a bad thing. However, some level of stress can actually be helpful—without it, the motivation to perform can decline. Researchers have found that stress has positive effects on performance

Table 14.2 :: Life Stress Inventories for the General Adult Population and for University Students

ORIGINAL SOCIAL READJUSTMENT RATING SCALE (HOLMES & RAHE, 1967)	
RATING	ITEM
100	Death of a spouse
73	Divorce
65	Marital separation
63	Jail term
63	Death of a close family member
53	Personal injury or illness
50	Marriage
47	Fired at work
45	Marital reconciliation
45	Retirement
44	Change in health of family member
40	Pregnancy
39	Sex difficulties
39	Gain of new family member
39	Business readjustment
38	Change in financial state
37	Death of close friend
36	Change to different line of work
35	Change in number of arguments with spouse
31	Mortgage exceeding $10 000
30	Foreclosure of mortgage or loan
29	Change in responsibilities at work
29	Son or daughter leaving home
29	Trouble with in-laws
28	Outstanding personal achievement
26	Wife begins or stops work
26	Begin or end school
25	Change in living conditions
24	Revision of personal habits
23	Trouble with boss
20	Change in work hours or conditions
20	Change in residence
20	Change in schools
19	Change in recreation
19	Change in church activities
18	Change in social activities
17	Mortgage or loan less than $10 000
16	Change in sleeping habits
15	Change in number of family get-togethers
15	Change in eating habits
13	Vacation
12	Christmas
11	Minor violations of the law
	Total

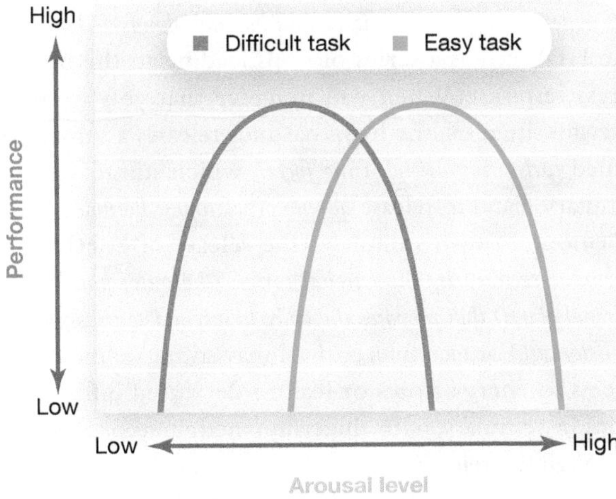

{FIG. 14.3} **Arousal and Performance** Performance is related to at least two critical factors—the difficulty of the task and the level of arousal/stress while they are being performed. For easy tasks, moderately high arousal helps; for difficult tasks, lower levels of arousal are optimal.

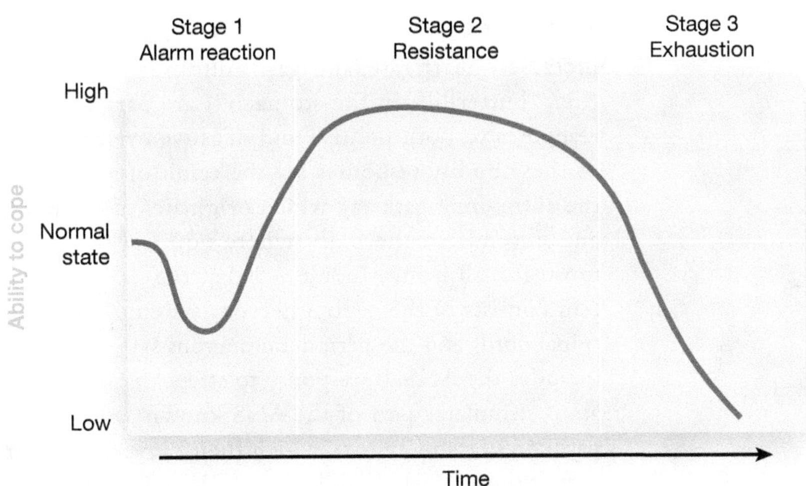

{FIG. 14.4} **The General Adaptation Syndrome** This graph depicts the body's resistance to stress. After the initial shock associated with the stressor (see the dip in resistance early in the Alarm phase), the body recruits resources to allow it to deal with the stressful situation or event. This ability to cope with the stressor peaks in the Resistance phase of the GAS. However, if the individual doesn't overcome the stressor, eventually he or she will be unable to resist the stress; this final phase is known as the Exhaustion Phase.

when the tasks being completed are relatively simple (see Figure 14.3). In this case, even if the stress consumes the person's cognitive resources, it will still be possible to complete the task. However, if a task is complex, stress will harm performance. This is because stress uses up many of our cognitive resources; a stressed-out person may find that she does not have the mental resources available to perform at the level she would be capable of if she were not experiencing stress. This pattern of data leads to the obvious question: *How* does a physiological response—stress—affect our mental life and cognitive abilities? In other words, what *is* stress?

Physiology of Stress

Think about the last time you experienced stress. How did you *feel*? Although stress depends upon our mental appraisal of a situation or event, the physiological response to stress occurs throughout most of the body. Indeed, you can literally feel yourself react to acute stressors, such as giving a presentation in class, as well as chronic stressors, such as the cumulative effect of a challenging school year. Walter Cannon, an early researcher into the phenomenon of stress (as well as emotion; see Module 11.4), noted that the physical responses to stressors were somewhat general, despite the fact that stress can come from a variety of sources that may be biological, cognitive, or social in nature. Cannon described this general reaction as a **fight-or-flight response**, *a set of physiological changes that occur in response to psychological or physical threats.* This discovery laid the foundation for the modern study of stress, with several researchers building upon Cannon's pioneering work.

Hans Selye (1950, 1956) of the Université de Montréal looked beyond the immediate fight-or-flight response and saw the unfolding of a larger pattern during responses to stress. He named this pattern the **general adaptation syndrome (GAS)**, *a theory of stress responses involving stages of alarm, resistance, and exhaustion* (see Figure 14.4). As GAS illustrates, a stressful event, such as a mild shock if you are a rat or a pop quiz (or a mild shock) if you are a university student, first elicits an *alarm* reaction. Alarm consists of your recognition of the threat and the physiological reactions that accompany it including increases in blood pressure, muscle tension, heart rate, and adrenaline release. As the stressful event continues, the individual enters the second part of this adaptive response, known as *resistance*. Resistance is characterized by an individual using his or her physical and mental resources to respond to the stressor in an appropriate way (e.g., furiously studying for a quiz or running away from predators). However, an animal (or student) can't maintain this level of energy use forever. The third and final stage of the GAS is often referred to as *exhaustion*; this occurs when the stressful experience depletes your physical resources and your physiological stress response declines.

Since the work of Cannon and Selye, psychologists have further uncovered the highly complex physiological interactions that occur during and after stress. In their search, two key pathways have been identified: the autonomic nervous system (ANS) pathway and the hypothalamic-pituitary-adrenal (HPA) axis.

Simulate
Will This Survey Stress You Out?

Listen
Pop Quiz

Explore
Virtual Brain: Emotion, Health, and Stress

THE STRESS PATHWAYS Sweaty palms, an increased heart rate, and gastrointestinal sensations (i.e., "butterflies in the stomach") are part of stress responses to both positive and negative events. Many of these bodily responses are the result of activity in the autonomic pathway, which originates in the brain and extends to the body where you *feel* stress the most. Recall from Module 3.3 that the nervous system consists of the central nervous system (brain and spinal cord) and the peripheral nervous system, which includes the ANS. In response to stress, the hypothalamus stimulates part of the ANS known as the sympathetic nervous system, which then causes the inner part of the adrenal glands known as the adrenal medulla (found on top of the kidneys) to release epinephrine and norepinephrine (also known as adrenaline and noradenaline). These chemicals then trigger the bodily changes associated with the fight-or-flight response (see Figure 14.5).

Another physiological system involved in the stress response is the **hypothalamic–pituitary–adrenal (HPA) axis**, *a neural and endocrine circuit that provides communication between the nervous system (the hypothalamus) and the endocrine system (pituitary and adrenal glands).* Think of the HPA axis as a series of steps leading to the body's stress response. When you perceive that you are in a stressful situation, the hypothalamus releases a substance called *corticotrophin-releasing factor*, which stimulates the pituitary gland to release *adrenocorticotrophic hormone*. This hormone in turn stimulates the release of **cortisol**, *a hormone secreted by the adrenal cortex (the outer part of the adrenal gland) that prepares the body to respond to stressful circumstances.* For example, cortisol may stimulate increased access to energy stores or lead to decreased inflammation. In summary, both the sympathetic nervous system (through the release of epinephrine and norepinephrine) and the HPA axis (through the release of cortisol) function to prepare us to respond to stress.

With rare medical exceptions, humans mount both autonomic and HPA axis responses to stress. These responses are highly adaptive and promote behaviours that help our survival (e.g., being more vigilant or running extra fast). However, as we will see later, chronic stress responses, which can occur under circumstances such as having legal or financial problems, impact long-term health (Chrousos & Gold, 1992). Also, individuals differ in how their ANS responds to stress. These individual differences may be traceable to our early experiences with stressful events. Human and animal studies reveal that childhood stress, such as deprivation of maternal care, has lasting effects on the stress response system (Chrousos, 2009) as well as on some neurotransmitter systems (Robbins et al., 1996).

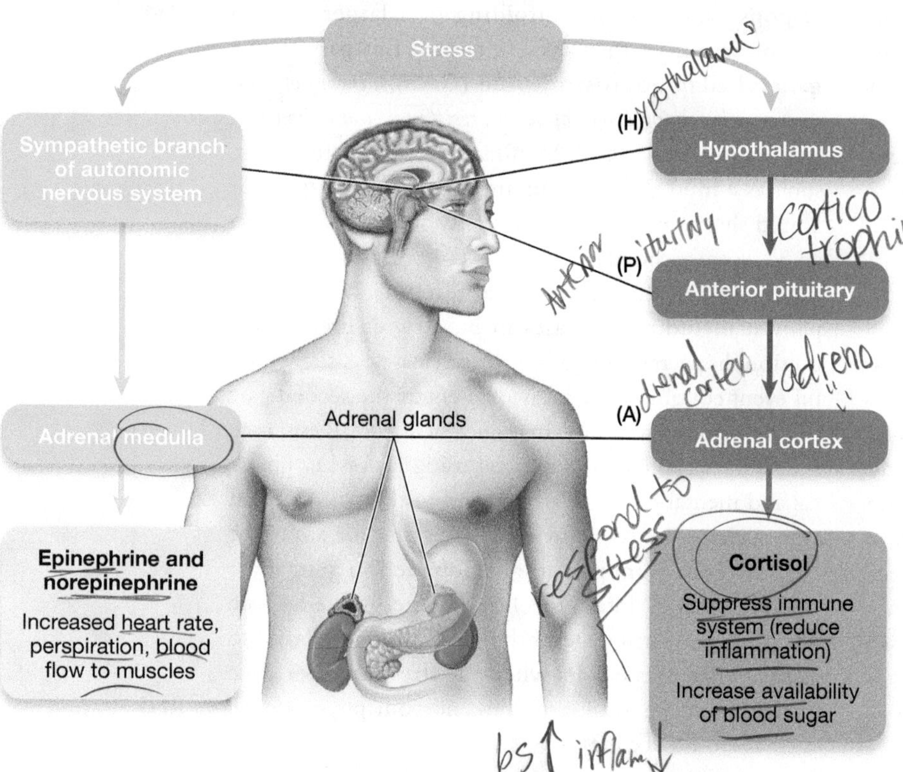

{FIG. 14.5} **Stress Pathways of the Body** The stress pathways of the body include the autonomic nervous system and the HPA axis. Both systems converge on the adrenal glands. The autonomic response involves stimulation of the adrenal medulla by the sympathetic nervous system, resulting in the release of epinephrine and norepinephrine—chemicals that stimulate the fight-or-flight response. Activity of the HPA axis results in stimulation of the adrenal cortex, which releases cortisol into the bloodstream. **Click on this figure in your eText to see more details.**

Researchers have also discovered that the release of chemicals called glucocorticoids (cortisol is a type of glucocorticoid), which are a part of the HPA axis, is affected by social stressors such as being excluded from a conversation (Kirschbaum et al., 1993). These cortisol responses to social stressors are larger in individuals with depression or a history of childhood maltreatment (Harkness et al., 2011), suggesting that these factors may interact in some psychological disorders. In a study investigating the relationship between glucocorticoids and childhood stress, researchers conducted autopsies on people who had experienced extensive childhood abuse and eventually committed suicide. The researchers were specifically interested in the number of glucocorticoid receptors in the hippocampus. They assumed that if an individual experienced a lot of stress during childhood, glucocorticoid receptors in the brain would start to become inactive. This response sounds strange, but it actually makes sense; if these receptors were being overstimulated due to the child's awful experiences, his or her brain would respond by trying to bring the glucocorticoid activity back down to normal levels. Because the brain couldn't control the stress from the outside world, its only option would be to reduce the number of places (receptors) that the stress could have its effect. If there were fewer glucocorticoid receptors available to stimulate HPA activity, then the high levels of stress experienced by abuse victims wouldn't continuously use up their body's resources. The results of this study were consistent with the researchers' expectations. Compared with the autopsies of controls, the brains of the deceased individuals who had been abused had significantly fewer receptors for glucocorticoids (McGowan et al., 2009). Fewer receptors for these chemicals have also been found in well-controlled rat studies involving maternal deprivation. Thus, the experiences that we have during development can influence how our brains and bodies respond to stress in adulthood.

OXYTOCIN: TO TEND AND BEFRIEND One observation you have likely made is that males and females respond to stress and threat in different ways. Although people are often cautious about making claims about sex differences, there are in fact some differences in the HPA axis of males and females (Kudielka & Kirschbaum, 2005). Shelley Taylor and her colleagues at UCLA have suggested that whereas men are more likely to react to stress or threats with a fight-or-flight response, women are more likely to have a more social *tend-and-befriend* response (Taylor et al., 2000; Taylor, 2006). This view makes sense if you think about the history of our species. Over the course of our species' evolution, females have had to care for dependent and vulnerable children. Running away from a stressful situation would have required abandoning offspring; getting into a fight risked the possibility of death or injury. Both of these responses would have reduced the likelihood that their offspring would have survived. Instead, it made more sense to seek out stable friendship networks for support during times of stress. Doing so provided comfort, but also the potential for additional resources to help with offspring. This is not to say that women don't have any instinctive fight-or-flight response or that men have no need to tend and befriend; rather, these researchers are suggesting that there are sex differences in which response is more likely to occur.

The tend-and-befriend reaction may be promoted by the release of **oxytocin**, *a stress-sensitive hormone that is typically associated with maternal bonding and social relationships*. Oxytocin influences a number of behaviours including the contraction of the uterus when a woman is in labour, romantic attachment, social bonding, trust, wound healing, and orgasm (although not all at the same time; Caldwell & Young III, 2006; Lee et al., 2009). Although oxytocin is clearly involved in a number of behaviours, its role in stress is particularly important. Animal studies have shown that stimulating the release of oxytocin reduces activity in the sympathetic nervous system (one of the parts of the stress network) and blood pressure (Carter et al., 1998). In humans, women who are breast-feeding and thus have high levels of oxytocin show lower stress responses to physical and psychological stress (Light et al., 2000); similar findings were reported in men who were given doses of oxytocin (Heinrichs et al., 2003). And, most relevant to the tend-and-befriend hypothesis, women who receive more frequent hugs from their romantic partners also have higher oxytocin levels and lower stress responses (Light et al., 2005). That's something to think about when studying for exams.

Quick Quiz 14.2a

Physiology of Stress

KNOW ...

1 Which of the following is not a component of Selye's general adaptation syndrome?

A Resistance **C** Flight

B Alarm **D** Exhaustion

2 Which of the following is a major player in the chemical response comprising the autonomic fight-or-flight stress response system?

A Cortisol **C** Dopamine

B Epinephrine **D** Oxytocin

UNDERSTAND ...

3 A major difference between the tend-and-befriend stress response and the responses mediated by the autonomic pathway and the HPA axis is that

A the tend-and-befriend response involves cortisol activity.

B men are more likely to express the tend-and-befriend response.

C the tend-and-befriend response facilitates care for offspring and others in a social group.

D the tend-and-befriend response is a negative stress reaction, whereas the autonomic pathway and HPA axis responses are positive reactions.

4 High ________ levels and low ________ levels are associated with elevated stress.

A epinephrine; cortisol

B epinephrine; oxytocin

C cortisol; oxytocin

D cortisol; testosterone

APPLY ...

5 According to the Social Readjustment Rating Scale (SRRS), which of the following is most likely to cause you the most stress?

A A jail term

B The death of a family member

C A pregnancy

D A divorce

Answers can be found on page ANS-4.

Simulate How Stressed Are You?

Stress, Immunity, and Illness

Stress and physical health are closely related. The immune system, which is responsible for protecting the body against infectious disease, has numerous connections with the nervous system, including the stress response systems just discussed (Maier & Watkins, 1998; Selye, 1955). **Psychoneuroimmunology** *is the study of the relationship between immune system and nervous system functioning.* You have likely had the unfortunate experience of getting sick in the midst of a period of high stress. In fact, one study suggests that final exams may be bad for you. In this investigation, medical students provided blood samples during the term and again during the final exam period. Analysis of these blood samples showed reduced immune responses during the high-stress period at the end of the term (Kiecolt-Glaser, 1984). This is not an isolated phenomenon; dozens of experimental and correlational studies have shown, for example, that stress increases the likelihood that people will succumb to the cold virus (Cohen et al., 1998).

Watch Basics: Stress and Your Health

Psychologists are finding that the stress–illness relationship is a very complex one, involving numerous physiological systems. Also, the effects of mental stress on physical functioning are diverse. Recall that stress can come in a variety of forms—at the very least, we can divide it into acute and chronic variations. It appears that stress also has dual influences on immunity. Acute stressors tend to activate the immune system, whereas chronic exposure to stress generally causes suppression of the immune system (Segerstrom & Miller, 2004).

Importantly, the interactions between stress and immunity are influenced by social factors: specifically, the intimate relationships that play such an important part of our lives.

WORKING THE SCIENTIFIC LITERACY MODEL

Hormones, Relationships, and Health

Social relationships can be a major source of both positive and negative stress, and they can provide a great deal of support during our most stressful times. Given the links between stress and health, it seems reasonable to ask: How do our personal relationships relate to health?

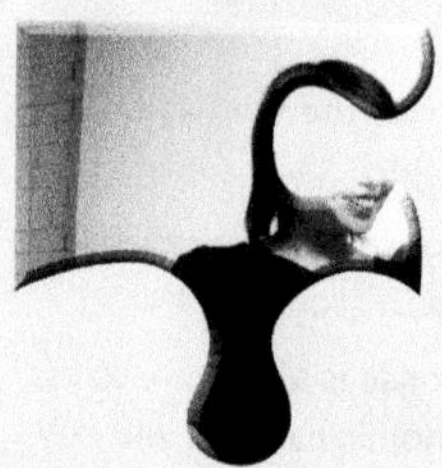

What do we know about hormones, relationships, and health?

Many family events and relationships can be stressful. Almost everyone has argued with their parents or siblings. Holidays and weddings can be fun, but they also involve a lot of planning and, at times, "intense discussion." Sometimes relationships—particularly with close friends or romantic partners—become very difficult and tense, and may even lead to chronic stress responses that adversely affect a person's health. However, other relationships can be quite fulfilling, and can lead to strong social bonds that will last a lifetime. These positive relationships have been linked to specific hormonal responses in the body. Two hormones, oxytocin and vasopressin, are involved in social behaviour and bonding. We previously discussed the role of oxytocin in moderating stress responses, particularly in females. Oxytocin has been shown to inhibit activity in the amygdala, a brain region involved with fear and threat responses (Kirsch et al., 2005). It may also prevent the release of both adrenocorticotropic hormone and cortisol, hormones related to stress (Heinrichs et al., 2003). Vasopressin also has stress-reducing functions. Like oxytocin, the release of vasopressin is controlled by the hypothalamus and pituitary gland; it also affects the levels of stress hormones released by the adrenal gland (Goland et al., 1991). People with high vasopressin levels tend to report better relationship quality with their spouses (Walum et al., 2008). However, oxytocin and vasopressin have health functions that go beyond improving social bonds. Both of these hormones also interact with the immune system, specifically to reduce inflammation.

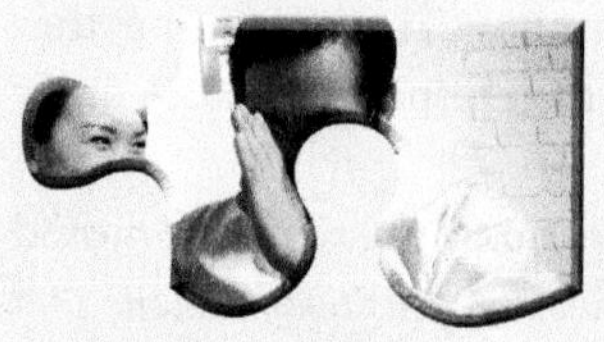

How can science explain connections between hormones, relationships, and health?

A common, if not surprising method for measuring immunity and health is to see how quickly people recover from a minor wound. In one study, the effect of marital stress on

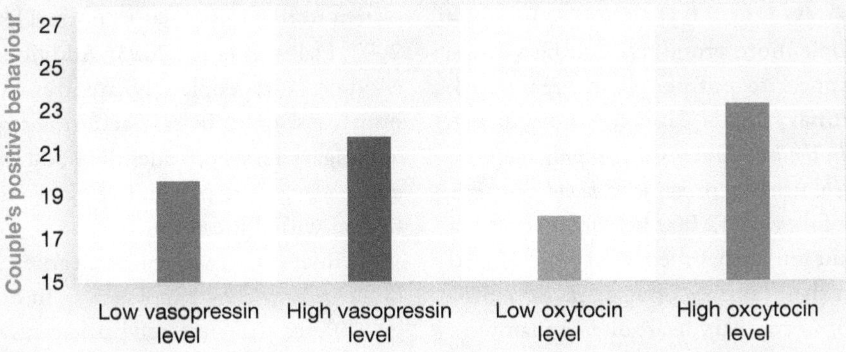

{FIG. 14.6} **Relationship Quality Is Related to Physiological Responses** Higher oxytocin and vasopressin levels are associated with positive social interactions between married couples.

wound healing was tested in a group of 37 married couples (Gouin et al., 2010). Each couple was asked to sit together with no other couples or researchers present and complete a series of marital interaction tasks, including a discussion of the history of their marriage and a task in which both spouses were instructed to discuss something they wished to change about themselves. These interactions were videotaped. The researchers also took blood samples to measure oxytocin and vasopressin levels. Additionally, each participant consented to receiving a suction blister on the forearm, which is a very minor wound created with a medical vacuum pump.

During the marital interaction tasks, those who engaged their partner with positive responses including acceptance, support, and self-disclosure had higher levels of oxytocin and vasopressin. Those who responded with hostility, withdrawal, and distress had lower levels (Figure 14.6). In addition, the suction blister wounds healed more quickly over an eight-day period in individuals with high oxytocin and vasopressin levels. (Suction wounds heal to 100% within 12 days.)

The health-promoting effects of oxytocin are also evident from placebo-controlled studies. In another experiment, married couples were given either an intranasal solution of oxytocin or a placebo. The couples then engaged in discussion about conflict within their marriage. Those who received a boost of oxytocin showed more positive, constructive behaviour during their discussion compared to couples in the placebo group. The researchers also measured cortisol levels from saliva samples obtained from each individual. Those in the oxytocin group had lower levels of this stress hormone compared to couples in the placebo group (Ditzen et al., 2009).

Can we critically evaluate this evidence?

It might be tempting to conclude that a boost of oxytocin or vasopressin could be the key to marital happiness, stress reduction, and physical health. Although the studies you just read about are related to these important qualities, it is important to avoid oversimplifying what their results mean. Claims that homeopathic oxytocin remedies can make anyone happier and better at love, marriage, sex, and even "mind reading" should be looked at with skepticism. Advertisements for such products are not hard to find. However, scientists are still in the relatively early stages of learning just how oxytocin and vasopressin affect social behaviour in humans, and how they are related to immune system function (Gouin et al., 2010; Macdonald & Macdonald, 2010).

Why is this relevant?

Although these studies were conducted with married couples, the physiological and physical healing benefits of close, positive social relationships extend to romantic relationships, friendships, and family. Procedures for healing physical injury currently focus on repair to damaged areas and preventing infection from setting in. In addition to these critical steps, it appears that managing psychological stress is also important for facilitating recovery from wounds (Gouin & Kiecolt-Glaser, 2011). As we shall see, stress can also affect a number of other aspects of our physical health.

DAJ/Glow Images

STRESS, FOOD, AND HEART DISEASE In addition to making people more prone to catching viruses, high stress levels appear to put people at greater risk for developing **coronary heart disease**—*a condition in which plaques form in the blood vessels that supply the heart with blood and oxygen, resulting in restricted blood flow.* For example, one study followed 12 000 healthy males for a nine-year period and found that men who experienced ongoing stress with their families or at work were 30% more likely to die from coronary heart disease than were men who were not chronically stressed (Matthews & Gump, 2002). Coronary heart disease begins when injury and infection damage the arteries of the heart. This damage triggers the inflammatory response by the immune system—white blood cells travel to affected areas in an attempt to repair the damaged tissue. These cells gather cholesterol and form dangerous plaques, which can rupture, break off, and block blood flow. So how does stress fit into this picture? Stress causes an increased release of those molecules that cause the inflammation that leads to heart complications (Segerstrom & Miller, 2004).

Stress influences heart functioning in other, indirect, ways as well. Survey research has consistently shown that people are drawn toward sweet and fatty foods when they are stressed (Oliver & Wardle, 1999; Steptoe et al., 1998). Laboratory-based studies have shown similar trends. In one experiment, female participants were given anagram puzzles to solve (e.g., turning YOGHPOSCYL into PSYCHOLOGY). The women who had the highest levels of the stress hormone cortisol ate more sweet, high-fat snacks than did the less-stressed women (Epel et al., 2001). The relationship between stress and unhealthy food extends to other species as well. Low-status females in a colony of monkeys are often bullied and harassed by high-status females; researchers have noted that the low-status females ate more banana-flavoured pellets than their social superiors (Wilson et al., 2008). Interestingly, similar results were found when monkeys had the opportunity to self-administer cocaine; the subordinate monkeys pressed a lever much more often than the dominant monkeys who presumably had less stress (Morgan et al., 2002).

Obviously, overeating unhealthy food (or doing cocaine) is not a good long-term solution to stress. So, why do some people (and monkeys) use food and drugs to deal with stress? Although it is possible that these substances directly affect the hormones and brain areas associated with stress, most scientists agree that food (and drugs) influence the brain's dopamine reward system (see Modules 5.3 and 6.2). Some research suggests that chronic stress suppresses the reward system (so stressed people would find less joy in things). It is possible that eating rewarding foods increases the activity in this system so that it is closer to normal levels (Adam & Epel, 2007; Dallman et al., 2003). Additionally, as discussed in Module 11.1, people who are stressed are mobilizing the body's resources in case action is required; eating fatty and sugary foods provides the body with extra calories *in anticipation* of the person having to use additional energy to deal with a stressor.

However, as we learned earlier, males and females differ in how they handle stress. In one study, psychologists offered male research participants snacking options of healthy foods (peanuts and grapes) or unhealthy options (M&Ms and potato chips) while they were given an unsolvable anagram puzzle (stressful) or a solvable anagram (nonstressful). Consistent with what you've read in this module, female participants ate more junk food when

MYTHS IN MIND

Stress and Ulcers

The link between stress and eating is not the only health issue that is oversimplified or misunderstood. People typically associate ulcers—open sores in the lining of the esophagus, stomach, and small intestine—with people working in high-stress jobs, such as police officers or air traffic controllers. The belief that stress causes people to develop ulcers is widespread. In actuality, most ulcers are caused by a bacterium, *Helicobacter pylori*, which can cause inflammation of the lining of various regions of the digestive tract. This bacterium is surprisingly common, and approximately 10% to 15% of people who are exposed to it will develop an ulcer resulting from inflammation. Thus stress does not cause ulcers, although it can worsen their symptoms. Also, smoking, alcohol, pain relievers, and a poor diet—anything that can irritate the digestive system—increases problems associated with ulcers.

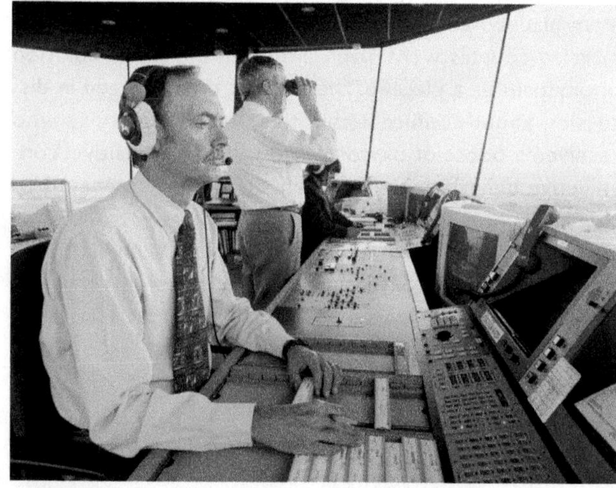

Contrary to popular belief, chronic stress, like that experienced by air traffic controllers, will not cause a stomach ulcer.

they were stressed (Zellner et al., 2006). In contrast, male participants at more M&Ms and chips in the easy anagram condition (Zellner et al., 2007). While this difference was surprising, the experimenters quickly found an explanation: Unlike the male participants, many of the female participants were on diets. Stress caused the females to yield to temptation and eat chocolate and chips. Males, on the other hand, snacked more in the easy condition because they finished the puzzle quickly and therefore had more time left to eat (men are wonderfully simple sometimes). These results show us that the relationship between stress and unhealthy behaviours is not simple, but can also be influenced by a number of outside social factors.

AIDS Although stress is often linked to cardiovascular problems like heart attacks and strokes, its negative effect on the immune system makes stress a factor in other conditions as well. Acquired immune deficiency syndrome (AIDS) is a disease caused by infection with the human immunodeficiency virus (HIV). This disease saps the immune system's ability to fight off infections, to such an extent that even conditions that are relatively harmless to most of the population can be devastating to an individual with AIDS. Patients in industrialized countries with more medical options have a better prognosis than those living in impoverished areas. Retroviral therapies have greatly increased the longevity, health, and overall quality of life of patients. However, people who are HIV positive need regular vaccination treatments. Unfortunately, stress impedes the body's ability to respond to vaccinations. In turn, studies have shown that those who experience serious emotional distress are less responsive to HIV treatments. Stress-induced elevation of the neurotransmitter norepinephrine—which is involved in emotional arousal and stress responses—can also worsen the condition of the various illnesses associated with AIDS. Patients who have elevated activity of the autonomic nervous system are slower to respond to antiretroviral therapies, which increases their risks of developing certain types of cancer such as B-cell lymphoma (Cole et al., 1998).

CANCER Researchers are also finding numerous links between psychosocial factors and cancer progression (Antoni & Lutgendorf, 2007). Several factors, such as the type of cancer and an individual's age, account for why some people rapidly succumb to cancer while others are able to win the battle. In addition, stress levels affect the progression of cancer. Why is this? It appears that norepinephrine supports cancer cell growth, and that cortisol magnifies this effect. Hormones from the autonomic nervous system stimulate cells that reside in tumours, which ultimately results in growth and proliferation of these masses (Antoni et al., 2006). Thus, when someone experiences stress, the autonomic nervous system and HPA axis naturally respond, but their reactions compromise how well the individual can fight the disease.

For many people, stress levels can be changed and the course of a disease such as cancer can be slowed. For example, individuals who have undergone assertiveness training and learn anger management techniques show reduced autonomic activity and hormonal activity associated with the HPA axis (Antoni et al., 2007). Also, those who are optimistic, cope by using humour, and have a positive outlook on the disease (and thus less stress) show physiological benefits such as greater immune responses (Lutgendorf et al., 2007). This suggests that a person's personality can influence the effect stress has on her immune system.

Quick Quiz 14.2b
Stress, Immunity, and Illness

KNOW ...

1 What is psychoneuroimmunology?
- **A** A condition in which plaques form in the blood vessels that supply the heart with blood and oxygen, resulting in restricted blood flow
- **B** The study of both the positive and negative effects that our behaviour and decisions have on health, survival, and well-being
- **C** The study of the relationship between immune system and nervous system functioning
- **D** A hormone secreted by the adrenal gland

UNDERSTAND ...

2 A direct effect of stress on coronary health would be
- **A** a stress-related increase in inflammation that results in buildup of cholesterol in the arteries.
- **B** eating more fattening foods in response to stress.
- **C** engaging in increased risky behaviour due to stress.
- **D** increased moodiness during periods of stress.

3 How does stress affect cancer?
- **A** Stress decreases the number of white blood cells in the body, which results in cancer progression.
- **B** Hormones from the autonomic nervous system stimulate cells that reside in tumours, which can in turn stimulate growth and proliferation of the tumours.
- **C** Stress decreases the growth of cancer cells.
- **D** Stress does not affect cancer.

ANALYZE ...

4 Researchers have concluded that the actual cause of ulcers is ________.
- **A** stress
- **B** bacterial infection
- **C** genetics
- **D** poor diet

Answers can be found on page ANS-4.

Explore AIDS Timeline

Watch IT Video: AIDS

Stress, Personality, and Illness

How people handle and cope with stress often depends on their personality. This relationship is evident very early in life, even during infancy. Children who are easily distressed tend to be more prone to illness during adulthood. Even cognitive activity in our early years is related to adult health. For example, children who are able to better focus their attention on tasks tend to be healthier in adulthood (Kubzansky et al., 2009). Furthermore, infants who are securely attached to their mothers show reduced activity in their sympathetic nervous systems when their mothers are absent (Frigerio et al., 2009). As personality takes shape in adulthood, we can further see how different personalities deal with stress and how stress relates to health.

Watch
Thinking Like a Psychologist: Personality and Health

First consider your own responses to a common stressful event. Imagine you have a one-hour break between classes, during which you need to get lunch and also visit one of your professors across campus. When you arrive at your professor's office, you see a line of other students awaiting their turn, and the current occupant is blathering on and on about something completely unrelated to schoolwork (busy professors love this, by the way). How would you tend to react in this situation? Would you become agitated, angry, resentful, and fidgety? Or would you be more inclined to strike up a conversation with others in line to help pass the time? Your answer will likely depend on various factors—but each of us tends to have a common style of responding to stressful events.

Simulate
How Healthy Are You?

The **Type A personality** *describes people who tend to be impatient and worry about time, and are easily angered, competitive, and highly motivated.* In contrast, the **Type B personality** *describes people who are more laid back and characterized by a patient, easygoing, and relaxed disposition* (Friedman & Rosenman, 1974). The concept of Type A and B did not originate in psychology. Rather, cardiologists suspected that people who were prone to stress had poorer physical health. They identified these individuals as Type A, and their studies revealed that people who fall in the Type A category are far more likely to have heart attacks than are Type B people. This initial finding has been replicated many times, though the correlation between levels of Type A characteristics and coronary heart disease is only moderate. This less-than-strong relationship likely reflects the fact that other factors, not just how a person copes with stress, may further elevate the risk of coronary heart disease. People who have a Type A personality also engage in behaviours that compromise physical health, such as drinking large quantities of alcohol, smoking, and sleeping less than people with a Type B personality. Thus, numerous correlated factors may explain the relationship between Type A personality and risk of coronary heart disease.

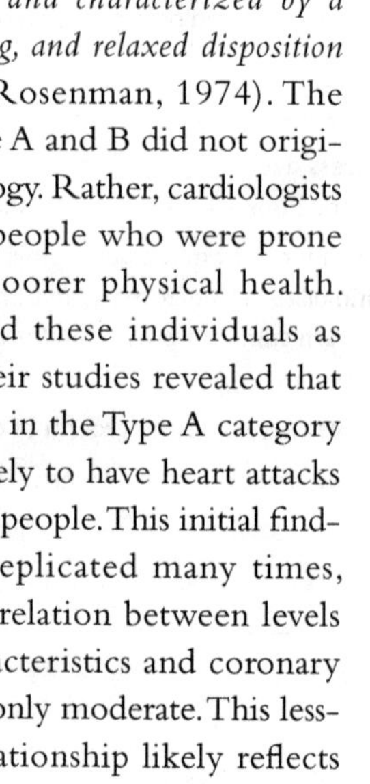

Syda Productions/Fotolia LLC

People with Type A personalities are often successful. However, they are also much more likely to experience heart attacks and strokes than are more relaxed, less hostile individuals.

The distinction between Type A and B personalities has not satisfied all behavioural scientists and physicians. Being quick to anger is a characteristic of Type A individuals, but so is being hyper-motivated to succeed at work. Perhaps there is something more specific about personality that increases one's risk for developing heart disease. More recent research has shown that people who are prone to hostility and anger are at greater risk for developing coronary heart disease (Razzini et al., 2008). Other personality characteristics linked to coronary heart disease include anxiety and depression (Barger & Sydeman, 2005; Lett et al., 2004).

Together, these studies show us that stress can affect us in a number of different ways ranging from our heart rate and blood pressure to our survival rates when fighting long-term illnesses. But these studies show us something else as well: that how we mentally react to the stressors can dramatically influence how our body responds. In the next module, we will pull this research together to show how you can draw from psychology research to help you cope with stress. Doing so will make you happier—and healthier.

Quick Quiz 14.2c Stress, Personality, and Illness

KNOW ...

1 People with ________ personality are patient and easygoing, and have a relaxed disposition, whereas ________ personality individuals tend to be impatient and are easily angered, competitive, and highly motivated.

- **A** Type A; Type B
- **B** stressed; relaxed
- **C** Type B; Type A
- **D** relaxed; stressed

2 The health risk most likely to be associated with Type A personality is ________.

- **A** AIDS
- **B** cancer
- **C** coronary heart disease
- **D** the cold virus

ANALYZE ...

3 Which of the following observations is a fair critique of the Type A and Type B categorization of personality types?

- **A** They were not developed by psychologists.
- **B** They apply only to hospital patients.
- **C** They reflect the fact that people tend to lie on personality tests.
- **D** Their connection to health outcomes may be more reflective of lifestyle factors such as sleep and alcohol consumption than of personality style.

Answers can be found on page ANS-4.

Module Summary

Module 14.2

Now that you have read this module you should

Imagesource/Glow Images

KNOW ...

- ***The key terminology associated with stress and illness:***

coronary heart disease (p. 606)
cortisol (p. 602)
fight-or-flight response (p. 601)
general adaptation syndrome (GAS) (p. 601)
hypothalamic–pituitary–adrenal (HPA) axis (p. 602)
oxytocin (p. 603)
psychoneuroimmunology (p. 604)
stress (p. 599)
Type A personality (p. 608)
Type B personality (p. 608)

UNDERSTAND ...

- ***The physiological reactions that occur under stress.*** When a person encounters a stressor, the hypothalamus stimulates the sympathetic nervous system to act, triggering the release of epinephrine and norepinephrine from the adrenal medulla. This reaction is often referred to as the fight-or-flight response. Another part of the stress response system is the HPA axis, in which the hypothalamus stimulates the pituitary gland to release hormones that in turn stimulate the adrenal cortex to release cortisol, which prepares the body to deal with stressful situations.
- ***How the immune system is connected to stress responses.*** Cortisol suppresses the immune system, leaving people more vulnerable to illness and slowing recovery time from illness and injury.

APPLY ...

- ***You can compare your own life stress experiences with those of others.*** To complete this activity, look at **Table 14.2** on page 600. Using the values next to each stressful event listed, add up the numbers that apply to your experiences and compute your total stress score. Holmes and Rahe (1968) found that a score of 300 or more puts people at significant risk for illness, while a score of 150–299 puts people at a moderate risk.

  Years later, Renner and Mackin (1998) developed a similar scale for college and university students based on data gathered from a sample of 257 undergraduate students (range: 17–45 years; mean: 19.75 years). Do an Internet search for Renner and Mackin's College Undergraduate Stress Scale and calculate your own stress score. They reported an average stress score of 1247 (standard deviation: 441), with scores ranging from 182 to 2571. How did you compare with their sample?

ANALYZE ...

- ***The claim that ulcers are caused by stress.*** Ulcers are damaged areas of the digestive tract often caused by infection with the bacterium *Helicobacter pylori*. Stress and other factors, such as diet and alcohol consumption, can worsen the condition of ulcers, but stress alone does not cause them.

John Lund/Stephanie Roeser/Glow Images

Module 14.3

Coping and Well-Being

Learning Objectives

After reading this module you should

KNOW ...	UNDERSTAND ...	APPLY ...	ANALYZE ...
The key terminology associated with coping and well-being	How control over the environment influences coping and outlook Positive and negative styles of coping	Your knowledge of the beneficial effects of optimism to help you reframe stressful situations as positive opportunities	Whether activities such as relaxation techniques, meditation, and biofeedback actually help people cope with stress and problems

What is the best way to cope with a personal disaster, such as losing your job? Writing about how the event makes you feel may not seem like a priority, but according to psychologist James Pennebaker, it may be one of the best strategies for coping and regaining the emotional resources needed to move on. Pennebaker, a leading researcher on the psychological benefits of writing, decided to intervene when a local computing and electronics firm laid off 60 professional workers. All he asked the workers to do was to write, but their instructions on how to write were different: Half the volunteers were randomly assigned to write about their "deepest thoughts and feelings surrounding the job loss, and how their lives, both personal and professional, had been affected" (Spera et al., 1994, p. 725). In contrast, the control group members were told to write about their plans for the day and how they planned to find another job, which is much less personal and emotional. After a month of weekly 20-minute writing sessions, the group members who were writing about their emotions were getting hired much more frequently than the control group members. The participants were randomly assigned to the two groups, so the differences between the groups can be traced to the writing rather than to pre-existing personality differences. Similar methods have been used in Pennebaker's studies of first-year university students, people grieving the loss of a loved one, and other groups experiencing stressful transitions. The result was the same each time—group members who wrote meaningful narratives of their emotions and thoughts came out ahead, not just in terms of mental health, but physically and in terms of their performance at work or school.

Focus Questions

 What are the different ways people cope with stress?

 Which factors make coping especially challenging?

This module is designed to help you. In it, you will read about some widely used solutions for coping with stress and behavioural methods that may potentially help in improving health. We will also discuss some topics that might be less familiar, but may prove useful in how you cope with stress and negative events. Finally, we will discuss how stress and successful coping are closely related to your sense of control.

Coping

Although understanding how stress works—both physically and mentally—is important, it is the ability to cope with that stress that will dictate whether or not you are happy. **Coping** *refers to the processes used to manage demands, stress, and conflict.* Some of us approach a problem or stressor, such as large monetary debt or a setback at work, by taking a problem-solving approach. In other words, we cope by defining the problem and working toward a solution. If you are stressed out by school demands, you could address the problem by setting up a study schedule, dropping a course, or finding a tutor, among many other possible solutions. However, there are times when it is more important to focus on the emotional effects of a stressor than on attempting to find an immediate solution to a problem—in fact, not all stressors are brought about by problems that have identifiable solutions. For example, imagine that your beloved family pet has passed away. In such a situation, you obviously cannot make a list to deal with your grief; however, you *can* find ways to reduce the negative effects your emotions are having, both on yourself and on others. Neither of these styles of coping is necessarily superior to the other—their suitability depends on the nature of the problem (Folkman & Lazarus, 1980). In many instances, both *problem-focused coping* and *emotion-focused coping* are used to deal with a stressor.

Of course, not all coping techniques actually help; some may simply replace one problem with another. For example, some people turn to alcohol or drugs to temporarily avoid feelings of stress, and some turn to food. Unfortunately, sitting in front of the television and eating a litre of Häagen-Dazs® ice cream from the container is not a healthy method of coping. In this section, we will examine both the positive and negative methods of coping, and then describe several techniques that can be used to improve one's well-being.

POSITIVE COPING STRATEGIES Psychology may have a reputation for focusing on the negative, including how damaging stress can be. In reality, psychologists also study what makes people thrive, even in the face of extreme stress. This area of study, **positive psychology**, uses scientific methods to study human strengths and potential. Research in this area has identified numerous adaptive and constructive ways in which people cope with problems. These researchers have found that one of the most powerful tools for coping is also one of the simplest: focusing on positive emotions.

Although it may seem difficult to imagine experiencing positive emotions during times of stress, doing something simple like watching a funny movie can actually help you cope with stress and negative life experiences. Barbara Fredrickson and her colleagues at the University of North Carolina (Chapel Hill) have shown that positive emotions can affect how we perceive and think about the world. For example, these researchers have shown that a negative mood narrows your focus of attention so that you attend to a small part of your environment, whereas positive moods cause the focus of your attention to expand (Fredrickson & Branigan, 2005). Other scientists have demonstrated that positive moods can also increase a person's creativity. In one experiment, participants were shown groups of three words (e.g., falling, actor, dust) and were asked to find a word that related all three items (e.g., star). Individuals in the positive mood condition scored higher than other participants (Isen, 1987). This increase in flexible thinking is crucial during coping, as it would help people experiencing negative emotions reframe their stressors into something less upsetting.

Although the effects of positive emotion on our ability to perceive and think are interesting, the most stunning effect of positive emotions is their effect on our autonomic nervous system. When most of us watch a scary movie, our heart rates increase as we experience fear. Then, after a little while, our heart rates return to normal. But, the speed that this recovery occurs can be influenced by positive emotions. Researchers have found that when participants watched positive films after seeing a scary movie clip, their heart rate returned to normal faster than when participants viewed a sad or neutral film (see Figure 14.7). The positive emotions seemed to

Explore Coping Strategies and Their Effects

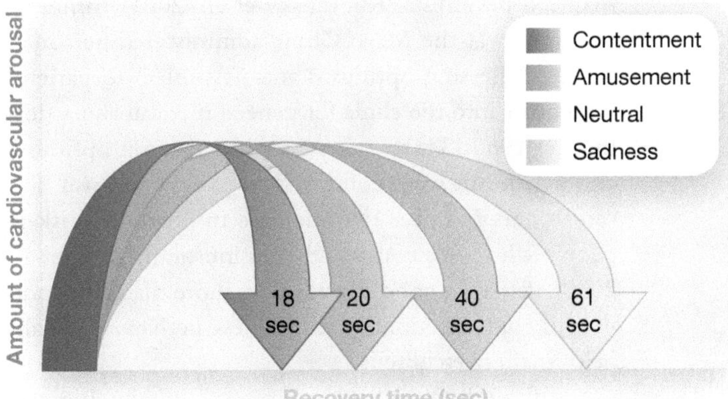

{FIG. 14.7} **Positive Moods and Recovery from Negative Emotional Events** Research shows that positive moods speed a person's recovery from negative events. In this study, viewing a video depicting positive emotions (amusement or contentment) caused heart rates to return to normal levels faster than a neutral or sad video (Fredrickson & Levenson, 1998).

defuse the effects of the negative emotions, thus decreasing the amount of damage that stress and negative emotions can have on the body (Fredrickson & Levenson, 1998). Because positive emotions allow people to broaden their thought processes and to build new intellectual, social, and physical resources, these results are now described as the *broaden-and-build theory* of positive emotions (Fredrickson, 2001, 2003).

OPTIMISM AND PESSIMISM Closely linked to positive emotions is the concept of **optimism**, *the tendency to have a favourable, constructive view on situations and to expect positive outcomes.* People who are optimistic tend to initially perceive situations in a positive way and are also more likely to find positive elements in situations. In contrast, **pessimists** *tend to have a negative perception of life and expect negative outcomes.* These individuals often have what is known as **pessimistic explanatory style**, *which is the tendency to interpret and explain negative events as internally based (i.e., as being due to that person rather than to an external situation) and as a constant, stable quality* (Burns & Seligman, 1989). For example, a laid-off employee who struggles to find a job may attribute the problem to his perceived inability to network properly rather than to the fact that it is tough to find jobs in his field.

Watch
Grieving a Loss Part 1: Bob, 81 Years Old

Watch
Grieving a Loss Part 2: Bob, 81 Years Old

As you might expect after reading the previous section, optimism is correlated with better physical health than pessimism. For example, scientists have shown that women who tend toward pessimism and test positive for the HPV virus (a papilloma virus known to cause cervical cancer) have lower counts of white blood cells that fight disease than do optimistic women with the HPV virus. Long-term studies show similar effects of optimism. In the U.S. Veterans Affairs Normative Aging Study involving a large cohort of male participants, optimists had a lower incidence of coronary heart disease than did pessimists (Kubzansky et al., 2001). Similarly, researchers at the Mayo Clinic administered personality tests assessing optimism and pessimism to patients who came into the clinic for general medical issues during the 1960s. Thirty years later, the data on optimism and pessimism were compared to patient survival. The researchers found a 19% increase in mortality risk in people who were consistently pessimistic (Maruta et al., 2000). Perhaps a good attitude does more than help individuals cope emotionally with illness; perhaps it actually helps them overcome it.

Although these studies present a convincing case for optimism, there is an alternative explanation for the results: Optimists and pessimists may simply have had different lifestyles. One of these other lifestyle variables (e.g., diet) could potentially explain the health differences between optimists and pessimists. In order to control for this possibility, a group of U.S. researchers conducted longitudinal (long-term) studies of a group of females with nearly identical lifestyles: nuns. The Nun Study, as it is now known, was exceptional in that it allowed researchers to examine how personality factors such as optimism and pessimism affected people over the course of their lifetime while controlling for variables such as diet, work demands, and stress. As part of this study (which is part of a longitudinal study about factors leading to Alzheimer's disease), the researchers examined the handwritten autobiographies of 180 nuns; these documents were written by the nuns when they were entering the order in their early-to-mid twenties. The emotional content of the autobiographies were coded by the researchers to see if positive emotions predicted how long the nuns lived. Here are two excerpts from the study (Danner et al., 2001, p. 806):

Judith Collins/Alamy

Is the glass half full or half empty? Long-term studies have shown that people who have a pessimistic view tend to have increased medical problems and reduced longevity compared to optimists.

> *Sister 1 (low positive emotion): I was born on September 26, 1909, the eldest of seven children, five girls and two boys . . . My candidate year was spent in the Motherhouse, teaching Chemistry and Second Year Latin at Notre Dame Institute. With God's grace, I intend to do my best for our Order, for the spread of religion and for my personal sanctification.*

> *Sister 2 (high positive emotion): God started my life off well by bestowing upon me a grace of inestimable value . . . The past year which I have spent as a candidate studying at Notre Dame College has been a very happy one. Now I look forward with eager joy to receiving the Holy Habit of Our Lady and to a life of union with Love Divine.*

The researchers found a strong correlation between positive emotions during young adulthood and the longevity of the nuns—people who were more positive during their twenties lived longer than less positive people (Danner et al., 2001). Similar results have been found with less-controlled populations (Maruta et al., 2000; Peterson et al., 1998), suggesting that the results of the Nun Study are due to optimism and positivity, not to an act of divine intervention.

PERSONALITY AND COPING Optimism and pessimism provide a nice continuum for how different individuals emotionally respond to the situations and people that they will encounter in their lives. Of course, as you read in Module 12.1, our personalities cannot simply be described along one dimension. Over the past twenty years, a number of studies have examined the effect of different personality traits on coping. They have found that each of the Big Five personality traits has its own effect on how a person copes with stress and adversity.

- *Neuroticism:* People high in neuroticism have **negative affectivity**, *the tendency to respond to problems with a pattern of anxiety, hostility, anger, guilt, or nervousness.* These negative emotions make it difficult for these individuals to choose an appropriate coping strategy for a given problem (DeLongis & Holtzman, 2005; O'Brien & DeLongis, 1996). For instance, someone with high levels of negativity may deal with a difficult breakup by socially withdrawing from others, becoming angry and resentful, and possibly growing hostile enough to threaten and harass the other person with phone calls, repeated texting, or the spreading of rumours. This personality trait has been linked to frequent physical complaints and illnesses such as headaches, chronic pain, stomach aches, and coronary heart disease (Friedman & Booth-Kewley, 1987; Watson & Pennebaker, 1989).
- *Extraversion:* People high in extraversion are relatively outgoing and social. Their social nature also has benefits when it comes to coping with stress. Extraverts are more likely than introverts to actively seek out help from others rather than trying to solve a problem on their own. They are also more likely to listen to the advice of others and to try to reframe the stress in a way that is more positive or constructive (Lee-Baggley et al., 2005).
- *Agreeableness:* Agreeable people want to get along with the people around them. Like extraverts, people who are high on the trait of agreeableness are willing to seek help from others. Although this trait does not seem to be related to problem-related coping, it does play a major role in how people experiencing stress interact with others (Newth & DeLongis, 2004). Therefore, agreeableness is a trait that may help people avoid additional interpersonal stresses (e.g., not arguing with friends when everyone is already stressed out about a camping trip that is going poorly).
- *Conscientiousness:* People with high levels of conscientiousness tend to be quite disciplined and focused on what is expected of them. When coping, these individuals are less likely to show their emotions than people with low levels of conscientiousness, perhaps so that they can reduce the effect that stress is having on their other responsibilities (Newth & DeLongis, 2004). This method of coping has been referred to as *distancing,* because people attempt to distance themselves from their own emotions.
- *Openness to experience:* People high on this trait tend to be intellectually curious and aware of their emotions. In terms of coping, researchers have found them to respond with empathy when stressful situations involved other people (O'Brien & DeLongis, 1996). They are also less likely to use emotional distancing as a method of coping with interpersonal stressors such as family issues (Lee-Baggley et al., 2005).

Although these summaries tell us how different traits are related to how different people cope with stressors, it is important to remember that everyone has elements of all five of these traits. This combination of personality traits influences how prone we are to stress, how we appraise different stressful situations, and, most importantly, whether we are able to overcome or cope with the stress.

RESILIENCE Thus far, we have discussed a number of factors that can reduce the effects of stress and promote well-being. However, there are times when negative life events are unavoidable. As you have likely noticed in your own life, individuals differ in their ability to bounce back from events such as disaster, disease, or major loss. This trait is known as **resilience**, *the ability to effectively recover from illness or adversity.* Resilient people tend to have one or more factors stacked in their favour. Financial and social resources, opportunities for rest and relaxation, and other positive life circumstances contribute to resiliency. Even so, amazing stories of resiliency can be found among individuals living with unimaginable stress. Thus, the personality and emotional characteristics discussed earlier are also important contributors to resiliency in the face of adversity.

Watch Optimism and Resilience

One amazing example is that of Viktor Frankl, an early- and mid-20th-century Austrian psychiatrist. Frankl was already an influential physician and therapist when he, his wife, and family were forced into concentration camps during World War II. Frankl found himself in the role of helping people adjust to life in the concentration camp, even while he himself struggled to survive each day. He encouraged others to tap into whatever psychological resources they had left to cope with very bleak circumstances. Frankl found that one of the most critical parts of surviving in these camps was finding some sort of meaning in life. For some, this could be the desire to reunite with their family when the war eventually ended. For others, it was a love of poetry (astoundingly, some prisoners were able to write poetry in the concentration camps). But, if a prisoner seemed to lose this sense of meaningfulness in his life, Frankl could tell that this prisoner would soon die. As Frankl later noted, "Despair equals Suffering minus Meaning" (Gelman et al., 2000, p. 625). A key challenge, then, was to maintain this sense of meaningfulness so that people had a purpose in their lives. Doing so allowed them to cope and remain resilient while witnessing terrifying events. Eventually Frankl's wife and parents were deported to different concentration camps, where they were murdered. Despite his own enormous losses, Frankl continued helping others to cope and find solace under the worst of circumstances (Frankl, 1959).

Watch
Emotional Longevity

Imagno/Hulton Archive/Getty Images

Stories of survival like Viktor Frankl's experiences in Nazi concentration camps show us the power of human resilience. Frankl went on to become an influential psychiatrist who developed a new method of therapy focused on finding meaning in life.

Listen
Psychology in the News: Neurofeedback for ASD

Psychologists have long focused on the negative outcomes of stress, but stories such as Frankl's demonstrate that stress and trauma can also lead people to recognize how strong they really are. In fact, psychologists describe the phenomenon of **post-traumatic growth**, *the capacity to grow and experience long-term positive effects in response to negative events* (Tedeschi & Calhoun, 2004). It happens in response to events such as automobile accidents, sexual and physical assault, combat, and severe and chronic illnesses. Individuals who experience post-traumatic growth often report feeling a greater sense of vulnerability, yet over time develop an increased inner strength. They also report finding greater meaning and depth in their relationships, a greater sense of appreciation for what they have, and an increased sense of spirituality (Tedeschi & Calhoun, 2004).

Post-traumatic growth is not an alternative reaction to post-traumatic stress. Rather, the two conditions occur together. Clinicians recognize that the growth occurs during the process of coping, not because of the event itself. Often a clinical psychologist trained in working with trauma victims helps facilitate the growth process and assists the individual in finding the interpersonal and social resources needed for healing. Some of these resources include medications and some form of counselling. It is also becoming increasingly common for people to use other techniques to reduce responses to stress and negative events including meditation and yoga.

MEDITATION, RELAXATION, AND BIOFEEDBACK

As you have been reading this chapter, your circulatory system has been pumping blood and maintaining blood pressure, your lungs have been breathing in air, and your digestive system may have been working on a recent meal, all without the tiniest bit of conscious effort. Certainly you can intentionally hold your breath for a moment, but can you hold your heartbeat or change your blood pressure? If you are like most of us, you cannot control all of these autonomic functions, but that does not mean it is impossible.

Biofeedback *is a therapeutic technique involving the use of physiological recording instruments to provide feedback that increases awareness of bodily responses.* The psychologists who developed this technique believed that by seeing or hearing a machine's representation of bodily processes, people could gain awareness of stress responses and bring them under voluntary control. For example, a patient with chronic stress could use feedback on his blood pressure, heart rate, and tension of his facial muscles to monitor and, possibly, control his stress responses. As you can imagine, this ability would have very useful applications to clinical psychology. However, after some very promising findings, the excitement over biofeedback faded, in part because it was found that simple relaxation techniques were just as useful.

Many people report significant benefits by using relaxation and meditation techniques to cope with stress and life's difficult periods. Both techniques are designed to calm emotional responses as well as physiological reactions to stress. People frequently regard meditation as either a religious or new-age ritual—something that takes years of practice from which only "experts" can benefit. This is not the case—anyone can meditate. Health benefits are often observed in novices, although the time it takes for this to occur varies from person to person and across meditation techniques. As discussed in Module 5.2, meditation comes in two general varieties: (1) *concentrative* or *focused attention meditation*, in which the individual focuses on a specific thought or sensation, such as an image or a repeated sound, and (2) *mindfulness* or *open monitoring (OA) meditation*, which involves attending to all thoughts, sensations, and feelings without attempting to judge or control them (Cahn & Polich, 2006). Several studies have shown that both types of meditation are very effective in reducing blood pressure, which reduces the potential for long-term problems with hypertension and cardiovascular disease (Rainforth et al., 2007).

Mindfulness-based stress reduction (MBSR) is a structured relaxation program based on elements of mindfulness meditation. The primary goal of MBSR is to help people to cope and to relax by increasing the link between one's body and one's mind. A common meditative technique used in MSBR is a body scan in which participants pay attention to the sensation of their toes, then their feet, ankles, calves, and so on. By attempting to focus on bodily sensations for 15–20 minutes, the participants engage in a great deal of attentional control; if someone's mind wanders, she is simply asked to bring it back to the body scan without judging herself for the slip-up. During these relaxation exercises, participants are instructed to recognize and become aware of any emotions they may experience, but to then let it go so that the emotion is not part of their identity. Studies using MSBR have found that it reduces stress (Baer et al., 2012) and increases a sense of meaningfulness in life (Dobkin, 2008). Not surprisingly, MSBR also leads to increased brain activity in the insula, a brain area related to perceiving bodily sensations; this area is involved with a person's ability to focus on the present moment (Farb et al., 2013).

Altered brain activity has also been found after people learned a complex form of meditation called integrated mind–body training (IMBT). This technique, developed from traditional Chinese medicine, involves a combination of relaxation and posture correction, as well as instructions for heightening one's awareness of one's body (Tang, 2011). Similar to MBSR, this technique has been shown to enhance the control of attention (Tang et al., 2007). IMBT has also been linked to an increased ability to control bodily physiology. In one study, researchers compared participants who had completed either five days of IMBT or five days of a simpler relaxation training program. The IMBT group showed lower heart rates, breathing rates, and skin conductance responses (a measure of stress) than did the relaxation training group. These differences appear to be due to activity in a region of the midfrontal cortex called the anterior cingulate gyrus; this area is involved in controlling attention as well as in some emotional responses. In this study, activity within the anterior cingulate was

Bonnie Kamin/PhotoEdit

Biofeedback involves the use of physiological monitoring, which allows the patient to see and sometimes hear the output of his or her physiological reactions.

Tyler Olson/Shutterstock

Meditation is practised in many cultures, typically to serve the function of promoting health and stress reduction.

Watch In the Real World: Reducing Stress, Improving Health

associated with the participants' increased control over parasympathetic nervous system responses. The increased parasympathetic activity accounted for the heightened sense of relaxation experienced while meditating (Tang et al., 2009). Interestingly, later studies showed a strengthening of the white-matter connections between the anterior cingulate and emotional structures in the base of the brain (Tang et al., 2010), suggesting that IMBT can change how different neural regions interact.

Although meditation does appear to have a number of health benefits, training procedures like MBSR and IMBT might not be for everyone. However, there is a relaxation technique that many people in your class already perform: yoga. According to various organizations, approximately 1.5 million Canadians regularly practise yoga (in one of its many forms). Yoga involves directed breathing while participants move their bodies into specific poses. This voluntary breathing can influence activity in the parasympathetic nervous system, leading to a decrease in emotional arousal (Sovik, 2000). Consistent with this view, U.S. college students who performed directed breathing had lower levels of physical and mental stress than did control participants (Cappo & Holmes, 1984). Yoga may also help your immune system; when compared to people in a simple relaxation condition (nature walks and soft music), people who performed yoga had greater changes in gene expression in the immune cells circulating in the bloodstream (Qu et al., 2013).

Thus, scientific studies of meditation and relaxation training in all their forms appear to confirm their health benefits, and are also bringing us closer to understanding precisely *how* these changes to the brain and body help us cope with stress and negativity.

Elena Ray/Fotolia

Approximately one in twenty Canadians performs yoga. However, the stress-related benefits of yoga have not been researched as thoroughly as other relaxation and meditation techniques.

PSYCH @ Church

Stress-reduction techniques like mindfulness are sometimes associated with spiritualism, as many arose as part of different Buddhist traditions; however, a belief in a higher power is not a requirement of these techniques. In contrast, many people use religion as their primary coping mechanism during stressful situations, both large and small. They may use any combination of religious practices, depending on the specific nature of the faith: prayer, meditation, religious counselling, and social support from family and congregations. All of these efforts can provide strength and comfort during difficult times, but they may also be associated with greater overall happiness. Many psychologists have become increasingly curious about the possible health benefits associated with religion and spirituality. Numerous studies have found that people who are very religious and are actively engaged with religious practices do, in fact, live a bit longer than do people who are less religious or nonreligious; in fact, they were 29% more likely to be alive at any given follow-up point during the study (McCullough et al., 2000).

A hasty interpretation of these results might lead one to conclude that religion causes people to live longer—that the experiences of prayer and of attending church lead to the greater longevity. However, the studies in this area actually produce correlational, not experimental, data—psychologists cannot randomly assign people to be religious or not. Consequently, we must consider alternative explanations. For example, lifestyle factors are also at play. Younger and older people of Muslim, Jewish, or Christian faith are more likely to engage in healthy behaviours, including wearing seatbelts, visiting the dentist, and avoiding both the consumption of alcohol and cigarette smoking (reviewed in McCullough & Willoughby, 2009). Religions also tend to have negative views of criminal activity, drug abuse, and risky sexual activity. Thus, the increased longevity is probably related to the greater self-control and self-regulation that are characteristic of many religious belief systems.

Generally, people who are religious show greater well-being and lower levels of depression (Smith et al., 2003). The determination of whether religion protects people from depression depends on the point of view taken, however. People who cope with problems using positive aspects of religion (e.g., viewing stressors with kindness or collaborating with others in solving problems) are less prone to depression than religious people who adopt negative appraisals of their problems and concerns, such as viewing problems as a result of a wrathful God's punishment (Ano & Vasconcelles, 2005; McCullough & Willoughby, 2009).

EXERCISE Relaxation training and religious study both require discipline; individuals must follow instructions or teachings in a fairly consistent manner. Staying in good physical condition requires similar devotion, and also produces considerable physical and psychological benefits. However, even short bursts of exercise can be useful. For example, researchers in Germany asked university student participants either to do all-out sprints, to jog, or to do nothing. The students who sprinted were able to learn 20% more items on a vocabulary list than the students who jogged or were inactive (Winter et al., 2007). Why did this occur? Perhaps the sprinters were more motivated than the others. This explanation sounds plausible, but the researchers randomly assigned healthy participants to the three groups—so there should not be anything inherent to the sprinter group that would lead them to learn more words. It appears that the type of exercise they engaged in led to increased cognitive performance. Which physiological processes might account for the cognitive edge the sprinters gained from their intense physical activity? The researchers discovered that the students who engaged in intense exercising had increased levels of dopamine, epinephrine, and **brain-derived neurotrophic factor (BDNF)**—*a protein in the nervous system that promotes survival, growth, and the formation of new synapses.* Cardiovascular exercise also provides immediate benefits in cognitive processing speed, again as measured in university-aged students (Hillman et al., 2003). But, these immediate benefits of exercise are not limited to younger people. When sedentary adults between 60 and 85 years of age take up weekly exercise, they show improved brain functioning and cognitive performance (Hillman et al., 2008; Kramer et al., 1999).

One important issue to address is whether these short-term effects translate into lifelong cognitive benefits from exercise. Results from long-term studies indicate that a lifestyle that includes regular exercise helps preserve cognitive function and the brain systems that support it (van Praag, 2009). Researchers have found that older people who are at genetic risk for developing Alzheimer's disease and who show cognitive impairments can slow the rate of memory decline by exercising (Lautenschlager et al., 2008). It appears that levels of brain chemicals such as BDNF are boosted by exercise, which helps explain the changes in the brain that account for the cognitive benefits. Furthermore, exercise supports the development of new nerve cells in the hippocampus, a critical area for memory and cognitive activity (van Praag, 2008). Together, these studies tell us that the benefits of exercise go far beyond helping you look good.

Quick Quiz 14.3a

Coping

KNOW ...

1 ________ is the tendency to respond to problems with a pattern of anxiety, hostility, anger, guilt, or nervousness.

- **A** A coping style
- **B** Negative affectivity
- **C** Pessimism
- **D** An aggression complex

2 What is brain-derived neurotrophic factor (BDNF)?

- **A** A protein in the nervous system that promotes survival, growth, and formation of new synapses
- **B** A calorie-restricted diet that may involve eating approximately 60% of the normal amount of calories, while continuing to take in the needed nutrients
- **C** A neurotransmitter that reduces stress and increases overall well-being
- **D** A hormone that is released in those individuals with a healthy diet

UNDERSTAND ...

3 ________ is a positive coping strategy, while ________ is a negative style of coping.

- **A** Meditation; resilience
- **B** Pessimistic explanatory style; negative affectivity
- **C** Meditation; alcohol
- **D** Post-traumatic growth; resilience

APPLY ...

4 Your partner suddenly broke up with you and did not offer an explanation. If you attribute the breakup to your not being a very outgoing person, you are demonstrating ________.

- **A** negative affectivity
- **B** a pessimistic explanatory style
- **C** resilience
- **D** a coping style

ANALYZE ...

5 What is the most accurate conclusion regarding the effects of meditation on stress and well-being?

- **A** Meditation is the absolute best way to combat stress and protect your body from disease.
- **B** Advanced training in meditation will decrease stress in a manner similar to simple relaxation techniques.
- **C** Meditation helps the practitioner control his or her physiological responses, thereby decreasing stress and preventing health problems such as cardiovascular disease.
- **D** Meditation is not a commonly used way of managing stress.

Answers can be found on page ANS-4.

Perceived Control

As Dr. Pennebaker's story from the beginning of this module illustrates, the most stressful of circumstances are the ones that people have little or no control over. For example, children who reside in abusive homes have no control over their circumstances, nor do the victims of natural disasters. Each situation can result in people acquiring a sense that their behaviour has little effect on external events.

Laboratory experiments have demonstrated the negative impact that a lack of control has on health and behaviour. A classic example comes from work on avoidance learning in dogs conducted in the 1960s by Martin Seligman and his colleagues (Seligman & Maier, 1967). In this study, dogs received electrical shocks while strapped into a harness. Half of the dogs learned to press a panel in order to escape the shock, thus providing them some control over their stressor. The other half of the dogs received the same number of shocks as the first group, but had no control over when the shocks would occur. After a delay, each dog was placed in a device known as a shuttle box consisting of two small areas separated by a low divider that the animal could easily jump across (see Figure 14.8). On each experimental trial, a tone was sounded before the section of the box that the animal was standing on became electrified, thus providing a shock similar to the one experienced in the earlier part of the study. Through trial and error, animals that were in the controllable stress condition learned that they could jump over the divider to the other side of the shuttle box to get away from the shock; after a few trials, this behaviour occurred immediately after the warning tone was presented, which allowed them to avoid the shock altogether. In contrast, the dogs who had experienced the uncontrollable shocks had difficulties learning to escape. Instead, they would lie down, whine, and appear resigned to receive the shock. This finding was described as **learned helplessness**—*an acquired suppression of avoidance or escape behaviour in response to unpleasant, uncontrollable circumstances.*

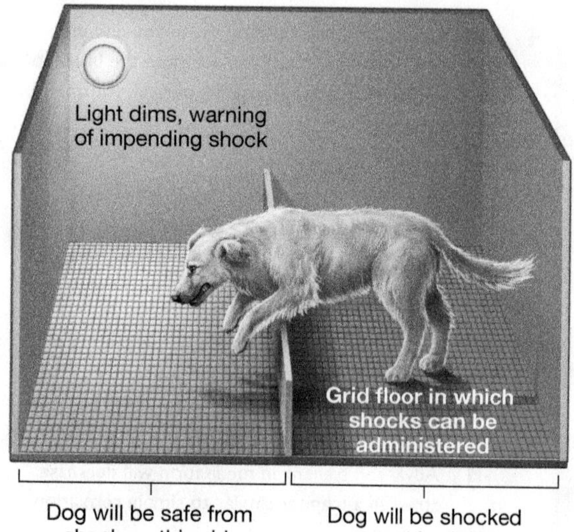

{FIG. 14.8} **The Learned Helplessness Procedure** In Seligman and Maier's study, dogs that could avoid a painful shock would quickly learn to do so. Conversely, dogs that initially learned they could not avoid a shock remained passive when the opportunity to do so was given. The acquired failure to avoid or escape unpleasant circumstances that are perceived as uncontrollable is referred to as learned helplessness. **Click on this figure in your eText to see more details.**

Later studies provided some interesting insights into learned helplessness, with some potentially important implications for how humans respond to stress. Researchers found that stress responses involve nuclei in the brainstem as well as the ventral (lower) regions of the frontal lobes. When a stressful event is controllable (e.g., being shocked, but having a way to escape), the brainstem produces a stress response such as increased heart rate and blood pressure; however, this response is then inhibited by the frontal lobes (Amat et al., 2005). When a stressful event is not controllable, the brainstem provides a stress response without being inhibited. This finding suggests that the degree to which a person *perceives* a stressor to be controllable will influence whether the stress response will be inhibited, and whether the person will experience an event as being stressful.

The important point about learned helplessness is that the animal, or person, *learns* that their actions cannot remove the stress in one situation (e.g., the harness) and then *generalizes* that helplessness to other situations (e.g., the shuttle box). This is similar to the thought processes of some people with depression. People with depression are prone to hold beliefs that their actions have no influence on external events, and that their environment and circumstances dictate outcomes. Learned helplessness also has similarities to anxiety disorders; namely, increased nervousness and a feeling of being unable to escape a stressor (Maier & Watkins, 2005). Clearly, both aspects of learned helplessness can negatively affect mental and physical well-being. This phenomenon shows that the perception of control can have a dramatic effect on our ability to cope. Without it, many humans and some nonhuman species will endure pain and stress rather than initiating ways to avoid or escape it.

WORKING THE SCIENTIFIC LITERACY MODEL

Compensatory Control and Health

The idea of a random world in which people lack personal control over events can be discomforting. For example, hurricanes and tornados are often referred to as "acts of God," rather than the result of an unfortunate confluence of meteorological events and human-populated areas. But does having a sense of control lead to better health?

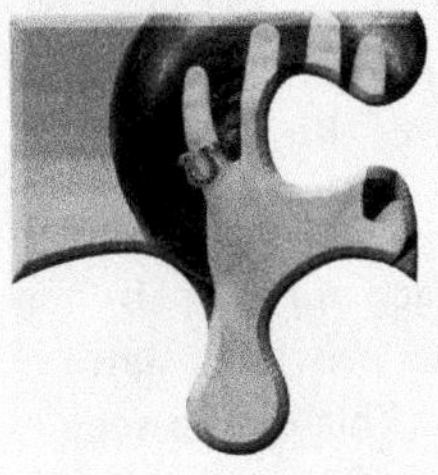

What do we know about how people cope with seemingly random events?

Some people feel as if they are the victims of random events, while others believe themselves to be the beneficiaries of the whims of life. However, the idea that randomness dictates worldly events can create anxiety in people. Even if a person believes randomness is the rule, he or she can become highly motivated to find meaning in the world and, through this search, a sense that the course of events is determined by the will of individuals or God (Kay et al., 2009). In this way, many people cope with stressful life events through **compensatory control**—*psychological strategies people use to preserve a sense of nonrandom order when personal control is compromised* (Kay et al., 2009). For example, people who are skeptical of any divine purpose in the world may change their view in the wake of personal or societal tragedy. These observations are primarily correlational, but researchers have conducted experiments to determine causal relationships between sense of control and beliefs about randomness versus orderliness.

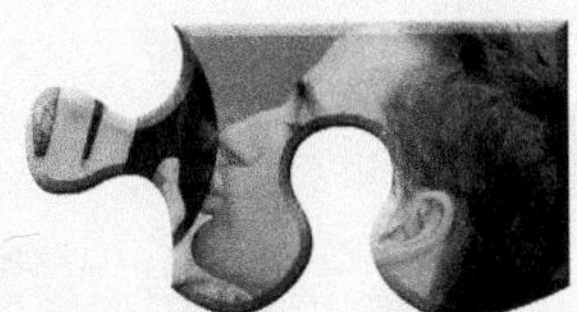

How can science explain compensatory control?

To study compensatory control, researchers have developed a laboratory task that manipulates people's sense of personal control over a situation (Whitson & Galinsky, 2008). In one study, participants completed a concept identification task in which two symbols were presented on a computer screen, and the participant had to guess which symbol correctly represented the concept that the computer had chosen (e.g., the colour of the symbol, its shape). The computer provided feedback on whether the participants chose the correct or incorrect symbol after each trial. Half of the participants received accurate feedback, while the other half received completely random feedback—sometimes their correct answers were recorded as incorrect, and vice versa. Participants receiving random feedback reported feeling a lower sense of control on a self-report measure.

Following the concept identification task, the participants then viewed multiple pictures, such as those shown in Figure 14.9. If you look closely, you will see that one of the pictures has a horse-like figure in it, whereas the other image has no discernible pattern. Participants in both conditions reported seeing faintly drawn figures, such as the horse. However, participants who had a diminished sense of control induced by the random feedback they received on the computer task were more likely to report seeing patterns within completely random images (Whitson & Galinsky, 2008).

It appears that when people feel their sense of control is undermined, they compensate by heightening their search for structure in the world, to the point of calling upon their imagination. This is evident in other domains as well, not just detecting patterns in random, snowy images. People also gain a greater need for structure and become increasingly willing to believe in superstitious rituals and conspiracy theories

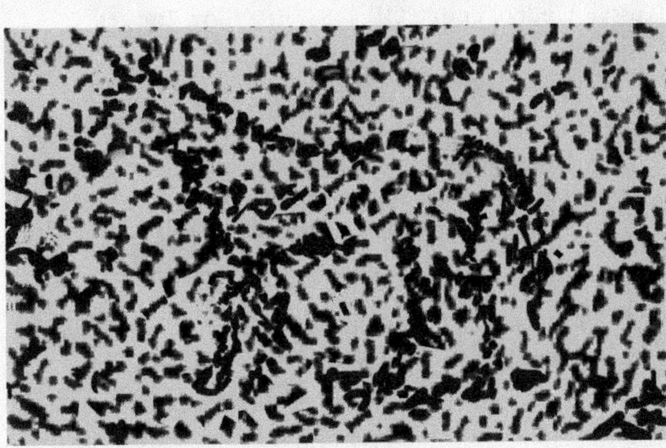

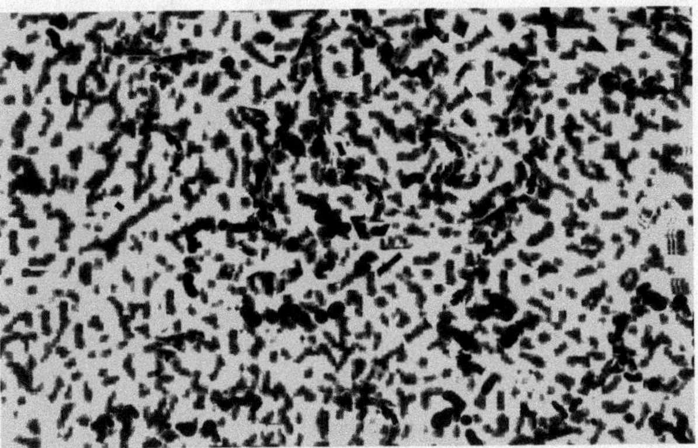

{FIG. 14.9} **Seeing Images Where There Are None** Do you see a figure in the image on the left? You may see a figure resembling a horse. What about on the right? There is no discernible image intended for this image. Psychologists have found that individuals who feel as though they lack control are more likely to detect patterns in the image at right than are people who feel a greater sense of control (Whitson & Galinsky, 2008).

when their sense of control is diminished (Figure 14.9; Kay et al., 2009; Whitson & Galinksy, 2008).

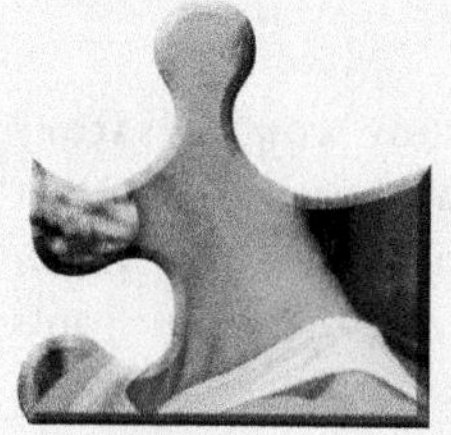

Can we critically evaluate this evidence?

A major advantage of the study described here is that the researchers were able to experimentally induce a perceived lack of control in the participants who received random feedback on their performance on the computerized task. The observation that these participants then perceived images within randomness and showed a heightened belief in superstition and conspiracies may help to explain how people respond to lost control outside of the laboratory. Of course, one limitation is that a real-world lack of control, such as that which occurs in the face of a natural disaster or the loss of a job, has far greater consequences. Thus, as with any laboratory experiment, there is a limit to the degree to which the results generalize.

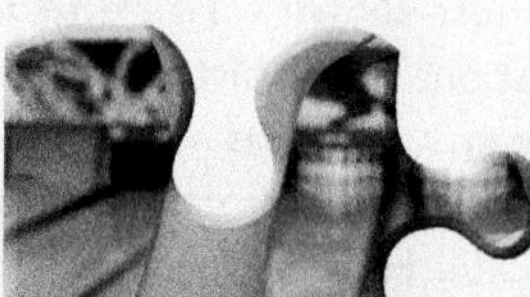

Why is this relevant?

Having a sense of control greatly affects how we think about and interpret the world. In addition, it affects our health. Individuals who believe they can predict and influence present and future events tend to have improved physical and mental well-being compared to people who believe the opposite. For example, patients who are scheduled to undergo medical procedures, such as a colonoscopy, have reduced anxiety for the procedure if they are given clear, informative tutorials about the procedure before it occurs (Luck et al., 1999).

Researchers have found that when people perceive that they have lost a sense of control during an experimental procedure, they report a greater need for structure, perceive images in random arrays, become more superstitious, and endorse conspiracy theories (Kay et al., 2009). These researchers have also suggested that religion is sometimes used as a form of compensatory control (Kay et al., 2010). What do you think?

Jyoti Sarkar/Shutterstock.com

People may also compensate for their lack of control by performing superstitious rituals, which can provide a sense of at least partial control over outcomes. This can be seen in everyday examples, such as among athletes who follow the same steps when preparing for a game (see Module 6.2), as well as in extreme, maladaptive forms, such as in obsessive–compulsive disorder (covered in Module 15.3).

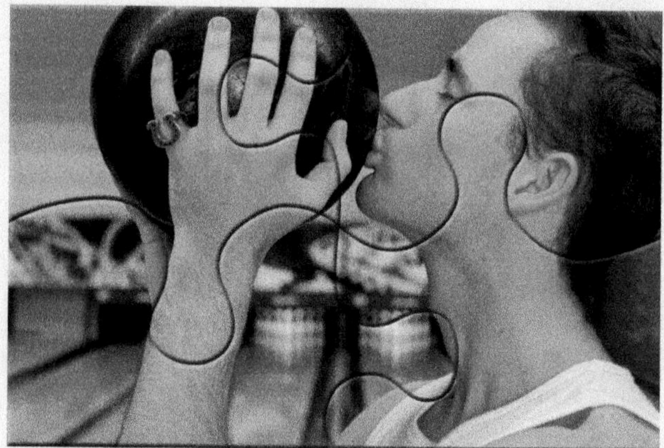

Russell Underwood/CORBIS/Flirt/Glow Images

Quick Quiz 14.3b

Perceived Control

KNOW ...

1 ________ is an acquired suppression of avoidance or escape behaviour in response to unpleasant, uncontrollable circumstances.

- **A** Compensatory control
- **B** Learned helplessness
- **C** Coping
- **D** Resilience

UNDERSTAND ...

2 People often turn to religion to explain natural disasters. This behaviour demonstrates the concept of ________ .

- **A** compensatory control
- **B** learned helplessness
- **C** coping
- **D** resilience

3 A mentally healthy person who is prone to claiming that patterns exist where there are none

- **A** is showing negative affectivity.
- **B** is showing signs of post-traumatic growth.
- **C** probably feels a lost sense of control over a problem or situation.
- **D** has a pessimistic explanatory style.

Answers can be found on page ANS-4.

Module 14.3

Module Summary

Now that you have read this module you should

KNOW ...

- ***The key terminology associated with coping and well-being:***

biofeedback (p. 614)
brain-derived neurotrophic factor (BDNF) (p. 617)
compensatory control (p. 619)
coping (p. 611)
learned helplessness (p. 618)
negative affectivity (p. 613)
optimism (p. 612)
pessimism (p. 612)
pessimistic explanatory style (p. 612)
positive psychology (p. 611)
post-traumatic growth (p. 614)
resilience (p. 613)

UNDERSTAND ...

- ***How control over the environment influences coping and outlook.*** Psychologists have discovered that people (and dogs) become more willing to allow unpleasant events to occur if they learn (or believe) that their behaviour brings no change. Having at least some degree of control helps people with coping and outlook. When control is threatened, people use compensatory responses, such as detecting order within random images.
- ***Positive and negative styles of coping.*** Whether someone copes using a positive or negative style is related to personality (e.g., optimism versus pessimism). Positive coping includes the concept of resilience—the ability to recover from adversity, and even benefit from the experience, as is the case with post-traumatic growth. Coping via negative affectivity and pessimism can have both psychological and physiological disadvantages.

John Lund/Stephanie Roeser/Glow Images

APPLY ...

- ***Your knowledge of the beneficial effects of optimism to help you reframe stressful situations as positive opportunities.*** For each of the following four situations, try to think of both a pessimistic and an optimistic way of interpreting the event.

  1. You find out that you are one of four people to be scheduled for an interview for a job you really want.
  2. Your flight home from Europe is overbooked, so your return home is delayed by a day.
  3. Your car has a flat tire and you have to bike 10 km to get to school in time for your 10 A.M. class.
  4. Your friend decides to stop attending the kickboxing class that you really enjoy.

  How did you feel after each optimistic and pessimistic interpretation? Did you feel better after putting a positive spin on things?

ANALYZE ...

- ***Whether activities such as relaxation techniques, meditation, and biofeedback actually help people cope with stress and problems.*** Meditation and other relaxation methods have been found to be quite effective in reducing stress. While some training and practice may be necessary, these techniques are by no means inaccessible to those who are motivated to pursue them.

Work the Scientific Literacy Model :: Stress and Health

1 What do we know about the nature of stress?

Review **Figure 14.5** on **page 602**, which outlined the pathways of stress in the body. All stress starts with an event, so it is important to know the difference between a stressor and stress. Recall that a stressor is an *event* that causes us to experience stress. This event can be either negative, such as getting stuck in traffic, or positive, such as becoming a parent. It is not even necessary for the event to actually occur—just the thought of an upcoming presentation can exert pressure on some students. Our *reaction* to the event is called stress, and it can take physical, emotional, mental, and behavioural forms. **Table 14.2** on **page 600** lists several possible stressors; you may want to try coming up with examples of your own, along with possible stress reactions. One example of a stressor would be taking your psychology final exam. A possible stress reaction: increased heart rate at the thought of the exam, and worrying about the exam the night before. Keep in mind that the same stressor can affect people differently.

On **page 599**, we covered Lazarus and Folkman's cognitive appraisal theory of stress. This theory predicts that we evaluate a stressor in terms of its stakes or importance, and then consider our resources for coping *before* we have a stress reaction.

2 How can science help explain stress and health?

The effects of stress on the immune system have been the focus of some interesting recent research. On **page 602**, we explained how the autonomic nervous system's response to stress can differ depending on the individual. Human and animal studies suggest that chronic stress, like parental deprivation during childhood and trauma, can have negative effects on brain development. Other research has linked chronic stress to coronary heart disease and the progression of various cancers. Even if you are dealing with stressors that seem more mundane, you may have a reduced immune response; this finding came out of a study in which medical students were shown to exhibit reduced immune responses during the stressful period of final exams. Personality also seems to play a role in the stress response, with research on people with Type A and Type B personalities suggesting that highly motivated, competitive, and quick-to-anger people (Type A) are more likely to have heart attacks than laid-back, easygoing Type B people.

Ase/Shutterstock

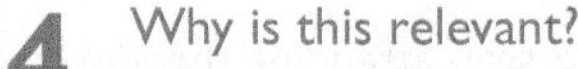

4 Why is this relevant?

Watch the accompanying video excerpt on reducing stress. You can access the video at MyPsychLab or by clicking the play button in the centre of your eText. If your instructor assigns this video as a homework activity, you will find additional content to help you in MyPsychLab. You can also view the video by using your smart phone and the QR code below, or you can go to the YouTube link provided.

After you have read this chapter and watched the video, imagine a friend has just lost a job that helped him cover tuition costs. Apply Lazarus and Folkman's cognitive theory of stress and describe his potential reactions to this job loss. In your answer, be sure to describe the following: Stressful Event; Primary Appraisal; Secondary Appraisal; Stress Response.

3 Can we critically evaluate claims about stress and health?

While it is true that Type A people tend to have more heart attacks, people who fall into that category are also more likely to engage in other risky behaviours, such as excessive alcohol consumption and smoking—both of which are also risk factors for heart disease. Similarly, in the **Myths in Mind** feature on **page 606**, we debunked the idea that chronic stress causes ulcers. Ulcers are caused by infection with a type of bacteria, but high levels of stress can certainly worsen their symptoms.

An important consideration when assessing much of the research relating stress to physical and mental health in humans is the fact that it is correlational. However, experiments using animals often do confirm the existence of cause-and-effect relationships between stress and health.

MyPsychLab **Your turn to Work the Scientific Literacy Model:** Watch the accompanying video on YouTube, or on your phone (using the Layar app or QR code). If your instructor has assigned this as a homework activity, you can find the video clip and additional content at MyPsychLab. Answer the questions that accompany the video clip to test your understanding.

15

Psychological Disorders

Irmak Akcadogan/Shutterstock

MPI/Archive Photos/Getty Images

Module 15.1

Defining and Classifying Psychological Disorders

Learning Objectives

After reading this module you should

KNOW ...	UNDERSTAND ...	APPLY ...	ANALYZE ...
The key terminology associated with defining and classifying psychological disorders	The differences between the concepts of psychological disorders and insanity	Your knowledge to understand the symptoms, stereotypes, and stigma surrounding psychological disorders	Whether the benefits of labelling psychological disorders outweigh the disadvantages

Over the centuries, our understanding of psychological disorders has come a very, very long way. The unfortunate people who had experiences that were out of the ordinary, from odd behaviours to visions to hallucinations, may well have been judged to be under the sway of evil spirits inhabiting their bodies (Hunter & Macalpine, 1963). By the 16th century, this led to the witch scares, which for at least two centuries created mass paranoia as the public sought protection from witches who gained power through allegiance to the devil. Armed with the *Malleus Maleficarum (Hammer of the Witches)*, a 1486 German text filled with detailed instructions for identifying witches, countless people were subjected to "tests," such as looking for the "Devil's mark" on the body, a visible spot such as a mole or birthmark that could be interpreted as a sign of allegiance with the Devil.

"Treatments" for mental illness were directly based on this model of illness as possession by evil. Brutal imprisonment, torture, and demon exorcism were not designed with human psychology in mind, as ways of rehabilitating dysfunctional thoughts, emotions, and behaviours. The focus was on driving the demon out of the person's body, or simply executing them, as in the witch-hunting craze which saw the execution of tens of thousands of innocent people (almost all of whom were women).

Thankfully, times have changed.

Focus Questions

 Are psychological disorders fundamentally different from physical illnesses, or should we view them the same way?

 Which guidelines or criteria allow psychologists to diagnose a mental disorder such as post-traumatic stress disorder (PTSD)?

As the ascension of scientific thought began to displace the religious domination of the Middle Ages, explanations for mental illness shifted from demon possession to physical illnesses, believing that the person was suffering from some sort of health affliction.

Asylums, *residential facilities for the mentally ill*, were set up across Europe, with the general goal of curing the patients' bodily afflictions that gave rise to their symptoms. Their treatments would certainly not meet modern standards of medical care and were generally ineffective, such as draining up to 40% of a person's total blood volume! There were even treatments such as throwing the person into a pit of snakes. As unbelievable as that seems (not to mention how difficult it would be for doctors to make house calls . . .), the hope was to shock the person out of the diseased state (Szasz, 2006).

A fortunate change in society's approach to treating mental illness came with the courageous activism of two heroic figures, Philippe Pinel, a physician in France, and Dorothea Dix, a schoolteacher in the United States. Their tireless advocacy for the mentally ill led to widespread reforms that ushered in a new approach, called *moral treatment,* which led to patients being treated with kindness and decency, able to roam the hospital halls and get outside for fresh air. However, there were still virtually no effective treatments, and many people afflicted with mental illness were permanently incarcerated.

By the 1950s, over half a million people were in psychiatric hospitals in the United States, mostly long-term, but in 1955, everything changed. Chlorpromazine (called Thorazine in the U.S.) was introduced, and suddenly, people with schizophrenia and other disorders involving being "out of touch" with reality were able to function independently, even holding down jobs and living at home with their families. The success of chlorpromazine and other medications led to widespread deinstitutionalization, which saw the number of psychiatric inpatients drop by over 80% over the next three decades (Torrey, 1997).

The return of hundreds of thousands of people to regular life had its down sides, however, greatly increasing the number of homeless people as a result of former inpatients quitting their medications and slipping back into their disorders. Also, although these treatments made a substantial difference to many people's symptoms, they were not cures; as a result, there were countless challenges to overcome in order to reintegrate people with schizophrenia and similar disorders into their families and communities.

Unfortunately, helping people reintegrate into regular life has never been a central part of the psychiatric approach to treating mental illnesses. Of course, many mental health workers help people at the practical level, but this level of "treatment" is generally secondary; the emphasis is overwhelmingly on the person's symptoms, and treating the symptoms directly. The problem that prevents the field from sufficiently focusing on the larger, systemic challenge of helping people with mental illness learn to function effectively in the world is essentially a problem in the whole approach to mental illness, a problem that is so fundamental to the discipline that it remains almost invisible much of the time. The problem is basically that the guiding paradigm for mental health and mental illness is the medical model, which has held sway since the end of the Middle Ages. The **medical model** *sees psychological conditions through the same lens as Western medicine tends to see physical conditions—as sets of symptoms, causes, and outcomes, with treatments aimed at changing physiological processes in order to alleviate symptoms.* Through this lens, psychological disorders such as depression, post-traumatic stress disorder, or autism can be approached in the same manner as conventional medicine would approach diabetes or cancer. What the medical model is generally missing is an appreciation for the whole system of factors that affects the person's overall functioning. Thus, the medical model could be critiqued as being overly narrow, more focused on "cure" than on promoting wellness and helping the person become stronger more generally.

In recent decades, the medical model has begun to be overturned in favour of the biopsychosocial model, which includes physiological processes within a more holistic view of the person as a set of multiple interacting systems (Table 15.1). For example, depression involves biological factors (e.g., the neurotransmitter serotonin), psychological factors (e.g., negative beliefs about the self and feelings of hopelessness), and social factors (e.g., social isolation or conflictual relationships). Understanding the multiple systems that underlie disorders such as depression gives us greater insight into how to develop

Table 15.1 :: Biological, Psychological, and Sociocultural Factors Influence Both Physical and Mental Disorders

	DIABETES	MAJOR DEPRESSION
Biological	Genetic influences on pancreatic function; excessive refined sugars	Genetic influences on neurotransmitter production and function; sleep disruption; lack of positive emotional arousal
Psychological	Poor food choices; sedentary lifestyle; alcohol abuse	Negative self-concept; pessimism; negative life experiences
Sociocultural	Familial and cultural foods and traditions; limited budget for groceries; lack of physical and nutritional education in the schools; lack of role models	Lack of social support; social withdrawal; lack of psychological services; stigma regarding psychological treatments

more effective treatments; in particular, it becomes easier to see how important it is to use convergent treatment approaches, treating more than one system at a time so as to affect the person's overall functioning.

Despite the advances of the biopsychosocial model, one of the thorniest problems in the mental health field remains how to reliably identify who has a mental disorder in the first place! Given the immense range of "normal" human behaviour and experience, how can we determine what is "abnormal?"

Defining Abnormal Behaviour

In some ways, you might expect it to be simple to decide whether or not someone has a disorder—you just have to figure out whether or not they are "normal." However, what is considered normal has an enormous range, particularly across time and culture. Think about what is considered normal in different cultures; the sheer diversity is staggering. One of the main insights to have come into our collective awareness from the study of anthropology is just how incredibly diverse human cultures and cultural practices can be. "Normal" can be owning slaves, or it can be living in a religious farming commune; normal can be daily drug trafficking and regular violence on a particular city block; it can be repressive boarding schools, or religiously influenced societies that hold strict gender norms and provide very different amounts of freedom and power to men and women. Normal can be village dances where everyone links arms and dances together mostly naked, or it can be the current club culture of North American youth (which is similar in some respects to the village culture, minus the linking of arms).

Simulate Survey: Are You Normal?

It is amazing to pause for a moment and think about this diversity, and how, from the "inside" perspective of the people living in that culture, their practices seem perfectly normal and even right, the way things should be; but take just a small step outside that cultural framework, and look at it from a different perspective, and everything changes.

Of course, this means that from the "inside" perspective of your own mind, your own beliefs and values and lifestyle are also culturally bound, and would look very different from other perspectives. It can be easy to forget this as we go through life, because the way we see things seems to make so much sense that we often become trapped in a particular perspective. Remembering to appreciate just how constructed our perspectives are can be quite liberating.

However, this does create a real challenge for the clinical psychologist, who is trying to determine whether a person's behaviour and experience are abnormal—whether they have a disorder that needs to be treated. It is obviously problematic to be judging normalcy by using your own particular cultural framework, although it is also practically impossible not to do so, as we are always operating within our cultural framework. Overcoming this challenge requires that each person works hard to understand the ways her own perspective may bias her, as well as directly learning about alternative perspectives, as much as possible. But there is no easy path to judging someone as being "abnormal."

One possible solution to this problem would be to first understand the appropriate cultural framework and perspective, and then find out whether most people in that culture or having that perspective would have similar experiences. If so, then even though the behaviour pattern might seem problematic from one perspective, it would be appropriately judged from within its own framework. This makes a good deal of sense, but consider the problem that the way that "most people" experience things may itself not be very healthy or desirable, or the way that a small subgroup experiences things may be quite healthy or desirable. For example, only a minority of the population practises regular meditation, exercises vigorously, follows a vegetarian diet, or completely abstains from drugs and alcohol during adolescence. Yet each of these practices can be seen to be healthy or desirable, in that they make people healthier, stronger, and generally happier. However, such "abnormal" behaviours are often judged negatively; consider the fact that in past decades, there were various sexual disorders with which individuals could be diagnosed as a result of having non-heterosexual preferences; now, psychologists' perspectives have changed, and alternatives to heterosexuality are no longer considered disorders, although they are still, *statistically speaking*, "abnormal."

In sum, determining what is normal and what is abnormal is fraught with difficulty and subjective bias; making this judgment is a process one should approach sensitively and with a great deal of self-awareness.

The key criterion used by psychologists in deciding whether a person has a disorder is whether the person's thoughts, feelings, or behaviours are **maladaptive**, which, according to the American Psychiatric Association (2000), is determined by three key criteria, *whether it causes distress to oneself or others, impairs day-to-day functioning, or increases the risk of injury or harm to oneself or others.*

However, there are many exceptions, behaviours that would fulfill these criteria but not necessarily indicate mental illness. Consider the following:

- Heavy drug users and people with psychopathic tendencies may not think they have a problem.
- Family members may be concerned about a person's involvement in a new relationship, or may disapprove of body modifications such as tattoos or piercings.

- Mourning the loss of a loved one or having a religious conversion may interfere with one's day-to-day activities.
- Activists may get arrested for protesting government actions and extreme sports enthusiasts may risk death or injury out of passion for their sport.

Obviously, the criteria are not perfect and do not account for all circumstances, as noted in the examples above. But generally speaking, when a person's behaviour and experience meet these criteria, there is cause for possible concern; thus, these guiding principles are a useful starting point for the diagnostic process. In order to make more specific diagnoses and determine exactly what type of disorder a person may have, mental health professionals rely on a carefully designed system.

PSYCHOLOGY'S PUZZLE: HOW TO DIAGNOSE PSYCHOLOGICAL DISORDERS The attempt to develop a rigorous system for diagnosing mental illness goes back to at least 1840, when the U.S. government wanted to collect data on mental illness in the country and included in the official census a single category to denote mental illness, "idiocy/insanity." By 1917, this had evolved into a guide for mental hospitals, called the "Statistical Manual for the Use of Institutions for the Insane." In World War II, American psychiatrists were hired in large numbers by the U.S. military to aid in the selection of soldiers and treatment for mental disturbances as a result of military duty.

Building on the military's diagnostic system, as well as the sixth edition of the World Health Organization's International Statistical Classification of Disease (which included mental disorders), the American Psychiatric Association created the **Diagnostic and Statistical Manual of Mental Disorders (DSM)**, *a standardized manual to aid in the diagnosis of disorders*; this edition described the symptoms of 106 different "mental disorders." The purpose for developing the DSM was to provide mental health workers with a reliable method for diagnosing mental illness and to ensure consistency across different institutions and hospitals.

It is worth noting that from the very beginning, the DSM was rooted in a psychobiological view, which argued that mental disorders represented specific reactions that an individual's personality had to psychological, social, and biological processes. However, other emphases changed over the years, from an initial focus on psychodynamic views to a later focus on cognitive and biological perspectives. By the mid-1990s, the DSM had gone through several revisions, and expanded to include a much greater number of disorders (more than 350!).

Why are there so many more disorders (about four times more) now than half a century ago? The answer to this question may depend on your perspective. Some would argue that as clinical science has progressed we are now better able to diagnose people, and the new disorders are entirely valid categorizations of symptoms. Another more disturbing possibility is that the creation of ever-more categories of disorders has been engineered in part by pharmaceutical companies as a way of increasing the number of disorders people will need to be treated for. This topic has become a battlefield between those who believe science is continually improving our understanding of mental illness, and those who believe that more aspects of human experience are being pathologized in order to feed the profits of pharmaceutical companies.

Whatever the ultimate reason, the DSM remains the standard reference manual in the mental health field, particularly in North America. The latest edition, the DSM-5, was published in May 2013. In order to aid in the process of diagnosis, the DSM-5 describes three important pieces of information for each disorder: a set of symptoms and the number of symptoms that must be met in order to have the disorder; the **etiology** (*origins or causes*) of symptoms; and a prognosis or prediction of how these symptoms will persist or change over time.

One of the big changes in the DSM-5 compared to previous versions is that it discarded the five-axis system that was used in the past. Until DSM-5 clinicians guided by the DSM made their evaluations along five separate axes or dimensions of functioning, the assumption being that integrating these different types of information would result in a more complete diagnostic understanding of the individual. The five axes were as follows: Axis I: clinical disorders (including depression, anxiety disorders, ADHD, or substance abuse problems); Axis II: personality disorders and mental retardation; Axis III: general medical conditions; Axis IV: psychosocial and environmental problems (i.e., life circumstances, such as relationship or work problems, which can impact psychological functioning); and Axis V: the global assessment of functioning (GAF).

Simulate
Overview of Clinical Assessment Methods

Simulate
Overview of Clinical Assessment Tools

In place of this system, the DSM-5 has separate categories for the different disorders that used to appear under different axes (especially axes I and II). Also, several disorders were reorganized or renamed; for example, mental retardation was replaced with the term *intellectual disability* (or *intellectual developmental disorder*), and obsessive-compulsive and related disorders became their own category, whereas in the past they were subtypes of anxiety disorders.

The creation of the DSM-5 was a highly contentious process that received a great deal of criticism within the field of mental health. In particular, critics of the new approach have argued that pharmaceutical companies have had too much influence over the guidelines described in the DSM (the net result being to make it easier for individuals to be given a diagnosis, thereby increasing the demand for pharmacological treatments). The overall impact of these changes remains to be determined, as the mental health community is only now at the beginning of transitioning from using the DSM-IV to the DSM-5.

Furthermore, the DSM-5 does not resolve the critiques that have been lodged against past versions. For one, the diagnosis of specific disorders is often not highly reliable, definitions are not always based on empirical evidence, and different disorders often share many common symptoms. This leads to a lack of agreement among mental health professionals about how to classify many disorders, and the frequent possibility that a given person will receive a different diagnosis if she goes to different therapists or doctors. The DSM also sends the implicit message that disorders can be objectively defined, although the entire process of deciding a given pattern of behaviour implies mental illness is highly subjective and depends upon prevailing beliefs and norms operating in a given time and culture; consider, for example, that homosexuality was once considered a disorder, and as we discussed earlier, there is no objectively correct way to determine whether a person's symptoms are indicative of a mental illness or not.

Critics also express concern that giving mental health workers more labels with which to diagnose clients is not necessarily a good thing and may lead to overdiagnoses. This is especially problematic in certain contexts, because the diagnosis provides both an explanation for what is happening with a person who is struggling, and that there is hope that the problem can be treated. Think of how powerful the temptation would be in many situations to reach for readily available solutions, such as drugs that purport to treat the disorder, without fully considering the costs that might result, or alternative perspectives and potential solutions to the problems one is experiencing.

As one example, consider attention deficit/hyperactivity disorder (ADHD), which is commonly applied to children who are having problems adjusting to elementary school (especially boys, who are at least three times more likely to be diagnosed with ADHD than girls; Barkley, 1998). For most children, by the time their parents and teachers decide to get them assessed for a psychological disorder such as ADHD, they will all likely have been witnessing an accumulation of problematic behaviours on the part of the child—getting in trouble for being restless or misbehaving in class, forgetting to do homework, interrupting frequently during conversations, not paying attention in class, and steadily falling behind in school. Imagine how welcome such a diagnosis would be, especially perhaps to the parents or teachers who would appreciate having some help in the form of medication that can help children function effectively and, ideally, reach their full potential, or at the very least, become more manageable.

Interestingly, since being included in the DSM, ADHD diagnoses have skyrocketed, although only in North America; in Europe, ADHD only seems to occur 10% as often. Also, there is a very wide range of estimates as to how many children have ADHD, ranging from the most common rate of 3–5% up to about 20% (Shaywitz & Shaywitz, 1991). Whether North Americans are massively overdiagnosing ADHD, or whether Europeans and others are missing the vast numbers of people with ADHD in their population, is not something we can know, but it is worth thinking about, because if ADHD is so highly subjective and susceptible to being used as a way of pharmacologically controlling people, then this would be a problem.

Along this line of reasoning, critics charge that the handy availability of the ADHD diagnosis makes it too easy to pathologize children and then medicate them to fix the pathology. The critics' argument that generations of children are being exposed to the long-term effects of stimulant medications that are generally used for treating ADHD is especially troublesome in light of studies showing that many children, between 20% to 70% of children diagnosed with ADHD, no longer meet the criteria once they reach adulthood (Weiss & Hechtman, 1993). Given that medications inevitably bring increased risk of a wide variety of problems, particularly when relied upon over time, it is of utmost importance to ensure that diagnoses are made in as careful and unbiased a manner as possible.

Perhaps one solution for improving the diagnostic accuracy of the DSM is to develop more objective, biological indicators such as genetic markers, indicators of neurotransmitter dysfunction, or brain abnormalities, that are involved in the symptoms and functional deficits experienced by the individual. These efforts are under way, although the field has a long way to go before such biological markers can be substantially incorporated into diagnostic criteria (Hyman, 2007). A focus on the biological markers of functional deficits and symptoms would also potentially help to shift mental health practitioners away from the reliance on classifying people into particular disorder categories, and instead develop more individualized approaches for understanding the particular manifestation of symptoms for each individual. In other words, by understanding what is not working for a person, we can develop ways of fixing the necessary systems, thereby "fixing" the disorder. There is a subtle shift in this line of reasoning, away from thinking in terms of disorders themselves, as though there are "diseases of the mind" that we must cure, and instead thinking in terms of actual processes (cognitive, emotional, neurological) that are being affected.

One additional weakness of the DSM approach is that there is a fine, and essentially arbitrary, line between whether a person is considered to have a disorder or not. For each disorder, the DSM provides a list of possible symptoms, and guidelines as to how many of the symptoms the person must have before being given the diagnosis. If a person seems to have the necessary number (e.g., five out of nine possible symptoms), then he has the disorder, but with one symptom less, he doesn't. In practice, what this means is that the diagnosis a person receives, and even whether a person receives any diagnosis at all, can depend on a single symptom. The accuracy problem this creates is then compounded by the fact that symptoms themselves are often thought of by a clinician in an either/or fashion: Either you have the symptom or you do not. However, many symptoms consist of quite normal thoughts and behaviours (e.g., difficulty sleeping, anxious thoughts), but to be considered actual symptoms of a disorder they must be more severe or longer-lasting than usual, or occur in inappropriate contexts or without any clear reason. Obviously, making such judgment calls is a highly subjective process that may be fraught with error, leaving it very likely that a given person might be deemed mentally ill by one doctor who checks off symptom boxes a little more readily, but be deemed normal by another doctor who has more strict and conservative interpretations of people's symptoms. The long-term effects of this can be substantial. Imagine a person with a considerable amount of anxiety, odd behaviour patterns, and a strong need to control the environment who is evaluated by a clinician in early adulthood when these patterns are just starting to develop. Depending on exactly what had been happening in that person's life and recent experiences, coupled with that clinician's particular biases and ways of interpreting things, several different diagnoses might be possible, such as obsessive-compulsive disorder, or generalized anxiety disorder, or potentially borderline personality disorder; or he could be seen as "sub-clinical," meaning that his symptoms do not quite meet the criteria for diagnosis, from which the person may conclude that he is "normal" and be resistant to ever admitting that he has problems he would benefit from working on.

As people enter the world of mental health care, they enter a system that offers very powerful treatments and ways of managing what can otherwise be devastating psychological conditions. However, they also enter a decision-making system that is less accurate than we would like. This can be a serious problem, because once a person has been labelled as having a disorder, the label itself may change how that person is viewed by others, and how subsequent behaviours are interpreted.

WORKING THE SCIENTIFIC LITERACY MODEL

Labelling and Mental Disorders

What are the outcomes of diagnosing and labelling the disorder a person is believed to be experiencing? On the positive side, it is hoped that receiving a diagnosis of mental illness should make people more likely to seek and receive effective treatment; also, receiving a diagnosis of a specific disorder should facilitate communication among mental health professionals: A label indicates a set of symptoms, probable causes, and potential treatments, thus helping to summarize a given person's experience and highlight the important pieces of information that will be useful for understanding and treating the person. However, these diagnostic labels can also have their drawbacks, such as biasing how people will subsequently interpret the person's actions or experiences, or changing how people feel about themselves.

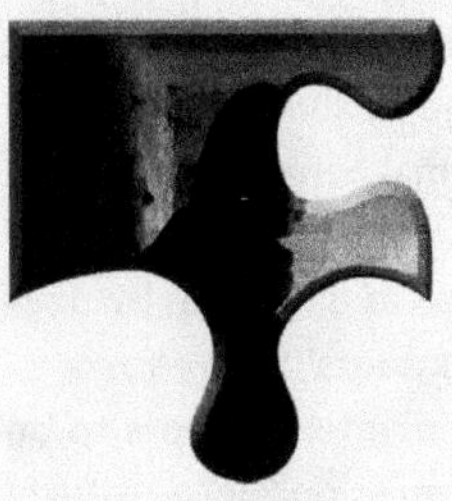

What do we know about how labels affect people?

It is important to put the following information in the proper context, which is the recognition that diagnostic labels can be very helpful; they can help people understand their experiences and communicate in a standardized way with whoever they may need to as they manage their symptoms and navigate the mental health-care system. Understanding the precise disorder can, ideally, help clinicians to prescribe effective treatments.

However it is also, unfortunately, the case that being labelled with a mental illness can potentially damage a person's material, social, and psychological well-being in a variety of ways (Link et al., 1989; Rosenfield, 1997). For example, seeing oneself as "mentally ill" has been shown to be associated with low self-esteem or feelings of helplessness; in some cases, a diagnosis may lead a person to indulge in even more extreme or destructive behaviour patterns. Further problems arise because of the ways in which society's general views toward the mentally ill become experienced and often internalized by the mentally ill themselves. People may begin to expect others to reject and devalue them, which feeds the tendency to withdraw from social contact (Kroska & Harkness, 2006; Link, 1987). People may also become demoralized about their capabilities and themselves in general, which then interferes with their motivations and goal-related striving. Sadly, in a classic self-fulfilling prophecy (see Module 13.2), the long-term effects can be that people end up experiencing the social rejection and stigmatization they initially feared (Kroska & Harkness, 2006).

How can science explain how labels may affect perceptions of another person's behaviour?

One of the most surprising and daring studies ever conducted in psychology occurred in the early 1970s, when eight people, volunteering with David Rosenhan, decided to get themselves committed to psychiatric hospitals. None of the eight were experiencing any symptoms of mental illness, but when they went to their doctors and complained that they were hearing voices, they received diagnoses for schizophrenia or bipolar disorder, and were admitted to a psychiatric hospital for observation and treatment. Once they were in the hospital, the challenge was to convince the doctors that there was, in fact, nothing wrong with them and they could be released back to their regular lives.

Once admitted, the volunteers exhibited no further symptoms and simply tried to behave "normally." Nevertheless, their behaviours were often interpreted as abnormal in some way by their doctors, so that even normal behaviours such as asking a question to a doctor, or talking about one's relatively normal childhood, would be interpreted as abnormal by doctors or hospital staff. Despite the volunteers' best efforts to be released, it took from 7 to 59 days for their doctors to be convinced their symptoms were "in remission"; interestingly, in that time period, they were also given a total of 2100 pills to take (which they merely pretended to take but were able to dispose of when nobody was looking) (Rosenhan, 1973).

Watch

Special Topics: Diagnosing Mental Disorders

Can we critically evaluate this information?

It is tempting to ask whether the labels applied to psychological disorders are beneficial or harmful, but this question may actually oversimplify the situation. For one, the advantages of this system are clear for professionals: Labels are a necessary means of identifying and describing the problems they encounter. There is also evidence to suggest that labels help individuals understand their own situation, and the labels may hold out hope for successful treatment. Some psychologists who are in favour of labels have argued that Rosenhan's study fails to address the larger issue of labels, because the symptoms he used were so marked and severe; auditory hallucinations are such a hallmark of disorders such as schizophrenia that it would be virtually impossible, perhaps even irresponsible, for a doctor to fail to diagnose an appropriate disorder and to use this diagnosis in judging the person's subsequent behaviours. Thus, it seems that labels can be both helpful and harmful in certain instances. In an ideal world, we would be able to keep the labels and get rid of the stigma. That may not be entirely possible, but it is a goal for psychologists and community groups to work toward.

Why is this relevant?

Many of the potential costs or risks associated with being diagnosed with a psychological disorder stem from the more general problem of stigma toward mental illness. Researchers from a number of academic areas have identified some techniques that work in reducing stigmatization. For example, research shows that personal contact and knowledge of biopsychosocial explanations of mental illness are associated with lower stigma (Boyd et al., 2010). Education seems to matter, too: When individuals are instructed about the first-person experience of mental illness, they show greater acceptance than groups that simply learn the facts about mental illness (Mann & Himelien, 2008). On campus, you might find a chapter of a student organization known as Active Minds, a group that operates in several countries including Canada and the United States, and has had success in reducing the stigma associated with mental illness at some campuses (McKinney, 2009). Keep these findings in mind as you read the rest of this chapter; as an informed student you will be less likely to judge others and more likely to seek help yourself, or recommend it to others, if it is ever needed.

Michael Mercer/Alamy

Quick Quiz 15.1a
Defining Abnormal Behaviour

KNOW ...

1 Rosenhan's classic study "On Being Sane in Insane Places" showed that

A psychiatric institutions actually make disorders more likely, because they reinforce odd behaviour and they offer ready-made labels that people use to "pathologize" themselves.

B therapists who come from a Freudian, psychoanalytic background can easily be tricked into believing people have a disorder that they do not in fact have, whereas therapists who are trained in a modern cognitive-behavioural-therapy type of framework do not make this same mistake.

C once people have been labelled with a specific disorder, this will change how other people interpret their behaviour and behave toward them.

D the presence of a mentally healthy person in a group of mentally ill patients can dramatically improve the functional scores of the patients.

UNDERSTAND ...

2 One problem with the DSM is that

A there is no objectively definable line separating normal from abnormal; thus, determining whether a person has a disorder or not relies upon criteria for distinguishing normal from abnormal, and those criteria are essentially arbitrary.

B the construction of the DSM may reflect the influence of the pharmaceutical industry.

C it may lead to overdiagnoses, because it provides diagnostic labels that can be appealing to people for a variety of reasons (such as offering hope that treatment is possible, or making a child's behaviour more manageable).

D all of the above.

3 Which of the following is not a psychiatric criterion for mental illness?

A Expression of behaviour that causes distress to self or others

B The condition must be categorical

C Impairment of functioning

D Increased amount of high-risk behaviours (e.g., drug use, speeding)

Answers can be found on page ANS-4.

Applications of Psychological Diagnoses

Perhaps one of the most important things to appreciate about psychological disorders is that there is no perfect test for identifying them, nor a rigid line separating "normal" from "abnormal" when it comes to human psychology. Being able to reliably diagnose particular disorders is a central and ongoing challenge to the mental health fields, having an impact on problems that range from individuals knowing how to effectively navigate the mental health system (i.e., getting the appropriate treatment they need), to the stigmatization of the mentally ill (i.e., the problem of being misdiagnosed or having labels misapplied), to the use of the insanity defence in criminal trials (i.e., being able to accurately determine whether or not a person is criminally responsible for a crime they committed). Each of these issues is made more difficult to deal with by the fact that our measurements of psychological disorders are not nearly as accurate as we would like; in many cases, we cannot even say with confidence whether someone is mentally ill and what psychological illness or disorder they have.

THE MENTAL DISORDER DEFENCE (AKA THE INSANITY DEFENCE) This lack of diagnostic accuracy plays a big role in the criminal justice system. You have no doubt heard that in some trials a defendant will plead "not guilty by reason of insanity," which is now called the **mental disorder defence** in Canada. This defence does not deny that the person committed the offence, but *claims that the defendant was in such an extreme, abnormal state of mind when committing the crime that he or she could not discern that the actions were legally or morally wrong.* For example, a person could cause a car accident or commit murder when in a severely dissociated state, such as could occur due to schizophrenia or PTSD.

Thus, whether or not we can objectively and accurately measure "sanity" is extremely important, potentially making the difference between a person being a convicted felon or being in a psychiatric treatment program. However, determining that a person was not "sane" when committing a crime is not an easy thing to do, and the legal definition of sanity doesn't always reflect our intuitions.

Consider the following cases:

On June 20, 2001, Andrea Yates drowned all five of her children in the bathtub, one by one, carefully laying their bodies on her bed, side by side. This horrific murder seems impossible to comprehend. How could a person do such a thing? Surely she must be "insane!" As her psychological history was revealed to the public, it became apparent that in the years preceding the murders, Andrea Yates had experienced bouts of severe post-partum depression and psychosis, with multiple suicide attempts and psychiatric hospitalizations, and had been put on anti-psychotic medications. Although her initial trial resulted in a guilty verdict and life sentence, she was able to successfully appeal, and in 2006 was found not guilty by reason of insanity. Assuming that such a verdict is accurate, one can see the value of this defence; it would be horrific beyond belief to murder one's own children in a state of uncontrollable psychosis, and then, after the fact, to be found guilty of their murders and the rest of your life is to be spent behind bars. The amount of suffering such a person would go through is practically inconceivable.

Between 1978 and 1991, Jeffrey Dahmer murdered at least 15 men, committing utterly horrific acts to them both before and after they died. He engaged in sexual and cannibalistic acts with the corpses of his victims, and fully dismembered and dissected them, keeping various body parts in his refrigerator. With some of the victims, Dahmer had drilled holes into their skulls while they were still alive, and injected acid or boiling water into their brains.

It seems necessary to pause for a moment and reflect on just how outrageous the above paragraph is. To think that a human being could be so disconnected from normal human connection that he could commit such atrocities and to think of just what happened in his little apartment over those years is the worst of nightmares. Surely such a person must be "insane!" However, in 1992, the jury rejected Dahmer's insanity defence. Dahmer's crimes had been carefully orchestrated and planned, and were undertaken with his full intention to commit the harm that he did. He was aware that what he was doing was legally wrong, and he took steps to hide his actions and abduct his victims carefully so that they would not be able to get away. Dahmer also drank very heavily, and seemed to use alcohol as a way of lowering his inhibitions in many of the cases of his most horrific acts. He had a long history of alcohol and drug abuse and behaviour patterns consistent with extreme borderline personality disorder, various sexual paraphilias, and a profound self-hatred that he projected onto his victims. There is no doubt that Jeffrey Dahmer was severely psychologically disturbed. But in terms of his legal status, he was sane. Dahmer was sentenced to 15 consecutive life terms in prison. Two years later, in 1994, he was murdered by a fellow inmate.

Steve Ueckert/Pool/ZUMA Press/Newscom

Andrea Yates was found not guilty by reason of insanity. The jury believed she could not distinguish right from wrong at the time of the murders.

ALLEN FREDRICKSON/Reuters/Landov

Jeffrey Dahmer, however, was found to be sane. His admission of guilt and remorse suggested he did understand that what he did was wrong.

The reasoning behind these decisions about why Jeffrey Dahmer is considered sane while Andrea Yates is considered "insane" is based on the M'Naghten rule. That case happened in 1843 in Great Britain. Daniel M'Naghten was found to have assassinated the Prime Minister's secretary, but a jury was convinced that he was not to be found guilty, and they did not send him to jail. They believed that he had been incapable of knowing that what he did was wrong, so M'Naghten was committed to a mental institution, and the plea "not guilty by reason of insanity" entered the legal profession.

Applying the M'Naghten rule is extremely tricky, and indeed, it is rarely used. One study showed that this defence is used in fewer than 1% of federal cases in the United States—and it has a success rate of only 20% (Melton et al., 2007).

BIOPSYCHOSOCIAL PERSPECTIVES

Symptoms, Treatments, and Culture

Another key issue with diagnosing psychological disorders is that they may not present the same across different cultures, and a lack of appreciation for these cultural differences can potentially lead to misdiagnoses. For example, posttraumatic stress disorder (PTSD) is a common psychological

illness affecting almost 10% of the Canadian population (Van Ameringen et al., 2008). The disorder can be very long-lasting and debilitating, interfering with many aspects of a person's life because of recurring thoughts, images, and nightmares that induce symptoms of tension and often severe anxiety. And as the world is showing no signs of exposing people to fewer disasters, wars, and trauma, PTSD is going to be an unfortunate companion for many on the road of life.

Despite the seemingly universal physiological symptoms of PTSD, researchers have found interesting differences in the cognitive and emotional symptoms between some samples of people. For example, people who experienced trauma in the U.S.-led war in Afghanistan and the 2004 tsunami in the Indian Ocean showed somewhat different symptoms, depending on whether they were Americans or natives to the region (i.e., Afghans during the war, or Sri Lankans during the tsunami). Americans tended to report difficult internal experiences such as flashbacks, whereas Afghans and Sri Lankans were more likely to experience worries about the welfare of their families and communities more generally. Thus, recurring personal flashbacks seem to be more of an individualistic phenomenon, whereas recurring worries about others seem to be more of a collectivistic phenomenon (Fernando, 2008; Miller et al., 2006). It is important for mental health professionals to be sensitive to the cultural differences that may arise in the experience of a particular psychological disorder, and factoring such cultural differences into diagnostic research and practice remains an ongoing challenge.

Cultural differences play a role in treatments as well, in many different ways. For example, one of the more controversial possible breakthroughs in the treatment of PTSD involves psychological therapy combined with carefully prescribed doses of MDMA (the psychoactive component in the street drug ecstasy). Thus far, MDMA, in combination with psychological therapy, has proven to be an effective treatment for cases of PTSD that resist other forms of treatment (Mithoefer et al., 2013; Oehen et al., 2013). The effectiveness seems due to multiple mechanisms. For example, the oxytocin release induced by MDMA helps with the emotional bonding and trust that is essential to the therapeutic alliance between therapist and client (see Module 16.1), and the effects on serotonin seem beneficial for helping to reduce the anxiety that is key to PTSD. In short, MDMA helps people attain an open and secure state of mind so that they can more effectively face the trauma and begin to address, through therapy, the reactions it provokes. Of course, there are large cultural and sub-cultural differences in the acceptance of drugs such as MDMA, which is illegal in the United States and is associated with "rave culture," widespread abuse, and even occasional deaths in the minds of many. Andrew Feldmar, a psychologist in Vancouver involved in the research of MDMA, who advocates strongly for the potential benefits of psychedelics, has been permanently banned from entering the United States.

In sum, fully understanding disorders, from diagnosis to treatment, involves understanding the multiple systems involved in determining the individual's psychological health, from broad cultural attitudes and perspectives to the physiological mechanisms operating within individuals. As we become better at developing a full-systems understanding of disorders, by integrating the insights from the biological, psychological, and social levels of analysis, we should become better at learning to properly identify, manage, and ideally cure people of their psychological afflictions.

Hou Yu/ZUMAPRESS/Newscom

Survivors of major disasters are at risk for developing PTSD. Cultural factors influence the nature of the anxiety that people experience in the wake of such disasters.

Quick Quiz 15.1b

Applications of Psychological Diagnoses

UNDERSTAND ...

1 As described in this section, insanity

A is itself a psychological disorder.

B describes a person with any psychological disorder.

C is not recognized by the legal profession or judicial system.

D means that an individual could not distinguish between right and wrong when he or she broke a law.

APPLY ...

2 Which of the following statements about PTSD is true?

A People of all cultures experience the exact same concerns after trauma.

B Some cultures are immune to stress reactions.

C Physiological symptoms of PTSD may be common among people of different cultures, but the specific concerns people have can vary.

D PTSD occurs only in cultures that use a medical model.

Answers can be found on page ANS-4.

Module Summary

Module **15.1**

Now that you have read this module you should

KNOW ...

- ***The key terminology associated with defining and classifying psychological disorders***:

asylums (p. 625)
Diagnostic and Statistical Manual of Mental Disorders (DSM) (p. 627)
etiology (p. 627)
maladaptive (p. 626)
medical model (p. 625)
mental disorder defence (insanity defence) (p. 631)

UNDERSTAND ...

- ***The differences between the concepts of psychological disorders and insanity.*** It is important to make distinctions between the psychological concept of a disorder and the legal concept of insanity. The legal consideration of sanity hinges on whether people know, at the time when committing a crime, that their actions are wrong, in a legal or a moral sense. Thus, to be found legally insane is much more severe than being given a diagnosis for a psychological disorder. Obviously, the vast majority of people with disorders are considered sane, and even if people have a disorder and commit a crime, the disorder by no means excuses them from their actions. It is important to remember that, in order to have a disorder, the primary criterion is whether the behaviour is maladaptive, whereas in order to be found criminally not responsible, the primary criterion is whether the person knew what they were doing was wrong.

APPLY ...

- ***Your knowledge to understand the symptoms, stereotypes, and stigma surrounding psychological disorders.*** Researchers have created some simple measures of stigma. See how you compare to others by completing the scale in **Table 15.2**.

MPI/Archive Photos/Getty Images

ANALYZE ...

- ***Whether the benefits of labelling psychological disorders outweigh the disadvantages.*** To evaluate the importance of the DSM-5's labels, it would be helpful to consider their functions. They organize large amounts of information about symptoms, causes, and outcomes into terminology that mental health professionals can work with. From a practical point of view, this system meets the requirements of the insurance companies that pay for psychological services. One downside to this process is that once the label is applied, people have the tendency to misinterpret behaviours that are perfectly normal. Another downside is that if insurance and pharmaceutical companies have influence over how the guidelines are decided, then the whole system could be biased in favour of over-diagnosing and over-medicating people.

Table 15.2 :: Attitudes toward Mental Illness

Complete the following scale to measure your attitude toward mental illness. For each of the items, circle the number that best describes how much you agree or disagree with the statement.

ITEM	COMPLETELY DISAGREE			COMPLETELY AGREE	
If I had a mentally ill relative, I wouldn't want anyone to know.	1	2	3	4	5
Most of my friends would see me as being weak if they thought that I had a mental illness.	1	2	3	4	5
I would be very embarrassed if I were diagnosed as having a mental illness.	1	2	3	4	5
Mentally ill people scare me.	1	2	3	4	5
I would cross the street if I saw a mentally ill person coming in order to avoid passing him/her.	1	2	3	4	5
I think that mentally ill people are strange and weird.	1	2	3	4	5
Find your total score by adding up the numbers you circled and dividing by 6.					

Interpretation: This scale measures stigma toward individuals who have a mental illness. Compare your score to a large sample of high school students. Their average on this same scale was 2.13, with higher scores indicating greater levels of stigma. For those with a family member diagnosed with a mental disorder, the mean dropped to 2.05.

Source: Watson et al., 2005.

News-Journal/AP images

Module 15.2

Personality and Dissociative Disorders

Learning Objectives

After reading this module you should

KNOW ...	UNDERSTAND ...	APPLY ...	ANALYZE ...
The key terminology associated with personality and dissociative disorders	The phenomenon of dissociation and how a dissociative disorder might occur	The biopsychosocial model to understand the causes of personality disorders	The status of dissociative identity disorder as a legitimate diagnosis

Often, the people who commit harm to others have themselves suffered substantial harm from others; the abused person becomes the abuser, and the person with the angry father becomes an angry father himself. Of course, this may not always happen, because experiences that we have in life can also motivate us to change; the child of alcoholic parents becomes a non-drinker, or the survivor of childhood abuse becomes a deeply compassionate person who counsels others. Both patterns, stability and change, are possible. One of the distinct features of personality disorders are their stability, generally over the person's entire life, and as these patterns unfold in an individual's life, damage is invariably done to many others.

Consider the appallingly sad case of Aileen Wuornos (note: this story is potentially triggering or upsetting, particularly to people who have experienced abuse themselves). Aileen's life was one of those saddest of human stories, so relentlessly tragic that it became the inspiration for the 2003 movie, *Monster*, in which Charlize Theron won an Oscar for her portrayal of Aileen.

Aileen Wuornos grew up in a complete chaos of abuse and mental illness. Her father was incarcerated and mentally ill, thus being absent from her life. Her mother abandoned her, leaving her adopted, at age 4, by her grandparents. Wuornos later described a childhood of being sexually abused and beaten by her grandfather, of prostituting herself for money and cigarettes to others, and being raped and impregnated at age 13 by a friend of her grandfather's. The baby was given up for adoption, and by age 15, Aileen had been thrown out of the house and was supporting herself through prostitution.

With no stable home or healthy family relationships, she had very little capacity to develop trust in others or emotionally connect with others. When she was 20, she was, suddenly and surprisingly, wed to a wealthy yacht club owner; this might have been her ticket to a better life, but within weeks it had devolved into violence and conflict, and the marriage was eventually annulled. Over the next decade, Aileen struggled to keep her life together, but was arrested numerous times for offences ranging from forging cheques to armed robbery and car theft, leading her to spend some time in prison.

Then, when she was 33 years old, Aileen Wuornos's life of pain and trauma came spilling back out of her in a murderous frenzy. Over a one-year period spanning 1989 and 1990, she murdered seven men across the state of Florida. She initially claimed to have killed them in self-defence, in response to each of them attempting to rape her. Although diagnosed with borderline personality disorder and antisocial personality disorder, Wuornos was determined to be sane at the time of her killings and fit to stand trial. She was convicted and sentenced to death in the state of Florida (*Wuornos v. State of Florida*, 1994). In 2002, she was executed by lethal injection.

Focus Questions

 What are personality disorders, and how do they differ from normal personality traits?

 What are the key characteristics of dissociative disorders? Why does a person develop a dissociative disorder?

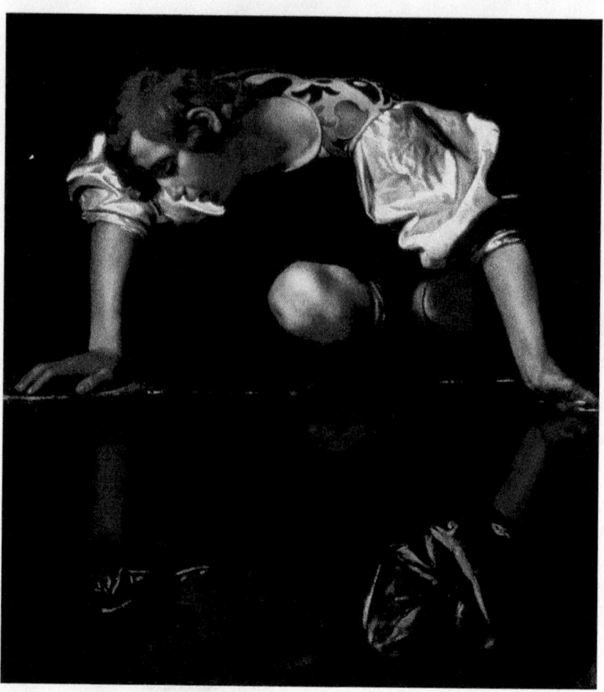

Narcissus, c.1597–99 (oil on canvas), Caravaggio, Michelangelo Merisi da (1571–1610)/Palazzo Barberini, Rome, Italy/The Bridgeman Art Library

According to Greek mythology, Narcissus discovered his image reflecting from the surface of a pool of water. Unable to tear himself away from the beauty of his own face, Narcissus wasted away and died at the water's edge. In modern times, narcissism describes a person who has an inflated sense of self-importance.

Chapter 12 described the psychological approaches to personality—the relatively stable patterns of thinking, behaving, and relating to others that make each person unique and are bound up with that person's identity. In certain unusual cases, personality patterns can become deeply entrenched and maladaptive or destructive, which is described as developing a personality disorder (PD).

Defining and Classifying Personality Disorders

Mental health professionals identify **personality disorders** as *particularly unusual patterns of behaviour (relative to one's cultural context) that are maladaptive, distressing to oneself or others, and resistant to change.* For example, some people feel no empathy toward others, even those in great distress. Others have intense needs and high expectations for receiving the attention and admiration of others, and tend to feel severely rejected if their expectations are not met. Other people may become rapidly and obsessively attached to another person, only to reject that individual at a future time. Obviously, many people experience these basic patterns of behaviour in varying degrees; it is important to remember that personality disorders represent extreme and persistent cases.

The DSM-5 identifies 10 distinct personality disorders, which are categorized into three different clusters based on shared features. Cluster A disorders are characterized by odd or eccentric behaviour, and include Paranoid Personality Disorder, Schizoid Personality Disorder, and Schizotypal Personality Disorder. Cluster B disorders are indicated by dramatic, emotional, and erratic behaviour, and include Antisocial Personality Disorder, Borderline Personality Disorder, Histrionic Personality Disorder, and Narcissistic Personality Disorder. Cluster C disorders are characterized by anxious, fearful, and inhibited behaviour, and include Avoidant Personality Disorder, Dependent Personality Disorder, and Obsessive-Compulsive Personality Disorder. In addition to these 10 disorders, the DSM-5 also identifies Personality Disorder Not Otherwise Specified, which is a diagnosis given to individuals who exhibit patterns of behaviour consistent with that of a personality disorder, but which does not fit into any of the personality disorder categories described above.

Although each personality disorder deserves to be expanded upon, we are going to explore the four disorders in Cluster B to get a sense of the overarching commonalities shared by disorders in a given cluster, as well as the specific factors that differentiate between them.

BORDERLINE PERSONALITY One of the clearest examples of the emotional dysfunction that lies at the core of personality disorders is found in borderline personality disorder (Blashfield & Intoccia, 2000). **Borderline personality disorder (BPD)** *is characterized by intense extremes between positive and negative emotions, an unstable sense of self, impulsivity, and difficult social relationships.* People with BPD experience a wide range of emotions including extremely positive states such as joy, excitement, and love, but also including negative and destructive emotions such as anger, despair, and shame.

Relationships are characterized by instability and intensity. A person with BPD may fall in love quickly and passionately, but also be highly fearful of abandonment and thus react intensely to any sign of rejection or criticism, and easily become disgusted with or rejecting of their partner. They also are often manipulative in relationships, attempting to keep the person attached to them and under their control. In fact, their emotional reactions and ability to be emotionally manipulative in relationships are so strong that many therapists will limit themselves to only one or a very small number of clients with BPD, because they can be so emotionally intense and exhausting.

It is believed that borderline personality disorder arises out of the person's attempts to deal with deeply rooted insecurity and severe emotional disturbances that are ultimately rooted in traumatic or emotionally difficult experiences, such as inconsistent, abusive, or neglectful parenting. To cope with or escape from negative emotions, the person often engages in impulsive, risky, or self-destructive behaviour, including substance abuse, indiscriminate sex, self-injury such as cutting or burning oneself, and even suicide (American Psychiatric Association, 2013; Linehan, 1993).

NARCISSISTIC PERSONALITY **Narcissistic personality disorder (NPD)** *is characterized by an inflated sense of self-importance and an excessive need for attention and admiration, as well as intense self-doubt and fear of abandonment.* The central focus on the narcissistic person's own feelings and self-importance leaves little room for empathy for others, and instead, they will tend to be manipulative, putting themselves first and ensuring that their own needs are met in their relationships, regardless of the toll it takes on others. In many public situations, such as school, people with NPD have a strong sense of "entitlement," believing that people should satisfy their demands, and being likely to do whatever it takes, including cheating, in order to ensure their own success (Brunell et al., 2011).

Watch
Janna: Borderline Personality Disorder

HISTRIONIC PERSONALITY Emotional dysfunction can also be seen in **histrionic personality disorder (HPD)**, *which is characterized by excessive attention seeking and dramatic behaviour.* "Histrionic" comes from a Latin word meaning "like an actor or like a theatrical performance"—an apt label for this disorder. People who have HPD are typically high-functioning because their dramatic nature makes them seem vibrant and attractive in social situations, and they readily use flirtatiousness, sexuality, and flattery to garner the social attention they crave. Similar to the other personality disorders discussed in this section, the histrionic person often engages in indulgent and risky behaviours, and tends to be highly sensitive to criticism and generally manipulative in relationships. The key difference between histrionic and the other personality disorders in this cluster is the flamboyance and exhibitionistic tendencies in histrionic behaviour.

WORKING THE SCIENTIFIC LITERACY MODEL

Antisocial Personality Disorder

The diagnosis of **antisocial personality disorder (APD)** is given to individuals who have a *profound lack of empathy or emotional connection with others, a disregard for others' rights or preferences, and a tendency toward inserting their own desires, often violently, onto others regardless of the consequences for other people or, often when younger, other animals.* As a psychological condition, it is highly resistant to treatment, in part because individuals with APD are not alarmed or distressed by their actions (although others frequently are), and they are thus rarely, if ever, motivated to change.

What do we know about antisocial personality disorder?

People with APD tend to be physically and verbally abusive, destructive, and frequently find themselves in trouble with the law. Symptoms of the disorder typically appear during childhood and adolescence, including harming or torturing people or animals, destroying property, stealing, and being deceitful (Lynam & Gudonis, 2005). The term "psychopath" is often used colloquially to describe a person who exhibits these types of behaviour, and indeed, the cold-blooded, remorseless murderer often fits the category of APD.

For some people with severe APD, the antisocial acts they commit are severe, and their lack of guilt or remorse is truly disturbing. This tendency was clearly evident in the words of Aileen Wuornos when she refused to appeal her death sentence:

> *I killed those men, robbed them as cold as ice. And I'd do it again, too. . . . There's no chance in keeping me alive or anything, because I'd kill again. I have hate crawling through my system. (CNN, 2002)*

Keep in mind that serial killers represent only a very small subset of people with antisocial tendencies. In fact, people with APD are often very successful, particularly in business, which often rewards the kind of calculating, aggressive disposition of the person with APD, particularly when coupled with the charm and social skills that many people with APD also possess. In fact, business managers often score highly on measures of antisocial personality tendencies, rivalling the scores of people with APD who are in jail. It is interesting to speculate for a moment on the implications for society if we construct our business and economic systems to reward antisocial qualities such as manipulativeness and lack of empathy.

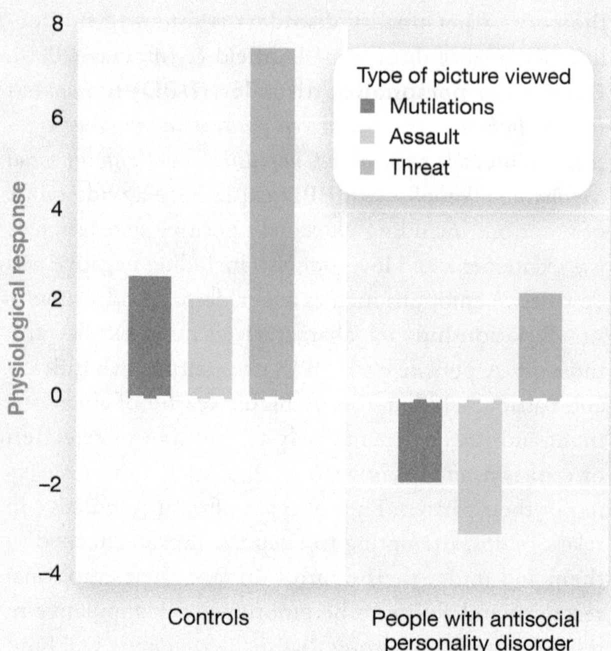

{FIG. 15.1} **Emotional Responses of Individuals with Antisocial Personality Disorder** This graph shows the strength of autonomic response to three types of pictures: mutilations, assault, and threat. Responses are much greater among control subjects (those who do not have APD; the three bars on the left) than among the individuals with antisocial personality disorder (the three bars on the right).

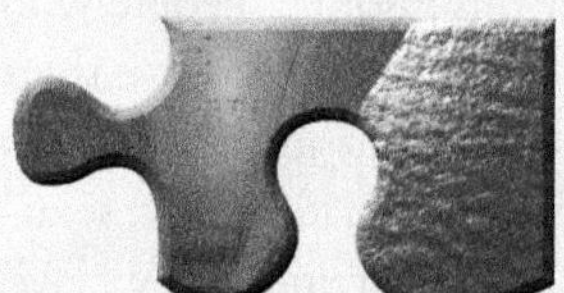

How can science explain antisocial personality disorder?

You may have heard stories of people who have "snapped" under stress and committed horrific acts—however, this type of extreme stress response does not at all characterize APD. In fact, researchers have discovered that people with antisocial personality disorder are under-reactive to stress. For example, a flash of light, a loud sound, or the sudden appearance of an angry face will startle most people. In contrast, people with APD show very weak startle responses—such as blinking—when exposed to unpleasant stimuli. In one study, researchers recorded the electrical signals of the eyeblink muscles while presenting disturbing images to a group of people with APD and a control group without APD. You can see the results in Figure 15.1, in which the strength of the startle response is indicated by the height of the bars. The group of people with APD (the bars on the right side) have much weaker responses than the group without APD (on the left; Levenston et al., 2000).

This reduced reactivity to stress is part of a larger system of emotion regulation processes, which corresponds to a neurological system of brain areas that tie together thinking and reasoning, agency and will, and emotion. Central brain areas include parts of the prefrontal cortex (in particular the orbitofrontal cortex), amygdala, anterior cingulate cortex, and other regions (Davidson et al., 2000); see Figure 15.2.

The amygdala is centrally involved in the experience of one's own emotions and those of other people. As a result, extremely important functions, including feeling empathy for others, and learning through fear and punishment, are dependent on the amygdala (Rolls, 1999). When the amygdala is not functioning properly, people are less able to empathically connect with others, to feel the impact of negative emotions, and to be less responsive to negativity in general. Without the negative emotional information and control provided by the amygdala, the person becomes desensitized to the environment and the general experiences of life, and may therefore seek more extreme experiences in order to *feel something.* Less able to empathize with others, it may be easier for people with APD to be manipulative, abusive, or otherwise cruel; they may veer toward antisocial activities because of the feeling of excitement, arousal, and power it gives them, in conjunction with the fact that they are unaffected by the guilt and other moral emotions that would normally restrain people from committing harm.

This sets them on a developmental trajectory that commonly leads to committing violent and antisocial acts; engaging in aggressive, risky, or self-destructive behaviours; and having volatile and generally dysfunctional interpersonal relationships.

Although all of us "lose control" at some point in our lives, most of the time, people without APD are able to control their negative emotional reactions and are responsive to cues in the environment, such as signs of fear or anger in the faces or behaviour of others (Davidson et al., 2000).

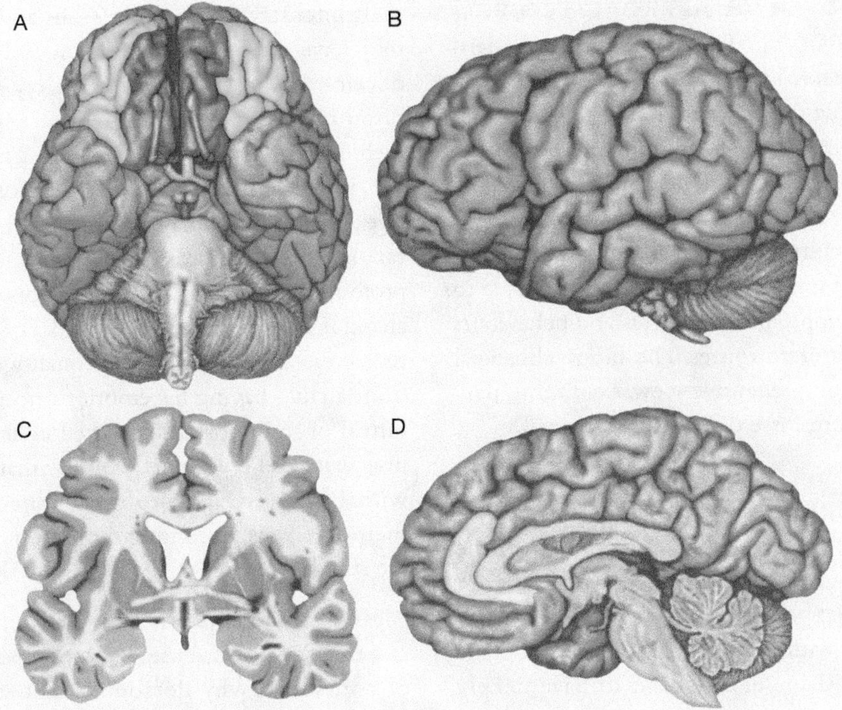

{FIG. 15.2} **Emotion Regulation in the Brain**

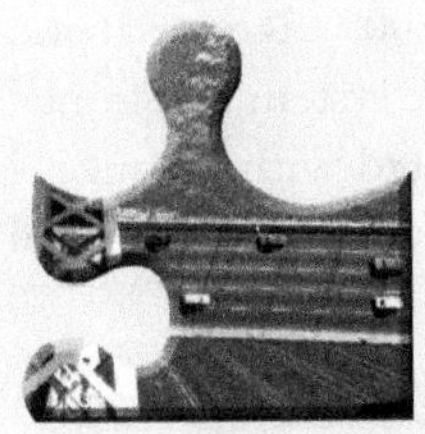

Can we critically evaluate this information?

One cautionary note to keep in mind when reading about antisocial personality disorder is that we must be careful not to assume that all people with APD are violent criminals, gleefully harming others indiscriminantly. Ironically, many of the characteristics of APD may themselves be highly desirable in our competitive corporate culture. The ability to emotionally detach from people, to be manipulative and able to deceive or lie without any moral reservations, to be charming and charismatic so as to appear to connect with people even though you can easily see people as tools to be used to satisfy your own desires, may well be rewarded in the worlds of CEOs, lawyers, salespeople, and undoubtedly many other social environments. These personality traits give people great power over others, because they are able to use others for their own personal gain without being held back by moral constraints (Lykken, 1995). Thus, the abusive boyfriend, the charming corporate ladder-climber, the intensely focused surgeon, the serial killer, or the socially inhibited hermit may all be outcomes of antisocial personality disorder.

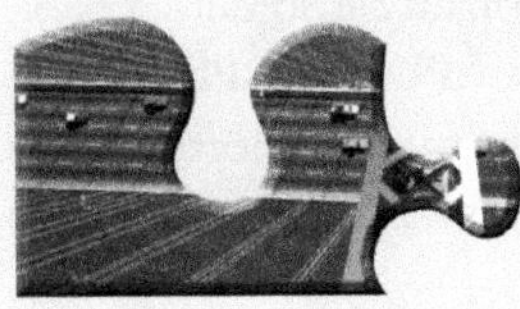

Why is this relevant?

Identifying how physiology and brain function differ in people with APD is certainly helpful for psychologists who are trying to understand the underlying basis for these disturbing behavioural patterns. People with APD tend to be highly resistant to psychological therapies, making it even more critical to understand the underlying biological processes. Also, antisocial patterns are often detectable during childhood and adolescence, which are critical periods of brain development. If a system of early diagnosis and treatment could be instituted, it might be possible to more effectively intervene before the person develops the full manifestation of the disorder, and before committing much harm.

From a larger perspective, the possibility that so much of our current post-industrial, globalizing culture rewards traits associated with APD seems to warrant taking a pause and asking, does this make sense? Are these the tendencies that we want to be encouraging in our society?

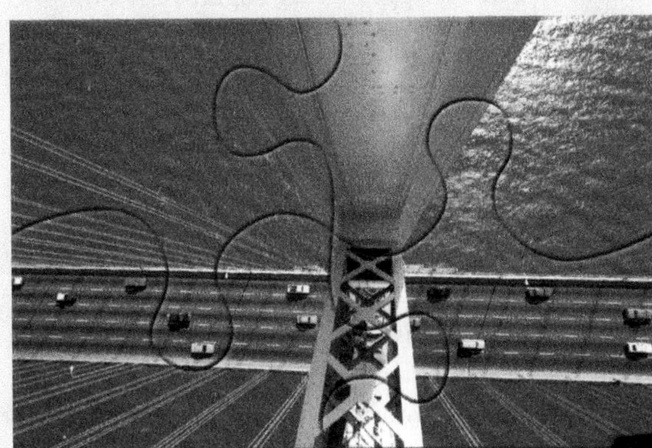

mark downey/Alamy

THE BIOPSYCHOSOCIAL APPROACH TO PERSONALITY DISORDERS It is often difficult to identify the causes of personality disorders because they seem to arise from multiple causes over a long period of time. Rather than pinpointing the exact moment a disorder began, psychologists speak in general terms about the types of events that contribute to personality disorders. Adding to the difficulty is the fact that multiple causes are likely at play, and it may be possible for two people to develop the same symptomatic thoughts and behaviours through entirely different routes. The biopsychosocial model provides a comprehensive view, examining personality disorders from three different perspectives.

Psychological Factors Do people with personality disorders think differently from normal people? Persistent beliefs about the self are a major part of the human personality, and the attempt to compensate for and cope with negative beliefs about oneself is a key part of APD. People with narcissistic (NPD) or histrionic (HPD) personality disorder also tend to have deeply rooted negative beliefs about the self, how they are regarded, and whether they are loved by others. Much of their dysfunctional behaviour patterns stem from attempts to compensate for these negative self-beliefs. For example, the person with NPD may continually seek attention, adoration, and reassurance from others, avoiding negative information about the self at all costs. A similar pattern may be apparent in someone who has a histrionic personality. Attention seeking through engaging in flattery and wearing provocative clothing may help individuals with HPD avoid the negative feelings they associate with being unnoticed.

Adults with APD and children with conduct disorders (often a precursor to APD) have difficulty learning tasks that require decision making and following complex rules. Brain-imaging studies show that children with conduct disorders perform worse at these tasks and have reduced activity in the frontal lobes compared with healthy controls and even children with ADHD (Finger et al., 2008). Thus it appears that cognitive factors and their underlying brain systems are involved in personality disorders.

Sociocultural Factors Children begin to develop social skills and emotional attachments at home and in their local neighbourhood and community. Not surprisingly, then, troubled homes and communities can contribute to the development of psychopathy or antisocial personality disorder (Meier et al., 2008). Such individuals have often themselves experienced trauma or abuse, and with this history of themselves being treated as objects rather than as sensitive human beings, and their need to defend themselves against and dissociate from their intensely negative emotions and experiences, they may have effectively shut down and never sufficiently developed the emotional circuitry for empathy. This often results in aggression and cruelty toward others, including animals.

In general, personality disorders often involve extensive emotional damage from childhood experiences, ranging from physical violence and sexual abuse to the profound invalidation and insecurity of being repeatedly abandoned or neglected as a child. For example, even less severe cases of borderline personality disorder may arise from a child having his emotions treated as if they were unreal or unimportant (Crowell et al., 2009). The deep insecurity and emotional volatility that result leave adults with BPD never able to master the ability to control their emotions, becoming more vulnerable to everyday life stressors (Glaser et al., 2008).

Biological Factors Not everyone who experiences extreme stress and abuse develops a personality disorder, of course. So why do some adapt successfully while others develop personality disorders? The answer may lie in how stress interacts with biological predispositions for personality disorders. A number of specific genes seem to contribute to emotional instability through serotonin systems in the brain (Crowell et al., 2009). Research also points to unique activity in the limbic system and frontal lobes—brain regions that are associated with emotional responses and impulse control, respectively (Brendel et al., 2005).

COMORBIDITY AND PERSONALITY DISORDERS Personality disorders present serious challenges to mental health professionals, who have struggled to reach consensus on how to categorize specific subtypes. One issue is the high levels of comorbidity among personality disorders. **Comorbidity** is *the presence of two disorders simultaneously.* In some cases, the presence of the two disorders interferes with their functioning or treatment. For example, a person who is being treated for heart disease may also have diabetes, and the presence of both diseases in the same individual can complicate treatment. Similarly, substance abuse is often comorbid with personality disorders (Goldstein et al., 2007; Gudonis et al., 2009). Their intertwining presents a challenge for treatment: Is it the personality disorder or the substance abuse that is at the root of the problem? Comorbidity rates between the personality disorder subtypes have led some psychologists to suggest that the DSM-IV identified far too many different types of personality disorders (Clark, 2007). These disagreements aside, APD and BPD are the most reliable to diagnose; that is, two or more mental health professionals are highly likely to agree on whether someone has APD or BPD.

Quick Quiz 15.2a
Defining and Classifying Personality Disorders

KNOW ...

1 Which of the following is not a characteristic of personality disorders?

A Traits that are inflexible and maladaptive

B Significant functional impairment or subjective distress

C Marked deviation from cultural expectations

D Typically diagnosed with medical tests

2 Which of the following individuals demonstrates the definition of comorbidity?

A A person who has both borderline personality disorder and a substance abuse disorder

B A person who is histrionic who both seeks excessive attention and is emotionally hyper-reactive

C A person with borderline personality disorder who is impulsive and tends to be in unstable relationships

D A person who experiences a personality disorder that turns out to be fatal

UNDERSTAND ...

3 ________ refers to a condition marked by a habitual pattern of willingly violating others' personal rights, with very little sign of empathy or remorse.

A Borderline personality disorder

B Narcissistic personality disorder

C Histrionic personality disorder

D Antisocial personality disorder

4 ________ involves intense extremes between positive and negative emotions, an unstable sense of self, impulsivity, and difficult social relationships.

A Borderline personality disorder

B Narcissistic personality disorder

C Histrionic personality disorder

D Antisocial personality disorder

APPLY ...

5 Which of the following biopsychosocial factors is least likely to be related to personality disorders?

A Stress reactivity

B History of abuse

C Decreased activity of the frontal lobes

D Enjoyment of pain

Answers can be found on page ANS-4.

Dissociative Identity Disorder

Have you ever been so engaged in driving, reading a book, or playing a game that you were totally unaware of what was going on around you? Have you ever had difficulty determining whether an event, perhaps some long ago story, really happened the way you now remember it, or whether it was a story that happened to someone else, or even a dream? These types of experiences can be thought of as dissociative experiences, because they are characterized by a sense of separation—a dissociation—between the person and her surroundings. Dissociative experiences may arise while you are intensely focused on one activity, or when you drift off while not doing anything in particular, such as daydreaming during a long lecture. People differ in their tendencies to dissociate, but such experiences seem completely normal.

In a few cases, some people have such extreme dissociative experiences that they may be diagnosed with a **dissociative disorder**, *a category of mental disorders characterized by a split between conscious awareness from feeling, cognition, memory, and identity* (Kihlstrom, 2005). Dissociative disorders include the following conditions:

- *Dissociative fugue:* A period of profound autobiographical memory loss. People in fugue states may go so far as to develop a new identity in a new location with no recollection of their past.
- *Depersonalization disorder:* A strong sense of the surreal, the feeling that one is not connected to one's body, the feeling of disconnection from one's regular identity and awareness.
- *Dissociative amnesia:* A severe loss of memory, usually for a specific stressful event, when no biological cause for amnesia is present.

Probably the most familiar member of this category is **dissociative identity disorder (DID**; sometimes referred to as **multiple personality disorder)**, *in which a person experiences a split in identity such that they feel different aspects of themselves as though they were separated from each other. This can be severe enough that the person constructs entirely separate personalities, only one of which will generally be in control at a time.*

Explore Dissociative Identity Disorder

These distinct personalities, or alters, may be so different from one another as to have different genders, sexual orientations, memories, personality, and autobiographical sense of self and "who they are." The dissociation of alter identities can be so strong that one alter may have no memory of events experienced by other alters. From Dr. Jekyll and Mr. Hyde to Tyler Durden in *Fight Club*, we have been both fascinated and frightened by the possibility that a single individual can house radically different personalities within that individual's consciousness.

In most cases, dissociative disorders such as DID are thought to be brought on by extreme stress. Some psychologists have hypothesized that, during a traumatic event, such as being a victim of violence, individuals may cope with the experience by shifting their consciousness to a different perspective, possibly going to another place in their mind, or feeling as though they are standing back from their physical selves watching what was happening to them, as though it was happening to somebody else. With repeated experiences, this type of dissociation could become an individual's habitual way of coping with the trauma, as well as other stressful situations, producing a tendency to enter a completely different kind of consciousness, as though one had become a different person or developed a distinct personality (van der Kolk, 1994). Consistent with this, most cases of DID do include reports of a stressful event or series of events that precipitated the onset of the condition (Putnam, 1989).

DID is a very rare condition, affecting only about 1% of psychiatric patients, and therefore only a very small fraction of 1% of the general population (Rifkin et al., 1998). There has been a longstanding controversy surrounding whether DID is "real" or whether the symptoms are created by people. For example, many of the different characteristics of different alters can be faked, either through people explicitly adopting different personas, through hypnosis, or other means. A related critique is that the personalities are "real" insofar as the person believes them and they do describe different patterns of behaviour, but those personalities themselves were formed through the collusion of the person and therapists; in a sense then, the alters are mere inventions, but inventions that have begun to function like real personalities. A key problem in this debate is that a condition like DID is very difficult to test for in a rigorous fashion, given how personal and subjective the experience of identity is.

One approach to testing for DID is to check for memory dissociations between alter identities. For example, in one study, patients viewed words and pictures and were tested for recall of the stimuli either when they were experiencing the same alter as when they learned them, or when they were experiencing a different alter. The results suggested that some types of learning do not transfer between alter identities (Eich et al., 1997). This finding would suggest that the two alters are truly separate identities.

Another approach to examining DID is to record patterns of brain activity. One study using positron emission tomography (PET) actually found differing frontal lobe activity for people with DID while they were experiencing each of their alters (Reinders et al., 2003). (In case you wondered, the researchers obtained consent to participate in the study by both alters.) Although the results of both of these studies are thought provoking, they do not provide solid evidence for a biological basis of DID. After all, any different state of mind or emotional experience will involve different patterns of brain activity; the fact that the two "alters" produce different patterns of brain activation may simply reflect that the person is thinking about and experiencing things differently in the two states of mind, not that the alters are actually distinct personalities.

Another questionable aspect of DID is the huge change in the number of cases over time. By 1970, there were only 79 documented cases of DID (then referred to as multiple personality disorder). In 1986, there were around 6000; by 1998, the number had risen to more than 40 000 (Lilienfeld & Lynn, 2003). Also, 80% of patients diagnosed with DID were unaware of having the disorder before starting therapy (Putnam, 1989). These observations suggest that DID may have its origins in the context of therapy, rather than being a response to trauma. Also interesting, the number of alters changed dramatically; in the early decades up to the 1970s, a person would typically have only one alter; but by the 1980s, people generally had many different alters, even dozens or hundreds!

Why did the rate of DID skyrocket from 79 cases to more than 40 000 cases in fewer than three decades? This increased prevalence could simply be a product of awareness: After professionals learned how to identify the disorder, they could begin to diagnose it more effectively. Or it could simply be too easy for therapists who believe in DID to steer their clients in that direction, even unintentionally, creating a way for clients to interpret their experience in terms of multiple alters, and using highly suggestive practices such as hypnosis. A more plausible explanation is that a small subset of psychologists find the disorder compelling and are more willing to diagnose it, so they interpret symptoms through that framework, and may (even unintentionally) provoke dissociative symptoms in the context of therapy (Frankel, 1993).

Researchers have examined social and therapist effects on DID by observing what happens when the disorder is introduced to other parts of the world. In these cases it appears that DID—whether a disorder or not—has a strong sociocultural component. For example, the disorder was nonexistent in Japan in 1990 (Takahashi, 1990), but Japanese psychologists began diagnosing patients with DID when the disorder was described by North Americans (An et al., 1998). In India, the disorder is recognized, but how the disorder manifests itself is different from in America: Americans with DID switch from alters upon suggestion, whereas people in India who have DID switch alters only upon awakening (North et al., 1993). These observations point to a predominantly sociocultural disorder in which cultural beliefs and therapists determine how the symptoms are manifested (Lilienfeld et al., 1999).

Quick Quiz 15.2b Dissociative Identity Disorder

KNOW ...

1 Dissociative identity disorder is best described as

- **A** a lost grasp on reality.
- **B** a lack of regard for the feelings of others.
- **C** a splitting of identity.
- **D** a problem with memory, attention, and the ability to form coherent thoughts.

UNDERSTAND ...

2 Fugue is a form of dissociative disorder most commonly associated with

- **A** a belief that you no longer exist or are real.
- **B** loss of sensation in an appendage with no physical or neurological evidence.
- **C** housing multiple personalities in one body.
- **D** loss of identity and memories of the self.

3 Which of the following is believed to typically bring on dissociative identity disorder?

- **A** A physical injury to the head
- **B** Extreme stress or trauma
- **C** Old age
- **D** Genetics

ANALYZE ...

4 Skeptics have argued against the validity of DID in a number of different cases. What is their reasoning?

- **A** The disorder appears to be based on cultural expectations.
- **B** Most people who experience trauma do not dissociate.
- **C** The vast majority of cases come from a very small number of therapists.
- **D** Skeptics have cited all of these arguments.

Answers can be found on page ANS-4.

Module Summary

Module 15.2

News-Journal/AP images

Now that you have read this module you should

KNOW ...

- ***The key terminology associated with personality and dissociative disorders:***

antisocial personality disorder (APD) (p. 637)
borderline personality disorder (BPD) (p. 637)
comorbidity (p. 640)
dissociative disorder (p. 641)
dissociative identity disorder (DID) (multiple personality disorder) (p. 641)
histrionic personality disorder (HPD) (p. 637)
narcissistic personality disorder (NPD) (p. 637)
personality disorders (p. 636)

UNDERSTAND ...

- ***The phenomenon of dissociation and how a dissociative disorder might occur.*** Dissociation can be explained in everyday phenomena such as daydreaming. However, a dissociative disorder may occur when perceptions of mind, body, and surroundings are severely and chronically separated, such that the person loses his or her previously stable sense of self and identity.

APPLY ...

- ***The biopsychosocial model to understand the causes of personality disorders.*** Take antisocial personality disorder and psychopathy for example:
  1. Can you name one or two biological influences associated with APD and psychopathy?
  2. What is at least one psychological factor, consisting of emotions, thoughts, and experiences?
  3. What are at least two social or cultural factors, including relationships, cultural expectations, and so on?

  Check your answers on page ANS-4.

ANALYZE ...

- ***The status of dissociative identity disorder as a legitimate diagnosis.*** The lack of a physical basis for the disorder and its unusual rate and patterns of diagnosis bring about skepticism as to whether DID is "real" or is manufactured, perhaps unwittingly, by the person. It is important to find evidence for differences between alternate personalities that cannot be faked by people or created artificially. Recent research in brain imaging is beginning to look for different patterns of neurological activity that could denote distinct personalities, but this work is in its infancy.

Matsunaka Takeya/Aflo/Glow Images

Module 15.3

Anxiety, Depressive, and Obsessive-Compulsive Disorders

Learning Objectives After reading this module you should	KNOW ...	UNDERSTAND ...	APPLY ...	ANALYZE ...
	The key terminology related to anxiety, depressive, and obsessive-compulsive disorders	The different types of anxiety disorders How anxiety or depressive disorders can be self-perpetuating	Your knowledge of anxiety, depressive, and obsessive-compulsive disorders, so as to be alert to people who may benefit from some help	Whether maladaptive aspects of psychological disorders might arise from perfectly normal, healthy behaviours

Of all the things to be afraid of in life, surely one of them is not the possibility that you can "catch" a mental illness, waking up one morning mentally ill because of some bacteria or germ that you were exposed to. This is generally true; we are pretty safe. In most cases, psychological disorders develop over a period of time. There may be some initial signs that everything is "not quite right" with a person, and then there is a gradual unfolding of more noticeable personality, behavioural, or emotional problems.

Unfortunately, there are documented cases of sudden onset obsessive-compulsive disorder (OCD), in which young children suddenly and without prior warning developed symptoms of OCD, including repetitive behaviours and irrational fears and obsessions. Surprisingly, this sudden surge of OCD-like tendencies came after these children were exposed to bacterial streptococcal infections (Snider & Swedo, 2004). How is it possible that this particular infection seems capable of triggering a sudden-onset psychological disorder in some children?

The answer seems to be that when the immune system mounts its reaction to the bacterial infection, it also damages cells in the caudate, a part of the brain near its centre, related to many different functions including the control of one's impulses. As we will see in this module, one theory about OCD is that compulsive, repetitive behaviours (such as hand washing) are ways of dealing with a lost sense of impulse control, the sort of loss that occurs when the caudate is damaged (Huyser et al., 2009). If this theory is correct, then, at least in this case, a psychological disorder can be acquired virtually overnight.

Focus Questions

 The experience of anxiety drives many different disorders. What are some of the ways that problems with anxiety can manifest?

 Depression is another very common disorder. Why do people seem to develop depression?

If you have had any personal experiences with psychological disorders—maybe you, a family member, a friend, or a co-worker has experienced one—then there is a good chance you will come across a description of it in this module, because anxiety and mood disorders are extremely common.

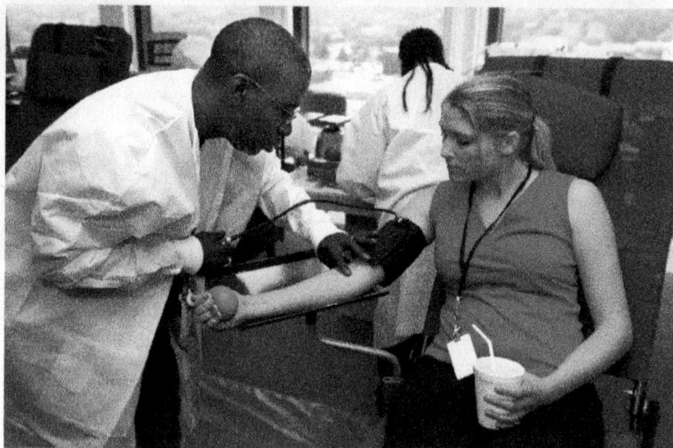

Top: Darren Bridges Photography/Alamy; bottom: dlewis33/iStockphoto

Fight or flight . . . or freeze or faint? In addition to fight-or-flight responses, mammals can also react by freezing—as in the "deer in the headlights" response—or by fainting, as some will do at the sight of blood (Bracha et al., 2004).

Anxiety Disorders

Anxiety disorders are *a category of disorders involving fear or nervousness that is excessive, irrational, and maladaptive.* They also are among the most frequently diagnosed disorders, affecting approximately one in every eight Canadians (Public Health Agency of Canada, 2002), and often occurring with other disorders, such as depressive or obsessive-compulsive disorders, substance abuse, or problematic behaviour patterns such as an excessive need to always be in control of situations.

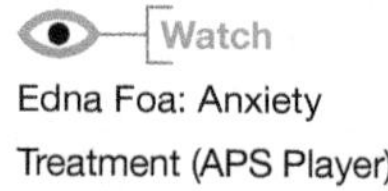

Watch
Anxiety Disorders

Although everyone experiences feelings of anxiety at times, and indeed, anxiety can be functional in certain circumstances, the experience of anxiety can become highly maladaptive, even crippling. People often cope with anxiety by limiting themselves to environments, activities, and people that make them feel safe and secure, and by developing rigid habits and ways of doing things so as to keep life predictable and under control. These patterns evolve in order to help the anxious person manage his or her fear, but they become imprisoning, stifling people's growth and experience of life in countless ways.

Watch
Edna Foa: Anxiety Treatment (APS Player)

In most people's common experience, anxiety occurs as a natural part of the fight-or-flight response (Nesse & Ellsworth, 2009). We experience this response as a racing, pounding heartbeat with increased respiration, as our autonomic systems prepare our bodies for quick action. Some people may notice a knot in the stomach and sweaty or clammy hands. These physical changes reflect a shift in energy away from non-emergency tasks like digestion and toward fighting or fleeing. This basic fight-or-flight response seems to be common to all mammals, implying that it has long been evolutionarily adaptive to have an easily triggered system that can quickly arouse the body for action in the face of an emergency. However, living in our modern, stressed-out society, we activate this stress response system repeatedly throughout our days of hustling and bustling and trying to get ahead in the world, and at this point, this system is no longer functional, but ends up actually being harmful to us. The constant wear and tear on the human body as a result of being continually prepped for action accumulates over time and causes a host of stress-related illnesses (see Module 14.2).

Clearly, it is important to identify specific symptoms that indicate that one's anxiety is becoming maladaptive. As discussed in Module 15.1, the distinction between a typical psychological state and a disorder depends on assessments of duration and severity of symptoms, and maladaptive impact on the lives of the person themselves or others.

VARIETIES OF ANXIETY DISORDERS

I had to cross that bridge twice a day to drop off my daughter at school. One Friday traffic slowed to a crawl and I noticed my heart thumping. Out of nowhere, the idea hit me: I was going to die on that bridge and there was nothing I could do about it. . . . The more I tried to calm myself, the worse it got. Everything was a blur. I somehow made it the last 50 feet and pulled over. That whole experience couldn't have been more than five minutes but it seemed like forever. Next Monday I felt skittish approaching the bridge. I kept thinking about my heart beating even though I tried paying attention to other things. Next thing I know I'm thinking, "I'm having a heart attack—a real heart attack this time."

For a while, I avoided the bridge by having my wife make the trip, but that didn't solve the problem. . . . I was in a meeting in the library when I thought I felt my heart racing again. Before long, I'd locked myself in the restroom wondering if this would be the time it killed me.

—JMD, a 44-year-old journalist

Table 15.3 :: What Are We So Afraid of?

	CURRENTLY EXPERIENCING THE PHOBIA	HAVE EXPERIENCED THE PHOBIA AT ONE TIME
Animals (snakes, birds, or other animals)	4.7%	50.3%
Natural environment (e.g., heights, storms, water)	5.9%	62.7%
Blood or bodily injury (including injections)	4.0%	42.5%
Situations (e.g., dentists, hospitals, crowded places)	5.2%	55.6%
Other specific objects	1.0%	10.6%

Source: Stinson et al., 2007.

What separates anxiety disorders from other forms of anxiety is a combination of an unjustifiable degree, duration, and source of anxiety. In all anxiety disorders, the experience creates distress for the individual and interferes with normal daily functioning at work, at school, and in personal relationships.

As you can see in the description of JMD's experiences, there does not seem to be any real source for his anxiety, but it certainly causes distress. Anxiety is interfering with his daily functioning, including his family life and his work. Therefore, it does seem like some type of anxiety disorder. Psychologists have identified distinct patterns of experience that have given rise to several major types of anxiety disorders.

Generalized Anxiety Disorder **Generalized anxiety disorder (GAD)** *involves frequently elevated levels of anxiety, generally from the normal challenges and stresses of everyday life.* The person with GAD fears disaster lurking around every corner, and may experience symptoms ranging from difficulty sleeping or breathing to difficulty concentrating because of intrusive thoughts. However, because the anxiety arises out of the ongoing situations and circumstances of life, people often have difficulty understanding their experience, and cannot identify specific reasons for which they are anxious (Turk et al., 2005). It is also impossible to ever sufficiently resolve the anxiety by controlling situations and trying to attend to every detail so that nothing goes wrong. Instead, as one detail is dealt with, the anxiety shifts to another source, and the control-oriented person is locked into a never-ending scramble to manage life perfectly so as to keep anxiety at bay. Not surprisingly, people with GAD often have unstable, irritable moods, experience difficulty concentrating, and have sleep problems. Although there are many different types of factors that increase the probability of developing GAD, ranging from innate, genetic components to current habitual thinking patterns, a convergence of stresses, such as occurs during major life changes, commonly precede the onset of the disorder (Newman & Llera, 2011).

Panic Disorder **Panic disorder** is *an anxiety disorder marked by occasional episodes of sudden, very intense fear.* This condition is distinct from GAD because the anxiety occurs in short segments, but can be much more severe. The key feature of this disorder is panic attacks—brief moments of extreme anxiety that include a rush of physical activity paired with frightening thoughts. A panic attack escalates when the fear of death causes increased physical arousal, and the increased physical symptoms feed the frightening thoughts. The escalation rarely goes on for more than 10 minutes, after which the individual will eventually return to a more relaxed state.

A substantial subset of people with panic disorder develop a recurring fear that the panic will strike again, particularly in an environment in which they would be exposed and unable to escape from people, such as a shopping mall or other public space. This fear can result in **agoraphobia** (which is often associated with panic disorder), *resulting from an intense fear of having a panic attack in public; as a result of this fear, the individual may begin to avoid public settings and increasingly isolate himself or herself.* In its most extreme forms, agoraphobia leads an individual to stay inside his or her home almost all the time.

WORKING THE SCIENTIFIC LITERACY MODEL

Specific Phobias

In contrast to GAD, where an individual's anxiety can be applied to just about any situation, a **phobia** is *a severe, irrational fear of a very specific object or situation*. Some of the most common phobias are listed in Table 15.3. The best-known form of phobia is a **specific phobia**, which involves *an intense fear of a specific object, activity, or organism*. For example, the person may be afraid of specific animals, heights, thunder, blood, and injections or other medical procedures. Social phobias, which are very common, are a different category of phobias, related to interpersonal situations and relationships; we will discus social phobias later.

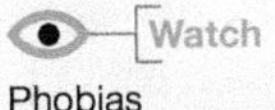

Phobias

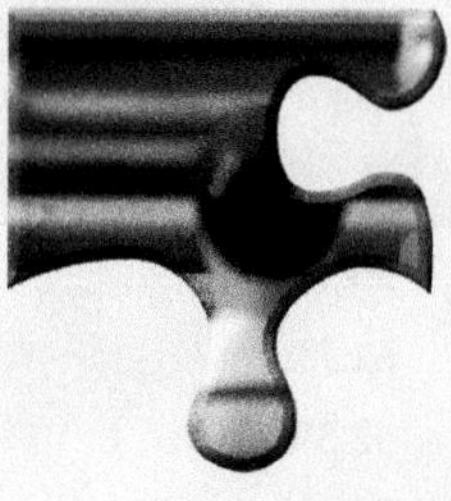

What do we know about specific phobias?

Phobias are often developed through unpleasant or frightening experiences—for example, a person who is bitten by a dog might develop a phobia of dogs. Phobias can also develop without direct, personal experience. Phobias can arise out of the patterns of anxiety that develop as children's fears give rise to thoughts, emotions, physiological responses (e.g., arousal), and behavioural reactions (e.g., avoidance) that can, in turn, feed back to reinforce the fear. This self-reinforcing nature of anxiety is extremely important to understand, in order to appreciate why disorders like phobias develop to the extreme degrees that they sometimes do (Merckelbach et al., 1996).

These patterns are sensitive to the social environment as well; if children are exposed to models, such as parents who exhibit fearful behaviours toward certain objects, this may reinforce the children's fears. There are likely many factors that influence whether or not a given person develops a phobia from a given set of experiences; after all, lots of people get bitten by dogs without developing a phobia.

It is important to understand that phobias are not a fundamentally different sort of experience, but rather, phobias develop out of the very normal set of negative, fear-based responses that people have to certain things in the environment. For example, if a person goes through a very negative experience in a certain environment, then cues related to that environment may trigger negative reactions. This is perfectly normal; children face many of these types of fears because of actual experiences but also because of their fertile imaginations (just think about hiding under the covers when you were a kid, afraid of what might be lurking in the dark . . .). Children end up, at different times, having fears of many different things; as just one example, almost half of children six to eight years old report being at least somewhat afraid of blood (Merckelbach et al., 1996; Öst, 1987). These mild to moderate fears, which are rampant in childhood, are the metaphoric soil out of which specific phobias may grow. It is in this early to middle childhood phase that many specific phobias seem to develop, including animal and blood-injury phobias (Öst, 1987); also, people with fear of heights or water usually report that they have always had the fear (Menzies & Clark, 1993). Claustrophobia, which involves more of social awareness components, tends to start later in life, in the late teens and early adulthood (Öst, 1987).

For most people, as they develop cognitively and as they mature over time, their childhood fears subside, but for a subset of people, perhaps those who are genetically prone to a stronger fear response, some of these fears become stable patterns of emotion, thought, and behaviour, and transfer into adulthood. This is what becomes a phobia.

Interestingly, some researchers have argued that the majority of the triggers for phobias are objects or situations that we, as a species, have reason to fear, or at the very least be cautious about. For example, people readily develop fears of spiders, snakes, heights, and drowning—dangers that would have been important over evolutionary time. On the other hand, people less readily develop the same type of fear response to guns, automobile accidents, and other such dangers of our modern environment. Psychologists arguing from an evolutionary perspective believe that the human species has evolved to be biologically predisposed to develop certain fears, based on our evolutionary history (Öhman & Mineka, 2001; see also Module 6.1). This of course does not argue that other phobias will be impossible to develop, but rather that people will generally tend to find that they have a stronger innate response toward categories of objects that are part of our evolutionary heritage.

How can science explain why some people are more likely than others to develop specific phobias?

Research on the characteristics of people who develop specific phobias has shown that there are, as you might expect, many potential causes of specific phobias, which determine for each individual whether he develops a phobia or not. For example, some of the risk factors for phobias include shyness and temperamental inhibition, both of which are, interestingly enough, partly genetically determined (Biederman et al., 1990; DiLalla, Kagan, & Reznick, 1994).

Recently, scientists have been piecing together the genetic factors that biologically predispose some people to experience more fear than others. One of the first questions to answer is simply whether or not the tendency to learn fear associations can be transmitted genetically. One group of researchers attempted to answer this using selective breeding techniques with mice. The researchers tested a strain of mice for how easily they could learn a fear association (an auditory tone coupled with an electrical shock). The fear response was measured by the length of time the mice held still—mice typically show fear by freezing in place (Ponder et al., 2007).

By selectively breeding the most fearful mice with each other, and the least fearful mice with each other, researchers could see whether the fear-association response would differ across the generations of these mice families. As Figure 15.3 shows, across four generations, fear responses became more and more distinct, with the third and fourth generations being very different from each other—the mice bred from the most fearful families became even more easily conditioned than their great-grandparents. Thus the fear-based learning system is, at least in part, genetically determined.

Can we critically evaluate this information?

Learning that fear responses in mice are genetically transmissible does not, in truth, contribute much to our understanding of phobias, in particular to our functional understanding of how a phobia develops in a specific person and how it might best be treated. Any level of analysis must, of course, be integrated with others into a full understanding of how disorders work. Furthermore, although identifying specific genes in mice that are related to fear responses may point to genes that are involved in human fear responses as well, the full manifestation of a phobia involves many processes and, therefore, would only be partially explained by a genetic understanding.

Why is this relevant?

Understanding the genetic contributions to fear responses and anxiety disorders is clearly important, opening up whole fields of possible treatment options and enhancing our biological understanding of how disorders work. A challenge for the future remains to understand the interaction between the genetic and other levels of analysis, leading to genetic testing possibilities, matching treatments to key genetic markers in order to make therapy as effective as possible.

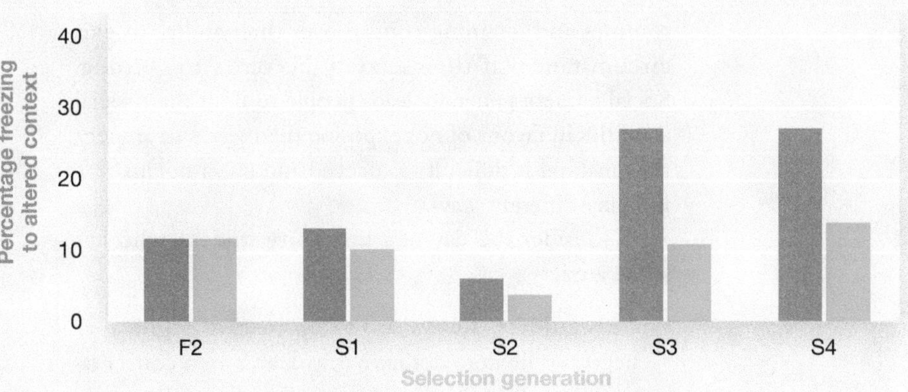

{FIG. 15.3} **Anxiety Levels Are Inherited in an Animal Model** Over the course of just a few generations, mice from the highly fearful genetic strain show increasingly strong fear responses as indicated by the height of the red bars.

Sergio Azenha/Alamy

Everett Collection

In the novel and miniseries *It*, by Stephen King, an evil life form would become a clown to lure children into a trap. This type of imagery can be the basis for which many people come to experience fear of certain objects—even clowns.

Think back to the case of JMD from the beginning of this section, the 44-year-old having problems with sudden attacks of anxiety. What information do you think is relevant to diagnosing JMD?

The overall extent of his fears and the fact that they are short term and limited in scope rather than general and long-lasting suggests that GAD is not a good match. The fact that his reaction seems to be triggered in various locations rather than being associated with something specific suggests that this is not a phobia. JMD's diagnosis would likely be a panic disorder, best characterized by the sudden and overwhelming attacks of fear and anxiety that strike him occasionally.

In reality, of course, this is a diagnosis that only a professionally trained clinical psychologist or psychiatrist would be able to make, but given what we know, panic disorder is the closest match.

Social Phobias **Social anxiety disorder** is *a very strong fear of being judged by others or being embarrassed or humiliated in public.* People who experience social anxiety deal with going out in public by developing familiar routines and retaining control over their ability to exit circumstances if their anxiety becomes too strong. Social anxiety generally leads people to limit their social activities in favour of not exposing themselves to anxiety, thus making it difficult to succeed and live a normal life in many different ways.

Consider the day of a university student who has social anxiety:

- This student always shows up to class right as it begins so he does not have to risk awkward conversation with classmates he does not know, or potentially worse, sitting conspicuously alone and unable to connect to anyone around him.
- Despite being hungry, the student will not go into the cafeteria because his roommate is not around. He cannot face the prospect of sitting with strangers, especially without his roommate. He finds a quiet spot near the library and gets lunch from a vending machine.
- Walking across a quiet part of campus, he sees his professor approaching. Not knowing if the professor would recognize him, he wonders if he should say hello. Thinking about this issue makes him so tense, he pretends to stop and read a text message to avoid eye contact.

As you can see, the day is a series of very unpleasant, tense moments in situations that most people would find completely ordinary, and it is a series of sacrificed opportunities as the person fails over and over again to take advantage of potential opportunities for connection and social contact. The distress the student feels and the degree to which he shapes his life around his social phobia suggest that he has social anxiety disorder. Of course, to make a formal diagnosis of this disorder, a psychologist would need to evaluate the student's full set of symptoms and their duration.

THE VICIOUS CYCLE OF ANXIETY DISORDERS

One of the most dangerous aspects of anxiety disorders is that they tend to be self-perpetuating (Figure 15.4), with anxiety leading to circumstances that provoke further anxiety (Hofmann, 2007). For example, people with social anxiety disorder may avoid many social situations because they feel awkward and insecure and don't want to embarrass themselves. As a result, they become even less confident about their ability to socially interact with people, making them even more likely to avoid social contact in the future, or if it is unavoidable, to be so overly anxious and incapable of functioning effectively that the social opportunity turns into a negative experience, further reinforcing the anxiety. Through many of these self-fulfilling prophecy types of processes, anxiety disorders tend to reinforce themselves over time.

Watch
Margo: Obsessive-Compulsive Disorder

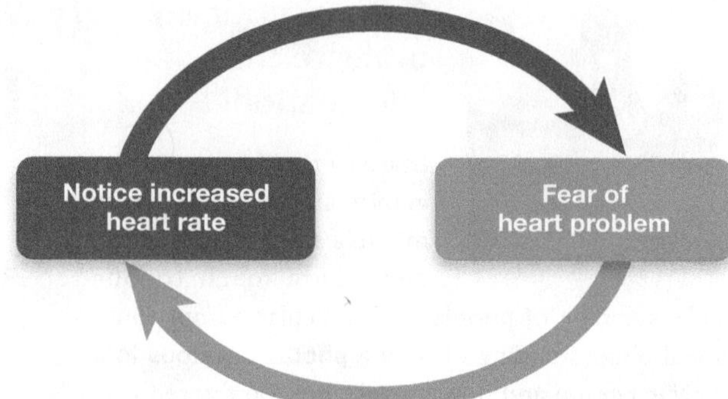

{FIG. 15.4} **The Vicious Cycle of Panic Attacks** **Click on this figure in your eText to see more details.**

Avoiding or interrupting this vicious cycle is central to the treatment of anxiety disorders. Instead of trying to minimize contact with feared situations, which only serves to reinforce the fear, the person must begin to practise confronting the fear. Only through exposing themselves to fear can people learn how to manage their responses or learn how to effectively manage the feared situation. For example, imagine a young girl who gets scratched by the neighbour's cat while trying to pet it. The girl may avoid cats in the future and, years later, still feel nervous and unsure of herself around cats. Only by learning to tolerate and eventually interact with cats will the girl be able to reduce her anxiety. It is unsurprising that the most important part of psychological therapy for anxiety disorders is **exposure**, in which the person is *repeatedly and in stages exposed to the object of his fear so that he can work past his emotional reactions.*

OBSESSIVE–COMPULSIVE DISORDER (OCD)

Until 2013, **obsessive–compulsive disorder (OCD)** was categorized as one of the anxiety disorders, although in the DSM-5 OCD was placed into its own category. Individuals with OCD are often *plagued by unwanted, inappropriate, and persistent thoughts (obsessions), and tend to engage in repetitive almost ritualistic behaviours (compulsions).* Generally, the obsessions and compulsions are linked together, with the compulsive behaviour serving as a means of coping with the anxiety produced by the obsessive thoughts (see Table 15.4). For example, a common manifestation of OCD is a person who is extremely concerned about germs and cleanliness; he may wash his hands many times each day, insist on only touching other objects through gloves, or become extremely vigilant about the chemicals in food and cleaning products. Although everybody has unwanted thoughts that seem to stick in their heads from time to time, obsessions take root and can last for a very long time, even many years. Also, these thoughts tend to be distressing or generally inappropriate.

We introduced this disorder at the outset by describing how it can occur suddenly in children. This is obviously

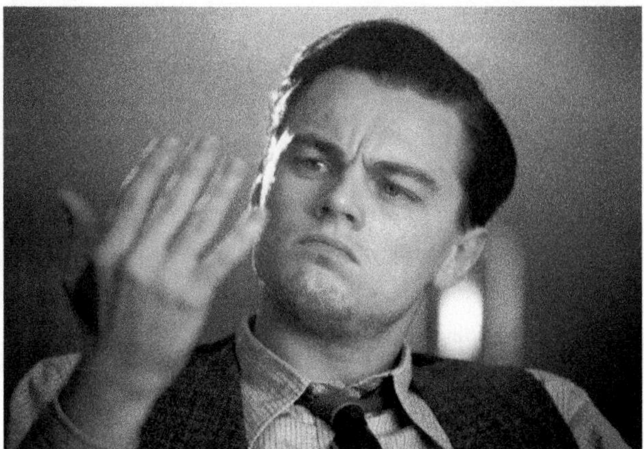

Miramax/courtesy Everett Collection

The Aviator (2004) depicted Howard Hughes's struggles with OCD.

exceedingly rare, and not at all representative of the way that OCD develops. OCD generally develops over time, ranging from childhood into early adulthood, by which time most cases of OCD will have manifested themselves.

The two components of OCD, obsessions and compulsions, are easy enough to understand on their own, because they are simply more extreme versions of experiences we all have had in varying degrees.

For example, you may have struggled with jealous thoughts in your relationship, or you may occasionally be plagued with thoughts of death and the meaninglessness of existence, or self-defeating thoughts like "I am a loser; I can't do anything right." Or maybe you have been left alone at night and images from horror movies or scary stories have come to your mind, leaving you beginning to panic and wonder if you should cower in your closet clutching a kitchen knife. And certainly you have had an annoying song stuck in your head at some point, going around and around in your mind despite your attempts to think about other things. In these ways and many others, all of us have experienced obsessive thinking.

As these types of intrusive thinking patterns develop and become more extreme and ever-present, they begin to increasingly interfere with the person's life. Imagine people who obsessively think about cleanliness and germs; everywhere they go in life, they encounter new microbiological terrors, forcing them to adopt elaborate rituals for how to sufficiently clean themselves and how to avoid making contact with germs in many different situations.

This is how compulsions arise, stemming from anxiety related to the obsessive thoughts. These types of feelings are also familiar to all of us, in some way. Have you ever experienced any kind of reaction about walking under a ladder, or spilling salt, or seeing a black cat cross your path? Have you ever had the almost uncontrollable urge that you just had to say something to that person, or you just didn't want to get on that elevator, or drive home with that person? Or you've found yourself packing your suitcase in just a certain way, or arranging your desk in just a certain way, or checking the stove just one more time before leaving the house.

Many psychologists believe that the compulsive behaviours that people with OCD engage in are ways of asserting control over their anxiety. Compulsive behaviours often arise from specific obsessions. Someone who worries about starting a fire might develop compulsive checking behaviours. For example, before she can leave her house, she might check that all lamps and appliances are unplugged. She may make the rounds two more times, ensuring that the electrical cords are secured by fasteners at least two feet from the outlet. Finally, she might turn off the light to leave but, to avoid the possibility that the light switch is halfway between on and off, she might count out a series of one to seven in which she turns the light off repeatedly, followed by one last downward swipe to ensure the switch is fully off. Only then can she feel secure in leaving the house.

Simulate The Obsessive-Compulsive Test

Although the compulsive behaviour patterns associated with OCD can create all sorts of problems, such as

Table 15.4 :: Prevalence of Symptoms in a Survey of 293 Individuals with Obsessive–Compulsive Disorder

PERCENTAGE OF SAMPLE EXPERIENCING OBSESSION	SPECIFIC TYPES OF OBSESSIONS
58%	A fear of being contaminated
56%	Persistent doubting
48%	Need to arrange things in a symmetrical pattern
45%	Aggressive thoughts
PERCENTAGE OF SAMPLE EXPERIENCING COMPULSION	**SPECIFIC TYPES OF OBSESSIONS**
69%	Checking
60%	Cleaning
56%	Repeating actions

Source: Pinto et al., 2006.

conflict and irritation within the family, these patterns also tend to be quite responsive to treatment. The anxious thought patterns and emotional reactions that give OCD a great deal of its emotional energy can also be substantially improved through appropriate treatment, in many cases.

In fact, anxiety, depressive, and obsessive-compulsive disorders are all generally amenable to treatment. Of course, there are exceptions, but most individuals who experience one of these disorders will find that they have multiple treatment possibilities available to them that can make a difference.

Quick Quiz 15.3a

Anxiety Disorders

KNOW ...

1 Which of the following is not classified as an anxiety disorder?

- **A** Panic attack
- **B** GAD
- **C** Depression
- **D** Social phobia

2 The difference between obsessions and compulsions is that

- **A** obsessions are repetitive behaviours, whereas compulsions are fears about specific events.
- **B** obsessions are repetitive, unwanted thoughts, whereas compulsions are repetitive behaviours.
- **C** obsessions are temporary, whereas compulsions are practically permanent.
- **D** obsessions and compulsions are the same thing.

UNDERSTAND ...

3 Allison has an intense fear of flying, so much so that she cannot even bear to close her eyes and imagine that she is on a plane. From this brief description, Allison may be experiencing

- **A** a specific phobia.
- **B** a social phobia.
- **C** a generalized phobia.
- **D** normal levels of anxiety.

4 Which condition is marked by a strong feeling of tension and worry, no matter what the situation may be?

- **A** A specific phobia
- **B** A panic attack
- **C** Generalized anxiety disorder
- **D** Normal feelings of anxiety

5 The idea that anxiety disorders can be self-perpetuating means that

- **A** anxiety in one situation always causes anxiety in another situation, regardless of what is happening in those situations.
- **B** the emotions associated with anxiety lead to physiological responses, which in turn lead to more anxious emotions, creating a vicious cycle.
- **C** you choose when and what to be anxious about.
- **D** anxiety is always limited to one situation or place.

ANALYZE ...

6 If anxiety leads to the onset of so many different disorders, how can it be a beneficial, adaptive process?

- **A** It cannot be an adaptive process.
- **B** The physiological response underlying anxiety prepares us to fight or flee.
- **C** Anxiety is a good way to gain sympathy.
- **D** The anxiety response evolved to help attract mates.

Answers can be found on page ANS-4.

Mood Disorders

There was a two-week period when I was on top of the world. I thought I could do anything. I took on extra tasks at work that I had no idea how to do and had no time to do them. I went around boasting about how well my work was going, bought a car I couldn't afford or didn't even want. I was so energized that I couldn't fall asleep. I wound up taking four or five people out for drinks and buying rounds for everyone, sometimes having 18 to 20 drinks a day before passing out for an hour or two and then waking up to start all over again. But I didn't think it was slowing me down. The only ill effect it seemed to have was that I was getting really annoyed with everyone—everyone was slowing me down. It was like having road rage but it occurred in my house, at my work, at the store. Nobody could move fast enough. And I started to get so annoyed that I decided I just needed to sleep. So I took a few sleeping pills, but that didn't do it. The next night I took about twice as many and I finally succeeded in getting myself admitted to the hospital—the psychiatric unit to be exact.

Then everything crashed. I just started crying nonstop for about three days; they put me on medication and said it would take about two weeks to work. In that time, I lost

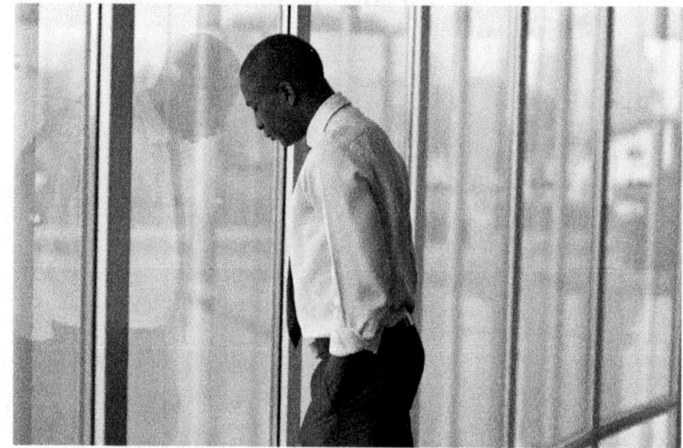

stefanolunardi/Shutterstock

Many people have experienced problems with a mood disorder. Those with depression may experience extended periods of sadness and hopelessness that have no apparent cause.

about 5 or 10 pounds from my total lack of appetite. Even when they decided I was okay to go home, I wasn't really ready to function. I lay in bed; I refused to answer the phone or respond to emails from friends. I guess I hit bottom when I was halfway up the stairs in my house. I was so confused: I couldn't figure out if I really wanted to go all the way up, or if I just wanted to go back down. I was so confused by that simple decision that I just sat down and cried on the middle steps.

—NS, 35-year-old research scientist

Statistics show that NS is not alone with his experiences, which are symptoms of a condition known as bipolar disorder: Mood disorders such as bipolar disorder and depression are particularly common, affecting almost 10% of adults in Canada and the U.S. (Health Canada, 2002; Kessler et al., 2005). Due to a combination of biological, cognitive, and sociocultural differences, rates of depression are twice as high among women as among men, and three times as high among people living in poverty (Hyde et al., 2008). There is also a genetic susceptibility to mood disorders. In this section we discuss the two major types of mood disorders—major depression and bipolar disorder.

MAJOR DEPRESSION AND BIPOLAR DISORDER

Feelings of sadness and depression are normal aspects of human experience. By comparison, major depression can be very severe and may occur even when there are no events or circumstances we normally associate with depressed mood. **Major depression** is *a disorder marked by prolonged periods of sadness, feelings of worthlessness and hopelessness, social withdrawal, and cognitive and physical sluggishness.* With this definition, it should be clear that depression involves more than just feeling sad for a long period of time; cognitive activities such as concentrating and making decisions are affected as well, while memories shift toward unpleasant and unhappy events. Physiologically, affected individuals may be lethargic and sleepy, yet also experience insomnia. They may experience changes in appetite and the onset of digestive problems such as constipation or loss of appetite.

To fully understand depression requires considering the cumulative, daily impact of life spiralling down into despair, problems piling up at work or at home, relationships being strained or crumbling, bills being unpaid and financial problems starting to interfere with daily life. People deep in depression may find it almost impossible to find the energy to answer the phone or to take care of more than the barest necessities of their lives; their social lives begin to suffer the strain as well, as they stop returning phone calls or emails. Other people start to notice, get annoyed, or have hurt feelings, which the depressed person likely knows, which then leads the depressed person to feel even worse about himself, as well as publicly exposed and perhaps embarrassed—and you begin to understand how depression becomes such a monster in people's lives, and leads to so many tragic stories.

Bipolar disorder (formerly referred to as *manic depression*) is *characterized by extreme highs and lows in mood, motivation, and energy.* It shares many symptoms with major depression—some distinguish the two by referring to major depression as unipolar—but it occurs only 38% as often as depression (NIMH, 2008). Bipolar disorder involves depression at one end and mania (an extremely energized, positive mood) at the other end. Mania may take several forms: talking excessively fast, racing thoughts, impulsive and spontaneous decisions, or high-risk behaviours. The experience of a manic episode can be exhilarating and parts of it can be highly enjoyable, but the costs of such excessive, indiscriminate, risky behaviour can be very high. Unfortunately, during a manic state, individuals feel little concern about the potential consequences of their actions. Later, as they come into a more normal frame of mind, they may feel a great deal of remorse and embarrassment for their actions, which contributes to their counterswing into depression.

Bipolar disorder encompasses both ends of an emotional continuum, and individuals with bipolar disorder can move from one end to the other at different rates. Some people with bipolar disorder experience only a few manic episodes in their lives, whereas others go through several episodes each year. A small number of "rapid cyclers" experience very abrupt mood swings, even within a matter of hours.

Watch
Speaking Out: Feliziano: Living With Bipolar Disorder

Watch
Nathan: Bipolar Disorder

COGNITIVE AND NEUROLOGICAL ASPECTS OF DEPRESSION

Depression affects cognition as well as emotion. People with depression can become confused and have difficulty concentrating and making decisions, all of which contribute to the growing feeling of helplessness and feeling incapable of doing anything right. As the depressed person begins to emphasize negative, self-defeating, and self-critical thoughts, they develop a characteristic depressive, or *pessimistic explanatory style* (Abramson, Seligman, & Teasdale, 1978; Sweeney et al., 1986). This describes *a set of habitual ways of explaining events to oneself which tend to be dysfunctional.* When something bad happens, such as the person failing to succeed at a task or a project, she makes internal, or *personal attributions,* for the event, blaming herself excessively for what happened ("It's all my fault! I did everything wrong! I messed the whole thing up!"). Depressed individuals also tend to make *stable attributions,* assuming that

Watch
Helen: Major Depression

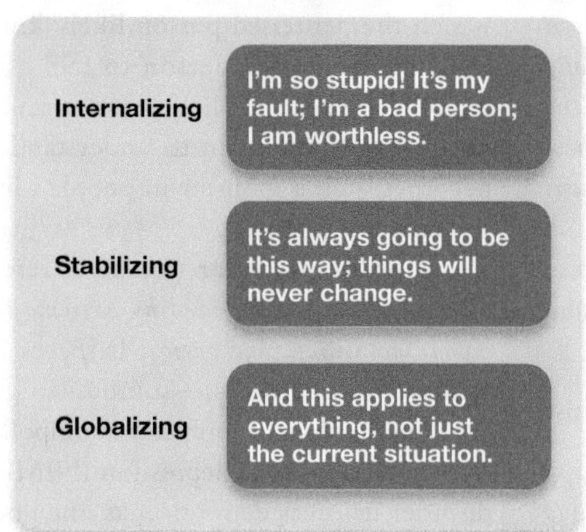

{FIG. 15.5} **Three Elements of the Depressive Explanatory Style** The three elements of the depressive explanatory style are internalizing, stabilizing, and globalizing.

the situation is going to persist ("It's always going to be like this. The problem is fundamental and is never going to change."). And as they spiral into catastrophic ways of thinking, they make *global attributions*, expanding the impact of the negative event into other domains or into overall life ("I just can't do anything right; I'm going to mess up everything"; or "This relationship is ruined; it's horrible; this has fundamentally changed how I see you and it affects everything about us!").

Watch
Jutta Joormann: Interaction of Cognition and Emotion (APS Player)

Explanatory style is important as a psychological precursor to psychological problems. People with a pessimistic explanatory style tend to take the inevitable negative events of life, and instead of making the best of them, they make the worst of them, drawing the most negative conclusions possible, adding as much stress and draining as much energy as they can. Thus, explanatory style tends to predict a huge host of life outcomes from stress and health to success and relationships. To get a sense of how this might work in specific events during a person's day, imagine an individual with depression who does something as minor as losing his keys; refer to Figure 15.5 to see the depressive explanatory style at work. Then extrapolate that same set of patterns across many different events, throughout one's life, and you will get a sense of the cumulative burden that this places on the individual, potentially leading to depression.

There is a substantial amount of research on the biological aspects of depression. For example, twin studies suggest an underlying genetic risk for developing major depression (Figure 15.6). In addition, brain-imaging research has identified two primary regions of interest related to depression: (1) the limbic system, which is active in emotional responses and processing, and (2) the dorsal (back) of the frontal cortex, which generally plays a role in controlling thoughts and concentrating. As is the case with panic disorder, a vicious cycle appears to occur with depression. The overactive limbic system responds strongly to emotions and sends signals that lead to a decrease in frontal lobe activity, and the decrease in frontal lobe functioning reduces the ability to concentrate and control what one thinks about (Gotlib & Hamilton, 2008).

Various neurotransmitters—especially serotonin, dopamine, and norepinephrine—appear to be involved in depression. In Module 16.3, we will discuss drug therapies that are used to alter these neurotransmitters. These brain regions and their neurotransmitters tie in to other physiological systems. The negative emotions of depression co-occur with stress reactions throughout the body, thereby involving the endocrine system, the digestive system, and the immune system. As a result, individuals with depression are at higher risk for a variety of illnesses, as well as cardiovascular disease and higher risk of mortality in given time periods; this link to mortality even persists once researchers statistically account for health behaviours and suicide (Penninx et al., 1999; Roblaes et al., 2005). Clearly, depression has implications for a person's health.

Research at the genetic level is also uncovering factors that contribute to the likelihood of being diagnosed with depression. For example, people who inherit "short" copies of a gene responsible for serotonin (5-HTT) activity are predisposed to depressive

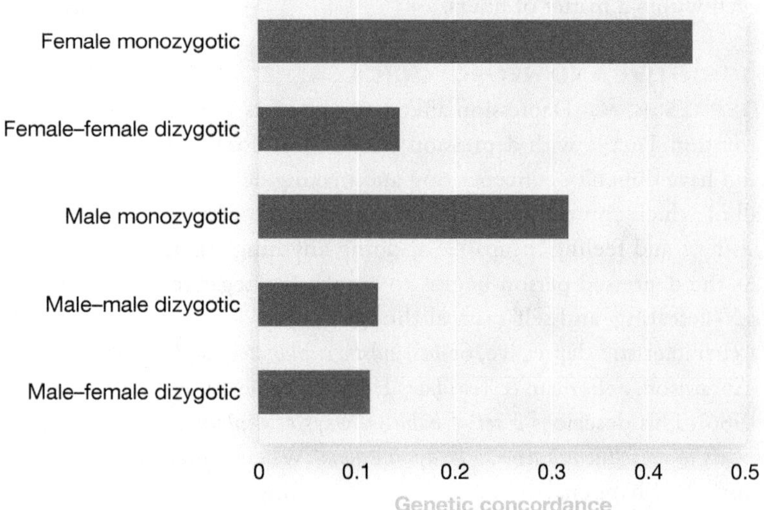

{FIG. 15.6} **Genetic Relatedness and Major Depression** Identical (monozygotic) twins have a greater chance of both developing major depression compared to fraternal (dizygotic) twins. Notice that the genetic correlation is highest for female monozygotic twins.

episodes in response to stress, whereas those who inherit "long" copies are less prone to depression ("short" and "long" refer to the structure of the different versions of the genes). Individuals who inherit short copies of the 5-HTT gene are also more prone to suicide attempts (Caspi et al., 2003; see also Module 3.1). Thus, one of the differences between people who thrive after adversity and people who develop depression may be hard-wiring that starts in the genes.

SOCIOCULTURAL INFLUENCES ON MOOD DISORDERS Biological and cognitive factors of depression interact with environmental influences. In particular, socioeconomic and environmental factors leave some individuals more vulnerable to mood disorders. Just living in a specific neighbourhood can be a risk factor for three main reasons (Cutrona et al., 2006). First, poor neighbourhoods are associated with higher daily stress levels due to substandard housing and facilities, increased crime rates, and other difficulties. Second, people living in these neighbourhoods are more vulnerable to stressors such as unemployment because they often lack connections, mentors, and job opportunities that professionals have access to in high-income neighbourhoods. Third, social ties tend not to be as strong in poor neighbourhoods. Low rates of home ownership combined with difficulty making rent can lead to high turnover; people may not know their neighbours very well and, therefore, take less interest in one another's well-being.

SUICIDE It is difficult to imagine a worse outcome from a mood disorder than suicide. For many people, it is equally difficult to imagine how anyone could reach such a low point. Nonetheless, suicide remains a serious public health concern. Particularly among Canadian youth, suicide is the second leading cause of death (behind transportation accidents).

There is significant variation in who is most likely to die by suicide. Suicide is four times more likely among males than among females, and two to three times more likely among Native Americans and European Americans than among individuals of other ethnicities. In addition, many people believe that adolescents are particularly vulnerable to suicide, but the highest suicide rates are actually observed among the elderly population: The suicide rate for people 65 and older is nearly 60% higher than the rate for teens (CDC, 2010). Fortunately, research, treatment, and public awareness have significantly reduced the suicide rate among youth since the 1980s (Gould et al., 2003).

Suicide often comes as a surprise to the family and friends of the victim, although in some cases clear warning signs are evident (Table 15.5). Among people in their teens and early 20s, the most significant risk factors are mood disorders, recent and extremely stressful life events, a family history of mood disorders (with or without suicide), easy access to a lethal means of suicide (most significantly, firearms), and the presence of these factors in conjunction with substance abuse (Gould et al., 2003; Moscicki, 2001). For younger individuals, being the victim of bullying and ostracism is a risk factor, but it is a greater concern when youth are both the victims and the perpetrators of bullying (Klomek et al., 2007). Family and friends have reported that in the weeks before a suicide, individuals have behaved in ways that are now recognized as warning signs. For example, an individual may verbally express despair and hopelessness (I just want to give up; Nothing matters anymore; They'll be sorry when I'm gone), give away personal possessions, suddenly withdraw from work or school, have crying spells, or obtain a means of committing the act.

Table 15.5 :: Warning Signs of Suicide

Learn how to recognize the danger signals. Be concerned if someone you know

- Talks about committing suicide
- Has trouble eating or sleeping
- Exhibits drastic changes in behaviour
- Withdraws from friends or social activities
- Loses interest in school, work, or hobbies
- Prepares for death by writing a will and making final arrangements
- Gives away prized possessions
- Has attempted suicide before
- Takes unnecessary risks
- Has recently experienced serious losses
- Seems preoccupied with death and dying
- Loses interest in his or her personal appearance
- Increases alcohol or drug use

Source: American Psychological Association, 2011.

PSYCH @

The Suicide Helpline

Thousands of people contact suicide telephone helplines every day. Is there even a "best practice" when it comes to helping an individual who is suicidal? The first telephone suicide helplines were operated by religious organizations and emphasized empathy and active listening. Although this may certainly be a helpful approach, it may not meet the needs of every caller. Modern suicide helplines are staffed by well-trained volunteers with access to suicide prevention specialists who can aid in effectively helping the distressed person, assess the level of risk, and get the appropriate medical or psychological help.

It turns out that good crisis telephone responders effectively use both styles, depending on the circumstances. First-time callers tend to benefit more from an active listener, who will be nonjudgmental, compassionate, and reflective. Repeat callers also need compassion, but tend to benefit more if the listener engages in problem-solving strategies (Mishara et al., 2007; Mishara & Daigle, 1997).

Some helpful resources can be found at http://www.suicidepreventionlifeline.org/.

Quick Quiz 15.3b Mood Disorders

KNOW ...

1 ________ is characterized by periods of intense depression as well as periods with elevated mood and energy levels.

A Major depression

B Unipolar depression

C Bipolar disorder

D Generalized anxiety disorder

UNDERSTAND ...

2 Depression is associated with lower activity in the frontal lobe, which may result in

A lack of appetite.

B difficulty concentrating and thinking.

C periods of elevated mood and energy.

D constipation.

APPLY ...

3 First-time callers to suicide prevention lines benefit most from

A empathy and active listening.

B firm, demanding instructions.

C extensive problem-solving interventions.

D direct referral to the hospital.

Answers can be found on page ANS-4.

Module Summary

Module 15.3

Matsunaka Takeya/Aflo/Glow Images

Now that you have read this module you should

KNOW ...

- ***The key terminology related to anxiety, depressive, and obsessive-compulsive disorders*:**

agoraphobia (p. 647)
anxiety disorders (p. 646)
bipolar disorder (p. 653)
exposure (p. 650)
generalized anxiety disorder (GAD) (p. 647)
major depression (p. 653)
obsessive–compulsive disorder (OCD) (p. 650)
panic disorder (p. 647)
phobia (p. 647)
social anxiety disorder (p. 649)
specific phobia (p. 647)

UNDERSTAND ...

- ***The different types of anxiety disorders.*** Although anxiety disorders share many similarities in symptoms, they differ in terms of what brings about the symptoms and the intensity of the symptoms. The cues that trigger anxiety range widely: In generalized anxiety disorder, just about anything may cause anxiety; in specific phobias, an individual fears only certain objects. Likewise, the intensity can range from near-constant worrying to brief periods of highly intense anxiety in phobias and panic disorder.
- ***How anxiety or depressive disorders can be self-perpetuating.*** Both depression and anxiety are characterized by a vicious cycle: With anxiety, anxious or fearful thoughts can lead to physiological arousal; physiological arousal can lead to escape and avoidance to get rid of the immediate fear, which in turn reinforces the anxious thoughts. In depression, a similar pattern can occur with depressed thoughts, self-blame, and social withdrawal.

APPLY ...

- ***Your knowledge of anxiety, depressive, and obsessive–compulsive disorders, so as to be alert to people who may benefit from some help.*** To do so, write down at least five warning signs for suicide, and identify the number of the suicide helpline. Check your answers on page ANS-4.

ANALYZE ...

- ***Whether maladaptive aspects of psychological disorders might arise from perfectly normal, healthy behaviours.*** To analyze this issue, we need to examine the specific symptoms that occur in someone who has a phobia and is showing an adaptive response (fear, anxiety) but to an inappropriate stimulus or situation. It is perfectly reasonable and healthy to be cautious about heights, for example, in the sense that falls can be dangerous, even life-threatening. This reaction is maladaptive only when the fear response is so intense or out of context that it interferes with daily life. Imagine a house painter who cannot climb a ladder or scaffold; unless he overcomes his fear (or finds very short houses to work on), he will have to make major adjustments to accommodate his fear.

Mark Owen/Blackout Concepts/Alamy

Module 15.4

Schizophrenia

Learning Objectives

After reading this module you should

KNOW ...	UNDERSTAND ...	APPLY ...	ANALYZE ...
The key terminology associated with schizophrenia	How different neurotransmitters affect individuals with schizophrenia The genetic and environmental contributions to schizophrenia	Your knowledge to identify different forms of schizophrenia	Claims that schizophrenia is related to genius or violent behaviour

John Nash is a remarkable story in many ways. He is remarkable for being the inspiration for a movie, *A Beautiful Mind*. He is remarkable for being a genius, a mathematician, and winner of a Nobel Prize for his mathematical work on game theory (Google "Nash equilibrium"), which has become a cornerstone of modern economics and has immense importance in understanding society. He is also remarkable for being an underachiever, you might say, in the sense that Nash undoubtedly has not risen to his full potential, or anything close to it. The world was, at least partially, deprived of one of its most brilliant minds, because Nash also has the remarkable characteristic of having schizophrenia.

In 1959, while a professor at MIT, and with his wife expecting their first child, Nash started experiencing delusional patterns of thought, developing strange and rigid beliefs, feeling that he was playing some sort of special role as a messenger of some kind, hearing and seeing things that weren't there, even thinking he was being contacted by aliens who were leaving messages for him in newspapers. His ability to function in daily life fluctuated greatly, as he veered between his lucid, brilliant mind and the confused, schizophrenic mind into which he was also developing. His marriage ended shortly thereafter, and Nash eventually spent almost a decade in a psychiatric institution. The voices in his head continued to haunt him for decades. But eventually, he learned how to manage his symptoms and function again in the world. He was able to return to work, and even remarried his original wife (in 2001). He remains an active mathematician and frequent speaker today.

John Nash's case raises some central questions about schizophrenia. What are the underlying neurological and cognitive processes that are affected by the disorder and produce the symptoms a person experiences? Are there ways of gaining control over symptoms, by strengthening the underlying systems in other ways? What factors contribute to better management of schizophrenia symptoms, and to slowing or halting its long-term progression?

Nash's story also challenges some common assumptions about schizophrenia, such as the belief that it is a one-way ticket to insanity and the person is going to get steadily worse. Or the belief that people with schizophrenia are to be feared, because they are perpetually unstable and likely to do random, unpredictable, even violent or dangerous things. Nash himself managed to live a productive, quiet, peaceful, and generally happy life. There are obviously not always such happy endings that people with schizophrenia can look forward to, but it is encouraging to know that it is possible.

Focus Questions

 Why do some people develop schizophrenia? What are its causal factors?

 What brain changes are associated with schizophrenia?

Schizophrenia is often regarded as one of the more devastating psychological illnesses, and indeed, severe cases of schizophrenia involve a shocking loss of basic functioning. Although schizophrenia is not common (affecting only between approximately 4 to 8 out of every 1000 adults worldwide [Bhugra, 2005; Saha et al., 2005]), schizophrenia seems to be universal, appearing in cultures all over the world and across history. Some of our earliest writings describe people who seem to have lost touch with reality, who hear voices from within, and produce bizarre speech and behaviours. At the time, it may have been thought that they were possessed by demons or spirits. Now, we would likely diagnose schizophrenia.

Symptoms and Types of Schizophrenia

Schizophrenia refers to what many psychologists and psychiatrists believe is *a brain disease that causes the person to experience significant breaks from reality, a lack of integration of thoughts and emotions, and problems with attention and memory*. Symptoms may begin to occur and escalate very gradually, remaining unnoticeable for a long time before family members start to perceive a pattern. In other cases, however, symptoms can begin and escalate very rapidly.

There are many popular but misguided beliefs regarding schizophrenia. For example, people believe that people have schizophrenia when they have more than one personality; however, this is dissociative identity disorder (see Module 15.2). Nor is schizophrena solely an organic brain disease that only responds to medication. In fact, schizophrenia is strongly affected by social factors such as family support and life events that cause stress. Also, as we saw with John Nash, schizophrenia does not necessarily get steadily worse. In most cases, the person's symptoms fluctuate over time, sometimes throwing the person into acute psychosis in which he is not in touch with reality in different ways, whereas at other times symptoms could be in remission and the person capable of functioning normally.

In most cases of schizophrenia, there are three distinct phases: prodromal, active, and residual. These tend to occur in sequence, although individuals may cycle through all three many times.

In the **prodromal phase**, *people may become easily confused and have difficulty organizing their thoughts, they may lose interest and begin to withdraw from friends and family, and they may lose their normal motivations, withdraw from life, and spend increasing amounts of time alone, often deeply engrossed in their own thoughts*. It is not uncommon for other people to get upset as a result of these behaviours, assuming the person is lazy or otherwise being irresponsible.

In the **active phase**, *people typically experience delusional thoughts, hallucinations, or disorganized patterns of thoughts, emotions, and behaviour*. This phase usually transitions into the **residual phase**, *in which people's predominant symptoms have disappeared or lessened considerably, and they may simply be withdrawn, have trouble concentrating, and generally lack motivation*.

There is huge variety in terms of the progression of schizophrenia. Some people cycle through the three stages only a couple of times in their lives, whereas others may cycle repeatedly through the three stages; typically, the severity of their withdrawal in the residual phase tends to increase with repeated episodes, and their ability to function normally seems to decrease after each active phase they go through.

The most significant and characteristic symptoms of schizophrenia are the tendency to experience hallucinations, delusions, and disorganized patterns of thinking, feeling, and behaving. These are most pronounced in the active phase of the disease, but one must always remember that the transitions between these phases will not be perfectly clean, so that the hallucinations and delusions, for example, are either consistently there or are completely gone. The person with schizophrenia may experience short-term resurgences of symptoms, perhaps associated with stressful periods or other factors and, in general, may experience fluctuations in symptoms due to any number of possible reasons.

Simulate Schizophrenia Overview

Explore Types and Symptoms of Schizophrenia

Hallucinations are *alterations in perception, such that a person hears, sees, smells, feels, or tastes something that does not actually exist, except in that person's own mind*.

Delusions are *beliefs that are not based on reality (at least from the perspective of the person's general culture)*. For example, people may believe that they are someone famous, like Jesus or the president of the United States, or that their bodies are not under their own control but are being controlled by alien beings. They may find special significance in common events in the world, and feel like they have a special connection with reality or some sort of unusual power, like the ability to control the wind.

Consider the following personal account of a man named Kurt Snyder, who wrote a book about his experiences with schizophrenia during college:

> *I thought about fractals and infinity for many years. I always told myself I was on the verge of discovery, but I simply had to think a little bit harder about it. I just wasn't thinking hard enough. The reality is that the problems I was trying to solve were far beyond my mental abilities, but I didn't recognize this fact. Even though I had no evidence to substantiate my self-image, I knew in my heart that I was just like Einstein, and that someday I would get a flash of inspiration. I didn't recognize the truth—that I am not a genius. I kept most of my mathematical ideas to myself and spoke to very few people about them. I was paranoid that someone else would solve the riddle first if I provided the right clues. (Snyder, 2006, p. 209)*

Kurt's experiences, and those of many other individuals diagnosed with schizophrenia, attest to the mind-altering experiences that characterize this disorder.

Disorganized behaviour *describes the considerable difficulty people with schizophrenia may have completing the tasks of everyday life*—cooking, taking care of one's hygiene, socializing. They have great difficulty organizing their behaviour enough to complete tasks before getting distracted by other thoughts or things to do, and never being able to follow a project to completion, or even a train of thought, finding their minds jumping from thought to thought uncontrollably.

Provided by Kurt Snyder, author

Kurt Snyder began experiencing schizophrenia in college. *Me, Myself, and Them* is his personal account of living with schizophrenia.

In addition to disorganized thinking, numerous other symptoms accompany schizophrenia. For some individuals, the symptoms cluster into different patterns, leading mental health professionals in the past to identify subtypes of the disorder. These subtypes were dropped from official practice in 2013 (at least, according to the DSM-5), but they are still commonly used:

- **Paranoid schizophrenia**: *Symptoms include delusional beliefs that one is being followed, watched, or persecuted, and may also include delusions of grandeur or the belief that one has some secret or insight or power or some other characteristic that makes one particularly special.*
- **Disorganized schizophrenia**: *Symptoms include thoughts, speech, behaviour, and emotion that are poorly integrated and incoherent. People with disorganized schizophrenia may also show inappropriate, unpredictable mannerisms.*
- **Catatonic schizophrenia**: *Symptoms include episodes in which a person remains mute and immobile—sometimes in bizarre positions—for extended periods. Individuals may also exhibit repetitive, purposeless movements.*
- **Undifferentiated schizophrenia**: *This category includes individuals who show a combination of symptoms from more than one type of schizophrenia.*
- **Residual schizophrenia**: *This category reflects individuals who show some symptoms of schizophrenia but are either in transition to a full-blown episode or in remission.*

Another distinction is often made between positive and negative symptoms (Harvey & Walker, 1987). **Positive symptoms** refer to *the presence of maladaptive behaviours, such as confused and paranoid thinking, and inappropriate emotional reactions*. In contrast, **negative symptoms** involve *the absence of adaptive behaviour, such as absent or flat emotional reactions, lack of interacting with others in a social setting, and lack of motivation.*

Individuals with schizophrenia experience several problems with cognitive functioning. These range from basic, low-level physiological responses, such as excessive eye blinking in response to stimulation (Perry et al., 2002), to more complex cognitive skills, such as those required for standardized achievement tests—test scores tend to drop during adolescence as the disorder begins and progresses (Fuller et al., 2002). Many complex

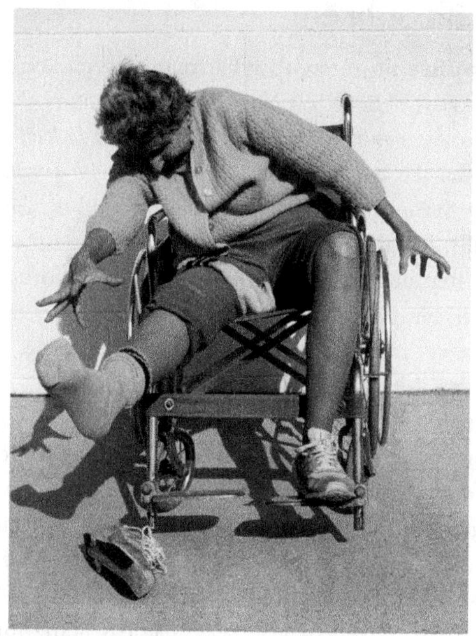

Grunnitus Studio/Science Source

People who experience catatonic schizophrenia will remain immobile, even if in a bizarre position, for extended periods of time.

cognitive abilities involve the prefrontal cortex, a brain region that shows significant neurological decline in individuals with schizophrenia (Wright et al., 2000). This may be the reason for deficits in working memory that connect to symptoms associated with schizophrenia, such as the inability to keep track of a train of thought, organize the sequence of a conversation, and handle multiple memory tasks for a short period of time. Working memory deficits may partially explain the disorganized thoughts and speech characteristic of schizophrenia (Park et al., 1999).

Social interaction is often very difficult for many people with schizophrenia. They typically have difficulty reasoning about social situations and show relatively poor social adjustment (Done et al., 1994). In addition, their emotional expressions and ability to react to the emotions of others may be impaired (Penn & Combs, 2000). For example, people with schizophrenia may maintain a neutral mask-like expression on their faces, and show little response to smiles or other expressions from people around them. As a result, the person with schizophrenia generally is not as socially competent and strikes others as a little "odd"; this can set social feedback processes in motion (such as others then avoiding eye contact or extended discussions with the schizophrenic person), which then cause the person with schizophrenia to become aware of this negative social feedback, to feel self-conscious and uncomfortable, and to be more likely to socially withdraw in the future.

Social withdrawal and isolation is a very common consequence of schizophrenia and may even be related to the long-term outcomes of the disease; helping people with schizophrenia deal with their own social behaviours and skills, as well as working to further reduce stigma in society so that people may not behave as negatively toward people with schizophrenia, are important challenges for society to address in helping individuals with this disorder. Unfortunately, a great deal of stigma does remain toward schizophrenia, in part because of common misunderstandings that many have of the disease.

MYTHS IN MIND

Schizophrenia Is Not a Sign of Violence or Genius

Although schizophrenia is a widely recognized term, it is also widely misunderstood. As was mentioned in the opening story about John Nash, people may believe that schizophrenia makes people violent or dangerous, or causes people to have different personalities (which is actually called dissociative identity disorder; see Module 15.2). People also commonly believe that the "madness" of schizophrenia is also associated with being a genius. It can be difficult to dispel such myths, especially with high-profile cases that provide an example of the myth, such as John Nash or Ted Kaczynski (aka the "Unabomber"). Similar to Nash, Kaczynski was a very bright mathematician, who seemed to slip into schizophrenic delusions. Contrary to Nash, however, Kaczynski's delusions led him to take violent actions against what he perceived to be the evil system of our society. This earned him his Unabomber nickname, because he sent bombs, through the mail, to prominent researchers at various universities.

The truth is that schizophrenia is not associated with genius but, in fact, with cognitive deficits as noted earlier in this module. Contrary to Ted Kaczynski and John Nash, people with schizophrenia typically score slightly below average on IQ tests (Woodberry et al., 2008). Also, people with schizophrenia are only rarely violent, and in almost all cases in which they are, other factors such as substance abuse play a big role; their overall propensity for violence is not meaningfully different from the rest of the population (Douglas et al., 2009; Fazel et al., 2009). Rather than being violent, people with schizophrenia are likely to isolate themselves and end up in situations in which they are likely to get harmed themselves. In fact, ironically, it's the people with schizophrenia who should perhaps fear the rest of society; people with mental illnesses are approximately 10 times more likely to be victims of crime than the non-mentally ill (Teplin et al., 2005).

Elaine Thompson/AP Images

Ted Kaczynski's case is unusual because his illness led him to send bombs to researchers through the mail. Most people with schizophrenia do not present a threat to others.

Robert P. Matthews/Princeton University/Getty Images

John Nash is a math genius and the subject of *A Beautiful Mind*. Stories like Nash's lead some to incorrectly associate genius with certain types of mental illness, including schizophrenia.

Quick Quiz 15.4a

Symptoms and Types of Schizophrenia

KNOW ...

1 A person with schizophrenia who experiences delusions that she is royalty is experiencing a(n) ________ symptom.

A positive
B negative
C catatonic
D undifferentiated

APPLY ...

2 A patient who is nonresponsive and remains still in odd postures may be diagnosed with which subtype of schizophrenia?

A Disorganized
B Undifferentiated
C Catatonic
D Residual

3 An individual showing poor integration of thinking and emotion visits a psychiatrist claiming that all of her neighbours are watching her. Into which category of schizophrenia might the psychiatrist classify the individual?

A Residual
B Undifferentiated
C Disorganized
D Paranoid

ANALYZE ...

4 Which of the following statements best summarizes the relationship between schizophrenia and violence?

A Generally, people with schizophrenia are no more likely to become violent than non-mentally ill people, and if violence occurs, other factors, such as substance abuse, are likely to contribute to its cause.
B People with schizophrenia are twice as likely to be violent as non-mentally ill people.
C People with schizophrenia are far more peaceful than non-mentally ill people.
D People with schizophrenia cannot differentiate right from wrong, and therefore are prone to violence.

5 There have been several famous cases of people with superior intellectual abilities as well as schizophrenia. Does this mean that schizophrenia is the cause or the result of genius?

A No; in fact, the average IQ of people with schizophrenia may be slightly lower than average.
B Yes; in fact, the average IQ of people with schizophrenia is approximately 15% higher than average.
C Yes, because people who are that smart are likely to develop schizophrenia simply because they know too much.
D No, because schizophrenia is associated with very low IQs.

Answers can be found on page ANS-4.

Explaining Schizophrenia

So far we have described schizophrenia based on its psychological and physical characteristics. Researchers are also very curious about the underlying sources of these characteristics and have employed a wide range of techniques to discover what causes schizophrenia. Although a single definitive answer has not yet emerged, a holistic understanding is emerging through the application of the biopsychosocial model.

GENETICS Studies using twin, adoption, and family history methods have shown that as genetic relatedness increases, the chance that a relative of a person with schizophrenia will also develop the disorder increases (see Figure 15.7). For example, if one identical twin has schizophrenia, the other twin has a 25% to 50% chance of developing it. This rate is significantly higher than the 10% to 17% rate found in dizygotic (fraternal) twin pairs (Gottesman, 1991).

Watch: Genetics Research in Schizophrenia

For decades, behavioural genetic studies have shown that genes contribute to schizophrenia, but they cannot identify the specific genes that contribute to the disorder. However, with the benefit of recent technological advances and the data from the Human Genome Project, researchers are beginning to make progress at the molecular level. For example, scientists have discovered a distinct pattern of genetic irregularities that is found in 15% of individuals with schizophrenia, compared with

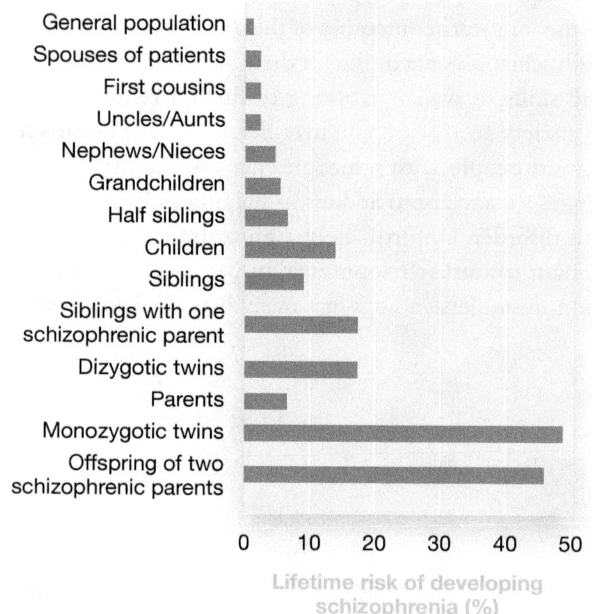

{FIG. 15.7} **Genetic Influences for Schizophrenia** The more genetic similarity an individual has to a person with schizophrenia, the more likely that he or she will also develop the disorder.

only 5% of healthy controls (Walsh et al., 2008). On the one hand, this relationship suggests a possible genetic contribution to schizophrenia. On the other hand, the genetic abnormality was not found in 85% of the individuals with schizophrenia. Thus, like most disorders, schizophrenia cannot be diagnosed by testing for a single gene, and the search for the complex genetic combinations that may underlie schizophrenia has barely begun.

Researchers at the University of Alberta have made major contributions to this search. Their first breakthrough came by chance, as is often the case. Researcher Diane Cox was looking at samples of genetic material for research that had nothing to do with schizophrenia, but she noticed samples from a mother-daughter pair that showed a remarkable similarity; each sample had a break in one of the genes on a specific chromosome, #14 (Kamnasaran et al., 2003), and as it turned out, both of them had schizophrenia. This important clue led to further breakthroughs about genetic contributions to schizophrenia and the mechanisms through which genes affect the development of the disease (Wong et al., 2013).

Another way to examine the biological factors involved in schizophrenia is to examine brain anatomy and chemistry.

SCHIZOPHRENIA AND THE NERVOUS SYSTEM

One important neurological characteristic of people with schizophrenia is the size of the brain ventricles, the fluid-filled spaces in the core of the brain. People with schizophrenia have ventricular spaces that are 20% to 30% larger than people without schizophrenia (see Figure 15.8; Gottesman & Gould, 2003). The reason for these larger ventricular spaces is a loss of brain matter, which amounts to a reduction of total brain volume by approximately 2% in those individuals with schizophrenia. In particular, the reduced volume can be found in structures such as the amygdala and hippocampus (Wright et al., 2000).

The brains of people with schizophrenia are not just different in size; they also function differently. People with schizophrenia have a lower level of activity in their frontal lobes than those without schizophrenia. People who have a long history with the disorder show lower levels of activity in their frontal lobes during a resting state, and even when their frontal lobes are activated by a cognitive task (Hill et al., 2004). Also, as mentioned above, they also tend to have smaller amygdala and hippocampal regions, which are also less active during tasks that would normally activate those brain areas (Hempel et al., 2003).

Not only changes in brain regions, but also in brain chemistry, are part of the development of schizophrenia. Specifically, individuals with schizophrenia have overactive dopamine receptors (Heinz & Schlagenhauf, 2010), and excess dopamine can produce the types of positive symptoms associated with schizophrenia, such as hallucinations and delusions; however, dopamine levels cannot account for the negative symptoms such as flattened emotion and lack of speech (Andreasen et al., 1995).

Glutamate, another neurotransmitter, appears to be underactive in certain brain regions, including the hippocampus and the frontal cortex, of individuals with schizophrenia. Glutamate is a primary excitatory neurotransmitter, so a reduction of glutamate in those areas would correspond to a reduction of their functioning. Interestingly, glutamate receptor activity is also inhibited

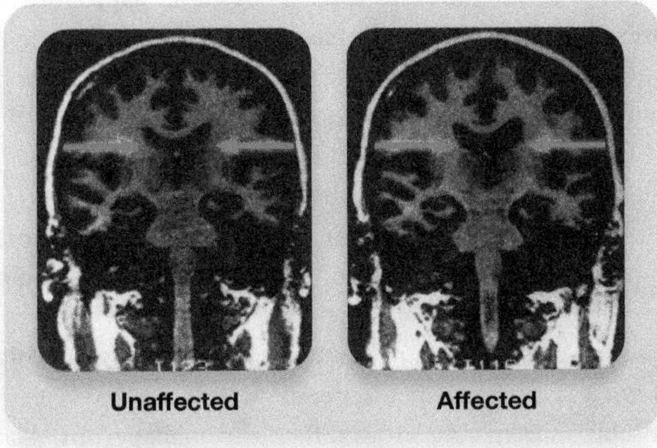

Courtesy of E. Fuller Torrrey and Daniel Weinberger

{FIG. 15.8} **Brain Volume in One Monozygotic Twin with Schizophrenia and Another without Schizophrenia** The brains of two genetically identical individuals, one affected with schizophrenia and the other unaffected, are shown here. The arrows point to the spaces created by the ventricles of the brain. Note the significant loss of brain matter in the affected individual.

Werner Bachmeier/imagebroker/Alamy

Psychologists have long noted that individuals who are being treated with antipsychotic drugs that block dopamine tend to be heavy smokers. One possible reason is that both the rewarding experiences and the impaired concentration associated with dopamine are reduced by the medication. Heavy nicotine use stimulates the reward and cognitive centres of the brain, thereby helping compensate for the dampening effects the medication has on dopamine (Winterer, 2010).

by the drug PCP (angel dust), which in high doses can cause symptoms that mirror those of schizophrenia.

In summary, scientists have found several neurological differences associated with schizophrenia, although researchers are still far from having a clear picture about the biological basis of this disorder. To further our understanding of the disorder we need to examine how these biological variables interact with environmental influences.

ENVIRONMENTAL AND CULTURAL INFLUENCES ON SCHIZOPHRENIA Research on the neuroscience of schizophrenia has made inroads toward discovering its causes. But remember a few observations: First, many people who do not have mutant versions of the genes involved in schizophrenia may still develop the disorder. Second, an identical twin has roughly a 50% chance of developing schizophrenia if her twin has it, despite sharing 100% of her genes. Finally, although approximately 1% of the world population may have the disorder, as much as 10% of the population is at a genetic risk for developing schizophrenia (Meehl, 1990). Taken together, these observations are reminders that a genetic, or even complete biological, understanding will not tell the full story of schizophrenia; in order to fully understand this disease, we must consider the role of environmental factors.

Environmental and Prenatal Factors As discussed in Module 10.1, environmental influences shape our development even before birth, while we are still in the womb. One intriguing finding in the literature is that people with schizophrenia are more likely to have been born during winter months (Tochigi et al., 2004). One hypothesis is that winter births carry a higher risk of eventual schizophrenia because the fetus's brain is developing a great deal during the second trimester, which coincides with the onset of flu season; maternal exposure to the influenza virus at such a critical time of neurological development may be one contributing factor. More generally, environmental factors that cause stress for the mother while pregnant, such as losing her spouse or experiencing trauma such as war or violence, can impact fetal development; the massive release of stress hormones during such difficult events has a variety of neurological and cognitive effects on the developing fetus (see Module 10.1), which could increase the risk of developing schizophrenia (Brown & Derkits, 2010; King et al., 2010). Clearly, more research needs to be done on the environmental contributions to schizophrenia, which might give us greater ability to understand the sorts of emotional support pregnant women need, which then might serve to prevent cases of schizophrenia from developing in the first place.

Long after prenatal development, certain events can increase one's risk of developing schizophrenia. For example, some research suggests that a very small proportion of people who use marijuana develop psychotic symptoms, possibly because the drug interacts with the genes involved in schizophrenia (Caspi et al., 2005). Head injuries occurring prior to age 10 also put people who are genetically vulnerable to schizophrenia at greater risk for developing the disorder (AbdelMalik et al., 2003). Also, being raised in an environment where psychosocial stressors (e.g., interpersonal conflict, social isolation, poverty) are more abundant, such as modern urban environments, puts individuals at greater risk for developing schizophrenia (van Os et al., 2004), because schizophrenic episodes are often triggered by acutely stressful circumstances.

Social Factors One of the big findings in the schizophrenia literature has been that the progression of the disease seems to be highly related to psychosocial factors, and in particular by how emotionally supportive or critical members in the family are toward the person with schizophrenia. Families high in "emotional expressiveness" (EE) tend to be overly critical and controlling, whereas families low in EE tend to be more supportive, accepting, and non-judging. As several teams of researchers have found, there are huge differences between people with schizophrenia who live in high-EE versus low-EE families. In high-EE families, people with schizophrenia are three to four times more likely to experience a relapse of their symptoms within a nine-month period (Brown et al., 1972; King & Dixon, 1999). This has led to the creation of therapeutic interventions designed to help families reduce their negative behaviours and learn to be more appropriately assertive. The assumption has been that the amount of emotional expressiveness in families causes the relapse of symptoms, presumably because in high-EE families the schizophrenic person would be much more stressed, and the stress then exacerbates their symptoms.

However, it is not clear exactly what the relationship between EE and schizophrenia may be. One line of research, headed by Suzanne King of McGill University, has shown that the causal pathway might be the opposite of what is assumed; that is, people with more severe cases of schizophrenia are more difficult to manage, put more stress on the family, and therefore end up causing greater emotional expression in their families (King, 2000). Nevertheless, research that has examined the impact of therapeutic interventions on families has shown that changing the EE of the family has a causal influence on the likelihood of schizophrenic relapse (Lam, 1991). Thus, the full relationship between schizophrenia and emotional expressiveness may involve a two-way causal process, with each factor affecting the other over time; untangling this causal story remains a challenge for future research.

Cultural Factors In Module 15.1, we introduced the topic of cultural perceptions of mental illness. Differing cultural perspectives are evident when it comes to schizophrenia. For example, ethnicity influences the types of experiences that individuals report having. Anglo-Americans tend to focus on the mental experiences of the disorder, such as disorganized thinking and emotions. In contrast, Mexican Americans focus more on how schizophrenia affects the body, such as by producing tension or tiredness. They conceive of the disorder as any other form of illness, whereas Americans tend to view mental disorders as separate from other types of illness (Weisman et al., 2000).

You have probably heard the term "running amok" to describe violent and out-of-control behaviour. This term is actually Indonesian in origin. Psychiatrist Emil Kraepelin concluded that amok is more similar to what we call psychosis, albeit with some notable differences. For example, auditory hallucinations—a very common symptom of schizophrenia as Westerners know it—seem to be virtually absent in Indonesians. Kraepelin attributed this difference to the low use of speech in this culture (Jilek, 1995).

Beliefs about mental illness are linked to varying cultural views of the world (McGruder, 2004). Many people throughout the world, such as the Swahili of Tanzania, believe that what we call schizophrenia is really a sign that spirits have invaded the body. In many cultures, the self is not perceived to be as separate and self-contained as in Western culture, but rather it is understood that the self is "permeable" to other entities or beings. Spirits, which are thought to overpower humans, can therefore invade the mind and body.

As you think about the different ways that a person with schizophrenia would be treated in these different cultural contexts, and the presumed sophistication of our scientific understanding of what we call "schizophrenia," consider one surprising fact—the long-term outcomes for people who have symptoms that would be diagnosed as schizophrenia are actually better in developing countries and traditional cultures that have been minimally influenced by the Western medical system. Understanding why that may be is a discussion for another time, but for now, just think about that for a moment . . .

WORKING THE SCIENTIFIC LITERACY MODEL

The Neurodevelopmental Hypothesis

Schizophrenia is obviously a complex disorder, and no one explanation has been able to account for all the variations in symptoms, severity, and duration of this disorder. Perhaps a combination of factors is to blame. One of the leading perspectives on the causes of schizophrenia is the neurodevelopmental hypothesis.

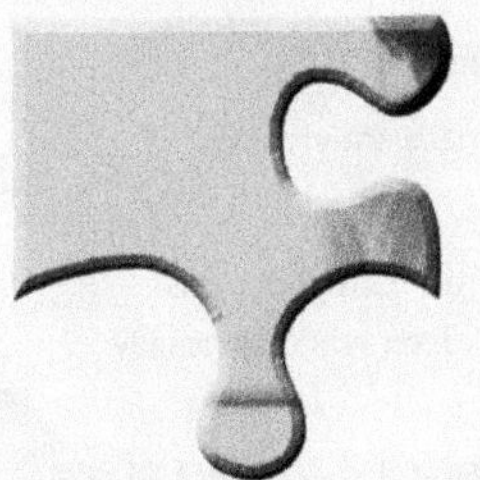

What do we know about the neurodevelopmental hypothesis?

As with most disorders, schizophrenia is best explained by interactions between various biopsychosocial factors. Much research has shown that people who develop schizophrenia likely exhibited certain patterns of behaviour earlier in life, suggesting that *the adult manifestation of what we call "schizophrenia" is the outgrowth of disrupted neurological development early in the person's life.* This is the **neurodevelopmental hypothesis**. In fact, schizophrenia may even be set in motion through environmental factors while the person is still in the womb, such as exposure to flu viruses. The sensitivity to environmental conditions exhibited by schizophrenia may indicate that *the development of schizophrenia in adulthood can be traced back to the disruption of brain development early in life*, even during prenatal development.

How can science test the neurodevelopmental hypothesis?

The neurodevelopmental hypothesis draws from research on genetics and prenatal factors. However, the developmental emphasis of the hypothesis gains strength from behavioural evidence collected during childhood and adolescence, which shows that people who develop schizophrenia showed warning signs when they were very young. For example, when psychologists viewed home movies of infants and children who subsequently developed schizophrenia, they noted that these children showed some unusual motor patterns, primarily on the left side of the body, such as jerky, repeated, and unnecessary arm movements (Walker et al., 1994). Siblings who did not have schizophrenia did not show these same motor patterns. This evidence suggests that a schizophrenic propensity already exists very early in life, setting in motion the processes and shaping the patterns of brain activity that lead further into the development of the disorder.

In adolescence, psychologists can detect the schizophrenia prodrome, a collection of characteristics that resemble mild forms of schizophrenia symptoms. For example, a teenager might become increasingly socially withdrawn and have some difficulty with depression and anxiety. But the most telling—and most perplexing—problems include experiences that resemble hallucinations and delusions, with the exception that the affected individual does not fully believe them. For example, a teen might say, "I seem to keep hearing my mother calling my name before I fall asleep, even when I know she isn't home. It is strange . . ." (Walker et al., 2010, p. 206).

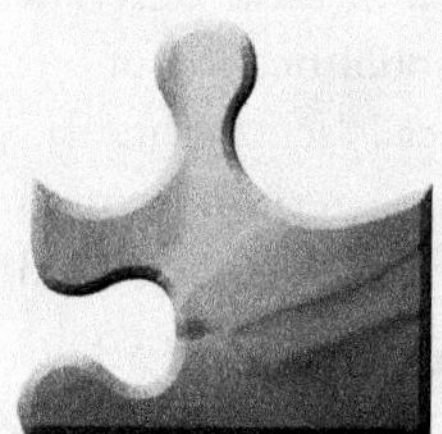

Can we critically evaluate this information?

Perhaps the most interesting challenge to this research, and one that has huge implications for our understanding of developmental disorders, is that the precursors to schizophrenia are not unique to that disorder, but in fact are precursors to a variety of neurodevelopmental disorders. In fact, the traditional view that the neurodevelopmental disorders are separate and discrete categories is being challenged; instead, the developmental disorders of intellectual disability, autism, ADHD, schizophrenia, and bipolar disorder may in fact be part of a larger syndrome of dysfunction that is rooted in common causes (Owen et al., 2011). The fact that cognitive deficits play such a central role in all these disorders fits with this possibility.

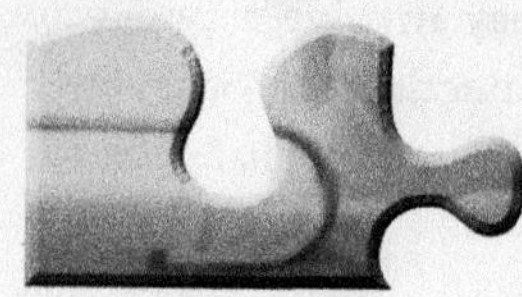

Why is this relevant?

What might be some advantages to understanding the early development of schizophrenia? By identifying developmental patterns and catching them early, it may be possible to alter the progression of the disorder, thereby preventing schizophrenia from developing, or at least controlling its severity. In recent years, a number of attempts to prevent schizophrenia from developing in high-risk populations have been made, but have not proved effective (McGlashan et al., 2006; McGorry et al., 2002). To accomplish this goal, researchers will have to rely on all levels of explanation: genetics, the function and structure of the brain, neurotransmitters, prenatal influences, and psychosocial factors.

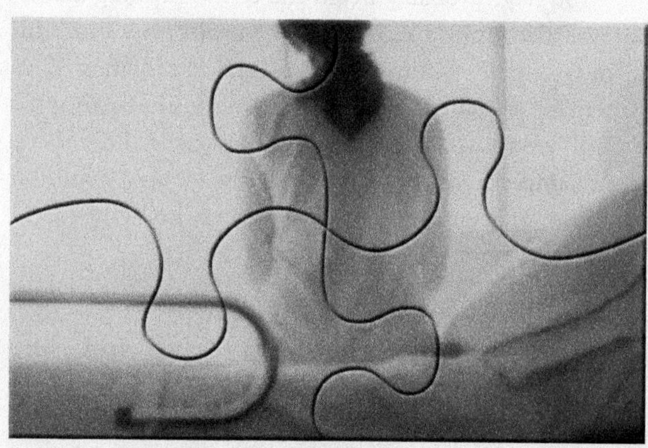

Michele Constantini/Glow Images

Quick Quiz 15.4b Explaining Schizophrenia

KNOW ...

1 The neurodevelopmental hypothesis states that

- **A** biological factors are solely responsible for schizophrenia.
- **B** social factors are solely responsible for schizophrenia.
- **C** irregular biological and environmental factors interact during early development and are responsible for schizophrenia.
- **D** prenatal exposure to the influenza virus definitely causes schizophrenia.

UNDERSTAND ...

2 Which of the following statements is most accurate concerning the biochemical basis of schizophrenia?

- **A** The neurotransmitter dopamine is overly active.
- **B** Dopamine is underactive.
- **C** Serotonin levels are too low.
- **D** There is too much glutamate activity.

3 Evidence for the neurodevelopmental hypothesis includes the fact that young children who eventually develop schizophrenia

- **A** report hallucinations as early as four years of age.
- **B** show unusual motor patterns such as jerky, repeated movements.
- **C** lapse into periods of catatonia.
- **D** had the flu during preschool.

Answers can be found on page ANS-4.

Module Summary

Module 15.4

Now that you have read this module you should

KNOW ...

- ***The key terminology associated with schizophrenia:***

active phase (p. 659)
catatonic schizophrenia (p. 660)
delusions (p. 659)
disorganized behaviour (p. 660)
disorganized schizophrenia (p. 660)
hallucinations (p. 659)
negative symptoms (p. 660)
neurodevelopmental hypothesis (of schizophrenia) (p. 665)
paranoid schizophrenia (p. 660)
positive symptoms (p. 660)
prodromal phase (p. 659)
residual phase (p. 659)
residual schizophrenia (p. 660)
schizophrenia (p. 659)
undifferentiated schizophrenia (p. 660)

UNDERSTAND ...

- ***How different neurotransmitters affect individuals with schizophrenia.*** Part of how we can explain schizophrenia is by identifying the neurotransmitters that are affected by the disorder. Abnormal dopamine and glutamate levels are found in schizophrenia; review the effects of these neurotransmitters on page 663.
- ***The genetic and environmental contributions to schizophrenia.*** The neurodevelopmental hypothesis claims that at least some neurological abnormalities are present at birth, although it does not state to what degree these abnormalities are genetic or environmental. Nevertheless, some research suggests that prenatal exposure to the flu or to significant amounts of stress hormones are risk factors for this type of mental illness. Genetics seem to play a role, as twin studies show that if one identical twin has schizophrenia, the other has a 50% chance of developing the disorder—a substantial increase over the 1% occurrence rate in the general population.

Mark Owen/Blackout Concepts/Alamy

APPLY ...

- ***Your knowledge to identify different forms of schizophrenia.*** Try the activity in **Table 15.6**: Identify which symptoms in the left column most closely match the form of schizophrenia (if any) in the right column.

  Check your answers on page ANS-4.

ANALYZE ...

- ***Claims that schizophrenia is related to genius or violent behaviour.*** As you have read, some high-profile cases highlight people with schizophrenia who are intellectually brilliant. In reality, however, research tells us that the average intelligence of people with schizophrenia is similar to, although a little bit lower than, the norm. Similarly, the belief that schizophrenia leads to violence derives from a small group of high-profile examples. In truth, there does not seem to be increased risk of violence associated with schizophrenia alone.

Table 15.6 :: Application Activity for Module 15.4

1. Rosalita was helped to a chair and she has sat there, virtually motionless, for about two hours.	A. This is not schizophrenia.
2. Eyanna refuses to go to the dentist. "Last time I went," she said, "they put a transmitter in my teeth so that the agents can control my thoughts."	B. Paranoid schizophrenia
3. Jeff has begun experiencing extreme dissociations. He even has started acting differently and referring to himself as "Steve."	C. Catatonic schizophrenia
4. Jinhai's language is very difficult to understand. He seems to be talking perfectly well but many of the words he is using are made up and other words are totally out of place.	D. Disorganized schizophrenia
	E. Residual schizophrenia

Work the Scientific Literacy Model :: Understanding Schizophrenia

1 What do we know about schizophrenia?

Recall that psychologists evaluate mental disorders such as schizophrenia using two complementary models. The medical model assumes that, like diseases of the body, psychological disorders have a standard set of symptoms, probable causes, and likely outcomes. On **page 660**, you can review the several subtypes of schizophrenia, such as paranoid, catatonic, or disorganized schizophrenia, each of which has its own set of symptoms. **Table 15.1 on page 625** offers a snapshot of another approach that psychologists use to develop a comprehensive view of each disorder—the biopsychosocial model. It is likely that genetics, environment, and the brain all play key roles in the development of the disorder.

When diagnosing most mental disorders, psychiatrists and psychologists rely on the DSM-5, which offers a set of guidelines for identifying the symptoms and severity of mental illnesses. For example, two symptoms experienced by individuals with schizophrenia are hallucinations and delusions. These terms are sometimes used interchangeably, but they mean different things. Recall that hallucinations are false perceptions of reality (hearing voices), whereas delusions are false or erroneous beliefs about reality (believing that one is God).

2 How can science help explain schizophrenia?

The disorganized thought processes characteristic of schizophrenia may be explained by brain research that suggests a decline in the functioning of the prefrontal cortex in people with this disease (**page 663**). Twin studies suggest a strong genetic influence in the emergence of schizophrenia, although specific genes cannot entirely explain why some people develop the disease. Biological research, as shown in **Figure 15.8**, demonstrates that people with schizophrenia have larger ventricle spaces, which correspond to a loss of brain matter. Research has also revealed that imbalances of chemicals in the brain may account in part for some symptoms of the disorder. Research on prenatal factors indicates that babies born in the winter months are statistically more likely to develop schizophrenia, suggesting a possible link between the effects of influenza season and fetal brain development. When it comes to environmental factors, those who are genetically at risk for the disorder and who suffer head injuries before the age of 10 years have an increased chance of developing the disease, as do those individuals who are raised in an environment characterized by psychosocial stress.

4 Why is this relevant?

Watch the accompanying video excerpt on psychological disorders. You can access the video at MyPsychLab or by clicking the play button in the centre of your eText. You can also view the video by using your smart phone and the QR code below, or you can go to the YouTube link provided.

Irmak Akcadogan/Shutterstock

After you have read this chapter and watched the video, consider the following questions: Why do most researchers consider schizophrenia a brain disorder? Which evidence suggests that schizophrenia could begin in the womb?

3 Can we critically evaluate claims about schizophrenia?

The complexity of schizophrenia seems to call for an approach that uses multiple perspectives. On **page 664**, we explored the neurodevelopmental hypothesis, which proposes that a combination of genetic and environmental factors work together during infant and child development to make people more susceptible to the disease. For instance, psychologists can identify symptoms in adolescence that predict schizophrenia. Detecting early precursors to the disorder might allow people to alter the progression of schizophrenia.

While schizophrenia is a familiar disorder to most people, it is often misunderstood. **Myths in Mind on page 661** dispels the notion that, despite famous cases such as those of John Nash and Ted Kaczynski, people with schizophrenia are likely to be either geniuses or violent offenders. To the contrary, people with schizophrenia tend to score below average on standardized intelligence tests and are less likely to be perpetrators of crime (and more likely to be victims of it).

MyPsychLab **Your turn to Work the Scientific Literacy Model:** Watch the accompanying video on YouTube, or on your phone (using the Layar app or QR code). If your instructor has assigned this as a homework activity, you can find the video clip and additional content at MyPsychLab. Answer the questions that accompany the video clip to test your understanding.

youtube.com/workthemodel

SCAN WITH LAYAR

16

Therapies

Gts/Shutterstock

Ambrophoto/Alamy

Module 16.1

Treating Psychological Disorders

Learning Objectives

After reading this module you should

KNOW ...	UNDERSTAND ...	APPLY ...	ANALYZE ...
The key terminology associated with mental health treatment	The major barriers to seeking help for psychological disorders The arguments for and against involuntary treatment	Your knowledge to suggest what approach to therapy is likely most appropriate for a given situation	Whether self-help options, such as popular books, are a useful therapy option

"The Power of Vulnerability" has become one of the most popular TED (Teaching, Entertainment, Design) talks ever given. This simple, from the heart talk involves a confident, brilliant, personable, and completely vulnerable woman, talking about how she went to a therapist because she was having a breakdown (although according to her therapist it was a spiritual awakening). Brene Brown's talk on shame courageously exposed to millions of TED viewers the deeply moving admission that so many millions of us struggle with shame, and that it is normal and indeed healthy for a person to go to a therapist. By being so open about her experiences, and letting the public know that therapists themselves go to therapists, she set an example for the rest of us that a key step toward overcoming the stigma that too many people still associate with mental illness and therapy is to talk about it. In our DIY culture, with a strong individualistic belief that people need to "pull themselves up by their own bootstraps," it is all too common to view mental illness as a sign of weakness, and to view therapists as "quacks" and "shrinks," lost in their psycho-babble and out of touch with reality. There are countless examples, from the brain-frying terror of *One Flew Over the Cuckoo's Nest*, to Frasier dispensing psychological "wisdom" on his radio show, to real-life pop-culture psychologists or therapists such as Dr. Laura Schlessinger or Dr. Phil McGraw providing therapeutic advice to people they have just met and have known for only minutes as part of their programs. To the casual viewer, it may start to seem like psychologists have about as much credibility as Lucy from Peanuts, sitting in her booth providing "psychological" advice to Charlie Brown for a nickel.

Thus, it is worth paying attention when an extremely popular cultural event, like Brene Brown's TED talk, shows the public that therapy is a normal part of many people's lives. Perhaps the stigma associated with mental illness and attending therapy is finally being overcome.

Focus Questions

 What are the major barriers that hold people back from seeking psychological help?

 What are the settings in which psychological therapy typically occurs?

In Chapter 15 we described some of the psychological disorders that affect people. Given that approximately one in five people will experience a psychological disorder in their lifetime (Narrow et al., 2002), disorders touch everyone's life, either directly or indirectly through friends, family, neighbours, or co-workers. Furthermore, if you consider the term "disorder" more broadly, to include experiences like shame that can markedly reduce or limit a person's overall functioning, then far more than 20% of us are limiting ourselves and could benefit from having our "issues" effectively treated. Clearly, there is a pervasive need for effective psychological treatments. In this module, we provide an overarching view of the approach our society takes to treating psychological disorders, discussing who tends to seek treatment, who provides it, and how treatment approaches are evaluated.

Over the past several decades, attitudes toward therapy have indeed changed, as Brene Brown's TED talk illustrates. It is now commonplace for celebrities to be open about their traumatic childhoods, relationship problems, drug abuse, and other psychological struggles. Similarly, bookstores have entire sections devoted to psychology, chock-full of advice and insight for people seeking to help themselves or someone they care about. These changes reflect a general normalization of the whole idea of psychological disorders and a lessening of the stigma toward mental illness. This shift is reflected in the high number of people who seek psychological services; each year in Canada, approximately 10% of the population seeks treatment for mental health issues (Lesage et al., 2006).

Nevertheless, not all groups of people are equally likely to seek psychological treatment. In general, women participate in therapy more often than men, and people aged 35 through 55 seek treatment more often than younger adults and the elderly (Addis & Mahalik, 2003; Olfson & Marcus, 2010). People from certain cultural groups are less likely to use psychological services; in Canada, Asian Canadians and people of Native descent are both less likely to seek mental health treatment than Caucasians (Sue & Lam, 2002). Therapy is also a more popular choice for Canadians and Americans in general relative to people from many other countries such as Israel, Hungary, Japan, and Korea (Cohen et al., 1998; Masuda et al., 2005; Yoo & Skovholt, 2001). There are many possible reasons for these differences, ranging from the degree of stigma toward mental illness in different cultures to financial and other barriers that make access to treatment more difficult.

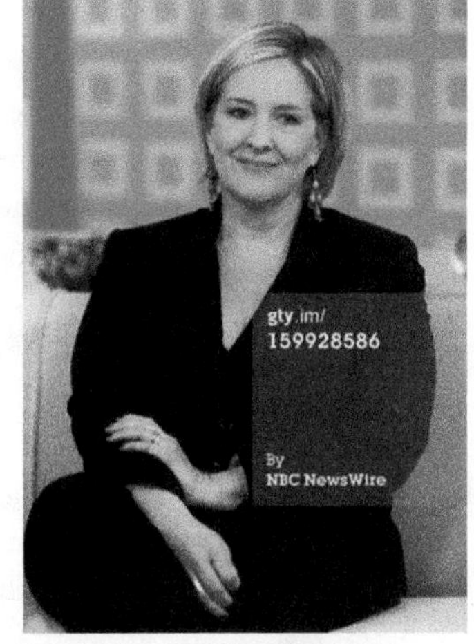

Peter Kramer/NBC/NBC NewsWire via Getty Images

Brene Brown's TED talk on shame challenges the stigma of mental illness and attending therapy.

Barriers to Psychological Treatment

Despite the optimism with which we opened this chapter, it is still the case that many people with a disorder do not receive help. For example, in one study, of 1600 adults who had been diagnosed with depression or an anxiety disorder, only 30% were receiving some form of therapy (Young et al., 2001). In both Canada and the U.S., surveys show that approximately two-thirds of people with mental health issues do not seek help from the mental health system (Lesage et al., 2006; NIMH, 2011). Furthermore, even when people do seek therapy, about half of them significantly delay doing so after first becoming aware of their mental health issues, often for years (DiClemente & Prochaska, 1985; Prochaska & DiClemente, 1984). Why would people choose not to seek help?

There are many barriers that prevent or delay people from seeking psychological treatment. One problem that almost everyone struggles with is that disorders themselves are inherently ambiguous; there is no objective, easily definable line between "mentally healthy" and "mentally ill" and no litmus test that can tell a person with a high degree of certainty that they need to seek help. Thus, a person may believe he is simply "sad," not depressed, and of course, sadness is a regular part of life, and not everyone who is sad needs to go see a therapist. Or a person may believe she is merely stressed or a bit worried about things, not that she has an anxiety disorder. This inescapable ambiguity makes it unclear exactly when it's desirable for a person to seek treatment.

Also, people very commonly are motivated to not see themselves as mentally ill, so much so that they minimalize their symptoms, basically tricking themselves and others to think that they are healthier than they really are. To some, such a label would feel like a sign of weakness or a personal failing. Or people may be concerned that others may view or treat them negatively, or be unwilling to risk the social stigma that they fear might embarrass either themselves or their families. Or they may not trust the psychological or psychiatric professions, and be skeptical of the efficacy and safety of different treatments (Craske et al., 2005; Mansfield et al., 2005; Vanheusdan et al., 2008).

Overcoming such skepticism may make a big difference in helping people seek treatment; for example, in one study, 99% of respondents said they would seek mental health treatment if they believed it would be helpful (Fox et al., 2001). There is an important role to be played by educational programs that help people become aware of what problems can be treated and help to build confidence in the mental health profession (Fox et al., 2001; Sharp et al., 2006).

The cumulative impact of the different barriers to psychological treatment leaves millions of people delaying or simply never receiving the kind of therapy and support that could, literally, change their lives (Wang et al., 2005). Understanding these barriers is an important step toward overcoming them.

STIGMA ABOUT MENTAL ILLNESS One common barrier that we alluded to earlier is stigma toward mental illness and toward the process of therapy itself (Corrigan, 2004; Vogel et al., 2009). You may already understand the effects of stigma—just imagine a business executive needing to take some time off work to undergo an operation. Imagine the support he would receive from his colleagues, the openness with which he would be able to talk to people about his health. Now imagine that same executive needing to take some time off for mental health issues, and as you do so, the whole situation changes! Very few people may be told; the person will have very little support because people generally won't know what is going on. Think of the impact this could have on, for example, a person trying for a promotion, or trying to find new employment. In many professions, mental illness carries a strong stigma, resulting in people with psychological disorders experiencing discrimination at the workplace. There may also be social costs, such as being treated differently by friends, family, or potential romantic partners. For example, one out of every two Canadians admits that they would likely not socialize with a friend who had a serious mental illness, and one in four Canadians admits that they are afraid to be around people with serious mental illnesses (Canadian Medical Association, 2008). Obviously, we still have a long way to go before mental illnesses are viewed in the same way as physical ailments.

Simulate
How Do You Take Care of Your Mental Health?

Watch
Alan Kazdin: What sort of treatments have you been developing for clinical problems?

GENDER ROLES In many countries with strong gender norms, including Canada and the U.S., there are extra pressures on men to avoid treatment, because "needing help" and going to therapy seem incompatible with the idea of being "strong" and independent, key aspects of the male gender role. This emphasis on strength and independence leads people to deny that they have any problems, or to believing that they need to "just get over it," as though people can be expected to overcome mental health issues through sheer force of will. These traditionally male gender roles certainly don't promote talking about emotions and acknowledging vulnerabilities, steps that would put people on a path toward healing (Berger et al., 2005; Mahalik et al., 2003). Getting men to see therapy differently has presented such a challenge that the NIMH has staged public awareness campaigns, such as the "Real Men, Real Depression" campaign. Initial evidence indicates that social marketing messages such as this do succeed in increasing the likelihood people will seek help, perhaps partially overcoming resistance based on traditional gender roles (Bell et al., 2010; Rochlen et al., 2006).

LOGISTICAL BARRIERS: EXPENSE AND AVAILABILITY Two of the main barriers to mental health treatment are about access—whether people can afford the money and the time (Colonna-Pydyn et al., 2007; Craske et al., 2005). Money has a particularly profound influence on the way that the mental health system functions, and the kinds of treatments that are available for many people. For example, psychotherapy can be very expensive, generally costing more than $100 per hour, and often much more than that. Therapy is also associated with numerous indirect costs, such as time away from work, transportation, and possibly child care. Unfortunately, government health-care coverage in Canada generally only includes treatment by psychiatrists, leaving counsellors, psychologists, and many types of therapists less able to reach many people who can't afford their services. The net result of these sorts of funding decisions is to give a heavy advantage toward the medical approaches, and treatment providers, for psychological disorders. In practice, this means that most of the money flows toward the pharmaceutical industries and hospitals, and medically-based treatments retain their dominance over the field. What often happens, especially for individuals from lower-income families, is that they simply attempt to cope with their lives, while all too often their situation becomes increasingly dysfunctional and ready to collapse until finally, a major problem occurs and they can no longer avoid it. This often results in the treatment process beginning in a hospital emergency room, which places an extra burden on the public health-care system (Snowdon, 1999).

To help overcome these barriers, some community organizations provide offices in lower-income areas where private psychotherapists are scarce and needed. Community mental health centres often provide therapy on a sliding scale, which means the cost of a one-hour session varies depending on the patient's income and insurance status. Drug treatments can also be made more affordable by using generic products as opposed to brand-name ones, although this tends to be resisted by pharmaceutical companies who spend huge sums of money researching and promoting their drugs.

INVOLUNTARY TREATMENT In some cases, people are required (that is, forced) to enter the mental health system against their will. In Canada and the United States, as well as many other countries, people can be compelled through the courts or on the advice of social service agencies or doctors to be treated for mental illness. The majority of these cases arise due to the person engaging in highly erratic or disturbing behaviour, which results in legal trouble and the perception that the person may be a risk to themselves or others. Involuntary treatment can also be required after the person commits harm to others, as in some cases of domestic violence.

This "outpatient commitment" is a highly contentious issue in the field of mental health and in the legal system, because it effectively strips people of some of their basic rights. Proponents of this practice argue that it improves mental health, reduces the costs of mental illness on society, and increases the effectiveness of treatment by ensuring that people with severe disorders receive treatment that they might otherwise avoid; it also may protect society from people who may otherwise commit harm. People who are opposed are concerned that this practice is unethical because it can restrict the freedom and take away the rights of people who have not done anything harmful to themselves or others, force people to receive medications that may alter brain function and have dangerous side effects, and can easily be misapplied to certain ethnic groups and lower socioeconomic classes (Kisely et al., 2011).

Research has thus far failed to clear up the controversy. For example, some studies show that a significant number of people benefit from mandated treatment, as indicated by their adherence to treatment and reduced encounters with law enforcement (Hough & O'Brien, 2005; Pollack et al., 2005). On the other hand, many people placed in involuntary treatment programs feel coerced and resentful, and not everyone benefits. The concern that involuntary treatment decisions can be biased has also been backed up by research. A survey of records in the U.S. indicated that individuals who are lower in socioeconomic status and from African-American or Latino backgrounds are significantly more likely to receive court-ordered treatment (Takeuchi & Cheung, 1998). Some of this bias may be due to fairly benevolent reasons; for example, if poorer individuals are unable to afford treatment, then a court-ordered treatment may be relied upon to get people the help that they need. But much of this bias may be due to more undesirable reasons, such as prejudice and the general lack of legal power wielded by people of lower socioeconomic status or from marginalized ethnic groups. Thus, supporters of involuntary treatment continue to point to its apparent benefits for some people, whereas opponents point to its apparent costs for others. The debate continues.

Quick Quiz 16.1a

Barriers to Psychological Treatment

KNOW ...

1 People who would argue against the practice of involuntary commitment tend to believe that

- **A** committing people against their will is wrong because it removes people's basic human rights and freedoms.
- **B** imposing treatments, such as drug treatments, onto people is unethical because the side effects and unintended consequences of the treatment itself may further harm the person.
- **C** the decision to commit people to treatment can be biased due to prejudice and stereotypes that exist in society.
- **D** all of the above

UNDERSTAND ...

2 Which type of barrier is in evidence when people believe their problems are not important enough for a therapist?

- **A** Financial
- **B** Minimalizing
- **C** Skepticism about therapy
- **D** Procrastination

APPLY ...

3 People's fears that they may be stigmatized for having a mental illness

- **A** are unfounded; our society has advanced too far to still be stigmatizing mental illness.
- **B** are based on fear that they may be exposed to severe treatments against their will.
- **C** are the sign of delusions, possibly indicating schizophrenia.
- **D** are understandable; unfortunately, there may often be professional or social costs when others know someone has had a psychological disorder.

Answers can be found on page ANS-4.

Mental Health Providers and Settings

A wide variety of treatment settings are available for people in need of mental health care. The type of treatment people receive depends on several factors, including their age, the type and severity of the disorder, and the existence of any legal issues and concerns that coincide with the need for treatment. Mental health services

Guildhall Library & Art Gallery/Heritage Images/Glow Images

Today, some people with severe mental disorders reside in an institution or hospital that specializes in mental health care. These settings are dramatically different than they were just a few decades ago, when they were called "insane asylums" and other unfortunate names.

Watch

Alan Kazdin: How do we reach out to people who need help for mental illness?

Explore

Psychotherapy Practitioners and Their Activities

include inpatient care, outpatient office visits, the use of prescription drugs, attending therapy sessions, and taking part in support groups. Different types of care tend to be delivered by professionals with different training and skill sets.

MENTAL HEALTH PROVIDERS In popular culture, the terms psychologist and psychiatrist are often (and erroneously) used as if they mean the same thing. In fact, there are some major differences between the two, and even within a category there can be huge differences; certainly not every psychologist nor every psychiatrist takes the same approach as their peers.

Clinical psychologists are perhaps the best-known type of psychologist in the mental health field. **Clinical psychologists** *have received Ph.D. level of training, and are able to formally diagnose and treat mental health issues ranging from the everyday and mild to the chronic and severe.* **Counselling psychologists** are *mental health professionals who typically work with people needing help with more common problems such as stress, coping, and mild forms of anxiety and depression, rather than severe mental disorders*; counselling psychologists may have either a Master's or Ph.D. level of training. Practitioners of clinical and counselling psychology work in many capacities and settings. They may provide individual or group therapy in an office or institution such as a hospital, or they may conduct psychological testing and research. Other people with different levels of training and background also conduct therapy; for example, clinical social workers and psychiatric nurses conduct therapy to help people cope with psychological problems.

Psychiatrists are *medical doctors who specialize in mental health and who are allowed to diagnose and treat mental disorders through prescribing medications.* It is important to note that many psychiatrists also work within an integrative biopsychosocial perspective, and perform psychological counselling and therapy, or work closely with other professionals who provide such services. In Canada and most U.S. states, clinical psychologists cannot prescribe medications, so in many settings psychologists and psychiatrists work together and offer an approach combining medications with psychological therapies. Like clinical psychologists, psychiatrists work in a variety of settings, but they are most frequently found in hospitals and other institutional settings, treating people with relatively severe psychological disorders.

INPATIENT TREATMENT AND DEINSTITUTIONALIZATION Throughout much of human history, people experiencing severe disorders—such as the profound disturbances associated with schizophrenia or Alzheimer's disease—were often separated from society. They may have been physically removed from the city or, in the 1800s and 1900s, locked in an asylum. These actions hardly qualify as treatments because there was no hope that the individuals would get better. Instead, the goals were to protect the public and to provide basic care for individuals whose families could not do so (Wright, 1997).

Sadly, many of the mental institutions of past generations were terrible places for the patients. The creation of large institutions for housing the mentally unwell began around the 14th century due to a rapidly growing population and mass migration to the cities; these trends tended to disrupt the normal family and community traditions that would have provided structure to individuals' lives and the bonds of collective responsibility that people would have had for the mentally ill members of their families. As a result, society's outcasts grew in number, until institutions were built to house them. For the next few centuries, the inmates of these institutions were subjected to brutal confinement, torture, and an almost complete lack of humane conditions. In fact, the modern word *bedlam* derives from this time. In 1403, St. Mary of Bethlehem, a hospital in London, England, began admitting patients with mental issues; the hospital's treatment of these patients was so awful and the hospital's operations were so chaotic that a mispronunciation of Bethlehem as "bedlam" stuck, thereafter referring to chaos and madness in general (Foucault, 1975).

In the late 1700s, attitudes toward mental illness finally started to change; two key figures emerge from this period as heroes who helped to re-humanize the institutionalized inmates of psychological hospitals. Philippe Pinel, in 1792, was the first to be granted permission to remove the chains from the inmates of French hospitals. Slowly, people began to think that the psychologically disturbed would benefit from more humane treatment. In the mid-1800s in North America, Dorothea Dix campaigned heroically to improve the conditions of institutionalized patients and was highly instrumental in shifting society's attitudes. By the end of the 19th century, psychology was gaining credibility as a science, and asylums were built both to house the mentally ill and to attempt to treat their conditions. Unfortunately, these asylums quickly became overcrowded, and there were not many effective treatments at the time for most disorders, and so in practical terms, the asylums became little more than giant warehouses that separated the mentally ill from the rest of society.

This pattern continued until the 1960s, when people started to take a dim view toward merely housing those with disorders in dismal asylums. Effective treatments also started to be developed for some disorders, largely in the form of medications that were useful for alleviating different symptoms. As patients' symptoms became more treatable, a society-wide movement toward **deinstitutionalization** occurred, *whereby mental health patients were released back into their communities, generally after having their symptoms alleviated through medication.* The next three decades saw about an 85% decrease in the number of psychiatric inpatients (Sealy & Whitehead, 2004), both in Canada and many other countries (Fakhoury & Priebe, 2002). Although a small subset of people remained who required inpatient care, the vast majority of patients now entered the hospital for a very short stay before they were stabilized, given medication, and sent back to the care of their families.

In the decades since this movement began, mental health care providers have gathered together many resources and strategies to help people in some form of distress. For example, in as little as three or four days, a patient admitted after a suicide attempt may be fully evaluated, begin medication and therapy, receive education about emergency resources such as suicide hotlines, and then be released. Thus, whereas the goal in the past seemed to be to remove the mentally ill from society, now inpatient treatment is geared more toward protecting the individual patient from harm, and providing as quick a return to society as possible.

Of course, some people still require more intensive, long-term care, although in place of the asylum, many chronic inpatients live in residential treatment centres, which tend to resemble a dormitory or motel more than an asylum. Low-level **residential treatment centres** are *housing facilities in which residents receive psychological therapy and life skills training, with the explicit goal of helping residents become re-integrated into society as well as they can.* Medium- to high-level centres have the same emphasis as low-level centres, but also place restrictions on individuals' freedoms. These centres function like hospitals inside medium-security prisons, with a high staff-to-resident ratio ensuring that residents remain under control, residents' movements and freedom under restriction, and escape prevented by a security system and physical barriers (e.g., locked doors that bar escape). These facilities are intended for individuals with a more dangerous history—perhaps people who have committed physical or sexual assault.

OUTPATIENT TREATMENT AND PREVENTION Outpatient therapy and inpatient housing simultaneously grew in popularity through the early 20th century. Their emergence paved the way for deinstitutionalization, which was essentially a call to move the mentally ill to the community where they could receive outpatient treatment. After deinstitutionalization began, however, homelessness and substance abuse became a major problem for the severely mentally ill, who were not always able to reintegrate into society or were not cared for by their families.

To meet these needs, some psychologists began spending time away from individual, one-on-one therapy to see what they could do for the community at large—thus arose a field now known as **community psychology**, *an area of psychology that focuses on identifying how individuals' mental health is influenced by the neighbourhood, economics and community resources, social groups, and other community-based variables.* By operating at this level, community psychologists work to prevent the development of disorders, seeking to enhance the factors, such as healthy family relationships, that strengthen people and make them more resilient to the kinds of stresses that can otherwise undermine mental health. For example, to prevent depression, community psychologists may conduct research into the environmental and neighbourhood factors that contribute to stress, anxiety, and depression, and then work with community groups to resolve these problems. In addition, they may develop programs to counter negative cognitive patterns and bolster positive thinking in schools and in afterschool programs. Community psychologists, such as those at Wilfrid Laurier University in Waterloo, Ontario, are involved with issues other than mental health as well, such as environmental sustainability and social justice. Regardless of the focal issue, their basic approach involves applying psychology to the whole socio-ecological context in which individuals live, and seeking to improve human welfare by improving this larger context through collaboration with community organizations.

PSYCH @

The University Mental Health Counselling Centre

In many workplace or education-based communities, mental health services are available to the population through the institution's own services. A good example is university campuses. As you are no doubt aware, it is not at all uncommon that the stresses of university life can bring about temporary struggles with mental well-being. Most university students experience the stresses of managing a heavy workload, beginning a career path, developing an adult identity, and finding a way to pay for college, also often juggling work and family obligations along with school. Also, some students face lifelong struggles with mental illness. Approximately 15% of university students exhibit symptoms of depression; one study on first-year students at Acadia University found that 7% of male and 14% of female students experienced a major depressive disorder in their first year at school alone (Price et al., 2006)! In general, mental health issues seem to be on the rise in university students; over the past two decades, rates of depression have increased more than 50%, with anxiety disorders and other issues also increasing (American College Health Association, 2007).

Watch What's in It for Me?: Finding a Therapist if You Need One

University counselling centres typically employ a resident psychologist or psychiatrist, along with a staff of counsellors trained to help with psychological problems. These counselling centres are in great demand; some are so busy they even have waiting lists. Counsellors are well trained to help with the more common student issues, such as stress, anxiety, time management, depression, and relationship issues, but they also often encounter students with more severe disorders than most counselling centres are designed to accommodate (Gallagher, 2007; Voelker, 2003). In these cases, counsellors are trained to provide information that can help the student seek the appropriate mental health professional and, potentially, advocate on their behalf.

Quick Quiz 16.1b

Mental Health Providers and Settings

KNOW ...

1 Which type of provider is generally permitted to prescribe medications?

A Psychiatrist
B Clinical psychologist
C Clinical social worker
D Medical psychologist

2 ________ study how individuals' mental health is influenced by the neighbourhood, economics, social groups, and other community-based variables.

A Residential treatment centres
B Community psychologists
C Psychiatrists
D Social workers

3 The social movement against keeping the mentally ill in asylums is known as ________.

A empirically validated treatments
B social work
C deinstitutionalization
D community psychology

Answers can be found on page ANS-4.

Evaluating Treatments

Given the diversity of treatment approaches and settings that are available, it is important to know which approaches are effective. Aside from the obvious economic logic of society not wasting money on ineffective treatments, it is important for individuals seeking help to get help that actually, well, helps! In the mid-1990s, the American Psychological Association set up task forces to evaluate different therapy practices; as of 2005, these task forces had made their findings and recommendations available online (APA, 2009). The general philosophy is that properly designed research studies are needed to examine the effectiveness of different therapeutic approaches, and these approaches should evolve depending on what research suggests does and does not work.

EMPIRICALLY SUPPORTED TREATMENTS

Empirically supported treatments (also called evidence-based therapies) are *treatments that have been tested and evaluated* (Chambless & Ollendick, 2001; De Los Reyes & Kazdin, 2008). The most rigorous way of testing whether a certain therapy works is through an experiment. Recall from Module 2.2 that an experiment would involve randomly assigning volunteers to a treatment group (e.g., a type of therapy) and to a control group. Ideally, experiments are also double-blind, which in this case means that neither the patient nor the individual evaluating the patient is aware of which treatment the patient is receiving. However, this level of rigour is often close to impossible to attain when evaluating therapies. One common problem is that it is ethically problematic to place people into a control group, because it effectively denies them treatment that they need. It is also generally impossible to use double-blind procedures, given that a therapist, of course, knows which type of treatment she administers, and many clients likely do as well.

Also, testing the effectiveness of therapy using some therapists may not generalize to others, because some therapists will be much more skilled than others. Each client and therapist is unique, and much of the effectiveness of therapy comes from the therapeutic alliance—the relationship that emerges in therapy. In fact, the specific type of therapy used is actually less important than these "common factors" of therapist and client building a relationship. Establishing a positive relationship therefore depends on various qualities of the therapist and client, as well as the "fit" between the two. Therapists who are more socially skilled, who show warmth, concern, and empathy, tend to be more effective. Similarly, clients who are more open to the process, more willing to trust the therapist, and more willing to recognize and work on their issues are more likely to benefit from therapy (Prochaska & Norcross, 2002).

Therefore, even though a therapist may implement the same steps and procedures in a therapy, each session is different and each combination of client and therapist is unique. As a result, it is very difficult to adequately test the effectiveness of many therapeutic approaches to the rigorous extent required for empirical support (DeRubeis & Crits-Cristoph, 1998).

Many psychologists believe that evaluating psychological therapies in the same way we evaluate, for example, the efficacy of drugs ignores many of the nuances and complexity that exist in the process of therapy (Westen & Bradley, 2005), and provides a misleading picture of how effective therapy can be in specific instances. This same problem has held back research on the effectiveness of self-help treatments, because of course, any individual book or approach may work differently for different individuals. What benefits one person, at a certain time in her life, may be useless to someone else. Nevertheless, some research tries to address this issue, given the explosion of self-help literature in the past few decades.

WORKING THE SCIENTIFIC LITERACY MODEL

Can Self-Help Treatments Be Effective?

Many people opt to address their psychological problems by using resources that do not involve visiting an actual therapist, such as self-help books, online information, or community workshops. Are these approaches helpful?

What do we know about the availability of self-help treatments?

There is a huge variety of self-help materials available to the public. Just walk down to your local bookstore and check out the psychology section, where you will find books on everything from anxiety and depression to how to raise children, deal with divorce, and optimize your well-being. A quick perusal will reveal that many of these books are written by people with Ph.D.s in the relevant fields (although many are not), but the books also do not always agree with one another as to how to best approach whatever issue they are discussing. For example, if you read the popular literature on how to help children deal with emotional struggles, you could catalogue several approaches that were not only different, but actually would work against each other. How can one know which approach is right? How can one know whether the use of self-help literature is effective in general? There is some research on this issue, examining whether **bibliotherapy**, *the use of self-help books and other reading materials as a form of therapy*, improves people's symptoms.

How can science test the effectiveness of self-help treatments?

One study attempted to assess the effectiveness of bibliotherapy over a three-month period in 170 elderly primary care patients who were experiencing depression. The patients were evenly divided into two groups: both groups received a "standard care" approach, but the self-help group also read a self-help book on depression. After three months,

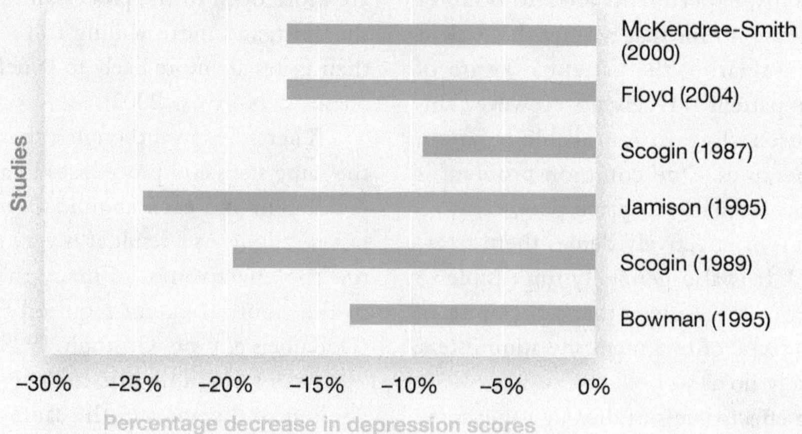

{FIG. 16.1} **Results of Six Studies Evaluating the Self-Help Book *Feeling Good*** Research on the book *Feeling Good* shows successful results in reducing symptoms of depression. Comparisons across six studies (identified by author name and publication date) indicate statistically significant improvement in each case (Anderson et al., 2005).

the group who read the self-help book in addition to the standard care showed no signs of reduced depression compared to the control group (Joling et al., 2010). However, as discussed earlier, this is hardly a definitive test of the effectiveness of self-help. Maybe that particular book wasn't effective for this population, but a different one could have been. Or maybe different books would appeal to different people, so testing a single book on a whole group may show no overall improvement, but a few individuals could have benefited substantially.

A slightly stronger approach to this question is to perform a meta-analysis, combining numerous studies testing a similar hypothesis. One such analysis combined six separate studies that had tested whether the book *Feeling Good* reduced depressive symptoms. The researchers found that over four weeks, those who read the book had reduced depression compared to those who did not (see Figure 16.1; Anderson et al., 2005). Thus, there may be reason to believe that bibliotherapy can be helpful.

Can we critically evaluate this evidence?

It may strike you as impersonal to turn to a computer, television, or book for assistance with mental health problems. However, this impersonal nature of these treatments may be an important advantage, helping people to gather information anonymously (Rainie & Packel, 2001).

Another issue is that it is always important to consider the source. Self-help gurus may be focused more on the business and entertainment side of things rather than on producing long-term positive benefits to those in need. In addition, some of these individuals do not have professional degrees in psychology or other mental health fields. As a consequence, we should not expect all self-help materials to have the same success rates; it is even possible that some could do more harm than good. Before judging a specific self-help treatment as effective or not, we should determine whether it is supported by sound scientific research.

Why is this relevant?

Major advantages of using self-help options include that they are typically low in cost, are convenient, and provide anonymity for those who want it. Self-help options are easy to find. In fact, many people consult online resources to get help for depression, anxiety, substance-abuse problems, and sexual health (Fox, 2005). If you do turn to self-help resources for your psychological problems, remember to choose wisely, which means to look into the credibility of the sources and the extent to which their claims seem based on solid research. It is also important to not merely read the book, but to also apply the exercises it recommends. As we know from research on neural plasticity (see Module 3.3), people can change their brains (and therefore their well-being) enormously through practice, but simply reading a book and expecting to be mentally healthier is not much different from reading a workout book and expecting to get bigger muscles. In both cases, you have to do the exercises described in order to reap the benefits. Research does suggest that putting insights into practice tends to be lower for self-help approaches than face-to-face therapy sessions (O'Kearney et al., 2006), which likely limits the effectiveness of these approaches. If you are experiencing psychological distress, it is probably advisable to speak with a mental health professional at least once—especially if symptoms are severe—to find out whether self-help is appropriate for your situation. They may also be able to suggest resources that they believe are high quality, which can save you a great deal of wasted energy wading through the burgeoning self-help literature to find quality information.

Emilio Ereza/Alamy

Quick Quiz 16.1c Evaluating Treatments

KNOW ...

1 ________ is the relationship that emerges in therapy between the therapist and client, and is an important determinant of the therapy's effectiveness.

- **A** Client insight
- **B** Bibliotherapy
- **C** Therapeutic alliance
- **D** Friendship

UNDERSTAND ...

2 What does it mean to say that a therapy has "empirical support"?

- **A** Insurance companies prefer it.
- **B** Therapists prefer to use it.
- **C** Research studies confirm that it is effective compared to no treatment and possibly compared to other alternatives.
- **D** Research studies demonstrate that it can do a better job than drugs.

3 Which of the following conclusions best summarizes the effectiveness of bibliotherapy?

- **A** It has no benefit whatsoever.
- **B** It is more effective than other forms of therapy.
- **C** It works, but is addictive.
- **D** It may be helpful to many people, but its results are not consistent.

Answers can be found on page ANS-4.

Module Summary

Module 16.1

Ambrophoto/Alamy

Now that you have read this module you should

KNOW ...

- ***The key terminology associated with mental health treatment:***

bibliotherapy (p. 677)
clinical psychologist (p. 674)
community psychology (p. 675)
counselling psychologist (p. 674)
deinstitutionalization (p. 675)
empirically supported treatments (p. 676)
psychiatrist (p. 674)
residential treatment centre (p. 675)

UNDERSTAND ...

- ***The major barriers to seeking help for psychological disorders.*** These barriers include expense, availability, gender, and attitudes toward therapy, which are often influenced by the stigma against therapy that may be held by a particular group (e.g., males in general).
- ***The arguments for and against involuntary treatment.*** Proponents of involuntary treatment argue that it helps to protect innocent people who may otherwise end up being victims of violence at the hands of a psychologically disturbed individual. Proponents also argue that such treatment improves mental health, and ensures that people with severe disorders receive the appropriate treatment. Opponents argue that there is no good evidence that involuntary treatment benefits the individual, and instead, receiving involuntary treatment may result in the patient feeling coerced or resentful, suggesting that such treatments are not without cost.

APPLY ...

- ***Your knowledge to suggest what approach to therapy is likely most appropriate for a given situation.*** The appropriate kind of therapeutic setting depends on a host of factors, from what is available and within the person's means to afford to what sorts of issues the person is experiencing. For common problems such as stress and milder forms of depression and anxiety, seeing a counselling psychologist is likely the best first step; for students, most universities offer counselling services on campus. For more severe and debilitating problems, such as severe anxiety, depression, or schizophrenia, a clinical psychologist or psychiatrist is likely most appropriate. A psychologist will likely engage in a form of psychological therapy, whereas a psychiatrist will likely take a more physiological approach involving prescribing medication.

ANALYZE ...

- ***Whether self-help options, such as popular books, are a useful therapy option.*** Self-help books alone are not likely to be life-changing or stand-alone treatments for serious problems with depression, anxiety, and substance abuse, for example. Even so, research on bibliotherapy indicates that in some cases, when used in conjunction with other methods, reading self-help books can bring about modest improvements. It is, of course, always possible that for a specific individual, any specific self-help book may be profoundly helpful and even life-changing; however, on average, reading self-help books has only a small therapeutic benefit.

i love images/Alamy

Module 16.2

Psychological Therapies

Learning Objectives

After reading this module you should

KNOW ...	UNDERSTAND ...	APPLY ...	ANALYZE ...
The key terminology related to psychological therapies	The general approaches to conducting major types of psychological therapy	Your knowledge to identify major therapeutic techniques	The pros and cons of the major types of psychological therapy

Medical doctors are generally required to follow the Hippocratic Oath—an agreement that states they will cause no harm to their patients. One way of honouring this oath is to use the safest and most effective treatments. We do not generally associate the Hippocratic Oath with psychologists, but they also follow the basic tenet. Like physicians, psychologists must be aware of the possibility that a specific type of treatment might worsen a condition and, therefore, should be avoided.

For example, Scared Straight was a program developed in the 1970s that involved exposing at-risk youth to prisons and prisoners. The interventions were based on the premise that shocking or scaring the youths with the harsh realities of prison life would deter criminal activity. These scare tactics involved blunt descriptions of prison violence, along with verbal aggression directed at adolescents attending the sessions. The program may have succeeded in scaring and shocking adolescents, but the youths who attended these sessions did not necessarily go down a straight path. Many were later convicted of crimes and incarcerated. In fact, if anything, the program seemed to backfire; according to some analyses, participation in the program is associated with an increased chance that adolescents would commit crimes (Petrosino et al., 2003).

Scared Straight and other methods for helping people can, in fact, do more harm than good (Lilienfeld, 2007). Although a rare case, this example reminds us that therapy can be done in many different ways, and we should be cautious in determining which ones are best.

Focus Questions

 Which options for therapy are available?

 Are all well-established options equally effective at treating problems?

In Module 16.1, we introduced psychological therapy as a set of processes for resolving personal, emotional, behavioural, and social problems and improving well-being. Psychological therapy is a broad term, and mental health providers have a veritable smorgasbord of therapeutic approaches to choose from. In this module, we will study several of these approaches. Although the methods are diverse, they share the common feature of each being a type of psychological therapy, rather than biological or medical therapy. In psychological approaches, techniques for resolving problems rely heavily upon communication between client and therapist.

Most forms of psychological therapy work best with a specific type of disorder. It is therefore important to match the client's symptoms to the appropriate therapeutic technique.

Insight Therapies

Psychologists have long believed that self-knowledge and understanding can lead to positive changes in behaviour. This is certainly the case for **insight therapies**, which is *a general term referring to therapy that involves dialogue between client and therapist for the purposes of gaining awareness and understanding of psychological problems and conflicts*. Historically, the formal beginning of insight therapy came with the development of psychoanalysis by Sigmund Freud and its evolution into **psychodynamic therapies**, *forms of insight therapy that emphasize the need to discover and resolve unconscious conflicts*.

Explore Key Components of Therapies

PSYCHOANALYSIS: EXPLORING THE UNCONSCIOUS Psychoanalysis sprung out of Freud's understanding of consciousness. As described in Module 12.3, Freud hypothesized that much of our consciousness occurs at the unconscious level, outside of our conscious awareness. In particular, many fundamental urges, such as sexuality, appetites, and aggression, were thought to be constantly influencing how we think and behave, although we would not be explicitly aware of these processes. In fact, because these urges are generally socially unacceptable, we would actively protect ourselves from becoming aware of them through a variety of psychological defences. As a result, the true causes of our behaviour, and thus of our psychological issues, lie in the unconscious. This led Freud to emphasize the importance of "making the unconscious conscious," believing that the process of bringing material from the unconscious into consciousness allowed clients to gain insight into their problems and the past experiences from which they stem. This understanding was believed to liberate clients from the grips of the previously unknown forces that were impacting their lives.

Freud and his followers based their practice on some core ideas summarized in Table 16.1. These core ideas may sound straightforward, except for one crucial point: Accessing the unconscious mind is tricky business. The client cannot tell you much about it because, by definition, people are not consciously aware of the contents of their unconscious. Freud and his associates came up with several methods they believed would help them access the mysterious unconscious realm.

1) During the practice of **free association**, *clients are encouraged to talk or write without censoring their thoughts in any way*, just allowing everything that pops into the mind to come spilling out, no matter how odd or meaningless it may seem. Freud believed that this uncensored thought barrage would reveal clues to aspects of the unconscious that clients normally wouldn't allow to be expressed.

2) Dreams were also believed to be useful sources of information about unconscious conflicts. Freud believed that in the relatively unguarded dreaming mind, the unconscious would be better able to express itself; however, because the unconscious doesn't communicate through the same language-based way of thinking that the conscious mind uses, it expresses itself through symbols that need to be properly interpreted. **Dream analysis** is *a method for understanding the unconscious by examining the details of what happens during a dream (the manifest content), in order to gain insight into the true meaning of the dream, the emotional, unconscious material that is communicated symbolically (the latent content)*. Dreams take the form of imagery (sometimes bizarre and nonsensical imagery) and loose storylines, but within this confusing jumble, symbolic truths are hidden. The psychoanalyst's role was to help clients properly understand these symbolic truths in order to gain insight into their unconscious conflicts.

Table 16.1 :: Core Ideas Forming the Basis of Psychoanalysis

Core Ideas Forming the Basis of Psychoanalysis
Adults' psychological conflicts have their origins in early experiences.
These conflicts affect the thoughts and emotions of the individual, and their source often remains outside of conscious awareness.
The unconscious conflicts and their effects are called neuroses (anxieties).
By accessing the unconscious mind, the analyst and client can gain a better understanding of the early conflicts that lead to neuroses.
Once the conflicts are brought to the surface, the analyst and the client can work through them together.

For example, consider one of Freud's dream analyses: A client dreamed he was riding his bicycle down a street when suddenly a dachshund ran him down and bit his ankle as he attempted to pedal away. Meanwhile, two elderly ladies sat by and laughed at the incident.

Those details are the manifest content, but what might the dream mean—what is the latent content? Freud pointed out that in his waking life the client had repeatedly seen a woman walking a dog and, although he was very attracted to her, he felt great anxiety about approaching her. The man had consciously devised a plan to use the dog as an excuse to strike up a conversation with the woman. Unfortunately, the anxiety caused by fear of rejection manifested itself in an unpleasant dream about being attacked by a dog, accompanied by the humiliation of being laughed at (Freud, 1920, pp. 165–166).

3) **Resistance** *occurs as the treatment brings up unconscious material that the client wishes to avoid, and the client engages in strategies for keeping the information out of conscious awareness.* Resistance may be subtle, such as the client using humour to avoid talking about something painful, or it may be obvious, such as the client skipping sessions, becoming angry at the therapist, or becoming cynical about the whole process. Ironically, this is considered a promising signal for the psychoanalyst because it means that they are beginning to access the unconscious motives of clients' present difficulties. Psychoanalysts then attempt to push through the resistance by making clients aware of how and what they are resisting.

4) **Transference** is *a psychoanalytic process whereby clients direct the emotional experiences that they are reliving toward the therapist, rather than the original person involved in the experiences (e.g., their parents).* For example, if the patient is addressing a hidden sexual conflict, then her transference may involve developing sexual feelings for the analyst. As another example, if the client's mother made him feel criticized, he may begin to feel criticized by the analyst and respond defensively. Thus, the client's interaction with the analyst becomes a kind of stage on which conflicts with other people are revealed and explored. Transference is a significant milestone in the process of psychotherapy. Once it is reached, the therapist and client can begin to work through specific problems and discuss ways of coping with them.

MODERN PSYCHODYNAMIC THERAPIES Today, Freudian-based psychoanalysis is practised by a relatively small number of therapists. Nevertheless, Freud's ideas have remained influential and several newer therapies have evolved from traditional psychoanalysis. Diverting from Freud, these approaches are more concerned with the client's conscious rather than unconscious experience. They also acknowledge the effect of cultural and interpersonal influences on individual behaviour, as well as the impact of important needs such as love, power, belonging, security, and status. Finally, they are more optimistic about people's ability to reach healthy functioning.

One example is **object relations therapy**, *a variation of psychodynamic therapy that focuses on how early childhood experiences and emotional attachments influence later psychological functioning* (which we discussed in Module 10.2). In contrast to psychoanalysis, object relations therapy does not centre on repressed sexual and aggressive conflicts. Instead, the focus is on "objects," which are the clients' mental representations of themselves and others. The early relations between the child and these "objects" results in the development of a mental model for the child; as a consequence, she will form and maintain relationships as an adult based on her representations of childhood relationships. The object relations therapist's job is to help the client understand these underlying patterns in relationships, which often involve issues of trust, fear of abandonment, or dependence on others. Once therapy produces insight, then the client and the therapist can work through any problems they may have identified.

Both object relations therapy and psychoanalysis share the goal of helping individuals gain insight into how and why their current functioning was affected by early events. In addition to these approaches, other variations on the process of therapy have been developed.

A strong emphasis on interpersonal relationships informed Harry Stack Sullivan's *interpersonal psychotherapy.* In this approach, the therapist assumes the role of *participant observer,* through which the therapist both interacts with and observes the client over time in order to understand any unrealistic expectations the client may have toward their relationships as well as other situations in daily life. Sullivan's work influenced Interpersonal Therapy (IPT; Klerman et al., 1984). IPT was originally developed as a treatment for depression that would work quickly, focusing on improving clients' social skills and guiding them through their interpersonal issues and life transitions. IPT has been found to effectively treat depression, substance abuse, and eating disorders (Klerman & Weissman, 1993; Weissman et al., 2000).

HUMANISTIC-EXISTENTIAL PSYCHOTHERAPY

One important movement in psychotherapy arose during the 1950s, when humanistic psychologists broke from psychoanalytic approaches, creating a new discipline based on at least five fundamental differences (listed in Table 16.2). Therapies operating within this orientation emphasize individual strengths and the potential

Table 16.2 :: Contrasting Psychoanalytic and Humanistic Views of Major Psychological Issues and Debates

ISSUE	PSYCHOANALYSIS	HUMANISTIC THERAPY
Conscious versus unconscious	Focuses on unconscious drives	Focuses on conscious experience
Determinism versus free will	Behaviour is determined by repressed sexual and aggressive instincts	Behaviour is chosen freely
Weaknesses versus strengths	Everyone has neuroses	Everyone has strengths
Responsibility for change	The analyst interprets and explains to the client what is wrong	The therapist asks the client what is wrong and attempts to help clarify issues
Mechanism of change	Insight into unconscious conflicts allows problems to be worked through	Unconditional positive regard allows a person to develop and heal

for growth, as well as the belief that human nature is essentially positive, rather than the essentially negative perspective advanced by psychoanalytic approaches. This shift toward the positive was believed to help individuals access their own personal power and agency for overcoming their problems.

Humanistic and existential therapies share many similarities: to help people express their authentic selves, to overcome alienation, to become more loving, and to take responsibility for their experiences so that they learn to dwell fully in the present. The major difference between them is that humanistic therapists focus on removing the obstacles that prevent self-actualization from unfolding naturally, whereas existential therapists emphasize the importance of facing painful experiences such as feelings about isolation, death, and meaninglessness, believing that self-actualization involves transforming by facing one's fears and negativity. Even though attaining insight is still an important aspect of these therapies, rather than interpreting the hidden meanings of dreams and free associations, the therapist's role is to listen empathically in order to understand the clients' internal world. This is referred to as a **phenomenological approach**, which means that *the therapist addresses the clients' feelings and thoughts as they unfold in the present moment, rather than looking for unconscious motives or dwelling in the past.*

American psychologist Carl Rogers (1902–1987) developed a version of humanistic therapy called **client-centred therapy (or person-centred therapy)**, *which focuses on individuals' abilities to solve their own problems and reach their full potential with the encouragement of the therapist.* As a humanist, Rogers believed that all individuals could develop and reach their full potential. However, people experience psychological problems when others impose conditions of worth, meaning that they appear to judge or lose affection for a person who does not live up to expectations. Conditions of worth are imposed, for example, by a father who is never satisfied with his child's report card or a wife who gets angry at her spouse over failing to keep his promises; interestingly, conditions of worth are also imposed by parents who show excessive attention and praise when their children behave in desired ways, sending the message that the child is only lovable when she is "good." If people give the impression that their respect and love for a person are contingent upon the person behaving in certain ways or meeting certain expectations, then they have imposed conditions of worth. Conditions of worth can produce long-term consequences to psychological health because they increase insecurities within the individual; as a result, the individual is likely to change his behaviour in an attempt to regain affection. If this happens frequently, then the individual's behaviour starts to be primarily about gaining affection and approval, living in order to please others rather than being able to express his own authentic self. That, to Carl Rogers, is a key aspect of most psychological dysfunction.

The most important aspect of client-centred therapy lies within the dialogue that unfolds between therapist and client. The therapist must show unconditional positive regard through genuine, empathetic, and non-judgmental attention. If the therapist can remove all conditions of worth, clients may begin to express themselves without fear and begin to develop inner strength. Finally, with self-confidence and strength, clients can accept disagreements with others and focus on living their lives to the fullest.

EVALUATING INSIGHT THERAPIES As discussed in Module 16.1, therapies should be used only if there is empirical support that they actually work, although it is worth remembering that a given approach may work for a given individual, even if it doesn't work for most people. Thus, even though it is important to generally practise empirically supported approaches to treatment, it is also important to balance this with the idiosyncratic needs and beliefs of particular clients. Just because a therapy doesn't work for most people, doesn't mean it won't work for some people.

Psychodynamic therapies meet some of the rigorous criteria for empirically supported therapies, though surprisingly few studies in this area have been conducted with proper research design and control conditions. Ultimately, the effectiveness of insight therapies depends on the condition being treated. Studies that have used the most rigorous research designs have shown that psychodynamic therapy has not been effective in treating severe depression or schizophrenia, but it has shown promise for treating panic disorder, dependence on opiate drugs (e.g., heroin), and borderline personality disorder (Gibbons et al., 2008). Psychodynamic therapy may help with major depression if combined with drug treatment—an approach we will describe in greater detail in Module 16.3.

Insight therapies can help people gain understanding and awareness of the nature of their psychological problems. As we will soon read, many people with psychological disorders are able to successfully learn to function effectively without digging into the possible "root causes" by instead cultivating new, adaptive behaviours (Weisz et al., 1995). Some people are also not well suited to insight therapy, such as young children or people with severe disorders such as schizophrenia.

Research shows that Carl Rogers was accurate in emphasizing the importance of the therapeutic relationship for successful therapy (Horvath & Bedi, 2002; Wampold, 2001). In fact, a strong alliance is a good predictor of successful therapy *over and above* the specific type of therapy delivered (Bohart et al., 2002). Positive regard (Farber & Lane, 2002) and empathy (Bohart et al., 2002) are modestly related to the outcome of therapy, although Rogers may have overemphasized their importance somewhat (Bohart, 2003).

Research on the effectiveness of person-centred therapy is somewhat inconsistent. In general, it is more effective than no treatment at all (Greenberg et al., 1994). However, some studies have found it to be no more effective than a placebo treatment (Smith et al., 1980), whereas others have found it to be as effective as cognitive behavioural therapy (Elliott, 2002; Greenberg & Watson, 1998). One complicating factor in this research may be the skill of therapists themselves; some therapists are likely much better able to connect with clients and establish the proper kind of rapport in therapy, and thus may be far more effective than others at this kind of therapy. This difference in therapists' skill could account for these mixed findings.

One very promising type of person-centred therapy has evolved from the humanistic-existential tradition and is being heavily researched today; emotion-focused therapy is based on the well-supported belief that it is better to face and accept difficult emotions and thoughts rather than bottle them inside (Greenberg, 2004; Hayes et al., 2003). Therapists employing this form of therapy aim to help clients overcome their tendency to suppress disturbing thoughts and emotions. Research suggests that this is about as effective at treating mood disorders as cognitive behaviour therapy, part of the group of therapies we examine next.

Quick Quiz 16.2a

Insight Therapies

KNOW ...

1 ______ refers to a phenomenon of psychoanalysis in which the client begins directing emotional responses toward the therapist.

A Resistance
B Befriending
C Objectifying
D Transference

2 In psychoanalysis, resistance occurs when

A a client develops sexual attraction for the analyst.
B a client begins to divert the analysis by joking, becoming cynical, or perhaps just refusing to answer questions.
C a therapist begins to have the same feelings as the client.
D the therapist refuses to continue a therapy session.

UNDERSTAND ...

3 In psychoanalysis, treatment for psychological problems seems to come from

A the client becoming more conscious of the workings of their unconscious.
B the client receiving unconditional positive regard.
C the therapist understanding and explaining the manifest content of a dream.
D the therapist diagnosing the psychological disorder and providing appropriate drug therapy.

APPLY ...

4 A kindergarten teacher (unintentionally) places conditions of worth on her students. What does this mean?

A She always lets her students know how much she values them.
B She regularly tries to draw compliments out of her students.
C She acts as if a student no longer matters to her or the school if he misbehaves.
D She provides monetary rewards for good behaviour.

ANALYZE ...

5 What has research concluded in regard to the effectiveness of insight therapies?

A Insight therapies are always very effective.
B Insight therapies are never effective.
C Insight therapies do not help people gain awareness of the nature of their psychological problems, so they tend to not be effective.
D The effectiveness of insight therapies depends on the conditions that are being treated.

Answers can be found on page ANS-4.

Behavioural, Cognitive, and Group Therapies

Behavioural therapies *address problem behaviours, and the environmental factors that trigger them, as directly as possible.* At the heart of behavioural therapies is the belief that patterns of behaviour are the result of conditioning and learning that have led to the automatization of maladaptive habits. Thus, behavioural approaches seek to recondition clients, training them to adopt different behavioural responses to situations until they develop new, more functional, habits.

Therapy

SYSTEMATIC DESENSITIZATION How behavioural therapy works is clearly illustrated by examining how it is applied to one of the most common types of social anxiety, public speaking. Most people experience at least some anxiety about public speaking, but for some, their reaction is so intense that even thinking about making a speech can bring on major anxiety, physiological arousal, and even panic attacks. As the moment to give the speech approaches, environmental cues, such as the professor standing at the front, the dreaded podium, the ticking clock, can all trigger anxious feelings and heighten the person's arousal.

Listen
IT Audio: Hierarchy of Fears

Watch
IT Video: Public Speaking

To help people learn to handle such fear-inducing situations, therapists may choose the behavioural technique known as **systematic desensitization**, in which *gradual exposure to a feared stimulus or situation is coupled with relaxation training* (Wolpe, 1990). First, the client may be exposed to a very mild version of the fear-inducing situation, such as merely imagining walking up to the front of the room where he is going to give the speech, and as he does so, the client practises relaxing in order to counteract the mild anxiety he may feel. Then he progresses to more realistic and concrete manifestations of the situation, each time practising relaxing until he can learn to tolerate his feelings and counteract them with a relaxation response. Eventually, he can handle the real thing. Behavioural therapists and their clients follow three main steps in conducting systematic desensitization, which are outlined in Table 16.3.

In some cases, the client may elect to undergo a process called flooding. In this procedure, the client goes straight to the most challenging part of the hierarchy, exposing himself to the scenario that causes the most anxiety and panic. For example, he may elect to give a long speech in front of 100 strangers. The idea here is that, rather than avoiding the anxiety-provoking situation, the client dives right in and (one hopes) discovers that there are no truly negative consequences to giving a well-prepared speech.

Fear and anxiety responses can be acquired through observing others (Olsson & Phelps, 2007). Fortunately, these responses can also be reversed by observation. Thus another technique is based on observational learning or "modelling" (Module 6.3; Bandura, 1977). With this method, the client observes another person engage with the feared object or situation. For example, an ophidiophobe (a person with a phobia of snakes) might observe another person as he handles a snake. In some cases, such as with a fear of heights or flying, virtual reality technology has been used to provide exposure treatments.

Table 16.3 :: Applying Steps of Systematic Desensitization to Fear of Public Speaking

1. Build an anxiety hierarchy. This involves the therapist assisting the client in creating a list of stimuli that arouse fear responses, starting with the stimulus or situation that evokes the least amount of anxiety and ending with the stimulus that elicits the most anxiety.

   Think about and visualize:

   1. Doing library research for a presentation
   2. Preparing slides and note cards
   3. Practising the presentation alone
   4. Practising the presentation with a small group of friends
   5. Leaving for campus on the day of the presentation
   6. Class starting
   7. Being called up to give the presentation
   8. Setting up and looking out at the audience
   9. Beginning to speak
   10. Delivering the presentation

2. Relaxation training. During this phase, the client learns to respond to relaxation suggestions from the therapist as they work through the hierarchy. This is typically done using mental imagery while the client is visiting the therapist's office.
3. Work through the hierarchy. Steps 1 and 2 are combined here as the therapist works through the hierarchy with the client while engaging in relaxation techniques.

WORKING THE SCIENTIFIC LITERACY MODEL

Virtual Reality Therapies

Systematic desensitization techniques have long been a part of behavioural treatments for fear and anxiety. However, there are some key barriers that can prevent them from being effective. For one, people with fear and anxiety about a specific object or situation usually avoid any contact with it—so even taking the first step toward a therapist's office can be challenging. This helps to explain why most people with post-traumatic stress disorder (PTSD) never seek treatment (Kessler, 2000). Also, although mental imagery is typically the method employed with these therapeutic techniques, it may not transfer well to the actual anxiety-provoking situation because mental imagery often doesn't have the same power as the much more vivid, real situation. One way to address these problems is being discovered through technology.

Erika Schultz/MCT/Newscom

{FIG. 16.2} **Virtual Reality Exposure** Combat veterans diagnosed with PTSD have participated in virtual reality therapies involving simulated exposure to traumatic events. Therapists work with clients to help them process and cope with their fears.

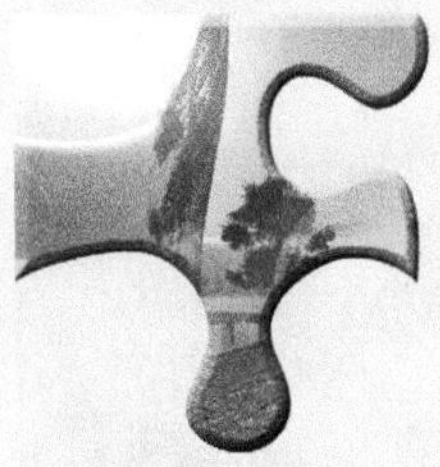

What do we know about virtual reality exposure?

Virtual reality exposure (VRE) is *a treatment that uses graphical displays to create an experience in which the client seems to be immersed in an actual environment.* This much more vivid environment maps on more easily to the real thing, and shows promise for helping people learn to relax in the face of their fears. Also, virtual reality therapy may help to reduce the tendency for people's avoidance strategies. Over the past decade, this technology has become increasingly common in helping soldiers returning from the military conflicts in Iraq and Afghanistan—many of whom have developed PTSD.

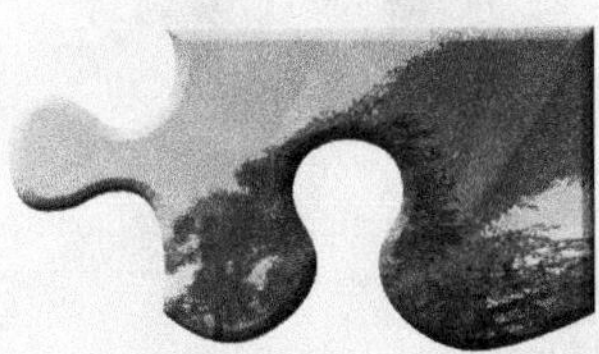

How can scientists study virtual reality exposure?

Psychologists at Emory University in Atlanta have been using a simulator called Virtual Iraq, which was developed to deliver two possible scenarios—being in a Middle Eastern city or driving a Humvee through a desert road in simulated war conditions (Figure 16.2). The weather, time of day, background noise, civilians, aerial craft, and ground vehicles can be programmed by the therapist to change as desired during the exposure sessions. There is also the option to provide simulated gunfire and bomb explosions. Smell cues are available using an air compressor that pumps in odours of burning rubber, garbage, diesel fuel, and gunpowder (Cukor et al., 2009). Using this technology, psychologists have conducted VRE sessions with combat veterans.

In one set of trials, 20 active-duty soldiers who were diagnosed with PTSD following combat activity underwent VRE therapy. Their PTSD symptoms were measured before and after therapists guided them through VRE treatment in the Virtual Iraq simulator. At the conclusion of their therapy, the soldiers' PTSD symptoms declined by 50%, with 16 of the soldiers no longer meeting the criteria for the disorder (Rizzo et al., 2010). The results included fewer disturbing thoughts about stressful events that occurred during military service; fewer disturbing dreams; reduced physical reactions such as heart pounding, sweating, and trouble breathing; and less avoidance of activities that trigger memories of military service. VRE using the Virtual Iraq simulator appears to work.

Can we critically evaluate this evidence?

From an experimental standpoint, this study should have used a placebo (control) group that received no treatment, or a comparison group that received some other treatment method. In fact, such studies have recently occurred; in one study of veterans who had served in Iraq or Afghanistan, the effectiveness of VRE sessions was compared to the standard approaches (e.g., prolonged exposure therapy, among other standard treatments), and the VRE approach outperformed the standard approaches (McLay et al., 2011).

It's also not clear from this one study whether VRE therapy would be beneficial for disorders other than PTSD. However, other research has shown that virtual reality approaches are useful for helping people in many different types of circumstances, including symptom reduction in people with various phobias (Opris et al., 2012; Powers & Emmelkamp, 2008), stress management in patients with cancer (Schneider et al., 2011), and body image issues in clients with eating disorders (Riva, 2005).

Why is this relevant?

Virtual reality technologies seem to help overcome key barriers to therapeutic effectiveness. As discussed earlier regarding PTSD, clients typically avoid any stimuli associated with the original trauma, and therefore may be resistant to therapy which will expose them to the trauma; VRE approaches can get around this resistance because the therapist has extremely high control over the precise way in which the client will be exposed to the feared situation and can therefore easily tailor the approach to the client's needs (Hodges et al., 2001).

Carol and Mike Werner/Alamy

AVERSIVE CONDITIONING Behavioural therapies can also be used to extinguish unwanted behaviours. Most people have at least one behaviour they would like to reduce or eliminate, perhaps a nervous habit such as fingernail biting, or a serious health concern such as smoking. Behavioural principles tell us that these habits are maintained because they bring rewards in some fashion. As long as they are enjoyable or reduce stress, these habits will be difficult to break.

Aversive conditioning is *a behavioural technique that involves replacing a positive response to a stimulus with a negative response, typically by using punishment.* One aversive conditioning treatment involves using the drug Antabuse (disulfiram) to reduce problem alcohol consumption. Antabuse causes nausea and vomiting when combined with alcohol, so the drug classically conditions an aversion to alcohol. Antabuse works for some individuals, but there are several reasons why it is not entirely effective (Garbutt, 2009). As you can imagine, the client must have a fairly strong motivation to quit, and must be willing to take the drug knowing that it would make her ill. If she cheats and skips the drug one day, then the treatment will not have much chance of working. Thus, even though aversive conditioning can help people quit, it still requires willpower to complete the treatments.

Monika Olszewska/Shutterstock

The drug Antabuse is used in aversive conditioning for alcohol consumption. When it is taken and the person subsequently consumes alcohol, Antabuse causes nausea and vomiting. If successful, Antabuse treatment leads to a conditioned aversion to alcohol.

COGNITIVE-BEHAVIOURAL THERAPIES Behavioural therapies, despite their effectiveness at changing problem behaviours, do not directly address problematic thoughts. This is extremely important because some disorders, most notably depression, are caused in part by dysfunctional habits of thinking. Two psychodynamically trained psychologists, Albert Ellis (1962) and Aaron Beck (1963), found that people with depression tend to interpret and think about their lives in a negative light. As Ellis, Beck, and others learned more about these thought patterns, it became apparent that therapies should be directed at changing negative cognitions into more realistic and rational thought patterns, as well as helping people learn to control the physiological processes (e.g., arousal) that reinforce negative thinking. Over time, this new approach became known as cognitive-behavioural therapy.

Cognitive-behavioural therapy (CBT) *is a form of therapy that consists of procedures such as cognitive restructuring, stress inoculation training, and exposing people to experiences they may have a tendency to avoid*, as in systematic desensitization (NIMH, 2009). Because avoiding thoughts and stressful situations tends to reinforce the negative feelings that would arise, helping clients to face negativity allows them the opportunity to gain insight into their feelings, to practise a courageous response to negativity, and to learn methods for coping when negativity arises. This type of therapy is far more about the present than about the past; rather than excavating past traumas or conflicts, CBT therapists help clients become more aware of the thought, emotion, and behaviour patterns that arise in their current lives; through this heightened self-awareness, clients learn to identify their habitual dysfunctional tendencies, and then work on building more functional cognitive and behavioural habits.

At the behavioural end of CBT, clients are given exercises and guidance in gaining skills they may be lacking. For example, as with systematic desensitization, clients may learn relaxation techniques, enabling them to better tolerate negative feelings when they arise. As another example, a person with social anxiety who has difficulty integrating into social situations may learn and practise certain social skills, such as making "small talk" with people at parties or learning to be more responsive to people's non-verbal cues, rather than the socially anxious person's current tendency to not express himself and generally withdraw from social settings.

At the cognitive end of CBT, clients are given exercises and strategies to build more functional cognitive habits. Cognitive restructuring involves learning to challenge their negative thought patterns, to question their self-defeating beliefs, and to view situations in a different light. For example, people with depression or anxiety disorders often hold extreme and irrational beliefs, such as "I can't do anything right," "I have nothing worthwhile to say," "If I fail, it's going to be a total disaster." As they become more aware of these negative beliefs, they can question or dispute them, helping themselves appreciate that these beliefs are far more negative than reality warrants. After all, nobody can do *everything* wrong; nobody has literally nothing to say that is worthwhile; and any failure is not "the end of the world," so to speak, but is also an opportunity to learn and improve.

One set of dysfunctional thinking patterns that powerfully reinforces depression is *the tendency to make internal, stable, and global attributions for negative events*. This **negative explanatory style** results in people making the worst out of many situations. **Internal attributions** are the *thoughts that say "it's all my fault"; blaming oneself excessively for negative things that happen, rather than appreciating that, even though one may bear some responsibility, there were also other factors that contributed to the negative event, such as bad luck or the behaviour of other people.* **Stable attributions** are *thoughts like "it's never going to change"; coming to see the situation as permanent and irreversible.* **Global events** are *thoughts like "my whole life is ruined"; blowing things out of proportion rather than seeing a negative event as simply that, one negative event and not something that needs to spiral into greater problems* (Seligman et al., 1979). Once these self-defeating cognitive habits have been identified, a therapist and client can work on developing more functional and healthy ways of thinking. After that, it's the client's job to put the therapy into practice—noting her automatic thought tendencies as they occur, and then actually practising her cognitive principles, such as restructuring as we discussed earlier. As the client practises interrupting old thought patterns and actively cultivating new, healthier ones, these healthier patterns should become more easily activated, until eventually they become automatic behavioural habits. In contrast, the depressive thought patterns should fade with disuse, becoming less easily activated over time.

Watch
In the Real World: Cognitive-Behavioural Therapy

The fact that these exercises change people's functioning has been dramatically demonstrated through recent neuroimaging studies, which show substantial changes to neurological function after CBT (Frewen et al., 2008). For example, one study at L'Institut universitaire de gériatrie de Montréal showed that, before being treated with CBT, people suffering from spider phobia showed activation in certain brain areas when viewing pictures of spiders: part of the prefrontal cortex (right dorsolateral PFC) which is involved with controlling emotional responses, and part of the hippocampus (the parahippocampal gyrus) which is involved in contextual fear memories. The activation of these two areas likely reflects the automatic reactivation of fear memories that underlie the phobia, plus the person's attempt to override the fear response. After receiving CBT, these areas were no longer active when subjects viewed spider pictures, suggesting that CBT not only helped people subjectively, but also functionally "rewired" the brain (Paquette et al., 2003).

MINDFULNESS-BASED COGNITIVE THERAPY One of the biggest recent advances in therapeutic practice, spearheaded by researchers at the Centre for

Addiction and Mental Health in Toronto, is the integration of meditation-based practices, such as mindfulness, with traditional cognitive-behavioural approaches. In this groundbreaking area of research, East meets West and ancient meets modern, as traditional Eastern meditation and spiritual practices merge with Western psychological therapies and neuroscientific understanding.

Mindfulness practice and cognitive-behavioural therapy begin in somewhat similar ways—the goal of each is to get the client better acquainted with her thoughts and feelings, in the present moment of experiencing them. Each approach emphasizes greater self-awareness, which comes from the practice of observing oneself. At this very basic level, mindfulness and CBT are similar to each other.

Otherwise, the two approaches differ significantly. In CBT, there is a basic orientation of "fixing oneself." The purpose of becoming aware of one's patterns of thoughts, feelings, and behaviour is to gain greater control so that the negative thought patterns get replaced with more positive ones. In contrast, the practice of mindfulness involves consciously adopting an orientation of "accepting" oneself, fully, in the present moment. Strictly speaking, from a mindfulness perspective, you don't necessarily have to "do" anything about problematic thoughts and feelings; instead, you make the active choice to accept them as they are, to simply observe them without reacting to them.

It may sound like "just watching yourself" is a pretty mild and unimpressive thing to do. Just watching yourself sounds like, basically, doing nothing. However, it is in fact a highly active and intentional process. In order to be able to watch yourself without reacting to the different thoughts and feelings that arise, you must consciously choose, again and again, to take an attitude of openness and acceptance toward yourself. Dr. Daniel Siegel (2007) describes this attitude as COAL—curious, open, accepting, and loving. COAL is, essentially, the same attitude that parents take toward children in order to help them develop emotional security (Module 10.2). As people develop emotional security through being involved in loving and accepting relationships, this is reflected in the development of certain brain areas that Siegel calls the "social circuitry." These areas, such as the medial prefrontal cortex, are involved in experiencing and managing emotions, feeling empathy and taking the perspective of others, and generally speaking, reflect an *interpersonal attunement* between oneself and other people. The practice of mindfulness is believed to be a kind of *intrapersonal attunement,* a relationship between oneself and oneself; it seems to involve the same social circuitry, and lead to the same emotional and neurological outcomes as the development of secure attachment. Basically, by practising attending openly and non-reactively to yourself, you become your own best friend or healthy parent. As Siegel describes it, mindfulness is like re-parenting yourself; it's an opportunity to rebuild yourself, actually changing your own biological structures that are involved in emotional security.

A second key way in which mindfulness affects a person is through the experience of **decentring**, *which occurs when one is able to "step back" from one's normal consciousness and observe oneself more objectively, as an observer.* You have no doubt had the experience decentring many times, such as when you become aware that you are "talking to yourself" as though there is a private voice in your mind that you can "speak" with, or you may have had the experience of becoming aware of yourself having an experience while you are having the experience. For example, you may be dancing but then you suddenly become aware of yourself dancing, as though you are looking at yourself from a third-person perspective.

The ability to decentre is a powerful antidote to difficult thoughts and feelings. By "stepping back" from your own thoughts and feelings and observing them dispassionately, you become able to detach yourself from any damaging or troubling consequences of your thoughts. It's similar to what you might do if someone were attacking you and trying to hit you; if you could step away from their blows, you wouldn't be harmed by their anger. In the same way, when you are able to mentally step away from a difficult thought, you become less attached to the emotional consequences of the thought, and thus, less harmed by your own negative thinking patterns.

Mindfulness-based cognitive therapy (MBCT) *involves combining mindfulness meditation with standard cognitive-behavioural therapy tools.* The goals are to reap the benefits of mindfulness practice described above, and then to work on changing dysfunctional patterns using CBT. Many independent controlled trials have shown that MBCT has powerful effects on people who have experienced a major depressive disorder. After the person emerges from a depressive episode, the practice of MBCT substantially reduces the likelihood of experiencing a relapse, lengthens the amount of time that passes between depressive episodes, and reduces residual depressive symptoms for years after treatment (Bondolfi et al., 2010; Kuyken et al., 2008, 2010).

MBCT seems to have great promise as a therapy for many different conditions. Initial studies suggest it is beneficial for social anxiety disorder and generalized anxiety (Evans et al., 2008; Piet et al., 2010), bipolar disorder (Weber et al., 2010; Williams et al., 2008), depression (Kingston et al., 2007; Williams et al., 2007), hypochondriasis (McManus et al., 2012), and suicidal ideation (Crane & Williams, 2010). Mindfulness exercises are excellent tools for encouraging people to become more growth-oriented, and they are adaptable to both individual therapy and therapy in group settings.

GROUP AND FAMILY THERAPIES In some situations, clients may benefit by participating in group therapy sessions. Group members share their personal stories and experiences, and the bonding and support that occur in this context can be very powerful. To encourage people to open up to each other, therapists may group people together based on the issue that they are dealing with (e.g., alcohol addiction, divorce), or other similarities (e.g., age, ethnicity, gender, sexual orientation, etc.). A final, logistic advantage to group therapy is the cost, which is usually much cheaper than individual therapy. This makes group therapy accessible to a broad range of people across society.

In other situations, psychologists may conduct family therapy. This may occur if a client's difficulties stem from or are reinforced by unhealthy dynamics within the family; for example, people with schizophrenia are far less likely to have their symptoms stay in remission if their families exhibit negative patterns of communication and emotional involvement (Hooley, 2007). Thus, family therapy may be extremely effective for helping people with schizophrenia, generally in conjunction with anti-psychotic drug treatments. Family therapy may also be used to help families deal with specific family members who are highly dysfunctional in some way, such as being addicted or having poor emotional control.

Family therapists generally take a **systems approach**, *an orientation that encourages therapists to see an individual's symptoms as being influenced by many different interacting systems*; one important system is the family system, which can play a big role in the development and maintenance of psychological disorders. For example, imagine a family in which one person is emotionally abusive and controls the other family members through becoming excessively angry; a therapist taking a systems approach would see that behaviour pattern as stemming not only from the individual themselves, but also from the other family members. For example, the other family members may constantly monitor that person and carefully choose their own behaviours so as to avoid making that person angry. Or the family may stop inviting other people to the house, allowing the angry person to isolate the family within the community. Or the family members may be too quick to forgive or to apologize themselves and accept the blame whenever the angry person loses his temper, rather than challenging the person and being clear about what the family will and will not tolerate. There are many different ways in which family members contribute to the maintenance of a dysfunctional pattern of behaviour, and a family systems therapist would therefore treat the individual by also working with the other family members to change the larger patterns that reinforce the problematic behaviours.

EVALUATING COGNITIVE-BEHAVIOURAL THERAPIES Behavioural therapies have been shown to be particularly effective at treating symptoms associated with anxiety disorders, such as obsessive-compulsive disorder and specific phobias (Chambless & Ollendick, 2001). They have also proved useful for increasing behavioural skills (e.g., social skills) and decreasing problematic behaviours (e.g., social withdrawal).

Watch
Cognitive-Behavioural Therapy

Cognitive-behavioural therapy has been quite effective in treating depression, which is not too surprising given that this method of therapy was specifically developed for this purpose (Hollon et al., 2002). In addition, cognitive-behavioural therapies have been successful in treating such conditions as anxiety, obesity, and eating disorders. In fact, CBT is the most effective treatment currently available for anxiety disorders, particularly over the long term, outperforming anti-anxiety medications for most adult anxiety disorders (Hofmann & Smits, 2008), and the effects last much longer than the effects of drugs, which often are effective only so long as the person remains on the medication (Hollon et al., 2006). Neuroimaging research on people with obsessive-compulsive disorder showed that both SSRI and CBT treatments effect the same changes in neural activity (Schwartz et al., 1996), suggesting that these different approaches target similar neural processes. In many cases, rather than taking an either/or approach, the best outcomes have been found by combining drug treatments with cognitive behavioural therapy; this has been found for several different disorders, including panic disorder with agoraphobia (Starcevic et al., 2004), and depression (McCullough, 2000).

Generally speaking, cognitive and behavioural therapies are the workhorses of psychological treatments; they are quite versatile in their applications and can help to treat a wide variety of disorders. They also take much less time (and are therefore much less expensive) than psychodynamic approaches, and have none of the undesirable side effects of drug treatments. Nevertheless, different treatments work best for different people, and it is worth remembering that for any given person, it is currently impossible to know ahead of time which treatment or combination of treatments may work the best.

Quick Quiz 16.2b Behavioural, Cognitive, and Group Therapies

KNOW ...

1 ______ involves a process in which the client faces feared situations gradually and under controlled conditions.

A Client-centred therapy **C** Insight therapy

B Family therapy **D** Exposure therapy

2 ________ consists of key procedures including exposure, cognitive restructuring, and stress inoculation training.

A Cognitive-behavioural therapy

B Family therapy

C Virtual reality exposure therapy

D Exposure therapy

UNDERSTAND ...

3 The key difference between mindfulness and cognitive behavioural therapy is that

A only mindfulness involves decentring.

B CBT is supported by empirical research, whereas mindfulness is just a practice that comes from Buddhism but has little empirical support.

C in CBT, clients practise replacing their dysfunctional thoughts with more functional thoughts; whereas in mindfulness practice, clients simply watch their thoughts and accept them as they are.

D CBT can be combined with drug treatments, but mindfulness cannot.

APPLY ...

4 Neil is facing difficulties with anger and depression, and his parents are having trouble managing his behaviours and responding appropriately. To address all of these concerns, the most beneficial treatment in this situation would be ________.

A cognitive-behavioural therapy

B family therapy

C virtual reality exposure therapy

D exposure therapy

ANALYZE ...

5 A major strength of cognitive-behavioural therapy is that

A it has been particularly effective in treating depression, anxiety, and eating disorders.

B it prevents resistance from occurring.

C it is not affected by the quality of the client–therapist relationship.

D it develops transference between client and therapist.

6 Cognitive-behavioural therapies seem to be effective because they

A help individuals restructure their maladaptive thoughts and beliefs.

B teach individuals to brood over problems effectively.

C systematically desensitize phobias.

D none of the above.

Answers can be found on page ANS-4.

Module Summary

Module 16.2

Now that you have read this module you should

KNOW ...

- ***The key terminology related to psychological therapies:***

aversive conditioning (p. 688)
behavioural therapy (p. 686)
client-centred therapy (or person-centred therapy) (p. 684)
cognitive-behavioural therapy (CBT) (p. 689)
decentring (p. 690)
dream analysis (p. 682)
free association (p. 682)
global events (p. 689)
insight therapy (p. 682)
internal attribution (p. 689)
mindfulness-based cognitive therapy (MBCT) (p. 690)
negative explanatory style (p. 689)
object relations therapy (p. 683)
phenomenological approach (p. 684)
psychodynamic therapy (p. 682)
resistance (p. 683)
stable attributions (p. 689)
systematic desensitization (p. 686)
systems approach (p. 691)
transference (p. 683)
virtual reality exposure (VRE) (p. 687)

UNDERSTAND ...

- ***The general approaches to conducting major types of psychological therapy.*** Each therapy seems to be different. Psychoanalysis, for example, works by uncovering hidden conflicts, whereas humanistic therapy focuses on removing conditions of worth that can hinder a person's growth. Behavioural and cognitive therapies target dysfunctional thought and behaviour patterns, seeking to replace undesirable patterns with more functional ones that clients then practise regularly. Group and family therapies have also been developed, working with social systems that are larger than one individual.

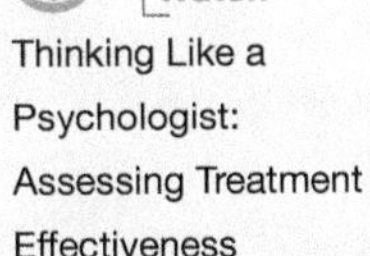
Thinking Like a Psychologist: Assessing Treatment Effectiveness

APPLY ...

- ***Your knowledge to identify major therapeutic techniques.*** Imagine you are helping someone with a phobia find a therapist for treatment, and you speak with three professionals about the approach each would take. Match their response with the corresponding school of thought. Note: Not all the schools of therapy will be used. Check your answers on page ANS-4.

1. I would ask the individual to describe his train of thought when he encounters the feared object. Then I would ask him to explain why it is irrational to think that way, and we would try to replace his irrational thoughts with more reasonable, less anxiety-provoking beliefs.
2. I would ask the patient to think about his earliest childhood experiences with the object, and then to speak freely about those memories at length. We would try to discover the significance of that object in his early development.
3. We would take an active approach. One important step is to teach the client how to be calm and relaxed while gradually introducing the feared stimulus.

A. Humanistic therapy
B. Cognitive-behavioural therapy
C. Psychodynamic therapy
D. Family therapy
E. Behavioural therapy

i love images/Alamy

ANALYZE ...

- ***The pros and cons of the major types of psychotherapy.*** See **Table 16.4** below.

Table 16.4 :: Pros and Cons of the Major Types of Therapy

	PROS	CONS
Insight therapies	• Can provide deep understanding of the self • Can facilitate substantial personal growth and personal transformation	• Often (but not always) involve long-term therapy, often very expensive • Can have limited application to people with serious disorders
Behavioural and cognitive therapies	• Typically time- and cost-efficient • Addresses immediate thoughts and behavioural problems • Addresses both mild and severe problems	• Does not necessarily offer deeper understanding of psychological problems • When used alone, may not be effective for some severe cases and certain disorders (e.g., schizophrenia)
Group/family therapies	• Allows individuals to empathize and relate to others with similar problems • Gives family members insight into how each individual contributes to both positive and negative aspects of family life • Can change the larger social dynamics that reinforce and maintain the disorder • Can enable individuals to change who would otherwise not be able to (e.g., many cases of addiction)	• Does not fully address individual issues (although group and family therapies are often used in combination with individualized therapy)

Image Courtesy of The Advertising Archives

Module 16.3

Biomedical Therapies

Learning Objectives

After reading this module you should

KNOW ...	UNDERSTAND ...	APPLY ...	ANALYZE ...
The key terminology associated with biological treatments	How the drugs described in this module affect brain functioning The other major medical approaches to therapy	Your knowledge of drug therapies to different psychological conditions	Whether St. John's wort, a popular herbal remedy for depression, works

The word "depression" used to be taboo. Although depression likely affected a large proportion of people, it was not socially acceptable to admit to it; if you did, you risked being labelled as someone who was weak and simply needed "to get it together." Then in 1987 Prozac hit the market, and everything changed. When Eli Lilly (the manufacturer of Prozac) found that it seemed to help a sample of people with mild depression, suddenly, it seemed there was a miracle cure for the untold millions who are suffering silently. Millions of dollars were spent on marketing campaigns, familiarizing doctors with this wonder drug, and teaching the general public about the symptoms of depression. Rates of depression diagnoses skyrocketed, and sales of Prozac kept pace. Within a decade after its release, Prozac was making $2.5 *billion* per year for Eli Lilly (Couzin, 2004).

Unfortunately, a growing number of people started to voice concerns about this wonder drug and its "sister" drugs, the selective serotonin reuptake inhibitors (SSRIs) known by their brand names like Paxil and Zoloft. For some people, these drugs were alleged to cause a wide range of side effects, from relatively "mild" problems such as sexual dysfunction, weight gain, and skin rashes, to very serious problems such as seizures, breathing problems, and even thoughts of committing suicide.

Many of these side effects were acknowledged by the drugs' manufacturers, but it was the ironic, and terrifying, possibility that anti-depressant drugs could actually increase the risk of suicide which caught the public's attention, and which the manufacturers denied. Dr. David Healy, author of the book, *Let Them Eat Prozac*, not only made the claim that Prozac increased the risk of suicidal behaviours, but also alleged that Eli Lilly's own research showed this, but the findings had been suppressed. This seems to be backed up by documents leaked to CNN in 2005, showing that Eli Lilly knew back in the 1980s that patients on Prozac were more than 1200% more likely to attempt suicide than patients on several other antidepressants.

This controversy generated a great deal of bad press for the SSRIs. Then, things got even worse, as research on the efficacy of these drugs turned out to be unimpressive. A recent meta-analysis concluded that the impact of SSRIs on symptoms of depression, compared to a placebo, is extremely small (and not "clinically significant") for moderately or even severely depressed patients; only among the most depressed group did the SSRIs have a clinically meaningful impact greater than placebos, and that was merely because such severely depressed people were less responsive to placebos, not because of any increase in the impact of the SSRIs. In short, SSRIs appear to have only a very small positive effect for most people. In fact, the authors conclude, "Given these data, there seems little evidence to support the prescription of antidepressant medication to any but the most severely depressed patients, unless alternative treatments have failed to provide benefit" (Kirsch et al., 2008).

Nevertheless, these drugs are prescribed to tens of millions of people in North America alone, making billions of dollars for the companies that produce them. Drug companies also fund the vast majority of the research on their product's effectiveness, making for a difficult regulatory situation, when the academic researchers who are "independently" testing the drugs are, in fact, dependent on the drug manufacturers for much of their funding.

Where does this leave you, as a potential consumer of these drugs? We hope that it leaves you with the awareness that there are important decisions to be made when taking any prescription medication. For one, they don't work the same way with everybody; Prozac undoubtedly helps many people, but it also fails to work for many others, and causes its own problems in many cases. Armed with this knowledge and a better understanding that there are many different ways to treat a psychological condition such as depression, consumers should be a little more wary, more likely to do their homework and find out just how effective a drug is likely to be, and what other options may be available.

Focus Questions

1. What medical techniques are available for influencing psychological disorders, and how do they work?
2. What are the risks and benefits associated with different biomedical approaches?

All of the psychological disorders that we have covered in this text involve brain chemistry, because everything that occurs in consciousness involves brain chemistry. The biomedical approach to treating disorders involves using drugs, surgery, or other medical procedures in order to alter the functioning of the central nervous system and correct what is believed to be the underlying biological problem. **Psychopharmacotherapy**—*the use of drugs to attempt to manage or reduce clients' symptoms*—is by far the most frequently used biomedical option, and is often employed in conjunction with some form of therapy. Other options, such as surgery or electrically stimulating the brain, are typically used only in situations where no other available treatments have succeeded. In this module, we explore and evaluate each of these biomedical treatment options, and examine how they may be used in conjunction with other forms of therapy.

Explore Biomedical Therapies

Drug Treatments

Psychotropic drugs are *medications designed to alter psychological functioning*. Drug approaches were first predominantly used in institutional and clinical settings, generally targeting very severe cases. However, in more recent decades, drug treatments have become mainstream practice for many people experiencing even relatively mild psychological problems and symptoms. This expansion has made certain psychotropic drugs, such as those used to treat depression, among the most prescribed forms of medicine (Olfson & Marcus, 2009).

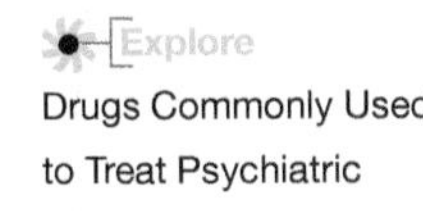

Drugs Commonly Used to Treat Psychiatric Disorders

Psychotropic drugs have been developed to take many different courses of action. First, all psychotropic drugs are designed to cross the **blood–brain barrier,** *a network of tightly packed cells that only allow specific types of substances to move from the bloodstream to the brain in order to protect delicate brain cells against harmful infections and other substances* (see Figure 16.3). Psychotropic drugs are designed to cross this barrier and then affect one or more specific neurotransmitters. The specific neurotransmitters

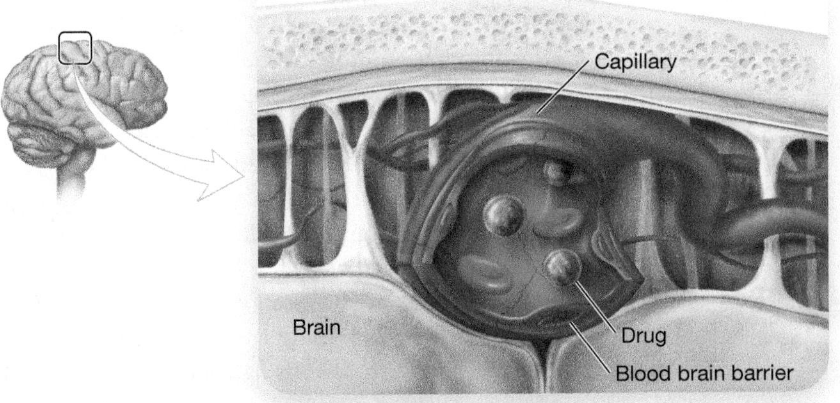

{FIG. 16.3} **How Psychotropic Drugs Reach the Brain** In order to affect the brain in the desired way, psychotropic drugs must cross the blood–brain barrier, a network of densely packed cells that restrict the flow of substances between the capillaries and brain cells.

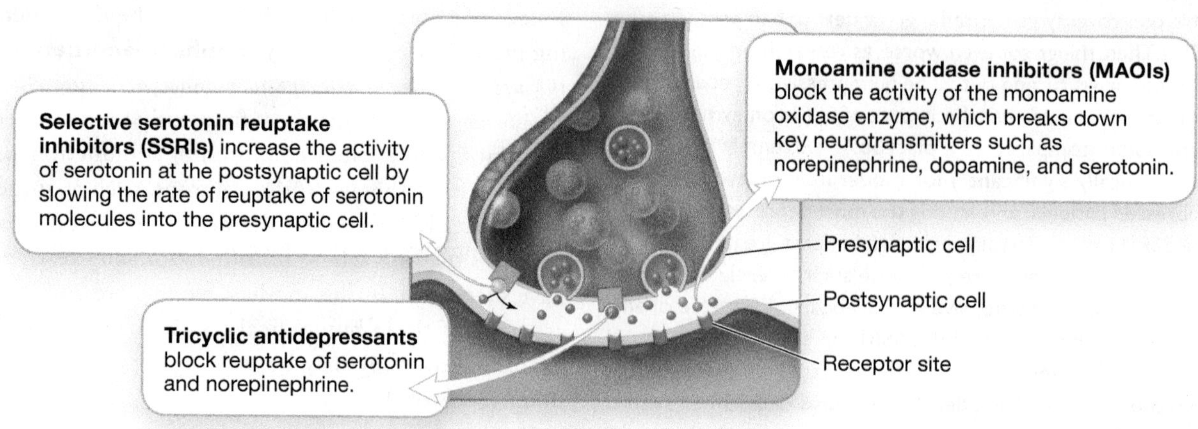

{FIG. 16.4} **Antidepressant Effects at the Synapse** The major antidepressant drugs have different ways of increasing the transmission of neurotransmitters such as serotonin, dopamine, and norepinephrine at the synapses.

that are targeted depend on the underlying disorder that is believed to best account for the client's symptoms.

ANTIDEPRESSANTS AND MOOD STABILIZERS

As the name suggests, **antidepressant drugs** are *medications designed to elevate mood and reduce other symptoms of depression.* In general, antidepressant drugs target areas of the brain that, when functioning normally, are rich in monoamine neurotransmitters—serotonin, norepinephrine, and dopamine. With multiple neurotransmitters involved, antidepressants come in several varieties, each with its own way of altering brain chemistry (Figure 16.4).

Monoamine oxidase inhibitors (MAOIs) were the first type of antidepressant that was developed and widely used. They *work by deactivating monoamine oxidase (MAO), an enzyme that breaks down serotonin, dopamine, and norepinephrine at the synaptic clefts of nerve cells* (see Figure 16.4). When MAO is inhibited, fewer dopamine, serotonin, and norepinephrine neurotransmitters are metabolized, which in turn leaves more of them available at the synapses. Although MAOIs are often effective at relieving the symptoms of depression, they are used less frequently than other antidepressants, in part because they can have dangerous interactions with fermented foods (e.g., aged cheeses, smoked meats, alcoholic beverages) and other medications, causing severely high blood pressure if mixed with the wrong foods or medications. If you look at the label of just about any over-the-counter medication, you will probably find listed warnings against using MAOIs when taking the nonprescription drug. MAOIs have a host of other more minor side effects as well, such as diarrhea, weight gain, and sexual dysfunction.

Tricyclic antidepressants were among the earliest types of antidepressants on the market and *appear to work by blocking the reuptake of serotonin and norepinephrine* (Figure 16.4). Unfortunately, as with MAOIs, many side effects are associated with tricyclic antidepressants, including nausea, weight gain, sexual dysfunction and, in some cases, seizures.

Selective serotonin reuptake inhibitors (SSRIs) are *a class of antidepressant drugs that block the reuptake of the neurotransmitter serotonin.* Among the most common of these are Prozac (fluoxetine), Zoloft (sertraline), and Paxil (paroxetine). These antidepressants successfully alleviate some proportion of the symptoms of depression in some clients, although they also come with certain side effects, as discussed in the opening vignette of this module.

Keep in mind that enhancing mood through increasing serotonin function is just a hypothesis about how these drugs work, not a fact. There are other possible mechanisms; for example, increasing serotonin amounts has been shown to cause the brain stem to diminish activation in order to reduce arousal, which could be one way that SSRIs reduce negative emotions in general (Maier & Watkins, 2005). SSRIs also decrease the extent to which parts of the amygdala are activated, which has been shown to be hyperaroused in people with depression; reducing this amygdala activity would reduce the person's tendency to activate negative emotions in response to various stimuli (Sheline et al., 2001). SSRIs have been shown to lead to neurogenesis—the growth of brand-new neurons—in the hippocampus, which may help alleviate depression because reduced hippocampal volume has been connected to depression (Jacobs, 2004). Any given drug generally has multiple effects on the brain, and researchers are constantly searching for a better understanding of these multiple effects, so as to develop a better understanding of the processes that cause and maintain disorders, and to become better able to precisely target those processes in designing treatments.

Mood stabilizers are *drugs used to prevent or reduce the severity of mood swings experienced by people with bipolar disorder.* **Lithium** was *one of the first mood stabilizers to be prescribed regularly in psychiatry, and from the 1950s to the 1980s, was the standard drug treatment for depression and bipolar disorder.* Lithium, a salt compound, can be quite effective, but it can also be toxic to the kidneys and endocrine system. Today, doctors generally prefer to prescribe other drugs because they seem to be more effective and safer than lithium (Thase & Denko, 2008). For example, people with bipolar disorder now often take anticonvulsant medications such as valproate or anti-psychotic medications. Although these medicines can be effective in preventing manic episodes, they are also associated with significant side effects, including weight gain, nausea, and fatigue; there are also a host of more rare and serious side effects, including brain damage due to elevated levels of ammonia in the blood (Wadzinski et al., 2007).

MYTHS IN MIND

Antidepressant Drugs Are Happiness Pills

A common belief is that antidepressants are happiness in pill form—that their chemical magic not only causes depression to disappear, but also brings on optimism and a rush of positive emotion. In reality, antidepressant drugs can alleviate depression (in some individuals), but they do not make people happier than they were before becoming depressed.

The "happiness pill" misconception about antidepressants has led some individuals to believe that taking a high dose of antidepressants will induce a euphoric high, much like cocaine or heroin. This is also a myth. Although some people have attempted to abuse antidepressants by taking high doses (even crushing and snorting them for quicker delivery to the brain), there is no evidence that an intense rush of happiness results. In fact, SSRIs typically take a couple of weeks to work. Taking a high dose, or snorting crushed-up pills, neither magnifies their effects nor reduces the two-week waiting period before effects become evident.

In short, individuals without depression should not expect to feel greater happiness if they take the drugs.

WORKING THE SCIENTIFIC LITERACY MODEL

Is St. John's Wort Effective?

People often make the assumption that biomedical therapies are limited to prescription drugs or procedures that only a physician can provide. In reality, people often self-prescribe and administer treatments for depression consisting of over-the-counter remedies. As with any other treatment, we should examine the evidence to determine the effectiveness of these options. In this case, we will examine St. John's wort.

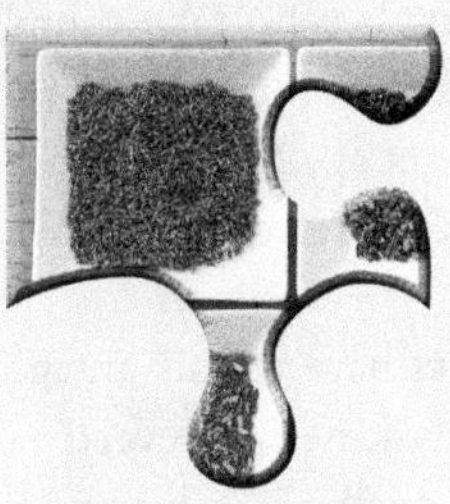

What do we know about St. John's wort?

St. John's wort (*Hypericum perforatum*) is an herbal remedy available in drugstores that has a long history of use as a treatment for various conditions. It is very popular in European countries, and is commonly purchased in Canada and the United States. Despite its widespread use as a mood enhancer, medical opinion on its effectiveness for depression has generally been mixed.

What have scientific studies found about St. John's wort and depression?

Several groups of researchers have been testing whether St. John's wort can alleviate depression. The most recent meta-analysis of this research combined the results of 29 different studies with over 5400 patients (Linde et al., 2008). The results indicate that St. John's wort is indeed more effective than a placebo, and equally as effective as prescription antidepressant drugs, at alleviating the symptoms of major depression. Most studies have looked at mild to moderate levels of depression, although there is some initial evidence that St. John's wort can work as effectively as SSRIs for more severe cases of depression as well (Jurcic et al., 2007). And as an added bonus, St. John's wort has fewer and less severe potential side effects than the prescription drug alternatives.

Can we critically evaluate this evidence?

St. John's wort, just like prescription antidepressant drugs, produces mixed results. For some people, it seems to be effective; for others, it does little or nothing. However, due to conflicting results, we should consider one of the most important confounds: Because herbal supplements are not regulated by government agencies, the quality may vary a great deal among brands, which could explain the conflicting results (Klaus et al., 2008). Standardizing the quality of St. John's wort for research purposes would help to overcome this problem and allow its effectiveness to be tested more precisely.

Why is this relevant?

Knowledge about alternative treatments such as St. John's wort can help individuals with depression make fully informed choices about what treatment is best for them. However, individuals considering the herbal remedy still need to consult with their doctors. The FDA warns that St. John's wort can produce unfavourable reactions with medications used to treat heart disease, seizures, and some cancers. Also, drug treatments, whether herbal or prescription, may not be the only therapeutic option—especially for people experiencing relatively mild or moderate levels of depression. Indeed, while the efficacy of St. John's wort has been compared to common drug treatments, research has not sufficiently tested how it compares to psychological therapies for depression.

Fancy/Alamy

ANTIANXIETY DRUGS Sometimes referred to as tranquilizers, **antianxiety drugs** are prescribed to alleviate nervousness and tension, and to prevent and reduce panic attacks. Widely prescribed examples include Xanax (alprazolam), Valium (diazepam), and Ativan (lorazepam). These drugs *affect the activity of gamma-aminobutyric acid (GABA), an inhibitory neurotransmitter that reduces neural activity* (see Module 3.2). They appear to temporarily alter the structure of GABA receptors, allowing more GABA molecules to inhibit neural activity. The effects of antianxiety drugs are relatively short-lived. They take effect within minutes of ingestion and may last for only a few hours. Given that these drugs facilitate inhibition of the nervous system, it is not surprising that their side effects include drowsiness, tiredness, and impaired attention, especially when they are taken at high doses. More serious side effects include memory impairments, depression, decreased sex drive, and many other possible effects. These drugs also have the potential to induce abuse and withdrawal symptoms.

ANTIPSYCHOTIC DRUGS **Antipsychotic drugs** *are generally used to treat symptoms of psychosis, including delusions, hallucinations, and severely disturbed or disorganized thought.* Antipsychotics are the common treatment for schizophrenia and are sometimes prescribed to people with severe mood disorders. There are several classes of antipsychotic drugs.

As discussed in Module 15.4, symptoms of schizophrenia are related to increased activity of dopamine, possibly because of the presence of an overabundance of receptors for dopamine in key brain regions. The first generation of antipsychotic medications (e.g., Thorazine, Halodol) was designed to block dopamine receptors. However, these drugs had significant side effects, such as seizures, anxiety, nausea, and impotence. One of the more severe and often permanent side effects, **tardive dyskinesia**, is *a movement disorder involving involuntary movements and facial tics.*

The newer generation of medications is referred to as **atypical antipsychotics** or second-generation antipsychotics. *Makers of atypical antipsychotics claim that these drugs are less likely to produce extrapyramidal side effects including movement disorders that commonly occur when first-generation antipsychotics are prescribed.* The various atypical antipsychotics on the market vary in their exact effects, but generally speaking they primarily seem to reduce dopamine and serotonin activity. Atypical antipsychotics work for almost half of the individuals who take them, reducing the severity of symptoms but not necessarily eliminating them altogether (Leucht et al., 2009). Unfortunately, studies show that their effects weaken over time, such that symptoms can return.

Second-generation antipsychotics have the advantage of carrying a lower risk for tardive dyskinesia. Nevertheless, they are not without risk. For example, Clozapine, which is a very effective antipsychotic drug, is known to compromise the body's white blood cells, and patients must have their blood regularly monitored or the consequences can be extremely severe, even leading to death.

Unfortunately, finding out exactly how psychiatric drugs affect people is not always easy to do, and requires that large numbers of people end up being unwitting guinea pigs, before the true effects of some medications are made known to the public. For example, one of the bigger scandals in the pharmaceutical industry in recent years involved another of the atypical antipsychotic drugs, Zyprexa. Initially, Zyprexa was hailed as a major breakthrough for individuals with schizophrenia and it was prescribed to massive numbers of people (eventually more than 20 million people around the world).

Then people began to allege that Zyprexa caused drastic weight gain, and evidence started to accumulate that Zyprexa was linked to the onset of diabetes, hyperglycemia, and pancreatitis. Although Eli Lilly officially denied that Zyprexa caused these consequences, as of 2007, the drug's manufacturer, Eli Lilly, had paid more than $1.2 billion to settle lawsuits brought against it by almost 30 000 people (Berenson, 2007).

Much of the testing of drugs, and their promotion and marketing to physicians, occurs behind a curtain of secrecy, making it difficult for the public to always know whether drugs are being used appropriately. Again, Zyprexa is a good example. In 2009, Eli Lilly pled guilty to charges involving the "off-label marketing" of Zyprexa. To understand just how much potential harm can occur due to such practices, consider first of all the possible side effects that were discussed above. Then consider some of the details of the case:

> *Zyprexa had received approval by the Food and Drug Administration (FDA) as a treatment for schizophrenia and bipolar disorder. However, Eli Lilly admitted that they marketed the drug illegally, promoting it to doctors as a treatment for other conditions.*
>
> *The general media reported that Eli Lilly admitted to illegally marketing Zyprexa for "off-label uses," which are uses that have not been approved by the FDA. According to the U.S. Department of Justice, Eli Lilly concentrated these illegal marketing efforts to doctors who treat the elderly in nursing homes and other assisted living situations, and primary care physicians. In addition to schizophrenia and bipolar disorder, doctors were encouraged to prescribe Zyprexa for dementia, Alzheimer's, agitation, aggression, hostility, depression, and generalized sleep disorder, all of which are common symptoms in elderly populations. Zyprexa also has the side effect of sedation, which was promoted as a therapeutic benefit for the elderly, helping to deal with any behavioural issues. Their sales slogan "5 at 5" was used to symbolize how 5 milligrams of Zyprexa given at 5 p.m. would help put elderly patients to sleep for the night.*
>
> *Following these efforts, Eli Lilly expanded its marketing efforts to primary care physicians, recommending that Zyprexa be prescribed to all adult patients with behavioural symptoms ranging from sleep disorders to aggression, and agitation to depression. Eli Lilly created marketing materials promoting Zyprexa for these off-label uses, and trained its sales force how to promote the drug illegally and how to respond to doctors' concerns or resistance.*

The company was fined a total of $1.4 billion. In 2010 alone, Eli Lilly made more than $5 billion from Zyprexa (Stastna, 2013).

EVALUATING DRUG THERAPIES Many people believe that drugs are designed to target the root physical causes of psychological disorders, and that they should therefore be more effective than psychological approaches to therapy. This set of beliefs is not warranted, on both counts. For one, it is not necessarily the case that the physical processes targeted by drugs are in fact the "root causes" of disorders; they may be involved in reinforcing the disorder, but they may not be the original cause. Also, drugs are not more effective than psychological therapies in many cases. For example, with regard to depression, the use of antidepressants has become increasingly accepted among the general public, in part due to the pervasive marketing campaigns from drug companies. However, these drugs are not as effective as they are widely believed to be. Only approximately 50% to 60% of people who take antidepressants improve within a few months—compared to 30% of people who improve similarly by taking a placebo (Hollon et al., 2002). Interestingly, 50% to 60% of people also improve from psychological therapy used to treat depression. Thus, we cannot conclude that drugs either are more effective or should replace other approaches to therapy. In many situations, a combination of treatment approaches may work the best; for example, combining psychological therapy with antidepressants has been shown to be more effective in treating major depression than medication alone (Burnand et al., 2002; de Jonghe et al., 2001).

In other cases, such as most anxiety disorders, psychological treatments such as cognitive-behavioural therapy (Module 16.2) are generally the most effective treatment (Hofmann & Smits, 2008). A key advantage of CBT is that the effects last long after the treatment is completed (Hollon et al., 2006), whereas anti-anxiety medications typically are effective only as long as the client maintains the drug regimen, and of course, come with side effects and addictive potential. This superior long-term effect of CBT over drugs has been found for generalized anxiety disorder (Hofmann & Smits, 2008) and panic disorder (Barlow et al., 2000).

One highly promising area of therapeutic development concerns the generally superior effects of combining different forms of therapy, such as combining drugs and psychological treatments. Research generally shows that drugs are more effective when combined with other types of therapy. For example, combining drugs with CBT is more effective for panic disorder with agoraphobia than either treatment on its own (Starcevic et al., 2004).

Even schizophrenia, which is often viewed to be an organic "brain disease," is more effectively treated by combined approaches. People with schizophrenia tend to have difficulty in self-reflecting, projecting themselves into the past and future (D'Argembeau et al., 2008), engaging in basic self-care, and integrating into regular social life. Although drugs may reduce many symptoms, treating the symptoms just listed through psychological therapies has been shown to have a huge impact on reducing the likelihood of experiencing further schizophrenic episodes. Some research has shown that the likelihood of experiencing future schizophrenic episodes is affected even more strongly by social factors, such as how much negative emotion and hostility are experienced in the family, than even by whether the person with schizophrenia takes the prescribed medication (Hooley & Gotlib, 2000). Clearly, evaluating drug treatments, as well as the potential for developing integrative treatments that use multiple approaches in conjunction with one another, are vitally important areas of research.

Quick Quiz 16.3a

Drug Treatments

KNOW ...

1 Tardive dyskinesia is

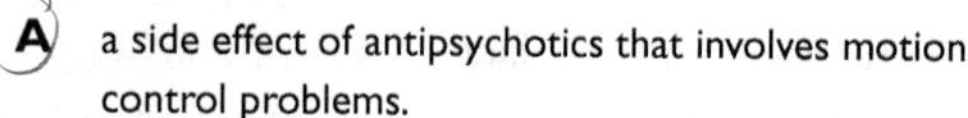

A a side effect of antipsychotics that involves motion control problems.

B an antidepressant that breaks down enzymes in the synapse.

C the growth of new neurons in the adult brain.

D a side effect of antidepressant drugs.

UNDERSTAND ...

2 ________ affect the nervous system by blocking reuptake of serotonin in neurons.

A MAOIs

B Antianxiety medications

C Mood stabilizers

D SSRIs

3 Monoamine oxidase inhibitor drugs work by

A boosting the ability of an enzyme to break down serotonin, dopamine, and norepinephrine molecules.

B inhibiting the ability of an enzyme to break down serotonin, dopamine, and norepinephrine molecules.

C selectively blocking the reuptake of serotonin.

D creating new dopamine molecules.

ANALYZE ...

4 Generally speaking, which of the following is the most accurate statement about psychotropic drugs?

A They are superior to talking therapy.

B Their effects are rarely evident until weeks after taking them.

C They are usually more effective if combined with some form of psychological treatment.

D Although drugs often had bad side effects in the past, modern drugs have largely fixed those problems.

5 Imagine that a friend asks you what you have heard about St. John's wort because he is considering using it to alleviate his depression. What would you say, based on the research?

A St. John's wort is as effective at treating depressive symptoms as antidepressants for many people.

B St. John's wort is superior to prescription antidepressant medications.

C Your friend may as well take a placebo: St. John's wort has never proved effective at reducing symptoms of depression.

D St. John's wort is superior to cognitive-behavioural therapies.

Answers can be found on page ANS-4.

BIOPSYCHOSOCIAL PERSPECTIVES

Exercise and Depression

One of the tricky things about "mental illness" is that the very label can be misleading because disorders such as major depressive disorder are not strictly "mental"; they also involve the body. This should be no surprise when you consider the multiple feedback pathways between the body and the brain. Consider the role that physiological arousal plays in emotional intensity (Module 11.4) and stress (Module 14.2). However, although we know that the body affects the mind, it is easy to forget this when considering psychological disorders; people often think that they are "all in your head." As a result, when we think of therapy, we generally think of psychological treatments and drug treatments that operate on neurotransmitters. But what if body-based treatments, such as physical exercise, could also be effective, even for serious disorders like major depressive disorder?

In fact, numerous studies have shown that exercise is more effective than placebos at relieving depressive symptoms, and is approximately as effective as standard SSRI medications, particularly for mild to moderate cases of depression (Carek et al., 2011). Furthermore, the "side effects" of

PictureArt/Fotolia

exercise are overwhelmingly positive, compared to the huge range of potential negative side effects associated with antidepressant medications. In contrast to medications that often induce side effects that detract from the person's quality of life, exercise brings a wide range of benefits that pretty much universally improve quality of life, and shows promise for preventing relapse of depressive symptoms better than medication (Babyak et al., 2000).

So what is it about exercise that alleviates depressive symptoms? Several mechanisms are probably at work. In the short term, many exercises, such as running, cause the release of endorphins, which reduce pain sensation and increase mood. Exercise also more generally increases people's energy levels and positive emotions, leading to greater participation in enjoyable activities, counteracting the tendencies toward social withdrawal and negative cognitive styles which are associated with depression. Neuroscience research even indicates that exercise increases activity in the brain's reward circuitry, thus counteracting the tendency for people to experience less pleasure in daily activities as they slide into a depressive episode.

Thus, there are more treatments available for depression than traditional psychological or psychiatric approaches. This takes "therapy" in a whole new direction, in which behaviour change and motivation become central foci for the therapist and client, and the focus starts to shift somewhat from managing symptoms to engaging in healthier ways of living in general.

Technological and Surgical Methods

Drugs are not the only method of biomedical therapy available to people seeking help for psychological problems. There are a variety of other approaches, ranging from direct surgical interventions to high-tech stimulation of brain areas by magnetic pulses. Today, these procedures are fairly safe and are carefully tested and scrutinized, although that has not always been the case.

You have likely heard of the **frontal lobotomy**. The story behind this procedure is chilling. Many neurologists of the 1800s and 1900s experimented with *surgically removing regions of the cortex* in the hope of "curing" psychological problems. In the 1930s, researchers started to discover that, by damaging the prefrontal areas of aggressive chimpanzees, they could make these unmanageable animals much calmer and more controllable. When Portuguese surgeon Antonio Moniz heard about this at a conference, he thought it might be useful for helping people with severe psychoses and other disorders. He helped to develop the **leucotomy**, *the surgical destruction of brain tissues in the prefrontal cortex*. Drilling small holes into the skull, Moniz would typically insert a small wire loop, a leucotome, through the holes and into the brain matter, and with a few flips of the wrist the damage is done and the patient is left to "recover."

Moniz himself had limited success, reporting a general improvement in the symptoms of several severely depressed, anxious, or otherwise disturbed people, and recommended it as a method of last resort when all else seems to have failed. The technique was popularized and turned into a veritable industry by an enterprising American surgeon, Dr. Walter Freeman, who also heard about the earlier work with chimpanzees at the same conference as Moniz. Freeman, with his surgical and research partner Dr. James Watts, further developed the "lobotomy" (as he called the procedure) for about a decade, until he learned of a new method, developed in Italy, for getting into the brain through the eye sockets, thereby avoiding drilling into the skull.

Freeman adapted this further into the trans-orbital lobotomy, which became known as the "icepick lobotomy." The name was well deserved. Freeman actually would insert a slender metal shaft, like an icepick, in between the eyeball and eyelid, then with a hammer, would tap it through the bony roof of the eye socket and into the brain. Then he would basically swish it around until the frontal lobes were detached from the rest of the brain (Valenstein, 1973). He was even able to perform this brain-slicing without anesthesia, by first inducing a seizure in the patient through an electroconvulsive shock. Freeman believed the procedure to be miraculously successful. He became a passionate

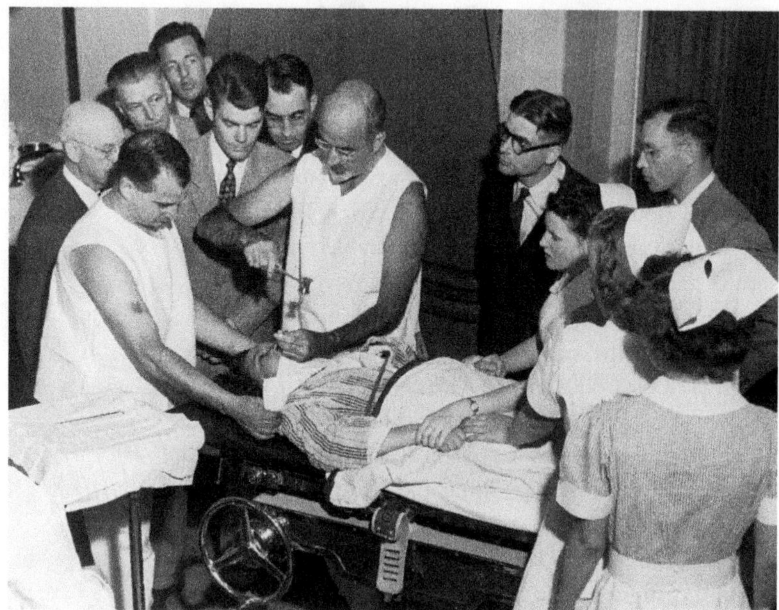

Bettmann/CORBIS

Walter Freeman performing a frontal lobotomy surgery.

advocate for the lobotomy, and because he was able to perform so many at a time, often more than a dozen in a single day, he travelled around the country in his van, the "lobotomobile," lobotomizing several thousand people in total. His procedure was always controversial, seen as a miraculous cure by some people and as a terrible barbaric practice by others, committing unknown amounts of harm and sometimes even ending in the patient's death from cerebral hemorrhaging. Nevertheless, Freeman was quite a medical celebrity for a while, and toured the country teaching his technique to many doctors and psychiatrists. In total, approximately 40 000 lobotomies are believed to have been performed in the United States and thousands more in western Europe. Freeman was eventually barred from practising, although not until 1967. And despite the protestations of many people, the man who started it all, Antonio Moniz, was awarded the Nobel Prize in Medicine.

By the 1950s, the popularity of the frontal lobotomy was dwindling rapidly. The inconsistent and often very negative results of the procedure, and the effectiveness of new psychotropic medications, convinced most of the field to move away from the lobotomy. Nevertheless, the basic practice of therapeutically destroying brain tissue survives to this day, although the techniques have gotten vastly more refined and precise.

FOCAL LESIONS One set of techniques involves performing **focal lesions**, *which are small areas of brain tissue that are surgically destroyed*. These brain lesions are only used in some severe cases, when all other treatments have not worked to satisfaction. For example, in some cases of depression, obsessive-compulsive disorder, and other anxiety disorders, lesion surgery has been targeted at a cluster of cells in the anterior cingulate cortex, an area that is overactive in people with these disorders (Cosgrove & Rauch, 2003; Fitzgerald et al., 2005; Steele et al., 2008). This procedure, which is called an anterior cingulotomy, has no more risks or side effects than do many of the drugs used to treat these disorders, and it can reduce symptoms successfully despite other treatments being ineffective. These cutting-edge techniques (no pun intended) have only become possible in recent years due to the surgical precision allowed by the use of brain-imaging technology, which allows surgeons to precisely target desired brain areas.

ELECTROCONVULSIVE THERAPY **Electroconvulsive therapy (ECT)** *involves passing an electrical current through the brain in order to induce a temporary seizure*. This procedure was introduced in the 1930s and has been viewed negatively for much of its history, in part because in its early days it was generally unsafe and easily abused; many people who have read the book or seen the movie *One Flew Over the Cuckoo's Nest* likely have a negative view of this procedure. In fact, many people believe that ECT causes lasting cognitive impairments, but the majority of research on people who have been treated with it suggests that this is not true (Rose et al., 2003).

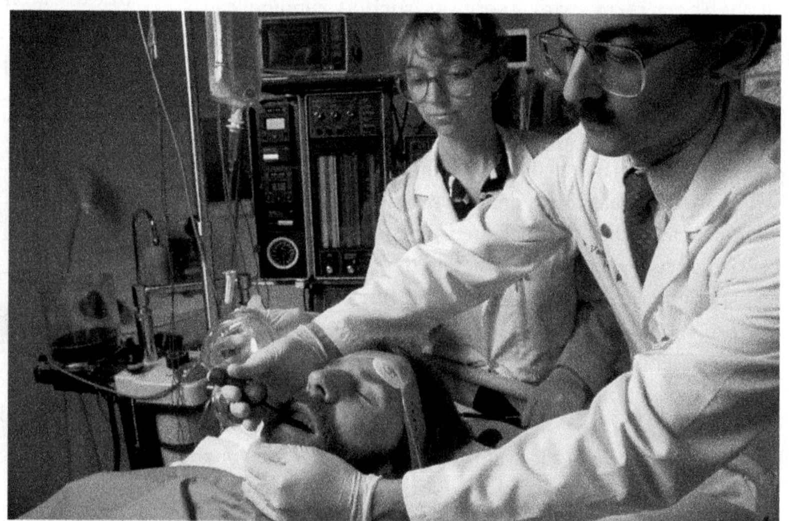

Will & Deni McIntyre/Science Source

People with depression or bipolar disorder may elect to undergo electroconvulsive therapy if other treatments have not been successful.

Over the years, ECT techniques have improved dramatically. Patients' experiences are much less negative as well, as a result of the fact they are now given sedatives and muscle relaxants to reduce the discomfort they may experience and to prevent injury related to the convulsions. Thus ECT has gone from being viewed as a torturous "shock treatment" to a relatively safe procedure, although it is still reserved for the most severe cases of disorders such as depression and bipolar disorder. The side effects are relatively mild, typically consisting of some amnesia, but only for events occurring around the time of the treatment.

Why does ECT work? Frankly, we don't know. Despite its use for decades, the mechanisms through which ECT affects the brain are largely unknown. There is some neuroimaging evidence that ECT changes the functional connectivity of the prefrontal cortices, diminishing some and enhancing others (Beall et al., 2012; Perrin et al., 2012). One possible interpretation of this emerging literature is that ECT may alter the patient's tendency to habitually engage in negative thoughts (see Module 15.3), thereby disrupting the dysfunctional thinking patterns that are characteristic of depression. More research is needed before we will fully understand why ECT works as mysteriously well as it does.

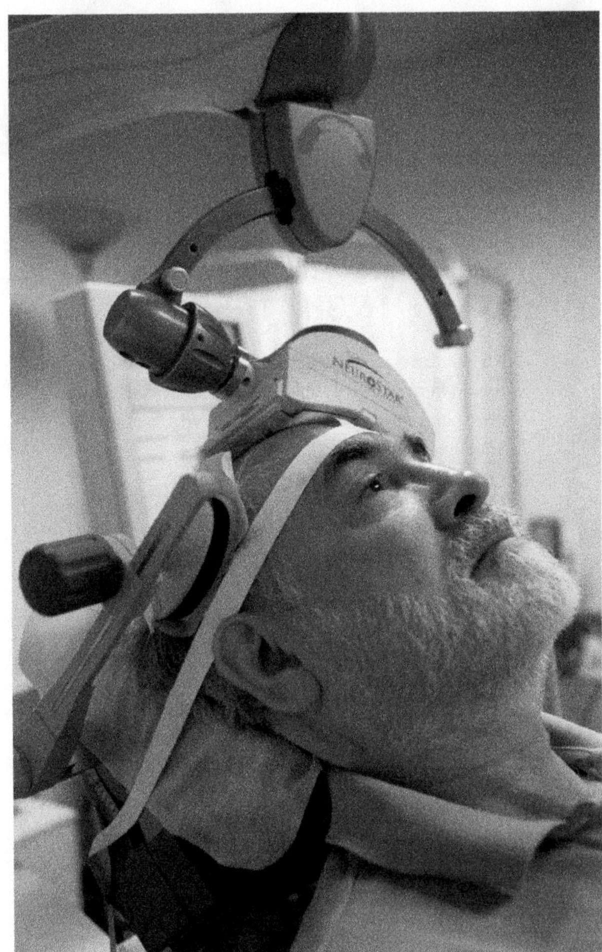

Bonnie Weller/staff/Newscom

Delivering brief pulses of a strong magnetic field to the cerebral cortex has been shown to help alleviate symptoms of severe depression, and possibly other disorders.

TRANSCRANIAL MAGNETIC STIMULATION **Transcranial magnetic stimulation (TMS)** is *a therapeutic technique in which a focal area of the brain is exposed to a powerful magnetic field* (see Module 3.4). TMS does not involve anesthesia nor induce a seizure. Clinical researchers have discovered that stimulating parts of the frontal lobes of the cortex reduces depressive symptoms (Chistyakov et al., 2005) and may hold considerable promise for reducing symptoms of other mental disorders, such as schizophrenia (Slotema et al., 2010; Zaman et al., 2008).

DEEP BRAIN STIMULATION **Deep brain stimulation (DBS)** is *a technique that involves electrically stimulating specific regions of the brain.* The procedure involves inserting thin electrode-tipped wires into the brain and carefully routing them to the targeted brain regions. A small battery connected to the wires is then inserted just beneath the skin surface. Unlike many of the drugs reviewed previously, DBS produces instantaneous results, and seems to work on even severe cases of depression that have been unresponsive to other treatments. As reported by researchers at the Rotman Research Institute in Toronto, who pioneered the application of DBS on depression, the effects seem almost miraculous; patients who are severely depressed report relief from their symptoms instantaneously, as soon as the electricity is applied (Mayberg et al., 2005; McNeely et al., 2008). Other researchers have shown DBS to be effective on symptoms of OCD as well (Aouizerate et al., 2009).

However, despite the stunning successes of DBS, there are some troublesome side effects to consider, such as internal bleeding and infection from the surgical insertion of the wires. Also, even though the wires and electrodes are placed with the utmost precision, it is possible that temporary behavioural side effects can occur. DPS can cause relatively benign experiences such as spontaneous laughter and penile erections, but it can also trigger more troublesome states of depression or aggression (Kringelbach et al., 2007).

WHEN ARE TECHNOLOGICAL AND SURGICAL METHODS USED? Technological and surgical methods are typically reserved for severe cases of disorders such as depression, schizophrenia, or obsessive-compulsive disorder. Some of these methods continue to be controversial because procedures such as the frontal lobotomy and ECT are the first examples to come to mind. Lobotomies are a thing of the past, however, and ECT is now a relatively safe procedure. Surgeries that involve destroying brain tissue are used in extreme cases, and as less invasive methods such as DBS and TMS become more extensively researched and widely available, they hold considerable promise for helping otherwise intractable cases.

Quick Quiz 16.3b Technological and Surgical Methods

UNDERSTAND ...

1 If a doctor wanted to activate a very specific brain region in the hope of alleviating symptoms of a mental disorder, she would most likely use which of the following procedures?

A Focal lesion

B Cingulotomy

C Electroconvulsive therapy

D Deep brain stimulation

2 Which of the following techniques results in intentionally killing nerve cells?

A Deep brain stimulation

B Electroconvulsive therapy

C Focal lesion

D Transcranial magnetic stimulation

ANALYZE ...

3 What is the key problem with a system that attempts to treat psychological disorders using the two predominant approaches of pharmacological treatments and psychological therapy?

A Psychological therapies are generally not effective and can be replaced by pharmacological treatments.

B Pharmacological treatments are often ineffective and carry side effects; thus, they should not be used.

C The current system of practice largely ignores other powerful factors that affect psychological health, such as exercise and nutrition.

D The system assumes that there is such a thing as a "disorder" in the first place, rather than simple variability in human experience.

Answers can be found on page ANS-4.

Module Summary

Module 16.3

Now that you have read this module you should

KNOW ...

- ***The key terminology associated with biological treatments:***

antianxiety drugs (p. 698)
antidepressant drugs (p. 696)
antipsychotic drugs (p. 698)
atypical antipsychotics (p. 698)
blood–brain barrier (p. 695)
deep brain stimulation (DBS) (p. 703)
electroconvulsive therapy (ECT) (p. 702)
focal lesions (p. 702)
frontal lobotomy (p. 701)
leucotomy (p. 701)
lithium (p. 697)
monoamine oxidase inhibitors (MAOIs) (p. 696)
mood stabilizers (p. 697)
psychopharmacotherapy (p. 695)
psychotropic drugs (p. 695)
selective serotonin reuptake inhibitors (SSRIs) (p. 696)
tardive dyskinesia (p. 698)
transcranial magnetic stimulation (TMS) (p. 703)
tricyclic antidepressants (p. 696)

UNDERSTAND ...

- ***How the drugs described in this module affect brain functioning.*** Antidepressant drugs typically target monoamine neurotransmitter activity, with differing mechanisms of action (review **Figure 16.4, p. 696**). Many of the antipsychotic drugs on the market reduce dopamine activity in the brain. Antianxiety drugs tend to target GABA receptors and increase activity of this inhibitory neurotransmitter.
- ***The other major medical approaches to therapy.*** Other procedures available for treating mental illness include electroconvulsive therapy, transcranial magnetic stimulation, deep brain stimulation, and focal lesions. In some cases, particularly ECT, researchers are still unsure about which aspect of the treatment produces the therapeutic results. Stimulation techniques increase the brain activity in targeted areas, whereas lesions prevent brain activity. By targeting the areas responsible for specific behaviours, thoughts, or emotions, treatments can have dramatic effects on the experience of someone with a psychological disorder.

Image Courtesy of The Advertising Archives

APPLY ...

- ***Your knowledge of drug therapies to different psychological conditions.*** Match the drugs listed in the left column with the condition they are typically prescribed to treat on the right. Check your answers on page ANS-4.

DRUG	CONDITION
1. Lithium	a. Anxiety
2. An SSRI	b. Depression
3. Xanax	c. Schizophrenia
4. Clozapine	d. Bipolar disorder

ANALYZE ...

- ***Whether St. John's wort, a popular herbal remedy for depression, works.*** Research into the effects of St. John's wort suggests it may be an effective treatment for many people. The herb works about as well as prescription antidepressants for at least mild to moderate levels of depression, but its efficacy for severe depression is not well established. Using St. John's wort carries the significant advantage of not exposing the person to nearly the same range of potential side effects as the prescription drugs, although it is also advisable to consult with a mental health professional rather than self-medicating without any professional support.

Work the Scientific Literacy Model :: Understanding Psychological Therapies

1 What do we know about treating psychological disorders?

Although we categorize disorders and define them separately, the reality is that clinicians often treat psychological disorders with a mixture of therapeutic techniques. **Table 16.4 (p. 693)** summarizes the major types of psychotherapies, and you can review the major psychotropic drugs and psychosurgeries on **pages 695–704**. If you are having trouble remembering the specifics of these therapies, you can think about them in terms of their treatment goals. For instance, while psychoanalysis and humanistic therapy are both insight therapies, the goal of psychoanalysis is to develop insight into the problem by revealing unconscious conflicts, whereas the humanistic approach attempts to gain a richer understanding of those factors that bring about personal growth and self-actualization by focusing on conscious and subjective experience. The cognitive-behavioural model aims to change the thoughts and feelings that lead to unwanted behaviours, and the goal of the behavioural approach is to change an unwanted behaviour through principles of classical conditioning and observational learning. Finally, biomedical therapies aim to alleviate symptoms and, potentially, treat the neurological basis of the client's problems.

2 How can science help explain psychological therapies?

First, it is important to note that many therapies stem from basic scientific research. For example, systematic desensitization comes directly out of basic research on classical conditioning. Similarly, drug treatments are derived from an understanding of neurotransmitter functioning in the brain. Thus, one important way that science helps to explain psychological therapies is by providing a theoretical and empirically informed understanding of the psychological and physiological processes underlying specific disorders.

In order to test the effectiveness of treatments themselves, the most rigorous scientific approach would be double-blind experiments; ideally, such investigations would involve control groups and follow patients over a long period of time. These methods are certainly used with the biologically based treatments, but great difficulties arise when researchers think about implementing these methods with psychotherapy. In particular, the therapist cannot be blinded to the type of treatment being provided, and the client often cannot as well. In addition, testing the effectiveness of psychotherapy in a standardized way may be difficult, because the effectiveness of the therapy depends so heavily on the therapeutic alliance—the unique relationship between therapist and patient, which is obviously impossible to standardize and difficult to manipulate with any precision.

Gts/Shutterstock

3 Can we critically evaluate claims about psychological therapies and treatments?

Psychotherapy is clearly a powerful tool in the treatment of psychological disorders. But what if someone cannot or will not see a mental health care professional? Encouraging research on self-help treatments suggests that these methods can be helpful if the treatment itself is valid, and combining the self-help treatment with at least one face-to-face therapy session would likely achieve a better rate of success.

The **Myths in Mind** feature on **page 697** discussed the misconception that antidepressants can alleviate depression and deliver a dose of euphoria in the form of a magic pill. While studies support the use of antidepressants across a range of psychological problems, they are by no means the first and only treatment for such patients. Herbal supplements such as St. John's wort might be effective for treating depression, but when considering studies of these products, we have to keep in mind confounding variables such as the strength of the supplement (most of these products are unregulated in Canada, and their precise strength and purity are generally unknown) and the degree of depression in the individual. Controlled and long-term studies of St. John's wort indicate that the supplement is no more effective than a placebo at treating people who are diagnosed with depression.

4 Why is this relevant?

Watch the accompanying video excerpt on psychological therapies. You can access the video at MyPsychLab or by clicking the play button in the centre of your eText. If your instructor assigns this video as a homework activity, you will find additional content to help you in MyPsychLab. You can also view the video by using your smart phone and the QR code below, or you can go to the YouTube link provided.

After you have read this chapter and watched the video, compare and contrast the following forms of psychotherapy: cognitive, humanistic, and behavioural. Identify the focus of each approach as well as areas of agreement and difference.

MyPsychLab **Your turn to Work the Scientific Literacy Model:** Watch the accompanying video on YouTube, or on your phone (using the Layar app or QR code). If your instructor has assigned this as a homework activity, you can find the video clip and additional content at MyPsychLab. Answer the questions that accompany the video clip to test your understanding.

YouTube
youtube.com/workthemodel

SCAN WITH LAYAR

Answer Key

CHAPTER 1

Quick Quiz 1.1a :: p. 5

1. B 2. C 3. D 4. C

Quick Quiz 1.1b :: p. 10

1. A 2. B 3. A

Module Summary Apply Activity 1.1 :: p. 11

1. The appeals to your wallet and to your environmental conscience sound great, but it might be too good to be true!
2. The manufacturer is trying to make money. That does not make the company evil, but it might lead its marketing staff to exaggerate the benefits offered by its products.
3. We do not have any evidence that the product works; we have only the manufacturer's claim. Until you find the evidence, you must tolerate ambiguity—you cannot say if it is effective or not.

Quick Quiz 1.2a :: p. 19

1. D 2. B 3. A 4. B

Quick Quiz 1.2b :: p. 27

1. A 2. D 3. A 4. C

Module Summary Apply Activity 1.2 :: p. 28

1. C 2. A 3. B 4. E 5. D

CHAPTER 2

Quick Quiz 2.1a :: p. 40

1. A 2. B 3. C 4. A

Quick Quiz 2.1b :: p. 42

1. B 2. C 3. A

Module Summary Apply Activity 2.1 :: p. 43

1. The problem with the instrumentation is one of reliability. One key measure of reliability in research is the degree to which a measurement provides consistent, stable responses. In this case, the recording device does not meet this criterion.
2. The problem with Dr. Nielson's happiness measure probably concerns its validity. The different observers were always in agreement on how they recorded the children's behaviour, so their measure is reliable. However, given what the second group of researchers found, it is possible that Dr. Nielson's group is actually measuring how energetic children are, rather than how happy they are. (As you may have thought, this could also go the other way around: The researcher who was recording whether children were energetic may have been unknowingly measuring whether they were happy.)

Quick Quiz 2.2a :: p. 49

1. B 2. C 3. D

Quick Quiz 2.2b :: p. 51

1. B (This is a strong negative correlation. The strength of the relationship is strongest because it is closer to −1.0 than either +.54 or +.10. Correlation coefficients cannot go above 1.0.)

2. A 3. C

Quick Quiz 2.2c :: p. 53

1. C 2. B 3. A 4. A

Module Summary Apply Activity 2.2 :: p. 54

1. independent; dependent
2. positive; negative

Quick Quiz 2.3a :: p. 61

1. B 2. C 3. B

Quick Quiz 2.3b :: p. 62

1. D 2. B

Module Summary Apply Activity 2.3 :: p. 63

1. It is not really informed consent if the volunteers are exposed to risks before signing the consent form. The "informed" part of informed consent means that individuals are fully informed about risks they may experience as a result of participating in the study.
2. This research design is unethical because it requires volunteers to answer all of the questions in a survey. Participants generally have the right to quit at any time, or to decline to answer any specific questions they choose. This issue is particularly important with sensitive topics such as sexuality.

Quick Quiz 2.4a :: p. 68

1. B 2. D 3. A 4. C

Quick Quiz 2.4b :: p. 71

1. C 2. A

Module Summary Apply Activity 2.4 :: p. 72

1. Negatively skewed 2. 90–94

3. 9 (4 between 80–84 and 5 between 85–89)

CHAPTER 3

Quick Quiz 3.1a :: p. 82

1. B 2. C 3. D 4. A

Quick Quiz 3.1b :: p. 90

1. C 2. B 3. D

Module Summary Apply Activity 3.1 :: p. 91

1. Evolutionary psychologists predict that males will be more jealous about sexual infidelity because they are more interested in the reproductive qualities in a mate. This statement does not mean that women will not experience jealousy; rather, it indicates that men will have a stronger response on average.
2. This graph does show that men have stronger responses to infidelity, so these results support the hypothesis.

Quick Quiz 3.2a :: p. 97

1. C 2. B 3. B 4. C

Quick Quiz 3.2b :: p. 103

1. B 2. B 3. D 4. A

Module Summary Apply Activity 3.2 :: p. 104

1. The monoamines are a group of neurotransmitters including serotonin, dopamine, and norepinephrine.
2. If monoamine oxidase breaks down the monoamine neurotransmitters, then an inhibitor would prevent it from breaking down the neurotransmitters. The result would be more monoamine neurotransmitters in the synapse.
3. Yes, an MAOI might produce effects resembling those of an SSRI, at least to the extent that both drugs have similar end results. Both types of drugs increase the amount of a neurotransmitter in the synapse, but do so in different ways.

Quick Quiz 3.3a :: p. 108

1. D 2. A 3. C

Quick Quiz 3.3b :: p. 118

1. C 2. A 3. D 4. A

Module Summary Apply Activity 3.3 :: p. 119

1. Occipital lobe
2. Broca's area (in the frontal lobe)
3. Movement and responses to rewarding stimuli
4. Problems with balance, coordination, and timing of movement

Quick Quiz 3.4a :: p. 122

1. C 2. D 3. B

Quick Quiz 3.4b :: p. 127

1. C 2. C 3. A 4. A

Module Summary Apply Activity 3.4 :: p. 128

1. EEG (It provides a continuous measure of brain activity.)
2. PET
3. fMRI
4. ERP or MEG

CHAPTER 4

Quick Quiz 4.1a :: p. 137

1. D 2. B 3. A 4. D 5. B

Quick Quiz 4.1b :: p. 141

1. B 2. D 3. B

Module Summary Apply Activity 4.1 :: p. 142

1. Correct rejection. There is no monster in the closet, and the child is confident that she has not heard anything.
2. Miss. There really are monsters in the closet, but the child has not heard them.
3. Hit. There really is a monster in the closet.
4. False alarm. There is no monster in the closet, but the child insists that she heard something.

Quick Quiz 4.2a :: p. 149

1. A 2. D 3. A 4. C

Quick Quiz 4.2b :: p. 157

1. A 2. C 3. C 4. D 5. C

Module Summary Apply Activity 4.2 :: p. 158

The pictorial depth cues include:

1. a linear perspective (the tracks converging as they reach the horizon);
2. a texture gradient (the rocks, grass, and other nearby objects can be seen in greater detail than objects farther away);
3. height in plane (the features that are in the top half of the picture are perceived as far away relative to objects in the bottom region of the photo); and
4. relative size. Railroad ties are known to be the same size, but the ones that are closer appear larger than those that are far off.

Quick Quiz 4.3a :: p. 162

1. A 2. C 3. D

Quick Quiz 4.3b :: p. 166

1. B 2. B 3. C 4. A

Quick Quiz 4.4a :: p. 173

1. B 2. A 3. C 4. A

Quick Quiz 4.4b :: p. 177

1. D 2. B 3. C 4. B 5. B

CHAPTER 5

Quick Quiz 5.1a :: p. 185

1. B 2. A 3. C

Quick Quiz 5.1b :: p. 189

1. C 2. A 3. B

Quick Quiz 5.1c :: p. 192

1. B 2. D 3. A

Quick Quiz 5.1d :: p. 196

1. B 2. D 3. B

Quick Quiz 5.2a :: p. 201

1. B 2. C 3. C 4. A

Quick Quiz 5.2b :: p. 203

1. A 2. C

Quick Quiz 5.2c :: p. 208

1. B 2. D

Module Summary Apply Activity 5.2 :: p. 208

1. False 2. True 3. True 4. False 5. False 6. True 7. True

Quick Quiz 5.3a :: p. 212

1. C 2. A 3. C

Quick Quiz 5.3b :: p. 219

1. D 2. A 3. C

Quick Quiz 5.3c :: p. 222

1. B 2. C 3. A

CHAPTER 6

Quick Quiz 6.1a :: p. 230

1. C 2. B 3. D 4. B

Quick Quiz 6.1b :: p. 232

1. B 2. C 3. A

Quick Quiz 6.1c :: p. 239

1. C 2. B 3. A

Quick Quiz 6.1d :: p. 241

1. A 2. B

Module Summary Apply Activity 6.1 :: p. 242

1. CS = theme song, US = kiss, UR = excitement, CR = excitement
2. CS = instrument used by the eye doctor, US = puff of air, UR = blinking, CR = blinking
3. CS = advertisement, US = delicious meal, UR = pleasure from the meal, CR = cravings

Quick Quiz 6.2a :: p. 250

1. D 2. C 3. B 4. A

Quick Quiz 6.2b :: p. 256

1. A 2. B 3. D 4. B

Module Summary Apply Activity 6.2 :: p. 257

1. Negative punishment explains Bill's change in behaviour. This process is considered punishment because Bill's behaviour of cheating stopped; it is considered negative punishment because the consequence was to remove something he found reinforcing (being at school).
2. Positive reinforcement explains Ericka's pursuit of math. The personal and social rewards are stimuli that added (positively related) to her doing math, which increased her interest in and pursuit of this subject.
3. We are negatively reinforced for closing the car doors, turning off lights, and fastening the seat belt. Each of these behaviours removes the unpleasant buzzing or dinging sound. In turn, the behaviours increase because they allow us to either avoid or escape the annoying sounds.
4. Hernan is using positive punishment. The nail and cuticle biting decrease because he introduces an unpleasant stimulus, the terrible-tasting lotion.

Quick Quiz 6.3a :: p. 260

1. C 2. A

Quick Quiz 6.3b :: p. 267

1. B 2. C 3. A 4. C

Module Summary Apply Activity 6.3 :: p. 267

1. Teaching a child how to kick a soccer ball properly will likely involve observational learning. A teacher (you) would show the child the different steps involved with kicking. If the child is having difficulties mastering each component (proper placement of the non-kicking foot, proper positioning of the kicking foot, etc.), you may use operant conditioning to shape the correct behaviours.
2. Improving efficiency in an office would likely involve mentoring. Efficient members of the office would likely model their behaviour for less efficient members. A system of rewards may be established to reinforce these newly learned behaviours. Remember, the different types of learning discussed in this chapter can be used together to change behaviour.
3. Improving sustainable behaviours requires that individuals have the necessary knowledge of what behaviours should be performed. This education phase would likely involve a series of examples from universities or cities that are doing a good job being environmentally friendly. The instructor would hope that these positive behaviours would be picked up by the students; rewards may help reinforce these behaviours.

CHAPTER 7

Quick Quiz 7.1a :: p. 277

1. D 2. C 3. C 4. A

Quick Quiz 7.1b :: p. 280

1. C 2. B 3. A 4. B

Quick Quiz 7.1c :: p. 282

1. C 2. D 3. B

Quick Quiz 7.1d :: p. 285

1. A 2. B 3. C

Module Summary Apply Activity 7.1 :: p. 286

1. If Dr. Richard blocks long-term potentiation, then the rat is unlikely to form any long-term memories. At best, they will be weak memories, and the rat will only partially remember the maze.
2. A damaged hippocampus can lead to anterograde amnesia. However, if the damage happens after the rat has committed the maze path to memory, then memory for this specific information should be unaffected by the procedure.

Quick Quiz 7.2a :: p. 293

1. B 2. A 3. B 4. B 5. A

Quick Quiz 7.2b :: p. 296

1. A 2. C 3. D

Quick Quiz 7.2c :: p. 299

1. B 2. B 3. A

Quick Quiz 7.3a :: p. 305

1. D 2. A 3. C

Quick Quiz 7.3b :: p. 310

1. B 2. A 3. A 4. D 5. B

Module Summary Apply Activity 7.3 :: p. 311

Of the 225 exonerations, 77% of the cases included erroneous eyewitness testimony—more than any other contributing factor. Given this high correlation, we believe research on eyewitness testimony should continue to find ways of reducing errors. The results of this research should be applied to investigative techniques used by law enforcement officers.

CHAPTER 8

Quick Quiz 8.1a :: p. 320

1. B 2. B 3. D 4. A

Quick Quiz 8.1b :: p. 322

1. C 2. B

Module Summary Apply Activity 8.1 :: p. 323

1. For most people, a trout would be a better example for a fish. Hammerheads and eels have unique shapes, but trout are very "fish-like"—they are better prototypes for this category.
2. For many Canadians, prototypical sports might include hockey, football, and baseball. For much of the rest of the world, the prototypical sport is probably soccer. Sports that are not considered prototypical by many would include golf, badminton, and equestrian competitions.
3. When people respond to this category, they usually settle on prototypical items that are difficult or impossible to replace—for example, photo albums and other memorabilia, prized possessions, and heirlooms.

Quick Quiz 8.2a :: p. 326

1. B 2. B 3. B

Quick Quiz 8.2b :: p. 334

1. D 2. C 3. D 4. C 5. A

Quick Quiz 8.3a :: p. 341

1. D 2. C 3. D 4. A

Quick Quiz 8.3b :: p. 344

1. B 2. A 3. A

Quick Quiz 8.3c :: p. 348

1. B 2. C 3. A

Module Summary Apply Activity 8.3 :: p. 349

1. This is a morpheme. We can tell in at least two ways. First, it contains multiple phonemes. Second, it can be added to words in a meaningful way such as in "dislike" and "disprove."
2. On one hand, you might consider /s/ a phoneme because it represents a single sound. On the other hand, you might consider it a morpheme because it can be added to words in a meaningful way (to make a noun plural). Thus, in this case /s/ can be either a phoneme or a morpheme.
3. This is a phoneme. It represents the sound of "c" in cat. However, /k/ is not a morpheme because it does not have any intrinsic meaning.

CHAPTER 9

Quick Quiz 9.1a :: p. 356

1. B 2. D 3. C 4. C

Quick Quiz 9.1b :: p. 362

1. B 2. C 3. D 4. D 5. D

Quick Quiz 9.2a :: p. 367

1. D 2. B 3. D

Quick Quiz 9.2b :: p. 374

1. C 2. B 3. A 4. D 5. C

Quick Quiz 9.2c :: p. 376

1. A 2. C

Module Summary Apply Activity 9.2 :: p. 376

Katrina obviously scores high in analytical intelligence—this is apparent in her academic success. She is also likely to score very high in creativity, as she has made significant discoveries and contributions to the field of chemistry. Unfortunately, she does not seem to do as well with practical intelligence. Katrina is probably about average because she may get by at work, but appears to be quite dependent on others at home, or she may be below average, given that she is unable to even cook for herself.

Quick Quiz 9.3a :: p. 382

1. B 2. A 3. D

Quick Quiz 9.3b :: p. 386

1. A 2. B 3. D

Quick Quiz 9.3c :: p. 388

1. C 2. B 3. D

CHAPTER 10

Quick Quiz 10.1a :: p. 394

1. C 2. D 3. A

Quick Quiz 10.1b :: p. 399

1. A 2. B 3. D 4. C

Quick Quiz 10.1c :: p. 403

1. A 2. C

Quick Quiz 10.2a :: p. 411

1. C 2. A 3. C 4. B 5. C

Quick Quiz 10.2b :: p. 417

1. C 2. B 3. D

Quick Quiz 10.3a :: p. 423

1. B 2. A 3. C

Quick Quiz 10.3b :: p. 429

1. B 2. B 3. C 4. B

Module Summary Apply Activity 10.3 :: p. 430

1. Jeff displays conventional reasoning in his decision. Although you would likely regard what he did as wrong, his reasoning for engaging in the behaviour is based on whether the act breaks a law.
2. Margaret displays postconventional moral reasoning because she is not personally affected, but is looking out for the well-being of innocent strangers.

Quick Quiz 10.4a :: p. 433

1. C 2. B

Quick Quiz 10.4b :: p. 440

1. D 2. B

CHAPTER 11

Quick Quiz 11.1a :: p. 447

1. A 2. C 3. B

Quick Quiz 11.1b :: p. 449

1. B 2. C 3. A 4. B

Quick Quiz 11.1c :: p. 453

1. B 2. C 3. C

Quick Quiz 11.2a :: p. 458

1. A 2. D

Quick Quiz 11.2b :: p. 461

1. B 2. B 3. A

Quick Quiz 11.2c :: p. 464

1. C 2. D 3. A

Quick Quiz 11.3a :: p. 470

1. B 2. B 3. C 4. A

Quick Quiz 11.3b :: p. 475

1. A 2. B 3. C

Quick Quiz 11.4a :: p. 480

1. C 2. B 3. C

Quick Quiz 11.4b :: p. 485

1. A 2. C 3. C

Quick Quiz 11.4c :: p. 488

1. B 2. C 3. C

CHAPTER 12

Quick Quiz 12.1a :: p. 502

1. A 2. A 3. C 4. B 5. C

Quick Quiz 12.1b :: p. 504

1. A 2. B 3. A

Quick Quiz 12.2a :: p. 510

1. B 2. D 3. C

Quick Quiz 12.2b :: p. 514

1. B 2. B 3. C

Quick Quiz 12.2c :: p. 516

1. B 2. B 3. A

Quick Quiz 12.2d :: p. 519

1. C 2. C 3. B

Quick Quiz 12.3a :: p. 531

1. A 2. D 3. A 4. C 5. C 6. B

Quick Quiz 12.3b :: p. 533

1. D 2. C 3. D

Quick Quiz 12.3c :: p. 534

1. B 2. A 3. A

CHAPTER 13

Quick Quiz 13.1a :: p. 548

1. A 2. D 3. A 4. D 5. D

Quick Quiz 13.1b :: p. 556

1. A 2. C 3. D

Quick Quiz 13.2a :: p. 564

1. B 2. B 3. B 4. C

Quick Quiz 13.2b :: p. 569

1. A 2. D 3. B 4. B

CHAPTER 14

Quick Quiz 14.1a :: p. 590

1. D 2. C 3. A

Quick Quiz 14.1b :: p. 594
1. B 2. C 3. D 4. D
Quick Quiz 14.1c :: p. 596
1. B 2. D 3. D
Quick Quiz 14.2a :: p. 603
1. C 2. B 3. C 4. C 5. D
Quick Quiz 14.2b :: p. 607
1. C 2. A 3. B 4. B
Quick Quiz 14.2c :: p. 609
1. C 2. C 3. D
Quick Quiz 14.3a :: p. 617
1. B 2. A 3. C 4. B 5. C
Quick Quiz 14.3b :: p. 620
1. B 2. A 3. C

CHAPTER 15

Quick Quiz 15.1a :: p. 631
1. C 2. D 3. B
Quick Quiz 15.1b :: p. 633
1. D 2. C
Quick Quiz 15.2a :: p. 641
1. D 2. A 3. D 4. A 5. D
Quick Quiz 15.2b :: p. 643
1. C 2. D 3. B 4. D
Module Summary Apply Activity 15.2 :: p. 644

1. People with psychopathy show reduced startle reflex and reduced activity in the frontal lobes.
2. Individuals with psychopathy have difficulty learning and following rules.
3. People who develop psychopathy or APD are more likely to grow up in distressed homes or neighborhoods where prosocial rules are not easily learned. A history of childhood sexual, physical, or emotional abuse at the hands of adults is also associated with APD and psychopathy.

Quick Quiz 15.3a :: pp. 652
1. C 2. B 3. A 4. C 5. B 6. B
Quick Quiz 15.3b :: p. 656
1. C 2. B 3. A
Module Summary Apply Activity 15.3 :: p. 657

If someone you know is considering suicide, he or she can call 1-800-273-TALK (8255). Five key signs of suicidal thinking are (1) talking about suicide; (2) withdrawing from friends or social activities; (3) losing interest in school, work, or hobbies; (4) preparing for death by writing a will, making final arrangements, or giving away prized possessions; and (5) losing interest in personal appearance. See Table 15.6 for additional signs.

Quick Quiz 15.4a :: p. 662
1. A 2. C 3. D 4. A 5. A
Quick Quiz 15.4b :: p. 666
1. C 2. A 3. B
Module Summary Apply Activity 15.4 :: p. 667

1. C: The statuesque behaviour is catatonia.
2. B: The overly suspicious delusions are signs of paranoia.
3. A: This sounds like dissociative disorder (see Module 15.2).
4. D: The scrambled language and thoughts represent disorganized schizophrenia.

CHAPTER 16

Quick Quiz 16.1a :: p. 673
1. D 2. B 3. D
Quick Quiz 16.1b :: p. 676
1. A 2. B 3. C
Quick Quiz 16.1c :: p. 679
1. C 2. C 3. D
Quick Quiz 16.2a :: p. 685
1. D 2. B 3. A 4. C 5. D
Quick Quiz 16.2b :: p. 692
1. D 2. A 3. C 4. B 5. A 6. A
Module Summary Apply Activity 16.2 :: p. 693

1. B: cognitive-behavioral therapy, because it is aimed at addressing irrational thought patterns and cognitive restructuring.
2. C: psychodynamic therapy, because the emphasis is on gaining insight into early childhood experiences.
3. E: behavioural therapy, because the focus is on modifying observable behaviour patterns.

Quick Quiz 16.3a :: p. 700
1. A 2. D 3. B 4. C 5. A
Quick Quiz 16.3b :: p. 704
1. D 2. C 3. C
Module Summary Apply Activity 16.3 :: p. 705
1. D 2. B 3. A 4. C

Glossary

3,4-methylenedioxy-*N*-methylamphetamine :: see *ecstasy* 214

absolute threshold :: the minimum amount of energy or quantity of a stimulus required for it to be reliably detected at least 50% of the time it is presented 134

accommodation :: a creative process whereby people modify their belief structures based on experience 406

acetylcholine :: one of the most widespread neurotransmitters within the body, found at the junctions between nerve cells and skeletal muscles; it is very important for voluntary movement 99

achievement motivation :: the drive to perform at high levels and to accomplish significant goals 470

acquisition :: the initial phase of learning in which a response is established 230

acronyms :: pronounceable words whose letters represent the initials of an important phrase or set of items 298

action potential :: a wave of electrical activity that originates at the base of the axon and rapidly travels down its length 96

activation–synthesis hypothesis :: suggests that dreams arise from brain activity originating from bursts of excitatory messages from the pons, a part of the brainstem 189

active phase :: phase of schizophrenia during which people typically experience delusional thoughts, hallucinations, or disorganized patterns of thoughts, emotions, and behaviour 659

adrenal glands :: a pair of endocrine glands located adjacent to the kidneys that release stress hormones, such as cortisol and epinephrine 102

affiliation motivation :: see *need to belong* 467

agonists :: drugs that enhance or mimic the effects of a neurotransmitter's action 101

agoraphobia :: often associated with panic disorder, agoraphobia results from an intense fear of having a panic attack in public; as a result of this fear, the individual may begin to avoid public settings and increasingly isolate himself or herself 647

algorithms :: problem-solving strategies based on a series of rules 325

all-or-none principle :: individual nerve cells fire at the same strength every time an action potential occurs 97

allostasis :: motivation is not only influenced by current needs, but also by the anticipation of future needs 445

Alzheimer's disease :: a degenerative and terminal condition resulting in severe damage of the entire brain 433

amnesia :: a profound loss of at least one form of memory 283

amotivational :: a feeling of having little or no motivation to perform a behaviour 472

amygdala :: a group of nuclei in the medial portion (near the middle) of the temporal lobes in each hemisphere of the brain that facilitates memory formation for emotional events, mediates fear responses, and appears to play a role in recognizing and interpreting emotional stimuli, including facial expressions 111

analytic system :: operates at the explicit level of consciousness, is slower and methodical, and uses logic and discursive thinking (i.e., reasoning using language) 575

analytical psychology :: focuses on the role of unconscious archetypes in personality development 532

anchoring effect :: occurs when an individual attempts to solve a problem involving numbers and uses previous knowledge to keep (i.e., anchor) the response within a limited range 329

anecdotal evidence :: an individual's story or testimony about an observation or event that is used to make a claim as evidence 41

anorexia nervosa :: an eating disorder that involves (1) self-starvation, (2) intense fear of weight gain and dissatisfaction with one's body, and (3) a denial of the serious consequences of severely low weight 450

antagonists :: inhibit neurotransmitter activity by blocking receptors or preventing synthesis of a neurotransmitter 101

anterograde amnesia :: the inability to form new memories for events occurring after a brain injury 283

anthropometrics :: (literally, "the measurement of people") methods of measuring physical and mental variation in humans 353

antianxiety drugs :: affect the activity of gamma-aminobutyric acid (GABA), an inhibitory neurotransmitter that reduces neural activity 698

antidepressant drugs :: medications designed to elevate mood and reduce other symptoms of depression 696

antipsychotic drugs :: generally used to treat positive symptoms of psychosis, including delusions, hallucinations, and severely disturbed or disorganized thought 698

antisocial personality disorder (APD) :: a profound lack of empathy or emotional connection with others, a disregard for others' rights or preferences, and a tendency toward inserting their own desires, often violently, onto others regardless of the consequences for other people or, often when younger, other animals 637

anxiety disorders :: a category of disorders involving fear or nervousness that is excessive, irrational, and maladaptive 646

APD :: see *antisocial personality disorder* 637

aphasia :: a language disorder caused by damage to the brain structures that support using and understanding language 337

appeal to authority :: the belief in an "expert's" claim even when no supporting data or scientific evidence is present 41

appeal to common sense :: a claim that appears to be sound, but lacks supporting scientific evidence 42

approach goal :: an enjoyable and pleasant incentive that a person is drawn toward, such as praise, financial reward, or a feeling of satisfaction 470

ARAS :: see *ascending reticular activating system* 517

archetypes :: images and symbols that reflect common "truths" held across cultures, such as universal life experiences or types of people 532

arousal theory of extraversion :: extraversion is determined by people's threshold for arousal 517

ascending reticular activating system (ARAS) :: plays a central role in controlling this arousal response 517

assimilation :: a conservative process, whereby people fit new information into the belief systems they already possess 406

asylums :: residential facilities for the mentally ill 625

attachment :: the enduring emotional bond formed between individuals 411

attachment behavioural system :: focused on meeting our own needs for security 416

attention :: selects which information will be passed on to STM 272

attitude inoculation :: a strategy for strengthening attitudes and making them more resistant to change by first exposing people to a weak counter-argument and then refuting that argument 577

atypical antipsychotics :: drugs that reduce positive symptoms of schizophrenia and are less likely to produce extrapyramidal side effects including movement disorders that commonly occur when first-generation antipsychotics are prescribed 698

autonomic nervous system :: the portion of the peripheral nervous system responsible for regulating the activity of organs and glands 107

availability heuristic :: entails estimating the frequency of an event based on how easily examples of it come to mind 328

aversive conditioning :: a behavioural technique that involves replacing a positive response to a stimulus with a negative response, typically by using punishment 688

avoidance goal :: an attempt to avoid an unpleasant outcome such as shame, embarrassment, losing money, or feeling emotional pain 47

avoidance learning :: a specific
reinforcement that rem
stimulus will

axon :: transports information in the form of electrochemical reactions from the cell body to the end of the neuron 94

BAS :: see *behavioural activation system* 518

basal ganglia :: a group of three structures that are involved in facilitating planned movements, skill learning, and integrating sensory and movement information with the brain's reward system 110

behavioural activation system (BAS) :: a "GO" system, arousing the person to action in the pursuit of desired goals 518

behavioural genetics :: the study of how genes and the environment influence behaviour 79

behavioural genomics :: the study of how specific genes, in their interactions with the environment, influence behaviour 78

behavioural inhibition system (BIS) :: a "danger" system, motivating the person to action in order to avoid punishments or other negative outcomes 518

behavioural therapies :: address problem behaviours, and the environmental factors that trigger them, as directly as possible 686

behaviourism :: an approach that dominated the first half of the 20th century of North American psychology and had a singular focus on studying only observable behaviour, with little to no reference to mental events or instincts as possible influences on behaviour 21

belief perseverance :: occurs when an individual believes he or she has the solution to the problem or the correct answer for a question and accepts only evidence that will confirm those beliefs 331

bell curve :: see *normal distribution* 65

between-subjects design :: an experimental design in which we compare the performance of participants who are in different groups 52

bibliotherapy :: the use of self-help books and other reading materials as a form of therapy 677

binocular depth cues :: distance cues that are based on the differing perspectives of both eyes 154

biofeedback :: a therapeutic technique involving the use of physiological recording instruments to provide feedback that increases awareness of bodily responses 614

biopsychosocial model :: a means of explaining behaviour as a product of biological, psychological, and sociocultural factors 5

bipolar disorder :: characterized by extreme highs and lows in mood, motivation, and energy 653

BIS :: see *behavioural inhibition system* 518

blood–brain barrier :: a network of tightly packed cells that only allow specific types of substances to move from the bloodstream to the brain in order to protect delicate brain cells against harmful infections and other substances 695

BMI :: see *body mass index* 591

body mass index (BMI) :: a statistic commonly used for estimating a healthy body weight given an individual's height 591

borderline personality disorder (BPD) :: characterized by intense extremes between positive and negative emotions, an unstable sense of self, impulsivity, and difficult social relationships 637

bottom-up processing :: occurs when we perceive individual bits of sensory information (e.g., sounds) and use them to construct a more complex perception (e.g., a message) 139

BPD :: see *borderline personality disorder* 637

brain death :: a condition in which the brain, specifically including the brainstem, no longer functions 204

brain stem :: the "stem" or bottom of the brain and consists of two structures: the medulla and the pons 108

brain-derived neurotrophic factor (BDNF) :: a protein in the nervous system that promotes survival, growth, and formation of new synapses 617

Broca's area :: region of the left frontal lobe that controls our ability to articulate speech sounds that compose words 337

bulimia nervosa :: an eating disorder that is characterized by periods of food deprivation, binge-eating, and purging 450

bystander effect :: the presence of other people actually reduces the likelihood of helping behaviour 549

Cannon-Bard theory of emotion :: the brain interprets a situation and generates subjective emotional feelings, and that these representations in the brain trigger responses in the body 481

caregiving behavioural system :: focused on meeting the needs of others 416

case study :: an in-depth report about the details of a specific case 45

catatonic schizophrenia :: Symptoms include episodes in which a person remains mute and immobile—sometimes in bizarre positions—for extended periods. Individuals may also exhibit repetitive, purposeless movements. 660

categories :: clusters of interrelated concepts 315

CBT :: see *cognitive-behavioural therapy* 689

cell body :: the part of a neuron that contains the nucleus that houses the cell's genetic material 93

central executive :: the control centre of working memory; it coordinates attention and the exchange of information among the three storage components 279

central nervous system (CNS) :: consists of the brain and the spinal cord 106

central route to persuasion :: occurs when people pay close attention to the content of a message, evaluate the evidence presented, and examine the logic of the arguments 573

central tendency :: a measure of the central point of a distribution 65

cerebellum :: (Latin for "little brain") the lobe-like structure at the base of the brain that is involved in the monitoring of movement, maintaining balance, attention, and emotional responses 109

cerebral cortex :: the convoluted, wrinkled outer layer of the brain that is involved in multiple higher functions, such as thought, language, and personality 111

chameleon effect :: people copy others' behaviours even without realizing it 541

chromosomes :: structures in the cellular nucleus that are lined with all of the genes an individual inherits 76

chunking :: organizing smaller units of information into larger, more meaningful units 273

circadian rhythms :: internally driven daily cycles of approximately 24 hours affecting physiological and behavioural processes 182

classical categorization :: a theory that claims that objects or events are categorized according to a certain set of rules or by a specific set of features 315

classical conditioning :: learning that occurs when a neutral stimulus elicits a response that was originally caused by another stimulus 227

client-centred therapy :: focuses on individuals' abilities to solve their own problems and reach their full potential with the encouragement of the therapist 684

clinical psychologists :: have received Ph.D. level of training and are able to formally diagnose and treat mental health issues ranging from the everyday and mild to the chronic and severe 674

clinical psychology :: the field of psychology that concentrates on the diagnosis and treatment of psychological disorders 16

cochlea :: a fluid-filled membrane that is coiled in a snail-like shape and contains the structures that convert sound into neural impulses 161

cognitive-behavioural therapy (CBT) :: a form of therapy that consists of procedures such as cognitive restructuring, stress inoculation training, and exposing people to experiences they may have a tendency to avoid 689

cognitive development :: the study of changes in memory, thought, and reasoning processes that occur throughout the lifespan 406

cognitive dissonance theory :: when we hold inconsistent beliefs, this creates a kind of aversive inner tension, or "dissonance"; we are then motivated to reduce this tension in whatever way we can 580

cohort effect :: differences between people that result from being born in different time periods 393

collective unconscious :: a separate, nonpersonal realm of the unconscious that holds the collective memories and mythologies of humankind, stretching deep into our ancestral past 532

coma :: a state marked by a complete loss of consciousness 204

community psychology :: an area of psychology that focuses on identifying how individuals' mental health is influenced by the neighbourhood, economics and community resources, social groups, and other community-based variables 675

comorbidity :: the presence of two disorders simultaneously, or the presence of a second disorder that affects the one being treated 640

companionate love :: related to tenderness, and to the affection we feel when our lives are intertwined with another person 469

compensatory control :: psychological strategies people use to preserve a sense of nonrandom order when personal control is compromised 619

computerized tomography (or CT scans) :: a structural neuroimaging technique in which x-rays are sent through the brain by a tube that rotates around the head 123

concept :: the mental representation of an object, event, or idea 315

concrete operational stage :: (ages 7 to 11 years) children develop skills in logical thinking, and manipulating numbers 408

conditioned emotional responses :: consist of emotional and physiological responses that develop to a specific object or situation 232
conditioned response (CR) :: the learned response that occurs to the conditioned stimulus 228
conditioned stimulus (CS) :: a once-neutral stimulus that later elicits a conditioned response because it has a history of being paired with an unconditioned stimulus 228
conditioned taste aversion :: acquired dislike or disgust of a food or drink because it was paired with illness 235
cones :: photoreceptors that are sensitive to the different wavelengths of light that we perceive as colour 146
confirmation bias :: occurs when an individual searches for only evidence that will confirm his or her beliefs instead of evidence that might disconfirm them 331
confounding variable :: a variable outside of the researcher's control that might affect or provide an alternative explanation for the results 52
conscious mind :: your current awareness, containing everything you are aware of right now 523
consciousness :: a person's subjective awareness, including thoughts, perceptions, experiences of the world, and self-awareness 181
conservation :: the knowledge that the quantity or amount of an object is not the same as the physical arrangement and appearance of that object 407
consolidation :: the process of converting short-term memories into long-term memories in the brain 283
construal-level theory :: describes how information affects us differently depending on our psychological distance from the information 574
constructive memory :: a process by which we first recall a generalized schema and then add in specific details 303
contact hypothesis :: social contact between members of different groups is extremely important to overcoming prejudice 569
continuous reinforcement :: every response made results in reinforcement 251
control group :: the group that does not receive the treatment or stimuli targeting a specific behaviour; this group therefore serves as a baseline to which the experimental group is compared 52
control processes :: shift information from one memory store to another 271
convenience samples :: samples of individuals who are the most readily available 35
conventional morality :: regards social conventions and rules as guides for appropriate moral behaviour 426
convergence :: occurs when the eye muscles contract so that both eyes focus on a single object 154
coping :: the processes used to manage demands, stress, and conflict 611
core knowledge hypothesis :: infants have inborn abilities for understanding some key aspects of their environment 409
cornea :: the clear layer that covers the front portion of the eye and also contributes to the eye's ability to focus 145
coronary heart disease :: a condition in which plaques form in the blood vessels that supply the heart with blood and oxygen, resulting in restricted blood flow 606
corpus callosum :: a collection of neural fibers connecting the two hemispheres 115
correlational research :: involves measuring the degree of association between two or more variables 49
cortisol :: a hormone secreted by the adrenal cortex (the outer part of the adrenal gland) that prepares the body to respond to stressful circumstances 602
counselling psychologists :: mental health professionals who typically work with people needing help with more common problems such as stress, coping, and mild forms of anxiety and depression, rather than severe mental disorders 674
CR :: see *conditioned response* 228
critical thinking :: involves exercising curiosity and skepticism when evaluating the claims of others, and with our own assumptions and beliefs 9
cross-fostered :: being raised as a member of a family that was not of the same species 346
cross-sectional design :: used to measure and compare samples of people at different ages at a given point in time 393
crystallized intelligence (Gc) :: a type of intelligence that draws upon past learning and experience 369
CS :: see *conditioned stimulus* 228
CT scan :: see *computerized tomography* 123
dark adaptation :: the process by which the rods and cones become increasingly sensitive to light under low levels of illumination 147
Dark Triad :: three traits— Machiavellianism, Psychopathy, and Narcissism—that describe a person who is socially destructive, aggressive, dishonest, and likely to commit harm in general 497
DBS :: see *deep brain stimulation* 703
debriefing :: the researchers should explain the true nature of the study, and especially the nature of and reason for the deception 58
decentring :: occurs when one is able to "step back" from one's normal consciousness and observe oneself more objectively, as an observer 690
deception :: misleading or only partially informing participants of the true topic or hypothesis under investigation 57
declarative memories :: memories that we are consciously aware of and that can be verbalized, including facts about the world and one's own personal experiences 280
deep brain stimulation (DBS) :: a technique that involves electrically stimulating specific regions of the brain 703
defence mechanisms :: unconscious strategies the ego uses to reduce or avoid anxiety 525
deinstitutionalization :: a social movement in North America in the 1960s which sought to relocate the mentally ill from living in institutions to living within their community 675
delaying gratification :: putting off immediate temptations in order to focus on longer-term goals 422
delusions :: beliefs that are not based on reality (at least from the perspective of the person's general culture) 659
demand characteristics :: inadvertent cues given off by the experimenter or the experimental context that provide information about how participants are expected to behave 36
dementia :: mild to severe disruption of mental functioning, memory loss, disorientation, poor judgment, and decision making 432
dendrites :: small branches radiating from the cell body that receive messages from other cells and transmit those messages toward the rest of the cell 93
dependent variable :: the observation or measurement that is recorded during the experiment and subsequently compared across all groups 52
descriptive statistics :: a set of techniques used to organize, summarize, and interpret data 65
determinism :: the belief that all events are governed by lawful, cause-and-effect relationships 13
developmental psychology :: the study of human physical, cognitive, social, and behavioural characteristics across the lifespan 393
Diagnostic and Statistical Manual of Mental Disorders (DSM) :: a standardized manual to aid in the diagnosis of disorders 627
DID :: see *dissociative identity disorder* 641
difference threshold :: the smallest difference between stimuli that can be reliably detected at least 50% of the time 134
diffusion of responsibility :: the responsibility for taking action is spread across more than one person, thus making no single individual feel personally responsible 549
diffusion tensor imaging (or DTI) :: a form of structural neuroimaging allowing researchers or medical personnel to measure white-matter pathways in the brain 124
discrimination :: (1) occurs when an organism learns to respond to one original stimulus but not to new stimuli that may be similar to the original stimulus; (2) behaviour that disfavours or disadvantages members of a certain social group in some way 232
discriminative stimulus :: a cue or event that indicates that a response, if made, will be reinforced 248
dishabituation :: the recovery of responsiveness to a habituated stimulus as the result of the presentation of a new stimulus 409
disorganized behaviour :: the considerable difficulty people with schizophrenia may have completing the tasks of everyday life 660
disorganized schizophrenia :: Symptoms include thoughts, speech, behaviour, and emotion that are poorly integrated and incoherent. People with disorganized schizophrenia may also show inappropriate, unpredictable mannerisms. 660
display rules :: the unwritten expectations we have regarding when it is appropriate to show a certain emotion 487
dispositional attribution :: see *internal attribution* 562
dissociation theory :: explains hypnosis as a unique state in which consciousness is divided into two parts: an observer and a hidden observer 199
dissociative disorder :: a category of mental disorders characterized by a split between conscious awareness from feeling, cognition, memory, and identity 641

dissociative identity disorder (DID; sometimes referred to as multiple personality disorder) :: a person experiences a split in identity such that they feel different aspects of themselves as though they were separated from each other. This can be severe enough that the person constructs entirely separate personalities, only one of which will generally be in control at a time. 641

divided attention :: paying attention to more than one stimulus or task at the same time 140

dizygotic twins :: fraternal twins who come from two separate eggs fertilized by two different sperm cells that share the same womb; these twins have approximately 50% of their genetics in common 79

DNA (deoxyribonucleic acid) :: a molecule formed in a double-helix shape that contains four amino acids: adenine, cytosine, guanine, and thymine 76

doctrine of specific nerve energies :: first proposed in 1826 by the German physiologist Johannes Muller, the doctrine states that the different senses are separated in the brain 133

door-in-the-face technique :: involves asking for something relatively big, then following with a request for something relatively small 579

dopamine :: a monoamine neurotransmitter involved in such varied functions as mood, control of voluntary movement, and processing of rewarding experiences 99

double-blind study :: a study in which neither the participant nor the experimenter knows the exact treatment for any individual 39

dream analysis :: a method for understanding the unconscious by examining the details of what happens during a dream (the manifest content), in order to gain insight into the true meaning of the dream, the emotional, unconscious material that is communicated symbolically (the latent content) 682

drive :: a biological trigger that tells us we may be deprived of something and causes us to seek out what is needed, such as food or water 445

DRM procedure :: participants study a list of highly related words called semantic associates 308

DSM :: see *Diagnostic and Statistical Manual of Mental Disorders* 627

DTI :: see *diffusion tensor imaging* 124

dual coding :: occurs when information is stored in more than one form 298

dual-process models :: models of behaviour that account for both implicit and explicit processes 559

ecological validity :: the results of a laboratory study can be applied to or repeated in the natural environment 35

ecstasy (3,4-methylenedioxy-*N*-methylamphetamine or MDMA) :: a drug that is typically classified as a stimulant, but also has hallucinogenic effects 214

ECT :: see *electroconvulsive therapy* 702

EEG :: see *electroencephalogram* 124

ego :: the decision maker, frequently under tension, trying to reconcile the opposing urges of the id and superego 524

egocentric :: seeing the world only from one's own perspective 414

elaboration likelihood model :: a model of persuasion that states when audiences are sufficiently motivated to pay attention to a message (i.e., they care about the issue) and they have the opportunity for careful processing (i.e., they have the cognitive resources available to understand the message), they will be persuaded by the facts of the argument, the substance; when either of these two factors, motivation and opportunity, are missing, people will tend to be persuaded by other factors 573

elaborative rehearsal :: prolonging exposure to information by thinking about its meaning 289

electroconvulsive therapy (ECT) :: involves passing an electrical current through the brain in order to induce a temporary seizure 702

electroencephalogram (or EEG) :: measures patterns of brain activity with the use of multiple electrodes attached to the scalp 124

embryonic stage :: spans weeks two through eight of the gestational period, during which time the embryo begins developing major physical structures such as the heart and nervous system, as well as the beginnings of arms, legs, hands, and feet 395

emotion :: a behaviour with the following three components: (a) a subjective thought and/or experience with (b) accompanying patterns of neural activity and physical arousal and (c) an observable behavioural expression (e.g., an emotional facial expression or changes in muscle tension) 478

emotional dialects :: variations across cultures in how common emotions are expressed 487

empirically supported treatments :: treatments that have been tested and evaluated 676

empiricism :: a philosophical tenet that knowledge comes through experience 13

encoding specificity principle :: retrieval is most effective when it occurs in the same context as encoding 290

encoding :: the process of storing information in the LTM system 272

endogenous rhythms :: biological rhythms that are generated by our body independent of external cues such as light 182

endorphin :: a hormone produced by the pituitary gland and the hypothalamus that functions to reduce pain and induce feelings of pleasure 102

entity theory :: the belief that intelligence is a fixed characteristic and relatively difficult (or impossible) to change 361

entrainment :: when biological rhythms become synchronized to external cues such as light, temperature, or even a clock 182

epigenetics :: changes in gene expression that occur as a result of experience and that do not alter the genetic code 81

episodic buffer :: a storage component of working memory that combines the images and sounds from the other two components into coherent, story-like episodes 279

episodic memories :: declarative memories for personal experiences that seem to be organized around "episodes" and are recalled from a first-person ("I" or "my") perspective 280

escape learning :: occurs if a response removes a stimulus that is already present 246

etiology :: origins or causes 627

evidence-based therapies :: see *empirically supported treatments* 676

evolution :: the change in the frequency of genes occurring in an interbreeding population over generations 82

experiential system :: operates implicitly, quickly, and intuitively and is predominantly emotional 575

experimental group :: the group in the experiment that receives a treatment or the stimuli targeting a specific behaviour 52

explicit memories :: see *declarative memories* 280

explicit processes :: correspond to "conscious" thought: deliberative, effortful, relatively slow, and generally under our intentional control 559

exposure :: repeatedly and in stages exposing an individual to the object of his fear so that he can work past his emotional reactions 650

external attribution :: the observer explains the actor's behaviour as the result of the situation 562

extinction :: (1) in classical conditioning, the loss or weakening of a conditioned response when a conditioned stimulus and unconditioned stimulus no longer occur together; (2) in operant conditioning, the weakening of an operant response when reinforcement is no longer available 231

extrinsic motivation :: motivation geared toward gaining rewards or public recognition, or avoiding embarrassment 471

facial feedback hypothesis :: our emotional expressions can influence our subjective emotional states 481

factor analysis :: a statistical technique that examines correlations between variables to find clusters of related variables, or "factors" 365, 494

FAE :: see *fundamental attribution error* 563

false consensus effect :: tendency to project the self-concept onto the social world 562

false memory :: remembering events that did not occur, or incorrectly recalling details of an event 305

falsifiable :: the hypothesis is precise enough that it could be proven false 41

fast mapping :: the ability to map words onto concepts or objects after only a single exposure 342

fetal alcohol syndrome :: abnormalities in mental functioning, growth, and facial development in the offspring of women who use alcohol during pregnancy 396

fetal stage :: spans week eight through birth of the gestational period, during which time the skeletal, organ, and nervous systems become more developed and specialized 395

fight-or-flight response :: a set of physiological changes that occur in response to psychological or physical threats 601

first-letter technique :: uses the first letters of a set of items to spell out words that form a sentence 298

Five Factor Model :: a trait-based theory of personality based on the finding that personality can be described using five major dimensions 494

fixation :: becoming preoccupied with obtaining the pleasure associated with a particular stage 527

fixed-interval schedule :: reinforces the first response occurring after a set amount of time passes 253

fixed-ratio schedule :: reinforcement is delivered after a specific number of responses have been completed 252

flashbulb memory :: an extremely vivid and detailed memory about an event and the conditions surrounding how one learned about the event 295

fluid intelligence (Gf) :: a type of intelligence used in learning new information and solving new problems not based on knowledge the person already possesses 369

Flynn effect :: the steady population level increases in intelligence test scores over time 385

fMRI :: see *functional magnetic resonance imaging* 125

focal lesions :: small areas of brain tissue that are surgically destroyed 702

foot-in-the-door technique :: involves making a simple request followed by a more substantial request 579

forebrain :: the most visibly obvious region of the brain, consists of all of the neural structures that are located above the midbrain, including all of the folds and grooves on the outer surface of the brain; the multiple interconnected structures in the forebrain are critical to such complex processes as emotion, memory, thinking, and reasoning 110

formal operational stage :: (ages 11 to adulthood) the development of advanced cognitive processes such as abstract reasoning and hypothetical thinking 408

fovea :: the central region of the retina 146

free association :: clients are encouraged to talk or write without censoring their thoughts in any way 682

frequency :: the number of observations that fall within a certain category or range of scores 65

frequency theory :: the perception of pitch is related to the frequency at which the basilar membrane vibrates 163

frontal lobes :: important in numerous higher cognitive functions, such as planning, regulating impulses and emotion, language production, and voluntary movement 113

frontal lobotomy :: surgically removing regions of the cortex 701

functional fixedness :: occurs when an individual identifies an object or technique that could potentially solve a problem, but can think of only its most obvious function 326

functional magnetic resonance imaging (fMRI) :: measures brain activity by detecting the influx of oxygen-rich blood into neural areas that were just active 125

functional neuroimaging :: a type of brain scanning that provides information about which areas of the brain are active when a person performs a particular behaviour 124

functionalism :: the study of the purpose and function of behaviour and conscious experience 21

fundamental attribution error (FAE) :: tendency to over-emphasize internal (dispositional) attributions, and under-emphasize external (situational) factors 563

g :: see *general intelligence factor* 365

GABA (gamma-amino butyric acid) :: the primary inhibitory neurotransmitter of the nervous system, meaning that it prevents neurons from generating action potentials 98

GAD :: see *generalized anxiety disorder* 647

GAS :: see *general adaptation syndrome* 601

gate-control theory :: explains our experience of pain as an interaction between nerves that transmit pain messages and those that inhibit these messages 170

Gc :: see *crystallized intelligence* 369

gender roles :: the accepted attitudes and behaviours of males and females in a given society 461

gene knockout (KO) studies :: involve removing a specific gene and comparing the characteristics of animals with and without that gene 380

general adaptation syndrome (GAS) :: a theory of stress responses involving stages of alarm, resistance, and exhaustion 601

general intelligence factor (g) :: a basic cognitive trait comprising the ability to learn, reason, and solve problems, regardless of their nature 365

generalizability :: the degree to which one set of results can be applied to other situations, individuals, or events 34

generalization :: a process in which a response that originally occurs to a specific stimulus also occurs to different, though similar, stimuli 231

generalized anxiety disorder (GAD) :: involves frequently elevated levels of anxiety, generally from the normal challenges and stresses of everyday life 647

generativity :: being engaged in meaningful and productive work, as well as making contributions to future generations 439

genes :: the basic units of heredity; genes are responsible for guiding the process of creating the proteins that make up our physical structures and regulate development and physiological processes throughout the lifespan 76

genotype :: the genetic makeup of an organism—the unique set of genes that comprise that individual's genetic code 76

germinal stage :: the first phase of prenatal development, which spans from conception to two weeks 395

gestalt psychology :: an approach emphasizing that psychologists need to focus on the whole of perception and experience, rather than its parts 25

Gf :: see *fluid intelligence* 369

glial cells :: specialized cells of the nervous system that are involved in mounting immune responses in the brain, removing waste, and synchronizing the activity of the billions of neurons that constitute the nervous system 94

global events :: thoughts like "my whole life is ruined"; blowing things out of proportion rather than seeing a negative event as simply that, one negative event and not something that needs to spiral into greater problems 689

glucose :: a sugar that serves as a primary energy source for the brain and the rest of the body 446

glutamate :: most common excitatory neurotransmitter in the brains of vertebrates 98

graded membership :: the observation that some concepts appear to make better category members than others 315

groupthink :: the stifling of diversity that occurs when individuals are not able to express their true perspectives, instead having to focus on agreeing with others and maintaining harmony in the group 544

gustatory system :: functions in the sensation and perception of taste 173

habituation :: a decrease in responding with repeated exposure to a stimulus or event 409

hallucinations :: alterations in perception, such that a person hears, sees, smells, feels, or tastes something that does not actually exist, except in that person's own mind 659

hallucinogenic drugs :: substances that produce perceptual distortions 214

haptics :: the active, exploratory aspect of touch sensation and perception 169

Hawthorne effect :: behaviour change that occurs as a result of being observed 35

heritability :: statistic, expressed as a number between zero and one, that represents the degree to which genetic differences between individuals contribute to individual differences in a behaviour or trait found in a population 79

heuristics :: problem-solving strategies that stem from prior experiences and provide an educated guess as to what is the most likely solution 325

HEXACO model of personality :: a six-factor theory that generally replicates the five factors of the Five Factor Model and adds one additional factor: Honesty–Humility 497

hippocampus :: critical for learning and memory, particularly the formation of new memories 111

histrionic personality disorder (HPD) :: characterized by excessive attention seeking and dramatic behaviour 637

homeostasis :: the body's physiological processes that allow it to maintain consistent internal states in response to the outer environment 445

hormones :: chemicals secreted by the glands of the endocrine system 102

HPA axis :: see *hypothalamic–pituitary–adrenal axis* 602

HPD :: see *histrionic personality disorder* 637

humanistic psychology :: focuses on the unique aspects of each individual human, each person's freedom to act, his or her rational thought, and the belief that humans are fundamentally different from other animals 23

humourism :: explained both physical illnesses and disorders of personality as resulting from imbalances in key fluids in the body 517

hypnosis :: a procedure of inducing a heightened state of suggestibility 199

hypothalamic–pituitary–adrenal (HPA) axis :: a neural and endocrine circuit that provides communication between the nervous system (the hypothalamus) and the endocrine system (pituitary and adrenal glands) 602

hypothalamus :: a brain structure that regulates basic biological needs and motivational systems 102

hypothesis :: (plural: hypotheses) a testable prediction about processes that can be observed and measured 3

hypothesis test :: a statistical method of evaluating whether differences among groups are meaningful, or could have been arrived at by chance alone 69

IAT :: see *Implicit Associations Test* 566

id :: a collection of basic biological drives, including those directed toward sex and aggression 524

identifiable victim effect :: people are powerfully moved to action by the story of a single suffering person compared to information about a whole group of people 575

identity :: a clear sense of what kind of person you are, what types of people you belong with, and what roles you should play in society 428

idiographic approach :: creating detailed descriptions of a specific person's unique personality characteristics 493

imagination inflation :: the increased confidence in a false memory of an event following repeated imagination of the event 307

imitation :: recreating someone else's motor behaviour or expression, often to accomplish a specific goal 263

Implicit Associations Test (IAT) :: measures how fast people can respond to images or words flashed on a computer screen 566

implicit memories :: see *nondeclarative memories* 280

implicit processes :: correspond to "unconscious" thought: intuitive, automatic, effortless, very fast, and operate largely outside of our intentional control 559

inattentional blindness :: a failure to notice clearly visible events or objects because attention is directed elsewhere 141

incremental theory :: the belief that intelligence can be shaped by experiences, practice, and effort 361

independent variable :: the variable that the experimenter manipulates to distinguish between two or more groups 52

inductive discipline :: involves explaining the consequences of a child's actions on other people, activating empathy for others' feelings 418

inferiority complex :: the struggle many people have with feelings of inferiority, which stem from experiences of helplessness and powerlessness during childhood 532

informational influence :: occurs when people internalize the values and beliefs of the group, coming to believe the same things and feel the same ways themselves 545

informed consent :: a potential volunteer must be informed (know the purpose, tasks, and risks involved in the study) and give consent (agree to participate based on the information provided) without pressure 57

ingroup bias :: as positive biases toward the self get extended to include one's ingroups, people become motivated to see their ingroups as superior to their outgroup 563

ingroups :: groups we feel positively toward and identify with 563

insight therapies :: a general term referring to therapy that involves dialogue between client and therapist for the purposes of gaining awareness and understanding of psychological problems and conflicts 682

insomnia :: a disorder characterized by an extreme lack of sleep 192

intelligence :: the ability to think, understand, reason, and adapt to or overcome obstacles 354

intelligence quotient, or IQ :: a measure of intelligence computed using a standardized test and calculated by taking a person's mental age, dividing it by his chronological age, and then multiplying by 100 354

intermittent reinforcement :: see *partial reinforcement* 251

internal attribution :: the observer explains the behaviour of the actor in terms of some innate quality of that person 562, 689

intersexual selection :: a situation in which members of one sex select a mating partner based on their desirable traits 84

intrasexual selection :: a situation in which members of the same sex compete in order to win the opportunity to mate with members of the opposite sex 83

intrinsic motivation :: the process of being internally motivated to perform behaviours and overcoming challenges (e.g., a genuine desire to master a task rather than being motivated by a reward) 472

introjection :: the internalization of the conditional regard of significant others 418

iris :: a round muscle that adjusts the size of the pupil; it also gives the eyes their characteristic colour 145

James-Lange theory of emotion :: our physiological reactions to stimuli (e.g., a racing heart) precede the emotional experience (e.g., the fear) 481

jet lag :: the discomfort a person feels when sleep cycles are out of synchronization with light and darkness 188

kinesthesis :: the sense of bodily motion and position 169

KO :: see *gene knockout studies* 380

language :: a form of communication that involves the use of spoken, written, or gestural symbols that are combined in a rule-based form 338

latent content :: the actual symbolic meaning of a dream built on suppressed sexual or aggressive urges 189

latent learning :: learning that is not immediately expressed by a response until the organism is reinforced for doing so 259

learned helplessness :: an acquired suppression of avoidance or escape behaviour in response to unpleasant, uncontrollable circumstances 618

learning :: a process by which behaviour or knowledge changes as a result of experience 226

lens :: a clear structure that focuses light onto the back of the eye 145

lesioning :: a technique in which researchers intentionally damage an area in the brain 121

leucotomy :: the surgical destruction of brain tissues in the pre-frontal cortex 701

libido :: the motivation for sexual activity and pleasure 456

limbic system :: an integrated network involved in emotion and memory 111

linguistic relativity :: the theory that the language we use determines how we understand the world 321

lithium :: one of the first mood stabilizers to be prescribed regularly in psychiatry, and from the 1950s to the 1980s, was the standard drug treatment for depression and bipolar disorder 697

locked-in syndrome :: a disorder in which the patient is aware and awake but, because of an inability to move his or her body, appears unconscious 207

longitudinal design :: follows the development of the same set of individuals through time 393

long-term memory (LTM) :: holds information for extended periods of time, if not permanently 275

long-term potentiation (LTP) :: demonstrated that there is an enduring increase in connectivity and transmission of neural signals between nerve cells that fire together 282

LTM :: see *long-term memory* 275

LTP :: see *long-term potentiation* 282

magnetic resonance imaging (MRI) :: a structural imaging technique in which clear images of the brain are created based on how different neural regions absorb and release energy while in a magnetic field 123

magnetoencephalography (MEG) :: a neuroimaging technique that measures the tiny magnetic fields created by the electrical activity of nerve cells in the brain 125

maintenance rehearsal :: prolonging exposure to information by repeating it 288

major depression :: a disorder marked by prolonged periods of sadness, feelings of worthlessness and hopelessness, social withdrawal, and cognitive and physical sluggishness 653

manifest content :: the images and storylines that we dream about 189

MAOIs :: see *monoamine oxidase inhibitors* 696

marijuana :: a drug comprising the leaves and buds of the *Cannabis* plant that produces a combination of hallucinogenic, stimulant, and relaxing (narcotic) effects 216

mastery motive :: see *intrinsic motivation* 472

materialism :: the belief that humans, and other living beings, are composed exclusively of physical matter 14

MBCT :: see *mindfulness-based cognitive therapy* 690

MCS :: see *minimally conscious state* 207

MDMA :: see *ecstasy* 214

mean :: the arithmetic average of a set of numbers 66

median :: the 50th percentile—the point on the horizontal axis at which 50% of all observations are lower, and 50% of all observations are higher 66

medical model :: sees psychological conditions through the same lens as Western medicine tends to see physical conditions—as sets of symptoms, causes, and outcomes, with treatments aimed at changing physiological processes in order to alleviate symptoms 625

meditation :: any procedure that involves a shift in consciousness to a state in which an individual is highly focused, aware, and in control of mental processes 202

MEG :: see *magnetoencephalography* 125

menarche :: the onset of menstruation 421

menopause :: the termination of the menstrual cycle and reproductive ability in women 432

mental age :: the average intellectual ability score for children of a specific age 354
mental disorder defence :: claims that the defendant was in such an extreme, abnormal state of mind when committing the crime that he or she could not discern that the actions were legally or morally wrong 631
mental set :: a cognitive obstacle that occurs when an individual attempts to apply a routine solution to what is actually a new type of problem 326
method of loci :: a mnemonic that connects words to be remembered to locations along a familiar path 297
midbrain :: resides just above the hindbrain, primarily functions as a relay station between sensory and motor areas 109
mimicry :: taking on for ourselves the behaviours, emotional displays, and facial expressions of others 540
mindfulness-based cognitive therapy (MBCT) :: involves combining mindfulness meditation with standard cognitive-behavioural therapy tools 690
minimal group paradigm :: a description of how easily people will form social categories, Us vs. Them, even using criteria that are meaningless 564
minimally conscious state (MCS) :: a disordered state of consciousness marked by the ability to show some behaviours that suggest at least partial consciousness, even if on an inconsistent basis 207
misinformation effect :: when information occurring after an event becomes part of the memory for that event 306
mnemonic :: a technique intended to improve memory for specific information 297
mode :: the category with the highest frequency (that is, the category with the most observations) 66
monoamine oxidase inhibitors (MAOIs) :: work by deactivating monoamine oxidase (MAO), an enzyme that breaks down serotonin, dopamine, and norepinephrine at the synaptic clefts of nerve cells 696
monocular cues :: depth cues that we can perceive with only one eye 155
monozygotic twins :: twins who come from a single ovum (egg), which makes them genetically identical (almost 100% genetic similarity) 79
mood stabilizers :: drugs used to prevent or reduce the severity of mood swings experienced by people with bipolar disorder 697
morphemes :: the smallest meaningful unit of a language 339
motivation :: concerns the physiological and psychological processes underlying the initiation of behaviours that direct organisms toward specific goals 444
MRI :: see *magnetic resonance imaging* 123
multimodal integration :: the ability to combine sensation from different modalities such as vision and hearing into a single integrated perception 175
multiple intelligences :: a model claiming that there are eight (now updated to at least nine) different forms of intelligence, each independent from the others 372
multiple personality disorder :: see *dissociative identity disorder* 641
myelin :: a fatty sheath that insulates axons from one another, resulting in increased speed and efficiency of neural communication 95
naive realism :: the assumption that the way we see things is the way that they are 562
narcissistic personality disorder (NPD) :: characterized by an inflated sense of self-importance and an excessive need for attention and admiration, as well as intense self-doubt and fear of abandonment 637
narcolepsy :: a disorder in which a person experiences extreme daytime sleepiness and even sleep attacks 195
natural selection :: the process by which favourable traits become increasingly common in a population of interbreeding individuals, while traits that are unfavourable become less common 82
naturalistic observations :: observations that unobtrusively observe and record behaviour as it occurs in the subject's natural environment 47
nature and nurture relationships :: the inquiry into how heredity (nature) and environment (nurture) influence behaviour and mental processes 18
need to belong :: the motivation to maintain relationships that involve pleasant feelings such as warmth, affection, appreciation, and mutual concern for each person's well-being 467
negative affectivity :: the tendency to respond to problems with a pattern of anxiety, hostility, anger, guilt or nervousness 613
negative explanatory style :: the tendency to make internal, stable, and global attributions for negative events 689
negative punishment :: occurs when a behaviour decreases because it removes or diminishes a particular stimulus 247
negative reinforcement :: involves the strengthening of a behaviour because it removes or diminishes a stimulus 246
negative symptoms :: the absence of adaptive behaviour, such as absent or flat emotional reactions, lack of interacting with others in a social setting, and lack of motivation 660
negatively skewed distribution :: a distribution in which the curve has an extended tail to the left of the cluster 65
neurodevelopmental hypothesis :: the adult manifestation of what we call "schizophrenia" is the outgrowth of disrupted neurological development early in the person's life 665
neurons :: one of the major types of cells found in the nervous system, which are responsible for sending and receiving messages throughout the body 93
neuroplasticity :: the capacity of the brain to change and rewire itself based on individual experience 116
neurotransmitters :: the chemicals that function as messengers allowing neurons to communicate with each other 94
night terrors :: intense bouts of panic and arousal that awaken the individual, typically in a heightened emotional state 193
nightmares :: particularly vivid and disturbing dreams that occur during REM sleep 193
nociception :: the activity of nerve pathways that respond to uncomfortable stimulation 170
nomothetic approach :: examines personality in large groups of people, with the aim of making generalizations about personality structure 493
nondeclarative memories :: include actions or behaviours that you can remember and perform without awareness 280
nootropic substances :: substances that are believed to beneficially affect intelligence 387
noradrenaline :: see *norepinephrine* 99
norepinephrine :: (also known as noradrenaline) a monoamine synthesized from dopamine molecules that is involved in regulating stress responses, including increasing arousal, attention, and heart rate 99
normal distribution :: a symmetrical distribution with values clustered around a central, mean value 65
normative influence :: a social pressure to adopt a group's perspective in order to be accepted, rather than rejected, by a group 545
NPD :: see *narcissistic personality disorder* 637
obesity :: a disorder of positive energy balance, in which energy intake exceeds energy expenditure 450
object permanence :: the ability to understand that objects exist even when they cannot be directly perceived 407
object relations therapy :: a variation of psychodynamic therapy that focuses on how early childhood experiences and emotional attachments influence later psychological functioning 683
objective measurements :: the measure of an entity or behaviour that, within an allowed margin of error, is consistent across instruments and observers 32
observational learning :: involves changes in behaviour and knowledge that result from watching others 260
obsessive–compulsive disorder (OCD) :: plagued by unwanted, inappropriate, and persistent thoughts (obsessions), and tend to engage in repetitive almost ritualistic behaviours (compulsions) 650
occipital lobes :: located at the rear of the brain and are where visual information is processed 112
OCD :: see *obsessive–compulsive disorder* 650
olfactory epithelium :: a thin layer of cells that are lined by sensory receptors called cilia 175
olfactory system :: involved in smell—the detection of airborne particles with specialized receptors located in the nose 175
operant conditioning :: a type of learning in which behaviour is influenced by consequences 244
operational definitions :: statements that describe the procedures (or operations) and specific measures that are used to record observations 33
opiates :: (also called narcotics) drugs such as heroin and morphine that reduce pain and induce extremely intense feelings of euphoria 218
opponent-process theory :: a theory of colour perception stating that we perceive colour in terms of opposing pairs: red to green, yellow to blue, and white to black 148
optic nerve :: a dense bundle of fibres that connect to the brain 146

optimism :: the tendency to have a favourable, constructive view on situations and to expect positive outcomes 612

outgroups :: those "other" groups that we don't identify with 563

oxytocin :: a stress-sensitive hormone that is typically associated with maternal bonding and social relationships 603

panic disorder :: an anxiety disorder marked by occasional episodes of sudden, very intense fear 647

paranoid schizophrenia :: Symptoms include delusional beliefs that one is being followed, watched, or persecuted, and may also include delusions of grandeur or the belief that one has some secret or insight or power or some other characteristic that makes one particularly special. 660

parasympathetic nervous system :: helps maintain homeostatic balance in the presence of change; following sympathetic arousal, it works to return the body to a baseline, nonemergency state 107

parietal lobes :: involved in our experiences of touch as well our bodily awareness 112

partial reinforcement effect :: a phenomenon in which organisms that have been conditioned under partial reinforcement resist extinction longer than those conditioned under continuous reinforcement 253

partial reinforcement :: only a certain number of responses are rewarded, or a certain amount of time must pass before reinforcement is available 251

passionate love :: associated with a physical and emotional longing for the other person 468

peer review :: a process in which papers submitted for publication in scholarly journals are read and critiqued by experts in the specific field of study 39

perception :: involves attending to, organizing, and interpreting stimuli that we sense 132

perceptual constancy :: the ability to perceive objects as having constant shape, size, and colour despite changes in perspective 153

performance motive :: see *extrinsic motivation* 471

peripheral nervous system (PNS) :: a division of the nervous system that transmits signals between the brain and the rest of the body and is divided into two subcomponents, the somatic system and the autonomic system 106

peripheral route to persuasion :: depends upon features that are not directly related to the message itself, such as the attractiveness of the person delivering the information 573

persistent vegetative state :: state of minimal to no consciousness in which the patient's eyes may be open, and the individual will develop sleep–wake cycles without clear signs of consciousness 204

person perception :: the processes by which individuals categorize and form judgments about other people 560

personal unconscious :: a vast repository of experiences and patterns that were absorbed during the entire experiential unfolding of the person's life 532

personality :: a characteristic pattern of thinking, feeling, and behaving that is unique to each individual, and remains relatively consistent over time and situations 493

personality disorders :: particularly unusual patterns of behaviour (relative to one's cultural context), that are maladaptive, distressing to oneself or others, and resistant to change 636

personality trait :: a person's habitual patterns of thinking, feeling, and behaving 493

person-centred perspective :: founded on the assumption that people are basically good, and given the right environment their personality will develop fully and normally 533

person-centred therapy :: see *client-centred therapy* 684

pessimism :: the tendency to have a negative perception of life and expect negative outcomes 612

pessimistic explanatory style :: the tendency to interpret and explain negative events as internally based (i.e., as being due to that person rather than to an external situation) and as a constant, stable quality 612

PET :: see *positron emission tomography* 125

phenomenological approach :: the therapist addresses the clients' feelings and thoughts as they unfold in the present moment, rather than looking for unconscious motives or dwelling in the past 684

phenotype :: physical traits or behavioural characteristics that show genetic variation, such as eye colour, the shape and size of facial features, and even personality 76

phobia :: a severe, irrational fear of a very specific object or situation 647

phonemes :: the most basic of unit of speech sounds 339

phonological loop :: a storage component of working memory that relies on rehearsal and that stores information as sounds, or an auditory code 278

phrenology :: the theory that personality characteristics could be assessed by carefully measuring the outer skull 517

physical dependence :: the need to take a drug to ward off unpleasant physical withdrawal symptoms 211

pitch :: the perceptual experience of sound wave frequencies 160

pituitary gland :: the master gland of the endocrine system that produces hormones and sends commands about hormone production to the other glands of the endocrine system 102

place theory of hearing :: how we perceive pitch is based on the location (place) along the basilar membrane that sound stimulates 163

placebo effect :: a measurable and experienced improvement in health or behaviour that cannot be attributable to a medication or treatment 38

pluralistic ignorance :: occurs when there is a disjunction between the private beliefs of individuals and the public behaviour they display to others 550

polysomnography :: a set of objective measurements used to examine physiological variables during sleep 183

population :: the group that researchers want to generalize about 35

positive psychology :: uses scientific methods to study human strengths and potential 611

positive punishment :: a process in which a behaviour decreases in frequency because it was followed by a particular, usually unpleasant, stimulus 247

positive reinforcement :: the strengthening of behaviour after potential reinforcers such as praise, money, or nourishment follow that behaviour 246

positive symptoms :: the presence of maladaptive behaviours, such as confused and paranoid thinking, and inappropriate emotional reactions 660

positively skewed distribution :: a distribution in which the long tail is on the right of the cluster 65

positron emission tomography (or PET) :: a type of scan in which a low level of a radioactive isotope is injected into the blood, and its movement to regions of the brain engaged in a particular task is measured 125

postconventional morality :: considers rules and laws as relative 426

post-traumatic growth :: the capacity to grow and experience long-term positive effects in response to negative events 614

pragmatics :: the study of nonlinguistic elements of language use 340

preconventional morality :: characterized by self-interest in seeking reward or avoiding punishment 426

prejudice :: an affective, emotionally driven process, including negative attitudes toward and critical judgments of other groups 565

preoperational stage :: (ages two to seven) language development, using symbols, pretend play, and mastering the concept of conservation 407

preparedness :: the biological predisposition to rapidly learn a response to a particular class of stimuli 235

preserve and protect hypothesis :: suggests that two more adaptive functions of sleep are preserving energy and protecting the organism from harm 186

preterm infant :: an infant born earlier than 36 weeks of gestation 397

primary auditory cortex :: a major perceptual centre of the brain involved in perceiving what we hear 164

primary reinforcers :: reinforcing stimuli that satisfy basic motivational needs—needs that affect an individual's ability to survive (and, if possible, reproduce) 247

primary sex traits :: changes in the body that are part of reproduction 421

proactive interference :: a process in which the first information learned (e.g., in a list of words) occupies memory, leaving fewer resources left to remember the newer information 276

problem solving :: accomplishing a goal when the solution or the path to the solution is not clear 325

problem-solving theory :: the theory that thoughts and concerns are continuous from waking to sleeping, and that dreams may function to facilitate finding solutions to problems encountered while awake 190

procedural memories :: patterns of muscle movements (motor memory) 281

processing fluency :: the ease with which information is processed 578

prodromal phase :: phase of schizophrenia during which people may become easily confused and have difficulty organizing their thoughts, they may lose interest and begin to withdraw from friends and family, and they may lose their normal motivations, withdraw from life, and spend increasing amounts of time alone, often deeply engrossed in their own thoughts 659

projective tests :: personality tests in which ambiguous images are presented to an individual to elicit responses that reflect unconscious desires or conflicts 529

prototypes :: mental representations of an average category member 316

pseudoscience :: an idea that is presented as science but does not actually utilize basic principles of scientific thinking or procedure 4

psychiatrists :: medical doctors who specialize in mental health and who are allowed to diagnose and treat mental disorders primarily through prescribing medications 674

psychoactive drugs :: substances that affect thinking, behaviour, perception, and emotion 213

psychoanalysis :: a psychological approach that attempts to explain how behaviour and personality are influenced by unconscious processes 17

psychodynamic therapies :: forms of insight therapy that emphasize the need to discover and resolve unconscious conflicts 682

psychological dependence :: occurs when addiction develops without any physical symptoms of withdrawal 211

psychology :: the scientific study of behaviour, thought, and experience, and how they can be affected by physical, mental, social, and environmental factors 3

psychoneuroimmunology :: the study of the relationship between immune system and nervous system functioning 604

psychopharmacotherapy :: the use of drugs to attempt to manage or reduce clients' symptoms 695

psychophysics :: the study of the relationship between the physical world and the mental representation of that world 14

psychotropic drugs :: medications designed to alter psychological functioning 695

punisher :: a stimulus that is contingent upon a response, and that results in a decrease in behaviour 245

punishment :: a process that decreases the future probability of a response 245

pupil :: regulates the amount of light that enters by changing its size; it dilates (expands) to allow more light to enter and constricts (shrinks) to allow less light into the eye 145

quasi-experimental research :: a research technique in which the two or more groups that are compared are selected based on predetermined characteristics, rather than random assignment 52

random assignment :: a technique for dividing samples into two or more groups in which participants are equally likely to be placed in any condition of the experiment 51

random sample :: a sampling technique in which every individual of a population has an equal chance of being included 35

Raven's Progressive Matrices :: an intelligence test that is based on pictures, not words, thus making it relatively unaffected by language or cultural background 356

reciprocal determinism :: behaviour, internal (personal) factors, and external (situational) factors interact to determine one another, and that our personalities are based on interactions among these three aspects 503

recovered memory :: a memory of a traumatic event that is suddenly recovered after blocking the memory of that event for a long period of time 309

recovered memory controversy :: a heated debate among psychologists about the validity of recovered memories 310

reflexes :: involuntary muscular reactions to specific types of stimulation 400

refractory period :: (1) brief period in which a neuron cannot fire; (2) a time period during which erection and orgasm are not physically possible 95, 458

rehearsal :: repeating information until you do not need to remember it anymore 278

reinforcement :: a process in which an event or reward that follows a response increases the likelihood of that response occurring again 244

reinforcer :: a stimulus that is contingent upon a response, and that increases the probability of that response occurring again 245

reliability :: consistent and stable answers across multiple observations and points in time 34

REM sleep :: a stage of sleep characterized by quickening brain waves, inhibited body movement, and rapid eye movements (REM) 185

replication :: the process of repeating a study and finding a similar outcome each time 40

representativeness heuristic :: making judgments of likelihood based on how well an example represents a specific category 327

research ethics board (REB) :: a committee of researchers and officials at an institution charged with the protection of human research participants 56

residential treatment centres :: housing facilities in which residents receive psychological therapy and life skills training, with the explicit goal of helping residents become re-integrated into society as well as they can 675

residual phase :: phase of schizophrenia during which people's predominant symptoms have disappeared or lessened considerably, and they may simply be withdrawn, have trouble concentrating, and generally lack motivation 659

residual schizophrenia :: This category reflects individuals who show some symptoms of schizophrenia but are either in transition to a full-blown episode or in remission. 660

resilience :: the ability to effectively recover from illness or adversity 613

resistance :: occurs as the treatment brings up unconscious material that the client wishes to avoid, and the client engages in strategies for keeping the information out of conscious awareness 683

resting potential :: relatively stable state during which the cell is not transmitting messages 95

restless legs syndrome :: a persistent feeling of discomfort in the legs and the urge to continuously shift them into different positions 193

restore and repair hypothesis :: the idea that the body needs to restore energy levels and repair any wear and tear experienced during the day's activities 185

retina :: lines the inner surface of the eye and consists of specialized receptors that absorb light and send signals related to the properties of light to the brain 146

retinal disparity :: (also called binocular disparity) the difference in relative position of an object as seen by both eyes, which provides information to the brain about depth 154

retrieval :: brings information from LTM back into STM 272

retroactive interference :: the most recently learned information overshadows some older memories that have not yet made it into long-term memory 276

retrograde amnesia :: a condition in which memory for the events preceding trauma or injury is lost 285

reuptake :: a process whereby neurotransmitter molecules that have been released into the synapse are reabsorbed into the axon terminals of the presynaptic neuron 97

Right-Wing Authoritarianism (RWA) :: a highly problematic set of personality characteristics that involve three key tendencies: 1) obeying orders and deferring to the established authorities in a society; 2) supporting aggression against those who dissent or differ from the established social order; and 3) believing strongly in maintaining the existing social order 497

rods :: photoreceptors that occupy peripheral regions of the retina; they are highly sensitive under low light levels 146

Rorschach inkblot test :: a test in which people are asked to describe what they see on the inkblot, and psychologists interpret this description using a standardized scoring and interpretation method 529

RWA :: see *Right-Wing Authoritarianism* 497

sample :: a select group of population members 35

satiation :: the point in a meal when we are no longer motivated to eat 446

savant :: an individual with low mental capacity in most domains but extraordinary abilities in other specific areas such as music, mathematics, or art 364

scaffolding :: a highly attentive approach to teaching in which the teacher matches guidance to the learner's needs 411

schedules of reinforcement :: rules that determine when reinforcement is available 251

schemas :: organized clusters of memories that constitute one's knowledge about events, objects, and ideas 302

schizophrenia :: a brain disease that causes the person to experience significant breaks from reality, a lack of integration of thoughts and emotions, and problems with attention and memory 659

scientific literacy :: the ability to understand, analyze, and apply scientific information 6

scientific method :: a way of learning about the world through collecting observations, developing theories to explain them, and using the theories to make predictions 3

sclera :: is the white, outer surface of the eye 145
secondary reinforcers :: stimuli that acquire their reinforcing effects only after we learn that they have value 247
secondary sex traits :: changes in the body that are not part of reproduction 421
sedative drugs :: sometimes referred to as "downers," depress activity of the central nervous system 219
selective attention :: involves focusing on one particular event or task 140
selective serotonin reuptake inhibitors (SSRIs) :: a class of antidepressant drugs that block the reuptake of the neurotransmitter serotonin 696
self-actualization :: the drive to grow and fulfill one's potential 533
self-awareness :: the ability to recognize one's individuality 414
self-determination theory :: an individual's ability to achieve their goals and attain psychological well-being is influenced by the degree to which he or she is in control of the behaviours necessary to achieve those goals 471
self-efficacy :: an individual's confidence that he or she can plan and execute a course of action in order to solve a problem 471
self-fulfilling prophecies :: a first impression (or an expectation) affects one's behaviour, and then that affects other people's behaviour, leading one to "confirm" the initial impression or expectation 561
self-reporting :: a method in which responses are provided directly by the people who are being studied, typically through face-to-face interviews, phone surveys, paper and pencil tests, and web-based questionnaires 48
self-serving biases :: biased ways of processing self-relevant information to enhance our positive self-evaluation 562
semantic memories :: declarative memories that include facts about the world 280
semantic network :: an interconnected set of nodes (or concepts) and the links that join them to form a category 316
semantics :: the study of how people come to understand meaning from words 339
sensation :: the process of detecting external events by sense organs and turning those stimuli into neural signals 132
sensitive period :: a window of time during which exposure to a specific type of environmental stimulation is needed for normal development of a specific ability 393
sensorimotor stage :: from birth to two years, a time during which infants' thinking about and exploration of the world are based on immediate sensory (e.g., seeing, feeling) and motor (e.g., grabbing, mouthing) experiences 407
sensory adaptation :: the reduction of activity in sensory receptors with repeated exposure to a stimulus 133
sensory memory :: a memory store that accurately holds perceptual information for a very brief amount of time 272
serial position effect :: in general, most people will recall the first few items from a list and the last few items, but only an item or two from the middle 275
serotonin :: a monoamine involved in regulating mood, sleep, aggression, and appetite 99
set point :: a hypothesized mechanism that serves to maintain body weight around a physiologically programmed level 591
sex guilt :: negative emotional feelings for having violated culturally accepted standards of appropriate sexual behaviour 462
sexual orientation :: the consistent preference for sexual relations with members of the opposite sex (heterosexuality), same sex (homosexuality), or either sex (bisexuality) 459
sexual response cycle :: the phases of physiological change during sexual activity, which comprises four primary stages: excitement, plateau, orgasm, and resolution 458
sexual scripts :: the set of rules and assumptions about the sexual behaviours of males and females 461
shaping :: a procedure in which a specific operant response is created by reinforcing successive approximations of that response 251
short-term memory (STM) :: a memory store with limited capacity and duration (less than a minute) 273
signal detection theory :: whether a stimulus is perceived depends on both sensory experience and judgment made by the subject 135
single-blind study :: a study in which participants do not know the true purpose of the study, or else do not know which type of treatment they are receiving (for example, a placebo or a drug) 39
situational attributions :: see *external attribution* 562
sleep apnea :: a disorder characterized by the temporary inability to breathe during sleep 194
sleep deprivation :: occurs when an individual cannot or does not sleep 186
sleep displacement :: occurs when an individual is prevented from sleeping at the normal time although she may be able to sleep earlier or later in the day than usual 187
social anxiety disorder :: a very strong fear of being judged by others or being embarrassed or humiliated in public 649
social contagion :: the often subtle, unintentional spreading of a behaviour as a result of social interactions 596
social desirability (or socially desirable responding) :: research participants respond in ways that increase the chances that they will be viewed favourably 36
social facilitation :: occurs when one's performance is affected by the presence of others 543
social loafing :: occurs when an individual puts less effort into working on a task with others 542
social norms :: the (usually unwritten) guidelines for how to behave in social contexts 542
social roles :: are more specific sets of expectations for how someone in a specific position should behave 551
social-cognitive theory :: explains hypnosis by emphasizing the degree to which beliefs and expectations contribute to increased suggestibility 200
soma :: see *cell body* 93
somatic nervous system :: consists of nerves that control skeletal muscles, which are responsible for voluntary and reflexive movement; it also consists of nerves that receive sensory input from the body 107
somnambulism :: or sleepwalking, a disorder that involves wandering and performing other activities while asleep 194
sound localization :: the process of identifying where sound comes from 162
specific phobia :: an intense fear of a specific object, activity, or organism 647
spermarche :: during puberty, a male's first ejaculation of sperm 421
spontaneous recovery :: the reoccurrence of a previously extinguished conditioned response, typically after some time has passed since extinction 231
SSRIs :: see *selective serotonin reuptake inhibitors* 696
stable attributions :: thoughts like "it's never going to change"; coming to see a situation as permanent and irreversible 689
standard deviation :: a measure of variability around the mean 68
Stanford-Binet test :: a test intended to measure innate levels of intelligence 354
state :: a temporary physical or psychological engagement that influences behaviour 501
statistical significance :: the means of the groups are farther apart than you would expect them to be by random chance alone 70
stereotype :: a cognitive structure, a set of beliefs about the characteristics that are held by members of a specific social group; these beliefs function as schemas, serving to guide how we process information about our social world 565
stimulants :: a category of drugs that speed up the nervous system, typically enhancing wakefulness and alertness 213
STM :: see *short-term memory* 273
storage :: the time and manner in which information is retained between encoding and retrieval 288
stores :: retain information in memory without using it for any specific purpose 271
strange situation :: a way of measuring infant attachment by observing how infants behave when exposed to different experiences that involve anxiety and comfort 413
stress :: a psychological and physiological reaction that occurs when perceived demands exceed existing resources to meet those demands 599
structural neuroimaging :: a type of brain scanning that produces images of the different structures of the brain 123
structuralism :: an attempt to analyze conscious experience by breaking it down into basic elements, and to understand how these elements work together 20
Substance P :: a neurotransmitter involved in the experience of pain 100
superego :: comprised of our values and moral standards 524
sympathetic nervous system :: responsible for the fight-or-flight response of an increased heart rate, dilated pupils, and decreased salivary flow—responses that prepare the body for action 107
synapses :: the microscopically small spaces that separate individual nerve cells 96
synaptic cleft :: the minute space between the axon terminal (terminal button) and the dendrite 97

synaptic pruning :: the loss of weak nerve cell connections 402

synaptogenesis :: the forming of new synaptic connections 402

syntax :: the rules for combining words and morphemes into meaningful phrases and sentences 340

systematic desensitization :: gradual exposure to a feared stimulus or situation is coupled with relaxation training 686

systems approach :: an orientation that encourages therapists to see an individual's symptoms as being influenced by many different interacting systems 691

tardive dyskinesia :: a movement disorder involving involuntary movements and facial tics 698

TAT :: see *Thematic Apperception Test* 529

temporal lobes :: located at the sides of the brain near the ears and are involved in hearing, language, and some higher-level aspects of vision such as object and face recognition 112

teratogens :: substances, such as drugs or environmental toxins, that impair the process of fetal development 396

testing effect :: the finding that taking practice tests can improve exam performance, even without additional studying 299

testosterone :: a hormone that is involved in the development of sex characteristics and the motivation of sexual behaviour 461

thalamus :: a set of nuclei involved in relaying sensory information to different regions of the brain 111

Thematic Apperception Test :: (TAT) a test in which respondents are asked to tell stories about ambiguous pictures involving various interpersonal situations 529

theory :: an explanation for a broad range of observations that also generates new hypotheses and integrates numerous findings into a coherent whole 4

theory of mind :: the ability to recognize the thoughts, beliefs, and expectations of others, and to understand that these can be different from one's own 415

thin slices of behaviour :: very small samples of a person's behaviour 560

third variable problem :: the possibility that a third, unmeasured variable is actually responsible for a well-established correlation between two variables 50

TMS :: see *transcranial magnetic stimulation* 123, 703

tolerance :: when repeated use of a drug results in a need for a higher dose to get the intended effect 211

top-down processing :: when our perceptions are influenced by our expectations or by our prior knowledge 139

transcranial magnetic stimulation (TMS) :: a procedure in which an electromagnetic pulse is delivered to a targeted region of the brain in order to increase or decrease its activity; it is sometimes used as a therapeutic technique to help treat the symptoms of psychological disorders like depression 122, 703

transduction :: takes place when specialized receptors transform the physical energy of the outside world into neural impulses 132

transference :: a psychoanalytic process whereby clients direct the emotional experiences that they are reliving toward the therapist, rather than the original person involved in the experiences (e.g., their parents) 683

triarchic theory of intelligence :: a theory that divides intelligence into three distinct types: analytical, practical, and creative 371

trichromatic theory :: maintains that colour vision is determined by three different cone types that are sensitive to short, medium, and long wavelengths of light 147

tricyclic antidepressants :: appear to work by blocking the reuptake of serotonin and norepinephrine 696

two-factor theory :: patterns of physical arousal and the cognitive labels we attach to them form the basis of our emotional experiences 483

Type A personality :: people who tend to be impatient and worry about time, and are easily angered, competitive, and highly motivated 608

Type B personality :: people who are more laid back and characterized by a patient, easygoing, and relaxed disposition 608

unconditioned response (UR) :: a reflexive, unlearned reaction to an unconditioned stimulus 227

unconditioned stimulus (US) :: a stimulus that elicits a reflexive response without learning 227

unconscious mind :: a vast and powerful but inaccessible part of your consciousness, operating without your conscious endorsement or will to influence and guide your behaviours 523

undifferentiated schizophrenia :: This category includes individuals who show a combination of symptoms from more than one type of schizophrenia. 660

unit bias :: the tendency to assume that the unit of sale or portioning is an appropriate amount to consume 448

UR :: see *unconditioned response* 227

US :: see *unconditioned stimulus* 227

validity :: the degree to which an instrument or procedure actually measures what it claims to measure 34

variability :: the degree to which scores are dispersed in a distribution 67

variable :: the object, concept, or event being measured 33

variable-interval schedule :: the first response is reinforced following a variable amount of time 253

variable-ratio schedule :: the number of responses required to receive reinforcement varies according to an average 252

video deficit :: young children do not learn very much from information presented on screens 386

virtual reality exposure (VRE) :: a treatment that uses graphical displays to create an experience in which the client seems to be immersed in an actual environment 687

visuospatial sketchpad :: a storage component of working memory that maintains visual images and spatial layouts in a visuospatial code 278

Wernicke's area :: the area of the brain most associated with finding the meaning of words 337

Whorfian hypothesis :: see *linguistic relativity* 321

within-subjects design :: an experimental design in which the same participants respond to all types of stimuli or experience all experimental conditions 52

working memory :: a model of short-term remembering that includes a combination of memory components that can temporarily store small amounts of information for a short period of time 278

Young-Helmholtz theory :: see *trichromatic theory* 147

zeitgeist :: refers to a general set of beliefs of a particular culture at a specific time in history 14

zone of proximal development :: the set of new skills that an individual is ready to attain based on his or her current skill set 410

zygote :: the initial cell formed when the nuclei of egg and sperm fuse 394

References

AbdelMalik, P., Husted, J., Chow, E. W., & Bassett, A. S. (2003). Childhood head injury and expression of schizophrenia and multiply affected families. *Archives of General Psychiatry, 60,* 231–236.

Abouguendia, M., & Noels, K. A. (2001). General and acculturation-related daily hassles and psychological adjustment in first- and second-generation South Asian immigrants to Canada. *International Journal of Psychology, 36,* 163–173.

Abraham, W. (2006). Memory maintenance: The changing nature of neural mechanisms. *Current Directions in Psychological Science, 15,* 5–8.

Abramowitz, E., Barak, Y., Ben-Avi, I., & Knobler, H. (2008). Hypnotherapy in the treatment of chronic combat-related PTSD patients suffering from insomnia: A randomized, zolpidem-controlled clinical trial. *International Journal of Clinical and Experimental Hypnosis, 56,* 270–280.

Abramson, L. Y., Seligman, M. E., & Teasdale, J. D. (1978). Learned helplessness in humans: Critique and reformulation. *Journal of Abnormal Psychology, 87,* 49.

Acevedo-Garcia, D., Osypuk, T. L., McArdle, N., & Williams, D. R. (2008). Towards a policy relevant analysis of geographic and racial/ethnic disparities in child health. *Health Affairs, 27,* 321–333.

Ackerman, P. L., et al. (2002). Individual differences in working memory within a nomological network of cognitive and perceptual speed abilities. *Journal of Experimental Psychology: General, 131,* 567–589.

Adair, G. (1984). The Hawthorne effect: A reconsideration of the methodological artifact. *Journal of Applied Psychology, 69,* 334–345.

Adam, T. C., & Epel, E. S. (2007). Stress, eating, and the reward system. *Physiology and Behavior, 91,* 449–458.

Adams, H. E., Wright, L. W., & Lohr, B. A. (1996). Is homophobia associated with homosexual arousal? *Journal of Abnormal Psychology, 105,* 440–445.

Addis, M. E., & Mahalik, J. R. (2003). Men, masculinity, and the contexts of help seeking. *American Psychologist, 58,* 5–14.

Adelstein, J. S., Shehzad, Z., Mennes, M., DeYoung, C. G., Zuo, X.-N., et al. (2011). Personality is reflected in the brain's intrinsic functional architecture. *PLoS ONE, 6,* e27633.

Adolphs, R., Tranel, D., & Buchanan, T. W. (2005). Amygdala damage impairs emotional memory for gist but not details of complex stimuli. *Nature Neuroscience, 8,* 512–518.

Adorno, T. W., Frenkel-Brunswik, E., Levinson, D. J., & Sanford, R. N. (1950). *The authoritarian personality.* New York: Harper and Row.

Aggleton, J. P., & Waskett, L. (1999). The ability of odours to serve as state-dependent cues for real-world memories: Can Viking smells aid the recall of Viking experiences? *British Journal of Psychiatry, 90,* 1–7.

Ahlfinger, N. R., & Esser, J. K. (2001). Testing the groupthink model: Effects of promotional leadership and conformity predisposition. *Social Behavior and Personality, 29,* 31–41.

Ainsworth, M. D. S. (1978). The development of infant–mother attachment. In B. M. Caldwell & H. N. Ricciuti (Eds.), *Review of child development research* (Vol. 3, pp. 1–94). Chicago: University of Chicago Press.

Aknin, L. B., Hamlin, J. K., & Dunn, E. W. (2012). Giving leads to happiness in young children. *PLoS One, 7,* e39211.

Albert, S. (1977). Temporal comparison theory. *Psychological Review, 84,* 485–503.

Aldous, J., & Ganey, R. F. (1999). Family life and the pursuit of happiness: The influence of gender and race. *Journal of Family Issues, 20,* 155–180.

Alicke, M. D., & Govorun, O. (2005). The better-than-average effect. In M. D. Alicke, D. A. Dunning, & J. I. Krueger (Eds.), *The self in social judgment (Studies in self and identity)* (pp. 85–106). New York: Psychology Press.

Alladin, A., & Alibhai, A. (2007). Cognitive hypnotherapy for depression: An empirical investigation. *International Journal of Clinical and Experimental Hypnosis, 55,* 147–166.

Allen, J. S., Bruss, J., Brown, C. K., & Damasio, H. (2005). Normal neuroanatomical variation due to age: The major lobes and a parcellation of the temporal region. *Neurobiology of Aging, 26*(9), 1245–1260.

Allen, R. (2004). Dopamine and iron in the pathophysiology of restless legs syndrome. *Sleep Medicine, 5,* 385–391.

Allen, S. W., Norman, G. R., & Brooks, L. R. (1992). Experimental studies of learning dermatologic diagnosis: The impact of examples. *Research Basic to Medical Education, 4,* 35–44.

Allport, G. W. (1954). *The nature of prejudice.* Cambridge, MA: Perseus Books.

Allport, G. W. (1955). *Becoming: Basic considerations for a psychology of personality.* New Haven, CT: Yale University Press.

Allport, G., & Odbert, H. W. (1936). Trait names: A psycholexical study. *Psychological Monographs, 47,* 211.

Altemeyer, B. (1996). *The authoritarian specter.* Cambridge, MA: Harvard University Press.

Altemeyer, B. (2006). *The authoritarians.* Self-published book downloaded at http://members.shaw.ca/jeanaltemeyer/drbob/TheAuthoritarians.pdf

Amaral, D. G., Capitanio, J. P., Jourdain, M., Mason, W. A., Mendoza, S. P., & Prather, M. (2003). The amygdala: Is it an essential component of the neural network for social cognition? *Neuropsychologia, 41,* 235–240.

Amat, J., Baratta, M. V., Paul, E., Bland, S. T., Watkins, L. R., & Maier, S. F. (2005). Medial prefrontal cortex determines how stressor controllability affects behavior and dorsal raphe nucleus. *Nature Neuroscience, 8,* 365–371.

Amato, P. R. (2001). Children of divorce in the 1990s: An update of the Amato and Keith (1991) meta-analysis. *Journal of Family Psychology, 15,* 355–370.

Ambady, N., & Rosenthal, R. (1993). Half a minute: Predicting teacher evaluations from thin slices of nonverbal behavior and physical attractiveness. *Journal of Personality and Social Psychology, 64,* 431–441.

American Academy of Neurology Quality Standards Subcommittee. (1995). Practice parameters for determining brain death in adults. *Neurology, 45,* 1012–1014.

American Academy of Pediatrics. (1999). Media education. *Pediatrics, 104,* 341–342.

American College Health Association. (2007). The American College Health Association National College Health Assessment (ACHA-NCHA) spring 2006 reference group data report (abridged). *Journal of American College Health, 53,* 195–206.

American Psychiatric Association. (2000). *Diagnostic and statistical manual of mental disorders* (4th ed.). Washington, DC: Author.

American Psychiatric Association. (2000). *Diagnostic and statistical manual of mental disorders* (4th ed., text revision). Washington, DC: Author.

American Psychiatric Association. (2013). *Diagnostic and statistical manual of mental disorders* (5th ed.). Arlington, VA: American Psychiatric Publishing.

American Psychological Association. (2004, September). Getting a good night's sleep with the help of psychology. Retrieved June 10, 2011, from http://www.apa.org/research/action/sleep.aspx

American Psychological Association (APA). (2009). Task force on evidence-based practice. Retrieved from http://www.apa.org/practice/ebp.html

American Psychological Association. (2010). Psychology and global climate change: Addressing a multifaceted phenomenon and set of challenges. Retrieved December 31, 2013, from http://www.apa.org/ science/about/publications/climate-change.aspx

American Psychological Association. (2011). Suicide warning signs. Retrieved from http://www.apa.org/topics/suicide/signs.aspx

Amichai-Hamburger, Y., & Ben-Artzi, E. (2003). Loneliness and Internet use. *Computers in Human Behavior, 19*, 71–80.

An, K., Kobayashi, S., Tanaka, K., Kaneda, H., Su-gibayashi, M., & Okazaki, J. (1998). Dissociative identity disorder and childhood trauma in Japan. *Psychiatry and Clinical Neurosciences, 52*, 111–114.

Anastasi, A., & Urbina, S. (1996). *Psychological testing.* New York: Prentice Hall.

Anderson, B., & Harvey, T. (1996). Alterations in cortical thickness and neuronal density in the frontal cortex of Albert Einstein. *Neuroscience Letters, 210,* 161–164.

Anderson, C. A., Berkowitz, L., Donnerstein, E., Huesmann, L. R., Johnson, J. D., Linz, D., Malamuth, N. M., & Wartella, E. (2003). The influence of media violence on youth. *Psychological Science in the Public Interest, 4,* 81–110.

Anderson, C. A., Shibuya, A., Ihori, N., Swing, E. L., Bushman, B. J., Sakamoto, A., et al. (2010). Violent video game effects on aggression, empathy, and prosocial behavior in Eastern and Western countries: A meta-analytic review. *Psychological Bulletin, 136*, 151–173.

Anderson, D. R., Huston, A. C., Schmitt, K. L., Linebarger, D. L., & Wright, J. C. (2001). Early childhood television viewing and adolescent behavior. *Monographs of the Society for Research in Child Development, 68*(1, Serial No. 264).

Anderson, L., Lewis, G., Araya, R., Elgie, R., Harrison, G., Proudfoot, J., Schmidt, U., Sharp, D., Weightman, A., & Williams, C. (2005). Self-help books for depression: How can practitioners and patients make the right choice? *British Journal of General Practice, 55,* 387–392.

Andreasen, N. C., Arndt, S., Alliger, R., Miller, D., & Flaum, M. (1995). Symptoms of schizophrenia: Methods, meaning, and mechanisms. *Archives of General Psychiatry, 52,* 341–351.

Angus Reid Poll. (2012, September 5). Britons and Canadians more likely to endorse evolution than Americans. Retrieved from http://www.angus-reid.com/wp-content/uploads/2012/09/2012.09.05_CreEvo.pdf

Ano, G. G., & Vasconcelles, E. B. (2005). Religious coping and psychological adjustment to stress: A meta-analysis. *Journal of Clinical Psychology, 61*, 461–480.

Antoni, M., & Lutgendorf, S. (2007). Psychosocial factors and disease progression in cancer. *Current Directions in Psychological Science, 16*, 42–46.

Antoni, M., Lutgendorf, S., Cole, S., Dhabhar, F., Sephton, S., McDonald, P., et al. (2006). The influence of biobehavioral factors on tumor biology, pathways and mechanisms. *Nature Reviews Cancer, 6*, 240–248.

Antoni, M., Schneiderman, N., & Penedo, F. (2007). Behavioral interventions and psychoneuroimmunology. In R. Ader, R. Glaser, N. Cohen, & M. Irwin (Eds.), *Psychoneuroimmunology* (4th ed., pp. 615–703). New York: Academic Press.

Aouizerate, B., Cuny, E., Bardinct, E., Yelnik, J., Martin-Guehl, C., Rotge, J. Y., et al. (2009). Distinct striatal targets in treating obsessive-compulsive disorder and major depression. *Journal of Neurosurgery, 111*, 775–779.

Arendt, J. (2009). Managing jet lag: Some of the problems and possible new solutions. *Sleep Medicine Reviews, 13*, 249–256.

Arguin, M., Bub, D., & Dudek, G. (1996). Shape integration for visual object recognition and its implication in category-specific visual agnosia. *Visual Cognition, 3*, 221–275.

Ariely, D., & Berns, G. S. (2011). Neuromarketing: the hope and hype of neuroimaging in business. *Nature Reviews Neuroscience, 11*, 284–292.

Arnett, J. (1992). Reckless behavior in adolescence: A developmental perspective. *Developmental Review, 12,* 339–373.

Arnett, J. J. (2000). Emerging adulthood: A theory of development from the late teens through the twenties. *American Psychologist, 55*, 469–480.

Aron, A., Fisher, H., Mashek, D. J., Strong, G., Li, H., & Brown, L. L. (2005). Reward, motivation, and emotion systems associated with early-stage intense romantic love. *Journal of Neurophysiology, 94,* 327–337.

Aronson, E., & Gonzales, M. H. (1990). Alternative social influence processes applied to energy conservation. In J. Edwards, R. S. Tindale, L. Heath, & E. J. Posaval (Eds.), *Social influences: Processes and prevention* (pp. 301–325). New York: Plenum.

Asch, S. E. (1951). Effects of group pressure upon the modification and distortion of judgments. In H. Guetzkow (Ed.), *Groups, leadership and men: Research in human relations* (pp. 177–190). Oxford, UK: Carnegie Press.

Asch, S. E. (1955). Opinions and social pressure. *Scientific American, 193*, 31–35.

Asch, S. E. (1956). Studies of independence and conformity: A minority of one against a unanimous majority. *Psychological Monographs, 70* (9, No. 416).

Aschoff, J. (1965). Circadian rhythms in man. *Science, 148,* 1427–1432.

Aschoff, J., & Wever, R. (1962). Spontanperidik des menschen bei ausschluss aller zeitgeber. *Naturwissenschaftern, 49,* 337–342.

Aschoff, J., Gerecke, U., & Wever, R. (1967). Desynchronization of human circadian rhythms. *Japanese Journal of Physiology, 17,* 450–457.

Aserinsky, E., & Kleitman, N. (1953). Regularly occurring periods of eye motility, and concomitant phenomena, during sleep. *Science, 118*, 273–274.

Ashby, F. G., Isen, A. M., & Turken, A. U. (1999). A neuropsychological theory of positive affect and its influence on cognition. *Psychological Review, 106,* 529–550.

Ashton, M. C., & Lee, K. (2007). Empirical, theoretical, and practical advantages of the HEXACO model of personality structure. *Personality and Social Psychology Review, 11*, 150–166.

Ashton, M. C., & Lee, K. (2008). The HEXACO Model of Personality Structure and the importance of the H factor. *Social and Personality Psychology Compass, 2*, 1952–1962.

Aslin, R. N. (2007). What's in a look? *Developmental Science, 10,* 48–53.

Assor, A., Roth, G., & Deci, E. L. (2004). The emotional costs of parents' conditional regard: A self-determination theory analysis. *Journal of Personality, 72*, 47–88.

Atkinson, R. C., & Shiffrin, R. M. (1968). Human memory: A proposal system and it control processes. In K.W.S.A.J.T. Spence (Ed.), *The psychology of learning and motivation 8.* London: Academic Press.

Aubrey, J. B., Armstrong, B., Arkin, A., Smith, C. T., & Rose, G. (1999). Total sleep deprivation affects memory for a previously learned route. *Sleep, 22*, S246.

Avolio, B. J., & Waldman, D. A. (1994). Variations in cognitive, perceptual, and psychomotor abilities across the working life span: Examining the effects of race, sex, experience, education, and occupational type. *Psychology and Aging, 9,* 430–442.

Awh, E., Barton, B., & Vogel, E. K. (2007). Visual working memory represents a fixed number of items, regardless of complexity. *Psychological Science, 18*, 622–628.

Aylward, E. H., Park, J. E., Field, K. M., Parsons, A. C., Richards, T. L., Cramer, S. C., & Meltzoff, A. N. (2005). Brain activation during face perception: Evidence of a developmental change. *Journal of Cognitive Neuroscience, 17,* 308–319.

Azar, B. (2011). Positive psychology advances, with growing pains. *Monitor on Psychology, 42,* 32.

Babyak, M. A., Blumenthal, J. A., Herman, S., Khatri, P., Doraiswamy, P. M., Moore, K. A., Craighead, W. E., Baldewicz, T. T., & Krishnan, K. R. (2000). Exercise treatment for major depression: Maintenance of therapeutic benefit at 10 months. *Psychosomatic Medicine, 62,* 633–638.

Bachman, J. G., Wadsworth, K. N., O'Malley, P. M., & Johnston, L. D. (1997). *Smoking, drinking, and drug use in young adulthood: The impacts of new freedoms and new responsibilities.* Hillsdale, NJ: Lawrence Erlbaum Associates.

Baddeley, A. (2001). Is working memory still working? *American Psychologist, 56,* 851–864.

Baddeley, A. D., Thomson, N., & Buchanan, M. (1975). Word length and the structure of short-term memory. *Journal of Verbal Learning & Verbal Behavior, 14,* 575–589.

Badman, M. K., & Flier, J. S. (2005). The gut and energy balance: Visceral allies in the obesity wars. *Science, 307,* 1909–1914.

Baer, R. A., Carmody, J., & Hunsinger, M. (2012). Weekly change in mindfulness and perceived stress in a mindfulness-based stress reduction program. *Journal of Clinical Psychology, 68,* 755–765.

Bahrick, H. (1984). Semantic memory content in permastore: Fifty years of memory for Spanish learned in school. *Journal of Experimental Psychology: General, 113,* 1–29.

Bahrick, L. E., & Watson, J. S. (1985). Detection of intermodal proprioceptive–visual contingency as a potential basis of self-perception in infancy. *Developmental Psychology, 21,* 963–973.

Bailenson, J. N., Shum, M. S., Atran, S., Medin, D., & Coley, J. D. (2002). A bird's eye view: Biological categorization and reasoning within and across cultures. *Cognition, 84,* 1–53.

Bailey, J. M., & Pillard, R. C. (1995). Genetics of human sexual orientation. *Annual Review of Sex Research, 6,* 126–150.

Bailey, J. M., Dunne, M. P., & Martin, N. G. (2000). Genetic and environmental influences on sexual orientation and its correlates in an Australian twin sample. *Journal of Personality and Social Psychology, 78,* 524–536.

Bailey, J. M., Pillard, R. C., Neale, M. C., & Agyei, Y. (1993). Heritable factors influence sexual orientation in women. *Archives of General Psychiatry, 50,* 217–223.

Baker, J. R., Bezance, J. B., Zellaby, E., & Aggleton, J. P. (2004). Chewing gum can produce context-dependent effects upon memory. *Appetite, 43,* 207–210.

Balch, W., Myers, D., & Papotto, C. (1999). Dimensions of mood in mood-dependent memory. *Journal of Experimental Psychology: Learning, Memory, and Cognition, 25,* 70–83.

Ball, K., & Lee, C. (2002). Psychological stress, coping, and symptoms of disordered eating in a community sample of young Australian women. *International Journal of Eating Disorders, 31,* 71–81.

Baltes, P. B., & Lindenberger, U. (1997). Emergence of a powerful connection between sensory and cognitive functions across the adult life span: A new window to the study of cognitive aging? *Psychology and Aging, 12,* 12–21.

Bandura, A. (1973). *Aggression: A Social Learning Analysis.* Engelwood Cliffs, NJ: Prentice-Hall.

Bandura, A. (1977). *Social learning theory.* Englewood Cliffs, NJ: Prentice Hall.

Bandura, A. (1997). *Self-efficacy: The exercise of control.* New York: W.H. Freeman.

Bandura, A., & Walters, R. H. (1963). *Social learning and personality development.* New York: Holt, Rinehart, and Winston.

Bandura, A., Ross, D., & Ross, S. A. (1961). Transmission of aggression through imitation of aggressive models. *Journal of Abnormal and Social Psychology, 63,* 575–582.

Bandura, A., Ross, D., & Ross, S. A. (1963). Imitation of film-mediated aggressive models. *Journal of Abnormal and Social Psychology, 66,* 3–11.

Banse, R., Seise, J., & Zerbes, N. (2001). Implicit attitudes toward homosexuality: Reliability, validity, and controllability of the IAT. *Zeitschrift fur Experimentelle Psychologie, 48,* 145–160.

Barabasz, M. (2007). Efficacy of hypnotherapy in the treatment of eating disorders. *International Journal of Clinical and Experimental Hypnosis, 55,* 318–335.

Barbanoj, M. J., Riba, J., Clos, S., Giménez S., Grasa E., & Romero S. (2008). Daytime Ayahuasca administration modulates REM and slow-wave sleep in healthy volunteers. *Psychopharmacology (Berl.), 196,* 315–326.

Bard, K. A., Todd, B., Bernier, C., Love, J., & Leavens, D. A. (2006). Self-awareness in human and chimpanzee infants: What is measured and what is meant by the mirror-and-mark test? *Infancy, 9,* 185–213.

Barger, L. K., Cade, B. E., Ayas, N. Y., Cronin, J. W., Rosner, B., Speizer, F. E., & Czeisler, C. A. (2005). Extended work shifts and the risk of motor vehicle crashes among interns. *The New England Journal of Medicine, 352,* 125–134.

Barger, S. D., & Sydeman, S. J. (2005). Does generalized anxiety disorder predict coronary heart disease risk factors independently of major depressive disorder? *Journal of Affective Disorders, 88,* 87–91.

Bargh, J. A. (1999). The cognitive monster. In S. Chaiken & Y. Trope (Eds.), *Dual process theories in social psychology* (pp. 361–382). New York: Guilford Press.

Bar-Haim, Y., Lamy, D., Pergamin, L., Bakermans-Kranenburg, M. J., & van Ijzendoorn, M. H. (2007). Threat-related attentional bias in anxious and nonanxious individuals: A metaanalytic study. *Psychological Bulletin, 133,* 1–24.

Barkley, R. A. (1998). *Attention-deficit/hyperactivity disorder.* Chicago: Guilford Press.

Barlow, D. H., Gorman, J. M., Shear, M. K., & Woods, S. W. (2000). Cognitive-behavioral therapy, imipramine, or their combination for panic disorder: A randomized controlled trial. *Journal of the American Medical Association, 283,* 2529–2536.

Barnea-Goraly, N., Menon, V., Eckert, M., Tamm, L., Bammer, R., Karchemskiy, A., et al. (2005). White matter development during childhood and adolescence: A cross-sectional diffusion tensor imaging study. *Cerebral Cortex, 15,* 1848–1854.

Barnes, C., & Wagner, D. (2009). Changing to Daylight Saving Time cuts into sleep and increases workplace injuries. *Journal of Applied Psychology, 94,* 1305–1317.

Baron-Cohen, S., Burt, L., Smith-Laittan, F., Harrison, J., & Bolton, P. (1996). Synaesthesia: Prevalence and familiality. *Perception, 25,* 1073–1079.

Barr, R. (2010). Transfer of learning between 2D and 3D sources during infancy: Informing theory and practice. *Developmental Review, 30,* 128–154.

Barr, R., & Hayne, H. (1999). Developmental changes in imitation from television during infancy. *Child Development, 70,* 1067–1081.

Barrett, L. F., & Salovey, P. (Eds.). (2002). *The wisdom in feeling: Psychological processes in emotional intelligence.* New York: Guilford Press.

Bartels, S., & Zeki, S. (2004). The neural correlated of maternal and romantic love. *Neuroimage, 21,* 1155–1166.

Bartlett, F. C. (1932). *Remembering: A study in experimental and social psychology.* Cambridge, UK: Cambridge University Press.

Bateman, D. (2001). Neurological assessment of coma. *Journal of Neurology, Neurosurgery & Psychiatry, 71,* i13–i17.

Battaglia, M., Ogliari, A., Zanoni, A., Citterio, A., Pozzoli, U., Giorda, R., Maffei, C., & Marino, C. (2005). Influence of the serotonin transporter promoter gene and shyness on children's cerebral responses to facial expressions. *Archives of General Psychiatry, 62,* 85–94.

Baum, A., & Valins, S. (1977). *Architecture of social behavior: Psychological studies of social density.* Hillsdale, NJ: Erlbaum.

Baumeister, R. F., & Leary, M. R. (1995). The need to belong: Desire for interpersonal attachments as a fundamental human motivation. *Psychological Bulletin, 117,* 497–529.

Bauserman, R., & Davis, C. (1996). Perceptions of early sexual experiences and adult sexual adjustment. *Journal of Psychology and Human Sexuality, 8,* 37–59.

Bavelier, D., Green, C. S., & Dye, M. W. G. (2010). Children, wired: For better and for worse. *Neuron, 67,* 692–701.

Beall, E. B., Malone, D. A., Dale, R. M., Muzina, D. J., Koenig, K. A., et al. (2012). Effects of electroconvulsive therapy on brain functional activation and connectivity in depression. *Journal of ECT, 28,* 234–241.

Beauchamp, G. K., & Mennella, J. A. (2009). Early flavor learning and its impact on later feeding behavior. *Journal of Pediatric Gastroenterology and Nutrition, 48,* S25–S30.

Beauregard, M., Courtemanche, J., Paquette, V., & St-Pierre, E. (2009). The neural basis of unconditional love. *Psychiatry Research: Neuroimaging, 172,* 93–98.

Bechara, A., Damasio, A. R., Damasio, H., & Anderson, S. W. (1994). Insensitivity to future consequences following damage to human prefrontal cortex. *Cognition, 50,* 7–15.

Beck, A. T. (1963). Thinking and depression: I. Idiosyncratic content and cognitive distortions. *Archives of General Psychiatry, 9,* 324–333.

Beck, A. T., & Steer, R. A. (1977). *Manual for the Beck Depression Inventory.* San Antonio, TX: Psychology Corporation.

Beck, D. M., & Kastner, S. (2009). Top-down and bottom-up mechanisms in biasing competition in the human brain. *Vision Research, 49,* 1154–1165.

Beck, H. P., Levinson, S., & Irons, G. (2009). Finding little Albert: A journey to John B. Watson's infant laboratory. *American Psychologist, 64,* 605–614.

Beebe, B., Jaffe, J., Markese, S., Buck, K., Chen, H., Cohen, P., and Feldstein, S. (2010). The origins of 12-month attachment: A microanalysis of 4-month mother–infant interaction. *Attachment & Human Development, 12,* 6–141.

Beebe, B., Lachmann, F., & Jaffe, J. (1997). Mother–infant interaction structures and presymbolic self and object representations. *Psychoanalytic Dialogues, 7,* 133–182.

Beilock, S. L. (2008). Math performance in stressful situations. *Current Directions in Psychological Science, 17,* 339–343.

Beilock, S. L. (2010). *Choke: What the secrets of the brain reveal about getting it right when you have to.* New York: Free Press.

Beiser, M., & Gotowiec, A. (2000). Accounting for native/non-native differences in IQ scores. *Psychology in the Schools, 37,* 237–252.

Béjot, Y., Jeunet, N., Garrouty, R., Maltaverne, D., Nicolleau, L., Giroud, M., & Didi-Roy, R. (2010). Sexsomnia: An uncommon variety of parasomnia. *Clinical Neurology and Neurosurgery, 112,* 72–75.

Bekinschtein, T. A., Cardozo, J., & Manes, F. F. (2008). Strategies of Buenos Aires waiters to enhance memory capacity in a real-life setting. *Behavioural Neurology, 20,* 65–70.

Bell, P. A., & Yee, L. A. (1989). Skill level and audience effects on performance of a karate drill. *Journal of Social Psychology, 129,* 191–200.

Bell, R. A., Paterniti, D. A., Azari, R., Duberstein, P. R., & Epstein, R. M. (2010). Encouraging patients with depressive symptoms to seek care: A mixed methods approach to message development. *Patient Education and Counseling, 78,* 198–205.

Bellebaum, C., Jokisch, D., Gizewski, E. R., Forsting, M., & Daum, I. (2012). The neural coding of expected and unexpected monetary performance outcomes: Dissociations between active and observational learning. *Behavioural Brain Research, 227,* 241–251.

Belsky, J., & Rovine, M. (1990). Patterns of marital change across the transition to parenthood. *Journal of Marriage and the Family, 52,* 109–123.

Benbow, C. P., & Stanley, J. C. (1983). Sex differences in mathematical reasoning ability: More facts. *Science, 222,* 1029–1031.

Benedict, R. (1938). Continuities and discontinuities in cultural conditioning. *Psychiatry: Journal for the Study of Interpersonal Processes, 2,* 161–167.

Benet-Martinez, V., & John, O. P. (1998). Los Cinco Grandes across cultures and ethnic groups: Multitrait method analyses of the Big Five in Spanish and English. *Journal of Personality and Social Psychology, 75,* 729–750.

Bennett, G. G., Wolin, K. Y., Robinson, E. L., Fowler, S., & Edwards, C. L. (2005). Racial/ethnic harassment and tobacco use among African American young adults. *American Journal of Public Health, 95,* 238–240.

Berger, J. M., Levant, R., McMillan, K. K., Kelleher, W., & Sellers, A. (2005). Impact of gender role conflict, traditional masculinity ideology, alexithymia, and age on men's attitudes towards psychological help seeking. *Psychology of Men & Masculinity, 6,* 73–78.

Berger, R., & Phillips, N. (1995). Energy conservation and sleep. *Behavioural Brain Research, 69,* 65–73.

Berkman, L. F., & Breslow, L. (1983). *Health and ways of living: The Alameda county study.* New York: Oxford University Press.

Berlin, B. (1974). *Principles of Tzeltal plant classification.* New York: Academic Press.

Berns, G. S., Chappelow, J., Fink, C. F., Pagnoni, G., Martin-Skurski, M. E., & Richards, J. (2005). Neurobiological correlates of social conformity and independence during mental rotation. *Biological Psychiatry, 58,* 245–253.

Berquier, A., & Ashton, R. (1992). Characteristics of the frequent nightmare sufferer. *Journal of Abnormal Psychology, 101,* 246–250.

Berry, S. L., Beatty, W. W., & Klesges, R. C. (1985). Sensory and social influences on ice-cream consumption by males and females in a laboratory setting. *Appetite, 6,* 41–45.

Bertram, L., Lill, C. M., & Tanzi, R. E. (2010). The genetics of Alzheimer's disease: Back to the future. *Neuron, 68,* 270–281.

Best, D. (2009). Secondhand and prenatal tobacco smoke exposure. *Pediatrics, 123,* e1017–e1044.

Bezeau, S., & Graves, R. (2001). Statistical power and effect sizes of clinical neuropsychology research. *Journal of Clinical and Experimental Neuropsychology, 23,* 399–406.

Bhatara, A., Tirovolas, A., Duan, L. M., Levy, B., & Levitin, D. J. (2011). Perception of emotional expression in musical performance. *Journal of Experimental Psychology: Human Perception and Performance, 37,* 921–934.

Bhattacharya, J., & Bundorf, M. K. (2005). The incidence of healthcare costs of obesity. Working Paper #11303. National Bureau of Economic Research.

Bhugra, D. (2005). The global prevalence of schizophrenia. *PloS Medicine, 2,* 372–373.

Bialystok, E. (2009). International symposium on bilingualism lecture. *Bilingualism: Language and Cognition, 12,* 3–11.

Bialystok, E. (2011a). Reshaping the mind: The benefits of bilingualism. *Canadian Journal of Experimental Psychology, 65,* 229–235.

Bialystok, E. (2011b). Coordination of executive functions in monolingual and bilingual children. *Journal of Experimental Child Psychology, 110,* 461–468.

Bialystok, E., Craik, F. I. M., & Freedman, M. (2007). Bilingualism as a protection against the onset of symptoms of dementia. *Neuropsychologia, 45,* 459–464.

Bialystok, E., Craik, F. I. M., Klein, R., & Viswanathan, M. (2004). Bilingualism, aging, cognitive control: Evidence from the Simon task. *Psychology & Aging, 19,* 290–303.

Biederman, J., Rosenbaum, J. F., Hirshfeld, D. R., Faraone, S. V., Bolduc, E. A., Gersten, M., et al. (1990). Psychiatric correlates of behavioral inhibition in young children of parents with and without psychiatric disorders. *Archives of General Psychiatry, 47,* 21.

Bigelow, H. J. (1850). Dr. Harlow's case of recovery from the passage of an iron bar through the head. *American Journal of Medical Sciences, 20,* 13–22.

Birbaumer, N., Veit, R., Lotze, M., Erb, M., Hermann, C., Grodd, W., & Flor, H. (2005). Deficient fear conditioning in psychopathy: A functional magnetic resonance imaging study. *Archives of General Psychiatry, 62,* 799–805.

Bjork, R. A., & Whitten, W. B. (1974). Recency-sensitive retrieval processes in long-term free recall. *Cognitive Psychology, 6,* 173–189.

Black, S. M., & Hill, C. E. (1984). The psychological well-being of women in their middle years. *Psychology of Women Quarterly, 9,* 282–292.

Blackwell, L., Trzesniewski, K., & Dweck, C. (2007). Implicit theories of intelligence predict achievement across an adolescent transition: A longitudinal study and an intervention. *Child Development, 78,* 246–263.

Blair, C. (2006). How similar are fluid cognition and general intelligence? A developmental neuroscience perspective on fluid cognition as an aspect of human cognitive ability. *Behavioral and Brain Sciences, 29,* 109–160.

Blair, C., & Razza, R. P. (2007). Relating effortful control, executive function, and false belief understanding to emerging math and literacy ability in kindergarten. *Child Development, 78,* 64–663.

Blair, R. J. R., & Cipolotti, L. (2000). Impaired social response reversal: A case of acquired sociopathy. *Brain, 123,* 1122–1141.

Blake, R., Palmeri, T. J., Marois, R., & Kim, C.-Y. (2005). On the perceptual reality of synesthetic color. In L. C. Robertson & N. Sagiv (Eds.), *Synesthesia* (pp. 47–73). Oxford, UK: Oxford University Press.

Blandin, Y., & Proteau, L. (2000). On the cognitive basis of observational learning: Development of mechanisms for the detection and correction of errors. *Quarterly Journal of Experimental Psychology: Human Experimental Psychology, 53,* 846–867.

Blashfield, R. K., & Intoccia, V. (2000). Growth of the literature on the topic of personality disorders. *American Journal of Psychiatry, 157,* 3.

Blesa, J., Phani, S., Jackson-Lewis, V., & Pzedborski, S. (2012). Classic and new animal models of Parkinson's Disease. *Journal of Biomedicine and Biotechnology, 2012,* 1–10.

Bliss, T., & Lømo, T. (1973). Long-lasting potentiation of synaptic transmission in the dentate area of the anaesthetized rabbit following stimulation of the perforant path. *Journal of Physiology, 232,* 331–356.

Block, R. I., O'Leary, D. S., Hichwa, R. D., Augustinack, J. C., Ponto, L. L. B., Ghoneim, M. M., et al. (2002). Effects of frequent marijuana use on memory-related regional cerebral blood flow. *Pharmacology Biochemistry and Behavior, 72,* 237–250.

Boesch, C. (1991). Teaching among wild chimpanzees. *Animal Behaviour, 41,* 530–532.

Bogaert, A. F. (2008). Menarche and father absence in a national probability sample. *Journal of Biosocial Sciences, 40,* 623–636.

Bogle, K. E., & Smith, B. H. (2009). Illicit methylphenidate use: A review of prevalence, availability, pharmacology, and consequences. *Current Drug Abuse Reviews, 2,* 157–176.

Bohart, A., Elliott, R., Greenberg, L., & Watson, J. (2002). Empathy. In J. C. Norcross (Ed.), *Psychotherapy relationships that work: Therapist contributions and responsiveness to patients* (pp. 89–108). New York: Oxford University Press.

Bohart, A. C. (2003). *Person-centered psychotherapy and related experiential approaches* (pp. 107–148). New York: Guilford Press.

Boldizar, J. P., Wilson, K. L., & Deemer, D. K. (1989). Gender, life experiences, and moral judgment development: A process-oriented approach. *Journal of Personality and Social Psychology, 57,* 229–238.

Bolla, K. I., Brown, K., Eldreth, D., Tate, K., & Cadet, J. L. (2002). Dose-related neurocognitive effects of marijuana use. *Neurology, 59,* 1337–1343.

Boly, M., Faymonville, M. E., Peigneux, P., Lambermont, B., Damas, P., Del Fiore, G., et al. (2004). Auditory processing in severely brain injured patients: Differences between the minimally conscious state and the persistent vegetative state. *Archives of Neurology, 61,* 233–238.

Bondolfi, G., Jermann, F., Van der Linden, M., Gex-Fabry, M., Bizzini, L., Rouget, B. W., et al. (2010). Depression relapse prophylaxis with mindfulness-based cognitive therapy: Replication and extension in the Swiss health care system. *Journal of Affective Disorders, 122,* 224–231.

Bonebakker, A. E., Bonke, B., Klein, J., Wolters, G., Stijen, T., Passchier, J., et al. (1996). Information processing during general anesthesia: Evidence for unconscious memory. *Memory & Cognition, 24,* 766–776.

Bonnano, G. A. (2004). Loss, trauma, and human resilience: Have we underestimated the human capacity to thrive after extremely aversive events? *American Psychologist, 59,* 20–28.

Borland, D. C. (1982). A cohort analysis approach to the empty-nest syndrome among three ethnic groups of women: A theoretical position. *Journal of Marriage and the Family, 44,* 117–129.

Born, J., Lange, T., Hansen, K., Molle, M., & Fehm, H. L. (1997). Effects of sleep and circadian rhythm on human circulating immune cells. *The Journal of Immunology, 158,* 4454–4464.

Bouchard, T. J., Lykken, D. T., McGue, M., Segal, N. L., & Tellegen, A. (1990). Sources of human psychological differences: The Minnesota study of twins reared apart. *Science, 250,* 223–228.

Bourdage, J. S., Lee, K., Ashton, M. C., & Perry, A. (2007). Big Five and HEXACO model personality correlates of sexuality. *Personality and Individual Differences, 43,* 1506–1516.

Bouton, M. E. (1994). Context, ambiguity, and classical conditioning. *Current Directions in Psychological Science, 3,* 49–53.

Bouton, M. E. (2002). Context, ambiguity, and unlearning: Sources of relapse after behavioral extinction. *Biological Psychiatry, 52,* 976–986.

Bower, G. H. (1981). Mood and memory. *American Psychologist, 36,* 129–148.

Bowker, A., Boekhoven, B., Nolan, A., Bauhaus, S., Glover, P., Powell, T., & Taylor, S. (2009). Naturalistic observations of spectator behavior at youth hockey games. *The Sport Psychologist, 23,* 301–316.

Bowlby, J. (1951). Maternal care and mental health. *World Health Organization Monograph,* Serial No. 2.

Bowlby, J. (1980). *Attachment and loss, Vol. 3: Loss: Sadness and depression.* New York: Basic Books.

Boyce, W., Doherty-Poirier, M., MacKinnon, D., Fortin, C., Saab, H., King, M., & Gallupe, O. (2006). Sexual health of Canadian youth: Findings from the Canadian youth, sexual health and HIV/AIDS study. *Canadian Journal of Human Sexuality, 15,* 59–68.

Boyd, J. E., Katz, E. P., Link, B. G., & Phelan, J. C. (2010). The relationship of multiple aspects of stigma and personal contact with someone hospitalized for mental illness, in a nationally representative sample. *Social Psychiatry and Psychiatric Epidemiology, 45,* 1063–1070.

Bracha, H., Ralston, T., Matsukawa, J., Williams, A., & Bracha, A. (2004, October). Does "fight or flight" need updating? *Psychosomatics: Journal of Consultation Liaison Psychiatry, 45,* 448–449.

Bradley, R. H., Whiteside, L., Caldwell, B., Casey, P. H., Kelleher, K., et al. (1993). Maternal IQ, the home environment, and child IQ in low birthweight, premature children. *International Journal of Behavioral Development, 16,* 61–74.

Branch, C. H., & Eurman, L. J. (1980). Social attitudes towards patients with anorexia nervosa. *The American Journal of Psychiatry, 137,* 631–632.

Bransford, J. D., & Johnson, M. K. (1973). Considerations of some problems of comprehension. In W. Chase (Ed.), *Visual information processing* (pp. 383–438). Oxford, UK: Academic.

Braver, T. S., & Barch, D. M. (2002). A theory of cognitive control, aging cognition, and neuromodulation. *Neuroscience and Biobehavioral Reviews, 26,* 809–817.

Brefczynski-Lewis, J. A., Lutz, A., Schaefer, H. S., Levinson, D. B., & Davidson, R. J. (2007). Neural correlates of attentional expertise in long-term meditation practitioners. *Proceeding of the National Academy of Sciences, 104,* 11483–11488.

Brendel, G. R., Stern, E., & Silbersweig, D. (2005). Defining the neuro-circuitry of borderline personality disorder: Functional neuroimaging approaches. *Development and Psychopathology, 17,* 1197–1206.

Brion, M.J.,Victora, C., Matijasevich, A., Horta, B., Anselmi, L., Steer, C., Menezes, A. M., Lawlor, D. A., & Davey Smith, G. (2010). Maternal smoking and child psychological problems: Disentangling causal and noncausal effects. *Pediatrics, 126,* e57–e65.

Broca, P. (1861). Remarques sur le siège de la faculté du langage articule, suivies dune observation daphémie (Perte de la Parole). *Bulletin de la Societé Anatomique de Paris, 6,* 330–357.

Brondolo, E., Brady, N., Thompson, S., Contrada, R. J., Cassells, A., Tobin, J., & Sweeney, M. (2008b). Perceived racism and negative affect: Analyses of trait and state measures of affect in a community sample. *Journal of Social and Clinical Psychology*, 27,150–173.

Brondolo, E., Libby, D. J., Denton, E., Thompson, S., Schwartz, J., Sweeney, M., et al. (2008a). Racism and ambulatory blood pressure in a community sample. *Psychosomatic Medicine*, 70, 49–56.

Brook, J. S., Stimmel, M. A., Zhang, C., & Brook, D. W. (2008). The association between earlier marijuana use and subsequent academic achievement and health problems: A longitudinal study. *American Journal of Addiction, 17,* 155–160.

Brooks, D. C., Palmatier, M. I., Garcia, E. O., & Johnson, J. L. (1999). An extinction cue reduced spontaneous recovery of a conditioned taste aversion. *Animal Learning & Behavior, 27,* 77–88.

Brooks, L. R. (1978). Nonanalytic concept formation and memory for instances. In E. Rosch & B. Lloyd (Eds.), *Cognition and categorization* (pp. 169–211). Hillsdale, NJ: Erlbaum.

Brooks, L. R. & Hannah, S. D. (2006). Instantiated features and the use of "rules." *Journal of Experimental Psychology: General, 135,* 133–151.

Brotto, L. A., Chik, H. M., Ryder, A. G., Gorzalka, B. B., & Seal, B. N. (2005). Acculturation and sexual function in Asian women. *Archives of Sexual Behavior, 34,* 613–626.

Brown, A. (2002). Consolidation theory and retrograde amnesia in humans. *Psychonomic Bulletin & Review, 9,* 403–425.

Brown, A. S. (2003). A review of the déjà vu experience. *Psychological Bulletin, 129,* 394–413.

Brown, A. S., & Derkits, E. J. (2010). Prenatal infection and schizophrenia: A review of epidemiologic and translational studies. *American Journal of Psychiatry, 167,* 261–280.

Brown, A. S., & McNeil, D. (1966). The "tip of the tongue" phenomenon. *Journal of Verbal Learning and Verbal Behavior, 5,* 325–337.

Brown, G. W., Birley, J. L., & Wing, J. K. (1972). Influence of family life on the course of schizophrenic disorders: A replication. *The British Journal of Psychiatry, 121,* 251–258.

Brown, J. (1958). Some tests of decay theory of immediate memory. *Quarterly Journal of Experimental Psychology, 10,* 12–24.

Brown, J. M. (2003). Eyewitness memory for arousing events: Putting things into context. *Applied Cognitive Psychology, 17,* 93–106.

Brown, M., Keyner, R., & Lumsden, A. (2001). *The developing brain.* Oxford, UK: Oxford University Press.

Brown, R. E., & Milner, P. M. (2003). The legacy of Donald O. Hebb: More than the Hebb Synapse. *Nature Reviews Neuroscience, 4,* 1013–1019.

Brown, R. E., Basheer, R., McKenna, J. T., Strecker, R. E., & McCarley, R. W. (2012). Control of sleep and wakefulness. *Physiology Review, 92,* 1087–1187.

Brown, R. P., & Gerbarg, P. L. (2009). Yoga breathing, meditation, and longevity. *Longevity, Regeneration, and Optimal Health. 1172,* 54–62.

Brown, R., & Kulik, J. (1977). Flashbulb memories. *Cognition, 5,* 73–99.

Bruck, M., & Ceci, S. J. (1999). The suggestibility of children's memory. *Annual Review of Psychology, 50,* 419–439.

Brunell, A. B., Staats, S., Barden, J., & Hupp, J. M. (2011). Narcissism and academic dishonesty: The exhibitionism dimension and the lack of guilt. *Personality and Individual Differences, 50,* 323–328.

Buck, L. B., & Axel, R. (1991). A novel multigene family may encode odorant receptors: A molecular basis for odor recognition. *Cell, 65,* 175–187.

Buckholtz, J. W., Treadway, M. T., Cowan, R. L., Woodward, N. D., Li, R., Ansari, M. S., Baldwin, R. M., et al. (2010). Dopaminergic network differences in human impulsivity. *Science, 329,* 532.

Bugg, J. M., Zook, N. A., DeLosh, E. L., Davalos, D. B., & Davis, H.P. (2006). Age differences in fluid intelligence: Contributions of general slowing and frontal decline. *Brain and Cognition, 62,* 9–16.

Bukach, C. M., Bub, D. N., Masson, M. E. J., & Lindsay, D. S. (2004) Category specificity in normal episodic learning: Applications to object recognition and category-specific agnosia. *Cognitive Psychology, 48,* 1–46.

Bunn, E. M., Tyler, L. K., & Moss, H. E. (1998). Category-specific semantic deficits: The role of familiarity and property type reexamined. *Neuropsychology, 12,* 367–379.

Burger, J. M. (1999). The foot-in-the-door compliance procedure: A multiple-process analysis and review. *Personality and Social Psychology Review, 3,* 303–325.

Burkam, D. T., Ready, D. D., Lee, V. E., & LoGerfo, L. F. (2004). Social-class differences in summer learning between kindergarten and first grade: Model specification and estimation. *Sociology of Education, 77,* 1–31.

Burnand, Y., Andreoli, A., Kolatte, E., Venturini A., & Rosset, N. (2002). Psychodynamic psychotherapy and clomipramine in the treatment of major depression. *Psychiatric Services, 53,* 585–580.

Burns, M., & Seligman, M. (1989). Explanatory style across the life span: Evidence for stability over 52 years. *Journal of Personality and Social Psychology, 56,* 471–477.

Buschkuehl, M., Jaeggi, S. M., Hutchison, S., Perrig-Chiello, P., Däpp, C., Müller, M., et al. (2008). Impact of working memory training on memory performance in old-old adults. *Psychology and Aging, 23,* 743–753.

Bushman, B. J., & Anderson, C. A. (2007). Measuring the strength of the effect of violent media on aggression. *American Psychologist, 62,* 253–254.

Bushman, B. J., Moeller, S. J., & Crocker, J. (2011). Sweets, sex, or self-esteem? Comparing the value of self-esteem boosts with other pleasant rewards. *Journal of Personality, 79,* 993–1012.

Buston, P. M., & Emlen, S. T. (2003). Cognitive processes underlying human mate choice: The relationship between self-perception and mate preference in Western society. *Proceedings of the National Academy of Sciences, 100,* 8805–8810.

Butcher, L. M., Davis, O. S. P., Craig, I. W., & Plomin, R. (2008). Genome-wide quantitative trait locus association scan of general cognitive ability using pooled DNA and 500K single nucleotide polymorphism microarrays. *Genes, Brains and Behavior, 7,* 435–446.

Butler, A., Kang, S., & Roediger, H. (2009). Congruity effects between materials and processing tasks in the survival processing paradigm. *Journal of Experimental Psychology: Learning, Memory, and Cognition, 35,* 1477–1486.

Butler, B., & Klein, R. (2009). Inattentional blindness for ignored words: Comparison of explicit and implicit memory tasks. *Consciousness & Cognition, 18,* 811–819.

Button, E. J., Sonuga-Barke, E. J., Davies, J., & Thompson, M. (1996). A prospective study of self-esteem in the rediction of eating problems in adolescent schoolgirls: Questionnaire findings. *British Journal of Clinical Psychology, 35,* 193–203.

Cabeza, R. (2002). Hemispheric asymmetry reduction in older adults: The HAROLD model. *Psychology and Aging, 17,* 85–100.

Caci, H., Deschaux, O., Adan, A., & Natale, V. (2009). Comparing three morningness scales: Age and gender effects, structure and cut-off criteria. *Sleep Medicine, 10,* 240–245.

Cacioppo, J. T., & Hawkley, L. C. (2003). Social isolation and health, with an emphasis on underlying mechanisms. *Perspectives in Biology and Medicine, 46,* S39–S52.

Cacioppo, J. T., Hawkley, L. C., & Berntson, G. G. (2003). The anatomy of loneliness. *Current Directions in Psychological Science, 12,* 71–74.

Cacioppo, J. T., Hawkley, L. C., Norman, G. J., & Berntson, G. G. (2011). Social isolation. *Annuals of the New York Academy of Sciences, 1231,* 17–22.

Cacioppo, J. T., Hughes, M. E., Waite, L. J., Hawkley, L. C., & Thisted, R. A. (2006). Loneliness as a specific risk factor for depressive symptoms: Cross-sectional and longitudinal analyses. *Psychology and Aging, 21,* 140–151.

Cacioppo, J. T., Petty, R. E., Kao, C., & Rodriguez, R. (1986). Central and peripheral routes to persuasion: An individual difference perspective. *Journal of Personality and Social Psychology, 51,* 1032–1043.

Cahn, B. R., & Polich, J. (2006). Meditation states and traits: EEG, ERP and neuroimaging studies. *Psychological Bulletin, 132,* 180–211.

Cairns, R., & Cairns, B. (1994). *Lifelines and risks: Pathways of youth in our time.* New York: Cambridge University Press.

Caldwell, H. K., & Young, W. S. (2006). Oxytocin and vasopressin: Genetics and behavioral implications. In A. Lajtha & R. Lim (Eds.), *Handbook of Neurochemistry and Molecular Neurobiology* (pp. 573–607). Berlin: Springer-Verlag.

Campos, J. J., Bertenthal, B. I., & Kermoian, R. (1992). Early experience and emotional development: The emergence of wariness of heights. *Psychological Science, 3,* 61–64.

Canadian Medical Association, 8th Annual National Report Card on Health Care, August 2008. Ottawa, ON: Author.

Canli, T., Sivers, H., Whitfield, S. L., Gotlib, I. H., & Gabrieli, J. D. E. (2002). Amygdala response to happy faces as a function of extraversion. *Science, 296,* 2191.

Canli, T., Zhao, Z., Brewer, J., Gabrieli, J. D. E., & Cahill, L. (2000). Event-related activation in the human amygdala associates with later memory for individual emotional experience. *The Journal of Neuroscience, 20,* RC99.

Cao, X., Cui, Z., Feng, R., Tang, Y., Qin, Z., Mei, B., & Tsien, J. (2007). Maintenance of superior learning and memory function in NR2B transgenic mice during ageing. *European Journal of Neuroscience, 25,* 1815–1822.

Capafons, A., Mendoza, M., Espejo, B., Green, J., Lopes-Pires, C., Selma, M., et al. (2008). Attitudes and beliefs about hypnosis: A multicultural study. *Contemporary Hypnosis, 25,* 141–155.

Cappa, S. F., Perani, D., Schnur, T., Tettamanti, M., & Fazio, F. (1998). The effects of semantic category and knowledge type on lexical-semantic access: A PET study. *Neuroimage. 8,* 350–359.

Cappo, B. M., & Holmes, D. S. (1984). The utility of prolonged respiratory exhalation for reducing physiological and psychological arousal in non-threatening and threatening situation. *Journal of Psychosomatic Research, 28,* 265–273.

Caramazza, A., & Mahon, B. Z. (2003). The organization of conceptual knowledge: The evidence from category-specific semantic deficits. *Trends in Cognitive Sciences, 7,* 354–361.

Caramazza, A., & Shelton, J. R. (1998). Domain-specific knowledge systems in the brain: The animate-inanimate distinction. *Journal of Cognitive Neuroscience, 10,* 1–34.

Carek, P. J., Laibstain, S. E., & Care, S. M. (2011). Exercise for the treatment of depression and anxiety. *International Journal of Psychiatry in Medicine, 41,* 15–28.

Carise, D., Dugosh, K. L., McLellan, A. T., Camilleri, A., Woody, G. E., & Lynch, K. G. (2007). Prescription oxycotin abuse among patients entering addiction treatment. *American Journal of Psychiatry, 164,* 1750–1756.

Carmichael, M. S., Warburton, V. L., Dixen, J. & Davidson, J. M. (1994). Relationships among cardiovascular, muscular, and oxytocin responses during human sexual activity. *Archives of Sexual Behavior, 23,* 59–79.

Carmody, T. P., Duncan, C., Simon, J. A., Solkowitz, S., Huggins, J., Lee, S., & Delucchi, K. (2008). Hypnosis for smoking cessation: A randomized trial. *Nicotine & Tobacco Research, 10,* 811–818.

Carnagey, N. L., Anderson, C. A., & Bushman, B. J. (2007). The effect of video game violence on physiological desensitization to real-life violence. *Journal of Experimental Social Psychology, 43,* 489–496.

Carpendale, J. I. (2000). Kohlberg and Piaget on stages and moral reasoning. *Developmental Review, 20,* 181–205.

Carpendale, J. I., & Lewis, C. (2004). Constructing an understanding of mind: The development of children's social understanding within social interaction. *Behavioral and Brain Sciences, 27,* 79–96.

Carroll, J. B. (1993). *Human cognitive abilities: A survey of factor analytic studies.* Cambridge, U.K.: Cambridge University Press.

Carstensen, L. L., Isaacowitz, D., & Charles, S. T. (1999). Taking time seriously: A theory of socioemotional selectivity. *American Psychologist, 54,* 165–181.

Carston, R. (2002). *Thoughts and utterances: The pragmatics of explicit conversation.* New York: Blackwell.

Carter, A. C., Brandon, K., & Goldman, M. S. (2010). The college and noncollege experience: A review of the factors that influence drinking behavior in young adulthood. *Journal of Studies on Alcohol and Drugs, 71,* 742–750.

Carter, C. S. (1998). Neuroendocrine perspectives on social attachment and love. *Psychoneuroendocrinology, 23,* 779–818.

Carter, C. S., Braver, T. S., Barch, D. M., Botvinick, M. M., Noll, D., & Cohen, J. D. (1998). Anterior cingulate cortex, error detection, and the online monitoring of performance. *Science, 280,* 747–749.

Cartwright, R., Agargun, M., Kirkby, J., & Friedman, J. K. (2006). Relation of dreams to waking concerns. *Psychiatry Research, 141,* 261–270.

Caruso, E. M., Waytz, A., & Epley, N. (2010). The intentional mind and the hot hand: Perceiving intentions makes streaks seem likely to continue. *Cognition, 116,* 149–153.

Casey, B. J., Jones, R. M., & Hare, T. A. (2008). The adolescent brain. *Annals of the New York Academy of Sciences, 1124*(1), 111–126.

Cason, G. R., Lavond, D. G., & Thompson, R. F. (1922). The conditioned eyelid reaction. *Journal of Experimental Psychology, 5,* 153–196.

Caspi, A. (2000). The child is father of the man: Personality continuities from childhood to adulthood. *Journal of Personality and Social Psychology, 78,* 158–172.

Caspi, A., Moffitt, T. E., Cannon, M., Taylor, A., Craig, I. W., Harrington, H., McClay, J., Mill, J., Martin, J. Braithwaite, A., & Poulton, R. (2005). Moderation of the effect of adolescent-onset cannabis use on adult psychosis by a functional polymorphism in the catechol-O-methyltransferase gene: Longitudinal evidence of a gene X environment interaction. *Biological Psychiatry, 57,* 1117–1127.

Caspi, A., Sugden, K., Moffitt, T. E., Taylor, A., Craig, I.W., Harrington, H., et al. (2003). Influence of life stress on depression: Moderation by a polymorphism in the 5-HTT gene. *Science, 301,* 386–389.

Cattell, R.B. (1971). *Abilities: Their structure, growth, and action.* Boston: Houghton Mifflin.

Cattell, R. B. (1946). *The description and measurement of personality.* New York: Harcourt, Brace & World.

Cavallera, G., & Giudici, S. (2008). Morningness and eveningness personality: A survey in literature from 1995 up till 2006. *Personality and Individual Differences, 44*, 3–21.

Ceci, S. J. (1991). How much does schooling influence general intelligence and its cognitive components? A reassessment of the evidence. *Developmental Psychology, 27*, 703–722.

Ceci, S. J. (1999). The suggestibility of children's memory. *Annual Review of Psychology, 50*, 419–439.

Ceci, S. J., & Williams, W. M. (1997). Schooling, intelligence, and income. *American Psychologist, 52*, 1051–1058.

Centers for Disease Control and Prevention (CDC). (2002). Annual smoking-attributable mortality, years of potential life lost, and productivity losses—United States, 1995–1999. *Morbidity and Mortality Weekly Report, 51*, 300–303.

Centers for Disease Control and Prevention (CDC). (2009). Tobacco use and pregnancy. Retrieved August 1, 2010, from http://www.cdc.gov/reproductivehealth/tobaccousepregnancy/index.htm

Centers for Disease Control and Prevention (CDC). (2009a, April 17). *National Vital Statistics Reports, 57*.

Centers for Disease Control and Prevention (CDC). (2009b). Smoking & tobacco use. Retrieved June 20, 2011, from http://www.cdc.gov/tobacco/data_statistics/fact_sheets/fast_facts/index.htm

Centers for Disease Control and Prevention (CDC). (2010). Youth risk behavior surveillance—United States, 2009. *Morbidity and Mortality Weekly Report, 59*(No. SS-5). Retrieved from http://www.cdc .gov/mmwr/pdf/ss/ss5905.pdf

Cepeda, N. N., Pashler, H., Vul, E., et al. (2006). Distributed practice in verbal recall tasks: A review and quantitative synthesis. *Psychological Bulletin, 132*, 354–380.

Certain, L. K., & Kahn, R. S. (2003). Prevalence, correlates, and trajectory of television viewing among infants and toddlers. *Pediatrics, 109*, 634–642.

Chabris, C. F., Weinberger, A., Fontaine, M., & Simons, D. J. (2011). You do not talk about Fight Club if you do not notice Fight Club: Inattentional blindness for a simulated real-world assault. *i-Perception, 2*, 150–153.

Chaiken, S., & Trope, Y. (1999). *Dual-process theories in social psychology*. New York: Guilford Press.

Chambers, R. A., & Potenza, M. N. (2003). Neurodevelopment, impulsivity, and adolescent gambling. *Journal of Gambling Studies, 19*(1), 53–84.

Chambers, R. A., Taylor, J. R., & Potenza, M. N. (2003). Developmental neurocircuitry of motivation in adolescence: A critical period of addiction vulnerability. *The American Journal of Psychiatry, 160*, 1041–1052.

Chambers, R., Chuen Yee Lo, B., & Allen, N. B. (2008). The impact of intensive mindfulness training on attentional control, cognitive style, and affect. *Cognitive therapy and research, 32*, 303–322.

Chambless, D., & Ollendick, T. (2001). Empirically supported psychological interventions: Controversies and evidence. *Annual Review of Psychology, 52*, 685–716.

Chan, B. L., Witt, R., Charrow, A. P., Magee, A., Howard, R., Pasquina, P. F., & Heilman, K. M. (2007). Mirror therapy and phantom limb pain. *New England Journal of Medicine, 357*, 2206–2207.

Changizi, M. A., Zhang, Q., & Shimojo, S. (2006). Bare skin, blood, and the evolution of primate colour vision. *Biology Letters, 2*, 217–221.

Chapman, H. A., Kim, D. A., Susskind, J. M., & Anderson, A. K. (2009). In bad taste: Evidence for the oral origins of moral disgust. *Science, 323*, 1222–1226.

Chappel, J. N., Veach, T. L., & Krug, R. S. (1985). The Substance Abuse Attitude Survey: An instrument for measuring attitudes. *Journal of Studies on Alcohol, 46*, 48–52.

Charles, S. T., & Carstensen, L. L. (2009). Social and emotional aging. *Annual Review of Psychology, 61*, 383–409.

Charles, S. T., Mather, M., & Carstensen, L. L. (2003). Focusing on the positive: Age differences in memory for positive, negative, and neutral stimuli. *Journal of Experimental Psychology, 85*, 163–178.

Charness, N. (1981). Search in chess: Age and skill differences. *Journal of Experimental Psychology: Human Perception and Performance, 7*, 467–476.

Chartrand, T. L., & Bargh, J. A. (1999). The chameleon effect: The perception–behavior link and social interaction. *Journal of Personality and Social Psychology, 76*, 893–910.

Chase, W. G., & Simon, H. A. (1973). Perception in chess. *Cognitive Psychology, 4*, 55–81.

Chaudhari, N., Landin, A. M., & Roper, S. D. (2000). A metabotropic glutamate receptor variant functions as a taste receptor. *Nature Neuroscience, 3*, 113–119.

Cheesman, J., & Merikle, P. M. (1986). Distinguishing conscious from unconscious perceptual processes. *Canadian Journal of Psychology, 40*, 343–367.

Chen, I., Vorona, R., Chiu, R., & Ware, J. (2008). A survey of subjective sleepiness and consequences in attending physicians. *Behavioral Sleep Medicine, 6*, 1–15.

Chen, J. L., Penhune, V. B., & Zatorre, R. J. (2008). Listening to musical rhythms recruits motor regions of the brain. *Cerebral Cortex, 18*, 2844–2854.

Chen, J. P., Paredes, W., Li, J., Smith, D., Lowinson, J., & Gardner, E. L. (1990). Delta 9-tetrahydrocannabinol produces naloxone-blockable enhancement of presynaptic basaldopamine efflux in nucleus accumbens of conscious, freely-moving rats as measured by intracerebral microdialysis. *Psychopharmacology, 102*, 156–162.

Chen, K. W., Berger, C. C., Manheimer, E., Forde, D., Magidson, J., Dachman, L., & Lejuez, C. W. (2012). Meditative therapies for reducing anxiety: A systematic review and meta-analysis of randomized controlled trials. *Depression & Anxiety, 29*, 545–562.

Chen, S. C. (1937). Social modification of the activity of ants in nest-building. *Physiological Zoology, 10*, 420–436.

Cheng, H., & Riffe, D. (2008). Attention, perception, and perceived effects: Negative political advertising in a battleground state of the 2004 presidential election. *Mass Communication & Society, 11*, 177–196.

Chentsova-Dutton, Y. E., & Tsai, J. L. (2007). Cultural factors influence the expression of psychopathology. In S. O. Lilienfeld & W. T. O'Donohue (Eds.), *The great ideas of clinical science: 17 principles that every mental health professional should understand* (pp. 375–396). New York: Routledge/Taylor & Francis Group.

Chentsova-Dutton, Y. E., & Tsai, J. L. (2007). Gender differences in emotional responding among European Americans and Hmong Americans. *Cognition and Emotion, 21*, 162–181.

Cheung, B. Y., Chudek, M., & Heine, S. J. (2011). Evidence for a sensitive period for acculturation: Younger immigrants report acculturating at a faster rate. *Psychological Science, 22*, 147–152.

Cheung, F. M., Leung, K., Fan, R. M., Song, W., Zhang J.-X., & Zhang J.-P. (1996). Development of the Chinese Personality Assessment Inventory. *Journal of Cross-Cultural Psychology, 27*, 181–199.

Chiao, J. Y., Harada, T., Komeda, H., Li, Z., Mano, Y., Saito, D., Parrish, T. B., Sadato, N., & Iidaka, T. (2009). Neural basis of individualistic and collectivistic views of self. *Human Brain Mapping, 30*, 2813–2820.

Chiesa, A., & Serretti, A. (2011). Mindfulness based cognitive therapy for psychiatric disorders: A systematic review and meta-analysis. *Psychiatry Research, 187*, 441–453.

Chirkov, V. I., Safdar, S., de Guzman, J., & Playfoird, K. (2008). Further examining the role motivation to study abroad plays in the adaptation of intentional students in Canada. *International Journal of Intercultural Relations,* 32, 427–440.

Chirkov, V. I., Vansteenkiste, M., Tao, R., & Lynch, M. (2007). The role of motivation to study abroad in the adaptation of international students: A self-determination theory approach. *International Journal of Intercultural Relations, 31,* 199–222.

Chistyakov, A.V., Kaplan, B., Rubicheck, O., Kreinin, I., Koren, D., Feinsod, M., & Klein, E. (2005). Antidepressant effects of different schedules of repetitive transcranial magnetic stimulation vs. clomipramine in patients with major depressions: Relationship to changes in cortical excitability. *International Journal of Neuropsychopharmacology, 8,* 223–233.

Choi, I., Nisbett, R. E., & Norenzayan, A. (1999). Causal attribution across cultures: Variation and universality. *Psychological Bulletin, 125,* 47–63.

Choi, Y., Shamosh, N. A., Cho, S., DeYoung, C. G., Lee, M., Lee, J., & Lee, K. (2008). Multiple bases of human intelligence revealed by cortical thickness and neural activation. *The Journal of Neuroscience, 28,* 10323–10329.

Chopra, I. C., & Chopra, R.W. (1957). The use of cannabis drugs in India. *Bulletin of Narcotics, 9,* 4–29.

Chou, H., & Lien, B. (2011). What does a negative political ad really say? The effects of different content dimensions. *Journal of Marketing Communications, 17,* 281–295.

Christakis, D. A. (2009). The effects of media usage: What do we know and what should we learn? *Acta Paediatrica, 98,* 8–16.

Christakis, D. A., Zimmerman, F. J., DiGiuseppe, D. L., & McCarthy, C. A. (2004). Early television exposure and subsequent attentional problems in children. *Pediatrics, 113,* 708–713.

Christakis, N. A., & Fowler, J. H. (2007). The spread of obesity in a large social network over 32 years. *New England Journal of Medicine, 357,* 370–379.

Christakis, N. A., & Fowler, J. H. (2008). The collective dynamics of smoking in a large social network. *New England Journal of Medicine, 358,* 2249–2258.

Christensen, C., Silberberg, A., Hursh, S., Huntsberry, M., & Riley, A. (2008). Essential value of cocaine and food in rats: Tests of the exponential model of demand. *Psychopharmacology, 198,* 221–229.

Christian, K. M., & Thompson, R. F. (2003). Neural substrates of eyeblink conditioning: Acquisition and retention. *Learning & Memory, 10,* 427–455.

Christie, R., & Geis, F. L. (1970). *Studies in Machiavellianism.* New York: Academic Press.

Chrousos, G. P. (2009). Stress and disorders of the stress system. *Nature Reviews Endocrinology, 5,* 374–381.

Chrousos, G. P., & Gold, P. (1992). The concepts of stress and stress system disorders: Overview of physical and behavioral homeostasis. *Journal of the American Medical Association, 267,* 1244–1252.

Chuang, P.-C. (2006). Political spot advertising: A cross-cultural comparison of the 1996-2004 presidential campaigns in Taiwan and the U.S. *Intercultural Communication Studies, XV,* 65–76.

Chung, S., & Hernstein, R. J. (1967). Choice and delay of reinforcement. *Journal of Experimental Analysis of Behavior, 10,* 67–74.

Church, T. A. (2001). Culture and personality: Toward an integrated cultural trait psychology. *Journal of Personality, 68,* 651–703.

Cialdini, R. B. (2000). *Persuasion: Influence and practice* (4th ed.). New York: Allyn & Bacon.

Cialdini, R. B. (2001). Harnessing the science of persuasion. *Harvard Business Review, 79,* 72–81.

Cialdini, R. B., Vincent, J. E., Lewis, S. K., Catalan, J., Wheeler, D., & Darby, B. (1975). Reciprocal concessions procedure for inducing compliance: The door-in-the-face technique. *Journal of Personality and Social Psychology, 31,* 206–215.

Clancy, S. A. (2005). *Abducted: How people come to believe they were kidnapped by aliens.* Cambridge, MA: Harvard University Press.

Claparède, E. (1911/1951). Recognition and me-ness. Translated in D. Repaport (Ed.), *Organization and pathology of thought* (pp. 58–75). New York: Columbia University Press. (Originally published 1911.)

Clark, J. M., & Paivio, A. (1991). Dual coding theory and education. *Educational Psychology Review, 3,* 149–210.

Clark, L. A. (2007). Assessment and diagnosis of personality disorder: Perennial issues and an emerging reconceptualization. *Annual Review of Psychology, 58,* 227–257.

Clarke, D., Pulford, J., Bellringer, M., Abbott, M., & Hodgins, D. C. (2012). An exploratory study of problem gambling on casino versus non-casino electronic gaming machines. *International Journal of Mental Health and Addiction, 10,* 107–121.

Cleary, A. (2008). Recognition memory, familiarity, and déjà vu experiences. *Current Directions in Psychological Science, 17,* 353–357.

Clopton, N. A., & Sorell, G. T. (1993). Gender differences in moral reasoning: Stable or Situational? *Psychology of Women Quarterly, 17*(1), 85–101.

CNN. (2002). 'Wuornos' last words: I'll be back. Retrieved December 21, 2010, from http://archives.cnn.com/2002/LAW/10/09/wuornos.execution/index.html

Cohen, A. J. (2002). Music cognition and the cognitive psychology of film structure. *Canadian Psychology, 43,* 215–232.

Cohen, B., Guttmann, D., & Lazar, A. (1998). The willingness to seek help: A cross-national comparison. *Cross-Cultural Research: The Journal of Comparative Social Science, 32,* 342–357.

Cohen, J. (1988). *Statistical power analysis for the behavioral sciences (2nd ed.).* Hillsdale, NJ: Lawrence Erlbaum Associates.

Cohen, J. (1994). The earth is round ($p < 0.05$). *American Psychologist, 49,* 997–1003.

Cohen, N. J., Eichenbaum, H., Deacedo, B. S., & Corkin, S. (1985). Different memory systems underlying acquisition of procedural and declarative knowledge. In D. S. Olton, E. Gamzu, & S. Corkin (Eds.), *Memory dysfunctions: An integration of animal and human research from preclinical and clinical perspectives* (pp. 54–71). New York: New York Academy of Sciences.

Cohn, M. A., Fredrickson, B. F., Brown, S. L., Mikels, J. A., & Conway, A. M. (2009). Happiness unpacked: Positive emotions increase life satisfaction by building resilience. *Emotion, 9,* 361–368.

Cole, S., Korin, Y., Fahey, J., & Zack, J. (1998). Nor-epinephrine accelerates HIV replication via protein kinase A–dependent effects on cytokine production. *Journal of Immunology, 161,* 610–616.

Collins, A. (1988). *In the sleep room: The story of CIA brainwashing experiments in Canada.* Toronto: Key Porter Books.

Collins, A. M., & Loftus, E. F. (1975). A spreading-activation theory of semantic processing. *Psychological Review, 82,* 407–428.

Colonna-Pydyn, C., Gjesfjeld, C., & Greeno, C. (2007). The factor structure of the Barriers to Treatment Participation Scale (BTPS): Implications for future barriers scale development. *Administration and Policy in Mental Health and Mental Health Services Research, 34,* 563–569.

Colwill, R. M., & Recorla, R. A. (1985). Post-conditioning devaluation of a reinforce affects instrumental responding. *Journal of Experimental Psychology: Animal Behavior Processes, 11,* 120–132.

Colwill, R. M., & Rescorla, R. A. (1990). Effect of reinforce devaluation on discriminative control of instrumental behaviour. *Journal of Experimental Psychology, 16,* 40–47.

Comings, D. E., & Blum, K. (2000). Reward deficiency syndrome: Genetic aspects of behavioural disorders. *Progress in Brain Research, 126,* 325–341.

Compton, J. A., & Pfau, M. W. (2005). *Inoculation theory of resistance to influence at maturity: Recent progress in theory development and application and suggestions for future research* (pp. 97–145). Mahwah, NJ: Lawrence Erlbaum Associates.

Conde-Agudelo, A., Belizan, J. M., & Diaz-Rossello, J. (2011). Kangaroo mother care to reduce morbidity and mortality in low birthweight infants. *Cochrane Database of Systematic Reviews, 3.*

Connelly, M. (2000, February 29). Poll finds that half in state disagree with Diallo verdict. *New York Times.* Retrieved from http://www.nytimes.com/2000/02/29/nyregion/poll-finds-that-half-in-state-disagree-with-diallo-verdict.html

Conway, A. R. A., et al. (2002). A latent variable analysis of working memory capacity, short term memory capacity, processing speed, and general fluid intelligence. *Intelligence, 30,* 163–183.

Conway, M., & Ross, M. (1984). Getting what you want by revising what you had. *Journal of Personality and Social Psychology, 47,* 738–748.

Cook, E. W., Hodes, R. L., & Lang, P. J. (1986). Preparedness and phobia: Effects of stimulus content on human visceral conditioning. *Journal of Abnormal Psychology, 95,* 195–207.

Cook, I. A., Warren, C., Pajot, S. K., Schairer, D., & Leuchter, A. F. (2011). Regional brain activation with advertising images. *Journal of Neuroscience, Psychology, and Economics, 4,* 147–160.

Coombs, R. H. (1991). Marital status and personal wellbeing: A literature review. *Family Relations, 40,* 97–102.

Cooper, H. M., Charlton, K., Valentine, J. C., & Muhlenbruck, L. (2000). Making the most of summer school: A meta-analytic and narrative review. *Monographs of the Society for Research in Child Development, 65*(1, Serial No. 260).

Cooper, S. J. (2005). Donald O. Hebb's synapse and learning rule: A history and commentary. *Neuroscience and Biobehavioral Reviews, 28,* 851–874.

Cordner, G., & Shain, C. (2011). The changing landscape of police education and training. *Police Practice and Research, 12,* 281–285.

Coren, S. (1996a). Daylight savings time and traffic accidents. *New England Journal of Medicine, 334,* 924.

Coren, S. (1996b). Accidental death and the shift to daylight savings time. *Perceptual and Motor Skills, 83,* 921–922.

Corkin, S. (2002). What's new with the amnesic patient H.M.? *Nature Reviews Neuroscience, 3,* 153–160.

Correll, J., Park, B., Judd, C. M., & Wittenbrink, B. (2007). The influence of stereotypes on decisions to shoot. *European Journal of Social Psychology, 37*(6), 1102–1117.

Correll, J., Urland, G. R., & Ito, T. A. (2006). Event-related potentials and the decision to shoot: The role of threat perception and cognitive control. *Journal of Experimental Social Psychology, 42,* 120–128.

Corrigan, P. (2004). How stigma interferes with mental health care. *American Psychologist, 59,* 614–625.

Cosgrove, G. R., & Rauch, S. L. (2003). Stereotactic cingulotomy. *Neurosurgery Clinics of North America, 13,* 225–235.

Costa, A., Hernández, M., & Sebastián-Gallés, N. (2008). Bilingualism aids conflict resolution: Evidence from the ANT task. *Cognition, 106,* 59–86.

Cote, K. A., Milner, C. E., Osip, S. L., Baker, M. L., & Cuthbert, B. P. (2008). Physiological arousal and attention during a week of continuous sleep restriction. *Physiology & Behavior, 95,* 353–364.

Couzin, J. (2004). Volatile chemistry: Children and antidepressants. *Science, 305,* 468–470.

Cowan, C. P., & Cowan, P. A. (2000). *When partners become parents: The big life change for couples.* Mahwah, NJ: Lawrence Erlbaum Associates.

Cowan, N., Lichty, W., & Grove, T. R. (1990). Properties of memory for unattended spoken syllables. *Journal of Experimental Psychology: Learning, Memory, and Cognition, 16,* 258–269.

Cowan, R. L., Lyoo, I. K., Sung, S. M., Ahn, K. H., Kim, M. J., Hwang, J., et al. (2003). Reduced cortical gray matter density in human MDMA (Ecstasy) users: A voxel-based morphology study. *Drug and Alcohol Dependence, 72,* 225–235.

Cowan, R. L., Roberts, D. M., & Joers, J. M. (2008). Neuroimaging in humans MDMA (Ecstasy) users: A cortical model. *Annals of the New York Academy of Sciences, 1139,* 291–298.

Craig, I., & Plomin, R. (2006). Quantitative trait loci for IQ and other complex traits: Single-nucleotide polymorphism genotyping using pooled DNA and microarrays. *Genes, Brain and Behavior, 5*(suppl 1), 32–37.

Craik, F., & Lockhart, R. (1972). Levels of processing: A framework for memory research. *Journal of Verbal Learning & Verbal Behavior, 11,* 671–684.

Craik, F., & Tulving, E. (1975). Depth of processing and the retention of words in episodic memory. *Journal of Experimental Psychology: General, 104,* 268–294.

Craik, F., & Watkins, M. (1973). The role of rehearsal in short-term memory. *Journal of Verbal Learning & Verbal Behavior, 12,* 599–607.

Crane, C., & Williams, J. M. G. (2010). Factors associated with attrition from mindfulness based cognitive therapy for suicidal depression. *Mindfulness, 1,* 10–20.

Cranford, R. (2005). Facts, lies, and videotapes: The permanent vegetative state and the sad case of Terri Schiavo. *The Journal of Law, Medicine & Ethics, 33,* 363–371.

Craske, M., Edlund, M., Sullivan, G., Sherbourne, C., Stein, M., & Bystritsky, A. (2005). Perceived unmet need for mental health treatment and barriers to care among patients with panic disorder. *Psychiatric Services, 56,* 988–994.

Crean, R. D., Crane, N. A., & Mason, B. J. (2011). An evidence-based review of acute and long-term effects of cannabis use on executive cognitive functions. *Journal of Addictive Medicine, 5,* 1–8.

Crescentini, C., Seved-Allaei, S., De Pisapia, N., Jovicich, J., Amati, D., & Shallice, T. (2011). Mechanisms of rule acquisition and rule following in inductive reasoning. *The Journal of Neuroscience, 31,* 7763–7774.

Critchley, H., Daly, E., Phillips, M., Brammer, M., Bullmore, E., Williams, S., et al. (2000). Explicit and implicit neural mechanisms for processing of social information from facial expressions: A functional magnetic resonance imaging study. *Human Brain Mapping, 9,* 93–105.

Crowell, S. E., Beauchaine, T. P., & Linehan, M. M. (2009). A biosocial developmental model of borderline personality: Elaborating and extending Linehan's theory. *Psychological Bulletin, 125,* 495–510.

Crumpton, H. (1997). Persuasive entertainment: Top ten best and worst dressed lists. Paper presented at the Northwest Communication Association Conference, Coeur D'Alene, ID, April 19.

Cruse, D., Chennu, S., Chatelle, C., Bekinschtein, T. A., Fernandez-Espejo, D., Pickard, J. D., et al. (2011). Bedside detection of awareness in the vegetative state: A cohort study. *The Lancet, 378,* 2088–2094.

Cryan, J. F., Markou, A., & Lucki, I. (2002). Assessing antidepressant activity in rodents: Recent developments and future needs. *Trends in Pharmacological Sciences, 23,* 238–245.

Csibra, G., Davis, G., Spratling, M. W., & Johnson, M. H. (2000). Gamma oscillations and object processing in the infant brain. *Science, 290,* 1582–1585.

Cukor, J., Spitalnick, J., Difede, J., Rizzo, A., & Rothbaum, B. O. (2009). Emerging treatments for PTSD. *Clinical Psychology Review, 29,* 715–726.

Cunningham, W. A., Johnson, M. K., Raye, C. L., Gatenby, J. C., Gore, J. C., & Banaji, M. R. (2004). Separable neural components in the processing of Black and White faces. *Psychological Science, 15,* 806–813.

Cutrona, C., Wallace, G., & Wesner, K. (2006). Neighborhood characteristics and depression: An examination of stress processes. *Current Directions in Psychological Science, 15*(4), 188–192.

Cytowic, R. E. (1993). *The man who tasted shapes.* New York: G. P. Putnam's Sons.

D'Argembeau, A., Raffard, S., & Van der Linden, M. (2008). Remembering the past and imaging the future in schizophrenia. *Journal of Abnormal Psychology, 117,* 247–251.

Dagher, A. (2012). Functional brain imaging of appetite. *Trends in Endocrinology and Metabolism, 23,* 250–260.

Dahl, D. W., Sengupta, J., & Vohs, K. D. (2009). Sex in advertising: Gender differences and the role of relationship commitment. *Journal of Consumer Research, 36,* 215–231.

Dahl, R. E. (2001). Affect regulation, brain development, and behavioral/emotional health in adolescence. *CNS Spectrums, 6,* 60–72.

Dal Cin, S., Gibson, B., Zanna, M. P., Shumate, R., & Fong, G. T. (2007). Smoking in the movies, implicit associations of smoking with the self, and intentions to smoke. *Psychological Science, 18,* 559–563.

Dallman, M. F., Pecoraro, N., Akana, S. F., La Fleur, S. E., Gomez, F., Houshyar, H., et al. (2003). Chronic stress and obesity: A new view of "comfort food." *Proceedings of the National Academy of Sciences of the United States of America, 100,* 11696–11701.

Damasio, A. R. (1994). *Descartes' error: Emotion, reason, and the human brain.* New York: Putnam Publishing.

Damisch, L., Stoberock, B., & Mussweiler, T. (2010). Keep your fingers crossed! How superstition improves performance. *Psychological Science, 21,* 1014–1020.

Daneback, K., Cooper, A., & Månsson, S. (2005). An Internet study of cybersex participants. *Archives of Sexual Behavior, 34,* 321–328.

Dani, C., Poggi, C., Romagnoli, C., & Bertini, G. (2009). Survival and major disability rate in infant born at 22–25 weeks of gestation. *Journal of Perinatal Medicine, 37,* 599–608.

Danner, D. D., Snowdon, D. A., & Friesen, W. V. (2001). Positive emotions in early life and longevity: Findings from the nun study. *Journal of Personality and Social Psychology, 80,* 804–813.

DARA. (2012). Climate vulnerability monitor, 2nd Edition: A guide to the cold calculus of a hot planet. Fundacion DARA Internacional 2012, Madrid.

Darley, J. M., & Latané, B. (1968). Bystander intervention in emergencies: Diffusion of responsibility. *Journal of Personality and Social Psychology, 8,* 377–383.

Darmon, N., Briend, A., & Drewmowski, A. (2004). Energy-dense diets are associated with lower diet costs: A community study of French adults. *Public Health Nutrition, 7,* 21–27.

Dar-Nimrod, I., Rawn, C. D., Lehman, D. R., & Schwartz, B. (2009). The maximization paradox: The costs of seeking alternatives. *Personality and Individual Differences, 46,* 631–635.

Darwin, C. (1872). *The expression of the emotions in man and animals.* London: John Murray.

Davidson, R. J., Kabat-Zinn, J., Schumacher, J., Rosenkranz, M., Muller, D., Santorelli, S. F., et al. (2003). Alterations in brain and immune system function produced by mindfulness meditation. *Psychosomatic Medicine, 65,* 564–570.

Davidson, R. J., Putnam, K. M., & Larson, C. L. (2000). Dysfunction in the neural circuitry of emotion regulation: A possible prelude to violence. *Science, 289,* 591–594.

Davis, C., & Scott-Robertson, L. (2000). A psychological comparison of females with anorexia nervosa and competitive male bodybuilders: Body-shape ideals in the extreme. *Eating Behaviors, 1,* 33–46.

Davis, D., & Loftus, E. F. (2009) Expectancies, emotion and memory reports of visual events. In J. R. Brockmole (Ed.), *The Visual World in Memory* (pp. 178–214). New York: Psychology Press.

Dawson, D., & Reid, K. (1997). Fatigue, alcohol and performance impairment. *Nature, 388,* 235.

de Araujo, I. E., & Rolls, E. T. (2004). Representation in the human brain of food texture and oral fat. *Journal of Neuroscience, 24,* 3086–3093.

De Bruin, E., Beersma, D., & Daan, S. (2002). Sustained mental workload does not affect subsequent sleep intensity. *Journal of Sleep Research, 11,* 113–121.

de Gelder, B., & Hadjikhani, N. (2006). Nonconscious recognition of emotional body language. *NeuroReport, 17,* 583–586.

De Irala-Estevez, J., & Groth, M.V. (2000). A systematic review of socioeconomic differences in food habits in Europe: Consumption of fruit and vegetables. *European Journal of Clinical Nutrition, 54,* 706–714.

de Jonghe, F., Kool, S., van Aalst, G., Dekker J., & Peen J. (2001). Combining psychotherapy and antidepressants in the treatment of depression. *Journal of Affective Disorders, 64,* 217–229.

De Los Reyes, A., & Kazdin, A. (2008). When the evidence says, "yes, no, and maybe so": Attending to and interpreting inconsistent findings among evidence-based interventions. *Current Directions in Psychological Science, 17,* 47–51.

de Martino, B., Harrison, N. A., Knafo, S., Bird, G., & Dolan, R. J. (2008). Explain enhances logical consistency during decision making in autism. *The Journal of Neuroscience, 28,* 10746–10750.

de Martino, B., Kumaran, D., Seymour, B., & Dolan, R. J. (2006). Frames, biases, and rational decision-making in the human brain. *Science, 4,* 684–687.

de Vries, R. E., & van Kampen, D. (2010). The HEXACO and 5DPT models of personality: A comparison and their relationships with psychopathy, egoism, pretentiousness, immorality and Machiavelliansim. *Journal of Personality Disorders, 24,* 244–257.

de Waal, F. B. M., & Lanting, F. (1997) *Bonobo: The forgotten ape.* Berkeley and Los Angeles, CA: University of California Press.

De Young, R. (2000). New ways to promote proenvironmental behavior: Expanding and evaluating motives for environmentally responsible behavior. *Journal of Social Issues, 56,* 509–526.

Deary, I. J., & Stough, C. (1996). Intelligence and inspection time: Achievements, prospects, and problems. *American Psychologist, 51,* 599–608.

Deary, I. J., Penke, L., & Johnson, W. (2010). The neuroscience of human intelligence differences. *Nature Reviews Neuroscience, 11,* 201–211.

Deary, I., Strand, S., Smith, P., & Fernandes, C. (2007). Intelligence and educational achievement. *Intelligence, 35,* 13–21.

DeCasper, A. J., & Prescott, P. A. (1984). Human newborns' perception of male voices: Preference, discrimination, and reinforcing value. *Developmental Psychobiology, 17,* 481–491.

DeCasper, A. J., & Spence, M. J. (1986). Prenatal maternal speech influences newborns' perception of speech sounds. *Infant Behavior and Development, 9,* 133–150.

Deci, E. L. (1971). Effects of externally mediated rewards on intrinsic motivation. *Journal of Personality and Social Psychology, 18,* 105–115.

Deci, E. L., & Vansteenkiste, M. (2004). Self-determination theory of basic need satisfaction: Understanding human development in positive psychology. *Risershe di Psicologia, 27,* 23–40.

Deci, E. L., Eghrari, H., Patrick, B. C., & Leone, D. R. (1994). Facilitating internalization: The self-determination theory perspective. *Journal of Personality, 62,* 119–142.

Deci, E. L., Koestner, R., & Ryan, R. M. (1999). A meta-analytic review of experiments examining the effects of extrinsic rewards on intrinsic motivation. *Psychological Bulletin, 125,* 627–668.

Deese, J. (1959). On the prediction of occurrence of particular verbal intrusions in immediate recall. *Journal of Experimental Psychology, 58,* 17–22.

Deese, J., & Kaufman, R. A. (1957). Serial effects in recall of unorganized and sequentially organized verbal material. *Journal of Experimental Psychology, 54,* 180–187.

Delgado, J. M. R., & Anand, B. K. (1952). Increase of food intake induced by electrical stimulation of the lateral hypothalamus. *American Journal of Physiology, 172,* 162–168.

DeLoache, J. S. (1995). Early understanding and use of symbols: The model model. *Current Directions in Psychological Science, 4,* 109–113.

DeLoache, J. S., Uttal, D. H., & Rosengren, K. S. (2004). Scale errors offer evidence for a perception–action dissociation early in life. *Science, 304,* 1027–1029.

DeLongis, A., & Holtzman, S. (2005). Coping in context: The role of stress, social support, and personality in coping. *Journal of Personality, 73,* 1633–1656.

Dennis, N. A., Bowman, C. R., & Vandekar, S. N. (2012). True and phantom recollection: An fMRI investigation of similar and distinct neural correlates and connectivity. *NeuroImage, 59,* 2982–2993.

Depue, R. A., & Collins, P. F. (1999). Neurobiology of the structure of personality: Dopamine, facilitation of incentive motivation, and extraversion. *Behavioral and Brain Sciences, 22,* 491–569.

DeRubeis, R., & Crits-Christoph, P. (1998). Empirically supported individual and group psychological treatments for adult mental disorders. *Journal of Consulting and Clinical Psychology, 66,* 37–52.

Desroches, A. S., & Joanisse, M. (2009). Dyslexia. In E. Goldstein (Ed.), *Encyclopedia of perception* (pp. 371–373). Thousand Oaks, CA: Sage Publications.

Desroches, A. S., Cone, N. E., Bolger, D. J., Bitan, T., Burman, D. D., & Booth, J. R. (2010). Children with reading difficulties show differences in brain regions associated with orthographic processing during spoken language processing. *Brain Research, 1356,* 73–84.

DeYoung, C. G., Hirsh, J. B., Shane, M. S., Papademetris, X., Rajeevan, N., & Gray, J. R. (2010). Testing predictions from personality neuroscience: Brain structure and the Big Five. *Psychological Science, 21,* 820–828.

di Pellegrino, G., Fadiga, I., Fogassi, I., Gallese, V., & Rizzolatti, G. (1992). Understanding motor events: A neurophysiological study. *Experimental Brain Research, 91,* 176–180.

Diamond, M. C., Krech, D., & Rosenzweig, M. R. (1964). The effects of an enriched environment on the histology of the rat cerebral cortex. *Journal of Comparative Neurology, 123,* 111–120.

Diamond, M. C., Scheibel, A. B., Murphy, G. M. Jr., & Harvey, T. (1985). On the brain of a scientist: Albert Einstein. *Experimental Neurology, 88,* 198–204.

DiClemente, C. C., & J. O. Prochaska (1985). Processes and stages of self-change: Coping and competence in smoking behavior change. In Shiffman & T. A. Wills (Eds.), *Coping and substance use.* New York: Academic Press.

DiLalla, L. F., Kagan, J., & Reznick, J. S. (1994). Genetic etiology of behavioral inhibition among 2-year-old children. *Infant Behavior and Development, 17,* 405–412.

Dilworth-Bart, J. E., & Moore, C. F. (2006). Mercy mercy me: Social injustice and the prevention of environmental pollutant exposures among ethnic minority and poor children. *Child Development, 77,* 247–265.

Dingemanse, N. J., Both, C., Drent, P. J., & Tinbergen, J. M. (2004). Fitness consequences in a fluctuating environment. *Proceedings of the Royal Society of London, Series B, 271,* 847–852.

Dinges, D. F. (2006). The state of sleep deprivation: From functional biology to functional consequences. *Sleep Medicine Review, 10,* 303–305.

Dinges, D. F., Maislin, G., Brewster, R. M., Krueger, G. P., & Carroll, R. J. (2005). Pilot test of fatigue management technologies. *Journal of the Transportation Research Board No. 1922, Transportation Research Board of the National Academies, Washington, DC,* 175–182. Retrieved from: http://www .med.upenn.edu/uep/user_documents/ Dingesetal.–TRBProceedingspaper05-1234.pdf

DiPaola, S., Caitlin Riebe, C., & Enns, J. T. (2011). Rembrandt's textural agency: A shared perspective in visual art and science. *Leonardo, 43,* 145–151.

Ditzen, B., Schaer, M., Gabriel, B., Bodenmann, G., Ehlert, U., & Heinrichs, M. (2009). Intranasal oxytocin increases positive communication and reduces cortisol levels during couple conflict. *Biological Psychiatry, 65,* 728–731.

Dixon, M. J., Bub, D. N., & Arguin, M. (1997). The interaction of object form and object meaning in the identification performance of a patient with category specific visual agnosia. *Cognitive Neuropsychology, 14,* 1085–1130.

Dixon, M. J., Desmarais, G., Goimerac, C., Schweizer, T. A., & Bub, D. N. (2002). The role of premorbid expertise on object identification in category-specific visual agnosia. *Cognitive Neuropsychology, 19,* 401–419.

Dixon, M. J., Smilek, D., Cudahy, C., & Merikle, P. M. (2000). Five plus two equals yellow. *Nature, 406,* 365.

Dobkin, P. L. (2008). Mindfulness-based stress reduction: What processes are at work? *Complementary Therapies in Clinical Practice, 14,* 8–16.

Dolcos, F., LaBar, K. S., & Cabeza, R. (2004). Interaction between the amygdala and the medial temporal lobe memory system predicts better memory for emotional events. *Neuron, 42,* 855–863.

Domjan, M., Cusato, B., & Krause, M. A. (2004). Learning with arbitrary versus ecological conditioned stimuli: Evidence from sexual conditioning. *Psychonomic Bulletin and Review, 11,* 232–246.

Done, D. J., Crow, T. J., Johnstone, E. C., & Sacker, A. (1994). Childhood antecedents of schizophrenia and affective illness: Social adjustment at ages 7 and 11. *British Medical Journal, 309,* 699–703.

Douglas, K. S., Guy, L. S., & Hart, S. D. (2009). Psychosis as a risk factor for violence to others: A meta-analysis. *Psychological Bulletin, 135,* 679–706.

Dozois, D., Bieling, P., Patelis-Siotis, I., Hoar, L., Chudzik, S., McCabe, K., et al. (2009). Changes in self-schema structure in cognitive therapy for major depressive disorder: A randomized clinical trial. *Journal of Consulting and Clinical Psychology, 77,* 1078–1088.

Duckitt, J., & Farre, B. (1994). Right-wing authoritarianism and political intolerance among Whites in the future majority-rule South Africa. *Journal of Social Psychology, 134,* 735–741.

Duka, T., Weissenborn, R., & Dienes, Z. (2001). State-dependant effects of alcohol on recollective experience, familiarity and awareness of memories. *Psychopharmacology, 153,* 295–306.

Dunn, K. M., Cherkas, L. F., & Spector, T. D. (2005). Genetic influences on variation in female orgasmic function: A twin study. *Biology Letters, 1,* 260–263.

Durgin, F. H., Baird, J. A., Greenburg, M., Russell, R., Shaughnessy, K., & Waymouth, S. (2009). Who is being deceived? The experimental demands of wearing a backpack. *Psychonomic Bulletin and Review, 16,* 964–969.

Durmer, J. S., & Dinges, D. F. (2005). Neurocognitive consequences of sleep deprivation. *Seminars in Neurology, 25,* 117–129.

Durrant, J., & Ensom, R. (2012). Physical punishment of children: Lessons from 20 years of research. *Canadian Medical Association Journal, 184,* 1373–1376.

Dutton, D. G., & Aron, A. (1974. Some evidence for heightened sexual attraction under conditions of high anxiety. *Journal of Personality and Social Psychology, 30,* 510–517.

Dutton, D. J., & McLaren, L. (2011). Explained and unexplained regional variation in Canadian obesity. *Obesity, 19,* 1460–1468.

Dweck, C. (2002). Beliefs that make smart people dumb. In R. J. Sternberg (Ed.), *Why smart people can be so stupid* (pp. 24–41). New Haven, CT: Yale University Press.

Dykiert, D., Gale, C., & Deary, I. (2009). Are apparent sex differences in mean IQ scores created in part by sample restriction and increased male variance? *Intelligence, 37,* 42–47.

Dzirasa, K., & Covington, H. E. III. (2012). Increasing the validity of experimental models for depression. *Annals of the New York Academy of Sciences, 1265,* 36–45.

Ebbinghaus, H. (1885/1913). *Memory: A contribution to experimental psychology.* [Online]. Retrieved from http://psychclassics.yorku.ca/Ebbinghaus/

Eberhardt, J. L. (2005). Imaging race. *American Psychologist, 60,* 181–190.

Eccles, J. S., & Wigfield, A. (2002). Motivational beliefs, values, and goals. *Annual Review of Psychology, 53,* 109–132.

Edwards, A. S. (1917). The distribution of time in learning small amounts of material. In *Studies in Psychology: Titchener Commemorative Volume* (pp. 209–213). Worcester, MA: Wilson.

Edwards, J. G., Gibson, H. E., Jensen, T., Nugent, F., Walther, C., Blickenstaff, J., & Kauer, J. (2012). A novel non-CB1/TRPV1 endocannabinoid-mediated mechanism depresses excitatory synapses on hippocampal CA1 interneurons. *Hippocampus, 22,* 209–221.

Efrain, M. G., & Patterson, E. W. J. (1974). Voters vote beautiful: The effect of physical appearance on a national election. *Canadian Journal of Behavioural Science/Revue canadienne des sciences du comportement, 6,* 352.

Ehrlich, P. R., & Ehrlich, A. H. (2013). Can a collapse of global civilization be avoided? *Proceedings of the Royal Society B: Biological Sciences, 280,* 1754.

Eich, E., & Metcalfe, J. (1989). Mood dependent memory for internal versus external events. *Journal of Experimental Psychology, 15,* 443–455.

Eich, E., Macaulay, D., & Ryan, L. (1994). Mood dependent memory for events of the personal past. *Journal of Experimental Psychology, 123,* 201–215.

Eich, E., Macaulay, D., Lowenstein, R. J., & Dihle, P. H. (1997). Memory, amnesia, and dissociative identity disorder. *Psychological Science, 8,* 417–422.

Eisenberg, N. (2005). The development of empathy-related responding. In G. Carlo & C. P. Edwards (Eds.), *Moral motivation through the life span* (pp. 73–117). Lincoln, NE: University of Nebraska Press.

Eisenberger, N. I., & Lieberman, M. D. (2004). Why rejection hurts: A common neural alarm system for physical and social pain. *Trends in Cognitive Sciences, 8,* 294–300.

Eiser, A. S. (2005). Physiology and psychology of dreams. *Seminars in Neurology, 25,* 97–105.

Ekman, P., & Friesen, W. V. (1969). The repertoire of nonverbal behavior: Categories, origins, usage, and coding. *Semiotica, 1,* 49–98.

Ekman, P., O'Sullivan, M., & Frank, M. G. (1999). A few can catch a liar. *Psychological Science, 10,* 263–266.

Ekos Research Associates Inc. (2003). Canadian attitudes towards climate change: Spring 2003 tracking study. Retrieved from http://www .queensu .ca/cora/_files/CATCC-2003.pdf

Eldreth, D. A., Matochick, J. A., Cadet, J. L., & Bolla, K. I. (2004). Abnormal brain activity in prefrontal regions in abstinent marijuana users. *NeuroImage, 23,* 914–920.

Elfenbein, H. A., & Ambady, N. (2003). Universals and cultural differences in recognizing emotions. *Current Directions in Psychological Science, 12,* 159–164.

Elfenbein, H. A., Beaupré, M., Lévesque, M., & Hess, U. (2007). Toward a dialect theory: Cultural differences in the expression and recognition of posed facial expressions. *Emotion, 7,* 131–146.

Elkins, G., Marcus, J., Stearns, V., Perfect, M., Rajab, M. H., Ruud, C., et al. (2008). Randomized trial of a hypnosis intervention of hot flashes among breast cancer survivors. *Journal of Clinical Oncology, 26,* 5022–5026.

Elkins, S. R., & Moore, T. M. (2011). A time-series study of the treatment of panic disorder. *Clinical Case Studies, 10,* 3–22.

Elliot, A. J., & McGregor, H. A. (2001). A 2 × 2 achievement goal framework. *Journal of Personality and Social Psychology, 80,* 501–519.

Elliott, R. (2002). The effectiveness of humanistic therapies: A meta-analysis. In D. J. Cain (Ed.), *Humanistic psychotherapies: Handbook of research and practice* (pp. 57–81). Washington, DC: American Psychological Association.

Elliott, R., Bohart, A., Watson, J., & Greenberg, L. (2011). Empathy. *Psychotherapy, 48,* 43–49.

Elliott, R., Friston, K. J., & Dolan, R. J. (2000). Dissociable neural responses in human rewards systems. *Journal of Neuroscience, 20,* 6159–6165.

Elliott, R., Sahakian, B. J., Matthews, K., Bannerjea, A., Rimmer, J., & Robbins, T. W. (1997). Effects of methylphenidate on spatial working memory and planning in healthy young adults. *Psychopharmacology, 131,* 196–206.

Ellis, A. (1962). *Reason and emotion in psychotherapy.* New York: Lyle Stuart.

Ellis, B. J., & Garber, J. (2000). Psychosocial antecedents of variation in girls' pubertal timing: Maternal depression, stepfather presence, and marital and family stress. *Child Development, 71,* 485–501.

Ellis, L., & Ames, M. (1987). Neurohormonal functioning and sexual orientation: A theory of homosexuality–heterosexuality. *Psychological Bulletin, 101,* 233–258.

Environics Research Group. (2005a). 2005 public opinion survey on contaminated sites. Retrieved from http://www.queensu.ca/cora/_files/ECCC- 2005.pdf

Environics Research Group. (2005b). 2005 Environics focus Canada survey (No.EFC051). Retrieved from http://www.queensu.ca/cora/5data.html

Environics Research Group. (2007). Testing of mock-ups of health warning messages and warning notices on tobacco product advertisements for smokeless tobacco. Retrieved from http://www.tobaccolabels.ca/health/canada2007w2

Epel, E., Lapidus, R., McEwen, B., & Brownell, K. (2001). Stress may add bite to appetite in women: A laboratory study of stress-induced cortisol and eating behavior. *Psychoneuroendocrinology, 26,* 37–49.

Epley, N., & Gilovich, T. (2006). The anchoring-and-adjustment heuristic: Why the adjustments are insufficient. *Psychological Science, 17,* 311–318.

Epstein, S. (1994). Integration of the cognitive and the psychodynamic unconscious. *American Psychologist, 49*(8), 709–724.

Ericsson, K. A., & Polson, P. G. (1988). Memory for restaurant orders. In M. Chi, R. Glaser, & M. Farr (Eds.), *The nature of expertise* (pp. 23–70). Hillsdale, NJ: Erlbaum.

Erikson, E. (1963). *Childhood and society.* New York: Norton.

Evans, D., & Rothbart, M. K. (2007). Developing a model for adult temperament. *Journal of Research in Personality, 41,* 868–888.

Evans, G. W., & Schamberg, M. A. (2009). Childhood poverty, chronic stress, and adult working memory. *Proceedings of the National Academy Sciences, 106*(16), 6545–6549.

Evans, G. W., & Stecker, R. (2004). Motivational consequences of environmental stress. *Journal of Environmental Psychology, 24,* 143–165.

Evans, J. M. M., Newton, R. W., Ruta, D. A., MacDonald, T. M., & Morris, A. D. (2000). Socio-economic status, obesity and prevalence of Type 1 and Type 2 diabetes mellitus. *Diabetic Medicine, 17,* 478–480.

Evans, S., Ferrando, S., Findler, M., Stowell, C., Smart, C., & Haglin, D. (2008). Mindfulness-based cognitive therapy for anxiety. *Journal of Anxiety Disorders, 22,* 716–721.

Ewen, S. (1996). *PR! A Social History of Spin.* New York: Basic Books.

Exner, J. E. (1991). *The Rorschach: A comprehensive system. Vol. 2: Interpretation* (2nd ed.). New York: Wiley.

Eysenck, H. J. (1967). *The biological basis of personality.* Springfield, IL: Charles C. Thomas.

Eysenck, H. J. (1994). Personality: Biological foundations. In P. A. Vernon (Ed.), *The neuropsychology of individual differences.* London: Academic Press.

Fairclough, S. H., & Graham, R. (1999). Impairment of driving performance caused by sleep deprivation or alcohol: A comparative study. *Human Factors, 41,* 118–128.

Fakhoury, W., & Priebe, S. (2002) . The process of de-institutionalisation: An international overview. *Current Opinion in Psychiatry, 15,* 187–192.

Falk, E. B., Berkman, E. T., Mann, T., Harrison, B., & Lieberman, M. D. (2010). Predicting persuasion-induced behaviour change from the brain. *The Journal of Neuroscience, 30,* 8521–8424.

Fancher, R. E. (1985). *The intelligence men: Makers of the IQ controversy*. New York: W. W. Norton.

Fancher, R. E. (1990). *Pioneers of psychology*. New York: W. W. Norton & Company.

Fantz, R. L. (1961). The origin of form perception. *Scientific American, 47,* 627–638.

Farb, N. A. S., Segal, Z. V., Mayberg, H., Bean, J., McKeon, D., Fatima, Z., & Anderson, A. K. (2007). Attending to the present: Mindfulness meditation reveals distinct neural modes of self-reference. *Social Cognitive and Affective Neuroscience, 2,* 313–322.

Farb, N. A., Segal, Z. V., & Anderson, A. K. (2013). Mindfulness meditation training alters cortical representations of interoceptive attention. *Social, Cognitive & Affective Neuroscience, 8,* 15–26.

Farber, B. A., & Lane, J. S. (2002). Positive regard. In J. C. Norcross (Ed.), *Psychotherapy relationships that work* (pp. 175–194). New York: Oxford University Press.

Fazel, S., Långström, N., Hjern, A., Grann, M., & Lichtenstein, P. (2009). Schizophrenia, substance abuse, and violent crime. *Journal of the American Medical Association, 301,* 2016–2023.

Fehr, B. (1988). Prototype analysis of the concepts of love and commitment. *Journal of Personality and Social Psychology, 55,* 557–579.

Fein, S., & Spencer, S. J. (1997). Prejudice as self-image maintenance: Affirming the self through derogating others. *Journal of Personality and Social Psychology, 73,* 31–44.

Feinberg, D. R., DeBruine, L. M., Jones, B. C., & Perret, D. I. (2008). The role of femininity and averageness of voice pitch in aesthetic judgements of women's voices. *Perception, 37,* 615–623.

Feinberg, D. R., Jones, B. C., DeBruine, L. M., Moore, F. R., Smith, M. J. L., Cornwell, E. R., et al. (2005). The voice and face of woman: One ornament that signals quality? *Evolution and Human Behavior, 26,* 298–408.

Feldman, J. (2003). The simplicity principle in human concept learning. *Current Directions in Psychological Science, 12,* 227–232.

Fernandez, A., & Alonso, M. A. (2001). The relative value of environmental context reinstatement in free recall. *Psicologica, 22,* 253–266.

Fernando, G. A. (2008). Assessing mental health and psychosocial status in communities exposed to traumatic events: Sri Lanka as an example. *American Journal of Orthopsychiatry, 78,* 229–239.

Ferrer, E., & McArdle, J. J. (2004). An experimental analysis of dynamic hypotheses about cognitive abilities and achievement from childhood to early adulthood. *Developmental Psychology, 40,* 935–952.

Ferster, C. B., & Skinner, B. F. (1957). *Schedules of reinforcement*. Englewood Cliffs, NJ: Prentice Hall.

Festinger, L., & Carlsmith, J. M. (1959). Cognitive consequences of forced compliance. *Journal of Abnormal and Social Psychology, 58,* 203–210.

Festinger, L. (1957). *A theory of cognitive dissonance.* Redwood City, CA: Stanford University Press.

Festinger, L., Reicken, H., & Schachter, S. (1956). *When prophecy fails: A social and psychological study of a modern group that predicted the destruction of the world.* New York: Harper-Torchbooks.

Field, A. E., Austin, S. B., Taylor, C. B., Malspeis, S., Rosner, B., Rockett, H. R., et al. (2003). Relation between dieting and weight change among preadolescents and adolescents. *Pediatrics, 112,* 900–906.

Field, T., Diego, M. A., Hernandez-Reif, M., Deeds, O., & Figuereido, B. (2006). Moderate versus light pressure massage therapy leads to greater weight gain in preterm infants. *Infant Behavior and Development, 29,* 574–578.

Finger, E. C., Marsh, A. A., Mitchell, D. G., Reid, M. E., Sims, C., Budhani, S., et al. (2008). Abnormal ventromedial prefrontal cortex function in children with psychopathic traits during reversal learning. *Archives of General Psychiatry, 65,* 586–594.

Fiscella, K., Tancredi, D., & Franks, P. (2009). Adding socioeconomic status to Framingham scoring to reduce isparities in coronary risk assessment. *American Heart Journal, 157,* 988–994.

Fischer, P., & Greitemeyer, T. (2006). Music and aggression: The impact of sexual-aggressive song lyrics on aggression-related thoughts, emotions, and behaviour toward the same and the opposite sex. *Personality and Social Psychology Bulletin, 32,* 1165–1176.

Fischer, P., Kastenmüller, A., & Greitmeyer, T. (2010). Media violence and the self: The impact of personalized gaming characters in aggressive video games on aggressive behavior. *Journal of Experimental Social Psychology, 46,* 192–195.

Fisher, C., Byrne, J., Edwards, A., & Kahn, E. (1970). A psychophysiological study of nightmares. *Journal of the American Psychoanalytic Association, 18,* 747–782.

Fisher, H. E., Brown, L. L., Aron, A., Strong, G., & Mashek, D. (2010). Reward, addiction, and emotional regulation systems associated with rejection in love. *Journal of Neurophysiology, 104,* 51–60.

Fisher, R. A. (1925). Theory of statistical estimation. *Proceedings of the Cambridge Philosophical Society 22,* 700–725.

Fitzgerald, K. D., Welsh, R. C., Gehring, W. J., Abelson, J. L., Himle, J. A., Liberzon, I., & Taylor, S. F. (2005). Error-related hyperactivity of the anterior cingulate cortex in obsessive–compulsive disorder. *Biological Psychiatry, 57,* 287–294.

Fitzpatrick, E. M., Johnson, E., & Durieux-Smith, A. (2011). Exploring factors that affect age of cochlear implantation in children. *International Journal of Pediatric Otolaryngology, 75,* 1082–1087.

Fivush, R., & Nelson, K. (2004). Culture and language in the emergence of autobiographical memory. *Psychological Science, 15,* 573–577.

Flett, G. L., Krames, L., & Vredenburg, K. (2009). Personality traits in clinical and remitted depression: An analysis of instrumental-agentic and expressive-communal traits. *Current Psychology, 28,* 240–248.

Flora, C. (July 2005). The grandmaster experiment. *Psychology Today Magazine.* Retrieved from http://www.psychologytoday.com/articles/ 200506/the-grandmaster-experiment

Flynn, J. R. (1987). Massive IQ gains in 14 nations: What IQ tests really measure. *Psychological Bulletin, 101,* 171–191.

Flynn, J. R. (2007). *What is intelligence? Beyond the Flynn effect.* New York: Cambridge University Press.

Flynn, J. R., & Rossi-Casé, L. (2011). Modern women match men on Raven's Progressive Matrices. *Personality and Individual Differences, 50,* 799–803.

Flyvbjerg, B. (2006). Five misunderstandings about case-study research. *Qualitative Inquiry, 12,* 219–245.

Foer, J., & Siffre, M. (2008). Caveman: An interview with Michel Siffre. *Cabinet, 30.* Retrieved from http://www.cabinetmagazine .org/issues/30/foer.php

Fogel, S. M., Nader, R., Cote, K. A., & Smith, C. T. (2007). Sleep spindles and learning potential. *Behavioral Neuroscience, 121,* 1–10.

Folkman, S., & Lazarus, R. S. (1980). An analysis of coping in a middle-aged community sample. *Journal of Health and Social Behavior, 21,* 219–239.

Fonagy, P., & Target, M. (1997). Attachment and reflective function: Their role in self-organization. *Development and Psychopathology, 9,* 679–700.

Fonagy, P., Steele, M., Steele, H., Leigh, T., Kennedy, R., Mattoon, G., & Target, M. (1995). Attachment, the reflective self, and borderline states: The predictive specificity of the Adult Attachment Interview and pathological emotional development. In *Attachment theory: Social, developmental, and clinical perspectives* (pp. 233–278). Hillsdale, NJ: Analytic Press.

Fong, G. T., Hammond, D., & Hitchman, S. C. (2009). The impact of pictures on the effectiveness of tobacco warnings. *Bulletin of the World Health Organization, 87*, 640–643.

Fontanilla, D., Johannessen, M., Hajipour, A. R., Cozzi, N. V., Meyer, B. J., & Ruoho, A. E. (2009). The hallucinogen N, N-dimethyltryptamine (DMT) is an endogenous sigma-1 receptor regulator. *Science, 323*, 934–937.

Ford, D. (2002). *The dark side of the light chasers.* New York, NY: Riverhead Books.

Forer, B. R. (1949). The fallacy of personal validation: A classroom demonstration of gullibility. *Journal of Abnormal and Social Psychology* (American Psychological Association); *44*, 118–123.

Forgas, J. P. (Ed.). (2000). *Handbook of affect and social cognition.* Mahwah, NJ: Lawrence Erlbaum Associates Publishers.

Forlini, C., Gauthier, S., & Racine, E. (2013). Should physicians prescribe cognitive enhancers to healthy individuals? *Canadian Medical Association Journal, 185,* 1047–1050.

Foroud, T., Edenberg, H. J., & Crabbe, J. C. (2010). Genetic research: Who is at risk for alcoholism? *Alcohol Research & Health, 33,* 64–75.

Foster, E. M., & Watkins, S. (2010). The value of reanalysis: Television viewing and attention problems. *Child Development, 81*, 368–375.

Foucault, M. (1975). *Discipline and punish: The birth of the prison.* New York: Random House.

Fournier, A. K., Ehrhart, I. J., Glindemann, K. E., & Geller, E. (2004). Intervening to decrease alcohol abuse at university parties: Differential reinforcement of intoxication level. *Behavior Modification, 28*, 167–181.

Fouts, R. S. (1997). *Next of kin: What chimpanzees tell us about who we are.* New York: Avon Books.

Fowler, J. H., & Christakis, N. A. (2008). Dynamic spread of happiness in a large social network: Longitudinal analysis over 20 years in the Framingham Heart Study. *British Medical Journal, 337*, a2338.

Fox, E., Ridgewell, A., & Ashwin, C. (2009). Looking on the bright side: Biased attention and the human serotonin transporter gene. *Proceedings of the Royal Society, B., 276,* 1747–1751.

Fox, J., Blank, M., Rovnyak, V., & Barnett, R. (2001). Barriers to help seeking for mental disorders in a rural impoverished population. *Community Mental Health Journal, 37,* 421–436.

Fox, S. (2005). Health information online. Pew Internet and American Life Project. Retrieved from http://www.pewinternet.org

Fraley, R. C., Brumbaugh, C. C., & Marks, M. J. (2005). The evolution and function of adult attachment: A comparative and phylogenetic analysis. *Journal of Personality and Social Psychology, 89,* 731–746.

Frankel, F. H. (1993). Adult reconstruction of childhood events in the multiple personality literature. *American Journal of Psychiatry, 150,* 954–958.

Frankl, V. (1959). *Man's search for meaning.* New York: Washington Square Press.

Franks, N., & Richardson, T. (2006). Teaching in tandem-running ants. *Nature, 439*, 153.

Fredrickson, B. L. (2001). The role of positive emotions in positive psychology. *American Psychologist, 56,* 218–226.

Fredrickson, B. L. (2003). The value of positive emotions. *American Scientist, 91*, 330–335.

Fredrickson, B. L., & Branigan, C. (2005). Positive emotions broaden the scope of attention and thought-action repertoires. *Cognition and Emotion, 19*, 313–332.

Fredrickson, B. L., & Levenson, R. W. (1998). Positive emotions speed recovery from the cardiovascular sequelae of negative emotions. *Cognition and Emotion, 12*, 191–220.

Freud, A. (1936). *The ego and the mechanisms of defense.* London: Hogarth Press & Institute of Psycho-Analysis.

Freud, A. (1958). Adolescence. *Psychoanalytic Study of the Child, 13*, 255–278.

Freud, S. (1899/2011). *The interpretation of dreams.* New York: Avon.

Freud, S. (1905/2000). *Three essays on the theory of sexuality.* New York: Basic Books Classics.

Freud, S. (1920). *A general introduction to psychoanalysis.* New York: Liveright Publishing.

Frewen, P. A., Dozois, D. J., & Lanius, R. A. (2008). Neuroimaging studies of psychological interventions for mood and anxiety disorders: Empirical and methodological review. *Clinical Psychology Review, 28,* 228–246.

Frias, A., Watkins, P. C., Webber, A. C., & Froh, J. J. (2011). Death and gratitude: Death reflection enahnces gratitude. *The Journal of Positive Psychology, 6*, 154–162.

Fridlund, A. J., Beck, H. P., Goldie, W. D., & Irons, G. (2012). Little Albert: A neurologically impaired child. *History of Psychology, 15,* 302–327.

Fried, P., Watkinson, B., James, D., & Gray, R. (2002). Current and former marijuana use: Preliminary findings of a longitudinal study of the effects on IQ in young adults. *Canadian Medical Association Journal, 166,* 887–891.

Friederich, H. C., Brooks, S., Uher, R., Campbell, I. C., Giampietro, V., Brammer, M., et al. (2010). Neural correlated of body dissatisfaction in anorexia nervosa. *Neuropsychologia, 48,* 2878–2885.

Friedman, H. S., & Booth-Kewley, S. (1987). The "disease-prone personality": A meta-analytic view of the construct. *American Psychologist, 42*, 539–555.

Friedman, M., & Rosenman, R. H. (1974). *Type A behavior and your heart.* New York: Knopf.

Frigerio, A., Ceppi, E., Rusconi, M., Giorda, R., Raggi, M. E., & Fearon, P. (2009). The role played by the interaction between genetic factors and attachment in the stress response in infancy. *Journal of Child Psychology and Psychiatry, 50*, 1513–1522.

Frijters, J. C., Lovett, M. W., Sevcik, R. A., & Morris, R. D. (2013). For methods of identifying change in the context of a multiple component reading intervention for struggling middle school readers. *Reading and Writing, 26,* 539–563.

Frisch, R. E., & Barbieri, R. L. (2002). *Female fertility and body fat connection.* Chicago: University of Chicago Press.

Frodi, A., Bridges, L., & Grolnick, W. (1985). Correlates of mastery-related behavior: A short-term longitudinal study of infants in their second year. *Child Development, 56*, 1291–1298.

Fu, C. H., Abel, K. M., Allin, M. P., Gasston, D., Costafreda, S. G., Suckling, J., et al. (2005). Effects of ketamine on prefrontal and striatal regions in an overt verbal fluency task: A functional magnetic resonance imaging study. *Psychopharmacology, 183,* 92–102.

Fujioka, T., Mourad, N., & Trainor, L. J. (2011). Development of auditory-specific brain rhythm in infants. *European Journal of Neuroscience, 33,* 521–529.

Fukushima, H., Terasawa, Y., & Umeda, S. (2011). Association between interoception and empathy: Evidence from heartbeat-evoked brain potential. *International Journal of Psychophysiology, 79,* 259–265.

Fulda, S., & Schulz, H. (2003). Cognitive dysfunction in sleep-related breathing disorders: A meta-analysis. *Sleep Research Online, 5,* 13–43.

Fuller, R., Nopoulos, P., Arndt, S., O'Leary, D., Ho, B. C., & Andreasen, N. C. (2002). Longitudinal assessment of premorbid cognitive functioning in patients with schizophrenia through examination of standardized scholastic test performance. *American Journal of Psychiatry, 159,* 1183–1189.

Furley, P., Memmert, D., & Heller, C. (2010). The dark side of visual awareness in sport—inattentional blindness in a real-world basketball task. *Attention, Perception, & Psychophysics, 72,* 1327–1337.

Gaertner, S. L., & Dovidio, J. F. (2000). *Reducing intergroup bias: The common ingroup identity model.* New York: Psychology Press.

Gais, S., Molle, M., Helms, K., & Born, J. (2002). Learning-dependent increases in sleep spindle density. *Journal of Neuroscience, 22*, 6830–6834.

Galaburda, A. M., & Pandya, D. N. (1982). Role of architectonics and connections in the study of primate brain evolution. In E. Armstrong et al. (Eds.), *Primate brain evolution* (pp. 203–216). New York: Plenum Press.

Galanter, E. (1962). Contemporary psychophysics. In R. Brown, E. Galanter, E. H. Hess, & G. Mandler (Eds.), *New directions in psychology* (p. 231). New York: Holt, Rinehart, & Winston.

Gallagher, M., Graham, P. W., & Holland, P. C. (1990). The amygdala central nucleus and appetitive Pavlovian conditioning: Lesions impair one of conditioned behavior. *The Journal of Neuroscience, 10,* 1906–1911.

Gallagher, R. P. (2007). *National Survey of Counseling Center Directors (2007).* Washington, DC: International Association of Counseling Services. Retrieved from http://www.iacsinc.org/

Gallo, D., Roberts, M., & Seamon, J. (1997). Remembering words not presented in lists: Can we avoid creating false memories? *Psychonomic Bulletin & Review, 4,* 271–276.

Gallup Poll. (2005, November 1). Paranormal beliefs come (super)naturally to some. Retrieved from http://www.gallup.com/poll/19558/paranormal-beliefs-come-supernaturally-some.aspx

Gallup Poll. (2009, February 11). On Darwin's birthday, only 4 in 10 believe in evolution. Retrieved from http://www.gallup.com/poll/114544/ darwin-birthday-believe-evolution.aspx

Galobardes, B., Smith, G. D., & Lynch, J. W. (2006). Systematic review of the influence of childhood socioeconomic circumstances on risk for cardiovascular disease in adulthood. *Annals of Epidemiology, 16,* 91–104.

Galton, F. (1869). *Hereditary genius.* London: Macmillan.

Galvan, A., Hare, T. A., Parra, C. E., Penn, J., Voss, H., Glover, G., & Casey, B. J. (2006). Earlier development of the accumbens relative to orbitofrontal cortex might underlie risk-taking behavior in adolescents. *The Journal of Neuroscience, 26,* 6885–6892.

Garb, H. N., Wood, J. M., Lilienfeld, S. O., & Nezworski, M. T. (2005). Roots of the Rorschach controversy. *Clinical Psychology Review, 25,* 97–118.

Garbutt, J. (2009). The state of pharmacotherapy for the treatment of alcohol dependence. *Journal of Substance Abuse Treatment, 36,* S15–S23.

Garcia, J., Ervin, F. R., & Koelling, R. A. (1966). Learning with prolonged delay of reinforcement. *Psychonomic Science, 5,* 121–122.

Gardner, D. (2008). *Risk.* Toronto: McClelland & Stewart.

Gardner, H. (1983). *Frames of mind: The theory of multiple intelligences.* New York: Basic Books.

Gardner, H. (1999). *Intelligence reframed: Multiple intelligences for the 21st century.* New York: Basic Books.

Gardner, R. A., Gardner, B. T., & VanCantfort, T. E. (1989). *Teaching sign language to chimpanzees.* Albany, NY: State University of New York Press.

Garland, E. L., Fredrickson, B. L., Kring, A. M., Johnson, D. P., Meyer, P. S., & Penn, D. L. (2010). Upward spirals of positive emotions counter downward spirals of negativity: Insights from the broaden-and-build theory and affective neuroscience on the treatment of emotion dysfunctions and deficits in psychopathology. *Clinical Psychology Review, 30,* 849–864.

Garrow, J. S., & Stalley, S. (1975). Is there a "set point" for human body weight? *Proceedings of the Nutrition Society, 34,* 84–85.

Garry, M., & Polaschek, D. (2000). Imagination and memory. *Current Directions in Psychological Science, 9,* 6–10.

Garry, M., Manning, C., Loftus, E., & Sherman, S. (1996). Imagination inflation: Imagining a childhood event inflates confidence that it occurred. *Psychonomic Bulletin & Review, 3,* 208–214.

Gaudet, S., Clement, R., & Deuzeman, K. (2005). Daily hassles, ethnic identity and psychological adjustment among Lebanese-Canadians. *International Journal of Psychology, 40,* 157–168.

Gauthier, I., & Tarr, M. J. (*1997*). Becoming a "Greeble" expert: Exploring mechanisms for face recognition. *Vision Research, 37,* 1673–1682.

Gauthier, I., Skudlarski, P., Gore, J. C., & Anderson, A. W. (2000). Expertise for cars and birds recruits brain areas involved in face recognition. *Nature Neuroscience, 3,* 191–197.

Gauthier, I., Tarr, M. J., Anderson, A. W., Skudlarski, P., & Gore, J. C. (1999). Activation of the middle fusiform "face area" increases with expertise in recognizing novel objects. *Nature Neuroscience, 2,* 568–573.

Gawronski, B., Deutsch, R., & Seidel, O. (2005). Contextual influences on implicit evaluation: Additive versus contrastive effects of evaluative context stimuli in affective priming. *Personality and Social Psychology Bulletin, 31,* 1226–1236.

Gawryluk, J. R., D'arcy, R. C. N., Connolly, J. F., & Weaver, D. F. (2010). Improving the clinical assessment of consciousness with advances in electrophysiological and neuroimaging techniques. *Neurology, 10,* 1–7.

Geake, J. G., & Hansen, P. C. (2010). Functional neural correlates of fluid and crystallized intelligence. *Neuroimage, 49,* 3489–3497.

Geier, A., Rozin, P., & Doros, G. (2006). Unit bias: A new heuristic that helps explain the effect of portion size on food intake. *Psychological Science, 17,* 521–525.

Geller, E. S., Winett, R. A., & Everett, P. B. (1982). *Preserving the environment: New strategies for behavior change.* New York: Pergamon Press.

Geller, J., Cockell, S. J., Hewitt, P. L., Goldner, E. M., & Flett, G. L. (2000). Inhibited expression of negative emotions and interpersonal orientation in anorexia nervosa. *International Journal of Eating Disorders, 28,* 8–19.

Gelman, M., Kosma, L., Wurm, C. S., & Keks, N. (2000). Viktor Emil Frankl 1905–1997. *American Journal of Psychiatry, 157,* 625.

Gershoff, E. T. (2002). Parental corporal punishment and associated child behaviors and experiences: A meta-analytic and theoretical review. *Psychological Bulletin, 128,* 539–579.

Gershoff, E. T., & Bitensky, S. H. (2007). The case against corporal punishment of children: Converging evidence from social science research and international human rights law and implications for U.S. public policy. *Psychology, Public Policy, and the Law, 13,* 231–272.

Geschwind, N., Peeters, F., Drukker, M., van Os, J., & Wichers, M. (2011). Mindfulness training increases momentary positive emotions and reward experience in adults vulnerable to depression: A randomized controlled trial. *Journal of Consulting and Clinical Psychology, 79,* 618–628.

Gibbons, M., Crits-Christoph, P., & Hearon, B. (2008). The empirical status of psychodynamic therapies. *Annual Review of Clinical Psychology, 4,* 93–108.

Gibson, E. J., & Walk, R. D. (1960). The "visual cliff." *Scientific American, 202,* 67–71.

Giedd, J. N. (2008). The teen brain: Insights from neuroimaging. *Journal of Adolescent Health, 42,* 335–343.

Gigerenzer, G. (2004). Dread risk, September 11, and fatal traffic accidents. *Psychological Science, 15,* 286–287.

Gillham, N. W. (2001). *A life of Sir Francis Galton: From African exploration to the birth of eugenics.* New York: Oxford University Press.

Gilligan, C. (1982). *In a different voice: Psychological theory and women's development.* Cambridge, MA: Harvard University Press.

Gilovich, T., & Griffin, D. (2002). Introduction: Heuristics and biases: Then and now. In T. Gilovich, D. Griffin, & D. Kahneman (Eds.), *Heuristics and biases: The psychology of intuitive judgment* (pp. 1–18). New York: Cambridge University Press.

Gilovich, T., Vallone, R., & Tversky, A. (1985). The hot hand in basketball: On the misperception of random sequences. *Cognitive Psychology, 17,* 295–314.

Glaser, J. P., Os, J. V., Mengelers, R., & Myin-Germeys, I. (2008). A momentary assessment study of the reputed emotional phenotype associated with borderline personality disorder. *Psychological Medicine, 30,* 1–9.

Glenberg, A., Smith, S., & Green, C. (1977). Type I rehearsal: Maintenance and more. *Journal of Verbal Learning & Verbal Behavior, 16,* 339–352.

Glenn, N. D. (1990). Quantitative research on marital quality in the 1980s: A critical review. *Journal of Marriage and the Family, 52,* 818–831.

Glick, P., & Fiske, S. T. (1996). The ambivalent sexism inventory: Differentiating hostile and benevolent sexism. *Journal of Personality and Social Psychology, 70,* 491–512.

Glick, P., & Fiske, S. T. (2001). An ambivalent alliance: Hostile and benevolent sexism as complementary justifications for gender inequality. *American Psychologist, 56,* 109–118.

Glindemann, K. E., Ehrhart, I. J., Drake, E. A., & Geller, E. S. (2007). Reducing excessive alcohol consumption at university fraternity parties: A cost-effective incentive/reward intervention. *Addictive Behaviors, 32,* 39–48.

Gobet, F., & Simon, H. A. (1998). Expert chess memory: Revisiting the chunking hypothesis. *Memory, 6,* 225–255.

Godden, D. R., & Baddeley, A. D. (1975). Context-dependent memory in two environments: On land and underwater. *British Journal of Psychology, 66,* 325–331.

Godfrin, K. A., & van Heeringen, C. (2010). The effects of mindfulness-based cognitive therapy on recurrence of depressive episodes, mental health and quality of life: A randomized controlled study. *Behaviour Research and Therapy, 48,* 738–746.

Goel, V., & Dolan, R. J. (2004). Differential involvement of left parietal cortex in inductive and deductive reasoning. *Cognition, 93,* B109–121.

Goff, L.M., & Roediger III, H. L. (1998). Imagination inflation for action events: Repeated imaginings lead to illusory recollections. *Memory & Cognition, 26,* 20–33.

Gogtay, N., Giedd, J. N., Lusk, L., Hayashi, K. M., Greenstein, D., Vaituzis, C., et al. (2004). Dynamic mapping of human cortical development during childhood through early adulthood. *Proceedings of the National Academy of Sciences, 101,* 8174–8179.

Goh, J. O., Chee, M. W., Tan, J. C., Venkatraman, V., Hebrank, A., Leshikar, E. D., et al. (2007). Age and culture modulate object processing and object-scene binding in the ventral visual area. *Cognitive, Affective, & Behavioral Neuroscience, 7,* 44–52.

Goland, R. S., Wardlaw, S. L., MacCarter, G., Warren, W. B., & Stark, R. I. (1991). Adrenocorticotropin and cortisol responses to vasopressin during pregnancy. *Journal of Clinical Endocrinology and Metabolism, 73,* 257–261.

Golden, W. L. (2007). Cognitive-behavioral hypnotherapy in the treatment of irritable-bowel-syndrome-induced agoraphobia. *International Journal of Clinical and Experimental Hypnosis, 55,* 131–146.

Goldstein, A., & Flett, G. L. (2009). Personality, alcohol use, and drinking motives: A comparison of independent and combined internal drinking motives groups. *Behavior Modification, 33,* 182–198.

Goldstein, A. L., Flett, G. L., Wekerle, C., & Wall, A-M. (2009). Personality, child maltreatment, and substance use: Examining correlates of deliberate self-harm among university students. *Canadian Journal of Behavioural Sciences, 41,* 241–251.

Goldstein, R. B., Compton, W. M., Pulay, A. J., Ruan, W. J., Pickering, R. P., Stinson, F. S., & Brant, B. F. (2007). Antisocial behavioral syndromes and DSM-IV drug use disorders in the United States: Results from the National Epidemiologic Survey on Alcohol Related Conditions. *Drug and Alcohol Dependence, 90,* 145–158.

Gollan, T. H., & Acenas, L. R. (2004). What is a TOT? Cognate and translation effects on tip-of-the-tongue states in Spanish-English and Tagalog-English bilinguals. *Journal of Experimental Psychology: Learning, Memory, and Cognition, 30,* 246–269.

Gollwitzer, P. M. (1999). Implementation intentions: Strong effects of simple plans. *American Psychologist, 54,* 493–503.

Gomez, R., Cooper, A., & Gomez, A. (2000). Susceptibility to positive and negative mood states: Test of Eysenck's, Gray's, and Newman's theories. *Personality and Individual Differences, 29,* 351–365.

Goodale, M. A., Milner, A. D., Jakobson, L. S., & Carey, D. P. (1991). A neurological dissociation between perceiving objects and grasping them. *Nature, 349,* 154–156.

Goodall, J., & Berman, P. (1999). *A reason for hope: A spiritual journey.* New York: Warner Books.

Goodman, M. B. & Moradi, B. (2008). Attitudes and behaviors toward lesbian and gay persons: Critical correlates and mediated relations. *Journal of Counseling Psychology, 55,* 371–384.

Goodwin, D. W., Powell, B., Bremer, D., Hoine, H., & Stern, J. (1969). Alcohol and recall: State-dependent effects in man. *Science, 163,* 1358–1360.

Gopnik, A. (2010). *The philosophical baby.* New York: Farrar, Straus, & Giroux.

Gorn, G. J. (1982). The effects of music on advertising on choice behavior: A classical conditioning approach. *Journal of Marketing, 46,* 94–101.

Gosling, S. D. (2001). From mice to men: What can we learn about personality from animal research? *Psychological Bulletin, 127,* 45–86.

Gosling, S. D. (2008). *Snoop: What your stuff says about you.* New York: Basic Books.

Gosling, S. D., Ko, S. J., Mannarelli, T., & Morris, M. E. (2002). A room with a cue: Personality judgments based on offices and bedrooms. *Personality Processes and Individual Differences, 82,* 379–398.

Gosselin, N., Peretz, I., Noulhiane, M., Hasboun, D., Beckett, C., Baulac, M., & Samson, S. (2005). Impaired recognition of scary music following unilateral temporal lobe excision. *Brain, 128,* 628–640.

Gotlib, I., & Hamilton, J. (2008). Neuroimaging and depression: Current status and unresolved issues. *Current Directions in Psychological Science, 17,* 159–163.

Gottesman, I. (1991). *Schizophrenia genesis.* New York: W. H. Freeman.

Gottesman, I., & Gould, T. D. (2003). The endophenotype concept in psychiatry: Etymology and strategic intentions. *American Journal of Psychiatry, 160,* 636–645.

Gottfredson, L. S. (2003). On Sternberg's "Reply to Gottfredson." *Intelligence, 31,* 415–424.

Gottfredson, L. S. (2005). What if the hereditarian hypothesis is true? *Psychology, Public Policy, and Law, 11,* 311–319.

Gottfredson, L. S., & Deary, I. J. (2004). Intelligence predicts health and longevity, but why? *Current Directions in Psychological Science, 13,* 1–4.

Gottlieb, B. H., Still, E., & Newby-Clark, I. R. (2007). Types and precipitants of growth and decline in emerging adulthood. *Journal of Adolescent Research, 22,* 1–24.

Gottman, J. M., & Levenson, R. W. (1992). Marital processes predictive of later dissolution: Behavior, physiology and health. *Journal of Personality and Social Psychology, 63,* 221–233.

Gottman, J., & Levenson, R. W. (2002). A two-factor model for predicting when a couple will divorce: Exploratory analyses using 14-year longitudinal data. *Family Process, 41,* 83–96.

Gouin, J.-P., & Kiecolt-Glaser, J. K. (2011). The impact of psychological stress on wound healing: Methods and mechanisms. *Immunology and Allergy Clinics of North America, 31,* 81–93.

Gouin, J.-P., Carter, C. S., Pournajafi-Nazarloo, H., Glaser, R., Malarkey, W. B., Loving, T. J., et al. (2010). Marital behavior, oxytocin, vasopressin, and wound healing. *Psychoneuroendocrinology, 35,* 1082–1090.

Gould, M. S., Greenberg, T., Velting, D. M., & Shaffer, D. (2003). Youth suicide risk and preventive interventions: A review of the past 10 years. *Journal of the American Academy of Child and Adolescent Psychiatry, 42,* 386–405.

Gould, S. J. (1981). *The mismeasure of man.* New York: W. W. Norton.

Grabner, R. H., Stern, E., & Neubauer, A. C. (2003). When intelligence loses its impact: Neural efficiency during reasoning in a familiar area. *International Journal of Psychophysiology, 49,* 89–98.

Graf, P., & Schacter, D. L. (1985). Implicit and explicit memory for new associations normal and amnesic subjects. *Journal of Experimental Psychology: Learning, Memory, and Cognition, 11,* 501–518.

Graham, E. R., & Burke, D. M. (2011). Aging increases inattentional blindness to the gorilla in our midst. *Psychology and Aging, 26,* 162–166.

Graham, K., & Wells, S. (2004). Aggression among young adults in the social context of the bar. *Addiction Research and Theory, 9,* 193–219.

Grahn, J. A. (2009). The role of the basal ganglia in beat perception. *The Neurosciences and Music III—Disorders and Plasticity, 1169,* 35–45.

Grahn, J. A., & McAuley, J. D. (2009). Neural bases of individual differences in beat perception. *NeuroImage, 47,* 1894–1903.

Granpeesheh, D., Tarbox, J., & Dixon, D. R. (2009). Applied behavior analytic interventions for children with autism: A description and review of treatment research. *Annals of Clinical Psychiatry, 21,* 162–173.

Grant, H. M., Bredahl, L. C., Clay, J., Ferrie, J., Groves, J. E., McDorman, T. A., & Dark, V. J. (1998). Context-dependent memory for meaningful material: Information for students. *Applied Cognitive Psychology, 12,* 617–623.

Grant, J. A., & Rainville, P. (2009). Pain sensitivity and analgesic effects of mindful states in Zen meditators: A cross-sectional study. *Psychosomatic Medicine, 71,* 106–114.

Gray, J. (1992). *Men are from Mars, women are from Venus.* New York: Harper-Collins.

Gray, J. A. (1991). Neural systems, emotion and personality. In J. Madden IV (Ed.), *Neurobiology of learning, emotion and affect.* New York: Raven Press.

Gray, J. A., & McNaughton, N. (2000). *The neuropsychology of anxiety: An enquiry into the functions of the septo-hippocampal system.* New York: Oxford University Press.

Green, A. E., Fugelsang, J. A., & Dunbar, K. N. (2006). Automatic activation of categorical and abstract analogical relations in analogical reasoning. *Memory & Cognition, 34,* 1414–1421.

Greenberg, L., Elliott, R., & Lietaer, G. (1994). Research on experiential psychotherapies. In A. E. Bergin & S. L. Garfield (Eds.), *Handbook of psychotherapy and behavior change* (4th ed., pp. 509–542). New York: Guilford.

Greenberg, L. S. (2004). Emotion-focused therapy. *Clinical Psychology & Psychotherapy, 11,* 3–16.

Greenberg, L. S., & Watson, J. C. (1998). Experiential therapy of depression: Differential effects of client-centered relationship conditions and process-experiential interventions. *Psychotherapy Research, 8,* 210–224.

Green-Demers, I., Pelletier, L. G., & Menard, S. (1997). The impact of behavioural difficulty on the saliency of the association between self-determined motivation and environmental behaviours. *Canadian Journal of Behavioural Science, 29,* 157–166.

Greene, J. D., Sommerville, R. B., Nystrom, L. E., Darley, J. M., & Cohen, J. D. (2001). An fMRI investigation of emotional engagement in moral judgment. *Science, 293,* 2105–2108.

Greene, J., & Haidt, J. (2002). How (and where) does moral judgment work? *Trends in Cognitive Sciences, 6,* 517–523.

Greenwald, A. G., & Banaji, M. R. (1995). Implicit social cognition: Attitudes, self-esteem, and stereotypes. *Psychological Review, 102,* 4–27.

Greenwald, A. G., McGhee, D. E., & Schwartz, J. L. K. (1998). Measuring individual differences in implicit cognition: The implicit association test. *Journal of Personality and Social Psychology, 74,* 1464–1480.

Greenwald, A. G., Spangenberg, E. R., Pratkanis, A. R., & Eskenazi, J. (1991). Double-blind tests of subliminal self-help audiotapes. *Psychological Science, 2,* 119–122.

Greenwood, C. E., & Winocur, G. (2005). High-fat diets, insulin resistance and declining cognitive function. *Neurobiology of Aging, 26,* 42–45.

Gregory, W. L., Cialdini, R. B., & Carpenter, K. M. (1982). Self-relevant scenarios as mediators of likelihood estimates and compliance: Does imagining make it so? *Journal of Personality and Social Psychology, 43,* 89–99.

Greven, C. U., Harlaar, N., Kovas, Y., Chamorro-Premuzic, T., & Plomin, R. (2009). More than just IQ: School achievement is predicted by self-perceived abilities—but for genetic rather than environmental reasons. *Psychological Science, 20,* 753–762.

Grice, P. (1975). Logic and conversation. In P. Cole & J. Morgan (Eds.), *Syntax and semantics* (p. 3). New York: Academic Press.

Griffin, D. W., & Ross, L. (1991). Subjective construal, social inference, and human misunderstanding. In M. P. Zanna (Ed.), *Advances in experimental social psychology* (Vol. 24, pp. 319–359). New York: Academic Press.

Griffin, J. A., Umstattd, M. R., & Usdan, S. (2010). Alcohol use and high-risk sexual behaviour among collegiate women: A review of research on alcohol myopia theory. *Journal of American College Health, 58,* 523–532.

Griffiths, R. R., Richards, W. A., Johnson, M. W., McCann, U. D., & Jesse, R. (2008). Mystical-type experiences occasioned by psilocybin mediate the attribution of personal meaning and spiritual significance 14 months later. *Journal of Psychopharmacology, 22,* 621–632.

Grolnick, W. S., & Apostoleris, N. H. (2002). What makes parents controlling? In E. L. Deci & R. M. Ryan (Eds.), *Handbook of self determination research* (pp. 161–181). Rochester, NY: University of Rochester Press.

Grolnick, W. S., & Ryan, R. M. (1989). Parent styles associated with children's self-regulation and competence in school. *Journal of Educational Psychology, 81,* 143–153.

Gropper, S. S., Simmons, K. P., Gaines, A., Drawdy, K., Saunders, D., Ulrich, P., & Connell, L. J. (2009). The freshman 15: A closer look. *Journal of American College Health, 58,* 223–231.

Gross, C. G. (1998). *Brain, vision, memory: Tales in the history of neuroscience.* Cambridge, MA: MIT Press.

Gross, E. F. (2004). Adolescent Internet use: What we expect, what teens report. *Applied Developmental Pscyhology, 25,* 633–649.

Gruber, S. A., & Yurgelun-Todd, D. A. (2005). Neuroimaging of marijuana smokers during inhibitory processing: A pilot investigation. *Cognitive Brain Research, 23,* 107–118.

Gudonis, L. C., Derefinko, K., & Giancola, P. R. (2009). The treatment of substance misuse in psychopathic individuals: Why heterogeneity matters. *Substance Use & Misuse, 44*(9–10), 1415–1433.

Gustaffson, J. E. (1988). Hierarchical models of individual differences in cognitive abilities. In R. J. Sternberg (Ed.), *Advances in the psychology of human intelligence, Vol. 4* (pp. 35–71). Hillsdale, NJ: Erlbaum.

Gutchess, A. H., Hedden, T., Ketay, S., Aron, A., & Gabrieli, J. D. (2010). Neural differences in the processing of semantic relationships across cultures. *Social Cognitive and Affective Neuroscience, 5,* 254–263.

Guthrie, E. R. (1952). *The psychology of learning.* New York: Harper & Row.

Haber, J., & Jacob, T. (2007). Alcoholism risk moderation by a socio-religious dimension. *Journal of Studies on Alcohol and Drugs, 68,* 912–922.

Haddock, G., & Zanna, M. P. (1997). Impact of negative advertising on evaluations of political candidates: The 1993 Canadian federal election. *Basic and Applied Social Psychology, 19,* 205–223.

Haddock, G., Zanna, M. P., & Esses, V. M. (1993). Assessing the structure of prejudicial attitudes: The case of attitudes toward homosexuals. *Journal of Personality and Social Psychology, 65,* 1105–1118.

Hahn, C., Cowell, J. M., Wiprzycka, U. J., Goldstein, D., Ralph, M., Heasher, L., & Zelazo, P. D. (2012). Circadian rhythms in executive function during the transition to adolescence: The effect of synchrony between chronotype and time of day. *Developmental Science, 15,* 408–416.

Haidt, J. (2001). The emotional dog and its rational tail: A social intuitionist approach to moral judgment. *Psychological Review, 108,* 814–834.

Haier, R. J., Jung, R., Yeo, R. A., Head, K., & Alkire, M. T. (2005). The neuroanatomy of general intelligence: Sex matters. *NeuroImage, 25,* 320–327.

Haier, R. J., Siegel, B. V., Tang, C., Abel, L., & Buchsbaum, M. S. (1992). Intelligence and changes in regional cerebral glucose metabolic rate following learning. *Intelligence 16,* 415–426.

Hakuta, K., Bialystok, E., & Wiley, E. (2003). Critical evidence: A test of the critical-period hypothesis for second-language acquisition. *Psychological Science, 14,* 31–38.

Halberg, F., Peterson, R. E., & Silber, R. H. (1959). Phase relations of 24-hour periodicities in blood corticosterone, mitoses in cortical adrenal parenchyma and total body activity. *Endocrinology, 64,* 222–230.

Hall, G. S. (1904). *Adolescence* (Vols. 1 & 2). New York: Appleton.

Halpern, D. F. (1996). *Thought and knowledge: An introduction to critical thinking.* Mahwah, NJ: Lawrence Erlbaum.

Halpern, D. F., & Lamay, M. L. (2000). The smarter sex: A critical review of sex differences in intelligence. *Educational Psychology Review, 12,* 229–246.

Halpern-Fisher, B. L., Cornell, J. L., Kropp, R. Y., & Tschann, J. M. (2005). Oral versus vaginal sex among adolescents: Perceptions, attitudes, and behavior. *Pediatrics, 4,* 845–851.

Hamlin, J. K., Wynn, K., & Bloom, P. (2007). Social evaluation by preverbal infants. *Nature, 450,* 557–560.

Hamlin, J. K., Wynn, K., & Bloom, P. (2010). Three-month-olds show a negativity bias in their social evaluations. *Developmental Science, 13,* 923–929.

Hamlin, J. K., Wynn, K., Bloom, P., & Mahajan, N. (2011). How infants and toddlers react to antisocial others. *Proceedings of the National Academy of Sciences, 108,* 19931–19936.

Hammond, D. (2011). Health warning messages on tobacco products: A review. *Tobacco Control, 20,* 327–337.

Hammond, D., Ahmed, R., Burkhalter, R., Sae Yang, W., & Leatherdale, S. (2010). Illicit substance use among Canadian youth: Trends between 2002 and 2008. *Canadian Journal of Public Health, 102,* 7–12.

Hammond, D., Fong, G. T., Borland, R., Cummings, K. M., McNeill, A., & Driezen, P (2007). Communicating risk to smokers: The impact of health warnings on cigarette packages. *American Journal of Preventive Medicine, 32,* 202–209.

Hammond, D., Fong, G. T., McDonald, P. W., Cameron, R., & Brown, K. S. (2003). Impact of thegraphic Canadian warning labels on adult smoking behavior. *Tobacco Control, 12,* 391–395.

Hane, A. A., Feldstein, S., & Dernetz, V. H. (2003). The relation between coordinated interpersonal timing and maternal sensitivity in four-month-old infants. *Journal of Psycholinguistic Research, 32,* 525–539.

Hannah, S. (2005). Feature representations and analytic/nonanalytic processing. *Canadian Journal of Experimental Psychology, 59,* 41–46.

Hardisty, D. J., Johnson, E. J., & Weber, E. U. (2010). A dirty word or a dirty world? Attribute framing, political affiliation, and query theory. *Psychological Science, 21,* 86–92.

Hare, R. D. (1985). Comparison of procedures for the assessment of psychopathy. *Journal of Consulting and Clinical Psychology, 53,* 7–16.

Harkness, K. L., Stewart, J. S., & Wynne-Edwards, K. E. (2011). Cortisol reactivity to social stress in adolescents: Role of depression severity and child maltreatment. *Psychoneuroendocrinology, 36,* 173–181.

Harlow, J. M. (1848). Passage of an iron rod through the head. *Boston Medical and Surgical Journal, 39,* 389–393.

Harlow, J. M. (1849). Letter in "medical miscellany." *Boston Medical and Surgical Journal, 39,* 506–507.

Harlow, J. M. (1868). Recovery from the passage of an iron bar through the head. *Publications of the Massachusetts Medical Society, 2,* 327–347.

Harris, J. L., Bargh, J. A., & Brownell, K. D. (2009). Priming effects of television food advertising on eating behavior. *Health Psychology, 28,* 404–413.

Harris, R. B. (1990). Role of set-point theory in regulation of body weight. *The Journal of the Federation of American Societies for Experimental Biology, 4,* 3310–3318.

Hart, B., & Risley, T. R. (1995). *Meaningful differences in the everyday experience of young American children.* Baltimore: Paul H. Brookes.

Hart, J., Berndt, R. S., & Caramazza, A. (1985). Category-specific naming deficit following cerebral infarction. *Nature, 316,* 439–440.

Hartman, E., & Brezler, T. (2008). A systematic change in dreams after 9/11/01. *Sleep, 31,* 213–218.

Harvey, P., & Walker, E. (Eds.). (1987). *Positive and negative symptoms of psychosis: Description, research, and future directions.* Hillsdale, NJ: Lawrence Erlbaum Associates.

Hasher, L., Chung, C., May, C. P., & Foong, N. (2002). Age, time of testing, and proactive interference. *Canadian Journal of Experimental Psychology, 56,* 200–207.

Hatfield, E., & Rapson, R. L. (2009). The neuropsychology of passionate love and sexual desire. In E. Cuyler, & M. Ackart (Eds.), *Psychology of social relationships.* Hauppauge, NY: Nova Science.

Havas, D. A., Glenberg, A. M., Gutowski, K. A., Lucarelli, M. J., & Davidson, R. J. (2010). Cosmetic use of Botulinum toxin-A affects processing of emotional language. *Psychological Science, 21,* 895–900.

Hawkins, R. D. (1984). A cellular mechanism of classical conditioning in *aplysia. Journal of Experimental Biology, 112,* 113–128.

Hawkley, L. C., Burleson, M. H., Berntson, G. G., & Cacioppo, J. T. (2003). Loneliness in everyday life: Cardiovascular activity, psychosocial context, and health behaviors. *Journal of Personality & Social Psychology, 85,* 105–120.

Hayes, K. J., & Hayes, C. (1951). The intellectual development of a home-raised chimpanzee. *Proceedings of the American Philosophical Society, 95,* 105–109.

Hayes, S. C., Luoma, J. B., Bond, F. W., Masuda, A., & Lillis, J. (2006). Acceptance and commitment therapy: Model, processes and outcomes. *Behaviour Research and Therapy, 44,* 1–25.

Hayes, S., Young, R., & Sciortino, M. (2012). *The ACEEE 2012 international energy efficiency scorecard: Report Number E12A.* Washington, D: American Council for an Energy-Efficient Economy.

Hayne, H., Herbert, J., & Simcock, G. (2003). Imitation from television by 24- and 30-month-olds. *Developmental Science, 6,* 254–261.

He, C., Hotson, L., & Trainor, L. J. (2007). Mismatch responses to pitch changes in early infancy. *Journal of Cognitive Neuroscience, 19,* 878–892.

He, C., Hotson, L., & Trainor, L. J. (2009). Development of infant mismatch responses to auditory pattern changes between 2 and 4 months old. *European Journal of Neuroscience, 29,* 861–867.

Health Canada. (2002). *A report on mental illness in Canada.* Ottawa, ON:, Canada.

Health Canada. (2008). Canadian Tobacco Use Monitoring Survey (CTUMS). Retrieved from http://www.hc-sc.gc.ca/hc-ps/tobac-tabac/research-recherche/stat/ctums-esutc_2008-eng.php

Health Canada. (2010). Canadian alcohol and drug use monitoring survey: Summary of results for 2009. Retrieved from http://www.hc-sc.gc.ca/hc-ps/drugs-drogues/stat/_2009/summary-sommaire-eng.php

Health Canada. (2012). Canadian alcohol and drug use monitoring survey: Summary of results for 2011. Retrieved from http://www.hc-sc.gc.ca/hc-ps/drugs-drogues/stat/_2011/ summary-sommaire-eng.php

Healy, J. M. (2004). Early television exposure and subsequent attention problems in children. *American Academy of Pediatrics, 113,* 917–918.

Heath, C., & Heath, D. (2007). *Made to stick: Why some ideas survive and others die.* New York: Random House.

Heatherton, T. F., & Sargent, J. D. (2009). Does watching smoking in movies promote teenage smoking? *Current Directions in Psychological Science, 18,* 63–67.

Heatherton, T. F., & Weinberger, J. L. (Eds.). (1994). *Can personality change?* Washington, DC: American Psychological Association.

Hebb, D. O. (1947). The effects of early experience on problem solving at maturity. *American Psychologist, 2,* 306–307.

Hebb, D. O. (1949). *Organization of behavior: A Neuropsychological theory.* New York: John Wiley.

Hébert, S., & Peretz, I. (1997). Recognition of music in long-term memory: Are melodic and temporal patterns equal partners? *Memory & Cognition, 25,* 518–533.

Heider, F. (1958). *The psychology of interpersonal relations.* New York: Wiley.

Heine, S. J. (2003). An exploration of cultural variation in self-enhancing and self-improving motivations. In V. Murphy-Berman & J. J. Berman (Eds.), *Nebraska symposium on motivation: Vol. 49. Cross-cultural differences in perspectives on the self* (pp. 101–128). Lincoln: University of Nebraska Press.

Heine, S. J., & Buchtel, E. E. (2009). Personality: The universal and the culturally specific. *Annual Review of Psychology, 60,* 369–394.

Heinrichs, M., Baumgartner, T., Kirchbaum, C., & Ehlert, U. (2003). Social support and oxytocin interact to suppress cortisol and subjective responses to psychosocial stress. *Biological Psychiatry, 54,* 1389–1398.

Heinz, A., & Schlagenhauf, F. (2010). Dopaminergic dysfunction in schizophrenia: Salience attribution revisited. *Schizophrenia Bulletin, 36,* 472–485.

Hempel, A., Hempel, E., Schönknecht, P., Stippich, C., & Schröder, J. (2003). Impairment in basal limbic function in schizophrenia during affect cognition. *Psychiatry Research, 122,* 115–124.

Hemphill, E., Raine, K., Spence, J. C., & Smoyer-Tomic, K. E. (2008). Exploring obesogenic food environments in Edmonton, Canada: The association between socioeconomic factors and fast-food outlet access. *American Journal of Health Promotion, 22,* 426–432.

Hendrick, C., Hendrick, S. S., & Reich, D. A. (2006). The brief sexual attitudes scale. *Journal of Sex Research, 43,* 76–86.

Hendrickson, A. E., Wagoner, N., & Cowan, M. (1972). An autoradiographic and electron microscopic study of retino-hypothalamic connections. *Zeitschrift für Zellforschung und Mikroskopische Anatomie, 135,* 1–26.

Henrich, J., Heine, S. J., & Norenzayan, A. (2010) The weirdest people in the world? *Behavioral and Brain Sciences, 33,* 61–135.

Herd, D. (2009). Changing images of violence in rap music lyrics: 1979-1997. *Journal of Public Health Policy, 30,* 395–406.

Herlitz, J., Wiklund, I., Caidahl, K., Hartford, M., Haglid, M., & Karlsson, B. W. (1998). The feeling of loneliness prior to coronary artery bypass grafting might be a predictor of short- and long-term postoperative mortality. *European Journal of Vascular and Endovascular Surgery, 16,* 120–125.

Herman, C. P., Roth, D. A., & Polivy, J. (2003). Effects of the presence of others on food intake: A normative interpretation. *Psychological Bulletin, 129,* 873–886.

Herman, L. M. (2002). Vocal, social, and self-imitation by bottlenosed dolphins. In C. Nehaniv & K. Dautenhahn (Eds.), *Imitation in animals and artifacts* (pp. 63–108). Cambridge, MA: MIT Press.

Herman, L. M., Kuczai, S., & Holder, M. D. (1993). Responses to anomalous gestural sequences by a language-trained dolphin: Evidence for processing of semantic relations and syntactic information. *Journal of Experimental Psychology: General, 122,* 184–194.

Herman-Giddens, M. E., Slora, E. J., Wasserman, R. C., Bourdony, C. J., Bhapkar, M. V., Koch, G. G., & Hasemeier, C. M. (1997). Secondary sexual characteristics and menses in young girls seen in office practice: A study from the Pediatric Research in Office Settings network. *Pediatrics, 99,* 505–512.

Hermann, D., Sartorius, A., Welzel, H., Walter, S., Skopp, G., Ende, G., & Mann, K. (2007). Dorsolateral prefrontal cortex N-Acetylaspartate/total creatine (NAA/tCr) loss in male recreational cannabis users. *Biological Psychiatry, 61,* 1281–1289.

Hernandez, A. E., & Li, P. (2007). Age of acquisition: Its neural and computational mechanisms. *Psychological Bulletin, 133,* 638–650.

Hernandez-Reif, M., Diego, M., & Field, T. (2007). Preterm infants show reduced stress behaviors and activity after 5 days of massage therapy. *Infant Behavior and Development, 30,* 557–561.

Herrnstein, R., & Murray, C. (1994). *The bell curve: Intelligence and class structure in American life.* New York: Free Press.

Hershkowitz, I., Orbach, Y., Lamb, M. E., Sternberg, K. J., Horowitz, D., & Hovav, M. (1998). Visiting the scene of the crime: Effects on children's recall of alleged abuse. *Legal and Criminological Psychology, 3,* 195–207.

Hertenstein, M. J., Keltner, D., App, B., Bulleit, B. A., & Jaskolka, A. R. (2006). Touch communicated distinct emotions. *Emotion, 6,* 528–533.

Hetherington, E. M., Bridges, M., & Insabella, G. M. (1998). What matters? What does not? Five perspectives on the association between marital transitions and children's adjustment. *American Psychologist, 53,* 167–184.

Heyes, C. M., & Galef, B. G. Jr. (Eds.). (1996). *Social learning in animals: The roots of culture.* San Diego: Academic Press.

Heyser, C. J., Hampson, R. E., & Deadwyler, S. A. (1993). Effects of delta-9-tetrahydrocannabinol on delayed match to sample performance in rats: Alterations in short-term memory associated with changes in task specific firing of hippocampal cells. *Journal of Pharmacology and Experimental Therapeutics, 264,* 294–307.

Higgins, D. M., Peterson, J. B., Lee, A. and Pihl, R. O. (2007). Prefrontal cognitive ability, intelligence, Big Five personalityand the prediction of advanced academic and workplace performance. *Journal of Personality and Social Psychology, 93,* 298–319.

Hilgard, E. R (1986). *Divided consciousness: Multiple controls in human thought and action.* New York: Wiley.

Hill, K. E., Mann, L., Laws, K. R., Stippich, C., & Schröder, J. (2004). Hypofrontality in schizophrenia: A meta-analysis of functional imaging studies. *Acta Psychiatrica Scandinavica, 110,* 243–256.

Hill, S. Y., Schwin, R., Powell, B., & Goodwin, D. W. (1973). State-dependent effects of marihuana on human memory. *Nature, 243,* 241–242.

Hillary, F. G., Schultheis, M. T., Challis, B. H., Millis, S. R., Carnevale, G. J., Galshi, T., & Deluca, J. (2003). Spacing of repetitions improves learning and memory after moderate and severe TBI. *Journal of Clinical Experimental Neuropsychology, 25,* 49–58.

Hillman, C. H., Erickson, K. I., & Kramer, A. F. (2008). Be smart, exercise your heart: Exercise effects on brain and cognition. *Nature Reviews Neuroscience, 9,* 58–65.

Hillman, C. H., Snook, E. M., & Jerome, G. J. (2003). Acute cardiovascular exercise and executive control function. *International Journal of Psychophysiology, 48,* 307–314.

Hingson, R. W., Zha, W., & Weitzman, E. R. (2009, July). Magnitude of and trends in alcohol-related mortality and morbidity among U.S. college students ages 18–24, 1998–2005. *Journal of Studies on Alcohol and Drugs, 16* (suppl), 12–20.

Hirschfeld, R. M. A., Klerman, G. L., Lavori, P., et al. (1989). Premorbid personality assessments of first onset of major depression. *Archives of General Psychiatry, 46,* 345–350.

Hirsh, J. B. (2010). Personality and environmental concern. *Journal of Environmental Psychology, 30,* 245–248.

Hirsh, J. B., & Dolderman, D. (2007). Personality predictors of consumerism and environmentalism: A preliminary study. *Personality and Individual Differences, 43,* 1583–1593.

Hirst, W., Phelps, E., Buckner, R., Budson, A., Cuc, A., Gabrieli, J., et al. (2009). Long-term memory for the terrorist attack of September 11: Flashbulb memories, event memories, and the factors that influence their retention. *Journal of Experimental Psychology: General, 138,* 161–176.

Hobson, J. A., & McCarley, R. W. (1977). The brain as a dream state generator: An activation-synthesis hypothesis of the dream process. *The American Journal of Psychiatry, 134,* 1335–1348.

Hobson, J., Pace-Schott, E., & Stickgold, R. (2000). Dreaming and the brain: Toward a cognitive neuroscience of conscious states. *Behavioral and Brain Sciences, 23,* 793–842.

Hodges, L. F., Anderson, P., Burdea, G. C., Hoffman, H. G., & Rothbaum, B. O. (2001). VR as a tool in the treatment of psychological and physical disorders. *IEEE Computer Graphics and Applications, 21,* 25–33.

Hodges, N. J., Williams, A. M., Hayes, S. J., & Breslin, G. (2007). What is modelled during observational learning? *Journal of Sport Sciences, 25,* 531–545.

Hodgins, D. C., Stea, J. N., & Grant, J. E. (2011). Gambling disorders. *The Lancet, 378,* 1874–1884.

Hodson, G., & Sorrentino, R. M. (2001). Just who favours the in-group? Personality differences in reactions to uncertainty in the minimal group paradigm. *Group Dynamics: Theory, Research and Practice, 5,* 92–101.

Hoeft, F., Gabriele, J. D. E., Whitfield-Gabrieli, S., Haas, B. W., Bammer, R., Menon, V., & Spiegel, D. (2012). Functional brain basis of hypnotizability. *Archives of General Psychiatry, 69,* 1064–1072.

Hofer, M. A. (2006). Psychobiological roots of early attachment. *Current Directions in Psychological Science, 15,* 84–88.

Hoffman, M. L., & Saltzstein, H. D. (1967). Parent discipline and the child's moral development. *Journal of Personality and Social Psychology, 5,* 45–57.

Hoffman, S. G., Grossman, P., & Hinton, D. E. (2011). Loving-kindness and compassion meditation: Potential for psychological interventions. *Clinical Psychology Review, 31,* 1126–1132.

Hofmann, S. (2007). Cognitive factors that maintain social anxiety disorder: A comprehensive model and its treatment implications. *Cognitive Behaviour Therapy, 36,* 193–209.

Hofmann, S. G., & Smits, J. A. J. (2008). Cognitive-behavioral therapy for adult anxiety disorders: A meta-analysis of randomized placebo-controlled trials. *Journal of Clinical Psychiatry, 69,* 621–632.

Hofmann, W., Houwer, J. D., Pergini, M., Baeyens, F., & Crombez, G. (2010). Evaluative conditioning in humans: A meta-analysis. *Psychological Bulletin, 136,* 390–421.

Hofschire, L. J., & Greenberg, B. S. (2002). Media's impact on adolescents' body dissatisfaction. In J. D. Brown, J. R. Steele., & K. Walsh-Childers (Eds.), *Sexual teens, sexual media.* Mahwah, NJ: Lawrence Erlbaum Associates.

Hofstede, G. (1984). The cultural relativity of the quality of life concept. *Academy of Management Review, 9,* 389–398.

Hogan, M. J., Kelly, C. A. M., Verrier, D., Newell, J., Hasher, L., & Robertson, I. H. (2009). Optimal time-of-day and consolidation of learning in younger and older adults. *Experimental Aging Research, 35,* 107–128.

Hojnoski, R. L., Morrison, R., Brown, M., & Matthews, W. J. (2006). Projective test use among school psychologists: A survey and critique. *Journal of Psychoeducational Assessment, 24,* 145–159.

Holleran, S. E., Mehl, M. R., & Levitt, S. (2009). Eavesdropping on social life: The accuracy of stranger ratings of daily behavior from thin slices of natural conversations. *Journal of Research in Personality, 43,* 660–672.

Hollerman, J. R., & Schultz, W. (1996). Activity of dopamine neurons during learning in a familiar task context. *Society for Neuroscience Abstracts, 22,* 1388.

Hollon, S. D., Stewart, M. O., & Strunk, D. (2006). Enduring effects for cognitive behavior therapy in the treatment of depression and anxiety (pp. 285–315). Annual Reviews, Palo Alto, CA. Retrieved from http://search.proquest.com/docview/621155442?accountid=14771

Hollon, S., Thase, M., & Markowitz, J. (2002). Treatment and prevention of depression. *Psychological Science in the Public Interest, 3,* 39–77.

Holmes, T. H., & Rahe, R. H. (1967). The social readjustment rating scale. *Journal of Psychosomatic Research, 11,* 213–218.

Holstege, G., Georgiadis, J. R., Paans, A. M. J., Meiners, L.C., van der Graaf, F. H. C. E., &, Reinders, A. A. T. (2003). Brain activation during human male ejaculation. *Journal of Neuroscience, 23,* 9185–9193.

Holyoak, K. J., & Morrison R. G. (2005). Thinking and reasoning: A reader's guide. In K. J. Holyoak & R. G. Morrison (Eds.), *The Cambridge handbook of thinking and reasoning* (pp. 1–9). New York: Cambridge University Press.

Hooker, W. D., & Jones, R.T. (1987). Increased susceptibility to memory intrusions and the Stroop interference effect during acute marijuana intoxication. *Psychopharmacology, 91,* 20–24.

Hooley, J. (2007). Expressed emotion and relapse of psychopathology. *Annual Review of Clinical Psychology, 3,* 329–352.

Hooley, J. M., & Gotlib, I. H. (2000). A diathesis-stress conceptualization of expressed emotion and clinical outcome. *Journal of Applied and Preventive Psychology, 9,* 135–151.

Hoover, A. E., Démonet, J. F., & Steeves, J. K. (2010). Superior voice recognition in a patient with acquired prosopagnosia and object agnosia. *Neuropsychologia, 48,* 3725–3732.

Hopkins, B., & Westra, T. (1989). Maternal expectations of their infants' development: Some cultural differences. *Developmental Medicine and Child Neurology, 31,* 384–390.

Horn, J. L., & Cattell, R. B. (1967). Age differences in fluid and crystallized intelligence. *Acta Psychologica, 26,* 107–129.

Horn, L. R., & Ward, G. (2004). *The handbook of pragmatics.* Malden, MA: Blackwell.

Horne, J., & Minard, A. (1985). Sleep and sleepiness following a behaviourally "active" day. *Ergonomics, 28,* 567–575.

Horne, P. J., & Erjavec, M. (2007). Do infants show generalized imitation of gestures? *Journal of the Experimental Analysis of Behavior, 87,* 63–87.

Horner, V., & Whiten, A. (2005). Causal knowledge and imitation/emulation switching in chimpanzees (Pan troglodytes) and children (Homo sapiens). *Animal Cognition, 8,* 164–181.

Horvath, A. O., & Bedi, R. P. (2002). The alliance. In J. C. Norcross (Ed.), *Psychotherapy relationships that work: Therapist contributions and responsiveness to patients* (pp. 37–69). New York: Oxford University Press.

Hoshino-Browne, E., Zanna, A. S., Spencer, S. J., Zanna, M. P., Kitayama, S., & Lackenbauer, S. (2005). On the cultural guises of cognitive dissonance: The case of easterners and westerners. *Journal of Personality and Social Psychology, 89,* 294–310.

Hough, W., & O'Brien, K. (2005). The effect of community treatment orders on offending rates. *Psychiatry, Psychology and Law, 12,* 411–423.

House, J. S., Landis, K. R., & Umberson, D. (1988). Social relationships and health. *Science, 241,* 540–545.

Howe, M. L. (2003). Memories from the cradle. *Current Directions in Psychological Science, 12,* 62–65.

Hrobjartsson, A., & Gotzsche, P. (2010). Placebo interventions for all clinical conditions. *Cochrane Database of Systematic Reviews, 1,* CD003974.

Huang, C. (2012). Outcome-based observational learning in human infants. *Journal of Comparative Psychology, 126,* 139–149.

Hubel, D. H., & Weisel, T. N. (1959). Receptive fields of single neurons in the cat's striate cortex. *Journal of Physiology, 148,* 574–591.

Hubel, D. H., & Wiesel, T. N. (1962). Receptive fields, binocular interaction and functional architecture in the cat's visual cortex. *Journal of Physiology, 160,* 106–154.

Hudson, J., Hiripi, E., Pope, H., & Kessler, R. (2007). The prevalence and correlates of eating disorders in the National Comorbidity Survey replication. *Biological Psychiatry, 61,* 348–358.

Huesmann, L. R. (2007). The impact of electronic media violence: Scientific theory and research. *Journal of Adolescent Health, 41,* S6–S13.

Huffman, M. A. (1996). Acquisition of innovative cultural behaviors in nonhuman primates: A case study of stone handling, a socially transmitted behavior in Japanese macaques. In C. M. Heyes & B. Galef (Eds.), *Social learning in animals: The roots of culture* (pp. 267–289). San Diego: Academic Press.

Hull, C. L. (1952). *A behavior system: An introduction to behavior theory concerning the individual organism.* New Haven, CT: Yale University Press.

Hunter, J. E., & Hunter, R. F. (1984). Validity and utility of alternative predictors of job performance. *Psychological Bulletin, 96,* 72–98.

Hunter, R. A., & Macalpine, I. (Eds.). (1963). *Three hundred years of psychiatry, 1535–1860: A history presented in selected English texts.* New York: Oxford University Press.

Huyser, C., Veltman, D. J., de Haan, E., & Boer, F. (2009). Paediatric obsessive–compulsive disorder, a neurodevelopmental disorder? Evidence from neuroimaging. *Neuroscience and Biobehavioral Reviews, 33,* 818–830.

Hyde, J., Mezulis, A., & Abramson, L. (2008). The ABCs of depression: Integrating affective, biological, and cognitive models to explain the emergence of the gender difference in depression. *Psychological Review, 115,* 291–313.

Hyde, K. L., Peretz, I., & Zatorre, R. J. (2007). Evidence for the role of the right auditory cortex in fine pitch resolution. *Neuropsychologia, 46,* 632–639.

Hyman, S. E. (2007). Can neuroscience be integrated into the DSM-V? *Nature Reviews Neuroscience, 8,* 725–732.

Iacoboni, M., Molnar-Szakacs, I., Gallese V., Buccino, G., Mazziotta, F. C., & Rizzolatti, G. (2005). Grasping the intentions of others with one's own mirror neuron system. *PLoS Biology, 3,* e79.

Inlow, J. K., & Restifo, L. L. (2004). Molecular and comparative genetics of mental retardation. *Genetics, 166,* 835–881.

Inn, A., Wheeler, A. C., & Sparling, C. L. (1977). The effects of suspect race and situation hazard on police officer shooting behavior. *Journal of Applied Social Psychology, 7,* 27–37.

Innocence Project. (2010, November). Retrieved from http://www.innocenceproject.org/ Content/Eyewitness_Identification_Reform.php

International Narcotics Control Board. (2004). Report of the Interational Narcotics Control Board 2004. Retrieved from: http:// www.incb.org/incb/en/publications/annual-reports/ annual-report-2004.html

Isen, A. M., Daubman, K. A., & Nowicki, G. P. (1987). Positive affect facilitates creative problem solving. *Journal of Personality and Social Psychology, 52,* 112–1131.

Isenberg, D. J. (1986). Group polarization: A critical review and meta-analysis. *Journal of Personality and Social Psychology, 50,* 1141–1151.

Ito, T. A., & Urland, G. R. (2003). Race and gender on the brain: Electrocortical measures of attention to the race and gender of multiply categorizable individuals. *Journal of Personality and Social Psychology, 85,* 616–626.

Iyengar, S. S., Wells, R. E., & Schwartz, B. (2006). Doing better but feeling worse: Looking for the "best" job undermines satisfaction. *Psychological Science, 17,* 143–150.

Izard, V., Sann, C., Spelke, E. S., & Streri, A. (2009). Newborn infants perceive abstract numbers. *Proceedings of the National Academy of Sciences, 106,* 10382–10385.

Jacobs, B. (2004). Depression: The brain finally gets into the act. *Current Directions in Psychological Science, 13,* 103–106.

Jacoby, L. L., & Brooks, L. R. (1984). Nonanalytic cognition: Memory, perception and concept learning. In G. Bower (Ed.), *The psychology of learning and motivation: Advances in research and theory* (pp. 1–46). San Diego, CA: Academic Press.

Jaeggi, S. M., Buschkuehl, M., Jonides, J., & Perrig, W. J. (2008). Improving fluid intelligence with training on working memory. *Proceedings of the National Academy of Sciences of the United States of America, 105,* 6829–6833.

Jaeggi, S. M., Buschkuehl, M., Jonides, J., & Shah, P. (2011). Short- and long-term benefits of cognitive training. *Proceedings of the National Academy of Sciences of the United States of America, 108*(25), 10081–10086.

Jaffee, S., & Hyde, J. S. (2000). Gender differences in moral orientation: A meta-analysis. *Psychological Bulletin, 126,* 703–726.

Jager, G., Kahn, R. S., Ven Den Brink, W., Van Ree, J. M., & Ramsey, N. F. (2006). Long-term effects of frequent cannibus use on working memory and attention: An fMRI study. *Psychopharmacology, 185,* 358–368.

Jager, G., Van Kell, H. H., De Win, M. M. L., Kahn, R. S., Van Den brink, W., Van Ree, J. M., & Ramsey, N. F. (2007). Effects of frequent cannabis use on hippocampal activity during an associative memory task. *European Neuropsychopharmacology, 17,* 289–297.

James, T. W., Cullham, J., Humphrey, G. K., Milner, A. D., & Goodale, M. A. (2003). Ventral occipital lesions impair object recognition but not object-directed grasping: An fMRI study. *Brain, 126,* 2463–2475.

James, W. (1890). *The principles of psychology.* New York: Henry Holt and Company.

Jamieson, G. A., & Sheehan, P. W. (2004). An empirical test of Woody and Bower's dissociated-control theory of hypnosis. *The International Journal of Clinical and Experimental Hypnosis, 52,* 232–249.

Jang, K. L., Livesley, W. J., Ando, J., Yamagata, S., Suzuki, A., Angleitner, A., Ostendorf, F., Riemann, R., & Spinath, F. (2006). Behavioral genetics of the higher-order factors of the Big Five. *Personality and Individual Differences, 41,* 261–272.

Janis, I. L. (1972). *Victims of groupthink: A psychological study of foreign policy decisions and fiascoes.* Boston: Houghton Mifflin.

Jencks, C., Smith, M., Acland, H., Bane, M. J., Cohen, D., Gintis, H., Heyns, B., & Michelson, S. (1972). *Inequality: A reassessment of the effect of family and schooling in America.* New York: Harper & Row.

Jensen, A. R. (1993). Test validity: *g* versus "tacit knowledge." *Current Directions in Psychological Science, 2,* 53–56.

Jensen, R. (2006). Behaviorism, latent learning, and cognitive maps: Needed revisions in introductory psychology textbooks. *Behavioral Analysis, 29,* 187–209.

Jewanski, J., Day, S. A., & Ward, J. (2009). A colorful albino: The first documented case of synaesthesia, by Georg Tobias Ludwig Sachs in 1812. *Journal of the History of the Neuroscience: Basic and Clinical Perspectives, 18,* 293–303.

Jha, A. P., Stanley, E. A., Kiyonaga, A., Wong, L., & Gelfand, L. (2010). Examining the protective effects of mindfulness training on working memory capacity and affective performance. *Emotion, 10,* 54–64.

Jilek, W. G. (1995). Emil Kraepelin and comparative sociocultural psychiatry. *European Archives of Psychiatry and Clinical Neuroscience, 245,* 231–238.

John, E. R., Chesler, P., Bartlett, F., & Victor, I. (1968). Observational learning in cats. *Science, 29,* 1489–1491.

John, O. P., & Srivastava, S. (1999). The Big Five trait taxonomy: History, measurement, and theoretical perspectives. In L. A. Pervin &

O. P. John (Eds.), *Handbook of personality: Theory and research* (2nd ed., pp. 102–138). New York, NY: Guilford.

Johns, M. W. (1991). A new method for measuring daytime sleepiness: The Epworth sleepiness scale. *Sleep, 14*, 540–545.

Johnson, W., te Nijenhuis, J., & Bouchard, T. (2008). Still just 1 *g*: Consistent results from five test batteries, *Intelligence, 36*, 81–95.

Johnson, A. M., Reed, T. E., & Vernon, P. A. (2005). Nerve conduction velocity (NCV) is a valid and useful construct for studying human cognitive abilities: A reply to Saint-Amour et al. *Neuropsychologia, 43,* 1845–1846.

Johnson, B. B. (2012). Climate change communication: A provocative inquiry into motives, meanings, and means. *Risk Analysis, 32*, 973–991.

Johnson, K. E., & Mervis, C. B. (1997). Effects of varying levels of expertise on the basic level of categorization. *Journal of Experimental Psychology: General, 126*, 248–277.

Johnson, M. H., Dziurawiec, S., Ellis, H., & Morton, J. (1991). Newborns' preferential tracking of face-like stimuli and its subsequent decline. *Cognition, 40,* 1–19.

Johnson, M. K., Raye, C. L., Mitchell, K. J., & Ankudowich, E. (2012). The cognitive neuroscience of true and false memories. *Nebraska Symposium on Motivation, 58*, 15–52.

Johnson, W., & Bouchard, T. J., Jr. (2007). Sex differences in mental abilities: *g* masks the dimensions on which they lie. *Intelligence, 35,* 23–39.

Joling, K. J., van Hout, H. P., Van't Veer-Tazelaar, P. J., van der Horst, H. E., Cuijpers, P., van de Ven, P. M., & van Marwijk, H. W. (2011). How effective is bibliotherapy for very old adults with subthreshold depression? Randomized controlled trial. *American Journal of Geriatric Psychiatry, 19*, 256–265.

Jones, A., Gublis, A., & Baker, E. H. (2010). Differences in tobacco use between Canada and the United States. *International Journal of Public Health*, 55,167–75.

Jones, D. N., & Paulhus, D. L. (2010). Different provocations trigger aggression in narcissists and psychopaths. *Social and Personality Psychology Science, 1*, 12–18.

Jones, H. P., Karuri, S., Cronin, C. M., Ohlsson, A., Peliowski, A., Synnes, A., & Lee, S. K. (2005). Actuarial survival of a large Canadian cohort of preterm infants. *BMC Pediatrics, 5*, 1–13.

Jones, K. L., & Smith, D. W. (1973). Recognition of the fetal alcohol syndrome in early infancy. *Lancet, 2,* 999–1001.

Jonides, J., Lacey, S., & Nee, D. (2005). Processes of working memory in mind and brain. *Current Directions in Psychological Science, 14*, 2–5.

Josephson, W. L. (1987). Television violence and children's aggression: Testing the priming, social script, and disinhibition predictions. *Interpersonal Relations and Group Processes, 53,* 882–890.

Juda, M. N., Campbell, L., & Crawford, C. B. (2004). Dieting symptomatology in women and perceptions of social support: An evolutionary approach. *Evolution and Human Behavior, 25,* 200–208.

Julius, D., & Basbaum, A. I. (2001). Molecular mechanisms of nociception. *Nature, 413,* 203–210.

Jurcic, J., Pereira, J. A., & Kavanaugh, D. (2007). St John's wort versus paroxetine for depression. *Canadian Family Physician, 53,* 1511–1513.

Jusczyk, P. W., Friederici, A. D., Wessels, J., Svenkerud, V. Y., & Jusczyk, A. M. (1993). Infants' sensitivity to the sound patterns of native language words. *Journal of Memory and Language, 32*, 402–420.

Kahneman, D. (2003). A perspective on judgment and choice: Mapping bounded rationality. *American Psychologist, 58*, 697–720.

Kahneman, D., & Miller, D. T. (1986). Norm theory: Comparing reality to its alternatives. *Psychological Review, 93*, 136–153.

Kales, A., Soldatos, C. R., Bixler, E. O., Ladda, R. L., Charney, D. S., Weber, G., & Schweitzer, P. K. (1980). Hereditary factors in sleepwalking and night terrors. *The British Journal of Psychiatry, 137,* 111–118.

Kalisch, R., Korenfeld, E., Stephan, K. E., Weiskopf, N., Seymour, B., & Dolan, R. J. (2006). Context-dependent human extinction memory is mediated by a ventromedial prefrontal and hippocampal network. *The Journal of Neuroscience, 26*, 9503–9511.

Kalnin, A. J., Edwards, C. R., Wang, Y., Kato, J., Ide, H., Kabashima, I., et al. (2009). Neural correlates of attitude change following positive and negative advertisements. *Frontiers in Behavioral Neuroscience, 3,* 1–13.

Kaminski, J., Call, J., & Fischer, J. (2004). Word learning in a domestic dog: Evidence for "fast mapping." *Science, 304*, 1682–1683.

Kamnasaran, D., Muir, W. J., Ferguson-Smith, M. A., & Cox, D. W. (2003). Disruption of the neuronal PAS3 gene in a family affected with schizophrenia. *Journal of Medical Genetics, 40,* 325–332.

Kanayama, G., Rogowska, J., Pope, H. G., Gruber, S. A., & Yurgelun-Todd, D. A. (2004). Spatial working memory in heavy cannabis users: A functional magnetic resonance imaging study. *Psychopharmacology, 176,* 239–247.

Kanwisher, N., McDermott, J., & Chun, M. (1997). The fusiform face area: A module in human extrastriate cortex specialized for the perception of faces. *Journal of Neuroscience, 17,* 4302–4311.

Kaplan, S. (2000). New ways to promote proenvironmental behavior: Human nature and environmentally responsible behavior. *Journal of Social Issues, 56*, 491–508.

Karakashian, L. M., Walter, M. I., & Christopher, A. N. (2006). Fear of negative evaluation affects helping behavior: The bystander effect revisited. *North American Journal of Psychology, 8,* 13–32.

Karam, M., Russo, F. A., & Fels, D. I. (2009). Designing the model human cochlea: An ambient crossmodal audio-tactile display. *IEEE Transactions on Haptics, 2,* 1–10.

Karau, S. J., & Williams, K. D. (2001). Understanding individual motivation in groups: The collective effort model. In M. E. Turner (Ed.), *Groups at work: Theory and research* (pp. 113–141). Mahwah, NJ: Lawrence Erlbaum Associates.

Kaufman, A. S. (2001). WAIS-III IQs, Horn's theory, and generational changes from young adulthood to old age. *Intelligence, 29*, 131–167.

Kawai, M. (1965). Newly acquired pre-cultural behavior of a natural troop of Japanese monkeys on Koshima Island. *Primates, 6,* 1–30.

Kawakami, K., Dovidio, J. F., Moll, J., Hermsen, S., & Russim, A. (2000). Just say no (to stereotyping): Effects of training in negation of stereotypic associations on stereotype activation. *Journal of Personality and Social Psychology, 78,* 871–888.

Kay, A. C., Gaucher, D., McGregor, I., & Nash, K. (2010). Religious belief as compensatory control. *Personality and Social Psychology Review, 14,* 37–48.

Kay, A. C., Whitson, J. A., Gaucher, D., & Galinsky, A. D. (2009). Compensatory control: Achieving order through the mind, our institutions, and the heavens. *Current Directions in Psychological Science, 18*, 264–268.

Kaye, W. H., Gwirtsman, H. E., George, D. T., Weiss, S. R., & Jimerson, D. C. (1986). Relationship of mood alterations to bingeing behaviour in bulimia. *The British Journal of Psychiatry, 149,* 479–485.

Kebbell, M., Milne, R., & Wagstaff, G. (1999). The cognitive interview: A survey of its forensic effectiveness. *Psychology, Crime, & Law, 5,* 101–115.

Keel, P. K., & Klump, K. L. (2003). Are eating disorders culture-bound syndromes? Implications for conceptualizing their etiology. *Psychological Bulletin, 129*, 747–769.

Keenan, J. P., Wheeler, M. A., Gallup Jr, G. G., & Pascual-Leone, A. (2000). Self-recognition and the right prefrontal cortex. *Trends in Cognitive Sciences, 4*, 338–344.

Kelemen, W. L., & Creeley, C. E. (2003). State-dependent memory effects using caffeine and placebo do not extend to metamemory. *Journal of General Psychology, 13D,* 70–86.

Kellet, J., & Kokkinidis, L. (2004). Extinction deficit and fear reinstatement after electrical stimulation of the amygdala: Implications for kindling-associated fear and anxiety. *Neuroscience, 127,* 277–287.

Kenny, D. A. (2004). PERSON: A general model of interpersonal perception. *Personality and Social Psychology Review, 8,* 265–280.

Kernis, M. H., Paradise, A. W., Whitaker, D. J., Wheatman, S. R., & Goldman, B. N. (2000). Master of one's psychological domain? Not likely if one's self-esteem is unstable. *Personality and Social Psychology Bulletin, 26,* 1297–1305.

Kershaw, T. C., Hemmerich, J. A., & Ahmed, S. (2009). Flashbulb memory for September 11 and the Columbia space shuttle disaster. In M.R. Kelley, *Applied memory* (pp. 129–146). Hauppage, NY: Nova Science Publishers.

Kessler, R. C. (2000). Posttraumatic stress disorder: The burden to the individual and to society. *Journal of Clinical Psychiatry, 61*(suppl. 5), 4–12.

Kessler, R. C., Chiu, W. T., Demler, O., & Walters, E. E. (2005). Prevalence, severity, and comorbidity of twelve-month DSM-IV disorders in the National Comorbidity Survey Replication (NCS-R). *Archives of General Psychiatry, 62,* 617–627.

Kevles, D. J. (1985). *In the name of eugenics: Genetics and the uses of human heredity.* University of California Press.

Kiecolt-Glaser, J. (1984). Psychosocial modifiers of immunocompetence in medical students. *Psychosomatic Medicine, 46,* 7–14.

Kiecolt-Glaser, J. K., & Newton, T. L. (2001). Marriage and health: His and hers. *Psychological Bulletin, 127,* 472–503.

Kielburger, C., & Kielburger, M. (2006). *Me to we: Finding meaning in a material world.* New York: Fireside.

Kigar, D. L., Witelson, S. F., Glezer, I. I., & Harvey, T. (1997). Estimates of cell number in temporal neocortex in the brain of Albert Einstein. *Social Neurosciences Abstracts, 23,* 88–89.

Kihlstrom, J. F. (1997). Hypnosis, memory and amnesia. *Philosophical Transactions of the Royal Society of London B: Biological Sciences, 352,* 1727–1732.

Kihlstrom, J. F. (2005). Dissociative disorders. *Annual Review of Clinical Psychology, 1,* 227–253.

Kim, H., Shimojo, S., & O'Doherty, J. P. (2006). Is avoiding an aversive outcome rewarding? Neural substrates of avoidance learning in the human brain. *PLoS Biology, 4,* e233.

Kim, J. J., & Fanselow, M. S. (1992). Modality-specific retrograde amnesia of fear. *Science, 256,* 675–677.

King, D. B., & DeCicco, T. L. (2007). The relationships between dream content and physical health, mood, and self-construal. *Dreaming, 17,* 127–139.

King, S. (2000). Is expressed emotion cause or effect in the mothers of schizophrenic young adults? *Schizophrenia Research, 45,* 65–78.

King, S., & Dixon, M. J. (1999). Expressed emotion and relapse in young schizophrenia outpatients. *Schizophrenia Bulletin, 25,* 377–386.

King, S., St. Hilaire, A., & Heidkamp, D. (2010). Prenatal factors in schizophrenia. *Current Directions in Psychological Science, 19,* 209–213.

Kingston, T., Dooley, B., Bates, A., Lawlor, E., & Malone, K. (2007). Mindfulness-based cognitive therapy for residual depressive symptoms. *Psychology and Psychotherapy: Theory, Research and Practice, 80,* 193–203.

Kinsey, A. C., Pomeroy, W. B., & Martin, C. E. (1948). *Sexual behaviour in the human male.* Philadelphia: W.B. Saunders.

Kinsey, A. C., Pomeroy, W. B., & Matin, C. E. (1953). *Sexual behaviour in the human female.* Philadelphia: W.B. Saunders.

Kirk, K. M., Bailey, J. M., Dunne, M. P., & Martin, N. G. (2000). Measurement models for sexual orientation in a community twin sample. *Behavioral Genetics, 30,* 345–356.

Kirkham, T. C. (2009). Cannabinoids and appetite: Food craving and food pleasure. *International Review of Psychiatry, 21,* 163–171.

Kirsch, I., & Lynn, S. (1998). Dissociation theories of hypnosis. *Psychological Bulletin, 123,* 100–115.

Kirsch, I., Deacon, B. J., Huedo-Medina, T., Scoboria, A., Moore, T. J., & Johnson, B. T. (2008). Initial severity and antidepressant benefits: A meta-analysis of data submitted to the food and drug administration. *PLoS Medicine, 5,* 1.

Kirsch, P., Esslinger, C., Chen, Q., Mier, D., Lis, S., Siddhanti, S., Gruppe, H., Mattay, V. S., Gallhofer, B., & Meyer-Lindenberg, A. (2005). Oxytocin modulates neural circuitry for social cognition and fear in humans. *Journal of Neuroscience, 25,* 11489–11493.

Kirschbaum, C., Pirke, K.-M., & Hellhammer, D. K. (1993). The "Trier Social Stress Test"—A tool for investigating psychobiological stress in a laboratory setting. *Neuropsychobiology, 28,* 76–81.

Kirschbaum, C., Wust, S., & Hellhammer, D. (1992). Consistent sex differences in cortisol responses to psychological stress. *Psychosomatic Medicine, 54,* 648–657.

Kisely, S. R., Campbell, L. A., & Preston, N. J. (2011). Compulsory community and involuntary outpatient treatment for people with severe mental disorders. *Cochrane Database of Systematic Reviews, 2.*

Kisilevsky, B. S., Hains, S. M., Lee, K., Xie, X., Huang, H., Ye, H. H., et al. (2003). Effects of experience on fetal voice recognition. *Psychological Science, 14,* 220–224.

Klaus, L., Berner, M. M., & Levente, K. (2008). St. John's wort for major depression. In *Cochrane Database of Systematic Reviews: Reviews 2008, 4.* Chichester, UK: John Wiley & Sons.

Kleider, H., Pezdek, K., Goldinger, S., & Kirk, A. (2008). Schema-driven source misattribution errors: Remembering the expected from a witnessed event. *Applied Cognitive Psychology, 22,* 1–20.

Klein, N. (2007). *The shock doctrine: The rise of disaster capitalism.* New York: Picador.

Klerman, G. L., & Weissman, M. M. (1993). *New applications of interpersonal psychotherapy.* Washington DC: American Psychiatric Press.

Klerman, G. L., Weissman, M. M., Rounsaville, B. J., et al. (1984). *Interpersonal psychotherapy of depression.* Northvale, NJ: Jason Aronson Inc.

Klingberg, T., Fernell, E., Olesen, P. J., Johnson, M., Gustafsson, P., Dahlstrom, K., Gillberg, C. G., Forssberg, H., & Westerberg, H. (2005). Computerized training of working memory in children with ADHD—a randomized, controlled trial. *Journal of the American Academy of Child and Adolescent Psychiatry, 44,* 177–186.

Klomek, A., Marrocco, F., Kleinman, M., Schonfeld, I., & Gould, M. (2007). Bullying, depression, and suicidality in adolescents. *Journal of the American Academy of Child & Adolescent Psychiatry, 46,* 40–49.

Knutson, B., Fong, G. W., Bennett, S. M., Adams, C. M., & Hommer, D. (2003). A region of mesial prefrontal cortex tracks monetarily rewarding outcomes: Characterization with rapid event-related fMRI. *NeuroImage, 18,* 263–272.

Knutson, B., Rick, S., Wimmer, G. E., Prelec, D., & Loewenstein, G. (2007). Neural predictors of purchases. *Neuron, 53,* 147–156.

Koball, H. L., Moiduddin, E., Henderson, J., Goesling, B., & Besculides, M. (2010). What do we know about the link between marriage and health? *Journal of Family Issues, 31,* 1019–1040.

Kohlberg, I. (1984). *The psychology of moral development: Essays on moral development* (Vol. II). San Francisco: Harper & Row.

Köksal, F., Domjan, M., Kurt, A., Sertel, Ö., Örüng, S., Bowers, R., & Kumru, G. (2004). An animal model of fetishism. *Behaviour Research and Therapy, 42,* 1421–1434.

Kolb, B. (1989). Brain development, plasticity, and behavior. *American Psychologist, 44,* 1203–1212.

Kolb, B. (1995). *Brain plasticity and behavior.* Florence, KT: Routledge.

Komisaruk, B. R. (2005). Functional MRI of the brain during orgasm in women. *Annual Review of Sex Research, 16,* 62–86.

Koob, G. F. (1992). Neural mechanisms of drug reinforcement. *Annals of the New York Academy of Sciences, 654,* 171–191.

Kornell, N. (2009). Optimising learning using flashcards: Spacing is more effective than cramming. *Applied Cognitive Psychology, 23,* 1297–1317.

Kornell, N., & Bjork, R. A. (2007). The promise and perils of self-regulated study. *Psychonomic Bulletin & Review, 14,* 219–224.

Kotchoubey, B., Kaiser, J., Bostanov, V., Lutzenberger, W., & Birbaumer, N. (2009). Recognition of affective prosody in brain-damaged patients and healthy controls: A neurophysiological study using EEG and whole-head MEG. *Cognitive, Affective, & Behavioral Neuroscience, 9,* 153–167.

Kovacs, A. M., & Mehler, J. (2009). Cognitive gains in 7-month-old bilingual infants. *Current Issue, 106,* 6556–6560.

Kramer, A F., Hahn, S., Cohen, N. J., Banich, M. T., McAuley, E., Harrison, C. R., et al. (1999). Ageing, fitness and neurocognitive function. *Nature, 400,* 418–419.

Kramer, M., Schoen, L. S., & Kinney, L. (1984). Psychological and behavioral features of disturbed dreamers. *Psychiatric Journal of the University of Ottawa, 9,* 102–106.

Kramer, T. H., Buckhout, R., & Eugenio, P. (1990). Weapon focus, arousal, and eyewitness memory. *Law and Human Behavior, 14,* 167–184.

Kraus, M. W., Huang, C., & Keltner, D. (2010). Tactile communication, cooperation, and performance: An ethological study of the NBA. *Emotion, 10,* 745–749.

Krevans, J., & Gibbs, J. C. (1996). Parents' use of inductive discipline: Relations to children's empathy and prosocial behavior. *Child Development, 67,* 3263–3277.

Kringelbach, M. L., Jenkinson, N., Owen, S. L. F., & Aziz, T. Z. (2007). Translational principles of deep brain stimulation. *Nature Reviews Neuroscience, 8,* 623–635.

Kristensen, P., & Bjerkedal, T. (2007). Explaining the relation between birth order and intelligence. *Science, 316,* 1717–1718.

Kristensson, E., Sundqvist, M., Astin, M., Kjerling, M., Mattsson, H., Dornonville, et al. (2006). Acute psychological stress raises plasma ghrelin in the rat. *Regulatory Peptides, 134,* 114–117.

Kronenberger, W. G., Hummer, T. A., Moiser, K. M., Dunn, D. W., & Mathews, V. P. (2011). The interacting role of media violence exposure and aggressive-disruptive behaviour in adolescent brain activation during an emotional stroop task. *Psychiatry Research, Neuroimaging, 192,* 12–19.

Kroska, A., & Harkness, S. K. (2006). Stigma sentiments and self-meanings: Exploring the modified labeling theory of mental illness. *Social Psychology Quarterly, 69,* 325–348.

Krueger, R. F., Caspi, A., Moffitt, T. E., et al. (1996). Personality traits are differentially linked to mental disorders: A multi-trait—multi-diagnosis study of an adolescent birth cohort. *Journal of Abnormal Psychology, 105,* 299–312.

Kruger, J., Wirtz, D., & Miller, D. (2005). Counterfactual thinking and the first instinct fallacy. *Journal of Personality and Social Psychology, 88,* 725–735.

Krystal, A. (2009). A compendium of placebo-controlled trials of the risks/benefits of pharmacological treatments for insomnia: The empirical basis for U.S. clinical practice. *Sleep Medicine Reviews, 13,* 265–274.

Kubzansky, L. D., Martin, L. T., & Buka, S. L. (2009). Early manifestations of personality and adult health: A life course perspective. *Health Psychology, 28,* 364–372.

Kubzansky, L. D., Sparrow, D., Vokonas, P., & Kawachi, I. (2001). Is the glass half empty or half full? A prospective study of optimism and coronary heart disease in the normative aging study. *Psychosomatic Medicine, 63,* 910–916.

Kudielka, B. M., & Kirschbaum, C. (2005). Sex differences in HPA axis responses to stress: A review. *Biological Psychology, 69,* 113–132.

Kuran, T. (1995). The inevitability of future revolutionary surprises. *American Journal of Sociology, 100,* 1528–1551.

Kurdek, L. A. (2005). Gender and marital satisfaction early in marriage: A growth curve approach. *Journal of Marriage and Family, 67,* 68–84.

Kuyken, W., Byford, S., Taylor, R. S., Watkins, E., Holden, E., White, K., et al. (2008). Mindfulness-based cognitive therapy to prevent relapse in recurrent depression. *Journal of Consulting and Clinical Psychology, 76,* 966–978.

Kuyken, W., Watkins, E., Holden, E., White, K., Taylor, R. S., Byford, S., et al. (2010). How does mindfulness-based cognitive therapy work? *Behaviour Research and Therapy, 48,* 1105–1112.

La Guardia, J. G. (2009). Developing who I am: A self-determination theory approach to the establishment of healthy identities. *Educational Psychologist, 44,* 90–104.

LaBar, K. S., & Cabeza, R. (2006). Cognitive neuroscience of emotional memory. *Nature Neuroscience, 7,* 54–64.

LaBar, K. S., & Phelps, E. A. (1998). Arousal-mediated memory consolidation: Role of the medial temporal lobe in humans. *Psychological Science, 9,* 490–493.

Lakin, J. L., & Chartrand, T. L. (2003). Using nonconscious behavioral mimicry to create affiliation and rapport. *Psychological Science, 14,* 334–339.

Lakin, J. L., Jefferis, V. E., Cheng, C. M., & Chartrand, T. L. (2003). The chameleon effect as social glue: Evidence for the evolutionary significance of nonconscious mimicry. *Journal of Nonverbal Behavior, 27,* 145–162.

Lakoff, G., & Johnson, M. (1999). *Philosophy in the flesh: The embodied mind and its challenge to Western thought.* New York: Basic Books.

Lalumière, M. L., & Quinsey, C. L. (1998). Pavlovian conditioning of sexual interest in human males. *Archives of Sexual Behavior, 27,* 241–252.

Lam, D. H. (1991). Psychosocial family intervention in schizophrenia: A review of empirical studies. *Psychological Medicine, 21,* 423–441.

Lam, L. T., & Peng, Z. (2010). Effect of pathological use of the Internet on adolescent mental health: A prospective study. *Archives of Pediatric and Adolescent Medicine, 164,* 901–906.

Laming, D. (2010). Serial position curves in free recall. *Psychological Review, 117,* 93–133.

Landrigan, C. P., Rothschild, J. M., Cronin, J. W., Kaushal, R., Burdick, E., Katz, J. T., et al. (2004). Effect of reducing interns' work hours on serious medical errors in intensive care units. *New England Journal of Medicine, 351,* 1838–1848.

Landrine, H., & Klonoff, E. A. (1996). The schedule of racist events: A measure of racial discrimination and a study of its negative physical and mental health consequences. *Journal of Black Psychology, 22,* 144–168.

Laney, C., Heuer, F., & Reisberg, D. (2003). Thematically-induced arousal in naturally-occurring emotional memories. *Applied Cognitive Psychology, 17,* 995–1004.

Langford, D. J., Crager, S. E., Shehzad, Z., Smith, S. B., Sotocinal, S. G., Levenstadt, J. S., et al. (2006). Social modulation of pain as evidence for empathy in mice. *Science, 312,* 1967–1970.

Langford, D. J., Tuttle, A. H., Briscoe, C., Harvey-Lewis, C., Baran, I., Gleeson, P., et al. (2011). Varying perceived social threat modulates pain behavior in male mice. *The Journal of Pain, 12,* 125–132.

Langhans, W. (1996a). Metabolic and glucostatic control of feeding. *Proceedings of the Nutritional Society, 55,* 497–515.

Langhans, W. (1996b). Role of the liver in the metabolic control of eating: What we know—and what we do not know. *Neuroscience and Biobehavioral Review, 20,* 145–153.

Langston, J. W., Ballard, P., Tetrud, J. W., & Irwin, I. (1983). Chronic parkinsonism in humans due to a product of meperidine-analog synthesis. *Science, 219,* 979–980.

Långström, N., Rahman, Q., & Carlstrom, E. (2010). Genetic and environmental effects on same-sex sexual behavior: A population study of twins in Sweden. *Archives of Sexual Behavior, 39,* 75–80.

Larsen, R. J., Kasimatis, M., & Frey, K. (1992). Facilitating the furrowed brow: An unobtrusive test of the facial feedback hypothesis applied to unpleasant affect. *Cognition & Emotion, 6,* 321–338.

Lasco, M. S., Jordan, T. J., Edgar, M. A., Petito, C. K., & Byne, W. (2002). A lack of dimorphism of sex or sexual orientation in the human anterior commissure. *Brain Research, 936,* 95–98.

Lashley, K. S. (1950). In search of the engram. *Society of Experimental Biology, Symposium, 4,* 454–482.

Latané B., & Darley, J. M. (1968). Group inhibition of bystander intervention in emergencies. *Journal of Personality and Social Psychology, 10,* 215–221.

Latané B., Williams, K., & Harkins, S. (2006). Many hands make the light work: The causes and consequences of social loafing. In J. M. Levine & R. L. Moreland (Eds.), *Small groups* (pp. 297–308). New York: Psychology Press.

Lattal, K. A. (2010). Delayed reinforcement of operant behaviour. *Journal of the Experimental Analysis of Behavior, 93,* 129–139.

Laureys, S., Owen, A. M., & Schiff, N. D. (2004). Brain function in coma, vegetative state, and related disorders. *Lancet Neurology, 3,* 537–546.

Lautenschlager, N. T., Cox, K. L., Flicker, L., Foster, J. K., van Bockxmeer, F. M., Xiao, J., et al. (2008). Effect of physical activity on cognitive function in older adults at risk for Alzheimer disease. *The Journal of the American Medical Association, 300,* 1027–1037.

Lavie, P. (2001). Sleep–wake as a biological rhythm. *Annual Review of Psychology, 5,* 277–303.

Laws, K. R., & Kokkalis, J. (2007). Ecstasy (MDMA) and memory function: A meta-analytic update. *Human Psychopharmacology, 22,* 381–388.

Lay, C. H., & Safdar, A. F. (2003). Daily hassles and distress among college students in relation to immigrant and minority status. *Current Psychology, 22,* 3–22.

Lazar, S. W., Kerr, C. E., Wasserman, R. H., Gray, J. R., Greve, D. N., Treadway, M. T., et al. (2005). Meditation experience is associated with increased cortical thickness. *Neuroreport 16,* 1893–1897.

Lazarus, R. S., & Folkman, S. (1984). *Stress, appraisal, and coping.* New York: Springer Publishing Company.

Le Grand, R., Barrie, I., & Tanaka, J. (2005). Testing the face-like versus geometric properties of the NI70 component. *Journal of Cognitive Neuroscience, 12,* 112.

Le Grand, R., Mondloch, C. J., Mauer, D., & Brent, H. P. (2004). Impairment in holistic face processing following early visual deprivation. *Psychological Science, 15,* 762–768.

Leary, M. R., Kowalski, R. M., Smith, L., & Phillips, S. (2003). Teasing, rejection, and violence: Case studies of the school shootings. *Aggressive Behavior, 29,* 202–214.

Lebens, H., Roefs, A., Martijn, C., Houben, K., Nederkoorn, C., & Jansen, A. (2011). Making implicit measures of associations with snack foods more negative through evaluative conditioning. *Eating Behaviors, 12,* 249–253.

Leblanc, V. R., Norman, G. R., & Brooks, L. R. (2001). Effect of a diagnostic suggestion on diagnostic accuracy and identification of clinical features. *Academic Medicine, 76,* S18–S20.

Leboe, J. P., & Whittlesea, B. W. A. (2002). The inferential basis of familiarity and recall. *The Journal of Memory and Language, 46,* 804–829.

Lederman, S. J., & Klatzky, R. L. (2004). Haptic identification of common objects: Effects of constraining the manual exploration process. *Perception and Psychophysics, 66,* 618–628.

Lederman, S. J., Kilgour, A., Kitada, R., Klatzky, R. I., & Hamilton, C. (2007). Haptic face processing. *Canadian Journal of Experimental Psychology, 61,* 230–241.

LeDoux, J. E. (1995). Emotion: Clues from the brain. *Annual Review of Psychology, 46,* 209–235.

LeDoux, J. E. (2000). Emotion circuits in the brain. *Annual Review of Neuroscience, 23,* 155–184.

Lee, H. J., Macbeth, A. H., Pagani, J. H., & Young, W. S. (2009). Oxytocin: The great facilitator of life. *Progress in Neurobiology, 88,* 127–151.

Lee, J. L. C. (2010). Memory reconsolidation mediates the updating of hippocampal memory content. *Frontiers in Behavioural Neuroscience, 11,* 168.

Lee, T. D., & Genovese, E. D. (1988). Distribution of practice in motor skills acquisition: Learning and performance effects reconsidered. *Research Quarterly for Exercise and Sport, 59,* 277–287.

Lee, K., & Ono, H. (2012). Marriage, cohabitation, and happiness: A cross-national analysis of 27 countries. *Journal of Marriage and Family, 74*(5), 953–972.

Lee-Baggley, D., Preece, M., & DeLongis, A. (2005). Coping with interpersonal stress: Role of the big five traits. *Journal of Personality and Social Psychology, 73,* 9–46.

Lefkowitz, E. S. (2005). "Things have gotten better": Developmental changes among emerging adults after the transition to university. *Journal of Adolescent Research, 20,* 40–63.

Lehman, P. K., & Geller, E. S. (2004). Behavior analysis and environmental protection: Accomplishments and potential for more. *Behavior and Social Issues, 13,* 13–32.

Leichtman, M. D., & Ceci, S. J. (1995). The effects of stereotypes and suggestions on preschoolers' reports. *Developmental Psychology, 31,* 568–578.

Leighton, J. P., & Sternberg, R. J. (2003). Reasoning and problem solving. In A. F. Healy & R. W. Proctor (Eds.), *Handbook of psychology: Experimental psychology* (Vol. 4, pp. 623–648). Hoboken, NJ: John Wiley & Sons.

Leiserowitz, A., Maibach, E., Roser-Renouf, C., & Smith, N. (2010). *Climate change in the American mind: Americans' global warming beliefs and attitudes in January 2010.* Yale University and George Mason University. New Haven, CT: Yale Project on Climate Change Communication.

Lejuez, C. W., Magidson, J. F., Mitchell, S. H., Sinha, R., Stevens, M. C., & de Wit, H. (2010). Behavioral and biological indicators of impulsivity in the development of alcohol use, problems, and disorders. *Alcoholism: Clinical and Experimental Research, 34,* 1334–1345.

Lepper, M. P., Greene, D., & Nisbett, R. E. (1973). Undermining children's intrinsic interest with extrinsic reward: A test of the "overjustification" hypothesis. *Journal of Personality and Social Psychology, 28,* 129–137.

Lesage, A., Vasiliadis, H.-M., Gagné, M.-A., Dudgeon, S., Kasman, N., & Hay, C. (2006). *Prevalence of mental illness and related service utilization in Canada: An analysis of the Canadian Community Health Survey.* Mississauga, ON: Canadian Collaborative Mental Health Initiative..

Lesch, K-P., Bengel, D., Heils, A., et al. (1996). Association of anxiety-related traits with a polymorphism in the serotonin transporter gene regulatory region. *Science, 273,* 1527–1531.

Lett, H. S., Blumenthal, J. A., Babyak, M. A., Sherwood, A., Strauman, T., Robins, C., & Newman, M.F. (2004). Depression as a risk factor for coronary artery disease: Evidence, mechanisms, and treatment. *Psychosomatic Medicine, 66,* 303–315.

Leucht, S., Arbter, D., Engel, R., Dienel, A., & Kieser, M. (2009). How effective are second-generation antipsychotic drugs? A meta-analysis of placebo-controlled trials. *Molecular Psychiatry, 14,* 429–447.

LeVay, S. (1991). A difference in hypothalamic structure between heterosexual and homosexual men. *Science, 253,* 1034–1037.

Levenston, G. K., Patrick, C. J., Bradley, M. M., & Lang, P. J. (2000). The psychopath as observer: Emotion and attention in picture processing. *Journal of Abnormal Psychology, 109,* 373–385.

Leventhal, H. (1970). Findings and theory in the study of fear communications. *Advances in Experimental Social Psychology, 5,* 119–186.

Levin, R. (1994). Sleep and dreaming characteristics of frequent nightmare subjects in a university population. *Dreaming, 4,* 127–137.

Levin, R., & Fireman, G. (2002). Nightmare prevalence, nightmare distress, and self-reported psychological disturbance. *Sleep, 25,* 205–212.

Levin, R., & Nielson, T. A. (2007). Disturbed sleeping, posttraumatic disorder, and affect distress: A review and neurocognitive model. *Psychological Bulletin, 133,* 482–528.

Levine, B., Svoboda, E., Hay, J. F., Winocur, G., & Moscovitch, M. (2002). Aging and autobiographical memory: Dissociating episodic from semantic retrieval. *Psychology and Aging, 17,* 677–689.

Levine, M. P., Smolak, L., & Hayden, H. (1994). The relation of sociocultural factors to eating attitudes and behaviors among middle school girls. *The Journal of Early Adolescence, 14,* 471–490.

Levinger, G. (1965). Marital cohesiveness and dissolution: An integrative review. *Journal of Marriage and the Family, 27,* 19–28.

Levinson, B. W. (1965). States of awareness during general anaesthesia. *British Journal of Anaethesia, 37,* 544–546.

Levitin, D. (2006). *This is your brain on music: The science of a human obsession.* New York: Dutton Books.

Levy, S. R., Chiu, C., & Hong, Y. (2006). Lay theories and intergroup relations. *Group Processes & Intergroup Relations, 9,* 5–24.

Lewin, K. (1936). *Principles of topological psychology.* New York: McGraw-Hill.

Lewin, T. (2009, October 23). No Einstein in your crib? Get a refund. *The New York Times.*

Li, C. (2010). Primacy effect or recency effect? A long-term memory test of Super Bowl commercials. *Journal of Consumer Behaviour, 9,* 32–44.

Li, L., & Yong, H. H. (2009). Tobacco advertising on the street in Kunming, China. *Tobacco Control, 18,* 63.

Liberman, N., & Trope, Y. (2008). The psychology of transcending the here and now. *Science, 322,* 1201–1205.

Lieberman, L. (2001). How "Caucasoids" got such big crania and why they shrank: From Morton to Rushton. *Current Anthropology, 42,* 69–95.

Lieberman, P. (1984). *The biology and evolution of language.* Cambridge, MA: Harvard University Press.

Liebowitz, M. R. (1983). *The chemistry of love.* Boston: Little, Brown, & Co.

Liégeois, F., Badeweg, T., Connelly, A., Gadian, D. G., Mishkin, M., & Vargha-Khadem, F. (2003). Language fMRI abnormalities associated with FOXP2 gene mutation. *Nature Neuroscience, 6,* 1230–1237.

Light, K. C., Grewen, K. M., & Amico, J. A. (2005). More frequent partner hugs and higher oxytocin levels are linked to lower blood pressure and heart rate for women in premenopausal women. *Biological Psychology, 69,* 5–21.

Light, K. C., Smith, T. E., Johns, J. M., Brownley, K. A., Hofheimer, J. A., & Amico, J. A. (2000). Oxytocin responsivity in mothers of infants: A preliminary study of relationship with BP during laboratory stress and normal ambulatory activity. *Health Psychology, 19,* 560–567.

Lilienfeld, S. (2007). Psychological treatments that cause harm. *Perspectives on Psychological Science, 2,* 53–70.

Lilienfeld, S. O., & Arkowitz, H. (2009, February). Lunacy and the full moon. *Scientific American, 20,* 64–65.

Lilienfeld, S. O., & Lynn, S. J. (2003). Dissociative identity disorder: Multiple personality, multiple controversies. In S. O. Lilienfeld, J. M. Lohr, & S. J. Lynn (Eds.), *Science and pseudoscience in clinical psychology* (pp. 109–142). New York: Guilford Press.

Lilienfeld, S. O., Lynn, S. J., Kirsch, I., Chaves, J. F., Sarbin, T. R., Ganaway, G. K., & Powell, R. A. (1999). Dissociative identity disorder and the sociocognitive model: Recalling the lessons of the past. *Psychological Bulletin, 125,* 507–523.

Lilienfeld, S. O., Wood, J. M., & Garb, H. N. (2000). The scientific status of projective techniques. *Psychological Science in the Public Interest, 1,* 27–66.

Lillard, A. (1998). Ethnopsychologies: Cultural variations in theories of mind. *Psychological Bulletin, 123,* 3–32.

Lin, C., Davidson, T., & Ancoli-Israel, S. (2008). Gender differences in obstructive sleep apnea and treatment implications. *Sleep Medicine Reviews, 12,* 481–496.

Lindau, S. T., Schumm, L. P., Laumann, E. O., Levinson, W., O'Muircheartaigh, C. A., & Waite, L. J. (2007). A study of sexuality and health among older adults in the United States. *New England Journal of Medicine, 357,* 762–774.

Linde, K., Berner, M. M., & Kriston, L. S. (2008). John's wort for major depression. *Cochrane Database of Systemic Reviews, 4,* CD000448.

Lindstrom, M., & Underhill, P. (2010). *Buy•ology, truth and lies about why we buy.* New York: Broadway Books.

Linehan, M. (1993). *Cognitive behavioral treatment of borderline personality disorder.* New York: Guilford Press.

Link, B. G. (1987). Understanding labeling effects in the area of mental disorders: An assessment of the effects of expectations of rejection. *American Sociological Review, 52,* 96–112.

Link, B. G., Cullen, F. T., Struening, E., Shrout, P. E., & Dohrenwend, B. P. (1989). A modified labeling theory approach to mental disorders: An empirical assessment. *American Sociological Review, 54,* 400–423.

Liszkowski, U., Carpenter, M., Striano, T., & Tomasello, M. (2006). 12-and 18-month-olds point to provide information for others. *Journal of Cognition and Development, 7,* 173–187.

Livingstone, M. S., & Conway, B. R. (2004). Was Rembrandt stereoblind? *The New England Journal of Medicine, 351,* 1264–1265.

Ljungberg, T., Apicella, P., & Schultz, W. (1992). Responses of monkey dopamine neurons during learning of behavioral reactions. *Journal of Neurophysiology, 67,* 145–163.

LoBue, V., Rakison, D. H., & DeLoache, J. S. (2010). Threat perception across the life span: Evidence for multiple converging pathways. *Current Directions in Psychological Science, 19,* 375–379.

Locksley, A., Ortiz, V., & Hepburn, C. (1980). Social categorization and discriminatory behavior: Extinguishing the minimal intergroup discrimination effect. *Journal of Personality and Social Psychology, 39,* 773–783.

Loewenstein, G. F., Weber, E. U., Hsee, C. K., & Welch, N. (2001). Risk as feelings. *Psychological Bulletin, 127,* 267–286.

Loftus, E. F. (1975). Leading questions and the eyewitness report. *Cognitive Psychology, 7,* 560–572.

Loftus, E. F. (1997). Creating false memories. *Scientific America, 277,* 70–75.

Loftus, E. F., & Davis, D. (2006). Recovered memories. *Annual Review of Clinical Psychology, 2,* 469–498.

Loftus, E. F., Loftus, G. R., & Lesso, J. (1987). Some facts about "weapon focus." *Law and Human Behavior, 11,* 55–62.

Loftus, E. F., & Palmer, J. C. (1974). Reconstruction of automobile destruction: An example of the interaction between language and memory. *Journal of Verbal Learning and Verbal Behavior, 13,* 585–589.

Logan, J. M., Sanders, A. L., Snyder, A. Z., Morris, J. C., & Buckner, R. L. (2002). Under-recruitment and nonselective recruitment: Dissociable neural mechanisms associated with aging. *Neuron, 33,* 827–840.

Logel, C., & Cohen, G. L. (2012). The role of the self in physical health: Testing the effect of a cause-affirmation intervention on weight loss. *Psychological Science, 23,* 53–55.

Loggia, M. L., Mogil, J. S., & Bushnell, M. C. (2008a). Empathy hurts: Compassion for another increases both sensory and affective components of pain perception. *Pain, 136,* 168–176.

Loggia, M. L., Mogil, J. S., & Bushnell, M. C. (2008b). Experimentally induced mood changes preferentially affect pain unpleasantness. *The Journal of Pain, 9,* 784–791.

Lomber, S. G., & Malhotra, S. (2008). Double dissociation of "what" and "where" processing inauditory cortex. *Nature Neuroscience, 11,* 609–616.

Lømo, T. (1966). Frequency potentiation of excitatory synaptic activity in the dentate area of the hippocampal formation. *Acta Physiological Scandinavica, 68,* 128.

Lorber, M. F. (2004). Psychophysiology of aggression, psychopathy, and conduct problems: A meta-analysis. *Psychological Bulletin, 130,* 531.

Lorenzoni, I., & Pidgeon, N. F. (2006). Public views on climate change: European and USA perspectives. *Climatic Change, 77,* 73–95.

Lorrain, D. S., Matuszewich, L., Friedman, R. D., & Hull, E. M. (1997). Extracellular serotonin in the lateral hypothalamic area is increased during the postejaculatory interval and impairs copulation in male rats. *The Journal of Neuroscience, 17,* 9361–9366.

Losin, E. A. R., Dapretto, M., & Lacoboni, M. (2010). Culture and neuroscience: Additive or synergistic? *Social, Cognitive, and Affective Neuroscience, 5,* 148–158.

Lougheed, J. P., & Hollenstein, T. (2012). A limited repertoire of emotion regulation strategies is associated with internalizing problems in adolescence. *Social Development, 21,* 704–721.

Lovett, M. W., Lacerenza, L., De Palma, M., & Frijters, J. C. (2012). Evaluating the efficacy of remediation for struggling readers in high school. *Journal of Learning Disabilities, 45,* 151–169.

Lowenstein, L. F. (2002). Fetishes and their associated behavior. *Sexuality and Disability, 20,* 135–147.

Lubow, R. E., & Moore, A. U. (1959). Latent inhibition: The effect of non-reinforced preexposure to the conditioned stimulus. *Journal of Comparative and Physiological Psychology, 52,* 415–419.

Lucas, R. E., Diener, E., Grob. A., Suh, E. M., & Shao, L. (2000). Cross-cultural evidence for the fundamental features of extraversion. *Journal of Personality and Social Psychology, 79,* 452–468.

Luck, A., Pearson, S., Maddern, G., & Hewett, P. (1999). Effects of video information on precolonoscopy anxiety and knowledge: A randomised trial. *Lancet, 354,* 2032–2035.

Luders, E., Narr, K., Bilder, R., Szeszko, P., Gurbani, M., Hamilton, L., Toga, A. W., & Gaser, C. (2008). Mapping the relationship between cortical convolution and intelligence: Effects of gender. *Cerebral Cortex, 18,* 2019–2026.

Luo, L., & Craik, F. I. (2008). Aging and memory: A cognitive approach. *Canadian Journal of Psychiatry, 53,* 346–353.

Lutgendorf, S. K., Costanzo, E., & Siegel, S. (2007). Psychosocial influences in oncology: An expanded model of biobehavioral mechanisms. In R. Ader, R. Glaser, N. Cohen, & M. Irwin (Eds.), *Psychoneuroimmunology* (4th ed., pp. 869–895). New York: Academic Press.

Lutz, A., Slagter, H. A., Dunne, J. D., & Davidson, R. J. (2008). Attention regulation and monitoring in meditation. *Trends in Cognitive Sciences, 12,* 163–169.

Lykken, D. T. (1995). *The antisocial personalities.* Mahwah, NJ: Lawrence Erlbaum Associates.

Lyles, J., & Cadet, J. L. (2003). Methylenedioxymethamphetamine (MDMA, Ecstasy) neurotoxicity: Cellular and molecular mechanisms. *Brain Research, 42,* 155–168.

Lynam, D. R., & Gudonis, L. (2005). The development of psychopathology. *Annual Review of Clinical Psychology, 1,* 381–407.

Lynn, R., & Irving, P. (2004). Sex differences on the Progressive Matrices: A meta-analysis. *Intelligence, 32,* 481–498.

Lynn, S. J., & Kirsch, I. (1996). False memories, hypnosis, and fantasy-proneness. *Psychological Inquiry, 7,* 151–155.

Lynn, S., Nash, M., Rhue, J., Frauman, D., & Sweeney, C. (1984). Nonvolition, expectancies, and hypnotic rapport. *Journal of Abnormal Psychology, 93,* 295–303.

Lyons, B. D., Hoffman, B. J., & Michel, J. W. (2009). Not much more than g? An examination of the impact of intelligence on NFL performance. *Human Performance, 22,* 225–245.

Lyons, N. P. (1983). Two perspectives: On self, relationships, and morality. *Harvard Educational Review, 53,* 125–145.

Lyznicki, J. M., Doege, T. C., Davis, R. M., & Williams, M. A. (1998). Sleepiness, driving, and motor vehicle crashes. *Journal of the American Medical Association, 279,* 1908–1913.

MacCracken, M. J., & Stadulis, R. E. (1985). Social facilitation of young children's dynamic balance performance. *Journal of Sport Psychology, 7,* 150–165.

Macdonald, K., & Macdonald, T. M. (2010). The peptide that binds: A systematic review of oxytocin and its prosocial effects in humans. *Harvard Review of Psychiatry, 18,* 1–21.

MacDonald, T. K., & Martineau, A. M. (2002). Self-esteem, mood, and intentions to use condoms: When does low self-esteem lead to risky health behaviors? *Journal of Experimental Social Psychology, 38,* 299–306.

Machado Rocha, F. C., Stéfano, S. C., De Cássia Haiek, R., Rosa Oliveira, L. M., & Da Silveira, D. X. (2008). Therapeutic use of Cannabis sativa on chemotherapy-induced nausea and vomiting among cancer patients: Systematic review and meta-analysis. *European Journal of Cancer Care, 17,* 431–443.

Mack, A., & Rock, I. (1998). *Inattentional blindness.* Cambridge, MA: MIT Press.

Macmillan, M. (2008). Phineas Gage: Unravelling the myth. *The Psychologist, 21,* 828–839.

Madden, D.J., Turkington, T. G., Coleman, R. E., Provenzale, J. M., DeGrado, T. R., & Hoffman, J. M. (1996). Adult age differences in regional cerebral blood flow during visual world identification: Evidence from $H_2^{15}O$ PET. *NeuroImage, 3,* 127–142.

Maddux, W. W., Mullen, E., & Galinsky, A. D. (2008). Chameleons bake bigger pies and take bigger pieces: Strategic behavioral mimicry facilitates negotiation outcomes. *Journal of Experimental Social Psychology, 44,* 461–468.

Maes, H. H., Neale, M. C., & Eaves, L. J. (1997). Genetic and environmental factors in relative body weight and human adiposity. *Behavioral Genetics, 27,* 325–351.

Maguire, E. A., Gadian, D. G., Johnsrude, I. S., Good, C. D., Ashburner, J., Frackowiak, R. S., & Frith, C. D. (2000). Navigation-related structural changes in the hippocampus of taxi drivers. *Proceedings of the National Academy of Sciences, 97,* 4398–4403.

Mahalik, J., Good, G., & Englar-Carlson, M. (2003). Masculinity scripts, presenting concerns, and help seeking: Implications for practice and training. *Professional Psychology: Research and Practice, 34,* 123–131.

Mahon, M., & Crutchley, A. (2006). Performance of typically-developing school-age children with English as an additional language on the British Picture Vocabulary Scales II. *Child Language Teaching and Therapy,* 22, 333–351.

Maier, N. F. (1931). Reasoning in humans. II. The solution of a problem and its appearance in consciousness. *Journal of Comparative Psychology, 12,* 181–194.

Maier, N. R. F. (1930). Reasoning in humans: On direction. *Journal of Comparative Psychology, 10,* 115–143.

Maier, S. F., & Watkins, L. R. (1998). Cytokines for psychologists: Implications of bidirectional immune-to-brain communication for understanding behavior, mood, and cognition. *Psychological Review, 105,* 83–107.

Maier, S. F., & Watkins, L. R. (2005). Stressor controllability and learned helplessness: The roles of the dorsal raphe nucleus, serotonin, and corticotrophin-releasing factor. *Neuroscience and Behavioral Reviews, 29,* 829–841.

Main, M., & Solomon, J. (1990). Procedures for identifying disorganized/disoriented infants during the Ainsworth Strange Situation. In M. Greenberg, D. Cicchetti, & M. Cummings

(Eds.), *Attachment in the preschool years*, (pp. 121–160). Chicago: University of Chicago Press.

Makin, J., Fried, P. A., & Watkinson, B. (1991). A comparison of active and passive smoking during pregnancy: Long-term effects. *Neurotoxicology and Teratology, 13*, 5–12.

Mampe, B., Friederici, A. D., Christophe, A., & Wermke, K. (2009). Newborns' cry melody is shaped by their native language. *Current Biology, 19*, 1994–1997.

Mandai, O., Guerrien, A., Sockeel, P., Dujardin, K., & Leconte, P. (1989). REM sleep modifications following a Morse code learning session in humans. *Physiology & Behavior, 46*, 639–642.

Mangels, J. A., Butterfield, B., Lamb, J., Good, C., & Dweck, C. S. (2006). Why do beliefs about intelligence influence learning success? A social cognitive neuroscience model. *Social Cognitive and Affective Neuroscience, 1*, 75–86.

Mann, C. E., & Himelein, M. J. (2008). Putting the person back into psychopathology: An intervention to reduce mental illness stigma in the classroom. *Social Psychiatry and Psychiatric Epidemiology, 43*, 545–551.

Manning, R., Levine, M., & Collins, A. (2007). The Kitty Genovese murder and the social psychology of helping: The parable of the 38 witnesses. *American Psychologist, 62*, 555–562.

Mansfield, A. K., Addis, M. E., & Courtenay, W. (2005). Measurement of men's help seeking: Development and evaluation of the barriers to help seeking scale. *Psychology of Men & Masculinity, 6*, 95–108.

Maquet, P., Peters, J., Aerts, J., Delfiore, G., Dequeldre, C., Luxen, A., & Franck, G. (1996). Functional neuroanatomy of human rapid-eye-movement sleep and dreaming. *Nature, 383*, 163–166.

Marcia, J. E. (2002). Identity and psychosocial development in adulthood. *Identity: An International Journal of Theory and Research, 2*, 7–28.

Maren, S. (2001). Neurobiology of Pavlovian fear conditioning. *Annual Review of Neuroscience, 24*, 897–931.

Marino, L. (2002). Convergence of complex cognitive abilities in cetaceans and primates. *Brain, Behavior, and Evolution, 59*, 21–32.

Marks, G., & Miller, N. (1987). Ten years of research on the false-consensus effect: An empirical and theoretical review. *Psychological Bulletin, 102*, 72–90.

Marks, L. V. (2001). *Sexual chemistry: A history of the contraceptive pill*. New Haven: Yale University Press.

Markus, H. (1977). Self-schema and processing information about the self. *Personality and Social Psychology Bulletin, 35*, 63–78.

Markus, H. R., & Kitayama, S. (1991). Culture and the self: Implications for cognition, emotion, and motivation. *Psychological Review, 98*, 224–253.

Markus, H., Uchida, Y., Omoregie, H., Townsend, S., & Kitayama, S. (2006). Going for the gold: Models of agency in Japanese and American contexts. *Psychological Science, 17*, 103–112.

Marois, R., & Ivanoff, J. (2005). Capacity limits of information processing in the brain. *Trends in Cognitive Sciences, 46*, 774–785.

Marotta, J. J., Genovese, C. R., & Behrmann, M. (2001). A functional MRI study of face recognition in patients with prosopagnosia. *Neuroreport, 12*, 1581–1587.

Marshall, K. (2011). Gambling 2011. Component of Statistics Canada Catalogue no. 75-001-X, 1–7.

Martin, A., Wiggs, C. L., Ungerleider, L. G., & Haxby, J. V. (1996). Neural correlates of category-specific knowledge. *Nature, 379*, 649–652.

Martin, L. (1986). "Eskimo words for snow": A case study in the genesis and decay of an anthropological example. *American Anthropologist, 88*, 418–423.

Martin, R. A. (2002). Is laughter the best medicine? Humor, laughter and physical health. *Current Directions in Psychological Science, 11*, 216–220.

Martin, R. A. (2007). *The psychology of humor: An integrative approach*. Burlington, MA: Elsevier Academic Press.

Martin-Santos, R., Fagundo, A. B., Crippa, J. A., Atakan, Z., Bhattacharyya, S., Allen, P., et al. (2010). Neuroimaging in cannabis use: A systematic review of the literature. *Psychological Medicine, 40*, 383–398.

Maruff, P., Falleti, M. G., Collie, A., Darby, D., & McStephen, M. (2005). Fatigue-related impairment in the speed, accuracy and variability of psychomotor performance: Comparison with blood alcohol levels. *Journal of Sleep Research, 14*, 21–27.

Maruta, T., Colligan, R. C., Malinchoc, M., & Offord, K. P. (2000). Optimists vs pessimists: Survival rate among medical patients over a 30-year period. *Mayo Clinic Proceedings, 75*, 140–143.

Mascolo, M. E., & Fischer, K. W. (2007). The codevelopment of self and sociomoral emotions during the toddler years. In C. A. Brownell, & C. B. Kopp (Eds.), *Socioemotional development in the toddler years: transitions and transformations* (pp. 66–99). New York: Guilford Press.

Maslow, A. (1943). A theory of human motivation. *Psychological Review, 50*, 370–396.

Maslow, A. (1954). *Motivation and Personality*. New York: Harper and Row.

Maslow, A. (1968). *Toward a psychology of being* (2nd ed.). New York: Van Nostrand.

Maslow, A. (1970). *Motivation and personality*,. New York: Harper & Row.

Masters, W., & Johnson, V. (1966). *Human sexual response*. Oxford, UK: Little, Brown.

Masuda, T., Ellsworth, P. C., Mesquita, B., Leu, J., Tanida, S., & van de Veerdonk, E. (2008). Placing the face in context: Cultural differences in the perception of facial emotion. *Journal of Personality and Social Psychology, 94*, 365–381.

Mather, J. A., & Anderson, R. C. (1993). Personalities of octopuses (*Octopus rubescens*). *Journal of Comparative Psychology, 107*, 336–340.

Matsunaga, H., Kaye, W. H., McConaha, C., Plotnicov, K., Pollice, C., & Rao, R. (2000). Personality disorders among subjects recovered from eating disorders. *International Journal of Eating Disorders, 27*, 353–357.

Matthews, K., & Gump, B. B. (2002). Chronic work stress and marital dissolution increase risk of posttrial mortality in men from the Multiple Risk Factor Intervention Trial. *Archives of Internal Medicine, 162*, 309–315.

Mattson, M. P. (2000) Neuroprotective signaling and the aging brain: Take away my food and let me run. *Brain Research, 886*, 47–53.

Maurer, D., Lewis, T. L., Brent, H. P., & Levin, A. V. (1999). Rapid improvement in the acuity of infants after visual input. *Science, 286*, 108–110.

Maurer, D., & Maurer, C. (1988). *The world of the newborn*. New York: Basic Books.

Mayberg, H. S., Liotti, M., Brannan, S. K., McGinnis, S., Mahurin, R. K., Jerabek, P. A., Silva, J. A., Tekell, J. L., Martin, C. C., Lancaster, J. L., & Fox, P. T. (1999). Reciprocal limbic-cortical function and negative mood: Converging PET findings in depression and normal sadness. *The American Journal of Psychiatry, 156*, 675–682.

Mayberg, H. S., Lozano, A. M., Voon, V., McNeely, H. E., Seminowicz, D., Hamani, C., et al. (2005). Deep brain stimulation for treatment-resistant depression. *Neuron, 45*, 651–660.

Mayberg, H. S., Silva, J. A., Brannan, S. K., Tekell, J. L., Mahurin, R. K., McGinnis, S., & Jerabek, P. A. (2002). The functional neuroanatomy of the placebo effect. *American Journal of Psychiatry, 159*, 728–737.

Mayer, G. (2012). The use of sodium oxybate to treat narcolepsy. *Expert Review of Neurotherapeutics, 12*, 519–529.

Mazzoni, G., & Memon, A. (2003). Imagination can create false autobiographical memories. *Psychological Science, 14*, 186–188.

McAnulty, G., Duffy, F. H., Butler, S., Bernstein, J. H., Zurakowski, D., & Als, H. (2010). Effects of newborn individualized developmental care and assessment program (NIDCAP) at age 8 years: Preliminary data. *Clinical Pediatrics (Philadelphia), 49*, 258–270.

McAnulty, G., Duffy, F. H., Butler, S., Parad, R., Ringer, S., Zurakowski, D., & Als, H. (2009). Individualized developmental care for a large sample of very preterm infants: Health, neurobehaviour and neurophysiology. *Acta Paediatrica, 98,* 1920–1926.

McClure, S. M., Laibson, D. I., Loewenstein, G., & Cohen, J. D. (2004). Separate neural systems value immediate and delayed monetary rewards. *Science, 306,* 503–507.

McCormick, L. M., Keel, P. K., Brumm, M. C., Bowers, W., Swayze, V., Andersen, A., & Andreasen, N. (2008). Implications of starvation-induced change in right dorsal anterior cingulate volume in anorexia nervosa. *International Journal of Eating Disorders, 41,* 602–610.

McCoy, A. (2006). *A question of torture: CIA interrogation from the Cold War to the War on Terror.* New York: Metropolitan Books.

McCracken, L. M., Gauntlett-Gilbert, J., & Vowles, K. E. (2007). The role of mindfulness in a contextual cognitive–behavioral analysis of chronic pain-related suffering and disability. *Pain, 131,* 63–69.

McCrae, R. R. (2001). Trait psychology and culture. *Journal of Personality, 69,* 819–846.

McCrae, R. R., & Costa, P. (1987). Validation of the Five-Factor Model of personality across instruments and observers. *Journal of Personality and Social Psychology, 52,* 81–90.

McCrae, R. R., & Costa, P. T. (1990). *Personality in adulthood.* New York: The Guildford Press.

McCrae, R. R., Terracciano, A., et al. (2005). Personality profiles of cultures: Aggregate personality traits. *Journal of Personality and Social Psychology, 89,* 407–425.

McCullough, J. P. (2000). *Treatment for chronic depression: Cognitive behavioral analysis system of psychotherapy (CBASP).* New York: Guilford Press.

McCullough, M. E., & Willoughby, B. L. (2009). Religion, self-regulation, and self-control: Associations, explanations, and implications. *Psychological Bulletin, 135,* 69–93.

McCullough, M. E., Hoyt, W. T., Larson, D. B., Koenig, H. G., & Thoresen, C. E. (2000). Religious involvement and mortality: A meta-analytic review. *Health Psychology, 19,* 211–222.

McDaid, C., Duree, K. H., Griffin, S. C., Weatherly, H. L. A., Stradling, J. R., Davies, J. O., et al. (2009). A systematic review of continuous positive airway pressure for obstructive sleep apnoea–hypopnoea syndrome. *Sleep Science Reviews, 13,* 427–436.

McDaniel, M. A. (2005). Big-brained people are smarter: A meta-analysis of the relationship between in vivo brain volume and intelligence. *Intelligence, 33,* 337–346.

McEwen, B. S. (2000). The neurobiology of stress: From serendipity to clinical relevance. *Brain Research, 886,* 172–189.

McGeown, W. J., Mazzoni, G., Venneri, A., Kirsch, I. (2009). Hypnotic induction decreases anterior default mode activity. *Consciousness and Cognition, 18,* 848–855.

McGlashan, T. H., Zipursky, R. B., Perkins, D., Addington, J., Miller, T., & Woods, S. W. (2006). Randomized double-blind clinical trial of olanzapine versus placebo in patients prodromally symptomatic for psychosis. *American Journal of Psychiatry, 163,* 790–799.

McGorry, P. D., Yung, A. R., Phillips, L. J., Yuen, H. P., Francey, S., & Cosgrave, E. M. (2002). Randomized controlled trial of interventions designed to reduce the risk of progression to first-episode psychosis in a clinical sample with subthreshold symptoms. *Archives of General Psychiatry, 59,* 921–928.

McGowan, P. O., Sasaki, A., D'Alessio, A. C., Dymov, S., Labonte, B., Szyf, M., et al. (2009). Epigenetic regulation of the glucocorticoid receptor in human brain associates with childhood abuse. *Nature Neuroscience, 12,* 342–348.

McGruder, J. (2004). Disease models of mental illness and aftercare patient education: Critical observations from meta-analyses, cross-cultural practice and anthropological study. *British Journal of Occupational Therapy, 67,* 310–318.

McGuire, W. J. (1961). The effectiveness of supportive and refutational defenses in immunizing defenses. *Sociometry, 24,* 184–197.

McKenzie-Mohr, D. (2000). Fostering sustainable behavior through community-based social marketing. *American Psychologist, 55,* 531–537.

McKinney, K. G. (2009). Initial evaluation of Active Minds: A student organization dedicated to reducing the stigma of mental illness. *Journal of College Student Psychotherapy, 23,* 281–301.

McLaughlin, K. A., Hatzenbuehler, M. L., Mennin, D. S., & Nolen-Hoeksema, S. (2011). Emotion dysregulation and adolescent psychopathology: A prospective study. *Behaviour research and therapy, 49,* 544–554.

McLay, R. N., Wood, D. P., Webb-Murphy, J. A., Spira, J. L., Wiederhold, M. D., Pyne, J. M., & Wiederhold, B. K. (2011). A randomized, controlled trial of virtual reality exposure therapy for post-traumatic stress disorder in active duty service members with combat-related post-traumatic stress disorder. *Cyberpsychology, Behavior, and Social Networking, 14,* 223–229.

McManus, F., Surawy, C., Muse, K., Vazquez-Montes, M., & Williams, J. M. G. (2012). A randomized clinical trial of mindfulness-based cognitive therapy versus unrestricted services for health anxiety (hypochondriasis). *Journal of Consulting and Clinical Psychology, 80,* 817–828.

McNally, R. J., Lasko, N. B., Clancy, S. A., Macklin, M. L., Pitman, R. K., & Orr, S. P. (2004). Psychophysiological responding during script-driven imagery in people reporting abduction by space aliens. *Psychological Science, 15,* 493–497.

McNeely, H. E., Mayberg, H. S., Lozano, A. M., & Kennedy, S. H. (2008). Neuropsychological impact of Cg25 deep brain stimulation for treatment-resistant depression: Preliminary results over 12 months. *Journal of Nervous and Mental Disease, 196,* 405–410.

McVey, G. L., Gusella, J., Tweed, S., & Ferrari, M. (2009). A controlled evaluation of web-based training for teachers and public health practitioners on the prevention of eating disorders. *Eating Disorders: Journal of Treatment and Prevention, 17,* 1–26.

Mead, M. (1928). *Coming of age in Samoa: A psychological study of primitive youth for Western civilization.* Oxford, UK: William Morrow.

Meehl, P. (1990). Toward an integrated theory of schizotaxia, schizotypy, and schizophrenia. *Journal of Personality Disorders, 4,* 1–99.

Meehl, P. E. (1967). Theory-testing in psychology and physics: A methodological paradox. *Philosophy of Science, 34,* 103–115.

Mehl, M. R., Gosling, S. D., & Pennebaker, J. W. (2006). Personality in its natural habitat: Manifestations and implicit folk theories of personality in daily life. *Journal of Personality and Social Psychology, 90,* 862–877.

Mehler, J., & Bever, T. G. (1967). Cognitive capacity of very young children. *Science, 158,* 141–142.

Meier, M. H., Slutske, W. S., Arndt, S., & Cadoret, R. J. (2008). Impulsive and callous traits are more strongly associated with delinquent behavior in higher risk neighborhoods among boys and girls. *Journal of Abnormal Psychology, 117,* 377–385.

Melton, G. B., Petrila, J., Poythress, N. G., & Slobogin, C. (2007). *Psychological evaluations for the courts: A handbook for mental health professionals and lawyers* (3rd ed.). New York: Guilford Press.

Meltzoff, A. N. (1988). Infant imitation and memory: Nine-month-olds in immediate and deferred tests. *Child Development, 59,* 217–225.

Meltzoff, A. N., & Moore, M. K. (1977). Imitation of facial and manual gestures by human neonates. *Science, 198,* 75–78.

Melzack, R., & Wall, P. D. (1965). Pain mechanisms: A new theory. *Science, 150,* 971–979.

Melzack, R., & Wall, P. D. (1982). *The challenge of pain.* New York: Basic Books.

Memmert D., & Furley, P. (2007). "I spy with my little eye!": Breadth of attention, inattentional blindness, and tactical decision making in team sports. *Journal of Sport and Exercise Psychology, 29,* 365–347.

Menzies, R. G., & Clarke, J. C. (1993). The etiology of childhood water phobia. *Behaviour Research and Therapy, 31,* 499–501.

Merckelbach, H., de Jong, P. J., Muris, P., & van den Hout, M. A. (1996). The etiology of specific phobias. *Clinical Psychology Review, 16,* 337–361.

Merikle, P. M., & Daneman, M. (1996). Memory for unconsciously perceived events: Evidence from anesthetized patients. *Consciousness and Cognition, 5,* 525–541.

Merikle, P. M., & Joordens, S. (1997). Parallels between perception without attention and perception without awareness. *Consciousness and Cognition, 6,* 219–236.

Merikle, P. M., & Skanes, H. E. (1992). Subliminal self-help audiotapes: A search for placebo effects. *Journal of Applied Psychology, 77,* 772–776.

Messer, D. (2000). State of the art: Language acquisition. *The Psychologist, 13,* 138–143.

Meston, C. M., & Ahrold, T. (2010). Ethnic, gender, and acculturation influences on sexual behaviors. *Archives of Sexual Behavior, 39,* 179–189.

Meston, C. M., & Buss, D. M. (2007). Why humans have sex. *Archives of Sexual Behavior, 36,* 477–507.

Meston, C. M., Hamilton, L. D., & Harte, C. B. (2009). Sexual motivation in women as a function of age. *International Society for Sexual Medicine, 6,* 3305–3319.

Mezulis, A. H., Abramson, L. Y., Hyde, J. S., & Hankin, B. L. (2004). Is there a universal positivity bias in attributions? A meta-analytic review of individual, developmental, and culture differences in the self-serving attributional bias. *Psychological Bulletin, 130,* 711–747.

Michael, E. B., & Gollan, T. H. (2005). Being and becoming bilingual: Individual differences and consequences for language production. In J.F. Kroll & A. M. B. de Groot (Eds.), *Handbook of bilingualism: Psycholinguistic approach* (pp. 389–407). New York: Oxford University Press.

Mikulincer, M., & Shaver, P. R. (2005). Attachment security, compassion, and altruism. *Current directions in psychological science, 14,* 34–38.

Milfont, T. L. (2010). Global warming, climate change, and human psychology. In V. Corral-Verdugo, C. Garcia-Cadana, & M. Frjas-Arment (Eds.), *Psychological approaches to sustainability: Current trends in theory, research and practice.* New York: Nova Science.

Milgram, S. (1963). Behavioral study of obedience. *Journal of Abnormal and Social Psychology, 67,* 371–378.

Milgram, S. (1974). *Obedience to authority: An experimental view.* New York: Harpercollins.

Miller, D.T., & Ross, M. (1975). Self-serving biases in the attribution of causality: Fact or fiction? *Psychological Bulletin, 82,* 213–225.

Miller, G. (1956). The magical number seven, plus or minus two: Some limits on our capacity for processing information. *Psychological Review, 63,* 81–97.

Miller, I. J., Jr., & Reedy, F. E. (1990). Variations in human taste bud density and intensity perception. *Physiology and Behavior, 47,* 1213–1219.

Miller, K. E., Omidian, P., Quraishy, A., Quraishy, N., Nasiry, M., Nasiry, S., Karyar, N. M., & Yaqubi, A. (2006). The Afghan Symptom Checklist: A culturally grounded approach to mental health assessment in a conflict zone. *American Journal of Orthopsychiatry, 76,* 423–433.

Miller, L. J., Myers, A., Prinzi, L., & Mittenberg, W. (2009). Changes in intellectual functioning associated with normal aging. *Archives of Clinical Neuropsychology, 24,* 681–688.

Miller, L. L., & Cornett, T. L. (1978). Marijuana: Dose effects on pulse rate, subjective estimates of intoxication, free recall and recognition memory. *Pharmacology Biochemistry and Behavior, 9,* 573–577.

Miller, L. L., McFarland, D., Cornett, T. L., & Brightwell, D. (1977). Marijuana and memory impairment: Effect on free recall and recognition memory. *Pharmacology Biochemistry and Behavior, 7,* 99–103.

Milling, L. (2009). Response expectancies: A psychological mechanism of suggested and placebo analgesia. *Contemporary Hypnosis, 26,* 93–110.

Mills, D., Coffey-Corina, S., & Neville, H. (1997). Language comprehension and cerebral specialization from 13 to 20 months. *Developmental Neuropsychology, 13,* 397–445.

Mills, J. N. (1964). Circadian rhythms during and after three months in solitude underground. *Journal of Physiology, 174,* 217–231.

Milner, B. (1962). Les troubles de la mémoire accompagnant des lésions hippocampiques bilatérales. In P. Passouant (Ed.), *Physiologie de l'Hippocampe* (pp. 257–272). Paris: Centre Nationale de la Recherche Scientifique.

Milner, B., Corkin, S., & Teuber, H. L. (1968). Further analysis of the hippocampal amnesic syndrome: 14-year follow-up study of H.M. *Neuropsychologia 6,* 215–234.

Milner, D., & Goodale, M. A. (2006). *The visual brain in action* (2nd ed). Oxford, UK: Oxford University Press.

Mischel, W. (1968). *Personality and assessment.* New York: Wiley.

Mischel, W. (1981). *Introduction to personality.* New York: Holt, Rinehart and Winston.

Mischel, W., & Ebbesen, E. B. (1970). Attention in delay of gratification. *Journal of Personality and Social Psychology, 16,* 329–337.

Mischel, W., & Shoda, Y. (1998). Reconciling processing dynamics and personality dispositions. *Annual Review of Psychology, 49,* 229–258.

Mishara, B. L., & Daigle, M. S. (1997). Effects of different telephone intervention styles with suicidal callers at two suicide prevention centers: An empirical investigation. *American Journal of Community Psychology, 5,* 861–885.

Mishara, B. L., Chagnon, F., Daigle, M., Balan, B., Raymond, S., Marcoux, I., Bardon, C., Campbell, J. K., & Berman, A. (2007). Which helper behaviors and intervention styles are related to better short-term outcomes in telephone crisis intervention? Results from a silent monitoring study of calls to the U.S. 1-800-SUICIDE Network. *Suicide and Life Threatening Behavior, 37,* 308–321.

Mishra, S., Gregson, M., & Lalumiere, M. L. (2012). Framing effects and risk-sensitive decision making. *British Journal of Psychology, 103,* 83–87.

Mistry, K. B., Minkovitz, C. S., Strobino, D. M., & Borzekowski, D. (2007). Children's television exposure and behavioral and social outcomes at 5.5 years: Does timing of exposure matter? *Pediatrics, 120,* 762–769.

Mitchell, R. W. (1987). A comparative-developmental approach to understanding imitation. In P. P. G. Bateson & P. H. Klopfer (Eds.), *Perspectives in Ethology* (pp. 183–215). New York: Springer.

Mithoefer, M. C., Wagner, M. T., Mithoefer, A. T., Jerome, L., Martin, S. F., Yazar-Klosinski, B., et al. (2013). Durability of improvement in post-traumatic stress disorder symptoms and absence of harmful effects or drug dependency after 3, 4-methylenedioxymethamphetamine-assisted psychotherapy: A prospective long-term follow-up study. *Journal of Psychopharmacology, 27,* 28–39.

Miyake, Y., Okamoto, Y., Onoda, K., Shirao, N., Okamoto, Y., Otagaki, Y., & Yamawaki, S. (2010). Neural processing of negative word stimuli concerning body image in patients with eating disorders: An fMRI study. *Neuroimage, 15,* 1333–1339.

Mizushige, T., Inoue, K., & Fushiki, T. (2007). Why is fat so tasty? Chemical reception of fatty acid on the tongue. *Journal of Nutritional Science and Vitaminology, 53,* 1–4.

Molina, J., & Mendoza, M. (2006). Change of attitudes towards hypnosis after a training course. *Australian Journal of Clinical & Experimental Hypnosis, 34,* 146–161.

Molteni, R., Barnard, R. J., Ying, Z., Roberts, C. K., & Gómez-Pinilla, F. (2002). A high-fat, refined sugar dient reduces hippocampal brain-derived neurotrophic factor, neuronal plasticity and learning. *Neuroscience, 112,* 803–814.

Mondloch, C. J., Maurer, D., & Ahola, S. (2006). Becoming a face expert. *Psychological Science, 17,* 930–934.

Monk-Turner, E., Wren, K., McGill, L., Matthiae, C., Brown, S., & Brooks, D. (2008). Who is giving at whom? A look at how sex is used in magazine advertisements. *Journal of Gender Studies, 17,* 201–209.

Montgomery, G. H., DuHamel, K. N., & Redd, W. H. (2000). A metaanalysis of hypnotically induced analgesia: How effective is hypnosis? *International Journal of Clinical and Experimental Hypnosis, 48,* 138–153.

Montgomery, I., Trinder, J., Fraser, G., & Paxton, S. (1987). Aerobic fitness and exercise: Effect on the sleep of younger and older adults. *Australian Journal of Psychology, 39,* 259–271.

Monti, M. M., Vanhaudenhuyse, A., Coleman, M. R., Boly, M., Pickard, J. D., Tshibanda, L., et al. (2010). Willful modulation of brain activity in disorders of consciousness. *The New England Journal of Medicine, 362,* 579–589.

Moore, B., Mischel, W., & Zeiss, A. (1976). Comparative effects of the reward stimulus and its cognitive representation in voluntary delay. *Journal of Personality and Social Psychology, 34,* 419–424.

Moore, L. P., Moore, J. W., & Hauck, W. E. (1982). Conditioning children's attitudes toward alcohol, smoking, and drugs. *Journal of Experimental Education, 50,* 154–158.

Morgan, C. J., Muetzelfeldt, L., & Curran, H. V. (2010). Consequences of chronic ketamine self-administration upon neurocognitive function and psychological wellbeing: A 1-year longitudinal study. *Addiction, 105,* 12–33.

Morgan, D., Grant, K. A., Gage, H. D., Mach, R. H., Kaplan, J. R., Prioleau, O., et al. (2002). Social dominance in monkeys: Dopamine D2 receptors and cocaine self-administration. *Nature Neuroscience, 5,* 169–174.

Morgane, P. J., Mokler, D. J., & Galler, J. R. (2002). Effects of prenatal protein malnutrition on the hippocampal formation. *Neuroscience and Biobehavioral Reviews, 26,* 471–483.

Morin, C., Bootzin, R., Buysse, D., Edinger, J., Espie, C., & Lichstein, K. (2006). Psychological and behavioral treatment of insomnia: Update of the recent evidence (1998–2004). *Sleep: Journal of Sleep and Sleep Disorders Research, 29,* 1398–1414.

Morin, L. P. (2013). Neuroanatomy of the extended circadian rhythm system. *Experimental Neurology, 243,* 4–20.

Morleo, M., Woolfall, K., Dedman, D., Mukherjee, R., Bellis, M. A., & Cook, P. A. (2011). Underreporting of foetal alcohol spectrum disorders: An analysis of hospital episode statistics. *BMC Pediatrics, 11,* 14.

Morris, G., Nevet, A., Arkadir, D., Vaadia, E., & Bergman, H. (2006). Midbrain dopamine neurons encode decisions for future action. *Nature Neuroscience, 9,* 1057–1063.

Morris, M. W., & Peng, K. (1994). Culture and cause: American and Chinese attributions for social and physical events. *Journal of Personality and Social Psychology, 67,* 949–971.

Moscicki, E. K. (2001). Epidemiology of completed and attempted suicide: Toward a framework for prevention. *Clinical Neuroscience Research, 1,* 310–323.

Motet, A. (1897). *Accès de somnambulisme spontané et provoqué. Annales d'Hygiene et de Médecine Légale, 3e série, 37,* 502–525. Cited in L. Thoinot (1911), *Medicolegal aspects of moral offenders.* Philadelphia, PA: Weysse A. David and Company.

Müller, J. (1826). *Zer vergleichenden Physiologie des Gesichtssinnes des Menschen und her Thiere.* Leipzig: Cnobloch.

Müller, N. G., & Knight, R. T. (2006). The functional neuroanatomy of working memory: Contributions of human brain lesion studies. *Neuroscience, 139,* 51–58.

Munt, S. (1998). *Heroic desire: Lesbian identity and cultural space.* New York: New York University Press.

Murdock, B. B. (1962). The serial position effect of free recall. *Journal of Experimental Psychology, 64,* 482–488.

Murphy, C., Cain, W. S., & Bartoshuk, L. M. (1977). Mutual action of taste and olfaction. *Sensory Processes, 1,* 204–211.

Murphy, G. G., & Glanzman, D. L. (1997). Mediation of classical conditioning in *Aplysia californica* by LTP of sensorimotor synapses. *Science, 278,* 467–471.

Murphy, M. R., Checkley, S. A., Seckl, J. R., & Lightman, S. L. (1990). Naloxone inhibits oxytocin release at orgasm in man. *Journal of Clinical Endocrinology and Metabolism, 71,* 1056–1058.

Murtagh, D. R., & Greenwood, K. M. (1995). Identifying effective psychological treatments for insomnia: A meta-analysis. *Journal of Consulting and Clinical Psychology, 63,* 79–89.

Myers, C. E., McGlinchey-Berroth, R., Warren, S., Monti, L., Brawn, C. M., & Gluck, M. A. (2000). Latent learning in medial temporal amnesia: Evidence for disrupted representational but preserved attentional processes. *Neuropsychology, 14,* 3–15.

Myers, D. G., & Diener, E. (1995). Who is happy? *Psychological Science, 6,* 10–19.

Naëgelé, B., Thouvard, V., Pépin, J. L., Lévy, P., Bonnet, C., Perret, J. E., et al. (1995). Deficits of cognitive executive functions in patients with sleep apnea syndrome. *Sleep, 18,* 43–52.

Nairne, J. S. (1996). Short-term/working memory. In E. Bjork & R. A. Bjork (Eds.), *Memory* (pp. 101–126). San Diego, CA: Academic Press.

Nakamura, M., Kanbayashi, T., Sugiura, T., & Inoue, Y. (2011). Relationship between clinical characteristics of narcolepsy and CSF orexin-A levels. *Journal of Sleep Research, 20,* 45–49.

Narby, D. J., Cutler, B. L., & Moran, G. (1993). A meta-analysis of the association between authoritarianism and jurors' perceptions of defendant culpability. *Journal of Applied Psychology, 78,* 34–42.

Narrow, W. E., Rae, D. S., Robins, L. N., & Regier, D. A. (2002). Revised prevalence based estimates of mental disorders in the United States: Using a clinical signficance criterion to reconcile 2 surveys' estimates. *Archives of General Psychiatry, 59,* 115–123.

Nash, M. R., Perez, N., Tasso, A., & Levy, J. L. (2009). Clinical research on the utility of hypnosis in the prevention, diagnosis, and treatment of medical and psychiatric disorders. *International Journal of Clinical and Experimental Hypnosis, 57,* 443–450.

Nash, R., Wade, K., & Lindsay, D. (2009). Digitally manipulating memory: Effects of doctored videos and imagination in distorting beliefs and memories. *Memory & Cognition, 37,* 414–424.

National Eating Disorders Association. (2002). *National eating disorders association statistics: Eating disorders and their precursors.* Retrieved from http://www.nationaleatingdisorders.org/nedaDir/ files/documents/handouts/Stats.pdf

National Institute of Mental Health (NIMH). (2008). The numbers count: Mental disorders in America. Retrieved from http://www.nimh.nih.gov/health/publications/the-numbers-count-mental-disorders-in-america/index.shtml

National Institute of Mental Health (NIMH). (2009). Post-traumatic stress disorder (PTSD). Retrieved from http://www.nimh.nih.gov/health/publications/post-traumatic-stress-disorder-ptsd/psychotherapy.shtml

National Institute of Mental Health (NIMH). (2011). Use of mental health services and treatment among adults. Retrieved from http://www.nimh.nih.gov/statistics/3USE_MT_ADULT.shtml

Neisser., U. (1967). *Cognitive psychology.* New York: Appleton-Century-Crofts.

Neisser, U. (2000). Snapshots or benchmarks? In U. Neisser & I. Hyman (Eds.), *Memory observed: Remembering in natural contexts* (2nd ed., pp. 68–74). New York: Worth Publishing.

Neisser, U., & Harsch, N. (1992). Phantom flashbulbs: False recollections of hearing the news about Challenger. In E. Winograd & U. Neisser

(Eds.), *Affect and accuracy in recall: Studies in flashbulb memories* (pp. 9–31). Cambridge, UK: Cambridge University Press.

Neisser, U., Boodoo, G., Bouchard, T. J., Boykin, A. W., Brody, N., Ceci, S. J., Halpern, D. F., Loehlin, J. C., Perloff, R., Sternberg, R. J., & Urbina, S. (1996). Intelligence: Knowns and unknowns. *American Psychologist, 51,* 77–101.

Nesse, R., & Ellsworth, P. (2009). Evolution, emotions, and emotional disorders. *American Psychologist, 64,* 129–139.

Nestler, E. J., & Hyman, S. E. (2010). Animal models of neuropsychiatric disorders. *Nature Neuroscience, 13,* 1161–1169.

Neugebauer, R., Hoek, H.W., & Susser, E. (1999). Prenatal exposure to wartime famine and development of antisocial personality disorder in early adulthood. *The Journal of the American Medical Association, 282,* 455–462.

Neville, H. J. (1995). Developmental specificity in neurocognitive development in humans. In M. Gazzaniga (Ed.), *The cognitive neurosciences* (pp. 219–231). Cambridge, MA: MIT Press.

Newcombe, N. S., Drummey, A., Fox, N. A., et al. (2000). Remembering early childhood: How much, how, and why (or why not). *Current Directions in Psychological Science, 9,* 55–58.

Newman, M. G., & Llera, S. J. (2011). A novel theory of experiential avoidance in generalized anxiety disorder: A review and synthesis of research supporting a contrast avoidance model of worry. *Clinical Psychology Review, 31,* 371–382.

Newth, S., & DeLongis, A. (2004). Individual differences, mood, and coping with chronic pain in rheumatoid arthritis: A daily process analysis. *Psychology and Health, 19,* 283–305.

Newton, E. L. (1991). The rocky road from actions to intentions. Dissertation. Available from ProQuest Information and Learning.

Nicki, R. M., Gallagher, T. M., & Cormier, A. E. (2007). Attractiveness of video lottery terminal (VLT) games for problem and non-problem gamblers. *Gambling Research: Journal of the National Association for Gambling Studies (Australia), 19,* 21–35.

Nielsen, M., & Tomaselli, K. (2010). Overimitation in Kalahari Bushman children and the origins of human cultural cognition. *Psychological Science, 21,* 729–736.

Nielsen Research. (April 28, 2010). U.S. homes add even more TV sets in 2010. Retrieved from http://www.nielsen.com/us/en/newswire/2010/u-s-homes-add-even-more-tv-sets-in-2010.html

Nielsen, T. A., & Levin, R. (2007). Nightmares: A new neurocognitive model. *Sleep Medicine Reviews, 11,* 295–310.

Nielsen, T. A., & Zadra, A. L. (2005). Nightmares and other common dream disturbances. In M. Kryger, N. Roth, & W. C. Dement (Eds.), *Principles and practice of sleep medicine* (pp. 926–935). Philadelphia, PA: Elsevier Saunders.

Nielsen, T. A., Laberge, L., Paquet, J., Tremblay, R. E., Vitaro, F., & Montplaisir, J. (2000). Development of disturbing dreams during adolescence and their relation to anxiety symptoms. *Sleep, 23,* 1–10.

Nielsen, T. A., Stenstrom, P., & Levin, R. (2006). Nightmare frequency as a function of age, gender, and September 11, 2001: Findings from an Internet questionnaire. *Dreaming, 16,* 145–158.

Nielsen, T. A., Zadra, A. L., Simard, V., Saucier, S., Stentrom, P., Smith, C., & Kuiken, D. (2003). The typical dreams of Canadian university students. *Dreaming, 13,* 211–235.

Nielson, K., Yee, D., & Erickson, K. (2005). Memory enhancement by a semantically unrelated emotional arousal source induced after learning. *Neurobiology of Learning and Memory, 84,* 49–56.

Nisbett, R. E. (2003). *The geography of thought: How Asians and Westerners think differently . . . and why.* New York: Free Press.

Nisbett, R. E. (2005). Heredity, environment, and race differences in IQ: A commentary on Rushton and Jensen (2005). *Psychology, Public Policy, and Law, 11,* 302–310.

Nisbett, R. E. (2009). *Intelligence and how to get it: Why schools and cultures count.* New York: Norton.

Nisbett, R. E., & Masuda, T. (2003). Culture and point of view. *Proceedings of the National Academy of Sciences, 100,* 11163–11170.

Nisbett, R. E., & Wilson, T. D. (1977). Telling more than we can know: Verbal reports on mental processes. *Psychological Review, 84,* 231.

Nisbett, R. E., Aronson, J., Blair, C., Dickens, W., Flynn, J., Halpern, D. F., & Turkheimer, E. (2012). Intelligence: New findings and theoretical developments. *American Psychologist, 67,* 130–159.

Noels, K. A., Pelletier, L. G., Clement, R., & Vallerand, R. J. (2000). Why are you learning a second language? Motivational orientations and self-determination theory. *Language Learning, 50,* 57–85.

Nolan, J. M., Schultz, P. W., Cialdini, R. B., Goldstein, N. J., & Griskevicius, V. (2008). Normative social influence is underdetected. *Personality and Social Psychology Bulletin, 34,* 913–923.

Norman, D., & Shallice, T. (1986). Attention to action. In R.J. Davidson, G. E. Schwartz, & D. Shapiro (Eds.), *Consciousness and self-regulation* (pp. 1–18). New York: Plenum Press.

Norman, G. R., Brooks, L. R., & Allen, S. W. (1989a). Recall by expert medical practitioners and novices as a record of processing. *Journal of Experimental Psychology: Learning, Memory, and Cognition, 15,* 1166–1174.

Norman, G. R., Rosenthal, D., Brooks, L. R., Allen, S. W., & Muzzin, L. J. (1989b). The development of expertise in dermatology. *Archives of Dermatology, 125,* 1063–1068.

North, C. S., Ryall, J. E. M., Ricci, D. A., & Wetzel, R. D. (1993). *Multiple personalities, multiple disorders.* New York: Oxford University Press.

Northstone, K., Joinson, C., Emmett, P., Ness, A., & Paus, T. (2012). Are dietary patterns in childhood associated with IQ at 8 years of age? A population-based cohort study. *Journal of Epidemiology and Community Health, 66,* 624–628.

Nosek, B. A. (2007). Implicit–explicit relations. *Current Directions in Psychological Science, 16,* 65–69.

Nosek, B. A., Banjai, M., & Greenwald, A. G. (2002). Harvesting implicit group attitudes and beliefs from a demonstration web site. *Group Dynamics: Theory, Research, and Practice, 6,* 101–115.

Nosyk, B., Marshall, B. D. L., Fischer, B., Montaner, J. S. G., Wood, E., & Kerr, T. (2012). Increases in the availability of prescribed opioids in a Canadian setting. *Drug and Alcohol Dependence, 126,* 7–12.

Nunn, J. A., Gregory, L. J., Brammer, M., Williams, S. C., Parslow, D. M., Morgan, M. J., et al. (2002). Functional magnetic resonance imaging of synesthesia: Activation of V4/V8 by spoken words. *Nature Neuroscience, 5,* 371–375.

Nuttin, J. M. (1985). Narcissism beyond Gestalt and awareness: The name–letter effect. *European Journal of Social Psychology, 15,* 353–361.

Nyi, P. P., Lai, E. P., Lee, D. Y., Biglete, S. A., Torrecer, G. I., & Anderson, I. B. (2010). Influence of age on Salvia divinorum use: Results of an Internet survey. *Journal of Psychoactive Drugs, 42,* 385–392.

O'Brien, T. B., & DeLongis, A. (1996). The interactional context of problem-, emotion-, and relationship-focused coping: The role of the Big Five personality factors. *Journal of Personality, 64,* 775–813.

O'Connor, A. R., & Moulin, C. J. (2010). Recognition without identification, erroneous familiarity, and déjà vu. *Current Psychiatry Reports, 12,* 165–173.

O'Kearney, R., Gibson, M., Christensen, H., & Griffiths, K. M. (2006). Effects of a cognitive-behavioural Internet program on depression, vulnerability to depression and stigma in adolescent males: A school-based controlled trial. *Cognitive Behavior Therapy, 35,* 43–54.

O'Leary, C. M., Nassar, N., Kurinczuk, J. J., de Klerk, N., Geelhoed, E., Elliot, E. J., & Bower, C. (2010). Prenatal alcohol exposure and risk of birth defects. *Pediatrics, 126,* e843–e850.

Ochsner, K. N., & Gross, J. J. (2005). The cognitive control of emotion. *Trends in Cognitive Sciences, 9,* 242–249.

Oehen, P., Traber, R., Widmer, V., & Schnyder, U. (2013). A randomized, controlled pilot study of MDMA (±3, 4-Methylenedioxymethamphetamine)-assisted psychotherapy for treatment of resistant, chronic post-traumatic stress disorder (PTSD). *Journal of Psychopharmacology, 27*(1), 40–52.

Öhman, A., & Mineka, S. (2001). Fears, phobias, and preparedness: Toward an evolved module of fear and fear learning. *Psychological Review, 108,* 483–522.

O'Keefe, D. J. (1999). Variability of persuasive message effects: Meta-analytic evidence and implications. *Document Design, 1,* 87–97.

Olfson, M., & Marcus, S. C. (2010). National trends in outpatient psychotherapy. *American Journal of Psychiatry, 167,* 1456–1463.

Olfson, M., & Marcus, S. C. (2009). National patterns in antidepressant medication treatment. *Archives of General Psychiatry, 66,* 848–856.

Oliver, G., & Wardle, J. (1999). Perceived effects of stress on food choice. *Physiology and Behavior, 66,* 511–515.

Olivo, E., Dodson-Lavelle, B., Wren, A., Fang, Y., & Oz, M. (2009). Feasibility and effectiveness of a brief meditation-based stress management intervention for patients diagnosed with or at risk for coronary heart disease: A pilot study. *Psychology, Health & Medicine, 14,* 513–523.

Olsen, G. D. (2002). Salient stimuli in advertising: The effect of contrast interval length and type on recall. *Journal of Experimental Psychology: Applied, 8,* 168–179.

Olshansky, S. J., Passaro, D. J., Hershow, R. C., Layden, J., Carnes, B. A., Brody, J., et al. (2005). A potential decline in life expectancy in the United States in the 21st century. *New England Journal of Medicine, 352,* 1138–1145.

Olson, H. C., Streissguth, A. P., Sampson, P. D., Barr, H. M., Bookstein, F. L., & Thiede, K. (1997). Association of prenatal alcohol exposure with behavioral and learning problems in early adolescence. *Journal of the American Academy of Child & Adolescent Psychiatry, 36,* 1187–1194.

Olson, K. R., Lambert, A. J., & Zacks, J. M. (2004). Graded structure and the speed of category verification: On the moderating effects of anticipatory control for social vs. non-social categories. *Journal of Experimental Social Psychology, 40,* 239–246.

Olson, M. A., & Fazio, R. H. (2001). Implicit attitude formation through classical conditioning. *Psychological Science, 12,* 413–417.

Olsson, A., & Phelps, E. (2007). Social learning of fear. *Nature Neuroscience, 10,* 1095–1102.

Opriş, D., Pintea, S., García-Palacios, A., Botella, C., Szamosközi, Ş., & David, D. (2011). Virtual reality exposure therapy in anxiety disorders: A quantitative meta-analysis. *Depression and Anxiety, 29,* 85–93.

O'Reilly, T., & Tennant, M. (2009). *The age of persuasion: How marketing ate our culture.* Toronto: Knopf.

Orne, M. T. (1962). On the social psychology of the pyschological experiment: With particular reference to demand characteristics and their implications. *American Psychologist, 17,* 776–783.

Ortner, C. N. M., Kilner, S. J., & Zelazo, P. D. (2007). Mindfulness meditation and reduced emotional interference on a cognitive task. *Motivation and Emotion, 31,* 271–283.

Oskamp, S., Edwards, T. C., Sherwood, D. L., Okuda, S. M., & Swanson, D. C. (1991). Factors influencing household recycling behavior. *Environment and behavior, 23,* 494–519.

Öst, L. G. (1987). Age of onset in different phobias. *Journal of Abnormal Psychology, 96,* 223.

Ostafin, B. D., Marlatt, G., & Greenwald, A. G. (2008). Drinking without thinking: An implicit measure of alcohol motivation predicts failure to control alcohol use. *Behaviour Research and Therapy, 46,* 1210–1219.

Overgaard, M., & Overgaard, R. (2011). Measurements of consciousness in the vegetative state. *The Lancet, 378,* 2052–2054.

Owen, A. M., & Coleman, M. R. (2008). Functional neuroimaging of the vegetative state. *Nature Reviews Neuroscience, 9,* 235–243.

Owen, A. M., Coleman, M. R., Boly, M., et al. (2006). Detecting awareness in the vegetative state. *Science, 313,* 1402.

Owen, M. J., O'Donovan, M. C., Thapar, A., & Craddock, N. (2011). Neurodevelopmental hypothesis of schizophrenia. *The British Journal of Psychiatry, 198,* 173–175.

Oxford English Dictionary. (2011). Retrieved June 16, 2011, from http://dictionary.oed.com/entrance.dtl

Packer, D. J. (2008). Identifying systematic disobedience in Milgram's obedience experiments: A meta-analytic review. *Perspectives on Psychological Science, 3,* 301–304.

Pagnoni, G., & Cekic, M. (2007). Age effects on gray matter volume and attentional performance in Zen meditation. *Neurobiology of Aging, 28,* 1623–1627.

Paller, K. (2004). Electrical signals of memory and of the awareness of remembering. *Current Directions in Psychological Science, 13,* 49–55.

Pallesen, S., Hilde, I., Havik, O., & Nielsen, G. (2001). Clinical assessment and treatment of insomnia. *Professional Psychology: Research and Practice, 32,* 115–124.

Pan, A., Malik, V. S., & Hu, F. B. (2012). Exporting diabetes mellitus to Asia: The impact of Western-style fast food. *Circulation, 126,* 163–165.

Paparrigopoulos, T. J. (2005). REM sleep behaviour disorder: Clinical profiles and pathophysiology. *International Review of Psychiatry, 17,* 293–300.

Paquette, V., Levesque, J., Mensour, B., Leroux, J. M., Beaudoin, G., Bourgouin, P., & Beauregard, M. (2003). "Change the mind and you change the brain": Effects of cognitive-behavioral therapy on the neural correlates of spider phobia. *Neuroimage, 18,* 401–409.

Paradis, C., Solomon, L. Z., Florer, F., & Thompson, T. (2004). Flashbulb memories of personal events of 9/11 and the day after for a sample of New York City residents. *Psychological Reports, 95,* 304–310.

Paris, B. J. (1994). *Karen Horney: A psychoanalyst's search for self-understanding.* New Haven, CT: Yale University Press.

Park, D. C., & Huang, C-M. (2010). Culture wires the brain: A cognitive neuroscience perspective. *Perspectives on Psychological Science, 5,* 391–400.

Park, S., Püschel, J., Sauter, B. H., Rentsch, M., & Hell, D. (1999). Spatial working memory deficits and clinical symptoms of schizophrenia: A 4-month follow-up study. *Biological Psychiatry, 46,* 392–400.

Parrott, M. D., & Greenwood, C. E. (2007). Dietary influences on cognitive function with aging. *Annals of the New York Academy of Sciences, 1114,* 389–397.

Parsons, H. M. (1974). What happened at Hawthorne?: New evidence suggests the Hawthorne effect resulted from reinforcement contingencies. *Science, 183,* 922–932.

Pasher, H., McDaniel, M., Rohrer, D., & Bjork, R. (2008). Learning styles: Concepts and evidence. *Psychological Science in the Public Interest, 9,* 105–119.

Pashler, H. (1998). *The psychology of attention.* Cambridge, MA: MIT Press.

Patrick, G. T. W., & Gilbert, J. A. (1896). Studies from the psychological laboratory of the University of Iowa: On the effects of loss of sleep. *Psychological Review, 3,* 469–483.

Patterson, C. M., & Newman, J. P. (1993). Reflectivity and learning from aversive events: Toward a psychological mechanism for the syndromes of disinhibition. *Psychological Review, 100,* 716–736.

Patterson, D., & Jensen, M. (2003). Hypnosis and clinical pain. *Psychological Bulletin, 129,* 495–521.

Paul, D. B., & Blumenthal, A. L. (1989). On the trail of little Albert. *Psychological Record, 39,* 547–553.

Paulesu, E., Frith, C., & Frackowiak, R. (1993). The neural correlates of the verbal component of working memory. *Nature, 362*, 342–345.

Paulhus, D. L., & Williams, K. (2002). The dark triad of personality: Narcissism, Machiavellianism, and psychopathy. *Journal of Research in Personality, 36*, 556–568.

Pearson, P., & Schaefer, E. (2005). Toupee or not toupee? The role of instructional set, centrality, and relevance in change blindness. *Visual Cognition, 12,* 1528–1543.

Pelham, B. W., Carvallo, M., & Jones, J. T. (2005). Implicit egoism. *Current Directions in Psychological Science, 14*, 106–110.

Pelletier, L. G., & Sharp, E. (2008). Persuasive communication and proenvironmental behaviours: How message tailoring and message framing can improve the integration of behaviours through self-determined motivation. *Canadian Psychology, 49,* 210–217.

Pelletier, L. G., Tuson, K. M., Green-Demers, I., Noels, K., & Beaton, A. M. (1998). Why are you doing things for the environment? The motivation toward the environment scale (MTES). *Journal of Applied Social Psychology, 28,* 437–468.

Pelphrey, K. A., & Morris, J. P. (2006). Brain mechanisms for interpreting the actions of others from biological-motion cues. *Current Directions in Psychological Science, 15,* 136–140.

Penfield, W., & Jasper, H. H. (1951). *Epilepsy and the functional anatomy of the human brain.* New York: Little, Brown, and Company.

Penn, D. L., & Combs, D. (2000). Modification of affect perception deficits in schizophrenia. *Schizophrenia Research, 46,* 217–229.

Penninx, B., Geerlings, S., Deeg, D., van Eijk, J., van Tilburg, W., & Beekman, A. (1999). Minor and major depression and the risk of death in older persons. *Archives of General Psychiatry, 56,* 889–895.

Pereira, E. A. C., Lu, G., Wang, S., Schweder, P. M., Hyam, J. A., Stein, J. F., Paterson, D. J., Aziz, T. Z., & Green, A. L. (2010). Ventral periaqueductal grey stimulation alters heart rate variability in humans with chronic pain. *Experimental Neurology, 223,* 574–581.

Perloff, R. M. (2002). The third-person effect. In J. Bryant & D. Zillmann (Eds.), *Media effects: Advances in theory and research* (2nd ed., pp. 489–506). Mahwah, NJ: Erlbaum.

Perrin, J. S., Merz, S., Bennett, D. M., Currie, J., Steele, D. J., et al. (2012). Electroconvulsive therapy reduces frontal cortical connectivity in severe depressive disorder. *Proceedings of the National Academy of Sciences, USA, 109,* 5464–5468.

Perry, J. L., & Carroll, M. E. (2008). The role of impulsive behavior in drug abuse. *Psychopharmacology, 200,* 1–26.

Perry, W., Feifel, D., Minassian, A., Bhattacharjie, B. S., & Braff, D. L. (2002). Information processing deficits in acutely psychotic schizophrenia patients medicated and unmedicated at the time of admission. *American Journal of Psychiatry, 159,* 1375–1381.

Pertwee, R. G., & Ross, R. A. (2002). Cannabinoid receptors and their ligands. *Prostaglandins, Leukotrienes and Essential Fatty Acids, 66,* 101–121.

Peters, R. M., Hackeman, E., & Goldreich, D. (2009). Diminutive digits discern delicate details: Fingertip size and the sex difference in tactile spatial acuity. *The Journal of Neuroscience, 29,* 15756–15761.

Peterson, C., Seligman, M. E. P., Yurko, K. H., Martin, L. R., & Friedman, H. S. (1998). Catastrophizing and untimely death. *Psychological Science, 9*, 49–52.

Peterson, L., & Peterson, M. (1959). Short-term retention of individual verbal items. *Journal of Experimental Psychology, 58*, 193–198.

Peterson, N. R., Pisoni, D. B., & Miyamoto, R. T. (2010). Cochlear implants and spoken language processing abilities: Review and assessment of the literature. *Restorative Neurology and Neuroscience, 28,* 237–250.

Petrosino, A., Turpin-Petrosino, C., & Buehler, J. (2003). Scared Straight and other juvenile awareness programs for preventing juvenile delinquency: A systematic review of the randomized experimental evidence. *Annals of the American Academy of Political and Social Science, 589*, 41–62.

Pettigrew, T. F. (1997). Generalised intergroup contact effects on prejudice. *Personality and Social Psychology Bulletin, 23,* 173–185.

Pettigrew, T. F. (1998). Intergroup contact theory. *Annual review of psychology, 49*, 65–85.

Pettigrew, T. F., & Tropp, L. R. (2006). A meta-analytic test of intergroup contact theory. *Journal of Personality and Social Psychology, 90*, 751.

Pfaus, J. G., & Scepkowski, L. A. (2005). The biologic basis for libido. *Current Sexual Health Reports, 2,* 95–100.

Pfaus, J. G., Kippin, T. E., Coria-Avila, G. A., Gelez, H., Afonso, V. M., Ismail, N., & Parade, M. (2012). Who, what, where, when (and maybe even why)? How the experience of sexual reward connects sexual desire, preference, and performance. *Archives of Sexual Behavior, 41,* 31–62.

Pfefferbaum, A., Darley, C. F., Tinklenberg, J. R., Walton, R. T., & Kopell, B. S. (1977). Marijuana and memory intrusions. *Journal of Nervous & Mental Disease, 165,* 165–172.

Phelps, E. A. (2004). Human emotion and memory: Interactions of the amygdala and hippocampal complex. *Current Opinion in Neurobiology, 14,* 198–202.

Phelps, E. A., O'Connor, K. J., Cunningham, W. A., Funayama, S., Gatenby, J. C., Gore, J. C., & Mahzarin R. Banaji, M. R. (2000). Performance on indirect measures of race evaluation predicts amygdala activation. *Journal of Cognitive Neuroscience 12*, 729–738.

Phillips, D. I. W. (2006). External influences on the fetus and their long-term consequences. *Lupus, 15*, 794–800.

Phillips, M., Brooks-Gunn, J., Duncan, G. J., Klebanov, P. K., & Crane, J. (1998). Family background, parenting practices, and the Black–White test score gap. In C. Jencks & M. Phillips (Eds.), *The Black–White test score gap* (pp. 102–145). Washington, DC: Brookings Institution Press.

Phillips, R. G., & LeDoux, J. E. (1992). Differential contribution of amygdala and hippocampus to cued and contextual fear conditioning. *Behavioral Neuroscience, 106,* 274–285.

Piaget, J., & Inhelder, B. (1956). *The child's conception of space.* Boston: Routledge & Kegan Paul.

Pica, P., Jackson, S., Blake, R., & Troje, N. F. (2011). Comparing biological motion perception in two distinct human societies. *PLoS One, 6*, e28391.

Pickens, C. L., Saddoris, M. P., Setlow, B., Gallager, M., Holland, P. C., & Schoenbaum, G. (2003). Different roles for orbitofrontal cortex and basolateral amygdala in a reinforcer devaluation task. *The Journal of Neuroscience, 23,* 11078–11064.

Piet, J., Hougaard, E., Hecksher, M. S., & Rosenberg, N. K. (2010). A randomized pilot study of mindfulness-based cognitive therapy and group cognitive-behavioral therapy for young adults with social phobia. *Scandinavian Journal of Psychology, 51*, 403–410.

Pinker, S. (1994). *The language instinct.* New York: William Morrow.

Pinker, S. (1999). *Words and rules: The ingredients of language.* New York: Basic Books.

Pinkleton, B. (1997). The effects of negative comparative political advertising on candidate evaluations and advertising evaluations: An exploration. *Journal of Advertising, 24,* 19–31.

Piñon, A., & Gambara, H. (2005). A meta-analytic review of framing effect: Risky, attribute and goal framing. *Psicothema, 17,* 325–331.

Pinsker, H., Kupfermann, I., Castellucci, V., & Kandel, E. (1970). Habituation and dishabituation of the gill-withdrawal reflex in *Aplysia. Science, 167*, 1740–1742.

Pinto, A., Mancebo, M., Eisen, J., Pagano, M., & Rasmussen, S. (2006). The Brown longitudinal obsessive compulsive study: Clinical features and symptoms of the sample at intake. *Journal of Clinical Psychiatry, 67,* 703–711.

Pistis, M., Porcu, G., Melis, M., Diana, M., & Gessa, G. L. (2001). Effects of cannabinoids on prefrontal neuronal responses to ventral tegmental area stimulation. *European Journal of Neuroscience, 14,* 96–102.

Pizzagalli, D. A., Lehmann, D., Hendrick, A. M., Regard, M., Pascual-Marqui, R. D., & Davidson, R. J. (2002). Affective judgments of faces modulate early activity (~160 ms) within the fusiform gyri. *NeuroImage, 16,* 663–677.

Plant, E. A., & Peruche, B. (2005). The consequences of race for police officers' responses to criminal suspects. *Psychological Science, 16,* 180–183.

Plomin, R., & Caspi, A. (1999). Behavioral genetics and personality. In L. A. Pervin & O. P. John (Eds.), *Handbook of personality: Theory and research* (2nd ed., pp. 251–276). New York, NY: Guilford Press.

Plomin, R., & Spinath, F. M. (2004). Intelligence: Genetics, genes, and genomics. *Journal of Personality and Social Psychology, 86,* 112–129.

Polansky, J. R., Titus, K., Lanning, N., & Glantz, S. A. (2013). *Smoking in top-grossing US movies, 2012.* San Francisco: Center for Tobacco Control Research and Education.

Polivy, J., & Herman, C. P. (2002). Causes of eating disorders. *Annual Review of Psychology, 53,* 187–213.

Polivy, J., Herman, C. P., & Coelho, J. S. (2008). Caloric restriction in the presence of attractive food cues: External cues, eating, and weight. *Physiology & Behavior, 94,* 729–733.

Pollack, D., McFarland, B., Mahler, J., & Kovas, A. (2005). Outcomes of patients in a low-intensity, short-duration involuntary outpatient commitment program. *Psychiatric Services, 56,* 863–866.

Ponder, C. A., Kliethermes, C. L., Drew, M. R., Mul-ler, J. J., Das, K. K., Risbrough, V. B., Crabbe, J. C., Gilliam, T.C., & Palmer, A. A. (2007). Selection for contextual fear conditioning affects anxiety-like behaviors and gene expression. *Genes, Brain & Behavior, 6,* 736–749.

Pope, H. G., Gruber, A. J., Hudson, J. I., Cohane, G., Huetis, M. A., & Yurgelun-Todd, D. (2003). Early-onset cannabis use and cognitive deficits: What is the nature of the association? *Drug and Alcohol Dependence, 69,* 303–310.

Porter, R. H., & Winberg, J. (1999). Unique salience of maternal breast odors for newborn infants. *Neuroscience and Biobehavioral Reviews, 23,* 439–449.

Porter, S., ten Brinke, L., & Gustaw, C. (2010). Dangerous decisions: The impact of first impressions of trustworthiness on the evaluation of legal evidence and defendant culpability. *Psychology, Crime & Law, 16,* 1–15.

Poulin-Dubois, D., Blaye, A., Coutya, J., & Bialystok, E. (2011). The effects of bilingualism on toddlers' executive functioning. *Journal of Experimental Child Psychology, 108,* 567–579.

Powell, J. L. (2012). Why climate deniers have no scientific credibility—in one pie chart. Retrieved from http://www.desmogblog.com/2012/11/15/why-climate-deniers-have-no-credibility-science-one-pie-chart

Powers, M. B., & Emmelkamp, P. M. G. (2008). Virtual reality exposure therapy for anxiety disorders: A meta-analysis. *Journal of Anxiety Disorders 39,* 250–261.

Prentice, D. A., & Miller, D. T. (1993). Pluralistic ignorance and alcohol use on campus: Some consequences of misperceiving the social norm. *Journal of Personality and Social Psychology, 64,* 243.

Price, E. L., McLeod, P. J., Gleich, S. S., & Hand, D. (2006). One-year prevalence rates of major depressive disorder in first-year university students. *Canadian Journal of Counselling, 40,* 68–81.

Prochaska, J. O., & DiClemente, C. C. (1984). Self change processes, self efficacy and decisional balance across five stages of smoking cessation. *Advances in cancer control–1983* (pp. 131–140). New York: Alan R. Liss, Inc.

Prochaska, J. O., & DiClemente, C. C. (1985). Common processes of self-change in smoking, weight control, and psychological distress. In S. Shiffman & T. Wills. (Eds.), *Coping and substance abuse: A conceptual framework* (pp. 345–363). New York: Academic Press.

Prochaska, J. O., & Norcross, J. C. (2002). Stage of change. In J. C. Norcross (Ed.), *Psychotherapy relationships that work* (pp. 303–313). New York: Oxford.

Propper R. E., Stickgold, R., Keeley, R., & Christman, S. D. (2007). Is television traumatic? Dreams, stress, and media exposure in the aftermath of September 11, 2001. *Psychological Science, 18,* 334–340.

Public Health Agency of Canada. (2002). *A report on mental illnesses in Canada.* Retrieved from http://www.phac-aspc.gc.ca/publicat/miic-mmac/chap_4-eng.php.

Pujol, J., Soriano-Mas, C., Ortiz, H., Sebastian-Galles, N., Losilla, J. M., & Deus, J. (2006). Myelination of language-related areas in the developing brain. *Neurology, 66,* 339–343.

Putnam, F. W. (1989). *Diagnosis and treatment of multiple personality disorder.* New York: Guilford Press.

Qu, S., Olafsrud, S. M., Meza-Zepeda, L. A., & Saatcioglu, F. (2013). Rapid gene expression changes in peripheral blood lymphocytes upon practice of a comprehensive yoga program. *Public Library of Science One, 8,* 1–8.

Quirk, G. J., & Beer, J. S. (2006). Prefrontal involvement in the regulation of emotion: Convergence of rat and human studies. *Current Opinion in Neurobiology, 16,* 723–727.

Quirk, G. J., Repa, J. C., & Ledoux, J. E. (1995). Fear conditioning enhances short-latency auditory responses of lateral amygdala neurons: Parallel recording in the freely behaving rat. *Neuron, 15,* 1029–1039.

Rachman, S. (1966). Sexual fetishism: An experimental analogue. *Psychological Record, 16,* 293–296.

Rada, P., Avena, N. M., & Hoebel, B. G. (2005). Daily bingeing on sugar repeatedly releases dopamine in the accumbens shell. *Neuroscience, 134,* 737–744.

Raffi, A. R., Rondini, M., Grandi, S., & Fava, G. A. (2000). Life events and prodromal symptoms in bulimia nervosa. *Psychological Medicine, 30,* 727–731.

Rainforth, M. V., Schneider, R. H., Nidich, S. I., Gaylord-King, C., Salerno, J. W., & Anderson, J. W. (2007). Stress reduction programs in patients with elevated blood pressure: A systematic review and meta-analysis. *Current Hypertension Reports, 9,* 520–528.

Rainie, L., & Packel, D. (2001). More online, doing more: The Pew Internet & American Life Project. Retrieved from http://www.pewinternet.org

Raji, C. A., Ho, A. J., Parikshak, N. N., Becker, J. T., Lopez, O. L., Kuller, L. H., Hua, X., Leow, A. D., Toga, A. W., & Thompson, P. M. (2010). Brain structure and obesity. *Human Brain Mapping, 31,* 353–364.

Ramachandran, V. S., & Altschuler, E. L. (2009). The use of visual feedback, in particular mirrorvisual feedback, in restoring brain function. *Brain, 132,* 1693–1710.

Ramachandran, V. S., & Gregory, R. L. (1991). Perceptual filling in of artificially induced scotomas in human vision. *Nature, 350,* 699–702.

Ramachandran, V. S., & Hubbard, E. M. (2003). The phenomenology of synaesthesia. *Journal of Consciousness Studies, 10,* 49–57.

Ramaekers, J. G., Kauert, G., van Ruitenbeek, P., Theunissen, E. L., Schneider, E., & Moeller, M. R. (2006). High-potency marijuana impairs executive function and inhibitory motor control. *Neuropsychopharmacology, 31,* 2296–2303.

Ramakrishnan, U., Manjrekar, R., Rivera, J., Gonzáles-Cossío, T., & Martorell, R. (1999). Micronutrients and pregnancy outcome: A review of the literature. *Nutrition Research, 19,* 103–159.

Ranganath, C., Johnson, M. K., & D'Esposito, M. (2003). Prefrontal activity associated with working memory and episodic long-term memory. *Neuropsychologia, 41,* 378–389.

Ranganathan, M., & D'Souza, D. C. (2006). The acute effects of cannabinoids on memory in humans: A review. *Psychopharmacology, 188,* 425–444.

Ransdell, S. E., & Fischler, I. (1987). Memory in a momlingual mode: When are bilinguals at a disadvantage. *Journal of Memory and Language, 26,* 392–405.

Rasmussen, E. B., & Newland, M. C. (2008). Asymmetry of reinforcement and punishment in human choice. *Journal of the Experimental Analysis of Behavior, 89,* 157–167.

Rauscher, F. H., & Shaw, G. L. (1998). Key components of the "Mozart effect." *Perceptual and Motor Skills, 86,* 835–841.

Rauscher, F. H., Shaw, G. L., & Ky, K. N. (1993). Music and spatial task performance. *Nature, 365,* 611.

Raynor, H. A., & Epstein, L. (2003). The relative-reinforcing value of food under differing levels of food deprivation and restriction. *Appetite, 40,* 15–24.

Raz, A., Fan, J., & Posner, M. I. (2005). Hypnotic suggestion reduces conflict in the human brain. *Proceedings of the National Academy of Sciences, 102,* 9978–9983.

Raz, N. (2000). Aging of the brain and its impact on cognitive performance: Integration of structural and functional findings. In F. I. M. Craik & T. A. Salthouse (Eds.), *Handbook of aging and cognition—II.* (pp. 1–90). Mahwah, NJ: Lawrence Erlbaum Associates.

Razzini, C., Bianchi, F., Leo, R., Fortuna, E., Siracusano, A., & Romeo, F. (2008). Correlations between personality factors and coronary artery disease: From type A behaviour pattern to type D personality. *Journal of Cardiovascular Medicine, 9,* 761–768.

Rechtschaffen, A. (1998). Current perspectives on the function of sleep. *Perspectives in Biological Medicine, 41,* 359–390.

Reed, T. E., & Jensen, A. R. (1992). Conduction velocity in a brain nerve pathway of normal adults correlates with intelligence level. *Intelligence, 16,* 259–272.

Reed, T. E., Vernon, P. A., & Johnson, A. M. (2004). Confirmation of correlation between brain nerve conduction velocity and intelligence level in normal adults. *Intelligence, 32,* 563–572.

Regan, B. C., Julliot, C., Simmen, B., Vienot, F., Charles-Dominique, P., & Mollon, J. D. (2001). Frutis, foliage and the evolution of primate colour vision. *Philosophical Transactions of the Royal Society B: Biological Sciences, 356,* 229–283.

Rehm, J., Baliunas, D., Brochu, S., Fischer, B., Gnam, W., Patra, J., et al. (2006). *The costs of substance abuse in Canada 2002.* Ottawa: Canadian Centre on Substance Abuse.

Reichert, T. (2003). *The erotic history of advertising.* Amherst, NY: Prometheus.

Reichert, T. (2012). Sex in advertising research: A review of content, effects, and functions of sexual information in consumer advertising. *Annual Review of sex Research, 13,* 241–273.

Reichert, T., & Alvaro, E. (2001). The effects of sexual information on ad and brand processing and recall. *Southwestern Mass Communication Journal, 17,* 9–17.

Reichert, T., Childers, C. C., & Reid, L. N. (2012). How sex in advertising varies by product category: An analysis of three decades of visual sexual imagery in magazine advertising. *Journal of Current Issues & Research in Advertising, 33,* 1–19.

Reichert, T., Heckler, S. E., & Jackson, S. (2001). The effects of sexual social marketing appeals on cognitive processing and persuasion. *Journal of Advertising, 30,* 13–27.

Reilly, S., & Bornovalova, M. A. (2005). Conditioned taste aversion and amygdala lesions in the rat: A critical review. *Neuroscience & Biobehavioral Reviews, 29,* 1067–1088.

Reinders, A. T. S., Nijenhuis, E. R. S., Paans, A. M. J., Korf, J., Willemsen, A. T. M., & den Boer, J. A. (2003). One brain, two selves. *NeuroImage, 20,* 2119–2125.

Reingen, P. H., & Kernan, J. B. (1993). Social perception and interpersonal influence: Some consequences of the physical attractiveness stereotype in a personal selling setting. *Journal of Consumer Psychology, 2,* 25–38.

Reisenzen, R., & Studtman, M. (2007). On the expression and experience of surprise: No evidence for facial feedback, but evidence for a reverse self-inference effect. *Emotion, 7,* 612–627.

Reissland, N. (1988). Neonatal imitation in the first hour of life: Observations in rural Nepal. *Developmental Psychology, 24,* 464–469.

Reiter, E. O., & Lee, P. A. (2001). Have the onset and tempo of puberty changed? *Archives of Pediatrics & Adolescent Medicine, 155,* 988–989.

Remafedi, G., Resnick, M., Blum, R., & Harris, L. (1992). Demography of sexual orientation in adolescents. *Pediatrics, 89,* 714–721.

Rendell, L., & Whitehead, H. (2001). Culture in whales and dolphins. *Behavioral and Brain Sciences, 24,* 309–382.

Renner, M., & Mackin, R. (1998). A life stress instrument for classroom use. *Teaching of Psychology, 25,* 46–48.

Rensink, R. A., O'Regan, J. K., & Clark J. J. (2000). On the failure to detect changes in scenes across brief interruptions. *Visual Cognition, 7,* 127–145.

Rensink, R. A., O'Regan, J. K., & Clark, J. J. (1997). To see or not to see: The need for attention to perceive changes in scenes. *Psychological Science, 8,* 368–373.

Renvoise, P., & Morin, C. (2007). *Neuromarketing.* Nashville, TN: Thomas Nelson.

Report of the Federal/Provincial/Territorial Heads of Prosecutions Subcommittee on the Prevention of Wrongful Convictions. (2011). The path to justice: Preventing wrongful convictions.Retrieved from http://www.ppsc-sppc.gc.ca/eng/pub/ ptj-spj/ptj-spj-eng.pdf

Ricciardelli, L. A., & McCabe, M. P. (2004). A biopsychosocial model of disordered eating and the pursuit of muscularity in adolescent boys. *Psychological Bulletin, 130,* 179–205.

Richert, R. A., Robb, M. B., Fender, J. G., & Wartella, E. (2010). Word learning from baby videos. *Archives of Pediatrics & Adolescent Medicine, 164,* 432–437.

Richmond, D., & Hartman, P. T. (1982). Sex appeal in advertising. *Journal of Advertising Research, 22,* 53–61.

Rideout, V., & Hamel, E. (2006). *The media family: Electronic media in the lives of infants, toddlers, preschoolers, and their parents.* Menlo Park, CA: Henry J. Kaiser Foundation.

Rieber, R., & Robinson, D. (Eds.). (1980). *Wilhelm Wundt and the making of a scientific psychology.* New York: Kluwer Academic/Plenum Publishers.

Rieger, G., & Savin-Williams, R. C. (2011, February 25). Gender nonconformity, sexual orientation, and psychological well-being [Electronic publication ahead of print]. *Archives of Sexual Behavior.*

Rifkin, A., Ghisalbert, D., Dimatou, S., Jin, C., & Sethi, M. (1998). Dissociative identity disorder in psychiatric inpatients. *American Journal of Psychiatry, 155,* 844–845.

Ritterband, L., Thorndike, F., Gonder-Frederick, L., Magee, J., Bailey, E., Saylor, D., et al. (2009). Efficacy of an Internet-based behavioral intervention for adults with insomnia. *Archives of General Psychiatry, 66,* 692–698.

Riva, G. (2005). Virtual reality in psychotherapy: Review. *CyberPsychology & Behavior, 8*(3), 220–240.

Rivera, S. M., Wakeley, A., & Langer, J. (1999). The drawbridge phenomenon: Representational reasoning or perceptual preference. *Developmental Psychology, 35,* 427–435.

Rizzo, A. S., Difede, J., Rothbaum, B. O., Reger, G., Spitalnick, J., Cukor, J., & McLay, R. (2010). Development and early evaluation of the Virtual Iraq/Afghanistan exposure therapy system for combat-related PTSD. *Annals of the New York Academie of Sciences, 1208,* 114–125.

Rizzolatti, G., & Craighero, L. (2004). The mirror-neuron system. *Annual Review of Neuroscience, 27,* 169–192.

Rizzolatti, G., Fadiga, L., Fogassi, L., & Gallese, V. (1996). Premotor cortex and the recognition of motor actions. *Cognitive Brain Research, 3,* 131–141.

Robb, M. B., Richert, R. A., & Wartella, E. A. (2009). Just a talking book? Word learning from watching baby videos. *British Journal of Developmental Psychology, 27,* 27–45.

Robbins, T. W., Jones, G. H., & Wilkinson, L. S. (1996). Behavioural and neurochemical effects of early social deprivation in the rat. *Journal of Psychopharmacology, 10,* 39–47.

Roberson, D. M. J., & Davidoff, J. (2000). The "categorical perception" of colors and facial expressions: The effect of verbal interference. *Memory & Cognition,* 28, 977–986.

Roberson, D. M. J., Davies, I. R. L., & Davidoff, J. (2000). Color categories are not universal: Replications and new evidence in favor of linguistic relativity. *Journal of Experimental Psychology: General, 129,* 369–398.

Roberts, B. W., & DelVecchio, W. F. (2000). The rank-order consistency of personality from childhood to old age: A quantitative review of longitudinal studies. *Psychological Bulletin, 126,* 3–25.

Roberts, B., Walton, K., & Viechtbauer, W. (2006). Patterns of mean-level change in personality traits across the life course: A meta-analysis of longitudinal studies. *Psychological Bulletin, 132,* 1–25.

Roberts, P. M., Garcia, L. J., Desrochers, A., & Hernandez, D. (2002). English performance of proficient bilingual adults on the Boston Naming Test. *Aphasiology, 16,* 635–645.

Roberts, R., Roberts, C., & Duong, H. (2009). Sleepless in adolescence: Prospective data on sleep deprivation, health and functioning. *Journal of Adolescence, 32,* 1045– 1057.

Robertson, S. I. (2001). *Problem solving.* New York: Psychology Press.

Robinson, L., Platt, B., & Riedel, G. (2011, February 16). Involvement in the cholinergic system in conditioning and perceptual memory. *Behavioral and Brain Research, 221,* 443–465.

Roblaes, T., Glaser, R., & Kiecolt-Glaser, J. (2005). Out of balance: A new look at chronic stress, depression, and immunity. *Current Directions in Psychological Science, 14,* 111–115.

Robleto, K., Poulos, A. M, & Thompson, R. F. (2004). Brain mechanisms of extinction of the classically conditioned eyeblink response. *Learning & Memory, 11,* 517–524.

Rochlen, A., McKelley, R., & Pituch, K. (2006). A preliminary examination of the "Real Men. Real Depression" campaign. *Psychology of Men & Masculinity, 7,* 1–13.

Roe, D., & Finger, S. (1996). Gustave Dax and his fight for recognition: An overlooked chapter in the early history of cerebral dominance. *Journal of the History of the Neurosciences, 5,* 228–240.

Roediger, H. L., & McDermott, K. B. (1995). Creating false memories: Remembering words not presented in lists. *Journal of Experimental Psychology: Learning, Memory, and Cognition, 21,* 803–814.

Roediger, H., Agarwal, P. K., Kang, S. K., & Marsh, E. J. (2010). Benefits of testing memory: Best practices and boundary conditions. In G. M. Davies & D. B. Wright (Eds.), *Current issues in applied memory research* (pp. 13–49). New York: Psychology Press.

Rogers, J. M. (2009). Tobacco and pregnancy. *Reproductive Toxicology, 28,* 152–160.

Rogers, J., Kochunov, P., Zilles, K., et al. (2010). On the genetic architecture of cortical folding and brain volume in primates. *Neuroimage, 53,* 1103–1108.

Rogoff, B., Mistry, J., Goncu, A., & Mosier, C. (1993). Guided participation in cultural activity by toddles and caregivers. *Monographs for the Society of Research in Child Development, 58* (serial no. 236).

Rollins, B. C. (1989). Marital quality at midlife. In S. Hunter & M. Sundel (Eds.), *Midlife myths* (pp. 184–194). Newbury Park, CA: Sage.

Rolls, E. T. (1999). *The brain and emotion* (Vol. 4, p. 16190). Oxford, UK: Oxford University Press.

Rolls, E. T. (2010). *Neural representation of fat texture in the mouth.* In J-P. Montmayeur & J. le Coutre (Eds.), Fat detection: Taste, texture, and post ingestive effects (pp. 197–223). Boca Raton, FL: CRC Press.

Rorty, M., Yager, J., Rossotto, E., & Buckwalter, G. (2000). Parental intrusiveness in adolescence recalled by women with a history of bulimia nervosa and comparison women. *International Journal of Eating Disorders, 28,* 202–208.

Rosch, E. H. (1973). Natural categories. *Cognitive Psychology, 4,* 328–350.

Rosch, E., & Mervis, C. B. (1975). Family resemblances: Studies in the internal structure of categories. *Cognitive Psychology,* 7, 573–605.

Rosch, E., Mervis, C. B., Gray, W., Johnson, D., & Boyes-Braem, P. (1976). Basic objects in natural categories. *Cognitive Psychology, 8,* 382–439.

Rose, D., Wykes, T., Leese, M., Bindman, J., & Fleischmann, P. (2003). Patients' perspectives on electroconvulsive therapy: Systematic review. *British Medical Journal, 326,* 1363–1368.

Rose, N., Myerson, J., Roediger, H., & Hale, S. (2010). Similarities and differences between working memory and long-term memory: Evidence from the levels-of-processing span task. *Journal of Experimental Psychology: Learning, Memory, and Cognition, 36,* 471–483.

Roselli, C. E., & Stormshak, F. (2009). Prenatal programming of sexual partner preference: The ram model. *Journal of Neuroendocrinology, 21,* 359–364.

Roselli, C. E., Larkin, K., Schrunk, J. M., & Stormshak, F. (2004). Sexual partner preference, hypothalamic morphology and aromatase in rams. *Physiology and Behavior, 83,* 233–245.

Rosenbaum, R. S., Kohler, S., Schacter, D. L., Moscovitch, M., Westmacott, R., Black, S. E., et al. (2005). The case of K.C.: Contributions of a memory-impaired person to memory theory. *Neuropsychologia, 43,* 989–1021.

Rosenblum, G. D., & Lewis, M. (2003). Emotional development in adolescence. In G. D. Rosenblum & M. Lewis (Eds.), *Blackwell Handbook of Adolescence* (pp. 269–289). Malden: Blackwell Publishing.

Rosenfield, S. (1997). Labeling mental illness: The effects of received services and perceived stigma on life satisfaction. *American Sociological Review, 62,* 660–672.

Rosenhan, D. L. (1973). On being sane in insane places. *Science, 179,* 250–258.

Rosenthal, R. (1974). *On the social psychology of the self-fulfilling prophecy: Further evidence for Pygmalion effects and their mediating mechanisms.* New York: MSS Modular Publications.

Rosenthal, R., & Fode, K. L. (1963). The effect of experimenter bias on the performance of the albino rat. *Behavioral Science, 8,* 183–189.

Rosenthal, R., & Jacobson, L. (1966). Teachers' expectancies: Determinates of pupils' IQ gains. *Psychological Reports, 19,* 115–118.

Rosenthal, R., & Jacobson, L. (1968). *Pygmalion in the classroom: Teacher expectation and pupils' intellectual development.* New York: Holt, Rinehart & Winston.

Rosenzweig, M. R., Krech, D., Bennett, E. L., & Diamond, M. C. (1962). Effects of environmental complexity and training on brain chemistry and anatomy: A replication and extension. *Journal of Comparative and Physiological Psychology, 55,* 429–437.

Ross, C. E., Mirowsky, J., & Goldsteen, K. (1990). The impact of the family on health: The decade in review. *Journal of Marriage and the Family, 52,* 1059–1078.

Ross, L. (1977). The intuitive psychologist and his shortcomings: Distortions in the attribution process. In L. Berkowitz (Ed.), *Advances in experimental social psychology* (Vol. 10). New York: Academic Press.

Ross, L., & Ward, A. (1996). Naive realism in everyday life: Implications for social conflict and misunderstanding. In T. Brown, E. S. Reed, & E. Turiel (Eds.), *Values and knowledge* (pp. 103–135). Hillsdale, NJ: Erlbaum.

Ross, M., & Wang, Q. (2010). Why we remember and what we remember: Culture and autobiographical memory. *Perspectives on Psychological Science, 5,* 401–409.

Ross, M., & Wilson, A. E. (2000). Constructing and appraising past selves. In D. L. Schacter & E. Scarry (Eds.), *Memory, brain and belief* (pp. 231–258). Cambridge, MA: Harvard University Press.

Rosselli, M., Ardila, A., Araujo, K., Weekes, V. A., Caracciolo, V., Padilla, M., et al. (2000). Verbal fluency and repetition skills in healthy older Spanish–English bilinguals. *Applied Neuropsychology, 7,* 17–24.

Rossini, P. M., Altamura, C., Ferretti, A., Vernieri, F., Zappasodi, F., Caulo, M., et al. (2004). Does cerebrovascular disease affect the coupling between neuronal activity and local haemodynamics? *Brain, 127,* 99–110.

Rotermann, M. (2008). Trends in teen sexual behaviour and condom use. *Health Reports, 19,* 53–57.

Roth, S. H., Fleischmann, R. M., Burch, F. X., Dietz, F., Bockow, B., Rapoport, R. J., et al. (2000). Around-the-clock, controlled-release oxycodone therapy for osteoarthritis-related pain: Placebo-controlled trial and long-term evaluation. *Archives of Internal Medicine, 160,* 853–860.

Rothbart, M. K., & Bates, J. E. (2006). Temperament. In W. Damon, R. Lerner, & N. Eisenberg (Eds.), *Handbook of child psychology: Vol. 3. Social, emotional, and personality development* (6th ed., pp. 99–166). New York: Wiley.

Rothman, A., & Salovey, P. (1997). Shaping perceptions to motivate health behavior: The role of message framing. *Psychological Bulletin, 121,* 3–19.

Rouder, J. N., & Ratcliff, R. (2004). Comparing categorization models. *Journal of Experimental Psychology: General, 133,* 63–82.

Rouder, J. N., & Ratcliff, R. (2006). Comparing exemplar- and rule-based theories of categorization. *Current Directions in Psychological Science, 15,* 9–13.

Rozanski, A., Blumenthal, J. A., & Kaplan, J. (1999). Impact of psychological factors on the pathogenesis of cardiovascular disease and implications for therapy. *Circulation, 99,* 2192–2217.

Rubin, D., & Wenzel, A. (1996). One hundred years of forgetting: A quantitative description of retention. *Psychological Review, 103,* 734–760.

Rudman, L. A., Feinburg, J., & Fairchild, K. (2002). Minority members' implicit attitudes: Automatic ingroup bias as a function of group status. *Social Cognition, 20,* 294–320.

Ruffman, T., Slade, L., Devitt, K., & Crowe, E. (2006). What mothers say and what they do: The relation between parenting, theory of mind, language and conflict/cooperation. *British Journal of Developmental Psychology, 24,* 105–124.

Rule, N. O., & Ambady, N. (2008). Brief exposures: Male sexual orientation is accurately perceived at 50 ms. *Journal of Experimental Social Psychology, 44,* 1100–1105.

Rule, N. O., & Ambady, N. (2010). Democrats and Republicans can be differentiated from their faces. *PLoS ONE, 5,* e8733.

Rule, N. O., Macrae, C. N., & Ambady, N. (2009). Ambiguous group membership is extracted automatically from faces. *Psychological Science, 20*(4), 441–443.

Rushton, J. P., & Jensen, A. R. (2005). Thirty years of research on race differences in cognitive ability. *Psychology, Public Policy, and Law, 11,* 235–294.

Ryan, R. M., & Deci, E. L. (2000). Self-determination theory and the facilitation of intrinsic motivation, social development, and well-being. *American Psychologist, 55,* 68–78.

Sacerdote, B. (2001). Peer effects with random assignment: Results for Dartmouth roommates. *Quarterly Journal of Economics, 116,* 681–704.

Sachs, G. T. L. (1812). *Historiae naturalis duorum leucaetiopum: Auctoris ipsius et sororis eius.* Erlangen. [Online]. Retrieved from http://mdz10.bib-bvb.de/~db/0001/bsb00012567/images/

Sack, K. (1998). Georgia's governor seeks musical start for babies. *The New York Times,* January 15, 1998, p. A12.

Safdar, S. F., & Lay, C. H. (2003). The relations of immigrant-specific and immigrant-nonspecific daily hassles to distress controlling for psychological adjustment and cultural competence. *Journal of Applied Social Psychology, 33,* 299–320.

Saffran, E. M., & Schwartz, M. F. (1994). Impairment of sentence comprehension. *Philosophical transactions of the Royal Scoiety of London, Series B, Biological Sciences, 346,* 47–53.

Sagberg, F. (1999). Road accidents caused by drivers falling asleep. *Accident Analysis & Prevention, 31,* 639–649.

Saha, S., Chant, D., Welham, J., & McGrath, J. (2005). A systematic review of the prevalence of schizophrenia. *PLoS Medicine, 2*(5), e141.

Sahakian, B., & Morein-Zamir, S. (2007). Professor's little helper. *Nature, 450,* 1157–1159.

Sahdra, B. K., MacLean, K. A., Ferrer, E., Shaver, P. R., Rosenberg, E. L., Jabocs, T. L., et al. (2011). Enhanced response inhibition during intensive meditation training predicts improvements in self-reported adaptive socioemotional functioning. *Emotion, 11,* 299–312.

Salo, R., Ursu, S., Buonocore, M. H., Leamon, M. H., & Carter, C. (2010). Impaired prefrontal cortical functioning disrupted adaptive cognitive control in methamphetamine abusers: An fMRI study. *Biological Psychiatry, 65,* 706–709.

Salthouse, T. A. (1987). The role of representations in age differences in analogical reasoning. *Psychology and Aging, 2,* 357–362.

Salvatore, J. E., I-Chun Kuo, S., Steele, R. D., Simpson, J. A., & Collins, W. A. (2011). Recovering from conflict in romantic relationships: A developmental perspective. *Psychological Science, 22,* 376–383.

Samson, D., & Pillon, A. (2003). A case of impaired conceptual knowledge for fruit and vegetables. *Cognitive Neuropsychology, 20,* 373–400.

Sargent, J. D. (2005). Smoking in the movies: Impact on adolescent smoking. *Adolescent Medicine, 16,* 345–370.

Saucier, G., Bel-Bahar, T., & Fernandez, C. (2007). What modifies the expression of personality tendencies? Defining basic domains of situation variables. *Journal of Personality, 75,* 479–504.

Saus, E., Johnsen, B., Eid, J., Riisem, P., Andersen, R., & Thayer, J. (2006). The effect of brief situational awareness training in a police shooting simulator: An experimental study. *Military Psychology, 18,* s3–s21.

Savage-Rumbaugh, S., & Lewin, R. (1994). *Kanzi: The ape at the brink of the human mind.* New York: Wiley.

Savin-Williams, R. C., & Cohen, K. M. (2004). Homoerotic development during childhood and adolescence. *Child Adolescent Psychiatric Clinics of North America, 13,* 529–549.

Saxon, A. H. (1989). *P. T. Barnum: The legend and the man.* New York: Columbia University Press.

Schachter, S., & Singer, J. (1962). Cognitive, social, and physiological determinants of emotional state. *Psychological Review, 69,* 379–399.

Schacter, D. L. (1985). Priming of old and new knowledge in amnesic patients and normal subjects. *Annals of the New York Academy of Sciences, 444,* 41–53.

Schaie, K. W. (1994). The course of adult intellectual development. *American Psychologist, 49*(4), 304–313.

Scheier, M. F., & Carver, C. S. (1985). Optimism, coping, and health: Assessment and implications of generalized outcome expectancies. *Health Psychology, 4,* 219–247.

Schenck, C. H., & Mahowald, M. (2002). REM sleep behavior disorder: Clinical, developmental, and neuroscience perspectives 16 years after its formal identification. *Sleep, 25,* 120–138.

Schenck, C. H., Arnulf, I., & Mahowald, M. W. (2007). Sleep and sex: what can go wrong? A review of the literature on sleep-related disorders and abnormal sexual behaviours and experiences. *Sleep, 30,* 683–702.

Schenck, C. H., Lee, S. A., Bornemann, M. A., & Mahowald, M. W. (2009). Potentially lethal behaviors associated with rapid eye movement sleep behavior disorder: Review of the literature and forensic implications. *Journal of Forensic Science, 54,* 1475–1484.

Schenck, C. H., Milner, D. M., Hurwitz, T. D., et al. (1989). A polysomnographic and clinical report on sleep-related injury in 100 adult patients. *American Journal of Psychiatry, 146,* 1166–1173.

Schierenbeck, T., Riemann, D., Berger, M., & Hornyak, M. (2008). Effect of illicit recreational drugs upon sleep: Cocaine, ecstasy and marijuana. *Sleep Medicine Reviews, 12,* 381–389.

Schinka, J. A., Busch, R. M., & Robichaux-Keene, N. (2004). A meta-analysis of the association between the serotonin transporter gene polymorphism (5HTTLPR) and trait anxiety. *Molecular Psychiatry, 9,* 197–202.

Schmader, T., Johns, M., & Forbes, C. (2008). An integrated process model of stereotype threat effects on performance. *Psychological Review, 115,* 336–356.

Schmidt, F. L., & Hunter, J. E. (1993). Tacit knowledge, practical intelligence, general mental ability and job knowledge. *Current Directions in Psychological Science, 2,* 8–9.

Schmidt, F. L., & Hunter, J. E. (1998). The validity and utility of selection methods in personnel psychology: Practical and theoretical implications of 85 years of research findings. *Psychological Bulletin, 124,* 262–274.

Schmidt, F. L., Hunter, J. E., & Pearlman, K. (1981). Task differences as moderators of aptitude test validity in selection: A red herring. *Journal of Applied Psychology, 66,* 166–185.

Schmidt, M. E., Pempek, T. A., Kirkorian, H. L., Lund, A. F., & Anderson, D. R. (2008). The effect of background television on the toy play behavior of very young children. *Child Development, 79,* 1137–1151.

Schmidt, M. E., Rich, M., Rifas-Shiman, S. L., Oken, E., & Traveras, E. M. (2009). Viewing television in infancy and child cognition at 3 years of age in a US cohort. *Pediatrics, 123,* e370–e375.

Schmidt, U., Humfress, H., & Treasure, J. (1997). The role of general family environment and sexual and physical abuse in the origins of eating disorders. *European Eating Disorders Review, 5,* 184–207.

Schmitt, D. P., Allik, J., McCrae, R. R., Benet-Mar-tinez, V., et al. (2007). The geographic distribution of Big Five personality traits: Patterns and profiles of human self-descriptions across 56 nations. *Journal of Cross-Cultural Psychology, 38,* 173–212.

Schmitt, D. P., Realo, A., Voracek, M., & Allik, J. (2008). Why can't a man be more like a woman? Sex differences in Big Five personality traits across 55 cultures. *Journal of Personality and Social Psychology, 94,* 168–182.

Schmolk, H., Buffalo, E. A., & Squire, L. R. (2000). Memory distortions develop over time: Recollections of the O. J. Simpson trial verdict after 15 and 32 months. *Psychological Science, 11,* 39–45.

Schnakers, C., Vanhaudenhuyse, A., Giacino, J., Ventura, M., Boly, M., Majerus, S., et al. (2009). Diagnostic accuracy of the vegetative and minimally conscious state: Clinical consensus versus standardized neurobehavioral assessment. *BMC Neurology, 9,* 35.

Schnall, S., Haidt, J., Clore, G. L., & Jordan, A. H. (2008). Disgust as embodied moral judgment. *Personality and Social Psychology Bulletin, 34,* 1096–1109.

Schneider, S. M., Kisby, C. K., & Flint, E. P. (2011). Effect of virtual reality on time perception in patients receiving chemotherapy. *Support Care Cancer, 19,* 555–564.

Schoenberger, N. E., Kirsch, I., Gearan, P., Montgomery, G., Pastyrnak, S., et al. (1997). Hypnotic enhancement of a cognitive behavioral treatment for public speaking anxiety. *Behavior Therapy, 28,* 127–140.

Schottenbauer, M. A., Momenan, R., Kerick, M., & Hommer, D. W. (2007). Relationships among aging, IQ, and intracranial volume in alcoholics and control subjects. *Neuropsychology, 21,* 337–345.

Schredl, M. (2001). Night terrors in children: Prevalence and influencing factors. *Sleep and Hypnosis, 3,* 68–72.

Schredl, M. (2003). Effects of state and trait factors on nightmare frequency. *European Archives of Psychiatry and Clinical Neuroscience, 253,* 241–247.

Schreurs, B. G. (1993). Long-term memory and extinction of the classically conditioned rabbit nictitating membrane response. *Learning and Motivation, 24,* 293–302.

Schreurs, B. G., Gusev, P. A., Tomsic, D., Alkon, D. L., & Shi, T. (1998). Intracellular correlates of acquisition and long-term memory of classical conditioning in Purkinje cell dendrites in slices of rabbit cerebellar lobule HVI. *Journal of Neuroscience, 18,* 5498–5507.

Schroeder, D. A., Penner, L. A., Dovidio, J. F., & Piliavin, J. A. (1995). *The psychology of helping and altruism: Problems and puzzles.* New York: McGraw-Hill.

Schroers, M., Prigot, J., & Fagen, J. (2007). The effect of a salient odor context on memory retrieval in young infants. *Infant Behavior and Development, 30,* 685–689.

Schultheiss, O. C., & Brunstein, J. C. (2001). Assessing implicit motives with a research version of the TAT: Picture profiles, gender differences, and relations to other personality measures. *Journal of Personality Assessment, 77,* 71–86.

Schultz, P. W., & Zelezny, L. (2003). Reframing environmental messages to be congruent with American values. *Human Ecology Review, 10*(2), 126–136.

Schultz, W. (1998). Predictive reward signal of dopamine neurons. *Journal of Neurophysiology, 80,* 1–27.

Schultz, W., & Dickinson, A. (2000). Neuronal coding of prediction errors. *Annual Review of Neuroscience, 23,* 473–500.

Schultz, W., & Romo, R. (1987). Responses of nigrostriatal dopamine neurons to high intensity somatosensory stimulation in the anesthetized monkey. *Journal of Neurophysiology, 57,* 201–217.

Schultz, W., & Romo, R. (1990). Dopamine neurons of the monkey mid-brain: Contingencies of responses to stimuli eliciting immediate behavioral reactions. *Journal of Neurophysiology, 63,* 607–624.

Schultz, W., Tremblay, L., & Hollerman, J. R. (2000). Reward processing in primate orbitofrontal cortex and basal ganglia. *Cerebral Cortex, 10,* 272–283.

Schulz-Hardt, S., Frey, D., Luthgens, C., & Moscovici, S. (2000). Biased information search in group decision making. *Journal of Personality and Social Psychology, 78,* 655–669.

Schutter, D. J. L. G., Hofman, D., & Van Honk, J. (2008). Fearful faces selectively increase corticospinal motor tract excitability: A transcranial magnetic stimulation study. *Psychophysiology, 45,* 345–348.

Schwartz, B., Ward, A., Monterosso, J., Lyubomirsky, S., White, K., & Lehman, D. R. (2002). Maximizing versus satisficing: Happiness is a matter of choice. *Journal of Personality and Social Psychology, 83,* 1178–1197.

Schwartz, J. M., Stoessel, P. W., Baxter, L. R., Martin, K. M., & Phelps, M. E. (1996). Systematic changes in cerebral glucose metabolic rate after successful behavior modificiation treatment of obsessive-compulsive disorder. *Archives of General Psychiatry, 53,* 109–113.

Schwartz, S. H. (1994). Are there universal aspects in the structure and contents of human values? *Journal of Social Issues, 50,* 19–45.

Schwartz, T. A., Ware, J., Fischer, C. E., Craik, F. I. M., & Bialystok, E. (2012). Bilingualism as a contributor to cognitive reserve: Evidence from brain atrophy in Alzheimer's disease. *Cortex, 48,* 991–996.

Scoboria, A., Mazzoni, G., Kirsch, I., & Jimenez, S. (2006). The effects of prevalence and script information on plausibility belief and memory of autobiographical events. *Applied Cognitive Psychology, 20,* 1049–1064.

Scoville, W. B., & Milner, B. (1957). Loss of recent memory after bilateral hippocampal lesions. *Journal of Neurology, Neurosurgery, and Psychiatry, 20,* 11–21.

Seale, J. P., Shellenberger, S., Rodriguez, C., Seale, J. D., & Alvarado, M. (2002). Alcohol use and cultural change in and indigenous population: A case study from Venezuela. *Alcohol and Alcoholism, 37,* 603–608.

Sealy, P., & Whitehead, P. C. (2006). The impact of deinstitutionalization of psychiatric hospitals on psychological distress of the community in Canada. *Journal of Health & Social Policy, 21,* 73–94.

Sears, H. A., & Byers, E. S. (2010). Adolescent girls' and boys' experiences of psychologically, physically, and sexually aggressive behaviors in their dating relationships: Co-occurrence and emotional reaction. *Journal of Aggression, Maltreatment & Trauma, 19,* 517–539.

Sedikides, C., & Strube, M. J. (1995). The multiply motivated self. *Personality and Social Psychology Bulletin, 21,* 1330–1335.

Segal Z. V., Williams J. M. G., & Teasdale J. D. (2002). *Mindfulness-based cognitive therapy for depression: A new approach to preventing relapse.* New York: Guilford.

Segerstrom, S. C., & Miller, G. E. (2004). Psychological stress and the immune system: A meta-analytic study of 30 years of inquiry. *Psychological Bulletin, 130,* 601–630.

Seidenberg, M. S., & Pettito, L. A. (1979). Signing behavior in apes: A critical review. *Cognition, 7,* 177–215.

Seligman, M. E. P. (1971). Phobias and preparedness. *Behavior Therapy, 2,* 307–320.

Seligman, M. E. P., & Csikszentmihalyi, M. (2000). Positive psychology: An introduction. *American Psychologist, 55,* 5–14.

Seligman, M. E. P., Abramson, L. Y., Semmel, A., & von Baeyer, C. (1979). Depressive attributional style. *Journal of Abnormal Psychology, 88,* 242–247.

Seligman, M. E., & Maier, S. F. (1967). Failure to escape traumatic shock. *Journal of Experimental Psychology, 74,* 1–9.

Selye, H. (1950). Stress and the general adaptation syndrome. *British Medical Journal,* 1385–1392.

Selye, H. (1955). Stress and disease. *Science, 122,* 625–631.

Selye, H. (1956). *The stress of life.* New York: McGraw-Hill.

Senghas, A. (2003). Intergenerational influence and ontogenetic development in the emergence of spatial grammar in Nicaraguan Sign Language. *Cognitive Development, 18,* 511–531.

Senghas, A., Kita, S., & Ozyurek, A. (2004). Children creating core properties of language: Evidence from an emerging sign language in Nicaragua. *Science, 305,* 1779–1782.

Sengupta, J., & Dahl, D. W. (2008). Gender-related reactions to gratuitous sex appeals in advertising. *Journal of Consumer Psychology, 18,* 62–78.

Shad, M. U., Bidesi, A. S., Chen, L-A., Thomas, B. P., Ernst, M., & Rao, U. (2011). Neurobiology of decision-making in adolescents. *Behavioural Brain Research, 217,* 67–76.

Shamosh, N. A., DeYoung, C. G., Green, A. E., Reis, D. L., Johnson, M. R., Conway, A. R. A., et al. (2008). Individual differences in delay discounting: Relation to intelligence, working memory, and anterior prefrontal cortex. *Psychological Science, 19,* 904–911.

Shapiro, A. F., Gottman, J. M. & Carrère, S. (1999). The baby and the marriage: Identifying factors that buffer against decline in marital satisfaction after the baby arrives. *Journal of Family Psychology, 14,* 59–70.

Shapiro, C. M., Tranjanovic, N. N., & Fedoroff, J. P. (2003). Sexsomnia—a new parasomnia? *Canadian Journal of Psychiatry, 48,* 311–317.

Sharot, T., & Phelps, E. A. (2004). How emotional arousal modulates memory: Disentangling the effects of attention and retention. *Cognitive Affective Behavioural Neuroscience, 4,* 294–306.

Sharot, T., Martorella, E. A., Delgado, M. R., & Phelps, E. A. (2007). How personal experience modulates the neural circuitry of memories of September 11. *Proceedings of the National Academy of Sciences of the United States of America, 104,* 389–394.

Sharp, W., Hargrove, D., Johnson, L., & Deal, W. (2006). Mental health education: An evaluation of a classroom based strategy to modify help seeking for mental health problems. *Journal of College Student Development, 47,* 419–438.

Shaywitz, S. E. (1998). Dyslexia. *Current Concepts, 338,* 307–312.

Shaywitz, S. E., & Shaywitz, B. A. (1991). Introduction to the special series on attention deficit disorder. *Journal of Learning Disabilities, 24,* 68–71.

Sheldon, K. M., Arndt, J., & Houser-Marko, L. I. (2003). In search of the organismic valuing process: The human tendency to move towards beneficial goal choices. *Journal of Personality, 71,* 835–869.

Sheline, Y. I., Barch, D. M., Donnelly, J. M., Ollinger, J. M. Snyder, A. Z., & Mintun, M. A. (2001). Increased amygdala response to masked emotional faces in depressed subjects resolves with antidepressant treatment: An fMRI study. *Biological Psychiatry, 50,* 651–658.

Shepperd, J. A., & Koch, E. (2005). Pitfalls in teaching judgment heuristics. *Teaching of Psychology, 32,* 43–46.

Sheridan, M A., Fox, N. A., Zeanah, C. H., McLaughlin, K. A., & Nelson, C. A. (2012). Variation in neural development as a result of exposure to institutionalization early in childhood. *Proceedings of the National Academy of Sciences of the United States of America, 109,* 12927–12932.

Sherif, M. (1961). *The robbers cave experiment: Intergroup conflict and cooperation.* Middletown, CT: Wesleyan University Press.

Shi, R., & Werker, J. F. (2001). Six-month-old infants' preferences for lexical words. *Psychological Science, 12,* 70–75.

Shi, R., Werker, J. F., & Morgan, J. L. (1999). Newborn infants' sensitivity to perceptual cues to lexcial and grammatical words. *Cognition, 72,* B11–B21.

Shields, M., & Tjepkema, M. (2006). Regional differences in obesity. *Health Reports, 17,* 61–67.

Shields, M., Carroll, M. D., & Ogden, C. L. (2011). Adult obesity prevalence in Canada and the United States. *Advances in Nutrition, 2,* 368–369.

Shin, L. M., Orr, S. P., Carson, M. A., Rauch, S. L., Macklin, M. L., Lasko, N. B., Peters, P. M., Metzger, L. J., Dougherty, D. D., Cannistraro, P. A., Alpert, N. M., Fischman, A. J., & Pitman, R. K. (2004). Regional cerebral blood flow in the amygdala and medial prefrontal cortex during traumatic imagery in male and female Vietnam veterans with PTSD. *Archives of General Psychiatry, 6,* 168–176.

Shin, L. M., Rauch, S. L., & Pitman, R. K. (2006). Amygdala, medial prefrontal cortex, and hippocampal function in PTSD. *Annals of the New York Academy of Sciences, 1071,* 67–79.

Shoda, Y., Mischel, W., & Peake, P. K. (1990). Predicting adolescent cognitive and self-regulatory competencies from preschool delay of gratification: Identifying diagnostic conditions. *Developmental Psychology, 26,* 978–986.

Sibley, C. G., & Duckitt, J. (2008). Personality and prejudice: A meta-analysis and theoretical review. *Personality and Social Psychology Review, 12,* 248–279.

Siegel, D. (2007). *The mindful brain: Reflection and attunement in the cultivation of well-being.* New York: W. W. Norton & Company.

Siegel, J. (1995). Phylogeny and the function of REM sleep. *Behavioural Brain Research, 69,* 29–34.

Siegel, J. (2005). Clues to the functions of mammalian sleep. *Nature, 437,* 1264–1271.

Siegel, S. (1984). Pavlovian conditioning and heroin overdose: Reports by overdose victims. *Bulletin of the Psychonomic Society, 22,* 428–430.

Siegel, S., Baptista, M. A. S., Kim, J. A., McDonald, R. V., & Weise-Kelly, L. (2000). Pavlovian psychopharmacology: The associative basis of tolerance. *Experimental and Clinical Psychopharmacology, 8,* 276–293.

Siegel, S., Hinson, R. E., Krank, M. D., & McCully, J. (1982). Heroin "overdose" death: Contribution of drug-associated environmental cues. *Science, 216,* 436–437.

Siegler, R. S. (1992). The other Alfred Binet. *Developmental Psychology, 28*, 179–190.

Silva, A. J., Paylor, R., Wehner, J. M., & Tonegawa, S. (1992). Impaired spatial learning in alpha-calcium-calmodulin kinase II mutant mice. *Science, 257*, 206–211.

Silva, M., Groeger, J., & Bradshaw, M. (2006). Attention–memory interactions in scene perception. *Spatial Vision, 19*, 9–19.

Simons, D. J., & Chabris, C. F. (1999). Gorillas in our midst: Sustained inattentional blindness for dynamic events. *Perception, 28*, 1059–1074.

Simons, D. J., & Levin, D. T. (1997). Change blindness. *Trends in Cognitive Sciences, 1*, 261–267.

Singer T., Kiebel, S. J., Winston, J. S., Dolan, R. J., & Frith, C. D. (2004). Brain responses to the acquired moral status of faces. *Neuron, 41*, 653–662.

Singer, M. A., & Goldin-Meadow, S. (2005). Children learn when their teacher's gestures and speech differ. *Psychological Science, 16*, 85–89.

Singer, R. N. (1965). Massed and distributed practice effects on the acquisition and retention of a novel basketball skill. *The Research Quarterly, 36*, 68–77.

Sinha, R. (2009). Modeling stress and drug craving in the laboratory: Implications for addiction treatment development. *Addiction Biology, 14*, 84–98.

Sireteanu, R. (1999). Switching on the infant brain. *Science, 286*, 59–61.

Skinner, B. F. (1948). Superstition in the pigeon. *Journal of Experimental Psychology, 38*, 168–172.

Skinner, B. F. (1985). Cognitive science and behaviorism. *British Journal of Psychology, 76*, 291–301.

Slater, A., Morison, V., & Somers, M. (1988). Orientation discrimination and cortical function in the human newborn. *Perception, 17*, 597–602.

Slotema, C. W., Blom, J. D., Hoek, H. W., & Sommer, I. E. (2010). Should we expand the toolbox of psychiatric treatment methods to include repetitive transcranial magnetic stimulation (rTMS)? A meta-analysis of the efficacy of rTMS in psychiatric disorders. *Journal of Clinical Psychiatry, 71*, 873–884.

Slovic, P. (2007). If I look at the mass I will never act: Psychic numbing and genocide. *Judgment and Decision Making, 2*, 79–95.

Slovic, P., Finucane, M., Peters, E., & MacGregor, D. G. (2002). Rational actors or rational fools: Implications of the affect heuristic for behavioral economics. *Journal of Socio-economics, 31*, 329–342.

Small, D. A., Loewenstein, G., & Slovic, P. (2007). Sympathy and callousness: The impact of deliberative thought on donations to identifiable and statistical victims. *Organizational Behavior and Human Decision Processes, 102*, 143–153.

Small, D. M., Jones-Gotman, M., Zatorre, R. J., Petrides, M., Evans, A. C. (1997). Flavor processing: More than the sum of its parts. *Neuroreport, 8*, 3913–3917.

Small, D. M., Zatorre, R. J., Dagher, A., Evans, A. C., & Jones-Gotman, M. (2001). Changes in brain activity related to eating chocolate. *Brain, 124*, 1720–1733.

Small, G. W., Siddarth, P., Kepe, V., Ercoli, L. M., Burggren, A. C., Bookheimer, S. Y., Miller, K. J., et al. (2012). Prediction of cognitive decline by positron emission tomography of brain amyloid and tau. *Archives of Neurology, 69*, 215–222.

Smilek, D., Moffatt, B. A., Pasternak, J., White, B. N., Dixon, M. J., & Merikle, P. M. (2002). Synaesthesia: A case study of discordant monozygotic twins. *Neurocase, 8*, 338–342.

Smith, B. W. (2004). Structural and organizational predictors of homicide by police. *Policing: An International Journal of Police Strategies and Management, 27*, 539–557.

Smith, B., Fowler, D. G., Freeman, D., Bebbington, P., Bashforth, H., Garety, P., et al. (2006). Emotion and psychosis: links between depression, self-esteem, negative schematic beliefs and delusions and hallucinations. *Schizophrenia Research, 86*, 181–188.

Smith, C. (1993). Sleep and learning: Some recent findings. In A. Moffit, M. Kramer, & R. Hoffmann (Eds.), *The functions of dreaming.* Albany: SUNY.

Smith, C. (2001). Sleep states and memory processes in humans: Procedural versus declarative memory systems. *Sleep Medicine Reviews, 5*, 491–506.

Smith, C. T., Nixon, M. R., & Nadar, R. S. (2004). Posttraining increases in REM sleep intensity implicate REM sleep in memory processing and provide a biological marker of learning potential. *Learning & Memory, 11*, 714–719.

Smith, C., & Lapp, L. (1991). Increases in number of REMs and REM density in humans following an intensive learning period. *Journal of Sleep Research & Sleep Medicine, 14*, 325–330.

Smith, C., & MacNeil, C. (1994). Impaired motor memory for a pursuit rotor task following Stage 2 sleep loss in college students. *Journal of Sleep Research, 3*, 206–213.

Smith, E., & Delargy, M. (2005). Locked-in syndrome. *British Medical Journal, 330*, 406–409.

Smith, J. E., & Tolson, J. M. (2008). Recognition, diagnosis, and treatment of restless legs syndrome. *Journal of the American Academy of Nurse Practitioners, 20*, 396–401.

Smith, M. L., Glass, G. V., & Miller, T. I. (1980). *The benefits of psychotherapy.* Baltimore: John Hopkins University Press.

Smith, S. D., & Kornelsen, J. (2011). Emotion-dependent responses in spinal cord neurons: A spinal fMRI study. *Neuroimage, 58*, 269–274.

Smith, T. B., McCullough, M. E., & Poll, J. (2003). Religiousness and depression: Evidence for a main eff ect and the moderating influence of stressful life events. *Psychological Bulletin, 129*, 614–636.

Smith, T. C., Ryan, M. A. K., Wingard, D. L., Slymen, D. J., Sallis, J. F., & Kirtz-Silverstein, D. (2008). New onset and persistent symptoms of post-traumatic stress disorder self-reported after deployment and combat exposures: Prospective population based US military cohort study. *British Medical Journal, 336*, 366–371.

Snider, L. A., & Swedo, S. E. (2004). PANDAS: Current status and directions for research. *Molecular Psychiatry, 9*, 900–907.

Snowdon, L. R. (1999). African American service use for mental health problems. *Journal of Community Psychology, 27*, 303–313.

Snyder, K. (2006). Kurt Snyder's personal experience with schizophrenia. *Schizophrenia Bulletin, 32*, 209–211.

Söderlund, H., Moscovitch, M., Kumar, N., Mandic, M., & Levine, B. (2012). As time goes by: Hippocampal connectivity changes with remoteness of autobiographical memory retrieval. *Hippocampus, 22*, 670–679.

Solomon, K. D., Fernández de Castro, L. E., Sandoval, H. P., Biber, J. M., Groat, B., Neff, K. D., et al. (2009). LASIK world literature review: Quality of life and patient satisfaction. *Ophthalmology, 116*, 691–701.

Solutions Research Group. (2006). *Fast Forward (TM) Trend Analysis: Report prepared for the CRTC.* Data retrieved from http://www.crtc.gc.ca/eng/ publications/reports/radio/srg.pdf

Son Hing, L. S., Bobocel, D. R., Zanna, M. P., & McBride, M. V. (2007). Authoritarian dynamics and unethical decision making: High SDO leaders and high RWA followers. *Journal of Personality and Social Psychology, 92*, 67–81.

Sousa-Poza, A., & Sousa-Poza, A. A. (2000). Well-being at work: A cross-national analysis of the levels and determinants of job satisfaction. *Journal of Socio-Economics, 29*, 517–538.

Sovik, R. (2000). The science of breathing—The yoga view. *Progress in Brain Research, 122*, 491–505.

Sowell, E. R., Peterson, B. S., Thompson, P. M., Welcome, S. E., Henkenius, A. L., & Toga, A. W. (2003). Mapping cortical change across the human life span. *Nature neuroscience, 6*, 309–315.

Spanos, N. P., Burgess, C. A., & Burgess, M. F. (1994). Past-life identities, UFO abductions, and satanic ritual abuse: The social construction of memories. *International Journal of Clinical and Experimental Hypnosis, 42*, 433–446.

Spanos, N., Cobb, P., & Gorassini, D. (1985). Failing to resist hypnotic test suggestions: A strategy for self-presenting as deeply hypnotized. *Psychiatry: Journal for the Study of Interpersonal Processes, 48*, 282–292.

Spearman, C. (1923). *The nature of intelligence and the principles of cognition*. London: Macmillan.

Spearman, C. (1939). Thurstone's work re-worked. *The Journal of Educational Psychology, 30*, 1–16.

Spector, F., & Maurer, D. (2009). Synesthesia: A new approach to understanding the development of perception. *Developmental Psychology, 45*, 175–189.

Spelke, E. S., & Kinzler, K. D. (2007). Core knowledge. *Developmental Science, 10*, 89–96.

Spence, A., Poortinga, W., & Pidgeon, N. (2012). The psychological distance of climate change. *Risk Analysis, 32*, 957–972.

Spencer, S. J., Steele, C. M., & Quinn, D. M. (1999). Stereotype threat and women's math performance. *Journal of Experimental Social Psychology, 35*(1), 4–28.

Spera, S. P., Buhrfeind, E. D., & Pennebaker, J. W. (1994). Expressive writing and coping with job loss. *Academy of Management Journal, 37*, 722–733.

Sperling, G. (1960). The information available in brief visual presentations. *Psychological Monographs, 74*, 1–29.

Spires-Jones, T., & Knafo, S. (2012). Spines, plasticity, and cognition in Alzheimer's model mice. *Neural Plasticity, 2012*, 1–10.

Sproule, B., Brands, B., Li, S., & Catz-Biro, L. (2009). Changing patterns in opioid addiction. *Canadian Family Physician, 55*, 68–69, e1–5.

Squeglia, L. M., Jacobus, J., & Tapert, S. F. (2009). The influence of substance use on adolescent brain development. *Clinical EEG and Neuroscience, 40*, 31–38.

Squire, L. R. (1986). Mechanisms of memory. *Science, 232*, 1612–1619.

Squire, L. R. (1989). On the course of forgetting in very long-term memory. *Journal of Experimental Psychology: Learning, Memory, and Cognition, 15*, 241–245.

Stack, S. & Eshleman, J. R. (1998). Marital status and happiness: A 17-nation study. *Journal of Marriage and Family, 60*, 527–536.

Staffen, W., Kronbichler, M., Aichhorn, M., Mair, A., & Ladurner, G. (2006). Selective brain activity in response to one's own name in the persistent vegetative state. *Journal of Neurology, Neurosurgery, and Psychiatry, 77*, 1383–1384.

Stafford, L. D., Salchi, S., & Waller, B. M. (2009). Odors cur memory for odor-associated words. *Chemosensory Perception, 2*, 59–69.

Stanhope, N., Cohen, G., & Conway, M. (1993). Very long-term retention of a novel. *Applied Cognitive Psychology, 7*, 239–256.

Stanovich, K. E., & West, R. F. (2000). Individual differences in reasoning: Implications for the rationality debate? *Behavioral and Brain Sciences, 23*, 645–665.

Starcevic, V., Linden, M., Uhlenhuth, E. H., Kolar, D., & Latas, M. (2004). Treatment of panic disorder with agoraphobia in an anxiety disorders clinic: Factors influencing psychiatrists' treatment choices. *Psychiatry Research, 125*, 41–52.

Starin, E. D. (2004). Masturbation observations in Temminck's red colobus. *Folia Primatologica, 75*, 114–117.

Stark, C. E., Okado, Y., & Loftus, E. F. (2010). Imaging the reconstruction of true and false memories using sensory reactivation and the misinformation paradigms. *Learning and Memory, 17*, 485–488

Stastna, K. (2013). Eli Lilly files $500M NAFTA suit against Canada over drug patents. Retrieved from: http://www.cbc.ca/news/business/eli-lilly-files-500m-nafta-suit-against-canada-over-drug-patents-1.1829854

Statistics Canada. (2003). Canadian community health survey: Mental health and well-being 2002. Retrieved from http://www.statcan.gc.ca/pub/82-617-x/index-eng.htm

Statistics Canada. (2003). Sources of workplace stress. Perspective on labour and income, 4. Retrieved from http://www.statcan.gc.ca/pub/75-001-x/00603/6533-eng.html

Statistics Canada. (2004). Table 101-6511 - 30 and 50 year total divorce rates per 1,000 marriages, Canada, provinces and territories, annual (rate per 1,000 marriages), CANSIM (database). (Accessed 2013-11-05).

Statistics Canada. (2007). *Canadian community health survey, cycle 4.1, 2007* [computer file]. Ottawa, ON: Statistics Canada. Health Statistics Division [producer]; Statistics Canada. Data Liberation Initiative [distributor], July 2007. (STC cat. no. 82M0013XCB)

Statistics Canada. (2008). Households report. Data retrieved from http://www45.statcan.gc.ca/2008/cgco_2008_006-eng.htm

Statistics Canada. (2008). Sedentary behavior and obesity. *Health Reports, 29*, 18–30. Retrieved from http://www.statcan.gc.ca/pub/82-003-x/2008002/article/10599-eng.htm

Statistics Canada. (2010). Overweight and obese adults (self-reported), 2010. Retrieved from http://www.statcan.gc.ca/pub/82-625-x/2011001/article/11464-eng.htm

Statistics Canada. (2011). Adult obesity prevalence in Canada and the United States. Health facts sheet. Retrieved from http://www.statcan.gc.ca/pub/82-625-x/2012001/article/11664-eng.htm

Statistics Canada. (2012a). Leading causes of death, by sex. Retrieved from http://www.statcan.gc.ca/tables-tableaux/sum-som/l01/cst01/hlth36a-eng.htm

Statistics Canada. (2012b). Current smoking trends. Retrieved from http://www.statcan.gc.ca/pub/82-624-x/2012001/article/11676-eng.pdf

Statistics Canada. (2012). *Portrait of families and living arrangements in Canada.* http://www12.statcan.gc.ca/census-recensement/2011/as-sa/ 98-312-x/98-312-x2011001-eng.pdf

Statistics Canada. (2013). Select health indicators of First Nations people living off reserve, Metis and Inuit. Retrieved from http://www.statcan.gc.ca/pub/82-624-x/2013001/article/11763-eng.htm

Steele, C. (1997). A threat in the air: How stereotypes shape intellectual identity and performance. *American Psychologist, 52*, 613–629.

Steele, C. M., & Josephs, R. A. (1990). Alcohol myopia: Its prized and dangerous effects. *American Psychologist, 45*, 921–933.

Steele, J. D., Christmas, D., Eliamel, M. S., & Matthews, K. (2008). Anterior cingulotomy for major depression: Clinical outcome and relationship to lesion characteristics. *Biological Psychiatry, 63*, 670–677.

Steele, K. M., Ball, T. N., & Runk, R. (1997). Listening to Mozart does not enhance backwards digit span performance. *Perceptual and Motor Skills, 84*, 1179–1184.

Steele, K. M., Bass, K. E., & Crook, M. D. (1999). The mystery of the Mozart effect: Failure to replicate. *Psychological Science, 10*, 366–369.

Steffen, P. R., McNeilly, M., Anderson, N., & Sherwood, A. (2003). Effects of perceived racism and anger inhibition on ambulatory lood pressure in African Americans. *Psychosomatic Medicine, 65*, 746–750.

Stein, Z., Susser, M., Saenger, G., & Marolla, F. (1975). Famine and human development: The Dutch hunger winter of 1944–1945.

Steinberg, L. (2004). Risk taking in adolescence: What changes, and why? *Annals of the New York Academy of Sciences, 1021*, 51–58.

Steinberg, L. (2007). Risk taking in adolescence: New perspectives from brain and behavioral science. *Current Directions in Psychological Science, 16*, 55–59.

Steinberg, L. (2008). A social neuroscience perspective on adolescent risk-taking. *Developmental Review, 28*, 78–106.

Steptoe, A., Lipsey, Z., & Wardle, J. (1998). Stress, hassles and variations in alcohol consumption, food choice and physical exercise: A dairy study. *British Journal of Health Psychology, 3*, 51–63.

Sterling, P. (2011). Allostasis: A model of predictive regulation. *Physiology & Behavior, 106,* 5–15.

Stern, P. C., & Dietz, T. (1994). The value basis of environmental concern. *Journal of Social Issues 50,* 65–84.

Sternberg, R. J. (1983). Components of human intelligence. *Cognition, 15,* 1–48.

Sternberg, R. J. (1988). *The triarchic mind: A new theory of human intelligence.* New York: Penguin Books.

Sternberg, R. J. (2003). Intelligence. In I. B. Weiner & D. K. Freedheim (Eds.), *Comprehensive handbook of psychology, Vol. 1.* New York: Wiley.

Sternberg, R. J., Castejón, J. L., Prieto, M. D., Hautamäki, J., & Grigorenko, E. L. (2001). Confirmatory factor analysis of the Sternberg Triarchic Abilities Test in three international samples: An empirical test of the triarchic theory of intelligence. *European Journal of Psychological Assessment, 17,* 1–16.

Sternberg, R. J., Wagner, R. K., Williams, W. M., & Horvath, J. A. (1995). Testing common sense. *American Psychologist, 60,* 46–59.

Stettler, N., Signer, T., & Paolo, S. (2004). Electronic games and childhood obesity. *Nutrition Research Newsletter, 23,* 7–8.

Stevenson, R. A., Schlesinger, J. J., & Wallace, M. T. (2013). Effects of divided attention and operating room noise on perception of pulse oximeter pitch changes: A laboratory study. *Anesthesiology, 118,* 376–381.

Stevenson, R. J., Oaten, M. J., Caste, T. I., Repacholi, B. M., & Wagland, P. (2010). Children's response to adult disgust elicitors: Development and acquisition. *Developmental Psychology, 46,* 165–177.

Stewart, D. W., & Punj, G. N. (1998). Effects of using a nonverbal (musical) cue on recall and playback of television advertising: Implications for advertising tracking. *Journal of Business Research, 42,* 39–51.

Stewart, T. L., Latu, I. M., Kawakami, K., & Myers, A. C. (2010). Consider the situation: Reducing automatic stereotyping through Situational Attribution Training. *Journal of Experimental Social Psychology, 46,* 221–225.

Stice, E. (1998). Relations of restraint and negative affect to bulimic pathology: A longitudinal test of three competing models. *International Journal of Eating Disorders, 23,* 243–260.

Stice, E., & Shaw, H. E. (1994). Adverse effects of the media portrayed thin-ideal on women and linkages to bulimic symptomatology. *Journal of Social and Clinical Psychology, 13,* 288–308.

Stice, E., Presnell, K., Shaw, H., & Rohde, P. (2005). Psychological and behavioral risk factors for obesity onset in adolescent girls: A prospective study. *Journal of Consulting and Clinical Psychology, 73,* 195–202.

Stice, E., Spoor, S., Bohon, C., Veldhuizen, M. G., & Small, D. M. (2008). Relation of reward from food intake and anticipated food intake to obesity: A functional magnetic resonance imaging study. *Journal of Abnormal Psychology, 117,* 924–935.

Stickgold, R., LaTanya, J., & Hobson, A. (2000). Visual discrimination learning requires sleep after training. *Nature Neuroscience, 3,* 1237–1238.

Stickgold, R., Scott, L., Rittenhouse, C., & Hobson, J. A. (1999). Sleep-induced changes in associative memory. *Journal of Cognitive Neuroscience, 11,* 182–193.

Stigler, S. (2008). Fisher and the 5% level. *Chance, 21,* 12.

Stillman, R. C., Weingartner, H., Wyatt, R. J., Gillin, J. C., & Eich, J. (1974). State-dependent (dissociative) effects of marihuana on human memory. *Arch Gen Psychiatry, 31,* 81–85.

Stine-Morrow, E. A. L. (2007). The Dumbledore hypothesis of cognitive aging. *Current Directions in Psychological Science, 16,* 295–299.

Stinson, F. S., Dawson, D. A., Chou, P. S., et al. (2007). The epidemiology of DSM-IV specific phobia in the USA: Results from the National Epidemiologic Survey on Alcohol and Related Conditions. *Psychological Medicine, 37,* 1047–1059.

Stokoe, W. C., Casterline, D. C., & Croneberg, C. G. (1976). *A dictionary of American Sign Language on linguistic principles* (2nd ed.). Linstok Press: Silver Spring, MD.

Stouffer, E. M. (2010). The entorhinal cortex, but not the dorsal hippocampus, is necessary for single-cue latent learning. *Hippocampus, 20,* 1061–1071.

Stouffer, E. M., & White, N. M. (2006). Neural circuits mediating latent learning and conditioning for salt in the rat. *Neurobiology of Learning and Memory, 86,* 91–99.

Strack, F., Martin, L. L., & Stepper, S. (1988). Inhibiting and facilitating conditions of the human smile: A nonobtrusive test of the facial feedback hypothesis. *Journal of Personality and Social Psychology, 54,* 768–777.

Strahan, E. J., Lafrance, A., Wilson, A. E., Ethier, N., Spencer, S. J., & Zanna, M. J. (2008). Victoria's dirty secret: How sociocultural norms influence adolescent girls and women. *Personality and Social Psychology Bulletin, 34,* 288–301.

Strahan, E. J., Spencer, S. J., & Zanna, M. P. (2002). Subliminal priming and persuasion: Striking while the iron is hot. *Journal of Experimental Social Psychology, 38,* 556–568.

Strahan, E. J., Wilson, A. E., Cressman, K. E., & Bruote, V. M. (2006). Comparing to perfection: How cultural norms for appearance affect social comparisons and self-image. *Body Image, 3,* 211–227.

Strassman, R. (2001). *DMT: Spirit molecule.* Rochester, VT: Park Street Press.

Streissguth, A. P., & Connor, P. D. (2001). Fetal alcohol syndrome and other effects of prenatal alcohol: Developmental cognitive neuroscience implications. In C. A. Nelson & M. Luciana (Eds.), *Handbook of developmental cognitive neuroscience* (pp. 505–518). Cambridge, MA: MIT Press.

Streissguth, A. P., Barr, H. M., Bookstein, F. L., Sampson, P. D., & Olson, H. C. (1999). The long-term neurocognitive consequences of prenatal alcohol exposure: A 14-year study. *Psychological Science, 10,* 186–190.

Strenziok, M., Krueger, F., Deshpande, G., Lenroot, R.K., van der Meer, E., & Grafman, J. (2011). Fronto-parietal regulation of media violence exposure in adolescents: A multi-method study. *Social, Cognitive, and Affective Neuroscience, 6,* 537–547.

Streppel, M. T., Boshuizen, H. C., Ocke, M. C., Kok, F. J., & Kromhout, D. (2007). Mortality and life expectancy in relation to long-term cigarette, cigar, and pipe smoking: The Zutphen study. *Tobacco Control, 16,* 107–113.

Strick, M., van Baaren, R. B., Holland, R. W., & van Knippenberg, A. (2009). Humor in advertisements enhances product liking by mere association. *Journal of Experimental Psychology: Applied, 15,* 35–45.

Stuart, E. W., Shimp, T. A., & Engle, R. W. 1990. Classical conditioning of negative attitudes. *Advances in Consumer Research, 17,* 536–540.

Substance Abuse and Mental Health Services Administration (SAMHSA). (2010). Results from the 2009 National Survey on Drug Use and Health: National findings (Office of Applied Studies, NSDUH Series H-38A, HHS Publication No. SMA 10-4586 Findings). Rockville, MD: SAMHSA.

Sue S., & Lam A. G. (2002). Cultural and demographical diversity. In J. Norcross (Ed.), *Psychotherapy relations that work: Therapist contributions and responsiveness to patients.* Oxford, UK: Oxford University Press.

Sumnall, H. R., Measham, F., Brandt, S. D., & Cole, J. C. (2011). Salvia divinorum use and phenomenology: Results from an online survey. *Journal of Psychopharmacology, 25,* 1496–1507.

Super, D. E., Savickas, M. L., & Super, C. M. (1996). The life-span, life-space approach to careers. In D. Brown, L. Brooks, & Associates (Eds.), *Career choice and development: Applying contemporary theories to practice* (3rd ed., pp. 121–178). San Francisco: Jossey-Bass.

Supreme Court of Canada. (2001). *R. v. Sharpe,* [2001] 1 S.C.R. 45, 2001 SCC 2.

Supreme Court of Canada. (2007). *R. v. Trochym,* [2007] 1 S.C.R., 2007 SCC 239.

Supreme Court of Canada. *Canadian Foundation for Children, Youth and the Law v. Canada (Attorney General),* [2004] 1 S.C.R. 76, 2004 SCC 4.

Susser, E. B., Brown, A., & Matte, T. D. (1999). Prenatal factors and adult mental and physical health. *Canadian Journal of Psychiatry, 44,* 326–334.

Susskind, J. M., & Anderson, A. K. (2008). Facial expression form and function. *Nature Neuroscience, 11,* 843–850.

Susskind, J. M., Lee, D. H., Cusi, A., Feiman, R., Grabski, W., & Anderson, A. K. (2008). Expressing fear enhances sensory acquisition. *Nature Neuroscience, 11,* 843–850.

Sutherland, R., & Hayne, H. (2001). The effect of postevent information on adults' eyewitness reports. *Applied Cognitive Psychology, 15,* 249–263.

Süβ, H. M. et al. (2002). Working-memory capacity explains reasoning ability—and a little bit more. *Intelligence, 30,* 261–288.

Sweeney, P. D., Anderson, K., & Bailey, S. (1986). Attributional style in depression: A meta-analytic review. *Journal of Personality and Social Psychology, 50,* 974.

Swithers, S. E., & Davidson, T. L. (2005). Obesity: Outwitting the wisdom of the body? *Current Neurology and Neuroscience Reports, 5,* 159–162.

Swithers, S. E., Baker, C. R., & Davidson, T. L. (2009). General and persistent effects of high-intensity sweeteners on body weight gain and caloric compensation in rats. *Behavioral Neuroscience, 123,* 772–780.

Symons, C. S., & Johnson, B. T. (1997). The self-reference effect in memory: A meta-analysis. *Psychological Bulletin, 121,* 371–394.

Szasz, T. (2006). Mental illness as brain disease: A brief history lesson. *Freeman, 56,* 24.

Szelenberfer, W., Niemcewicz, S., & Dabrowska, A. J. (2005). Sleepwalking and night terrors: Psychopathological correlates. *International Review of Psychology, 17,* 263–270.

Tajfel, H. (1970). Experiments in intergroup discrimination. *Scientific American, 223,* 96–102.

Tajfel, H., & Turner, J. C. (1986). The social identity theory of intergroup behaviour. In S. Worchel & W. G. Austin (Eds.), *Psychology of intergroup relations* (2nd ed., pp. 7–24). Chicago: Nelson-Hall.

Tajfel, H., & Turner, J. C. (2004). *The social identity theory of intergroup behavior.* New York: Psychology Press.

Tajfel, H., Billig, M. G., Bundy, R. P., & Flament, C. (1971). Social categorization and intergroup behaviour. *European Journal of Social Psychology, 1,* 149–178.

Takahashi, Y. (1990). Is multiple personality really rare in Japan? *Dissociation, 3,* 57–59.

Takashima, A., Nieuwenhuis, I. L., Rijpkema, M., Petersson, K. M., Jensen, O., & Fernández, G. (2007). Memory trace stabilization leads to large-scale changes in the retrieval network: A functional MRI study on associative memory. *Learning and Memory, 14,* 472–479.

Takeuchi, D., & Cheung, M. (1998). Coercive and voluntary referrals: How ethnic minority adults get into mental health treatment. *Ethnicity & Health, 3,* 149–158.

Talarico, J., & Rubin, D. (2003). Confidence, not consistency, characterizes flashbulb memories. *Psychological Science, 14,* 455–461.

Talmi, D., Grady, C., Goshen-Gottstein, Y., & Moscovitch, M. (2005). Neuroimaging the serial position curve: A test of single-store versus dual-store models. *Psychological Science, 16,* 716–723.

Tanaka, J. W., & Farah, M. J. (1993). Parts and wholes in face recognition. *The Quarterly Journal of Experimental Psychology, 46A,* 225–245.

Tang, Y. (2011). Mechanisms of integrative body-mind training. *Neuroscience Bulletin, 27,* 383–388.

Tang, Y., Lu, Q., Geng, X., Stein, E. A., Yang, Y., & Posner, M. I. (2010). Short-term meditation induces white matter changes in the anterior cingulate. *Proceedings of the National Academy of Sciences of the USA, 107,* 15649–15652.

Tang, Y., Ma, Y., Fan, Y., Feng, H., Wang, J., Feng, S., et al. (2009). Central and autonomic nervous system interaction is altered by short-term meditation. *Proceedings of the National Academy of Sciences, 106,* 8864–8870.

Tang, Y., Ma., Y., Wang, J., Fan, Y., Feng, S., Lu, Q., et al. (2007). Short-term meditation training improves attention and self-regulation. *Proceedings of the National Academy of Science of the United States of America, 104,* 17152–17156.

Tang, Y., Shimizu, E., Dube, G. R., Rampon, C., Kerchner, G. A., Zhuo, M., Liu, G., & Tsien, J. Z. (1999). Genetic enhancement of learning and memory in mice. *Nature, 401,* 63–69.

Tangney, J. P., & Dearing, R. L. (2002). *Shame and guilt.* New York: Guilford Publications.

Tashiro, A., Hiroshi, M., & Gage, F. H. (2007). Experience-specific functional modification of the dentate gyrus through adult neurogenesis: A critical period during an immature stage. *The Journal of Neuroscience, 27,* 3252–3259.

Taylor, A. J., & Hort, J. (2004). Measuring proximal stimuli involved in flavour perception. In A. J. Taylor & D. R. Roberts (Eds.), *Flavor perception* (pp. 1–38). Oxford, UK: Blackwell.

Taylor, S. E. (2006). Tend and befriend: Biobehavioral bases of affiliation under stress. *Current Directions in Psychological Science, 15,* 273–277.

Taylor, S. E., Klein, L. C., Lewis, B. P., Gruenewald, T. L., Gurung, R. A. R., & Updegraff, J. A. (2000). Biobehavioral responses to stress in females: Tend-and-befriend, not fight-or-flight. *Psychological Review, 107,* 411–429.

Taylor, V. A., Grant, J., Daneault, V., Scavone, G., Breton, E., Roffe-Vidal, S., et al. (2011). Impact of mindfulness on the neural responses to emotional pictures in experienced and beginner meditators. *NeuroImage, 57,* 1524–1533.

Tedeschi, R. G., & Calhoun, L. G. (2004). Post-traumatic growth: Conceptual foundations and empirical evidence. *Psychological Inquiry, 15,* 1–18.

Tellegen, A., Lykken, D. T., Bouchard, T. J., Wilcox, K. J., Segal, N. L., & Rich, S. (1998). Personality similarity in twins reared apart and together. *Journal of Personality and Social Psychology, 54,* 1031–1039.

Teplin, L. A., McClelland, G. M., Abram, K. M., & Weiner, D. A. (2005). Crime victimization in adults with severe mental illness: Comparison with the National Crime Victimization Survey. *Archives of General Psychiatry, 62,* 911–921.

Terman, L. M. (1916). *The uses of intelligence tests.* Boston: Houghton Mifflin.

Terracciano, A., Abdel-Khalek, A. M., Adám, N., et al. (2005). National character does not reflect mean personality trait levels in 49 cultures. *Science, 310,* 96–100.

Terracciano, A., Sanna, S, Uda, M., et al. (2010). Genome-wide association scan for five major dimensions of personality. *Molecular Psychiatry, 15,* 647–656.

Terry, W. S. (1982). Recognition of sentences from text after massed Vs spaced readings. *The Journal of General Psychology, 109,* 67–71.

Thase, M. E., & Denko, T. (2008). Pharmacotherapy of mood disorders. *Annual Review of Clinical Psychology, 4,* 53–91.

Thibault, J. W., & Kelley, H. H. (1959). *The social psychology of groups.* New York: John Wiley.

Thøgersen, J., & Ölander, F. (2003). Spillover of environment-friendly consumer behaviour. *Journal of Environmental Psychology, 23,* 225–236.

Thoinot, L. (1913). *Medicolegal aspects of moral offenses.* A. W. Weysse (translator). Philadelphia: F. A. Davis and Company Publishers.

Thomas, A., & Chess, S. (1977). *Temperament and development.* New York: Brunder/Mazel.

Thompson, W. C., Clarke-Stewart, A., & Lepore, S. J. (1997). What did the janitor do? Suggestive interviewing and the accuracy of children's accounts. *Law and Human Behavior, 21,* 405–426.

Thompson, W. F., Russo, F. A., & Quinto, L. (2008). Audio-visual integration of emotional cues in song. *Cognition and Emotion, 22,* 1457–1470.

Thorndike, E. I. (1911). *Animal intelligence.* New York: Macmillan.

Thorndike, E. L. (1905). *The elements of psychology.* New York: Seiler.

Thornton, A., & Raihani, N. J. (2010). Identifying teaching in wild animals. *Learning & Behavior, 38,* 297–309.

Thurstone, L. L. (1938). *Primary mental abilities.* Chicago: University of Chicago Press.

Tirri, K., & Nokelainen, P. (2008). Identification of multiple intelligences with the Multiple Intelligence Profiling Questionnaire III. *Psychology Science, 50,* 206–221.

Tobias, M. C., O'Neill, J., Hudkins, M., Bartzokis, G., Dean, A. C., & London, E. D. (2010). White-matter abnormalities in brain during early abstinence from methamphetamine abuse. *Psychopharmacology, 209,* 13–24.

Tochigi, M., Okazaki, Y., Kato, N., & Sasaki, T. (2004). What causes seasonality of birth in schizophrenia? *Neuroscience Research, 48,* 1–11.

Todman, D. (2008). Wilder Penfield. *Journal of Neurology, Neurosurgery, & Psychiatry, 255,* 1104–1105.

Todorov, A., Mandisodza, A. N., Goren, A., & Hall, C. (2005). Inferences of competence from faces predict election outcomes. *Science, 308,* 1623–1626.

Tokar, D. M., & Subich, L. M. Relative contributions of congruence and personality dimensions to job satisfaction. *Journal of Vocational Behavior, 50,* 482–491.

Tolman, E. C., & Honzik, C. H. (1930). Degrees of hunger, reward and non-reward, and maze learning in rats. *University of California Publications in Psychology,* 4241–4256.

Tom, G., Tong, S., & Hesse, C. (2010). Thick slice and thin slice teaching evaluations. *Social Psychology of Education, 13,* 129–136.

Tomarken, A. J., Davidson, R. J., & Henriques, J. B. (1990). Resting frontal brain asymmetry predicts affective responses to films. *Journal of Personality and Social Psychology, 59,* 791–801.

Tomblin, J. B., O'Brien, M., Shriberg, L. D., Williams, C., Murray, J., Patil, S., et al. (2009). Language features in a mother and daughter of a chromosome 7;13 translocation involving FOXP2. *Journal of Speech, Language, and Hearing Research, 52,* 1157–1174.

Torrey, E. F. (1997). *Out of the shadows: Confronting America's mental illness crisis.* New York: John Wiley & Sons.

Tottenham, L. S., Saucier, D. M., Elias, L. J., & Gutwin, C. (2005). Men are more accurate than women in aiming at targets in both near space and extrapersonal space. *Perceptual and Motor Skills, 101,* 3–12.

Tracy, M., Zimmerman, F. J., Galea, S., et al. (2008). What explains the relation between family poverty and childhood depressive symptoms? *Journal of Psychiatric Research, 42,* 1163–1175.

Trainor, L. J. (2010). Using electroencephalography (EEG) to measure maturation of auditory cortex in infants: Processing pitch, duration and sound location. In R. E. Trembley, R. G. Barr, RDeV. Peters, & M. Bovin (Eds.), *Encyclopedia on early childhood development.* Montreal, QC: Centre of Excellence for Early Childhood Development.

Trainor, L. J., McFadden, M., Hodgson, L., Darragh, L., Barlow, J., Matsos, L., & Sonnadara, R. (2003). Changes in auditory cortex and the development of mismatch negativity between 2 and 6 months of age. *International Journal of Psychophysiology, 51,* 5–15.

Tranel, D., Damasio, H., & Damasio, A. R. (1997). A neural basis for the retrieval of conceptual knowledge. *Neuropsychologia 35,* 1319–1327.

Triplett, N. (1898). The dynamogenic factors in pacemaking and competition. *The American Journal of Psychology, 9,* 507–533.

Trivers, R. L. (1972). Parental investment and sexual selection. In B. Campbell (Ed.), *Sexual selection and the descent of man: 1871–1971* (pp. 136–179). Chicago, IL: Aldine.

Troje, N. F. (2002a). Decomposing biological motion: A framework for analysis and synthesis of human gait patterns. *Journal of Vision, 2,* 371–387.

Troje, N. F. (2002b). The little difference: Fourier based gender classification from biological motion. In R.P. Wurtz & M. Lappe (Eds.), *Dynamic perception.* Berlin: Aka Press.

Troje, N. F. (2008). Retrieving information from human movement patterns. In T. F. Shipley & J. M. Zacks (Eds.), *Understanding events: How humans see, represent, and act on events* (pp. 308–334). New York: Oxford University Press.

Troop, N. A. (1998). Eating disorders as coping strategies: A critique. *European Eating Disorders Review, 6,* 229–237.

Trope, Y., & Liberman, N. (2010). Construal-level theory of psychological distance. *Psychological Review, 117,* 440–463.

Tropp, L. R., & Pettigrew, T. F. (2005). Relationships between intergroup contact and prejudice among minority and majority status groups. *Psychological Science, 16,* 951–957.

Troseth, G. L. (2010). Is it life or is it Memorex? Video as a representation of reality. *Developmental Review, 30,* 155–175.

Tse, D., Takeuchi, T., Kakeyama, M., Kajii, Y., Okuno, H., Tohyama, C., et al. (2011). Schema-dependent gene activation and memory encoding in neocortex. *Science, 333,* 891–895.

Tsuchiya, N., Moradi, F., Felsen, C., Yamazaki, M., & Adolphs, R. (2009). Intact rapid detection of fearful faces in the absence of the amygdala. *Nature Neuroscience, 12,* 1224–1225.

Tulving E., & Watkins, M. J. (1975). Structure of memory traces. *Psychological Review, 82,* 261–275.

Tulving, E. (1972). Episodic and semantic memory. In E. Tulving & W. Donaldson (Eds.), *Organization of memory* (pp. 381–402). New York: Academic Press.

Tulving, E. (1974). Cue-dependent forgetting. *American Scientist, 62,* 74–82.

Tulving, E., & Markowitsch, H. J. (1998). Episodic and declarative memory: Role of the hippocampus. *Hippocampus, 8,* 198–203.

Tulving, E., & Thompson, D. M. (1973). Encoding specificity and retrieval processes in episodic memory. *Psychological Review, 80,* 352–373.

Tulving, E., Kapur, S., Craik, F. I. M., Moscovitch, M., & Houle, S. (1994). Hemispheric encoding/retrieval asymmetry in episodic memory: Positron emission tomography findings. *Proceedings of the National Academy of Sciences, 91,* 2016–2020.

Tulving, E., Schacter, D. L., & Stark, H. A. (1982). Priming effects in word-fragment completion are independent of recognition memory. *Journal of Experimental Psychology, 8,* 336–342.

Tulving, E., Schacter, D. L., McLachlan, D. R., & Moscovitch, M. (1988). Priming of semantic autobiographical knowledge: A case study of retrograde amnesia. *Brain and Cognition, 8,* 3–20.

Turk, C., Heimberg, R., Luterek, J., Mennin, D., & Fresco, D. (2005). Emotion dysregulation in generalized anxiety disorder: A comparison with social anxiety disorder. *Cognitive Therapy and Research, 29,* 89–106.

Turkheimer, E., Haley, A., Waldron, M., D'Onofrio, B., & Gottesman, I. I. (2003). Socioeconomic status modifies heritability of IQ in young children. *Psychological Science, 14,* 623–628.

Turner, D. C., Robbins, L. C., Aron, A. R., Dowson, J., & Sahakian, B. J. (2003). Cognitive enhancing effects of modafinil in healthy volunteers. *Psychopharmacology, 165,* 260–269.

Tversky, A., & Kahneman, D. (1973). Availability: A heuristic for judging frequency and probability. *Cognitive Psychology, 5,* 207–232.

Tversky, A., & Kahneman, D. (1982). The framing of decisions and the psychology of choice. *Science, 211,* 453–458.

Tversky, A., & Kahneman, D. (1986). Rational choice and the framing of decisions. *The Journal of Business, 59,* S521–S278.

Tweed, R. G., & Tweed, C. J. (2011). Positive emotion following spousal bereavement: Desirable or pathological? *Journal of Positive Psychology, 6,* 131–141.

U.S. Department of Justice. (2001). *Policing and homicide, 1976–98: Justifiable homicide by police, police officers murdered by felons* (NCJ180987). Washington, DC: Bureau of Justice Statistics.

Ungerleider, L. G., & Mishkin, M. (1982). Object vision and spatial vision: Two cortical pathways. In D. J. Ingle, M. A. Goodale, & R. J. W. Mansfield (Eds.), *Analysis of visual behaviour* (pp. 296–302). Cambridge, MA: MIT Press.

United States Federal Trade Commission. (2011). Federal Trade Commission Cigarette Report for 2007 and 2008. Retrieved from http://www.ftc.gov/os/2011/07/110729cigarettereport.pdf

Uziel, L. (2007). Individual differences in the social facilitation effect: A review and meta-analysis. *Journal of Research in Personality, 41*, 579–601.

Vadhan, N. P., Hart, C. L., van Gorp, W. G., Gunderson, E. W., Haney, M., & Foltin, R. W. (2007). Acute effects of smoked marijuana on decision making, as assessed by modified gambling task, in experienced marijuana users. *Journal of Clinical and Experimental Neuropsychology, 29*, 357–364.

Valenstein, E. S. (1973). *Brain control: A critical examination of brain stimulation and psychosurgery.* London: Wiley-Interscience.

Valentin, V., & O'Doherty, J. P. (2009). Overlapping prediction errors in dorsal striatum during instrumental learning with juice and money reward in the human brain. *Journal of Neurophysiology, 102*, 3384–3391.

Van Ameringen, M., Mancini, C., Patterson, B., & Boyle, M. H. (2008). Post-traumatic stress disorder in Canada. *CNS Neuroscience and Therapeutics, 14*, 171–181.

Van Damme, S., Lorenz, J., Eccleston, C., Koster, E. H., De Clercq, A., & Crombez, G. (2004). Fear-conditioned cues of impending pain facilitate attentional engagement. *Journal of Clinical Neurophysiology, 34*, 33–39.

Van den Bussche, E., Van den Noortgate, W., & Reynvoet, B. (2009). Mechanisms of masked priming: A meta-analysis. *Psychological Bulletin, 135*, 452–477.

van der Kolk, B. A. (1994). The body keeps score: Memory and the evolving psychobiology of posttraumatic stress. *Harvard Review of Psychiatry, 1*, 253–265.

van Kesteren, M. T. R., Fernandez, G., Norris, D. G., & Hermans, E. J. (2010b). Persistent schema-dependent hippocampal-neocortical connectivity during memory encoding and postencoding rest in humans. *Proceedings of the National Academy of Sciences, 107*, 7550–7555.

van Kesteren, M. T. R., Rijpkema, M., Ruiter, D. J., & Fernandez, G. (2010a). Retrieval of associative information congruent with prior knowledge is related to increased medial prefrontal activity and connectivity. *Journal of Neuroscience, 30*, 15888–15894.

van Kesteren, M. T. R., Ruiter, D. J., Fernandez, G., & Henson, R. N. (2012). How schema and novelty augment memory formation. *Trends in Neuroscience, 35*, 211–219.

Van Oort, F. V. A., Greaves-Lord, K., Verhulst, F. C., Ormel, J., & Huizink, A. C. (2009). The developmental course of anxiety symptoms during adolescence: The TRAILS study. *Journal of Child Psychology and Psychiatry, 50*(10), 1209–1217.

van Os, J., Pedersen, C. B., & Mortensen, P. B. (2004). Confirmation of synergy between urbanicity and familial liability in the causation of psychosis. *American Journal of Psychiatry, 161*, 2312–2314.

van Praag, H. (2008). Neurogenesis and exercise: Past and future directions. *Neuromolecular Medicine, 10*, 128–140.

van Praag, H. (2009). Exercise and the brain: Something to chew on. *Trends in Neuroscience, 32*, 283–290.

van Straten, A., & Cuijpers, P. (2009). Self-help therapy for insomnia: A meta-analysis. *Sleep Medicine Reviews, 13*, 61–71.

Vance, E. B., & Wagner, N. N. (1976). Written descriptions of orgasm: A study of sex differences. *Archives of Sexual Behavior, 5*, 87–98.

Vanheusden, K., Mulder, C. L., van der Ende, J., van Lenthe, F. J., et al. (2008). Young adults face major barriers to seeking help from mental health services. *Patient Education and Counseling 73*(1), 97–104.

Vansteenkiste, M., Lens, W., & Deci, E. L. (2006). Intrinsic versus extrinsic goal contents in self-determination theory: Another look at the quality of academic motivation. *Educational Psychology, 41*, 19–31.

Vargha-Khadem, F., Gadian, D. G., Copp, A., & Mishkin, M. (2005). FOXP2 and the neuroanatomy of speech and language. *Nature Reviews Neuroscience, 6*, 131–138.

Verwey, M., & Amir, S. (2009). Food-entrainable circadian oscillators in the brain. *European Journal of Neuroscience, 30*, 1650–1657.

Villar, J., Merialdi, M., Gülmezoqlu, A. M., Abalos, E., Carroli, G., Kulier, R., & de Onis, M. (2003). Characteristics of randomized controlled trials included in systematic reviews of nutritional interventions reporting maternal morbidity, mortality, preterm delivery, intrauterine growth restriction and small for gestational age and birth weight outcomes. *Journal of Nutrition, 133*, 1632–1639.

Virdee, K., Cumming, P., Caprioli, D., Jupp, B., Rominger, A., Aigbirhio, F. I., et al. (2012). Applications of positron emissions tomography in animal models of neurological and neuropsychiatric disorders. *Neuroscience and BioBehavioral Reviews, 36*, 1188–1216.

Voelker, R. (2003). Mounting student depression taxing campus mental health services. *Journal of the American Medical Association, 289*, 2055–2056.

Vogel, D. L., Wade, N. G., & Ascheman, P. (2009). Measuring perceptions of stigmatization by others for seeking psychological help: Reliability and validity of a new stigma scale with college students. *Journal of Counseling Psychology, 56*, 301–308.

Vogel, E., Woodman, G., & Luck, S. (2001). Storage of features, conjunctions, and objects in visual working memory. *Journal of Experimental Psychology: Human Perception and Performance, 27*, 92–114.

Vohs, K. D., Bardone, A. M., Joiner, T. E., & Abramson, L. Y. (1999). Perfectionism, perceived weight status, and self-esteem interact to predict bulimic symptoms: A model of bulimic symptoms development. *Journal of Abnormal Psychology, 108*, 695–700.

Vokey, J. R., & Read, J. D. (1985). Subliminal messages. *American Psychologist, 40*, 1231–1239.

Volkow, N. D. (2010). Congressional Caucus on Prescription Drug Abuse. Retrieved November 24, 2010, from http://nida.nih.gov/Testimony/ 9-22-10Testimony.html

Volkow, N. D., Fowler, J. S., Wang, G. J., Baler, R., & Telang, F. (2009). Imaging dopamine's role in drug abuse and addiction. *Neuropharmacology, 56 Supplement 1*, 3–8.

von Frisch, K. (1967). *The dance language and orientation of bees.* Cambridge, MA: Harvard University Press.

Vouloumanos, A., & Werker, J. F. (2004). Tuned to the signal: The privileged status of speech for young infants. *Developmental Science, 3*, 270–276.

Voyer, D., Bowes, A., & Techentin, C. (2008). On the perception of sarcasm in dichotic listening. *Neuropsychology, 22*, 390–399.

Vygotsky, L. (1978). *Mind in society: The development of higher psychological processes.* (M. Cole, V. John-Steiner, S. Scribner, & E. Soubermen, Eds.). Cambridge MA: Harvard University Press.

Wade, K. A., Garry, M., Read, J. D., & Lindsay, D. S. (2002). A picture is worth a thousand lies: Using false photographs to create false childhood memories. *Psychonomic Bulletin & Review, 9*, 597–603.

Wadzinski, J., Franks, R., Roane, D., & Bayard, M. (2007). Valproate-associated hyperammonemic encephalopathy. *Journal of the American Board of Family Medicine, 20*, 499–502.

Wagar, B. M., & Thagard, P. (2004). Spiking Phineas Gage: A neurocomputational theory of cognitive-affective integration in decision making. *Psychological Review, 111*, 67–69.

Wagenaar, W. A., & Groeneweg, J. (1990). The memory of concentration camp survivors. *Applied Cognitive Psychology, 4*, 77–87.

Wagner, A. D., Desmond, J. E., Glover, G. H., & Gabrieli, J. D. E. (1998). Prefrontal cortex and recognition memory: Functional-MRI evidence for context-dependent retrieval processes. *Brain, 121*, 1985–2002.

Wagner, G. A., & Morris, E. K. (1987). "Superstitious" behavior in children. *Psychological Record, 37*, 471–488.

Wahba, M. A., & Bridwell, L. G. (1976). Maslow reconsidered: A review of research on the need hierarchy theory. *Organizational Behavior and Human Performance, 15*, 212–240.

Wahlsten, D. (1997). Leilani Muir versus the philosopher king: Eugenics on trial in Alberta. *Genetica, 99,* 185–198.

Wai, J., Cacchio, M., Putallaz, M., & Makel, M. C. (2010). Sex differences in the right tail of cognitive abilities: A 30 year examination. *Intelligence, 38,* 412–423.

Waite, L. J., & Gallagher, M. (2000). *The case for marriage: Why married people are happier, healthier and better off financially.* New York: Doubleday.

Wakefield, A. J., Murch, S. H., Anthony, A., Linnell, J., Casson, D. M., Malik, M., et al. (1998). Retracted: Ileal-lymphoid-nodular hyperplasia, non-specific colitis, and pervasive developmental disorder in children. *Lancet, 351,* 637–641.

Walker, E. G., Savole, T., & Davis, D. (1994). Neuromotor precursors of schizophrenia. *Schizophrenia Bulletin, 20,* 441–451.

Walker, E. G., Shapiro, D., Esterberg, M., & Trotman, H. (2010). Neurodevelopment and schizophrenia: Broadening the focus. *Current Directions in Psychological Science, 19,* 204–208.

Walker, L. J., & Frimer, J. A. (2007). Moral personality of brave and caring exemplars. *Journal of Personality and Social Psychology, 93,* 845–860.

Walker, L. J., Frimer, J. A., & Dunlop, W. L. (2010). Varieties of moral personality: Beyond the banality of heroism. *Journal of Personality, 78,* 907–942.

Walker, M. P., Liston, C., Hobson, J. A., & Stickgold, R. (2002). Cognitive flexibility across the sleep-wake cycle: REM-sleep enhancement of anagram problem solving. *Cognitive Brain Research, 14,* 317–324.

Waller, G. P., & Hodgson, S. (1996). Body image distortion in Anorexia and Bulimia Nervosa: The role of perceived and actual control. *Journal of Nervous & Mental Disease, 184,* 213–219.

Wallston, K. A., Wallston, B. S., & DeVellis, R. (1978). Development of the multidimentsional health locus of control (MHLC) Scales. *Health Education & Behavior, 6,* 160–170.

Walsh, T., McClellan, J. M., McCarthy, S. E., Addington, A. M., Pierce, S. B., et al. (2008). Rare structural variants disrupt multiple genes in neurodevelopmental pathways in schizophrenia. *Science, 320,* 539–543.

Walther, E., & Grigoriadis, S. (2004). Why sad people like shoes better: The influence of mood on the evaluative conditioning of consumer attitudes. *Psychology and Marketing, 21,* 755–773.

Walum, H., Westberg, L., Henningsson, S., et al. (2008). Genetic variation in vasopressin receptor 1a gene (AVPR1A) associated with pair-bonding behavior in humans. *Proceedings of the National Academy of Sciences, 105,* 14153–14156.

Wampold, B. E. (2001). *The great psychotherapy debate: Model, methods, and findings.* Mahwah, NJ: Lawrence Erlbaum Associates.

Wang, P. S., Berglund, P., Olfson, M., Pincus, H. A., Wells, K. B., & Kessler, R. C. (2005). Failure and delay in initial treatment contact after first onset of mental disorders in the National Comorbidity Survey Replication. *Archives of General Psychiatry, 62,* 603–613.

Wang, S. H., & Morris, R .G. (2010). Hippocampal-neocortical interactions in memory formation, consolidation, and reconsolidation. *Annual Review of Psychology, 61,* 49–79.

Wang, X., Lu, T., Snider, R. K., & Liang, L. (2005). Sustained firing in auditory cortex evoked by preferred stimuli. *Nature, 435,* 341–346.

Wansink, B. (1996). Can package size accelerate usage volume? *Journal of Marketing, 60,* 1–14.

Wansink, B., & Cheney, M. M. (2005). Superbowls: Serving bowl size and food consumption. *Journal of American Medical Association, 293,* 1727–1728.

Wansink, B., & Kim, J. (2005). Bad popcorn in big buckets: Portion size can influence intake as much as taste. *Journal of Nutrition Education and Behavior, 37,* 242–245.

Wansink, B., & Wansink, C. S. (2010). The largest last supper: Depictions of food portions and plate size increased over the millennium. *International Journal of Obesity, 34,* 943–944.

Wansink, B., Painter, J. E., & North, J. (2005). Bottomless bowls: Why visual cues of portion size may influence intake. *Obesity Research, 13,* 93–100.

Ward, C. D., & Cooper, R. P. (1999). A lack of evidence in 4-month-old human infants for paternal voice preference. *Developmental Psychobiology, 35,* 49–59.

Ware, M. A., Wang, T., Shapiro, S., Robinson, A., Dubruet, T., Huynh, T., et al. (2010). Smoked cannabis for chronic neuropathic pain: A randomized controlled trial. *Canadian Medical Association Journal, 182,* E694–E701.

Warneken F., & Tomasello, M. (2007). Helping and cooperation at 14 months of age. *Infancy, 11,* 271–294.

Warneken, F., & Tomasello, M. (2009). The roots of human altruism. *British Journal of Psychology, 100,* 455–471.

Warneken, F., & Tomasello, M. (2013). The emergence of contingent reciprocity in young children. *Journal of Experimental Child Psychology, 116,* 338–350.

Warren, M. P., & Brooks-Gunn, J. (1989). Mood and behavior during adolescence: Evidence for hormonal factors. *Journal of Clinical Endocrinology and Metabolism, 69,* 77–83.

Warrington, E. K., & Shallice, T. (1979). Semantic access dyslexia. *Brain, 102,* 43–63.

Warrington, E. K., & McCarthy, R. (1987). Categories of knowledge: Further fractionations and an attempted integration. *Brain, 110,* 1273–1296.

Wasser, S. K., & Barash, D. P. (1983). Reproductive suppression among female mammals: Implication for biomedicine and sexual selection theory. *Quarterly Review of Biology, 58,* 523–538.

Watkins, C. E., Campbell, V. L., Neiberding, R., & Hallmark, R. (1995). Contemporary practice of psychological assessment by clinical psychologists. *Professional Psychology: Research and Practice, 26,* 54–60.

Watson, A. C., Miller, F. E., & Lyons, J. S. (2005). Adolescent attitudes toward serious mental illness. *Journal of Nervous and Mental Disease, 193,* 769–772.

Watson, D., & Pennebaker, J. W. (1989). Health complaints, stress and distress: Exploring the central role of negative affectivity. *Psychological Review, 96,* 234–264.

Watson, J. B. (1913). Psychology as the behaviorist views it. *Psychological Review, 20,* 158–177.

Watson, J. B. (1930). *Behaviorism.* Chicago: University of Chicago Press.

Watson, J. B., & Rayner, R. R. (1920). Conditioned emotional reactions. *Journal of Experimental Psychology, 3,* 1–14.

Watson, J. C., Gordon, L. B., Stermac, L., Kalogerakos, F., & Steckley, P. (2003). Comparing the effectiveness of process-experiential with cognitive-behavioral psychotherapy in the treatment of depression. *Journal of Consulting and Counseling Psychology, 71,* 773–781.

Watson, M. W., & Getz, K. (1990). The relationship between Oedipal behaviors and children's family role concepts. *Merrill-Palmer Quarterly, 36,* 487–505.

Watts, R. E. (2000). Adlerian counseling: A viable approach for contemporary practice. *TCA Journal, 28,* 11–23.

Wayment, H. A., & Peplau, L. A. (1995). Social support and well-being among lesbian and heterosexual women: A structural modeling approach. *Personality and Social Psychology Bulletin, 21,* 1189–1199.

Webb, W. B., & Cartwright, R. D. (1978). Sleep and dreams. *Annual Review of Psychology, 29,* 223–252.

Weber, B., Jermann, F., Gex-Fabry, M., Nallet, A., Bondolfi, G., & Aubry, J. M. (2010). Mindfulness-based cognitive therapy for bipolar disorder: A feasibility trial. *European Psychiatry, 25,* 334–337.

Wechsler, D. (1939). *The measurement of adult intelligence.* Baltimore: Williams & Witkins.

Weeks, D. L., & Anderson, L. P. (2000). The interaction of observational learning with overt practice: Effects on motor skill learning. *Acta Psychologica, 104,* 259–271.

Weinsier, R. L., Hunter, G. R., Desmond, R. A., Byrne, N. M., Zuckerman, P. A., & Darnell, B. (2002). Free-living activity expenditure in women successful and unsuccessful at maintaining a normal body weight. *American Journal of Clinical Nutrition, 75,* 499–504.

Weisman, A. G., Lopez, S. R., Ventura, J., Nuechterlein, K. H., Goldstein, M. J., & Hwang, S. (2000). A comparison of psychiatric symptoms between Anglo-Americans and Mexican-Americans with schizophrenia. *Schizophrenia Bulletin, 26,* 817–824.

Weiss, A., King, J. E., & Hopkins, W. D. (2007). A cross-setting study of chimpanzee (*Pan troglodytes*) personality structure and development: Zoological parks and Yerkes National Primate Research Center. *American Journal of Primatology, 69,* 1264.

Weiss, C., & Disterhoft, J. F. (2011). Exploring prefrontal cortical memory mechanisms with eyeblink conditioning. *Behavioral Neuroscience, 125,* 318–326.

Weiss, E., Kemmler, G., Deisenhammer, E., Fleischhacker, W., & Delazer, M. (2003). Sex differences in cognitive functions. *Personality and Individual Differences, 35,* 863–875.

Weiss, G., & Hechtman, L. T. (1993). *Hyperactive children grown up: ADHD in children, adolescents, and adults.* New York: Guilford Press.

Weissman, M. M., Markowitz, J. C., Klerman, G. L. (2000). *Comprehensive guide to interpersonal psychotherapy.* New York: Basic Books.

Weisz, J. R., Weiss, B., Han, S. S., Granger, D. A., & Morton, T. (1995). Effects of psychotherapy with children and adolescents revisited: A meta-analysis of treatment outcome studies. *Psychological Bulletin, 117,* 450–468.

Weitzer, R., & Tuch, S. A. (2004). Race and perceptions of police misconduct. *Social Problems, 51,* 305–325.

Wells, B., & Corts, D. P. (2008). Attitudes towards fraternities and sororities: Evidence of implicit, ingroup favoritism. *College Student Journal.*

Wells, G. L., & Quinlivan, D. S. (2009). Suggestive eyewitness identification procedures and the Supreme Court's reliability test in light of eyewitness science: 30 years later. *Law and Human Behavior, 33,* 1–24.

Wenk, G. (2010). *Your brain on food: How chemicals control your thoughts and feelings.* Oxford, UK: Oxford University Press.

Werker, J. F. (2003). Baby steps to learning language. *Journal of Pediatrics (Supplement: Special Issue), 143,* S62–S69.

Werker, J. F., & Lalonde, C. E. (1988). Cross-language speech perception: Initial capabilities and developmental change. *Developmental Psychology, 24,* 672–683.

Werker, J. F., & Tees, R. C. (1984). Phonemic and phonetic factors in adult cross-language speech perception. *Journal of the Acoustical Society of America, 75,* 1866–1878.

Werker, J. F., Yeung, H. H., & Yoshida, K. A. (2012). How do infants become experts at native-speech perception. *Current Directions in Psychological Science, 21,* 221–226.

Wernicke, C. (1874). *Der aphasische symptomencomplex.* Breslau: Kohn and Weigert.

West, E. A., Forcelli, P. A., McCue, D. L., & Malkova, L. (2013). Differential effects of serotonin-specific and excitotoxic lesions of OFC on conditioned reinforce devaluation and extinction in rats. *Behavioral Brain Research, 246,* 10–14.

Westen, D. (1998). The scientific legacy of Sigmund Freud: Toward a psychodynamically informed psychological science. *Psychological Bulletin, 124,* 333–371.

Westen, D., & Bradley, R. (2005). Empirically supported complexity: Rethinking evidence-based practice in psychotherapy. *Current Directions in Psychological Science, 14,* 266–271.

Westen, D., Blagov, P. S., & Harenski, K. (2006). Neural bases for motivated reasoning: An fMRI study of emotional constraints on partisan political judgment in the 2004 U.S. presidential election. *Journal of Cognitive Neuroscience, 18,* 1974–1958.

Wever, R. A., Polasek, J., & Wildgruber, C. M. (1983). Bright light affects human circadian rhythms. *European Journal of Physiology, 396,* 85–87.

Whishaw, I. Q. (1991). Latent learning in a swimming pool place task by rats: Evidence for the use of associative and not cognitive mapping processes. *Quarterly Journal of Experimental Psychology B, 43,* 83–103.

Whiten, A. (2000). Primate culture and social learning. *Cognitive Science, 24,* 477–508.

Whitson, J. A., & Galinsky, A. D. (2008). Lacking control increases illusory pattern perception. *Science, 322,* 115–117.

Whorf, B. L. (1973). *Language, thought, and reality: Selected writings of Benjamin Whorf.* J. B. Carroll (Ed.). Oxford, UK: Technology Press of MIT.

Wiens, S. (2005). Interoception in emotional experience. *Current Opinion in Neurology, 18,* 442–447.

Wijdicks, E. F. (2006). Minimally conscious state vs. persistent vegetative state: The case of Terry (Wallis) vs. the case of Terri (Schiavo). *Mayo Clinic Proceedings, 81,* 1155–1158.

Wijnen, V. J. M., van Boxtel, G. J. M., Eilander, H. J., & de Gelder, B. (2007). Mismatch negativity predicts recovery from the vegetative state. *Clinical Neurophysiology, 118,* 597–605.

Williams, J. M. G., Alatiq, Y., Crane, C., Barnhofer, T., Fennell, M. J. V., Duggan, D. S., et al. (2007). Mindfulness-based cognitive therapy (MBCT) in bipolar disorder: Preliminary evaluation of immediate effects on between-episode functioning. *Journal of Affective Disorders, 107,* 275–279.

Williams, J. M. G., Duggan, D. S., Crane, C., & Fennell, M.J.V. (2006). Mindfulness-based cognitive therapy for prevention of recurrence of suicidal behaviour. *Journal of Clinical Psychology, 62,* 201–210.

Williams, K. M., Nathanson, C., & Paulhus, D. L. (2010). Identifying and profiling scholastic cheaters: Their personality, cognitive ability, and motivation. *Journal of Experimental Psychology: Applied, 16,* 293–307.

Williams, L. E., & Bargh, J. A. (2008). Experiencing physical warmth promotes interpersonal warmth. *Science, 322,* 606–607.

Williamson, A. M., & Feyer, A. (2000). Moderate sleep deprivation produces impairments in cognitive and motor performance equivalent to legally prescribed levels of alcohol intoxication. *Occupational & Environmental Medicine, 57,* 649–655.

Willingham, D. T. (2004). Reframing the mind: How Howard Gardner became a hero among educators by simply by redefining talents as "intelligences." *Education Next, 4,* 19–24.

Willis, J., & Todorov, A. (2006). First impressions: Making up your mind after a 100-ms exposure to a face. *Psychological Science, 17,* 592–598.

Willner, P., Towell, A., Sampson, D., Sophokleous, S., & Muscat, R. (1987). Reduction of sucrose preference by chronic unpredictable mild stress, and its restoration by a tricyclic antidepressant. *Psychopharmacology, 93,* 358–364.

Willoughby, T. (2008). A short-term longitudinal study of Internet and computer game use by adolescent boys and girls: Prevalence, frequency of use, and psychosocial predictors. *Developmental Psychology, 44,* 195–204.

Wilson, A. E., & Ross, M. (2003). The identity function of autobiographical memory: Time is on our side. *Memory, 11,* 137–149.

Wilson, M. E., Fisher, J., Fischer, A., Lee, V., Harris, R. B., & Bartness, T. J. (2008). Quantifying food intake in socially housed monkeys: Social status effects on caloric consumption. *Physiology & Behavior,* 94, 586–594.

Wilson, P. M., Mack, D. E., & Grattan, K. P. (2008). Understanding motivation for exercise: A self-determination theory perspective. *Canadian Psychology, 49,* 250–256.

Wimmer, F., Hoffmann, R. F., Bonato, R. A., & Moffitt, A. R. (1992). The effects of sleep deprivation on divergent thinking and attention processes. *Journal of Sleep Research, 1,* 223–230.

Wimmer, H., & Perner, J. (1983). Beliefs about beliefs: Representation and constrained function of wrong beliefs in young children's understanding of deceptions. *Cognition, 13,* 103–128.

Winkielman, P., Schwarz, N., & Nowak, A. (2002). Affect and processing dynamics: Perceptual fluency enhances evaluations. In *Emotional cognition: From brain to behaviour* (pp. 111–135). Amsterdam, Netherlands: John Benjamins Publishing Company.

Winter, B., Breitenstein, C., Mooren, F. C., Voelker, K., Fobker, M., Lechtermann, A., et al. (2007). High impact running improves learning. *Neurobiology of Learning and Memory, 87,* 597–609.

Winterer, G. (2010). Why do patients with schizophrenia smoke? *Current Opinion in Psychiatry, 23,* 112–119.

Witelson, S. F., Beresh, H., & Kigar, D. L. (2006). Intelligence and brain size in 100 postmortem brains: Sex, lateralization and age factors. *Brain: A Journal of Neurology, 129,* 386–398.

Witelson, S. F., Kigar, D. L., & Harvey, T. (1999). The exceptional brain of Albert Einstein. *The Lancet, 353,* 2149–2153.

Wolpe, J. (1990). *The practice of behavior therapy.* Elmsford, NY: Pergamon Press.

Wong, C. K., & Read, J. D. (2011). Positive and negative effects of physical context reinstatement on eyewitness recall and identification. *Applied Cognitive Psychology, 25,* 2–11.

Wong, J., Rothmond, D. A., Webster, M. J., & Weickert, C. S. (2013). Increases in two truncated TrkB isoforms in the prefrontal cortex of people with schizophrenia. *Schizophrenia Bulletin, 39*(1), 130–140.

Woo, J. S. T., Brotto, L. A., & Gorcalka, B. (2010). Sex guilt and culture-linked barriers to testicular examinations. *International Journal of Sexual Health, 22,* 144–154.

Woo, J. S.T., Brotto, L. A., & Gorzalka, B. (2012). The relationship between sex guilt and sexual desire in a community sample of Chinese and Euro-Canadian women. *Journal of Sex Research, 49,* 290–298.

Wood, D., Harms, P., & Vazire, S. (2010). Perceiver effects as projective tests: What your perceptions of others say about you. *Journal of Personality and Social Psychology, 99,* 174–190.

Woodberry, K. A., Giuliano, A. J., & Seidman, L. J. (2008). Premorbid IQ in schizophrenia. *American Journal of Psychiatry, 165,* 579–587.

Woodworth, R. S. (1929). *Psychology: A study of mental life* (2nd ed.). [Online]. Retrieved from http://www.gutenberg.org/files/31382/31382-h/31382-h.htm

Woody, E. Z., & Bowers, K. (1994). A frontal assault on dissociated control. In S. J. Lynn & J. W. Rhue (Eds.), *Dissociation: Clinical and theoretical perspectives* (pp. 52–79). New York: Guilford Press

Word, C. O., Zanna, M. P., & Cooper, J. (1974). The nonverbal mediation of self-fulfilling prophecies in interracial interaction. *Journal of Experimental Social Psychology, 10,* 109–120.

World Health Organization (WHO). (2009). Global strategy on diet, physical activity and health. Retrieved November 23, 2009, from http://www.who.int/dietphysicalactivity/publications/facts/obesity/en/

Wright, D. (1997). Getting out of the asylum: Understanding the confinement of the insane in the nineteenth century. *Social History of Medicine, 10,* 137–155.

Wright, I. C., Rabe-Hesketh, S., Woodruff, P. W., David, A. S., Murray, R. M., & Bullmore, E. T. (2000). Meta-analysis of regional brain volumes in schizophrenia. *American Journal of Psychiatry, 157,* 16–25.

Wright, J. C., Huston, A. C., Scantlin, R., & Kotler, J. (2001). The Early Window Project: "Sesame Street" prepares children for school. In S. M. Fisch & R. T. Truglio (Eds.), *"G" is for "growing": Thirty years of research on children and* Sesame Street (pp. 97–114). Mahwah, NJ: Lawrence Erlbaum.

Wright, S. C., Aron, A., McLaughlin-Volpe, T., & Ropp, S. A. (1997). The extended contact effect: Knowledge of cross-group friendships and prejudice. *Journal of Personality and Social Psychology, 73,* 73–90.

Wuornos v. State of Florida, 19 Fla. Law W. S 455 (September 22, 1994).

Yalch, R. F. (1991). Memory in a jingle jungle: Music as a mnemonic device in communicating advertising slogans. *Journal of Applied Psychology, 76,* 268–275.

Yamamoto, T. (2007). Brain regions responsible for the expression of conditioned taste aversion in rats. *Chemical Senses, 32,* 105–109.

Yamamoto, T., & Fujimoto, Y. (1991). Brain mechanisms of taste aversion learning in the rat. *Brain Research Bulletin, 27,* 403–306.

Yamamoto, T., Matsuo, R., Kiyomitsu, Y., & Kitamura, R. (1989). Taste responses of cortical neurons in freely ingesting rats. *Journal of Neurophysiology, 61,* 1244–1258.

Yasoshima, Y., Scott, T. R., & Yamamoto, T. (2006). Memory-dependent c-Fos expression in the nucleus accumbens and extended amygdala following the expression of a conditioned taste aversion in the rat. *Neuroscience, 141,* 35–45.

Ybarra, O., Burnstein, E., Winkielman, P., Keller, M., Manis, M., Chan, E., & Rodriguez, J. (2008). Mental exercising through simple socializing: Social interaction promotes general cognitive functioning. *Personality and Social Psychology Bulletin, 34,* 248–259.

Yoo, S. K., & Skovholt, T. M. (2001). Cross-cultural examination of depression expression and help-seeking behavior: A comparative study of American and Korean college students. *Journal of College Counseling, 4,* 10–19.

Young, A. S., Klap, R., Sherbourne, C. D., & Wells, K. B. (2001). The quality of care for depressive and anxiety disorders in the United States. *Archives of General Psychiatry, 58,* 55–61.

Youssef, A. B., & Youssef, H. B. (2011). Social networking on web 2.0: From emotional intelligence to cyber emotional intelligence. *Management Information Systems, 6,* 21–28.

Yuile, A., & McVey, G. L. (2009). The role of social influence in the prevention of disordered eating among young adolescent females. *Journal of School Mental Health, 2,* 47–60.

Zadra, A., & Donderi, D. C. (2000). Nightmares and bad dreams: Their prevalence and relationship to well-being. *Journal of Abnormal Psychology, 109,* 273–281.

Zahn-Waxler, C., & Radke-Yarrow, M. (1990). The origins of empathic concern. *Motivation and Emotion, 14,* 107–130.

Zahn-Waxler, C., Radke-Yarrow, M., Wagner, E., & Chapman, M. (1992). Development of concern for others. *Developmental Psychology, 28,* 126–136.

Zajonc, R. B., Heingartner, A., & Herman, E. M. (1969). Social enhancement and impairment of performance in the cockroach. *Journal of Personality and Social Psychology, 13,* 83–92.

Zajonc, R. B. (1976). Family configuration and intelligence. *Science, 192,* 227–236.

Zak, P. J. (2008, June). The neurobiology of trust. *Scientific American, 298,* 88–92.

Zaman, R., Thind, D., & Kocmur, M. (2008). Transcranial magnetic stimulation in schizophrenia. *Neuroendocrinological Letters, 1,* 147–160.

Zanna, M. P., Kiesler, C. A., & Pikonis, P. A. (1970). Positive and negative attitudinal affect established by classical conditioning. *Journal of Personality and Social Psychology, 14,* 321–328.

Zeidan, F., Gordon, N., Merchant, J., & Goolkasian, P. (2010). The effects of brief mindfulness meditation training on experimentally induced pain. *Journal of Pain, 11,* 199–209.

Zelazo, N. A., Zelazo, P. R., Cohen, K. M., & Zelazo, P. D. (1993). Specificity of practice effects on elementary neuromotor patterns. *Developmental Psychology, 29,* 686–691.

Zellner, D. A., Loaiza, S., Gonzalez, Z., Pita, J., Morales, J., Pecora, D., & Wolf, A. (2006). Food selection changes under stress. *Physiology and Behavior, 87,* 789–793.

Zellner, D. A., Saito, S., & Gonzalez, J. (2007). The effect of stress on men's food selection. *Appetite, 49,* 696–699.

Zentall, T. R. (2012). Perspectives on observational learning in animals. *Journal of Comparative Psychology, 126,* 114–128.

Zimbardo, P. G. (2004). *A situationist perspective on the psychology of evil: Understanding how good people are transformed into perpetrators.* New York: Guilford Press.

Zimbardo, P. G. (2007). *The lucifer effect: Understanding how good people turn evil.* New York: Random House.

Zimmerman, F. J., & Christakis, D. A. (2005). Children's television viewing and cognitive outcomes: A longitudinal analysis of national data. *Archives of Pediatric and Adolescent Medicine, 159,* 619–625.

Zimmerman, F. J., Christakis, D. A., & Meltzoff, A. N. (2007). Association between media viewing and language development in children under 2 years. *Journal of Pediatrics, 151,* 354–368.

Zucker, R. A., Donovan, J. E., Masten, A. S., Mattson, M. E., & Moss, H. B. (2008). Early developmental processes and the continuity of risk for underage drinking and problem drinking. *Pediatrics, 121,* 5252–5272.

Zuroff, D. C., Fournier, M. A., Patall, E. A., & Leybman, M. J. (2010). Steps toward an evolutionary personality psychology: Individual differences in the social rank domain. *Canadian Psychology, 51,* 58–66.

Credits

Text Credits

CHAPTER 1

Page 17: "A Phrenology Map" From p. 106 in *Psychology: From Inquiry to Understanding*, 2nd ed. by Scott O. Lilienfeld, Steven J. Lynn, Laura L. Namy, & Nancy J. Woolf. Copyright © 2011. Printed and electronically reproduced by permission of Pearson Education, Inc., Upper Saddle River, New Jersey.; **22:** Watson, J. B. (1930). *Behaviorism*. Chicago: University of Chicago Press.

CHAPTER 2

Page 41: SOURCE: http://www.jamespowell.org/ Reprinted with permission of James Powell.

CHAPTER 3

Page 76: Figure 3.22, p. 114 in *Psychology: From Inquiry to Understanding*, 2nd ed. by Scott O. Lilienfeld, Steven J. Lynn, Laura L. Namy, & Nancy J. Woolf. Copyright © 2011. Printed and electronically reproduced by permission of Pearson Education, Inc., Upper Saddle River, New Jersey.; **77:**http://ghr.nlm.nih.gov/handbook/illustrations/normalkaryotype; **81:** SOURCE: Adapted from Caspi, A., et al. (2003). Influence of life stress on depression: Moderation by a polymorphism in the 5-HTT gene. *Science, 301,* 386–389. Copyright © 2003 by American Association for the Advancement of Science. Reprinted by Rightslink on behalf of the publisher.; **85:** SOURCE: Data are from Elliott, A. J., & Pazda, A. D. (2012). Dressed for Sex: Red as a Female Sexual Signal in Humans. *PLoS One*, 7, e34607.; **87:** Kenrick, D.T., Sadalla, E.K. Groth, G., & Trost, M.R. (1990). "Evolution, traits and the stages of human courtship: Qualifying the parental investment model." *Journal of Personality, 58,* 97–116. Reprinted with permission of John Wiley & Sons.; **89:** Based on Fuster, J.M., *The Prefrontal Cortex: Anatomy, Physiology, and Neuropsychology of the Frontal Lobe*, 2nd edition. New York: Raven Press, 1989.; **89:** From p. 344 in *Psychology: From Inquiry to Understanding*, 2nd ed. by Scott O. Lilienfeld, Steven J. Lynn, Laura L. Namy, & Nancy J. Woolf. Copyright © 2011. Printed and electronically reproduced by permission of Pearson Education, Inc., Upper Saddle River, New Jersey.; **90:** Reprinted with permission.; **91:** Adapted from Cramer, R., Lipinski, R., Meteer, J., & Houska, J. (2008). Sex differences in subjective distress to unfaithfulness: Testing competing evolutionary and violation of infidelity expectations hypotheses. *The Journal of Social Psychology, 148*(4), 389–405. Copyright © 2008. Reprinted by permission of Taylor & Francis Group, http://www.informaworld.com.; **94:** Adapted from Figure 3.16, p. 101 in *Psychology: From Inquiry to Understanding*, 2nd ed. by Scott O. Lilienfeld, Steven J. Lynn, Laura L. Namy, & Nancy J. Woolf. Copyright © 2011. Printed and electronically reproduced by permission of Pearson Education, Inc., Upper Saddle River, New Jersey.; **96:** Adapted from Figure 3.3, p. 88 in *Psychology: From Inquiry to Understanding*, 2nd ed. by Scott O. Lilienfeld, Steven J. Lynn, Laura L. Namy, & Nancy J. Woolf. Copyright © 2011. Printed and electronically reproduced by permission of Pearson Education, Inc., Upper Saddle River, New Jersey.; **97:** "The Lock and Key Analogy for how Neurotransmitters and Receptors Match" Figure 3.11, p. 89 in *Psychology: From Inquiry to Understanding*, 2nd ed. by Scott O. Lilienfeld, Steven J. Lynn, Laura L. Namy, & Nancy J. Woolf. Copyright © 2011. Printed and electronically reproduced by permission of Pearson Education, Inc., Upper Saddle River, New Jersey.; **102:** Slightly adapted from Figure 3.18, p. 103 in *Psychology: From Inquiry to Understanding*, 2nd ed. by Scott O. Lilienfeld, Steven J. Lynn, Laura L. Namy, & Nancy J. Woolf. Copyright © 2011. Printed and electronically reproduced by permission of Pearson Education, Inc., Upper Saddle River, New Jersey.; **106:** Figure 2.1, p. 38 from *Psychology: An Exploration*, 1st ed. by Saundra Ciccarelli & J. Noland White. Copyright © 2010. Reprinted and electronically reproduced by permission of Pearson Education, Inc., Upper Saddle River, New Jersey.; **107:** Figure 3.17, p. 102 in *Psychology: From Inquiry to Understanding*, 2nd ed. by Scott O. Lilienfeld, Steven J. Lynn, Laura L. Namy, & Nancy J. Woolf. Copyright © 2011. Printed and electronically reproduced by permission of Pearson Education, Inc., Upper Saddle River, New Jersey.; **108:** Adapted from Figure 3.15, p. 100 in *Psychology: From Inquiry to Understanding*, 2nd ed. by Scott O. Lilienfeld, Steven J. Lynn, Laura L. Namy, & Nancy J. Woolf. Copyright © 2011. Printed and electronically reproduced by permission of Pearson Education, Inc., Upper Saddle River, New Jersey; **110:** Carlson, Neil R., Psychology of Behavior, 11th ed., Copyright © 2013, pp. 29, 72. Reprinted and electronically reproduced by permission of Pearson Education, Inc., Upper Saddle River, New Jersey; **110:** Pearson Education; **111:** Slightly adapted from Figure 3.14, p. 99 in *Psychology: From Inquiry to Understanding*, 2nd ed. by Scott O. Lilienfeld, Steven J. Lynn, Laura L. Namy, & Nancy J. Woolf. Copyright © 2011. Printed and electronically reproduced by permission of Pearson Education, Inc., Upper Saddle River, New Jersey.; **112:** Adaptation of Morieb, 2001 as reprinted in *Psychology: From Inquiry to Understanding*,1st ed. by Scott O. Lilienfeld, Steven J. Lynn, Laura L. Namy, and Nancy J. Woolf. Copyright © 2009. Printed and electronically reproduced by permission of Pearson Education, Inc., Upper Saddle River, New Jersey.; **112:** Slightly adapted from Figure 3.11, p. 95 in *Psychology: From Inquiry to Understanding*, 2nd ed. by Scott O. Lilienfeld, Steven J. Lynn, Laura L. Namy, & Nancy J. Woolf. Copyright © 2011. Printed and electronically reproduced by permission of Pearson Education, Inc., Upper Saddle River, New Jersey.; **113:** Images courtesy of Masud Husain (from Hemispatial Neglect, Parton, Malhotra & Husain) (2004) *J Neurol Neurosurg Psychiatry*, *75*:13–21; **114:** Figure 12.9, p. 438 from *Human Anatomy and Physiology*, 7th ed. by Elaine N. Marieb & Katja Hoehn. Copyright © 2007. Printed and electronically reproduced by permission of Pearson Education, Inc., Upper Saddle River, New Jersey.; **115:** Slightly adapted from Figure 3.10, p. 95 in *Psychology: From Inquiry to Understanding*, 2nd ed. by Scott O. Lilienfeld, Steven J. Lynn, Laura L. Namy, & Nancy J. Woolf. Copyright © 2011. Printed and electronically reproduced by permission of Pearson Education, Inc., Upper Saddle River, New Jersey.; **115:** Slightly adapted from Figure 3.20, p. 111 in *Psychology: From Inquiry to Understanding*, 2nd ed. by Scott O. Lilienfeld, Steven J. Lynn, Laura L. Namy, & Nancy J. Woolf. Copyright © 2011. Printed and electronically reproduced by permission of Pearson Education, Inc., Upper Saddle River, New Jersey.; **121:** Pearson Canada; **124:** Figure 3.19, p. 107 in *Psychology: From Inquiry to Understanding*, 2nd ed. by Scott O. Lilienfeld, Steven J. Lynn, Laura L. Namy, & Nancy J. Woolf. Copyright © 2011. Printed and electronically reproduced by permission of Pearson Education, Inc., Upper Saddle River, New Jersey.

CHAPTER 4

Page 140: From "The Role of Frequency in Developing Perceptual Sets" by D. A. Alampay & B. R. Bugelski (1961) *Canadian Journal of Psychology, 15,* 205–211. Copyright © 1961 by Canadian Psychological Association, by permission.; **144:** Figure 3.1, p. 79 from *Psychology: An Exploration*, 1st ed. by Saundra Ciccarelli and J. Noland White. Copyright © 2010. Reprinted and electronically reproduced by permission of Pearson Education, Inc., Upper Saddle River, New Jersey; **146:** Figure 3.4(a), p. 81 from *Psychology: An Exploration*, 1st ed. by Saundra Ciccarelli and J. Noland White. Copyright © 2010. Reprinted and electronically reproduced by permission of Pearson Education, Inc., Upper Saddle River, NJ.; **148:** Adapted from Figure 4.16, p. 138 in *Psychology: From Inquiry to Understanding*, 2nd ed. by Scott O. Lilienfeld, Steven J. Lynn, Laura L. Namy, and Nancy J. Woolf. Copyright © 2011. Printed and electronically reproduced by permission of Pearson Education, Inc., Upper Saddle River, New Jersey.; **148:** Figure 4.24, p. 143 in *Psychology: From Inquiry to Understanding*, 2nd ed. by Scott O. Lilienfeld, Steven J. Lynn, Laura L. Namy, and Nancy J. Woolf. Copyright © 2011. Printed and electronically reproduced by permission of Pearson Education, Inc., Upper Saddle River, New Jersey.; **149:** (Fig. 3.4, p. 96) from *Psychology*, 3rd edition by Saundra Ciccarelli & J. Noland White. Copyright © 2012. Printed and electronically reproduced by permission of Pearson Education, Inc., Upper Saddle River, New Jersey.; **150:** Figure 4.18, p. 139 in *Psychology: From Inquiry to Understanding*, 2nd ed. by Scott O. Lilienfeld, Steven J. Lynn, Laura L. Namy, and Nancy J. Woolf. Copyright

© 2011. Printed and electronically reproduced by permission of Pearson Education, Inc., Upper Saddle River, New Jersey.; 152: Expertise and the Fusiform Face Area. Reprinted with permission of Dr. Isabel Gauthier.; 153: Figure 4.7, p. 128 in *Psychology: From Inquiry to Understanding*,2nd ed. by Scott O. Lilienfeld, Steven J. Lynn, Laura L. Namy, and Nancy J. Woolf. Copyright © 2011. Printed and electronically reproduced by permission of Pearson Education, Inc., Upper Saddle River, New Jersey.; 154: Reprinted by permission of Melvyn Goodale; 160: Figure 4.27, p. 148 in *Psychology: From Inquiry to Understanding*, 2nd ed. by Scott O. Lilienfeld, Steven J. Lynn, Laura L. Namy, and Nancy J. Woolf. Copyright © 2011. Printed and electronically reproduced by permission of Pearson Education, Inc., Upper Saddle River, New Jersey.; 163: Figure 4.31, p. 151 in *Psychology: From Inquiry to Understanding*, 2nd ed. by Scott O. Lilienfeld, Steven J. Lynn, Laura L. Namy, and Nancy J. Woolf. Copyright © 2011. Printed and electronically reproduced by permission of Pearson Education, Inc., Upper Saddle River, New Jersey.; 170: Figure 3.12, p. 109 from *Psychology*, 3rd edition by Saundra Ciccarelli & J. Noland White. Copyright © 2012. Printed and electronically reproduced by permission of Pearson Education, Inc., Upper Saddle River, NJ.; 170: From Kalat. *Biological Psychology*, 10th ed. Copyright © 2009 South–Western, a part of Cengage Learning, Inc. Reproduced by permission. www.cengage.com/permissions; 172: Adapted from p. 157 in *Psychology: From Inquiry to Understanding*, 2nd ed. by Scott O. Lilienfeld, Steven J. Lynn, Laura L. Namy, and Nancy J. Woolf. Copyright © 2011. Printed and electronically reproduced by permission of Pearson Education, Inc., Upper Saddle River, New Jersey. Pearson adaptation derived from Ramachandran and Rogers–Ramachandran (1996). Synaesthesia in phantom limbs induced with mirrors. *Proceedings of the Royal Society of London*, 263, 377–386.; 173: From Chan, Brenda L., et al, "Mirror Therapy for Phantom Limb Pain," *The New England Journal of Medicine, 357*(21), 2206. Copyright © 2007 Massachusetts Medical Society. Reprinted by permission of The Massachusetts Medical Society.; 174: Adapted from p. 153 in *Psychology: From Inquiry to Understanding*, 2nd ed. by Scott O. Lilienfeld, Steven J. Lynn, Laura L. Namy, and Nancy J. Woolf. Copyright © 2011. Printed and electronically reproduced by permission of Pearson Education, Inc., Upper Saddle River, New Jersey.; 174: Figure 4.32, p. 152 in *Psychology: From Inquiry to Understanding*, 2nd ed. by Scott O. Lilienfeld, Steven J. Lynn, Laura L. Namy, and Nancy J. Woolf. Copyright © 2011. Printed and electronically reproduced by permission of Pearson Education, Inc., Upper Saddle River, New Jersey.

CHAPTER 5

Page 183: SOURCE: "How Sleep Requirements Change with Age" From Roffwarg, H. P., Defazio, J. N., and Dement, W. C., (1966), "Ontogenetic Development of the Human Sleep–Dream Cycle" in *Science*, April 29, 1966, 152(3722):604–619. Copyright © 1966 by AAAS. Reprinted by permission of AAAS.; 187: From Coren, Stanley, "Daylight Savings Time and Traffic Accidents," *The New England Journal of Medicine,344*(14), 924. Copyright © 1996 the Massachusetts Medical Society. Reprinted by permission of The Massachusetts Medical Society; 188: From "Effect of Reducing Interns' Work Hours on Serious Medical Errors in Intensive Care Units" by C. P. Landrigan et al. (2004) *New England Journal of Medicine,351*(18), 1838–1848. Copyright © 2004. Reprinted by permission of Massachusetts Medical Society.; 204: SOURCE: Garyluk et al., Improving the Clinical Assessment of Consciousness With Advances in Electrophysiological and Neuroimaging Techniques (2010), *BMC Neurology*, 10:11. From BioMed Central.; 223: From Chappel, J. N., Veach, T. L., & Krug, R. S., "The Substance Abuse Attitude Survey: An instrument for measuring attitudes," *Journal of Studies on Alcohol, 46*(1), 48–52. Copyright © 1985 Alcohol Research Documentation, Inc. Republished by permission.

CHAPTER 6

Page 229: CARLSON, Neil R., Psychology Of Behavior, 11th ed., Copyright © 2013, pp. 29, 72. Reprinted and electronically reproduced by permission of Pearson Education, Inc., Upper Saddle River, New Jersey; 259: Figure 4.9, p. 141 from *Psychology: An Exploration*, 1st ed. by Saundra Ciccarelli & J. Noland White. Copyright © 2010. Adapted by permission of Pearson Education, Inc., Upper Saddle River, NJ.

CHAPTER 7

Page 271: Based on McGill; 292: Wong, C. K., & Read, J. D. (2011). Positive and negative effects of physical context reinstatement on eyewitness recall and identification. *Applied Cognitive Psychology,25,* 2–11. Figure 2 (p. 7). Reprinted by permission of John Wiley & Sons, Inc.; 297: "Ebbinghaus's Forgetting Curve" Ebbinghaus, 1885.; 297: From Bahrick, H. P. (1984). Semantic memory content in permastore: Fifty years of memory for Spanish learned in school. *Journal of Experimental Psychology: General, 113* (1), 1–29. American Psychological Association.; 302: Bransford, J. D., & Johnson, M. K. (1973). Considerations of some problems of comprehension. In W. Chase (ed.), *Visual information processing* (pp. 383–438). Oxford, UK Academic.; 303: SOURCE: Kleider, H., Pezdek, K., Goldinger, S., & Kirk, A. (2008). Schema–driven source misattribution errors: Remembering the expected from a witnessed event. *Applied Cognitive Psychology, 22*(1), 1–20. Copyright © 2008 by John Wiley & Sons. Reprinted by permission of John Wiley & Sons.; 306: Based on data from Loftus, E. F., & Palmer, J. C. (1974). Reconstruction of automobile destruction: An Example of the interaction between language and memory. *Journal of Verbal Learning and Verbal Behavior*, 13, 585–589. (p. 586.); 308: From Roediger, H., & McDermott, K. (1995). Creating false memories: Remembering words not presented in lists. *Journal of Experimental Psychology: Learning, Memory, and Cognition, 21,* 803–814. American Psychological Association.

CHAPTER 8

Page 330: Wade, Carol; Tavris, Carol, *Invitation to Psychology,* 2nd Ed., Copyright © 2002, p. 21. Adapted and electronically reproduced by permission of Pearson Education, Inc., Upper Saddle River, New Jersey; 331: SOURCE: Westen, D., Blagov, P. S., & Harenski, K. (2006). Neural bases for motivated reasoning: An fMRI study of emotional constraints on partisan political judgment in the 2004 U.S. presidential election. *Journal of Cognitive Neuroscience, 18,* 1974–1958. Reprinted with permission of MIT Press.

CHAPTER 9

Page 358: Terman, 1916, pp. 91–92; 361: "Implicit Theories of Intelligence Predict Achievement Across an Adult Transition: A Longitudinal Study and an Intervention," by L. S. Blackwell, K. H. Trzesniewski, & C. S. Dweck (2007), Child Development. Reprinted by permission of John Wiley & Sons, Inc.; 367: Craig and Mark Keilburger, *Free The Children* (2006; Me to We Books).

CHAPTER 10

Page 409: Testing Infants' Understanding of Quantity, from the Proceedings of the National Academy of Sciences of the United States of America. Reprinted with permission.; 412: Harlow, Harry F., The Nature of Love, *American Psychologist*, Vol 13(12), Dec 1958, 673–685. From the American Psychological Association.; 438: From Statistics Canada, Marriage and Divorce Trends in Canada.; 438: Recognizing the Four Horsemen of the (Relationship) Apocalypse. Reprinted with permission of the Gottman Institute at www.gottman.com; 440: Data from "At the Intersection of Emotion and Cognition: Aging and the Positivity Effect" by L. L. Carstensen & J. A. Mikels, (2005) *Current Directions in Psychological Science, 14*(3).

CHAPTER 11

Page 446: From Weiten. *Psychology*, 8th ed. Copyright © 2011 South–Western, a part of Cengage Learning, Inc. Reproduced by permission. www.cengage.com/permissions; 450: Data from Statistics Canada, Health Indicators, June 2004.; 451: Data from Hudson, J., Hiripi, E., Pope, H., & Kessler, R. (2007). The prevalence and correlates of eating disorders in the National Comorbidity Survey replication. *Biological Psychiatry, 61,* 348–358.; 469: From Aron, A., Fisher, H., Mashek, D. J., Strong, G., Li, H., & Brown, L. L., "Reward, motivation, and emotion systems associated with early–stage intense romantic love," *Journal of Neurophysiology, 94,* 327–337 (Fig 3). Copyright © 2005 American Physiological Society. Reprinted by permission; 480: Pearson; 484: Graph based on Schachter, S., & Singer, J. (1962). Cognitive, social, and physiological determinants of emotional state. *Psychological Review, 69,* 379–399. (Table 5, p. 392).

CHAPTER 12

521: Maslow, A. (1968). *Toward a psychology of being* (2nd ed.). New York: Van Nostrand.

CHAPTER 13

Page 555: Milgram, S. (1963). Behavioral study of obedience. *Journal of Abnormal and Social Psychology, 67,* 371–378.; 556: Stanley Milgram, *Obedience to Authority: An Experimental View* (New York: Harper & Row), 1974; 576: David Fetherstonhaugh, Paul Slovic, Stephen Johnson, James Friedrich, "Insensitivity to the Value of Human Life: A Study of Psychophysical Numbing," *Journal of Risk and Uncertainty,* May 1997, Volume 14, Issue 3, pp 283–300.

CHAPTER 14

Page 587: CDC, 2009b; Rehm et al., 2006; Statistics Canada, 2012b.; 589: Based on Hans Selye's General Adaptation Syndrome.; 601: Based on "Stress and the General Adaptation Syndrome" by Hans Selye, *British Medical Journal,* June 17, 1950.; 611: Based on Fredrickson, B. L., & Levenson, R. W (1998). Positive emotions speed recovery from the cardiovascular sequelae of negative emotions. *Cognition & Emotion, 12,* 191–220. Figure 3, p. 205.; **619:** SOURCE: Whitson, J. A., & Galinsky, A. D. (2008). Lacking control increases illusory pattern perception. *Science,322,* 115–117. Copyright © 2008 by AAAS. Reprinted through Rightslink, by permission of the AAAS.

CHAPTER 15

Page 638: "Emotional Responses of Individuals with Anti–Social Personality Disorder" from "The psychopath as observer: Emotion and attention in picture processing" Adapted from Levenston, G. K., Patrick, C. J., Bradley, M. M., & Lang, P. J. (2000). The psychopath as observer: Emotion and attention in picture processing. *Journal of Abnormal Psychology, 109* (3), 373–385.; **638:**http://edition.cnn.com/2002/LAW/10/09/wuornos.execution/; **646:** JMD; **647:** Frederick S. Stinson et al., "The epidemiology of DSM–IV specific phobia in the USA: results from the National Epidemiologic Survey on Alcohol and Related Conditions," *Psychological Medicine*, Volume 37, Issue 07 (July 2007), pp. 1047–1059 (p. 1053, Table 3). Copyright © 2007 Cambridge University Press. Reprinted with the permission of Cambridge University Press.; **649:** From "Selection for Contextual Fear Conditioning Affects Anxiety–Like Behaviors and Gene Expression" by C.A. Ponder, C. L. Kliethermes, M. R. Drew, J. Muller, K. Das, V. B. Risbrough, J. C. Crabbe, T. C. Gilliam, & A. A. Palmer (2007) *Genes, Brain & Behavior, 6*(8), 736–749. Copyright © 2007 by John Wiley and Sons. Reprinted by permission of John Wiley and Sons.; **654:** Pearson; **655:** American Psychological Association, 2011; **660:** Kurt Snyder, "Kurt Snyder's Personal Experience with Schizophrenia," *Schizophr Bull* 32 (2): 209–211. Copyright © 2006 Oxford University Press. Reprinted by permission.

Name Index

Note: Boldface page numbers indicate figures, photos, and tables.

T

U

V

Subject Index

Note: Boldface page numbers indicate figures, photos, and tables.

F

L

M

N

Q

R

S